# THEME AND FORM

PRENTICE-HALL ENGLISH LITERATURE SERIES

MAYNARD MACK, *Editor*

**MONROE BEARDSLEY**
*Swarthmore College*

**ROBERT DANIEL**
*University of Tennessee*

**GLENN LEGGETT**
*University of Washington*

# THEME AND FORM

## An Introduction to Literature

*Englewood Cliffs, N. J.*
PRENTICE-HALL, INC.

Ⓒ—Copyright, 1956, by
PRENTICE-HALL, INC.
Englewood Cliffs, N.J.

Library of Congress
Catalog Card No: 56-9171

*First printing* .......... *April, 1956*
*Second printing* ....... *January, 1957*
*Third printing* ........ *August, 1957*
*Fourth printing* .......... *July, 1958*
*Fifth printing* ....... *September, 1958*
*Sixth Printing* ........ *August, 1959*

PRINTED IN THE UNITED STATES OF AMERICA

91404

# PREFACE

THE reader of this anthology will encounter in it specimens of all the chief *genres,* or modes, of literature: the essay, including brief biographies; prose fiction; poetry; and the drama, represented not only by plays, in verse and prose, but also by a film scenario. These literary works are arranged in ten chapters, each concerned with a certain kind of experience or situation; but within the chapters the representatives of each mode are grouped together. An introduction gives a succinct account of the generic nature of literature, emphasizing the elemental unity underlying its various species. For the reader's guidance in understanding and enjoying literature in no matter what mode he encounters it, the book concludes with analyses of an essay, a story, a play, and a poem, together with explanations of the critical terms commonly used in discussing them.

The title, *Theme and Form,* is designed to suggest the close connection between the two fundamental aspects of literature, as well as the direction that the reader is advised to follow in continuing his study of literature. Most readers rightly consider that the subject of a literary work implies a theme, or themes, which they can relate to their own lives and experiences of the world. But the formal elements of the work have this degree of importance: without them the subject could not have been presented at all, and the themes would not have been precisely what they are. This book offers the reader a means of understanding how the individual substance and particular thematic concerns of a literary work are developed through its aesthetic form, including all its levels and types of order.

The choice and arrangement of the contents has been governed by this view of literature, more fully explained in the introduction, and by its corollary, that to understand and feel the relationships among theme, form, and experience is the principal problem of literary studies. We believe that an arrangement combining thematic and formal groupings is the most illuminating method of helping the reader to solve the problem.

To our many colleagues whose assistance we have requisitioned, we once again most gratefully acknowledge our indebtedness, wishing that space allowed us to name each one. More particularly we thank, for unflagging help and support, Professor Maynard Mack of Yale University, our series editor; Mr. William A. Pullin; Messrs. Donald R. Hammonds and William W. Worcester of Prentice-Hall, Inc.; and our patient and encouraging wives.

M. B.

R. D.

G. L.

# TABLE OF CONTENTS

# ANALYTIC CONTENTS

## Essays and Exposition: Nonfiction

### EXPOSITORY NARRATIVE AND DESCRIPTION

#### AUTOBIOGRAPHICAL NARRATIVE

#### HISTORICAL NARRATIVE

# EXPOSITORY NARRATIVE AND DESCRIPTION (CONT.)

# EXPOSITORY ANALYSIS

# EXPOSITORY ARGUMENT AND PERSUASION

# Prose Fiction

# Drama

# Poetry

## BALLADS AND NARRATIVES

# SONNETS AND SHORT LYRICS (CONT.)

# ODES AND ELEGIAC VERSE

# DRAMATIC PORTRAIT AND SELF-PORTRAIT

# REFLECTION AND RESOLUTION

# THE STUDY OF LITERATURE

COLLEGE students enroll for many subjects that are new to them—psychology and calculus, perhaps, or nutrition and dress-designing—but literature is not one of these. Nobody gets to college without having learned something about the appreciation of literature from his English teachers in high school and before. Having been already made familiar with a number of literary works and some of the critical terms used in discussing them, the student should expect to acquire in college new ways of understanding and enjoying literature, and a better grasp of the reasons that it occupies an important place in everyone's formal education.

But no one's knowledge of literature is limited to what he has learned about it in school. Even if he left school after the fifth grade, even if he is illiterate, throughout his life he enjoys literature in some form or other. For "literature" means not only what is permanently interesting and enduring—*The Scarlet Letter* and the plays of Shakespeare, for instance—but an immense amount of transient writing also, much of it widely popular and some of it very crude. The words of the latest song on the juke-boxes are a poem; so are ballads, like "Frankie and Johnny" and "Death on the Highway"; and of course the articles and stories in the weekly magazines of mass circulation are essays and fiction. Even the jokes we tell each other, and never expect to meet written down, are composed of the same basic elements as novels and narrative poems, and may be considered literature in its simplest form. Thus, before his college career begins, the student knows what literature is, for he has experienced it in two different ways: through the poems, essays, and stories that he has chosen for himself, and through the works that he has encountered (and, we hope, enjoyed) as a result of the tastes of his teachers.

This previous familiarity with the subject has both advantages and disadvantages. It is pleasant to have passed beyond the elementary stages of a study: not to have to struggle with definitions of *cost* and *price*, *mass* and *energy*, or *cell*, or *valence*. But the very fact that we enjoy the words of popular songs and the stories in a weekly magazine, which nobody compels us to pay any attention to, inclines us to resent the difficulty of understanding, let alone admiring, certain other literary works that we are told we ought to appreciate and admire. And so we are apt to separate poems and other fictions into two utterly distinct classes: the ones the teacher likes, and the ones that are good. At the same time, most readers feel some curiosity about the writings that have interested other readers over a great number of years, for many generations perhaps. They would like to understand and enjoy these writings because other people seem to have made them the permanent possessions of their minds. Not only do these people enjoy them, they evidently find something of enduring value for their lives in literature of this sort. If only it weren't such hard work. . . .

The first step in breaking down the barrier between these supposedly distinct classes is to remember that our likes and dislikes are not fixed but changing; what we enjoy today may seem childish and silly tomorrow, and we are constantly experiencing the joy of finding that we can master new, more advanced subjects, whether in class or out. A second step is to learn why some of the things we read are more difficult than others, for in so doing we shall discover that the difference between them is one of degree, not of kind. This means that they are composed of similar parts and satisfy the same sort of desires, however different they may seem in the methods by which their parts are combined: as a T-Model Ford and the latest one may be said to differ in degree rather than in kind. They are different, of course; but they are alike in that both make power produce motion, and their motions are both useful and agreeable. Though it is well to know that T-Models and the most recent Fords are different, it would not be at all sensible to try to explain the difference by saying that one is more difficult to manage, the other to comprehend, and letting it go at that.

Literature also has its different forms, but it cannot usefully be divided into writings that are easy to understand and those that are hard. The ways in which writers and critics have classified literature are of great importance in its study, and we shall shortly point out what some of them are. But all literary works have some things in common, which cause them to be spoken of together as "literature"; and since these similarities are even more significant than the differences, we shall first of all consider what a literary work is. The term *literature* does not apply to street-signs, slogans written in smoke by airplanes, or many other fascinating uses of language; and so the question is how to distinguish these from "Sir Patrick Spens," *Othello, The Scarlet Letter,* and other works that everyone agrees are literature.

## THE LITERARY WORK

Whatever else we may say about a literary work, it is at least a series of words arranged in a grammatical order. It is, in short, a piece of verbal discourse. And the essence of a verbal discourse is that in it someone is talking about something.

There are, then, two elements that are part of the common denominator of all literary works: there is always an implicit *speaker,* who is the apparent or ostensible utterer of the words; and there is always a *subject* of some sort that he is referring to, or, as we usually say, that the work is about. Consider, for example, the anonymous poem that begins:

> Frankie and Johnny were lovers.
> O Lawdy how they did love!
> They swore to be true to each other,
> As true as the stars above.
> He was her man, but he done her wrong.

The subject, baldly summarized, is a love affair that turned out badly because one of the parties was unfaithful and the other jealous. The speaker is telling the story with sympathy for both lovers but implies that Johnny's behavior is pretty much to be expected from a man. Together, and in relation to each other, the subject and the speaker make up what we may, in the most general sense, call a *situation*: the speaker is confronted by these violent events, and the poem embodies his response to what he sees.

Let us consider each of these three terms, *subject, situation,* and *speaker,* a little further.

## THE SUBJECT

The subject of a literary work may be a thing, a person, a scene, a state of affairs, an event, a whole series of events, or all of the universe, time and eternity. When we ask what the work is about, one of the answers to this question is its subject: in Katherine Mansfield's "Her First Ball" and in Milton's "On His Blindness" the subject is indicated by the title. [1]

The people referred to in a literary work need not, of course, ever have existed; the events need not have occurred. The Charge of the Light Brigade really happened, but the cavalry charge described in *Arms and the Man* did not. It makes no difference. For the subject of the work is not something outside of it, something that the author perhaps read about before he began to write, or something that prompted him to write. It is just what is presented in the work itself.

## THE SITUATION

What is central to a literary work is always a human situation of some kind. It may, for example, be the situation of a man confronting his own imminent death, as in "The Bishop Orders His Tomb at Saint Praxed's Church," or Boswell's "The Death of Johnson." It may include a whole series of shifting problems and perplexities that make up a complex plot, as in *Othello.*

Even if the characters in a story are animals (Donald Duck or the Houyhnhnms in *Gulliver's Travels*), or strange nonhuman beings from Mars or Krypton or Metaluna, they can only act in ways that involve some reflections or distortions or exaggerations of human motives: even in such a work the situation is implicitly a human one.

The central situation, or the dominant central situation if there are many, partly determines the way we classify a literary work. We say it is a love story, a love poem or a love drama: in short, a literary work whose principal subject is love. Or it is a war story, or a sports story; it is a detective story or a science-fiction story.

---

[1] All examples except a few very familiar ones are in this book.

## THE SPEAKER

All literary works imply, more or less distinctly, but always to some degree, a speaker. Any understandable sentence or series of sentences has the appearance of having been uttered by a human being, and tells us something about the human being who might have uttered it. The parrot who says "Polly want a cracker" does not understand what he is saying; yet this demand, uttered in a peremptory tone, suggests a speaker who is rude and not very bright, and it is this implicit speaker, not the parrot, that we are referring to here.

The speaker of a literary work, in other words, is not to be confused with the actual living author—however similar they may be. No doubt Hazlitt really believed the things he wrote in his essay "On the Fear of Death"; and Yeats may actually have felt about his daughter the way the speaker in "A Prayer for My Daughter" does. But that is not inevitable, any more than it is inevitable that an actor who plays Richard III or Falstaff should resemble those characters in real life. And it is not to be taken for granted. The speaker in "Why I Live at the P.O." bears little resemblance to Eudora Welty; Browning's Fra Lippo Lippi is not Browning. Nor can we expect to learn more of these characters by studying the lives of their authors; all we can know about the postmistress or about Lippo is what they reveal about themselves in the way they talk about the situations they are in, especially the way they talk about other people.

The speaker of a literary work more or less clearly reveals himself in what he says and what he does not say. At one extreme, he may take part in the action, reporting it in the first person: as happens in "The Secret Sharer" and "Araby." Or, without being actually involved, he may write about the events in such a way as to imply some relationship to them: he lives in the same village and has heard the story, as in "The Girl in Arles," or "A Rose for Emily," and he shows some feeling about the people involved. Even where the speaker seems to be most detached and unwilling to give himself away, as in "The Undefeated" or "Act of Faith," the very withdrawal and distance give some hint, however vague and general, of the speaker's nature.

It is often convenient, though it is misleading, to refer to the speaker of a literary work by the name of the author. We say "Robert Frost" or "Wordsworth" or "Matthew Arnold" when we mean the speaker in one of their poems. It is obviously silly to say that Shakespeare advises us, "Neither a borrower nor a lender be," when in fact it is only one of his characters who says it. The speaker of a poem is similarly one of the author's characters, whether the author presents the same character in many poems, as does Frost, or presents many different characters, as does Browning. A poem or a short story is a *performance* of a certain kind: somebody is speaking about something, and thereby responding to a situation. The author is playing a role, like an actor on the stage.

It is worth noting here, though without pausing to dwell on it, that just as there is an implicit speaker in a literary work, so there may be an implicit auditor, or person to whom it is ostensibly addressed. That is, the speaker may show by the words he chooses, and his manner of address, and in other ways, what sort of person, or what class of people, he is aiming his words at. This can easily be seen in a speech such as Winston Churchill's on Dunkirk or Thoreau's "Plea for Captain John Brown" or the Sermon on the Mount, each of which is carefully designed for the audience and the occasion. But it may also be implicit less obviously in the level of difficulty and complexity of an essay or poem or story, the attention and education it presupposes, the "talking up" or "talking down" in it.

## ATTITUDE

If there is, then, always a speaker and always something spoken of (more specifically, a human situation to which the speaker gives his attention and calls ours), there is also some *attitude* of the speaker *toward* the situation he describes, or the events he narrates.

"Attitude" in this context may cover a good deal of ground. If the speaker reveals philosophic, moral, religious, or political beliefs, then these are included in the term: for example, the speaker's conclusions about the guilt for World War II in "September 1, 1939," the speaker's distinctions between various personality types in the chapter from *The Lonely Crowd,* the speaker's reflections upon the nature of moral evil in "Original Sin." It also includes the speaker's emotions: the horror expressed by the narrator of "The Black Cat," the calm religious faith of the speaker in "Easter Wings," or the ecstatic religious joy of the speaker in "The Windhover."

It is useful to make the distinction, where we can, between those elements of attitude that may be called "beliefs" and those that may be called "emotions," though sometimes they are so bound up together and intermingled that the distinction is not sharp. Beliefs may be stated, more or less adequately, in words, and can be abstracted from the work and discussed on their own merits.

We said earlier that to name the subject of a literary work is to give one answer to the question, "What is it about?" "Frankie and Johnny" is about a woman who shoots her lover because he is unfaithful. But there is another answer to this question. "Frankie and Johnny" is also about the extremes to which human beings may be driven by jealous passion; it is about the perilousness of love, and about moral evil, and perhaps other things as well. These are general concepts that come to the speaker's mind, though he does not name them as such but lets them come through the concrete images of the poem, its rhymes and rhythms, and its insistent refrain, "He was her man, but he done her wrong."

These concepts may be called the *themes* of the poem, and, in the same sense, we may say that "A Rose for Emily" shares some themes with "Frankie and Johnny," as *Othello* shares other themes with it. A literary work may have many themes, and these are often among its most important, though not most obvious, elements.

A speaker may dwell upon a theme, such as the shortness of life, the paradoxical character of evil, or the blindness of men to what is in each other's hearts, without going further to suggest a positive belief about the matter. But when we refer to the philosophical or social content of a literary work, its ideology or point of view, we mean more than its themes, we mean its *thesis*—or theses, if there are several. "Frankie and Johnny" seems to say, though tentatively and subtly, that Johnny is guilty and recognizes his own guilt, and that it is important for people to be true to each other. And such stories as "The Hint of an Explanation" and "The Black Cat" contain other implicit propositions definite enough to be called, for want of a better name, philosophical "theses," however vague and indistinct they may be, and however crude and unqualified they may appear when extracted from the works themselves.

Themes and theses emerge from all the other elements of a literary work, and may be the last to be fully understood. But as the outcome of the rest, they must be understood for full appreciation. They correspond roughly to what we call the point of a joke. As we expect a joke to have a point—that shaggy-dog stories have no point is their point—so do we expect that a literary work should have a theme. The simplest joke will illustrate the relation between the theme and the elements involved in the subject. Two men were passing a graveyard; one called the other's attention to a headstone which read, "Here lies John Jones, an honest man and a lawyer." The other said, "But what's the idea of burying three men in one grave?" Note first that the action, the two characters, and the setting are all essential to the joke, and second that out of these the point (the implicit sneer at lawyers' honesty) emerges. Without its point the joke would be nothing, but it is also obvious that if the point were stated explicitly, as in the previous parenthesis, the joke would be destroyed. Because the point must be inferred from the way in which the action, the characters, and the setting work together, the reader experiences a momentary difficulty of understanding; yet it is this very difficulty that gives the joke whatever value it possesses. Where more serious works are concerned, we must likewise expect that the themes will be left to the reader to infer, regardless of a certain amount of obscurity that may be the result.

## TONE

The speaker's attitude is embodied in what is called the *tone* of a literary work. When we say that a remark is bitter, envious, cheerful, carefree, angry, hurt, or disillusioned, we are describing its tone: that is, the state of mind which we should naturally expect a speaker to be in if he talks this way. And such adjectives as these may be applied in exactly the same way to literary works, as a whole or in part, though sometimes we find that there is no word that hits off the tone of a work exactly, so that we can only describe rather crudely what we nevertheless experience in its precise uniqueness. The tone of "Spotted Horses" is evidently quite different from the tone of "A Rose for Emily," though the same author wrote both. The tone of Wolcott Gibbs's humor in "Ring Out, Wild Bells" is different from that of Clarence Day's humor in "Father Interferes with the Twenty-Third Psalm," though both are humorous.

"Tone" is a general name for the pervasive quality of a work. To be understood, in a particular case, it must be analyzed into those components of style that create it. We shall come to style later.

So far, we have been considering certain fundamental aspects of literary works, aspects that are common to them all. A literary work, it seems clear, is inevitably a human document, in two senses: it involves some situation or event in which human beings are involved, and it is itself a dramatized, or objectified, response (emotional and intellectual) to that situation or event, whether real or imagined. Certain human situations are so inescapable a part of real life, and so rich in material for description and reflection, that they turn up constantly, endlessly varied, in literary works.

## FORM IN LITERATURE

Even the simplest literary work is made up of parts: of paragraphs or stanzas, of scenes or episodes, of sections or chapters. And its subject is made up of elements: few or many characters, who may change much or little or not at all as they are involved in incidents that are violent or calm, long or short, funny or sad. The *form* of a literary work is just the way these parts or elements are connected with one another.

For some purposes, it is convenient to speak of the connections among the parts as making up the *explicit* form of the work: *Arms and the Man* consists of three acts; "Ozymandias" is a sonnet. Then the connections among the elements of the subject may be said to make up the *implicit* form of the work: the change in the reader's conception of Bluntschli, in *Arms and the Man*, from one act to the next; the ironic contrast in "Ozymandias" between the pompous inscription and the present state of the statue. But we shall include both of these types of form in our discussion.

There are two main distinctions that we need here: distinctions that cut across each other, so that we have four types of thing to consider.

## SOUND AND SENSE

The first distinction has to do with the two ways in which every literary work exists. A literary work consists of words, and words are, roughly speaking, sounds with meaning. (The written characters are signs for the spoken sounds, and we shall for our present purposes treat words as audible entities.) Whether a literary work is read aloud or silently, it always has a *sound* and a *sense,* or meaning. We can, when we wish, talk about the sound of the work without referring at all to its meaning: as when we say that a sentence contains two hundred syllables or a line of verse five accents, or that a passage is harsh and jerky. We can also talk about the meaning of the work, without referring to its sound: as when we say that a line is witty or pathetic, or that a passage is comic or logical. And we can talk about the connection between the sound and the meaning: as when we say that the softness of the line fits the tenderness of the meaning.

To sum up, in a literary work there may exist sound-form (the connections among the sounds), and sense-form (the connections among the meanings), and sound-sense-form (the connections between sounds and meanings).

## STRUCTURE AND TEXTURE

The second distinction cannot be made as sharply as the first, but it is still very useful. When the parts of a literary work themselves consist of parts, and those parts of parts (as sections are made up of paragraphs, paragraphs of sentences, and sentences of words), we can speak of the dominant parts and of the subordinate parts. "The Beast in the Jungle" consists of six sections, describing six main episodes, connected by passages that bridge the gaps of time; these are the dominant parts. But within the first episode, for example, there is a whole series of conversational give-and-takes, each of which can be discussed on its own. Again, we can divide *The Rape of the Lock* into its main sections, or talk about individual couplets or lines.

Now, when we talk about the connections among the dominant parts of a literary work, we are talking about its *structure. Arms and the Man* consists of three acts, in which we see things successively from the points of view of the three main characters. The story of the Crucifixion from Matthew 26-28 consists of three episodes, in which an *ABA* pattern can be discerned (Christ with his disciples; Christ alone; Christ with his disciples again). Wordsworth's "Resolution and Independence" moves through three main moods: joy in life, fear, and confidence regained; in that respect, it also exhibits the *ABA* pattern. All these statements are statements about *structure*.

When on the other hand we talk about the connections among the subordinate parts of a literary work, we are talking about its *texture*. Henry James writes long sentences with many qualifying clauses; Hemingway tends to write short, clipped sentences. Pope uses parallel and antithetical constructions; Frost and Auden use familiar and colloquial phrases in a fresh and ironic way. All these statements are statements about *texture*.

When we study the form of a literary work, then, we can study the structure and the texture of its sound, and the structure and the texture of its sense. And there are many important things to be noticed about each.

We need not analyze the sound aspect of literature further here, except to illustrate the distinction between structure and texture. When we say that a poem is a sonnet, or that it consists of three stanzas with a certain rhyme scheme, we are talking about the structure of its sound. When we say that it is in iambic meter, or that it contains a high proportion of sibilants, or alliteration, we are talking about the texture of its sound. *Texture* and *structure* are correlative words, like *local* and *regional*.

There is more, however, to the subject of texture and structure, as regards the meaning of literature.

Consider texture first.

## STYLE

The texture of a literary work, the details of its workmanship, is usually called its *style*. The style of a writer includes his preference for a certain diction (that is, words of a certain sort), and his preference for certain syntactical constructions. But what is more important, it includes the devices he employs to obtain what we shall, in the most general sense, call *multiple meaning*.

Multiple meaning applies to sentences, and it applies to words and phrases. *Verbal irony* is an example of the first sort. An ironic statement is one made in such a way as to show that the speaker actually believes something much less than, or much more than, or opposed to, what he says. In Marvell's poem, "To His Coy Mistress," the lines:

> The grave's a fine and private place,
> But none, I think, do there embrace—

are an example of ironic understatement, for worse things might be said of the grave than that it does not permit of love-making—and indeed the speaker says some of these things in other lines of the poem.

Multiple meanings of the second sort are *figures of speech*. Roughly speaking, any use of a word that gives it, or fixes for it momentarily, an unusual meaning in a certain context may be called a figure of speech, but figures of speech vary in complexity. At one extreme, we have unexpected *images* (words that refer to things that can be perceived through the senses) that give the suggestion of some further meaning over and above the obvious one. In "Sir Patrick Spens":

> The king sits in Dumferling toune,
> Drinking the blude-reid wine.

The epithet "blood-red" hints that the upshot of this gathering will be something more than revelry. Somewhat more complex and rich in meaning is the *simile,* an explicit, figurative likening of one thing to another:

> and then my state,
> Like to the lark at break of day arising
> From sullen earth, sings hymns at heaven's gate

(Shakespeare, Sonnet 29). Here the comparison of the speaker's joy to the wakening of the lark helps characterize that joy precisely and in various ways at once. More complex still is the *metaphor,* in which something is called by a predicate that, on one level, actually contradicts it, so that, on other levels, various secondary senses come into play:

> We are the hollow men
> We are the stuffed men

(T. S Eliot, "The Hollow Men"). It is impossible for living and speaking men to be literally hollow, or to be stuffed, and it is even more impossible for them to be both at the same time, but the connotations of "hollow" and "stuffed," in the context of the poem, range over a whole set of spiritual lacks.

When the same object, or objects related to it, turn up several times in a literary work, in metaphorical ways, the object condenses into itself a number of meanings in the work, and becomes a kind of *symbol* there. For example, the china jar becomes a symbol of feminine chastity in *The Rape of the Lock,* the Black Cat a symbol of man's irrational impulse to evil in Poe's story, the cage a symbol of the artist's relation to society in Kafka's "Hunger Artist."

We may count *allusion* as another sort of multiple meaning, for when the speaker in one poem makes a reference to another literary work or to historical or mythological characters, he imports into the context the extra symbolic meanings of the things referred to. The speaker in "Dover Beach" refers to the dramas of Sophocles; the speaker in "Ode to a Nightingale" refers to Ruth, in the Old Testament; the speaker in "Adieu, Farewell Earth's Bliss" intensifies the bitterness and inevitability of death by reminding us that Helen, the fairest, and Hector, the bravest, of the Trojans could not evade it.

## TYPES OF STRUCTURE

To ask about the structure of a literary work is to ask what are its main binding-principles: what makes it hang together, connects its beginning with its end, and defines for it a shape that can be taken in by the reader's mind. There are four principal types of literary structure. A particular literary work may exhibit more than one of them, but they are all distinct and independent. Since their function is to unify the literary work, to make it, despite all its textural complexities, *one,* these four structures may be thought of as four kinds of unity.

(1) *Descriptive structure.* Nothing is more exasperating than a conversation that keeps hopping from one subject to another, without disposing satisfactorily of any of them. A literary work will have at least some degree of unity if it is all about the same person, place, or thing. This structure, which is the simplest of all, is found, for example, in Mumford's essay on the Manufacturers Trust Building and Prescott's account of Cortez.

There are, of course, various species of descriptive structure. The statements may be grouped in some scheme of *classification*, as in José Limon's essay "On Dance." Or they may be grouped in terms of an extended *comparison*, as in Bernard Shaw's essay on "Duse and Bernhardt."

(2) *Plot structure*. A literary work may or may not have a plot; but this is one of the important ways in which literary works are structured. A plot is more than a mere sequence of events, such as one might find in the almanac's topical summary of last year's notable happenings. It is a sequence that has a marked degree of coherence and completeness. It is coherent if the motivation is clear, so that once the initial conditions, the events that set off the train of action, are given, the others follow with psychological plausibility. It is complete if its beginning marks a break with the past, not taking for granted what it does not provide, and its ending seems a consummation or resolution of what has gone before.

(3) *Logical structure*. A literary work may or may not be an argument: that is, it may or may not set out to convince someone of something by presenting reasons for believing it. Russell's essay "Facts and Dreams," de Roussy de Sales' "Love in America," are examples of argument, but of course several of the other essays in this book that are primarily descriptive contain snatches of larger pieces of argument, as well.

Since to argue for something means to give reasons for it, there must be some connection between the reasons and that which they are reasons for (the conclusion); and this connection must be a logical one. It is the nature of this logical connection that determines the logical structure of an argument; it determines whether, for example, it is an inductive or a deductive argument, whether, if inductive, it is an argument from analogy or a generalization, and whether, if deductive, it is syllogistic or has some other form. We need not consider all these distinctions in detail here. But to grasp the unity of a work, even of a poem like "To His Coy Mistress" or "September 1, 1939," may involve seeing that it is an argument and what its conclusion is.

(4) *Symbolic structure*. If a literary work contains symbols, they may form a cluster or family of related symbols that appear here and there at crucial moments throughout the work; or they may be subordinated to a single dominant symbol that appears throughout the work. This is another way in which the work can be tied together, and a very important way in some works. The concept of "honesty" in *Othello* is kept constantly before the audience's mind, in a great variety of ironically related forms; in "Blackberry Winter" the flood and its consequences bring together the diverse symbols of irremediable change; the religious images and metaphors in "Fern Hill" run through the poem like a binding thread.

For present purposes, it is convenient to let the term *symbolic structure* cover *allegory* as well. On one level, an allegory is a narrative; what makes a narrative allegorical is that it suggests some fairly systematic identification of the characters and incidents with abstract qualities or general concepts. "Young Goodman Brown," for example, is allegorical, though the allegory is not worked out in detail: Faith, the wife, is also Religious Faith in the same sense that the characters and places in *Pilgrim's Progress* are symbols of phases of the moral and religious life. Kafka's story "A Hunger-Artist" approaches allegory, but the meanings of the artist, the cage, and so forth are less fixed and determinate than in a strict allegory.

## THE MODES OF LITERATURE

As we have seen, one literary work may differ from another in any of several ways: in the sort of situation it involves, in the speaker's relation to the situation, in its form, in its theme or thesis. Evidently if we counted all possible combinations of these, the variety would be great. But certain combinations of them have proved more valuable, and hence more durable, than others. We shall refer to them as different *modes* of literature. (Sometimes they are called "genres.") Literature exists in several chief modes.

Four of these modes are represented in this book, and we must now say a little about each: how they are distinguished from one another, what the notable characteristics of each one are. Not that all literary works must fall into one of the conventional or already known categories: writers have always been interested in exploring new modes, or new combinations of old modes, sometimes with such success as to open new chapters in the history of literature. And even where they have failed to produce valuable works, those works are not to be condemned merely because they did not follow a previously marked path.

The modes of literature to be found in this book are prose fiction, the drama (including a screen play), the essay, and poetry. Let us consider each of them.

### PROSE FICTION

Speaking accurately enough for our present purposes, we may say that a prose fiction is distinguished from other literary modes by four characteristics. (1) It is written in non-metrical language; that is, it does not follow regular rhythms. (2) It is a narrative; that is, it has a plot. (3) Its narrative is a *story*, not a *report;* in other words, it does not claim that the events actually happened, as does a newspaper report, but sets forth the events as something that might have happened, or that can, for the sake of the story, be supposed to have happened. It involves make-believe. (4) It is told in the past tense, as though the events were already gone by and the conclusion reached; it is, in this respect, make-believe history. This fact has certain important implications for prose fiction in general: it means, for example, that the story comes through the eyes and ears of an observer of, or actor in, the events. Thus there is always a point of view, or perspective from which the action is observed.

It is customary to distinguish three subspecies of prose fiction: the short story, the novelette, and the novel. These distinctions cannot be made very sharp, for definite word limits would be arbitrary. But between the typical short story and the typical novelette or novel, there is a significant difference in the shape of the plot. A short story, although it may include many scenes and cover a considerable period of time, shapes up to one outstanding climax; a novelette or novel has scope for more than one.

Let us now consider some of the main features of prose fiction and some of the terms we shall need if we wish to talk about it clearly.

The subject of fiction is always characters in action, as we have seen, and if we use the word "conflict" in a broad sense, we may say that it always involves conflict. It may be an overt conflict between different people, as in "Sredni Vashtar," or a conflict within the mind of one person, as in "Act of Faith." Sometimes the antagonist—that which the leading character, or protagonist, is up against—is so generalized as to be personified Evil, or the forces of change, or Time, as in "Blackberry Winter."

The conflict always takes place against a particular background, or *setting*, which helps to define the terms of the conflict, to sharpen its point (as does the setting of "Act of Faith"), and may symbolically represent the antagonist itself (as in "Blackberry Winter"). When we speak of the setting of the story, we mean the physical scene, the surrounding circumstances, the climate and the weather, and so forth.

The conflict is always, as we have said, viewed from a particular angle. Sometimes the narrator, though not himself a character in the story, sees everything from the point of view of one of the characters, so that although he reports the thoughts of that character, he speaks of all the other characters as seen from the outside only. This "fixed" point of view may be seen in "Her First Ball." Sometimes the narrator switches from one character to another, as in "The Blind Man"; and sometimes the narrator adopts a purely objective point of view, from which he speaks externally of what all the characters do or say, but never directly reports the thoughts of any of them, as in "The Undefeated."

The conflict always has a dramatic shape. It may get under way more or less rapidly; that is, it may involve a shorter or longer *exposition*, in which the characters are introduced, but before anything happens. "The Girl in Arles" takes a few paragraphs to introduce the main characters; "An Occurrence at Owl Creek Bridge" plunges into the first scene immediately, but later returns to tell the reader how Farquhar came to be on the bridge.

As a story moves on, the reader sometimes feels that the conflict is at a high degree of tension, when what is happening will be decisive for the future of some important character. At other times, the tension is relaxed, and the excitement is at a lower ebb. Such a moment of high tension, where threads previously laid down seem to be drawn together by the author, where some long-expected result is about to be consummated, where the action of the story reaches a turning-point or a point where something vital will be revealed about the characters—such a point is a *climax* of the story. The discovery of the nature of the necklace in Maupassant's story, Mrs. De Ropp's removal of the hen in "Sredni Vashtar," are such points of climax. In "The Beast in the Jungle" there are two such points: the scene in which we learn that May Bartram has realized the truth about John Marcher, and the scene in which John Marcher realizes the truth about himself.[2]

## THE DRAMA

For convenience we may use the term "drama" to cover not only the three stage plays that are included in this book, but also the motion-picture scenario. There are noteworthy differences between stage plays and motion pictures, but what we shall say here applies to both.

Like prose fiction, a drama is a narrative, and the things we have been saying about conflict, setting, and climax apply as well to the drama. The fundamental difference is in the perspective toward the events involved. Whereas fiction is in the past tense, as though it were a recollection after the event and hence seems like a memory, the drama is in the present tense. It is like a radio broadcast of a baseball game: the action is happening at the moment it is being described, and so the announcer uses the present tense. Imagine

[2] For further discussion of prose fiction, see page 691.

his using the past tense, and you feel the difference between a drama, whether you are seeing it acted or just reading it, and a story.

In a drama, the speaker withdraws as far as possible and presents the characters in action and in speech, with no connective tissue of plot-summary. The action in the drama is now, not then, and your attention is primarily on the future: what is to come, and how.[3]

## THE ESSAY

The term "essay" may be used to cover discursive writing of any length, from a few paragraphs to a book. What distinguishes an essay from fiction, even an essay which includes narrative, is that it makes an implicit claim to truth for all that it says. A story may make some claim to truth—not that all the incidents it describes really happened, but that the view of life it implies is a true view. But an essay claims that it is all true, except where it is avowedly being fanciful; for example, it may introduce a paragraph by the words, "Some people have said . . ." or "There is a story (probably a myth) that illustrates this point . . ."

Though no very sharp line can be drawn between the two species, it is convenient to distinguish the *narrative essay* from the *reflective essay* according to the main focus of attention. History is narrative (*e.g.,* "The Battle of Balaclava"); biographies (*e.g.,* "Cortez") and autobiographical reminiscences (*e.g.,* "A Miserable, Merry Christmas") are narrative essays, or parts of narrative essays that can stand by themselves. The narrative essay will usually have a thesis of some sort, however implicit—that parents can be too dominating, or that children often suffer from misunderstanding. But the main body of the essay is the narrative that conveys the point, and the point is not defended by an argument.

In the reflective essay, on the other hand, the thesis is explicitly stated, and reasons are given for it. Russell's "Facts and Dreams" and Freud's "Childhood and Concealing Memories" are reflective essays; they aim to prove, to convince someone of something.

Though the *formal oration* has some features that distinguish it from essays in general (features that follow from its being designed to be delivered aloud to an audience, rather than addressed to a single reader in his study), it may be considered as a special type of reflective essay. Thoreau's "Plea for Captain John Brown" and Winston Churchill's report on Dunkirk are speeches, and they arouse emotional as well as intellectual responses, as indeed most reflective essays do; what puts them in this category is that though they contain narrative elements, these are subordinated to their general theses.[4]

## POETRY

The distinction between poetry in general and other modes of literature is a double one. First, we must distinguish *verse,* or metrical discourse, from all other discourse; and though there will be borderline cases where nobody can say that something is verse or prose, in general the distinction is very useful.

The syllables that make up English words are either stressed or unstressed in speaking, and it is this fact that makes verse possible. In

Frank - ie and John - ny were lov - ers,

---

[3] For further discussion of the drama, see page 696.
[4] For further discussion of the essay, see page 686.

the stressed syllables are marked, the rest not. A passage in English is metrical, or in meter, when the stresses occur with enough regularity to be perceived as a pattern. *Verse* is metrical discourse, and may be more or less regular. *Free verse* is verse in which the patterns of stress vary from line to line, in an irregular way, as in "The Too-Late Born" and "Speaking of Poetry." In strict verse, every line may have the same number of stresses and approximately the same pattern of stresses; for example, *The Rape of the Lock* and "There Was a Boy." Or there may be a single pattern consisting of lines of various lengths, which together form a stanza-pattern. It may be a simple one, as in "Frankie and Johnny," or a complicated one, as in "Ode to a Nightingale."

The lines of a poem or their parts may be connected in another way by sound. Any similarity in the quality of sound between two words may be called *rhyme*, of which there are various sorts, the most familiar of which is the sort exhibited in "love-above" and "corn-forlorn." Unrhymed verse is called blank verse, but *blank verse* usually implies unrhymed lines of ten syllables, with the even-numbered syllables stressed, because this meter predominates in the plays of Shakespeare and many other famous poems.

But not all verse is poetry. For we do not call it poetry unless it involves some sustained multiple meaning. A verse that is a simple direct statement:

> Simple Simon met a pieman
>      Going to the Fair.
> Said Simple Simon to the pieman,
>      "Let me taste your ware,"

is not yet poetry; it is metrical fiction. But when, however simple the verse-pattern may be, there is metaphor or simile, or a pervasive irony, or an emergent theme that is carried by the imagery, then there is poetry. Even in the first verse of "Frankie and Johnny," there is a simile ("as true as the stars above"), a pungent colloquialism with a good deal of meaning ("He was her man"), and a sudden and dramatic shift ("but he done her wrong") that warns us from the beginning what the theme will be. If by some twist we could turn Simple Simon into a symbol of the Common Man faced with the stern economic doctrine of *caveat emptor,* we should give this verse another level of meaning, and that would make it a poem, though not necessarily a good one.

Poetry, then, is fairly concentrated verse, verse rich in meanings. To say much more about it than that we must make further subdivisions. Let us consider *lyric poetry, narrative poetry, reflective poetry*.

The lyric poem, of which "Spring and Fall" is an example, is distinguished by two features that go together. First, its situation is a state of affairs, or a momentarily arrested stage of some event. It does not tell a story, though a story may be implicit in the situation; for example, in "Ozymandias" there is a long history presupposed in the destruction of the statue. In "Dead Boy" the speaker confronts the fact of a boy's death; in "The Windhover" the speaker confronts the flight of a falcon. Second, though the lyric poem may include sentences in the past tense, as "The Windhover" does, or the present tense, as "The Second Coming" does, or may be largely questions and imperatives, like some of Donne's Holy Sonnets, yet essentially it is tenseless. It does not recreate a past as a story does, or aim at a future, like drama; it is a timeless confrontation, and when the word "is" occurs in it, it has something like the tenseless meaning it has in a mathematical statement: "2 is the square root of 4" does not mean now, today, as opposed to yesterday or tomorrow.

The narrative poem, such as "Frankie and Johnny," "Michael," or "Sir Patrick Spens," tells a story in verse. The questions that can be asked of prose fiction, about its point of view and setting and climax, can also be asked of narrative poetry.

The reflective poem, such as "September 1, 1939" or "The Spacious Firmament on High," is a kind of essay in verse. Most lyric poems, of course, contain some hint of reflection, for the speaker is interested in the possible general meaning of the object he is thinking of. Even a slight lyric like "Upon Julia's Clothes" may have just a hint of a general thesis. But we may distinguish reflective poetry by the predominance of the general ideas in it. Auden, for example, is not concerned merely to present the fact of the war's beginning, or to tell the story of it, but to explain it to himself, and Addison's poem is one version of a famous argument for the existence of God.[5]

## THE THEMATIC METHOD

There are several ways of studying literature. You can, for one, study it in chronological sequence, from *Beowulf* to *The Age of Anxiety;* in short, as literary history. Such a beginning would be difficult for the inexperienced reader; to get the most out of literary history, one ought first to study the primary modes of literature and the formal principles of design that they exhibit. But this second method—studying short stories, then essays, then poems, and so forth—is not, we believe, the best beginning either, for the human significance of those formal aspects of the work lies not in themselves but in the subjects they shape and the themes they embody and define.

### THE VALUES OF LITERATURE

The ultimate purpose of learning to read literature is to take possession of what is uniquely valuable in it, what literature is good for, and can do, that nothing else can do, or do so well. To define the special function of literature, to establish its human worth, would require more than a general introduction, which is supposed to lead on to the works themselves, with as little preliminary as is needed. But there are two fundamental values of literature that can be securely defended.

First, a literary work can evoke a complete, ordered, unified, and therefore inherently satisfying experience. This value it shares with the other arts, for a musical composition or a painting can also yield the sort of experience that we think of as "an experience." But though in some respects literature is weaker than the other arts, its resources of sound and multiple meaning, of emotional appeal and logical argument, of story and description make it capable of ranging over the whole of human thought, action, and feeling. Hence, the sort of experience that it can create may be far more complicated and profound than that afforded by any other art. The experience of reading a poem, for instance, does not come merely from recognizing that the words form a poem, or that they are about love, or are arranged in fourteen lines. No ticking off and labeling of any abstracted element or aspect of the poem is enough: it is the poem as a whole that creates the experience.

[5] For further discussion of poetry, see page 700.

Second, literature gives us insights into ourselves and our life and helps us to understand them. Not that poems, stories, and plays are capable of proving the insights they propose, but the insights are there to be tested in our own experience. They enlarge the scope of our experience of human nature. They can sharpen our perception of human motives and our discrimination between subtly different human feelings, and in this way make us capable of understanding ourselves better, by our own efforts, even when the literary work contains no abstract propositions that we can call knowledge.

The question is, then, how to study literature so as to realize these values most readily and most fully.

In order to give us its potential value, a literary work must act upon us with all its force. But it does not act like aspirin or Benzedrine, which have an effect upon you whether or not you know anything about chemistry. A literary work acts through the mind and the feelings; it acts by means of the understanding that you bring to it, and it requires a certain friendliness and affection if it is to do its best. It won't work completely unless you know something about the way it works.

Thus, appreciation cannot be wholly separated from understanding. To get the most from a short story, a poem, an essay, or a play, you must ask certain questions about it, at least in your own mind, and try to think out the answers, preferably with the help of others with whom you can discuss them. What is going on? What sort of speaker is involved, and what is his point of view and tone? What is the theme, and the thesis, if any? What is the literary mode, and what sorts of texture and structure help to hold the work together? These lead to other and more searching questions about the connections among the various aspects of the work: How do the details of language and setting and character help to define the theme? How does the theme emerge from the structure? What are the different ranges of potential meaning possible to literature in the different modes?

## THE PLAN OF THIS BOOK

Comparison is the great tool for analyzing literature, and for answering such questions as these; that is, making explicit the significant similarities and differences among literary works. Some light can be thrown on one work by comparing it with almost any other, but illuminating comparison requires that the things compared be similar in some respects, so that their differences are set off by contrast. Some characteristics of a literary work are highlighted most clearly by comparison with other works having similar formal features: a lyric with a lyric, an oration with an oration, a short story with a short story. Some characteristics show up most clearly when a work is compared with another that is nearly contemporary, some when it is compared with other works by the same author, or by another author of the same country.

All these comparisons may be employed to throw all possible light upon a particular work. But they should be made in the order that brings us most quickly to a comprehensive grasp of all its important aspects. What first strikes us, as a kind of solid center, and what is most likely to make one work remind us of another, is its central situation: its concern with childhood, or beauty, or love. It is this consideration that has led to the organization that we have adopted.

The selections in each chapter—essays, stories, poems, and in some chapters, a play—

are grouped together because they have the same or a similar subject, and a group of related themes that grow out of reflection upon that subject. One chapter deals with people in love, another with the experience of war, another with the arts. We suggest that the selections in each chapter be read and discussed together. A careful considera- tion of the similarities and differences in their treatment of the subject and their develop- ment of the themes will lead into discussion of the significant aspects of structure and texture that mould the subject and carry the themes. And the discussion of literary form can, if desired, be made the occasion for excursions into the history of literary modes. This way of gaining access to the selections may be called, for the sake of abbreviation, the thematic method of studying literature.

There has been no attempt to force literary works into arbitrarily defined categories: it will easily be seen that the situations that unify each chapter are subjects often dealt with in literature. Even less do we advocate a limited view of each work. If *Othello* is placed in the chapter on the experience of evil, it is because that seems to us a fruitful way of considering it, though it is also of course about love and about war, and might also be profitably studied with the selections in those chapters. Nor do we insist that the contents be read in a particular order, though the modes are kept distinct within each chapter; the easiest of the essays are put first, and so with the stories and the poems. The order of chapters is equally discretionary. In general, the themes become more complex and the writings more profound as the book moves on; the plays occur in the natural order of study, from the most accessible to the least.

Comparison of two short stories with a similar theme, such as "The Girl in Arles" and "Mateo Falcone," exposes the differences in the way the theme is worked out, and certain facts about the nature of the short story and its range of capacities also emerge. When a short story and a poem having a similar theme are compared, such as "A Hunger- Artist" and "Fra Lippo Lippi," the essential differences between stories and poems be- come clear. And reading a few essays—for example, those on the nature of evil—that deal with a subject in an abstract way, leads to a better grasp of the themes and theses that are implicit in stories and poems having the same subject.

For students and instructors who may prefer to consider these works in some other order—to deal with themes or formal patterns that we have not emphasized—we have provided an alternate table of contents in which the modes are grouped together. Indeed, we would urge the reader to experiment with various combinations, looking for illumi- nating comparisons that have not occurred to the editors. But whatever order he follows, it is our hope that the reader will terminate his study of this book with a strong sense of the unity of literature—the deep identity of substance, power, and worth that underlies all the differences.

We believe that the thematic method of study will give the greatest enjoyment from the selections in this book. We believe that it will endow the reader with a better under- standing of both the familiar masterpieces and the newer, contemporary works that are here. And we hope that through his increased understanding and enjoyment of these works, he will be better enabled to make literature one of his permanent possessions.

# THEME AND FORM

THEME AND FORM

# C H A P T E R   O N E

## EARLY YEARS

SOME ESSAYS, stories, and poems impress the reader as being very nearly reports of incidents that the authors either underwent themselves or heard about from others. But however strong this impression may be, it is a fact that when life becomes literature it is profoundly changed. The selections in this chapter, which focus on the experiences of childhood and youth, show the raw materials at various stages of transformation. Some of them (for example, Coleridge's letter and the chapter from Mark Twain's *Life on the Mississippi*) appear to be describing actual events, though pointing them up and giving them more meaning than they may have had for participants or spectators at the time. In others, the material is entirely reshaped and reordered: the sense of autobiography is almost absent from "Her First Ball" and "Blackberry Winter"; their incidents are so self-contained and so completely organized as imaginative literature that it hardly occurs to us to wonder whether Katherine Mansfield actually knew such a girl as Leila, or whether Robert Penn Warren ever met a tramp resembling the stranger in the story.

Nevertheless, as works of literature they do not lose their connection with life. On various levels of profundity, the writers are exploring perennial attitudes of youth toward the adult world (as in "Blackberry Winter" and "Gentlemen-Rankers") and of the adult toward his own lost childhood. The adult may search his memory to explain himself scientifically (as Freud does in "Childhood and Concealing Memories") or to make clearer to himself what it means to grow into the responsibilities and restrictions of adulthood (as do the speakers in "Birches," "The Retreat," and "Fern Hill").

1

The works in this chapter, then, invite discussion of an important question: how do real life, reporting, and literature differ from one another? Even if the reader does not finish this chapter with the conviction that he can answer this question satisfactorily, some wrestling with its complexities will help him understand the special values that such literary works as these have for him as an individual. Sometimes they may take his breath away by their likeness to his own experience. Sometimes they may engage his interest precisely by their strangeness to his own experience. Sometimes it may be a combination of the two that makes them worth reading, and that makes them memorable after they have been read.

*Wolcott Gibbs*

# RING OUT, WILD BELLS

When I finally got around to seeing Max Reinhardt's cinema version of "A Midsummer-Night's Dream," and saw a child called Mickey Rooney playing Puck, I remembered suddenly that long ago I had taken the same part.

Our production was given on the open-air stage at the Riverdale Country School, shortly before the war. The scenery was only the natural scenery of that suburban dell, and the cast was exclusively male, ranging in age from eleven to perhaps seventeen. While we had thus preserved the pure, Elizabethan note of the original, it must be admitted that our version had its drawbacks. The costumes were probably the worst things we had to bear, and even Penrod, tragically arrayed as Launcelot in his sister's stockings and his father's drawers, might have been embarrassed for us. Like Penrod, we were costumed by our parents, and like the Schofields, they seemed on the whole a little weak historically. Half of the ladies were inclined to favor the Elizabethan, and they had constructed rather bunchy ruffs and farthingales for their offspring; others, who had read as far as the stage directions and learned that the action took place in an Athenian wood, had produced something vaguely Athenian, usually beginning with a sheet. Only the fairies had a certain uniformity. For some reason their parents had all decided on cheesecloth, with here and there a little ill-advised trimming with tinsel.

My own costume was mysterious, but spectacular. As nearly as I have ever been able to figure things out, my mother found her inspiration for it in a Maxfield Parrish picture of a court jester. Beginning at the top, there was a cap with three stuffed horns; then, for the main part, a pair of tights that covered me to my wrists and ankles; and finally slippers with stuffed toes that curled up at the ends. The whole thing was made out of silk in alternate green and red stripes, and (unquestionably my poor mother's most demented stroke) it was covered from head to foot with a thousand tiny bells. Because all our costumes were obviously perishable, we never wore them in rehearsal, and naturally nobody knew that I was invested with these peculiar sound effects until I made my entrance at the beginning of the second act.

Our director was a man who had strong opinions about how Shakespeare should be played, and Puck was one of his favorite characters. It was his theory that Puck, being "the incarnation of mischief," never ought to be still a minute, so I had been coached to bound onto the stage, and once there to dance up and down, cocking my head and waving my arms.

"I want you to be a little whirlwind," this man said.

Even as I prepared to bound onto the stage, I had my own misgivings about those dangerously abundant gestures, and their probable effect on my bells. It was too late, however, to invent another technique for playing Puck, even if there had been room for anything but horror in my mind. I bounded onto the stage.

The effect, in its way, must have been superb. With every leap I rang like a thousand children's sleighs, my melodies foretelling God knows what worlds of merriment to the enchanted spectators. It was even worse when I came to the middle of the stage and went into my gestures. The other ringing had been loud but sporadic. This was persistent, varying only slightly in volume and pitch with the vehemence of my gestures. To a blind man, it must have sounded as though I had recklessly decided to accompany myself on a xylophone. A maturer actor would probably have made up his mind that an emergency existed, and abandoned his gestures as impracticable under the circumstances. I was thirteen, and incapable of innovations. I had been told by responsible authorities that gestures went with this part, and I continued to make them. I also continued to ring—a silvery music, festive and horrible.

If the bells were hard on my nerves, they were even worse for the rest of the cast, who were totally unprepared for my new interpretation. Puck's first remark is addressed to one of the fairies, and it is mercifully brief.

I said, "How now, spirit! Whither wander you?"

This unhappy child, already embarrassed by a public appearance in cheesecloth and tinsel, was also burdened with an opening speech of sixteen lines in verse. He began bravely:

> Over hill, over dale,
> Thorough bush, thorough brier,
> Over park, over pale,
> Thorough flood, thorough fire . . .

At the word "fire," my instructions were to bring my hands up from the ground in a long, wavery sweep, intended to represent fire. The bells pealed. To my startled ears, it sounded more as if they exploded. The fairy stopped in his lines and looked at me sharply. The jingling, however, had diminished; it was no more than as if a faint wind stirred my bells, and he went on:

> I do wander every where,
> Swifter than the moone's sphere . . .

Here again I had another cue, for a sort of swoop and dip indicating the swiftness of the moone's sphere. Again the bells rang out, and again the performance stopped in its tracks. The fairy was clearly troubled by these interruptions. He had, however, a child's strange acceptance of the inscrutable, and was even able to regard my bells as a last-minute adult addition to the program, nerve-racking but not to be questioned. I'm sure it was only this that got him through that first speech.

My turn, when it came, was even worse. By this time the audience had succumbed to a helpless gaiety. Every time my bells rang, laughter swept the spectators, and this mounted and mingled with the bells until everything else was practically inaudible. I began my speech, another long one, and full of incomprehensible references to Titania's changeling.

"Louder!" said somebody in the wings. "You'll have to talk louder."

It was the director, and he seemed to be in a dangerous state.

"And for heaven's sake, stop that jingling!" he said.

I talked louder, and I tried to stop the jingling, but it was no use. By the time I got to the end of my speech, I was shouting and so was the audience. It appeared that I had very little control over the bells, which continued to jingle in spite of my passionate efforts to keep them quiet.

All this had a very bad effect on the fairy, who by this time had many symptoms of a complete nervous collapse. However, he began his next speech:

> Either I mistake your shape and making quite,
> Or else you are that shrewd and knavish sprite
> Call'd Robin Goodfellow: are you not he
> That . . .

At this point I forgot that the rules had been changed and I was supposed to leave out the gestures. There was a furious jingling, and the fairy gulped.

"Are you not he that, that . . ."

He looked miserably at the wings, and the director supplied the next line, but the tumult was too much for him. The unhappy child simply shook his head.

"Say anything!" shouted the director desperately. "Anything at all!"

The fairy only shut his eyes and shuddered.

"All right!" shouted the director. "All right, Puck. *You* begin *your* next speech."

By some miracle, I actually did remember my next lines, and had opened my mouth to begin on them when suddenly the fairy spoke. His voice was a high, thin monotone, and there seemed to be madness in it, but it was perfectly clear.

"Fourscore and seven years ago," he began, "our fathers brought forth on this continent a new nation, conceived . . ."

He said it right through to the end, and it was certainly the most successful speech ever made on that stage, and probably one of the most successful speeches ever made on any stage. I don't remember, if I ever knew, how the rest of us ever picked up the dull, normal thread of the play after that extraordinary performance, but we must have, because I know it went on. I only remember that in the next intermission the director cut off my bells with his penknife, and after that things quieted down and got dull.

*Clarence Day*

# FATHER INTERFERES WITH THE TWENTY-THIRD PSALM

When we boys were little, we used to go to Mother's room Sunday evenings, on our way upstairs to bed, and sit in a circle around her, while she told us a story from the Bible or talked to us about how good we ought to be and how much we ought to love God. She loved God herself as much as she dared to, and she deeply loved us, and she was especially tender and dear on those Sunday evenings. One of my brothers told me years afterward how much they had meant to him in those days, and how he had cherished the memory of them all his life.

I was a little older than my brothers, though, and my feelings were mixed. I loved Mother and hated to disappoint her, but I couldn't respond as easily as the other boys to her gentle appeals. I never seemed to have the emotions that she waited for me to show. I wish now that I could have listened uncritically and have thought only of the look in her eyes. What difference need it have made to me whether we had the same ideas about God, or whether the stories Mother thought lovely seemed less so to me? But there I sat, staring uncomfortably at the carpet and trying to avoid answering questions.

One night she repeated the Twenty-third Psalm to us and asked us to learn it by heart.

FATHER INTERFERES WITH THE TWENTY-THIRD PSALM: From *Life with Father*, by Clarence Day. Copyright, 1935, by Clarence Day. Used by permission of Alfred A. Knopf, Inc.

"The Lord is my shepherd," she whispered softly. "He maketh me to lie down in green pastures: he leadeth me beside the still waters." She raised her eyes and went on bravely, although with a quiver of fear: "Thy rod and thy staff they comfort me." She had often felt the Lord's rod.

I heard Father going by in the hall. He looked in at the doorway and smiled affectionately at us and at Mother. Then he went off, and I heard his firm step as he walked on toward his room.

He hadn't meant to interfere with Mother's teachings. He hadn't spoken one word. But I found myself speculating all of a sudden on what his opinion would be of the Twenty-third Psalm.

I couldn't imagine Father being comforted by the Lord's rod and staff, or allowing anybody whatever to lead him to a pasture and get him to lie down somewhere in it. I could see him in my mind's eye, in his tailed coat and top hat, refusing point-blank even to enter a pasture. He would as soon have thought of wearing overalls. In spite of my admiring him for this attitude, it seemed wicked of him. I felt resentful about it. It would have been so much easier for me to be properly reverent if he had not been around. My idea was that if Mother was too religious, Father wasn't religious enough.

"Good night, Clarence," I heard Mother saying. "You won't forget, darling?"

I kissed her and went out, wondering what I was not to forget. Oh, yes—she had asked us to learn that psalm by heart.

Up in my bedroom, I got out my Bible. It was full of paper bookmarks, to help me find texts that I'd had to memorize, and these bookmarks in turn were full of pictures I had drawn of Biblical scenes. A picture of Adam looking doubtfully at the Tree of Knowledge in Eden, with a complete set of school books dangling heavily down from its boughs. A picture of Sarah "dealing hardly with Hagar," driving her out with a broomstick. A picture of the sun, moon, and stars bowing politely to Joseph.

I sat down and added to the collection a picture of Job in pajamas, weeping copiously as he endeavored, on top of all his other trials, to learn the Twenty-third Psalm. I also drew his three unsatisfactory friends, sitting in a row staring at Job. Each friend wore a sardonic expression and had a large mustache and imperial like Napoleon the Third.

I got out another Bible that Mother had lent me. This one was in French, and it sometimes shocked me deeply to read it. As my belief was that when God had created the world He had said, "Let there be light," it seemed to me highly irreverent to put French words in His mouth and have Him exclaim, *"Que la lumière soit!"* Imagine the Lord talking French! Aside from a few odd words in Hebrew, I took it completely for granted that God had never spoken anything but the most dignified English.

The French were notoriously godless, however. It made me laugh, though it frightened me, too, to see what liberties they had taken. In my English Bible, David was a fine Anglo-Saxon type, "a youth, ruddy and of a fair countenance." In the French, he was a revolting little snip from the boulevards, *"un enfant, blond, et d'une belle figure."* Where my Bible spoke of "leviathan," the French said *"le crocodile,"* which ruined the grandeur and mystery of that famous beast. And where mine said, "Behold now behemoth," they said, *"Voici l'hippopotame!"*

Instead of the children of Israel fearing lest the Lord should be wroth, the French said *"les enfants d'Israel"* were afraid lest *"le Seigneur"* should be *"irrité."* This word *"irrité"* appeared everywhere in the French version. It wasn't only the Lord. Cain was *"très irrité."* Moise (which seemed to me a very jaunty way of referring to Moses) was *"irrité"* again and again. Everybody was *"irrité."* When my regular Bible, the real one, impressively described men as "wroth," their anger seemed to have something stately and solemn about it. If they were full of mere irritation all the time, they were more like the Day family.

I turned at last to the Twenty-third Psalm. They had spoiled that, too. They had twisted it around until it read as though the scene were in Paris. "Green pastures" were changed into *"parcs herbeux,"* and "thy rod and thy staff" had become *"ton bâton,"* as though the Lord were leading David up and down the Bois de Boulogne like a drum major.

I decided to go to bed and let that psalm wait for a day or two. But before putting the books back on my shelf, I hunted up the one place in the French Bible that I really liked. "Blessed are the meek," my English Bible said,

"for they shall inherit the earth." I had always hated that verse. It made all religion so difficult. Uriah Heep typified the meek, to my mind. The meek were a snivelling, despicable, and uncomfortable lot. But in poring over the French Bible one evening, I had found to my delight that some daring Frenchman had altered this passage, and had changed the Sermon on the Mount into something that a fellow could stand. *"Heureux les débonnaires,"* he had represented Jesus as saying, *"car ils hériteront de la terre."*

The debonair! That was more like it! I cheerfully jumped into bed.

## Samuel Taylor Coleridge
# LETTER TO THOMAS POOLE

October 16, 1797.

DEAR POOLE,—From October, 1779, to October, 1781. I had asked my mother one evening to cut my cheese entire, so that I might toast it. This was no easy matter, it being a crumbly cheese. My mother, however, did it. I went into the garden for something or other, and in the mean time my brother Frank minced my cheese "to disappoint the favorite." I returned, saw the exploit, and in an agony of passion flew at Frank. He pretended to have been seriously hurt by my blow, flung himself on the ground, and there lay with outstretched limbs. I hung over him moaning, and in a great fright; he leaped up, and with a horse-laugh gave me a severe blow in the face. I seized a knife, and was running at him, when my mother came in and took me by the arm. I expected a flogging, and struggling from her I ran away to a hill at the bottom of which the Otter flows, about one mile from Ottery. There I stayed; my rage died away, but my obstinacy vanquished my fears, and taking out a little shilling book which had, at the end, morning and evening prayers, I very devoutly repeated them—thinking at the same time with inward and gloomy satisfaction how miserable my mother must be! I distinctly remember my feelings when I saw a Mr. Vaughan pass over the bridge, at about a furlong's distance, and how I watched the calves in the fields beyond the river. It grew dark and I fell asleep. It was towards the latter end of October, and it proved a dreadful stormy night. I felt the cold in my sleep, and dreamt that I was pulling the blanket over me, and actually pulled over me a dry thorn bush which lay on the hill. In my sleep I had rolled from the top of the hill to within three yards of the river, which flowed by the unfenced edge at the bottom. I awoke several times, and finding myself wet and stiff and cold, closed my eyes again that I might forget it.

In the mean time my mother waited about half an hour, expecting my return when the sulks had evaporated. I not returning, she sent into the churchyard and round the town. Not found! Several men and all the boys were sent to ramble about and seek me. In vain! My mother was almost distracted; and at ten o'clock at night I was cried by the crier in Ottery, and in two villages near it, with a reward offered for me. No one went to bed; indeed, I believe half the town were up all the night. To return to myself. About five in the morning, or a little after, I was broad awake, and attempted to get up and walk; but I could not move. I saw the shepherds and workmen at a distance, and cried, but so faintly that it was impossible to hear me thirty yards off. And there I might have lain and died; for I was now almost given over, the ponds and even the river, near where I was lying, having been dragged. But by good luck, Sir Stafford Northcote, who had been out all night, resolved to make one other trial, and came so near that he heard me crying. He carried me in his arms for near a quarter of a mile, when we met my father and Sir Stafford's servants. I remember and never shall forget my father's face as he looked upon me while I lay in the servant's arms—so calm, and the tears stealing down his face; for I was the child of his old age. My mother, as you may suppose, was outrageous with joy. [Meantime] in rushed a young lady, crying out, "I hope you'll whip him, Mrs. Coleridge!" This woman still lives in Ottery; and neither philosophy or religion have been able to conquer the antipathy which I feel towards her whenever I see her. I was put to bed and recovered in a day or so, but I was certainly injured. For I was weakly and subject to the ague for many years after.

My father (who had so little of parental ambition in him, that he had destined his children

to be blacksmiths, etc., and had accomplished his intention but for my mother's pride and spirit of aggrandizing her family)—my father had, however, resolved that I should be a parson. I read every book that came in my way without distinction; and my father was fond of me, and used to take me on his knee and hold long conversations with me. I remember that at eight years old I walked with him one winter evening from a farmer's house, a mile from Ottery, and he told me the names of the stars and how Jupiter was a thousand times larger than our world, and that the other twinkling stars were suns that had worlds rolling round them; and when I came home he shewed me how they rolled round. I heard him with a profound delight and admiration: but without the least mixture of wonder or incredulity. For from my early reading of fairy tales and genii, etc., etc., my mind had been habituated to the Vast, and I never regarded my senses in any way as the criteria of my belief. I regulated all my creeds by my conceptions, not by my sight, even at that age. Should children be permitted to read romances, and relations of giants and magicians and genii? I know all that has been said against it; but I have formed my faith in the affirmative. I know no other way of giving the mind a love of the Great and the Whole. Those who have been led to the same truths step by step, through the constant testimony of their senses, seem to me to want a sense which I possess. They contemplate nothing but parts, and all parts are necessarily little. And the universe to them is but a mass of little things. It is true, that the mind may become credulous and prone to superstition by the former method; but are not the experimentalists credulous even to madness in believing any absurdity, rather than believe the grandest truths, if they have not the testimony of their own senses in their favour? I have known some who have been rationally educated, as it is styled. They were marked by a microscopic acuteness, but when they looked at great things, all became a blank and they saw nothing, and denied (very illogically) that anything could be seen, and uniformly put the negation of a power for the possession of a power, and called the want of imagination judgment and the never being moved to rapture philosophy!

Towards the latter end of September, 1781, my father went to Plymouth with my brother

Francis, who was to go as midshipman under Admiral Graves, who was a friend of my father's. My father settled my brother, and returned October 4, 1781. He arrived at Exeter about six o'clock, and was pressed to take a bed there at the Harts', but he refused, and, to avoid their entreaties, he told them, that he had never been superstitious, but that the night before he had had a dream which had made a deep impression. He dreamt that Death had appeared to him as he is commonly painted, and touched him with his dart. Well, he returned home, and all his family, I excepted, were up. He told my mother his dream; but he was in high health and good spirits, and there was a bowl of punch made, and my father gave a long and particular account of his travel, and that he had placed Frank under a religious captain, etc. At length he went to bed, very well and in high spirits. A short time after he had lain down he complained of a pain in his bowels. My mother got him some peppermint water, and, after a pause, he said, "I am much better now, my dear!" and lay down again. In a minute my mother heard a noise in his throat, and spoke to him, but he did not answer; and she spoke repeatedly in vain. Her shriek awaked me, and I said, "Papa is dead!" I did not know of my father's return, but I knew that he was expected. How I came to think of his death I cannot tell; but so it was. Dead he was. Some said it was the gout in the heart;—probably it was a fit of apoplexy. He was an Israelite without guile, simple, generous, and taking some Scripture texts in their literal sense, he was conscientiously indifferent to the good and the evil of this world.

God love you and

S. T. COLERIDGE

*Mark Twain*

# I TAKE A FEW EXTRA LESSONS

During the two or two and a half years of my apprenticeship I served under many

I TAKE A FEW EXTRA LESSONS: From *Life on the Mississippi*, 1875, 1883, by Mark Twain. Used by permission of Harper and Brothers.

pilots, and had experience of many kinds of steamboatmen and many varieties of steamboats; for it was not always convenient for Mr. Bixby to have me with him, and in such cases he sent me with somebody else. I am to this day profiting somewhat by that experience; for in that brief, sharp schooling, I got personally and familiarly acquainted with about all the different types of human nature that are to be found in fiction, biography, or history. The fact is daily borne in upon me that the average shore-employment requires as much as forty years to equip a man with this sort of an education. When I say I am still profiting by this thing, I do not mean that it has constituted me a judge of men—no, it has not done that, for judges of men are born, not made. My profit is various in kind and degree, but the feature of it which I value most is the zest which that early experience has given to my later reading. When I find a well-drawn character in fiction or biography I generally take a warm personal interest in him, for the reason that I have known him before—met him on the river.

The figure that comes before me oftenest, out of the shadows of that vanished time, is that of Brown, of the steamer *Pennsylvania*—the man referred to in a former chapter, whose memory was so good and tiresome. He was a middle-aged, long, slim, bony, smooth-shaven, horse-faced, ignorant, stingy, malicious, snarling, fault-hunting, mote-magnifying tyrant. I early got the habit of coming on watch with dread at my heart. No matter how good a time I might have been having with the off-watch below, and no matter how high my spirits might be when I started aloft, my soul became lead in my body the moment I approached the pilot-house.

I still remember the first time I ever entered the presence of that man. The boat had backed out from St. Louis and was "straightening down." I ascended to the pilot-house in high feather, and very proud to be semi-officially a member of the executive family of so fast and famous a boat. Brown was at the wheel. I paused in the middle of the room, all fixed to make my bow, but Brown did not look around. I thought he took a furtive glance at me out of the corner of his eye, but as not even this notice was repeated, I judged I had been mistaken. By this time he was picking his way among some dangerous "breaks" abreast the woodyards; therefore it would not be proper to interrupt him; so I stepped softly to the high bench and took a seat.

There was silence for ten minutes; then my new boss turned and inspected me deliberately and painstakingly from head to heel for about —as it seemed to me—a quarter of an hour. After which he removed his countenance and I saw it no more for some seconds; then it came around once more, and this question greeted me:

"Are you Horace Bigsby's cub?"

"Yes, sir."

After this there was a pause and another inspection. Then:

"What's your name?"

I told him. He repeated it after me. It was probably the only thing he ever forgot; for although I was with him many months he never addressed himself to me in any other way than "Here!" and then his command followed.

"Where was you born?"

"In Florida, Missouri."

A pause. Then:

"Dern sight better stayed there!"

By means of a dozen or so of pretty direct questions, he pumped my family history out of me.

The leads were going now in the first crossing. This interrupted the inquest. When the leads had been laid in he resumed:

"How long you been on the river?"

I told him. After a pause:

"Where'd you get them shoes?"

I gave him the information.

"Hold up your foot!"

I did so. He stepped back, examined the shoe minutely and contemptuously, scratching his head thoughtfully, tilting his high sugar-loaf hat well forward to facilitate the operation, then ejaculated, "Well, I'll be dod derned!" and returned to his wheel.

What occasion there was to be dod derned about it is a thing which is still as much of a mystery to me now as it was then. It must have been all of fifteen minutes—fifteen minutes of dull, homesick silence—before that long horse-face swung round upon me again—and then what a change! It was as red as fire, and every muscle in it was working. Now came this shriek:

"Here! You going to set there all day?"

I lit in the middle of the floor, shot there by the electric suddenness of the surprise. As soon as I could get my voice I said apologetically: "I have had no orders, sir."

"You've had no *orders!* My, what a fine bird we are! We must have *orders!* Our father was a *gentleman*—owned slaves—and *we've* been to *school.* Yes, *we* are a gentleman, *too,* and got to have *orders!* ORDERS, is it? ORDERS is what you want! Dod dern my skin, *I'll* learn you to swell yourself up and blow around *here* about your dod-derned *orders!* G'way from the wheel!" (I had approached it without knowing it.)

I moved back a step or two and stood as in a dream, all my senses stupefied by this frantic assault.

"What you standing there for? Take that ice-pitcher down to the texas-tender! Come, move along, and don't you be all day about it!"

The moment I got back to the pilot-house Brown said:

"Here! What was you doing down there all this time?"

"I couldn't find the texas-tender; I had to go all the way to the pantry."

"Derned likely story! Fill up the stove."

I proceeded to do so. He watched me like a cat. Presently he shouted:

"Put down that shovel! Derndest numskull I ever saw—ain't even got sense enough to load up a stove."

All through the watch this sort of thing went on. Yes, and the subsequent watches were much like it during a stretch of months. As I have said, I soon got the habit of coming on duty with dread. The moment I was in the presence, even in the darkest night, I could feel those yellow eyes upon me, and knew their owner was watching for a pretext to spit out some venom on me. Preliminarily he would say:

"Here! Take the wheel."

Two minutes later:

"*Where* in the nation you going to? Pull her down! pull her down!"

After another moment:

"Say! You going to hold her all day? Let her go—meet her! meet her!"

Then he would jump from the bench, snatch the wheel from me, and meet her himself, pouring out wrath upon me all the time.

George Ritchie was the other pilot's cub. He was having good times now; for his boss, George Ealer, was as kind-hearted as Brown wasn't. Ritchie had steered for Brown the season before; consequently, he knew exactly how to entertain himself and plague me, all by the one operation. Whenever I took the wheel for a moment on Ealer's watch, Ritchie would sit back on the bench and play Brown, with continual ejaculations of "Snatch her! snatch her! Derndest mud-cat I ever saw!" "Here! Where are you going *now*? Going to run over that snag?" "Pull her *down!* Don't you hear me? Pull her *down!*" "There she goes! *Just* as I expected! I *told* you not to cramp that reef. G'way from the wheel!"

So I always had a rough time of it, no matter whose watch it was; and sometimes it seemed to me that Ritchie's good-natured badgering was pretty nearly as aggravating as Brown's dead-earnest nagging.

I often wanted to kill Brown, but this would not answer. A cub had to take everything his boss gave, in the way of vigorous comment and criticism; and we all believed that there was a United States law making it a penitentiary offense to strike or threaten a pilot who was on duty. However, I could *imagine* myself killing Brown; there was no law against that; and that was the thing I used always to do the moment I was abed. Instead of going over my river in my mind, as was my duty, I threw business aside for pleasure, and killed Brown. I killed Brown every night for months; not in old, stale, commonplace ways, but in new and picturesque ones—ways that were sometimes surprising for freshness of design and ghastliness of situation and environment.

Brown was *always* watching for a pretext to find fault; and if he could find no plausible pretext, he would invent one. He would scold you for shaving a shore, and for not shaving it; for hugging a bar, and for not hugging it; for "pulling down" when not invited, and for *not* pulling down when not invited; for firing up without orders, and for waiting *for* orders. In a word, it was his invariable rule to find fault with *everything* you did; and another invariable rule of his was to throw all his remarks (to you) into the form of an insult.

One day we were approaching New Madrid, bound down and heavily laden. Brown was at one side of the wheel, steering; I was at the other, standing by to "pull down" or "shove up." He cast a furtive glance at me every now and then. I had long ago learned what that meant; viz., he was trying to invent a trap for me. I wondered what shape it was going to take. By and by he stepped back from the wheel and said in his usual snarly way:

"Here! See if you've got gumption enough to round her to."

This was simply *bound* to be a success; nothing could prevent it; for he had never allowed me to round the boat to before; consequently, no matter how I might do the thing, he could find free fault with it. He stood back there with his greedy eye on me, and the result was what might have been foreseen: I lost my head in a quarter of a minute, and didn't know what I was about; I started too early to bring the boat around, but detected a green gleam of joy in Brown's eye, and corrected my mistake. I started around once more while too high up, but corrected myself again in time. I made other false moves, and still managed to save myself; but at last I grew so confused and anxious that I tumbled into the very worst blunder of all—I got too far *down* before beginning to fetch the boat around. Brown's chance was come.

His face turned red with passion; he made one bound, hurled me across the house with a sweep of his arm, spun the wheel down, and began to pour out a stream of vituperation upon me which lasted till he was out of breath. In the course of this speech he called me all the different kinds of hard names he could think of, and once or twice I thought he was even going to swear—but he had never done that, and he didn't this time. "Dod dern" was the nearest he ventured to the luxury of swearing, for he had been brought up with a wholesome respect for future fire and brimstone.

That was an uncomfortable hour; for there was a big audience on the hurricane-deck. When I went to bed that night, I killed Brown in seventeen different ways—all of them new.

## *Sigmund Freud*
## CHILDHOOD AND CONCEALING MEMORIES

I started with the remarkable fact that the earliest recollections of a person often seemed to preserve the unimportant and accidental, whereas (frequently though not universally) not a trace is found in the adult memory of the weighty and affective impressions of this period. As it is known that the memory exercises a certain selection among the impressions at its disposal, it would seem logical to suppose that this selection follows entirely different principles in childhood than at the time of intellectual maturity. However, close investigation points to the fact that such an assumption is superfluous. The indifferent childhood memories owe their existence to a process of displacement. It may be shown by psychoanalysis that in the reproduction they represent the substitute for other really significant impressions, whose direct reproduction is hindered by some resistance. As they do not owe their existence to their own contents, but to an associative relation of their contents to another repressed thought, they deserve the title of "concealing memories," by which I have designated them. . . .

How far back into childhood do our memories reach? I am familiar with some investigations on this question by V. and C. Henri and Potwin. They assert that such examinations show wide individual variations, inasmuch as some trace their reminiscences to the sixth month of life, while others can recall nothing of their lives before the end of the sixth or even the eighth year. But what connection is there between these variations in the behavior of childhood reminiscences, and what signification may be ascribed to them? It seems that it is

CHILDHOOD AND CONCEALING MEMORIES: From *Psychopathology of Everyday Life,* by Sigmund Freud. English Translation by A. A. Brill, 1914. Used by permission of The Macmillan Company and Ernest Benn, Ltd.

not enough to procure the material for this question by simple inquiry, but it must later be subjected to a study in which the person furnishing the information must participate.

I believe we accept too indifferently the fact of infantile amnesia—that is, the failure of memory for the first years of our lives—and fail to find in it a strange riddle. We forget of what great intellectual accomplishments and of what complicated emotions a child of four years is capable. We really ought to wonder why the memory of later years has, as a rule, retained so little of these psychic processes, especially as we have every reason for assuming that these same forgotten childhood activities have not glided off without leaving a trace in the development of the person, but that they have left a definite influence for all future time. Yet in spite of this unparalleled effectiveness they were forgotten! This would suggest that there are particularly formed conditions of memory (in the sense of conscious reproduction) which have thus far eluded our knowledge. It is quite possible that the forgetting of childhood may give us the key to the understanding of those amnesias which, according to our newer studies, lie at the basis of the formation of all neurotic symptoms.

Of these retained childhood reminiscences, some appear to us readily comprehensible, while others seem strange or unintelligible. It is not difficult to correct certain errors in regard to both kinds. If the retained reminiscences of a person are subjected to an analytic test, it can be readily ascertained that a guarantee for their correctness does not exist. Some of the memory pictures are surely falsified and incomplete, or displaced in point of time and place. The assertions of persons examined, that their first memories reach back perhaps to their second year, are evidently unreliable. Motives can soon be discovered which explain the disfigurement and the displacement of these experiences, but they also demonstrate that these memory lapses are not the result of a mere unreliable memory. Powerful forces from a later period have molded the memory capacity of our infantile experiences, and it is probably due to these same forces that the understanding of our childhood is generally so very strange to us.

The recollection of adults, as is known, proceeds through different psychic material. Some recall by means of visual pictures—their memories are of a visual character; other individuals can scarcely reproduce in memory the most paltry sketch of an experience; we call such persons *"auditifs"* and *"moteurs"* in contrast to the *"visuels,"* terms proposed by Charcot. These differences vanish in dreams; all our dreams are preponderatingly visual. But this development is also found in the childhood memories; the latter are plastic and visual, even in those people whose later memory lacks the visual element. The visual memory, therefore, preserves the type of the infantile recollections. Only my earliest childhood memories are of a visual character; they represent plastically depicted scenes, comparable only to stage settings.

In these scenes of childhood, whether they prove true or false, one usually sees his own childish person both in contour and dress. This circumstance must excite our wonder, for adults do not see their own persons in their recollections of later experiences. It is, moreover, against our experiences to assume that the child's attention during his experiences is centered on himself rather than exclusively on outside impressions. Various sources force us to assume that the so-called earliest childhood recollections are not true memory traces but later elaborations of the same, elaborations which might have been subjected to the influences of many later psychic forces. Thus the "childhood reminiscences" of individuals altogether advance to the signification of "concealing memories," and thereby form a noteworthy analogy to the childhood reminiscences as laid down in the legends and myths of nations.

Whoever has examined mentally a number of persons by the method of psychoanalysis must have gathered in this work numerous examples of concealing memories of every description. However, owing to the previously discussed nature of the relations of the childhood reminiscences to later life, it becomes extraordinarily difficult to report such examples. For, in order to attach the value of the concealing memory to an infantile reminiscence, it would be often necessary to present the entire life-history of the person concerned. Only seldom is it possible, as in the following good example, to take out from its context and report a single childhood memory.

A twenty-four-year-old man preserved the following picture from the fifth year of his life: In the garden of a summerhouse he sat on a stool next to his aunt, who was engaged in teaching him the alphabet. He found difficulty in distinguishing the letter *m* from *n,* and he begged his aunt to tell him how to tell one from the other. His aunt called his attention to the fact that the letter *m* had one whole portion (a stroke) more than the letter *n.* There was no reason to dispute the reliability of this childhood recollection; its meaning, however, was discovered only later, when it showed itself to be the symbolic representation of another boyish inquisitiveness. For just as he wanted to know the difference between *m* and *n* at that time, so he concerned himself later about the difference between boy and girl, and he would have been willing that just this aunt should be his teacher. He also discovered that the difference was a similar one; that the boy again had one whole portion more than the girl, and at the time of this recognition his memory awoke to the corresponding childish inquisitiveness.

I would like to show by one more example the sense that may be gained by a childhood reminiscence through analytic work, although it may seem to contain no sense before. In my forty-third year, when I began to interest myself in what remained in my memory of my own childhood, a scene struck me which for a long time, as I afterwards believed, had repeatedly come to consciousness, and which through reliable identification could be traced to a period before the completion of my third year. I saw myself in front of a chest, the door of which was held open by my half-brother, twenty years my senior: I stood there demanding something and screaming; my mother, pretty and slender, then suddenly entered the room, as if returning from the street.

In these words I formulated this scene so vividly seen, which, however, furnished no clue. Whether my brother wished to open or lock the chest (in the first explanation it was a "cupboard"), why I cried, and what bearing the arrival of my mother had, all these questions were dim to me; I was tempted to explain to myself that it dealt with the memory of a hoax by my older brother, which was interrupted by my mother. Such misunderstandings of childhood scenes retained in memory are not uncommon; we recall a situation, but it is not centralized; we do not know on which of the elements to place the psychic accent. Analytic effort led me to an entirely unexpected solution of the picture. I missed my mother and began to suspect that she was locked in this cupboard or chest, and therefore demanded that my brother should unlock it. As he obliged me, and I became convinced that she was not in the chest, I began to cry; this is the moment firmly retained in the memory, which was directly followed by the appearance of my mother, who appeased my worry and anxiety.

But how did the child get the idea of looking for the absent mother in the chest? Dreams which occurred at the same time pointed dimly to a nurse, concerning whom other reminiscences were retained; as for example, that she conscientiously urged me to deliver to her the small coins which I received as gifts, a detail which in itself may lay claim to the value of a concealing memory for later things. I then concluded to facilitate for myself this time the task of interpretation, and asked my now aged mother about that nurse. I found out all sorts of things, among others the fact that this shrewd but dishonest person had committed extensive robberies during the confinement of my mother, and that my half-brother was instrumental in bringing her to justice.

This information gave me the key to the scene from childhood, as through a sort of inspiration. The sudden disappearance of the nurse was not a matter of indifference to me; I had just asked this brother where she was, probably because I had noticed that he had played a part in her disappearance, and he, evasive and witty as he is to this day, answered that she was "boxed in." I understood this answer in the childish way, but asked no more, as there was nothing else to be discovered. When my mother left me shortly thereafter I suspected that the naughty brother had treated her in the same way as he did the nurse, and therefore pressed him to open the chest.

I also understand now why in the translation of the visual childhood scene my mother's slenderness was accentuated; she must have struck me as being newly restored. I am two and a half years older than the sister born at that time, and when I was three years of age I was separated from my half-brother.

*Katherine Mansfield*

# HER FIRST BALL

Exactly when the ball began Leila would have found it hard to say. Perhaps her first real partner was the cab. It did not matter that she shared the cab with the Sheridan girls and their brother. She sat back in her own little corner of it, and the bolster on which her hand rested felt like the sleeve of an unknown young man's dress suit; and away they bowled, past waltzing lamp-posts and houses and fences and trees.

"Have you really never been to a ball before, Leila? But, my child, how too weird—" cried the Sheridan girls.

"Our nearest neighbour was fifteen miles," said Leila softly, gently opening and shutting her fan.

Oh dear, how hard it was to be indifferent like the others! She tried not to smile too much; she tried not to care. But every single thing was so new and exciting. . . Meg's tuberoses, Jose's long loop of amber, Laura's little dark head, pushing above her white fur like a flower through snow. She would remember for ever. It even gave her a pang to see her cousin Laurie throw away the wisps of tissue paper he pulled from the fastenings of his new gloves. She would like to have kept those wisps as a keepsake, as a remembrance. Laurie leaned forward and put his hand on Laura's knee.

"Look here, darling," he said. "The third and the ninth as usual. Twig?"

Oh, how marvellous to have a brother! In her excitement Leila felt that if there had been time, if it hadn't been impossible, she couldn't have helped crying because she was an only child and no brother had ever said "Twig?" to her; no sister would ever say, as Meg said to Jose that moment, "I've never known your hair go up more successfully than it has to-night!"

But, of course, there was no time. They were at the drill hall already; there were cabs in front of them and cabs behind. The road was bright on either side with moving fan-like lights, and on the pavement gay couples seemed to float through the air; little satin shoes chased each other like birds.

"Hold on to me, Leila; you'll get lost," said Laura.

"Come on, girls, let's make a dash for it," said Laurie.

Leila put two fingers on Laura's pink velvet coat, and they were somehow lifted past the big golden lantern, carried along the passage, and pushed into the little room marked "Ladies." Here the crowd was so great there was hardly space to take off their things; the noise was deafening. Two benches on either side were stacked high with wraps. Two old women in white aprons ran up and down tossing fresh armfuls. And everybody was pressing forward trying to get at the little dressing-table and mirror at the far end.

A great quivering jet of gas lighted the ladies' room. It couldn't wait; it was dancing already. When the door opened again and there came a burst of tuning from the drill hall, it leaped almost to the ceiling.

Dark girls, fair girls were patting their hair, tying ribbons again, tucking handkerchiefs down the fronts of their bodices, smoothing marble-white gloves. And because they were all laughing it seemed to Leila that they were all lovely.

"Aren't there any invisible hairpins?" cried a voice. "How most extraordinary! I can't see a single invisible hairpin."

"Powder my back, there's a darling," cried someone else.

"But I must have a needle and cotton. I've torn simply miles and miles of the frill," wailed a third.

Then, "Pass them along, pass them along!" The straw basket of programmes was tossed from arm to arm. Darling little pink-and-silver programmes, with pink pencils and fluffy tassels. Leila's fingers shook as she took one out of the basket. She wanted to ask someone, "Am I meant to have one too?" but she had just time to read: "Waltz 3. *Two, Two in a Canoe*. Polka 4. *Making the Feathers Fly*," when Meg cried, "Ready, Leila?" and they pressed their way through the crush in the passage towards the big double doors of the drill hall.

Dancing had not begun yet, but the band had stopped tuning, and the noise was so great it seemed that when it did begin to play it would never be heard. Leila, pressing close to Meg, looking over Meg's shoulder, felt that even the little quivering coloured flags strung across the ceiling were talking. She quite forgot to be shy; she forgot how in the middle of dressing she had sat down on the bed with one shoe off and one shoe on and begged her mother to ring up her cousins and say she couldn't go after all. And the rush of longing she had had to be sitting on the veranda of their forsaken up-country home, listening to the baby owls crying "More pork" in the moonlight, was changed to a rush of joy so sweet that it was hard to bear alone. She clutched her fan, and, gazing at the gleaming, golden floor, the azaleas, the lanterns, the stage at one end with its red carpet and gilt chairs and the band in a corner, she thought breathlessly, "How heavenly; how simply heavenly!"

All the girls stood grouped together at one side of the doors, the men at the other, and the chaperones in dark dresses, smiling rather foolishly, walked with little careful steps over the polished floor towards the stage.

"This is my little country cousin Leila. Be nice to her. Find her partners; she's under my wing," said Meg, going up to one girl after another.

Strange faces smiled at Leila—sweetly, vaguely. Strange voices answered, "Of course, my dear." But Leila felt the girls didn't really see her. They were looking towards the men. Why didn't the men begin? What were they waiting for? There they stood, smoothing their gloves, patting their glossy hair and smiling among themselves. Then, quite suddenly, as if they had only just made up their minds that that was what they had to do, the men came gliding over the parquet. There was a joyful flutter among the girls. A tall, fair man flew up to Meg, seized her programme, scribbled something; Meg passed him on to Leila. "May I have the pleasure?" He ducked and smiled. There came a dark man wearing an eyeglass, then cousin Laurie with a friend, and Laura with a little freckled fellow whose tie was crooked. Then quite an old man—fat, with a big bald patch on his head—took her programme and murmured, "Let me see, let me see!" And he was a long time comparing his programme, which looked black with names, with hers. It seemed to give him so much trouble that Leila was ashamed. "Oh, please don't bother," she said eagerly. But instead of replying the fat man wrote something, glanced at her again. "Do I remember this bright little face?" he said softly. "Is it known to me of yore?" At that moment the band began playing; the fat man disappeared. He was tossed away on a great wave of music that came flying over the gleaming floor, breaking the groups up into couples, scattering them, sending them spinning. . . .

Leila had learned to dance at boarding school. Every Saturday afternoon the boarders were hurried off to a little corrugated iron mission hall where Miss Eccles (of London) held her "select" classes. But the difference between that dusty-smelling hall—with calico texts on the walls, the poor, terrified little woman in a brown velvet toque with rabbit's ears thumping the cold piano, Miss Eccles poking the girls' feet with her long white wand—and this, was so tremendous that Leila was sure if her partner didn't come and she had to listen to that marvellous music and to watch the others sliding, gliding over the golden floor, she would die at least, or faint, or lift her arms and fly out of one of those dark windows that showed the stars.

"Ours, I think—" Someone bowed, smiled, and offered her his arm; she hadn't to die after all. Someone's hand pressed her waist, and she floated away like a flower that is tossed into a pool.

"Quite a good floor, isn't it?" drawled a faint voice close to her ear.

"I think it's most beautifully slippery," said Leila.

"Pardon!" The faint voice sounded surprised. Leila said it again. And there was a tiny pause before the voice echoed, "Oh, quite!" and she was swung round again.

He steered so beautifully. That was the great difference between dancing with girls and men, Leila decided. Girls banged into each other and stamped on each other's feet; the girl who was gentleman always clutched you so.

The azaleas were separate flowers no longer; they were pink and white flags streaming by.

"Were you at the Bells' last week?" the voice came again. It sounded tired. Leila wondered whether she ought to ask him if he would like to stop.

"No, this is my first dance," said she.

Her partner gave a little gasping laugh. "Oh, I say," he protested.

"Yes, it is really the first dance I've ever been to." Leila was most fervent. It was such a relief to be able to tell somebody. "You see, I've lived in the country all my life up till now. . . ."

At that moment the music stopped and they went to sit on two chairs against the wall. Leila tucked her pink satin feet under and fanned herself, while she blissfully watched the other couples passing and disappearing through the swing doors.

"Enjoying yourself, Leila?" asked Jose, nodding her golden head.

Laura passed and gave her the faintest little wink; it made Leila wonder for a moment whether she was quite grown up after all. Certainly her partner did not say very much. He coughed, tucked his handkerchief away, pulled down his waistcoat, took a minute thread off his sleeve. But it didn't matter. Almost immediately the band started and her second partner seemed to spring from the ceiling.

"Floor's not bad," said the new voice. Did one always begin with the floor? And then, "Were you at the Neaves' on Tuesday?" And again Leila explained. Perhaps it was a little strange that her partners were not more interested. For it was thrilling. Her first ball! She was only at the beginning of everything. It seemed to her that she had never known what the night was like before. Up till now it had been dark, silent, beautiful very often—oh yes—but mournful somehow. Solemn. And now it would never be like that again—it had opened dazzling bright.

"Care for an ice?" said her partner. And they went through the swing doors, down the passage, to the supper-room. Her cheeks burned, she was fearfully thirsty. How sweet the ices looked on little glass plates and how cold the frosted spoon was, iced too! And when they came back to the hall there was the fat man waiting for her by the door. It gave her quite a shock again to see how old he was; he ought to have been on the stage with the fathers and mothers. And when Leila compared him with her other partners he looked shabby. His waistcoat was creased, there was a button off his glove, his coat looked as if it was dusty with French chalk.

"Come along, little lady," said the fat man. He scarcely troubled to clasp her, and they moved away so gently, it was more like walking than dancing. But he said not a word about the floor. "Your first dance, isn't it?" he murmured.

"How *did* you know?"

"Ah," said the fat man, "that's what it is to be old!" He wheezed faintly as he steered her past an awkward couple. "You see, I've been doing this kind of thing for the last thirty years."

"Thirty years?" cried Leila. Twelve years before she was born!

"It hardly bears thinking about, does it?" said the fat man gloomily. Leila looked at his bald head, and she felt quite sorry for him.

"I think it's marvellous to be still going on," she said kindly.

"Kind little lady," said the fat man, and he pressed her a little closer and hummed a bar of the waltz. "Of course," he said, "you can't hope to last anything like as long as that. No-o," said the fat man, "long before that you'll be sitting up there on the stage, looking on, in your nice black velvet. And these pretty arms will have turned into little short fat ones, and you'll beat time with such a different kind of fan—a black ebony one." The fat man seemed to shudder. "And you'll smile away like the poor old dears up there, and point to your daughter, and tell the elderly lady next to you how some dreadful man tried to kiss her at the club ball. And your heart will ache, ache"—the fat man squeezed her closer still, as if he really was sorry for that poor heart—"because no one wants to kiss you now. And you'll say how unpleasant these polished floors are to walk on, how dangerous they are. Eh, Mademoiselle Twinkletoes?" said the fat man softly.

Leila gave a light little laugh, but she did not feel like laughing. Was it—could it all be true? It sounded terribly true. Was this first ball only the beginning of her last ball, after all? At that the music seemed to change; it sounded sad, sad; it rose upon a great sigh. Oh, how quickly things changed! Why didn't happiness last for ever? For ever wasn't a bit too long.

"I want to stop," she said in a breathless voice. The fat man led her to the door.

"No," she said, "I won't go outside. I won't sit down. I'll just stand here, thank you." She leaned against the wall, tapping with her foot,

pulling up her gloves and trying to smile. But deep inside her a little girl threw her pinafore over her head and sobbed. Why had he spoiled it all?

"I say, you know," said the fat man, "you mustn't take me seriously, little lady."

"As if I should!" said Leila, tossing her small dark head and sucking her underlip. . . .

Again the couples paraded. The swing doors opened and shut. Now new music was given out by the bandmaster. But Leila didn't want to dance any more. She wanted to be home, or sitting on the veranda listening to those baby owls. When she looked through the dark windows at the stars they had long beams like wings. . . .

But presently a soft, melting, ravishing tune began, and a young man with curly hair bowed before her. She would have to dance, out of politeness, until she could find Meg. Very stiffly she walked into the middle; very haughtily she put her hand on his sleeve. But in one minute, in one turn, her feet glided, glided. The lights, the azaleas, the dresses, the pink faces, the velvet chairs, all became one beautiful flying wheel. And when her next partner bumped her into the fat man and he said, 'Par*don*,' she smiled at him more radiantly than ever. She didn't even recognize him again.

## *James Joyce*

# ARABY

North Richmond Street, being blind, was a quiet street except at the hour when the Christian Brothers' School set the boys free. An uninhabited house of two stories stood at the blind end, detached from its neighbors in a square ground. The other houses of the street, conscious of decent lives within them, gazed at one another with brown imperturbable faces.

The former tenant of our house, a priest, had died in the back drawing room. Air, musty from having been long enclosed, hung in all the rooms, and the waste room behind the kitchen was littered with old useless papers. Among these I found a few paper-covered books, the pages of which were curled and damp: *The Abbot,* by Walter Scott, *The Devout Communicant,* and *The Memoirs of Vidocq.* I liked the last best because its leaves were yellow. The wild garden behind the house contained a central apple tree and a few straggling bushes under one of which I found the late tenant's rusty bicycle pump. He had been a very charitable priest; in his will he had left all his money to institutions and the furniture of his house to his sister.

When the short days of winter came dusk fell before we had well eaten our dinners. When we met in the street the houses had grown somber. The space of sky above us was the color of ever-changing violet and towards it the lamps of the street lifted their feeble lanterns. The cold air stung us and we played till our bodies glowed. Our shouts echoed in the silent street. The career of our play brought us through the dark muddy lanes behind the houses where we ran the gauntlet of the rough tribes from the cottages, to the back doors of the dark dripping gardens where odors arose from the ashpits, to the dark odorous stables where a coachman smoothed and combed the horse or shook music from the buckled harness. When we returned to the street, light from the kitchen windows had filled the areas. If my uncle was seen turning the corner we hid in the shadow until we had seen him safely housed. Or if Mangan's sister came out on the doorstep to call her brother in to his tea we watched her from our shadow peer up and down the street. We waited to see whether she would remain or go in and, if she remained, we left our shadow and walked up to Mangan's steps resignedly. She was waiting for us, her figure defined by the light from the half-opened door. Her brother always teased her before he obeyed and I stood by the railings looking at her. Her dress swung as she moved her body and the soft rope of her hair tossed from side to side.

Every morning I lay on the floor in the front parlor watching her door. The blind was pulled down to within an inch of the sash so that I could not be seen. When she came out on the doorstep my heart leaped. I ran to the hall, seized my books and followed her. I kept her brown figure always in my eye and, when we came near the point at which our ways di-

verged, I quickened my pace and passed her. This happened morning after morning. I had never spoken to her, except for a few casual words, and yet her name was like a summons to all my foolish blood.

Her image accompanied me even in places the most hostile to romance. On Saturday evenings when my aunt went marketing I had to go to carry some of the parcels. We walked through the flaring streets, jostled by drunken men and bargaining women, amid the curses of laborers, the shrill litanies of shop boys who stood on guard by the barrels of pigs' cheeks, the nasal chanting of street singers, who sang a *come-all-you* about O'Donovan Rossa, or a ballad about the troubles in our native land. These noises converged in a single sensation of life for me: I imagined that I bore my chalice safely through a throng of foes. Her name sprang to my lips at moments in strange prayers and praises which I myself did not understand. My eyes were often full of tears (I could not tell why) and at times a flood from my heart seemed to pour itself out into my bosom. I thought little of the future. I did not know whether I would ever speak to her or not or, if I spoke to her, how I could tell her of my confused adoration. But my body was like a harp and her words and gestures were like fingers running upon the wires.

One evening I went into the back drawing room in which the priest had died. It was a dark rainy evening and there was no sound in the house. Through one of the broken panes I heard the rain impinge upon the earth, the fine incessant needles of water playing in the sodden beds. Some distant lamp or lighted window gleamed below me. I was thankful that I could see so little. All my senses seemed to desire to veil themselves and, feeling that I was about to slip from them, I pressed the palms of my hands together until they trembled, murmuring: *"O love! O love!"* many times.

At last she spoke to me. When she addressed the first words to me I was so confused that I did not know what to answer. She asked me was I going to *Araby.* I forgot whether I answered yes or no. It would be a splendid bazaar, she said; she would love to go.

"And why can't you?" I asked.

While she spoke she turned a silver bracelet round and round her wrist. She could not go, she said, because there would be a retreat that week in her convent. Her brother and two other boys were fighting for their caps and I was alone at the railings. She held one of the spikes, bowing her head towards me. The light from the lamp opposite our door caught the white curve of her neck, lit up her hair that rested there and, falling, lit up the hand upon the railing. It fell over one side of her dress and caught the white border of a petticoat, just visible as she stood at ease.

"It's well for you," she said.

"If I go," I said, "I will bring you something."

What innumerable follies laid waste my waking and sleeping thoughts after that evening! I wished to annihilate the tedious intervening days. I chafed against the work of school. At night in my bedroom and by day in the classroom her image came between me and the page I strove to read. The syllables of the word *Araby* were called to me through the silence in which my soul luxuriated and cast an Eastern enchantment over me. I asked for leave to go to the bazaar on Saturday night. My aunt was surprised and hoped it was not some Freemason affair. I answered few questions in class. I watched my master's face pass from amiability to sternness; he hoped I was not beginning to idle. I could not call my wandering thoughts together. I had hardly any patience with the serious work of life which, now that it stood between me and my desire, seemed to me child's play, ugly monotonous child's play.

On Saturday morning I reminded my uncle that I wished to go to the bazaar in the evening. He was fussing at the hall stand, looking for the hat brush, and answered me curtly:

"Yes, boy, I know."

As he was in the hall I could not go into the front parlor and lie at the window. I left the house in bad humor and walked slowly towards the school. The air was pitilessly raw and already my heart misgave me.

When I came home to dinner my uncle had not yet been home. Still it was early. I sat staring at the clock for some time and, when its ticking began to irritate me, I left the room. I mounted the staircase and gained the upper part of the house. The high cold empty gloomy rooms liberated me and I went from room to room singing. From the front window I saw my companions playing below in the street. Their cries reached me weakened and indistinct and,

leaning my forehead against the cool glass, I looked over at the dark house where she lived. I may have stood there for an hour, seeing nothing but the brown-clad figure cast by my imagination, touched discreetly by the lamplight at the curved neck, at the hand upon the railings and at the border below the dress.

When I came downstairs again I found Mrs. Mercer sitting at the fire. She was an old garrulous woman, a pawnbroker's widow, who collected used stamps for some pious purpose. I had to endure the gossip of the tea table. The meal was prolonged beyond an hour and still my uncle did not come. Mrs. Mercer stood up to go: she was sorry she couldn't wait any longer, but it was after eight o'clock and she did not like to be out late, as the night air was bad for her. When she had gone I began to walk up and down the room, clenching my fists. My aunt said:

"I'm afraid you may put off your bazaar for this night of Our Lord."

At nine o'clock I heard my uncle's latchkey in the hall door. I heard him talking to himself and heard the hall stand rocking when it had received the weight of his overcoat. I could interpret these signs. When he was midway through his dinner I asked him to give me the money to go to the bazaar. He had forgotten.

"The people are in bed and after their first sleep now," he said.

I did not smile. My aunt said to him energetically:

"Can't you give him the money and let him go? You've kept him late enough as it is."

My uncle said he was very sorry he had forgotten. He said he believed in the old saying: "All work and no play makes Jack a dull boy." He asked me where I was going and, when I had told him a second time he asked me did I know *The Arab's Farewell to His Steed.* When I left the kitchen he was about to recite the opening lines of the piece to my aunt.

I held a florin tightly in my hand as I strode down Buckingham Street towards the station. The sight of the streets thronged with buyers and glaring with gas recalled to me the purpose of my journey. I took my seat in a third-class carriage of a deserted train. After an intolerable delay the train moved out of the station slowly. It crept onward among ruinous houses and over the twinkling river. At Westland Row Station a crowd of people pressed to the carriage doors; but the porters moved them back, saying that it was a special train for the bazaar. I remained alone in the bare carriage. In a few minutes the train drew up beside an improvised wooden platform. I passed out on to the road and saw by the lighted dial of a clock that it was ten minutes to ten. In front of me was a large building which displayed the magical name.

I could not find any sixpenny entrance and, fearing that the bazaar would be closed, I passed in quickly through a turnstile, handing a shilling to a weary-looking man. I found myself in a big hall girdled at half its height by a gallery. Nearly all the stalls were closed and the greater part of the hall was in darkness. I recognized a silence like that which pervades a church after a service. I walked into the center of the bazaar timidly. A few people were gathered about the stalls which were still open. Before a curtain, over which the words *Café Chantant* were written in colored lamps, two men were counting money on a salver. I listened to the fall of the coins.

Remembering with difficulty why I had come I went over to one of the stalls and examined porcelain vases and flowered tea sets. At the door of the stall a young lady was talking and laughing with two young gentlemen. I remarked their English accents and listened vaguely to their conversation.

"O, I never said such a thing!"

"O, but you did!"

"O, but I didn't!"

"Didn't she say that?"

"Yes. I heard her."

"O, there's a . . . fib!"

Observing me, the young lady came over and asked me did I wish to buy anything. The tone of her voice was not encouraging; she seemed to have spoken to me out of a sense of duty. I looked humbly at the great jars that stood like eastern guards at either side of the dark entrance to the stall and murmured:

"No, thank you."

The young lady changed the position of one of the vases and went back to the two young men. They began to talk of the same subject. Once or twice the young lady glanced at me over her shoulder.

I lingered before her stall, though I knew my stay was useless, to make my interest in her wares seem the more real. Then I turned away slowly and walked down the middle of the bazaar. I allowed the two pennies to fall against the sixpence in my pocket. I heard a voice call from one end of the gallery that the light was out. The upper part of the hall was now completely dark.

Gazing up into the darkness I saw myself as a creature driven and derided by vanity; and my eyes burned with anguish and anger.

## Robert Penn Warren
# BLACKBERRY WINTER

It was getting into June and past eight o'clock in the morning, but there was a fire— even if it wasn't a big fire, just a fire of chunks —on the hearth of the big stone fireplace in the living room. I was standing on the hearth, almost into the chimney, hunched over the fire, working my bare toes slowly on the warm stone. I relished the heat which made the skin of my bare legs warp and creep and tingle, even as I called to my mother, who was somewhere back in the dining room or kitchen, and said: "But it's June, I don't have to put them on!"

"You put them on if you are going out," she called.

I tried to assess the degree of authority and conviction in the tone, but at that distance it was hard to decide. I tried to analyze the tone, and then I thought what a fool I had been to start out the back door and let her see that I was barefoot. If I had gone out the front door or the side door she would never have known, not till dinner time anyway, and by then the day would have been half gone and I would have been all over the farm to see what the storm had done and down to the creek to see the flood. But it had never crossed my mind that they would try to stop you from going barefoot in June, no matter if there had been a gully-washer and a cold spell.

Nobody had ever tried to stop me in June as long as I could remember, and when you are nine years old, what you remember seems forever; for you remember everything and everything is important and stands big and full and fills up Time and is so solid that you can walk around and around it like a tree and look at it. You are aware that time passes, that there is a movement in time, but that is not what Time is. Time is not a movement, a flowing, a wind then, but is, rather, a kind of climate in which things are, and when a thing happens it begins to live and keeps on living and stands solid in Time like the tree that you can walk around. And if there is a movement, the movement is not Time itself, any more than a breeze is climate, and all the breeze does is to shake a little the leaves on the tree which is alive and solid. When you are nine, you know that there are things that you don't know, but you know that when you know something you know it. You know how a thing has been and you know that you can go barefoot in June. You do not understand that voice from back in the kitchen which says that you cannot go barefoot outdoors and run to see what has happened and rub your feet over the wet shivery grass and make the perfect mark of your foot in the smooth, creamy, red mud and then muse upon it as though you had suddenly come upon that single mark on the glistening auroral beach of the world. You have never seen a beach, but you have read the book and how the footprint was there.

The voice had said what it had said, and I looked savagely at the black stockings and the strong, scuffed brown shoes which I had brought from my closet as far as the hearth rug. I called once more, "But it's June," and waited.

"It's June," the voice replied from far away, "but it's blackberry winter."

I had lifted my head to reply to that, to make one more test of what was in that tone, when I happened to see the man.

The fireplace in the living room was at the end; for the stone chimney was built, as in so many of the farmhouses in Tennessee, at the end of a gable, and there was a window on each side of the chimney. Out of the window on the north side of the fireplace I could see the man. When I saw the man I did not call out what I had intended, but, engrossed by the strangeness of the sight, watched him, still far off, come along the path by the edge of the woods.

What was strange was that there should be a man there at all. That path went along the yard fence, between the fence and the woods which came right down to the yard, and then on back past the chicken runs and on by the woods until it was lost to sight where the woods bulged out and cut off the back field. There the path disappeared into the woods. It led on back, I knew, through the woods and to the swamp, skirted the swamp where the big trees gave way to sycamores and water oaks and willows and tangled cane, and then led on to the river. Nobody ever went back there except people who wanted to gig frogs in the swamp or to fish in the river or to hunt in the woods, and those people, if they didn't have a standing permission from my father, always stopped to ask permission to cross the farm. But the man whom I now saw wasn't, I could tell even at that distance, a sportsman. And what would a sportsman have been doing down there after a storm? Besides, he was coming from the river, and nobody had gone down there that morning. I knew that for a fact, because if anybody had passed, certainly if a stranger had passed, the dogs would have made a racket and would have been out on him. But this man was coming up from the river and had come up through the woods. I suddenly had a vision of him moving up the grassy path in the woods, in the green twilight under the big trees, not making any sound on the path, while now and then, like drops off the eaves, a big drop of water would fall from a leaf or bough and strike a stiff oak leaf lower down with a small, hollow sound like a drop of water hitting tin. That sound, in the silence of the woods, would be very significant.

When you are a boy and stand in the stillness of woods, which can be so still that your heart almost stops beating and makes you want to stand there in the green twilight until you feel your very feet sinking into and clutching the earth like roots and your body breathing slow through its pores like the leaves—when you stand there and wait for the next drop to drop with its small, flat sound to a lower leaf, that sound seems to measure out something, to put an end to something, to begin something, and you cannot wait for it to happen and are afraid it will not happen, and then when it has happened, you are waiting again, almost afraid.

But the man whom I saw coming through the woods in my mind's eye did not pause and wait, growing into the ground and breathing with the enormous, soundless breathing of the leaves. Instead, I saw him moving in the green twilight inside my head as he was moving at that very moment along the path by the edge of the woods, coming toward the house. He was moving steadily, but not fast, with his shoulders hunched a little and his head thrust forward, like a man who has come a long way and has a long way to go. I shut my eyes for a couple of seconds, thinking that when I opened them he would not be there at all. There was no place for him to have come from, and there was no reason for him to come where he was coming, toward our house. But I opened my eyes, and there he was, and he was coming steadily along the side of the woods. He was not yet even with the back chicken yard.

"Mama," I called.

"You put them on," the voice said.

"There's a man coming," I called, "out back."

She did not reply to that, and I guessed that she had gone to the kitchen window to look. She would be looking at the man and wondering who he was and what he wanted, the way you always do in the country, and if I went back there now she would not notice right off whether or not I was barefoot. So I went back to the kitchen.

She was standing by the window. "I don't recognize him," she said, not looking around at me.

"Where could he be coming from?" I asked.

"I don't know," she said.

"What would he be doing down at the river? At night? In the storm?"

She studied the figure out the window, then said, "Oh, I reckon maybe he cut across from the Dunbar place."

That was, I realized, a perfectly rational explanation. He had not been down at the river in the storm, at night. He had come over this morning. You could cut across from the Dunbar place if you didn't mind breaking through a lot of elder and sassafras and blackberry bushes which had about taken over the old cross path, which nobody ever used any more. That satisfied me for a moment, but only for a moment. "Mama," I asked, "what would he be doing over at the Dunbar place last night?"

Then she looked at me, and I knew I had made a mistake, for she was looking at my bare feet. "You haven't got your shoes on," she said.

But I was saved by the dogs. That instant there was a bark which I recognized as Sam,

the collie, and then a heavier, churning kind of bark which was Bully, and I saw a streak of white as Bully tore round the corner of the back porch and headed out for the man. Bully was a big, bone-white bull dog, the kind of dog that they used to call a farm bull dog but that you don't see any more, heavy chested and heavy headed, but with pretty long legs. He could take a fence as light as a hound. He had just cleared the white paling fence toward the woods when my mother ran out to the back porch and began calling, "Here you, Bully! Here you!"

Bully stopped in the path, waiting for the man, but he gave a few more of those deep, gargling, savage barks that reminded you of something down a stone-lined well. The red clay mud, I saw, was splashed up over his white chest and looked exciting, like blood.

The man, however, had not stopped walking even when Bully took the fence and started at him. He had kept right on coming. All he had done was to switch a little paper parcel which he carried from the right hand to the left, and then reach into his pants pocket to get something. Then I saw the glitter and knew that he had a knife in his hand, probably the kind of mean knife just made for devilment and nothing else, with a blade as long as the blade of a frog-sticker, which will snap out ready when you press a button in the handle. That knife must have had a button in the handle, or else how could he have had the blade out glittering so quick and with just one hand?

Pulling his knife against the dogs was a funny thing to do, for Bully was a big, powerful brute and fast, and Sam was all right. If those dogs had meant business, they might have knocked him down and ripped him before he got a stroke in. He ought to have picked up a heavy stick, something to take a swipe at them with and something which they could see and respect when they came at him. But he apparently did not know much about dogs. He just held the knife blade close against the right leg, low down, and kept on moving down the path.

Then my mother had called, and Bully had stopped. So the man let the blade of the knife snap back into the handle, and dropped it into his pocket, and kept on coming. Many women would have been afraid with the strange man who they knew had that knife in his pocket. That is, if they were alone in the house with nobody but a nine-year-old boy. And my mother was alone, for my father had gone off, and Dellie, the cook, was down at her cabin because she wasn't feeling well. But my mother wasn't afraid. She wasn't a big woman, but she was clear and brisk about everything she did and looked everybody and everything right in the eye from her own blue eyes in her tanned face. She had been the first woman in the county to ride a horse astride (that was back when she was a girl and long before I was born), and I have seen her snatch up a pump gun and go out and knock a chicken hawk out of the air like a busted skeet when he came over her chicken yard. She was a steady and self-reliant woman, and when I think of her now after all the years she has been dead, I think of her brown hands, not big, but somewhat square for a woman's hands, with square-cut nails. They looked, as a matter of fact, more like a young boy's hands than a grown woman's. But back then it never crossed my mind that she would ever be dead.

She stood on the back porch and watched the man enter the back gate, where the dogs (Bully had leaped back into the yard) were dancing and muttering and giving sidelong glances back to my mother to see if she meant what she had said. The man walked right by the dogs, almost brushing them, and didn't pay them any attention. I could see now that he wore old khaki pants, and a dark wool coat with stripes in it, and a gray felt hat. He had on a gray shirt with blue stripes in it, and no tie. But I could see a tie, blue and reddish, sticking in his side coat-pocket. Everything was wrong about what he wore. He ought to have been wearing blue jeans or overalls, and a straw hat or an old black felt hat, and the coat, granting that he might have been wearing a wool coat and not a jumper, ought not to have had those stripes. Those clothes, despite the fact that they were old enough and dirty enough for any tramp, didn't belong there in our back yard, coming down the path, in Middle Tennessee, miles away from any big town, and even a mile off the pike.

When he got almost to the steps, without having said anything, my mother, very matter-of-factly, said, "Good morning."

"Good morning," he said, and stopped and looked her over. He did not take off his hat, and under the brim you could see the perfectly unmemorable face, which wasn't old and wasn't young, or thick or thin. It was grayish and covered with about three days of stubble. The eyes were a kind of nondescript, muddy hazel, or something like that, rather bloodshot. His teeth, when he opened his mouth, showed yellow and uneven. A couple of them had been knocked out. You knew that they had been knocked out, because there was a scar, not very old, there on the lower lip just beneath the gap.

"Are you hunting work?" my mother asked him.

"Yes," he said—not "yes, mam"—and still did not take off his hat.

"I don't know about my husband, for he isn't here," she said, and didn't mind a bit telling the tramp, or whoever he was, with the mean knife in his pocket, that no man was around, "but I can give you a few things to do. The storm has drowned a lot of my chicks. Three coops of them. You can gather them up and bury them. Bury them deep so the dogs won't get at them. In the woods. And fix the coops the wind blew over. And down yonder beyond that pen by the edge of the woods are some drowned poults. They got out and I couldn't get them in. Even after it started to rain hard. Poults haven't got any sense."

"What are them things—poults?" he demanded, and spat on the brick walk. He rubbed his foot over the spot, and I saw that he wore a black, pointed-toe low shoe, all cracked and broken. It was a crazy kind of shoe to be wearing in the country.

"Oh, they're young turkeys," my mother was saying. "And they haven't got any sense. I oughtn't to try to raise them around here with so many chickens, anyway. They don't thrive near chickens, even in separate pens. And I won't give up my chickens." Then she stopped herself and resumed briskly on the note of business. "When you finish that, you can fix my flower beds. A lot of trash and mud and gravel has washed down. Maybe you can save some of my flowers if you are careful."

"Flowers," the man said, in a low, impersonal voice which seemed to have a wealth of meaning, but a meaning which I could not fathom. As I think back on it, it probably was not pure contempt. Rather, it was a kind of impersonal and distant marveling that he should be on the verge of grubbing in a flower bed. He said the word, and then looked off across the yard.

"Yes, flowers," my mother replied with some asperity, as though she would have nothing said or implied against flowers. "And they were very fine this year." Then she stopped and looked at the man. "Are you hungry?" she demanded.

"Yeah," he said.

"I'll fix you something," she said, "before you get started." She turned to me. "Show him where he can wash up," she commanded, and went into the house.

I took the man to the end of the porch where a pump was and where a couple of wash pans sat on a low shelf for people to use before they went into the house. I stood there while he laid down his little parcel wrapped in newspaper and took off his hat and looked around for a nail to hang it on. He poured the water and plunged his hands into it. They were big hands, and strong looking, but they did not have the creases and the earth-color of the hands of men who work outdoors. But they were dirty, with black dirt ground into the skin and under the nails. After he had washed his hands, he poured another basin of water and washed his face. He dried his face, and with the towel still dangling in his grasp, stepped over to the mirror on the house wall. He rubbed one hand over the stubble on his face. Then he carefully inspected his face, turning first one side and then the other, and stepped back and settled his striped coat down on his shoulders. He had the movements of a man who has just dressed up to go to church or a party—the way he settled his coat and smoothed it and scanned himself in the mirror.

Then he caught my glance on him. He glared at me for an instant out of the bloodshot eyes, then demanded in a low, harsh voice, "What you looking at?"

"Nothing," I managed to say, and stepped back a step from him.

He flung the towel down, crumpled, on the shelf, and went toward the kitchen door and entered without knocking.

My mother said something to him which I could not catch. I started to go in again, then thought about my bare feet, and decided to go back of the chicken yard, where the man would have to come to pick up the dead chicks. I hung around behind the chicken house until he came out.

He moved across the chicken yard with a fastidious, not quite finicking motion, looking down at the curdled mud flecked with bits of chicken-droppings. The mud curled up over the soles of his black shoes. I stood back from him some six feet and watched him pick up the first of the drowned chicks. He held it up by one foot and inspected it.

There is nothing deader looking than a drowned chick. The feet curl in that feeble, empty way which back when I was a boy, even if I was a country boy who did not mind hog-killing or frog-gigging, made me feel hollow in the stomach. Instead of looking plump and fluffy, the body is stringy and limp with the fluff plastered to it, and the neck is long and loose like a little string of rag. And the eyes have that bluish membrane over them which makes you think of a very old man who is sick about to die.

The man stood there and inspected the chick. Then he looked all around as though he didn't know what to do with it.

"There's a great big old basket in the shed," I said, and pointed to the shed attached to the chicken house.

He inspected me as though he had just discovered my presence, and moved toward the shed.

"There's a spade there, too," I added.

He got the basket and began to pick up the other chicks, picking each one up slowly by a foot and then flinging it into the basket with a nasty, snapping motion. Now and then he would look at me out of the blood-shot eyes. Every time he seemed on the verge of saying something, but he did not. Perhaps he was building up to say something to me, but I did not wait that long. His way of looking at me made me so uncomfortable that I left the chicken yard.

Besides, I had just remembered that the creek was in flood, over the bridge, and that people were down there watching it. So I cut across the farm toward the creek. When I got to the big tobacco field I saw that it had not suffered much. The land lay right and not many tobacco plants had washed out of the ground. But I knew that a lot of tobacco round the country had been washed right out. My father had said so at breakfast.

My father was down at the bridge. When I came out of the gap in the osage hedge into the road, I saw him sitting on his mare over the heads of the other men who were standing around, admiring the flood. The creek was big here, even in low water; for only a couple of miles away it ran into the river, and when a real flood came, the red water got over the pike where it dipped down to the bridge, which was an iron bridge, and high over the floor and even the side railings of the bridge. Only the upper iron work would show, with the water boiling and frothing red and white around it. That creek rose so fast and so heavy because a few miles back it came down out of the hills, where the gorges filled up with water in no time when a rain came. The creek ran in a deep bed with limestone bluffs along both sides until it got within three quarters of a mile of the bridge, and when it came out from between those bluffs in flood it was boiling and hissing and steaming like water from a fire hose.

Whenever there was a flood, people from half the county would come down to see the sight. After a gully-washer there would not be any work to do anyway. If it didn't ruin your crop, you couldn't plow and you felt like taking a holiday to celebrate. If it did ruin your crop, there wasn't anything to do except to try to take your mind off the mortgage, if you were rich enough to have a mortgage, and if you couldn't afford a mortgage you needed something to take your mind off how hungry you would be by Christmas. So people would come down to the bridge and look at the flood. It made something different from the run of days.

There would not be much talking after the first few minutes of trying to guess how high the water was this time. The men and kids just stood around, or sat their horses or mules, as the case might be, or stood up in the wagon beds. They looked at the strangeness of the flood for an hour or two, and then somebody would say that he had better be getting on home to dinner and would start walking down the gray, puddled limestone pike, or would touch heel to his mount and start off. Everybody always knew what it would be like when he got down to the bridge, but people always came. It was like church or a funeral. They always came, that is, if it was summer and the flood unexpected. Nobody ever came down in winter to see high water.

When I came out of the gap in the bodock hedge, I saw the crowd, perhaps fifteen or twenty men and a lot of kids, and saw my father sitting his mare, Nellie Gray. He was a tall, limber man and carried himself well. I was always proud to see him sit a horse, he was so

quiet and straight, and when I stepped through the gap of the hedge that morning, the first thing that happened was, I remember, the warm feeling I always had when I saw him up on a horse, just sitting. I did not go toward him, but skirted the crowd on the far side, to get a look at the creek. For one thing, I was not sure what he would say about the fact that I was barefoot. But the first thing I knew, I heard his voice calling, "Seth!"

I went toward him, moving apologetically past the men, who bent their large, red or thin, sallow faces above me. I knew some of the men, and knew their names, but because those I knew were there in a crowd, mixed with the strange faces, they seemed foreign to me, and not friendly. I did not look up at my father until I was almost within touching distance of his heel. Then I looked up and tried to read his face, to see if he was angry about my being barefoot. Before I could decide anything from that impassive, high-boned face, he had leaned over and reached a hand to me. "Grab on," he commanded.

I grabbed on and gave a little jump, and he said, "Up-see-daisy!" and whisked me, light as a feather, up to the pommel of his McClellan saddle.

"You can see better up here," he said, slid back on the cantle a little to make me more comfortable, and then, looking over my head at the swollen, tumbling water, seemed to forget all about me. But his right hand was laid on my side, just above my thigh, to steady me.

I was sitting there as quiet as I could, feeling the faint stir of my father's chest against my shoulders as it rose and fell with his breath, when I saw the cow. At first, looking up the creek, I thought it was just another big piece of driftwood steaming down the creek in the ruck of water, but all at once a pretty good-size boy who had climbed part way up a telephone pole by the pike so that he could see better yelled out, "Golly-damn, look at that-air cow!"

Everybody looked. It was a cow all right, but it might just as well have been driftwood; for it was dead as a chunk, rolling and roiling down the creek, appearing and disappearing, feet up or head up, it didn't matter which.

The cow started up the talk again. Somebody wondered whether it would hit one of the clear places under the top girder of the bridge and get through or whether it would get tangled in the

drift and trash that had piled against the upright girders and braces. Somebody remembered how about ten years before so much driftwood had piled up on the bridge that it was
knocked off its foundations. Then the cow hit.
It hit the edge of the drift against one of the
girders, and hung there. For a few seconds it
seemed as though it might tear loose, but then
we saw it was really caught. It bobbed and
heaved on its side there in a slow, grinding, uneasy fashion. It had a yoke around its neck, the
kind made out of a forked limb to keep a
jumper behind fence.

"She shore jumped one fence," one of the
men said.

And another: "Well, she done jumped her
last one, fer a fack."

Then they began to wonder about whose cow
it might be. They decided it must belong to Milt
Alley. They said that he had a cow that was a
jumper, and kept her in a fenced-in piece of
ground up the creek. I had never seen Milt
Alley, but I knew who he was. He was a squatter and lived up the hills a way, on a shirt-tail
patch of set-on-edge land, in a cabin. He was
pore white trash. He had lots of children. I had
seen the children at school, when they came.
They were thin-faced, with straight, sticky-
looking, dough-colored hair, and they smelled
something like old sour buttermilk, not because
they drank so much buttermilk but because that
is the sort of smell which children out of those
cabins tend to have. The big Alley boy drew
dirty pictures and showed them to the little boys
at school.

That was Milt Alley's cow. It looked like the
kind of cow he would have, a scrawny, old,
sway-backed cow, with a yoke around her neck.
I wondered if Milt Alley had another cow.

"Poppa," I said, "do you think Milt Alley has
got another cow?"

"You say 'Mr. Alley,' " my father said
quietly.

"Do you think he has?"

"No telling," my father said.

Then a big gangly boy, about fifteen, who
was sitting on a scraggly little old mule with a
piece of croker sack thrown across the saw-
tooth spine, and who had been staring at the
cow, suddenly said to nobody in particular,
"Reckin anybody ever et drownt cow?"

He was the kind of boy who might just as
well as not have been the son of Milt Alley, with

his faded and patched overalls ragged at the
bottom of the pants and the mud-stiff brogans
hanging off his skinny, bare ankles at the level
of the mule's belly. He had said what he did,
and then looked embarrassed and sullen when
all the eyes swung at him. He hadn't meant to
say it, I am pretty sure now. He would have
been too proud to say it, just as Milt Alley
would have been too proud. He had just been
thinking out loud, and the words had popped
out.

There was an old man standing there on the
pike, an old man with a white beard. "Son," he
said to the embarrassed and sullen boy on the
mule, "you live long enough and you'll find a
man will eat anything when the time comes."

"Time gonna come fer some folks this year,"
another man said.

"Son," the old man said, "in my time I et
things a man don't like to think on. I was a
sojer and I rode with Gin'l Forrest, and them
things we et when the time come. I tell you. I
et meat what got up and run when you taken
out yore knife to cut a slice to put on the fire.
You had to knock it down with a carbeen butt,
it was so active. That-air meat would jump like
a bullfrog, it was so full of skippers."

But nobody was listening to the old man. The
boy on the mule turned his sullen sharp face
from him, dug a heel into the side of the mule
and went off up the pike with a motion which
made you think that any second you would hear
mule bones clashing inside that lank and scrof-
ulous hide.

"Cy Dundee's boy," a man said, and nodded
toward the figure going up the pike on the mule.

"Reckin Cy Dundee's young-uns seen times
they'd settle fer drownt cow," another man said.

The old man with the beard peered at them
both from his weak, slow eyes, first at one and
then at the other. "Live long enough," he said,
"and a man will settle fer what he kin git."

Then there was silence again, with the people
looking at the red, foam-flecked water.

My father lifted the bridle rein in his left
hand, and the mare turned and walked around
the group and up the pike. We rode on up to
our big gate, where my father dismounted to
open it and let me myself ride Nellie Gray
through. When he got to the lane that led off
from the drive about two hundred yards from
our house, my father said, "Grab on." I
grabbed on, and he let me down to the ground.

"I'm going to ride down and look at my corn," he said. "You go on." He took the lane, and I stood there on the drive and watched him ride off. He was wearing cowhide boots and an old hunting coat, and I thought that that made him look very military, like a picture. That and the way he rode.

I did not go to the house. Instead, I went by the vegetable garden and crossed behind the stables, and headed down for Dellie's cabin. I wanted to go down and play with Jebb, who was Dellie's little boy about two years older than I was. Besides, I was cold. I shivered as I walked, and I had gooseflesh. The mud which crawled up between my toes with every step I took was like ice. Dellie would have a fire, but she wouldn't make me put on shoes and stockings.

Dellie's cabin was of logs, with one side, because it was on a slope, set on limestone chunks, with a little porch attached to it, and had a little whitewashed fence around it and a gate with plow-points on a wire to clink when somebody came in, and had two big white oaks in the yard and some flowers and a nice privy in the back with some honeysuckle growing over it. Dellie and Old Jebb, who was Jebb's father and who lived with Dellie and had lived with her for twenty-five years even if they never had got married, were careful to keep everything nice around their cabin. They had the name all over the community for being clean and clever Negroes. Dellie and Jebb were what they used to call "white-folks' niggers." There was a big difference between their cabin and the other two cabins farther down where the other tenants lived. My father kept the other cabins weatherproof, but he couldn't undertake to go down and pick up after the litter they strewed. They didn't take the trouble to have a vegetable patch like Dellie and Jebb or to make preserves from wild plum, and jelly from crab apple the way Dellie did. They were shiftless, and my father was always threatening to get shed of them. But he never did. When they finally left, they just up and left on their own, for no reason, to go and be shiftless somewhere else. Then some more came. But meanwhile they lived down there, Matt Rawson and his family, and Sid Turner and his, and I played with their children all over the farm when they weren't working. But when I wasn't around they were mean sometimes to Little Jebb. That was because the other tenants down there were jealous of Dellie and Jebb.

I was so cold that I ran the last fifty yards to Dellie's gate. As soon as I had entered the yard, I saw that the storm had been hard on Dellie's flowers. The yard was, as I have said, on a slight slope, and the water running across had gutted the flower beds and washed out all the good black woods-earth which Dellie had brought in. What little grass there was in the yard was plastered sparsely down on the ground, the way the drainage water had left it. It reminded me of the way the fluff was plastered down on the skin of the drowned chicks that the strange man had been picking up, up in my mother's chicken yard.

I took a few steps up the path to the cabin, and then I saw that the drainage water had washed a lot of trash and filth out from under Dellie's house. Up toward the porch, the ground was not clean any more. Old pieces of rag, two or three rusted cans, pieces of rotten rope, some hunks of old dog dung, broken glass, old paper, and all sorts of things like that had washed out from under Dellie's house to foul her clean yard. It looked just as bad as the yards of the other cabins, or worse. It was worse, as a matter of fact, because it was a surprise. I had never thought of all that filth being under Dellie's house. It was not anything against Dellie that the stuff had been under the cabin. Trash will get under any house. But I did not think of that when I saw the foulness which had washed out on the ground which Dellie sometimes used to sweep with a twig broom to make nice and clean.

I picked my way past the filth, being careful not to get my bare feet on it, and mounted to Dellie's door. When I knocked, I heard her voice telling me to come in.

It was dark inside the cabin, after the daylight, but I could make out Dellie piled up in bed under a quilt, and Little Jebb crouched by the hearth, where a low fire simmered. "Howdy," I said to Dellie, "how you feeling?"

Her big eyes, the whites surprising and glaring in the black face, fixed on me as I stood there, but she did not reply. It did not look like Dellie, or act like Dellie, who would grumble and bustle around our kitchen, talking to herself, scolding me or Little Jebb, clanking pans, making all sorts of unnecessary noises and mutterings like an old-fashioned black steam thrasher engine when it has got up an extra head of steam and keeps popping the governor and rumbling and shaking on its wheels. But now Dellie just lay up there on the bed, under the patch-work quilt, and turned the black face, which I scarcely recognized, and the glaring white eyes to me.

"How you feeling?" I repeated.

"I'se sick," the voice said croakingly out of the strange black face which was not attached to Dellie's big, squat body, but stuck out from under a pile of tangled bedclothes. Then the voice added: "Mighty sick."

"I'm sorry," I managed to say.

The eyes remained fixed on me for a moment, then they left me and the head rolled back on the pillow. "Sorry," the voice said, in a flat way which wasn't question or statement of anything. It was just the empty word put into the air with no meaning or expression, to float off like a feather or a puff of smoke, while the big eyes, with the whites like the peeled white of hard-boiled eggs, stared at the ceiling.

"Dellie," I said after a minute, "there's a tramp up at the house. He's got a knife."

She was not listening. She closed her eyes.

I tiptoed over to the hearth where Jebb was and crouched beside him. We began to talk in low voices. I was asking him to get out his train and play train. Old Jebb had put spool wheels on three cigar boxes and put wire links between the boxes to make a train for Jebb. The box that was the locomotive had the top closed and a length of broom stick for a smoke stack. Jebb didn't want to get the train out, but I told him I would go home if he didn't. So he got out the train, and the colored rocks, and fossils of crinoid stems, and other junk he used for the load, and we began to push it around, talking the way we thought trainmen talked, making a chuck-chucking sound under the breath for the noise of the locomotive and now and then uttering low, cautious toots for the whistle. We got so interested in playing train that the toots got louder. Then, before he thought, Jebb gave a good, loud *toot-toot,* blowing for a crossing.

"Come here," the voice said from the bed.

Jebb got up slow from his hands and knees, giving me a sudden, naked, inimical look.

"Come here!" the voice said.

Jebb went to the bed. Dellie propped herself weakly up on one arm, muttering, "Come closer."

Jebb stood closer.

"Last thing I do, I'm gonna do it," Dellie said. "Done tole you to be quiet."

Then she slapped him. It was an awful slap, more awful for the kind of weakness which it came from and brought to focus. I had seen her slap Jebb before, but the slapping had always been the kind of easy slap you would expect from a good-natured, grumbling Negro woman like Dellie. But this was different. It was awful. It was so awful that Jebb didn't make a sound. The tears just popped out and ran down his face, and his breath came sharp, like gasps.

Dellie fell back. "Cain't even be sick," she said to the ceiling. "Git sick and they won't even let you lay. They tromp all over you. Cain't even be sick." Then she closed her eyes.

I went out of the room. I almost ran getting to the door, and I did run across the porch and down the steps and across the yard, not caring whether or not I stepped on the filth which had washed out from under the cabin. I ran almost all the way home. Then I thought about my mother catching me with the bare feet. So I went down to the stables.

I heard a noise in the crib, and opened the door. There was Big Jebb, sitting on an old nail keg, shelling corn into a bushel basket. I went in, pulling the door shut behind me, and crouched on the floor near him. I crouched there for a couple of minutes before either of us spoke, and watched him shelling the corn.

He had very big hands, knotted and grayish at the joints, with calloused palms which seemed to be streaked with rust with the rust coming up between the fingers to show from the back. His hands were so strong and tough that he could take a big ear of corn and rip the grains right off the cob with the palm of his hand, all in one motion, like a machine. "Work long as me," he would say, "and the good Lawd'll give you a hand lak cass-ion won't nuthin' hurt." And his hands did look like cast iron, old cast iron streaked with rust.

He was an old man, up in his seventies, thirty years or more older than Dellie, but he was strong as a bull. He was a squat sort of man, heavy in the shoulders, with remarkably long arms, the kind of build they say the river natives have on the Congo from paddling so much in their boats. He had a round bullet-head, set on powerful shoulders. His skin was very black, and the thin hair on his head was now grizzled like tufts of old cotton batting. He had small eyes and a flat nose, not big, and the kindest and wisest old face in the world, the blunt, sad, wise face of an old animal peering tolerantly out on the goings-on of the merely human creatures before him. He was a good man, and I loved him next to my mother and father. I crouched there on the floor of the crib and watched him shell corn with the rusty cast-iron hands, while he looked down at me out of the little eyes set in the blunt face.

"Dellie says she's mighty sick," I said.

"Yeah," he said.

"What's she sick from?"

"Woman-mizry," he said.

"What's woman-mizry?"

"Hit comes on 'em," he said. "Hit just comes on 'em when the time comes."

"What is it?"

"Hit is the change," he said. "Hit is the change of life and time."

"What changes?"

"You too young to know."

"Tell me."

"Time come and you find out everthing."

I knew that there was no use in asking him any more. When I asked him things and he said that, I always knew that he would not tell me. So I continued to crouch there and watch him. Now that I had sat there a little while, I was cold again.

"What you shiver fer?" he asked me.

"I'm cold. I'm cold because it's blackberry winter," I said.

"Maybe 'tis and maybe 'tain't," he said.

"My mother says it is."

"Ain't sayen Miss Sallie doan know and ain't sayen she do. But folks doan know everthing."

"Why isn't it blackberry winter?"

"Too late fer blackberry winter. Blackberries done bloomed."

"She said it was."

"Blackberry winter just a leetle cold spell. Hit come and then hit go away, and hit is growed summer of a sudden lak a gunshot. Ain't no tellen hit will go way this time."

"It's June," I said.

"June," he replied with great contempt. "That what folks say. What June mean? Maybe hit is come cold to stay."

"Why?"

"Cause this-here old yearth is tahrd. Hit is tahrd and ain't gonna perduce. Lawd let hit

come rain one time forty days and forty nights, 'cause He was tahrd of sinful folks. Maybe this-here old yearth say to the Lawd, Lawd, I done plum tahrd, Lawd, lemme rest. And Lawd say, Yearth, you done yore best, you give 'em cawn and you give 'em taters, and all they think on is they gut, and, Yearth, you kin take a rest."

"What will happen?"

"Folks will eat up everthing. The yearth won't perduce no more. Folks cut down all the trees and burn 'em cause they cold, and the yearth won't grow no more. I been tellen 'em. I been tellen folks. Sayen, maybe this year, hit is the time. But they doan listen to me, how the yearth is tahrd. Maybe this year they find out."

"Will everything die?"

"Everthing and everbody, hit will be so."

"This year?"

"Ain't no tellen. Maybe this year."

"My mother said it is blackberry winter," I said confidently, and got up.

"Ain't sayen nuthin' agin Miss Sallie," he said.

I went to the door of the crib. I was really cold now. Running, I had got up a sweat and now I was worse.

I hung on the door, looking at Jebb, who was shelling corn again.

"There's a tramp came to the house," I said. I had almost forgotten the tramp.

"Yeah."

"He came by the back way. What was he doing down there in the storm?"

"They comes and they goes," he said, "and ain't no tellen."

"He had a mean knife."

"The good ones and the bad ones, they comes and they goes. Storm or sun, light or dark. They is folks and they comes and they goes lak folks."

I hung on the door, shivering.

He studied me a moment, then said, "You git on to the house. You ketch yore death. Then what yore mammy say?"

I hesitated.

"You git," he said.

When I came to the back yard, I saw that my father was standing by the back porch and the tramp was walking toward him. They began talking before I reached them, but I got there just as my father was saying, "I'm sorry, but I haven't got any work. I got all the hands on the place I need now. I won't need any extra until wheat thrashing."

The stranger made no reply, just looked at my father.

My father took out his leather coin purse, and got out a half-dollar. He held it toward the man. "This is for half a day," he said.

The man looked at the coin, and then at my father, making no motion to take the money. But that was the right amount. A dollar a day was what you paid them back in 1910. And the man hadn't even worked half a day.

Then the man reached out and took the coin. He dropped it into the right side pocket of his coat. Then he said, very slowly and without feeling: "I didn't want to work on your —— farm."

He used the word which they would have frailed me to death for using.

I looked at my father's face and it was streaked white under the sunburn. Then he said, "Get off this place. Get off this place or I won't be responsible."

The man dropped his right hand into his pants pocket. It was the pocket where he kept the knife. I was just about to yell to my father about the knife when the hand came back out with nothing in it. The man gave a kind of twisted grin, showing where the teeth had been knocked out above the new scar. I thought that instant how maybe he had tried before to pull a knife on somebody else and had got his teeth knocked out.

So now he just gave that twisted, sickish grin out of the unmemorable grayish face, and then spat on the brick path. The glob landed just about six inches from the toe of my father's right boot. My father looked down at it, and so did I. I thought that if the glob had hit my father's boot something would have happened. I looked down and saw the bright glob, and on one side of it my father's strong cowhide boots, with the brass eyelets and the leather thongs, heavy boots splashed with good red mud and set solid on the bricks, and on the other side the pointed-toe, broken, black shoes, on which the mud looked so sad and out of place. Then I saw one of the black shoes move a little, just a twitch first, then a real step backward.

The man moved in a quarter circle to the end of the porch, with my father's steady gaze upon him all the while. At the end of the porch, the man reached up to the shelf where the wash pans were to get his little newspaper-wrapped parcel. Then he disappeared around the corner of the house and my father mounted the porch and went into the kitchen without a word.

I followed around the house to see what the man would do. I wasn't afraid of him now, no matter if he did have the knife. When I got around in front, I saw him going out the yard gate and starting up the drive toward the pike. So I ran to catch up with him. He was sixty yards or so up the drive before I caught up.

I did not walk right up even with him at first, but trailed him, the way a kid will, about seven or eight feet behind, now and then running two or three steps in order to hold my place against his longer stride. When I first came up behind him, he turned to give me a look, just a meaningless look, and then fixed his eyes up the drive and kept on walking.

When we had got around the bend in the drive which cut the house from sight, and were going along by the edge of the woods, I decided to come up even with him. I ran a few steps, and was by his side, or almost, but some feet off to the right. I walked along in this position for a while, and he never noticed me. I walked along until we got within sight of the big gate that let on the pike.

Then I said: "Where did you come from?"

He looked at me then with a look which seemed almost surprised that I was there. Then he said, "It ain't none of yore business."

We went on another fifty feet.

Then I said, "Where are you going?"

He stopped, studied me dispassionately for a moment, then suddenly took a step toward me and leaned his face down at me. The lips jerked back, but not in any grin, to show where the teeth were knocked out and to make the scar on the lower lip come white with the tension.

He said: "Stop following me. You don't stop following me and I cut yore throat, you little son-of-a-bitch."

Then he went on to the gate, and up the pike.

That was thirty-five years ago. Since that time my father and mother have died. I was still a boy, but a big boy, when my father got cut on the blade of a mowing machine and died of lockjaw. My mother sold the place and went to town to live with her sister. But she never took hold after my father's death, and she died within three years, right in middle life. My aunt always said, "Sallie just died of a broken heart, she was so devoted." Dellie is dead, too, but she died, I heard, quite a long time after we sold the farm.

As for Little Jebb, he grew up to be a mean and ficey Negro. He killed another Negro in a fight and got sent to the penitentiary, where he is yet, the last I heard tell. He probably grew up to be mean and ficey from just being picked on so much by the children of the other tenants, who were jealous of Jebb and Dellie for being thrifty and clever and being white-folks' niggers.

Old Jebb lived forever. I saw him ten years ago and he was about a hundred then, and not looking much different. He was living in town then, on relief—that was back in the Depression—when I went to see him. He said to me: "Too strong to die. When I was a young feller just comen on and seen how things wuz, I prayed the Lawd. I said, Oh, Lawd, gimme strength and meke me strong fer to do and to in-dure. The Lawd hearkened to my prayer. He give me strength. I was in-duren proud fer being strong and me much man. The Lawd give me my prayer and my strength. But now He done gone off and fergot me and left me alone with my strength. A man doan know what to pray fer, and him mortal."

Jebb is probably living yet, as far as I know.

That is what has happened since the morning when the tramp leaned his face down at me and showed his teeth and said: "Stop following me. You don't stop following me and I cut yore throat, you little son-of-a-bitch." That was what he said, for me not to follow him. But I did follow him, all the years.

*Phyllis McGinley*

# LAMENT OF THE NORMAL CHILD

*I was strolling past a schoolhouse when I spied a*
*   sobbing lad.*
*  His little face was sorrowful and pale.*

*"Come, tell me why you weep," I said, "and why*
*   you seem so sad."*
*  And thus the urchin lisped his tragic tale:*

The school where I go is a modern school
  With numerous modern graces.
And there they cling to the modern rule
  Of "Cherish the Problem Cases!"
From nine to three
I develop Me.     10
  I dance when I'm feeling dancy,
Or everywhere lay on
With creaking crayon
  The colors that suit my fancy.
But when the commoner tasks are done,
  Deserted, ignored, I stand.
For the rest have complexes, everyone;
  Or a hyperactive gland.
Oh, how can I ever be reconciled
  To my hatefully normal station?   20
Why couldn't I be a Problem Child
  Endowed with a small fixation?
Why wasn't I trained for a Problem Child
  With an Interesting Fixation?

I dread the sound of the morning bell.
  The iron has entered my soul.
I'm a square little peg who fits too well
  In a square little normal hole.
For seven years
In Mortimer Sears   30
  Has the Œdipus angle flourished;
And Jessamine Gray,
She cheats at play
  Because she is undernourished.
The teachers beam on Frederick Knipe
  With scientific gratitude,
For Fred, they claim, is a perfect type
  Of the Antisocial Attitude.
And Cuthbert Jones has his temper riled
  In a way professors mention.   40
But I am a Perfectly Normal Child,
  So I don't get any attention.
I'm nothing at all but a Normal Child,
  So I don't get the least attention.

The others jeer as they pass me by.
  They titter without forbearance.
"He's Perfectly Normal," they shrilly cry,
  "With Perfectly Normal parents."
For I learn to read
With a normal speed.   50

I answer when I'm commanded.
Infected antrums
Don't give me tantrums.
   I don't even write left-handed.
I build with blocks when they give me blocks.
   When it's busy hour, I labor.
And I seldom delight in landing socks
   On the ear of my little neighbor.

So here, by luckier lads reviled,
   I sit on the steps alone.                                    60
Why couldn't I be a Problem Child
   With a Case to call my own?
Why wasn't I born a Problem Child
   With a Complex of my own?


*Rudyard Kipling*

# GENTLEMEN-RANKERS

To the legion of the lost ones, to the cohort of the damned,
   To my brethren in their sorrow overseas,
Sings a gentleman of England cleanly bred, machinely crammed,
   And a trooper of the Empress, if you please.
Yes, a trooper of the forces who has run his own six horses,
   And faith he went the pace and went it blind,
And the world was more than kin while he held the ready tin,
   But to-day the Sergeant's something less than kind.
      We're poor little lambs who've lost our way,
        Baa! Baa! Baa!                                      10
      We're little black sheep who've gone astray,
        Baa–aa–aa!
      Gentlemen-rankers out on the spree,
      Damned from here to Eternity,
      God ha' mercy on such as we,
        Baa! Yah! Bah!

Oh, it's sweet to sweat through stables, sweet to empty kitchen slops,
   And it's sweet to hear the tales the troopers tell,
To dance with blowzy housemaids at the regimental hops
   And thrash the cad who says you waltz too well.                      20
Yes, it makes you cock-a-hoop to be "Rider" to your troop,
   And branded with a blasted worsted spur,
When you envy, O how keenly, one poor Tommy living cleanly
   Who blacks your boots and sometimes calls you "Sir."

If the home we never write to, and the oaths we never keep,
   And all we know most distant and most dear,
Across the snoring barrack-room return to break our sleep,
   Can you blame us if we soak ourselves in beer?
When the drunken comrade mutters and the great guard-lantern gutters
   And the horror of our fall is written plain,                        30
Every secret, self-revealing on the aching whitewashed ceiling,
   Do you wonder that we drug ourselves from pain?

GENTLEMEN-RANKERS: From *Departmental Ditties and Ballads and Barrack-Room Ballads*, by Rudyard Kipling. Reprinted by permission of Mrs. George Bambridge, Doubleday & Company, Inc., The Macmillan Company of Canada, and A. P. Watt & Son.

We have done with Hope and Honour, we are lost to Love and Truth,
    We are dropping down the ladder rung by rung,
And the measure of our torment is the measure of our youth.
    God help us, for we knew the worst too young!
Our shame is clean repentance for the crime that brought the sentence,
    Our pride it is to know no spur of pride,
And the Curse of Reuben holds us till an alien turf enfolds us
    And we die, and none can tell Them where we died.      40
        We're poor little lambs who've lost our way,
          Baa! Baa! Baa!
        We're little black sheep who've gone astray,
          Baa–aa–aa!
        Gentlemen-rankers out on the spree,
          Damned from here to Eternity,
        God ha' mercy on such as we,
          Baa! Yah! Bah!

## William Wordsworth
# THERE WAS A BOY

There was a Boy; ye knew him well, ye cliffs
And islands of Winander!—many a time,
At evening, when the earliest stars began
To move along the edges of the hills,
Rising or setting, would he stand alone,
Beneath the trees, or by the glimmering lake;
And there, with fingers interwoven, both hands
Pressed closely palm to palm and to his mouth
Uplifted, he, as through an instrument,
Blew mimic hootings to the silent owls,     10
That they might answer him.—And they would
   shout
Across the watery vale, and shout again,
Responsive to his call,—with quivering peals,
And long halloos, and screams, and echoes loud
Redoubled and redoubled; concourse wild
Of jocund din! And, when there came a pause
Of silence such as baffled his best skill:
Then sometimes, in that silence, while he hung
Listening, a gentle shock of mild surprise
Has carried far into his heart the voice     20
Of mountain-torrents; or the visible scene
Would enter unawares into his mind
With all its solemn imagery, its rocks,
Its woods, and that uncertain heaven received
Into the bosom of the steady lake.

This boy was taken from his mates, and died
In childhood, ere he was full twelve years old.
Pre-eminent in beauty is the vale
Where he was born and bred: the churchyard
   hangs
Upon a slope above the village-school;     30
And through that churchyard when my way has led
On summer-evenings, I believe that there
A long half-hour together I have stood
Mute—looking at the grave in which he lies!

## Robert Frost
# BIRCHES

When I see birches bend to left and right
Across the lines of straighter darker trees,
I like to think some boy's been swinging them.
But swinging doesn't bend them down to stay.
Ice-storms do that. Often you must have seen them
Loaded with ice a sunny winter morning
After a rain. They click upon themselves
As the breeze rises, and turn many-colored
As the stir cracks and crazes their enamel.
Soon the sun's warmth makes them shed crystal
   shells     10
Shattering and avalanching on the snowcrust—
Such heaps of broken glass to sweep away

You'd think the inner dome of heaven had fallen.
They are dragged to the withered bracken by the
    load,
And they seem not to break; though once they are
    bowed
So low for long, they never right themselves:
You may see their trunks arching in the woods
Years afterwards, trailing their leaves on the
    ground
Like girls on hands and knees that throw their hair
Before them over their heads to dry in the sun.   20
But I was going to say when Truth broke in
With all her matter-of-fact about the ice-storm
(Now am I free to be poetical?)
I should prefer to have some boy bend them
As he went out and in to fetch the cows—
Some boy too far from town to learn baseball,
Whose only play was what he found himself,
Summer or winter, and could play alone.
One by one he subdued his father's trees
By riding them down over and over again      30
Until he took the stiffness out of them,
And not one but hung limp, not one was left
For him to conquer. He learned all there was
To learn about not launching out too soon
And so not carrying the tree away
Clear to the ground. He always kept his poise
To the top branches, climbing carefully
With the same pains you use to fill a cup
Up to the brim, and even above the brim.
Then he flung outward, feet first, with a swish,   40
Kicking his way down through the air to the
    ground.
So was I once myself a swinger of birches.
And so I dream of going back to be.
It's when I'm weary of considerations,
And life is too much like a pathless wood
Where your face burns and tickles with the
    cobwebs
Broken across it, and one eye is weeping
From a twig's having lashed it open,
I'd like to get away from earth a while
And then come back to it and begin over.      50
May no fate wilfully misunderstand me
And half grant what I wish and snatch me away
Not to return. Earth's the right place for love:
I don't know where it's likely to go better.

I'd like to go by climbing a high birch tree,
And climb black branches up a snow-white trunk
*Toward* heaven, till the tree could bear no more,
But dipped its top and set me down again.
That would be good both going and coming back.
One could do worse than be a swinger of
    birches.                                    60


## Henry Vaughan
# THE RETREAT


Happy those early days, when **I**
Shined in my angel-infancy!
Before I understood this place
Appointed for my second race,
Or taught my soul to fancy aught
But a white, celestial thought,
When yet I had not walked above
A mile or two from my first love,
And looking back—at that short space—
Could see a glimpse of his bright face;      10
When on some gilded cloud or flower
My gazing soul would dwell an hour,
And in those weaker glories spy
Some shadows of eternity;
Before I taught my tongue to wound
My conscience with a sinful sound,
Or had the black art to dispense
A several sin to every sense,
But felt through all this fleshy dress
Bright shoots of everlastingness.            20
    O, how I long to travel back,
And tread again that ancient track!
That I might once more reach that plain,
Where first I left my glorious train;
From whence the enlightened spirit sees
That shady city of palm trees.
But ah! my soul with too much stay
Is drunk, and staggers in the way!
Some men a forward motion love,
But I by backward steps would move;          30
And when this dust falls to the urn,
In that state I came, return.

*Dylan Thomas*
# FERN HILL

Now as I was young and easy under the apple boughs
About the lilting house and happy as the grass was green,
    The night above the dingle starry,
      Time let me hail and climb
    Golden in the heydays of his eyes,
And honoured among wagons I was prince of the apple towns
And once below a time I lordly had the trees and leaves
      Trail with daisies and barley
    Down the rivers of the windfall light.

And as I was green and carefree, famous among the barns      10
About the happy yard and singing as the farm was home,
    In the sun that is young once only,
      Time let me play and be
    Golden in the mercy of his means,
And green and golden I was huntsman and herdsman, the calves
Sang to my horn, the foxes on the hills barked clear and cold,
      And the sabbath rang slowly
    In the pebbles of the holy streams.

All the sun long it was running, it was lovely, the hay–
Fields high as the house, the tunes from the chimneys, it was air      20
    And playing, lovely and watery
      And fire green as grass.
    And nightly under the simple stars
As I rode to sleep the owls were bearing the farm away,
All the moon long I heard, blessed among stables, the nightjars
      Flying with the ricks, and the horses
    Flashing into the dark.

And then to awake, and the farm, like a wanderer white
With the dew, come back, the cock on his shoulder: it was all
    Shining, it was Adam and maiden,      30
      The sky gathered again
    And the sun grew round that very day.
So it must have been after the birth of the simple light
In the first, spinning place, the spellbound horses walking warm
      Out of the whinnying green stable
    On to the fields of praise.

And honoured among foxes and pheasants by the gay house
Under the new made clouds and happy as the heart was long,
    In the sun born over and over,
      I ran my heedless ways,      40

My wishes raced through the house-high hay
And nothing I cared, at my sky blue trades, that time allows
In all his tuneful turning so few and such morning songs
       Before the children green and golden
         Follow him out of grace,

Nothing I cared, in the lamb white days, that time would take me
Up to the swallow thronged loft by the shadow of my hand,
       In the moon that is always rising,
         Nor that riding to sleep
       I should hear him fly with the high fields            50
And wake to the farm forever fled from the childless land.
Oh as I was young and easy in the mercy of his means,
        Time held me green and dying
       Though I sang in my chains like the sea.

# FAMILY LIFE

THE CHILD'S first relationships to other persons are formed within the family, and the success or failure, the richness or poverty, the closeness or distance, of these relationships have, we are told, a great deal to do with determining the pattern of all his later ones. Most of us wonder at some time or other how we became what we are, whether we would have been different if our parents had brought us up differently, or had not died when we were young, or had had a different job, place to live, income level. Writers have always wondered in the same way about themselves and others, and have sought to treat these matters with perspective and insight. This chapter shows how literature can help us to understand ourselves by reflecting upon the causes of our personalities.

Certain fundamental types of family conflict and family attitude that have often been explored in literature are found in this chapter. The dominating parent who wishes to cast the child into some preconceived mold is represented by Betsey Trotwood, though she is frustrated from the start. There is the loving parent who, wishing the younger generation to develop in its own way, is in harmony with the child: Naomi in the story of Ruth, and the father in Yeats's "Prayer." There are the parents and children who just don't understand one another: the family in "Sixteen." There is the well-meaning parent whose best intentions turn out wrong: Michael, in Wordsworth's poem, and the father of Lincoln Steffens. Mateo Falcone and the father of Jan in "The Girl in Arles" are fathers who face the problem of teaching their children the ways of the society into which they must go. These problems are also discussed by David Riesman, who points out significant changes in the way parents in our day conceive of their job of bringing up children. There are children who disappoint their parents in one way or another: Fortunato, Jan, Luke, and Edward.

The works that follow, then, concern various young people, not so much directly as in their relationships to others, particularly their parents and brothers and sisters. They call attention to the perpetually recurrent feelings of parents and children toward one another, and dramatize the emotions of love and hate, loyalty and envy, hope and disappointment, pride and humility. And whether or not they pronounce moral judgment upon the acts and attitudes they describe, they have, or can have, that indirect moral effect that is peculiar to good literature, for they broaden our experience and understanding of the range of good and evil that is possible in these fundamental human relationships.

*From the Bible*

# THE BOOK OF RUTH

Now it came to pass in the days when the judges ruled, that there was a famine in the land. And a certain man of Bethlehem-judah went to sojourn in the country of Moab, he, and his wife, and his two sons. And the name of the man was Elimelech, and the name of his wife Naomi, and the name of his two sons Mahlon and Chilion, Ephrathites of Bethlehem-judah. And they came into the country of Moab, and continued there.

And Elimelech Naomi's husband died; and she was left, and her two sons. And they took them wives of the women of Moab; the name of the one was Orpah, and the name of the other Ruth: and they dwelled there about ten years. And Mahlon and Chilion died also both of them; and the woman was left of her two sons and her husband.

Then she arose with her daughters-in-law, that she might return from the country of Moab; for she had heard in the country of Moab how that the Lord had visited his people in giving them bread. Wherefore she went forth out of the place where she was, and her two daughters-in-law with her; and they went on the way to return unto the land of Judah. And Naomi said unto her two daughters-in-law, "Go, return each to her mother's house; the Lord deal kindly with you, as ye have dealt with the dead, and with me. The Lord grant you that ye may find rest, each of you in the house of her husband." Then she kissed them; and they lifted up their voice, and wept. And they said unto her, "Surely we will return with thee unto thy people."

And Naomi said, "Turn again, my daughters; why will ye go with me? Are there yet any more sons in my womb, that they may be your husbands? Turn again, my daughters, go your way; for I am too old to have an husband. If I should say, 'I have hope,' if I should have an husband also to-night, and should also bear sons, would ye tarry for them till they were grown? Would ye stay for them from having husbands? Nay, my daughters; for it grieveth me much for your sakes that the hand of the Lord is gone out against me." And they lifted up their voice, and wept again, and Orpah kissed her mother-in-law; but Ruth clave unto her. And she said, "Behold, thy sister-in-law is gone back unto her people, and unto her gods; return thou after thy sister-in-law."

And Ruth said, "Intreat me not to leave thee, or to return from following after thee, for whither thou goest, I will go; and where thou lodgest, I will lodge. Thy people shall be my people, and thy God my God. Where thou diest, will I die, and there will I be buried. The Lord do so to me, and more also, if aught but death part thee and me."

When she saw that she was steadfastly minded to go with her, then she left speaking unto her. So they two went until they came to Bethlehem. And it came to pass, when they were come to Bethlehem, that all the city was moved about them, and they said, "Is this Naomi?"

And she said unto them, "Call me not Naomi, call me Mara; for the Almighty hath dealt very bitterly with me. I went out full, and the Lord hath brought me home again empty. Why then call ye me Naomi, seeing the Lord hath testified against me, and the Almighty hath afflicted me?"

So Naomi returned, and Ruth the Moabitess, her daughter-in-law, with her, which returned out of the country of Moab; and they came to Bethlehem in the beginning of barley harvest.

And Naomi had a kinsman of her husband's, a mighty man of wealth, of the family of Elimelech; and his name was Boaz. And Ruth the Moabitess said unto Naomi, "Let me now go to the field, and glean ears of corn after him in whose sight I shall find grace." And she said unto her, "Go, my daughter." And she went, and came, and gleaned in the field after the reapers; and her hap was to light on a part of the field belonging unto Boaz, who was of the kindred of Elimelech.

And, behold, Boaz came from Bethlehem, and said unto the reapers, "The Lord be with you." And they answered him, "The Lord bless thee."

Then said Boaz unto his servant that was set over the reapers, "Whose damsel is this?"

And the servant that was set over the reapers answered and said, "It is the Moabitish damsel that came back with Naomi out of the country of Moab; and she said, 'I pray you, let me glean and gather after the reapers among the sheaves.' So she came, and hath continued even from the morning until now, that she tarried a little in the house."

Then said Boaz unto Ruth, "Hearest thou not, my daughter? Go not to glean in another field, neither go from hence, but abide here fast by my maidens. Let thine eyes be on the field that they do reap, and go thou after them. Have I not charged the young men that they shall not touch thee? And when thou art athirst, go unto the vessels, and drink of that which the young men have drawn."

Then she fell on her face, and bowed herself to the ground, and said unto him, "Why have I found grace in thine eyes, that thou shouldest take knowledge of me, seeing I am a stranger?"

And Boaz answered and said unto her, "It hath fully been showed me, all that thou hast done unto thy mother-in-law since the death of thine husband; and how thou hast left thy father and thy mother, and the land of thy nativity, and art come unto a people which thou knewest not heretofore. The Lord recompense thy work, and a full reward be given thee of the Lord God of Israel, under whose wings thou art come to trust."

Then she said, "Let me find favour in thy sight, my lord; for that thou hast comforted me, and for that thou hast spoken friendly unto thine handmaid, though I be not like unto one of thine handmaidens."

And Boaz said unto her, "At mealtime come thou hither, and eat of the bread, and dip thy morsel in the vinegar."

And she sat beside the reapers; and he reached her parched corn, and she did eat, and was sufficed, and left. And when she was risen up to glean, Boaz commanded his young men, saying, "Let her glean even among the sheaves, and reproach her not; and let fall also some of the handfuls of purpose for her, and leave them, that she may glean them, and rebuke her not."

So she gleaned in the field until even, and beat out that she had gleaned; and it was about an ephah of barley. And she took it up, and went into the city. And her mother-in-law saw what she had gleaned; and she brought forth, and gave to her that she had reserved after she was sufficed. And her mother-in-law said unto her, "Where hast thou gleaned to-day? And where wroughtest thou? Blessed be he that did take knowledge of thee."

And she showed her mother-in-law with whom she had wrought, and said, "The man's name with whom I wrought to-day is Boaz."

And Naomi said unto her daughter-in-law, "Blessed be he of the Lord, who hath not left off his kindness to the living and to the dead." And Naomi said unto her, "The man is near of kin unto us, one of our next kinsmen."

And Ruth the Moabitess said, "He said unto me also, 'Thou shalt keep fast by my young men, until they have ended all my harvest.' "

And Naomi said unto Ruth her daughter-in-law, "It is good, my daughter, that thou go out with his maidens, that they meet thee not in any other field." So she kept fast by the maidens of Boaz to glean unto the end of barley harvest and of wheat harvest; and dwelt with her mother-in-law.

Then Naomi her mother-in-law said unto her, "My daughter, shall I not seek rest for thee, that it may be well with thee? And now is not Boaz of our kindred, with whose maidens thou wast? Behold, he winnoweth barley to-night in the threshing-floor. Wash thyself therefore, and anoint thee, and put thy raiment upon thee, and get thee down to the floor; but make not thyself known unto the man, until he shall have done eating and drinking. And it shall be, when he lieth down, that thou shalt mark the place where he shall lie, and thou shalt go in, and uncover his feet, and lay thee down; and he will tell thee what thou shalt do."

And she said unto her, "All that thou sayest unto me I will do."

And she went down unto the floor, and did according to all that her mother-in-law bade her. And when Boaz had eaten and drunk, and his heart was merry, he went to lie down at the end of the heap of corn; and she came softly, and uncovered his feet, and laid her down. And it came to pass at midnight, that the man was afraid, and turned himself; and, behold, a woman lay at his feet. And he said, "Who art thou?"

And she answered, "I am Ruth thine handmaid; spread therefore thy skirt over thine handmaid, for thou art a near kinsman."

And he said, "Blessed be thou of the Lord, my daughter, for thou hast showed more kindness in the latter end than at the beginning, inasmuch as thou followedst not young men, whether poor or rich. And now, my daughter, fear not; I will do to thee all that thou requirest, for all the city of my people doth know that thou art a virtuous woman. And now it is true that I am thy near kinsman; howbeit there is a kinsman nearer than I. Tarry this night, and it shall be in the morning, that if he will perform unto thee the part of a kinsman, well, let him do the kinsman's part; but if he will not do the part of a kinsman to thee, then will I do the part of a kinsman to thee, as the Lord liveth. Lie down until the morning."

And she lay at his feet until the morning, and she rose up before one could know another. And he said, "Let it not be known that a woman came into the floor." Also he said, "Bring the veil that thou hast upon thee, and hold it." And when she held it, he measured six measures of barley, and laid it on her; and she went into the city.

And when she came to her mother-in-law, she said, "Who art thou, my daughter?"

And she told her all that the man had done to her. And she said, "These six measures of barley gave he me; for he said to me, 'Go not empty unto thy mother-in-law.' "

Then said she, "Sit still, my daughter, until thou know how the matter will fall; for the man will not be in rest, until he have finished the thing this day."

Then went Boaz up to the gate, and sat him down there: and, behold, the kinsman of whom Boaz spake came by; unto whom he said, "Ho, such a one! turn aside, sit down here." And he turned aside, and sat down. And he took ten men of the elders of the city, and said, "Sit ye down here." And they sat down.

And he said unto the kinsman, "Naomi, that is come again out of the country of Moab, selleth a parcel of land, which was our brother Elimelech's; and I thought to advertise thee, saying, 'Buy it before the inhabitants, and before the elders of my people.' If thou wilt redeem it, redeem it. But if thou wilt not redeem it, then tell me, that I may know; for there is none to redeem it beside thee; and I am after thee."

And he said, "I will redeem it."

Then said Boaz, "What day thou buyest the field of the hand of Naomi, thou must buy it also of Ruth the Moabitess, the wife of the dead, to raise up the name of the dead upon his inheritance."

And the kinsman said, "I cannot redeem it for myself, lest I mar mine own inheritance. Redeem thou my right to thyself, for I cannot redeem it."

Now this was the manner in former time in Israel concerning redeeming and concerning changing, for to confirm all things: a man plucked off his shoe, and gave it to his neighbour; and this was a testimony in Israel. Therefore the kinsman said unto Boaz, "Buy it for thee." So he drew off his shoe.

And Boaz said unto the elders, and unto all the people, "Ye are witnesses this day, that I have bought all that was Elimelech's, and all that was Chilion's and Mahlon's, of the hand of Naomi. Moreover Ruth the Moabitess, the wife of Mahlon, have I purchased to be my wife, to raise up the name of the dead upon his inheritance, that the name of the dead be not cut off from among his brethren, and from the gate of his place: ye are witnesses this day."

And all the people that were in the gate, and the elders, said, "We are witnesses. The Lord make the woman that is come into thine house like Rachel and like Leah, which two did build the house of Israel; and do thou worthily in Ephratah, and be famous in Bethlehem. And let thy house be like the house of Pharez, whom Tamar bare unto Judah, of the seed which the Lord shall give thee of this young woman."

So Boaz took Ruth, and she was his wife. And when he went in unto her, the Lord gave her conception, and she bare a son. And the women said unto Naomi, "Blessed be the Lord, which hath not left thee this day without a kinsman, that his name may be famous in Israel. And he shall be unto thee a restorer of thy life, and a nourisher of thine old age; for thy daughter-in-law, which loveth thee, which is better to thee than seven sons, hath borne him."

And Naomi took the child, and laid it in her bosom, and became nurse unto it. And the women her neighbours gave it a name, saying, "There is a son born to Naomi"; and they called his name Obed: he is the father of Jesse, the father of David.

## Lincoln Steffens
# A MISERABLE, MERRY CHRISTMAS

What interested me in our new neighborhood was not the school, nor the room I was to have in the house all to myself, but the stable which was built back of the house. My father let me direct the making of a stall, a little smaller than the other stalls, for my pony, and I prayed and hoped and my sister Lou believed that that meant that I would get the pony, perhaps for Christmas. I pointed out to her that there were three other stalls and no horses at all. This I said in order that she should answer it. She could not. My father, sounded, said that some day we might have horses and a cow; meanwhile a stable added to the value of a house. "Some day" is a pain to a boy who lives in and knows only "now." My good little sisters, to comfort me, remarked that Christmas was coming, but Christmas was always coming and grown-ups were always talking about it, asking you what you wanted and then giving you what they wanted you to have. Though

everybody knew what I wanted, I told them all again. My mother knew that I told God, too, every night. I wanted a pony, and to make sure that they understood, I declared that I wanted nothing else.

"Nothing but a pony?" my father asked.

"Nothing," I said.

"Not even a pair of high boots?"

That was hard. I did want boots, but I stuck to the pony. "No, not even boots."

"Nor candy? There ought to be something to fill your stocking with, and Santa Claus can't put a pony into a stocking."

That was true, and he couldn't lead a pony down the chimney either. But no. "All I want is a pony," I said. "If I can't have a pony, give me nothing, nothing."

Now I had been looking myself for the pony I wanted, going to sales stables, inquiring of horsemen, and I had seen several that would do. My father let me "try" them. I chose several, but my father always found some fault with them. I was in despair. When Christmas was at hand I had given up all hope of a pony, and on Christmas Eve I hung up my stocking along with my sisters', of whom, by the way, I now had three. I haven't mentioned them or their coming because, you understand, they were girls, and girls, young girls, counted for nothing in my manly life. They did not mind me either; they were so happy that Christmas Eve that I caught some of their merriment. I speculated on what I'd get; I hung up the biggest stocking I had, and we all went reluctantly to bed to wait till morning. Not to sleep; not right away. We were told that we must not only sleep promptly, we must not wake up till seven-thirty the next morning—or if we did, we must not go to the fireplace for our Christmas. Impossible.

We did sleep that night, but we woke up at six A.M. We lay in our beds and debated through the open doors whether to obey till, say, half-past six. Then we bolted. I don't know who started it, but there was a rush. We all disobeyed; we raced to disobey and get first to the fireplace in the front room downstairs. And there they were, the gifts, all sorts of wonderful things, mixed-up piles of presents; only, as I disentangled the mess, I saw that my stocking was empty; it hung limp; not a thing in it; and under and around it—nothing. My sisters had knelt down, each by her pile of gifts; they were squealing with delight, till they looked up and saw me standing there in my nightgown with nothing. They left their piles to come to me and look with me at my empty place. Nothing. They felt my stocking: nothing.

I don't remember whether I cried at that moment, but my sisters did. They ran with me back to my bed, and there we all cried till I became indignant. That helped some. I got up, dressed, and driving my sisters away, I went alone out into the yard, down to the stable, and there, all by myself, I wept. My mother came out to me by and by; she found me in my pony stall, sobbing on the floor, and she tried to comfort me. But I heard my father outside; he had come part way with her, and she was having some sort of angry quarrel with him. She tried to comfort me; besought me to come to breakfast. I could not; I wanted no comfort and no breakfast. She left me and went on into the house with sharp words for my father.

I don't know what kind of a breakfast the family had. My sisters said it was "awful." They were ashamed to enjoy their own toys. They came to me, and I was rude. I ran away from them. I went around to the front of the house, sat down on the steps, and, the crying over, I ached. I was wronged, I was hurt—I can feel now what I felt then, and I am sure that if one could see the wounds upon our hearts, there would be found still upon mine a scar from that terrible Christmas morning. And my father, the practical joker, he must have been hurt, too, a little. I saw him looking out of the window. He was watching me or something for an hour or two, drawing back the curtain ever so little lest I catch him, but I saw his face, and I think I can see now the anxiety upon it, the worried impatience.

After—I don't know how long—surely an hour or two—I was brought to the climax of my agony by the sight of a man riding a pony down the street, a pony and a brand-new saddle; the most beautiful saddle I ever saw, and it was a boy's saddle; the man's feet were not in the stirrups; his legs were too long. The outfit was perfect; it was the realization of all my dreams, the answer to all my prayers. A fine new bridle, with a light curb bit. And the pony! As he drew near, I saw that the pony was really a small horse, what we called an Indian pony, a bay, with black mane and tail, and one white foot and a white star on his forehead. For such a horse as that I would have given, I could have forgiven, anything.

But the man, a disheveled fellow with a blackened eye and a fresh-cut face, came along, reading the numbers on the houses, and, as my hopes—my impossible hopes—rose, he looked at our door and passed by, he and the pony, and the saddle and the bridle. Too much. I fell upon the steps, and having wept before, I broke now into such a flood of tears that I was a floating wreck when I heard a voice.

"Say, kid," it said, "do you know a boy named Lennie Steffens?"

I looked up. It was the man on the pony, back again, at our horse block.

"Yes," I spluttered through my tears. "That's me."

"Well," he said, "then this is your horse. I've been looking all over for you and your house. Why don't you put your number where it can be seen?"

"Get down," I said, running out to him.

He went on saying something about "ought to have got here at seven o'clock; told me to bring the nag here and tie him to your post and leave him for you. But, hell, I got into a drunk—and a fight—and a hospital, and—"

"Get down," I said.

He got down, and he boosted me up to the saddle. He offered to fit the stirrups to me, but I didn't want him to. I wanted to ride.

"What's the matter with you?" he said, angrily. "What you crying for? Don't you like the horse? He's a dandy, this horse. I know him of old. He's fine at cattle; he'll drive 'em alone."

I hardly heard, I could scarcely wait, but he persisted. He adjusted the stirrups, and then, finally, off I rode, slowly, at a walk, so happy, so thrilled, that I did not know what I was doing. I did not look back at the house or the man, I rode off up the street, taking note of everything—of the reins, of the pony's long mane, of the carved leather saddle. I had never seen anything so beautiful. And mine! I was going to ride up past Miss Kay's house. But I noticed on the horn of the saddle some stains like rain-drops, so I turned and trotted home, not to the house but to the stable. There was the family, father, mother, sisters, all working for me, all happy. They had been putting in place the tools of my new business: blankets, currycomb, brush, pitchfork—everything, and there was hay in the loft.

"What did you come back so soon for?" somebody asked. "Why didn't you go on riding?"

I pointed to the stains. "I wasn't going to get my new saddle rained on," I said. And my father laughed. "It isn't raining," he said. "Those are not rain-drops."

"They are tears," my mother gasped, and she gave my father a look which sent him off to the house. Worse still, my mother offered to wipe away the tears, still running out of my eyes. I gave her such a look as she had given him, and she went off after my father, drying her own tears. My sisters remained and we all unsaddled the pony, put on his halter, led him to his stall, tied and fed him. It began really to rain; so all the rest of that memorable day we curried and combed that pony. The girls plaited his mane, forelock, and tail, while I pitchforked hay to him and curried and brushed, curried and brushed. For a change we brought him out to drink; we led him up and down, blanketed like a race-horse; we took turns at that. But the best, the most inexhaustible fun, was to clean him. When we went reluctantly to our midday Christmas dinner, we all smelt of horse, and my sisters had to wash their faces and hands. I was asked to, but I wouldn't, till my mother bade me look in the mirror. Then I washed up—quick. My face was caked with the muddy lines of tears that had coursed over my cheeks to my mouth. Having washed away that shame, I ate my dinner, and as I ate I grew hungrier and hungrier. It was my first meal that day, and as I filled up on the turkey and the stuffing, the cranberries and the pies, the fruit and the nuts—as I swelled, I could laugh. My mother said I still choked and sobbed now and then, but I laughed, too; I saw and enjoyed my sisters' presents till—I had to go out and attend to my pony, who was there, really and truly there, the promise, the beginning, of a happy double life. And—I went and looked to make sure—there was the saddle, too, and the bridle.

But that Christmas, which my father had planned so carefully, was it the best or the worst I ever knew? He often asked me that; I never could answer as a boy. I think now that it was both. It covered the whole distance from broken-hearted misery to bursting happiness— too fast. A grown-up could hardly have stood it.

*Edmund Gosse*

# MY FATHER AND MY MOTHER

It must have been my Father who taught me my letters. To my Mother, as I have said, it was distasteful to teach, though she was so prompt and skilful to learn. My Father, on the contrary, taught cheerfully, by fits and starts. In particular, he had a scheme for rationalising geography, which I think was admirable. I was to climb upon a chair, while, standing by my side, with a pencil and a sheet of paper, he was to draw a chart of the markings on the carpet. Then, when I understood the system, another chart on a smaller scale of the furniture in the room, then of a floor of the house, then of the backgarden, then of a section of the street. The result of this was that geography came to me of itself, as a perfectly natural miniature arrangement of objects, and to this day has always been the science which gives me least difficulty. My Father also taught me the simple rules of arithmetic, a little natural history, and the elements of drawing; and he laboured long and unsuccessfully to make me learn by heart hymns, psalms and chapters of Scripture, in which I always failed ignominiously and with tears. This puzzled and vexed him, for he himself had an extremely retentive textual memory. He could not help thinking that I was naughty, and would not learn the chapters, until at last he gave up the effort. All this sketch of an education began, I believe, in my fourth year, and was not advanced or modified during the rest of my Mother's life.

Meanwhile, capable as I was of reading, I found my greatest pleasure in the pages of books. The range of these was limited, for story-books of every description were sternly excluded. No fiction of any kind, religious or secular, was admitted into the house. In this it was to my Mother, not to my Father, that the prohibition was due. She had a remarkable,

I confess to me still somewhat unaccountable impression, that to "tell a story," that is, to compose fictitious narrative of any kind, was a sin. She carried this conviction to extreme lengths. My Father, in later years, gave me some interesting examples of her firmness. As a young man in America, he had been deeply impressed by *Salathiel,* a pious prose romance of that then popular writer, the Rev. George Croly. When he first met my Mother, he recommended it to her, but she would not consent to open it. Nor would she read the chivalrous tales in verse of Sir Walter Scott, obstinately alleging that they were not "true." She would read none but lyrical and subjective poetry. Her secret diary reveals the history of this singular aversion to the fictitious, although it cannot be said to explain the cause of it. As a child, however, she had possessed a passion for making up stories, and so considerable a skill in it that she was constantly being begged to indulge others with its exercise. But I will, on so curious a point, leave her to speak for herself:

When I was a very little child, I used to amuse myself and my brothers with inventing stories, such as I read. Having, as I suppose, naturally a restless mind and busy imagination, this soon became the chief pleasure of my life. Unfortunately, my brothers were always fond of encouraging this propensity, and I found in Taylor, my maid, a still greater tempter. I had not known there was any harm in it, until Miss Shore [a Calvinist governess], finding it out, lectured me severely, and told me it was wicked. From that time forth I considered that to invent a story of any kind was a sin. But the desire to do so was too deeply rooted in my affection to be resisted in my own strength [she was at that time nine years of age], and unfortunately I knew neither my corruption nor my weakness, nor did I know where to gain strength. The longing to invent stories grew with violence; everything I heard or read became food for my distemper. The simplicity of truth was not sufficient for me; I must needs embroider imagination upon it, and the folly, vanity and wickedness which disgraced my heart are more than I am able to express. Even now [at the age of twenty-nine], though watched, prayed and striven against, this is still the sin that most easily besets me. It has hindered my prayers and prevented my improvement, and therefore has humbled me very much.

This is, surely, a very painful instance of the repression of an instinct. There seems to have been, in this case, a vocation such as is rarely heard, and still less often wilfully disregarded and silenced. Was my Mother intended by nature to be a novelist? I have often thought so, and her talents and vigour of purpose, directed along the line which was ready to form "the chief pleasure of her life," could hardly have failed to conduct her to great success. She was a little younger than Bulwer Lytton, a little older than Mrs. Gaskell—but these are vain and trivial speculations!

My own state, however, was, I should think, almost unique among the children of cultivated parents. In consequence of the stern ordinance which I have described, not a single fiction was read or told to me during my infancy. The rapture of the child who delays the process of going to bed by cajoling "a story" out of his mother or his nurse, as he sits upon her knee, well tucked up, at the corner of the nursery fire —this was unknown to me. Never, in all my early childhood, did any one address to me the affecting preamble, "Once upon a time!" I was told about missionaries, but never about pirates; I was familiar with humming-birds, but I had never heard of fairies. Jack the Giant-Killer, Rumpelstiltskin and Robin Hood were not of my acquaintance, and though I understood about wolves, Little Red Ridinghood was a stranger even by name. So far as my "dedication" was concerned, I can but think that my parents were in error thus to exclude the imaginary from my outlook upon facts. They desired to make me truthful; the tendency was to make me positive and sceptical. Had they wrapped me in the soft folds of supernatural fancy, my mind might have been longer content to follow their traditions in an unquestioning spirit.

Having easily said what, in those early years, I did not read, I have great difficulty in saying what I did read. But a queer variety of natural history, some of it quite indigestible by my undeveloped mind; many books of travels, mainly of a scientific character, among them voyages of discovery in the South Seas, by which my brain was dimly filled with splendour; some geography and astronomy, both of them sincerely enjoyed; much theology, which I desired to appreciate but could never get my teeth into (if I may venture to say so), and over which my eye and tongue learned to slip without penetrating, so that I would read, and read aloud, and with great propriety of emphasis, page after page without having formed an idea or retained an expression. There was, for instance, a writer on prophecy called Jukes, of whose works each of my parents was inordinately fond, and I was early set to read Jukes aloud to them. I did it glibly, like a machine, but the sight of Jukes's volumes became an abomination to me, and I never formed the outline of a notion what they were about. Later on, a publication called *The Penny Cyclopaedia* became my daily, and for a long time almost my sole study; to the subject of this remarkable work I may presently return.

It is difficult to keep anything like chronological order in recording fragments of early recollection, and in speaking of my reading I have been led too far ahead. My memory does not, practically, begin till we returned from certain visits, made with a zoological purpose, to the shores of Devon and Dorset, and settled, early in my fifth year, in a house at Islington, in the north of London. Our circumstances were now more easy; my Father had regular and well-paid literary work; and the house was larger and more comfortable than ever before, though still very simple and restricted. My memories, some of which are exactly dated by certain facts, now become clear and almost abundant. What I do not remember, except from having it very often repeated to me, is what may be considered the only "clever" thing that I said during an otherwise unillustrious childhood. It was not startlingly "clever," but it may pass. A lady—when I was just four—rather injudiciously showed me a large print of a human skeleton, saying, "There! you don't know what that is, do you?" Upon which, immediately and very archly, I replied, "Isn't it a man with the meat off?" This was thought wonderful, and, as it is supposed that I had never had the phenomenon explained to me, it certainly displays some quickness in seizing an analogy. I had often watched my Father, while he soaked the flesh off the bones of fishes and small mammals. If I venture to repeat this trifle, it is only to point out that the system on which I was being educated deprived all things, human life among the rest, of their mystery.

The "bare-grinning skeleton of death" was to me merely a prepared specimen of that featherless plantigrade vertebrate, *homo sapiens*.

As I have said that this anecdote was thought worth repeating, I ought to proceed to say that there was, so far as I can recollect, none of that flattery of childhood which is so often merely a backhanded way of indulging the vanity of parents. My Mother, indeed, would hardly have been human if she had not occasionally entertained herself with the delusion that her solitary duckling was a cygnet. This my Father did not encourage, remarking, with great affection, and chucking me under the chin, that I was "a nice little ordinary boy." My Mother, stung by this want of appreciation, would proceed so far as to declare that she believed that in future times the F. R. S.[1] would be chiefly known as his son's father! (This is a pleasantry frequent in professional families.) To this my Father, whether convinced or not, would make no demur, and the couple would begin to discuss, in my presence, the direction which my shining talents would take. In consequence of my dedication to "the Lord's Service," the range of possibilities was much restricted. My Father, who had lived long in the Tropics, and who nursed a perpetual nostalgia for "the little lazy isles where the trumpet-orchids blow," leaned towards the field of missionary labour. My Mother, who was cold about foreign missions, preferred to believe that I should be the Charles Wesley of my age, "or perhaps," she had the candour to admit, "merely the George Whitefield." I cannot recollect the time when I did not understand that I was going to be a minister of the Gospel.

It is so generally taken for granted that a life strictly dedicated to religion is stiff and dreary, that I may have some difficulty in persuading my readers that, as a matter of fact, in these early days of my childhood, before disease and death had penetrated to our slender society, we were always cheerful and often gay. My parents were playful with one another, and there were certain stock family jests which seldom failed to enliven the breakfast table. My Father and Mother lived so completely in the atmosphere of faith, and were so utterly convinced of their intercourse with God, that, so long as that inter-

---

[1] Gosse's father was a Fellow of the Royal Society.

course was not clouded by sin, to which they were delicately sensitive, they could afford to take the passing hour very lightly. They would even, to a certain extent, treat the surroundings of their religion as a subject of jest, joking very mildly and gently about such things as an attitude at prayer or the nature of a supplication. They were absolutely indifferent to forms. They prayed, seated in their chairs, as willingly as, reversed, upon their knees; no ritual having any significance for them. My Mother was sometimes extremely gay, laughing with a soft, merry sound. What I have since been told of the guileless mirth of nuns in a convent has reminded me of the gaiety of my parents during my early childhood.

So long as I was a mere part of them, without individual existence, and swept on, a satellite, in their atmosphere, I was mirthful when they were mirthful, and grave when they were grave. The mere fact that I had no young companions, no story books, no outdoor amusements, none of the thousand and one employments provided for other children in more conventional surroundings, did not make me discontented or fretful, because I did not know of the existence of such entertainments. In exchange, I became keenly attentive to the limited circle of interests open to me. Oddly enough, I have no recollection of any curiosity about other children, nor of any desire to speak to them or play with them. They did not enter into my dreams, which were occupied entirely with grown-up people and animals. I had three dolls, to whom my attitude was not very intelligible. Two of these were female, one with a shapeless face of rags, the other in wax. But, in my fifth year, when the Crimean War broke out, I was given a third doll, a soldier, dressed very smartly in a scarlet cloth tunic. I used to put the dolls on three chairs, and harangue them aloud, but my sentiment to them was never confidential, until our maid-servant one day, intruding on my audience, and misunderstanding the occasion of it, said: "What? a boy, and playing with a soldier when he's got two lady-dolls to play with?" I had never thought of my dolls as confidants before, but from that time forth I paid a special attention to the soldier, in order to make up to him for Lizzie's unwarrantable insult.

The declaration of war with Russia brought the first breath of outside life into our Calvinistic cloister. My parents took in a daily newspaper, which they had never done before, and events in picturesque places, which my Father and I looked out on the map, were eagerly discussed. One of my vividest early memories can be dated exactly. I was playing about the house, and suddenly burst into the breakfast-room, where, close to the door, sat an amazing figure, a very tall young man, as stiff as my doll, in a gorgeous scarlet tunic. Quite far away from him, at her writing table, my Mother sat with her Bible open before her, and was urging the gospel plan of salvation on his acceptance. She promptly told me to run away and play, but I had seen a great sight. This guardsman was in the act of leaving for the Crimea, and his adventures—he was converted in consequence of my Mother's instruction—were afterwards told by her in a tract, called *The Guardsman of the Alma,* of which I believe more than half a million copies were circulated. He was killed in that battle, and this added an extraordinary lustre to my dream of him. I see him still in my mind's eye, large, stiff, and unspeakably brilliant, seated, from respect, as near as possible to our parlour door. This apparition gave reality to my subsequent conversations with the soldier doll.

That same victory of the Alma, which was reported in London on my fifth birthday, is also marked very clearly in my memory by a family circumstance. We were seated at breakfast, at our small round table drawn close up to the window, my Father with his back to the light. Suddenly, he gave a sort of cry, and read out the opening sentences from the *Times* announcing a battle in the valley of the Alma. No doubt the strain of national anxiety had been very great, for both he and my Mother seemed deeply excited. He broke off his reading when the fact of the decisive victory was assured, and he and my Mother sank simultaneously on their knees in front of their tea and bread-and-butter, while in a loud voice my Father gave thanks to the God of Battles. This patriotism was the more remarkable, in that he had schooled himself, as he believed, to put his "heavenly citizenship" above all earthly duties. To those who said: "Because you are a Christian, surely you are not less an Englishman?" he would reply by shaking his head, and

by saying: "I am a citizen of no earthly State."
He did not realise that, in reality, and, to use
a cant phrase not yet coined in 1854, there
existed in Great Britain no more thorough
Jingo than he.

Another instance of the remarkable way in
which the interests of daily life were mingled,
in our strange household, with the practice of
religion, made an impression upon my memory.
We had all three been much excited by a report
that a certain dark geometer-moth, generated
in underground stables, had been met with in
Islington. Its name, I think, is *boletobia fuligi-
naria,* and I believe that it is excessively rare
in England. We were sitting at family prayers,
on a summer morning, I think in 1855, when
through the open window a brown moth came
sailing. My Mother immediately interrupted the
reading of the Bible by saying to my Father,
"O! Henry, do you think that can be *boletobia?*" My Father rose up from the sacred
book, examined the insect, which had now
perched, and replied: "No! it is only the common Vapourer, *orgygia antiqua,*" resuming his
seat, and the exposition of the Word, without
any apology or embarrassment.

In the course of this, my sixth year, there
happened a series of minute and soundless
incidents which, elementary as they may seem
when told, were second in real importance to
none in my mental history. The recollection of
them confirms me in the opinion that certain
leading features in each human soul are inherent to it, and cannot be accounted for by suggestion or training. In my own case, I was most
carefully withdrawn, like Princess Blanchefleur
in her marble fortress, from every outside influence whatever, yet to me the instinctive life
came as unexpectedly as her lover came to her
in the basket of roses. What came to me was
the consciousness of self, as a force and as a
companion, and it came as the result of one or
two shocks, which I will relate.

In consequence of hearing so much about an
Omniscient God, a being of supernatural wisdom and penetration who was always with us,
who made, in fact, a fourth in our company,
I had come to think of Him, not without awe,
but with absolute confidence. My Father and
Mother, in their serene discipline of me, never
argued with one another, never even differed;
their wills seemed absolutely one. My Mother

always deferred to my Father, and in his absence
spoke of him to me, as if he were all-wise.
I confused him in some sense with God; at all
events I believed that my Father knew everything and saw everything. One morning in my
sixth year, my Mother and I were alone in the
morning-room, when my Father came in and
announced some fact to us. I was standing on
the rug, gazing at him, and when he made this
statement, I remember turning quickly, in embarrassment, and looking into the fire. The
shock to me was as that of a thunderbolt, for
what my Father had said *was not true.* My
Mother and I, who had been present at the
trifling incident, were aware that it had not happened exactly as it had been reported to him.
My Mother gently told him so, and he accepted
the correction. Nothing could possibly have
been more trifling to my parents, but to me it
meant an epoch. Here was the appalling discovery, never suspected before, that my Father
was not as God, and did not know everything.
The shock was not caused by any suspicion that
he was not telling the truth, as it appeared to
him, but by the awful proof that he was not,
as I had supposed, omniscient.

This experience was followed by another,
which confirmed the first, but carried me a
great deal further. In our little back-garden,
my Father had built up a rockery for ferns and
mosses, and from the water-supply of the house
he had drawn a leaden pipe so that it pierced
upwards through the rockery and produced,
when a tap was turned, a pretty silvery parasol
of water. The pipe was exposed somewhere
near the foot of the rockery. One day, two
workmen, who were doing some repairs, left
their tools during the dinner-hour in the back-
garden, and as I was marching about I suddenly thought that to see whether one of these
tools could make a hole in the pipe would be
attractive. It did make such a hole, quite easily,
and then the matter escaped my mind. But a
day or two afterwards, when my Father came
in to dinner, he was very angry. He had turned
the tap, and, instead of the fountain arching at
the summit, there had been a rush of water
through a hole at the foot. The rockery was
absolutely ruined.

Of course I realised in a moment what I had
done, and I sat frozen with alarm, waiting to
be denounced. But my Mother remarked on the

visit of the plumbers two or three days before, and my Father instantly took up the suggestion. No doubt that was it; the mischievous fellows had thought it amusing to stab the pipe and spoil the fountain. No suspicion fell on me; no question was asked of me. I sat there, turned to stone within, but outwardly sympathetic and with unchecked appetite.

We attribute, I believe, too many moral ideas to little children. It is obvious that in this tremendous juncture, I ought to have been urged forward by good instincts, or held back by naughty ones. But I am sure that the fear which I experienced for a short time, and which so unexpectedly melted away, was a purely physical one. It had nothing to do with the emotions of a contrite heart. As to the destruction of the fountain, I was sorry about that, for my own sake, since I admired the skipping water extremely, and had no idea that I was spoiling its display. But the emotions which now thronged within me, and which led me with an almost unwise alacrity, to seek solitude in the back-garden, were not moral at all, they were intellectual. I was not ashamed of having successfully—and so surprisingly—deceived my parents by my crafty silence; I looked upon that as a providential escape, and dismissed all further thought of it. I had other things to think of.

In the first place, the theory that my Father was omniscient or infallible was now dead and buried. He probably knew very little; in this case he had not known a fact of such importance that if you did not know that, it could hardly matter what you knew. My Father, as a deity, as a natural force of immense prestige, fell in my eyes to a human level. In future, his statements about things in general need not be accepted implicitly. But of all the thoughts which rushed upon my savage and undeveloped little brain at this crisis, the most curious was that I had found a companion and a confidant in myself. There was a secret in this world and it belonged to me and to a somebody who lived in the same body with me. There were two of us, and we could talk with one another. It is difficult to define impressions so rudimentary, but it is certain that it was in this dual form that the sense of my individuality now suddenly descended upon me, and it is equally certain that it was a great solace to me to find a sympathiser in my own breast.

## David Riesman
## THE ROLE OF PARENTS TODAY

[*The book from which this extract is taken is a study of recent and continuing changes in the American character. Though there is disagreement among sociologists about the truth of the author's main thesis, it is supported by new and valuable insights into the way Americans think, feel, and behave.*

*Riesman first distinguishes three phases of population growth in Western countries, including America: (1) the phase of high birth rate and high death rate, leading to a stable population that is poor and changes its customs and traditions very little; (2) the phase in which the birth rate continues but the death rate is decreased, leading to a rapidly increasing population, technological progress, and individualism; (3) the phase in which the birth rate declines, leading to a stable or slightly declining population, a high economic level, and considerable mutual awareness and mutual dependence among people.*

*To these three phases correspond three personality-types, each of which predominates at one of the phases—types that are expressed in various aspects of social and individual life; for example, ways of bringing up children, economic activities, politics, religion, art. The tradition-directed person tends to conform to the traditions and established customs of his society: he wants to live up to the role he is born into. The inner-directed person has his own individual set of purposes and ambitions that he strives to realize: he wants to "succeed". The other-directed person is highly sensitive to the expectations and preferences of other people: he wants to be liked.*

*These personality-types are only "ideal types"; that is, there may be no perfect examples of each type, but many people may approximate more or less closely to each. Riesman analyzes and contrasts the three types; it is his main thesis that the United States is in transition from a period in which the inner-directed type was dominant to a period in which the other-directed type will be dominant.]*

*Q. Do you think the teachers should punish the children for using make-up?*

*A. Yes, I think they should punish them, but understand, I'm a modern mother and while I'm strict with my daughters, I am still modern. You know you can't punish your children too much or they begin to think you are mean and other children tell them you are mean.*

*From an interview*

Population curves and economic structures are only a part of the ecology of character formation. Interposed between them and the resultant social character are the human agents of character formation: the parents, the teachers, the members of the peer-group, and the storytellers. These are the transmitters of the social heritage, and they wield great influence over the lives of children and hence on the whole society. For children live at the wave front of the successive population phases and are the partially plastic receivers of the social character of the future. In this chapter we consider the changing role of parents and teachers in socializing the young in each of the three population phases. . . .

We shall concentrate here on the shift from inner-direction to other-direction as the principal mode of insuring conformity in the urban American middle class. Perspective, however, requires a glance at societies in which tradition-direction is the principal mode of insuring conformity; and since the tradition-directed types have played a very minor role in America, we will take examples from primitive and medieval society. As we compare methods of socialization we shall see what is new about the newer types—and particularly what is new about other-direction.

There has been a tendency in current social research, influenced as it is by psychoanalysis, to overemphasize and overgeneralize the importance of very early childhood in character formation. Even within this early period an almost technological attention has sometimes been focused on what might be called the tricks of the child-rearing trade: feeding and toilet-training schedules. The view implicit in this emphasis happens to be both a counsel of optimism and of despair. It is an optimistic view because it seems to say that facile mechanical changes in what the parent does will profoundly alter the character of the progeny. It is pessimistic because it assumes that once the child has reached, say, the weaning stage its character structure is so formed that, barring intensive psychiatric intervention, not much that happens afterward will do more than bring out tendencies already set.

Increasingly it is recognized, however, that character may change greatly after this early period and that cultural agents other than the parents may play important roles. Cultures differ widely not only in their timing of the various steps in character formation but also in the agents they rely on at each step. Each new historical phase on the curve of population is marked by an increase in the length of life and in the period of socialization—that is, the period before full entry into one's adult social and economic role. At the same time there is an increase in the responsibility placed on character-forming agents outside the home, the clan, or the village.

### PARENTAL ROLE IN THE STAGE OF TRADITION-DIRECTION

In societies depending on tradition-direction children can be "finished off" at an early point to assume an adult role. Adult roles are almost unchanging from generation to generation, and apart from training toward technical and manual skill, which may often be intensive, grown-up life demands little in the way of complex and literate instruction. Children begin very early to learn how to act like adults simply by watching adults around them. In the population phase of high growth potential there are many children to imitate a comparatively small number of adult models. The children live, ordinarily, in a large family setting. What the adults do is simple enough for children to grasp, so simple that children can often understand and imitate it before they have the physical skills to take a full part. Social maturity waits on biological maturity. Yet the biological roles of adult life are, in many cases, not themselves remote, for since there is little inhibition of childhood play and curiosity, children know what there is to know about sex and other adult functions—even though certain ceremonial mysteries may remain to testify to adult power and child helplessness.

Physical living patterns are an important factor in this setting. Houses consist typically of one room, without walls to separate the age groups and their varied functions. The households are often also economic units; the man does not go off to office or factory—and he does not go far. People are not yet so worried about saving time that they feel children are a nuisance; indeed, they may not feel themselves to be so very different from children anyway.

Furthermore, societies in the phase of high growth potential are characterized by a very low degree of social mobility. The parents train the child to succeed *them,* rather than to "succeed" by rising in the social system. Within any given social class society is age ranked, so that a person rises as a cork does in water: it is simply a matter of time, and little *in him* needs to change.

The upper social groups in such a society mature almost as quickly as the lower ones; the roles to be learned by children in both ranks of society differ only slightly in complexity. Even so, it is likely that a greater degree of individualization occurs at an earlier historical point in the upper strata than in the lower—as seems to have been the case in the Middle Ages when nobles, wandering artists, and priests were often closer to inner-direction than to the peasant's type of tradition-direction. Yet while the training of the leaders is of course somewhat more prolonged and their characters are more individuated, the young at all social levels take their places quickly in work, ceremony, and sexual role.

In summary: the major agency of character formation in societies dependent on tradition-direction is the extended family and its environing clan or group. Models for imitation are apt to be generalized in terms of the adult group as a whole rather than confined to the parents. What is imitated is behavior and specific traits such as bravery or cunning. The growing child does not confront problems of choice very different from those he watched his elders face; and his growth is conceived as a process of becoming an older, and therefore wiser, interpreter of tradition.

## PARENTAL ROLE IN THE STAGE OF INNER-DIRECTION

*Character and social mobility.* With the onset of the transitional-growth phase of the population curve, opportunities open for a good deal of social and geographical mobility. People begin to pioneer on new frontiers: frontiers of production, of colonization, of intellectual discovery. Although this affects only a few directly, society as mediated by the primary group no longer proclaims unequivocally what one must do in order to conform. Rather, the growing child soon becomes aware of competing sets of customs—competing paths of life—from among which he is, in principle, free to choose. And while parentage and social origins are still all but determinative for most people, the wider horizon of possibilities and of wants requires a character which can adhere to rather generalized and more abstractly defined goals. Such a character must produce under its own motive power the appropriate specific means to gain these general ends.

To be sure, the goals and ideals that are held up to children and exemplified for them by their parents' own goals and ideals differ between, on the one hand, the confident, secular man of the Renaissance, glorying in his individuality and freedom from old restraints, and, on the other hand, the God-fearing puritan, driven by conscience and anxious about his salvation. Yet both types are very much individuals, both are internally driven, and both are capable of pioneering. Finally, a society in which many people are internally driven—and are driven toward values, such as wealth and power, which are by their nature limited—contains in itself a dynamic of change by the very competitive forces it sets up. Even those who do not care to compete for higher places must do so in order not to descend in the social system, which has become a more open and less age-graded and birth-graded one.

All these tendencies are reinforced when roles become more complicated as the division of labor progresses. The acceleration of the division of labor means that increasing numbers of children can no longer take their parents' roles as models. This is especially true on the male side; characterological change in the west seems to occur first with men. Mothers and grandmothers could until very recent times train daughters for the feminine role on the basis of tradition alone. Thus in the recent movie, *House of Strangers,* the Italian-born banker who, like Giannini or Ponzi, rises out of an immigrant setting and departs from his own father's pattern, sets for himself ambitious goals of power and money such as he believes to be characteristic of a true-born American, while his wife is a stereotype of the woman who clings to the tradition-directed ways of her early background.

Yet, while parents in the stage of transitional growth of population cannot be sure of what the adult working role and mode of life of their children will be, neither can conformity to that role be left to chance and behavioral opportunism. To possess the drive that is required to fulfill demanding and ever more demanding roles calls for greater attention to formal character training. Especially in the Protestant countries character training becomes an important part of education, though of course this does not mean that most parents consciously undertake to produce children to meet new social specifications.

The new situation created by increased social mobility implies that children must frequently be socialized in such a way as to be unfitted for their parents' roles, while being fitted for roles not as yet fully determined. Homing pigeons can be taught to fly home, but the inner-directed child must be taught to fly a straight course away from home, with destination unknown; naturally many meet the fate of Icarus. Nevertheless, the drive instilled in the child is to *live up to ideals* and to test his ability to be on his own by continuous experiments in self-mastery—instead of by following tradition.

*Character training as a conscious parental task.* In a society depending on tradition-direction to insure conformity, much of the parent's effort is directed toward keeping the child from being a nuisance to the adult world; and this task is regularly delegated to older brothers or sisters or to other adults. The child soon learns that behavioral conformity is the price of peace, and he learns to propitiate—or at least not to annoy—those around him. The inner-directed parent, on the other hand, asks more of his child, just as he asks more of himself. He can do this because, with the passing of the extended kinship family, the parent has his children much more under his own undivided and

intensive scrutiny and control. Not satisfied with mere behavioral conformity, such a parent demands conformity of a more subtle sort, conformity as evidence of characterological fitness and self-discipline. The Puritan, especially, relentlessly scrutinizes his children as well as himself for the signs of election, that is, of salvation by the predestining God. And with secularization these signs are translated into signs predicting social mobility—signs that indicate a future facility in "passing," not from hell to heaven, but in the status hierarchy. On the one hand the parent looks for signs of potential failure—this search arises in part from guilty and anxious preoccupation about himself. On the other hand he looks for signs of talent—this must not be wasted.

In this way begins the process we see in extravagant form in the forced-draft childhood of John Stuart Mill, who studied the classics and wrote long essays under the zealous eye of his father before he was ten. Even when parents are less self-consciously pedagogical than James Mill, they may unconsciously impose their demands on children merely by being forceful, tense, and highly charged themselves. Indeed, the inner-directed man is frequently quite incapable of casual relationships. For one thing, he is preoccupied with his own concerns and therefore worried about wasting time; conversely, by not wasting time he avoids anxious self-preoccupation. For another thing, his relation to people, his children included, is mediated by his continuing, character-conditioned need to test and discipline himself.

This process, in the Renaissance-Reformation character which we term inner-directed, is less tense in the Latin countries than in the Protestant or Jansenist north, and in the north less tense in Lutheran or Anglican communicants than in the Calvinistic and Pietistic sects. Wherever inner-direction has attained relatively undisputed sway in a significantly large middle class, however, the production of the character structures of the coming generation becomes increasingly rationalized, just as is production in the non-household economy. In both cases the responsibility for production is no longer left to an external group sanction or situational pressure but is installed as a drive in the individual, and tremendous energies are unleashed toward the alteration of the material, social, and intellectual environment and toward the alteration of the self.

The social and spatial arrangements of middle-class life make it hard for the child to see through, let alone evade, the pressures put upon him to become inner-directed. As compared with the one-room house of the peasant or the "long house" of many primitive tribes, he grows up within walls that are physical symbols of the privacy of parental dominance. Walls separate parents from children, office from home, and make it hard if not impossible for the children to criticize the parents' injunctions by an "undress" view of the parents or of other parents. What the parents say becomes more real in many cases than what they do—significant training for a society in which words become increasingly important as a means of exchange, direction, and control. The conversation between parents and children, interrupted by the social distance that separates them, is continued by the child with himself in private.

The very pressure applied to the process of socialization by strict child rearing prolongs, as compared with the earlier era, the period in which socialization takes place. Freud has described this situation wonderfully in his concept of the watchful superego as a socializing agency incorporated into the child and accompanying him throughout life with ever renewed injunctions. This concept, while less fruitful in application to other societies, does seem to fit the middle class during the heyday of inner-direction in the west. One might even say that the character structure of the inner-directed person consists of the tension between superego, ego, and id. In a current cliché children are "brought up" rather than, as some would have it, "loved up"; and even when they have left home they continue to bring themselves up. They tend to feel throughout life that their characters are something to be worked on. The diary-keeping that is so significant a symptom of the new type of character may be viewed as a kind of inner time-and-motion study by which the individual records and judges his output day by day. It is evidence of the separation between the behaving and the scrutinizing self.

*Passage from home.* As the growing child takes over from his parents the duty of self-observation and character training, he becomes prepared to face and meet situations that are novel. Indeed, if he rises in the occupational hierarchy that becomes increasingly elaborated in the phase of transitional growth or if he moves toward the various opening frontiers, he finds that he can flexibly adapt his behavior precisely because he need not change his character. He can separate the two by virtue of the fact that he is an *individual* with a historically new level of self-awareness.

This awareness of the self is cause and consequence of the fact that choice is no longer automatically provided—or, rather, excluded—by the social setting of the primary group. Under the new conditions the individual must decide what to do—and therefore what to do with himself. This feeling of personal responsibility, this feeling that he matters as an individual, apart from his family or clan, makes him sensitive to the signals emanating from his internalized ideal. If the idea, as in the puritan, is to be "good" or, as in the child of the Renaissance, to be "great," what must he do to fulfill the injunction? And how does he know that he has fulfilled these difficult self-demands? As Max Weber and R. H. Tawney saw very clearly in their portraits of the puritan, little rest is available to those who ask themselves such questions.

The relative uncomfortableness of the more powerfully inner-directed homes—the lack of indulgence and casualness in dealing with children—prepares the child for the loneliness and psychic uncomfortableness of such questions and of the social situations that he may confront. Or, more exactly, the child's character is such that he feels comfortable in an environment which, like his home, is demanding and which he struggles to master.

We may say, then, that parents who are themselves inner-directed install a psychological gyroscope in their child and set it going; it is built to their own and other authoritative specifications; if the child has good luck, the governor will spin neither too fast, with the danger of hysteric outcomes, nor too slow, with the danger of social failure.

### PARENTAL ROLE IN THE STAGE OF OTHER-DIRECTION

*Character and social mobility.* In the phase of incipient population decline, the conditions for advancement alter significantly.

The inner-directed person is able to see industrial and commercial possibilities and to work with the zeal and ruthlessness required by expanding frontiers in the phase of transitional growth of population. Societies in the phase of incipient population decline, on the other hand, need neither such zeal nor such independence. Business, government, the professions, become heavily bureaucratized, as we see most strikingly, for instance, in France. Such societies increasingly turn to the remaining refractory components of the industrial process: the men who run the machines. Social mobility under these conditions continues to exist. But it depends less on what one is and what one does than on what others think of one—and how competent one is in manipulating others and being oneself manipulated. To look at it from another point of view, when the basic physical plant of a society is felt to be built, or rather when the building can be routinized by management planning, there begins to be room at the top for the other-directed person who can see the subtle opportunities given in the human setting. Though material abundance becomes technologically possible, people continue to work—and do make-work—at a pace more in keeping with the earlier era of transitional growth: mobility drives are still imbedded in their character. *But the product now in demand is neither a staple nor a machine; it is a personality.*

To bring the other-directed personality type and his typical economic framework together it might be observed that there exists in the production of personality the same sort of "product differentiation" that is characteristic of monopolistic competition generally. The economists apply the term "product differentiation" to a firm's effort to distinguish products not by price but by small differences, sufficient, however, in connection with advertising, to take the product out of direct price competition with otherwise similar competing products. Thus one cigarette is made slightly longer, another nearly oval, while still another is given a cork tip or a green box. *Time* and *Newsweek* engage in product differentiation. So do the makers of automobiles, streamliners, and toothpastes, and the operators of hotels and universities. So, too, people who are competing for jobs in the hierarchies of business, government, and professional life try to differentiate their personalities (as contrasted with their actual technical skills) —without getting as far out of line, let us say, as a 1934 prematurely streamlined Chrysler. In this study, the social aspect of this competitive procedure, since it will be extended to cover persons and services as well as commodities, will be termed "marginal differentiation," and thus distinguished from the related concept used by the economists.

Freud coined the phrase "narcissism with respect to minor differences" for the pride which individuals, groups, and nations manifest about small insignia which distinguish them from other individuals, groups, and nations. Marginal differentiation sometimes does have this quality of pride or of what Veblen called "invidious distinction." But the phenomenon I have in mind is one of anxiety rather than pride, of veiled competition rather than openly rivalrous display; the narcissism is muted or, as we shall see, alloyed with other, stronger elements.

In these circumstances parents who try, in inner-directed fashion, to compel the internalization of disciplined pursuit of clear goals run the risk of having their children styled clear out of the personality market. Gyroscopic direction is just not flexible enough for the rapid adaptations of personality that are required, precisely because there will be other competitors who do not have gyroscopes. Inhibited from presenting their children with sharply silhouetted images of self and society, parents in our era can only equip the child to do his best, whatever that may turn out to be. What is best is not in their control but in the hands of the school and peer-group that will help locate the child eventually in the hierarchy. But even these authorities speak vaguely; the clear principles of selection that once guided people of inner-directed character no longer apply. For example, social climbing itself may be called into public question at the same time that it is no longer so unequivocally desirable in terms of private wish. As some *Fortune* surveys indicate, a safe and secure job may be preferred to a risky one involving high stakes. What is more, it is no longer clear which way is up even if one wants to rise, for with the growth of the new middle class the older, hierarchical patterns disintegrate, and it is not easy to compare ranks among the several sets of hierarchies that do exist. Does an army colonel "rank" the head of an international union? A physics professor, a bank vice-president? A commentator, the head of an oil company?

Increasingly in doubt as to how to bring up their children, parents turn to other contemporaries for advice; they also look to the mass media; and like the mother quoted at the outset of this chapter they turn, in effect, to the children themselves. They may, nevertheless, fasten on some inflexible scheme of child rearing and follow that. Yet they cannot help but show their children, by their own anxiety, how little they depend on themselves and how much on others. Whatever they may seem to be teaching the child in terms of content, they are passing on to him their own contagious, highly diffuse anxiety. They reinforce this teaching by giving the child approval—and approving themselves because of the child—when he makes good.

To be sure, inner-directed parents also often were able to "love" only those children who made good in the outer world. But at least the canons of success were reasonably clear. The other-directed child, however, faces not only the requirement that he make good but also the problem of defining what making good means. He finds that both the definition and the evaluation of himself depend on the company he keeps: first, on his schoolmates and teachers; later, on peers and superiors. But perhaps the company one keeps is itself at fault? One can then shop for other preferred companies in the mass circulation media.

Approval itself, irrespective of content, becomes almost the only unequivocal good in this situation: one makes good when one is approved of. Thus all power, not merely some power, is in the hands of the actual or imaginary approving group, and the child learns from his parents' reactions to him that nothing in his character, no possession he owns, no inheritance of name or talent, no work he has done is valued for itself but only for its effect on others. Making good becomes almost equivalent to making friends, or at any rate the right kind of friends. "To him that hath approval, shall be given more approval."

*From bringing up children to "Bringing up Father."* The typical other-directed child grows up in a small family, in close urban quarters, or in a suburb. Even more than in the earlier epoch the father leaves home to go to work, and he goes too far to return for lunch. Home, moreover, is no longer an area of solid privacy.

As the size and living space of the family diminish and as the pattern of living with older relatives declines, the child must directly face the emotional tensions of his parents. There is a heightening of awareness of the self in relation to others under these conditions, especially since the parents, too, are increasingly self-conscious.

Under the new social and economic conditions, the position of children rises. They are not subjected to a period of deprivation and hardship which leads to compensatory dreams of a life of ease and pleasure. Girls are not, as they were in some earlier societies, drudges at home until, at puberty, they were suddenly given the only "capital" they were ever likely to find—that of their bodies—to live on as income, or exhaust as principal. Even boys from comfortable homes were expected until recently to hit the sunrise trail with paper routes or other economically profitable and "character-building" chores.

The parents lack not only the self-assurance that successful inner-direction brings but also the strategy of withdrawal available to many unsuccessful inner-directed types. The loss of old certainties in the spheres of work and social relations is accompanied by doubt as to how to bring up children. Moreover, the parents no longer feel themselves superior to the children. While children no longer have immediate economic value, they are less numerous, "scarcer" in relation to the number of adults: the effort is made, and it is objectively possible, to want all children who are conceived and to raise very nearly all children who are born. More is staked on every single child than in the earlier epoch when many children were not raised to maturity. In addition, apart from the fact that the children may be better Americans than the parents, in ethnic or social terms—as Jiggs's daughter is more up to date than he—there are undoubtedly other solid reasons (which I shall not go into) for the general emphasis on youth which runs through all forms of popular culture.

Historical changes in the lives of adolescents can be seen most clearly, perhaps, if one looks back to those *Bildungsromane* of the nineteenth century that described the misunderstood youth who struggled against the harsh or hypocritical tyranny of his parents, particularly if one compares one of the best of such novels, Samuel

Butler's *The Way of All Flesh,* with one of the best of our contemporary examples, for instance Lionel Trilling's short story, "The Other Margaret." In Trilling's story we have a picture of a precocious young girl in the intellectual, urban, upper middle class. Margaret, who goes to a progressive school, believes that Negroes are exploited, and she resents the inferior position in the home of "the other Margaret," a Negro domestic. It is the daughter Margaret who is self-righteous, not the parents.

In the face of her criticism, buttressed as it is by the authority of the school, the parents, themselves progressive, are on the defensive. They are tense and very much concerned with what their daughter thinks—and thinks of them. Eventually, all three adults manage to destroy Margaret's illusion of the virtues of the other Margaret—the parents by reasoning; the other Margaret by bad behavior. But in the end the parents are anxious about their victory, lest it harm their sensitive child. They possess little of the certainty and security of Theobald's parents in *The Way of All Flesh.*

In this change of parental attitude the mass media of communication play a dual role. From the mass media—radio, movies, comics—as well as from their own peers, children can easily learn what the norm of parental behavior is, and hold it over their parents' heads. Thus a kind of realism is restored to the child which was his property much more simply in the societies depending on tradition-direction: the other-directed child is often more knowing than his parents—like the proverbial Harvard man, there is little they can tell *him.*

As already noted, the parents also have their sources of direction in the mass media. For in their uneasiness as to how to bring up children they turn increasingly to books, magazines, government pamphlets, and radio programs. These tell the already anxious mother to accept her children. She learns that there are no problem children, only problem parents; and she learns to look into her own psyche whenever she is moved to deny the children anything, including an uninterrupted flow of affection. If the children are cross then the mother must be withholding something. And while these tutors also tell the mother to "relax" and to "enjoy her children," even this becomes an additional injunction to be anxiously followed.

It may be that children today do not gain the strength that adults—no longer inner-directed—have lost. To be sure, this was often a factitious strength, as Samuel Butler saw; but it was usually sufficient both to crush the child's spontaneity and anesthetize his diffuse anxiety. "Shades of the prison-house begin to close upon the growing boy"—and the prisoner might feel oppressed, even guilty, but not too anxious behind his bars. In contrast, what the other-directed child does "learn" from his parents is anxiety—the emotional tuning appropriate to his other-directed adjustment.

*The rule of "reason."* Despite the diminution of their authority, the parents still try to control matters; but with the loss of self-assurance their techniques change. They can neither hold themselves up as exemplars—when both they and the child know better—nor resort, in good conscience, to severe corporal punishment and deprivations. At most there are token spankings, with open physical warfare confined to the lower classes.

The parents' recourse, especially in the upper middle class, is to "personnel" methods—to manipulation in the form of reasoning, or, more accurately, of rationalizing. The child responds in the same manner. One might summarize the historical sequence by saying that the tradition-directed child propitiates his parents; the inner-directed child fights or succumbs to them; the other-directed child manipulates them and is in turn manipulated.

A movie of several years ago, *The Curse of the Cat People,* while it testified to American preoccupation with certain child-rearing themes which do not directly concern us here, also provides an interesting example of these manipulative relations between parent and child. A little girl lives in a suburban, middle-class home with its typical neatness, garden, and Negro servant. As in "The Other Margaret," there is a terrific pressure of adult emotion focused around this one child from the parents and servant. The child is supposed to invite the other children in the neighborhood for her birthday party; but believing her father's joke that the big tree in the yard is a mailbox, she puts the invitations there and they never go out. When her birthday arrives, the other children whom she had said she would invite tease her and refuse to play with her. Her father scolds her for taking him seriously, and she is also in difficulties for not getting along better with the other children. But the parents (plus servant) decide to go ahead with the party anyway, "as if." There follows a "party" which tries to persuade the child that there has been no tragedy, that this party is just as good as the one which failed.

The parents insist that the child somehow know, without a formal etiquette, when things are supposed to be "real" and when "pretend." The tree as the mailbox is pretend; the party real. Feeling misunderstood and alone, the little girl discovers a real friend in a strange woman who lives almost as a recluse in a great house. The parents frown upon this "friend" and her gift of a ring to the child. The little girl then discovers an imaginary friend at the bottom of the yard, a beautiful older woman with whom she talks. The father cannot see, that is to say "see," this latter friend and punishes the child for lying.

Notice this fictional family's lack of privacy for the child. The discovery of the gift of the ring seems to be typical of the fact that few of her excitements escape parental scrutiny. Moreover, the very fact that the father suggests to the daughter the secret about the make-believe "mailbox tree" is symbolic of the intrusion of his knowledge: the daughter is not allowed her own make-believe but must share it with him, subject to his determination of when it applies. That the daughter and father finally come into open conflict over the little girl's fantasy friend is only to be expected; the girl cannot put a lock on the door of her room or the door of her mind. (In a lower-class home there would be, spatially at least, even less privacy; but there might be more psychic privacy because the parents would often be less interested in the child.)

Notice, in the second place, the "reasonable" but subtly manipulative tone of parent-child relations. This is evidenced by the parental planning of the party for the daughter and her peers and by the parental irritation when the plan miscarries. Still more significant is the way in which the family meets the crisis of blocked peer-group communication symbolized by the nonoperative mailbox—a failure that is itself occasioned by a blockage of understanding about the real and the unreal between daughter and parents.

The fiasco is, obviously enough, a matter that requires immediate corrective action; par-ents in this pass, it seems, should *do* something. The parents of the child in this movie do nothing; they prefer to talk away the situation, to manipulate the child into the acceptance of a formal illusion of party making. The result is to produce a sort of exaggeration and burlesque of the way in which other-directed persons, in parent-child as in all other relations, constantly resort to manipulation and countermanipulation.

As contrasted with all this, the inner-directed parent is not particularly worried by his child's resentment or hostility. Nor is he as apt to be as aware of it. He and the child are both protected by the gap that separates them. The other-directed parent, however, has to win not only his child's good behavior but also his child's good will. Therefore, he is tempted to use his superior dialectic skill to "reason" with the child. And when the child learns—this is part of his sensitive radar equipment—how to argue too, the parent is torn between giving in and falling uneasily back on the sterner methods of *his* inner-directed parents. The father in *The Curse of the Cat People,* after trying to reason away the little girl's belief in her fantasy friend, finally spanks her. But such scenes are always succeeded by parental efforts at reconciliation, turning the spanking itself into a step in the manipulative chain.

Finally, we must observe the change in the content of the issues at stake between parent and child. The more driving and tense inner-directed parents compel their children to work, to save, to clean house, sometimes to study, and sometimes to pray. Other less puritanical types of inner-directed parent want their boys to be manly, their girls to be feminine and chaste. Such demands make either economic or ideological sense in the population phase of transitional growth. The large home could absorb enormous amounts of labor; even today those who putter in small house and small garden can still find lots to do. The parents themselves often set the example, in which they are supported by the school, of work and study: these are believed to be the paths of upward mobility both in this world and in the next.

In the other-directed home, on the other hand, the issues between parent and child concern the nonwork side of life. For in the phase of incipient population decline—most markedly, of course, in America but elsewhere too

—there is no work for children to do inside the urban home, and little outside. They need not brush and clean (except themselves)—they are less efficient than a vacuum cleaner. Nor is there an array of younger brothers and sisters to be taken care of. The American mother, educated, healthy, and efficient, has high standards for care of the apartment or small home and would, where she is not working, often feel quite out of a job if the children took over the housework. Fortunately released from the quandary of the old woman who lived in a shoe, she faces—just, as we shall see, as her husband does—the problem of leisure; care for the house and children is frequently her self-justification and escape.

So parents and children debate over eating and sleeping time as later they will debate over use of the family car. And they argue tensely, as in *The Curse of the Cat People,* about the contacts of the child with the "others" and about the emotional hue of the argument itself. But by the nature of these discussions the parents have a less easy victory. In the population phase of transitional growth they can point to self-evident tasks that need doing—self-evident at least according to accepted standards that have survived from the still earlier epoch. In the phase of incipient decline, however, the consumption or leisure issues are no longer self-evident; to decide them, if they are to be decided, one has to resort to models outside the particular home—in search of the ever changing norms of the group in which the parents happen to live. And indeed the radio and print bring the models into the home, like a trial record from which the child and parent legalists prepare briefs.

To sum up: parents in the groups depending on other-direction install in their children something like a psychological radar set—a device not tuned to control movement in any particular direction while guiding and steadying the person from within but rather tuned to detect the action, and especially the symbolic action, of others. Thereafter, the parents influence the children's character only insofar as (a) their own signals mingle with others over the radar, (b) they can locate children in a certain social environment in order to alter to a very limited degree what signals they will receive, (c) they take the risks of a very partial and precarious censorship of incoming messages. Thus the parental role diminishes in importance as compared with the same role among the inner-directed.

*Charles Dickens*

# BETSEY TROTWOOD

I was born at Blunderstone, in Suffolk, or "thereby," as they say in Scotland. I was a posthumous child. My father's eyes had closed upon the light of this world six months, when mine opened on it. There is something strange to me, even now, in the reflection that he never saw me; and something stranger yet in the shadowy remembrance that I have of my first childish associations with his white grave-stone in the churchyard, and of the indefinable compassion I used to feel for it lying out alone there in the dark night, when our little parlour was warm and bright with fire and candle, and the doors of our house were—almost cruelly, it seemed to me sometimes—bolted and locked against it.

An aunt of my father's, and consequently a great-aunt of mine, of whom I shall have more to relate by and by, was the principal magnate of our family. Miss Trotwood, or Miss Betsey, as my poor mother always called her, when she sufficiently overcame her dread of this formidable personage to mention her at all (which was seldom), had been married to a husband younger than herself, who was very handsome, except in the sense of the homely adage, "handsome is, that handsome does"—for he was strongly suspected of having beaten Miss Betsey, and even of having once, on a disputed question of supplies, made some hasty but determined arrangements to throw her out of a two pair of stairs' window. These evidences of an incompatibility of temper induced Miss Betsey to pay him off, and effect a separation by mutual consent. He went to India with his capital, and there, according to a wild legend in our family, he was once seen riding on an elephant, in company with a Baboon; but I think it must have been a Baboo—or a Begum. Any how, from India tidings of his death

BETSEY TROTWOOD: From *David Copperfield,* Chapter I.

reached home, within ten years. How they affected my aunt, nobody knew; for immediately
upon the separation she took her maiden name
again, bought a cottage in a hamlet on the sea-
coast a long way off, established herself there
as a single woman with one servant, and was
understood to live secluded, ever afterwards, in
an inflexible retirement.

My father had once been a favourite of hers,
I believe; but she was mortally affronted by his
marriage, on the ground that my mother was
"a wax doll." She had never seen my mother,
but she knew her to be not yet twenty. My
father and Miss Betsey never met again. He was
double my mother's age when he married, and
of but a delicate constitution. He died a year
afterwards, and, as I have said, six months
before I came into the world.

This was the state of matters on the afternoon of, what *I* may be excused for calling,
that eventful and important Friday. I can make
no claim, therefore, to have known, at that
time, how matters stood; or to have any remembrance, founded on the evidence of my
own senses, of what follows.

My mother was sitting by the fire, but poorly
in health, and very low in spirits, looking at it
through her tears, and desponding heavily
about herself and the fatherless little stranger,
who was already welcomed by some grosses of
prophetic pins in a drawer up-stairs, to a world
not at all excited on the subject of his arrival;
my mother, I say, was sitting by the fire, that
bright, windy March afternoon, very timid and
sad, and very doubtful of ever coming alive out
of the trial that was before her, when, lifting
her eyes as she dried them, to the window
opposite, she saw a strange lady coming up
the garden.

My mother had a sure foreboding at the
second glance, that it was Miss Betsey. The
setting sun was glowing on the strange lady,
over the garden-fence, and she came walking
up to the door with a fell rigidity of figure and
composure of countenance that could have belonged to nobody else.

When she reached the house, she gave another proof of her identity. My father had often
hinted that she seldom conducted herself like
any ordinary Christian; and now, instead of
ringing the bell, she came and looked in at that
identical window, pressing the end of her nose
against the glass to that extent that my poor

dear mother used to say it became perfectly flat
and white in a moment.

She gave my mother such a turn, that I have
always been convinced I am indebted to Miss
Betsey for having been born on a Friday.

My mother had left her chair in her agitation, and gone behind it in the corner. Miss
Betsey, looking round the room, slowly and in-
quiringly, began on the other side, and carried
her eyes on, like a Saracen's Head in a Dutch
clock, until they reached my mother. Then she
made a frown and a gesture to my mother, like
one who was accustomed to be obeyed, to come
and open the door. My mother went.

"Mrs. David Copperfield, I *think,*" said Miss
Betsey; the emphasis referring, perhaps, to my
mother's mourning weeds, and her condition.

"Yes," said my mother, faintly.

"Miss Trotwood," said the visitor. "You
have heard of her, I dare say?"

My mother answered she had had that pleasure. And she had a disagreeable consciousness
of not appearing to imply that it had been an
overpowering pleasure.

"Now you see her," said Miss Betsey. My
mother bent her head, and begged her to walk
in.

They went into the parlour my mother had
come from, the fire in the best room on the
other side of the passage not being lighted—
not having been lighted, indeed, since my
father's funeral; and when they were both
seated, and Miss Betsey said nothing, my
mother, after vainly trying to restrain herself,
began to cry.

"Oh tut, tut, tut!" said Miss Betsey, in a
hurry. "Don't do that! Come, come!"

My mother couldn't help it notwithstanding,
so she cried until she had had her cry out.

"Take off your cap, child," said Miss Betsey,
"and let me see you."

My mother was too much afraid of her to
refuse compliance with this odd request, if she
had any disposition to do so. Therefore she did
as she was told, and did it with such nervous
hands that her hair (which was luxuriant and
beautiful) fell all about her face.

"Why, bless my heart!" exclaimed Miss
Betsey. "You are a very Baby!"

My mother was, no doubt, unusually youthful in appearance even for her years; she hung
her head, as if it were her fault, poor thing,
and said, sobbing, that indeed she was afraid

she was but a childish widow, and would be but a childish mother if she lived. In a short pause which ensued, she had a fancy that she felt Miss Betsey touch her hair, and that with no ungentle hand; but, looking at her, in her timid hope, she found that lady sitting with the skirt of her dress tucked up, her hands folded on one knee, and her feet upon the fender, frowning at the fire.

"In the name of Heaven," said Miss Betsey, suddenly, "why Rookery?"

"Do you mean the house, ma'am?" asked my mother.

"Why Rookery?" said Miss Betsey. "Cookery would have been more to the purpose, if you had had any practical ideas of life, either of you."

"The name was Mr. Copperfield's choice," returned my mother. "When he bought the house, he liked to think that there were rooks about it."

The evening wind made such a disturbance just now, among some tall old elm-trees at the bottom of the garden, that neither my mother nor Miss Betsey could forbear glancing that way. As the elms bent to one another, like giants who were whispering secrets, and after a few seconds of such repose, fell into a violent flurry, tossing their wild arms about, as if their late confidences were really too wicked for their peace of mind, some weather-beaten ragged old rooks'-nests burdening their higher branches, swung like wrecks upon a stormy sea.

"Where are the birds?" asked Miss Betsey.

"The——?" My mother had been thinking of something else.

"The rooks—what has become of them?" asked Miss Betsey.

"There have not been any since we have lived here," said my mother. "We thought— Mr. Copperfield thought—it was quite a large rookery; but the nests were very old ones, and the birds have deserted them a long while."

"David Copperfield all over!" cried Miss Betsey. "David Copperfield from head to foot! Calls a house a rookery when there's not a rook near it, and takes the birds on trust, because he sees the nests!"

"Mr. Copperfield," returned my mother, "is dead, and if you dare to speak unkindly of him to me——"

My poor dear mother, I suppose, had some momentary intention of committing an assault and battery upon my aunt, who could easily have settled her with one hand, even if my mother had been in far better training for such an encounter than she was that evening. But it passed with the action of rising from her chair; and she sat down again very meekly, and fainted.

When she came to herself, or when Miss Betsey had restored her, whichever it was, she found the latter standing at the window. The twilight was by this time shading down into darkness; and dimly as they saw each other, they could not have done that without the aid of the fire.

"Well?" said Miss Betsey, coming back to her chair, as if she had only been taking a casual look at the prospect; "and when do you expect——"

"I am all in a tremble," faltered my mother. "I don't know what's the matter. I shall die, I am sure!"

"No, no, no," said Miss Betsey. "Have some tea."

"Oh dear me, dear me, do you think it will do me any good?" cried my mother in a helpless manner.

"Of course it will," said Miss Betsey. "It's nothing but fancy. What do you call your girl?"

"I don't know that it will be a girl, yet, ma'am," said my mother innocently.

"Bless the Baby!" exclaimed Miss Betsey, unconsciously quoting the second sentiment of the pincushion in the drawer up-stairs, but applying it to my mother instead of me, "I don't mean that. I mean your servant."

"Peggotty," said my mother.

"Peggotty!" repeated Miss Betsey, with some indignation. "Do you mean to say, child, that any human being has gone into a Christian church, and got herself named Peggotty?"

"It's her surname," said my mother, faintly. "Mr. Copperfield called her by it, because her Christian name was the same as mine."

"Here, Peggotty!" cried Miss Betsey, opening the parlour-door. "Tea. Your mistress is a little unwell. Don't dawdle."

Having issued this mandate with as much potentiality as if she had been a recognised authority in the house ever since it had been a house, and having looked out to confront the amazed Peggotty coming along the passage with a candle at the sound of a strange voice, Miss Betsey shut the door again, and sat down as before, with her feet on the fender, the skirt of her dress tucked up, and her hands folded on one knee.

"You were speaking about its being a girl," said Miss Betsey. "I have no doubt it will be a girl. I have a presentiment that it must be a girl. Now, child, from the moment of the birth of this girl——"

"Perhaps boy," my mother took the liberty of putting in.

"I tell you I have a presentiment that it must be a girl," returned Miss Betsey. "Don't contradict. From the moment of this girl's birth, child, I intend to be her friend. I intend to be her godmother, and I beg you'll call her Betsey Trotwood Copperfield. There must be no mistakes in life with *this* Betsey Trotwood. There must be no trifling with *her* affections, poor dear. She must be well brought up, and well guarded from reposing any foolish confidences where they are not deserved. I must make that *my* care."

There was a twitch of Miss Betsey's head, after each of these sentences, as if her own old wrongs were working within her, and she repressed any plainer reference to them by strong constraint. So my mother suspected, at least, as she observed her by the low glimmer of the fire: too much scared by Miss Betsey, too uneasy in herself, and too subdued and bewildered altogether, to observe anything very clearly, or to know what to say.

"And was David good to you, child?" asked Miss Betsey, when she had been silent for a little while, and these motions of her head had gradually ceased. "Were you comfortable together?"

"We were very happy," said my mother. "Mr. Copperfield was only too good to me."

"What, he spoilt you, I suppose?" returned Miss Betsey.

"For being quite alone and dependent on myself in this rough world again, yes, I fear he did indeed," sobbed my mother.

"Well! Don't cry!" said Miss Betsey. "You were not equally matched, child—if any two people *can* be equally matched—and so I asked the question. You were an orphan, weren't you?"

"Yes."

"And a governess?"

"I was nursery-governess in a family where Mr. Copperfield came to visit. Mr. Copperfield

was very kind to me, and took a great deal of notice of me, and paid me a good deal of attention, and at last proposed to me. And I accepted him. And so we were married," said my mother simply.

"Ha! Poor Baby!" mused Miss Betsey, with her frown still bent upon the fire. "Do you know anything?"

"I beg your pardon, ma'am," faltered my mother.

"About keeping house, for instance," said Miss Betsey.

"Not much, I fear," returned my mother. "Not so much as I could wish. But Mr. Copperfield was teaching me——"

("Much he knew about it himself!") said Miss Betsey in a parenthesis.

——"And I hope I should have improved, being very anxious to learn, and he very patient to teach, if the great misfortune of his death"— my mother broke down again here, and could get no farther.

"Well, well!" said Miss Betsey.

——"I kept my housekeeping-book regularly, and balanced it with Mr. Copperfield every night," cried my mother in another burst of distress, and breaking down again.

"Well, well!" said Miss Betsey. "Don't cry any more."

——"And I am sure we never had a word of difference respecting it, except when Mr. Copperfield objected to my threes and fives being too much like each other, or to my putting curly tails to my sevens and nines," resumed my mother in another burst, and breaking down again.

"You'll make yourself ill," said Miss Betsey, "and you know that will not be good either for you or for my god-daughter. Come! You mustn't do it!"

This argument had some share in quieting my mother, though her increasing indisposition had perhaps a larger one. There was an interval of silence, only broken by Miss Betsey's occasionally ejaculating "Ha!" as she sat with her feet upon the fender.

"David had bought an annuity for himself with his money, I know," said she, by and by. "What did he do for you?"

"Mr. Copperfield," said my mother, answering with some difficulty, "was so considerate and good as to secure the reversion of a part of it to me."

"How much?" asked Miss Betsey.

"A hundred and five pounds a year," said my mother.

"He might have done worse," said my aunt.

The word was appropriate to the moment. My mother was so much worse that Peggotty, coming in with the teaboard and candles, and seeing at a glance how ill she was,—as Miss Betsey might have done sooner if there had been light enough,—conveyed her up-stairs to her own room with all speed; and immediately despatched Ham Peggotty, her nephew, who had been for some days past secreted in the house, unknown to my mother, as a special messenger in case of emergency, to fetch the nurse and doctor.

Those allied powers were considerably astonished, when they arrived within a few minutes of each other, to find an unknown lady of portentous appearance sitting before the fire, with her bonnet tied over her left arm, stopping her ears with jewellers' cotton. Peggotty knowing nothing about her, and my mother saying nothing about her, she was quite a mystery in the parlour; and the fact of her having a magazine of jewellers' cotton in her pocket, and sticking the article in her ears in that way, did not detract from the solemnity of her presence.

The doctor having been up-stairs and come down again, and having satisfied himself, I suppose, that there was a probability of this unknown lady and himself having to sit there, face to face, for some hours, laid himself out to be polite and social. He was the meekest of his sex, the mildest of little men. He sidled in and out of a room, to take up the less space. He walked as softly as the Ghost in *Hamlet,* and more slowly. He carried his head on one side, partly in modest depreciation of himself, partly in modest propitiation of everybody else. It is nothing to say that he hadn't a word to throw at a dog. He couldn't have *thrown* a word at a mad dog. He might have offered him one gently, or half a one, or a fragment of one; for he spoke as slowly as he walked; but he wouldn't have been rude to him, and he couldn't have been quick with him, for any earthly consideration.

Mr. Chillip, looking mildly at my aunt with his head on one side, and making her a little bow, said, in allusion to the jewellers' cotton, as he softly touched his left ear:

"Some local irritation, ma'am?"

"What!" replied my aunt, pulling the cotton out of one ear like a cork.

Mr. Chillip was so alarmed by her abruptness—as he told my mother afterwards—that it was a mercy he didn't lose his presence of mind. But he repeated sweetly:

"Some local irritation, ma'am?"

"Nonsense!" replied my aunt, and corked herself again, at one blow.

Mr. Chillip could do nothing after this, but sit and look at her feebly, as she sat and looked at the fire, until he was called up-stairs again. After some quarter of an hour's absence, he returned.

"Well?" said my aunt, taking the cotton out of the ear nearest to him.

"Well, ma'am," returned Mr. Chillip, "we are—we are progressing slowly, ma'am."

"Ba—a—ah!" said my aunt, with a perfect shake on the contemptuous interjection. And corked herself as before.

Really—really—as Mr. Chillip told my mother, he was almost shocked; speaking in a professional point of view alone he was almost shocked. But he sat and looked at her, notwithstanding, for nearly two hours, as she sat looking at the fire, until he was again called out. After another absence, he again returned.

"Well?" said my aunt, taking out the cotton on that side again.

"Well, ma'am," returned Mr. Chillip, "we are—we are progressing slowly, ma'am."

"Ya—a—ah!" said my aunt. With such a snarl at him, that Mr. Chillip absolutely could not bear it. It was really calculated to break his spirit, he said afterwards. He preferred to go and sit upon the stairs, in the dark and a strong draught, until he was again sent for.

Ham Peggotty, who went to the national school, and was a very dragon at his catechism, and who may therefore be regarded as a credible witness, reported next day, that happening to peep in at the parlour-door an hour after this, he was instantly descried by Miss Betsey, then walking to and fro in a state of agitation, and pounced upon before he could make his escape. That there were now occasional sounds of feet and voices overhead which he inferred the cotton did not exclude, from the circumstance of his evidently being clutched by the lady as a victim on whom to expend her superabundant agitation when the sounds were loudest. That, marching him constantly up and down by the collar (as if he had been taking too much laudanum), she, at those times, shook him, rumpled his hair, made light of his linen, stopped *his* ears as if she confounded them with her own, and otherwise touzled and maltreated him. This was in part confirmed by his aunt, who saw him at half-past twelve o'clock, soon after his release, and affirmed that he was then as red as I was.

The mild Mr. Chillip could not possibly bear malice at such a time, if at any time. He sidled into the parlour as soon as he was at liberty, and said to my aunt in his meekest manner:

"Well, ma'am, I am happy to congratulate you."

"What upon?" said my aunt, sharply.

Mr. Chillip was fluttered again, by the extreme severity of my aunt's manner; so he made her a little bow, and gave her a little smile, to mollify her.

"Mercy on the man, what's he doing!" cried my aunt, impatiently. "Can't he speak?"

"Be calm, my dear ma'am," said Mr. Chillip, in his softest accents. "There is no longer any occasion for uneasiness, ma'am. Be calm."

It has since been considered almost a miracle that my aunt didn't shake him, and shake what he had to say out of him. She only shook her own head at him, but in a way that made him quail.

"Well, ma'am," resumed Mr. Chillip, as soon as he had courage, "I am happy to congratulate you. All is now over, ma'am, and well over."

During the five minutes or so that Mr. Chillip devoted to the delivery of this oration, my aunt eyed him narrowly.

"How is she?" said my aunt, folding her arms with her bonnet still tied on one of them.

"Well, ma'am, she will soon be quite comfortable, I hope," returned Mr. Chillip. "Quite as comfortable as we can expect a young mother to be, under these melancholy domestic circumstances. There cannot be any objection to your seeing her presently, ma'am. It may do her good."

"And *she*. How is *she*?" said my aunt, sharply.

Mr. Chillip laid his head a little more on one side, and looked at my aunt like an amiable bird.

"The baby," said my aunt. "How is she?"

"Ma'am," returned Mr. Chillip, "I apprehended you had known. It's a boy."

My aunt said never a word, but took her bonnet by the strings, in the manner of a sling, aimed a blow at Mr. Chillip's head with it, put it on bent, walked out, and never came back. She vanished like a discontented fairy; or like one of those supernatural beings whom it was popularly supposed I was entitled to see: and never came back any more.

No. I lay in my basket, and my mother lay in her bed; but Betsey Trotwood Copperfield was for ever in the land of dreams and shadows, the tremendous region whence I had so lately travelled; and the light upon the window of our room shone out upon the earthly bourne of all such travellers, and the mound above the ashes and the dust that once was he, without whom I had never been.

## *Jessamyn West*
## SIXTEEN

The steam from the kettle had condensed on the cold window and was running down the glass in tear-like trickles. Outside in the orchard the man from the smudge company was refilling the pots with oil. The greasy smell from last night's burning was still in the air. Mr. Delahanty gazed out at the bleak darkening orange grove; Mrs. Delahanty watched her husband eat, nibbling up to the edges of the toast, then stacking the crusts about his tea cup in a neat fence-like arrangement.

"We'll have to call Cress," Mr. Delahanty said, finally. "Your father's likely not to last out the night. She's his only grandchild. She ought to be here."

Mrs. Delahanty pressed her hands to the bones above her eyes. "Cress isn't going to like being called away from college," she said.

"We'll have to call her anyway. It's the only thing to do." Mr. Delahanty swirled the last of his tea around in his cup so as not to miss any sugar.

"Father's liable to lapse into unconsciousness any time," Mrs. Delahanty argued. "Cress'll hate coming and Father won't know whether she's here or not. Why not let her stay at Woolman?"

Neither wanted, in the midst of their sorrow for the good man whose life was ending, to enter into any discussion of Cress. What was the matter with Cress? What had happened to her since she went away to college? She, who had been open and loving? And who now lived inside a world so absolutely fitted to her own size and shape that she felt any intrusion, even that of the death of her own grandfather, to be an unmerited invasion of her privacy. Black magic could not have changed her more quickly and unpleasantly and nothing except magic, it seemed, would give them back their lost daughter.

Mr. Delahanty pushed back his cup and saucer. "Her place is here, Gertrude. I'm going to call her long distance now. She's a bright girl and it's not going to hurt her to miss a few days from classes. What's the dormitory number?"

"I know it as well as our number," Mrs. Delahanty said. "But at the minute it's gone. It's a sign of my reluctance, I suppose. Wait a minute and I'll look it up."

Mr. Delahanty squeezed out from behind the table. "Don't bother. I can get it."

Mrs. Delahanty watched her husband, his usually square shoulders sagging with weariness, wipe a clear place on the steamy windowpane with his napkin. Some of the green twilight appeared to seep into the warm dingy little kitchen. "I can't ever remember having to smudge before in February. I expect you're right," he added as he went toward the phone. "Cress isn't going to like it."

Cress didn't like it. It was February, the rains had been late and the world was burning with a green fire; a green smoke rolled down the hills and burst shoulder-high in the cover crops that filled the spaces between the trees in the orange orchards. There had been rain earlier in the day and drops still hung from the grass blades, sickle-shaped with their weight. Cress, walking across the campus with Edwin, squatted to look into one of these crystal globes. "Green from the grass and red from the

sun," she told him. "The whole world right there in one raindrop."

"As Blake observed earlier about a grain of sand," said Edwin.

"O.K., show off," Cress told him. "You know it—but I saw it." She took his hand and he pulled her up, swinging her in a semicircle in front of him. "Down there in the grass the world winked at me."

"Don't be precious, Cress," Edwin said.

"I will," Cress said, "just to tease you. I love to tease you, Edwin."

"Why?" Edwin asked.

"Because you love to have me," Cress said confidently, taking his hand. Being older suited Edwin. She remembered when she had liked him in spite of his looks; but now spindly had become spare, and the dark shadow of his beard—Edwin had to shave every day while other boys were still just fuzzy—lay under his pale skin; and the opinions, which had once been so embarrassingly unlike anyone else's, were now celebrated at Woolman as being "Edwinian." Yes, Edwin had changed since that day when she had knocked his tooth out trying to rescue him from the mush pot. And had she changed? Did she also look better to Edwin, almost slender now and the freckles not noticeable except at the height of summer? And with her new-found ability for light talk? They were passing beneath the eucalyptus trees and the silver drops, falling as the wind shook the leaves, stung her face, feeling at once both cool and burning. Meadow larks in the fields which edged the campus sang in the quiet way they have after the rain has stopped.

"Oh, Edwin," Cress said, "no one in the world loves the meadow lark's song the way I do!"

"It's not a competition," Edwin said, "you against the world in an 'I-love-meadow-larks' contest. Take it easy, kid. Love em as much as in you lieth, and let it go at that."

"No," she said. "I'm determined to overdo it. Listen," she exclaimed, as two birds sang together. "Not grieving, nor amorous, nor lost. Nothing to read into it. Simply music. Like Mozart. Complete. Finished. Oh, it is rain to listening ears." She glanced at Edwin to see how he took this rhetoric. He took it calmly. She let go his hand and capered amidst the fallen eucalyptus leaves.

"The gardener thinks you've got St. Vitus' dance," Edwin said.

Old Boat Swain, the college gardener whose name was really Swain, was leaning on his hoe, watching her hopping and strutting. She didn't give a hoot about him or what he thought.

"He's old," she told Edwin. "He doesn't exist." She felt less akin to him than to a bird or toad.

There were lights already burning in the dorm windows. Cress could see Ardis and Nina still at their tables, finishing their *Ovid* or looking up a final logarithm. But between five and six most of the girls stopped trying to remember which form of the sonnet Milton had used or when the Congress of Vienna had met, and dressed for dinner. They got out of their sweaters and jackets and into their soft bright dresses. She knew just what she was going to wear when she came downstairs at six to meet Edwin—green silk like the merman's wife. They were going to the Poinsettia for dinner, escaping salmon-wiggle night in the college dining room.

"At six," she told him, "I'll fly down the stairs to meet you like a green wave."

"See you in thirty minutes," Edwin said, leaving her at the dorm steps.

The minute she opened the door, she began to hear the dorm sounds and smell the dorm smells—the hiss and rush of the showers, the thud of the iron, a voice singing, "Dear old Woolman we love so well," the slap of bare feet down the hall, the telephone ringing.

And the smells! Elizabeth Arden and Cashmere Bouquet frothing in the showers; talcum powder falling like snow; *Intoxication* and *Love Me* and *Devon Violet;* rubber-soled sneakers, too, and gym T-shirts still wet with sweat after basketball practice, and the smell of the hot iron on damp wool.

But while she was still listening and smelling, Edith shouted from the top of the stairs, "Long distance for you, Cress. Make it snappy."

Cress took the stairs three at a time, picked up the dangling receiver, pressed it to her ear.

"Tenant calling Crescent Delahanty," the operator said. It was her father: "Grandfather is dying, Cress. Catch the 7:30 home. I'll meet you at the depot."

"What's the matter—Cressie?" Edith asked.

"I have to catch the 7:30 Pacific Electric. Grandfather's dying."

"Oh, poor Cress," Edith cried and pressed her arm about her.

Cress scarcely heard her. Why were they calling her home to watch Grandpa die, she thought, angrily and rebelliously. An old man, past eighty. He'd never been truly alive for her, never more than a rough, hot hand, a scraggly mustache that repelled her when he kissed her, an old fellow who gathered what he called "likely-looking" stones and kept them washed and polished, to turn over and admire. It was silly and unfair to make so much of his dying.

But before she could say a word, Edith was telling the girls. They were crowding about her. "Don't cry," they said. "We'll pack for you. Be brave, darling Cress. Remember your grandfather has had a long happy life. He wouldn't want you to cry."

"Brave Cress—brave Cress," they said. "Just frozen."

She wasn't frozen. She was determined. She was not going to go. It did not make sense. She went downstairs to meet Edwin as she had planned, in her green silk, ready for dinner at the Poinsettia. The girls had told him.

"Are you wearing that home?" he asked.

"I'm not going home," she said. "It's silly and useless. I can't help Grandfather. It's just a convention. What *good* can I do him, sitting there at home?"

"He might do you some good," Edwin said. "Had you thought about that?"

"Why Edwin!" Cress said. "Why Edwin!" She had the girls tamed, eating out of her hand, and here was Edwin who loved her—he said so, anyway—cold and disapproving. Looking at herself through Edwin's eyes, she hesitated.

"Go on," Edwin said. "Get what you need and I'll drive you to the station."

She packed her overnight bag and went with him; there didn't seem—once she'd had Edwin's view of herself—anything else to do. But once on the train her resentment returned. The Pacific Electric was hot and smelled of metal and dusty plush. It clicked past a rickety Mexican settlement, through La Habra and Brea, where the pool hall signs swung in the night wind off the ocean. An old man in a spotted corduroy jacket, and his wife, with her hair straggling through the holes in her broken net, sat in front of her.

Neat, thought Cress, anyone can be neat, if he wants to.

Her father, bareheaded, but in his big sheepskin jacket, met her at the depot. It was after nine, cold and raw.

"This is a sorry time, Cress," he said. He put her suitcase in the back of the car and climbed into the driver's seat without opening the door for her.

Cress got in, wrapped her coat tightly about herself. The sky was clear, the wind had died down.

"I don't see any sense in my having to come home," she said at last. "What good can I do Grandpa? If he's dying, how can I help?"

"I was afraid that was the way you might feel about it. So was your mother."

"Oh, Mother," Cress burst out. "Recently she's always trying to put me . . . ."

Her father cut her off. "That'll be about enough, Cress. Your place is at home and you're coming home and keeping your mouth shut, whatever you think. I don't know what's happened to you recently. If college does this to you, you'd better stay home permanently."

There was nothing more said until they turned up the palm-lined driveway that led to the house. "Here we are," Mr. Delahanty told her.

Mrs. Delahanty met them at the door, tired and haggard in her Indian design bathrobe.

"Cress," she said, "Grandfather's conscious now. I told him you were coming and he's anxious to see you. You'd better go in right away—this might be the last time he'd know you."

Cress was standing by the fireplace holding first one foot then the other toward the fire. "Oh, Mother, what am I to say?" she asked. "What can I say? Or does Grandfather just want to see me?"

Her father shook his head as if with pain. "Aren't you sorry your grandfather's dying, Cress? Haven't you any pity in your heart? Don't you understand what death means?"

"He's an old man," Cress said obstinately. "It's what we must expect when we grow old," though she, of course, would never grow old.

"Warm your hands, Cress," her mother said. "Grandfather's throat bothers him and it eases

him to have it rubbed. I'll give you the ointment and you can rub it in. You won't need to say anything."

Cress slid out of her coat and went across the hall with her mother to visit her grandfather's room. His thin old body was hardly visible beneath the covers; his head, with its gray skin and sunken eyes, lay upon the pillow as if bodiless. The night light frosted his white hair but made black caverns of his closed eyes.

"Father," Mrs. Delahanty said. "Father." But the old man didn't move. There was nothing except the occasional hoarse rasp of an indrawn breath to show that he was alive.

Mrs. Delahanty pulled the cane-bottomed chair a little closer to the bed. "Sit here," she said to Cress, "and rub this into his throat and chest." She opened her father's nightshirt so that an inch or two of bony grizzled chest was bared. "He says that this rubbing relieves him, even if he's asleep or too tired to speak. Rub it in with a slow steady movement." She went out to the living room leaving the door a little ajar.

Cress sat down on the chair and put two squeamish fingers into the jar of gray ointment; but she could see far more sense to this than to any talking or being talked to. If they had brought her home from school because she was needed in helping to care for Grandpa, that she could understand—but not simply to be present at his death. What had death to do with her?

She leaned over him, rubbing, but with eyes shut, dipping her fingers often into the gray grease. The rhythm of the rubbing, the warmth and closeness of the room, after the cold drive, had almost put her to sleep when the old man startled her by lifting a shaking hand to the bunch of yellow violets Edith had pinned to the shoulder of her dress before she left Woolman. She opened her eyes suddenly at his touch, but the old man said nothing, only stroked the violets awkwardly with a trembling forefinger.

Cress unpinned the violets and put them in his hand. "There, Grandpa," she said, "there. They're for you."

The old man's voice was a harsh and faltering whisper and to hear what he said Cress had to lean very close.

"I used to—pick them—on Reservoir Hill. I was always sorry to—plow them up. Still—so sweet. Thanks," he said, "to bring them. To remember. You're like her. Your grandmother," he added after a pause. He closed his eyes, holding the bouquet against his face, letting the wilting blossoms spray across one cheek like a pulled-up sheet of flowering earth. He said one more word, not her name but her grandmother's.

The dikes about Cress's heart broke. "Oh, Grandpa, I love you," she said. He heard her. He knew what she said, his fingers returned the pressure of her hand. "You were always so good to me. You were young and you loved flowers." Then she said what was her great discovery. "And you still do. You still love yellow violets, Grandpa, just like me."

At the sound of her uncontrolled crying, Mr. and Mrs. Delahanty came to the door. "What's the matter, Cress?"

Cress turned, lifted a hand toward them. "Why didn't you tell me?" she demanded. And when they didn't answer, she said, "Edwin knew."

Then she dropped her head on to her grandfather's outstretched hand and said something, evidently to him, which neither her father nor her mother understood.

"It's just the same."

*Prosper Mérimée*

# MATEO FALCONE

Coming out of Porto-Vecchio, and turning northwest toward the interior of the island, the ground rises somewhat rapidly, and, after a three hours' walk along winding paths, blocked by huge rocky boulders, and sometimes cut by ravines, you come to the edge of a wide *mâquis*. The *mâquis*, or high plateau, is the home of the Corsican shepherds and of all those who wish to escape the police. I would have you understand that the Corsican peasant sets fire to a stretch of woodland to save himself the trouble of manuring his fields. If the flames spread further than they should, so much the worse. In any case, he is sure of a good crop if he sows on this ground, which has been fertilised by the

MATEO FALCONE: Translator unknown.

ashes of the trees which grew on it. When the corn has been harvested, they leave the straw, because it takes too much time to gather it up. The roots of the burned trees, which have been left in the ground undamaged, put forth very thick shoots in the following spring, and these shoots, before many years, attain a height of seven or eight feet. It is this sort of undergrowth which is called a *mâquis*. It is composed of all sorts of trees and shrubs mingled and tangled every whichway. A man has to hew his way through with an axe, and there are *mâquis* so thick and tangled that even wild rams cannot penetrate them.

If you have killed a man, go into the *mâquis* of Porto-Vecchio with a good gun and powder and shot. You will live there quite safely, but don't forget to bring along a brown cloak and hood for your blanket and mattress. The shepherds will give you milk, cheese, and chestnuts, and you need not trouble your head about the law or the dead man's relatives, except when you are compelled to go down into the town to renew your ammunition.

When I was in Corsica in 18—, Mateo Falcone's house stood half a league away from the *mâquis*. He was a fairly rich man for that country. He lived like a lord, that is to say, without toil, on the produce of his flocks, which the nomadic shepherds pastured here and there on the mountains. When I saw him, two years later than the incident which I am about to relate, he did not seem to be more than fifty years of age.

Picture a small, sturdy man, with jet-black curly hair, a Roman nose, thin lips, large piercing eyes, and a weather-beaten complexion. His skill as a marksman was extraordinary, even in this country, where everyone is a good shot. For instance, Mateo would never fire on a wild ram with small shot, but at a hundred and twenty paces he would bring it down with a bullet in its head or its shoulder, just as he fancied. He used his rifle at night as easily as in the daytime, and I was given the following illustration of his skill, which may seem incredible, perhaps, to those who have never travelled in Corsica. He placed a lighted candle behind a piece of transparent paper as big as a plate, and aimed at it from eighty paces away. He extinguished the candle, and a moment later, in utter darkness, fired and pierced the paper three times out of four.

With this extraordinary skill Mateo Falcone had gained a great reputation. He was said to be a good friend and a dangerous enemy. Obliging and charitable, he lived at peace with all his neighbors around Porto-Vecchio. But they said of him that once, at Corte, whence he had brought home his wife, he had quickly freed himself of a rival reputed to be as fearful in war as in love. At any rate, people gave Mateo the credit for a certain shot which had surprised his rival shaving in front of a small mirror hung up in his window. The matter was hushed up and Mateo married the girl. His wife Giuseppa presented him at first, to his fury, with three daughters, but at last came a son whom he christened Fortunato, the hope of the family and the heir to its name. The girls were married off satisfactorily. At a pinch their father could count on the daggers and rifles of his sons-in-law. The son was only ten years old, but already gave promise for the future.

One autumn day, Mateo and his wife set forth to visit one of his flocks in a clearing on the *mâquis*. Little Fortunato wanted to come along, but the clearing was too far off, and moreover, someone had to stay to look after the house. His father refused to take him. We shall see that he was sorry for this afterwards.

He had been gone several hours, and little Fortunato lay stretched out quietly in the sunshine, gazing at the blue mountains, and thinking that next Sunday he would be going to town to have dinner with his uncle, the magistrate, when he was suddenly startled by a rifle shot. He rose and turned toward the side of the plain whence the sound had come. Other shots followed, fired at irregular intervals, and they sounded nearer and nearer, till finally, he saw a man on the path which led from the plain up to Mateo's house. He wore a mountaineer's peaked cap, had a beard, and was clad in rags. He dragged himself along with difficulty, leaning on his gun. He had just been shot in the thigh. The man was an outlaw from justice, who, having set out at nightfall to buy ammunition in the town, had fallen on the way into an ambuscade of Corsican gendarmes. After a vigorous defense, he had succeeded in making his escape, but the gendarmes had pursued him closely and fired at him from rock to rock. He had been just ahead of the soldiers, and his wound made it impossible for him to reach the *mâquis* without being captured.

He came up to Fortunato and asked:

"Are you Mateo Falcone's son?"

"Yes, I am."

"I'm Gianetto Sanpiero. The yellow necks are after me. Hide me, for I can go no farther."

"But what will my father say, if I hide you without his permission?"

"He will say that you did the right thing."

"How can I be sure of that?"

"Quick! Hide me! Here they come!"

"Wait till my father comes back."

"How the devil can I wait? They'll be here in five minutes. Come now, hide me, or I shall kill you."

Fortunato replied as cool as a cucumber:

"Your rifle is not loaded, and there are no cartridges in your pouch."

"I have my stiletto."

"But can you run as fast as I can?"

He bounded out of the man's reach.

"You are no son of Mateo Falcone. Will you let me be captured in front of his house?"

The child seemed touched.

"What will you give me if I hide you?" he said, coming nearer to him.

The fugitive felt in a leather wallet that hung from his belt, and took out a five-franc piece which he had been saving, no doubt, to buy powder. Fortunato smiled when he saw the piece of silver. He snatched it and said to Gianetto:

"Have no fear."

He made a large hole at once in a haystack beside the house. Gianetto huddled down in it, and the boy covered him up so as to leave a little breathing space, and yet so that no one could possibly suspect that a man was hidden there. He showed his ingenious wild cunning by another trick. He fetched a cat and her kittens and put them on top of the haystack, so that anyone who passed would think that it had not been disturbed for a long time. Then he noticed some bloodstains on the path in front of the house and covered them over carefully with dust. When he had finished, he lay down again in the sun looking as calm as ever.

A few minutes later, six men in brown uniforms with yellow collars, led by an adjutant, stopped in front of Mateo's door. The adjutant was a distant cousin of Falcone. (You know that degrees of kindred are traced farther in Corsica than anywhere else.) His name was Tiodoro Gamba. He was an energetic man, much feared by the outlaws, many of whom he had already hunted down.

"Good morning, little cousin," he said, accosting Fortunato. "How you have grown! Did you see a man go by just now?"

"Oh, I'm not as tall as you are yet, cousin," replied the child with an innocent smile.

"It won't take long. But, tell me, didn't you see a man go by?"

"Did I see a man go by?"

"Yes, a man with a black velvet peaked cap and a waistcoat embroidered in red and yellow?"

"A man with a black velvet peaked cap, and a waistcoat embroidered in red and yellow?"

"Yes. Hurry up and answer me, and don't keep repeating my questions."

"Monsieur the Curé went by this morning on his horse Pierrot. He enquired after papa's health, and I said to him that——"

"You are making a fool of me, you limb of the devil! Tell me at once which way Gianetto went. He's the man we're looking for, and I'm sure he went this way."

"How do you know?"

"How do I know? I know you've seen him."

"Can I see people pass by in my sleep?"

"You weren't asleep, you rascal. Our shots would wake you."

"So you think, cousin, that your rifles make all that hullaballoo? My father's rifle makes much more noise."

"The devil take you, you little scamp. I am positive that you have seen Gianetto. Maybe you've hidden him, in fact. Here, boys, search the house and see if our man isn't there. He could only walk on one foot, and he has too much sense, the rascal, to try and reach the *mâquis* limping. Besides, the trail of blood stops here."

"What will papa say?" asked Fortunato. "What will he say when he discovers that his house has been searched during his absence?"

"Do you realise that I can make you change your tune, you rogue?" cried the adjutant, as he pulled his ear. "Perhaps you will have something more to say when I have thrashed you with the flat of my sword."

Fortunato laughed in derision.

"My father is Mateo Falcone," he said meaningly.

"Do you realise, you rascal, that I can haul you off to Corte or to Bastia? I shall put you

in a dungeon on straw, with your feet in irons, and I'll have your head chopped off unless you tell me where to find Gianetto Sanpiero."

The child laughed again derisively at this silly threat. He repeated:

"My father is Mateo Falcone."

"Adjutant, don't get us into trouble with Mateo," muttered one of the gendarmes.

You could see that Gamba was embarrassed. He whispered to his men, who had already searched the house thoroughly. This was not a lengthy matter, for a Corsican hut consists of one square room. There is no furniture other than a table, benches, chests, cooking utensils, and weapons. Meanwhile, little Fortunato was stroking the cat, and seemed to take a malicious satisfaction in the discomfiture of his cousin and the gendarmes.

One gendarme approached the haystack. He looked at the cat and carelessly stuck a bayonet into the hay, shrugging his shoulders as if he thought the precaution absurd. Nothing stirred, and the child's face remained perfectly calm.

The adjutant and his men were desperate. They looked seriously out across the plain, as if they were inclined to go back home, when their leader, satisfied that threats would make no impression on Falcone's son, decided to make a final attempt, and see what coaxing and gifts might do.

"Little cousin," said he, "I can see that your eyes are open. You'll get on in life. But you are playing a risky game with me, and, if it weren't for the trouble it would give my cousin Mateo, God help me if I wouldn't carry you off with me."

"Nonsense!"

"But, when my cousin returns, I am going to tell him all about it, and he'll horsewhip you till the blood comes because you've been telling me lies."

"How do you know?"

"You'll see! . . . But see here! Be a good boy, and I'll give you a present."

"I advise you to go and look for Gianetto in the *mâquis,* cousin. If you hang about here much longer, it will take a cleverer man than you to catch him." The adjutant took a silver watch worth ten dollars out of his pocket. He noticed that little Fortunato's eyes sparkled as he looked at it, and he dangled the watch out to him at the end of its steel chain as he said:

"You scamp, wouldn't you like to have a

watch like this hanging round your neck, and to strut up and down the streets of Porto-Vecchio as proud as a peacock? Folk would ask you what time it was and you would say, 'Look at my watch!' "

"When I'm a big boy, my uncle, the magistrate, will give me a watch."

"Yes, but your uncle's son has one already —not as fine as this, to be sure—but he is younger than you are."

The boy sighed.

"Well, would you like this watch, little cousin?"

Fortunato kept eyeing the watch out of the corner of his eye, like a cat that has been given a whole chicken to play with. It does not dare to pounce upon it, because it is afraid folk are laughing at it, but it turns its eyes away now and then so as to avoid temptation, and keeps licking its lips, as much as to say to its master: "What a cruel trick to play on a cat!" And yet Gamba seemed to be really offering him the watch. Fortunato did not hold out his hand, but said with a bitter smile:

"Why are you mocking me?"

"I swear that I am not mocking you. Only tell me where Gianetto is, and the watch is yours."

Fortunato smiled incredulously and fixed his dark eyes on those of the adjutant, trying to read them to see if the man could be trusted.

"May I lose my epaulettes," cried the adjutant, "if I do not give you the watch on this one condition! My men are witnesses, and I cannot back out of it."

As he spoke, he held the watch nearer and nearer till it almost touched the pale cheek of the boy, whose face clearly showed the struggle going on in his heart between greed and the claims of hospitality. His bare breast heaved till he was almost suffocated. Meanwhile the watch dangled and twisted and even touched the tip of his nose. Little by little, his right hand rose toward it, the tips of his fingers touched it, and the whole weight of it rested on his hand, although the adjutant still had it by the chain. ... The face of the watch was blue. ... The case was newly burnished. ... It flamed like fire in the sun. ... The temptation was too great.

Fortunato raised his left hand and pointed with his thumb over his shoulder to the haystack on which he was leaning. The adjutant

understood him at once and let go the end of the chain. Fortunato felt that he was now sole possessor of the watch. He leaped away like a deer, and paused ten paces from the haystack which the gendarmes began to tumble over at once.

It was not long before they saw the hay begin to stir and a bleeding man came out with a stiletto in his hand. But when he tried to rise to his feet, his congealed wound prevented him from standing. He fell down. The adjutant flung himself upon his prey and wrested the stiletto from his grasp. He was speedily trussed up, in spite of his resistance, bound securely, and flung on the ground like a bundle of sticks. He turned his head toward Fortunato who had drawn near again.

"Son of ...!" he exclaimed, more in contempt than in anger.

The child threw him the piece of silver, realising that he no longer deserved it, but the fugitive paid no attention to it. He merely said quietly to the adjutant:

"My dear Gamba, I cannot walk. You must carry me to town."

"You were running as fast as a kid just now," retorted his captor, roughly. "But don't worry! I'm so glad to have caught you that I could carry you a league on my own back without feeling it. Anyhow, my friend, we'll make a litter for you out of branches and your cloak. We'll find horses at the farm at Crespoli."

"Very well," said the prisoner. "I suppose you will put a little straw on the litter to make it easier for me."

While the gendarmes were busy, some making a crude litter of chestnut boughs, and others dressing Gianetto's wound, Mateo Falcone and his wife suddenly appeared at a turn of the path which led from the mâquis. His wife came first, bowed low beneath the weight of a huge sack of chestnuts, while her husband strolled along, carrying a gun in one hand, and another slung over his shoulder. It is beneath a man's dignity to carry any other burden than his weapons.

As soon as he saw the soldiers, Mateo's first thought was that they must have come to arrest him. But there was no reason for it. He had no quarrel with the forces of law and order. He had an excellent reputation. He was "well thought of," as they say, but he was a Corsican, and a mountaineer, and there are very few Corsican mountaineers who, if they search their past sufficiently, cannot find some peccadillo, a rifle shot or a thrust with a stiletto, or some other trifle. Mateo had a clearer conscience than most of his friends, for it was at least ten years since he had pointed a rifle at a man; but all the same it behooved him to be cautious, and he prepared to put up a good defence, if necessary.

"Wife," he said, "put down your sack and be on your guard."

She obeyed at once. He gave her the gun from his shoulder belt, as it seemed likely that it might be in his way. He cocked the other rifle, and advanced in a leisurely manner toward the house, skirting the trees beside the path, and ready, at the least sign of hostility, to throw himself behind the largest trunk and fire from cover. His wife followed close behind him, holding her loaded rifle and his cartridges. It was a good wife's duty, in case of trouble, to reload her husband's arms.

The adjutant, on his side, was much troubled at seeing Mateo advance upon him so with measured steps, pointing his rifle, and keeping his finger on the trigger.

"If it should happen," thought he, "that Gianetto turns out to be Mateo's relative or friend, and he wishes to defend him, two of his bullets will reach us as sure as a letter goes by post, and if he aims at me, in spite of our kinship . . . !"

In his perplexity, he put the best face he could on the matter, and went forward by himself to meet Mateo and tell him all that had happened, greeting him like an old friend. But the short distance between him and Mateo seemed fearfully long.

"Hello, there, old comrade!" he cried out. "How are you? I'm your cousin Gamba."

Mateo stood still and said not a word. As the other man spoke, he slowly raised the barrel of his rifle so that, by the time the adjutant came up to him, it was pointing to the sky.

"Good-day, brother," said the adjutant, holding out his hand. "It's an age since I've seen you."

"Good-day, brother."

"I just stopped by to pass the time of day with you and cousin Pepa. We've had a long march to-day, but we can't complain, for we've made a famous haul. We've just caught Gianetto Sanpiero."

"Heaven be praised!" exclaimed Giuseppa.

"He stole one of our milch goats a week ago."

Gamba was delighted at her words.

"Poor devil!" said Mateo, "he was hungry."

"The chap fought like a lion," pursued the adjutant, somewhat annoyed. "He killed one of my men, and as if that were not enough, broke Corporal Chardon's arm; not that it matters, he's only a Frenchman. . . . Then he hid himself so cleverly that the devil himself couldn't find him. If it hadn't been for my little cousin Fortunato, I should never have found him."

"Fortunato?" cried Mateo.

"Fortunato?" echoed Giuseppa.

"Yes! Gianetto was hidden in your haystack over there, but my little cousin soon showed up his tricks. I shall tell his uncle, the magistrate, and he'll send him a fine present as a reward. And both his name and yours shall be in the report that I'm sending to the Public Prosecutor."

"Damn you!" muttered Mateo under his breath.

They had now rejoined the gendarmes. Gianetto was already laid on his litter, and they were all ready to start. When he saw Mateo in Gamba's company, he smiled oddly; then, turning toward the door of the house, he spat at the threshold.

"The house of a traitor!"

It was asking for death to call Falcone a traitor. A quick stiletto thrust, and no need of a second, would have instantly wiped out the insult. But Mateo's only movement was to put his hand to his head as if he were stunned.

Fortunato had gone into the house when he saw his father coming. Presently he reappeared with a bowl of milk, which he offered with downcast eyes to Gianetto.

"Keep away from me!" thundered the outlaw.

Then, turning to one of the gendarmes, he said:

"Comrade, will you give me a drink?"

The gendarme put the flask in his hand, and the outlaw drank the water given him by the man with whom he had just been exchanging rifle shots. Then he requested that his hands might be tied crossed on his breast instead of behind his back.

"I would rather," he said, "lie comfortably."

They gratified his request. Then, at a sign from the adjutant, saying good-bye to Mateo, who vouchsafed no answer, they set off quickly toward the plain.

Ten minutes passed before Mateo opened his mouth. The child looked uneasily, first at his mother, then at his father, who was leaning on his gun and gazing at him with an expression of concentrated fury.

"You begin well," said Mateo at last, in a calm voice, terrifying enough to those who knew the man.

"Father!" cried the boy, with tears in his eyes, coming nearer as if to throw himself at his father's knee.

"Out of my sight!" Mateo shouted.

The child stopped short a few paces away from his father, and sobbed.

Giuseppa approached him. She had just noticed the watch-chain hanging out of his shirt.

"Who gave you that watch?" she asked sternly.

"My cousin, the adjutant."

Falcone snatched the watch and flung it against a stone with such violence that it was shattered into a thousand fragments.

"Woman," he said, "is this a child of mine?"

Giuseppa's brown cheeks flushed brick red.

"What are you saying, Mateo? Do you realise to whom you are speaking?"

"Yes, perfectly well. This child is the first traitor in my family."

Fortunato redoubled his sobs and choking, and Falcone kept watching him like a hawk. At last he struck the ground with the butt of his rifle, then flung it across his shoulder, returned to the path which led toward the *mâquis,* and commanded Fortunato to follow him. The child obeyed.

Giuseppa ran after Mateo and clutched his arm.

"He is your son," she said in a trembling voice, fixing her dark eyes on those of her husband, as if to read all that was passing in his soul.

"Leave me," replied Mateo. "I am his father."

Giuseppa kissed her son and went back weeping into the house. She flung herself on her knees before an image of the Blessed Virgin and prayed fervently. Falcone walked about two hundred paces along the path, and went down a little ravine where he stopped. He tested the ground with the butt of his rifle, and

found it soft and easy to dig. The spot seemed suitable for his purpose.

"Fortunato, go over to that big rock."

The boy did as he was told. He knelt down.

"Father, Father, do not kill me!"

"Say your prayers!" shouted Mateo in a terrible voice.

The boy, stammering and sobbing, recited the Our Father and the Apostles' Creed. The father said "Amen!" in a firm voice at the end of each prayer.

"Are those all the prayers you know?"

"I know the Hail Mary, too, and the Litany my aunt taught me, Father."

"It is long, but never mind."

The boy finished the Litany in a stifled voice.

"Have you finished?"

"Oh, Father, forgive me! Forgive me! I'll never do it again. I'll beg my cousin, the magistrate, ever so hard to pardon Gianetto!"

He kept beseeching his father. Mateo loaded his gun and took aim.

"God forgive you!" he said.

The boy made a desperate effort to rise and clasp his father's knees, but he had no time. Mateo fired and Fortunato fell stone-dead.

Without glancing at the body, Mateo returned to the house to fetch a spade with which to dig his son's grave. He had only gone a few steps along the path when he met Giuseppa, running, for she had been alarmed by the rifle shot.

"What have you done?" she cried.

"Justice!"

"Where is he?"

"In the ravine. I am going to bury him. He died a Christian. I shall have a Mass said for him. Send word to my son-in-law, Tiodoro Bianchi, that he is to come and live with us."

*Alphonse Daudet*

# THE GIRL IN ARLES

The road leading down from my mill to the village passes near a farmhouse at the other end of a big courtyard planted with hackberry trees. It is a typical Provençal farmer's house,

THE GIRL IN ARLES: Translated by Robert Daniel

with its red tiles, great brown irregular front, and, at the very top, the weathervane, the pulley for hoisting the hay, and some brown tufts of hay sticking out of the loft.

Why had this house arrested my attention? Why did its shut gate make my heart ache? Though I could not have explained why, the place gave me a chill. It was too quiet.... When you passed by, the dogs did not bark and the guinea-fowl ran away without a sound. On the inside not a word was spoken. No sound at all, not even the tinkle of a mule's bell. Had there not been white curtains at the windows and smoke rising above the roof, you would have thought the place deserted.

Yesterday, just at noon, I was returning from the village, and to get out of the sunlight I walked beside the wall of the farm in the shade of the hackberry trees. On the road in front of the house some farmhands were silently finishing the loading of a haywagon. The gate had been left open. I glanced in as I passed and saw, at the other end of the courtyard, with his elbows on a big stone table and his head in his hands, a tall, white-haired old man, wearing a vest that was too short and a pair of tattered breeches. I stopped. One of the men said to me in a low voice, "Shh. It's the master. He's been that way ever since his son's tragedy."

At this moment a woman and a little boy, dressed in black and carrying huge gilt prayer-books, passed by us and went into the farmhouse.

"... the mistress and the younger son coming home from mass," the man added. "They go every day, ever since the boy killed himself. Oh, sir, what an affliction! The father is still wearing his funeral clothes; we can't get him to take them off.... Get up, horse!"

The wagon began to move away. Wishing to hear more, I asked the driver if i might get up beside him, and it was there, atop the load of hay, that I learned the whole heart-breaking story....

His name was Jan. He was a fine peasant lad, twenty years old, discreet as a girl, steady and of an open countenance. As he was very good-looking, women would stare at him; but he had no thought for any of them but one— a little girl in Arles, dressed always in velvet and lace, whom he had once met in the stadium

there. At first nobody at the farm approved of this love affair. The girl was considered a flirt, and her family were not country people. But Jan wanted his Arlésienne, no matter what. He would say, "I'll die if they don't let me have her."

They had to give in. It was decided that the wedding should take place after the harvest.

One Sunday evening, in the courtyard of the farmhouse, the family were finishing dinner. It was almost a wedding feast. Jan's fiancée was not present but they had drunk her health many times.... A man came to the gate and in a shaky voice asked to speak to Master Estève, to him only. Estève got up and went out to the road.

"Master," said the man, "you are about to marry your boy to a deceiver, who for two years has been my mistress. I will prove what I say: here are her letters!... Her parents know all about it and had promised her to me; but since your son has been courting her, neither they nor that fine girl want any more of me.... It would seem to me, though, that after that she couldn't be anyone else's wife."

"Very well," said Master Estève after looking at the letters. "Come in and drink a glass of muscatel."

The man answered: "No, thanks! I am too unhappy to drink." And he went away.

The father came back in, his face expressionless, and resumed his place at the table. The feast ended cheerfully.

That evening Master Estève and his son went out together into the fields. They stayed out a long while; when they came back, the mother was waiting up for them.

"Wife," said the farmer, taking her son to her, "give him a kiss. He is unhappy...."

Jan spoke no more of the girl in Arles. He still loved her, however, all the more that he had been made to see her in someone else's arms. Only he was too proud to say anything; that is what killed him, poor fellow. Sometimes he would spend whole days alone in a corner, without moving. Other days he would rush out into the fields and by himself do the work of ten laborers. When evening came, he would set out towards Arles and walk straight ahead till he saw the slender spires of the town rising in the sunset. Then he would come back. He never went any farther.

Seeing him like this, always sad and lonely, the people at the farm did not know what to do. They were afraid something frightful would happen. At the table one day his mother, looking at him with her eyes full of tears, said to him:

"All right. Listen, Jan, if you want her in spite of everything, we'll let you have her. . . ."

His father, red-faced with shame, lowered his head. Jan made a gesture that meant "No," and went out.

From that day on he changed his manner, pretending to be gay all the time, so as to reassure his parents. Once more he was to be seen at dances, in the tavern, and at the fair. On election day at Fonvieille, he was the one who led the dancing of the *farandole*.

His father said, "He is cured." His mother, though, was still worried, and kept an eye on her child more carefully than ever. Jan slept with his younger brother, very near the silk-worm nursery; the poor old woman made a bed for herself near their room—she said that the silkworms might need her during the night.

The feast of Eloi, patron saint of farmers, came around. There was a great celebration at the farm: *château neuf* for everybody, and the mulled wine flowed like water. Fireworks of all sorts, the hackberry trees full of colored lanterns . . . hurrah for Saint Eloi! They almost farandoled themselves to death. The young brother burned a hole in his new blouse. Even Jan seemed to be happy; he tried to make his mother dance, and the poor woman cried for joy.

At midnight everybody went to bed. They needed sleep. Jan did not go to sleep, though. His brother said afterwards that he sobbed all night. Oh, he had it bad, let me tell you.

At dawn the next day his mother heard someone running across his room. She seemed to have a presentiment: "Jan, is that you?"

Jan did not reply; he was already on the ladder.

Instantly his mother got out of bed: "Jan, where are you going?"

He climbed up to the hayloft, she climbing after him.

"Son, in the name of heaven!"

He shut the door and bolted it.

"Jan, my little Jan, answer me. What are you going to do?"

She groped for the latch with her old, shaking hands. . . . A window opening, the thud of a body on the flagstones of the courtyard, and that was all.

The poor fellow had said to himself, "I love her too much; I am going away. . . ." Ah, wretched souls that we are! It is a pretty hard thing that contempt cannot extinguish love.

That morning the village people were asking each other who could be screaming that way, down at the Estève farm.

In front of the stone table in the courtyard, covered with dew and blood, the mother, quite naked, was wailing with her dead child in her arms.

## Eudora Welty
# WHY I LIVE AT THE P.O.

I was getting along fine with Mama, Papa-Daddy, and uncle Rondo until my sister Stella-Rondo just separated from her husband and came back home again. Mr. Whitaker! Of course I went with Mr. Whitaker first, when he first appeared here in China Grove, taking "Pose-Yourself" photos, and Stella-Rondo broke us up. Told him I was one sided. Bigger on one side than the other, which is a deliberate, calculated falsehood: I'm the same. Stella-Rondo is exactly twelve months to the day younger than I am and for that reason she's spoiled.

She's always had anything in the world she wanted and then she'd throw it away. Papa-Daddy gave her this gorgeous Add-a-Pearl necklace when she was eight years old and she threw it away playing baseball when she was nine, with only two pearls.

So as soon as she got married and moved away from home the first thing she did was separate! From Mr. Whitaker! This photographer with the pop-eyes she said she trusted. Came home from one of those towns up in Illinois and to our complete surprise brought this child of two.

Mama said she like to made her drop dead for a second. "Here you had this marvelous blonde child and never so much as wrote your mother a word about it," says Mama. "I'm thoroughly ashamed of you." But of course she wasn't.

Stella-Rondo just calmly takes off this *hat,* I wish you could see it. She says, "Why, Mama, Shirley-T's adopted, I can prove it."

"How?" says Mama, but all I says was, "H'm!" There I was over the hot stove, trying to stretch two chickens over five people and a completely unexpected child into the bargain, without one moment's notice.

"What do you mean—'H'm!'?" says Stella-Rondo, and Mama says, "I heard that, Sister."

I said that oh, I didn't mean a thing, only that whoever Shirley-T. was, she was the spit-image of Papa-Daddy if he'd cut off his beard, which of course he'd never do in the world. Papa-Daddy's Mama's papa and sulks.

Stella-Rondo got furious! She said, "Sister, I don't need to tell you you got a lot of nerve and always did have and I'll thank you to make no future reference to my adopted child whatsoever."

"Very well," I said. "Very well, very well. Of course I noticed at once she looks like Mr. Whitaker's side too. That frown. She looks like a cross between Mr. Whitaker and Papa-Daddy."

"Well, all I can say is she isn't."

"She looks exactly like Shirley Temple to me," says Mama, but Shirley-T. just ran away from her.

So the first thing Stella-Rondo did at the table was turn Papa-Daddy against me.

"Papa-Daddy," she says. He was trying to cut up his meat. "Papa-Daddy!" I was taken completely by surprise. Papa-Daddy is about a million years old and's got this long-long beard. "Papa-Daddy, Sister says she fails to understand why you don't cut off your beard."

So Papa-Daddy l-a-y-s down his knife and fork! He's real rich. Mama says he is, he says he isn't. So he says, "Have I heard correctly? You don't understand why I don't cut off my beard?"

"Why," I says, "Papa-Daddy, of course I understand, I did not say any such of a thing, the idea!"

He says, "Hussy!"

I says, "Papa-Daddy, you know I wouldn't any more want you to cut off your beard

than the man in the moon. It was the farthest thing from my mind! Stella-Rondo sat there and made that up while she was eating breast of chicken."

But he says, "So the postmistress fails to understand why I don't cut off my beard. Which job I got you through my influence with the government. 'Bird's nest'—is that what you call it?"

Not that it isn't the next-to-smallest P.O. in the entire state of Mississippi.

I says, "Oh, Papa-Daddy," I says, "I didn't say any such of a thing, I never dreamed it was a bird's nest, I have always been grateful though this is the next-to-smallest P.O. in the state of Mississippi, and I do not enjoy being referred to as a hussy by my own grandfather."

But Stella-Rondo says, "Yes, you did say it too. Anybody in the world could of heard you, that had ears."

"Stop right there," says Mama, looking at *me.*

So I pulled my napkin straight back through the napkin ring and left the table.

As soon as I was out of the room Mama says, "Call her back, or she'll starve to death," but Papa-Daddy says, "This is the beard I started growing on the Coast when I was fifteen years old." He would of gone on till nightfall if Shirley-T. hadn't lost the Milky Way she ate in Cairo.

So Papa-Daddy says, "I am going out and lie in the hammock, and you can all sit here and remember my words: I'll never cut off my beard as long as I live, even one inch, and I don't appreciate it in you at all." Passed right by me in the hall and went straight out and got in the hammock.

It would be a holiday. It wasn't five minutes before Uncle Rondo suddenly appeared in the hall in one of Stella-Rondo's flesh-colored kimonos, all cut on the bias, like something Mr. Whitaker probably thought was gorgeous.

"Uncle Rondo!" I says. "I didn't know who that was! Where are you going?"

"Sister," he says, "get out of my way, I'm poisoned."

"If you're poisoned stay away from Papa-Daddy," I says. "Keep out of the hammock. Papa-Daddy will certainly beat you on the head if you come within forty miles of him. He thinks I deliberately said he ought to cut off his beard after he got me the P.O., and I've told him and told him and told him, and he acts like he just don't hear me. Papa-Daddy must of gone stone deaf."

"He picked a fine day to do it then," says Uncle Rondo, and before you could say "Jack Robinson" flew out in the yard.

What he'd really done, he'd drunk another bottle of that prescription. He does it every single Fourth of July as sure as shooting, and it's horribly expensive. Then he falls over in the hammock and snores. So he insisted on zigzagging right on out to the hammock, looking like a half-wit.

Papa-Daddy woke up with this horrible yell and right there without moving an inch he tried to turn Uncle Rondo against me. I heard every word he said. Oh, he told Uncle Rondo I didn't learn to read till I was eight years old and he didn't see how in the world I ever got the mail put up at the P.O., much less read it all, and he said if Uncle Rondo could only fathom the lengths he had gone to to get me that job! And he said on the other hand he thought Stella-Rondo had a brilliant mind and deserved credit for getting out of town. All the time he was just lying there swinging as pretty as you please and looping out his beard, and poor Uncle Rondo was *pleading* with him to slow down the hammock, it was making him as dizzy as a witch to watch it. But that's what Papa-Daddy likes about a hammock. So Uncle Rondo was too dizzy to get turned against me for the time being. He's Mama's only brother and is a good case of a one-track mind. Ask anybody. A certified pharmacist.

Just then I heard Stella-Rondo raising the upstairs window. While she was married she got this peculiar idea that it's cooler with the windows shut and locked. So she has to raise the window before she can make a soul hear her outdoors.

So she raises the window and says, *"Oh!"* You would have thought she was mortally wounded.

Uncle Rondo and Papa-Daddy didn't even look up, but kept right on with what they were doing. I had to laugh.

I flew up the stairs and threw the door open! I says, "What in the wide world's the matter, Stella-Rondo? You mortally wounded?"

"No," she says, "I am not mortally wounded but I wish you would do me the favor of looking out that window there and telling me what you see."

So I shade my eyes and look out the window.

"I see the front yard," I says.

"Don't you see any human beings?" she says.

"I see Uncle Rondo trying to run Papa-Daddy out of the hammock," I says. "Nothing more. Naturally, it's so suffocating-hot in the house, with all the windows shut and locked, everybody who cares to stay in their right mind will have to go out and get in the hammock before the Fourth of July is over."

"Don't you notice anything different about Uncle Rondo?" asks Stella-Rondo.

"Why, no, except he's got on some terrible-looking flesh-colored contraption I wouldn't be found dead in, is all I can see," I says.

"Never mind, you won't be found dead in it, because it happens to be part of my trousseau, and Mr. Whitaker took several dozen photographs of me in it," says Stella-Rondo. "What on earth could Uncle Rondo *mean* by wearing part of my trousseau out in the broad open daylight without saying so much as 'Kiss my foot,' *knowing* I only got home this morning after my separation and hung my negligee up on the bathroom door, just as nervous as I could be?"

"I'm sure I don't know, and what do you expect me to do about it?" I says. "Jump out the window?"

"No, I expect nothing of the kind. I simply declare that Uncle Rondo looks like a fool in it, that's all," she says. "It makes me sick to my stomach."

"Well, he looks as good as he can," I says. "As good as anybody in reason could." I stood up for Uncle Rondo, please remember. And I said to Stella-Rondo, "I think I would do well not to criticize so freely if I were you and came home with a two-year-old child I had never said a word about, and no explanation whatever about my separation."

"I asked you the instant I entered this house not to refer one more time to my adopted child, and you gave me your word of honor you would not," was all Stella-Rondo would say, and started pulling out every one of her eyebrows with some cheap Kress tweezers.

So I merely slammed the door behind me and went down and made some green-tomato pickle. Somebody had to do it. Of course Mama had turned both the niggers loose; she always said no earthly power could hold one anyway on the Fourth of July, so she wouldn't even try. It turned out that Jaypan fell in the lake and came within a very narrow limit of drowning.

So Mama trots in. Lifts up the lid and says, "H'm! Not very good for your Uncle Rondo in his precarious condition, I must say. Or poor little adopted Shirley-T. Shame on you!"

That made me tired. I says, "Well, Stella-Rondo had better thank her lucky stars it was her instead of me came trotting in with that very peculiar-looking child. Now if it had been me that trotted in from Illinois and brought a peculiar-looking child of two, I shudder to think of the reception I'd of got, much less controlled the diet of an entire family."

"But you must remember, Sister, that you were never married to Mr. Whitaker in the first place and didn't go up to Illinois to live," says Mama, shaking a spoon in my face. "If you had I would of been just as overjoyed to see you and your little adopted girl as I was to see Stella-Rondo, when you wound up with your separation and came on back home."

"You would not," I says.

"Don't contradict me, I would," says Mama.

But I said she couldn't convince me though she talked till she was blue in the face. Then I said, "Besides, you know as well as I do that that child is not adopted."

"She most certainly is adopted," says Mama, stiff as a poker.

I says, "Why, Mama, Stella-Rondo had her just as sure as anything in this world, and just too stuck up to admit it."

"Why, Sister," said Mama. "Here I thought we were going to have a pleasant Fourth of July, and you start right out not believing a word your own baby sister tells you!"

"Just like Cousin Annie Flo. Went to her grave denying the facts of life," I remind Mama.

"I told you if you ever mentioned Annie Flo's name I'd slap your face," says Mama, and slaps my face.

"All right, you wait and see," I says.

"I," says Mama, "I prefer to take my children's word for anything when it's humanly possible." You ought to see Mama, she weighs two hundred pounds and has real tiny feet.

Just then something perfectly horrible occurred to me.

"Mama," I says, "can that child talk?" I simply had to whisper! "Mama, I wonder if that child can be—you know—in any way? Do you realize," I says, "that she hasn't spoken one single solitary word to a human being up to this minute? This is the way she looks," I says, and I looked like this.

Well, Mama and I just stood there and stared at each other. It was horrible!

"I remember well that Joe Whitaker frequently drank like a fish," says Mama. "I believed to my soul he drank *chemicals*." And without another word she marches to the foot of the stairs and calls Stella-Rondo.

"Stella-Rondo? O-o-o-o-o! Stella Rondo!"

"What?" says Stella-Rondo from upstairs. Not even the grace to get up off the bed.

"Can that child of yours talk?" asks Mama.

Stella-Rondo says, "Can she what?"

"Talk! Talk!" says Mama. "Burdyburdy-burdyburdy!"

So Stella-Rondo yells back, "Who says she can't talk?"

"Sister says so," says Mama.

"You didn't have to tell me, I know whose word of honor don't mean a thing in this house," says Stella-Rondo.

And in a minute the loudest Yankee voice I ever heard in my life yells out, "OE-m Pop-OE the Sailor-r-r-r Ma-a-an!" and then somebody jumps up and down in the upstairs hall. In another second the house would of fallen down.

"Not only talks, she can tap-dance!" calls Stella-Rondo. "Which is more than some people I won't name can do."

"Why, the little precious darling thing!" Mama says, so surprised. "Just as smart as she can be!" Starts talking baby talk right there. Then she turns on me. "Sister, you ought to be thoroughly ashamed! Run upstairs this instant and apologize to Stella-Rondo and Shirley-T."

"Apologize for what?" I says. "I merely wondered if the child was normal, that's all. Now that she's proved she is, why, I have nothing further to say."

But Mama just turned on her heel and flew out, furious. She ran right upstairs and hugged the baby. She believed it was adopted. Stella-Rondo hadn't done a thing but turn her against me from upstairs while I stood there helpless over the hot stove. So that made Mama, Papa-Daddy and the baby all on Stella-Rondo's side.

Next, Uncle Rondo.

I must say that Uncle Rondo has been marvelous to me at various times in the past and I was completely unprepared to be made to jump out of my skin, the way it turned out. Once Stella-Rondo did something perfectly horrible to him—broke a chain letter from Flanders Field—and he took the radio back he had given her and gave it to me. Stella-Rondo was furious! For six months we all had to call her Stella instead of Stella-Rondo, or she wouldn't answer. I always thought Uncle Rondo had all the brains of the entire family. Another time he sent me to Mammoth Cave, with all expenses paid.

But this would be the day he was drinking that prescription, the Fourth of July.

So at supper Stella-Rondo speaks up and says she thinks Uncle Rondo ought to try to eat a little something. So finally Uncle Rondo said he would try a little cold biscuits and ketchup, but that was all. So *she* brought it to him.

"Do you think it wise to disport with ketchup in Stella-Rondo's flesh-colored kimono?" I says. Trying to be considerate! If Stella-Rondo couldn't watch out for her trousseau, somebody had to.

"Any objections?" asks Uncle Rondo, just about to pour out all the ketchup.

"Don't mind what she says, Uncle Rondo," says Stella-Rondo. "Sister has been devoting this solid afternoon to sneering out my bedroom window at the way you look."

"What's that?" says Uncle Rondo. Uncle Rondo has got the most terrible temper in the world. Anything is liable to make him tear the house down if it comes at the wrong time.

So Stella-Rondo says, "Sister says, 'Uncle Rondo certainly does look like a fool in that pink kimono!'"

Do you remember who it was really said that?

Uncle Rondo spills out all the ketchup and jumps out of his chair and tears off the kimono and throws it down on the dirty floor and puts his foot on it. It had to be sent all the way to Jackson to the cleaners and re-pleated.

"So that's your opinion of your Uncle Rondo, is it?" he says. "I look like a fool, do I? Well, that's the last straw. A whole day in this house with nothing to do, and then to hear you come out with a remark like that behind my back!"

"I didn't say any such of a thing, Uncle Rondo," I says, "and I'm not saying who did, either. Why, I think you look all right. Just try to take care of yourself and not talk and eat at the same time," I says. "I think you better go lie down."

"Lie down my foot!" says Uncle Rondo. I ought to of known by that he was fixing to do something perfectly horrible.

So he didn't do anything that night in the precarious state he was in—just played casino with Mama and Stella-Rondo and Shirley-T. and gave Shirley-T. a nickel with a head on both sides. It tickled her nearly to death, and she called him "Papa." But at 6:30 A.M. the next morning, he threw a whole five-cent package of some unsold one-inch firecrackers from the store as hard as he could into my bedroom and they every one went off. Not one bad one in the string. Anybody else, there'd be one that wouldn't go off.

Well, I'm just terribly susceptible to noise of any kind, the doctor has always told me I was the most sensitive person he had ever seen in his whole life, and I was simply prostrated. I couldn't eat! People tell me they heard it as far as the cemetery, and old Aunt Jep Patterson, that had been holding her own so good, thought it was Judgment Day and she was going to meet her whole family. It's usually so quiet here.

And I'll tell you it didn't take me any longer than a minute to make up my mind what to do. There I was with the whole entire house on Stella-Rondo's side and turned against me. If I have anything at all I have pride.

So I just decided I'd go straight down to the P.O. There's plenty of room there in the back, I says to myself.

Well! I made no bones about letting the family catch on to what I was up to. I didn't try to conceal it.

The first thing they knew, I marched in where they were all playing Old Maid and pulled the electric oscillating fan out by the plug, and everything got real hot. Next I snatched the pillow I'd done the needlepoint on right off the davenport from behind Papa-Daddy. He went "Ugh!" I beat Stella-Rondo up the stairs and finally found my charm bracelet in her bureau drawer under a picture of Nelson Eddy.

"So that's the way the land lies," says Uncle

Rondo. There he was, piecing on the ham. "Well, Sister, I'll be glad to donate my army cot if you got any place to set it up, providing you'll leave right this minute and let me get some peace." Uncle Rondo was in France.

"Thank you kindly for the cot and 'peace' is hardly the word I would select if I had to resort to firecrackers at 6:30 A.M. in a young girl's bedroom," I says back to him. "And as to where I intend to go, you seem to forget my position as postmistress of China Grove, Mississippi," I says. "I've always got the P.O."

Well, that made them all sit up and take notice.

I went out front and started digging up some four-o'clocks to plant around the P.O.

"Ah-ah-ah!" says Mama, raising the window. "Those happen to be my four-o'clocks. Everything planted in that star is mine. I've never known you to make anything grow in your life."

"Very well," I says. "But I take the fern. Even you, Mama, can't stand there and deny that I'm the one watered that fern. And I happen to know where I can send in a box top and get a packet of one thousand mixed seeds, no two the same kind, free."

"Oh, where?" Mama wants to know.

But I says, "Too late. You 'tend to your house and I'll 'tend to mine. You hear things like that all the time if you know how to listen to the radio. Perfectly marvelous offers. Get anything you want free."

So I hope to tell you I marched in and got that radio, and they could of all bit a nail in two, especially Stella-Rondo, that it used to belong to, and she well knew she couldn't get it back, I'd sue for it like a shot. And I very politely took the sewing-machine motor I helped pay the most on to give Mama for Christmas back in 1929, and a good big calendar, with the first-aid remedies on it. The thermometer and the Hawaiian ukulele certainly were rightfully mine, and I stood on the stepladder and got all my watermelon-rind preserves and every fruit and vegetable I'd put up, every jar. Then I began to pull the tacks out of the bluebird wall vases on the archway to the dining room.

"Who told you you could have those, Miss Priss?" says Mama, fanning as hard as she could.

"I bought 'em and I'll keep track of 'em," I says. "I'll tack 'em up one on each side the post-office window, and you can see 'em when you come to ask me for your mail, if you're so dead to see 'em."

"Not I! I'll never darken the door to that post office again if I live to be a hundred," Mama says. "Ungrateful child! After all the money we spent on you at the Normal."

"Me either," says Stella-Rondo. "You can just let my mail lie there and rot, for all I care. I'll never come and relieve you of a single solitary piece."

"I should worry," I says. "And who you think's going to sit down and write you all those big fat letters and postcards, by the way? Mr. Whitaker? Just because he was the only man ever dropped down in China Grove and you got him—unfairly—is he going to sit down and write you a lengthy correspondence after you come home giving no rhyme nor reason whatsoever for your separation and no explanation for the presence of that child? I may not have your brilliant mind, but I fail to see it."

So Mama says, "Sister, I've told you a thousand times that Stella-Rondo simply got homesick, and this child is far too big to be hers," and she says, "Now, why don't you all just sit down and play Casino?"

Then Shirley-T. sticks out her tongue at me in this perfectly horrible way. She has no more manners than the man in the moon. I told her she was going to cross her eyes like that some day and they'd stick.

"It's too late to stop me now," I says. "You should have tried that yesterday. I'm going to the P.O. and the only way you can possibly see me is to visit me there."

So Papa-Daddy says, "You'll never catch me setting foot in that post office, even if I should take a notion into my head to write a letter some place." He says, "I won't have you reachin' out of that little old window with a pair of shears and cuttin' off any beard of mine. I'm too smart for you!"

"We all are," says Stella-Rondo.

But I said, "If you're so smart, where's Mr. Whitaker?"

So then Uncle Rondo says, "I'll thank you from now on to stop reading all the orders I get on postcards and telling everybody in China Grove what you think is the matter with them," but I says, "I draw my own conclusions and will continue in the future to draw them." I says, "If people want to write their inmost secrets on penny postcards, there's nothing in the wide world you can do about it, Uncle Rondo."

"And if you think we'll ever *write* another postcard, you're sadly mistaken," says Mama.

"Cutting off your nose to spite your face then," I says. "But if you're all determined to have no more to do with the U.S. mail, think of this: What will Stella-Rondo do now, if she wants to tell Mr. Whitaker to come after her?"

"Wah!" says Stella-Rondo. I knew she'd cry. She had a conniption fit right there in the kitchen.

"It will be interesting to see how long she holds out," I says. "And now—I am leaving."

"Good-by," says Uncle Rondo.

"Oh, I declare," says Mama, "to think that a family of mine should quarrel on the Fourth of July, or the day after, over Stella-Rondo leaving old Mr. Whitaker and having the sweetest little adopted child! It looks like we'd all be glad!"

"Wah!" says Stella-Rondo, and has a fresh conniption fit.

*"He* left *her*—you mark my words," I says. "That's Mr. Whitaker. I know Mr. Whitaker. After all, I knew him first. I said from the beginning he'd up and leave her. I foretold every single thing that's happened."

"Where did he go?" asks Mama.

"Probably to the North Pole, if he knows what's good for him," I says.

But Stella-Rondo just bawled and wouldn't say another word. She flew to her room and slammed the door.

"Now look what you've gone and done, Sister," says Mama. "You go apologize."

"I haven't got time, I'm leaving," I says.

"Well, what are you waiting around for?" asks Uncle Rondo.

So I just picked up the kitchen clock and marched off, without saying "Kiss my foot" or anything, and never did tell Stella-Rondo good-by.

There was a nigger girl going along on a little wagon right in front.

"Nigger girl," I says, "come help me haul these things down the hill, I'm going to live in the post office."

Took her nine trips in her express wagon. Uncle Rondo came out on the porch and threw her a nickel.

And that's the last I've laid eyes on any of my family or my family laid eyes on me for five solid days and nights. Stella-Rondo may be telling the most horrible tales in the world about Mr. Whitaker, but I haven't heard them. As I tell everybody, I draw my own conclusions.

But oh, I like it here. It's ideal, as I've been saying. You see, I've got everything cater-cornered, the way I like it. Hear the radio? All the war news. Radio, sewing machine, book ends, ironing board and that great big piano lamp—peace, that's what I like. Butter-bean vines planted all along the front where the strings are.

Of course, there's not much mail. My family are naturally the main people in China Grove, and if they prefer to vanish from the face of the earth, for all the mail they get or the mail they write, why, I'm not going to open my mouth. Some of the folks here in town are taking up for me and some turned against me. I know which is which. There are always people who will quit buying stamps just to get on the right side of Papa-Daddy.

But here I am, and here I'll stay. I want the world to know I'm happy.

And if Stella-Rondo should come to me this minute, on bended knees, and *attempt* to explain the incidents of her life with Mr. Whitaker, I'd simply put my fingers in both my ears and refuse to listen.

## *Ogden Nash*

## SONG TO BE SUNG BY THE FATHER OF INFANT FEMALE CHILDREN

My heart leaps up when I behold
A rainbow in the sky;
Contrariwise, my blood runs cold
When little boys go by.

For little boys as little boys,
No special hate I carry,
But now and then they grow to men,
And when they do, they marry.

No matter how they tarry,
Eventually they marry. 10
And, swine among the pearls,
They marry little girls.

Oh, somewhere, somewhere, an infant plays,
With parents who feed and clothe him.
Their lips are sticky with pride and praise,
But I have begun to loathe him.
Yes, I loathe with a loathing shameless
This child who to me is nameless.
This bachelor child in his carriage
Gives never a thought to marriage, 20
But a person can hardly say knife
Before he will hunt him a wife.

I never see an infant (male),
A-sleeping in the sun,
Without I turn a trifle pale
And think, is he the one?
Oh, first he'll want to crop his curls,
And then he'll want a pony,
And then he'll think of pretty girls
And holy matrimony. 30
He'll put away his pony,
And sigh for matrimony.
A cat without a mouse
Is he without a spouse.

Oh, somewhere he bubbles, bubbles of milk,
And quietly sucks his thumbs;
His cheeks are roses painted on silk,
And his teeth are tucked in his gums.
But alas, the teeth will begin to grow,
And the bubbles will cease to bubble; 40
Given a score of years or so,
The roses will turn to stubble.
He'll sell a bond, or he'll write a book,
And his eyes will get that acquisitive look,
And raging and ravenous for the kill,
He'll boldly ask for the hand of Jill.
This infant whose middle
Is diapered still
Will want to marry
My daughter Jill. 50

Oh sweet be his slumber and moist his middle!
My dreams, I fear, are infanticiddle.
A fig for embryo Lohengrins!
I'll open all of his safety pins,
I'll pepper his powder and salt his bottle,
And give him readings from Aristotle,
Sand for his spinach I'll gladly bring,

And tabasco sauce for his teething ring,
And an elegant, elegant alligator
To play with in his perambulator. 60
Then perhaps he'll struggle through fire and water
To marry somebody *else's* daughter!

## Theodore Roethke
# MY PAPA'S WALTZ

The whiskey on your breath
Could make a small boy dizzy;
But I hung on like death:
Such waltzing was not easy.

We romped until the pans
Slid from the kitchen shelf;
My mother's countenance
Could not unfrown itself.

The hand that held my wrist
Was battered on one knuckle 10
At every step you missed
My right ear scraped a buckle.

You beat time on my head
With a palm caked hard by dirt,
Then waltzed me off to bed
Still clinging to your shirt.

## Robert Frost
# "OUT, OUT—"

The buzz saw snarled and rattled in the yard
And made dust and dropped stove-lengths of wood,
Sweet-scented stuff when the breeze drew across it.
And from there those that lifted eyes could count
Five mountain ranges one behind the other
Under the sunset far into Vermont.

And the saw snarled and rattled, snarled and
  rattled,
As it ran light, or had to bear a load.
And nothing happened: day was all but done.
Call it a day, I wish they might have said     10
To please the boy by giving him the half hour
That a boy counts so much when saved from work.
His sister stood beside them in her apron
To tell them "Supper." At the word, the saw,
As if to prove saws knew what supper meant,
Leaped out at the boy's hand, or seemed to leap—
He must have given the hand. However it was,
Neither refused the meeting. But the hand!
The boy's first outcry was a rueful laugh,
As he swung toward them holding up the hand   20

Half in appeal, but half as if to keep
The life from spilling. Then the boy saw all—
Since he was old enough to know, big boy
Doing a man's work, though a child at heart—
He saw all spoiled. "Don't let him cut my hand
  off—
The doctor when he comes. Don't let him, sister!"
So. But the hand was gone already.
The doctor put him in the dark of ether.
He lay and puffed his lips out with his breath.
And then—the watcher at his pulse took fright.  30
No one believed. They listened at his heart.
Little—less—nothing!—and that ended it.
No more to build on there. And they, since they
Were not the one dead, turned to their affairs.

## William Wordsworth
# MICHAEL

If from the public way you turn your steps
Up the tumultuous brook of Green-head Ghyll,
You will suppose that with an upright path
Your feet must struggle; in such bold ascent
The pastoral mountains front you, face to face.
But, courage! for around that boisterous brook
The mountains have all opened out themselves,
And made a hidden valley of their own.
No habitation can be seen; but they
Who journey thither find themselves alone     10
With a few sheep, with rocks and stones, and kites
That overhead are sailing in the sky.
It is in truth an utter solitude;
Nor should I have made mention of this Dell
But for one object which you might pass by,
Might see and notice not. Beside the brook
Appears a straggling heap of unhewn stones!
And to that simple object appertains
A story—unenriched with strange events,
Yet not unfit, I deem, for the fireside,        20
Or for the summer shade. It was the first
Of those domestic tales that spake to me
Of Shepherds, dwellers in the valleys, men
Whom I already loved;—not verily
For their own sakes, but for the fields and hills
Where was their occupation and abode.
And hence this Tale, while I was yet a Boy
Careless of books, yet having felt the power
Of Nature, by the gentle agency
Of natural objects, led me on to feel          30
For passions that were not my own, and think

(At random and imperfectly indeed)
On man, the heart of man, and human life.
Therefore, although it be a history
Homely and rude, I will relate the same
For the delight of a few natural hearts;
And, with yet fonder feeling, for the sake
Of youthful Poets, who among these hills
Will be my second self when I am gone.

Upon the forest-side in Grasmere Vale                        40
There dwelt a Shepherd, Michael was his name;
An old man, stout of heart, and strong of limb.
His bodily frame had been from youth to age
Of an unusual strength: his mind was keen,
Intense, and frugal, apt for all affairs,
And in his shepherd's calling he was prompt
And watchful more than ordinary men.
Hence had he learned the meaning of all winds,
Of blasts of every tone; and oftentimes,
When others heeded not, he heard the South        50
Make subterraneous music, like the noise
Of bagpipers on distant Highland hills.
The Shepherd, at such warning, of his flock
Bethought him, and he to himself would say,
"The winds are now devising work for me!"
And, truly, at all times, the storm, that drives
The traveller to a shelter, summoned him
Up to the mountains: he had been alone
Amid the heart of many thousand mists,
That came to him, and left him, on the heights.        60
So lived he till his eightieth year was past.
And grossly that man errs, who should suppose
That the green valleys, and the streams and rocks,
Were things indifferent to the Shepherd's thoughts.
Fields, where with cheerful spirits he had breathed
The common air; hills, which with vigorous step
He had so often climbed; which had impressed
So many incidents upon his mind
Of hardship, skill or courage, joy or fear;
Which, like a book, preserved the memory        70
Of the dumb animals, whom he had saved,
Had fed or sheltered, linking to such acts
The certainty of honourable gain;
Those fields, those hills—what could they less? had laid
Strong hold on his affections, were to him
A pleasurable feeling of blind love,
The pleasure which there is in life itself.

His days had not been passed in singleness.
His Helpmate was a comely matron, old—
Though younger than himself full twenty years.        80
She was a woman of a stirring life,
Whose heart was in her house: two wheels she had

Of antique form; this large, for spinning wool;
That small, for flax; and, if one wheel had rest,
It was because the other was at work.
The Pair had but one inmate in their house,
An only Child, who had been born to them
When Michael, telling o'er his years, began
To deem that he was old,—in shepherd's phrase,
With one foot in the grave. This only Son,                    90
With two brave sheep-dogs tried in many a storm,
The one of an inestimable worth,
Made all their household. I may truly say,
That they were as a proverb in the vale
For endless industry. When day was gone,
And from their occupations out of doors
The Son and Father were come home, even then,
Their labour did not cease; unless when all
Turned to the cleanly supper-board, and there,
Each with a mess of pottage and skimmed milk,                100
Sat round the basket piled with oaten cakes,
And their plain home-made cheese. Yet when the meal
Was ended, Luke (for so the Son was named)
And his old Father both betook themselves
To such convenient work as might employ
Their hands by the fire-side; perhaps to card
Wool for the Housewife's spindle, or repair
Some injury done to sickle, flail, or scythe,
Or other implement of house or field.

Down from the ceiling, by the chimney's edge,               110
That in our ancient uncouth country style
With huge and black projection overbrowed
Large space beneath, as duly as the light
Of day grew dim the Housewife hung a lamp;
An aged utensil, which had performed
Service beyond all others of its kind.
Early at evening did it burn—and late,
Surviving comrade of uncounted hours,
Which, going by from year to year, had found,
And left, the couple neither gay perhaps                     120
Nor cheerful, yet with objects and with hopes,
Living a life of eager industry.
And now, when Luke had reached his eighteenth year,
There by the light of this old lamp they sate,
Father and Son, while far into the night
The Housewife plied her own peculiar work,
Making the cottage through the silent hours
Murmur as with the sound of summer flies.
This light was famous in its neighbourhood,
And was a public symbol of the life                          130
That thrifty Pair had lived. For, as it chanced,
Their cottage on a plot of rising ground
Stood single, with large prospect, north and south,
High into Easedale, up to Dunmail-Raise,

And westward to the village near the lake;
And from this constant light, so regular,
And so far seen, the House itself, by all
Who dwelt within the limits of the vale,
Both old and young, was named THE EVENING STAR.

Thus living on through such a length of years,                    140
The Shepherd, if he loved himself, must needs
Have loved his Helpmate; but to Michael's heart
This son of his old age was yet more dear—
Less from instinctive tenderness, the same
Fond spirit that blindly works in the blood of all—
Than that a child, more than all other gifts
That earth can offer to declining man,
Brings hope with it, and forward-looking thoughts,
And stirrings of inquietude, when they
By tendency of nature needs must fail.                           150
Exceeding was the love he bare to him,
His heart and his heart's joy! For oftentimes
Old Michael, while he was a babe in arms,
Had done him female service, not alone
For pastime and delight, as is the use
Of fathers, but with patient mind enforced
To acts of tenderness; and he had rocked
His cradle, as with a woman's gentle hand.

And in a later time, ere yet the Boy
Had put on boy's attire, did Michael love,                       160
Albeit of a stern unbending mind,
To have the Young-one in his sight, when he
Wrought in the field, or on his shepherd's stool
Sate with a fettered sheep before him stretched
Under the large old oak, that near his door
Stood single, and, from matchless depth of shade,
Chosen for the Shearer's covert from the sun,
Thence in our rustic dialect was called
The CLIPPING TREE, a name which yet it bears.
There, while they two were sitting in the shade,                 170
With others round them, earnest all and blithe,
Would Michael exercise his heart with looks
Of fond correction and reproof bestowed
Upon the Child, if he disturbed the sheep
By catching at their legs, or with his shouts
Scared them, while they lay still beneath the shears.

And when by Heaven's good grace the boy grew up
A healthy Lad, and carried in his cheek
Two steady roses that were five years old;
Then Michael from a winter coppice cut                           180
With his own hand a sapling, which he hooped
With iron, making it throughout in all
Due requisites a perfect shepherd's staff,
And gave it to the Boy; wherewith equipt

He as a watchman oftentimes was placed
At gate or gap, to stem or turn the flock;
And, to his office prematurely called,
There stood the urchin, as you will divine,
Something between a hindrance and a help;
And for this cause not always, I believe,                    190
Receiving from his Father hire of praise;
Though nought was left undone which staff, or voice,
Or looks, or threatening gestures, could perform.

But soon as Luke, full ten years old, could stand
Against the mountain blasts; and to the heights,
Not fearing toil, nor length of weary ways,
He with his Father daily went, and they
Were as companions, why should I relate
That objects which the Shepherd loved before
Were dearer now? that from the Boy there came               200
Feelings and emanations—things which were
Light to the sun and music to the wind;
And that the old Man's heart seemed born again?

Thus in his Father's sight the Boy grew up:
And now, when he had reached his eighteenth year,
He was his comfort and his daily hope.

While in this sort the simple household lived
From day to day, to Michael's ear there came
Distressful tidings. Long before the time
Of which I speak, the Shepherd had been bound              210
In surety for his brother's son, a man
Of an industrious life, and ample means;
But unforeseen misfortunes suddenly
Had prest upon him; and old Michael now
Was summoned to discharge the forfeiture,
A grievous penalty, but little less
Than half his substance. This unlooked-for claim,
At the first hearing, for a moment took
More hope out of his life than he supposed
That any old man ever could have lost.                      220
As soon as he had armed himself with strength
To look his trouble in the face, it seemed
The Shepherd's sole resource to sell at once
A portion of his patrimonial fields.
Such was his first resolve; he thought again,
And his heart failed him. "Isabel," said he,
Two evenings after he had heard the news,
"I have been toiling more than seventy years,
And in the open sunshine of God's love
Have we all lived; yet, if these fields of ours             230
Should pass into a stranger's hand, I think
That I could not lie quiet in my grave.
Our lot is a hard lot; the sun himself
Has scarcely been more diligent than I;

And I have lived to be a fool at last
To my own family. An evil man
That was, and made an evil choice, if he
Were false to us; and, if he were not false,
There are ten thousand to whom loss like this
Had been no sorrow. I forgive him;—but                                    240
'Twere better to be dumb than to talk thus.

   "When I began, my purpose was to speak
Of remedies and of a cheerful hope.
Our Luke shall leave us, Isabel; the land
Shall not go from us, and it shall be free;
He shall possess it, free as is the wind
That passes over it. We have, thou know'st,
Another kinsman—he will be our friend
In this distress. He is a prosperous man,
Thriving in trade—and Luke to him shall go,                               250
And with his kinsman's help and his own thrift
He quickly will repair this loss, and then
He may return to us. If here he stay,
What can be done? Where every one is poor,
What can be gained?"
                       At this the old Man paused,
And Isabel sat silent, for her mind
Was busy, looking back into past times.
There's Richard Bateman, thought she to herself,
He was a parish-boy—at the church-door
They made a gathering for him, shillings, pence,                          260
And halfpennies, wherewith the neighbours bought
A basket, which they filled with pedlar's wares;
And, with this basket on his arm, the lad
Went up to London, found a master there,
Who, out of many, chose the trusty boy
To go and overlook his merchandise
Beyond the seas; where he grew wondrous rich,
And left estates and monies to the poor,
And, at his birth-place, built a chapel floored
With marble, which he sent from foreign lands.                            270
These thoughts, and many others of like sort,
Passed quickly through the mind of Isabel,
And her face brightened. The old Man was glad,
And thus resumed:—"Well, Isabel! this scheme
These two days has been meat and drink to me.
Far more than we have lost is left us yet.
   We have enough—I wish indeed that I
Were younger;—but this hope is a good hope.
Make ready Luke's best garments, of the best
Buy for him more, and let us send him forth                               280
To-morrow, or the next day, or to-night:
   —If he *could* go, the Boy should go to-night."

   Here Michael ceased, and to the fields went forth
With a light heart. The Housewife for five days

Was restless morn and night, and all day long
Wrought on with her best fingers to prepare
Things needful for the journey of her son.
But Isabel was glad when Sunday came
To stop her in her work: for, when she lay
By Michael's side, she through the last two nights            290
Heard him, how he was troubled in his sleep:
And when they rose at morning she could see
That all his hopes were gone. That day at noon
She said to Luke, while they two by themselves
Were sitting at the door, "Thou must not go:
We have no other Child but thee to lose,
None to remember—do not go away,
For if thou leave thy Father he will die."
The Youth made answer with a jocund voice;
And Isabel, when she had told her fears,                      300
Recovered heart. That evening her best fare
Did she bring forth, and all together sat
Like happy people round a Christmas fire.

    With daylight Isabel resumed her work;
And all the ensuing week the house appeared
As cheerful as a grove in Spring: at length
The expected letter from their kinsman came,
With kind assurances that he would do
His utmost for the welfare of the Boy;
To which, requests were added, that forthwith                 310
He might be sent to him. Ten times or more
The letter was read over; Isabel
Went forth to show it to the neighbours round;
Nor was there at that time on English land
A prouder heart than Luke's. When Isabel
Had to her house returned, the old Man said,
"He shall depart to-morrow." To this word
The Housewife answered, talking much of things
Which, if at such short notice he should go,
Would surely be forgotten. But at length                      320
She gave consent, and Michael was at ease.

    Near the tumultuous brook of Green-head Ghyll,
In that deep valley, Michael had designed
To build a Sheep-fold; and, before he heard
The tidings of his melancholy loss,
For this same purpose he had gathered up
A heap of stones, which by the streamlet's edge
Lay thrown together, ready for the work.
With Luke that evening thitherward he walked:
And soon as they had reached the place he stopped,           330
And thus the old Man spake to him:—"My son,
To-morrow thou wilt leave me: with full heart
I look upon thee, for thou art the same
That wert a promise to me ere thy birth,
And all thy life hast been my daily joy.

I will relate to thee some little part
Of our two histories; 'twill do thee good
When thou art from me, even if I should touch
On things thou canst not know of.—After thou
First cam'st into the world—as oft befalls                            340
To new-born infants—thou didst sleep away
Two days, and blessings from thy Father's tongue
Then fell upon thee. Day by day passed on,
And still I loved thee with increasing love.
Never to living ear came sweeter sounds
Than when I heard thee by our own fireside
First uttering, without words, a natural tune;
While thou, a feeding babe, didst in thy joy
Sing at thy Mother's breast. Month followed month,
And in the open fields my life was passed                            350
And on the mountains; else I think that thou
Hadst been brought up upon thy Father's knees.
But we were playmates, Luke: among these hills,
As well thou knowest, in us the old and young
Have played together, nor with me didst thou
Lack any pleasure which a boy can know."
Luke had a manly heart; but at these words
He sobbed aloud. The old Man grasped his hand,
And said, "Nay, do not take it so—I see
That these are things of which I need not speak.                      360
—Even to the utmost I have been to thee
A kind and a good Father: and herein
I but repay a gift which I myself
Received at others' hands; for, though now old
Beyond the common life of man, I still
Remember them who loved me in my youth.
Both of them sleep together: here they lived,
As all their Forefathers had done; and when
At length their time was come, they were not loth
To give their bodies to the family mould.                            370
I wished that thou shouldst live the life they lived,
But 'tis a long time to look back, my Son,
And see so little gain from threescore years.
These fields were burthened when they came to me;
Till I was forty years of age, not more
Than half of my inheritance was mine.
I toiled and toiled; God blessed me in my work,
And till these three weeks past the land was free.
—It looks as if it never could endure
Another Master. Heaven forgive me, Luke,                             380
If I judge ill for thee, but it seems good
That thou shouldst go."
                                        At this the old Man paused;
Then, pointing to the stones near which they stood,
Thus, after a short silence, he resumed:
"This was a work for us; and now, my Son,
It is a work for me. But, lay one stone—
Here, lay it for me, Luke, with thine own hands.

Nay, Boy, be of good hope;—we both may live
To see a better day. At eighty-four
I still am strong and hale;—do thou thy part;                    390
I will do mine.—I will begin again
With many tasks that were resigned to thee:
Up to the heights, and in among the storms,
Will I without thee go again, and do
All works which I was wont to do alone,
Before I knew thy face.—Heaven bless thee, Boy!
Thy heart these two weeks has been beating fast
With many hopes; it should be so—yes—yes—
I knew that thou couldst never have a wish
To leave me, Luke: thou hast been bound to me                    400
Only by links of love: when thou art gone,
What will be left to us!—But I forget
My purposes. Lay now the corner-stone,
As I requested; and hereafter, Luke,
When thou art gone away, should evil men
Be thy companions, think of me, my Son,
And of this moment; hither turn thy thoughts,
And God will strengthen thee: amid all fear
And all temptation, Luke, I pray that thou
May'st bear in mind the life thy Fathers lived,                  410
Who, being innocent, did for that cause
Bestir them in good deeds. Now, fare thee well—
When thou return'st, thou in this place wilt see
A work which is not here: a covenant
'Twill be between us; but, whatever fate
Befall thee, I shall love thee to the last,
And bear thy memory with me to the grave."

    The Shepherd ended here; and Luke stooped down,
And, as his Father had requested, laid
The first stone of the Sheep-fold. At the sight                  420
The old Man's grief broke from him; to his heart
He pressed his Son, he kissèd him and wept;
And to the house together they returned.
—Hushed was that House in peace, or seeming peace,
Ere the night fell:—with morrow's dawn the Boy
Began his journey, and when he had reached
The public way, he put on a bold face;
And all the neighbours, as he passed their doors,
Came forth with wishes and with farewell prayers,
That followed him till he was out of sight.                      430

    A good report did from their Kinsman come,
Of Luke and his well-doing: and the Boy
Wrote loving letters, full of wondrous news,
Which, as the Housewife phrased it, were throughout
"The prettiest letters that were ever seen."
Both parents read them with rejoicing hearts.
So, many months passed on: and once again
The Shepherd went about his daily work

With confident and cheerful thoughts; and now
Sometimes when he could find a leisure hour                    440
He to that valley took his way, and there
Wrought at the Sheep-fold. Meantime Luke began
To slacken in his duty; and, at length,
He in the dissolute city gave himself
To evil courses: ignominy and shame
Fell on him, so that he was driven at last
To seek a hiding-place beyond the seas.

There is a comfort in the strength of love;
'Twill make a thing endurable, which else
Would overset the brain, or break the heart:                   450
I have conversed with more than one who well
Remember the old Man, and what he was
Years after he had heard this heavy news.
His bodily frame had been from youth to age
Of an unusual strength. Among the rocks
He went, and still looked up to sun and cloud,
And listened to the wind; and, as before,
Performed all kinds of labour for his sheep,
And for the land, his small inheritance.
And to that hollow dell from time to time                      460
Did he repair, to build the Fold of which
His flock had need. 'Tis not forgotten yet
The pity which was then in every heart
For the old Man—and 'tis believed by all
That many and many a day he thither went,
And never lifted up a single stone.

There, by the Sheep-fold, sometimes was he seen
Sitting alone, or with his faithful Dog,
Then old, beside him, lying at his feet.
The length of full seven years, from time to time,             470
He at the building of this Sheep-fold wrought,
And left the work unfinished when he died.
Three years, or little more, did Isabel
Survive her Husband: at her death the estate
Was sold, and went into a stranger's hand.
The Cottage which was named the EVENING STAR
Is gone—the ploughshare has been through the ground
On which it stood; great changes have been wrought
In all the neighbourhood:—yet the oak is left
That grew beside their door; and the remains                   480
Of the unfinished Sheep-fold may be seen
Beside the boisterous brook of Green-head Ghyll.

*Anonymous*
# LORD RANDAL

"O where ha you been, Lord Randal, my son?
And where ha you been, my handsome young man?"
"I ha been at the greenwood; mother, mak my bed soon,
For I'm wearied wi huntin, and fain wad lie down."

"And wha met ye there, Lord Randal, my son?
An wha met you there, my handsome young man?"
"I met wi my true-love; mother, mak my bed soon,
For I'm wearied wi huntin, and fain wad lie down."

"And what did she give you, Lord Randal, my son?
And what did she give you, my handsome young man?"                    10
"Eels fried in a pan; mother, mak my bed soon,
For I'm wearied wi huntin, and fain wad lie down."

"And wha gat your leavins, Lord Randal, my son?
And wha gat your leavins, my handsome young man?"
"My hawks and my hounds; mother, mak my bed soon,
For I'm wearied wi huntin, and fain wad lie down."

"And what becam of them, Lord Randal, my son?
And what becam of them, my handsome young man?"
"They stretched their legs out and died; mother, mak my bed soon,
For I'm wearied wi huntin, and fain wad lie down."                   20

"O I fear you are poisoned, Lord Randal, my son!
I fear you are poisoned, my handsome young man!"
"O yes, I am poisoned; mother, mak my bed soon,
For I'm sick at the heart, and I fain wad lie down."

"What d' ye leave to your mother, Lord Randal, my son?
What d' ye leave to your mother, my handsome young man?"
"Four and twenty milk kye; ² mother, mak my bed soon,
For I'm sick at the heart, and I fain wad lie down."

"What d' ye leave to your sister, Lord Randal, my son?
What d' ye leave to your sister, my handsome young man?"             30
"My gold and my silver; mother, mak my bed soon,
For I'm sick at the heart, and I fain wad lie down."

"What d' ye leave to your brother, Lord Randal, my son?
What d' ye leave to your brother, my handsome young man?"
"My houses and my lands; mother, mak my bed soon,
For I'm sick at the heart, and I fain wad lie down."

"What d' ye leave to your true-love, Lord Randal, my son?
What d' ye leave to your true-love, my handsome young man?"
"I leave her hell and fire; mother, mak my bed soon,
For I'm sick at the heart, and I fain wad lie down."                 40

---
² Kine, cows.

## *Anonymous*

# EDWARD

"Why dois your brand [3] sae drap wi bluid,
  Edward, Edward,
Why dois your brand sae drap wi bluid,
  And why sae sad gang [4] yee O?"
"O I hae killed my hauke sae guid,[5]
  Mither, mither,
O I hae killed my hauke sae guid,
  And I had nae mair bot [6] hee O."

"Your haukis bluid was nevir sae reid,
  Edward, Edward,          10
Your haukis bluid was nevir sae reid,
  My deir son I tell thee O."
"O I hae killed my reid-roan steid,
  Mither, mither,
O I hae killed my reid-roan steid,
  That erst was sae fair and frie [7] O."

"Your steid was auld, and ye hae got mair,
  Edward, Edward,
Your steid was auld and ye hae got mair,
  Sum other dule ye drie [8] O."     20
"O I hae killed my fadir deir,
  Mither, mither,
O I hae killed my fadir deir,
  Alas, and wae is mee O!"

"And whatten penance wul ye drie for that,
  Edward, Edward,
And whatten penance wul ye drie for that?
  My deir son, now tell me O."
"Ile set my feit in yonder boat,
  Mither, mither,          30
Ile set my feit in yonder boat,
  And Ile fare ovir the sea O."

"And what wul ye doe wi your towirs and your
  ha,[9]
  Edward, Edward,
And what wul ye doe wi your towirs and your
  ha,
  That were sae fair to see O?"
"Ile let thame stand tul they doun fa,[10]
  Mither, mither,

---

[3] Sword.  [4] Go.  [5] Good.  [6] No more but.  [7] Free.
[8] Some other sorrow you suffer.  [9] Hall.  [10] Fall
down.

Ile let thame stand tul they doun fa,
  For here nevir mair maun [11] I bee O."  40

"And what wul ye leive to your bairns [12] and your
  wife,
  Edward, Edward,
And what wul ye leive to your bairns and your
  wife,
  Whan ye gang ovir the sea O?"
"The warldis [13] room, late them beg thrae [14] life,
  Mither, mither,
The warldis room, late them beg thrae life
  For thame nevir mair wul I see O."

"And what wul ye leive to your ain mither deir,
  Edward, Edward,          50
And what wul ye leive to your ain mither deir?
  My deir son, now tell me O."
"The curse of hell frae [15] me sall [16] ye beir,
  Mither, mither,
The curse of hell frae me sall ye beir,
  Sic counseils ye gave to me O."

---

[11] Must.  [12] Children.  [13] World's.  [14] Through.
[15] From.  [16] Shall.

## *William Butler Yeats*

# A PRAYER FOR MY DAUGHTER

Once more the storm is howling, and half hid
Under this cradle-hood and coverlid
My child sleeps on. There is no obstacle
But Gregory's wood and one bare hill
Whereby the haystack- and roof-levelling wind,
Bred on the Atlantic, can be stayed;
And for an hour I have walked and prayed
Because of the great gloom that is in my mind.

I have walked and prayed for this young child an
  hour
And heard the sea-wind scream upon the tower, 10
And under the arches of the bridge, and scream

---

A Prayer for My Daughter: From *Collected Poems,* by William Butler Yeats. Copyright, 1903, 1906, 1907, 1912, 1916, 1918, 1919, 1924, 1928, 1931, 1933, 1934, 1935, 1940, 1944, 1945, 1946, 1950, by The Macmillan Company. Copyright, 1940, by Georgie Yeats. Used by permission of The Macmillan Company, U. S. A. and Canada, and A. P. Watt & Son.

In the elms above the flooded stream;
Imagining in excited reverie
That the future years had come,
Dancing to a frenzied drum,
Out of the murderous innocence of the sea.

May she be granted beauty and yet not
Beauty to make a stranger's eye distraught,
Or hers before a looking-glass, for such,
Being made beautiful overmuch,                          20
Consider beauty a sufficient end,
Lose natural kindness and maybe
The heart-revealing intimacy
That chooses right, and never find a friend.

Helen being chosen found life flat and dull
And later had much trouble from a fool,
While that great Queen, that rose out of the
    spray,[17]
Being fatherless could have her way,
Yet chose a bandy-leggèd smith for man.
It's certain that fine women eat                        30
A crazy salad with their meat,
Whereby the Horn of Plenty is undone.

In courtesy I'd have her chiefly learned;
Hearts are not had as a gift but hearts are earned
By those that are not entirely beautiful;
Yet many, that have played the fool
For beauty's very self, has charm made wise,
And many a poor man that has roved,
Loved and thought himself beloved,
From a glad kindness cannot take his eyes.             40

May she become a flourishing hidden tree
That all her thoughts may like the linnet be,
And have no business but dispensing round
Their magnanimities of sound,

---

[17] Aphrodite (or Venus), who became the wife of
Hephaestus (or Vulcan), ugliest of the gods.

Nor but in merriment begin a chase,
Nor but in merriment a quarrel.
O may she live like some green laurel
Rooted in one dear perpetual place.

My mind, because the minds that I have loved,
The sort of beauty that I have approved,               50
Prosper but little, has dried up of late,
Yet knows that to be choked with hate
May well be of all evil chances chief.
If there's no hatred in a mind
Assault and battery of the wind
Can never tear the linnet from the leaf.

An intellectual hatred is the worst,
So let her think opinions are accursed.
Have I not seen the loveliest woman born
Out of the mouth of Plenty's horn,                     60
Because of her opinionated mind
Barter that horn and every good
By quiet natures understood
For an old bellows full of angry wind?

Considering that, all hatred driven hence,
The soul recovers radical innocence
And learns at last that it is self-delighting,
Self-appeasing, self-affrighting,
And that its own sweet will is Heaven's will;
She can, though every face should scowl               70
And every windy quarter howl
Or every bellows burst, be happy still.

And may her bridegroom bring her to a house
Where all's accustomed, ceremonious;
For arrogance and hatred are the wares
Peddled in the thoroughfares.
How but in custom and in ceremony
Are innocence and beauty born?
Ceremony's a name for the rich horn,
And custom for the spreading laurel tree.             80

# MAN AND WOMAN

Such words as *love, hate,* and *fear* are general labels for phenomena of unlimited variety; the precise quality of the emotion depends on the person, the object, and the circumstances. We need such general ideas for many purposes, but, as this chapter shows, it is one of the functions of literature to take us back to the concrete and subtly different feelings from which the general ideas are only abstractions. De Roussy de Sales says that there are many kinds of love and marriage, not just a "de luxe" model; and what could be more different than Bob Topping's and Davy Crockett's ways of getting a wife? These selections remind us how the conventions, and the problems, of love and marriage have changed through the centuries. Yet behind the fantasy of *The Rape of the Lock* and the broad humor of the Wife of Bath's Prologue we can discern aspects of love and sex that appear to be eternal.

In "Sophistication," "The Kiss," "To His Coy Mistress," and "Dover Beach" we see some of the ways in which men and women are drawn together. In "The Necklace," "Hilda," and "As I Walked Out One Evening" we see what follows when love is subverted or denied.

In reading and discussing these selections, it may be fruitful to consider the meaning of the word *love*. Does George really love Helen in "Sophistication," or does he merely need her? Does Riabovitch love the unknown lady in "The Kiss"? Does M. Loisel love his wife? Did Hilda ever love George Bowling? Does the Wife of Bath love her fifth husband? When is love a commitment to a person, and when is it a projection of the self, a clutching dependence, a desire for domination, a day dream? Real life, of course, raises questions like these, but the literature of love, by concentration and focus, sharpens our perception of distinctions and our insight into underlying motives.

## *The Editors of* Life

# LANA TURNER'S FOURTH AND POSITIVELY LAST TIME

Lana Turner, for all her success in Hollywood, has had a sad time of it. She once married Band Leader Artie Shaw but had to divorce him after seven months because, as the testimony showed, he was very cruel. Then she married a broker named Crane, only to discover that he was insufficiently divorced at the time. She remarried him as soon as this embarrassment was removed but after one short year decided that he too was cruel. She was left with nothing but her $226,000-a-year salary, a daughter named Cheryl and half a dozen casual beaux.

Tinplate Heir Bob Topping has also been plagued by misfortune. He is considered very talented by the cafe-society, or cocktail-and-hotfoot, set of New York and Hollywood, for he inherited $7 million and plays a fine game of golf. But his marriages have always turned out badly. In rapid succession he tried a chorus girl, an heiress and finally Actress Arline Judge, who had once been wed to his brother. (This marriage made him stepfather to his own nephew, but fortunately the confusion was cleared up when he and Arline decided to call it quits before he had much time to get acquainted with the boy.)

Last week—to the great delight of millions of Americans who somehow get a vicarious pleasure out of the social events in the higher-priced restaurants on the two coasts—Lana Turner, now 27, and Bob Topping, 34, finally found lasting happiness. Their wedding was performed under the finest auspices. The host and best man was Billy Wilkerson, who moves in the upper circles by virtue of having risen from speakeasy manager to publisher of the *Hollywood Reporter,* a trade paper which carries considerable profitable advertising from movie people who like to be mentioned favorably in its news columns. Mr. Wilkerson is an expert on marriages, having engaged in five of them himself.

At the end of the ceremony the select circle of guests distinctly heard Bob Topping say, "This is forever." Lana said, "Yes, darling." Nobody with a spark of romance could help being touched.

## *David Crockett*

# CROCKETT IN LOVE

I had remained for some short time at home with my father, when he informed me that he owed a man, whose name was Abraham Wilson, the sum of thirty-six dollars, and that if I would set in and work out the note, so as to lift it for him, he would discharge me from his service, and I might go free. I agreed to do this, and went immediately to the man who held my father's note, and contracted with him to work six months for it. I set in, and worked with all my might, not losing a single day in the six months. When my time was out, I got my father's note, and then declined working with the man any longer, though he wanted to hire me mighty bad. The reason was, it was a place where heaps of bad company met to drink and gamble, and I wanted to get away from them, for I know'd very well if I staid there, I should get a bad name, as nobody could be respectable that would live there. I therefore returned to my father, and gave him up his paper, which seemed to please him mightily, for though he was poor, he was an honest man, and always tried mighty hard to pay off his debts.

I next went to the house of an honest old Quaker, by the name of John Kennedy, who had removed from North Carolina, and proposed to hire myself to him, at two shillings a day. He agreed to take me a week on trial; at the end of which he appeared pleased with my work, and informed me that he held a note on my father for forty dollars, and that he would give me that note if I worked for him six months. I was certain enough that I should never get any part of the note; but then I remembered it was my father that owed it, and I concluded it was my duty as a child to help him along, and ease his lot as much as I could. I told the Quaker I would take him up at his offer, and immediately went to work. I never visited my father's house during the whole time of this engagement, though he lived only fifteen miles off. But when it was finished, and I had got the note, I borrowed one of my employer's horses, and, on a Sunday evening, went to pay my parents a visit. Some time after I got there, I pulled out the note and handed it to my father, who supposed Mr. Kennedy had sent it for collection. The old man looked mighty sorry, and said to me he had not the money to pay it, and didn't know what he should do. I then told him I had paid it for him, and it was then his own; that it was not presented for collection, but as a present from me. At this, he shed a heap of tears; and as soon as he got a little over it, he said he was sorry he couldn't give me any thing, but he was not able, he was too poor.

The next day, I went back to my old friend, the Quaker, and set in to work for him for some clothes; for I had now worked a year without getting any money at all, and my clothes were nearly all worn out, and what few I had left were mighty indifferent. I worked in this way for about two months; and in that time a young woman from North Carolina, who was the Quaker's niece, came on a visit to his house. And now I am just getting on a part of my history that I know I never can forget. For though I have heard people talk about hard loving, yet I reckon no poor devil in this world was ever cursed with such hard love as mine has always been, when it came on me. I soon found myself head over heels in love with this girl, whose name the public could make no use of; and I thought that if all the hills about there were pure chink, and all belonged to me, I would give them if I could just talk to her as I wanted to; but I was afraid to begin, for when I would think of saying any thing to her, my heart would begin to flutter like a duck in a puddle; and if I tried to outdo it and speak, would get right smack up in my throat, and choak me like a cold potatoe. It bore on my mind in this way, till at last I concluded I must die if I didn't broach the subject; and so I determined to begin and hang on a trying to speak, till my heart would get out of my throat one way or t'other. And so one day at it I went, and after several trials I could say a little. I told her how well I loved her; that she was the darling object of my soul and body; and I must

have her, or else I should pine down to nothing, and just die away with the consumption.

I found my talk was not disagreeable to her; but she was an honest girl, and didn't want to deceive nobody. She told me she was engaged to her cousin, a son of the old Quaker. This news was worse to me than war, pestilence, or famine; but still I knowed I could not help myself. I saw quick enough my cake was dough, and I tried to cool off as fast as possible; but I had hardly safety pipes enough, as my love was so hot as mighty nigh to burst my boilers. But I didn't press my claims any more, seeing there was no chance to do any thing.

I began now to think, that all my misfortunes growed out of my want of learning. I had never been to school but four days, as the reader has already seen, and did not yet know a letter.

I thought I would try to go to school some; and as the Quaker had a married son, who was living about a mile and a half from him, and keeping a school, I proposed to him that I would go to school four days in the week, and work for him the other two, to pay my board and schooling. He agreed I might come on those terms; and so at it I went, learning and working back and forwards, until I had been with him nigh on to six months. In this time I learned to read a little in my primer, to write my own name, and to cypher some in the three first rules in figures. And this was all the schooling I ever had in my life, up to this day. I should have continued longer, if it hadn't been that I concluded I couldn't do any longer without a wife; and so I cut out to hunt me one.

I found a family of very pretty little girls that I had known when very young. They had lived in the same neighbourhood with me, and I had thought very well of them. I made an offer to one of them, whose name is nobody's business, no more than the Quaker girl's was, and I found she took it very well. I still continued paying my respects to her, until I got to love her as bad as I had the Quaker's niece; and I would have agreed to fight a whole regiment of wildcats if she would only have said she would have me. Several months passed in this way, during all of which time she continued very kind and friendly. At last, the son of the old Quaker and my first girl had concluded to bring their matter to a close, and my own little queen and myself were called on to wait on them. We went on the day, and performed our duty as attendants. This made me worse than ever; and after it was over, I pressed my claim very hard on her, but she would still give me a sort of evasive answer. However, I gave her mighty little peace, till she told me at last she would have me. I thought this was glorification enough, even without spectacles. I was then about eighteen years old. We fixed the time to be married; and I thought if that day come, I should be the happiest man in the created world, or in the moon, or any where else.

I had by this time got to be mighty fond of the rifle, and had bought a capital one. I most generally carried her with me wherever I went, and though I had got back to the old Quaker's to live, who was a very particular man, I would sometimes slip out and attend the shooting matches, where they shot for beef; I always tried, though, to keep it a secret from him. He had at the same time a bound boy living with him, who I had gotten into almost as great a notion of the girls as myself. He was about my own age, and was deeply smitten with the sister to my intended wife. I know'd it was in vain to try to get the leave of the old man for my young associate to go with me on any of my courting frolics; but I thought I could fix a plan to have him along, which would not injure the Quaker, as we had no notion that he should ever know it. We commonly slept up-stairs, and at the gable end of the house there was a window. So one Sunday, when the old man and his family were all gone to meeting, we went out and cut a long pole, and, taking it to the house, we set it up on one end in the corner, reaching up the chimney as high as the window. After this we would go up-stairs to bed, and then putting on our Sunday clothes, would go out at the window, and climb down the pole, take a horse apiece, and ride about ten miles to where his sweetheart lived, and the girl I claimed as my wife. I was always mighty careful to be back before day, so as to escape being found out; and in this way I continued my attentions very closely until a few days before I was to be married, or at least thought I was, for I had no fear that any thing was about to go wrong.

Just now I heard of a shooting match in the neighbourhood, right between where I lived and my girl's house; and I determined to kill two birds with one stone,—to go to the shooting match first, and then to see her. I therefore made the Quaker believe I was going to hunt for deer, as they were pretty plenty about in those parts; but, instead of hunting them, I went straight on to the shooting match, where I joined in with a partner, and we put in several shots for the beef. I was mighty lucky, and when the match was over I had won the whole beef. This was on a Saturday, and my success had put me in the finest humour in the world. So I sold my part of the beef for five dollars in the real grit, for I believe that was before bank-notes was invented; at least I had never heard of any. I now started on to ask for my wife; for, though the next Thursday was our wedding day, I had never said a word to her parents about it. I had always dreaded the undertaking so bad, that I had put the evil hour off as long as possible; and, indeed, I calculated they knowed me so well, they wouldn't raise any objections to having me for their son-in-law. I had a great deal better opinion of myself, I found, than other people had of me; but I moved on with a light heart, and my five dollars jingling in my pocket, thinking all the time there was but few greater men in the world than myself.

In this flow of good humour I went ahead, till I got within about two miles of the place, when I concluded I would stop awhile at the house of the girl's uncle; where I might enquire about the family, and so forth, and so on. I was indeed just about ready to consider her uncle, my uncle; and her affairs, my affairs. When I went in, tho', I found her sister there. I asked how all was at home? In a minute I found from her countenance something was wrong. She looked mortified, and didn't answer as quick as I thought she ought, being it was her *brother-in-law* talking to her. However, I asked her again. She then burst into tears, and told me her sister was going to deceive me; and that she was to be married to another man the next day. This was as sudden to me as a clap of thunder of a bright sunshiny day. It was the capstone of all the afflictions I had ever met with; and it seemed to me, that it was more than any human creature could endure. It struck me perfectly speechless for some time, and made me feel so weak, that I thought I should sink down. I however recovered from my shock after a little, and rose and started without any ceremony, or even bidding any body good-bye. The young woman followed me out to the gate, and entreated me to go on to her father's, and said she would go with me. She said the young man, who was going to marry her sister, had got his license, and had asked for her; but she assured me her father and mother both preferred me to him; and that she had no doubt but that, if I would go on, I could break off the match. But I found I could go no further. My heart was bruised, and my spirits were broken down; so I bid her farewell, and turned my lonesome and miserable steps back again homeward, concluding that I was only born for hardships, misery, and disappointment. I now began to think, that in making me, it was entirely forgotten to make my mate: that I was born odd, and should always remain so, and that nobody would have me.

But all these reflections did not satisfy my mind, for I had no peace day nor night for several weeks. My appetite failed me, and I grew daily worse and worse. They all thought I was sick; and so I was. And it was the worse kind of sickness,—a sickness of the heart, and all the tender parts, produced by disappointed love.

I continued in this down-spirited situation for a good long time, until one day I took my rifle and started hunting. While out, I made a call at the house of a Dutch widow, who had a daughter that was well enough as to smartness, but she was as ugly as a stone fence. She was, however, quite talkative, and soon begun to laugh at me about my disappointment.

She seemed disposed, though, to comfort me as much as she could; and, for that purpose, told me to keep in good-heart, that "there was as good fish in the sea as had ever been caught out of it." I doubted this very much; but whether or not, I was certain that she was not one of them, for she was so homely that it almost give me a pain in the eyes to look at her.

But I couldn't help thinking, that she had intended what she had said as a banter for me to court her!!!—the last thing in creation I could have thought of doing. I felt little inclined to talk on the subject, it is true; but, to pass off the time, I told her I thought I was born odd, and that no fellow to me could be found. She protested against this, and said if I would come to their reaping, which was not far off,

she would show me one of the prettiest little girls there I had ever seen. She added that the one who had deceived me was nothing to be compared with her. I didn't believe a word of all this, for I had thought that such a piece of flesh and blood as she was had never been manufactured, and never would again. I agreed with her, though, that the little varment had treated me so bad, that I ought to forget her, and yet I couldn't do it. I concluded the best way to accomplish it was to cut out again, and see if I could find any other that would answer me; and so I told the Dutch girl I would be at the reaping, and would bring as many as I could with me.

I employed my time pretty generally in giving information of it, as far as I could, until the day came; and I then offered to work for my old friend, the Quaker, two days, if he would let his bound boy go with me one to the reaping. He refused, and reproved me pretty considerable roughly for my proposition; and said, if he was in my place he wouldn't go; that there would be a great deal of bad company there; and that I had been so good a boy, he would be sorry for me to get a bad name. But I knowed my promise to the Dutch girl, and I was resolved to fulfil it; so I shouldered my rifle, and started by myself. When I got to the place, I found a large company of men and women, and among them an old Irish woman, who had a great deal to say. I soon found out from my Dutch girl, that this old lady was the mother of the little girl she had promised me, though I had not yet seen her. She was in an outhouse with some other youngsters, and had not yet made her appearance. Her mamma, however, was no way bashful. She came up to me, and began to praise my red cheeks, and said she had a sweetheart for me. I had no doubt she had been told what I come for, and all about it. In the evening I was introduced to her daughter, and I must confess, I was plaguy well pleased with her from the word go. She had a good countenance, and was very pretty, and I was full bent on making up an acquaintance with her.

It was not long before the dancing commenced, and I asked her to join me in a reel. She very readily consented to do so; and after we had finished our dance, I took a seat alongside of her, and entered into a talk. I found her very interesting; while I was setting by her, making as good a use of my time as I could, her mother came to us, and very jocularly called me her son-in-law. This rather confused me, but I looked on it as a joke of the old lady, and tried to turn it off as well as I could; but I took care to pay as much attention to her through the evening as I could. I went on the old saying, of salting the cow to catch the calf. I soon become so much pleased with this little girl, that I began to think the Dutch girl had told me the truth, when she said there was still good fish in the sea.

We continued our frolic till near day, when we joined in some plays, calculated to amuse youngsters. I had not often spent a more agreeable night. In the morning, however, we all had to part; and I found my mind had become much better reconciled than it had been for a long time. I went home to the Quaker's, and made a bargain to work with his son for a low-priced horse. He was the first one I had ever owned, and I was to work six months for him. I had been engaged very closely five or six weeks, when this little girl run in my mind so, that I concluded I must go and see her, and find out what sort of people they were at home. I mounted my horse and away I went to where she lived, and when I got there I found her father a very clever old man, and the old woman as talkative as ever. She wanted badly to find out all about me, and as I thought to see how I would do for her girl. I had not yet seen her about, and I began to feel some anxiety to know where she was.

In a short time, however, my impatience was relieved, as she arrived at home from a meeting to which she had been. There was a young man with her, who I soon found was disposed to set up claim to her, as he was so attentive to her that I could hardly get to slip in a word edgeways. I began to think I was barking up the wrong tree again; but I was determined to stand up to my rack, fodder or no fodder. And so, to know her mind a little on the subject, I began to talk about starting, as I knowed she would then show some sign, from which I could understand which way the wind blowed. It was then near night, and my distance was fifteen miles home. At this my little girl soon began to indicate to the other gentleman that his room would be the better part of his company. At

length she left him, and came to me, and insisted mighty hard that I should not go that evening; and, indeed, from all her actions and the attempt she made to get rid of him, I saw that she preferred me all holler. But it wasn't long before I found trouble enough in another quarter. Her mother was deeply enlisted for my rival, and I had to fight against her influence as well as his. But the girl herself was the prize I was fighting for; and as she welcomed me, I was determined to lay siege to her, let what would happen. I commenced a close courtship, having cornered her from her old beau; while he set off, looking on, like a poor man at a country frolic, and all the time almost gritting his teeth with pure disappointment. But he didn't dare to attempt any thing more, for now I had gotten a start, and I looked at him every once in a while as fierce as a wildcat. I staid with her until Monday morning, and then I put out for home.

It was about two weeks after this that I was sent for to engage in a wolf hunt, where a great number of men were to meet, with their dogs and guns, and where the best sort of sport was expected. I went as large as life, but I had to hunt in strange woods, and in a part of the country which was very thinly inhabited. While I was out it clouded up, and I began to get scared; and in a little while I was so much so, that I didn't know which way home was, nor any thing about it. I set out the way I thought it was, but it turned out with me, as it always does with a lost man, I was wrong, and took exactly the contrary direction from the right one. And for the information of young hunters, I will just say, in this place, that whenever a fellow gets bad lost, the way home is just the way he don't think it is. This rule will hit nine times out of ten. I went ahead, though, about six or seven miles, when I found night was coming on fast; but at this distressing time I saw a little woman streaking it along through the woods like all wrath, and so I cut on too, for I was determined I wouldn't lose sight of her that night any more. I run on till she saw me, and she stopped; for she was as glad to see me as I was to see her, as she was lost as well as me. When I came up to her, who should she be but my little girl, that I had been paying my respects to. She had been out hunting her father's horses, and had missed her way, and had no knowledge where she was, or how far it was to any house, or what way would take us there. She had been travelling all day, and was mighty tired; and I would have taken her up, and toated her, if it hadn't been that I wanted her just where I could see her all the time, for I thought she looked sweeter than sugar; and by this time I loved her almost well enough to eat her.

At last I came to a path, that I know'd must go somewhere, and so we followed it, till we came to a house, at about dark. Here we staid all night. I set up all night courting; and in the morning we parted. She went to her home, from which we were distant about seven miles, and I to mine, which was ten miles off.

I now turned in to work again; and it was about four weeks before I went back to see her. I continued to go occasionally, until I had worked long enough to pay for my horse, by putting in my gun with my work, to the man I had purchased from; and then I began to count whether I was to be deceived again or not. At our next meeting we set the day for our wedding; and I went to my father's, and made arrangements for an infair, and returned to ask her parents for her. When I got there, the old lady appeared to be mighty wrathy; and when I broached the subject, she looked at me as savage as a meat axe. The old man appeared quite willing, and treated me very clever. But I hadn't been there long, before the old woman as good as ordered me out of her house. I thought I would put her in mind of old times, and see how that would go with her. I told her she had called me her son-in-law before I had attempted to call her my mother-in-law, and I thought she ought to cool off. But her Irish was up too high to do any thing with her, and so I quit trying. All I cared for was, to have her daughter on my side, which I knowed was the case then; but how soon some other fellow might knock my nose out of joint again, I couldn't tell. I however felt rather insulted at the old lady, and I thought I wouldn't get married in her house. And so I told her girl, that I would come the next Thursday, and bring a horse, a bridle, and saddle for her, and she must be ready to go. Her mother declared I shouldn't have her; but I know'd I should, if somebody else didn't get her before Thursday. I then started, bidding them good-day, and

went by the house of a justice of the peace, who lived on the way to my father's, and made a bargain with him to marry me.

When Thursday came, all necessary arrangements were made at my father's to receive my wife; and so I took my eldest brother and his wife, and another brother, and a single sister that I had, and two other young men with me, and cut out to her father's house to get her. We went on, until we got within two miles of the place, where we met a large company that had heard of the wedding, and were waiting. Some of that company went on with my brother and sister, and the young man I had picked out to wait on me. When they got there, they found the old lady as wrathy as ever. However the old man filled their bottle, and the young men returned in a hurry. I then went on with my company, and when I arrived I never pretended to dismount from my horse, but rode up to the door, and asked the girl if she was ready; and she said she was. I then told her to light on the horse I was leading; and she did so. Her father, though, had gone out to the gate, and when I started he commenced persuading me to stay and marry there; that he was entirely willing to the match, and that his wife, like most women, had entirely too much tongue; but that I oughtn't to mind her. I told him if she would ask me to stay and marry at her house, I would do so. With that he sent for her, and after they had talked for some time out by themselves, she came to me and looked at me mighty good, and asked my pardon for what she had said, and invited me stay. She said it was the first child she had ever had to marry; and she couldn't bear to see her go off in that way; that if I would light, she would do the best she could for us. I couldn't stand every thing, and so I agreed, and we got down, and went in. I sent off then for my parson, and got married in a short time; for I was afraid to wait long, for fear of another defeat. We had as good treatment as could be expected; and that night all went on well. The next day we cut out for my father's, where we met a large company of people, that had been waiting a day and a night for our arrival. We passed the time quite merrily, until the company broke up; and having gotten my wife, I thought I was completely made up, and needed nothing more in the whole world. But I soon found this was all a mistake—for now having a wife, I wanted every thing else; and, worse than all, I had nothing to give for it.

## Sir Francis Bacon
## OF MARRIAGE AND SINGLE LIFE

He that hath wife and children hath given hostages to fortune; for they are impediments to great enterprises, either of virtue or mischief. Certainly the best works, and of greatest merit for the public, have proceeded from the unmarried or childless men, which both in affection and means have married and endowed the public. Yet it were great reason that those that have children should have greatest care of future times, unto which they know they must transmit their dearest pledges. Some there are who, though they lead a single life, yet their thoughts do end with themselves, and account future times impertinences. Nay, there are some other that account wife and children but as bills of charges. Nay more, there are some foolish rich covetous men, that take a pride in having no children, because they may be thought so much the richer. For perhaps they have heard some talk, "Such an one is a great rich man," and another except to it, "Yes, but he hath a great charge of children"; as if it were an abatement to his riches. But the most ordinary cause of a single life is liberty, especially in certain self-pleasing and humorous minds, which are so sensible of every restraint, as they will go near to think their girdles and garters to be bonds and shackles. Unmarried men are best friends, best masters, best servants, but not always best subjects, for they are light to run away, and almost all fugitives are of that condition. A single life doth well with churchmen, for charity will hardly water the ground where it must first fill a pool. It is indifferent for judges and magistrates, for if they be facile and corrupt, you shall have a servant five times worse than a wife. For soldiers, I find the generals commonly in their hortatives put men in mind of their wives and children; and I think the despising of marriage amongst the Turks maketh the vulgar soldier more base. Certainly wife and children are a kind of discipline of humanity; and single men, though they be many times more charitable, because their means are less exhaust, yet, on the other side, they are more cruel and hard-hearted (good to make severe inquisitors), because their tenderness is not so oft called upon. Grave natures, led by custom, and therefore constant, are commonly loving husbands, as was said of Ulysses, *Vetulam suam praetulit immortalitati.*[1] Chaste women are often proud and forward, as presuming upon the merit of their chastity. It is one of the best bonds, both of chastity and obedience, in the wife if she think her husband wise, which she will never do if she find him jealous. Wives are young men's mistresses, companions for middle age, and old men's nurses, so as a man may have a quarrel to marry when he will. But yet he was reputed one of the wise men that made answer to the question when a man should marry: "A young man not yet, an elder man not at all." It is often seen that bad husbands have very good wives; whether it be that it raiseth the price of their husbands' kindness when it comes, or that the wives take a pride in their patience. But this never fails, if the bad husbands were of their own choosing, against their friends' consent; for then they will be sure to make good their own folly.

[1] "He preferred his aged wife to immortality," which was offered to him by Calypso if he would stay with her.

## Raoul de Roussy de Sales
## LOVE IN AMERICA

America appears to be the only country in the world where love is a national problem.

Nowhere else can one find a people devoting so much time and so much study to the question of the relationship between men and women. Nowhere else is there such concern about the fact that this relationship does not always make for perfect happiness. The great majority of the Americans of both sexes seem

LOVE IN AMERICA: From *The Atlantic Monthly,* May, 1938. Used by permission of the publishers.

to be in a state of chronic bewilderment in the face of a problem which they are certainly not the first to confront, but which—unlike other people—they still refuse to accept as one of those gifts of the gods which one might just as well take as it is: a mixed blessing at times, and at other times a curse or merely a nuisance.

The prevailing conception of love, in America, is similar to the idea of democracy. It is fine in theory. It is the grandest system ever evolved by man to differentiate him from his ancestors, the poor brutes who lived in caverns, or from the apes. Love is perfect, in fact, and there is nothing better. But, like democracy, it does not work, and the Americans feel that something should be done about it. Their statesmen are intent on making democracy work. Everybody is trying to make love work, too.

In either case the result is not very satisfactory. The probable reason is that democracy and love are products of a long and complicated series of compromises between the desires of the heart and the exactions of reason. They have a peculiar way of crumbling into ashes as soon as one tries too hard to organize them too well.

The secret of making a success out of democracy and love in their practical applications is to allow for a fairly wide margin of errors, and not to forget that human beings are absolutely unable to submit to a uniform rule for any length of time. But this does not satisfy a nation that, in spite of its devotion to pragmatism, also believes in perfection.

For a foreigner to speak of the difficulties that the Americans encounter in such an intimate aspect of their mutual relationship may appear as an impertinence. But the truth is that no foreigner would ever think of bringing up such a subject of his own accord. In fact, foreigners who come to these shores are quite unsuspecting of the existence of such a national problem. It is their initial observation that the percentage of good-looking women and handsome men is high on this continent, that they are youthful and healthy in mind and body, and that their outlook on life is rather optimistic.

If the newcomers have seen enough American moving pictures before landing here—and they usually have—they must have gathered the impression that love in America is normally triumphant, and that, in spite of many unfortunate accidents, a love story cannot but end very well indeed. They will have noticed that these love stories which are acted in Hollywood may portray quite regrettable situations at times and that blissful unions get wrecked by all sorts of misfortunes. But they never remain wrecked: even when the happy couple is compelled to divorce, this is not the end of everything. In most cases it is only the beginning. Very soon they will remarry, sometimes with one another, and always—without ever an exception—for love.

The observant foreigner knows, of course, that he cannot trust the movies to give him a really reliable picture of the American attitude towards love, marriage, divorce, and remarriage. But they nevertheless indicate that in such matters the popular mind likes to be entertained by the idea (1) that love is the only reason why a man and a woman should get married; (2) that love is always wholesome, genuine, uplifting, and fresh, like a glass of Grade A milk; (3) that when, for some reason or other, it fails to keep you uplifted, wholesome, and fresh, the only thing to do is to begin all over again with another partner.

Thus forewarned, the foreigner who lands on these shores would be very tactless indeed if he started questioning the validity of these premises. Besides, it is much more likely that he himself will feel thoroughly transformed the moment he takes his first stroll in the streets of New York. His European skepticism will evaporate a little more at each step, and if he considers himself not very young any more he will be immensely gratified to find that maturity and even old age are merely European habits of thought, and that he might just as well adopt the American method, which is to be young and act young for the rest of his life—or at least until the expiration of his visa.

If his hotel room is equipped with a radio, his impression that he has at last reached the land of eternal youth and perfect love will be confirmed at any hour of the day and on any point of the dial. No country in the world consumes such a fabulous amount of love songs. Whether the song is gay or nostalgic, the tune catchy or banal, the verses clever or silly, the theme is always love and nothing but love.

Whenever I have gone back to France and listened to the radio, I have always been surprised to find that so many songs can be written on other subjects. I have no statistics on hand, but I think that a good 75 per cent of the songs one hears on the French radio programs deal with politics. There are love songs, of course, but most of them are far from romantic, and this is quite in keeping with the French point of view that love is very often an exceedingly comical affair.

In America the idea seems to be that love, like so much else, should be sold to the public, because it is a good thing. The very word, when heard indefinitely, becomes an obsession. It penetrates one's subconsciousness like the name of some unguent to cure heartaches or athlete's foot. It fits in with the other advertisements, and one feels tempted to write to the broadcasting station for a free sample of this thing called Love.

Thus the visitor from Europe is rapidly permeated with a delightful atmosphere of romanticism and sweetness. He wonders why Italy and Spain ever acquired their reputation of being the lands of romance. This, he says to himself, is the home of poetry and passion. The Americans are the real heirs of the troubadours, and station WXZQ is their love court.

To discover that all this ballyhoo about love (which is not confined to the radio or the movies) is nothing but an aspect of the national optimistic outlook on life does not take very long. It usually becomes evident when the foreign visitor receives the confidences of one or more of the charming American women he will chance to meet. This normally happens after the first or second cocktail party to which he has been invited.

[ 2 ]

I wish at this point to enter a plea in defense of the foreign visitor, against whom a great many accusations are often made either in print or in conversation. These accusations fall under two heads. If the foreigner seems to have no definite objective in visiting America, he is strongly suspected of trying to marry an heiress. If for any reason he cannot be suspected of this intention, then his alleged motives are considerably more sinister. Many American men, and quite a few women, believe that the art of wrecking a happy home is not indigenous to this continent, and that in Europe it has been perfected to such a point that to practice it has become a reflex with the visitors from abroad.

It is very true that some foreign visitors come over here to marry for money in exchange for a title or for some sort of glamour. But there are many more foreigners who marry American women for other reasons besides money, and I know quite a few who have become so Americanized that they actually have married for love and for nothing else.

As for the charge that the Europeans are more expert than the Americans in spoiling someone else's marital happiness, it seems to me an unfair accusation. In most cases the initiative of spoiling whatever it is that remains to be spoiled in a shaky marriage is normally taken by one of the married pair, and the wrecker of happiness does not need any special talent to finish the job.

What is quite true, however, is that the American woman entertains the delightful illusion that there *must* be some man on this earth who can understand her. It seems incredible to her that love, within legal bonds or outside of them, should not work out as advertised. From her earliest years she has been told that success is the ultimate aim of life. Her father and mother made an obvious success of their lives by creating her. Her husband is, or wants to be, a successful business man. Every day 130,000,-000 people are panting and sweating to make a success of something or other. Success—the constant effort to make things work perfectly and the conviction that they can be made to— is the great national preoccupation.

And what does one do to make a success?

Well, the answer is very simple: one learns how, or one consults an expert.

That is what her husband does when he wants to invest his money or improve the efficiency of his business. That is what she did herself when she decided to "decorate" her house. In the American way of life there are no insoluble problems. You may not know the answer yourself, but nobody doubts that the answer exists—that there is some method or perhaps some trick by which all riddles can be solved and success achieved.

And so the European visitor is put to the task on the presumption that the accumulation of experience which he brings with him may qualify him as an expert in questions of sentiment.

The American woman does not want to be understood for the mere fun of it. What she actually wishes is to be helped to solve certain difficulties which, in her judgment, impede the successful development of her inner self. She seldom accepts the idea that maladjustments and misunderstandings are not only normal but bearable once you have made up your mind that, whatever may be the ultimate aim of our earthly existence, perfect happiness through love or any other form of expression is not part of the program.

### [ 3 ]

One of the greatest moral revolutions that ever happened in America was the popularization of Freud's works.

Up to the time that occurred, as far as I am able to judge, America lived in a blissful state of puritanical repression. Love, as a sentiment, was glorified and sanctified by marriage. There was a general impression that some sort of connection existed between the sexual impulses and the vagaries of the heart, but this connection was not emphasized, and the consensus of opinion was that the less said about it the better. The way certain nations, and particularly the French, correlated the physical manifestations of love and its more spiritual aspects was considered particularly objectionable. Love, in other words,—and that was not very long ago,—had not changed since the contrary efforts of the puritanically-minded and the romantic had finally stabilized it midway between the sublime and the parlor game.

The important point is that up to then (and ever since the first Pilgrims set foot on this continent) love had been set aside in the general scheme of American life as the one thing which could not be made to work better than it did. Each one had to cope with his own difficulties in his own way and solve them as privately as he could. It was not a national problem.

Whether or not people were happier under that system is beside the point. It probably does not matter very much whether we live and die with or without a full set of childish complexes and repressions. My own view is that most people are neither complex nor repressed enough as a rule; I wish sometimes for the coming of the Anti-Freud who will complicate and obscure everything again.

But the fact is that the revelations of psychoanalysis were greeted in America as the one missing link in the general program of universal improvement.

Here was a system, at last, that explained fully why love remained so imperfect. It reduced the whole dilemma of happiness to sexual maladjustments, which in turn were only the result of the mistakes made by one's father, mother, or nurse, at an age when one could certainly not be expected to foresee the consequences. Psychoanalysis integrated human emotions into a set of mechanistic formulas. One learned with great relief that the failure to find happiness was not irreparable. Love, as a sublime communion of souls and bodies, was not a legend, nor the mere fancy of the poets. It was real, and—more important still —practically attainable. Anybody could have it, merely by removing a few obstructions which had been growing within himself since childhood like mushrooms in a dark cellar. Love could be made to work like anything else.

It is true that not many people are interested in psychoanalysis any more. As a fad or a parlor game, it is dead. Modern débutantes will not know what you are talking about if you mention the Œdipus complex or refer to the symbolic meaning of umbrellas and top hats in dreams. Traditions die young these days. But the profound effect of the Freudian revelation has lasted. From its materialistic interpretation of sexual impulses, coupled with the American longing for moral perfection, a new science has been born: the dialectics of love; and also a new urge for the American people—they want to turn out, eventually, a perfect product. They want to get out of love as much enjoyment, comfort, safety, and general sense of satisfaction, as one gets out of a well-balanced diet or a good plumbing installation.

### [ 4 ]

Curiously enough, this fairly new point of view which implies that human relationships are governed by scientific laws has not destroyed the romantic ideal of love. Quite the contrary. Maladjustments, now that they are supposed to be scientifically determined, have become much more unbearable than in the horse-and-buggy age of love. Husbands and wives and lovers have no patience with their troubles. They want to be cured, and when they think they are incurable they become very intolerant. Reformers always are.

Usually, however, various attempts at readjustment are made with devastating candor. Married couples seem to spend many precious hours of the day and night discussing what is wrong with their relationship. The general idea is that—according to the teachings of most modern psychologists and pedagogues—one should face the truth fearlessly. Husbands and wives should be absolutely frank with one another, on the assumption that if love between them is real it will be made stronger and more real still if submitted, at frequent intervals, to the test of complete sincerity on both sides.

This is a fine theory, but it has seldom been practiced without disastrous results. There are several reasons why this should be so. First of all, truth is an explosive, and it should be handled with care, especially in marital life. It is not necessary to lie, but there is little profit in juggling with hand grenades just to show how brave one is. Secondly, the theory of absolute sincerity presupposes that, if love cannot withstand continuous blasting, then it is not worth saving anyway. Some people want their love life to be a permanent battle of Verdun. When the system of defense is destroyed beyond repair, then the clause of hopeless maladjustment is invoked by one side, or by both. The next thing to do is to divorce and find someone else to be recklessly frank with for a season.

Another reason why the method of adjustment through truthtelling is not always wise is that it develops fiendish traits of character which might otherwise remain dormant.

I know a woman whose eyes glitter with virtuous self-satisfaction every time she has had a "real heart-to-heart talk" with her husband, which means that she has spent several hours torturing him, or at best boring him to distraction, with a ruthless exposure of the deplorable status of their mutual relationship to date. She is usually so pleased with herself after these periodical inquests that she tells most of her friends, and also her coiffeur, about it. "Dick and I had such a wonderful time last evening. We made a real effort to find out the real truth about each other—or, at least, I certainly did. I honestly believe we have found a new basis of adjustment for ourselves. What a marvelous feeling that is—don't you think so?"

Dick, of course, if he happens to be present, looks rather nervous or glum, but that is not the point. The point is that Dick's wife feels all aglow because she has done her bit in the general campaign for the improvement of marital happiness through truth. She has been a good girl scout.

A man of my acquaintance, who believes in experimenting outside of wedlock, is unable to understand why his wife would rather ignore his experiments. "If I did not love her and if she did not love me," he argues, "I could accept her point of view. But why can't she see that the very fact that I want her to know everything I do is a proof that I love her? If I have to deceive her or conceal things from her, what is the use of being married to her?"

Be it said, in passing, that this unfortunate husband believes that these extramarital "experiments" are absolutely necessary to prevent him from developing a sense of inferiority, which, if allowed to grow, would destroy not only the love he has for his wife, but also his general ability in his dealings with the outside world.

## [ 5 ]

The difference between an American cookbook and a French one is that the former is very accurate and the second exceedingly vague. A French recipe seldom tells you how many ounces of butter to use to make *crêpes Suzette,* or how many spoonfuls of oil should go into a salad dressing. French cookbooks are full of esoteric measurements such as a *pinch* of pepper, a *suspicion* of garlic, or a *generous sprinkling* of brandy. There are constant references to seasoning *to taste,* as if the recipe were merely intended to give a general direction, relying on the experience and innate art of the cook to make the dish turn out right.

American recipes look like doctors' prescriptions. Perfect cooking seems to depend on perfect dosage. Some of these books give you a table of calories and vitamins—as if that had anything to do with the problem of eating well!

In the same way, there is now flourishing in America a great crop of books which offer precise recipes for the things you should do, or avoid doing, in order to achieve happiness and keep the fires of love at a constant temperature. In an issue of *Time* magazine, four such books were reviewed together. Their titles are descriptive enough of the purpose of the authors as well as the state of mind of the readers: *Love and Happiness, So You're Going to Get Mar-*

*ried, Marriages Are Made at Home, Getting Along Together.*

I have not read all these books, but, according to the reviewer, they all tend to give practical answers to the same mysterious problem of living with someone of the opposite sex. They try to establish sets of little rules and little tricks which will guarantee marital bliss if carefully followed, in the same way that cookbooks guarantee that you will obtain pumpkin pie if you use the proper ingredients properly measured.

As the publisher of one of these books says on the jacket: "There is nothing in this book about the complicated psychological problems that send men and women to psychoanalysts, but there is a lot in it about the little incidents of daily married life—the things that happen in the parlor, bedroom and bath—that handled one way enable people to live together happily forever after, and handled another way lead to Reno."

*Time's* review of these books is very gloomy in its conclusion: "Despite their optimistic tone," it says, "the four volumes give a troubled picture of United States domestic life—a world in which husbands are amorous when wives are not, and vice versa; where conflicts spring up over reading in bed or rumpling the evening paper . . . the whole grim panorama giving the impression that Americans are irritable, aggravated, dissatisfied people for whom marriage is an ordeal that only heroes and heroines can bear."

But I believe that the editors of *Time* would be just as dejected if they were reviewing four volumes about American cooking, and for the same reasons. You cannot possibly feel cheerful when you see the art of love or the art of eating thus reduced to such automatic formulas, even if the experts in these matters are themselves cheerful and optimistic. Good food, the pleasures of love, and those of marriage depend on imponderables, individual taste, and no small amount of luck.

## [ 6 ]

Thus the problem of love in America seems to be the resultant of conflicting and rather unrealistic ways of approaching it. Too many songs, too many stories, too many pictures, and too much romance on the one hand, and too much practical advice on the other. It is as if the experience of being in love could only

be one of two things: a superhuman ecstasy, the way of reaching heaven on earth and in pairs; or a psychopathic condition to be treated by specialists.

Between these two extremes there is little room for compromise. That the relationship between men and women offers a wide scale of variations seldom occurs to the experts. It is not necessarily true that there is but one form of love worth bothering about, and that if you cannot get the de luxe model, with a life guarantee of perfect functioning, nothing else is worth-while. It is not true either that you can indefinitely pursue the same quest for perfection, or that if a man and a woman have not found ideal happiness together they will certainly find it with somebody else. Life unfortunately does not begin at forty, and when you reach that age, in America or anywhere else, to go on complaining about your sentimental or physiological maladjustments becomes slightly farcical.

It is not easy, nor perhaps of any use, to draw any conclusion from all this, especially for a European who has lost the fresh point of view of the visitor because he lives here, and who is not quite sure of what it means to be a European any more. I sometimes wonder if there is any real difference between the way men and women get along—or do not get along —together on this side of the Atlantic and on the other. There are probably no more real troubles here than anywhere else. Human nature being quite remarkably stable, why should there be? But there is no doubt that the revolt against this type of human inadequacy is very strong indeed here, especially among the women who imagine that the Europeans have found better ways of managing their hearts and their senses than the Americans.

If this is at all true, I believe the reason is to be found in a more philosophical attitude on the part of the Europeans towards such matters. There are no theories about marital bliss, no recipes to teach you how to solve difficulties which, in the Old World, are accepted as part of the common inheritance.

Men and women naturally want to be happy over there, and, if possible, with the help of one another; but they learn very young that compromise is not synonymous with defeat. Even in school (I am speaking more particularly of France now) they are taught, through

the literature of centuries, that love is a phenomenon susceptible of innumerable variations,
but that—even under the best circumstances—
it is so intertwined with the other experiences
of each individual life that to be overromantic
or too dogmatic about it is of little practical
use. *"La vérité est dans les nuances,"* [2] wrote
Benjamin Constant, who knew a good deal about
such matters.

And, speaking of the truly practical and
realistic nature of love, it is a very strange thing
that American literature contains no work of
any note, not even essays, on love as a psychological phenomenon. I know of no good study
of the process of falling in and out of love, no
analytical description of jealousy, coquettish-
ness, or the development of tediousness. No
classification of the various brands of love such
as La Rochefoucauld, Pascal, Stendhal, Proust,
and many others have elaborated has been
attempted from the American angle. The interesting combinations of such passions as ambition, jealousy, religious fervor, and so forth,
with love are only dimly perceived by most
people and even by the novelists, who, with
very few exceptions, seem to ignore or scorn
these complicated patterns. These fine studies
have been left to the psychiatrists, the charla-
tans, or the manufacturers of naïve recipes.

The reason for this neglect on the part of
real thinkers and essayists may be that for a
long time the standards imposed by the puritanical point of view made the whole study
more or less taboo with respectable authors.
And then the Freudian wave came along and
carried the whole problem out of reach of the
amateur observer and the artist. In other words,
conditions have been such that there has been
no occasion to fill this curious gap in American
literature.

Of course, nothing is lost. The field remains
open, and there is no reason to suppose that
love in America will not cease to be a national
problem, a hunting ground for the reformer,
and that it will not become, as everywhere else,
a personal affair very much worth the effort it
takes to examine it as such. All that is necessary is for someone to forget for a while love
as Hollywood—or the professor—sees it, and
sit down and think about it as an eternally
fascinating subject for purely human observation.

[2] "Truth lies in slight variations."

## *Sherwood Anderson*
# SOPHISTICATION

It was early evening of a day in the late
fall and the Winesburg County Fair had
brought crowds of country people into town.
The day had been clear and the night came on
warm and pleasant. On the Trunion Pike,
where the road after it left town stretched away
between berry fields now covered with dry
brown leaves, the dust from passing wagons
arose in clouds. Children, curled into little
balls, slept on the straw scattered on wagon
beds. Their hair was full of dust and their fingers black and sticky. The dust rolled away
over the fields and the departing sun set it
ablaze with colors.

In the main street of Winesburg crowds filled
the stores and the sidewalks. Night came on,
horses whinnied, the clerks in the stores ran
madly about, children became lost and cried
lustily, an American town worked terribly at
the task of amusing itself.

Pushing his way through the crowds in Main
Street, young George Willard concealed himself
in the stairway leading to Doctor Reefy's office
and looked at the people. With feverish eyes
he watched the faces drifting past under the
store lights. Thoughts kept coming into his head
and he did not want to think. He stamped
impatiently on the wooden steps and looked
sharply about. "Well, is she going to stay with
him all day? Have I done all this waiting for
nothing?" he muttered.

George Willard, the Ohio village boy, was
fast growing into manhood and new thoughts
had been coming into his mind. All that day,
amid the jam of people at the Fair, he had
gone about feeling lonely. He was about to
leave Winesburg to go away to some city where
he hoped to get work on a city newspaper and
he felt grown up. The mood that had taken
possession of him was a thing known to men
and unknown to boys. He felt old and a little
tired. Memories awoke in him. To his mind his

new sense of maturity set him apart, made of him a half-tragic figure. He wanted someone to understand the feeling that had taken possession of him after his mother's death.

There is a time in the life of every boy when he for the first time takes the backward view of life. Perhaps that is the moment when he crosses the line into manhood. The boy is walking through the street of his town. He is thinking of the future and of the figure he will cut in the world. Ambitions and regrets awake within him. Suddenly something happens; he stops under a tree and waits as for a voice calling his name. Ghosts of old things creep into his consciousness; the voices outside of himself whisper a message concerning the limitations of life. From being quite sure of himself and his future he becomes not at all sure. If he be an imaginative boy a door is torn open and for the first time he looks out upon the world, seeing, as though they marched in procession before him, the countless figures of men who before his time have come out of nothingness into the world, lived their lives and again disappeared into nothingness. The sadness of sophistication has come to the boy. With a little gasp he sees himself as merely a leaf blown by the wind through the streets of his village. He knows that in spite of all the stout talk of his fellows he must live and die in uncertainty, a thing blown by the winds, a thing destined like corn to wilt in the sun. He shivers and looks eagerly about. The eighteen years he has lived seem but a moment, a breathing space in the long march of humanity. Already he hears death calling. With all his heart he wants to come close to some other human, touch someone with his hands, be touched by the hand of another. If he prefers that the other be a woman, that is because he believes that a woman will be gentle, that she will understand. He wants, most of all, understanding.

When the moment of sophistication came to George Willard, his mind turned to Helen White, the Winesburg banker's daughter. Always he had been conscious of the girl growing into womanhood as he grew into manhood. Once on a summer night when he was eighteen, he had walked with her on a country road and in her presence had given way to an impulse to boast, to make himself appear big and significant in her eyes. Now he wanted to see her for another purpose. He wanted to tell her of the new impulses that had come to him. He had tried to make her think of him as a man when he knew nothing of manhood and now he wanted to be with her and to try to make her feel the change he believed had taken place in his nature.

As for Helen White, she also had come to a period of change. What George felt, she in her young woman's way felt also. She was no longer a girl and hungered to reach into the grace and beauty of womanhood. She had come home from Cleveland, where she was attending college, to spend a day at the Fair. She also had begun to have memories. During the day she sat in the grandstand with a young man, one of the instructors from the college, who was a guest of her mother's. The young man was of a pedantic turn of mind and she felt at once he would not do for her purpose. At the Fair she was glad to be seen in his company as he was well dressed and a stranger. She knew that the fact of his presence would create an impression. During the day she was happy, but when night came on she began to grow restless. She wanted to drive the instructor away, to get out of his presence. While they sat together in the grandstand and while the eyes of former schoolmates were upon them, she paid so much attention to her escort that he grew interested. "A scholar needs money. I should marry a woman with money," he mused.

Helen White was thinking of George Willard even as he wandered gloomily through the crowds thinking of her. She remembered the summer evening when they had walked together and wanted to walk with him again. She thought that the months she had spent in the city, the going to theaters and the seeing of great crowds wandering in lighted thoroughfares, had changed her profoundly. She wanted him to feel and be conscious of the change in her nature.

The summer evening together that had left its mark on the memory of both the young man and woman had, when looked at quite sensibly, been rather stupidly spent. They had walked out of town along a country road. Then they had stopped by a fence near a field of young corn and George had taken off his coat and let it hang on his arm. "Well, I've stayed here in Winesburg—yes—I've not yet gone away but

I'm growing up," he said. "I've been reading books and I've been thinking. I'm going to try to amount to something in life.

"Well," he explained, "that isn't the point. Perhaps I'd better quit talking."

The confused boy put his hand on the girl's arm. His voice trembled. The two started to walk back along the road to town. In his desperation George boasted, "I'm going to be a big man, the biggest that ever lived here in Winesburg," he declared. "I want you to do something, I don't know what. Perhaps it is none of my business. I want you to try to be different from other women. You see the point. It's none of my business I tell you. I want you to be a beautiful woman. You see what I want."

The boy's voice failed and in silence the two came back into town and went along the street to Helen White's house. At the gate he tried to say something impressive. Speeches he had thought out came into his head, but they seemed utterly pointless. "I thought—I used to think— I had it in my mind you would marry Seth Richmond. Now I know you won't," was all he could find to say as she went through the gate and toward the door of her house.

On the warm fall evening as he stood in the stairway and looked at the crowd drifting through Main Street, George thought of the talk beside the field of young corn and was ashamed of the figure he had made of himself. In the street the people surged up and down like cattle confined in a pen. Buggies and wagons almost filled the narrow thoroughfare. A band played and small boys raced along the sidewalk, diving between the legs of men. Young men with shining red faces walked awkwardly about with girls on their arms. In a room above one of the stores, where a dance was to be held, the fiddlers tuned their instruments. The broken sounds floated down through an open window and out across the murmur of voices and the loud blare of the horns of the band. The medley of sounds got on young Willard's nerves. Everywhere, on all sides, the sense of crowding, moving life closed in about him. He wanted to run away by himself and think. "If she wants to stay with that fellow she may. Why should I care? What difference does it make to me?" he growled and went along Main Street and through Hern's grocery into a side street.

George felt so utterly lonely and dejected that he wanted to weep but pride made him walk rapidly along, swinging his arms. He came to Westley Moyer's livery barn and stopped in the shadows to listen to a group of men who talked of a race Westley's stallion, Tony Tip, had won at the Fair during the afternoon. A crowd had gathered in front of the barn and before the crowd walked Westley, prancing up and down and boasting. He held a whip in his hand and kept tapping the ground. Little puffs of dust arose in the lamplight. "Hell, quit your talking," Westley exclaimed. "I wasn't afraid, I knew I had 'em beat all the time. I wasn't afraid."

Ordinarily George Willard would have been intensely interested in the boasting of Moyer, the horseman. Now it made him angry. He turned and hurried away along the street. "Old windbag," he sputtered. "Why does he want to be bragging? Why don't he shut up?"

George went into a vacant lot and as he hurried along, fell over a pile of rubbish. A nail protruding from an empty barrel tore his trousers. He sat down on the ground and swore. With a pin he mended the torn place and then arose and went on. "I'll go to Helen White's house, that's what I'll do. I'll walk right in. I'll say that I want to see her. I'll walk right in and sit down, that's what I'll do," he declared, climbing over a fence and beginning to run.

On the veranda of Banker White's house Helen was restless and distraught. The instructor sat between the mother and daughter. His talk wearied the girl. Although he had also been raised in an Ohio town, the instructor began to put on the airs of the city. He wanted to appear cosmopolitan. "I like the chance you have given me to study the background out of which most of our girls come," he declared. "It was good of you, Mrs. White, to have me down for the day." He turned to Helen and laughed. "Your life is still bound up with the life of this town?" he asked. "There are people here in whom you are interested?" To the girl his voice sounded pompous and heavy.

Helen arose and went into the house. At the door leading to a garden at the back she stopped and stood listening. Her mother began to talk. "There is no one here fit to associate with a girl of Helen's breeding," she said.

Helen ran down a flight of stairs at the back

of the house and into the garden. In the darkness she stopped and stood trembling. It seemed to her that the world was full of meaningless people saying words. Afire with eagerness she ran through a garden gate and turning a corner by the banker's barn, went into a little side street. "George! Where are you, George?" she cried, filled with nervous excitement. She stopped running, and leaned against a tree to laugh hysterically. Along the dark little street came George Willard, still saying words. "I'm going to walk right into her house. I'll go right in and sit down," he declared as he came up to her. He stopped and stared stupidly. "Come on," he said and took hold of her hand. With hanging heads they walked away along the street under the trees. Dry leaves rustled under foot. Now that he had found her George wondered what he had better do and say.

At the upper end of the fair ground, in Winesburg, there is a half decayed old grandstand. It has never been painted and the boards are all warped out of shape. The fair ground stands on top of a low hill rising out of the valley of Wine Creek and from the grandstand one can see at night, over a cornfield, the lights of the town reflected against the sky.

George and Helen climbed the hill to the fair ground, coming by the path past Waterworks Pond. The feeling of loneliness and isolation that had come to the young man in the crowded streets of his town was both broken and intensified by the presence of Helen. What he felt was reflected in her.

In youth there are always two forces fighting in people. The warm unthinking little animal struggles against the thing that reflects and remembers, and the older, the more sophisticated thing had possession of George Willard. Sensing his mood, Helen walked beside him filled with respect. When they got to the grandstand they climbed up under the roof and sat down on one of the long bench-like seats.

There is something memorable in the experience to be had by going into a fair ground that stands at the edge of a Middle Western town on a night after the annual fair has been held. The sensation is one never to be forgotten. On all sides are ghosts, not of the dead, but of living people. Here, during the day just passed, have come the people pouring in from the town

and the country around. Farmers with their wives and children and all the people from the hundreds of little frame houses have gathered within these board walls. Young girls have laughed and men with beards have talked of the affairs of their lives. The place has been filled to overflowing with life. It has itched and squirmed with life and now it is night and the life has all gone away. The silence is almost terrifying. One conceals oneself standing silently beside the trunk of a tree and what there is of a reflective tendency in his nature is intensified. One shudders at the thought of the meaninglessness of life while at the same instant, and if the people of the town are his people, one loves life so intensely that tears come into the eyes.

In the darkness under the roof of the grandstand, George Willard sat beside Helen White and felt very keenly his own insignificance in the scheme of existence. Now that he had come out of town where the presence of the people stirring about, busy with a multitude of affairs, had been so irritating the irritation was all gone. The presence of Helen renewed and refreshed him. It was as though her woman's hand was assisting him to make some minute readjustment of the machinery of his life. He began to think of the people in the town where he had always lived with something like reverence. He had reverence for Helen. He wanted to love and to be loved by her, but he did not want at the moment to be confused by her womanhood. In the darkness he took hold of her hand and when she crept close put a hand on her shoulder. A wind began to blow and he shivered. With all his strength he tried to hold and to understand the mood that had come upon him. In that high place in the darkness the two oddly sensitive human atoms held each other tightly and waited. In the mind of each was that same thought. "I have come to this lonely place and here is this other," was the substance of the thing felt.

In Winesburg the crowded day had run itself out into the long night of the late fall. Farm horses jogged away along lonely country roads pulling their portion of weary people. Clerks began to bring samples of goods in off the sidewalk and lock the doors of stores. In the Opera House a crowd had gathered to see a show and further down Main Street the fiddlers, their instruments tuned, sweated and worked to keep the feet of youth flying over a dance floor.

In the darkness of the grandstand Helen White and George Willard remained silent. Now and then the spell that held them was broken and they turned and tried in the dim light to see into each other's eyes. They kissed but that impulse did not last. At the upper end of the fair ground a half dozen men worked over horses that had raced during the afternoon. The men had built a fire and were heating kettles of water. Only their legs could be seen as they passed back and forth in the light. When the wind blew the little flames of the fire danced crazily about.

George and Helen arose and walked away into the darkness. They went along a path past a field of corn that had not yet been cut. The wind whispered among the dry corn blades. For a moment during the walk back into town the spell that held them was broken. When they had come to the crest of Waterworks Hill they stopped by a tree and George again put his hands on the girl's shoulders. She embraced him eagerly and then again they drew quickly back from that impulse. They stopped kissing and stood a little apart. Mutual respect grew big in them. They were both embarrassed and to relieve their embarrassment dropped into the animalism of youth. They laughed and began to pull and haul at each other. In some way chastened and purified by the mood they had been in they became, not man and woman, not boy and girl, but excited little animals.

It was so they went down the hill. In the darkness they played like two splendid young things in a young world. Once, running swiftly forward, Helen tripped George and he fell. He squirmed and shouted. Shaking with laughter, he rolled down the hill. Helen ran after him. For just a moment she stopped in the darkness. There is no way of knowing what woman's thoughts went through her mind but, when the bottom of the hill was reached and she came up to the boy, she took his arm and walked beside him in dignified silence. For some reason they could not have explained they had both got from their silent evening together the thing needed. Man or boy, woman or girl, they had for a moment taken hold of the thing that makes the mature life of men and women in the modern world possible.

*Anton Chekhov*

# THE KISS

On the twentieth of May, at eight o'clock in the evening, six batteries of the N Artillery Brigade arrived at the village of Miestetchki to spend the night, before going to their camp.

The confusion was at its height—some officers at the guns, others in the church square with the quartermaster—when a civilian upon a remarkable horse rode from the rear of the church. The small cob with well-shaped neck wobbled along, all the time dancing on its legs as if someone were whipping them. Reaching the officers, the rider doffed his cap with ceremony and said—

"His Excellency, General von Rabbek, requests the honor of the officers' company at tea in his house near-by. . . ."

The horse shook its head, danced, and wobbled backwards; its rider again took off his cap, and turning around disappeared behind the church.

"The devil!" the general exclaimed, the officers dispersing to their quarters. "We are almost asleep, yet along comes this von Rabbek with his tea! That tea! I remember it!"

The officers of the six batteries had vivid recollections of a past invitation. During recent maneuvers they had been asked, with their Cossack comrades, to tea at the house of a local country gentleman, a Count, retired from military service; and this hearty old Count overwhelmed them with attentions, fed them like gourmands, poured vodka into them and made them stay the night. All this, of course, was fine. The trouble was that the old soldier entertained his guests too well. He kept them up till daybreak while he poured forth tales of past adventures and pointed out valuable paintings, engravings, arms, and letters from celebrated men. And the tired officers listened, perforce, until he ended, only to find out that the time for sleep had gone.

THE KISS: From *The Party and Other Stories*, by Anton Chekhov. Translation by Constance Garnett. Used by permission of The Macmillan Company and Chatto & Windus, Ltd.

Was von Rabbek another old Count? It might easily be. But there was no neglecting his invitation. The officers washed and dressed, and set out for von Rabbek's house. At the church square they learnt that they must descend the hill to the river, and follow the bank till they reached the general's gardens, where they would find a path direct to the house. Or, if they chose to go uphill, they would reach the general's barns half a *verst* from Miestetchki. It was this route they chose.

"But who is this von Rabbek?" asked one. "The man who commanded the N Cavalry Division at Plevna?"

"No, that was not von Rabbek, but simply Rabbe—without the von."

"What glorious weather!"

At the first barn they came to, two roads diverged; one ran straight forward and faded in the dusk; the other, turning to the right, led to the general's house. As the officers drew near they talked less loudly. To right and to left stretched rows of red-roofed brick barns, in aspect heavy and morose as the barracks of provincial towns. In front gleamed the lighted windows of von Rabbek's house.

"A good omen, gentlemen!" cried a young officer. "Our setter runs in advance. There is game ahead!"

On the face of Lieutenant Lobuitko, the tall stout officer referred to, there was not one trace of hair though he was twenty-five years old. He was famed among comrades for the instinct which told him of the presence of women in the neighborhood. On hearing his comrade's remark, he turned his head and said—

"Yes. There are women there. My instinct tells me."

A handsome, well-preserved man of sixty, in mufti, came to the hall door to greet his guests. It was von Rabbek. As he pressed their hands, he explained that though he was delighted to see them, he must beg pardon for not asking them to spend the night; as guests he already had his two sisters, their children, his brother, and several neighbors—in fact, he had not one spare room. And though he shook their hands and apologized and smiled, it was plain that he was not half as glad to see them as was last year's Count, and that he had invited them merely because good manners demanded it. The officers climbing the soft-carpeted steps and listening to their host understood this per-

fectly well; and realized that they carried into the house an atmosphere of intrusion and alarm. Would any man—they asked themselves —who had gathered his two sisters and their children, his brother and his neighbors, to celebrate, no doubt, some family festival, find pleasure in the invasion of nineteen officers whom he had never seen before?

A tall elderly lady, with a good figure, and a long face with black eyebrows, who resembled closely the ex-Empress Eugénie, greeted them at the drawing-room door. Smiling courteously and with dignity, she affirmed that she was delighted to see the officers, and only regretted that she could not ask them to stay the night. But the courteous, dignified smile disappeared when she turned away, and it was quite plain that she had seen many officers in her day, that they caused not the slightest interest, and that she had invited them merely because an invitation was dictated by good breeding and by her position in the world.

In a big dining room, at a big table, sat ten men and women, drinking tea. Behind them, veiled in cigar smoke, stood several young men, among them one, red-whiskered and extremely thin, who spoke English loudly with a lisp. Through an open door the officers saw into a brightly lighted room with blue wallpaper.

"You are too many to introduce singly, gentlemen!" said the general loudly, with affected joviality. "Make one another's acquaintance, please—without formalities!"

The visitors, some with serious, even severe faces, some smiling constrainedly, all with a feeling of awkwardness, bowed, and took their seats at the table. Most awkward of all felt Staff-Captain Riabovitch, a short, round-shouldered, spectacled officer, whiskered like a lynx. While his brother officers looked serious or smiled constrainedly, his face, his lynx whiskers, and his spectacles seemed to explain: "I am the most timid, modest, undistinguished officer in the whole brigade." For some time after he took his seat at the table he could not fix his attention on any single thing. Faces, dresses, the cut-glass cognac bottles, the steaming tumblers, the molded cornices—all merged in a single, overwhelming sentiment which caused him intense fright and made him wish to hide his head. Like an inexperienced lecturer he saw everything before him, but could distinguish nothing, and was in fact the victim of what men of science diagnose as "psychical blindness."

But, slowly conquering his diffidence, Riabovitch began to distinguish and observe. As became a man both timid and unsocial, he remarked first of all the amazing temerity of his new friends. Von Rabbek, his wife, two elderly ladies, a girl in lilac, and the red-whiskered youth (who, it appeared, was a young von Rabbek) sat down among the officers as unconcernedly as if they had held rehearsals, and at once plunged into various heated arguments in which they soon involved their guests. That artillerists have a much better time than cavalrymen or infantrymen was proved conclusively by the lilac girl, while von Rabbek and the elderly ladies affirmed the converse. The conversation became desultory. Riabovitch listened to the lilac girl fiercely debating themes she knew nothing about and took no interest in, and watched the insincere smiles which appeared on and disappeared from her face.

While the von Rabbek family with amazing strategy inveigled their guests into the dispute, they kept their eyes on every glass and mouth. Had everyone tea, was it sweet enough, why didn't one eat biscuits, was another fond of cognac? And the longer Riabovitch listened and looked, the more pleased he was with this disingenuous, disciplined family.

After tea the guests repaired to the drawing room. Instinct had not cheated Lobuitko. The room was packed with young women and girls, and ere a minute had passed the setter-lieutenant stood beside a very young, fair-haired girl in black, and, bending down as if resting on an invisible sword, shrugged his shoulders coquettishly. He was uttering, no doubt, most unentertaining nonsense, for the fair girl looked indulgently at his sated face, and exclaimed indifferently, "Indeed!" And this indifferent "Indeed!" might have quickly convinced the setter that he was on a wrong scent.

Music began. As the notes of a mournful valse throbbed out of the open window, through the heads of all flashed the feeling that outside that window it was springtime, a night of May. The air was odorous of young poplar leaves, of roses and lilacs—and the valse and the spring were sincere. Riabovitch, with valse and cognac mingling tipsily in his head, gazed at the window with a smile; then began to follow the movements of the women; and it seemed that the smell of roses, poplars, and lilacs came not from the gardens outside, but from the women's faces and dresses.

They began to dance. Young von Rabbek valsed twice round the room with a very thin girl; and Lobuitko, slipping on the parqueted floor, went up to the girl in lilac, and was granted a dance. But Riabovitch stood near the door with the wallflowers, and looked silently on. Amazed at the daring of men who in sight of a crowd could take unknown women by the waist, he tried in vain to picture himself doing the same. A time had been when he envied his comrades their courage and dash, suffered from painful heart-searchings, and was hurt by the knowledge that he was timid, round-shouldered, and undistinguished, that he had lynx whiskers, and that his waist was much too long. But with years he had grown reconciled to his own insignificance, and now looking at the dancers and loud talkers, he felt no envy, but only mournful emotions.

At the first quadrille von Rabbek junior approached and invited two nondancing officers to a game of billiards. The three left the room; and Riabovitch, who stood idle, and felt impelled to join in the general movement, followed. They passed the dining room, traversed a narrow glazed corridor and a room where three sleepy footmen jumped from a sofa with a start; and after walking, it seemed, through a whole houseful of rooms, entered a small billiard room.

Von Rabbek and the two officers began their game. Riabovitch, whose only game was cards, stood near the table and looked indifferently on, as the players, with unbuttoned coats, wielded their cues, moved about, joked, and shouted obscure technical terms. Riabovitch was ignored, save when one of the players jostled him or nudged him with the cue, and turning towards him said briefly, "Pardon!" so that before the game was over he was thoroughly bored, and, impressed by a sense of his superfluity, resolved to return to the drawing room and turned away.

It was on the way back that his adventure took place. Before he had gone far he saw that he had missed his way. He remembered distinctly the room with the three sleepy footmen; and after passing through five or six rooms entirely vacant, he saw his mistake. Retracing his steps, he turned to the left, and found himself in an almost dark room which he had not seen before; and after hesitating a minute, he boldly opened the first door he saw, and found himself in complete darkness. Through a chink of the door in front peered a bright light; from afar throbbed the dullest music of a mournful mazurka. Here, as in the drawing room, the windows were open wide, and the smell of poplars, lilacs, and roses flooded the air.

Riabovitch paused in irresolution. For a moment all was still. Then came the sound of hasty footsteps; then, without any warning of what was to come, a dress rustled, a woman's breathless voice whispered "At last!" and two soft, scented, unmistakably womanly arms met round his neck, a warm cheek impinged on his, and he received a sounding kiss. But hardly had the kiss echoed through the silence when the unknown shrieked loudly, and fled away— as it seemed to Riabovitch—in disgust. Riabovitch himself nearly screamed, and rushed headlong towards the bright beam in the door chink.

As he entered the drawing room his heart beat violently, and his hands trembled so perceptibly that he clasped them behind his back. His first emotion was shame, as if everyone in the room already knew that he had just been embraced and kissed. He retired into his shell, and looked fearfully around. But finding that hosts and guests were calmly dancing or talking, he regained courage, and surrendered himself to sensations experienced for the first time in life. The unexampled had happened. His neck, fresh from the embrace of two soft, scented arms, seemed anointed with oil; near his left mustache, where the kiss had fallen, trembled a slight, delightful chill, as from peppermint drops; and from head to foot he was soaked in new and extraordinary sensations, which continued to grow and grow.

He felt that he must dance, talk, run into the garden, laugh unrestrainedly. He forgot altogether that he was round-shouldered, undistinguished, lynx-whiskered, that he had an "indefinite exterior"—a description from the lips of a woman he had happened to overhear. As Madame von Rabbek passed him he smiled so broadly and graciously that she came up and looked at him questioningly.

"What a charming house you have!" he said, straightening his spectacles.

And Madame von Rabbek smiled back, said that the house still belonged to her father, and

asked were his parents still alive, how long he had been in the Army, and why he was so thin. After hearing his answers she departed. But though the conversation was over, he continued to smile benevolently, and think what charming people were his new acquaintances.

At supper Riabovitch ate and drank mechanically what was put before him, heard not a word of the conversation, and devoted all his powers to the unraveling of his mysterious, romantic adventure. What was the explanation? It was plain that one of the girls, he reasoned, had arranged a meeting in the dark room, and after waiting some time in vain had, in her nervous tension, mistaken Riabovitch for her hero. The mistake was likely enough, for on entering the dark room Riabovitch had stopped irresolutely as if he, too, were waiting for someone. So far the mystery was explained.

"But which of them was it?" he asked, searching the women's faces. She certainly was young, for old women do not indulge in such romances. Secondly, she was not a servant. That was proved unmistakably by the rustle of her dress, the scent, the voice. . . .

When at first he looked at the girl in lilac she pleased him; she had pretty shoulders and arms, a clever face, a charming voice. Riabovitch piously prayed that it was she. But, smiling insincerely, she wrinkled her long nose, and that at once gave her an elderly air. So Riabovitch turned his eyes on the blonde in black. The blonde was younger, simpler, sincerer; she had charming kiss-curls, and drank from her tumbler with inexpressible grace. Riabovitch hoped it was she—but soon he noticed that her face was flat, and bent his eyes on her neighbor.

"It is a hopeless puzzle," he reflected. "If you take the arms and shoulders of the lilac girl, add the blonde's curls, and the eyes of the girl on Lobuitko's left, then—"

He composed a portrait of all these charms, and had a clear vision of the girl who had kissed him. But she was nowhere to be seen.

Supper over, the visitors, sated and tipsy, bade their entertainers good-by. Both host and hostess apologized for not asking them to spend the night.

"I am very glad, gentlemen!" said the general, and this time seemed to speak sincerely, no doubt because speeding the parting guest is a kindlier office than welcoming him unwelcomed. "I am very glad indeed! I hope you will visit me on your way back. Without ceremony, please! Which way will you go? Up the hill? No, go down the hill and through the garden. That way is shorter."

The officers took his advice. After the noise and glaring illumination within doors, the garden seemed dark and still. Until they reached the wicket gate all kept silence. Merry, half tipsy, and content, as they were, the night's obscurity and stillness inspired pensive thought. Through their brains, as through Riabovitch's, sped probably the same question: "Will the time ever come when I, like von Rabbek, shall have a big house, a family, a garden, the chance of being gracious—even insincerely—to others, of making them sated, tipsy, and content?"

But once the garden lay behind them, all spoke at once, and burst into causeless laughter. The path they followed led straight to the river, and then ran beside it, winding around bushes, ravines, and overhanging willow trees. The track was barely visible; the other bank was lost entirely in gloom. Sometimes the black water imaged stars, and this was the only indication of the river's speed. From beyond it sighed a drowsy snipe, and beside them in a bush, heedless of the crowd, a nightingale chanted loudly. The officers gathered in a group, and swayed the bush, but the nightingale continued his song.

"I like his cheek!" they echoed admiringly. "He doesn't care a *kopek!* The old rogue!"

Near their journey's end the path turned up the hill, and joined the road not far from the church enclosure; and there the officers, breathless from climbing, sat on the grass and smoked. Across the river gleamed a dull red light, and for want of a subject they argued the problem, whether it was a bonfire, a window light, or something else. Riabovitch looked also at the light, and felt that it smiled and winked at him as if it knew about the kiss.

On reaching home, he undressed without delay, and lay upon his bed. He shared the cabin with Lobuitko and a Lieutenant Merzliakoff, a staid, silent little man, by repute highly cultivated, who took with him everywhere *The Messenger of Europe* and read it eternally. Lobuitko undressed, tramped impatiently from corner to corner, and sent his servant for beer. Merzliakoff lay down, balanced the candle on his pillow, and hid his head behind *The Messenger of Europe.*

"Where is she now?" muttered Riabovitch, looking at the soot-blacked ceiling.

His neck still seemed anointed with oil, near his mouth still trembled the speck of peppermint chill. Through his brain twinkled successively the shoulders and arms of the lilac girl, the kiss-curls and honest eyes of the girl in black, the waists, dresses, brooches. But though he tried his best to fix these vagrant images, they glimmered, winked, and dissolved; and as they faded finally into the vast black curtain which hangs before the closed eyes of all men, he began to hear hurried footsteps, the rustle of petticoats, the sound of a kiss. A strong, causeless joy possessed him. But as he surrendered himself to this joy, Lobuitko's servant returned with the news that no beer was obtainable. The lieutenant resumed his impatient march up and down the room.

"The fellow's an idiot," he exclaimed, stopping first near Riabovitch and then near Merzliakoff. "Only the worst numbskull and blockhead can't get beer! *Canaille!*"

"Everyone knows there's no beer here," said Merzliakoff, without lifting his eyes from *The Messenger of Europe.*

"You believe that!" exclaimed Lobuitko. "Lord in heaven, drop me on the moon, and in five minutes I'll find both beer and women! I will find them myself! Call me a rascal if I don't!"

He dressed slowly, silently lighted a cigarette, and went out.

"Rabbek, Grabbek, Labbek," he muttered, stopping in the hall. "I won't go alone, devil take me! Riabovitch, come for a walk! What?"

As he got no answer, he returned, undressed slowly, and lay down. Merzliakoff sighed, dropped *The Messenger of Europe,* and put out the light. "Well?" muttered Lobuitko, puffing his cigarette in the dark.

Riabovitch pulled the bedclothes up to his chin, curled himself into a roll, and strained his imagination to join the twinkling images into one coherent whole. But the vision fled him. He soon fell asleep, and his last impression was that he had been caressed and gladdened, that into his life had crept something strange, and indeed ridiculous, but uncommonly good and radiant. And this thought did not forsake him even in his dreams.

When he awoke the feeling of anointment and peppermint chill was gone. But joy, as on the night before, filled every vein. He looked entranced at the windowpanes gilded by the rising sun, and listened to the noises outside. Someone spoke loudly under the very window. It was Lebedietsky, commander of his battery, who had just overtaken the brigade. He was talking to the sergeant-major, loudly, owing to lack of practice in soft speech.

"And what next?" he roared.

"During yesterday's shoeing, your honor, *Golubtchik* was pricked. The *Feldscher* [3] ordered clay and vinegar. And last night, your honor, mechanic Artemieff was drunk, and the lieutenant ordered him to be put on the limber of the reserve gun carriage."

The sergeant-major added that Karpoff had forgotten the tent pegs and the new lanyards for the friction tubes, and that the officers had spent the evening at General von Rabbek's. But here at the window appeared Lebedietsky's red-bearded face. He blinked his short-sighted eyes at the drowsy men in bed, and greeted them.

"Is everything all right?"

"The saddle wheeler galled his withers with the new yoke," answered Lobuitko.

The commander sighed, mused a moment, and shouted—

"I am thinking of calling on Alexandra Yegorovna. I want to see her. Good-by! I will catch you up before night."

Fifteen minutes later the brigade resumed its march. As he passed von Rabbek's barns, Riabovitch turned his head and looked at the house. The Venetian blinds were down; evidently all still slept. And among them slept she—she who had kissed him but a few hours before. He tried to visualize her asleep. He projected the bedroom window opened wide with green branches peering in, the freshness of the morning air, the smell of poplars, lilacs, and roses, the bed, a chair, the dress which rustled last night, a pair of tiny slippers, a ticking watch on the table— all these came to him clearly with every detail. But the features, the kind, sleepy smile—all, in short, that was essential and characteristic— fled his imagination as quicksilver flees the hand. When he had covered half a *verst* he again turned back. The yellow church, the

house, gardens, and river were bathed in light. Imaging an azure sky, the green-banked river specked with silver sunshine flakes was inexpressibly fair; and, looking at Miestetchki for the last time, Riabovitch felt sad, as if parting forever with something very near and dear.

By the road before him stretched familiar, uninteresting scenes; to the right and left, fields of young rye and buckwheat with hopping rooks; in front, dust and the napes of human necks; behind, the same dust and faces. Ahead of the column marched four soldiers with swords—that was the advance guard. Next came the bandsmen. Advance guard and bandsmen, like mutes in a funeral procession, ignored the regulation intervals and marched too far ahead. Riabovitch, with the first gun of Battery No. 5, could see four batteries ahead.

To a layman, the long, lumbering march of an artillery brigade is novel, interesting, inexplicable. It is hard to understand why a single gun needs so many men; why so many, such strangely harnessed horses are needed to drag it. But to Riabovitch, a master of all these things, it was profoundly dull. He had learned years ago why a solid sergeant-major rides beside the officer in front of each battery; why the sergeant-major is called the *unosni*,[4] and why the drivers of leaders and wheelers ride behind him. Riabovitch knew why the near horses are called saddle horses, and why the off horses are called led horses—and all of this was uninteresting beyond words. On one of the wheelers rode a soldier still covered with yesterday's dust, and with a cumbersome, ridiculous guard on his right leg. But Riabovitch, knowing the use of this leg guard, found it in no way ridiculous. The drivers, mechanically and with occasional cries, flourished their whips. The guns in themselves were unimpressive. The limbers were packed with tarpaulin-covered sacks of oats; and the guns themselves, hung round with teapots and satchels, looked like harmless animals, guarded for some obscure reason by men and horses. In the lee of the gun tramped six gunners, swinging their arms, and behind each gun came more *unosniye*, leaders, wheelers; and yet more guns, each as ugly and uninspiring as the one in front. And as every one of the six batteries in the brigade had four guns, the pro-

[3] Regimental doctor.

[4] Because he rides ahead of the leading team (*unos*).

cession stretched along the road at least half a *verst*. It ended with a wagon train, with which, its head bent in thought, walked the donkey Magar, brought from Turkey by a battery commander.

Dead to his surroundings, Riabovitch marched onward, looking at the napes ahead or at the faces behind. Had it not been for last night's event, he would have been half asleep. But now he was absorbed in novel, entrancing thoughts. When the brigade set out that morning he had tried to argue that the kiss had no significance save as a trivial though mysterious adventure; that it was without real import; and that to think of it seriously was to behave himself absurdly. But logic soon flew away and surrendered him to his vivid imaginings. At times he saw himself in von Rabbek's dining room, *tête-à-tête* with a composite being, formed of the girl in lilac and the blonde in black. At times he closed his eyes, and pictured himself with a different, this time quite an unknown, girl of cloudy feature; he spoke to her, caressed her, bent over her shoulders; he imagined war and parting . . . then reunion, the first supper together, children. . . .

"To the brakes!" rang the command as they topped the brow of each hill.

Riabovitch also cried "To the brakes!" and each time dreaded that the cry would break the magic spell, and recall him to realities.

They passed a big country house. Riabovitch looked across the fence into the garden, and saw a long path, straight as a ruler, carpeted with yellow sand, and shaded by young birches. In an ecstasy of enchantment, he pictured little feminine feet treading the yellow sand; and, in a flash, imagination restored the woman who had kissed him, the woman he had visualized after supper the night before. The image settled in his brain and never afterward forsook him.

The spell reigned until midday, when a loud command came from the rear of the column.

"Attention! Eyes right! Officers!"

In a *calèche* drawn by a pair of white horses appeared the general of the brigade. He stopped at the second battery, and called out something which no one understood. Up galloped several officers, among them Riabovitch.

"Well, how goes it?" The general blinked his red eyes, and continued, "Are there any sick?"

Hearing the answer, the little skinny general mused a moment, turned to an officer, and said—

"The driver of your third-gun wheeler has taken off his leg guard and hung it on the limber. *Canaille!* Punish him!"

Then raising his eyes to Riabovitch, he added—

"And in your battery, I think, the harness is too loose."

Having made several other equally tiresome remarks, he looked at Lobuitko, and laughed.

"Why do you look so downcast, Lieutenant Lobuitko? You are sighing for Madame Lopukhoff, eh? Gentlemen, he is pining for Madame Lopukhoff!"

Madame Lopukhoff was a tall, stout lady, long past forty. Being partial to big women, regardless of age, the general ascribed the same taste to his subordinates. The officers smiled respectfully; and the general, pleased that he had said something caustic and laughable, touched the coachman's back and saluted. The *calèche* whirled away.

"All this, though it seems to me impossible and unearthly, is in reality very commonplace," thought Riabovitch, watching the clouds of dust raised by the general's carriage. "It is an everyday event, and within everyone's experience. . . . This old general, for instance, must have loved in his day; he is married now, and has children. Captain Wachter is also married, and his wife loves him, though he has an ugly red neck and no waist. . . . Salmanoff is coarse, and a typical Tartar, but he has had a romance ending in marriage. . . . I, like the rest, must go through it all sooner or later."

And the thought that he was an ordinary man, and that his life was ordinary, rejoiced and consoled him. He boldly visualized *her* and his happiness, and let his imagination run mad.

Towards evening the brigade ended its march. While the other officers sprawled in their tents, Riabovitch, Merzliakoff, and Lobuitko sat round a packing case and supped. Merzliakoff ate slowly, and, resting *The Messenger of Europe* on his knees, read on steadily. Lobuitko, chattering without cease, poured beer into his glass. But Riabovitch, whose head was dizzy from uninterrupted daydreams, ate in silence. When he had drunk three glasses he felt tipsy and weak; and an overmastering impulse forced him to relate his adventure to his comrades.

"A most extraordinary thing happened to me at von Rabbek's," he began, doing his best to speak in an indifferent, ironical tone. "I was on my way, you understand, from the billiard room . . . ."

And he attempted to give a very detailed history of the kiss. But in a minute he had told the whole story. In that minute he had exhausted every detail; and it seemed to him terrible that the story required such a short time. It ought, he felt, to have lasted all the night. As he finished, Lobuitko, who as a liar himself believed in no one, laughed incredulously. Merzliakoff frowned, and, with his eyes still glued to *The Messenger of Europe,* said indifferently—

"God knows who it was! She threw herself on your neck, you say, and didn't cry out! Some lunatic, I expect!"

"It must have been a lunatic," agreed Riabovitch.

"I, too, have had adventures of that kind," began Lobuitko, making a frightened face. "I was on my way to Kovno. I traveled second-class. The carriage was packed, and I couldn't sleep. So I gave the guard a *rouble,* and he took my bag, and put me in a *coupé.* I lay down, and pulled my rug over me. It was pitch dark, you understand. Suddenly I felt someone tapping my shoulder and breathing in my face. I stretched out my hand, and felt an elbow. Then I opened my eyes. Imagine! A woman! Coal-black eyes, lips red as good coral, nostrils breathing passion, breasts—buffers!"

"Draw it mild!" interrupted Merzliakoff in his quiet voice. "I can believe about the breasts, but if it was pitch dark how could you see the lips?"

By laughing at Merzliakoff's lack of understanding, Lobuitko tried to shuffle out of the dilemma. The story annoyed Riabovitch. He rose from the box, lay on his bed, and swore that he would never again take anyone into his confidence.

Life in camp passed without event. The days flew by, each like the one before. But on every one of these days Riabovitch felt, thought, and acted as a man in love. When at daybreak his servant brought him cold water, and poured it over his head, it flashed at once into his half-awakened brain that something good and warm and caressing had crept into his life.

At night when his comrades talked of love and of women, he drew in his chair, and his face was the face of an old soldier who talks of battles in which he has taken part. And when the rowdy officers, led by setter Lobuitko, made Don Juanesque raids upon the neighboring "suburb," Riabovitch, though he accompanied them, was morose and conscience-struck, and mentally asked *her* forgiveness. In free hours and sleepless nights, when his brain was obsessed by memories of childhood, of his father, his mother, of everything akin and dear, he remembered always Miestetchki, the dancing horse, von Rabbek, von Rabbek's wife, so like the ex-Empress Eugénie, the dark room, the chink in the door.

On the thirty-first of August he left camp, this time not with the whole brigade but with only two batteries. As an exile returning to his native land, he was agitated and enthralled by daydreams. He longed passionately for the queer-looking horse, the church, the insincere von Rabbeks, the dark room; and that internal voice which so often cheats the lovelorn whispered an assurance that he should see *her* again. But doubt tortured him. How should he meet her? What must he say? Would she have forgotten the kiss? If it came to the worst—he consoled himself—if he never saw her again, he might walk once more through the dark room, and remember. . . .

Towards evening the white barns and well-known church rose on the horizon. Riabovitch's heart beat wildly. He ignored the remark of an officer who rode by, he forgot the whole world, and he gazed greedily at the river glimmering afar, at the green roofs, at the dove-cote, over which fluttered birds dyed golden by the setting sun.

As he rode towards the church, and heard again the quartermaster's raucous voice, he expected every second a horseman to appear from behind the fence and invite the officers to tea. . . . But the quartermaster ended his harangue, the officers hastened to the village, and no horseman appeared.

"When Rabbek hears from the peasants that we are back he will send for us," thought Riabovitch. And so assured was he of this, that when he entered the hut he failed to understand why his comrades had lighted a candle, and why the servants were preparing the samovar.

A painful agitation oppressed him. He lay on his bed. A moment later he rose to look for the horseman. But no horseman was in sight. Again he lay down; again he rose; and this time, impelled by restlessness, went into the street and walked towards the church. The square was dark and deserted. On the hill stood three silent soldiers. When they saw Riabovitch they started and saluted, and he, returning their salute, began to descend the well-remembered path.

Beyond the stream, in a sky stained with purple, the moon slowly rose. Two chattering peasant women walked in a kitchen garden and pulled cabbage leaves; behind them their log cabins stood out black against the sky. The river bank was as it had been in May; the bushes were the same; things differed only in that the nightingale no longer sang, that it smelt no longer of poplars and young grass.

When he reached von Rabbek's garden Riabovitch peered through the wicket gate. Silence and darkness reigned. Save only the white birch trunks and patches of pathway, the whole garden merged in a black, impenetrable shade. Riabovitch listened greedily, and gazed intent. For a quarter of an hour he loitered; then hearing no sound, and seeing no light, he walked wearily towards home.

He went down to the river. In front rose the general's bathing box; and white towels hung on the rail of the bridge. He climbed on to the bridge and stood still; then, for no reason whatever, touched a towel. It was clammy and cold. He looked down at the river which sped past swiftly, murmuring almost inaudibly against the bathing-box piles. Near the left bank glowed the moon's ruddy reflection, overrun by ripples which stretched it, tore it in two, and, it seemed, would sweep it away as twigs and shavings are swept.

"How stupid! How stupid!" thought Riabovitch, watching the hurrying ripples. "How stupid everything is!"

Now that hope was dead, the history of the kiss, his impatience, his ardor, his vague aspirations and disillusion appeared in a clear light. It no longer seemed strange that the general's horseman had not come, and that he would never again see *her* who had kissed him by accident instead of another. On the contrary, he felt, it would be strange if he did ever see her again. . . .

The water flew past him, whither and why no one knew. It had flown past in May; it had sped a stream into a great river; a river, into the sea; it had floated on high in mist and fallen again in rain; it might be, the water of May was again speeding past under Riabovitch's eyes. For what purpose? Why?

And the whole world—life itself—seemed to Riabovitch an inscrutable, aimless mystification. . . . Raising his eyes from the stream and gazing at the sky, he recalled how Fate in the shape of an unknown woman had once caressed him; he recalled his summer fantasies and images—and his whole life seemed to him unnaturally thin and colorless and wretched. . . .

When he reached the cabin his comrades had disappeared. His servant informed him that all had set out to visit "General Fonrabbkin," who had sent a horseman to bring them. . . . For a moment Riabovitch's heart thrilled with joy. But that joy he extinguished. He cast himself upon his bed, and wroth with his evil fate, as if he wished to spite it, ignored the invitation.

## Guy de Maupassant
## THE NECKLACE

She was one of those pretty and charming girls born, as though fate had blundered over her, into a family of artisans. She had no marriage portion, no expectations, no means of getting known, understood, loved, and wedded by a man of wealth and distinction; and she let herself be married off to a little clerk in the Ministry of Education.

Her tastes were simple because she had never been able to afford any other, but she was as unhappy as though she had married beneath her; for women have no caste or class, their beauty, grace, and charm serving them for birth or family. Their natural delicacy, their instinctive elegance, their nimbleness of wit, are their only mark of rank, and put the slum girl on a level with the highest lady in the land.

She suffered endlessly, feeling herself born for every delicacy and luxury. She suffered from the poorness of her house, from its mean

THE NECKLACE: From *The Collected Novels and Stories of Guy de Maupassant*. Translation by Ernest Boyd. Copyright, 1924, by Alfred A. Knopf, Inc. Used by permission of the publisher.

walls, worn chairs, and ugly curtains. All these things, of which other women of her class would not even have been aware, tormented and insulted her. The sight of the little Breton girl who came to do the work in her little house aroused heart-broken regrets and hopeless dreams in her mind. She imagined silent ante-chambers, heavy with Oriental tapestries, lit by torches in lofty bronze sockets, with two tall footmen in knee-breeches sleeping in large arm-chairs, overcome by the heavy warmth of the stove. She imagined vast saloons hung with antique silks, exquisite pieces of furniture supporting priceless ornaments, and small, charming, perfumed rooms, created just for little parties of intimate friends, men who were famous and sought after, whose homage roused every other woman's envious longings.

When she sat down for dinner at the round table covered with a three-days-old cloth, opposite her husband, who took the cover off the soup tureen, exclaimed delightedly: "Aha! Scotch broth! There's nothing better," she imagined delicate meals, gleaming silver, tapestries peopling the walls with folk of a past age and strange birds in faery forest; she imagined delicate food served in marvellous dishes, murmured gallantries, listened to with an inscrutable smile as one trifled with the rosy flesh of trout or wings of asparagus chicken.

She had no clothes, no jewels, nothing. And these were the only things she loved; she felt that she was made for them. She had longed so eagerly to charm, to be desired, to be wildly attractive and sought after.

She had a rich friend, an old school friend whom she refused to visit, because she suffered so keenly when she returned home. She would weep whole days, with grief, regret, despair, and misery.

One evening her husband came home with an exultant air, holding a large envelope in his hand.

"Here's something for you," he said.

Swiftly she tore the paper and drew out a printed card on which were these words: *The Minister of Education and Madame Rampon-neau request the pleasure of the company of Monsieur and Madame Loisel at the Ministry on the evening of Monday, January the 18th.*

Instead of being delighted, as her husband hoped, she flung the invitation petulantly across the table, murmuring:

"What do you want me to do with this?"

"Why, darling, I thought you'd be pleased. You never go out, and this is a great occasion. I had tremendous trouble to get it. Everyone wants one; it's very select, and very few go to the clerks. You'll see all the really big people there."

She looked at him out of furious eyes, and said impatiently:

"And what do you suppose I am to wear at such an affair?"

He had not thought about it; he stammered:

"Why, the dress you go to the theatre in. It looks very nice, to me. . . ."

He stopped, stupefied and utterly at a loss when he saw that his wife was beginning to cry. Two large tears ran slowly down from the corners of her eyes towards the corners of her mouth.

"What's the matter with you? What's the matter with you?" he faltered.

But with a violent effort she overcame her grief and replied in a calm voice, wiping her wet cheeks:

"Nothing. Only I haven't a dress and so I can't go to this party. Give your invitation to some friend of yours whose wife will be turned out better than I shall."

He was heart-broken.

"Look here, Mathilde," he persisted. "What would be the cost of a suitable dress, which you could use on other occasions as well, something very simple?"

She thought for several seconds, reckoning up prices and also wondering for how large a sum she could ask without bringing upon herself an immediate refusal and an exclamation of horror from the careful-minded clerk.

At last she replied with some hesitation: "I don't know exactly, but I think I could do it on four hundred francs."

He grew slightly pale, for this was exactly the amount he had been saving for a gun, intending to get a little shooting next summer on the plain of Nanterre with some friends who went lark-shooting there on Sundays.

Nevertheless he said: "Very well. I'll give you four hundred francs. But try and get a really nice dress with the money."

The day of the party drew near, and Madame Loisel seemed sad, uneasy and anxious. Her dress was ready, however. One evening her husband said to her: "What's the matter with you? You've been very odd for the last three days."

"I'm utterly miserable at not having any jewels, not a single stone, to wear," she replied. "I shall look absolutely no one. I would almost rather not go to the party."

"Wear flowers," he said. "They're very smart at this time of year. For ten francs you could get two or three gorgeous roses." She was not convinced.

"No . . . there's nothing so humiliating as looking poor in the middle of a lot of rich women."

"How stupid you are!" exclaimed her husband. "Go and see Madame Forestier and ask her to lend you some jewels. You know her quite well enough for that."

She uttered a cry of delight.

"That's true. I never thought of it."

Next day she went to see her friend and told her her trouble.

Madame Forestier went to her dressing-table, took up a large box, brought it to Madame Loisel, opened it, and said:

"Choose, my dear."

First she saw some bracelets, then a pearl necklace, then a Venetian cross in gold and gems, of exquisite workmanship. She tried the effect of the jewels before the mirror, hesitating, unable to make up her mind to leave them, to give them up. She kept on asking: "Haven't you anything else?"

"Yes. Look for yourself. I don't know what you would like best."

Suddenly she discovered, in a black satin case, a superb diamond necklace; her heart began to beat covetously. Her hands trembled as she lifted it. She fastened it round her neck, upon her high dress, and remained in ecstasy at sight of herself. Then, with hesitation, she asked in anguish:

"Could you lend me this, just this alone?"

"Yes, of course."

She flung herself on her friend's breast, embraced her frenziedly, and went away with her treasure.

The day of the party arrived. Madame Loisel was a success. She was the prettiest woman present, elegant, graceful, smiling, and quite above herself with happiness. All the men stared at her, inquired her name, and asked to be introduced to her. All the under-secretaries

of state were eager to waltz with her. The Minister noticed her.

She danced madly, ecstatically, drunk with pleasure, with no thought for anything, in the triumph of her beauty, in the pride of her success, in a cloud of happiness made up of this universal homage and admiration, of the desires she had aroused, of the completeness of a victory so dear to her feminine heart.

She left about four o'clock in the morning. Since midnight her husband had been dozing in a deserted little room, in company with three other men whose wives were having a good time.

He threw over her shoulders the garments he had brought for them to go home in, modest everyday clothes, whose poorness clashed with the beauty of the ball dress. She was conscious of this and was anxious to hurry away, so that she would not be noticed by the other women putting on their costly furs. Loisel restrained her.

"Wait a little. You'll catch cold in the open. I'm going to fetch a cab."

But she did not listen to him and rapidly descended the staircase. When they were out in the street they could not find a cab; they began to look for one, shouting at the drivers whom they saw passing in the distance.

They walked down towards the Seine, desperate and shivering. At last they found on the quay one of those old night-prowling carriages which are only to be seen in Paris after dark, as though they were ashamed of their shabbiness in the daylight.

It brought them to their door in the Rue des Martyrs, and sadly they walked up to their own apartment. It was the end, for her. As for him, he was thinking that he must be at the office at ten.

She took off the garments in which she had wrapped her shoulders, so as to see herself in all her glory before the mirror. But suddenly she uttered a cry. The necklace was no longer round her neck!

"What's the matter with you?" asked her husband, already half undressed.

She turned towards him in the utmost distress.

"I . . . I . . . I've no longer got Madame Forestier's necklace. . . ."

He started with astonishment. "What! . . . Impossible!"

They searched in the folds of her dress, in the folds of the coat, in the pockets, everywhere. They could not find it.

"Are you sure that you still had it on when you came away from the ball?" he asked.

"Yes, I touched it in the hall at the Ministry."

"But if you had lost it in the street, we should have heard it fall."

"Yes. Probably we should. Did you take the number of the cab?"

"No. You didn't notice it, did you?"

"No."

They stared at one another, dumbfounded. At last Loisel put on his clothes again.

"I'll go over all the ground we walked," he said, "and see if I can't find it."

And he went out. She remained in her evening clothes, lacking strength to get into bed, huddled on a chair, without volition or power of thought.

Her husband returned about seven. He had found nothing.

He went to the police station, to the newspapers, to offer a reward to the cab companies, everywhere that a ray of hope impelled him.

She waited all day long, in the same state of bewilderment at this fearful catastrophe.

Loisel came home at night, his face lined and pale; he had discovered nothing.

"You must write your friend," he said, "and tell her that you've broken the clasp of her necklace and are getting it mended. That will give us time to look about us."

She wrote at his dictation.

By the end of a week they had lost all hope.

Loisel, who had aged five years, declared:

"We must see about replacing the diamonds."

Next day they took the box which had held the necklace and went to the jeweller's whose name was inside. He consulted his books.

"It was not I who sold this necklace, madame; I must have merely supplied the clasp."

Then they went from jeweller to jeweller, searching for another necklace like the first, consulting their memories, both ill with remorse and anguish of mind.

In a shop at the Palais-Royal they found a string of diamonds which seemed to them exactly like the one they were looking for. It was worth forty thousand francs. They were allowed to have it for thirty-six thousand.

They begged the jeweller not to sell it for three days. And they arranged matters on the understanding that it would be taken back for thirty-four thousand francs, if the first one were found before the end of February.

Loisel possessed eighteen thousand francs left to him by his father. He intended to borrow the rest.

He did borrow it, getting a thousand from one man, five hundred from another, five louis here, three louis there. He gave notes of hand, entered into ruinous agreements, did business with usurers and the whole race of moneylenders. He mortgaged the whole remaining years of his existence, risked his signature without even knowing if he could honour it, and, appalled at the agonising face of the future, at the black misery about to fall upon him, at the prospect of every possible physical privation and mortal torture, he went to get the new necklace and put down upon the jeweller's counter thirty-six thousand francs.

When Madame Loisel took back the necklace to Madame Forestier, the latter said to her in a chilly voice:

"You ought to have brought it back sooner; I might have needed it."

She did not, as her friend had feared, open the case. If she had noticed the substitution, what would she have thought? What would she have said? Would she not have taken her for a thief?

Madame Loisel came to know the ghastly life of abject poverty. Right from the start she played her part heroically. This fearful debt must be paid off. She would pay it. The servant was dismissed. They changed their apartment; they took a garret under the roof.

She came to know the heavy work of the house, the hateful duties of the kitchen. She washed the plates, wearing out her pink nails on the coarse pottery and the bottoms of pans. She washed the dirty linen, the shirts and dishcloths, and hung them out to dry on a string; every morning she took the dustbin down into the street and carried up the water, stopping on each landing to get her breath. And, clad like a poor woman, she went to the fruiterer, to the grocer, to the butcher, a basket on her arm, haggling, insulted, fighting for every wretched halfpenny of her money.

Every month notes had to be paid off, others to be renewed, time to be gained.

Her husband worked in the evenings at putting straight a merchant's accounts, and often at night he did copying at twopence halfpenny a page.

And this life lasted ten years.

At the end of ten years everything was paid off, everything, the usurer's charges and the accumulation of superimposed interest.

Madame Loisel looked old now. She had become like all the other strong, hard, coarse women of poor households. Her hair was badly done, her skirts were awry, her hands were red. She spoke in a shrill voice, and the water slopped all over the floor when she scrubbed it. But sometimes, when her husband was at the office, she sat down by the window and thought of that evening long ago, of the ball at which she had been so beautiful and so much admired.

What would have happened if she had never lost those jewels? Who knows? Who knows? How strange life is, how fickle! How little is needed to ruin or to save!

One Sunday, as she had gone for a walk along the Champs-Elysées to freshen herself after the labours of the week, she caught sight suddenly of a woman who was taking a child out for a walk. It was Madame Forestier, still young, still beautiful, still attractive.

Madame Loisel was conscious of some emotion. Should she speak to her? Yes, certainly. And now that she had paid, she would tell her all. Why not?

She went up to her. "Good morning, Jeanne."

The other did not recognise her, and was surprised at being thus familiarly addressed by a poor woman. "But . . . madame . . ." she stammered. "I don't know . . . you must be making a mistake."

"No . . . I am Mathilde Loisel."

Her friend uttered a cry. "Oh! . . . . my poor Mathilde, how you have changed! . . ."

"Yes, I've had some hard times since I saw you last; and many sorrows . . . and all on your account."

"On my account! . . . How was that?"

"You remember the diamond necklace you lent me for the ball at the Ministry?"

"Yes. Well?"

"Well, I lost it."

"How could you? Why, you brought it back."

"I brought you another one just like it. And for the last ten years we have been paying for it. You realise it wasn't easy for us; we had no money . . . Well, it's paid for at last, and I'm mighty glad."

Madame Forestier had halted. "You say you bought a diamond necklace to replace mine?"

"Yes. You hadn't noticed it? They were very much alike." And she smiled in proud and innocent happiness.

Madame Forestier, deeply moved, took her two hands. "Oh, my poor Mathilde! But mine was imitation. It was worth at the very most only five hundred francs! . . ."

*George Orwell*

# HILDA

I was living in a boarding-house in Ealing. The years were rolling on, or crawling on. Lower Binfield had passed almost out of my memory. I was the usual young city worker who scoots for the 8:15 and intrigues for the other fellow's job. I was fairly well thought of in the firm and pretty satisfied with life. The post-war success dope had caught me, more or less. You remember the line of talk. Pep, punch, grit, sand. Get on or get out. There's plenty of room at the top. You can't keep a good man down. And the ads in the magazines about the chap that the boss clapped on the shoulder, and the keen-jawed executive who's pulling down the big dough and attributes his success to so and so's correspondence course. It's funny how we all swallowed it, even blokes like me to whom it hadn't the smallest application. Because I'm neither a go-getter nor a down-and-out, and I'm by nature incapable of being either. But it was the spirit of the time. Get on! Make good! If you see a man down, jump on his guts before he gets up again. Of course this was in the early 'twenties, when some of the effects of the war had worn off and the slump hadn't yet arrived to knock the stuffing out of us.

I had an "A" subscription at Boots and went to half-crown dances and belonged to a local tennis club. You know those tennis clubs in the genteel suburbs—little wooden pavilions

HILDA: From *Coming Up for Air*, by George Orwell. Copyright, 1950, by Harcourt, Brace and Company, Inc. Used by permission of the publishers and Brandt & Brandt.

and high wire-netting enclosures where young chaps in rather badly cut white flannels prance up and down, shouting "Fifteen forty!" and "Vantage all!" in voices which are a tolerable imitation of the Upper Crust. I'd learned to play tennis, didn't dance too badly and got on well with the girls. At nearly thirty I wasn't a bad-looking chap, with my red face and butter-coloured hair, and in those days it was still a point in your favour to have fought in the war. I never, then or at any other time, succeeded in looking like a gentleman, but on the other hand you probably wouldn't have taken me for the son of a small shopkeeper in a country town. I could keep my end up in the rather mixed society of a place like Ealing, where the office-employee class overlaps with the middling-professional class. It was at the tennis club that I first met Hilda.

At that time Hilda was twenty-four. She was a small, slim, rather timid girl, with dark hair, beautiful movements and—because of having very large eyes—a distinct resemblance to a hare. She was one of those people who never say much, but remain on the edge of any con-versation that's going on, and give the impres-sion that they're listening. If she said anything at all, it was usually "Oh, yes, I think so too," agreeing with whoever had spoken last. At ten-nis she hopped about very gracefully, and didn't play badly, but somehow had a helpless, childish air. Her surname was Vincent.

If you're married, there'll be times when you've said to yourself "Why the hell did I do it?" and God knows I've said it often enough about Hilda. And once again, looking at it across fifteen years, why did I marry Hilda?

Partly, of course, because she was young and in a way very pretty. Beyond that I can only say that because she came of totally dif-ferent origins from myself it was very difficult for me to get any grasp of what she was really like. I had to marry her first and find out about her afterwards, whereas if I'd married, say, Elsie Waters, I'd have known what I was mar-rying. Hilda belonged to a class I only knew by hearsay, the poverty-stricken officer class. For generations past her family had been sol-diers, sailors, clergymen, Anglo-Indian officials and that kind of thing. They'd never had any money, but on the other hand none of them had ever done anything that I should recognise as work. Say what you will, there's a kind of snob-

appeal in that, if you belong as I do to the God-fearing shopkeeper class, the low church and high-tea class. It wouldn't make any impression on me now, but it did then. Don't mistake what I'm saying. I don't mean that I married Hilda *because* she belonged to the class I'd once served across the counter, with some notion of jockeying myself up in the social scale. It was merely that I couldn't understand her and there-fore was capable of being goofy about her. And one thing I certainly didn't grasp was that the girls in these penniless middle-class families will marry anything in trousers, just to get away from home.

It wasn't long before Hilda took me home to see her family. I hadn't known till then that there was a considerable Anglo-Indian colony in Ealing. Talk about discovering a new world! It was quite a revelation to me.

Do you know these Anglo-Indian families? It's almost impossible, when you get inside these people's houses, to remember that out in the street it's England and the twentieth century. As soon as you set foot inside the front door you're in India in the 'eighties. You know the kind of atmosphere. The carved teak furniture, the brass trays, the dusty tiger-skulls on the wall, the Trichinopoly cigars, the red-hot pickles, the yellow photographs of chaps in sun-helmets, the Hindustani words that you're expected to know the meaning of, the everlast-ing anecdotes about tiger-shoots and what Smith said to Jones in Poona in '87. It's a sort of little world of their own that they've created, like a kind of cyst. To me, of course, it was all quite new and in some ways rather interesting. Old Vincent, Hilda's father, had been not only in India but also in some even more outlandish place, Borneo or Sarawak, I forget which. He was the usual type, completely bald, almost in-visible behind his moustache, and full of stories about cobras and cummerbunds and what the district collector said in '93. Hilda's mother was so colourless that she was just like one of the faded photos on the wall. There was also a son, Harold, who had some official job in Ceylon and was home on leave at the time when I first met Hilda. They had a little dark house in one of those buried back-streets that exist in Ealing. It smelt perpetually of Trichinopoly cigars and it was so full of spears, blow-pipes, brass orna-ments and the heads of wild animals that you could hardly move about in it.

Old Vincent had retired in 1910, and since then he and his wife had shown about as much activity, mental or physical, as a couple of shell-fish. But at the time I was vaguely impressed by a family which had had majors, colonels and once even an admiral in it. My attitude towards the Vincents, and theirs towards me, is an interesting illustration of what fools people can be when they get outside their own line. Put me among business people—whether they're company directors or commercial travellers—and I'm a fairly good judge of character. But I had no experience whatever of the officer-rentier-clergyman class, and I was inclined to kow-tow to these decayed throw-outs. I looked on them as my social and intellectual superiors, while they on the other hand mistook me for a rising young business man who before long would be pulling down the big dough. To people of that kind, "business," whether it's marine insurance or selling peanuts, is just a dark mystery. All they know is that it's something rather vulgar out of which you can make money. Old Vincent used to talk impressively about my being "in business"—once, I remember, he had a slip of the tongue and said "in trade"—and obviously didn't grasp the difference between being in business as an employee and being there on your own account. He had some vague notion that as I was "in" the Flying Salamander I should sooner or later rise to the top of it, by a process of promotion. I think it's possible that he also had pictures of himself touching me for fivers at some future date. Harold certainly had. I could see it in his eye. In fact, even with my income being what it is, I'd probably be lending money to Harold at the moment if he were alive. Luckily he died a few years after we were married, of enteric or something, and both the old Vincents are dead, too.

Well, Hilda and I were married, and right from the start it was a flop. Why did you marry her? you say. But why did you marry yours? These things happen to us. I wonder whether you'll believe that during the first two or three years I had serious thoughts of killing Hilda. Of course in practice one never does these things, they're only a kind of fantasy that one enjoys thinking about. Besides, chaps who murder their wives always get copped. However cleverly you've faked the alibi, they know perfectly well that it's you who did it, and they'll pin it on to you somehow. When a woman's

bumped off, her husband is always the first suspect—which gives you a little side-glimpse of what people really think about marriage.

One gets used to everything in time. After a year or two I stopped wanting to kill her and started wondering about her. Just wondering. For hours, sometimes, on Sunday afternoons or in the evening when I've come home from work, I've lain on my bed with all my clothes on except my shoes, wondering about women. Why they're like that, whether they're doing it on purpose. It seems to be a most frightful thing, the suddenness with which some women go to pieces after they're married. It's as if they were strung up to do just that one thing, and the instant they've done it they wither off like a flower that's set its seed. What really gets me down is the dreary attitude towards life that it implies. If marriage was just an open swindle—if the woman trapped you into it and then turned round and said, "Now, you bastard, I've caught you and you're going to work for me while I have a good time!"—I wouldn't mind so much. But not a bit of it. They don't want to have a good time, they merely want to slump into middle-age as quickly as possible. After the frightful battle of getting her man to the altar, the woman kind of relaxes, and all her youth, looks, energy and joy of life just vanish overnight. It was like that with Hilda. Here was this pretty, delicate girl, who'd seemed to me—and in fact when I first knew her she *was*—a finer type of animal than myself, and within only about three years she'd settled down into a depressed, lifeless, middle-aged frump. I'm not denying that I was part of the reason. But whoever she'd married it would have been much the same.

What Hilda lacks—I discovered this about a week after we were married—is any kind of joy in life, any kind of interest in things for their own sake. The idea of doing things because you enjoy them is something she can hardly understand. It was through Hilda that I first got a notion of what these decayed middle-class families are really like. The essential fact about them is that all their vitality has been drained away by lack of money. In families like that, which live on tiny pensions and annuities—that's to say on incomes which never get bigger and generally get smaller—there's more sense of poverty, more crust-wiping and looking twice at sixpence, than you'd find in any farm-labourer's family, let alone a family like mine. Hilda's often told me that almost the first thing she can remember is a ghastly feeling that there was never enough money for anything. Of course, in that kind of family, the lack of money is always at its worst when the kids are at the school-age. Consequently they grow up, especially the girls, with a fixed idea not only that one always *is* hard-up but that it's one's duty to be miserable about it.

At the beginning we lived in a poky little maisonette and had a job to get by on my wages. Later, when I was transferred to the West Bletchley branch, things were better, but Hilda's attitude didn't change. Always that ghastly glooming about money! The milk bill! The coal bill! The rent! The school fees! We've lived all our life together to the tune of "Next week we'll be in the workhouse." It's not that Hilda's mean, in the ordinary sense of the word, and still less that she's selfish. Even when there happens to be a bit of spare cash knocking about I can hardly persuade her to buy herself any decent clothes. But she's got this feeling that you *ought* to be perpetually working yourself up into a stew about lack of money. Just working up an atmosphere of misery from a sense of duty. I'm not like that. I've got more the prole's attitude towards money. Life's here to be lived, and if we're going to be in the soup next week—well, next week is a long way off. What really shocks her is the fact that I refuse to worry. She's always going for me about it. "But, George! You don't seem to *realize!* We've simply got no money at all! It's very *serious!*" She loves getting into a panic because something or other is "serious." And of late she's got that trick, when she's glooming about something, of kind of hunching her shoulders and folding her arms across her breast. If you made a list of Hilda's remarks throughout the day, you'd find three bracketed together at the top—"We can't afford it," "It's a great saving" and "I don't know where the money's to come from." She does everything for negative reasons. When she makes a cake she's not thinking about the cake, only about how to save butter and eggs. When I'm in bed with her all she thinks about is how not to have a baby. If she goes to the pictures she's all the time writhing with indignation about the price of the seats. Her methods of housekeeping, with all the emphasis on "using things up" and "making things do," would have

given Mother convulsions. On the other hand, Hilda isn't in the least a snob. She's never looked down on me because I'm not a gentleman. On the contrary, from her point of view I'm much too lordly in my habits. We never have a meal in a teashop without a frightful row in whispers because I'm tipping the waitress too much. And it's a curious thing that in the last few years she's become much more definitely lower-middle-class, in outlook and even in appearance, than I am. Of course all this "saving" business has never led to anything. It never does. We live just about as well or as badly as the other people in Ellesmere Road. But the everlasting stew about the gas bill and the milk bill and the awful price of butter and the kids' boots and school fees goes on and on. It's a kind of game with Hilda.

We moved to West Bletchley in '29 and started buying the house in Ellesmere Road the next year, a little before Billy was born. After I was made an Inspector I was more away from home and had more opportunities with other women. Of course I was unfaithful—I won't say all the time, but as often as I got the chance. Curiously enough, Hilda was jealous. In a way, considering how little that kind of thing means to her, I wouldn't have expected her to mind. And like all jealous women she'll sometimes show a cunning you wouldn't think her capable of. Sometimes the way she's caught me out would have made me believe in telepathy, if it wasn't that she's often been equally suspicious when I didn't happen to be guilty. I'm more or less permanently under suspicion, though, God knows, in the last few years—the last five years, anyway—I've been innocent enough. You have to be, when you're as fat as I am.

Taking it by and large, I suppose Hilda and I don't get on worse than about half the couples in Ellesmere Road. There've been times when I've thought of separation or divorce, but in our walk of life you don't do those things. You can't afford to. And then time goes on, and you kind of give up struggling. When you've lived with a woman for fifteen years, it's difficult to imagine life without her. She's part of the order of things. I dare say you might find things to object to in the sun and the moon, but do you really want to change them? Besides, there were the kids. Kids are a "link," as they say. Or a "tie." Not to say a ball and fetter.

Of late years Hilda has made two great

friends called Mrs. Wheeler and Miss Minns. Mrs. Wheeler is a widow, and I gather she's got very bitter ideas about the male sex. I can feel her kind of quivering with disapproval if I so much as come into the room. She's a faded little woman and gives you a curious impression that she's the same colour all over, a kind of greyish dust-colour, but she's full of energy. She's a bad influence on Hilda, because she's got the same passion for "saving" and "making things do," though in a slightly different form. With her it takes the form of thinking that you can have a good time without paying for it. She's for ever nosing out bargains and amusements that don't cost money. With people like that it doesn't matter a damn whether they want a thing or not, it's merely a question of whether they can get it on the cheap. When the big shops have their remnant sales Mrs. Wheeler's always at the head of the queue, and it's her greatest pride, after a day's hard fighting round the counter, to come out without having bought anything. Miss Minns is quite a different sort. She's really a sad case, poor Miss Minns. She's a tall thin woman of about thirty-eight, with black patent-leather hair and a very *good*, trusting kind of face. She lives on some kind of tiny fixed income, an annuity or something, and I fancy she's a left-over from the old society of West Bletchley, when it was a little country town, before the suburb grew up. It's written all over her that her father was a clergyman and sat on her pretty heavily while he lived. They're a special by-product of the middle classes, these women who turn into withered hags before they even manage to escape from home. Poor old Miss Minns, for all her wrinkles, still looks exactly like a child. It's still a tremendous adventure to her not to go to church. She's always burbling about "modern progress" and "the woman's movement," and she's got a vague yearning to do something she calls "developing her mind," only she doesn't quite know how to start. I think in the beginning she cottoned on to Hilda and Mrs. Wheeler out of pure loneliness, but now they take her with them wherever they go.

And the times they've had together, those three! Sometimes I've almost envied them. Mrs. Wheeler is the leading spirit. You couldn't name a kind of idiocy that she hasn't dragged them into at one time or another. Anything from theosophy to cat's-cradle, provided you can do it on the cheap. For months they went on for the food-crank business. Mrs. Wheeler had picked up a second-hand copy of some book called *Radiant Energy* which proved that you should live on lettuces and other things that don't cost money. Of course this appealed to Hilda, who immediately began starving herself. She'd have tried it on me and the kids as well, only I put my foot down. Then they had a go at faith-healing. Then they thought of tackling Pelmanism, but after a lot of correspondence they found that they couldn't get the booklets free, which had been Mrs. Wheeler's idea. Then it was hay-box cookery. Then it was some filthy stuff called bee wine, which was supposed to cost nothing at all because you made it out of water. They dropped that after they'd read an article in the paper saying that bee wine gives you cancer. Then they nearly joined one of those women's clubs which go for conducted tours round factories, but after a lot of arithmetic Mrs. Wheeler decided that the free teas the factories gave you didn't quite equal the subscription. Then Mrs. Wheeler scraped acquaintance with somebody who gave away free tickets for plays produced by some stage society or other. I've known the three of them sit for hours listening to some highbrow play of which they didn't even pretend to understand a word —couldn't even tell you the name of the play afterwards—but they felt that they were getting something for nothing. Once they even took up spiritualism. Mrs. Wheeler had run across some down-and-out medium who was so desperate that he'd give séances for eighteen pence, so that the three of them could have a glimpse beyond the veil for a tanner a time. I saw him once when he came to give a séance at our house. He was a seedy-looking old devil and obviously in mortal terror of D.T.s. He was so shaky that when he was taking his overcoat off in the hall he had a sort of spasm and a hank of butter-muslin dropped out of his trouser-leg. I managed to shove it back to him before the women saw. Butter-muslin is what they make the ectoplasm with, so I'm told. I suppose he was going on to another séance afterwards. You don't get manifestations for eighteen pence. Mrs. Wheeler's biggest find of the last few years is the Left Book Club. I think it was in '36 that the news of the Left Book Club got to West Bletchley. I joined it soon afterwards, and it's almost the only time I can remember spending money without Hilda protesting. She can see some sense in buying a book when you're getting it for a third of its proper price. These women's attitude is curious, really. Miss Minns certainly had a try at reading one or two of the books, but this wouldn't even have occurred to the other two. They've never had any direct connection with the Left Book Club or any notion what it's all about—in fact I believe at the beginning Mrs. Wheeler thought it had something to do with books which had been left in railway carriages and were being sold off cheap. But they do know that it means seven and sixpenny books for half a crown, and so they're always saying that it's "such a good idea." Now and again the local Left Book Club branch holds meetings and gets people down to speak, and Mrs. Wheeler always takes the others along. She's a great one for public meetings of any kind, always provided that it's indoors and admission free. The three of them sit there like lumps of pudding. They don't know what the meeting's about and they don't care, but they've got a vague feeling, especially Miss Minns, that they're improving their minds, and it isn't costing them anything.

Well, that's Hilda. You see what she's like. Take it by and large, I suppose she's no worse than I am. Sometimes when we were first married I felt I'd like to strangle her, but later I got so that I didn't care. And then I got fat and settled down. It must have been in 1930 that I got fat. It happened so suddenly that it was as if a cannon ball had hit me and got stuck inside. You know how it is. One night you go to bed, still feeling more or less young, with an eye for the girls and so forth, and next morning you wake up in the full consciousness that you're just a poor old fatty with nothing ahead of you this side the grave except sweating your guts out to buy boots for the kids.

## Robert Herrick
## UPON JULIA'S CLOTHES

Whenas in silks my Julia goes,
Then, then (me thinks) how sweetly flows
The liquefaction of her clothes.

Next, when I cast mine eyes and see
That brave vibration, each way free,
O how that glittering taketh me!

## William Wordsworth
## VAUDRACOUR IN LOVE

                He beheld
A vision, and adored the thing he saw.
Arabian fiction never filled the world
With half the wonders that were wrought for him.
Earth breathed in one great presence of the spring;
Life turned the meanest of her implements,
Before his eyes, to price above all gold;
The house she dwelt in was a sainted shrine;
Her chamber-window did surpass in glory
The portals of the dawn; all Paradise      10
Could, by the simple opening of a door,
Let itself in upon him:—pathways, walks,
Swarmed with enchantment, till his spirit sank,
Surcharged, within him, overblest to move
Beneath a sun that wakes a weary world
To its dull round of ordinary cares;
A man too happy for mortality!

## Edmund Waller
## GO, LOVELY ROSE

  Go, lovely rose,
Tell her that wastes her time and me,
  That now she knows,
When I resemble her to thee,
  How sweet and fair she seems to be.

  Tell her that's young,
And shuns to have her graces spied,
  That hadst thou sprung
In deserts, where no men abide,
  Thou must have uncommended died.    10

  Small is the worth
Of beauty from the light retired;
  Bid her come forth,
Suffer her self to be desired,
  And not blush so to be admired.

Then die, that she,
The common fate of all things rare,
  May read in thee;
How small a part of time they share,
  That are so wondrous sweet and fair.    20

## Andrew Marvell
# TO HIS COY MISTRESS

Had we but world enough, and time,
This coyness, Lady, were no crime.
We would sit down and think which way
To walk, and pass our long love's day.
Thou by the Indian Ganges' side
Shouldst rubies find; I by the tide
Of Humber [5] would complain. I would
Love you ten years before the Flood,
And you should, if you please, refuse
Till the conversion of the Jews.    10
My vegetable love should grow
Vaster than empires and more slow;
An hundred years should go to praise
Thine eyes and on thy forehead gaze;
Two hundred to adore each breast,
But thirty thousand to the rest;
An age at least to every part,
And the last age should show your heart.
For, Lady, you deserve this state,
Nor would I love at lower rate.    20
  But at my back I always hear
Time's wingèd chariot hurrying near;
And yonder all before us lie
Deserts of vast eternity.
Thy beauty shall no more be found,
Nor, in thy marble vault, shall sound
My echoing song; then worms shall try
That long-preserved virginity,
And your quaint honor turn to dust,
And into ashes all my lust:    30
The grave's a fine and private place,
But none, I think, do there embrace.
  Now therefore, while the youthful hue
Sits on thy skin like morning dew,
And while thy willing soul transpires
At every pore with instant fires,
Now let us sport us while we may,
And now, like amorous birds of prey,

---

[5] A river in eastern England.

Rather at once our time devour
Than languish in his slow-chapped power.[6]    40
Let us roll all our strength and all
Our sweetness up into one ball,
And tear our pleasures with rough strife
Thorough the iron gates of life;
Thus, though we cannot make our sun
Stand still, yet we will make him run.

---

[6] i.e., the power of his slow-moving jaws.

## Matthew Arnold
# DOVER BEACH

The sea is calm to-night.
The tide is full, the moon lies fair
Upon the straits;—on the French coast the light
Gleams and is gone; the cliffs of England stand,
Glimmering and vast, out in the tranquil bay.
Come to the window, sweet is the night-air!
Only, from the long line of spray
Where the sea meets the moon-blanched land,
Listen! you hear the grating roar
Of pebbles which the waves draw back, and
  fling,    10
At their return, up the high strand,
Begin, and cease, and then again begin,
With tremulous cadence slow, and bring
The eternal note of sadness in.

Sophocles long ago
Heard it on the Ægean, and it brought
Into his mind the turbid ebb and flow
Of human misery; we
Find also in the sound a thought,
Hearing it by this distant northern sea.    20

The Sea of Faith
Was once, too, at the full, and round earth's shore
Lay like the folds of a bright girdle furled.
But now I only hear
Its melancholy, long, withdrawing roar,
Retreating, to the breath
Of the night-wind, down the vast edges drear
And naked shingles [7] of the world.

Ah, love, let us be true
To one another! for the world, which seems    30
To lie before us like a land of dreams,

---

[7] A beach strewn with gravel.

So various, so beautiful, so new,
Hath really neither joy, nor love, nor light,
Nor certitude, nor peace, nor help for pain;
And we are here as on a darkling plain
Swept with confused alarms of struggle and flight,
Where ignorant armies clash by night.


## W. H. Auden
## AS I WALKED OUT ONE EVENING

As I walked out one evening,
    Walking down Bristol Street,
The crowds upon the pavement
    Were fields of harvest wheat.

And down by the brimming river
    I heard a lover sing
Under an arch of the railway:
    "Love has no ending.

I'll love you, dear, I'll love you
    Till China and Africa meet          10
And the river jumps over the mountain
    And the salmon sing in the street.

I'll love you till the ocean
    Is folded and hung up to dry
And the seven stars go squawking
    Like geese about the sky.

The years shall run like rabbits
    For in my arms I hold
The Flower of the Ages
    And the first love of the world."      20

But all the clocks in the city
    Began to whirr and chime:
"O let not Time deceive you,
    You cannot conquer Time.

In the burrows of the Nightmare
    Where Justice naked is,
Time watches from the shadow
    And coughs when you would kiss.

In headaches and in worry
    Vaguely life leaks away,              30
And Time will have his fancy
    To-morrow or to-day.

Into many a green valley
    Drifts the appalling snow;
Time breaks the threaded dances
    And the diver's brilliant bow.

O plunge your hands in water,
    Plunge them in up to the wrist;
Stare, stare in the basin
    And wonder what you've missed.         40

The glacier knocks in the cupboard,
    The desert sighs in the bed,
And the crack in the tea-cup opens
    A lane to the land of the dead.

Where the beggars raffle the banknotes
    And the Giant is enchanting to Jack,
And the Lily-white Boy is a Roarer
    And Jill goes down on her back.

O look, look in the mirror,
    O look in your distress;              50
Life remains a blessing
    Although you cannot bless.

O stand, stand at the window
    As the tears scald and start;
You shall love your crooked neighbour
    With your crooked heart."

It was late, late in the evening,
    The lovers they were gone;
The clocks had ceased their chiming
    And the deep river ran on.            60

## William Shakespeare
## SONNET 29

When, in disgrace with fortune and men's eyes,
I all alone beweep my outcast state,
And trouble deaf heaven with my bootless cries,
And look upon myself, and curse my fate,
Wishing me like to one more rich in hope,
Featured like him, like him with friends possessed,

Desiring this man's art and that man's scope,
With what I most enjoy contented least;
Yet in these thoughts myself almost despising,
Haply I think on thee, and then my state,          10
Like to the lark at break of day arising
From sullen earth, sings hymns at heaven's gate;
   For thy sweet love remembered such wealth
     brings
   That then I scorn to change my state with kings.

## SONNET 73

That time of year thou may'st in me behold
When yellow leaves, or none, or few, do hang
Upon those boughs which shake against the cold,
Bare ruined choirs, where late the sweet birds sang.
In me thou see'st the twilight of such day
As after sunset fadeth in the west,
Which by and by black night doth take away,
Death's second self, that seals up all in rest.
In me thou see'st the glowing of such fire,
That on the ashes of his youth doth lie,          10
As the death-bed whereon it must expire,
Consumed with that which it was nourished by.
   This thou perceiv'st, which makes thy love more
     strong
   To love that well which thou must leave ere
     long.

## SONNET 116

Let me not to the marriage of true minds
Admit impediments. Love is not love
Which alters when it alteration finds,
Or bends with the remover to remove:
O, no! it is an ever-fixèd mark,
That looks on tempests and is never shaken;
It is the star to every wandering bark,
Whose worth's unknown, although his height be
   taken.
Love's not Time's fool, though rosy lips and cheeks
Within his bending sickle's compass come;          10
Love alters not with his brief hours and weeks,
But bears it out even to the edge of doom.
   If this be error and upon me proved,
   I never writ, nor no man ever loved.

## SONNET 129

The expense of spirit in a waste of shame
Is lust in action; and till action, lust
Is perjured, murderous, bloody, full of blame,
Savage, extreme, rude, cruel, not to trust;
Enjoyed no sooner but despisèd straight;
Past reason hunted; and no sooner had,
Past reason hated, as a swallowed bait
On purpose laid to make the taker mad:
Mad in pursuit, and in possession so;
Had, having, and in quest to have, extreme;          10
A bliss in proof,—and proved, a very woe;
Before, a joy proposed; behind, a dream.
   All this the world well knows; yet none knows
     well
   To shun the heaven that leads men to this hell.

## *John Donne*

# A VALEDICTION: FORBIDDING MOURNING

As virtuous men pass mildly away,
   And whisper to their souls, to go,
Whilst some of their sad friends do say,
   The breath goes now, and some say, no:

So let us melt, and make no noise,
   No tear-floods, nor sigh-tempests move;
'Twere profanation of our joys
   To tell the laity our love.

Moving of th' earth brings harms and fears,
   Men reckon what it did and meant,          10
But trepidation of the spheres,
   Though greater far, is innocent.

Dull sublunary lovers' love
   (Whose soul is sense) cannot admit
Absence, because it doth remove
   Those things which elemented it.

But we by a love so much refined
   That our selves know not what it is,
Inter-assurèd of the mind,
   Care less, eyes, lips, and hands to miss.          20

Our two souls therefore, which are one,
   Though I must go, endure not yet
A breach, but an expansion,
   Like gold to airy thinness beat.

If they be two, they are two so
   As stiff twin compasses are two;
Thy soul, the fixed foot, makes no show
   To move, but doth, if th' other do.

And though it in the center sit,
   Yet when the other far doth roam,    30
It leans, and hearkens after it,
   And grows erect, as that comes home.

Such wilt thou be to me, who must
   Like th' other foot, obliquely run;
Thy firmness makes my circle just,
   And makes me end, where I begun.


### George Gordon, Lord Byron
# JUAN AND HAIDÉE

It was the cooling hour, just when the rounded
   Red sun sinks down behind the azure hill,
Which then seems as if the whole earth it bounded,
   Circling all nature, hushed, and dim, and still,
With the far mountain-crescent half surrounded
   On one side, and the deep sea calm and chill,
Upon the other, and the rosy sky,
With one star sparkling through it like an eye.

And thus they wandered forth, and hand in hand,
   Over the shining pebbles and the shells,    10
Glided along the smooth and hardened sand,
   And in the worn and wild receptacles
Worked by the storms, yet worked as it were
     planned,
   In hollow halls, with sparry roofs and cells,
They turned to rest; and, each clasped by an arm,
Yielded to the deep twilight's purple charm.

They looked up to the sky, whose floating glow
   Spread like a rosy ocean, vast and bright;
They gazed upon the glittering sea below,
   Whence the broad moon rose circling into
     sight;    20
They heard the waves splash, and the wind so low,
  And saw each other's dark eyes darting light

Into each other—and, beholding this,
   Their lips drew near, and clung into a kiss;

A long, long kiss, a kiss of youth, and love,
   And beauty, all concentrating like rays
Into one focus, kindled from above;
   Such kisses as belong to early days,
Where heart, and soul, and sense, in concert move,
   And the blood's lava, and the pulse a blaze,    30
Each kiss a heart-quake,—for a kiss's strength,
I think it must be reckoned by its length.

By length I mean duration; theirs endured
   Heaven knows how long—no doubt they never
     reckoned;
And if they had, they could not have secured
   The sum of their sensations to a second:
They had not spoken; but they felt allured,
   As if their souls and lips each other beckoned,
Which, being joined, like swarming bees they
     clung—
Their hearts the flowers from whence the honey
     sprung.    40

They were alone, but not alone as they
   Who shut in chambers think it loneliness;
The silent ocean, and the starlight bay,
   The twilight glow, which momently grew less,
The voiceless sands, and dropping caves, that lay
   Around them, made them to each other press,
As if there were no life beneath the sky
Save theirs, and that their life could never die.

They feared no eyes nor ears on that lone beach,
   They felt no terrors from the night; they
     were    50
All in all to each other; though their speech
   Was broken words, they *thought* a language
     there,—
And all the burning tongues the passions teach
   Found in one sigh the best interpreter
Of nature's oracle—first love,—that all
Which Eve has left her daughters since her fall.

Haidée spoke not of scruples, asked no vows,
   Nor offered any; she had never heard
Of plight and promises to be a spouse,
   Or perils by a loving maid incurred;    60
She was all which pure ignorance allows,
   And flew to her young mate like a young bird,
And never having dreamt of falsehood, she
Had not one word to say of constancy.

She loved, and was belovèd—she adored,
  And she was worshipped; after nature's fashion,
Their intense souls, into each other poured,
  If souls could die, had perished in that passion,—
But by degrees their senses were restored,
  Again to be o'ercome, again to dash on;        70
And, beating 'gainst *his* bosom, Haidée's heart
Felt as if never more to beat apart.

Alas! they were so young, so beautiful,
  So lonely, loving, helpless, and the hour
Was that in which the heart is always full,
  And, having o'er itself no further power,
Prompts deeds eternity cannot annul,
  But pays off moments in an endless shower,
Of hell-fire—all prepared for people giving
Pleasure or pain to one another living.          80

Alas! for Juan and Haidée! they were
  So loving and so lovely—till then never,
Excepting our first parents, such a pair
  Had run the risk of being damned for ever;
And Haidée, being devout as well as fair,
  Had, doubtless, heard about the Stygian river.[8]
And hell and purgatory—but forgot
Just in the very crisis she should not.

They look upon each other; and their eyes
  Gleam in the moonlight; and her white arm
    clasps                                        90
Round Juan's head, and his around her lies
  Half buried in the tresses which it grasps;
She sits upon his knee, and drinks his sighs,
  He hers, until they end in broken gasps;
And thus they form a group that's quite antique,
Half naked, loving, natural, and Greek.[9]

And when those deep and burning moments
    passed,
  And Juan sunk to sleep within her arms,
She slept not, but all tenderly, though fast,
  Sustained his head upon her bosom's charms;
And now and then her eye to heaven is cast,       100
  And then on the pale cheek her breast now
    warms,
Pillowed on her o'erflowing heart, which pants
With all it granted, and with all it grants.

An infant when it gazes on a light,
  A child the moment when it drains the breast,

A devotee when soars the Host in sight,
  An Arab with a stranger for a guest,
A sailor when a prize has been struck in fight,
  A miser filling his most hoarded chest,        110
Feel rapture; but not such true joy are reaping
As they who watch o'er what they love while
    sleeping.

For there it lies so tranquil, so beloved,
  All that it hath of life with us is living;
So gentle, stirless, helpless, and unmoved,
  And all unconscious of the joy 'tis giving;
All it hath felt, inflicted, passed, and proved,
  Hushed into depths beyond the watcher's
    diving;
There lies the thing we love with all its errors
And all its charms, like death without its
    terrors.                                      120

The lady watched o'er her lover—and that hour
  Of Love's, and Night's, and Ocean's solitude,
O'erflowed her soul with their united power;
  Amidst the barren sand and rocks so rude
She and her wave-born love had made their bower,
  Where nought upon their passion could intrude,
And all the stars that crowded the blue space
Saw nothing happier than her glowing face.

Alas! the love of women! it is known
  To be a lovely and a fearful thing;            130
For all of theirs upon that die is thrown,
  And if 'tis lost, life hath no more to bring
To them but mockeries of the past alone,
  And their revenge is as the tiger's spring,
Deadly, and quick, and crushing; yet, as real
Torture is theirs, what they inflict they feel.

They are right; for man to man so oft unjust,
  Is always so to women; one sole bond
Awaits them, treachery is all their trust;
  Taught to conceal, their bursting hearts despond
Over their idol, till some wealthier lust        140
  Buys them in marriage—and what rests beyond?
A thankless husband, next a faithless lover,
Then dressing, nursing, praying, and all's over.

Some take a lover, some take drams or prayers,
  Some mind their household, others dissipation,
Some run away, and but exchange their cares,
  Losing the advantage of a virtuous station;
Few changes e'er can better their affairs,
  Theirs being an unnatural situation,           150
From the dull palace to the dirty hovel:
Some play the devil, and then write a novel.

[8] The Styx, the boundary of the Lower World.
[9] The setting is one of the smaller Cyclades, a group of islands in the Ægean Sea.

Haidée was Nature's bride, and knew not this:
  Haidée was Passion's child, born where the sun
Showers triple light, and scorches even the kiss
  Of his gazelle-eyed daughters; she was one
Made but to love, to feel that she was his
  Who was her chosen: what was said or done
Elsewhere was nothing. She had nought to fear,
Hope, care, nor love beyond,—her heart beat
    *here*.                                                    160

And oh! that quickening of the heart, that beat!
  How much it costs us! yet each rising throb
Is in its cause as its effect so sweet,
  That Wisdom, ever on the watch to rob
Joy of its alchemy, and to repeat
  Fine truths; even Conscience, too, has a tough
    job
To make us understand each good old maxim,
So good—I wonder Castlereagh [10] don't tax 'em.

And now 'twas done—on the lone shore were
    plighted
  Their hearts; the stars, their nuptial torches,
    shed                                                    170
Beauty upon the beautiful they lighted:
  Ocean their witness, and the cave their bed,
By their own feelings hallowed and united,
  Their priest was Solitude, and they were wed:
And they were happy—for to their young eyes
Each was an angel, and earth Paradise.

---

[10] Leader of the House of Commons who in 1816
tried to tax incomes.

*Geoffrey Chaucer*

# PROLOGUE TO THE WIFE OF BATH'S TALE

"Experience, though all authority
Was lacking in the world, confers on me
The right to speak of marriage, and unfold
Its woes. For, lords, since I was twelve years old
—Thanks to eternal God in heaven alive—

---

PROLOGUE TO THE WIFE OF BATH'S TALE: From
*The Portable Chaucer,* modernized by Theodore Morrison. Copyright, 1949, by Theodore Morrison. Reprinted by permission of The Viking Press, Inc., New York.

I have married at church door no less than five
Husbands, provided that I can have been
So often wed, and all were worthy men.
But I was told, indeed, and not long since,
That Christ went to a wedding only once          10
At Cana, in the land of Galilee.
By this example he instructed me
To wed once only—that's what I have heard!
Again, consider now what a sharp word,
Beside a well, Jesus, both God and man,
Spoke in reproving the Samaritan:
'Thou hast had five husbands'—this for a certainty
He said to her—'and the man that now hath thee
Is not thy husband.' True, he spoke this way,
But what he meant is more than I can say          20
Except that I would ask why the fifth man
Was not a husband to the Samaritan?
To just how many could she be a wife?
I have never heard this number all my life
Determined up to now. For round and round
Scholars may gloze, interpret, and expound,
But plainly, this I know without a lie,
God told us to increase and multiply.
That noble text I can well understand.
My husband—this too I have well in hand—          30
Should leave both father and mother and cleave
    to me.
Number God never mentioned, bigamy,
No, nor even octogamy; why do men
Talk of it as a sin and scandal, then?
  "Think of that monarch, wise King Solomon.
It strikes me that *he* had more wives than one!
To be refreshed, God willing, would please me
If I got it half as many times as he!
What a gift he had, a gift of God's own giving,
For all his wives! There isn't a man now living 40
Who has the like. By all that I make out
This king had many a merry first-night bout
With each, he was so thoroughly alive.
Blessed be God that I have married five,
And always, for the money in his chest
And for his nether purse, I picked the best.
In divers schools ripe scholarship is made,
And various practice in all kinds of trade
Makes perfect workmen, as the world can see.
Five husbands have had turns at schooling me. 50
Welcome the sixth, whenever I am faced
With yet another. I don't mean to be chaste
At all costs. When a spouse of mine is gone,
Some other Christian man shall take me on,
For then, says the Apostle, I'll be free
To wed, in God's name, where it pleases me.
To marry is no sin, as we can learn

From him; better to marry than to burn,
He says. Why should I care what obloquy
Men heap on Lamech [11] and his bigamy?      60
Abraham was, by all that I can tell,
A holy man; so Jacob was as well,
And each of them took more than two as brides,
And many another holy man besides.
Where, may I ask, in any period,
Can you show in plain words that Almighty God
Forbade us marriage? Point it out to me!
Or where did he command virginity?
The Apostle, when he speaks of maidenhood,
Lays down no law. This I have understood      70
As well as you, milords, for it is plain.
Men may advise a woman to abstain
From marriage, but mere counsels aren't commands.
He left it to our judgment, where it stands.
Had God enjoined us all to maidenhood
Then marriage would have been condemned for good.
But truth is, if no seed were ever sown,
In what soil could virginity be grown?
Paul did not dare command a thing at best
On which his Master left us no behest.      80
   "But now the prize goes to virginity.
Seize it whoever can, and let us see
What manner of man shall run best in the race!
But not all men receive this form of grace
Except where God bestows it by his will.
The Apostle was a maid, I know; but still,
Although he wished all men were such as he,
It was only *counsel* toward virginity.
To be a wife he gave me his permission,
And so it is no blot on my condition      90
Nor slander of bigamy upon my state
If when my husband dies I take a mate.
A man does virtuously, St. Paul has said,
To touch no woman—meaning in his bed.
For fire and fat are dangerous friends at best.
You know what this example should suggest.
Here is the nub: he held virginity
Superior to wedded frailty,
And frailty I call it unless man
And woman both are chaste for their whole span.      100
   "I am not jealous if maidenhood outweighs
My marriages; I grant it all the praise.
It pleases them, these virgins, flesh and soul
To be immaculate. I won't extol

---

[11] First man to marry more than one wife; cf. Genesis 4:19.

My own condition. In a lord's household
You know that every vessel can't be gold.
Some are of wood, and serve their master still.
God calls us variously to do his will.
Each has his proper gift, of all who live,
Some this, some that, as it pleases God to give.      110
   "To be virgin is a high and perfect course,
And continence is holy. But the source
Of all perfection, Jesus, never bade
Each one of us to go sell all he had
And give it to the poor; he did not say
That all should follow him in this one way.
He spoke to those who would live perfectly,
And by your leave, lords, that is not for me!
The flower of my best years I find it suits
To spend on the acts of marriage and its fruits. . . .      120
   "Now, sirs, I will get onward with my tale.
If ever I hope to drink good wine or ale,
I'm speaking truth: the husbands I have had,
Three of them have been good, and two were bad.
The three were kindly men, and rich, and old.
But they were hardly able to uphold
The statute which had made them fast to me.
You know well what I mean by this, I see!
So help me God, I can't help laughing yet
When I think of how at night I made them sweat,      130
And I thought nothing of it, on my word!
Their land and wealth they had by then conferred
On me, and so I safely could neglect
Tending their love or showing them respect.
So well they loved me that by God above
I hardly set a value on their love.
A woman who is wise is never done
Busily winning love when she has none,
But since I had them wholly in my hand
And they had given me their wealth and land,      140
Why task myself to spoil them or to please
Unless for my own profit and my ease?
I set them working so that many a night
They sang a dirge, so grievous was their plight!
They never got the bacon, well I know,
Offered as prize to couples at Dunmow
Who live a year in peace, without repentance!
So well I ruled them, by my law and sentence,
They were glad to bring me fine things from the fair
And happy when I spoke with a mild air,      150
For God knows I could chide outrageously.
   "Now judge if I could do it properly!
You wives who understand and who are wise,

This is the way to throw dust in their eyes.
There isn't on the earth so bold a man
He can swear false or lie as a woman can.
I do not urge this course in every case,
Just when a prudent wife is caught off base;
Then she should swear the parrot's mad who
    tattled
Her indiscretions, and when she's once
    embattled                                                     160
Should call her maid as witness, by collusion.
But listen, how I threw them in confusion:
    " 'Sir dotard, this is how you live?' I'd say.
'How can my neighbor's wife be dressed so gay?
She carries off the honors everywhere.
I sit at home. I've nothing fit to wear.
What were you doing at my neighbor's house?
Is she so handsome? Are you so amorous?
What do you whisper to our maid? God bless me,
Give up your jokes, old lecher. They depress
    me.                                                           170
When I have a harmless friend myself, you balk
And scold me like a devil if I walk
For innocent amusement to his house.
You drink and come home reeling like a souse
And sit down on your bench, worse luck, and
    preach.
Taking a wife who's poor—this is the speech
That you regale me with—costs grievously,
And if she's rich and of good family,
It is a constant torment, you decide,
To suffer her ill humor and her pride.                            180
And if she's fair, you scoundrel, you destroy her
By saying that every lecher will enjoy her;
For chastity at best has frail protections
If a woman is assailed from all directions.
    " 'Some want us for our wealth, so you declare,
Some for our figure, some think we are fair,
Some want a woman who can dance or sing,
Some want kindness, and some philandering,
Some look for hands and arms well turned and
    small.
Thus, by your tale, the devil may take us all!    190
Men cannot keep a castle or redoubt
Longer, you tell me, than it can hold out.
Or if a woman's plain, you say that she
Is one who covets each man she may see,
For at him like a spaniel she will fly
Until she finds some man that she can buy.
Down to the lake goes never a goose so gray
But it will have a mate, I've heard you say.
It's hard to fasten—this too I've been told—
A thing that no man willingly will hold.           200
Wise men, you tell me as you go to bed,

And those who hope for heaven should never
    wed.
I hope wild lightning and a thunderstroke
Will break your wizened neck! You say that smoke
And falling timbers and a railing wife
Drive a man from his house. Lord bless my life!
What ails an old man, so to make him chide?
We cover our vices till the knot is tied,
We wives, you say, and then we trot them out.
Here's a fit proverb for a doddering lout!          210
An ox or ass, you say, a hound or horse,
These we examine as a matter of course.
Basins and also bowls, before we buy them,
Spoons, spools, and such utensils, first we try them,
And so with pots and clothes, beyond denial;
But of their wives men never make a trial
Until they are married. After that, you say,
Old fool, we put our vices on display.
    " 'I am in a pique if you forget your duty
And fail, you tell me, to praise me for my
    beauty,                                                       220
Or unless you are always doting on my face
And calling me "fair dame" in every place,
Or unless you give a feast on my birthday
To keep me in good spirits, fresh and gay,
Or unless all proper courtesies are paid
To my nurse and also to my chambermaid,
And my father's kin with all their family ties—
You say so, you old barrelful of lies!
    " 'Yet just because he has a head of hair
Like shining gold, and squires me everywhere,  230
You have a false suspicion in your heart
Of Jenkin, our apprentice. For my part
I wouldn't have him if you died tomorrow!
But tell me this, or go and live in sorrow:
That chest of yours, why do you hide the keys
Away from me? It's my wealth, if you please,
As much as yours. Will you make a fool of me,
The mistress of our house? You shall not be
Lord of my body and my wealth at once!
No, by St. James himself, you must renounce  240
One or the other, if it drives you mad!
Does it help to spy on me? You would be glad
To lock me up, I think, inside your chest.
"Enjoy yourself, and go where you think best,"
You ought to say; "I won't hear tales of malice.
I know you for a faithful wife, Dame Alice."
A woman loves no man who keeps close charge
Of where she goes. We want to be at large.
Blessed above all other men was he,
The wise astrologer, Don Ptolemy,                   250
Who has this proverb in his *Almagest*:
"Of all wise men his wisdom is the best

Who does not care who has the world in hand."
Now by this proverb you should understand,
Since you have plenty, it isn't yours to care
Or fret how richly other people fare,
For by your leave, old dotard, you for one
Can have all you can take when day is done.
The man's a niggard to the point of scandal
Who will not lend his lamp to light a candle;   260
His lamp won't lose although the candle gain.
If you have enough, you ought not to com-
     plain.
   " 'You say, too, if we make ourselves look
     smart,
Put on expensive clothes and dress the part,
We lay our virtue open to disgrace.
And then you try to reinforce your case
By saying these words in the Apostle's name:
"In chaste apparel, with modesty and shame,
So shall you women clothe yourselves," said he,
"And not in rich coiffure or jewelry,           270
Pearls or the like, or gold, or costly wear."
Now both your text and rubric, I declare,
I will not follow as I would a gnat!
   " 'You told me once that I was like a cat,
For singe her skin and she will stay at home,
But if her skin is smooth, the cat will roam.
No dawn but finds her on the neighbors calling
To show her skin, and go off caterwauling.
If I am looking smart, you mean to say,
I'm off to put my finery on display.           280
   " 'What do you gain, old fool, by setting spies?
Though you beg Argus with his hundred eyes
To be my bodyguard, for all his skill
He'll keep me only by my own free will.
I know enough to blind him, as I live!
   " 'There are three things, you also say, that give
Vexation to this world both south and north,
And you add that no one can endure the fourth.
Of these catastrophes a hateful wife—
You precious wretch, may Christ cut short your
     life!—                                     290
Is always reckoned, as you say, for one.
Is this your whole stock of comparison,
And why in all your parables of contempt
Can a luckless helpmate never be exempt?
You also liken woman's love to hell,
To barren land where water will not dwell.
I've heard you call it an unruly fire;
The more it burns, the hotter its desire
To burn up everything that burned will be.
You say that just as worms destroy a tree       300
A wife destroys her spouse, as they have found
Who get themselves in holy wedlock bound.'

"By these devices, lords, as you perceive,
I got my three old husbands to believe
That in their cups they said things of this sort,
And all of it was false; but for support
Jenkin bore witness, and my niece did too.
These innocents, Lord, what I put them through!
God's precious pains! And they had no recourse,
For I could bite and whinny like a horse.       310
Though in the wrong, I kept them well annoyed,
Or oftentimes I would have been destroyed!
First to the mill is first to grind his grain.
I was always the first one to complain,
And so our peace was made; they gladly bid
For terms to settle things they never did!
   "For wenching I would scold them out of hand
When they were hardly well enough to stand.
But this would tickle a man; it would restore him
To think I had so great a fondness for him!     320
I'd vow when darkness came and out I stepped,
It was to see the girls with whom he slept.
Under this pretext I had plenty of mirth!
Such wit as this is given us at our birth.
Lies, tears, and needlework the Lord will give
In kindness to us women while we live.
And thus in one point I can take just pride:
In the end I showed myself the stronger side.
By sleight or strength I kept them in restraint,
And chiefly by continual complaint.             330
In bed they met their grief in fullest measure.
There I would scold; I would not do their
     pleasure.
Bed was a place where I would not abide
If I felt my husband's arm across my side
Till he agreed to square accounts and pay,
And after that I'd let him have his way.
To every man, therefore, I tell this tale:
Win where you're able, all is up for sale.
No falcon by an empty hand is lured.
For victory their cravings I endured            340
And even feigned a show of appetite.
And yet in old meat I have no delight;
It made me always rail at them and chide them,
For though the pope himself sat down beside them
I would not give them peace at their own board.
No, on my honor, I paid them word for word.
Almighty God so help me, if right now
I had to make my last will, I can vow
For every word they said to me, we're quits.
For I so handled the contest of my wits         350
That they gave up, and took it for the best,
Or otherwise we should have had no rest.
Like a mad lion let my husband glare,
In the end he got the worst of the affair.

"Then I would say, 'My dear, you ought to keep
In mind how gentle Wilkin looks, our sheep.
Come here, my husband, let me kiss your cheek!
You should be patient, too; you should be meek.
Of Job and of his patience when you prate
*Your* conscience ought to show a cleaner slate. 360
He should be patient who so well can preach.
If not, then it will fall on me to teach
The beauty of a peaceful wedded life.
For one of us must give in, man or wife,
And since men are more reasonable creatures
Than women are, it follows that *your* features
Ought to exhibit patience. Why do you groan?
You want my body yours, and yours alone?
Why, take it all! Welcome to every bit!
But curse you, Peter, unless you cherish it!      370
Were I inclined to peddle my *belle chose,*
I could go about dressed freshly as a rose.
But I will keep it for your own sweet tooth.
It's your fault if we fight. By God, that's truth!'
    "This was the way I talked when I had need.
But now to my fourth husband I'll proceed.

    "This fourth I married was a roisterer.
He had a mistress, and my passions were,
Although I say it, strong; and altogether
I was young and stubborn, pert in every
        feather.                                  380
If anyone took up his harp to play,
How I could dance! I sang as merry a lay
As any nightingale when of sweet wine
I had drunk my draft. Metellius, the foul swine,
Who beat his spouse until he took her life
For drinking wine, had I only been his wife,
He'd never have frightened me away from drink-
        ing!
But after a drink, Venus gets in my thinking,
For just as true as cold engenders hail
A thirsty mouth goes with a thirsty tail.          390
Drinking destroys a woman's last defense
As lechers well know by experience.

    "But, Lord Christ, when it all comes back to me,
Remembering my youth and jollity,
It tickles me to the roots. It does me good
Down to this very day that while I could
I took my world, my time, and had my fling.
But age, alas, that poisons everything
Has robbed me of my beauty and my pith.
Well, let it go! Good-by! The devil with          400
What cannot last! There's only this to tell:
The flour is gone, I've only chaff to sell.
Yet I'll contrive to keep a merry cheek!
But now of my fourth husband I will speak.

"My heart was, I can tell you, full of spite
That in another he should find delight.
I paid him for this debt; I made it good.
I furnished him a cross of the same wood,
By God and by St. Joce—in no foul fashion,
Not with my flesh; but I put on such passion      410
And rendered him so jealous, I'll engage
I made him fry in his own grease for rage!
On earth, God knows, I was his purgatory;
I only hope his soul is now in glory.
God knows it was a sad song that he sung
When the shoe pinched him; sorely was he wrung!
Only he knew, and God, the devious system
By which outrageously I used to twist him.
He died when I came home from Jerusalem.
He is buried near the chancel, under the beam     420
That holds the cross. His tomb is less ornate
Than the sepulcher where Darius lies in state
And which the paintings of Appelles graced
With subtle work. It would have been a waste
To bury him lavishly. Farewell! God save
His soul and give him rest! He's in his grave.

    "And now of my fifth husband let me tell.
God never let his soul go down to hell
Though he of all five was my scourge and flail!
I feel it on my ribs, right down the scale,        430
And ever shall until my dying day.
And yet he was so full of life and gay
In bed, and could so melt me and cajole me
When on my back he had a mind to roll me,
What matter if on every bone he'd beaten me!
He'd have my love, so quickly he could sweeten
        me.
I loved him best, in fact; for as you see,
His love was a more arduous prize for me.
We women, if I'm not to tell a lie,
Are quaint in this regard. Put in our eye          440
A thing we cannot easily obtain,
All day we'll cry about it and complain.
Forbid a thing, we want it bitterly,
But urge it on us, then we turn and flee.
We are chary of what we hope that men will buy.
A throng at market makes the prices high;
Men set no value on cheap merchandise,
A truth all women know if they are wise.

    "My fifth, may God forgive his every sin,
I took for love, not money. He had been           450
An Oxford student once, but in our town
Was boarding with my good friend, Alison.
She knew each secret that I had to give
More than our parish priest did, as I live!
I told her my full mind, I shared it all.
For if my husband pissed against a wall

Or did a thing that might have cost his life,
To her, and to another neighbor's wife,
And to my niece, a girl whom I loved well,
His every thought I wouldn't blush to tell.      460
And often enough I told them, be it said.
God knows I made his face turn hot and red
For secrets he confided to his shame.
He knew he only had himself to blame.

  "And so it happened once that during Lent,
As I often did, to Alison's I went,
For I have loved my life long to be gay
And to walk out in April or in May
To hear the talk and seek a favorite haunt
Jenkin the student, Alice, my confidante,      470
And I myself into the country went.
My husband was in London all that Lent.
I had the greater liberty to see
And to be seen by jolly company.
How could I tell beforehand in what place
Luck might be waiting with a stroke of grace?
And so I went to every merrymaking.
No pilgrimage was past my undertaking.
I was at festivals, and marriages,
Processions, preachings, and at miracle plays,  480
And in my scarlet clothes I made a sight.
Upon that costume neither moth nor mite
Nor any worm with ravening hunger fell.
And why, you ask? It was kept in use too well.

  "Now for what happened. In the fields we
      walked,
The three of us, and gallantly we talked,
The student and I, until I told him he,
If I became a widow, should marry me.
For I can say, and not with empty pride,
I have never failed for marriage to provide      490
Or other things as well. Let mice be meek;
A mouse's heart I hold not worth a leek.
He has one hole to scurry to, just one,
And if that fails him, he is quite undone.

  "I let this student think he had bewitched me.
(My mother with this piece of guile enriched me!)
All night I dreamed of him—this too I said;
He was killing me as I lay flat in bed;
My very bed in fact was full of blood;
But still I hoped it would result in good,      500
For blood betokens gold, as I have heard.
It was a fiction, dream and every word,
But I was following my mother's lore
In all this matter, as in many more.

  "Sirs—let me see; what did I mean to say?
Aha! By God, I have it! When he lay,
My fourth, of whom I've spoken, on his bier,
I wept of course; I showed but little cheer,

As wives must do, since custom has its place,
And with my kerchief covered up my face.      510
But since I had provided for a mate,
I did not cry for long, I'll freely state.
And so to church my husband on the morrow
Was borne away by neighbors in their sorrow.
Jenkin, the student, was among the crowd,
And when I saw him walk, so help me God,
Behind the bier, I thought he had a pair
Of legs and feet so cleanly turned and fair
I put my heart completely in his hold.
He was in fact some twenty winters old      520
And I was forty, to confess the truth;
But all my life I've still had a colt's tooth.
My teeth were spaced apart; that was the seal
St. Venus printed, and became me well.
So help me God, I was a lusty one,
Pretty and young and rich, and full of fun.
And truly, as my husbands have all said,
I was the best thing there could be in bed.
For I belong to Venus in my feelings,
Though I bring the heart of Mars to all my
      dealings.                      530
From Venus come my lust and appetite,
From Mars I get my courage and my might,
Born under Taurus, while Mars stood therein.
Alas, alas, that ever love was sin!
I yielded to my every inclination
Through the predominance of my constellation;
This made me so I never could withhold
My chamber of Venus, if the truth be told,
From a good fellow; yet upon my face
Mars left his mark, and in another place.      540
For never, so may Christ grant me intercession,
Have I yet loved a fellow with discretion,
But always I have followed appetite,
Let him be long or short or dark or light.
I never cared, as long as he liked me,
What his rank was or how poor he might be.

  "What should I say, but when the month ran
      out,
This jolly student, always much about,
This Jenkin married me in solemn state.
To him I gave land, titles, the whole slate      550
Of goods that had been given me before;
But my repentance afterward was sore!
He wouldn't endure the pleasures I held dear.
By God, he gave me a lick once on the ear,
When from a book of his I tore a leaf,
So hard that from the blow my ear grew deaf.
I was stubborn as a lioness with young,
And by the truth I had a rattling tongue,
And I would visit, as I'd done before,

No matter what forbidding oath he swore.     560
Against this habit he would sit and preach me
Sermons enough, and he would try to teach
   me
Old Roman stories, how for his whole life
The man Sulpicius Gallus left his wife
Only because he saw her look one day
Bareheaded down the street from his doorway.
   "Another Roman he told me of by name
Who, since his wife was at a summer's game
Without his knowledge, thereupon forsook
The woman. In his Bible he would look     570
And find that proverb of the Ecclesiast
Where he enjoins and makes the stricture fast
That men forbid their wives to rove about.
Then he would quote me this, you needn't doubt:
'Build a foundation over sands or shallows,
Or gallop a blind horse across the fallows,
Let a wife traipse to shrines that some saint
   hallows,
And you are fit to swing upon the gallows.'
Talk as he would, I didn't care two haws
For his proverbs or his venerable saws.     580
Set right by him I never meant to be.
I hate the man who tells my faults to me,
And more of us than I do, by your pleasure.
This made him mad with me beyond all measure.
Under his yoke in no case would I go.
   "Now, by St. Thomas, I will let you know
Why from that book of his I tore a leaf,
For which I got the blow that made me deaf.
   "He had a book, *Valerius,* he called it,
*And Theophrastus,* and he always hauled it     590
From where it lay to read both day and night
And laughed hard at it, such was his delight.
There was another scholar, too, at Rome
A cardinal, whose name was St. Jerome;
He wrote a book against Jovinian.
In the same book also were Tertullian,
Chrysippus, Trotula, Abbess Héloïse
Who lived near Paris; it contained all these,
Bound in a single volume, and many a one
Besides; the Parables of Solomon     600
And Ovid's *Art of Love.* On such vacation
As he could snatch from worldly occupation
He dredged this book for tales of wicked wives.
He knew more stories of their wretched lives
Than are told about good women in the Bible.
No scholar ever lived who did not libel
Women, believe me; to speak well of wives
Is quite beyond them, unless it be in lives
Of holy saints; no woman else will do.
Who was it painted the lion, tell me who?     610

By God, if women had only written stories
Like wits and scholars in their oratories,
They would have pinned on men more wickedness
Than the whole breed of Adam can redress.
Venus's children clash with Mercury's;
The two work evermore by contraries.
Knowledge and wisdom are of Mercury's giving,
Venus loves revelry and riotous living,
And with these clashing dispositions gifted
Each of them sinks when the other is uplifted.     620
Thus Mercury falls, God knows, in desolation
In the sign of Pisces, Venus's exaltation,
And Venus falls when Mercury is raised.
Thus by a scholar no woman can be praised.
The scholar, when he's old and cannot do
The work of Venus more than his old shoe,
Then sits he down, and in his dotage fond
Writes that no woman keeps her marriage bond!
   "But now for the story that I undertook—
To tell how I was beaten for a book.     630
   "Jenkin, one night, who never seemed to tire
Of reading in his book, sat by the fire
And first he read of Eve, whose wickedness
Delivered all mankind to wretchedness
For which in his own person Christ was slain
Who with his heart's blood bought us all again.
'By this,' he said, 'expressly you may find
That woman was the loss of all mankind.'
   "He read me next how Samson lost his hair.
Sleeping, his mistress clipped it off for fair;     640
Through this betrayal he lost both his eyes.
He read me then—and I'm not telling lies—
How Deianeira, wife of Hercules,
Caused him to set himself on fire. With these
He did not overlook the sad to-do
Of Socrates with *his* wives—he had two.
Xantippe emptied the pisspot on his head.
This good man sat as patient as if dead.
He wiped his scalp; he did not dare complain
Except to say 'With thunder must come rain.'     650
   "Pasiphaë, who was the queen of Crete,
For wickedness he thought her story sweet.
Ugh! That's enough, it was a grisly thing,
About her lust and filthy hankering!
And Clytemnestra in her lechery
Who took her husband's life feloniously,
He grew devout in reading of her treason.
And then he told me also for what reason
Unhappy Amphiaraus lost his life.
My husband had the story of *his* wife,     660
Eriphyle, who for a clasp of gold
Went to his Grecian enemies and told
The secret of her husband's hiding place,

For which at Thebes he met an evil grace.
Livia and Lucilia, he went through
Their tale as well; they killed their husbands, too.
One killed for love, the other killed for hate.
At evening Livia, when the hour was late,
Poisoned her husband, for she was his foe.
Lucilia doted on her husband so                               670
That in her lust, hoping to make him think
Ever of her, she gave him a love-drink
Of such a sort he died before the morrow.
And so at all turns husbands come to sorrow!
    "He told me then how one Latumius,
Complaining to a friend named Arrius,
Told him that in his garden grew a tree
On which his wives had hanged themselves, all
    three,
Merely for spite against their partnership.
'Brother,' said Arrius, 'let me have a slip        680
From this miraculous tree, for, begging pardon,
I want to go and plant it in my garden.'
    "Then about wives in recent times he read,
How some had murdered husbands lying abed
And all night long had let a paramour
Enjoy them with the corpse flat on the floor;
Or driven a nail into a husband's brain
While he was sleeping, and thus he had been slain;
And some had given them poison in their drink.
He told more harm than anyone can think,       690
And seasoned his wretched stories with proverbs
Outnumbering all the blades of grass and
    herbs
On earth. 'Better a dragon for a mate,
Better,' he said, 'on a lion's whims to wait
Than on a wife whose way it is to chide.
Better,' he said, 'high in the loft to bide
Than with a railing wife down in the house.
They always, they are so contrarious,
Hate what their husbands like,' so he would say.
'A woman,' he said, 'throws all her shame
    away                                                              700
When she takes off her smock.' And on he'd go:
'A pretty woman, unless she's chaste also,
Is like a gold ring stuck in a sow's nose.'
Who could imagine, who would half suppose
The gall my heart drank, raging at each drop?
    "And when I saw that he would never stop
Reading all night from his accursed book,
Suddenly, in the midst of it, I took
Three leaves and tore them out in a great pique,
And with my fist I caught him on the cheek      710
So hard he tumbled backward in the fire.
And up he jumped, he was as mad for ire
As a mad lion, and caught me on the head

With such a blow I fell down as if dead.
And seeing me on the floor, how still I lay,
He was aghast, and would have fled away,
Till I came to at length, and gave a cry.
'Have you killed me for my lands? Before I die,
False thief,' I said, 'I'll give you a last kiss!'
    "He came to me and knelt down close at
    this,                                                              720
And said, 'So help me God, dear Alison,
I'll never strike you. For this thing I have
    done
You are to blame. Forgive me, I implore.'
So then I hit him on the cheek once more
And said, 'Thus far I am avenged, you thief.
I cannot speak. Now I shall die for grief.'
But finally, with much care and ado,
We reconciled our differences, we two.
He let me have the bridle in my hand
For management of both our house and land.  730
To curb his tongue he also undertook,
And on the spot I made him burn his book.
And when I had secured in full degree
By right of triumph the whole sovereignty,
And he had said, 'My dear, my own true wife,
Do as you will as long as you have life;
Preserve your honor and keep my estate,'
From that day on we had settled our debate.
I was as kind, God help me, day and dark
As any wife from India to Denmark,               740
And also true, and so he was to me.
I pray the Lord who sits in majesty
To bless his soul for Christ's own mercy dear.
And now I'll tell my tale, if you will hear."

## Alexander Pope

# THE RAPE OF THE LOCK

AN HEROI-COMICAL POEM

Nolueram, Belinda, tuos violare capillos;
Sed juvat, hoc precibus me tribuisse tuis.[12]
                                                        —MARTIAL

TO MRS. ARABELLA FERMOR

    MADAM,—It will be in vain to deny that
I have some regard for this piece, since I dedicate it to You. Yet you may bear me witness

---

[12] "I did not desire to profane your locks, Belinda,
but am glad to have yielded this much to your
prayers."

it was intended only to divert a few young ladies, who have good sense and good humour enough to laugh not only at their sex's little unguarded follies, but at their own. But as it was communicated with the air of a secret, it soon found its way into the world. An imperfect copy having been offered to a bookseller, you had the good-nature for my sake, to consent to the publication of one more correct: this I was forced to, before I had executed half my design, for the Machinery was entirely wanting to complete it.

The Machinery, Madam, is a term invented by the critics, to signify that part which the Deities, Angels, or Dæmons, are made to act in a poem: for the ancient poets are in one respect like many modern ladies; let an action be never so trivial in itself, they always make it appear of the utmost importance. These Machines I determined to raise on a very new and odd foundation, the Rosicrucian doctrine of Spirits.

I know how disagreeable it is to make use of hard words before a lady; but it is so much the concern of a poet to have his works understood, and particularly by your sex, that you must give me leave to explain two or three difficult terms The Rosicrucians are a people I must bring you acquainted with. The best account I know of them is in a French book called *La Comte de Gabalis,* which, both in its title and size, is so like a novel, that many of the fair sex have read it for one by mistake. According to these gentlemen, the four elements are inhabited by Spirits, which they call Sylphs, Gnomes, Nymphs, and Salamanders. The Gnomes, or Dæmons of earth, delight in mischief; but the Sylphs, whose habitation is in the air, are the best-conditioned creatures imaginable; for, they say, any mortal may enjoy the most intimate familiarities with these gentle spirits, upon a condition very easy to all true adepts,—an inviolate preservation of chastity.

As to the following cantos, all the passages of them are as fabulous as the Vision at the beginning, or the Transformation at the end (except the loss of your hair, which I always mention with reverence). The human persons are as fictitious as the airy ones; and the character of Belinda, as it is now managed, resembles you in nothing but in beauty.

If this poem had as many graces as there are in your person or in your mind, yet I could never hope it should pass thro' the world half so

uncensured as You have done. But let its fortune be what it will, mine is happy enough, to have given me this occasion of assuring you that I am, with the truest esteem, Madam,

> Your most obedient, humble servant,
> A. POPE.

### CANTO I

What dire offence from am'rous causes springs,
What mighty contests rise from trivial things,
I sing—This verse to *Caryll,* [13] muse! is due:
This, ev'n Belinda may vouchsafe to view:
Slight is the subject, but not so the praise,
If she inspire, and he approve my lays.
  Say what strange motive, Goddess! could compel
A well-bred Lord t' assault a gentle Belle?
O say what stranger cause, yet unexplored,
Could make a gentle Belle reject a Lord?    10
In tasks so bold can little men engage,
And in soft bosoms dwells such mighty rage?
  Sol thro' white curtains shot a tim'rous ray,
And oped those eyes that must eclipse the day.
Now lapdogs give themselves the rousing shake,
And sleepless lovers just at twelve awake:
Thrice rung the bell, the slipper knocked
    the ground,
And the pressed watch returned a silver sound.
Belinda still her downy pillow prest,
Her guardian Sylph prolonged the balmy rest.   20
'T was he had summoned to her silent bed
The morning-dream that hovered o'er her head;
A youth more glitt'ring than a Birthnight Beau [14]
(That ev'n in slumber caused her cheek to glow)
Seemed to her ear his winning lips to lay,
And thus in whispers said, or seemed to say:
"Fairest of mortals, thou distinguished care
Of thousand bright Inhabitants of Air!
If e'er one vision touched thy infant thought,
Of all the nurse and all the priest have taught—   30
Of airy elves by moonlight shadows seen,
The silver token,[15] and the circled green,
Or virgins visited by Angel-powers,
With golden crowns and wreaths of heav'nly
    flowers;
Hear and believe! thy own importance know,
Nor bound thy narrow views to things below.
Some secret truths, from learned pride concealed,
To maids alone and children are revealed:

---

[13] John Caryll, friend of Pope.
[14] *i.e.,* one dressed for a royal birthday ball.
[15] The sixpence that fairies leave in the shoe of a maid they approve.

What tho' no credit doubting Wits may give?
The fair and innocent shall still believe.          40
Know, then, unnumbered Spirits round thee fly,
The light militia of the lower sky:
These, tho' unseen, are ever on the wing,
Hang o'er the Box,[16] and hover round the Ring.[17]
Think what an equipage thou hast in air,
And view with scorn two pages and a chair.[18]
As now your own, our beings were of old,
And once inclosed in woman's beauteous mould;
Thence, by a soft transition, we repair
From earthly vehicles [19] to these of air.          50
Think not, when woman's transient breath is fled,
That all her vanities at once are dead;
Succeeding vanities she still regards,
And, tho' she plays no more, o'erlooks the cards.
Her joy in gilded chariots, when alive,
And love of Ombre,[20] after death survive.
For when the Fair in all their pride expire,
To their first elements their souls retire.
The sprites of fiery termagants in flame
Mount up, and take a Salamander's name.          60
Soft yielding minds to water glide away,
And sip, with Nymphs, their elemental tea.
The graver prude sinks downward to a Gnome
In search of mischief still on earth to roam.
The light coquettes in Sylphs aloft repair,
And sport and flutter in the fields of air.
    "Know further yet: whoever fair and chaste
Rejects mankind, is by some Sylph embraced;
For spirits, freed from mortal laws, with ease
Assume what sexes and what shapes they please.
What guards the purity of melting maids,          70
In courtly balls, and midnight masquerades,
Safe from the treach'rous friend, the daring
    spark,[21]
The glance by day, the whisper in the dark;
When kind occasion prompts their warm desires,
When music softens, and when dancing fires?
'T is but their Sylph, the wise Celestials know,
Tho' Honour is the word with Men below.
    "Some nymphs there are, too conscious of their
    face,
For life predestined to the Gnome's embrace.          80
These swell their prospects and exalt their pride,
When offers are disdained, and love denied:

---

16 Theater box.
17 Circular drive in Hyde Park where fashionable
ladies aired themselves in their coaches.
18 Sedan chair.
19 Bodies.
20 Card game.
21 Beau.

Then gay ideas crowd the vacant brain,
While peers, and dukes, and all their sweeping
    train,
And garters, stars, and coronets [22] appear,
And in soft sounds, 'Your Grace' salutes their ear.
'T is these that early taint the female soul,
Instruct the eyes of young coquettes to roll,
Teach infant cheeks a bidden blush to know,
And little hearts to flutter at a Beau.          90
    "Oft, when the world imagine women stray,
The Sylphs thro' mystic mazes guide their way;
Thro' all the giddy circle they pursue,
And old impertinence [23] expel by new.
What tender maid but must a victim fall
To one man's treat, but for another's ball?
When Florio speaks, what virgin could withstand,
If gentle Damon did not squeeze her hand?
With varying vanities, from every part,
They shift the moving toyshop of their heart;  100
Where wigs with wigs, with sword-knots [24] sword-
    knots strive,
Beaux banish beaux, and coaches coaches drive.
This erring mortals Levity may call;
Oh blind to truth! the Sylphs contrive it all.
    "Of these am I, who thy protection claim,
A watchful sprite, and Ariel is my name.
Late, as I ranged the crystal wilds of air,
In the clear mirror of thy ruling star
I saw, alas! some dread event impend,
Ere to the main this morning sun descend,          110
But Heav'n reveals not what, or how, or where.
Warned by the Sylph, O pious maid, beware!
This to disclose is all thy guardian can:
Beware of all, but most beware of Man!"
    He said; when Shock,[25] who thought she slept
    too long,
Leaped up, and waked his mistress with his tongue.
'T was then, Belinda, if report say true,
Thy eyes first opened on a billet-doux;
Wounds, charms, and ardours were no sooner
    read,
But all the vision vanished from thy head.          120
    And now, unveiled, the toilet stands displayed,
Each silver vase in mystic order laid.
First, robed in white, the nymph intent adores,
With head uncovered the Cosmetic powers.
A heav'nly image in the glass appears;
To that she bends, to that her eyes she rears.

---

22 Insignia of knights, peers, and dukes.
23 Folly.
24 The ribbons in sword hilts.
25 Belinda's dog.

Th' inferior priestess,[26] at her altar's side,
Trembling begins the sacred rites of Pride.
Unnumbered treasures ope at once, and here
The various off'rings of the world appear;      130
From each she nicely culls with curious toil,
And decks the Goddess with the glitt'ring spoil.
This casket India's glowing gems unlocks,
And all Arabia breathes from yonder box.
The tortoise here and elephant unite,
Transformed to combs, the speckled, and the
    white.
Here files of pins extend their shining rows,
Puffs, powders, patches, bibles, billet-doux.
Now awful Beauty puts on all its arms;
The Fair each moment rises in her charms,      140
Repairs her smiles, awakens every grace,
And calls forth all the wonders of her face;
Sees by degrees a purer blush arise,
And keener lightnings quicken in her eyes.
The busy Sylphs surround their darling care,
These set the head, and those divide the hair,
Some fold the sleeve, whilst others plait the gown;
And Betty's praised for labours not her own.

### CANTO II

Not with more glories, in th' ethereal plain,
The sun first rises o'er the purpled main,
Than, issuing forth, the rival of his beams
Launched on the bosom of the silver Thames.
Fair nymphs, and well-dressed youths around her
    shone,
But every eye was fixed on her alone.
On her white breast a sparkling cross she wore,
Which Jews might kiss, and infidels adore.
Her lively looks a sprightly mind disclose,
Quick as her eyes, and as unfixed as those:      10
Favours to none, to all she smiles extends;
Oft she rejects, but never once offends.
Bright as the sun, her eyes the gazers strike,
And, like the sun, they shine on all alike.
Yet graceful ease, and sweetness void of pride,
Might hide her faults, if belles had faults to hide;
If to her share some female errors fall,
Look on her face, and you'll forget 'em all.
   This nymph, to the destruction of mankind,
Nourished two locks, which graceful hung behind
In equal curls, and well conspired to deck      20
With shining ringlets the smooth iv'ry neck.
Love in these labyrinths his slaves detains,
And mighty hearts are held in slender chains.
With hairy springes we the birds betray,

Slight lines of hair surprise the finny prey,
Fair tresses man's imperial race ensnare,
And beauty draws us with a single hair.
   Th' adventurous Baron the bright locks admired;
He saw, he wished, and to the prize aspired.      30
Resolved to win, he meditates the way,
By force to ravish, or by fraud betray;
For when success a lover's toil attends,
Few ask if fraud or force attained his ends.
   For this, ere Phœbus[27] rose, he had implored
Propitious Heav'n, and every Power adored,
But chiefly Love—to Love an altar built
Of twelve vast French romances, neatly gilt.
There lay three garters, half a pair of gloves,
And all the trophies of his former loves;      40
With tender billet-doux he lights the pyre,
And breathes three am'rous sighs to raise the fire.
Then prostrate falls, and begs with ardent eyes
Soon to obtain, and long possess the prize:
The Powers gave ear, and granted half his prayer,
The rest the winds dispersed in empty air.
   But now secure the painted vessel glides,
The sunbeams trembling on the floating tides;
While melting music steals upon the sky,
And softened sounds along the waters die:      50
Smooth flow the waves, the zephyrs gently play,
Belinda smiled, and all the world was gay.
All but the Sylph—with careful thoughts opprest
Th' impending woe sat heavy on his breast.
He summons straight his denizens of air;
The lucid squadrons round the sails repair:
Soft o'er the shrouds aërial whispers breathe
That seemed but zephyrs to the train beneath.
Some to the sun their insect-wings unfold,
Waft on the breeze, or sink in clouds of gold;      60
Transparent forms too fine for mortal sight,
Their fluid bodies half dissolved in light.
Loose to the wind their airy garments flew,
Thin glitt'ring textures of the filmy dew,
Dipt in the richest tincture of the skies,
Where light disports in ever-mingling dyes,
While ev'ry beam new transient colours flings,
Colours that change whene'er they wave their
    wings.
Amid the circle, on the gilded mast,
Superior by the head[28] was Ariel placed;      70
His purple pinions opening to the sun,
He raised his azure wand, and thus begun:
   "Ye Sylphs and Sylphids, to your chief give ear.
Fays, Fairies, Genii, Elves, and Dæmons, hear!

---

[26] Belinda's maid, Betty.

[27] The sun.
[28] Taller by a head than the others.

Ye know the spheres and various tasks assigned
By laws eternal to th' aërial kind.
Some in the fields of purest ether play,
And bask and whiten in the blaze of day:
Some guide the course of wand'ring orbs on high,
Or roll the planets thro' the boundless sky:      80
Some, less refined, beneath the moon's pale light
Pursue the stars that shoot athwart the night,
Or suck the mists in grosser air below,
Or dip their pinions in the painted bow,
Or brew fierce tempests on the wintry main,
Or o'er the glebe distil the kindly rain.
Others, on earth, o'er human race preside,
Watch all their ways, and all their actions guide:
Of these the chief the care of nations own,
And guard with arms divine the British Throne.
    "Our humbler province is to tend the Fair,      90
Not a less pleasing, tho' less glorious care;
To save the Powder from too rude a gale;
Nor let th' imprisoned Essences exhale;
To draw fresh colours from the vernal flowers;
To steal from rainbows ere they drop in showers
A brighter Wash; to curl their waving hairs,
Assist their blushes and inspire their airs;
Nay oft, in dreams invention we bestow,
To change a Flounce, or add a Furbelow.      100
    "This day black omens threat the brightest Fair,
That e'er deserved a watchful spirit's care;
Some dire disaster, or by force or slight; [29]
But what, or where, the Fates have wrapt in night.
Whether the nymph shall break Diana's law, [30]
Or some frail China jar receive a flaw;
Or stain her honour, or her new brocade,
Forget her prayers, or miss a masquerade,
Or lose her heart, or necklace, at a ball;
Or whether Heav'n has doomed that Shock must
    fall.                                        110
Haste, then, ye Spirits! to your charge repair:
The flutt'ring fan be Zephyretta's [31] care;
The drops [32] to thee, Brillante, [33] we consign;
And, Momentilla, [34] let the watch be thine;
Do thou, Crispissa, [35] tend her fav'rite Lock;
Ariel himself shall be the guard of Shock.
    "To fifty chosen sylphs, of special note,
We trust th' important charge, the petticoat;
Oft have we known that sev'n-fold fence to fail,

Tho' stiff with hoops, and armed with ribs of
    whale:                                       120
Form a strong line about the silver bound,
And guard the wide circumference around.
    "Whatever spirit, careless of his charge,
His post neglects, or leaves the Fair at large,
Shall feel sharp vengeance soon o'ertake his sins:
Be stopped in vials, or transfixed with pins,
Or plunged in lakes of bitter washes lie,
Or wedged whole ages in a bodkin's eye;
Gums and pomatums shall his flight restrain,
While clogged he beats his silken wings in vain,
Or alum styptics with contracting power      130
Shrink his thin essence like a rivelled [36] flower:
Or, as Ixion fixed, the wretch shall feel
The giddy motion of the whirling mill, [37]
In fumes of burning chocolate shall glow,
And tremble at the sea that froths below!"
    He spoke; the spirits from the sails descend;
Some, orb in orb, around the nymph extend;
Some thrid [38] the mazy ringlets of her hair;
Some hang upon the pendants of her ear;      140
With beating hearts the dire event they wait,
Anxious, and trembling for the birth of Fate.

CANTO III

Close by those meads, for ever crowned with
    flowers,
Where Thames with pride surveys his rising towers,
There stands a structure [39] of majestic frame,
Which from the neighb'ring Hampton takes its
    name.
Here Britain's statesmen oft the fall foredoom
Of foreign tyrants, and of nymphs at home;
Here, thou, great ANNA! [40] whom three realms
    obey,
Dost sometimes counsel take—and sometimes tea.
    Hither the Heroes and the Nymphs resort,
To taste awhile the pleasures of a court;      10
In various talk th' instructive hours they passed,
Who gave the ball, or paid the visit last;
One speaks the glory of the British Queen,
And one describes a charming Indian screen;
A third interprets motions, looks, and eyes;
At every word a reputation dies.
Snuff, or the fan, supply each pause of chat,
With singing, laughing, ogling, *and all that.*

---

[29] Cunning.
[30] The moon-goddess's rule of chastity.
[31] *i.e.,* "fluttering."
[32] Earrings.
[33] *i.e.,* "sparkling."
[34] *i.e.,* "timing."
[35] *i.e.,* "curling."

---

[36] Shriveled.
[37] A beater for hot chocolate.
[38] Thread.
[39] Hampton Court, a royal palace.
[40] Queen Anne of England.

Meanwhile, declining from the noon of day,
The sun obliquely shoots his burning ray;        20
The hungry judges soon the sentence sign,
And wretches hang that jurymen may dine;
The merchant from th' Exchange returns in peace,
And the long labours of the toilet cease.
Belinda now, whom thirst of fame invites,
Burns to encounter two adventurous knights,
At Ombre singly to decide their doom,
And swells her breast with conquests yet to come.
Straight the three bands [41] prepare in arms to join,
Each band the number of the sacred Nine.[42]       30
Soon as she spreads her hand, th' aërial guard
Descend, and sit on each important card:
First Ariel perched upon a Matadore,[43]
Then each according to the rank they bore;
For Sylphs, yet mindful of their ancient race,
Are, as when women, wondrous fond of place.
    Behold four Kings in majesty revered,
With hoary whiskers and a forky beard;
And four fair Queens, whose hands sustain a
    flower
Th' expressive emblem of their softer power;     40
Four Knaves, in garbs succinct,[44] a trusty band,
Caps on their heads, and halberts in their hand
And party-coloured troops, a shining train,
Draw forth to combat on the velvet plain.[45]
    The skilful nymph reviews her force with care;
"Let Spades be trumps!" she said, and trumps they
    were.
Now move to war her sable Matadores,
In show like leaders of the swarthy Moors.
Spadillio [46] first, unconquerable lord!
Led off two captive trumps, and swept the
    board.                                                50
As many more Manillio [47] forced to yield,
And marched a victor from the verdant field.
Him Basto [48] followed, but his fate more hard
Gained but one trump and one plebeian card.
With his broad sabre next, a chief in years,
The hoary Majesty of Spades appears,
Puts forth one manly leg, to sight revealed;
The rest his many coloured robe concealed.
The rebel Knave, who dares his prince engage,
Proves the just victim of his royal rage.         60

[41] Hands of cards.
[42] The Muses.
[43] One of the three highest trump cards.
[44] Tucked up.
[45] Velvet covering on a card table.
[46] Ace of spades.
[47] Two of spades, the second Matadore.
[48] Ace of clubs, the third Matadore.

Ev'n mighty Pam,[49] that Kings and Queens
    o'erthrew,
And mowed down armies in the flights of Loo,
Sad chance of war! now destitute of aid,
Falls undistinguished by the victor Spade.
    Thus far both armies to Belinda yield;
Now to the Baron Fate inclines the field.
His warlike amazon her host invades,
Th' imperial consort of the crown of Spades.
The Club's black tyrant first her victim died,
Spite of his haughty mien and barb'rous pride:  70
What boots the regal circle on his head,
His giant limbs, in state unwieldy spread;
That long behind he trails his pompous robe,
And, of all monarchs, only grasps the globe?
    The Baron now his Diamonds pours apace;
Th' embroidered King who shows but half his face,
And his refulgent Queen, with powers combined,
Of broken troops an easy conquest find.
Clubs, Diamonds, Hearts, in wild disorder seen,
With throngs promiscuous strew the level green.
Thus when dispersed a routed army runs,           80
Of Asia's troops, and Afric's sable sons,
With like confusion diff'rent nations fly,
Of various habit, and of various dye;
The pierced battalions disunited fall
In heaps on heaps; one fate o'erwhelms them all.
    The Knave of Diamonds tries his wily arts,
And wins (oh shameful chance!) the Queen of
    Hearts.
At this, the blood the virgin's cheek forsook,
A livid paleness spreads o'er all her look;       90
She sees, and trembles at th' approaching ill,
Just in the jaws of ruin, and Codille.[50]
And now (as oft in some distempered state)
On one nice trick depends the gen'ral fate!
An Ace of Hearts steps forth: the King [51] unseen
Lurked in her hand, and mourned his captive
    Queen.
He springs to vengeance with an eager pace,
And falls like thunder on the prostrate Ace.
The nymph, exulting, fills with shouts the sky;
The walls, the woods, and long canals reply.  100
    Oh thoughtless mortals! ever blind to fate,
Too soon dejected, and too soon elate:
Sudden these honours shall be snatched away,
And cursed for ever this victorious day.
    For lo! the board with cups and spoons is
    crowned,

[49] Jack of clubs, top trump in the game of Loo.
[50] Being "set".
[51] Highest card in red suits in Ombre.

The berries [52] crackle, and the mill turns round;
On shining Altars of Japan they raise
The silver lamp; the fiery spirits blaze:
From silver spouts the grateful liquors glide,
While China's earth receives the smoking tide.   110
At once they gratify their scent and taste,
And frequent cups prolong the rich repast.
Straight hover round the Fair her airy band;
Some, as she sipped, the fuming liquor fanned,
Some o'er her lap their careful plumes displayed,
Trembling, and conscious of the rich brocade.
Coffee (which makes the politician wise,
And see thro' all things with his half-shut eyes)
Sent up in vapours to the Baron's brain
New stratagems, the radiant Lock to gain.   120
Ah, cease, rash youth! desist ere 't is too late,
Fear the just Gods, and think of Scylla's fate! [53]
Changed to a bird, and sent to flit in air,
She dearly pays for Nisus' injured hair!
  But when to mischief mortals bend their will,
How soon they find fit instruments of ill!
Just then, Clarissa drew with tempting grace
A two-edged weapon from her shining case:
So ladies in romance assist their knight,
Present the spear, and arm him for the fight.   130
He takes the gift with rev'rence, and extends
The little engine on his fingers' ends;
This just behind Belinda's neck he spread,
As o'er the fragrant steams she bends her head.
Swift to the Lock a thousand sprites repair;
A thousand wings, by turns, blow back the hair;
And thrice they twitched the diamond in her ear;
Thrice she looked back, and thrice the foe drew
    near.
Just in that instant, anxious Ariel sought
The close recesses of the virgin's thought:   140
As on the nosegay in her breast reclined,
He watched th' Ideas rising in her mind,
Sudden he viewed, in spite of all her art,
An earthly Lover lurking at her heart.
Amazed, confused, he found his power expired,
Resigned to fate, and with a sigh retired.
  The Peer now spreads the glitt'ring forfex [54]
    wide,
T' inclose the Lock; now joins it, to divide.

---

[52] Coffee beans.
[53] Scylla plucked from the head of her father,
Nisus, a purple hair upon which the prosperity of
his kingdom was said to depend, in order to give it to
an enemy of Nisus with whom she was in love. The
enemy repudiated her for this act, and both Scylla
and Nisus were changed into birds.
[54] Scissors.

Ev'n then, before the fatal engine closed,
A wretched Sylph too fondly interposed;   150
Fate urged the shears, and cut the Sylph in twain
(But airy substance soon unites again).
The meeting points the sacred hair dissever
From the fair head, for ever, and for ever!
  Then flashed the living lightning from her eyes,
And screams of horror rend th' affrighted skies.
Not louder shrieks to pitying Heav'n are cast,
When husbands, or when lapdogs breathe their
    last;
Or when rich China vessels, fall'n from high,
In glitt'ring dust and painted fragments lie!   160
"Let wreaths of triumph now my temples twine,"
The Victor cried, "the glorious prize is mine!
While fish in streams, or birds delight in air,
Or in a coach and six the British Fair,
As long as Atalantis [55] shall be read,
Or the small pillow grace a lady's bed,
While visits shall be paid on solemn days,
When numerous wax-lights in bright order blaze:
While nymphs take treats, or assignations give,
So long my honour, name, and praise shall
    live!                                          170
What Time would spare, from Steel receives its
    date,
And monuments, like men, submit to Fate!
Steel could the labour of the Gods destroy,
And strike to dust th' imperial towers of Troy;
Steel could the works of mortal pride confound
And hew triumphal arches to the ground.
What wonder, then, fair Nymph! thy hairs should
    feel
The conquering force of unresisted steel?"

CANTO IV

But anxious cares the pensive nymph opprest
And secret passions laboured in her breast.
Not youthful kings in battle seized alive,
Not scornful virgins who their charms survive,
Not ardent lovers robbed of all their bliss,
Not ancient ladies when refused a kiss,
Not tyrants fierce that unrepenting die,
Not Cynthia when her mantua's pinned awry,
E'er felt such rage, resentment, and despair,
As thou, sad Virgin! for thy ravished hair.   10
  For, that sad moment, when the Sylphs with-
    drew,
And Ariel weeping from Belinda flew,
Umbriel, a dusky, melancholy sprite
As ever sullied the fair face of light,

---

[55] A popular novel of the day.

Down to the central earth, his proper scene,
Repaired to search the gloomy cave of Spleen.

Swift on his sooty pinions flits the Gnome,
And in a vapour [56] reached the dismal dome.
No cheerful breeze this sullen region knows,
The dreaded East [57] is all the wind that blows.  20
Here in a grotto sheltered close from air,
And screened in shades from day's detested glare,
She sighs for ever on her pensive bed,
Pain at her side, and Megrim [58] at her head.
Two handmaids wait the throne; alike in place,
But diff'ring far in figure and in face.
Here stood Ill-nature, like an ancient maid,
Her wrinkled form in black and white arrayed!
With store of prayers for mornings, nights, and
        noons,
Her hand is filled; her bosom with lampoons.  30
  There Affectation, with a sickly mien,
Shows in her cheek the roses of eighteen,
Practised to lisp, and hang the head aside,
Faints into airs, and languishes with pride;
On the rich quilt sinks with becoming woe,
Wrapt in a gown for sickness and for show.
The fair ones feel such maladies as these,
When each new night-dress gives a new disease.
  A constant vapour o'er the palace flies; [59]
Strange phantoms rising as the mists arise;     40
Dreadful as hermits' dreams in haunted shades,
Or bright as visions of expiring maids:
Now glaring fiends, and snakes on rolling spires,
Pale spectres, gaping tombs, and purple fires;
Now lakes of liquid gold, Elysian scenes,
And crystal domes, and angels in machines.
  Unnumbered throngs on ev'ry side are seen,
Of bodies changed to various forms by Spleen.
Here living Teapots stand, one arm held out,
One bent; the handle this, and that the spout:   50
A Pipkin there, like Homer's Tripod walks;
Here sighs a Jar, and there a Goose-pie talks;
Men prove with child, as powerful fancy works,
And maids turned bottles call aloud for corks.
  Safe passed the Gnome thro' this fantastic band,
A branch of healing spleenwort in his hand.
Then thus addressed the Power: "Hail, wayward
        Queen!
Who rule the sex to fifty from fifteen:
Parent of Vapours and of female wit,

Who give th' hysteric or poetic fit,             60
On various tempers act by various ways,
Make some take physic, others scribble plays;
Who cause the proud their visits to delay,
And send the godly in a pet to pray.
A nymph there is that all your power disdains,
And thousands more in equal mirth maintains.
But oh! if e'er thy Gnome could spoil a grace,
Or raise a pimple on a beauteous face,
Like citron-waters [60] matrons' cheeks inflame,
Or change complexions at a losing game;          70
If e'er with airy horns [61] I planted heads,
Or rumpled petticoats, or tumbled beds,
Or caused suspicion when no soul was rude,
Or discomposed the head-dress of a prude,
Or e'er to costive lapdog gave disease,
Which not the tears of brightest eyes could ease,
Hear me, and touch Belinda with chagrin;
That single act gives half the world the spleen."
  The Goddess, with a discontented air,
Seems to reject him tho' she grants his prayer.  80
A wondrous Bag with both her hands she binds,
Like that where once Ulysses held the winds;
There she collects the force of female lungs,
Sighs, sobs, and passions, and the war of tongues.
A Vial next she fills with fainting fears,
Soft sorrows, melting griefs, and flowing tears.
The Gnome rejoicing bears her gifts away,
Spreads his black wings, and slowly mounts to day.
  Sunk in Thalestris' [62] arms the nymph he found,
Her eyes dejected, and her hair unbound.         90
Full o'er their heads the swelling Bag he rent,
And all the Furies issued at the vent.
Belinda burns with more than mortal ire,
And fierce Thalestris fans the rising fire.
"O wretched maid!" she spreads her hands, and
        cried
(While Hampton's echoes, "Wretched maid!"
        replied),
"Was it for this you took such constant care
The bodkin,[63] comb, and essence to prepare?
For this your locks in paper durance [64] bound?
For this with torturing irons wreathed around?
For this with fillets strained your tender head, 100
And bravely bore the double loads of lead? [65]
Gods! shall the ravisher display your hair,

---

[56] Used here in two senses: "mist" and "peevish-ness."

[57] The east wind was supposed to cause the "spleen."

[58] A migraine headache.

[59] The lines which follow describe the delusions of those suffering from the "spleen."

[60] A mild orange-flavored brandy.

[61] The symbol of cuckolds.

[62] Queen of the Amazons: in this case, Belinda's friend.

[63] In this case, a hairpin.

[64] Curlers.

[65] Curl-papers stiffened with lead.

While the fops envy, and the ladies stare!
Honour forbid! at whose unrivalled shrine
Ease, Pleasure, Virtue, all, our sex resign.
Methinks already I your tears survey,
Already hear the horrid things they say,
Already see you a degraded toast,
And all your honour in a whisper lost!                    110
How shall I, then, your hapless fame defend?
'T will then be infamy to seem your friend!
And shall this prize, th' inestimable prize,
Exposed thro' crystal to the gazing eyes,
And heightened by the diamond's circling rays,
On that rapacious hand for ever blaze?
Sooner shall grass in Hyde Park Circus [66] grow,
And Wits take lodgings in the sound of Bow; [67]
Sooner let earth, air, sea, to chaos fall,
Men, monkeys, lapdogs, parrots, perish all!"        120
   She said; then raging to Sir Plume repairs,
And bids her Beau demand the precious hairs
(Sir Plume, of amber snuff-box justly vain,
And the nice conduct of a clouded cane [68]):
With earnest eyes, and round unthinking face,
He first the snuff-box opened, then the case,
And thus broke out—"My Lord, why, what the
      devil!
Z—ds! damn the Lock! 'fore Gad, you must be
      civil!
Plague on 't! 't is past a jest—nay, prithee, pox!
Give her the hair"—He spoke, and rapped his
      box.                                                         130
   "It grieves me much," replied the Peer again,
"Who speaks so well should ever speak in vain:
But by this Lock, this sacred Lock, I swear
(Which never more shall join its parted hair;
Which never more its honours shall renew,
Clipped from the lovely head where late it grew),
That, while my nostrils draw the vital air,
This hand, which won it, shall for ever wear."
He spoke, and speaking, in proud triumph spread
The long-contended honours of her head.            140
   But Umbriel, hateful Gnome, forbears not so;
He breaks the Vial whence the sorrows flow.
Then see! the nymph in beauteous grief appears,
Her eyes half languishing, half drowned in tears;
On her heaved bosom hung her drooping head,
Which with a sigh she raised, and thus she said:
   "For ever cursed be this detested day,
Which snatched my best, my fav'rite curl away!
Happy! ah, ten times happy had I been,
If Hampton Court these eyes had never seen! 150

[66] The Ring; see note 17.
[67] An unfashionable, commercial section of London.
[68] Mottled walking-stick.

Yet am not I the first mistaken maid,
By love of courts to numerous ills betrayed.
O had I rather unadmired remained
In some lone isle, or distant northern land;
Where the gilt chariot never marks the way,
Where none learn Ombre, none e'er taste Bohea! [69]
There kept my charms concealed from mortal eye,
Like roses, that in deserts bloom and die.
What moved my mind with youthful lords to
      roam?
O had I stayed, and said my prayers at home;  160
'Twas this the morning omens seemed to tell,
Thrice from my trembling hand the patch-box fell;
The tott'ring china shook without a wind,
Nay, Poll sat mute, and Shock was most unkind!
A Sylph, too, warned me of the threats of fate,
In mystic visions, now believed too late!
See the poor remnants of these slighted hairs!
My hands shall rend what ev'n thy rapine spares.
These, in two sable ringlets taught to break,
Once gave new beauties to the snowy neck;        170
The sister-lock now sits uncouth alone,
And in its fellow's fate foresees its own;
Uncurled it hangs, the fatal shears demands,
And tempts once more thy sacrilegious hands.
O hadst thou, cruel! been content to seize
Hairs less in sight, or any hairs but these!"

CANTO V

She said: the pitying audience melt in tears;
But Fate and Jove had stopped the Baron's ears.
In vain Thalestris with reproach assails,
For who can move when fair Belinda fails?
Not half so fixed the Trojan [70] could remain,
While Anna begged and Dido raged in vain.
Then grave Clarissa graceful waved her fan;
Silence ensued, and thus the nymph began:
   "Say, why are beauties praised and honoured
      most,
The wise man's passion, and the vain man's
      toast?                                                        10
Why decked with all that land and sea afford,
Why angels called, and angel-like adored?
Why round our coaches crowd the white-gloved
      beaux?
Why bows the side-box from its inmost rows?
How vain are all these glories, all our pains,
Unless Good Sense preserve what Beauty gains;
That men may say when we the front-box grace,
'Behold the first in virtue as in face!'

[69] A fashionable kind of tea.
[70] Aeneas, who deserted Dido, Queen of Carthage,
despite the prayers of her sister.

Oh! if to dance all night, and dress all day,
Charmed the smallpox, or chased old age away; 20
Who would not scorn what housewife's cares
    produce,
Or who would learn one earthly thing of use?
To patch, nay, ogle, might become a saint,
Nor could it sure be such a sin to paint.
But since, alas! frail beauty must decay,
Curled or uncurled, since Locks will turn to gray;
Since painted, or not painted, all shall fade,
And she who scorns a man must die a maid;
What then remains, but well our power to use,
And keep good humour still whate'er we lose?    30
And trust me, dear, good humour can prevail,
When airs, and flights, and screams, and scolding
    fail.
Beauties in vain their pretty eyes may roll;
Charms strike the sight, but merit wins the soul."
    So spoke the dame, but no applause ensued;
Belinda frowned, Thalestris called her prude.
"To arms, to arms!" the fierce virago cries,
And swift as lightning to the combat flies.
All side in parties, and begin th' attack;
Fans clap, silks rustle, and tough whalebones
    crack;                                        40
Heroes' and heroines' shouts confusedly rise,
And bass and treble voices strike the skies.
No common weapons in their hands are found,
Like Gods they fight nor dread a mortal wound.
    So when bold Homer makes the Gods engage,
And heav'nly breasts with human passions rage;
'Gainst Pallas, Mars; Latona, Hermes arms;
And all Olympus rings with loud alarms;
Jove's thunder roars, Heav'n trembles all around,
Blue Neptune storms, the bellowing deeps
    resound:
Earth shakes her nodding towers, the ground gives
    way,                                          50
And the pale ghosts start at the flash of day!
    Triumphant Umbriel, on a sconce's [71] height,
Clapped his glad wings, and sat to view the fight:
Propped on their bodkin-spears, the sprites survey
The growing combat, or assist the fray.
    While thro' the press enraged Thalestris flies,
And scatters death around from both her eyes,
A Beau and Witling [72] perished in the throng,
One died in metaphor, and one in song:          60
"O cruel Nymph! a living death I bear,"
Cried Dapperwit, and sunk beside his chair.
A mournful glance Sir Fopling upwards cast,

---

[71] Wall bracket for candles.
[72] A young dandy or fop.

"Those eyes are made so killing"—was his last.
Thus on Mæander's flowery margin lies
Th' expiring swan, and as he sings he dies.
    When bold Sir Plume had drawn Clarissa down,
Chloe stepped in, and killed him with a frown;
She smiled to see the doughty hero slain,
But, at her smile, the Beau revived again.      70
Now Jove suspends his golden scales in air,
Weighs the men's wits against the lady's hair;
The doubtful beam long nods from side to side;
At length the wits mount up, the hairs subside.
    See fierce Belinda on the Baron flies,
With more than usual lightning in her eyes;
Nor feared the chief th' unequal fight to try,
Who sought no more than on his foe to die.
But this bold lord, with manly strength endued,
She with one finger and a thumb subdued:        80
Just where the breath of life his nostrils drew,
A charge of snuff the wily virgin threw;
The Gnomes direct, to every atom just,
The pungent grains of titillating dust.
Sudden, with starting tears each eye o'erflows,
And the high dome reëchoes to his nose.
    "Now meet thy fate," incensed Belinda cried,
And drew a deadly bodkin from her side.
(The same, his ancient personage to deck,
Her great-great-grandsire wore about his neck,  90
In three seal-rings; which after, melted down,
Formed a vast buckle for his widow's gown:
Her infant grandame's whistle next it grew,
The bells she jingled, and the whistle blew;
Then in a bodkin graced her mother's hairs,
Which long she wore and now Belinda wears.)
    "Boast not my fall," he cried, "insulting foe!
Thou by some other shalt be laid as low;
Nor think to die dejects my lofty mind:
All that I dread is leaving you behind!          100
Rather than so, ah, let me still survive,
And burn in Cupid's flames—but burn alive."
"Restore the Lock!" she cries; and all around
"Restore the Lock!" the vaulted roofs rebound.
Not fierce Othello in so loud a strain
Roared for the handkerchief that caused his pain.
But see how oft ambitious aims are crossed,
And chiefs contend till all the prize is lost!
The Lock, obtained with guilt, and kept with pain,
In ev'ry place is sought, but sought in vain:   110
With such a prize no mortal must be blest.
So Heav'n decrees! with Heav'n who can contest?
    Some thought it mounted to the lunar sphere,
Since all things lost on earth are treasured there.
There heroes' wits are kept in pond'rous vases,
And beaux' in snuffboxes and tweezer-cases.

There broken vows, and deathbed alms are found,
And lovers' hearts with ends of riband bound,
The courtier's promises, and sick man's prayers,
The smiles of harlots, and the tears of heirs,      120
Cages for gnats, and chains to yoke a flea,
Dried butterflies, and tomes of casuistry.

But trust the Muse—she saw it upward rise,
Tho' marked by none but quick poetic eyes
(So Rome's great founder to the heav'ns withdrew,
To Proculus [73] alone confessed in view):
A sudden star, it shot thro' liquid air,
And drew behind a radiant trail of hair.
Not Berenice's locks [74] first rose so bright,
The heav'ns bespangling with dishevelled
     light.                                                 130
The Sylphs behold it kindling as it flies,
And pleased pursue its progress thro' the skies.

This the beau monde [75] shall from the Mall [76]
     survey,

And hail with music its propitious ray;
This the blest lover shall for Venus take,
And send up vows from Rosamonda's lake; [77]
This Partridge [78] soon shall view in cloudless skies,
When next he looks thro' Galileo's eyes;
And hence th' egregious wizard shall foredoom
The fate of Louis, [79] and the fall of Rome.      140
    Then cease, bright Nymph! to mourn thy
     ravished hair,
Which adds new glory to the shining sphere!
Not all the tresses that fair head can boast
Shall draw such envy as the Lock you lost.
For after all the murders of your eye,
When, after millions slain, yourself shall die;
When those fair suns shall set, as set they must,
And all those tresses shall be laid in dust,
This Lock the Muse shall consecrate to fame,
And 'midst the stars inscribe Belinda's name.      150

---

[73] Roman senator who confirmed the translation of Romulus, founder of Rome, to heaven.
[74] The hair of the Egyptian queen Berenice became a constellation.
[75] The world of fashion.
[76] Fashionable promenade in St. James' Park.

---

[77] A pond in St. James' Park, often identified with unhappy lovers.
[78] An astrologer of the day.
[79] Louis XIV of France.

# IN TIME OF WAR

WAR MAY not be one of the inevitable activities of man, but it is one of the oldest. In this experience, conflict among human beings is overt, violent, exciting, and large in scale; passions are strong, and the extremes of possible relations among human beings are often set side by side. So it is not surprising that poets and other storytellers from the earliest times have found in war the material for great literature. They have sought to understand the motives that drive men to war; by holding up for contemplation the human elements that war brings into view, they have clarified the various responses to it; they have lamented its sadness and horror, and commemorated its victories for nation or tribe.

Many aspects of war, and themes built upon them, run through the selections of this chapter. The account of the battle of Balaclava and the poems by Owen and Yeats show its impact upon the men who fight it; Pirandello's story and Auden's poem concern its effect upon noncombatants. The idea of heroism is considered from various points of view, as in *Henry V* and "An Occurrence at Owl Creek Bridge" and "The Too-late Born." Swift and Auden and Hardy raise searching questions about the rootedness of war in human nature.

Still another aspect of war emerges with particular vividness from a reading of these works, and that is the way in which human beings differ about its meaning. There is, first, the romantic conception of war as glorious and heroic, well suited to exhibit the finest qualities of human nature—manliness and loyalty and courage. This conception appears repeatedly in the literature of war, though with differing emphases and with differing judg-

150

ments being passed upon it. It appears in such varied works as *Henry V*, in both Kinglake's and Tennyson's account of the charge of the Light Brigade, and in *Arms and the Man*. Another range of conceptions seems more realistic: war being a job like any other, there is no place in it, according to this view, for illusions or self-deception. This view ranges all the way from Homer's Agamemnon to Stephen Crane's lieutenant. Finally, and perhaps most characteristic of our century, there is that inverted romanticism which rests upon a positive disillusionment, where the warrior starts out as a romantic and then learns that war is not what he thought. Sergius, returning from the battle, illustrates this attitude; it became commonplace in the literature of the First World War, and is thought by many to have determined the outlook of the generation that fought the second one.

## A. W. Kinglake
# THE BATTLE OF BALACLAVA

[*The Battle of Balaclava, the most famous engagement of the Crimean War, was fought on September 26, 1854. The Russians under General Liprandi had earlier captured a number of fortifications held by a small force of Turkish soldiers and were thus threatening the strategic seaport of Balaclava. The English Heavy Brigade had repulsed one attack by the Russians, and Lord Raglan, leader of the British forces, ordered Lord Lucan, commander of both the Light and Heavy Brigades, to send his Light Brigade charging into one of the weak spots in the Russian line. Instead, Lord Lucan ordered the Light Brigade, led by Lord Cardigan, to charge the strongest Russian position.*]

Lord Raglan's vexation was great, for he felt all the evil of any delay in seizing the advantage which the fortune of war was offering.

Being in this strait, and judging also, with what we now know to have been a true foresight, that the weak chain of Russian infantry columns which stretched towards him endwise along the line of the redoubts would prove somewhat soft to the touch, he determined to use his cavalry. He did not so determine apparently because the cavalry arm was the one which he would most willingly have selected

for his purpose if he had any freedom of choice, but because his infantry reinforcements were not yet far enough in advance, and the time was too precious to be lost. Be that as it may, he despatched to Lord Lucan a written instruction which in the subsequent controversies was generally called "the third order." It ran thus: "Cavalry to advance and take advantage of any opportunity to recover the heights. They will be supported by the infantry which have been ordered [to] advance on two fronts." Whilst directing that actual attacks against the enemy on the heights should be made to depend upon opportunity, this order, it should be observed, was peremptory and unconditional in requiring that our cavalry should advance; and since it came, not from a distant commander, but from one who looked down upon the whole field, and had before his eyes all the requisite ingredients of a positive resolve, it is difficult to see how the words could become open to misconstruction.

Lord Lucan, however, so read the order as to conceive it his duty to do no more for the moment than mount his cavalry, move the Light Brigade to another position hard by across the North Valley, and cause his Heavy Dragoons to remain on the slope of the rise there awaiting the infantry, which, to use his own language, "had not yet arrived. . . ."

From the height which he had occupied during the whole morning, and with the officers of his Staff around him, Lord Raglan watched for the moment when his cavalry, in obedience to the orders he had despatched, would begin its advance, and he watched with the expectation —an expectation which we now know to have been well founded—that the movement would cause the enemy to abandon his already relax-

THE BATTLE OF BALACLAVA: From *The Invasion of the Crimea*, Vol. 5, ch. 1.

ing hold, and give up the captured redoubts. He watched in vain. His cavalry did not move forward. From the way in which he saw the Russians withdrawing their cavalry and artillery, but also from the general aspect of the field, he knew that the minutes then passing were minutes of depression to the enemy, and therefore of opportunity for the English. It may well be imagined that at such a time the delayed compliance with his order was provoking; and if his words and his features betrayed mere vexation, or, at all events, well-governed anger, the more youthful men of his Staff were not, I imagine, so careful as to suppress their murmurs of impatience and indignation.

In this temper the Headquarter Staff were gazing upon the field, when some of them who had been pointing their field-glasses along the line of the Causeway ridge perceived all at once, as they thought, that the enemy was bringing forward some teams of artillery horses, with the lasso tackle attached to them; and they did not doubt—what otherwise seemed very probable—that the enemy, who was evidently preparing to retreat, must be seeking to carry off with him as trophies the English guns taken from the Turks.

It seems probable that, before this, Lord Raglan's patience must have almost come to its end, and that, without any new motive, he would have presently despatched a reminding and accelerating message to Lord Lucan; but the announcement of the artillery-teams coming up to carry off English guns may well have determined his choice of the moment for taking the step, and it gave him an opportunity—which, even in a moment of anger, his kind and generous nature would incline him to seize—an opportunity of softening the communication he had to make to the commander of his cavalry; for evidently the pressure which was to be applied to Lord Lucan would be relieved in some measure of its inculpatory aspect, by basing the necessity for instant action upon a new fact. Accordingly, Lord Raglan determined to repeat with increased urgency his hitherto disobeyed order for the advance of the cavalry, and to give to its commander a fresh motive for despatch, by pressing upon him the special object of endeavouring to prevent the enemy from carrying off the guns. This determination he expressed in terms intimating that the Quartermaster-General, who was close at his side,

should give immediate effect to it. With a pencil, and a slip of paper rested upon his sabretash, General Airey quickly embodied in a written order the instruction thus given him; but before Lord Raglan allowed the paper to go, he dictated some additional words which Airey at once inserted. The paper when thus completed became what men have called "the fourth order."

It was supposed that Lieutenant Calthorpe (an officer of the cavalry, and one of Lord Raglan's aides-de-camp), who chanced to stand ready and expectant, would be charged with the mission; but Lord Raglan called for Captain Nolan (the aide-de-camp of the Quartermaster-General), and specially desired that the order should be entrusted to him.

Nolan was no common man. Surrounded as he was at Headquarters by men of the world whose pleasant society must have been apparently well calculated to moderate a too wild devotion to one idea, he yet was an enthusiast —an enthusiast unchilled and unshaken. His faith was that miracles of war could be wrought by squadrons of horse, that the limits of what could fairly be asked of the cavalry had been wrongly assigned, and that—if only it could be properly constituted and properly led—the cavalry, after all, was the arm which should govern the issue of battles. Then adding to this creed an unbounded trust in the warlike quality of our troopers, he went on to conclude that the dominion of England in the world could be best assured by the sabre. He knew that where the question of cavalry excellence could be narrowed to a question of cavalry fighting, the English horsemen had been used to maintain their ascendant. The great day of Blenheim, he knew, was won in the main by our cavalry. With a single brigade of our cavalry at Salamanca, Le Marchant had cut through a French army. Nolan imagined that nothing but perverse mismanagement and evil choice of men prevented England from having what he held to be her own—from having an ascendant among nations resting mainly, or at all events largely, upon the prowess of her squadrons. Because this faith was glowing within him, Nolan had sorrowed and chafed at the unobtrusive part taken by our cavalry in the earlier days of the invasion. His journal, going down to the 12th of October, lies open before me. It teems with impatience of the comparative inaction to which our cavalry had been condemned; and discloses a belief—a belief based apparently, in part, upon somewhat wild processes of reason—that the commander of our cavalry was the man upon whom blame should rest. Nolan must have been solaced, one may suppose, nay, enraptured, by the feat of our Heavy Dragoons;[1] but, on the other hand, he could not but be tortured by having to witness the inaction to which the Light Brigade stood condemned whilst their comrades were fighting, and for this (if he knew not that the commander of our cavalry was present elsewhere) he probably blamed Lord Lucan. Besides, at the moment we speak of, an occasion had been offering itself to the cavalry, and Lord Raglan, as we know, had been ordering it to advance without being yet obeyed. Upon the whole, therefore, it is easy to understand that Nolan must have been burning with anger and zeal.

This was the officer to whom, by Lord Raglan's direction, General Airey delivered the order. Without having had their observance quickened, at the time, by any foreboding sentiments, men still remember how swiftly the messenger sped on his errand. That acclivity of some seven or eight hundred feet, which divided our Headquarter Staff from the plain of Balaclava below, was of just such a degree of steepness that, whilst no rider of merely ordinary experience and boldness would like to go down it at a high rate of speed, and whilst few of those going slowly would refrain from somewhat easing the abruptness of the path by a more or less zig-zag descent, the ground still was not so precipitous as to defy the rapid purpose of a horseman who had accustomed himself, in such things, to approach the extreme of what is possible. The special skill gained by such trials, with the boldness needed for using it, Nolan had in full measure; and he was armed with cogent words for the man whom he had brought himself to condemn as the obstructor of cavalry enterprise. Straight, swift, and intent—descending, as it were, on sure prey—he swooped angering down into the plain where Lord Lucan and his squadrons were posted. . . .

Although a period of some thirty, forty, or fifty minutes had since elapsed, the position of the Russian army was still nearly the same that it had been when Lord Lucan received his third order. Jabrokritsky, with some 8 battalions, 4 squadrons, and 14 guns, was established on the slopes of the Fedioukine Hills; and Liprandi, with his infantry and field-artillery still lingering upon the sites of the captured redoubts, continued to protrude so far west along the chain of the Causeway Heights as to have one of his regiments—the regiment of Odessa—drawn up near the Arabtabia Redoubt; but the whole of his defeated cavalry had been withdrawn to a position so far down the North Valley as to be within less than a mile of the aqueduct, and almost a mile and a half from the ground where Lord Lucan was posted. Drawn up across the North Valley, far in rear of the foremost Russian battalions, this large but discomfited body of horse connected Liprandi's corps-army with the troops of General Jabrokritsky, but connected it only by the rear—connected it in such a way that these forces together were the three sides of an oblong, and could be likened, as we saw, to the hand of a man with the two centre fingers held back and the other two fingers extended. The Odessa regiment formed the tip of that lesser finger which represents the extension of Liprandi's column along the chain of the Causeway Heights. Except at their rear, the two columns thus protruding were divided the one from the other by the whole breadth of the North Valley; and without straying into surmise, it can be stated that they were, each of them, in a condition to be more or less completely rolled up by an attack of cavalry, or even—without waiting for actual collision—by the mere sight of squadrons approaching.

Close in advance of the discomfited Russian cavalry, and, like them, fronting up the North Valley, some twelve pieces of the Don Cossack ordnance were in battery.

At a later moment, the smoke from this battery served to screen the horsemen behind it from the sight of the English; but at the time now spoken of, this great body of Russian cavalry, though a mile and a half off, could be descried by one standing on the ground where Lord Cardigan was posted. From the effect of distance and close massing, the dusky, grey columns looked black. . . .

Such seems to have been the position and attitude of the forces now confronting Lord

[1] Their successful attack on the Russian cavalry, which had just been made.

Lucan, and such the condition of things that Lord Raglan had sought to deal with by the order which Nolan was bringing. Lord Raglan, as we know, had the advantage of seeing all from high, commanding ground; but nothing less than his peculiar and instinctive faculty for the reading of a battle-field could have enabled him at the instant to grasp the whole import of what to others was a dim, complex scene, devoid of expression, and to send down an order so closely adapted to the exigency as the one which he had despatched. To strike at the nearest of the Russians that could be found on the Causeway Heights—or, in other words, at those Odessa battalions which stood ranged in front of the Arabtabia—this plainly was the task which (by reason of there being no infantry division yet present on the ground) invited the enterprise of our squadrons; and this also, we shall see, was the task which the order now coming enjoined.

We shall see that the French, when so minded, could direct an attack with their cavalry upon the head of the Russian detachment now holding the Fedioukine Hills—an attack somewhat similar in its nature to the one which Lord Raglan desired to have made against the tip of Liprandi's position on the Causeway Heights. In truth, there were two ranges of heights, each affording to the cavalry of the Allies so good a point for attack, that the one was decisively chosen—though chosen in vain—by Lord Raglan, and the other by General Morris, the Commander of the French cavalry division.

But between the two ranges, thus each of them inviting attack, there unhappily lay a smooth valley, which offered itself to those horsemen who might either be weary of life, or compelled by a sense of duty to go down and commit self-destruction.

Our Heavy Dragoons were on one of the slopes of the Causeway ridge, not far from the scene of their late victory. Lord Cardigan's brigade [2] stood, drawn up in two lines, and so placed as to be fronting straight down the North Valley.

Lord Lucan was sitting in the saddle in front of his troops, and between the two brigades, when Nolan came speeding from the Commander-in-Chief, and made haste to deliver the

---

[2] *i.e.*, the Light Brigade.

paper with which we saw him entrusted. By pursuing a theory that he seems to have formed in regard to the real authorship of directions from the English Headquarters, Lord Lucan had taught himself to mistake the channel for the source, and to imagine that General Airey must be often the originator of orders which, in fact, he was only transmitting. For this reason, and as tending, perhaps, to account in some measure for the way in which the order was about to act upon the mind or the temper of the general to whom it was addressed, it is worth while to remember two circumstances which would have been otherwise unimportant. The bearer of the order, as it chanced, was the aide-de-camp of General Airey, and its words were in General Airey's handwriting.

The order ran thus: "Lord Raglan wishes the cavalry to advance rapidly to the front, and try to prevent the enemy carrying away the guns. Troop of horse-artillery may accompany. French cavalry is on your left. Immediate. (Signed) R. AIREY."

Whether taken alone, or as a command reinforcing the one before sent, this order has really no word in it which is either obscure or misleading. By assigning "the guns" as the object, Lord Raglan most pointedly fixed the line of the Turkish redoubts as the direction in which to advance; and it must not be said that the expression left room in the mind of Lord Lucan for a doubt as to what guns were meant. He well knew that the guns indicated by the "fourth order" were the English guns taken in the forts—in the forts crowning those very "heights" which, more than half an hour before, he had been ordered to retake if he could; and no one, indeed, had more poignant reason than Lord Lucan for knowing what the guns were; because he was the commander of the force which—rightly, perhaps, but not, of course, without mortification—had had to stand by and be witness whilst Liprandi effected the capture.

If collated with the third order, the written words brought down by Nolan seem to come with accumulated weight and decisiveness. By the third order, the commander of our cavalry had been directed to advance, and take any opportunity of recovering the heights—those heights, be it remembered, where the enemy was posted with the seven English guns he had captured; and now, by this fourth order, Lord

Lucan—being requested to advance rapidly to the front, and try to prevent the enemy from carrying away the guns—was, for the second time, told that he must operate against the Russians on the Causeway Heights, and was furnished with a new and special motive for energy and despatch. Construed singly, the fourth order looks clear as day; read along with the former direction it looks equally clear, but even more cogent; for, when so considered, it appears to visit Lord Lucan with something like an expression of impatience and displeasure for having allowed more than half an hour to pass after the receipt of the third order without trying to recover the "heights. . . ."

Lord Lucan, however, had no sooner read this order, than there was awakened in his mind that spirit of hostile criticism which so marred his usefulness as a subordinate. He proceeded to sit in judgment upon the command of his chief, and at once, without mercy, condemned it. His own account declares that he "read the order with much consideration"—"perhaps consternation," he says, "would be the better word—at once seeing its impracticability for any useful purpose whatever, and the consequent great unnecessary risk and loss to be incurred." The formation of this strangely decisive opinion upon the merits of an order sent him by his Commander-in-Chief, was rendered the more inappropriate by the fact that the Commander who sent the order had the whole field of battle before him, whilst the critic who undertook to condemn it was so placed (upon the lower ground) that to him neither enemy nor guns were in sight. . . .

But, unhappily, Lord Lucan did not restrict himself to a silent condemnation of the order. With the bearer of the note for his listener, he suffered himself to run out against the order of his chief. Conceiving (erroneously) that he rightly understood the nature of the enterprise which Lord Raglan's written words had enjoined, he urged the uselessness of such an attack, and the dangers attending it.

By this language apparently Lord Lucan challenged the messenger to encounter him in wordy dispute, and to defend, if he could, the order of the Commander-in-Chief.

Nolan was a man who had gathered in Continental service the habit of such extreme and such rigid deference to any general officer, that his comrades imagined him to be the very last man who in such points would ever prove wanting; but perhaps that very reverence for the military hierarchy which had hitherto rendered him so superlatively respectful to general officers, may have made him the more liable to be shocked by the reception which Lord Lucan was giving to the order of the Commander-in-Chief. Up to this moment, however, Nolan was not so ungovernably indignant as to be guilty of more than imparting an authoritative tone to the words in which he answered Lord Lucan's denunciation of the order. "Lord Raglan's orders," he said, "are, that the cavalry should attack immediately."

Then quickly, and in a tone of impatience, caused, it seems, by what he imagined to be the absurdity of the attack thus enjoined, Lord Lucan said to Nolan, "Attack, sir! attack what? What guns, sir?"

This angry, impatient question was destined to put an end to all prospect of eliciting from Nolan any quiet explanation of the mission with which he came charged, or any of that priceless information in regard to the enemy's position which, coming as he did from high ground, the aide-de-camp was well able to give. . . . Throwing his head back, and pointing with his hand in a direction which Lord Lucan says confidently was towards the left-front corner of the valley, the aide-de-camp replied, "There, my lord, is your enemy; there are your guns." Lord Lucan declares that these words were addressed to him in a "most disrespectful but significant manner"; and, even without too much relying upon gesture or cadence of voice, it is easy to see that the apostrophe thus uttered by Nolan was almost in the nature of an indignant rebuke—an indignant rebuke inflicted by a captain upon a lieutenant-general in front of his troops.

Just men will therefore acknowledge that this outbreak of Nolan's was only too well fitted to enrage a general officer, and, by enraging him, to disturb his judgment; but, apart from the effect they might produce upon the temper of Lord Lucan, the gestures and the words of the aide-de-camp cannot fairly be wrought into the kind of importance which was afterwards assigned to them in controversy. The tenor of the apostrophe as recorded by Lord Lucan himself shows plainly enough that, by pointing generally to the direction in which the enemy might be found, Nolan's gestures and words

were meant to convey a taunt, not to give topo-
graphical guidance; and this is made the more
evident by taking care to remember that, when
the words passed between the Lieutenant-
General and the Aide-de-camp, they were
neither of them on ground from which any
Russians could be seen; for a messenger who
was so blindly placed at the moment as not to
have a glimpse of the enemy could hardly have
so trusted to his own and his hearer's recollection of the local bearings as to think of attempting to designate a particular object of attack by
pointing to its supposed position.

The haze that was at one time engendered
by controversy carried on with imperfect materials is yet further cleared off by observing the
angle of difference between the route of the
Causeway Heights, which Lord Raglan had
enjoined, and the fatal way down the North
Valley. Vast and terrible as was the contrast in
point of consequences between taking the right
way and taking the wrong one, the divergence
of the one route from the other at the spot
where Nolan made the gesture is represented
by an angle of little more than twenty degrees.
How is it possible that, where the difference of
direction between the two routes at the point
of departure had so moderate a width, and
where also there was no sight of a Russian
battalion or squadron to guide the eye or the
hand, the aide-de-camp could have even seemed
to forbid the one route or to enjoin the other,
by the way in which—burning with anger—he
tauntingly pointed to the "enemy"? . . .

Lord Lucan now personally imparted his
resolve to Lord Cardigan. There is some difference between the impressions that were
formed of this interview by Lord Lucan on
the one hand and Lord Cardigan on the other;
Lord Lucan believing that with the "fourth
order" in his hand he imparted its contents, or
at all events the main tenor of it, to Lord
Cardigan, and directed him "to advance," without in terms enjoining an "attack"; whilst Lord
Cardigan's statement is that he was ordered "to
attack the Russians in the valley about three-
quarters of a mile distant with the 13th Light
Dragoons and the 17th Lancers."

Lord Lucan's idea as to the way in which
this direction of his ought to have been executed is as follows:—He says: "After giving
to Lord Cardigan the order brought to me from
Colonel Airey by Captain Nolan I urged his

Lordship to advance steadily, and to keep his
men well in hand. My idea was that he was to
use his discretion and act as circumstances
might show themselves; my opinion is that
keeping his four squadrons under perfect control he should have halted them so soon as he
found that there was no useful object to be
gained, but great risk to be incurred; it was
clearly his duty to have handled his brigade
as I did the Heavy Brigade,[3] and so saved them
from much useless and unnecessary loss."

Lord Cardigan did not so understand the task
which was devolving upon him. From the way
in which his brigade was fronting at the time,
he considered that an indefinite order to advance was an order to advance down the valley
against the far distant guns and black masses
of cavalry which were seen to be drawn up
across it; and whatever were the words really
used, Lord Cardigan certainly understood that
without assailing either of the enemy's two protruded columns he was ordered to run the
gauntlet between them for a distance of more
than a mile, with the purpose of then charging
the battery which crossed the lower end of the
valley, and charging it moreover in front.

Understanding that he was thus instructed,
Lord Cardigan judged it right to point out the
true import of an order to advance down the
valley. So, on hearing the words of his Divi-
sional General, he brought down his sword in
salute, and answered, "Certainly, Sir; but allow
me to point out to you that the Russians have
a battery in the valley in our front, and batteries
and riflemen on each flank." Lord Lucan, after
first expressing his concurrence in what he
gathered to be the tenor of Lord Cardigan's
observation, went on to intimate—he shrugged
his shoulders whilst speaking—"that there was
no choice but to obey. . . ."

Then, without further question or parley,
Lord Cardigan tacitly signified his respectful
submission to orders, and began that great act
of military obedience which is enshrined in the
memory of his fellow-countrymen. He turned
quietly to his people and said: "The brigade
will advance!" . . .

Lord Cardigan placed himself quite alone at
a distance of about two horses' lengths in ad-

---

[3] When the Light Brigade began its charge, Lord
Lucan led the Heavy Brigade in support, but withdrew before going far down the North Valley.

vance of his Staff, and some five horses' lengths in advance of the centre of his first line.

When once a body of cavalry has been launched upon a course which is to end in attack, it has to dispense for a while with reliance upon full, explicit orders conveyed by word of mouth; and although there may come the time when the trumpet shall be sounding "the gallop," and when afterwards it shall be sounding "the charge," yet, upon the whole, the troops of the first line obtain guidance mainly by carefully watching the leader who rides at the head of the force; and, the empire of words being thus superseded for the time by the signalling, if so one may call it, which is effected by the pace and the position of a single horseman, it seems right, by a kind of analogy, that one who would listen to the story of a cavalry onslaught extending along a great distance should be able—as well as may be in the mind's eye—to see and distinguish the leader. . . .

Lord Cardigan had so good a stature that, although somewhat long in the fork, he yet sat rather tall in the saddle, and notwithstanding his fifty-seven years, he had a figure which retained the slenderness of youth. His countenance, highly bred and of the aquiline cast, had not been without such humble share as a mere brother might be expected to have of that beauty which once made famous the ancient name of Brudenell. Far from disclosing the real faults of his character, the features of the man rather tended to confirm the first popular impression that was created by the tidings of the Light Cavalry charge, and to indicate a nature which might have in it something of chivalrous, nay even Quixotic exaltation. His blue, frank-looking, genial eyes revealed none of the narrowness of disposition which I have thought myself obliged to ascribe to him. As might be supposed, he had an excellent cavalry seat, and was erect—but also stiff—in the saddle. He wore the uniform of his old regiment, the 11th Hussars; but instead of dangling loose from the shoulders, his pelisse—richly burthened in front with gold lace—was worn closely put on like a coat, and did not at all break or mitigate the rigid outline of his figure. The charger he rode was a thorough-bred chestnut, with marks of a kind visible from afar, which in controversy it may be well to remember. On the near side before, as well as on the near side behind, the horse had one white leg. In the small group which represented the Brigade-Staff, Lieutenant Maxse, assistant aide-de-camp, and Sir George Wombwell, extra aide-de-camp to Lord Cardigan, were, it seems, the only officers present.

Although the part of the enemy's line which Lord Cardigan meant to attack lay as yet very distant before him, it was evident, from the position of the flanking batteries betwixt which he must pass, that his brigade would not long be in motion without incurring a heavy fire; and, upon the whole, he seems to have considered that almost from the first his advance was in the nature of a charge.

Followed immediately by his first line, and, at a greater distance, by the other regiments of his brigade, Lord Cardigan moved forward at a trot, taking strictly the direction in which his troops before moving had fronted, and making straight down the valley towards the battery which crossed it at the distance of about a mile and a quarter.

Before Lord Cardigan had ridden a hundred paces in advance, he encountered a sight which filled him with anger. Right before him he saw Captain Nolan audaciously riding across his front from left to right; but not content with a trespass which alone would have been shocking enough to Lord Cardigan's orderly mind, Captain Nolan, turning round in his saddle, was shouting, and waving his sword, as though he would address the brigade. . . .

Failing to surmise that Nolan's object might be that of averting mistake and supplying a much-needed guidance, Lord Cardigan, at the time, only saw in the appeal of the aide-de-camp a ridiculous and unseemly attempt to excite the brigade—nay, even to hurry it forward. Considering, however, that Nolan must have been acting with a full knowledge of the enemy's position, as well as of Lord Raglan's true meaning, and that at the time of his appealing thus eagerly to our Light Cavalry by gesture and voice, he was not only on the right front of our line, but was actually bearing away diagonally in the very direction of the Causeway Heights, there is plainly more room for surmising that the aide-de-camp's anxiety had been roused by seeing our squadrons advance without having first changed their front, and that what he now sought was to undo the mistake of Lord Lucan, to bend our troops from the path which led down the fatal North Valley, and make them incline to their right—make them so incline to their right as to strike the true point of attack which Lord Raglan had twice over assigned.

But a Russian shell bursting on the right front of Lord Cardigan now threw out a fragment which met Nolan full on the chest, and tore a way into his heart. The sword dropt from his hand; but the arm with which he was waving it the moment before still remained high uplifted in the air, and the grip of the practised horseman remaining as yet unrelaxed still held him firm in his saddle. Missing the perfect hand of his master, and finding the accustomed governance now succeeded by dangling reins, the horse all at once wheeled about, and began to gallop back upon the front of the advancing brigade. Then from what had been Nolan—and his form was still erect in the saddle, his sword-arm still high in the air—there burst forth a cry so strange and appalling that the hearer who rode the nearest to him has always called it "unearthly." And in truth, I imagine the sound resulted from no human will, but rather from those spasmodic forces which may act upon the bodily frame when life, as a power, has ceased. The firm-seated rider, with arm uplifted and stiff, could hardly be ranked with the living. The shriek men heard rending the air was scarce other than the shriek of a corpse. This dead horseman rode on till he had passed through the interval of the 13th Light Dragoons. Then at last he dropt out of the saddle. . . .

At first, as was natural, the enemy's gunners and riflemen were so far taken by surprise, as to be hardly in readiness to seize the opportunity which Lord Cardigan was presenting to them; and indeed for some time, the very extravagance of the operation masked its character from the intelligence of the enemy, preventing him from seeing at once that it must result from some stupendous mistake; but the Russians at length perceived that the distance between our Heavy Brigade and Lord Cardigan's squadrons was every moment increasing, and that, whatever might be the true meaning of the enterprise in which our Light Cavalry had engaged, the red squadrons [4] now every moment left further and further in rear were not under orders to give it that kind of support which the

----

[4] i.e., the Heavy Brigade.

Englishman calls "thoroughgoing." This once understood, the enemy had fair means of inferring that the phenomenon of ten beautiful squadrons moving down the North Valley in well-ordered lines, was not the commencement of anything like a general advance on the part of the Allies, and might prove, after all, to be hardly the result of design. Accordingly, with more or less readiness, the forces on the Causeway Heights, the forces on the Fedioukine Hills, and the twelve-gun battery which crossed the lower end of the valley, became all prepared to inflict upon our Light Cavalry the consequences of the fault which propelled it. . . .

Soon, the fated advance of the Light Brigade had proceeded so far as to begin to disclose its strange purpose—the purpose of making straight for the far distant battery which crossed the foot of the valley, by passing for a mile between two Russian forces, and this at such ugly distance from each as to allow of our squadrons going down under a doubly flanking fire of round-shot, grape, and rifle-balls, without the opportunity of yet doing any manner of harm to their assailants. Then, from the slopes of the Causeway Heights on the one side, and the Fedioukine Hills on the other, the Russian artillery brought its power to bear right and left, with an efficiency every moment increasing; and large numbers of riflemen on the slopes of the Causeway Heights who had been placed where they were in order to cover the retreat of the Russian battalions, found means to take their part in the work of destroying our horsemen. Whilst Lord Cardigan and his squadrons rode thus under heavy cross-fire, the visible object they had straight before them was the white bank of smoke, from time to time pierced by issues of flame, which marks the site of a battery in action; for in truth the very goal that had been chosen for our devoted squadrons— a goal rarely before assigned to cavalry—was the front of a battery—the front of that twelve-gun battery, with the main body of the Russian cavalry in rear of it, which crossed the lower end of the valley; and so faithful, so resolute, was Lord Cardigan in executing this part of what he understood to be his appointed task, that he chose out one of the guns which he judged to be about the centre of the battery, rode straight at its fire, and made this, from first to last, his sole guiding star.

Pressing always deeper and deeper into this

pen of fire, the devoted brigade, with Lord Cardigan still at its head, continued to move down the valley. The fire the brigade was incurring had not yet come to be of that crushing sort which mows down half a troop in one instant, and for some time a steady pace was maintained. As often as a horse was killed or disabled, or deprived of the rider, the fall, or his plunge, or his ungoverned pressure, had commonly the effect of enforcing upon the neighbouring charges more or less of lateral movement, and in this way there was occasioned a slight distension of the rank in which the casualty had occurred; but, in the next instant, when the troopers had ridden clear of the disturbing cause, they closed up, and rode on in a line as even as before, though reduced by the loss just sustained. The movement occasioned by each casualty was so constantly recurring, and so constantly followed by the same process,—the process of re-closing the ranks,—that to distant observers, the alternate distension and contraction of the line seemed to have the precision and sameness which belong to mechanic contrivance. Of these distant observers there was one—and that too a soldier—who so felt to the heart the true import of what he saw that, in a paroxysm of admiration and grief, he burst into tears. In well-maintained order, but growing less every instant, our squadrons still moved down the valley.

Their pace for some time was firmly governed. When horsemen, too valorous to be thinking of flight, are brought into straits of this kind, their tendency is to be galloping swiftly forward, each man at the greatest pace he can exact from his own charger, thus destroying, of course, the formation of the line; but Lord Cardigan's love of strict, uniform order was a propensity having all the force of a passion; and as long as it seemed possible to exert authority by voice or by gesture, the leader of this singular onset was firm in repressing the fault.

Thus when Captain White, of the 17th Lancers (who commanded the squadron of direction), became "anxious," as he frankly expressed it, "to get out of such a murderous fire, and into the guns, as being the best of the two evils," and endeavouring, with that view, to "force the pace," pressed forward so much as to be almost alongside of the chief's bridle-arm, Lord Cardigan checked this impatience by laying his sword across the Captain's breast, telling him at the same time not to try to force the pace, and not to be riding before the leader of the brigade. Otherwise than for this, Lord Cardigan, from the first to the last of the onset, did not speak nor make sign. Riding straight and erect, he never once turned in his saddle with the object of getting a glance at the state of the squadrons which followed him; and to this rigid abstinence—giving proof, as such abstinence did, of an unbending resolve—it was apparently owing that the brigade never fell into doubt concerning its true path of duty, never wavered (as the best squadrons will, if the leader, for even an instant, appears to be uncertain of purpose), and was guiltless of even inclining to any default except that of failing to keep down the pace. . . .

But although he rode singly, and although, as we have seen, he rigidly abstained from any retrograde glance, Lord Cardigan, of course, might infer from the tramp of the regiments close following, and from what (without turning in his saddle) he could easily see of their flanks, that the momentum now gathered and gathering was too strong to be moderated by a commander; and, rightly perhaps, avoiding the effort to govern it by voice or by gesture, he either became impatient himself, and drew the troops on more and more by first increasing his own speed, or else yielded (under necessity) to the impatience of the now shattered squadrons, and closely adjusted his pace to the flow of the torrent behind him. In one way or in the other, a right distance was always maintained between the leader and his first line. As before, when advancing at a trot, so now, whilst flinging themselves impetuously deep into the jaws of an army, these two regiments of the first line still had in their front the same rigid hussar for their guide, still kept their eyes fastened on the crimson-red overalls and the white near hind-leg of the chestnut which showed them the straight, honest way—the way down to the mouths of the guns. . . .

Lord Cardigan insists that he was not the originator of the high speed which they reached in this part of their onset; whilst some, on the other hand, say that the squadrons never ceased from their duty of studiously watching the leader, and that the swiftness of Lord Cardigan was the cause which hurried forward the line. The truth, perhaps, is intermediate; for it seems not unlikely that the rapid pace of the leader, and the eagerness of the squadrons behind him, were causes which acted and reacted alternately the one on the other; but with whomsoever originating, and whether dictated by a sound warlike judgment, or by mere human instinct, the desire to move more and more swiftly was not unwarranted. Even at the cost of sacrificing military order for the moment, it was seemingly wise, after all, in the straits to which our squadrons had been brought, to let every man close upon the battery with all the speed he could gather.

Alone, in a sense, though close followed, and with no regimental labour on his hands, Lord Cardigan had more leisure for thought than the chief part of those he was leading; and for that reason simply, if not for any other, there is an interest in hearing him say how it fared with him mentally at the time of undergoing this trial. He has not been reluctant to disclose the tenor of the ideas which possessed themselves of his mind whilst he thus led his troops down the valley. From moment to moment he was an expectant of death; and it seems that death by some cannonball dividing his body was the manner of coming to an end which his fancy most constantly harboured; but there is a waywardness in the human mind which often prevents it from laying a full stress on any one thought, however momentous; and despite the black prospect of what the next moment might bring, Lord Cardigan—not knowing that his anger was with the dead—still dwelt, as he rode, on the incident which had marked the commencement of the advance—still raged and raged against Nolan for having ridden in front of him, for having called out to his troops. By thus affording distraction to one who supposed himself doomed, hot anger for once, it would seem, did the work of faith and philosophy.

Lord Cardigan and his first line had come down to within about eighty yards of the mouths of the guns, when the battery delivered a fire from so many of its pieces at once as to constitute almost a salvo. Numbers and numbers of saddles were emptied, and along its whole length the line of the 13th Light Dragoons and 17th Lancers was subjected to the rending perturbance that must needs be created in a body of cavalry by every man who falls slain or wounded, by the sinking and the plunging of every horse that is killed or disabled, and again by the wild, piteous intrusion of the riderless charger appalled by his sudden freedom coming thus in the midst of a battle, and knowing not whither to rush, unless he can rejoin his old troop, and wedge himself into its ranks. . . . The extent to which a charger can apprehend the perils of a battle-field may be easily underrated by one who confines his observation to horses still carrying their riders; for, as long as a troop-horse in action feels the weight and the hand of a master, his deep trust in man keeps him seemingly free from great terror, and he goes through the fight, unless wounded, as though it were a field-day at home: but the moment that death or a disabling wound deprives him of his rider, he seems all at once to learn what a battle is—to perceive its real dangers with the clearness of a human being, and to be agonised with horror of the fate he may incur for want of a hand to guide him. Careless of the mere thunders of guns he shows plainly enough that he more or less knows the dread accent that is used by missiles of war whilst cutting their way through the air, for as often as these sounds disclose to him the near passage of bullet or round-shot, he shrinks and cringes. His eyeballs protrude. Wild with fright, he still does not most commonly gallop home into camp. His instinct seems rather to tell him that what safety, if any, there is for him must be found in the ranks; and he rushes at the first squadron he can find, urging piteously, yet with violence, that he too by right is a troop-horse— that he too is willing to charge, but not to be left behind—that he must and he will "fall in." Sometimes a riderless charger thus bent on aligning with his fellows, will not be content to range himself on the flank of the line, but dart at some point in the squadron which he seemingly judges to be his own rightful place, and strive to force himself in. Riding, as it is usual for the commander of a regiment to do, some way in advance of his regiment, Lord George Paget was especially tormented and pressed by the riderless horses which chose to turn round and align with him. At one time there were three or four of these horses advancing close abreast of him on one side, and as many as five on the other. Impelled by terror, by gregarious instinct, and by their habit of ranging in line, they so "closed" in upon Lord George as to besmear his overalls with blood from the gory flanks of the nearest intruders, and oblige him to use his sword.

Familiar pulpit reflections concerning man's frail tenure of life come to have all the air of fresh truths when they are pressed upon the attention of mortals by the "ping" of the bullet, by the sighing, the humming, and at last the "whang" of the round-shot, by the harsh "whirr" of the jagged iron fragments thrown abroad from a bursting shell, by the sound—most abhorred of all those heard in battle—the sound that issues from the moist plunge of the round-shot when it buries itself with a "slosh" in the trunk of a man or a horse. Under tension of this kind prolonged for some minutes, the human mind, without being flurried, may be wrought into so high a state of activity as to be capable of well-sustained thought; and a man, if he chose, whilst he rode down the length of this fatal North Valley, could examine and test and criticise—nay, even could change or restore that armour of the soul, by which he had been accustomed to guard his serenity in the trials and dangers of life.

One of the most gifted of the officers now acting with the supports was able, whilst descending the valley, to construct and adopt such a theory of the divine governance as he judged to be the best-fitted for the battle-field. Without having been hitherto accustomed to let his thoughts dwell very gravely on any such subjects of speculation—he now all at once, whilst he rode, encased himself body and soul in the iron creed of the fatalist; and, connecting destiny in his mind with the inferred will of God, defied any missile to touch him, unless it should come with the warrant of a providential and foregone decree. As soon as he had put on this armour of faith, a shot struck one of his holsters without harming him or his horse; and he was so constituted as to be able to see in this incident a confirmation of his new fatalist doctrine. Then, with something of the confidence often shown by other sectarians not engaged in a cavalry onset, he went on to determine that his, and his only, was the creed which could keep a man firm in battle. There, plainly, he erred; and, indeed, there is reason for saying that it would be ill for our cavalry regiments if their prowess were really dependent upon the adoption of any highly spiritual or philosophic theory. I imagine that the great body of our cavalry people, whether officers or men, were borne forward and sustained in their path of duty by moral forces of another kind—by sense of military obligation, by innate love of fighting and of danger—by the shame of disclosing weakness—by pride of nation and of race—by pride of regiment, of squadron, of troop—by personal pride; not least, by the power of that wheel-going mechanism which assigns to each man his task, and inclines him to give but short audience to distracting, irrelevant thoughts.

But, whatever might be the variety of the governing motives which kept every man to his duty through all the long minutes of this trying advance, there was no variety in the results; for what it was his duty to do, that every man did; and as often as a squadron was torn, so often the undisabled survivors made haste to repair it. The same words were ever recurring—"Close in! Close in!" "Close in to the centre!" "Close in!" . . .

Lord Cardigan and his first line, still descending at speed on their goal, had rived their way dimly through the outer folds of the cloud which lay piled up in front of the battery; but then there came the swift moment when, through what remained of the dimness, men at last saw the brass cannons gleaming with their muzzles towards the chests of our horses; and visibly the Russian artillerymen—unappalled by the tramp and the aspect of squadrons driving down through the smoke—were as yet standing fast to their guns.

By the material obstacle which they offer to the onset of horsemen, field-pieces in action, with their attendant limber-carriages and tumbrils behind them, add so sure a cause of frustration to the peril that there is in riding at the mouths of the guns, that, upon the whole, the expedient of attacking a battery in front has been forbidden to cavalry leaders by a recognised maxim of war. But the huge misconception of orders which had sent the brigade down this valley was yet to be fulfilled to its utmost conclusion; and the condition of things had now come to be such that, whatever might be the madness (in general) of charging a battery in front, there, by this time, was no choice of measures. By far the greater part of the harm which the guns could inflict had already been suffered; and I believe that the idea of stopping short on the verge of the battery did not even present itself for a moment to the mind of the leader.

Lord Cardigan moved down at a pace which he has estimated at seventeen miles an hour, and already he had come to within some two or three horses' lengths of the mouth of one of the guns—a gun believed to have been a twelve-pounder—but then, the piece was discharged; and its torrent of flame seemed to gush in the direction of his chestnut's off forearm. The horse was so governed by the impetus he had gathered, and by the hand and the heel of his rider, as to be able to shy only a little at the blaze and the roar of the gun; but Lord Cardigan being presently enwrapped in the new column of smoke now all at once piled up around him, some imagined him slain. He had not been struck. In the next moment, and being still some two horses' lengths in advance of his squadrons, he attained to the long-sought battery, and shot in between two of its guns.

There was a portion of the 17th Lancers on our extreme left which outflanked the line of the guns, but with this exception the whole of Lord Cardigan's first line descended on the front of the battery; and as their leader had just done before them, so now our horsemen drove in between the guns; and some then at the instant tore on to assail the grey squadrons drawn up in rear of the tumbrils. Others stopped to fight in the battery, and sought to make prize of the guns. After a long and disastrous advance against clouds and invisible foes, they grasped, as it were, at reality. What before had been engines of havoc dimly seen or only inferred from the jets of their fire and their smoke, were now burnished pieces of cannon with the brightness and the hue of red gold—cannon still in battery, still hot with the slaughter of their comrades. In defiance of our cavalry raging fiercely amongst them, the Russian artillerymen with exceeding tenacity still clung to their guns. Here and there indeed gunners were seen creeping under the wheels for safety, but in general they fought with rare devotion, striving all that men could, in such conditions of fight, against the sabres and lances of horsemen. They desired at all hazards to save their Czar's cannon from capture by removing them in haste from the front; and apparently it was to cover this operation—an operation they had already begun to attempt—that the gunners, with small means of resistance, stood braving the assaults of dragoons. . . .

Of those who swept on at the instant without staying to subdue the resistance of the artillerymen, Lord Cardigan from the first had been one. After charging into the battery, he continued his onset with but little remission of speed; and although the smoke was so thick as to put him in danger of crushing his legs against wheels, he pierced his way through at a gallop between the limber-carriages and the tumbrils by a gangway so narrow as hardly to allow a passage for two horsemen going abreast. Of necessity, therefore, his people who had hitherto followed him strictly now had to seek out other paths for their still continuing onslaught. Some, by bending a little, when necessary, to their right or to their left, found gangways more or less broad for their passage through the ranks of the artillery-carriages, and others made good their advance by sweeping round the flanks of the battery, but a few only were able to follow close on the track of their leader, and all these, sooner or later, were cut off from him by the incidents of battle.

In this way it happened that Lord Cardigan had already become almost entirely isolated, when, still pursuing his onward course, he found himself riding down singly towards a large body of Russian cavalry, then distant, as he has since reckoned, about eighty yards from the battery. This cavalry was retreating, but presently it came to a halt, went about, and fronted. . . .

It was right, of course, that instead of submitting to be taken prisoner, or to be butchered by overwhelming numbers, Lord Cardigan, being nearly alone, and altogether unaided, should disengage himself, if he could, from the reach of his assailants by a sufficing movement of retreat, and this he accordingly did. . . .

When Lord Cardigan had withdrawn himself from the reach of his Cossack assailants, he still continued to retire, and passed once more through the battery into which he had led his brigade. He then saw men of the 13th Light Dragoons and the 17th Lancers retreating in knots up the valley, and he apparently imagined that the horsemen whom he thus saw retiring constituted the entire remnants of his first line. . . .

In these circumstances, he satisfied himself that, so far as concerned the business of rallying or otherwise interfering with the shattered fragments of his first line, there was nothing he could usefully do, without first following their retreat. . . .

Resolved as he was from a sense of personal honour to execute to the letter, and without stint of life, whatever he might make out to be his clear duty, he yet never seemed to attain to such a height above the level of self as to feel what is called public care. And certainly his own account, if taken as being complete, would tend to make people think that, although, as might be expected, he was magnanimously regardless of his mere personal safety, yet in other respects, he much remembered himself, and all but forgot his brigade. It occurred to him, he says, at the time, that it was an anomalous thing for a General to be retreating in the isolated state to which he found himself reduced, and he therefore determined to move at a pace decorously slow.

Whatever were his governing motives, and whatever was his actual pace, he rode back alone towards the spot where Scarlett [5] at this time was halted. The first words he uttered were characteristic, and gave curious proof that the anger provoked by an apparent breach of military propriety had not been at all obliterated by even the Light Cavalry Charge. He began to run out against the officer who had galloped across his front at the commencement of the onset, and was continuing his invective when Scarlett stopped him by saying that he had nearly ridden over Captain Nolan's dead body. . . .

Amongst the remnants of our Light Cavalry, now once more gathered together, there was, of course, a sense of the havoc that had been made in what, half an hour before, was Lord Cardigan's splendid brigade; but, for a while, this feeling was much interrupted by the joy of seeing comrade after comrade trail in from out of the fight, and in spite of the ruin their force had incurred, the men were from time to time cheering.

When the remnants of the brigade had formed up, Lord Cardigan came forward and said, "Men! it is a mad-brained trick, but it is no fault of mine." Some of the men answered, "Never mind, my lord! we are ready to go again." Lord Cardigan replied, "No, no, men! you have done enough."

---

[5] Commander of the Heavy Brigade.

It was upon one of the slopes which look southward towards Balaclava that the muster took place; and, for some time, stragglers and riderless chargers were coming in at intervals; but at length there was a numbering of horses, and afterwards the melancholy roll-call began. As often as it appeared that to the name called out there was no one present to answer, men contributed what knowledge they had as to the fate of their missing comrade, saying when and where they last had seen him. More or less truly, if they knew it not before, men learned the fate of their friends from this dismal inquest. And then also came the time for the final and deliberate severance of many a friendship between the dragoon and his charger; for the farriers, with their pistols in hand, were busied in the task of shooting the ruined horses.

Upon counting the brigade, it appeared that the force, which numbered 673 horsemen when it went into action, had been reduced to a mounted strength of 195; and there was one regiment, it seems—namely, the 13th Light Dragoons, which, after the charge, mustered only ten mounted troopers. From a later examination it resulted that, in officers and men killed and wounded, the brigade had suffered losses to the number of 247, of whom 113 had been killed and 134 wounded; and that (including 43 horses shot as unserviceable on account of their wounds) the brigade had 475 horses killed, besides having 42 others wounded. . . .

It has been computed that the onset, the combat, and the retreat, which are popularly comprised under the name of the "Light Cavalry Charge," lasted twenty minutes.

## *Winston Churchill*

# DUNKIRK

From the moment that the French defences at Sedan and on the Meuse were broken at the end of the second week of May, only a

---

DUNKIRK: Address to Commons, June 4, 1940. Used by permission of G. P. Putnam's Sons, and McClelland and Stewart, Ltd.

rapid retreat to Amiens and the south could have saved the British and French Armies who had entered Belgium at the appeal of the Belgian King; but this strategic fact was not immediately realised. The French High Command hoped they would be able to close the gap, and the Armies of the north were under their orders. Moreover, a retirement of this kind would have involved almost certainly the destruction of the fine Belgian Army of over 20 divisions and the abandonment of the whole of Belgium. Therefore, when the force and scope of the German penetration were realised and when a new French Generalissimo, General Weygand, assumed command in place of General Gamelin, an effort was made by the French and British Armies in Belgium to keep on holding the right hand of the Belgians and to give their own right hand to a newly created French Army which was to have advanced across the Somme in great strength to grasp it.

However, the German eruption swept like a sharp scythe around the right and rear of the Armies of the north. Eight or nine armoured divisions, each of about four hundred armoured vehicles of different kinds, but carefully assorted to be complementary and divisible into small self-contained units, cut off all communications between us and the main French Armies. It severed our own communications for food and ammunition, which ran first to Amiens and afterwards through Abbeville, and it shore its way up the coast to Boulogne and Calais, and almost to Dunkirk. Behind this armoured and mechanized onslaught came a number of German divisions in lorries, and behind them again there plodded comparatively slowly the dull brute mass of the ordinary German Army and German people, always so ready to be led to the trampling down in other lands of liberties and comforts which they have never known in their own.

I have said this armoured scythe-stroke almost reached Dunkirk—almost but not quite. Boulogne and Calais were the scenes of desperate fighting. The Guards defended Boulogne for a while and were then withdrawn by orders from this country. The Rifle Brigade, the 60th Rifles, and the Queen Victoria's Rifles, with a battalion of British tanks and 1,000 Frenchmen, in all about four thousand strong, defended Calais to the last. The British Brigadier was given an hour to surrender. He spurned the

offer, and four days of intense street fighting passed before silence reigned over Calais, which marked the end of a memorable resistance. Only 30 unwounded survivors were brought off by the Navy, and we do not know the fate of their comrades. Their sacrifice, however, was not in vain. At least two armoured divisions, which otherwise would have been turned against the British Expeditionary Force, had to be sent to overcome them. They have added another page to the glories of the light divisions, and the time gained enabled the Graveline water lines to be flooded and to be held by the French troops.

Thus it was that the port of Dunkirk was kept open. When it was found impossible for the Armies of the north to reopen their communications to Amiens with the main French Armies, only one choice remained. It seemed, indeed, forlorn. The Belgian, British and French Armies were almost surrounded. Their sole line of retreat was to a single port and to its neighbouring beaches. They were pressed on every side by heavy attacks and far outnumbered in the air.

When, a week ago to-day, I asked the House to fix this afternoon as the occasion for a statement, I feared it would be my hard lot to announce the greatest military disaster in our long history. I thought—and some good judges agreed with me—that perhaps 20,000 or 30,000 men might be re-embarked. But it certainly seemed that the whole of the French First Army and the whole of the British Expeditionary Force north of the Amiens-Abbeville gap would be broken up in the open field or else would have to capitulate for lack of food and ammunition. These were the hard and heavy tidings for which I called upon the House and the nation to prepare themselves a week ago. The whole root and core and brain of the British Army, on which and around which we were to build, and are to build, the greatest British Armies in the later years of the war, seemed about to perish upon the field or to be led into an ignominious and starving captivity.

That was the prospect a week ago. But another blow which might well have proved final was yet to fall upon us. The King of the Belgians had called upon us to come to his aid. Had not this Ruler and his Government severed themselves from the Allies, who rescued their country from extinction in the late war,[6] and had they not sought refuge in what has proved to be a fatal neutrality, the French and British Armies might well at the outset have saved not only Belgium but perhaps even Poland. Yet at the last moment, when Belgium was already invaded, King Leopold called upon us to come to his aid, and even at the last moment we came. He and his brave, efficient Army, nearly half a million strong, guarded our left flank and thus kept open our only line of retreat to the sea. Suddenly, without prior consultation, with the least possible notice, without the advice of his Ministers and upon his own personal act, he sent a plenipotentiary to the German Command, surrendered his Army, and exposed our whole flank and means of retreat.

I asked the House a week ago to suspend its judgment because the facts were not clear, but I do not feel that any reason now exists why we should not form our own opinions upon this pitiful episode. The surrender of the Belgian Army compelled the British at the shortest notice to cover a flank to the sea more than 30 miles in length. Otherwise all would have been cut off, and all would have shared the fate to which King Leopold had condemned the finest Army his country had ever formed. So in doing this and in exposing this flank, as anyone who followed the operations on the map will see, contact was lost between the British and two out of the three corps forming the First French Army, who were still farther from the coast than we were, and it seemed impossible that any large number of Allied troops could reach the coast.

The enemy attacked on all sides with great strength and fierceness, and their main power, the power of their far more numerous Air Force, was thrown into the battle or else concentrated upon Dunkirk and the beaches. Pressing in upon the narrow exit, both from the east and from the west, the enemy began to fire with cannon upon the beaches by which alone the shipping could approach or depart. They sowed magnetic mines in the channels and seas; they sent repeated waves of hostile aircraft, sometimes more than a hundred strong in one formation, to cast their bombs upon the single pier that remained, and upon the sand dunes upon which the troops had their eyes for shelter.

---

[6] i.e., the First World War.

Their U-boats, one of which was sunk, and their motor launches took their toll of the vast traffic which now began. For four or five days an intense struggle reigned. All their armoured divisions—or what was left of them—together with great masses of infantry and artillery, hurled themselves in vain upon the ever-narrowing, ever-contracting appendix within which the British and French Armies fought.

Meanwhile, the Royal Navy, with the willing help of countless merchant seamen, strained every nerve to embark the British and Allied troops; 220 light warships and 650 other vessels were engaged. They had to operate upon the difficult coast, often in adverse weather, under an almost ceaseless hail of bombs and an increasing concentration of artillery fire. Nor were the seas, as I have said, themselves free from mines and torpedoes. It was in conditions such as these that our men carried on, with little or no rest, for days and nights on end, making trip after trip across the dangerous waters, bringing with them always men whom they had rescued. The numbers they have brought back are the measure of their devotion and their courage. The hospital ships, which brought off many thousands of British and French wounded, being so plainly marked were a special target for Nazi bombs; but the men and women on board them never faltered in their duty.

Meanwhile, the Royal Air Force, which had already been intervening in the battle, so far as its range would allow, from home bases, now used part of its main metropolitan fighter strength, and struck at the German bombers and at the fighters which in large numbers protected them. This struggle was protracted and fierce. Suddenly the scene has cleared, the crash and thunder has for the moment—but only for the moment—died away. A miracle of deliverance, achieved by valour, by perseverance, by perfect discipline, by faultless service, by resource, by skill, by unconquerable fidelity, is manifest to us all. The enemy was hurled back by the retreating British and French troops. He was so roughly handled that he did not hurry their departure seriously. The Royal Air Force engaged the main strength of the German Air Force, and inflicted upon them losses of at least four to one; and the Navy, using nearly 1,000 ships of all kinds, carried over 335,000 men, French and British, out of the jaws of death and shame, to their native land and to the tasks which lie immediately ahead. We must be very careful not to assign to this deliverance the attributes of a victory. Wars are not won by evacuations. But there was a victory inside this deliverance, which should be noted. It was gained by the Air Force. Many of our soldiers coming back have not seen the Air Force at work; they saw only the bombers which escaped its protective attack. They underrate its achievements. I have heard much talk of this; that is why I go out of my way to say this. I will tell you about it.

This was a great trial of strength between the British and German Air Forces. Can you conceive a greater objective for the Germans in the air than to make evacuation from these beaches impossible, and to sink all these ships which were displayed, almost to the extent of thousands? Could there have been an objective of greater military importance and significance for the whole purpose of the war than this? They tried hard, and they were beaten back; they were frustrated at their task. We got the Army away; and they have paid fourfold for any losses which they have inflicted. Very large formations of German aeroplanes—and we know that they are a very brave race—have turned on several occasions from the attack of one-quarter of their number of the Royal Air Force, and have dispersed in different directions. Twelve aeroplanes have been hunted by two. One aeroplane was driven into the water and cast away by the mere charge of a British aeroplane, which had no more ammunition. All of our types—the Hurricane, the Spitfire and the new Defiant—and all our pilots have been vindicated as superior to what they have at present to face.

When we consider how much greater would be our advantage in defending the air above this Island against an overseas attack, I must say that I find in these facts a sure basis upon which practical and reassuring thoughts may rest. I will pay my tribute to these young airmen. The great French Army was very largely, for the time being, cast back and disturbed by the onrush of a few thousands of armoured vehicles. May it not also be that the cause of civilisation itself will be defended by the skill and devotion of a few thousand airmen? There never has been, I suppose, in all the world, in all the history of war, such an opportunity for youth. The Knights of the Round Table, the Crusaders, all fall back into the past—not only distant but prosaic; these young men, going forth every morn to guard their native land and all that we stand for, holding in their hands these instruments of colossal and shattering power, of whom it may be said that

"Every morn brought forth a noble chance
And every chance brought forth a noble knight,"

deserve our gratitude, as do all of the brave men who, in so many ways and on so many occasions, are ready, and continue ready to give life and all for their native land.

I return to the Army. In the long series of very fierce battles, now on this front, now on that, fighting on three fronts at once, battles fought by two or three divisions against an equal or somewhat larger number of the enemy, and fought fiercely on some of the old grounds that so many of us knew so well—in these battles our losses in men have exceeded 30,000 killed, wounded and missing. I take occasion to express the sympathy of the House to all who have suffered bereavement or who are still anxious. The President of the Board of Trade is not here to-day. His son has been killed, and many in the House have felt the pangs of affliction in the sharpest form. But I will say this about the missing: We have had a large number of wounded come home safely to this country, but I would say about the missing that there may be very many reported missing who will come back home, some day, in one way or another. In the confusion of this fight it is inevitable that many have been left in positions where honour required no further resistance from them.

Against this loss of over 30,000 men, we can set a far heavier loss certainly inflicted upon the enemy. But our losses in material are enormous. We have perhaps lost one-third of the men we lost in the opening days of the battle of 21st March, 1918, but we have lost nearly as many guns—nearly one thousand—and all our transport, all the armoured vehicles that were with the Army in the north. This loss will impose a further delay on the expansion of our military strength. That expansion had not been proceeding as fast as we had hoped. The best of all we had to give had gone to the

British Expeditionary Force, and although they had not the numbers of tanks and some articles of equipment which were desirable, they were a very well and finely equipped Army. They had the first-fruits of all that our industry had to give, and that is gone. And now here is this further delay. How long it will be, how long it will last, depends upon the exertions which we make in this Island. An effort the like of which has never been seen in our records is now being made. Work is proceeding everywhere, night and day, Sundays and week days. Capital and Labour have cast aside their interests, rights, and customs and put them into the common stock. Already the flow of munitions has leaped forward. There is no reason why we should not in a few months overtake the sudden and serious loss that has come upon us, without retarding the development of our general programme.

Nevertheless, our thankfulness at the escape of our Army and so many men, whose loved ones have passed through an agonizing week, must not blind us to the fact that what has happened in France and Belgium is a colossal military disaster. The French Army has been weakened, the Belgian Army has been lost, a large part of those fortified lines upon which so much faith had been reposed is gone, many valuable mining districts and factories have passed into the enemy's possession, the whole of the Channel ports are in his hands, with all the tragic consequences that follow from that, and we must expect another blow to be struck almost immediately at us or at France. We are told that Herr Hitler has a plan for invading the British Isles. This has often been thought of before. When Napoleon lay at Boulogne for a year with his flat-bottomed boats and his Grand Army, he was told by someone, "There are bitter weeds in England." There are certainly a great many more of them since the British Expeditionary Force returned.

The whole question of home defence against invasion is, of course, powerfully affected by the fact that we have for the time being in this Island incomparably more powerful military forces than we have ever had at any moment in this war or the last. But this will not continue. We shall not be content with a defensive war. We have our duty to our Ally. We have to reconstitute and build up the British Expe-

ditionary Force once again, under its gallant Commander-in-Chief, Lord Gort. All this is in train; but in the interval we must put our defences in this Island into such a high state of organisation that the fewest possible numbers will be required to give effective security and that the largest possible potential of offensive effort may be realized. On this we are now engaged. It will be very convenient, if it be the desire of the House, to enter upon this subject in a secret Session. Not that the Government would necessarily be able to reveal in very great detail military secrets, but we like to have our discussions free, without the restraint imposed by the fact that they will be read the next day by the enemy; and the Government would benefit by views freely expressed in all parts of the House by Members with their knowledge of so many different parts of the country. I understand that some request is to be made upon this subject, which will be readily acceded to by His Majesty's Government.

We have found it necessary to take measures of increasing stringency not only against enemy aliens and suspicious characters of other nationalities, but also against British subjects who may become a danger or a nuisance should the war be transported to the United Kingdom. I know there are a great many people affected by the orders which we have made who are the passionate enemies of Nazi Germany. I am very sorry for them, but we cannot, at the present time and under the present stress, draw all the distinctions which we should like to do. If parachute landings were attempted and fierce fighting attendant upon them followed, these unfortunate people would be far better out of the way, for their own sakes as well as for ours. There is, however, another class, for which I feel not the slightest sympathy. Parliament has given us the powers to put down Fifth Column activities with a strong hand, and we shall use those powers, subject to the supervision and correction of the House, without the slightest hesitation until we are satisfied, and more than satisfied, that this malignancy in our midst has been effectively stamped out.

Turning once again, and this time more generally, to the question of invasion, I would observe that there has never been a period in all these long centuries of which we boast when an absolute guarantee against invasion, still less against serious raids, could have been given to our people. In the days of Napoleon the same wind which would have carried his transports across the Channel might have driven away the blockading fleet. There was always the chance, and it is that chance which has excited and befooled the imaginations of many Continental tyrants. Many are the tales that are told. We are assured that novel methods will be adopted, and when we see the originality of malice, the ingenuity of aggression, which our enemy displays, we may certainly prepare ourselves for every kind of novel stratagem and every kind of brutal and treacherous manoeuvre. I think that no idea is so outlandish that it should not be considered and viewed with a searching, but at the same time, I hope, with a steady eye. We must never forget the solid assurances of sea power and those which belong to air power if it can be locally exercised.

I have, myself, full confidence that if all do their duty, if nothing is neglected, and if the best arrangements are made, as they are being made, we shall prove ourselves once again able to defend our Island home, to ride out the storm of war, and to outlive the menace of tyranny, if necessary for years, if necessary alone. At any rate, that is what we are going to try to do. That is the resolve of His Majesty's Government—every man of them. That is the will of Parliament and the nation. The British Empire and the French Republic, linked together in their cause and in their need, will defend to the death their native soil, aiding each other like good comrades to the utmost of their strength. Even though large tracts of Europe and many old and famous States have fallen or may fall into the grip of the Gestapo and all the odious apparatus of Nazi rule, we shall not flag or fail. We shall go on to the end, we shall fight in France, we shall fight on the seas and oceans, we shall fight with growing confidence and growing strength in the air, we shall defend our Island, whatever the cost may be, we shall fight on the beaches, we shall fight on the landing grounds, we shall fight in the fields and in the streets, we shall fight in the hills; we shall never surrender, and even if, which I do not for a moment believe, this Island or a large part of it were subjugated and starving, then our Empire beyond the seas, armed and guarded by the British Fleet, would carry on the struggle, until, in God's good time, the New World, with all its power and might, steps forth to the rescue and the liberation of the old.

*Samuel Johnson*

# THE FABLE OF THE VULTURES

Many naturalists are of opinion that the animals which we commonly consider as mute have the power of imparting their thoughts to one another. That they can express general sensations is very certain; every being that can utter sounds has a different voice for pleasure and for pain. The hound informs his fellows when he scents his game; the hen calls her chickens to their food by her cluck, and drives them from danger by her scream.

Birds have the greatest variety of notes; they have indeed a variety which seems almost sufficient to make a speech adequate to the purposes of a life, which is regulated by instinct, and can admit little change or improvement. To the cries of birds, curiosity or superstition has been always attentive; many have studied the language of the feathered tribes, and some have boasted that they understood it.

The most skillful or most confident interpreters of the sylvan dialogues have been commonly found among the philosophers of the East, in a country where the calmness of the air and the mildness of the seasons allow the student to pass a great part of the year in groves and bowers. But what may be done in one place by peculiar opportunities may be performed in another by peculiar diligence. A shepherd of Bohemia has, by long abode in the forests, enabled himself to understand the voice of birds; at least he relates with great confidence a story, of which the credibility is left to be considered by the learned.

"As I was sitting," said he, "within a hollow rock, and watching my sheep that fed in the valley, I heard two vultures interchangeably

THE FABLE OF THE VULTURES: THE IDLER, Number 22, September 16, 1758.

crying on the summit of the cliff. Both voices were earnest and deliberate. My curiosity prevailed over my care of the flock; I climbed slowly and silently from crag to crag, concealed among the shrubs till I found a cavity where I might sit and listen without suffering, or giving disturbance.

"I soon perceived that my labor would be well repaid; for an old vulture was sitting on a naked prominence with her young about her, whom she was instructing in the arts of a vulture's life, and preparing by the last lecture for their final dismission to the mountains and the skies.

" 'My children,' said the old vulture, 'you will the less want my instructions because you have had my practice before your eyes; you have seen me snatch from the farm the household fowl; you have seen me seize the leveret [7] in the bush, and the kid in the pasture; you know how to fix your talons, and how to balance your flight when you are laden with your prey. But you remember the taste of more delicious food; I have often regaled you with the flesh of man.' 'Tell us,' said the young vultures, 'where man may be found, and how he may be known; his flesh is surely the natural food of a vulture. Why have you never brought a man in your talons to the nest?' 'He is too bulky,' said the mother; 'when we find a man, we can only tear away his flesh and leave his bones upon the ground.' 'Since man is so big,' said the young ones, 'how do you kill him? You are afraid of the wolf and of the bear; by what power are vultures superior to man? Is man more defenseless than a sheep?' 'We have not the strength of man,' returned the mother; 'and I am sometimes in doubt whether we have the subtlety; and the vultures would seldom feast upon his flesh, had not nature, that devoted him to our uses, infused into him *a strange ferocity* which I have never observed in any other being that feeds upon the earth. Two herds of men will often meet and shake the earth with noise, and fill the air with fire. When you hear noise and see fire, with flashes along the ground, hasten to the place with your swiftest wing, for men are surely destroying one another; you will then find the ground smoking with blood, and covered with carcasses, of which many are dis-

---

[7] Young rabbit.

membered and mangled for the convenience of the vulture.' 'But when men have killed their prey,' said the pupil, 'why do they not eat it? When the wolf has killed a sheep, he suffers not the vulture to touch it till he has satisfied himself. Is not man another kind of wolf?' 'Man,' said the mother, 'is the only beast who kills that which he does not devour, and this quality makes him so much a benefactor to our species.' 'If men kill our prey and lay it in our way,' said the young one, 'what need shall we have of laboring for ourselves?' 'Because man will, sometimes,' replied the mother, 'remain for a long time quiet in his den. The old vultures will tell you when you are to watch his motions. When you see men in great numbers moving close together like a flight of storks, you may conclude that they are hunting, and that you will soon revel in human blood.' 'But still,' said the young one, 'I would gladly know the reason of this mutual slaughter. I could never kill what I could not eat.' 'My child,' said the mother, 'this is a question which I cannot answer, though I am reckoned the most subtle bird of the mountain. When I was young, I used frequently to visit the aerie of an old vulture who dwelt upon the Carpathian rocks; he had made many observations; he knew the places that afforded prey round his habitation as far in every direction as the strongest wing can fly between the rising and setting of the summer sun; he had fed year after year on the entrails of men. His opinion was that men had only the appearance of animal life, being really *vegetables with a power of motion*; and that as the boughs of an oak are dashed together by the storm that swine may fatten upon the falling acorns, so men are by some unaccountable power driven one against another till they lose their motion that vultures may be fed. Others think they have observed something of contrivance and policy among these mischievous beings; and those that hover more closely round them, pretend that there is in every herd one that gives directions to the rest, and seems to be more eminently delighted with a wide carnage. What it is that entitles him to such preeminence we know not; he is seldom the biggest or the swiftest, but he shows by his eagerness and diligence that he is, more than any of the others, a friend to vultures.' "

*Jonathan Swift*

# WAR AMONG THE YAHOOS

The reader may please to observe that the following extract of many conversations I had with my master contains a summary of the most material points of which we discoursed at several times for above two years, his Honour often desiring fuller satisfaction as I further improved in the Houyhnhnm tongue. I laid before him, as well as I could, the whole state of Europe; I discoursed of trade and manufactures, of arts and sciences, and the answers I gave to all the questions he made, as they arose upon several subjects, were a fund of conversation not to be exhausted. But I shall here only set down the substance of what passed between us concerning my own country, reducing it into order as well as I can, without any regard to time or other circumstances, while I strictly adhere to truth. My only concern is that I shall hardly be able to do justice to my master's arguments and expressions, which must needs suffer by my want of capacity as well as by a translation into our barbarous English.

In obedience, therefore, to his Honour's commands, I related to him the Revolution under the Prince of Orange,[8] the long war with France entered into by the said Prince and renewed by his successor, the present Queen,[9] wherein the greatest powers of Christendom were engaged, and which still continued; I computed, at his request, that about a million of Yahoos[10] might have been killed in the whole progress of it, and perhaps a hundred or more cities taken, and thrice as many ships burnt or sunk.

He asked me what were the usual causes or motives that made one country go to war with another. I answered they were innumerable, but I should only mention a few of the chief. Sometimes the ambition of Princes, who never think they have land or people enough to govern; sometimes the corruption of Ministers, who engage their master in a war in order to stifle or divert the clamour of the subjects against their evil administration. Difference in opinions hath cost many millions of lives—for instance, whether flesh be bread or bread be flesh; whether the juice of a certain berry be blood or wine; whether whistling be a vice or a virtue; whether it be better to kiss a post or throw it into the fire; what is the best colour for a coat—whether black, white, red or gray; and whether it should be long or short, narrow or wide, dirty or clean, with many more. Neither are any wars so furious and bloody, or of so long continuance, as those occasioned by difference in opinion, especially if it be in things indifferent.

Sometimes the quarrel between two Princes is to decide which of them shall dispossess a third of his dominions, where neither of them pretend to any right. Sometimes one Prince quarrelleth with another for fear the other should quarrel with him. Sometimes a war is entered upon because the enemy is too strong, and sometimes because he is too weak. Sometimes our neighbours want the things which we have or have the things which we want, and we both fight till they take ours or give us theirs. It is a very justifiable cause of war to invade a country after the people have been wasted by famine, destroyed by pestilence, or embroiled by factions among themselves. It is justifiable to enter into war against our nearest ally when one of his towns lies convenient for us, or a territory of land that would render our dominions round and complete. If a Prince sends forces into a nation where the people are poor and ignorant, he may lawfully put half of them to death, and make slaves of the rest, in order to civilize and reduce them from their barbarous way of living. It is a very kingly, honourable, and frequent practice, when one Prince desires the assistance of another to secure him against an invasion, that the assistant, when he hath driven out the invader, should seize on the dominions himself, and kill, imprison, or banish the Prince he came to relieve. Alliance by blood or marriage is a frequent cause of war between Princes, and the nearer the kindred is, the greater is their disposition to quarrel. Poor

---

WAR AMONG THE YAHOOS: From *Gulliver's Travels*, Part IV, Chapter 5.

[8] William III, 1689–1702. Reference is to the "Glorious Revolution" of 1688 which deposed James II and brought William and Mary to the English throne.

[9] Queen Anne, 1702–1714.

[10] The name of the Houyhnhnms' beast-like slaves; Gulliver and his master apply it to human beings.

nations are hungry, and rich nations are proud, and pride and hunger will ever be at variance. For those reasons the trade of a soldier is held the most honourable of all others, because a soldier is a Yahoo hired to kill in cold blood as many of his own species who have never offended him as possibly he can.

There are likewise another kind of Princes in Europe, not able to make war by themselves, who hire out their troops to richer nations for so much a day to each man, of which they keep three-fourths to themselves, and it is the best part of their maintenance; such are those in many northern parts of Europe.

What you have told me (said my master) upon the subject of war does indeed discover most admirably the effects of that reason you pretend to; however, it is happy that the shame is greater than the danger, and that Nature has left you utterly incapable of doing much mischief.

For your mouths lying flat with your faces, you can hardly bite each other to any purpose, unless by consent. Then as to the claws upon your feet, before and behind, they are so short and tender that one of our Yahoos would drive a dozen of yours before him. And, therefore, in recounting the numbers of those who have been killed in battle, I cannot but think that you have said the thing that is not.

I could not forbear shaking my head and smiling a little at his ignorance. And being no stranger to the art of war, I gave him a description of cannons, culverins, muskets, carbines, pistols, bullets, powder, swords, bayonets, sieges, retreats, attacks, undermines, countermines, bombardments, sea-fights, ships sunk with a thousand men, twenty thousand killed on each side; dying groans, limbs flying in the air, smoke, noise, confusion, trampling to death under horses' feet; flight, pursuit, victory; fields strewed with carcases left for food to dogs, and wolves, and birds of prey; plundering, stripping, ravishing, burning, and destroying. And to set forth the valour of my own dear countrymen I assured him that I had seen them blow up a hundred enemies at once in a siege, and as many in a ship, and beheld the dead bodies come down in pieces from the clouds, to the great diversion of the spectators.

I was going on to more particulars, when my master commanded me silence. He said whoever understood the nature of Yahoos might easily believe it possible for so vile an animal to be capable of every action I had named if their strength and cunning equalled their malice. But as my discourse had increased his abhorrence of the whole species, so he found it gave him a disturbance in his mind, to which he was wholly a stranger before. He thought his ears, being used to such abominable words, might by degrees admit them with less detestation; that although he hated the Yahoos of this country, yet he no more blamed them for their odious qualities than he did a gnnayh (a bird of prey) for its cruelty or a sharp stone for cutting my hoof. But when a creature pretending to reason could be capable of such enormities, he dreaded lest the corruption of that faculty might be worse than brutality itself. He seemed, therefore, confident that instead of reason we were only possessed of some quality fitted to increase our natural vices, as the reflection from a troubled stream returns the image of an ill-shapen body, not only larger, but more distorted.

*Ambrose Bierce*

# AN OCCURRENCE AT OWL CREEK BRIDGE

A man stood upon a railroad bridge in northern Alabama, looking down into the swift water twenty feet below. The man's hands were behind his back, the wrists bound with a cord. A rope closely encircled his neck. It was attached to a stout cross-timber above his head and the slack fell to the level of his knees. Some loose boards laid upon the sleepers supporting the metals of the railway supplied a footing for him and his executioners—two private soldiers of the Federal army, directed by a sergeant who in civil life may have been a deputy sheriff. At a short remove upon the same temporary platform was an officer in the uniform of his rank, armed. He was a captain. A sentinel at each end of the bridge stood with his rifle in the position known as "support," that is to say, vertical in front of the left shoulder, the hammer resting on the forearm thrown straight across the chest—a formal and unnatural position, enforcing an erect carriage of the body.

It did not appear to be the duty of these two men to know what was occurring at the center of the bridge; they merely blockaded the two ends of the foot planking that traversed it.

Beyond one of the sentinels nobody was in sight; the railroad ran straight away into a forest for a hundred yards, then, curving, was lost to view. Doubtless there was an outpost farther along. The other bank of the stream was open ground—a gentle acclivity topped with a stockade of vertical tree trunks, loopholed for rifles, with a single embrasure through which protruded the muzzle of a brass cannon commanding the bridge. Midway of the slope between the bridge and fort were the spectators—a single company of infantry in line, at "parade rest," the butts of the rifles on the ground, the barrels inclining slightly backward against the right shoulder, the hands crossed upon the stock. A lieutenant stood at the right of the line, the point of his sword upon the ground, his left hand resting upon his right. Excepting the group of four at the center of the bridge, not a man moved. The company faced the bridge, staring stonily, motionless. The sentinels, facing the banks of the stream, might have been statues to adorn the bridge. The captain stood with folded arms, silent, observing the work of his subordinates, but making no sign. Death is a dignitary who when he comes announced is to be received with formal manifestations of respect, even by those most familiar with him. In the code of military etiquette silence and fixity are forms of deference.

The man who was engaged in being hanged was apparently about thirty-five years of age. He was a civilian, if one might judge from his habit, which was that of a planter. His features were good—a straight nose, firm mouth, broad forehead, from which his long, dark hair was combed straight back, falling behind his ears to the collar of his well-fitting frock coat. He wore a mustache and pointed beard, but no whiskers; his eyes were large and dark gray, and had a kindly expression which one would hardly have expected in one whose neck was in the hemp. Evidently this was no vulgar assassin. The liberal military code makes provision for hanging many kinds of persons, and gentlemen are not excluded.

The preparations being complete, the two private soldiers stepped aside and each drew away the plank upon which he had been standing. The sergeant turned to the captain, saluted and placed himself immediately behind that officer, who in turn moved apart one pace. These movements left the condemned man and the sergeant standing on the two ends of the same plank, which spanned three of the cross-ties of the bridge. The end upon which the civilian stood almost, but not quite, reached a fourth. This plank had been held in place by the weight of the captain; it was now held by that of the sergeant. At a signal from the former the latter would step aside, the plank would tilt and the condemned man go down between two ties. The arrangement commended itself to his judgment as simple and effective. His face had not been covered nor his eyes bandaged. He looked a moment at his "unsteadfast footing," then let his gaze wander to the swirling water of the stream racing madly beneath his feet. A piece of dancing driftwood caught his attention and his eyes followed it down the current. How slowly it appeared to move! What a sluggish stream!

He closed his eyes in order to fix his last thoughts upon his wife and children. The water, touched to gold by the early sun, the brooding mists under the banks at some distance down the stream, the fort, the soldiers, the piece of drift—all had distracted him. And now he became conscious of a new disturbance. Striking through the thought of his dear ones was a sound which he could neither ignore nor understand, a sharp, distinct, metallic percussion like the stroke of a blacksmith's hammer upon the anvil; it had the same ringing quality. He wondered what it was, and whether immeasurably distant or near by—it seemed both. Its recurrence was regular, but as slow as the tolling of a death knell. He awaited each stroke with impatience and—he knew not why—apprehension. The intervals of silence grew progressively longer; the delays became maddening. With their greater infrequency the sounds increased in strength and sharpness. They hurt his ear like the thrust of a knife; he feared he would shriek. What he heard was the ticking of his watch.

He unclosed his eyes and saw again the water below him. "If I could free my hands," he thought, "I might throw off the noose and spring into the stream. By diving I could evade the bullets and, swimming vigorously, reach the bank, take to the woods and get away home.

My home, thank God, is as yet outside their lines; my wife and little ones are still beyond the invader's farthest advance."

As these thoughts, which have here to be set down in words, were flashed into the doomed man's brain rather than evolved from it the captain nodded to the sergeant. The sergeant stepped aside.

Peyton Farquhar was a well-to-do planter, of an old and highly respected Alabama family. Being a slave owner and like other slave owners a politician, he was naturally an original secessionist and ardently devoted to the Southern cause. Circumstances of an imperious nature, which it is unnecessary to relate here, had prevented him from taking service with the gallant army that had fought the disastrous campaigns ending with the fall of Corinth, and he chafed under the inglorious restraint, longing for the release of his energies, the larger life of the soldier, the opportunity for distinction. That opportunity, he felt, would come, as it comes to all in war time. Meanwhile he did what he could. No service was too humble for him to perform in aid of the South, no adventure too perilous for him to undertake if consistent with the character of a civilian who was at heart a soldier, and who in good faith and without too much qualification assented to at least a part of the frankly villainous dictum that all is fair in love and war.

One evening while Farquhar and his wife were sitting on a rustic bench near the entrance to his grounds, a gray-clad soldier rode up to the gate and asked for a drink of water. Mrs. Farquhar was only too happy to serve him with her own white hands. While she was fetching the water her husband approached the dusty horseman and inquired eagerly for news from the front.

"The Yanks are repairing the railroads," said the man, "and are getting ready for another advance. They have reached the Owl Creek bridge, put it in order and built a stockade on the north bank. The commandant has issued an order, which is posted everywhere, declaring that any civilian caught interfering with the railroad, its bridges, tunnels or trains will be summarily hanged. I saw the order."

"How far is it to the Owl Creek bridge?" Farquhar asked.

"About thirty miles."

"Is there no force on this side the creek?"

"Only a picket post half a mile out, on the railroad, and a single sentinel at this end of the bridge."

"Suppose a man—a civilian and student of hanging—should elude the picket post and perhaps get the better of the sentinel," said Farquhar, smiling, "what could he accomplish?"

The soldier reflected. "I was there a month ago," he replied. "I observed that the flood of last winter had lodged a great quantity of driftwood against the wooden pier at this end of the bridge. It is now dry and would burn like tow."

The lady had now brought the water, which the soldier drank. He thanked her ceremoniously, bowed to her husband and rode away. An hour later, after nightfall, he re-passed the plantation, going northward in the direction from which he had come. He was a Federal scout.

As Peyton Farquhar fell straight downward through the bridge he lost consciousness and was as one already dead. From this state he was awakened—ages later, it seemed to him—by the pain of a sharp pressure upon his throat, followed by a sense of suffocation. Keen, poignant agonies seemed to shoot from his neck downward through every fiber of his body and limbs. These pains appeared to flash along well-defined lines of ramification and to beat with an inconceivably rapid periodicity. They seemed like streams of pulsating fire heating him to an intolerable temperature. As to his head, he was conscious of nothing but a feeling of fullness—of congestion. These sensations were unaccompanied by thought. The intellectual part of his nature was already effaced; he had power only to feel, and feeling was torment. He was conscious of motion. Encompassed in a luminous cloud, of which he was now merely the fiery heart, without material substance, he swung through unthinkable arcs of oscillation, like a vast pendulum. Then all at once, with terrible suddenness, the light about him shot upward with the noise of a loud plash; a frightful roaring was in his ears, and all was cold and dark. The power of thought was restored; he knew that the rope had broken and he had fallen into the stream. There was no additional strangulation; the noose about his neck was already suffocating him and kept the water from his lungs. To die of hanging at the bottom of a river!—the idea seemed to him ludicrous. He opened his eyes in the darkness and saw above him a gleam of light, but how distant, how inaccessible! He was still sinking, for the light became fainter and fainter until it was a mere glimmer. Then it began to grow and brighten, and he knew that he was rising toward the surface—knew it with reluctance, for he was now very comfortable. "To be hanged and drowned," he thought, "that is not so bad; but I do not wish to be shot. No; I will not be shot; that is not fair."

He was not conscious of an effort, but a sharp pain in his wrist apprised him that he was trying to free his hands. He gave the struggle his attention, as an idler might observe the feat of a juggler, without interest in the outcome. What splendid effort! What magnificent, what superhuman strength! Ah, that was a fine endeavor! Bravo! The cord fell away; his arms parted and floated upward, the hands dimly seen on each side in the growing light. He watched them with a new interest as first one and then the other pounced upon the noose at his neck. They tore it away and thrust it fiercely aside, its undulations resembling those of a water snake. "Put it back, put it back!" He thought he shouted these words to his hands, for the undoing of the noose had been succeeded by the direst pang that he had yet experienced. His neck ached horribly; his brain was on fire; his heart, which had been fluttering faintly, gave a great leap, trying to force itself out at his mouth. His whole body was racked and wrenched with an insupportable anguish! But his disobedient hands gave no heed to the command. They beat the water vigorously with quick, downward strokes, forcing him to the surface. He felt his head emerge; his eyes were blinded by the sunlight; his chest expanded convulsively, and with a supreme and crowning agony his lungs engulfed a great draught of air, which instantly he expelled in a shriek!

He was now in full possession of his physical senses. They were, indeed, preternaturally keen and alert. Something in the awful disturbance of his organic system had so exalted and refined them that they made record of things never before perceived. He felt the ripples upon his face and heard their separate sounds as they struck. He looked at the forest on the bank of the stream, saw the individual trees, the leaves and the veining of each leaf—saw the very insects upon them: the locusts, the brilliant-bodied flies, the gray spiders stretching their webs from twig to twig. He noted the prismatic colors in all the dewdrops upon a million blades of grass. The humming of the gnats that danced above the eddies of the stream, the beating of the dragonflies' wings, the strokes of the water spiders' legs, like oars which had lifted their boat—all these made audible music. A fish slid along beneath his eyes and he heard the rush of its body parting the water.

He had come to the surface facing down the stream; in a moment the visible world seemed to wheel slowly round, himself the pivotal point, and he saw the bridge, the fort, the soldiers upon the bridge, the captain, the sergeant, the two privates, his executioners. They were in silhouette against the blue sky. They shouted and gesticulated, pointing at him. The captain had drawn his pistol, but did not fire; the others were unarmed. Their movements were grotesque and horrible, their forms gigantic.

Suddenly he heard a sharp report and something struck the water smartly within a few inches of his head, spattering his face with spray. He heard a second report, and saw one of the sentinels with his rifle at his shoulder, a light cloud of blue smoke rising from the muzzle. The man in the water saw the eye of the man on the bridge gazing into his own through the sights of the rifle. He observed that it was a gray eye and remembered having read that gray eyes were keenest, and that all famous marksmen had them. Nevertheless, this one had missed.

A counter-swirl had caught Farquhar and turned him half round; he was again looking into the forest on the bank opposite the fort. The sound of a clear, high voice in a monotonous singsong now rang out behind him and came across the water with a distinctness that pierced and subdued all other sounds, even the beating of the ripples in his ears. Although no soldier, he had frequented camps enough to know the dread significance of that deliberate, drawling, aspirated chant; the lieutenant on shore was taking a part in the morning's work. How coldly and pitilessly—with what an even, calm intonation, presaging, and enforcing tranquillity in the men—with what accurately measured intervals fell those cruel words:

"Attention, company! . . . Shoulder arms! . . . Ready! . . . Aim! . . . Fire!"

Farquhar dived—dived as deeply as he could. The water roared in his ears like the voice of Niagara, yet he heard the dulled thunder of the volley and, rising again toward the surface, met shining bits of metal, singularly flattened, oscillating slowly downward. Some of them touched him on the face and hands, then fell away, continuing their descent. One lodged between his collar and neck; it was uncomfortably warm and he snatched it out.

As he rose to the surface, gasping for breath, he saw that he had been a long time under water; he was perceptibly farther down stream —nearer to safety. The soldiers had almost finished reloading; the metal ramrods flashed all at once in the sunshine as they were drawn from the barrels, turned in the air, and thrust into their sockets. The two sentinels fired again, independently and ineffectually.

The hunted man saw all this over his shoulder; he was now swimming vigorously with the current. His brain was as energetic as his arms and legs; he thought with the rapidity of lightning.

"The officer," he reasoned, "will not make that martinet's error a second time. It is as easy to dodge a volley as a single shot. He has probably already given the command to fire at will. God help me, I cannot dodge them all!"

An appalling plash within two yards of him was followed by a loud, rushing sound, *diminuendo,* which seemed to travel back through the air to the fort and died in an explosion which stirred the very river to its deeps! A rising sheet of water curved over him, fell down upon him, blinded him, strangled him! The cannon had taken a hand in the game. As he shook his head free from the commotion of the smitten water he heard the deflected shot humming through the air ahead, and in an instant it was cracking and smashing the branches in the forest beyond.

"They will not do that again," he thought; "the next time they will use a charge of grape. I must keep my eye upon the gun; the smoke will apprise me—the report arrives too late; it lags behind the missile. That is a good gun."

Suddenly he felt himself whirled round and round—spinning like a top. The water, the banks, the forests, the now distant bridge, fort and men—all were commingled and blurred. Objects were represented by their colors only;

circular horizontal streaks of color—that was all he saw. He had been caught in a vortex and was being whirled on with a velocity of advance and gyration that made him giddy and sick. In a few moments he was flung upon the gravel at the foot of the left bank of the stream—the southern bank—and behind a projecting point which concealed him from his enemies. The sudden arrest of his motion, the abrasion of one of his hands on the gravel, restored him, and he wept with delight. He dug his fingers into the sand, threw it over himself in handfuls and audibly blessed it. It looked like diamonds, rubies, emeralds; he could think of nothing beautiful which it did not resemble. The trees upon the bank were giant garden plants; he noted a definite order in their arrangement, inhaled the fragrance of their blooms. A strange, roseate light shone through the spaces among their trunks and the wind made in their branches the music of Æolian harps. He had no wish to perfect his escape—was content to remain in that enchanting spot until retaken.

A whiz and rattle of grapeshot among the branches high above his head roused him from his dream. The baffled cannoneer had fired him a random farewell. He sprang to his feet, rushed up the sloping bank, and plunged into the forest.

All that day he traveled, laying his course by the rounding sun. The forest seemed interminable; nowhere did he discover a break in it, not even a woodman's road. He had not known that he lived in so wild a region. There was something uncanny in the revelation.

By nightfall he was fatigued, footsore, famishing. The thought of his wife and children urged him on. At last he found a road which led him in what he knew to be the right direction. It was as wide and straight as a city street, yet it seemed untraveled. No fields bordered it, no dwelling anywhere. Not so much as the barking of a dog suggested human habitation. The black bodies of the trees formed a straight wall on both sides, terminating on the horizon in a point, like a diagram in a lesson in perspective. Overhead, as he looked up through this rift in the wood, shone great golden stars looking unfamiliar and grouped in strange constellations. He was sure they were arranged in some order which had a secret and malign significance. The wood on either side was full of singular noises, among which—once, twice, and again—he distinctly heard whispers in an un-known tongue.

His neck was in pain and lifting his hand to it he found it horribly swollen. He knew that it had a circle of black where the rope had bruised it. His eyes felt congested; he could no longer close them. His tongue was swollen with thirst; he relieved its fever by thrusting it forward from between his teeth into the cold air. How softly the turf had carpeted the untraveled ave-nue—he could no longer feel the roadway be-neath his feet!

Doubtless, despite his suffering, he had fallen asleep while walking, for now he sees another scene—perhaps he has merely recovered from a delirium. He stands at the gate of his own home. All is as he left it, and all bright and beautiful in the morning sunshine. He must have traveled the entire night. As he pushes open the gate and passes up the wide white walk, he sees a flutter of female garments; his wife, looking fresh and cool and sweet, steps down from the veranda to meet him. At the bottom of the steps she stands waiting, with a smile of ineffable joy, an attitude of matchless grace and dignity. Ah, how beautiful she is! He springs forward with extended arms. As he is about to clasp her he feels a stunning blow upon the back of the neck; a blinding white light blazes all about him with a sound like the shock of a cannon—then all is darkness and silence!

Peyton Farquhar was dead; his body, with a broken neck, swung gently from side to side beneath the timbers of the Owl Creek bridge.

## Luigi Pirandello

# WAR

The passengers who had left Rome by the night express had had to stop until dawn at the small station of Fabriano in order to continue their journey by the small old-fash-ioned local joining the main line with Sulmona.

At dawn, in a stuffy and smoky second-class

carriage in which five people had already spent the night, a bulky woman in deep mourning was hoisted in—almost like a shapeless bundle. Behind her—puffing and moaning, followed her husband—a tiny man, thin and weakly, his face death-white, his eyes small and bright and looking shy and uneasy.

Having at last taken a seat he politely thanked the passengers who had helped his wife and who had made room for her; then he turned round to the woman trying to pull down the collar of her coat, and politely inquired:

"Are you all right, dear?"

The wife, instead of answering, pulled up her collar again to her eyes, so as to hide her face.

"Nasty world," muttered the husband with a sad smile.

And he felt it his duty to explain to his traveling companions that the poor woman was to be pitied for the war was taking away from her her only son, a boy of twenty to whom both had devoted their entire life, even breaking up their home at Sulmona to follow him to Rome, where he had to go as a student, then allowing him to volunteer for war with an assurance, however, that at least for six months he would not be sent to the front and now, all of a sud-den, receiving a wire saying that he was due to leave in three days' time and asking them to go and see him off.

The woman under the big coat was twisting and wriggling, at times growling like a wild animal, feeling certain that all those explana-tions would not have aroused even a shadow of sympathy from those people who—most likely—were in the same plight as herself. One of them, who had been listening with particular attention, said:

"You should thank God that your son is only leaving now for the front. Mine has been sent there the first day of the war. He has already come back twice wounded and been sent back again to the front."

"What about me? I have two sons and three nephews at the front," said another passenger.

"Maybe, but in our case it is our *only* son," ventured the husband.

"What difference can it make? You may spoil your only son with excessive attentions, but you cannot love him more than you would all your other children if you had any. Paternal love is not like bread that can be broken into pieces and split amongst the children in equal shares. A father gives *all* his love to each one of his children without discrimination, whether it be one or ten, and if I am suffering now for my two sons, I am not suffering half for each of them but double . . ."

"True . . . true . . ." sighed the embarrassed husband, "but suppose (of course we all hope it will never be your case) a father has two sons at the front and he loses one of them, there is still one left to console him . . . while . . ."

"Yes," answered the other, getting cross, "a son left to console him but also a son left for whom he must survive, while in the case of the father of an only son if the son dies the father can die too and put an end to his distress. Which of the two positions is the worse? Don't you see how my case would be worse than yours?"

"Nonsense," interrupted another traveler, a fat, red-faced man with bloodshot eyes of the palest gray.

He was panting. From his bulging eyes seemed to spurt inner violence of an uncontrolled vitality which his weakened body could hardly contain.

"Nonsense," he repeated, trying to cover his mouth with his hand so as to hide the two missing front teeth. "Nonsense. Do we give life to our children for our own benefit?"

The other travelers stared at him in distress. The one who had had his son at the front since the first day of the war sighed: "You are right. Our children do not belong to us, they belong to the Country. . . ."

"Bosh," retorted the fat traveler. "Do we think of the Country when we give life to our children? Our sons are born because . . . well, because they must be born and when they come to life they take our own life with them. This is the truth. We belong to them but they never belong to us. And when they reach twenty they are exactly what we were at their age. We too had a father and mother, but there were so many other things as well . . . girls, cigarettes, illusions, new ties . . . and the Country, of course, whose call we would have answered—when we were twenty—even if father and mother had said no. Now at our age, the love of our Country is still great, of course, but stronger than it is the love for our children. Is there any one of us here who wouldn't gladly take his son's place at the front if he could?"

There was a silence all round, everybody nodding as to approve.

"Why then," continued the fat man, "shouldn't we consider the feelings of our children when they are twenty? Isn't it natural that at their age they should consider the love for their Country (I am speaking of decent boys, of course) even greater than the love for us? Isn't it natural that it should be so, as after all they must look upon us as upon old boys who cannot move any more and must stay at home? If Country exists, if Country is a natural necessity, like bread, of which each of us must eat in order not to die of hunger, somebody must go to defend it. And our sons go, when they are twenty, and they don't want tears, because if they die, they die inflamed and happy (I am speaking, of course, of decent boys). Now, if one dies young and happy, without having the ugly sides of life, the boredom of it, the pettiness, the bitterness of disillusion . . . what more can we ask for him? Everyone should stop crying; everyone should laugh, as I do . . . or at least thank God—as I do—because my son, before dying, sent me a message saying that he was dying satisfied at having ended his life in the best way he could have wished. That is why, as you see, I do not even wear mourning. . . ."

He shook his light fawn coat as to show it; his livid lip over his missing teeth was trembling, his eyes were watery and motionless, and soon after he ended with a shrill laugh which might well have been a sob.

"Quite so . . . quite so . . ." agreed the others.

The woman who, bundled in a corner under her coat, had been sitting and listening had—for the last three months—tried to find in the words of her husband and her friends something to console her in her deep sorrow, something that might show her how a mother should resign herself to send her son not even to death but to a probably dangerous life. Yet not a word had she found amongst the many which had been said . . . and her grief had been greater in seeing that nobody—as she thought—could share her feelings.

But now the words of the traveler amazed and almost stunned her. She suddenly realized that it wasn't the others who were wrong and could not understand her but herself who could not rise up to the same height of those fathers and mothers willing to resign themselves, without crying, not only to the departure of their sons but even to their death.

She lifted her head, she bent over from her corner trying to listen with great attention to the details which the fat man was giving to his companions about the way his son had fallen as a hero, for his King and his Country, happy and without regrets. It seemed to her that she had stumbled into a world she had never dreamt of, a world so far unknown to her and she was so pleased to hear everyone joining in congratulating that brave father who could so stoically speak of his child's death.

Then suddenly, just as if she had heard nothing of what had been said and almost as if waking up from a dream, she turned to the old man, asking him:

"Then . . . is your son really dead?"

Everybody stared at her. The old man, too, turned to look at her, fixing his great, bulging, horribly watery light gray eyes, deep in her face. For some little time he tried to answer, but words failed him. He looked and looked at her, almost as if only then—at that silly, incongruous question—he had suddenly realized at last that his son was really dead—gone for ever—for ever. His face contracted, became horribly distorted, then he snatched in haste a handkerchief from his pocket and, to the amazement of everyone, broke into harrowing, heart-rending, uncontrollable sobs.

*Stephen Crane*

# AN EPISODE OF WAR

The lieutenant's rubber blanket lay on the ground, and upon it he had poured the company's supply of coffee. Corporals and other representatives of the grimy and hot-throated men who lined the breast-work had come for each squad's portion.

The lieutenant was frowning and serious at this task of division. His lips pursed as he drew with his sword various crevices in the heap, until brown squares of coffee, astoundingly

equal in size, appeared on the blanket. He was on the verge of a great triumph in mathematics, and the corporals were thronging forward, each to reap a little square, when suddenly the lieutenant cried out and looked quickly at a man near him as if he suspected it was a case of personal assault. The others cried out also when they saw blood upon the lieutenant's sleeve.

He had winced like a man stung, swayed dangerously, and then straightened. The sound of his hoarse breathing was plainly audible. He looked sadly, mystically, over the breast-work at the green face of a wood, where now were many little puffs of white smoke. During this moment the men about him gazed statue-like and silent, astonished and awed by this catastrophe which happened when catastrophes were not expected—when they had leisure to observe it.

As the lieutenant stared at the wood, they too swung their heads, so that for another instant all hands, still silent, contemplated the distant forest as if their minds were fixed upon the mystery of a bullet's journey.

The officer had, of course, been compelled to take his sword into his left hand. He did not hold it by the hilt. He gripped it at the middle of the blade, awkwardly. Turning his eyes from the hostile wood, he looked at the sword as he held it there, and seemed puzzled as to what to do with it, where to put it. In short, this weapon had of a sudden become a strange thing to him. He looked at it in a kind of stupefaction, as if he had been endowed with a trident, a sceptre, or a spade.

Finally he tried to sheathe it. To sheathe a sword held by the left hand, at the middle of the blade, in a scabbard hung at the left hip, is a feat worthy of a sawdust ring. This wounded officer engaged in a desperate struggle with the sword and the wobbling scabbard, and during the time of it he breathed like a wrestler.

But at this instant the men, the spectators, awoke from their stone-like poses and crowded forward sympathetically. The orderly-sergeant took the sword and tenderly placed it in the scabbard. At the time, he leaned nervously backward, and did not allow even his finger to brush the body of the lieutenant. A wound gives strange dignity to him who bears it. Well men shy from this new and terrible majesty. It is as if the wounded man's hand is upon the curtain which hangs before the revelations of all existence—the meaning of ants, potentates, wars, cities, sunshine, snow, a feather dropped from a bird's wing; and the power of it sheds radiance upon a bloody form, and makes the other men understand sometimes that they are little. His comrades look at him with large eyes thoughtfully. Moreover, they fear vaguely that the weight of a finger upon him might send him headlong, precipitate the tragedy, hurl him at once into the dim, grey unknown. And so the orderly-sergeant, while sheathing the sword, leaned nervously backward.

There were others who proffered assistance. One timidly presented his shoulder and asked the lieutenant if he cared to lean upon it, but the latter waved him away mournfully. He wore the look of one who knows he is the victim of a terrible disease and understands his helplessness. He again stared over the breast-work at the forest, and then, turning, went slowly rearward. He held his right wrist tenderly in his left hand as if the wounded arm was made of very brittle glass.

And the men in silence stared at the wood, then at the departing lieutenant; then at the wood, then at the lieutenant.

As the wounded officer passed from the line of battle, he was enabled to see many things which as a participant in the fight were unknown to him. He saw a general on a black horse gazing over the lines of blue infantry at the green woods which veiled his problems. An aide galloped furiously, dragged his horse suddenly to a halt, saluted, and presented a paper. It was, for a wonder, precisely like a historical painting.

To the rear of the general and his staff a group, composed of a bugler, two or three orderlies, and the bearer of the corps standard, all upon maniacal horses, were working like slaves to hold their ground, preserve their respectful interval, while the shells boomed in the air about them, and caused their chargers to make furious quivering leaps.

A battery, a tumultuous and shining mass, was swirling toward the right. The wild thud of hoofs, the cries of the riders shouting blame and praise, menace and encouragement, and, last, the roar of the wheels, the slant of the glistening guns, brought the lieutenant to an intent pause. The battery swept in curves that stirred the heart; it made halts as dramatic as the crash of a wave on the rocks, and when it fled onward this aggregation of wheels, levers, motors had a beautiful unity, as if it were a missile. The sound of it was a war-chorus that reached into the depths of man's emotion.

The lieutenant, still holding his arm as if it were of glass, stood watching this battery until all detail of it was lost, save the figures of the riders, which rose and fell and waved lashes over the black mass.

Later, he turned his eyes toward the battle, where the shooting sometimes crackled like bush-fires, sometimes sputtered with exasperating irregularity, and sometimes reverberated like the thunder. He saw the smoke rolling upward and saw crowds of men who ran and cheered, or stood and blazed away at the inscrutable distance.

He came upon some stragglers, and they told him how to find the field hospital. They described its exact location. In fact, these men, no longer having part in the battle, knew more of it than others. They told the performance of every corps, every division, the opinion of every general. The lieutenant, carrying his wounded arm rearward, looked upon them with wonder.

At the roadside a brigade was making coffee and buzzing with talk like a girls' boarding-school. Several officers came out to him and inquired concerning things of which he knew nothing. One, seeing his arm, began to scold. "Why, man, that's no way to do. You want to fix that thing." He appropriated the lieutenant and the lieutenant's wound. He cut the sleeve and laid bare the arm, every nerve of which softly fluttered under his touch. He bound his handkerchief over the wound, scolding away in the meantime. His tone allowed one to think that he was in the habit of being wounded every day. The lieutenant hung his head, feeling, in this presence, that he did not know how to be correctly wounded.

The low white tents of the hospital were grouped around an old schoolhouse. There was here a singular commotion. In the foreground two ambulances interlocked wheels in the deep mud. The drivers were tossing the blame of it back and forth, gesticulating and berating, while from the ambulances, both crammed with wounded, there came an occasional groan. An interminable crowd of bandaged men were coming and going. Great numbers sat under the trees nursing heads or arms or legs. There was a dispute of some kind raging on the steps of the schoolhouse. Sitting with his back against a tree a man with a face as grey as a new army blanket was serenely smoking a corncob pipe. The lieutenant wished to rush forward and inform him that he was dying.

A busy surgeon was passing near the lieutenant. "Good-morning," he said, with a friendly smile. Then he caught sight of the lieutenant's arm, and his face at once changed. "Well, let's have a look at it." He seemed possessed suddenly of a great contempt for the lieutenant. This wound evidently placed the latter on a very low social plane. The doctor cried out impatiently: "What mutton-head had tied it up that way anyhow?" The lieutenant answered, "Oh, a man."

When the wound was disclosed the doctor fingered it disdainfully. "Humph," he said. "You come along with me and I'll 'tend to you." His voice contained the same scorn as if he were saying: "You will have to go to jail."

The lieutenant had been very meek, but now his face flushed, and he looked into the doctor's eyes. "I guess I won't have it amputated," he said.

"Nonsense, man! Nonsense! Nonsense!" cried the doctor. "Come along, now. I won't amputate it. Come along. Don't be a baby."

"Let go of me," said the lieutenant, holding back wrathfully, his glance fixed upon the door of the old schoolhouse, as sinister to him as the portals of death.

And this is the story of how the lieutenant lost his arm. When he reached home, his sisters, his mother, his wife, sobbed for a long time at the sight of the flat sleeve. "Oh, well," he said, standing shamefaced amid these tears, "I don't suppose it matters so much as all that."

*Alfred, Lord Tennyson*

# THE CHARGE OF
# THE LIGHT BRIGADE

I

Half a league, half a league,
Half a league onward,
All in the valley of Death
    Rode the six hundred.

"Forward, the Light Brigade!
Charge for the guns!" he said.
Into the valley of Death
    Rode the six hundred.

II

"Forward, the Light Brigade!"
Was there a man dismayed?                          10
Not though the soldier knew
    Some one had blundered.
Theirs not to make reply,
Theirs not to reason why,
Theirs but to do and die.
Into the valley of Death
    Rode the six hundred.

III

Cannon to right of them,
Cannon to left of them,
Cannon in front of them                            20
    Volleyed and thundered;
Stormed at with shot and shell,
Boldly they rode and well,
Into the jaws of Death,
Into the mouth of hell
    Rode the six hundred.

IV

Flashed all their sabres bare,
Flashed as they turned in air,
Sabring the gunners there,
Charging an army, while                             30
    All the world wondered.
Plunged in the battery-smoke
Right through the line they broke;
Cossack and Russian
Reeled from the sabre-stroke
    Shattered and sundered.
Then they rode back, but not,
    Not the six hundred.

V

Cannon to right of them,
Cannon to left of them,                             40
Cannon behind them
    Volleyed and thundered;
Stormed at with shot and shell,
While horse and hero fell,
They that had fought so well
Came through the jaws of Death,
Back from the mouth of hell,
All that was left of them,
    Left of six hundred.

VI

When can their glory fade?                50
O the wild charge they made!
    All the world wondered.
Honor the charge they made!
Honor the Light Brigade,
    Noble six hundred!

*Thomas Love Peacock*

# THE WAR-SONG OF
# DINAS VAWR

The mountain sheep are sweeter,
But the valley sheep are fatter;
We therefore deemed it meeter
To carry off the latter.
We made an expedition;
We met a host, and quelled it;
We forced a strong position,
And killed the men who held it.

On Dyfed's richest valley,
Where herds of kine were brousing,      10
We made a mighty sally,
To furnish our carousing.
Fierce warriors rushed to meet us;
We met them, and o'erthrew them:
They struggled hard to beat us;
But we conquered them, and slew them.

As we drove our prize at leisure,
The king marched forth to catch us:
His rage surpassed all measure,
But his people could not match us.      20
He fled to his hall-pillars;
And, ere our force we led off,
Some sacked his house and cellars,
While others cut his head off.

We there, in strife bewild'ring,
Spilt blood enough to swim in:
We orphaned many children,
And widowed many women.
The eagles and the ravens
We glutted with our foemen;              30
The heroes and the cravens,
The spearmen and the bowmen.

We brought away from battle,
And much their land bemoaned them,

Two thousand head of cattle,
And the head of him who owned them:
Ednyfed, king of Dyfed,
His head was borne before us;
His wine and beasts supplied our feasts,
And his overthrow, our chorus.          40

*William Shakespeare*

# ONCE MORE UNTO
# THE BREACH

Once more unto the breach, dear friends, once
    more;
Or close the wall up with our English dead.
In peace there's nothing so becomes a man
As modest stillness and humility:
But when the blast of war blows in our ears,
Then imitate the action of the tiger;
Stiffen the sinews, summon up the blood,
Disguise fair nature with hard-favoured [11] rage;
Then lend the eye a terrible aspect;
Let it pry through the portage [12] of the head    10
Like the brass cannon; let the brow o'erwhelm it
As fearfully as doth a gallèd [13] rock
O'erhang and jutty [14] his confounded [15] base,
Swilled with the wild and wasteful ocean.
Now set the teeth and stretch the nostril wide,
Hold hard the breath and bend up every spirit
To his full height. On, on, you noblest English,
Whose blood is fet [16] from fathers of war-proof! [17]
Fathers that, like so many Alexanders,
Have in these parts from morn till even fought,  20
And sheathed their swords for lack of argument:
Dishonour not your mothers; now attest
That those whom you called fathers did beget you.
Be copy now to men of grosser blood,
And teach them how to war. And you, good
    yeomen,
Whose limbs were made in England, show us here
The mettle of your pasture; let us swear

---

ONCE MORE UNTO THE BREACH: From *The Life of
King Henry V*, Act III, Scene 1.

[11] Grim.
[12] Porthole.
[13] Worn by sea water.
[14] Jut over.
[15] Worn.
[16] Fetched.
[17] Ancestors proved in war.

That you are worth your breeding; which I doubt
 not;
For there is none of you so mean and base,
That hath not noble lustre in your eyes.  30
I see you stand like greyhounds in the slips, [18]
Straining upon the start. The game's afoot:
Follow your spirit, and upon this charge
Cry "God for Harry, England, and Saint
 George!" [19]

------

[18] Collars for hunting dogs, quickly removable.
[19] Patron saint of England.

## Thomas Hardy
## CHANNEL FIRING

That night your great guns, unawares,
Shook all our coffins as we lay,
And broke the chancel window-squares,
We thought it was the Judgment-day

And sat upright. While drearisome
Arose the howl of wakened hounds:
The mouse let fall the altar–crumb,
The worms drew back into the mounds,

The glebe cow drooled. Till God called, "No;
It's gunnery practice out at sea    10
Just as before you went below;
The world is as it used to be:

"All nations striving strong to make
Red war yet redder. Mad as hatters
They do no more for Christés sake
Than you who are helpless in such matters.

"That this is not the judgment-hour
For some of them's a blessed thing,
For if it were they'd have to scour
Hell's floor for so much threatening. . . .  20

"Ha, ha. It will be warmer when
I blow the trumpet (if indeed
I ever do; for you are men,
And rest eternal sorely need)."

------

So we lay down again. "I wonder,
Will the world ever saner be,"
Said one, "than when He sent us under
In our indifferent century!"

And many a skeleton shook his head.
"Instead of preaching forty year,"   30
My neighbor Parson Thirdly said,
"I wish I had stuck to pipes and beer."

Again the guns disturbed the hour,
Roaring their readiness to avenge,
As far inland as Stourton Tower,
And Camelot, and starlit Stonehenge.

## Wilfred Owen
## DULCE ET DECORUM EST

Bent double, like old beggars under sacks,
Knock-kneed, coughing like hags, we cursed
 through sludge,
Till on the haunting flares we turned our backs,
And towards our distant rest began to trudge.
Men marched asleep. Many had lost their boots,
But limped on, blood-shod. All went lame, all
 blind;
Drunk with fatigue; deaf even to the hoots
Of gas-shells dropping softly behind.

Gas! Gas! Quick, boys!—An ecstasy of fumbling,
Fitting the clumsy helmets just in time,  10
But someone still was yelling out and stumbling
And floundering like a man in fire or lime.—
Dim through the misty panes and thick green light,
As under a green sea, I saw him drowning.

In all my dreams before my helpless sight
He plunges at me, guttering, choking, drowning.

If in some smothering dreams, you too could pace
Behind the wagon that we flung him in,
And watch the white eyes writhing in his face,
His hanging face, like a devil's sick of sin;  20
If you could hear, at every jolt, the blood
Come gargling from the froth-corrupted lungs,
Bitter as the cud

------

Of vile, incurable sores on innocent tongues,—
My friend, you would not tell with such high zest
To children ardent for some desperate glory,
The old Lie: Dulce et decorum est
Pro patria mori.

## Archibald MacLeish
## THE TOO-LATE BORN

We too, we too, descending once again
The hills of our own land, we too have heard
Far off—Ah, que ce cor a longue haleine—[20]
The horn of Roland [21] in the passages of Spain,
The first, the second blast, the failing third,
And with the third turned back and climbed once
    more
The steep road southward, and heard faint the
    sound
Of swords, of horses, the disastrous war,
And crossed the dark defile at last, and found
At Ronçevaux [22] upon the darkening plain      10
The dead against the dead and on the silent ground
The silent slain—

[20] Ah, how long that horn reverberates!
[21] Knight of Charlemagne, hero of *Song of Roland.*
[22] Scene of battle in Pyrenees where Roland was killed, 778 A.D.

## A. E. Housman
## MY DREAMS ARE OF A FIELD AFAR

My dreams are of a field afar
    And blood and smoke and shot.
There in their graves my comrades are,
    In my grave I am not.

I too was taught the trade of man
    And spelt the lesson plain;
But they, when I forgot and ran,
    Remembered and remain.

## William Butler Yeats
## AN IRISH AIRMAN FORESEES HIS DEATH

I know that I shall meet my fate
Somewhere among the clouds above;
Those that I fight I do not hate,
Those that I guard I do not love;
My country is Kiltartan Cross,
My countrymen Kiltartan's poor,
No likely end could bring them loss
Or leave them happier than before.
Nor law, nor duty bade me fight,
Nor public men, nor cheering crowds,      10
A lonely impulse of delight
Drove to this tumult in the clouds;
I balanced all, brought all to mind,
The years to come seemed waste of breath
A waste of breath the years behind
In balance with this life, this death.

## W. H. Auden
## SEPTEMBER 1, 1939

I sit in one of the dives
On Fifty-Second Street
Uncertain and afraid
As the clever hopes expire
Of a low dishonest decade:

Waves of anger and fear
Circulate over the bright
And darkened lands of the earth,
Obsessing our private lives;
The unmentionable odour of death          10
Offends the September night.

Accurate scholarship can
Unearth the whole offence
From Luther until now
That has driven a culture mad,
Find what occurred at Linz,
What huge imago made
A psychopathic god:
I and the public know
What all schoolchildren learn,          20
Those to whom evil is done
Do evil in return.

Exiled Thucydides knew
All that a speech can say
About Democracy,
And what dictators do,
The elderly rubbish they talk
To an apathetic grave;
Analysed all in his book,
The enlightenment driven away,          30
The habit-forming pain,
Mismanagement and grief:
We must suffer them all again.

Into this neutral air
Where blind skyscrapers use
Their full height to proclaim
The strength of Collective Man,
Each language pours its vain
Competitive excuse:
But who can live for long          40
In an euphoric dream;
Out of the mirror they stare,
Imperialism's face
And the international wrong.

Faces along the bar
Cling to their average day:
The lights must never go out,
The music must always play,
All the conventions conspire
To make this fort assume          50
The furniture of home;
Lest we should see where we are,

Lost in a haunted wood,
Children afraid of the night
Who have never been happy or good.

The windiest militant trash
Important Persons shout
Is not so crude as our wish:
What mad Nijinsky wrote
About Diaghilev          60
Is true of the normal heart;
For the error bred in the bone
Of each woman and each man
Craves what it cannot have,
Not universal love
But to be loved alone.

From the conservative dark
Into the ethical life
The dense commuters come,
Repeating their morning vow;          70
"I *will* be true to the wife,
I'll concentrate more on my work,"
And helpless governors wake
To resume their compulsory game:
Who can release them now,
Who can reach the deaf.
Who can speak for the dumb?

All I have is a voice
To undo the folded lie,
The romantic lie in the brain          80
Of the sensual man-in-the-street
And the lie of Authority
Whose buildings grope the sky:
There is no such thing as the State
And no one exists alone;
Hunger allows no choice
To the citizen or the police;
We must love one another or die.

Defenceless under the night
Our world in stupour lies;          90
Yet, dotted everywhere,
Ironic points of light
Flash out wherever the Just
Exchange their messages:
May I, composed like them
Of Eros and of dust,
Beleaguered by the same
Negation and despair,
Show an affirming flame.

*Homer*

# AGAMEMNON

Now Dawn rose from her bed, where she lay by haughty Tithonos,[23]
to carry her light to men and to immortals. Zeus sent down
in speed to the fast ships of the Achaians [24] the wearisome goddess
of Hate, holding in her hands the portent of battle.
She took her place on the huge-hollowed black ship of Odysseus [25]
which lay in the middle, so that she could cry out to both flanks,
either as far as the shelters of Telamonian Aias [26]
or to those of Achilleus; [27] since these had hauled their balanced ships up
at the ends, certain of their manhood and their hands' strength.
There the goddess took her place, and cried out a great cry                      10
and terrible and loud, and put strength in all the Achaians'
hearts, to go on tirelessly with their fighting of battles.
And now battle became sweeter to them than to go back
in their hollow ships to the beloved land of their fathers.
    And Atreus' son [28] cried out aloud and drove the Achaians
to gird them, while he himself put the shining bronze upon him.
First he placed along his legs the beautiful greaves [29] linked
with silver fastenings to hold the greaves at the ankles.
Afterwards he girt on about his chest the corselet
that Kinyras [30] had given him once, to be a guest present.             20
For the great fame and rumour of war had carried to Kypros [31]
how the Achaians were to sail against Troy in their vessels.
Therefore he gave the king as a gift of grace this corselet.
Now there were ten circles of deep cobalt upon it,
and twelve of gold and twenty of tin. And toward the opening
at the throat there were rearing up three serpents of cobalt
on either side, like rainbows, which the son of Kronos [32]
has marked upon the clouds, to be a portent to mortals.
Across his shoulders he slung the sword, and the nails upon it
were golden and glittered, and closing about it the scabbard        30
was silver, and gold was upon the swordstraps that held it.
And he took up the man-enclosing elaborate stark shield,
a thing of splendour. There were ten circles of bronze upon it,
and set about it were twenty knobs of tin, pale-shining,
and in the very centre another knob of dark cobalt.
And circled in the midst of all was the blank-eyed face of the Gorgon [33]

---

AGAMEMNON: From *The Iliad*, Book XI. Translated by Richmond Lattimore. Copyright,
1951, by the University of Chicago Press. Used by permission of the publishers.

[23] Brother of the Trojan king, Priam.
[24] The Greeks.
[25] Counsellor and friend to the leader of the Greek forces, Agamemnon.
[26] A Greek, son of Telemon.
[27] Achilles, strongest of the Greek warriors.
[28] Agamemnon.
[29] Armor for leg below the knee.
[30] King of the island of Cyprus.
[31] Cyprus.
[32] Zeus was the son of the Titan, Kronos, who personified Time.
[33] Monster who turned to stone all those who looked at her.

with her stare of horror, and Fear was inscribed upon it, and Terror.
The strap of the shield had silver upon it, and there also on it
was coiled a cobalt snake, and there were three heads upon him
twisted to look backward and grown from a single neck, all three.                    40
Upon his head he set the helmet, two-horned, four-sheeted,
with the horse-hair crest, and the plumes nodded terribly above it.
Then he caught up two strong spears edged with sharp bronze
and the brazen heads flashed far from him deep into heaven.
And Hera [34] and Athene [35] caused a crash of thunder about him,
doing honour to the lord of deep-golden Mykenai.[36]
    Thereupon each man gave orders to his charioteer
to rein in the horses once again by the ditch, in good order,
while they themselves, dismounted and armed in their war gear, swept onward
to the ditch, and their incessant clamour rose up in the morning.                    50
In battle array they came to the ditch well ahead of the horseman
and the horseman followed a little behind. And the son of Kronos
drove down the evil turmoil upon them, and from aloft cast
down dews dripping blood from the sky, since he was minded
to hurl down a multitude of strong heads to the house of Hades.
    On the other side of the ditch at the break of the plain the Trojans
gathered about tall Hektor [37] and stately Poulydamas [38]
and Aineias,[39] honoured by Trojans in their countryside as a god is,
and the three sons of Antenor,[40] Polybos, and brilliant Agenor,
and Akamas, a young man still, in the likeness of the immortals.                     60
And Hektor carried the perfect circle of his shield in the foremost,
as among the darkened clouds the bale star shows forth
in all shining, then merges again in the clouds and the darkness.
So Hektor would at one time be shining among the foremost,
and then once more urging on the last, and complete in bronze armour
glittered like the thunder-flash of Zeus of the aegis, our father.
    And the men, like two lines of reapers who, facing each other,
drive their course all down the field of wheat or of barley
for a man blessed in substance, and the cut swathes drop showering,
so Trojans and Achaians driving in against one another                               70
cut men down, nor did either side think of disastrous panic.
The pressure held their heads on a line, and they whirled and fought like
wolves, and Hate, the Lady of Sorrow, was gladdened to watch them.
She alone of all the immortals attended this action
but the other immortals were not there, but sat quietly
remote and apart in their palaces, where for each one of them
a house had been built in splendour along the folds of Olympos.[41]
All were blaming the son of Kronos, Zeus of the dark mists,
because his will was to give glory to the Trojans. To these gods
the father gave no attention at all, but withdrawn from them                         80
and rejoicing in the pride of his strength sat apart from the others
looking out over the city of Troy and the ships of the Achaians,

---

[34] Chief of the goddesses.
[35] Daughter of Zeus, goddess of wisdom, protector of the Greeks.
[36] Agamemnon's capital city.
[37] Hector, strongest of the Trojan warriors.
[38] Counsellor to the Trojans.
[39] Aeneas, one of the Trojan leaders.
[40] Counsellor to Priam.
[41] Mountain in Greece, home of the gods.

watching the flash of the bronze, and men killing and men killed.

So long as it was early morning and the sacred daylight increasing,
so long the thrown weapons of both took hold and men dropped under them.
But at that time when the woodcutter makes ready his supper
in the wooded glens of the mountains, when his arms and hands have grown weary
from cutting down the tall trees, and his heart has had enough of it,
and longing for food and for sweet wine takes hold of his senses;
at that time the Danaans [42] by their manhood broke the battalions          90
calling across the ranks to each other. First Agamemnon
drove on, and killed a man, Bienor, shepherd of the people,
himself, then his companion Oïleus, lasher of horses;
who, springing down from behind his horses, stood forth to face him,
but Agamemnon stabbed straight at his face as he came on in fury
with the sharp spear, nor did helm's bronze-heavy edge hold it,
but the spearhead passed through this and the bone, and the inward
brain was all spattered forth. So he beat him down in his fury,
and Agamemnon the lord of men left them lying there
and their white bodies showing, since he had stripped off their tunics.      100
Then he went on to kill and strip Isos and Antiphos,
two sons of Priam, bastard one and one lawful, both riding
in a single chariot. The bastard, Isos, was charioteer
and renowned Antiphos rode beside him. Before this Achilleus
had caught these two at the knees of Ida, [43] and bound them in pliant
willows as they watched by their sheep, and released them for ransom.
This time the son of Atreus, wide-powerful Agamemnon,
struck Isos with the thrown spear in the chest above the nipple
and hit Antiphos by the ear with the sword and hurled him from his horses,
and in eager haste he stripped off from these their glorious armour           110
which he knew; he had seen these two before by the fast ships
when Achilleus of the swift feet had brought them in from Ida.
And as a lion seizes the innocent young of the running
deer, and easily crunches and breaks them caught in the strong teeth
when he has invaded their lair, and rips out the soft heart from them,
and even if the doe be very near, still she has no strength
to help, for the ghastly shivers of fear are upon her also
and suddenly she dashes away through the glades and the timber
sweating in her speed away from the pounce of the strong beast;
so there was no one of the Trojans who could save these two                   120
from death, but they themselves were running in fear from the Argives. [44]

Next he caught Peisandros and Hippolochos stubborn in battle,
sons of Antimachos the wise, who beyond all others
had taken the gold of Alexandros, [45] glorious gifts, so that
he had opposed the return of Helen to fair-haired Menelaos. [46]
Powerful Agamemnon caught his two sons riding
in one chariot, who together guided the running horses.
Now the glittering reins escaped from the hands of both of them
and they were stunned with fear, for against them rose like a lion
Atreus' son, and they supplicated him out of the chariot:                    130

[42] The Greeks.
[43] Mountain range near Troy.
[44] Achaians: *i.e.,* the Greeks.
[45] Another name for Paris, son of Priam, abductor of Helen.
[46] King of Sparta; brother of Agamemnon and husband of Helen.

"Take us alive, son of Atreus, and take appropriate ransom.
In the house of Antimachos the treasures lie piled in abundance,
bronze is there, and gold, and difficultly wrought iron,
and our father would make you glad with abundant repayment
were he to hear we were alive by the ships of the Achaians."
      Thus these two cried out upon the king, lamenting
and in pitiful phrase, but they heard the voice that was without pity:
"If in truth you are the sons of wise Antimachos,
that man who once among the Trojans assembled advised them
that Menelaos, who came as envoy with godlike Odysseus,                     140
should be murdered on the spot nor let go back to the Achaians,
so now your mutilation shall punish the shame of your father."
      He spoke, and spurned Peisandros to the ground from the chariot
with a spear-stroke in the chest, and he crashed on his back to the ground. Then
Hippolochos sprang away, but Atreides [47] killed him dismounted,
cutting away his arms with a sword-stroke, free of the shoulder,
and sent him spinning like a log down the battle. Thereafter
he left them, and toward that place where the most battalions were shaken
drove, and beside him drove the rest of the strong-greaved Achaians,
and footmen killed footmen who fled under strong compulsion                 150
and riders killed riders, and a storm of dust rose up under them
out of the plain uplifted by the thundering feet of their horses.
They killed with the bronze, and among them powerful Agamemnon
went onward always slaying and urged on the rest of the Argives.
As when obliterating fire comes down on the timbered forest
and the roll of the wind carries it everywhere, and bushes
leaning under the force of the fire's rush tumble uprooted,
so before Atreus' son Agamemnon went down the high heads
of the running Trojans, and in many places the strong-necked horses
rattled their empty chariots along the causeways of battle,                 160
and longed for their haughty charioteers, who were lying
along the ground, to delight no longer their wives, but the vultures.
      But Zeus drew Hektor out from under the dust and the missiles,
out of the place where men were killed, the blood and confusion,
while Atreides followed urging the Danaans forever onward.
The Trojans swept in their flight past the barrow of ancient Ilos,[48]
Dardanos' son, to the centre of the level ground and the fig tree,
as they made for the city, and he followed them always, screaming,
Atreus' son, his invincible hands spattered with bloody filth.
But when they had made their way to the Skaian gates and the oak tree       170
the Trojans stood their ground, and each side endured the other,
while others still in the middle plain stampeded like cattle
when a lion, coming upon them in the dim night, has terrified
the whole herd, while for a single one sheer death is emerging.
First the lion breaks her neck caught fast in the strong teeth,
then gulps down the blood and all the guts that are inward;
so Atreus' son, powerful Agamemnon, went after them
killing ever the last of the men; and they fled in terror.
Many were hurled from behind their horses, face downward or sprawling
under the hands of Atreides who raged with his spear in the forefront.      180
But when he was on the point of making his way to the city

---

[47] "Son of Atreus," Agamemnon.
[48] Grandfather of Priam.

and the steep wall, the father of gods and of men descending
out of the sky took his place along the ridges of Ida
of the fountains, and held fast in his hands the thunderbolt.
He sent on her way Iris [49] of the golden wings with a message:
"Go on your way, swift Iris, and carry my word to Hektor:
as long as he beholds Agamemnon, shepherd of the people,
raging among the champions and cutting down the ranged fighters,
so long let him hold back and urge on the rest of his people
to fight against the enemy through this strong encounter.                190
But when, either struck with a spear or hit by a flying arrow,
he springs up behind his horses, then I guarantee power to Hektor
to kill men, till he makes his way to the strong-benched vessels,
until the sun goes down and the blessed darkness comes over."
He spoke, and swift wind-footed Iris did not disobey him,
but went down along the hills of Ida to sacred Ilion,[50]
and found the son of wise Priam, Hektor the brilliant,
standing among the compacted chariots and by the horses.
Iris the swift of foot came close beside and spoke to him:
"Hektor, o son of Priam and equal of Zeus in counsel,                   200
Zeus my father has sent me down to tell you this message.
As long as you behold Agamemnon, shepherd of the people,
raging among the champions and cutting down the ranged fighters,
so long hold back from the fighting, but urge on the rest of your people
to fight against the enemy through this strong encounter.
But when, either struck with a spear or hit by a flying arrow,
he springs up behind his horses, then Zeus guarantees power to you
to kill men, till you make your way to the strong-benched vessels,
until the sun goes down and the blessed darkness comes over."
Swift-foot Iris spoke to him thus and went away from him,               210
and Hektor in all his armour leapt to the ground from his chariot
and shaking two sharp spears in his hand ranged over the whole host
stirring them up to fight and waking the ghastly warfare.
So they whirled about and stood their ground against the Achaians,
and the Argives against them pulled together their battle lines.
So the fighting grew close and they faced each other, and foremost
Agamemnon drove on, trying to fight far ahead of all others.
Tell me now, you Muses who have your homes on Olympos,
who was the first to come forth and stand against Agamemnon
of the very Trojans, or their renowned companions in battle.           220
Iphidamas, Antenor's son, the huge and stalwart
who had been reared in generous Thrace, the mother of sheepflocks.
Kisses [51] had raised him in his own house when he was little,
his mother's father, whose child was Theano, the girl of the fair cheeks.
But when he had arrived at the stature of powerful manhood
Kisses detained him there and gave him his daughter. Married
he went away from the bride chamber, looking for glory
from the Achaians, with twelve curved ships that followed with him.
These balanced vessels he had left behind in Perkote [52]
and gone himself to fight on foot at Ilion; and there                   230

[49] Messenger of the gods.
[50] Another name for Troy.
[51] Father of Theano, the wife of Antenor and mother of Iphidamas.
[52] City near Troy.

he came face to face with Atreus' son, Agamemnon.
Now when these in their advance were close to each other
the son of Atreus missed with his throw, and the spear was turned past him,
but Iphidamas stabbed to the belt underneath the corselet
and leaned in on the stroke in the confidence of his strong hand
but could not get clean through the bright war belt, far sooner
the spearpoint pushed against the silver bent back, like soft lead.
And in his hand wide-powerful Agamemnon catching it
dragged it against him, raging like a lion, and tore it
out of his hand, then struck the neck with his sword, and unstrung him.          240
So Iphidamas fell there and went into the brazen slumber,
unhappy, who came to help his own people, and left his young wife
a bride, and had known no delight from her yet, and given much for her.
First he had given a hundred oxen, then promised a thousand
head of goats and sheep, which were herded for him in abundance.
Now Agamemnon, son of Atreus, stripped him and went back
to the throng of the Achaians bearing the splendid armour.
   When Koön, conspicuous among the fighters, perceived him,
he who was Antenor's eldest born, the strong sorrow
misted about his eyes for the sake of his fallen brother.                        250
He came from the side and unobserved at great Agamemnon
and stabbed with his spear at the middle arm, underneath the elbow,
and the head of the glittering spear cut its way clean through.
Agamemnon the lord of men shuddered with fear then
but even so did not give up the attack or his fighting
but sprang at Koön, gripping a spear that struck with the wind's speed.
Now Koön was dragging his father's son, his brother Iphidamas,
by the foot back eagerly, and cried out on all the bravest,
but as he dragged him into the crowd, Agamemnon thrust at him
with the smoothed bronze spear underneath the knobbed shield, and unstrung him,    260
then came up and hewed off his head over Iphidamas.
There under the king, Atreus' son, the sons of Antenor
filled out their destiny and went down to the house of the death god.
   But Agamemnon ranged the ranks of the other fighters
with spear and sword and with huge stones that he flung, for such time
as the blood was still running warm from the spear-wound.
But after the sore place was dry, and the flow of blood stopped,
the sharp pains began to break in on the strength of Atreides.
As the sharp sorrow of pain descends on a woman in labour,
the bitterness that the hard spirits of childbirth bring on,                      270
Hera's daughters, who hold the power of the bitter birthpangs,
so the sharp pains began to break in on the strength of Atreides.
He sprang back into the car, and called to his charioteer
to drive him back to the hollow ships, since his heart was heavy.
He lifted his voice and called in a piercing cry to the Danaans:
"Friends, o leaders and men of counsel among the Argives,
you must still continue to defend our seafaring vessels
from the wearying attack, since Zeus of the counsels would not
allow me to do battle daylong against the Trojans."
   He spoke, and the charioteer lashed on the bright-maned horses               280
back toward the hollow ships, and they winged their way unreluctant.
The foam ran down their chests, they were powdered with dust from beneath them
as they carried the stricken king away from the fighting.

*Bernard Shaw*

# ARMS AND THE MAN

## CHARACTERS

*in the order of their appearance*

RAINA PETKOFF, *a young Bulgarian lady*
CATHERINE PETKOFF, *her mother*
LOUKA, *Raina's maid*
CAPTAIN BLUNTSCHLI, *a Swiss in the Serbian army*
A RUSSIAN OFFICER *in the Bulgarian army*
NICOLA, *the Petkoffs' manservant*
MAJOR PETKOFF, *Raina's father*
MAJOR SERGIUS SARANOFF, *Raina's fiancé*

*The action takes place at the home of Major Petkoff, in a small town in Bulgaria, in the years 1885 and 1886.*

## ACT I

*Night: A lady's bedchamber in Bulgaria, in a small town near the Dragoman Pass, late in November in the year 1885. Through an open window with a little balcony a peak of the Balkans, wonderfully white and beautiful in the starlit snow, seems quite close at hand, though it is really miles away. The interior of the room is not like anything to be seen in the west of Europe. It is half rich Bulgarian, half cheap Viennese. Above the head of the bed, which stands against a little wall cutting off the left hand corner of the room, is a painted wooden shrine, blue and gold, with an ivory image of Christ, and a light hanging before it in a pierced metal ball suspended by three chains. The principal seat, placed towards the other side of the room and opposite the window, is a Turkish ottoman. The counterpane and hangings of the bed, the window curtains, the little carpet, and all the ornamental textile fabrics in the room are oriental and gorgeous; the paper on the walls is occidental and paltry. The washstand, against the wall on the side nearest the ottoman and window, consists of an enamelled iron basin with a pail beneath it in a painted metal frame,*

*and a single towel on the rail at the side. The dressing table, between the bed and the window, is a common pine table, covered with a cloth of many colors, with an expensive toilet mirror on it. The door is on the side nearest the bed; and there is a chest of drawers between. This chest of drawers is also covered by a variegated native cloth; and on it there is a pile of paper backed novels, a box of chocolate creams, and a miniature easel with a large photograph of an extremely handsome officer, whose lofty bearing and magnetic glance can be felt even from the portrait. The room is lighted by a candle on the chest of drawers, and another on the dressing table with a box of matches beside it.*

*The window is hinged doorwise and stands wide open. Outside, a pair of wooden shutters, opening outwards, also stand open. On the balcony a young lady, intensely conscious of the romantic beauty of the night, and of the fact that her own youth and beauty are part of it, is gazing at the snowy Balkans. She is in her nightgown, well covered by a long mantle of furs, worth, on a moderate estimate, about three times the furniture of the room.*

*Her reverie is interrupted by her mother,* CATHERINE PETKOFF, *a woman over forty, imperiously energetic, with magnificent black hair and eyes, who might be a very splendid specimen of the wife of a mountain farmer, but is determined to be a Viennese lady, and to that end wears a fashionable tea gown on all occasions.*

CATHERINE [*entering hastily, full of good news*] Raina! [*She pronounces it Rah-eena, with the stress on the ee*]. Raina! [*She goes to the bed, expecting to find* RAINA *there*]. Why, where—? [RAINA *looks into the room*]. Heavens, child! are you out in the night air instead of in your bed? Youll[53] catch your death. Louka told me you were asleep.

RAINA [*dreamily*] I sent her away. I wanted to be alone. The stars are so beautiful! What is the matter?

CATHERINE. Such news! There has been a battle.

---

[53] Shaw conducted a lifelong and vigorous campaign in his prefaces and plays against what he called the irrationalities of English spelling, particularly the "unnecessary" apostrophe. *Arms and the Man* illustrates what he thought should be universal practice.

RAINA [*her eyes dilating*] Ah! [*She comes eagerly to* CATHERINE].

CATHERINE. A great battle at Slivnitza! A victory! And it was won by Sergius.

RAINA [*with a cry of delight*] Ah! [*They embrace rapturously*] Oh, mother! [*Then, with sudden anxiety*] is father safe?

CATHERINE. Of course! he sends me the news. Sergius is the hero of the hour, the idol of the regiment.

RAINA. Tell me, tell me. How was it? [*Ecstatically*] Oh, mother! mother! mother! [*She pulls her mother down on the ottoman; and they kiss one another frantically*].

CATHERINE [*with surging enthusiasm*] You cant guess how splendid it is. A cavalry charge! think of that! He defied our Russian commanders—acted without orders—led a charge on his own responsibility—headed it himself—was the first man to sweep through their guns. Cant you see it, Raina: our gallant splendid Bulgarians with their swords and eyes flashing, thundering down like an avalanche and scattering the wretched Serbs and their dandified Austrian officers like chaff. And you! you kept Sergius waiting a year before you would be betrothed to him. Oh, if you have a drop of Bulgarian blood in your veins, you will worship him when he comes back.

RAINA. What will he care for my poor little worship after the acclamations of a whole army of heroes? But no matter: I am so happy! so proud! [*She rises and walks about excitedly*]. It proves that all our ideas were real after all.

CATHERINE [*indignantly*] Our ideas real! What do you mean?

RAINA. Our ideas of what Sergius would do. Our patriotism. Our heroic ideals. I sometimes used to doubt whether they were anything but dreams. Oh, what faithless little creatures girls are! When I buckled on Sergius's sword he looked so noble: it was treason to think of disillusion or humiliation or failure. And yet—and yet—[*She sits down again suddenly*] Promise me youll never tell him.

CATHERINE. Dont ask me for promises until I know what I'm promising.

RAINA. Well, it came into my head just as he was holding me in his arms and looking into my eyes, that perhaps we only had our heroic ideas because we are so fond of reading Byron and Pushkin, and because we were so delighted with the opera that season at Bucharest. Real life is so seldom like that! indeed never, as far as I knew it then. [*Remorsefully*] Only think, mother: I doubted him: I wondered whether all his heroic qualities and his soldiership might not prove mere imagination when he went into a real battle. I had an uneasy fear that he might cut a poor figure there beside all those clever officers from the Tsar's court.

CATHERINE. A poor figure! Shame on you! The Serbs have Austrian officers who are just as clever as the Russians; but we have beaten them in every battle for all that.

RAINA [*laughing and snuggling against her mother*] Yes: I was only a prosaic little coward. Oh, to think that it was all true! that Sergius is just as splendid and noble as he looks! that the world is really a glorious world for women who can see its glory and men who can act its romance! What happiness! what unspeakable fulfilment!

*They are interrupted by the entry of* LOUKA, *a handsome proud girl in a pretty Bulgarian peasant's dress with double apron, so defiant that her servility to* RAINA *is almost insolent. She is afraid of* CATHERINE, *but even with her goes as far as she dares.*

LOUKA. If you please, madam, all the windows are to be closed and the shutters made fast. They say there may be shooting in the streets. [*RAINA and* CATHERINE *rise together, alarmed*]. The Serbs are being chased right back through the pass; and they say they may run into the town. Our cavalry will be after them; and our people will be ready for them, you may be sure, now theyre running away. [*She goes out on the balcony, and pulls the outside shutters to; then steps back into the room*].

CATHERINE [*businesslike, housekeeping instincts aroused*] I must see that everything is made safe downstairs.

RAINA. I wish our people were not so cruel. What glory is there in killing wretched fugitives?

CATHERINE. Cruel! Do you suppose they would hesitate to kill you—or worse?

RAINA [*to* LOUKA] Leave the shutters so that I can just close them if I hear any noise.

CATHERINE [*authoritatively, turning on her way to the door*] Oh no, dear: you must keep them fastened. You would be sure to drop off to sleep and leave them open. Make them fast, Louka.

LOUKA. Yes, madam. [*She fastens them*].

RAINA. Dont be anxious about me. The moment I hear a shot, I shall blow out the candles and roll myself up in bed with my ears well covered.

CATHERINE. Quite the wisest thing you can do, my love. Good night.

RAINA. Goodnight. [*Her emotion comes back for a moment*]. Wish me joy [*They kiss*]. This is the happiest night of my life—if only there are no fugitives.

CATHERINE. Go to bed, dear; and dont think of them. [*She goes out*].

LOUKA [*secretly to* RAINA] If you would like the shutters open, just give them a push like this [*She pushes them: they open: she pulls them to again*]. One of them ought to be bolted at the bottom; but the bolt's gone.

RAINA [*with dignity, reproving her*] Thanks, Louka; but we must do what we are told. [LOUKA *makes a grimace*]. Goodnight.

LOUKA [*carelessly*] Goodnight. [*She goes out, swaggering*].

RAINA, *left alone, takes off her fur cloak and throws it on the ottoman. Then she goes to the chest of drawers, and adores the portrait there with feelings that are beyond all expression. She does not kiss it or press it to her breast, or shew it any mark of bodily affection; but she takes it in her hands and elevates it, like a priestess.*

RAINA [*looking up at the picture*] Oh, I shall never be unworthy of you any more, my soul's hero: never, never, never. [*She replaces it reverently. Then she selects a novel from the little pile of books. She turns over the leaves dreamily; finds her page; turns the book inside out at it; and, with a happy sigh, gets into bed and prepares to read herself to sleep. But before abandoning herself to fiction, she raises her eyes once more, thinking of the blessed reality, and murmurs*] My hero! my hero!

*A distant shot breaks the quiet of the night. She starts, listening; and two more shots, much nearer, follow, startling her so that she scrambles out of bed, and hastily blows out the candle on the chest of drawers. Then, putting her fingers in her ears, she runs to the dressing table, blows out the light there, and hurries back to bed in the dark, nothing being visible but the glimmer of the light in the pierced ball before the image, and the starlight seen through the slits at the top of the shutters. The firing breaks out again: there is a startling fusillade quite close at hand. Whilst it is still echoing, the shutters disappear, pulled open from without; and for an instant the rectangle of snowy starlight flashes out with the figure of a man silhouetted in black upon it. The shutters close immediately; and the room is dark again. But the silence is now broken by the sound of panting. Then there is a scratch; and the flame of a match is seen in the middle of the room.*

RAINA [*crouching on the bed*] Who's there? [*The match is out instantly*]. Who's there? Who is that?

A MAN'S VOICE [*in the darkness, subduedly, but threateningly*] Sh—sh! Dont call out; or youll be shot. Be good; and no harm will happen to you. [*She is heard leaving her bed, and making for the door*]. Take care: it's no use trying to run away.

RAINA. But who—

THE VOICE [*warning*] Remember: if you raise your voice my revolver will go off. [*Commandingly*]. Strike a light and let me see you. Do you hear. [*Another moment of silence and darkness as she retreats to the chest of drawers. Then she lights a candle; and the mystery is at an end. He is a man of about 35, in a deplorable plight, bespattered with mud and blood and snow, his belt and the strap of his revolver case keeping together the torn ruins of the blue tunic of a Serbian artillery officer. All that the candlelight and his unwashed unkempt condition make it possible to discern is that he is of middling stature and undistinguished appearance, with strong neck and shoulders, roundish obstinate looking head covered with short crisp bronze curls, clear quick eyes and good brows and mouth, hopelessly prosaic nose like that of a strong minded baby, trim soldierlike carriage and energetic manner, and with all his wits about him in spite of his desperate predicament: even with a sense of the humor of it, without, however, the least intention of trifling with it or throwing away a chance. Reckoning up what he can guess about* RAINA: *her age, her social position, her character, and the extent to which she is frightened, he continues, more politely but still most determinedly*] Excuse my disturbing you; but you recognize my uniform? Serb! If I'm caught I shall be killed. [*Menacingly*] Do you understand that?

RAINA. Yes.

THE MAN. Well, I don't intend to get killed if I can help it. [*Still more formidably*] Do you understand that? [*He locks the door quickly but quietly*].

RAINA [*disdainfully*] I suppose not. [*She draws herself up superbly, and looks him straight in the face, adding, with cutting emphasis*] Some soldiers, I know, are afraid to die.

THE MAN [*with grim goodhumor*] All of them, dear lady, all of them, believe me. It is our duty to live as long as we can. Now, if you raise an alarm—

RAINA [*cutting him short*] You will shoot me. How do you know that *I* am afraid to die?

THE MAN [*cunningly*] Ah; but suppose I dont shoot you, what will happen then? A lot of your cavalry will burst into this pretty room of yours and slaughter me here like a pig; for I'll fight like a demon: they shant get me into the street to amuse themselves with: I know what they are. Are you prepared to receive that sort of company in your present undress? [RAINA, *suddenly conscious of her nightgown, instinctively shrinks and gathers it more closely about her neck. He watches her and adds pitilessly*] Hardly presentable, eh? [*She turns to the ottoman. He raises his pistol instantly, and cries*] Stop! [*She stops*]. Where are you going?

RAINA [*with dignified patience*] Only to get my cloak.

THE MAN [*passing swiftly to the ottoman and snatching the cloak*] A good idea! I'll keep the cloak; and youll take care that nobody comes in and sees you without it. This is a better weapon than the revolver: eh? [*He throws the pistol down on the ottoman*].

RAINA [*revolted*] It is not the weapon of a gentleman!

THE MAN. It's good enough for a man with only you to stand between him and death. [*As they look at one another for a moment*, RAINA *hardly able to believe that even a Serbian officer can be so cynically and selfishly unchivalrous, they are startled by a sharp fusillade in the street. The chill of imminent death hushes the man's voice as he adds*] Do you hear? If you are going to bring those blackguards in on me you shall receive them as you are.

*Clamor and disturbance. The pursuers in the street batter at the house door, shouting* Open the door! Open the door! Wake up, will you! *A man servant's voice calls to them angrily from within* This is Major Petkoff's house: you cant come in here; *but a renewal of the clamor, and a torrent of blows on the door, end with his*

letting a chain down with a clank, followed by a rush of heavy footsteps and a din of triumphant yells, dominated at last by the voice of CATHERINE, *indignantly addressing an officer with* What does this mean, sir? Do you know where you are? *The noise subsides suddenly.*

LOUKA [*outside, knocking at the bedroom door*] My lady! my lady! get up quick and open the door. If you dont they will break it down.

*The fugitive throws up his head with the gesture of a man who sees that it is all over with him, and drops the manner he has been assuming to intimidate* RAINA.

THE MAN [*sincerely and kindly*] No use, dear: I'm done for. [*Flinging the cloak to her*] Quick! wrap yourself up: theyre coming.

RAINA. Oh, thank you. [*She wraps herself up with intense relief*].

THE MAN [*between his teeth*] Dont mention it.

RAINA [*anxiously*] What will you do?

THE MAN [*grimly*] The first man in will find out. Keep out of the way; and dont look. It wont last long; but it will not be nice. [*He draws his sabre and faces the door, waiting*].

RAINA [*impulsively*] I'll help you. I'll save you.

THE MAN. You cant.

RAINA. I can. I'll hide you. [*She drags him towards the window*]. Here! behind the curtains.

THE MAN [*yielding to her*] Theres just half a chance, if you keep your head.

RAINA [*drawing the curtain before him*] S-sh! [*She makes for the ottoman*].

THE MAN [*putting out his head*] Remember—

RAINA [*running back to him*] Yes?

THE MAN. —nine soldiers out of ten are born fools.

RAINA. Oh! [*She draws the curtain angrily before him*].

THE MAN [*looking out at the other side*] If they find me, I promise you a fight: a devil of a fight.

*She stamps at him. He disappears hastily. She takes off her cloak, and throws it across the foot of the bed. Then, with a sleepy, disturbed air, she opens the door.* LOUKA *enters excitedly.*

LOUKA. One of those beasts of Serbs has been seen climbing up the waterpipe to your balcony. Our men want to search for him; and they are so wild and drunk and furious. [*She makes for the other side of the room to get as far from the door as possible*]. My lady says you are to dress at once and to—[*She sees the revolver lying on the ottoman, and stops, petrified*].

RAINA [*as if annoyed at being disturbed*] They shall not search here. Why have they been let in?

CATHERINE [*coming in hastily*] Raina, darling, are you safe? Have you seen anyone or heard anything?

RAINA. I heard the shooting. Surely the soldiers will not dare come in here?

CATHERINE. I have found a Russian officer, thank Heaven: he knows Sergius. [*Speaking through the door to someone outside*] Sir: will you come in now. My daughter will receive you.

*A young Russian officer, in Bulgarian uniform, enters, sword in hand.*

OFFICER [*with soft feline politeness and stiff military carriage*] Good evening, gracious lady. I am sorry to intrude; but there is a Serb hiding on the balcony. Will you and the gracious lady your mother please to withdraw whilst we search?

RAINA [*petulantly*] Nonsense, sir: you can see that there is no one on the balcony. [*She throws the shutters wide open and stands with her back to the curtain where the man is hidden, pointing to the moonlit balcony. A couple of shots are fired right under the window; and a bullet shatters the glass opposite* RAINA, *who winks and gasps, but stands her ground; whilst* CATHERINE *screams, and the officer, with a cry of* Take care! *rushes to the balcony*].

THE OFFICER [*on the balcony, shouting savagely down to the street*] Cease firing there, you fools: do you hear? Cease firing, damn you! [*He glares down for a moment; then turns to* RAINA, *trying to resume his polite manner*]. Could anyone have got in without your knowledge? Were you asleep?

RAINA. No: I have not been to bed.

THE OFFICER [*impatiently, coming back into the room*] Your neighbors have their heads so full of runaway Serbs that they see them everywhere. [*Politely*] Gracious lady: a thousand pardons. Goodnight. [*Military bow, which* RAINA *returns coldly. Another to* CATHERINE, *who follows him out*].

RAINA *closes the shutters. She turns and sees* LOUKA, *who has been watching the scene curiously.*

RAINA. Dont leave my mother, Louka, until the soldiers go away.

LOUKA *glances at* RAINA, *at the ottoman, at the curtain; then purses her lips secretively, laughs insolently, and goes out.* RAINA, *highly offended by this demonstration, follows her to the door, and shuts it behind her with a slam, locking it violently. The man immediately steps out from behind the curtain, sheathing his sabre. Then, dismissing the danger from his mind in a businesslike way, he comes affably to* RAINA.

THE MAN. A narrow shave; but a miss is as good as a mile. Dear young lady: your servant to the death. I wish for your sake I had joined the Bulgarian army instead of the other one. I am not a native Serb.

RAINA [*haughtily*] No: you are one of the Austrians who set the Serbs on to rob us of our national liberty, and who officer their army for them. We hate them!

THE MAN. Austrian! not I. Dont hate me, dear young lady. I am a Swiss, fighting merely as a professional soldier. I joined the Serbs because they came first on the road from Switzerland. Be generous: youve beaten us hollow.

RAINA. Have I not been generous?

THE MAN. Noble! Heroic! But I'm not saved yet. This particular rush will soon pass through; but the pursuit will go on all night by fits and starts. I must take my chance to get off in a quiet interval. [*Pleasantly*] You dont mind my waiting just a minute or two, do you?

RAINA [*putting on her most genteel society manner*] Oh, not at all. Wont you sit down?

THE MAN. Thanks [*He sits on the foot of the bed*].

RAINA *walks with studied elegance to the ottoman and sits down. Unfortunately she sits on the pistol, and jumps up with a shriek. The man, all nerves, shies like a frightened horse to the other side of the room.*

THE MAN [*irritably*] Dont frighten me like that. What is it?

RAINA. Your revolver! It was staring that officer in the face all the time. What an escape!

THE MAN [*vexed at being unnecessarily terrified*] Oh, is that all?

RAINA [*staring at him rather superciliously as she conceives a poorer and poorer opinion of him, and feels proportionately more and more at her ease*] I am sorry I frightened you.

[*She takes up the pistol and hands it to him*]. Pray take it to protect yourself against me.

THE MAN [*grinning wearily at the sarcasm as he takes the pistol*] No use, dear young lady: theres nothing in it. It's not loaded. [*He makes a grimace at it, and drops it disparagingly into his revolver case*].

RAINA. Load it by all means.

THE MAN. Ive no ammunition. What use are cartridges in battle? I always carry chocolate instead; and I finished the last cake of that hours ago.

RAINA [*outraged in her most cherished ideals of manhood*] Chocolate! Do you stuff your pockets with sweets—like a schoolboy—even in the field?

THE MAN [*grinning*] Yes: isnt it contemptible? [*Hungrily*] I wish I had some now.

RAINA. Allow me. [*She sails away scornfully to the chest of drawers, and returns with the box of confectionery in her hand*]. I am sorry I have eaten them all except these. [*She offers him the box*].

THE MAN [*ravenously*] Youre an angel! [*He gobbles the contents*]. Creams! Delicious! [*He looks anxiously to see whether there are any more. There are none: he can only scrape the box with his fingers and suck them. When that nourishment is exhausted he accepts the inevitable with pathetic goodhumor, and says, with grateful emotion*] Bless you, dear lady! You can always tell an old soldier by the inside of his holsters and cartridge boxes. The young ones carry pistols and cartridges: the old ones, grub. Thank you. [*He hands back the box. She snatches it contemptuously from him and throws it away. He shies again, as if she had meant to strike him*]. Ugh! Dont do things so suddenly, gracious lady. It's mean to revenge yourself because I frightened you just now.

RAINA [*loftily*] Frighten me! Do you know, sir, that though I am only a woman, I think I am at heart as brave as you.

THE MAN. I should think so. You havnt been under fire for three days as I have. I can stand two days without shewing it much; but no man can stand three days: I'm as nervous as a mouse. [*He sits down on the ottoman, and takes his head in his hands*]. Would you like to see me cry?

RAINA [*alarmed*] No.

THE MAN. If you would, all you have to do is to scold me just as if I were a little boy and you my nurse. If I were in camp now, theyd play all sorts of tricks on me.

RAINA [*a little moved*] I'm sorry. I wont scold you. [*Touched by the sympathy in her tone, he raises his head and looks gratefully at her: she immediately draws back and says stiffly*] You must excuse me: our soldiers are not like that. [*She moves away from the ottoman*].

THE MAN. Oh yes they are. There are only two sorts of soldiers: old ones and young ones. Ive served fourteen years: half of your fellows never smelt powder before. Why, how is it that youve just beaten us? Sheer ignorance of the art of war, nothing else. [*Indignantly*] I never saw anything so unprofessional.

RAINA [*ironically*] Oh! was it unprofessional to beat you?

THE MAN. Well, come! is it professional to throw a regiment of cavalry on a battery of machine guns, with the dead certainty that if the guns go off not a horse or man will ever get within fifty yards of the fire? I couldnt believe my eyes when I saw it.

RAINA [*eagerly turning to him, as all her enthusiasm and her dreams of glory rush back on her*] Did you see the great cavalry charge? Oh, tell me about it. Describe it to me.

THE MAN. You never saw a cavalry charge, did you?

RAINA. How could I?

THE MAN. Ah, perhaps not. No: of course not! Well, it's a funny sight. It's like slinging a handful of peas against a window pane: first one comes; then two or three close behind him; and then all the rest in a lump.

RAINA [*her eyes dilating as she raises her clasped hands ecstatically*] Yes, first One! the bravest of the brave!

THE MAN [*prosaically*] Hm! you should see the poor devil pulling at his horse.

RAINA. Why should he pull at his horse?

THE MAN [*impatient of so stupid a question*] It's running away with him, of course: do you suppose the fellow wants to get there before the others and be killed? Then they all come. You can tell the young ones by their wildness and their slashing. The old ones come bunched up under the number one guard: they know that theyre mere projectiles, and that it's no use trying to fight. The wounds are mostly broken knees, from the horses cannoning together.

RAINA. Ugh! But I dont believe the first man is a coward. I know he is a hero!

THE MAN [*goodhumoredly*] Thats what youd have said if youd seen the first man in the charge today.

RAINA [*breathless, forgiving him everything*] Ah, I knew it! Tell me. Tell me about him.

THE MAN. He did it like an operatic tenor. A regular handsome fellow, with flashing eyes and lovely moustache, shouting his war-cry and charging like Don Quixote at the windmills. We did laugh.

RAINA. You dared to laugh!

THE MAN. Yes; but when the sergeant ran up as white as a sheet, and told us theyd sent us the wrong ammunition, and that we couldnt fire a round for the next ten minutes, we laughed at the other side of our mouths. I never felt so sick in my life; though Ive been in one or two very tight places. And I hadnt even a revolver cartridge: only chocolate. We'd no bayonets: nothing. Of course, they just cut us to bits. And there was Don Quixote flourishing like a drum major, thinking he'd done the cleverest thing ever known, whereas he ought to be courtmartialled for it. Of all the fools ever let loose on a field of battle, that man must be the very maddest. He and his regiment simply committed suicide; only the pistol missed fire: thats all.

RAINA [*deeply wounded, but steadfastly loyal to her ideals*] Indeed! Would you know him again if you saw him?

THE MAN. Shall I ever forget him!

*She again goes to the chest of drawers. He watches her with a vague hope that she may have something more for him to eat. She takes the portrait from its stand and brings it to him.*

RAINA. That is a photograph of the gentleman—the patriot and hero—to whom I am betrothed.

THE MAN [*recognizing it with a shock*] I'm really very sorry. [*Looking at her*] Was it fair to lead me on? [*He looks at the portrait again*] Yes: thats Don Quixote: not a doubt of it. [*He stifles a laugh*].

RAINA [*quickly*] Why do you laugh?

THE MAN [*apologetic, but still greatly tickled*] I didnt laugh, I assure you. At least I didnt mean to. But when I think of him charging the windmills and imagining he was doing the finest thing—[*He chokes with suppressed laughter*].

RAINA [*sternly*] Give me back the portrait, sir.

THE MAN [*with sincere remorse*] Of course. Certainly. I'm really very sorry. [*He hands her the picture. She deliberately kisses it and looks him straight in the face before returning to the chest of drawers to replace it. He follows her, apologizing*]. Perhaps I'm quite wrong, you know: no doubt I am. Most likely he had got wind of the cartridge business somehow, and knew it was a safe job.

RAINA. That is to say, he was a pretender and a coward! You did not dare say that before.

THE MAN [*with a comic gesture of despair*] It's no use, dear lady: I cant make you see it from the professional point of view. [*As he turns away to get back to the ottoman, a couple of distant shots threaten renewed trouble*].

RAINA [*sternly, as she sees him listening to the shots*] So much the better for you!

THE MAN [*turning*] How?

RAINA. You are my enemy; and you are at my mercy. What would I do if I were a professional soldier?

THE MAN. Ah, true, dear young lady: youre always right. I know how good youve been to me: to my last hour I shall remember those three chocolate creams. It was unsoldierly; but it was angelic.

RAINA [*coldly*] Thank you. And now I will do a soldierly thing. You cannot stay here after what you have just said about my future husband; but I will go out on the balcony and see whether it is safe for you to climb down into the street. [*She turns to the window*].

THE MAN [*changing countenance*] Down that waterpipe! Stop! Wait! I cant! I darent! The very thought of it makes me giddy. I came up it fast enough with death behind me. But to face it now in cold blood—! [*He sinks on the ottoman*]. It's no use: I give up: I'm beaten. Give the alarm. [*He drops his head on his hands in the deepest dejection*].

RAINA [*disarmed by pity*] Come: dont be disheartened. [*She stoops over him almost maternally: he shakes his head*]. Oh, you are a very poor soldier: a chocolate cream soldier! Come, cheer up! it takes less courage to climb down than to face capture: remember that.

THE MAN [*dreamily, lulled by her voice*] No: capture only means death; and death is sleep: oh, sleep, sleep, sleep, undisturbed sleep! Climbing down the pipe means doing something —exerting myself—thinking! Death ten times over first.

RAINA [*softly and wonderingly, catching the rhythm of his weariness*] Are you as sleepy as that?

THE MAN. Ive not had two hours undisturbed sleep since I joined. I havnt closed my eyes for forty-eight hours.

RAINA [*at her wit's end*] But what am I to do with you?

THE MAN [*staggering up, roused by her desperation*] Of course. I must do something. [*He shakes himself; pulls himself together; and speaks with rallied vigor and courage*]. You see, sleep or no sleep, hunger or no hunger, tired or not tired, you can always do a thing when you know it must be done. Well, that pipe must be got down: [*he hits himself on the chest*] do you hear that, you chocolate cream soldier? [*He turns to the window*].

RAINA [*anxiously*] But if you fall?

THE MAN. I shall sleep as if the stones were a feather bed. Goodbye. [*He makes boldly for the window; and his hand is on the shutter when there is a terrible burst of firing in the street beneath.*]

RAINA [*rushing to him*] Stop! [*She seizes him recklessly, and pulls him quite round*]. Theyll kill you.

THE MAN [*coolly, but attentively*] Never mind: this sort of thing is all in my day's work. I'm bound to take my chance. [*Decisively*] Now do what I tell you. Put out the candle; so that they shant see the light when I open the shutters. And keep away from the window, whatever you do. If they see me theyre sure to have a shot at me.

RAINA [*clinging to him*] Theyre sure to see you: it's bright moonlight. I'll save you. Oh, how can you be so indifferent! You want me to save you, dont you?

THE MAN. I really dont want to be troublesome. [*She shakes him in her impatience*]. I am not indifferent, dear young lady, I assure you. But how is it to be done?

RAINA. Come away from the window. [*She takes him firmly back to the middle of the room. The moment she releases him he turns mechanically towards the window again. She seizes him and turns him back, exclaiming*] Please! [*He becomes motionless, like a hypnotized rabbit, his fatigue gaining fast on him. She releases him, and addresses him patronizingly*]. Now listen. You must trust to our hospitality.

You do not yet know in whose house you are. I am a Petkoff.

THE MAN. A pet what?

RAINA [*rather indignantly*] I mean that I belong to the family of the Petkoffs, the richest and best known in our country.

THE MAN. Oh yes, of course. I beg your pardon. The Petkoffs, to be sure. How stupid of me!

RAINA. You know you never heard of them until this moment. How can you stoop to pretend!

THE MAN. Forgive me: I'm too tired to think; and the change of subject was too much for me. Dont scold me.

RAINA. I forgot. It might make you cry. [*He nods, quite seriously. She pouts and then resumes her patronizing tone*]. I must tell you that my father holds the highest command of any Bulgarian in our army. He is [*proudly*] a Major.

THE MAN [*pretending to be deeply impressed*] A Major! Bless me! Think of that!

RAINA. You shewed great ignorance in thinking that it was necessary to climb up to the balcony because ours is the only private house that has two rows of windows. There is a flight of stairs inside to get up and down by.

THE MAN. Stairs! How grand! You live in great luxury indeed, dear young lady.

RAINA. Do you know what a library is?

THE MAN. A library? A roomful of books?

RAINA. Yes. We have one, the only one in Bulgaria.

THE MAN. Actually a real library! I should like to see that.

RAINA [*affectedly*] I tell you these things to shew you that you are not in the house of ignorant country folk who would kill you the moment they saw your Serbian uniform, but among civilized people. We go to Bucharest every year for the opera season; and I have spent a whole month in Vienna.

THE MAN. I saw that, dear young lady. I saw at once that you knew the world.

RAINA. Have you ever seen the opera of Ernani?

THE MAN. Is that the one with the devil in it in red velvet, and a soldiers' chorus?

RAINA [*contemptuously*] No!

THE MAN [*stifling a heavy sigh of weariness*] Then I dont know it.

RAINA. I thought you might have remembered the great scene where Ernani, flying from his foes just as you are tonight, takes refuge in the castle of his bitterest enemy, an old Castilian noble. The noble refuses to give him up. His guest is sacred to him.

THE MAN [quickly, waking up a little] Have your people got that notion?

RAINA [with dignity] My mother and I can understand that notion, as you call it. And if instead of threatening me with your pistol as you did you had simply thrown yourself as a fugitive on our hospitality, you would have been as safe as in your father's house.

THE MAN. Quite sure?

RAINA [turning her back on him in disgust] Oh, it is useless to try to make you understand.

THE MAN. Dont be angry: you see how awkward it would be for me if there was any mistake. My father is a very hospitable man: he keeps six hotels; but I couldnt trust him as far as that. What about your father?

RAINA. He is away at Slivnitza fighting for his country. I answer for your safety. There is my hand in pledge of it. Will that reassure you? [She offers him her hand].

THE MAN [looking dubiously at his own hand] Better not touch my hand, dear young lady. I must have a wash first.

RAINA [touched] That is very nice of you. I see that you are a gentleman.

THE MAN [puzzled] Eh?

RAINA. You must not think I am surprised. Bulgarians of really good standing—people in our position—wash their hands nearly every day. So you see I can appreciate your delicacy. You may take my hand. [She offers it again].

THE MAN [kissing it with his hands behind his back] Thanks, gracious young lady: I feel safe at last. And now would you mind breaking the news to your mother? I had better not stay here secretly longer than is necessary.

RAINA. If you will be so good as to keep perfectly still whilst I am away.

THE MAN. Certainly. [He sits down on the ottoman].

RAINA goes to the bed and wraps herself in the fur cloak. His eyes close. She goes to the door. Turning for a last look at him, she sees that he is dropping off to sleep.

RAINA [at the door] You are not going asleep, are you? [He murmurs inarticulately: she runs to him and shakes him]. Do you hear? Wake up: you are falling asleep.

THE MAN. Eh? Falling aslee—? Oh no: not the least in the world: I was only thinking. It's all right: I'm wide awake.

RAINA [severely] Will you please stand up while I am away. [He rises reluctantly]. All the time, mind.

THE MAN [standing unsteadily] Certainly. Certainly: you may depend on me.

RAINA looks doubtfully at him. He smiles weakly. She goes reluctantly, turning again at the door, and almost catching him in the act of yawning. She goes out.

THE MAN [drowsily] Sleep, sleep, sleep, sleep, slee—[The words trail off into a murmur. He wakes again with a shock on the point of falling]. Where am I? Thats what I want to know: where am I? Must keep awake. Nothing keeps me awake except danger: remember that: [intently] danger, danger, danger, dan—[trailing off again: another shock] Wheres danger? Mus' find it. [He starts off vaguely round the room in search of it]. What am I looking for? Sleep—danger—dont know. [He stumbles against the bed]. Ah yes: now I know. All right now. I'm to go to bed, but not to sleep. Be sure not to sleep, because of danger. Not to lie down either, only sit down. [He sits on the bed. A blissful expression comes into his face]. Ah! [With a happy sigh he sinks back at full length; lifts his boots into the bed with a final effort; and falls fast asleep instantly].

CATHERINE comes in, followed by RAINA.

RAINA [looking at the ottoman] He's gone! I left him here.

CATHERINE. Here! Then he must have climbed down from the—

RAINA [seeing him] Oh! [She points].

CATHERINE [scandalized] Well! [She strides to the bed, RAINA following until she is opposite her on the other side]. He's fast asleep. The brute!

RAINA [anxiously] Sh!

CATHERINE [shaking him] Sir! [Shaking him again, harder] Sir!! [Vehemently, shaking very hard] Sir!!!

RAINA [catching her arm] Dont, mamma; the poor darling is worn out. Let him sleep.

CATHERINE [letting him go, and turning amazed to RAINA] The poor darling! Raina!!! [She looks sternly at her daughter].

THE MAN sleeps profoundly.

## ACT II

*The sixth of March, 1886. In the garden of* MAJOR PETKOFF'S *house. It is a fine spring morning: the garden looks fresh and pretty. Beyond the paling the tops of a couple of minarets can be seen, shewing that there is a valley there, with the little town in it. A few miles further the Balkan mountains rise and shut in the landscape. Looking towards them from within the garden, the side of the house is seen on the left, with a garden door reached by a little flight of steps. On the right the stable yard, with its gateway, encroaches on the garden. There are fruit bushes along the paling and house, covered with washing spread out to dry. A path runs by the house, and rises by two steps at the corner, where it turns out of sight. In the middle, a small table, with two bent wood chairs at it, is laid for breakfast with Turkish coffee pot, cups, rolls, etc.; but the cups have been used and the bread broken. There is a wooden garden seat against the wall on the right.*

LOUKA, *smoking a cigaret, is standing between the table and the house, turning her back with angry disdain on a man servant who is lecturing her. He is a middle-aged man of cool temperament and low but clear and keen intelligence, with the complacency of the servant who values himself on his rank in servitude, and the imperturbability of the accurate calculator who has no illusions. He wears a white Bulgarian costume: jacket with embroidered border, sash, wide knickerbockers, and decorated gaiters. His head is shaved up to the crown, giving him a high Japanese forehead. His name is* NICOLA.

NICOLA. Be warned in time, Louka: mend your manners. I know the mistress. She is so grand that she never dreams that any servant could dare be disrespectful to her; but if she once suspects that you are defying her, out you go.

LOUKA. I do defy her. I will defy her. What do I care for her?

NICOLA. If you quarrel with the family, I never can marry you. It's the same as if you quarrelled with me!

LOUKA. You take her part against me, do you?

NICOLA [*sedately*] I shall always be depend-ent on the good will of the family. When I leave their service and start a shop in Sofia, their custom will be half my capital: their bad word would ruin me.

LOUKA. You have no spirit. I should like to catch them saying a word against me!

NICOLA [*pityingly*] I should have expected more sense from you, Louka. But youre young: youre young!

LOUKA. Yes; and you like me the better for it, dont you? But I know some family secrets they wouldnt care to have told, young as I am. Let them quarrel with me if they dare!

NICOLA [*with compassionate superiority*] Do you know what they would do if they heard you talk like that?

LOUKA. What could they do?

NICOLA. Discharge you for untruthfulness. Who would believe any stories you told after that? Who would give you another situation? Who in this house would dare be seen speaking to you ever again? How long would your father be left on his little farm? [*She impatiently throws away the end of her cigaret, and stamps on it*]. Child: you dont know the power such high people have over the like of you and me when we try to rise out of our poverty against them. [*He goes close to her and lowers his voice*]. Look at me, ten years in their service. Do you think I know no secrets? I know things about the mistress that she wouldnt have the master know for a thousand levas. I know things about him that she wouldnt let him hear the last of for six months if I blabbed them to her. I know things about Raina that would break off her match with Sergius if—

LOUKA [*turning on him quickly*] How do you know? I never told you!

NICOLA [*opening his eyes cunningly*] So thats your little secret, is it? I thought it might be something like that. Well, you take my advice and be respectful; and make the mistress feel that no matter what you know or dont know, she can depend on you to hold your tongue and serve the family faithfully. Thats what they like; and thats how youll make most out of them.

LOUKA [*with searching scorn*] You have the soul of a servant, Nicola.

NICOLA [*complacently*] Yes: thats the secret of success in service.

*A loud knocking with a whip handle on a wooden door is heard from the stable yard.*

MALE VOICE OUTSIDE. Hollo! Hollo there! Nicola!

LOUKA. Master! back from the war!

NICOLA [*quickly*] My word for it, Louka, the war's over. Off with you and get some fresh coffee. [*He runs out into the stable yard*].

LOUKA [*as she collects the coffee pot and cups on the tray, and carries it into the house*] Youll never put the soul of a servant into me.

MAJOR PETKOFF *comes from the stable yard, followed by* NICOLA. *He is a cheerful, excitable, insignificant, unpolished man of about 50, naturally unambitious except as to his income and his importance in local society, but just now greatly pleased with the military rank which the war has thrust on him as a man of consequence in his town. The fever of plucky patriotism which the Serbian attack roused in all the Bulgarians has pulled him through the war; but he is obviously glad to be home again.*

PETKOFF [*pointing to the table with his whip*] Breakfast out here, eh?

NICOLA. Yes, sir. The mistress and Miss Raina have just gone in.

PETKOFF [*sitting down and taking a roll*] Go in and say Ive come; and get me some fresh coffee.

NICOLA. It's coming, sir. [*He goes to the house door.* LOUKA, *with fresh coffee, a clean cup, and a brandy bottle on her tray, meets him*]. Have you told the mistress?

LOUKA. Yes: she's coming.

NICOLA *goes into the house.* LOUKA *brings the coffee to the table.*

PETKOFF. Well: the Serbs havnt run away with you, have they?

LOUKA. No, sir.

PETKOFF. Thats right. Have you brought me some cognac?

LOUKA [*putting the bottle on the table*] Here, sir.

PETKOFF. Thats right. [*He pours some into his coffee*].

CATHERINE, *who, having at this early hour made only a very perfunctory toilet, wears a Bulgarian apron over a once brilliant but now half worn-out dressing gown, and a colored handkerchief tied over her thick black hair, comes from the house with Turkish slippers on her bare feet, looking astonishingly handsome and stately under all the circumstances.* LOUKA *goes into the house.*

CATHERINE. My dear Paul: what a surprise for us! [*She stoops over the back of his chair to kiss him*]. Have they brought you fresh coffee?

PETKOFF. Yes: Louka's been looking after me. The war's over. The treaty was signed three days ago at Bucharest; and the decree for our army to demobilize was issued yesterday.

CATHERINE [*springing erect, with flashing eyes*] Paul: have you let the Austrians force you to make peace?

PETKOFF [*submissively*] My dear: they didnt consult me. What could *I* do? [*She sits down and turns away from him*] But of course we saw to it that the treaty was an honorable one. It declares peace—

CATHERINE [*outraged*] Peace!

PETKOFF [*appeasing her*]—but not friendly relations: remember that. They wanted to put that in; but I insisted on its being struck out. What more could I do?

CATHERINE. You could have annexed Serbia and made Prince Alexander Emperor of the Balkans. Thats what I would have done.

PETKOFF. I dont doubt it in the least, my dear. But I should have had to subdue the whole Austrian Empire first; and that would have kept me too long away from you. I missed you greatly.

CATHERINE [*relenting*] Ah! [*She stretches her hand affectionately across the table to squeeze his*].

PETKOFF. And how have you been, my dear?

CATHERINE. Oh, my usual sore throats: thats all.

PETKOFF [*with conviction*] That comes from washing your neck every day. Ive often told you so.

CATHERINE. Nonsense, Paul!

PETKOFF [*over his coffee and cigaret*] I dont believe in going too far with these modern customs. All this washing cant be good for the health: it's not natural. There was an Englishman at Philippopolis who used to wet himself all over with cold water every morning when he got up. Disgusting! It all comes from the English: their climate makes them so dirty that they have to be perpetually washing themselves. Look at my father! he never had a bath in his life; and he lived to be ninety-eight, the healthiest man in Bulgaria. I dont mind a good wash once a week to keep up my position; but once a day is carrying the thing to a ridiculous extreme.

CATHERINE. You are a barbarian at heart still, Paul. I hope you behaved yourself before all those Russian officers.

PETKOFF. I did my best. I took care to let them know that we have a library.

CATHERINE. Ah; but you didnt tell them that we have an electric bell in it? I have had one put up.

PETKOFF. Whats an electric bell?

CATHERINE. You touch a button; something tinkles in the kitchen; and then Nicola comes up.

PETKOFF. Why not shout for him?

CATHERINE. Civilized people never shout for their servants. Ive learnt that while you were away.

PETKOFF. Well, I'll tell you something Ive learnt too. Civilized people dont hang out their washing to dry where visitors can see it; so youd better have all that [indicating the clothes on the bushes] put somewhere else.

CATHERINE. Oh, thats absurd, Paul: I dont believe really refined people notice such things.

SERGIUS [knocking at the stable gates] Gate, Nicola!

PETKOFF. Theres Sergius. [Shouting] Hollo, Nicola!

CATHERINE. Oh, dont shout, Paul: it really isnt nice.

PETKOFF. Bosh! [He shouts louder than before] Nicola!

NICOLA [appearing at the house door] Yes, sir.

PETKOFF. Are you deaf? Dont you hear Major Saranoff knocking? Bring him round this way. [He pronounces the name with the stress on the second syllable: Sarahnoff].

NICOLA. Yes, Major. [He goes into the stable yard].

PETKOFF. You must talk to him, my dear, until Raina takes him off our hands. He bores my life out about our not promoting him. Over my head, if you please.

CATHERINE. He certainly ought to be promoted when he marries Raina. Besides, the country should insist on having at least one native general.

PETKOFF. Yes; so that he could throw away whole brigades instead of regiments. It's no use, my dear: he hasnt the slightest chance of promotion until we're quite sure that the peace will be a lasting one.

NICOLA [at the gate, announcing] Major Sergius Saranoff! [He goes into the house and returns presently with a third chair, which he places at the table. He then withdraws].

MAJOR SERGIUS SARANOFF, the original of the portrait in RAINA'S room, is a tall romantically handsome man, with the physical hardihood, the high spirit, and the susceptible imagination of an untamed mountaineer chieftain. But his remarkable personal distinction is of a characteristically civilized type. The ridges of his eyebrows, curving with an interrogative twist round the projections at the outer corners; his jealously observant eye; his nose, thin, keen, and apprehensive in spite of the pugnacious high bridge and large nostril; his assertive chin would not be out of place in a Parisian salon, shewing that the clever imaginative barbarian has an acute critical faculty which has been thrown into intense activity by the arrival of western civilization in the Balkans. The result is precisely what the advent of nineteenth century thought first produced in England: to wit, Byronism. By his brooding on the perpetual failure, not only of others, but of himself, to live up to his ideals; by his consequent cynical scorn for humanity; by his jejune credulity as to the absolute validity of his concepts and the unworthiness of the world in disregarding them; by his wincings and mockeries under the sting of the petty disillusions which every hour spent among men brings to his sensitive observation, he has acquired the half tragic, half ironic air, the mysterious moodiness, the suggestion of a strange and terrible history that has left nothing but undying remorse, by which Childe Harold fascinated the grandmothers of his English contemporaries. It is clear that here or nowhere is RAINA'S ideal hero. CATHERINE is hardly less enthusiastic about him than her daughter, and much less reserved in shewing her enthusiasm. As he enters from the stable gate, she rises effusively to greet him. PETKOFF is distinctly less disposed to make a fuss about him.

PETKOFF. Here already, Sergius! Glad to see you.

CATHERINE. My dear Sergius! [She holds out both her hands].

SERGIUS [kissing them with scrupulous gallantry] My dear mother, if I may call you so.

PETKOFF [drily] Mother-in-law, Sergius: mother-in-law! Sit down; and have some coffee.

SERGIUS. Thank you: none for me. [He gets away from the table with a certain distaste for

PETKOFF'S *enjoyment of it, and posts himself with conscious dignity against the rail of the steps leading to the house*].

CATHERINE. You look superb. The campaign has improved you, Sergius. Everybody here is mad about you. We were all wild with enthusiasm about that magnificent cavalry charge.

SERGIUS [*with grave irony*] Madam: it was the cradle and the grave of my military reputation.

CATHERINE. How so?

SERGIUS. I won the battle the wrong way when our worthy Russian generals were losing it the right way. In short, I upset their plans, and wounded their self-esteem. Two Cossack colonels had their regiments routed on the most correct principles of scientific warfare. Two major-generals got killed strictly according to military etiquette. The two colonels are now major-generals; and I am still a simple major.

CATHERINE. You shall not remain so, Sergius. The women are on your side; and they will see that justice is done you.

SERGIUS. It is too late. I have only waited for the peace to send in my resignation.

PETKOFF [*dropping his cup in his amazement*] Your resignation!

CATHERINE. Oh, you must withdraw it!

SERGIUS [*with resolute measured emphasis, folding his arms*] I never withdraw.

PETKOFF [*vexed*] Now who could have supposed you were going to do such a thing?

SERGIUS [*with fire*] Everyone that knew me. But enough of myself and my affairs. How is Raina; and where is Raina?

RAINA [*suddenly coming round the corner of the house and standing at the top of the steps in the path*] Raina is here.

*She makes a charming picture as they turn to look at her. She wears an underdress of pale green silk, draped with an overdress of thin ecru canvas embroidered with gold. She is crowned with a dainty eastern cap of gold tinsel. Sergius goes impulsively to meet her. Posing regally, she presents her hand: he drops chivalrously on one knee and kisses it.*

PETKOFF [*aside to* CATHERINE, *beaming with parental pride*] Pretty, isnt it? She always appears at the right moment.

CATHERINE [*impatiently*] Yes; she listens for it. It is an abominable habit.

SERGIUS *leads* RAINA *forward with splendid gallantry. When they arrive at the table, she*

turns to him with a bend of the head: he bows; and thus they separate, he coming to his place and she going behind her father's chair.

RAINA [*stooping and kissing her father*] Dear father! Welcome home!

PETKOFF [*patting her cheek*] My little pet girl. [*He kisses her. She goes to the chair left by* NICOLA *for* SERGIUS, *and sits down*].

CATHERINE. And so youre no longer a soldier, Sergius.

SERGIUS. I am no longer a soldier. Soldiering, my dear madam, is the coward's art of attacking mercilessly when you are strong, and keeping out of harm's way when you are weak. That is the whole secret of successful fighting. Get your enemy at a disadvantage; and never, on any account, fight him on equal terms.

PETKOFF. They wouldnt let us make a fair stand-up fight of it. However, I suppose soldiering has to be a trade like any other trade.

SERGIUS. Precisely. But I have no ambition to shine as a tradesman; so I have taken the advice of that bagman of a captain that settled the exchange of prisoners with us at Pirot, and given it up.

PETKOFF. What! that Swiss fellow? Sergius: I've often thought of that exchange since. He over-reached us about those horses.

SERGIUS. Of course he over-reached us. His father was a hotel and livery stable keeper; and he owed his first step to his knowledge of horse-dealing. [*With mock enthusiasm*] Ah, he was a soldier: every inch a soldier! If only I had bought the horses for my regiment instead of foolishly leading it into danger, I should have been a field-marshal now!

CATHERINE. A Swiss? What was he doing in the Serbian army?

PETKOFF. A volunteer, of course: keen on picking up his profession. [*Chuckling*] We shouldnt have been able to begin fighting if these foreigners hadnt shewn us how to do it: we knew nothing about it; and neither did the Serbs. Egad, there'd have been no war without them!

RAINA. Are there many Swiss officers in the Serbian Army?

PETKOFF. No. All Austrians, just as our officers were all Russians. This was the only Swiss I came across. I'll never trust a Swiss again. He humbugged us into giving him fifty ablebodied men for two hundred worn out chargers. They werent even eatable!

SERGIUS. We were two children in the hands of that consummate soldier, Major: simply two innocent little children.

RAINA. What was he like?

CATHERINE. Oh, Raina, what a silly question!

SERGIUS. He was like a commercial traveller in uniform. Bourgeois to his boots!

PETKOFF [grinning] Sergius: tell Catherine that queer story his friend told us about how he escaped after Slivnitza. You remember. About his being hid by two women.

SERGIUS [with bitter irony] Oh yes: quite a romance! He was serving in the very battery I so unprofessionally charged. Being a thorough soldier, he ran away like the rest of them, with our cavalry at his heels. To escape their sabres he climbed a waterpipe and made his way into the bedroom of a young Bulgarian lady. The young lady was enchanted by his persuasive commercial traveller's manners. She very modestly entertained him for an hour or so, and then called in her mother lest her conduct should appear unmaidenly. The old lady was equally fascinated; and the fugitive was sent on his way in the morning, disguised in an old coat belonging to the master of the house, who was away at the war.

RAINA [rising with marked stateliness] Your life in the camp has made you coarse, Sergius. I did not think you would have repeated such a story before me. [She turns away coldly].

CATHERINE [also rising] She is right, Sergius. If such women exist, we should be spared the knowledge of them.

PETKOFF. Pooh! nonsense! what does it matter?

SERGIUS [ashamed] No, Petkoff: I was wrong. [To RAINA, with earnest humility] I beg your pardon. I have behaved abominably. Forgive me, Raina. [She bows reservedly]. And you too, madam. [CATHERINE bows graciously and sits down. He proceeds solemnly, again addressing RAINA] The glimpses I have had of the seamy side of life during the last few months have made me cynical; but I should not have brought my cynicism here: least of all into your presence, Raina. I—[Here, turning to the others, he is evidently going to begin a long speech when the MAJOR interrupts him].

PETKOFF. Stuff and nonsense, Sergius! Thats quite enough fuss about nothing: a soldier's daughter should be able to stand up without flinching to a little strong conversation. [He rises]. Come: it's time for us to get to business. We have to make up our minds how those three regiments are to get back to Philippopolis: theres no forage for them on the Sofia route. [He goes towards the house]. Come along. [SERGIUS is about to follow him when CATHERINE rises and intervenes].

CATHERINE. Oh, Paul, cant you spare Sergius for a few moments? Raina has hardly seen him yet. Perhaps I can help you to settle about the regiments.

SERGIUS [protesting] My dear madam, impossible: you—

CATHERINE [stopping him playfully] You stay here, my dear Sergius: theres no hurry. I have a word or two to say to Paul. [SERGIUS instantly bows and steps back]. Now, dear [taking PETKOFF's arm]: come and see the electric bell.

PETKOFF. Oh, very well, very well.

They go into the house together affectionately. SERGIUS, left alone with RAINA, looks anxiously at her, fearing that she is still offended. She smiles, and stretches out her arms to him.

SERGIUS [hastening to her] Am I forgiven?

RAINA [placing her hands on his shoulders as she looks up at him with admiration and worship] My hero! My king!

SERGIUS. My queen! [He kisses her on the forehead].

RAINA. How I have envied you, Sergius! You have been out in the world, on the field of battle, able to prove yourself there worthy of any woman in the world; whilst I have had to sit at home inactive—dreaming—useless—doing nothing that could give me the right to call myself worthy of any man.

SERGIUS. Dearest: all my deeds have been yours. You inspired me. I have gone through the war like a knight in a tournament with his lady looking down at him!

RAINA. And you have never been absent from my thoughts for a moment. [Very solemnly] Sergius: I think we two have found the higher love. When I think of you, I feel that I could never do a base deed, or think an ignoble thought.

SERGIUS. My lady and my saint! [He clasps her reverently].

RAINA [returning his embrace] My lord and my—

SERGIUS. Sh-sh! Let me be the worshipper, dear. You little know how unworthy even the best man is of a girl's pure passion!

RAINA. I trust you. I love you. You will never disappoint me, Sergius. [LOUKA *is heard singing within the house. They quickly release each other*]. I cant pretend to talk indifferently before her: my heart is too full. [LOUKA *comes from the house with her tray. She goes to the table, and begins to clear it, with her back turned to them*]. I will get my hat; and then we can go out until lunch time. Wouldnt you like that?

SERGIUS. Be quick. If you are away five minutes, it will seem five hours. [RAINA *runs to the top of the steps, and turns there to exchange looks with him and wave him a kiss with both hands. He looks after her with emotion for a moment; then turns slowly away, his face radiant with the loftiest exaltation. The movement shifts his field of vision, into the corner of which there now comes the tail of* LOUKA'S *double apron. His attention is arrested at once. He takes a stealthy look at her, and begins to twirl his moustache mischievously, with his left hand akimbo on his hip. Finally, striking the ground with his heels in something of a cavalry swagger, he strolls over to the other side of the table, opposite her, and says*] Louka: do you know what the higher love is?

LOUKA [*astonished*] No, sir.

SERGIUS. Very fatiguing thing to keep up for any length of time, Louka. One feels the need of some relief after it.

LOUKA [*innocently*] Perhaps you would like some coffee, sir? [*She stretches her hand across the table for the coffee pot*].

SERGIUS [*taking her hand*] Thank you, Louka.

LOUKA [*pretending to pull*] Oh, sir, you know I didnt mean that. I'm surprised at you!

SERGIUS [*coming clear of the table and drawing her with him*] I am surprised at myself, Louka. What would Sergius, the hero of Slivnitza, say if he saw me now? What would Sergius, the apostle of the higher love, say if he saw me now? What would the half dozen Sergiuses who keep popping in and out of this handsome figure of mine say if they caught us here? [*Letting go her hand and slipping his arm dexterously round her waist*] Do you consider my figure handsome, Louka?

LOUKA. Let me go, sir. I shall be disgraced.

[*She struggles: he holds her inexorably*]. Oh, will you let go?

SERGIUS [*looking straight into her eyes*] No.

LOUKA. Then stand back where we cant be seen. Have you no common sense?

SERGIUS. Ah! thats reasonable. [*He takes her into the stable yard gateway, where they are hidden from the house*].

LOUKA [*plaintively*] I may have been seen from the windows: Miss Raina is sure to be spying about after you.

SERGIUS [*stung: letting her go*] Take care, Louka. I may be worthless enough to betray the higher love; but do not you insult it.

LOUKA [*demurely*] Not for the world, sir, I'm sure. May I go on with my work, please, now?

SERGIUS [*again putting his arm round her*] You are a provoking little witch, Louka. If you were in love with me, would you spy out of windows on me?

LOUKA. Well, you see, sir, since you say you are half a dozen different gentlemen all at once, I should have a great deal to look after.

SERGIUS [*charmed*] Witty as well as pretty. [*He tries to kiss her*].

LOUKA [*avoiding him*] No: I dont want your kisses. Gentlefolk are all alike: you making love to me behind Miss Raina's back; and she doing the same behind yours.

SERGIUS [*recoiling a step*] Louka!

LOUKA. It shews how little you really care.

SERGIUS [*dropping his familiarity, and speaking with freezing politeness*] If our conversation is to continue, Louka, you will please remember that a gentleman does not discuss the conduct of the lady he is engaged to with her maid.

LOUKA. It's so hard to know what a gentleman considers right. I thought from your trying to kiss me that you had given up being so particular.

SERGIUS [*turning from her and striking his forehead as he comes back into the garden from the gateway*] Devil! devil!

LOUKA. Ha! ha! I expect one of the six of you is very like me, sir; though I am only Miss Raina's maid. [*She goes back to her work at the table, taking no further notice of him*].

SERGIUS [*speaking to himself*] Which of the six is the real man? thats the question that torments me. One of them is a hero, another a buffoon, another a humbug, another perhaps a bit of a blackguard. [*He pauses, and looks fur-*

*tively at* LOUKA *as he adds, with deep bitterness*] And one, at least, is a coward: jealous, like all cowards. [*He goes to the table*]. Louka.

LOUKA. Yes?

SERGIUS. Who is my rival?

LOUKA. You shall never get that out of me, for love or money.

SERGIUS. Why?

LOUKA. Never mind why. Besides, you would tell that I told you; and I should lose my place.

SERGIUS [*holding out his right hand in affirmation*] No! on the honor of a—[*He checks himself; and his hand drops, nerveless, as he concludes sardonically*]—of a man capable of behaving as I have been behaving for the last five minutes. Who is he?

LOUKA. I dont know. I never saw him. I only heard his voice through the door of her room.

SERGIUS. Damnation! How dare you?

LOUKA [*retreating*] Oh, I mean no harm: youve no right to take up my words like that. The mistress knows all about it. And I tell you that if that gentleman ever comes here again, Miss Raina will marry him, whether he likes it or not. I know the difference between the sort of manner you and she put on before one another and the real manner.

SERGIUS *shivers as if she had stabbed him. Then, setting his face like iron, he strides grimly to her, and grips her above the elbows with both hands.*

SERGIUS. Now listen you to me.

LOUKA [*wincing*] Not so tight: youre hurting me.

SERGIUS. That doesnt matter. You have stained my honor by making me a party to your eavesdropping. And you have betrayed your mistress.

LOUKA [*writhing*] Please—

SERGIUS. That shews that you are an abominable little clod of common clay, with the soul of a servant. [*He lets her go as if she were an unclean thing, and turns away, dusting his hands of her, to the bench by the wall, where he sits down with averted head, meditating gloomily*].

LOUKA [*whimpering angrily with her hands up her sleeves, feeling her bruised arms*] You know how to hurt with your tongue as well as with your hands. But I dont care, now Ive found out that whatever clay I'm made of, youre made of the same. As for her, she's a liar; and her fine airs are a cheat; and I'm

worth six of her. [*She shakes the pain off hardily; tosses her head; and sets to work to put the things on the tray*].

*He looks doubtfully at her. She finishes packing the tray, and laps the cloth over the edges, so as to carry all out together. As she stoops to lift it, he rises.*

SERGIUS. Louka! [*She stops and looks defiantly at him*]. A gentleman has no right to hurt a woman under any circumstances. [*With profound humility, uncovering his head*] I beg your pardon.

LOUKA. That sort of apology may satisfy a lady. Of what use is it to a servant?

SERGIUS [*rudely crossed in his chivalry, throws it off with a bitter laugh, and says slightingly*] Oh! you wish to be paid for the hurt! [*He puts on his shako, and takes some money from his pocket*].

LOUKA [*her eyes filling with tears in spite of herself*] No: I want my hurt made well.

SERGIUS [*sobered by her tone*] How?

*She rolls up her left sleeve; clasps her arm with the thumb and fingers of her right hand; and looks down at the bruise. Then she raises her head and looks straight at him. Finally, with a superb gesture, she presents her arm to be kissed. Amazed, he looks at her; at the arm; at her again; hesitates; and then, with shuddering intensity, exclaims* Never! *and gets away as far as possible from her.*

*Her arm drops. Without a word, and with unaffected dignity, she takes her tray, and is approaching the house when* RAINA *returns, wearing a hat and jacket in the height of the Vienna fashion of the previous year, 1885.* LOUKA *makes way proudly for her, and then goes into the house.*

RAINA. I'm ready. Whats the matter? [*Gaily*] Have you been flirting with Louka?

SERGIUS [*hastily*] No, no. How can you think such a thing?

RAINA [*ashamed of herself*] Forgive me, dear: it was only a jest. I am so happy today.

*He goes quickly to her, and kisses her hand remorsefully.* CATHERINE *comes out and calls to them from the top of the steps.*

CATHERINE [*coming down to them*] I am sorry to disturb you, children; but Paul is distracted over those three regiments. He doesnt know how to send them to Philippopolis; and he objects to every suggestion of mine. You must go and help him, Sergius. He is in the library.

RAINA [*disappointed*] But we are just going out for a walk.

SERGIUS. I shall not be long. Wait for me just five minutes. [*He runs up the steps to the door*].

RAINA [*following him to the foot of the steps and looking up at him with timid coquetry*] I shall go round and wait in full view of the library windows. Be sure you draw father's attention to me. If you are a moment longer than five minutes, I shall go in and fetch you, regiments or no regiments.

SERGIUS [*laughing*] Very well. [*He goes in*].

RAINA *watches him until he is out of her sight. Then, with a perceptible relaxation of manner, she begins to pace up and down the garden in a brown study.*

CATHERINE. Imagine their meeting that Swiss and hearing the whole story! The very first thing your father asked for was the old coat we sent him off in. A nice mess you have got us into!

RAINA [*gazing thoughtfully at the gravel as she walks*] The little beast!

CATHERINE. Little beast! What little beast?

RAINA. To go and tell! Oh, if I had him here, I'd cram him with chocolate creams till he couldnt ever speak again!

CATHERINE. Dont talk such stuff. Tell me the truth, Raina. How long was he in your room before you came to me?

RAINA [*whisking round and recommencing her march in the opposite direction*] Oh, I forget.

CATHERINE. You cannot forget! Did he really climb up after the soldiers were gone; or was he there when that officer searched the room?

RAINA. No. Yes: I think he must have been there then.

CATHERINE. You think! Oh, Raina! Raina! Will anything ever make you straightforward? If Sergius finds out, it will be all over between you.

RAINA [*with cool impertinence*] Oh, I know Sergius is your pet. I sometimes wish you could marry him instead of me. You would just suit him. You would pet him, and spoil him, and mother him to perfection.

CATHERINE [*opening her eyes very widely indeed*] Well, upon my word!

RAINA [*capriciously: half to herself*] I always feel a longing to do or say something dreadful to him—to shock his propriety—to scandalize the five senses out of him. [*To* CATHERINE, *perversely*] I dont care whether he finds out about the chocolate cream soldier or not. I half hope he may. [*She again turns and strolls flippantly away up the path to the corner of the house*].

CATHERINE. And what should I be able to say to your father, pray?

RAINA [*over her shoulder, from the top of the two steps*] Oh, poor father! As if he could help himself! [*She turns the corner and passes out of sight*].

CATHERINE [*looking after her, her fingers itching*] Oh, if you were only ten years younger! [LOUKA *comes from the house with a salver, which she carries hanging down by her side*]. Well?

LOUKA. Theres a gentleman just called, madam. A Serbian officer.

CATHERINE [*flaming*] A Serb! And how dare he—[*checking herself bitterly*] Oh, I forgot. We are at peace now. I suppose we shall have them calling every day to pay their compliments. Well: if he is an officer why dont you tell your master? He is in the library with Major Saranoff. Why do you come to me?

LOUKA. But he asks for you, madam. And I dont think he knows who you are: he said the lady of the house. He gave me this little ticket for you. [*She takes a card out of her bosom; puts it on the salver; and offers it to* CATHERINE].

CATHERINE [*reading*] "Captain Bluntschli"? Thats a German name.

LOUKA. Swiss, madam, I think.

CATHERINE [*with a bound that makes* LOUKA *jump back*] Swiss! What is he like?

LOUKA [*timidly*] He has a big carpet bag, madam.

CATHERINE. Oh Heavens! he's come to return the coat. Send him away: say we're not at home: ask him to leave his address and I'll write to him. Oh stop: that will never do. Wait! [*She throws herself into a chair to think it out.* LOUKA *waits*]. The master and Major Saranoff are busy in the library, arnt they?

LOUKA. Yes, madam.

CATHERINE [*decisively*] Bring the gentleman out here at once. [*Peremptorily*] And be very polite to him. Dont delay. Here [*impatiently snatching the salver from her*]: leave that here; and go straight back to him.

LOUKA. Yes, madam [*going*].

CATHERINE. Louka!

LOUKA. [*stopping*] Yes, madam.

CATHERINE. Is the library door shut?

LOUKA. I think so, madam.

CATHERINE. If not, shut it as you pass through.

LOUKA. Yes, madam [*going*].

CATHERINE. Stop [LOUKA *stops*]. He will have to go that way [*indicating the gate of the stable yard*]. Tell Nicola to bring his bag here after him. Dont forget.

LOUKA [*surprised*] His bag?

CATHERINE. Yes: here: as soon as possible. [*Vehemently*] Be quick! [LOUKA *runs into the house.* CATHERINE *snatches her apron off and throws it behind a bush. She then takes up the salver and uses it as a mirror, with the result that the handkerchief tied round her head follows the apron. A touch to her hair and a shake to her dressing gown make her presentable*]. Oh, how? how? how can a man be such a fool! Such a moment to select! [LOUKA *appears at the door of the house, announcing* Captain Bluntschli. *She stands aside at the top of the steps to let him pass before she goes in again. He is the man of the midnight adventure in* RAINA'S *room, clean, well brushed, smartly uniformed, and out of trouble, but still unmistakably the same man. The moment* LOUKA'S *back is turned,* CATHERINE *swoops on him with impetuous, urgent, coaxing appeal*]. Captain Bluntschli: I am very glad to see you; but you must leave this house at once. [*He raises his eyebrows*]. My husband has just returned with my future son-in-law; and they know nothing. If they did, the consequences would be terrible. You are a foreigner: you do not feel our national animosities as we do. We still hate the Serbs: the effect of the peace on my husband has been to make him feel like a lion baulked of his prey. If he discovers our secret, he will never forgive me; and my daughter's life will hardly be safe. Will you, like the chivalrous gentleman and soldier you are, leave at once before he finds you here?

BLUNTSCHLI [*disappointed, but philosophical*] At once, gracious lady. I only came to thank you and return the coat you lent me. If you will allow me to take it out of my bag and leave it with your servant as I pass out. I need

detain you no further. [*He turns to go into the house*].

CATHERINE [*catching him by the sleeve*] Oh, you must not think of going back that way. [*Coaxing him across to the stable gates*] This is the shortest way out. Many thanks. So glad to have been of service to you. Good-bye.

BLUNTSCHLI. But my bag?

CATHERINE. It shall be sent on. You will leave me your address.

BLUNTSCHLI. True. Allow me. [*He takes out his card-case, and stops to write his address, keeping* CATHERINE *in an agony of impatience. As he hands her the card,* PETKOFF, *hatless, rushes from the house in a fluster of hospitality, followed by* SERGIUS].

PETKOFF [*as he hurries down the steps*] My dear Captain Bluntschli—

CATHERINE. Oh Heavens! [*She sinks on the seat against the wall*].

PETKOFF [*too preoccupied to notice her as he shakes* BLUNTSCHLI'S *hand heartily*] Those stupid people of mine thought I was out here, instead of in the—haw!—library [*he cannot mention the library without betraying how proud he is of it*]. I saw you through the window. I was wondering why you didnt come in. Saranoff is with me: you remember him, dont you?

SERGIUS [*saluting humorously, and then offering his hand with great charm of manner*] Welcome, our friend the enemy!

PETKOFF. No longer the enemy, happily. [*Rather anxiously*] I hope youve called as a friend, and not about horses or prisoners.

CATHERINE. Oh, quite as a friend, Paul. I was just asking Captain Bluntschli to stay to lunch; but he declares he must go at once.

SERGIUS [*sardonically*] Impossible, Bluntschli. We want you here badly. We have to send on three cavalry regiments to Philippopolis; and we dont in the least know how to do it.

BLUNTSCHLI [*suddenly attentive and businesslike*] Philippopolis? The forage is the trouble, I suppose.

PETKOFF [*eagerly*] Yes: thats it. [*To* SERGIUS] He sees the whole thing at once.

BLUNTSCHLI. I think I can shew you how to manage that.

SERGIUS. Invaluable man! Come along! [*Towering over* BLUNTSCHLI, *he puts his hand on his shoulder and takes him to the steps,* PETKOFF *following*].

RAINA *comes from the house as* BLUNTSCHLI *puts his foot on the first step.*

RAINA. Oh! The chocolate cream soldier!

BLUNTSCHLI *stands rigid.* SERGIUS, *amazed, looks at* RAINA, *then at* PETKOFF, *who looks back at him and then at his wife.*

CATHERINE [*with commanding presence of mind*] My dear Raina, dont you see that we have a guest here? Captain Bluntschli: one of our new Serbian friends.

RAINA *bows:* BLUNTSCHLI *bows.*

RAINA. How silly of me! [*She comes down into the centre of the group, between* BLUNT- SCHLI *and* PETKOFF]. I made a beautiful orna- ment this morning for the ice pudding; and that stupid Nicola has just put down a pile of plates on it and spoilt it. [*To* BLUNTSCHLI, *winningly*] I hope you didnt think that you were the choc- olate cream soldier, Captain Bluntschli.

BLUNTSCHLI [*laughing*] I assure you I did. [*Stealing a whimsical glance at her*] Your ex- planation was a relief.

PETKOFF [*suspiciously, to* RAINA] And since when, pray, have you taken to cooking?

CATHERINE. Oh, whilst you were away. It is her latest fancy.

PETKOFF [*testily*] And has Nicola taken to drinking? He used to be careful enough. First he shews Captain Bluntschli out here when he knew quite well I was in the library; and then he goes downstairs and breaks Raina's choc- olate soldier. He must—[NICOLA *appears at the top of the steps with the bag. He descends; places it respectfully before* BLUNTSCHLI; *and waits for further orders. General amazement.* NICOLA, *unconscious of the effect he is pro- ducing, looks perfectly satisfied with himself. When* PETKOFF *recovers his power of speech, he breaks out at him with*] Are you mad, Nicola?

NICOLA [*taken aback*] Sir?

PETKOFF. What have you brought that for?

NICOLA. My lady's orders, major. Louka told me that—

CATHERINE [*interrupting him*] My orders! Why should I order you to bring Captain Bluntschli's luggage out here? What are you thinking of, Nicola?

NICOLA [*after a moment's bewilderment, picking up the bag as he addresses* BLUNTSCHLI *with the very perfection of servile discretion*] I beg your pardon, captain, I am sure. [*To* CATHERINE] My fault, madam: I hope youll

overlook it. [*He bows, and is going to the steps with the bag, when* PETKOFF *addresses him angrily*].

PETKOFF. Youd better go and slam that bag, too, down on Miss Raina's ice pudding! [*This is too much for* NICOLA. *The bag drops from his hand almost on his master's toes, eliciting a roar of*] Begone, you butter-fingered donkey.

NICOLA [*snatching up the bag, and escaping into the house*] Yes, major.

CATHERINE. Oh, never mind, Paul: dont be angry.

PETKOFF [*blustering*] Scoundrel! He's got out of hand while I was away. I'll teach him. Infernal blackguard! The sack next Saturday! I'll clear out the whole establishment—[*He is stifled by the caresses of his wife and daughter, who hang round his neck, petting him*].

CATHERINE } [*together*] { Now, now, now, it
RAINA                        { Wow, wow, wow: not
mustnt be angry. He meant no
on your first day at home. I'll
harm. Be good to please me,
make another ice pudding. Tch-
dear. Sh-sh-sh-sh!
ch-ch!

PETKOFF [*yielding*] Oh well, never mind. Come, Bluntschli: lets have no more nonsense about going away. You know very well youre not going back to Switzerland yet. Until you do go back youll stay with us.

RAINA. Oh, do, Captain Bluntschli.

PETKOFF [*to* CATHERINE] Now, Catherine: it's of you he's afraid. Press him; and he'll stay.

CATHERINE. Of course I shall be only too delighted if [*appealingly*] Captain Bluntschli really wishes to stay. He knows my wishes.

BLUNTSCHLI [*in his driest military manner*] I am at madam's orders.

SERGIUS [*cordially*] That settles it!

PETKOFF [*heartily*] Of course!

RAINA. You see you must stay.

BLUNTSCHLI [*smiling*] Well, if I must, I must. *Gesture of despair from* CATHERINE.

## ACT III

*In the library after lunch. It is not much of a library. Its literary equipment consists of a single fixed shelf stocked with old paper cov- ered novels, broken backed, coffee stained, torn and thumbed; and a couple of little hanging shelves with a few gift books on them: the rest* of the wall space being occupied by trophies of war and the chase. But it is a most comfortable sitting room. A row of three large windows shews a mountain panorama, just now seen in one of its friendliest aspects in the mellowing afternoon light. In the corner next the right hand window a square earthenware stove, a perfect tower of glistening pottery, rises nearly to the ceiling and guarantees plenty of warmth. The ottoman is like that in RAINA'S room, and similarly placed; and the window seats are luxurious with decorated cushions. There is one object, however, hopelessly out of keeping with its surroundings. This is a small kitchen table, much the worse for wear, fitted as a writing table with an old canister full of pens, an eggcup filled with ink, and a deplorable scrap of heavily used pink blotting paper.

At the side of this table, which stands to the left of anyone facing the window, BLUNTSCHLI is hard at work with a couple of maps before him, writing orders. At the head of it sits SERGIUS, who is supposed to be also at work, but is actually gnawing the feather of a pen, and contemplating BLUNTSCHLI'S quick, sure, businesslike progress with a mixture of envious irritation at his own incapacity and awestruck wonder at an ability which seems to him almost miraculous, though its prosaic character forbids him to esteem it. The MAJOR is comfortably established on the ottoman, with a newspaper in his hand and the tube of his hookah within easy reach. CATHERINE sits at the stove with her back to them, embroidering. RAINA, reclining on the divan, is gazing in a daydream out at the Balkan landscape, with a neglected novel in her lap.

The door is on the same side as the stove, farther from the window. The button of the electric bell is at the opposite side, behind BLUNTSCHLI.

PETKOFF [looking up from his paper to watch how they are getting on at the table] Are you sure I cant help in any way, Bluntschli?

BLUNTSCHLI [without interrupting his writing or looking up] Quite sure, thank you. Saranoff and I will manage it.

SERGIUS [grimly] Yes: we'll manage it. He finds out what to do; draws up the orders; and I sign em. Division of labor! [BLUNTSCHLI passes him a paper]. Another one? Thank you. [He plants the paper squarely before him; sets

his chair carefully parallel to it; and signs with his cheek on his elbow and his protruded tongue following the movements of his pen]. This hand is more accustomed to the sword than to the pen.

PETKOFF. It's very good of you, Bluntschli: it is indeed, to let yourself be put upon in this way. Now are you quite sure I can do nothing?

CATHERINE [in a low warning tone] You can stop interrupting, Paul.

PETKOFF [starting and looking round at her] Eh? Oh! Quite right. [He takes his newspaper up again, but presently lets it drop]. Ah, you havnt been campaigning, Catherine: you dont know how pleasant it is for us to sit here, after a good lunch, with nothing to do but enjoy ourselves. Theres only one thing I want to make me thoroughly comfortable.

CATHERINE. What is that?

PETKOFF. My old coat. I'm not at home in this one: I feel as if I were on parade.

CATHERINE. My dear Paul, how absurd you are about that old coat! It must be hanging in the blue closet where you left it.

PETKOFF. My dear Catherine, I tell you Ive looked there. Am I to believe my own eyes or not? [CATHERINE rises and crosses the room to press the button of the electric bell]. What are you shewing off that bell for? [She looks at him majestically, and silently resumes her chair and her needlework]. My dear: if you think the obstinacy of your sex can make a coat out of two old dressing gowns of Raina's, your waterproof, and my mackintosh, youre mistaken. Thats exactly what the blue closet contains at present.

NICOLA presents himself.

CATHERINE. Nicola: go to the blue closet and bring your master's old coat here: the braided one he wears in the house.

NICOLA. Yes, madame. [He goes out].

PETKOFF. Catherine.

CATHERINE. Yes, Paul?

PETKOFF. I bet you any piece of jewellery you like to order from Sofia against a week's housekeeping money that the coat isnt there.

CATHERINE. Done, Paul!

PETKOFF [excited by the prospect of a gamble] Come: heres an opportunity for some sport. Wholl bet on it? Bluntschli: I'll give you six to one.

BLUNTSCHLI [imperturbably] It would be robbing you, Major. Madame is sure to be right. [*Without looking up, he passes another batch of papers to* SERGIUS].

SERGIUS [*also excited*] Bravo, Switzerland! Major: I bet my best charger against an Arab mare for Raina that Nicola finds the coat in the blue closet.

PETKOFF [*eagerly*] Your best char—

CATHERINE [*hastily interrupting him*] Dont be foolish, Paul. An Arabian mare will cost you 50,000 levas.

RAINA [*suddenly coming out of her picturesque revery*] Really, mother, if you are going to take the jewellery, I dont see why you should grudge me my Arab.

NICOLA *comes back with the coat, and brings it to* PETKOFF, *who can hardly believe his eyes.*

CATHERINE. Where was it, Nicola?

NICOLA. Hanging in the blue closet, madame.

PETKOFF. Well, I am d—

CATHERINE [*stopping him*] Paul!

PETKOFF. I could have sworn it wasnt there. Age is beginning to tell on me. I'm getting hallucinations. [*To* NICOLA] Here: help me to change. Excuse me, Bluntschli. [*He begins changing coats,* NICOLA *acting as valet*]. Remember: I didnt take that bet of yours, Sergius. Youd better give Raina that Arab steed yourself, since youve roused her expectations. Eh, Raina? [*He looks round at her; but she is again rapt in the landscape. With a little gush of parental affection and pride, he points her out to them, and says*] She's dreaming, as usual.

SERGIUS. Assuredly she shall not be the loser.

PETKOFF. So much the better for her. *I* shant come off so cheaply, I expect. [*The change is now complete.* NICOLA *goes out with the discarded coat*]. Ah, now I feel at home at last. [*He sits down and takes his newspaper with a grunt of relief*].

BLUNTSCHLI [*to* SERGIUS, *handing a paper*] Thats the last order.

PETKOFF [*jumping up*] What! Finished?

BLUNTSCHLI. Finished.

PETKOFF [*with childlike envy*] Havnt you anything for me to sign?

BLUNTSCHLI. Not necessary. His signature will do.

PETKOFF [*inflating his chest and thumping it*] Ah well, I think weve done a thundering good day's work. Can I do anything more?

BLUNTSCHLI. You had better both see the fellows that are to take these. [SERGIUS *rises*] Pack them off at once; and shew them that Ive marked on the orders the time they should hand them in by. Tell them that if they stop to drink or tell stories—if theyre five minutes late, theyll have the skin taken off their backs.

SERGIUS [*stiffening indignantly*] I'll say so. [*He strides to the door*]. And if one of them is man enough to spit in my face for insulting him, I'll buy his discharge and give him a pension. [*He goes out*].

BLUNTSCHLI [*confidentially*] Just see that he talks to them properly, Major, will you?

PETKOFF [*officiously*] Quite right, Bluntschli, quite right. I'll see to it. [*He goes to the door importantly, but hesitates on the threshold*]. By the bye, Catherine, you may as well come too. Theyll be far more frightened of you than of me.

CATHERINE [*putting down her embroidery*] I daresay I had better. You would only splutter at them. [*She goes out,* PETKOFF *holding the door for her and following her*].

BLUNTSCHLI. What an army! They make cannons out of cherry trees; and the officers send for their wives to keep discipline! [*He begins to fold and docket the papers*].

RAINA, *who has risen from the divan, marches slowly down the room with her hands clasped behind her, and looks mischievously at him.*

RAINA. You look ever so much nicer than when we last met. [*He looks up, surprised*]. What have you done to yourself?

BLUNTSCHLI. Washed; brushed; good night's sleep and breakfast. Thats all.

RAINA. Did you get back safely that morning?

BLUNTSCHLI. Quite, thanks.

RAINA. Were they angry with you for running away from Sergius's charge?

BLUNTSCHLI [*grinning*] No: they were glad; because theyd all just run away themselves.

RAINA [*going to the table, and leaning over it towards him*] It must have made a lovely story for them: all that about me and my room.

BLUNTSCHLI. Capital story. But I only told it to one of them: a particular friend.

RAINA. On whose discretion you could absolutely rely?

BLUNTSCHLI. Absolutely.

RAINA. Hm! He told it all to my father and Sergius the day you exchanged the prisoners.

[*She turns away and strolls carelessly across to the other side of the room*].

BLUNTSCHLI [*deeply concerned, and half incredulous*] No! You dont mean that, do you?

RAINA [*turning, with sudden earnestness*] I do indeed. But they dont know that it was in this house you took refuge. If Sergius knew, he would challenge you and kill you in a duel.

BLUNTSCHLI. Bless me! then dont tell him.

RAINA. Please be serious, Captain Bluntschli. Can you not realize what it is to me to deceive him? I want to be quite perfect with Sergius: no meanness, no smallness, no deceit. My relation to him is the one really beautiful and noble part of my life. I hope you can understand that.

BLUNTSCHLI [*sceptically*] You mean that you wouldnt like him to find out that the story about the ice pudding was a—a—a—You know.

RAINA [*wincing*] Ah, dont talk of it in that flippant way. I lied: I know it. But I did it to save your life. He would have killed you. That was the second time I ever uttered a falsehood. [BLUNTSCHLI *rises quickly and looks doubtfully and somewhat severely at her*]. Do you remember the first time?

BLUNTSCHLI. I! No. Was I present?

RAINA. Yes; and I told the officer who was searching for you that you were not present.

BLUNTSCHLI. True. I should have remembered it.

RAINA [*greatly encouraged*] Ah, it is natural that you should forget it first. It cost you nothing: it cost me a lie! A lie!

*She sits down on the ottoman, looking straight before her with her hands clasped round her knee.* BLUNTSCHLI, *quite touched, goes to the ottoman with a particularly reassuring and considerate air, and sits down beside her.*

BLUNTSCHLI. My dear young lady, dont let this worry you. Remember: I'm a soldier. Now what are the two things that happen to a soldier so often that he comes to think nothing of them? One is hearing people tell lies [RAINA *recoils*]: the other is getting his life saved in all sorts of ways by all sorts of people.

RAINA [*rising in indignant protest*] And so he becomes a creature incapable of faith and of gratitude.

BLUNTSCHLI [*making a wry face*] Do you like gratitude? I dont. If pity is akin to love, gratitude is akin to the other thing.

RAINA. Gratitude! [*Turning on him*] If you are incapable of gratitude you are incapable of any noble sentiment. Even animals are grateful. Oh, I see now exactly what you think of me! You were not surprised to hear me lie. To you it was something I probably did every day! every hour!! That is how men think of women. [*She paces the room tragically*].

BLUNTSCHLI [*dubiously*] Theres reason in everything. You said youd told only two lies in your whole life. Dear young lady: isnt that rather a short allowance? I'm quite a straightforward man myself; but it wouldnt last me a whole morning.

RAINA [*staring haughtily at him*] Do you know, sir, that you are insulting me?

BLUNTSCHLI. I cant help it. When you strike that noble attitude and speak in that thrilling voice, I admire you; but I find it impossible to believe a single word you say.

RAINA [*superbly*] Captain Bluntschli!

BLUNTSCHLI [*unmoved*] Yes?

RAINA [*standing over him, as if she could not believe her senses*] Do you mean what you said just now? Do you know what you said just now?

BLUNTSCHLI. I do.

RAINA [*gasping*] I! I!!! [*She points to herself incredulously, meaning "I*, RAINA PETKOFF *tell lies!" He meets her gaze unflinchingly. She suddenly sits down beside him, and adds, with a complete change of manner from the heroic to a babyish familiarity*] How did you find me out?

BLUNTSCHLI [*promptly*] Instinct, dear young lady. Instinct, and experience of the world.

RAINA [*wonderingly*] Do you know, you are the first man I ever met who did not take me seriously?

BLUNTSCHLI. You mean, dont you, that I am the first man that has ever taken you quite seriously?

RAINA. Yes: I suppose I do mean that. [*Cosily, quite at her ease with him*] How strange it is to be talked to in such a way! You know, Ive always gone on like that.

BLUNTSCHLI. You mean the—?

RAINA. I mean the noble attitude and the thrilling voice. [*They laugh together*]. I did it when I was a tiny child to my nurse. She believed in it. I do it before my parents. They believe in it. I do it before Sergius. He believes in it.

BLUNTSCHLI. Yes: he's a little in that line himself, isnt he?

RAINA [startled] Oh! Do you think so?

BLUNTSCHLI. You know him better than I do.

RAINA. I wonder—I wonder is he? If I thought that—! [Discouraged] Ah, well; what does it matter? I suppose, now youve found me out, you despise me.

BLUNTSCHLI [warmly, rising] No, my dear young lady, no, no, no a thousand times. It's part of your youth: part of your charm. I'm like all the rest of them: the nurse, your parents, Sergius: I'm your infatuated admirer.

RAINA [pleased] Really?

BLUNTSCHLI [slapping his breast smartly with his hand, German fashion] Hand aufs Herz! Really and truly.

RAINA [very happy] But what did you think of me for giving you my portrait?

BLUNTSCHLI [astonished] Your portrait! You never gave me your portrait.

RAINA [quickly] Do you mean to say you never got it?

BLUNTSCHLI. No. [He sits down beside her, with renewed interest, and says, with some complacency] When did you send it to me?

RAINA [indignantly] I did not send it to you. [She turns her head away, and adds, reluctantly] It was in the pocket of that coat.

BLUNTSCHLI [pursing his lips and rounding his eyes] Oh-o-oh! I never found it. It must be there still.

RAINA [springing up] There still! for my father to find the first time he puts his hand in his pocket! Oh, how could you be so stupid?

BLUNTSCHLI [rising also] It doesnt matter: I suppose it's only a photograph: how can he tell who it was intended for? Tell him he put it there himself.

RAINA [bitterly] Yes: that is so clever! isnt it? [Distractedly] Oh! what shall I do?

BLUNTSCHLI. Ah, I see. You wrote something on it. That was rash.

RAINA [vexed almost to tears] Oh, to have done such a thing for you, who care no more—except to laugh at me—oh! Are you sure nobody has touched it?

BLUNTSCHLI. Well, I cant be quite sure. You see, I couldnt carry it about with me all the time: one cant take much luggage on active service.

RAINA. What did you do with it?

BLUNTSCHLI. When I got through to Pirot I had to put it in safe keeping somehow. I thought of the railway cloak room; but thats the surest place to get looted in modern warfare. So I pawned it.

RAINA. Pawned it!!!

BLUNTSCHLI. I know it doesnt sound nice: but it was much the safest plan. I redeemed it the day before yesterday. Heaven only knows whether the pawnbroker cleared out the pockets or not.

RAINA [furious: throwing the words right into his face] You have a low shopkeeping mind. You think of things that would never come into a gentleman's head.

BLUNTSCHLI [phlegmatically] Thats the Swiss national character, dear lady. [He returns to the table].

RAINA. Oh, I wish I had never met you. [She flounces away, and sits at the window fuming].

LOUKA comes in with a heap of letters and telegrams on her salver, and crosses, with her bold free gait, to the table. Her left sleeve is looped up to the shoulder with a brooch, shewing her naked arm, with a broad gilt bracelet covering the bruise.

LOUKA [to BLUNTSCHLI] For you. [She empties the salver with a fling on to the table]. The messenger is waiting. [She is determined not to be civil to an enemy, even if she must bring him his letters].

BLUNTSCHLI [to RAINA] Will you excuse me: the last postal delivery that reached me was three weeks ago. These are the subsequent accumulations. Four telegrams: a week old. [He opens one]. Oho! Bad news!

RAINA [rising and advancing a little remorsefully] Bad news?

BLUNTSCHLI. My father's dead. [He looks at the telegram with his lips pursed, musing on the unexpected change in his arrangements. LOUKA crosses herself hastily].

RAINA. Oh, how very sad!

BLUNTSCHLI. Yes: I shall have to start for home in an hour. He has left a lot of big hotels behind him to be looked after. [He takes up a fat letter in a long blue envelope]. Here's a whacking letter from the family solicitor. [He puts out the enclosures and glances over them]. Great Heavens! Seventy! Two hundred! [In a crescendo of dismay] Four hundred! Four thousand!! Nine thousand six hundred!!! What on earth am I to do with them all?

RAINA [*timidly*] Nine thousand hotels?

BLUNTSCHLI. Hotels! nonsense. If you only knew! Oh, it's too ridiculous! Excuse me: I must give my fellow orders about starting. [*He leaves the room hastily, with the documents in his hand*].

LOUKA [*knowing instinctively that she can annoy* RAINA *by disparaging* BLUNTSCHLI] He has not much heart, that Swiss. He has not a word of grief for his poor father.

RAINA [*bitterly*] Grief! A man who has been doing nothing but killing people for years! What does he care? What does any soldier care? [*She goes to the door, restraining her tears with difficulty*].

LOUKA. Major Saranoff has been fighting too; and he has plenty of heart left. [RAINA, *at the door, draws herself up haughtily and goes out*]. Aha! I thought you wouldnt get much feeling out of your soldier. [*She is following* RAINA *when* NICOLA *enters with an armful of logs for the stove*].

NICOLA [*grinning amorously at her*] Ive been trying all the afternoon to get a minute alone with you, my girl. [*His countenance changes as he notices her arm*]. Why, what fashion is that of wearing your sleeve, child?

LOUKA [*proudly*] My own fashion.

NICOLA. Indeed! If the mistress catches you, she'll talk to you. [*He puts the logs down, and seats himself comfortably on the ottoman*].

LOUKA. Is that any reason why you should take it on yourself to talk to me?

NICOLA. Come! dont be so contrairy with me. Ive some good news for you. [*She sits down beside him. He takes out some paper money*. LOUKA, *with an eager gleam in her eyes, tries to snatch it; but he shifts it quickly to his left hand, out of her reach*]. See! a twenty leva bill! Sergius gave me that, out of pure swagger. A fool and his money are soon parted. Theres ten levas more. The Swiss gave me that for backing up the mistress's and Raina's lies about him. He's no fool, he isnt. You should have heard old Catherine downstairs as polite as you please to me, telling me not to mind the Major being a little impatient; for they knew what a good servant I was—after making a fool and a liar of me before them all! The twenty will go to our savings; and you shall have the ten to spend if youll only talk to me so as to remind me I'm a human being. I get tired of being a servant occasionally.

LOUKA. Yes: sell your manhood for 30 levas, and buy me for 10! [*Rising scornfully*] Keep your money. You were born to be a servant. I was not. When you set up your shop you will only be everybody's servant instead of somebody's servant. [*She goes moodily to the table and seats herself regally in* SERGIUS's *chair*].

NICOLA [*picking up his logs, and going to the stove*] Ah, wait til you see. We shall have our evenings to ourselves; and I shall be master in my own house, I promise you. [*He throws the logs down and kneels at the stove*].

LOUKA. You shall never be master in mine.

NICOLA [*turning, still on his knees, and squatting down rather forlornly on his calves, daunted by her implacable disdain*] You have a great ambition in you, Louka. Remember: if any luck comes to you, it was I that made a woman of you.

LOUKA. You!

NICOLA [*scrambling up and going at her*] Yes, me. Who was it made you give up wearing a couple of pounds of false black hair on your head and reddening your lips and cheeks like any other Bulgarian girl? I did. Who taught you to trim your nails, and keep your hands clean, and be dainty about yourself, like a fine Russian lady? Me: do you hear that? me! [*She tosses her head defiantly; and he turns away, adding more coolly*] Ive often thought that if Raina were out of the way, and you just a little less of a fool and Sergius just a little more of one, you might come to be one of my grandest customers, instead of only being my wife and costing me money.

LOUKA. I believe you would rather be my servant than my husband. You would make more out of me. Oh, I know that soul of yours.

NICOLA [*going closer to her for greater emphasis*] Never you mind my soul; but just listen to my advice. If you want to be a lady, your present behavior to me wont do at all, unless when we're alone. It's too sharp and impudent; and impudence is a sort of familiarity: it shews affection for me. And dont you try being high and mighty with me, either. Youre like all country girls: you think it's genteel to treat a servant the way I treat a stableboy. Thats only your ignorance; and dont you forget it. And dont be so ready to defy everybody. Act as if you expected to have your own way, not as if you expected to be ordered about. The way to get on as a lady is the same as the way to get on as a servant: youve got to know your place: thats the secret of it. And you may depend on me to know my place if you get promoted. Think over it, my girl. I'll stand by you: one servant should always stand by another.

LOUKA [*rising impatiently*] Oh, I must behave in my own way. You take all the courage out of me with your cold-blooded wisdom. Go and put those logs on the fire: thats the sort of thing you understand.

*Before* NICOLA *can retort,* SERGIUS *comes in. He checks himself a moment on seeing* LOUKA; *then goes to the stove.*

SERGIUS [*to* NICOLA] I am not in the way of your work, I hope.

NICOLA [*in a smooth, elderly manner*] Oh no, sir: thank you kindly. I was only speaking to this foolish girl about her habit of running up here to the library whenever she gets a chance, to look at the books. Thats the worst of her education, sir: it gives her habits above her station. [*To* LOUKA] Make that table tidy, Louka, for the Major. [*He goes out sedately*].

LOUKA, *without looking at* SERGIUS, *pretends to arrange the papers on the table. He crosses slowly to her, and studies the arrangement of her sleeve reflectively.*

SERGIUS. Let me see: is there a mark there? [*He turns up the bracelet and sees the bruise made by his grasp. She stands motionless, not looking at him: fascinated, but on her guard*] Ffff! Does it hurt?

LOUKA. Yes.

SERGIUS. Shall I cure it?

LOUKA [*instantly withdrawing herself proudly, but still not looking at him*] No. You cannot cure it now.

SERGIUS [*masterfully*] Quite sure? [*He makes a movement as if to take her in his arms*].

LOUKA. Dont trifle with me, please. An officer should not trifle with a servant.

SERGIUS [*indicating the bruise with a merciless stroke of his forefinger*] That was no trifle, Louka.

LOUKA [*flinching; then looking at him for the first time*] Are you sorry?

SERGIUS [*with measured emphasis, folding his arms*] I am never sorry.

LOUKA [*wistfully*] I wish I could believe a man could be as unlike a woman as that. I wonder are you really a brave man?

SERGIUS [*unaffectedly, relaxing his attitude*] Yes: I am a brave man. My heart jumped like a woman's at the first shot; but in the charge I found that I was brave. Yes: that at least is real about me.

LOUKA. Did you find in the charge that the men whose fathers are poor like mine were any less brave than the men who are rich like you?

SERGIUS [*with bitter levity*] Not a bit. They all slashed and cursed and yelled like heroes. Psha! the courage to rage and kill is cheap. I have an English bull terrier who has as much of that sort of courage as the whole Bulgarian nation, and the whole Russian nation at its back. But he lets my groom thrash him, all the same. Thats your soldier all over! No, Louka: your poor men can cut throats; but they are afraid of their officers; they put up with insults and blows; they stand by and see one another punished like children: aye, and help to do it when they are ordered. And the officers!!! Well [*with a short harsh laugh*] *I* am an officer. Oh, [*fervently*] give me the man who will defy to the death any power on earth or in heaven that sets itself up against his own will and conscience: he alone is the brave man.

LOUKA. How easy it is to talk! Men never seem to me to grow up: they all have schoolboy's ideas. You dont know what true courage is.

SERGIUS [*ironically*] Indeed! I am willing to be instructed. [*He sits on the ottoman, sprawling magnificently*].

LOUKA. Look at me! How much am I allowed to have my own will? I have to get your room ready for you: to sweep and dust, to fetch and carry. How could that degrade me if it did not degrade you to have it done for you? But [*with subdued passion*] if I were Empress of Russia, above everyone in the world, then!! Ah then, though according to you I could shew no courage at all, you should see, you should see.

SERGIUS. What would you do, most noble Empress?

LOUKA. I would marry the man I loved, which no other queen in Europe has the courage to do. If I loved you, though you would be as far beneath me as I am beneath you, I would dare to be the equal of my inferior. Would you dare as much if you loved me? No: if you felt the beginnings of love for me you would not let it grow. You would not dare: you would marry a rich man's daughter because you would be afraid of what other people would say of you.

SERGIUS [*bounding up*] You lie: it is not so, by all the stars! If I loved you, and I were the Czar himself, I would set you on the throne by my side. You know that I love another woman, a woman as high above you as heaven is above earth. And you are jealous of her.

LOUKA. I have no reason to be. She will never marry you now. The man I told you of has come back. She will marry the Swiss.

SERGIUS [*recoiling*] The Swiss!

LOUKA. A man worth ten of you. Then you can come to me; and I will refuse you. You are not good enough for me. [*She turns to the door*].

SERGIUS [*springing after her and catching her fiercely in his arms*] I will kill the Swiss; and afterwards I will do as I please with you.

LOUKA [*in his arms, passive and steadfast*] The Swiss will kill you, perhaps. He has beaten you in love. He may beat you in war.

SERGIUS [*tormentedly*] Do you think I believe that she—she! whose worst thoughts are higher than your best ones, is capable of trifling with another man behind my back?

LOUKA. Do you think she would believe the Swiss if he told her now that I am in your arms?

SERGIUS [*releasing her in despair*] Damnation! Oh, damnation! Mockery! mockery everywhere! everything I think is mocked by everything I do. [*He strikes himself frantically on the breast*]. Coward! liar! fool! Shall I kill myself like a man, or live and pretend to laugh at myself? [*She again turns to go*]. Louka! [*She stops near the door*]. Remember: you belong to me.

LOUKA [*turning*] What does that mean? An insult?

SERGIUS [*commandingly*] It means that you love me, and that I have had you here in my arms, and will perhaps have you there again. Whether that is an insult I neither know nor care: take it as you please. But [*vehemently*] I will not be a coward and a trifler. If I choose to love you, I dare marry you, in spite of all Bulgaria. If these hands ever touch you again, they shall touch my affianced bride.

LOUKA. We shall see whether you dare keep your word. And take care. I will not wait long.

SERGIUS [*again folding his arms and standing motionless in the middle of the room*] Yes: we shall see. And you shall wait my pleasure.

BLUNTSCHLI, *much preoccupied, with his papers still in his hand, enters, leaving the door open for* LOUKA *to go out. He goes across to the table, glancing at her as he passes.* SERGIUS, *without altering his resolute attitude, watches him steadily.* LOUKA *goes out, leaving the door open.*

BLUNTSCHLI [*absently, sitting at the table as before, and putting down his papers*] Thats a remarkable looking young woman.

SERGIUS [*gravely, without moving*] Captain Bluntschli.

BLUNTSCHLI. Eh?

SERGIUS. You have deceived me. You are my rival. I brook no rivals. At six o'clock I shall be in the drilling-ground on the Klissoura road, alone, on horseback, with my sabre. Do you understand?

BLUNTSCHLI [*staring, but sitting quite at his ease*] Oh, thank you: thats a cavalry man's proposal. I'm in the artillery; and I have the choice of weapons. If I go, I shall take a machine gun. And there shall be no mistake about the cartridges this time.

SERGIUS [*flushing, but with deadly coldness*] Take care, sir. It is not our custom in Bulgaria to allow invitations of that kind to be trifled with.

BLUNTSCHLI [*warmly*] Pooh! dont talk to me about Bulgaria. You dont know what fighting is. But have it your own way. Bring your sabre along. I'll meet you.

SERGIUS [*fiercely delighted to find his opponent a man of spirit*] Well said, Switzer. Shall I lend you my best horse?

BLUNTSCHLI. No: damn your horse! thank you all the same, my dear fellow. [RAINA *comes in, and hears the next sentence*]. I shall fight you on foot. Horseback's too dangerous; I don't want to kill you if I can help it.

RAINA [*hurrying forward anxiously*] I have heard what Captain Bluntschli said, Sergius. You are going to fight. Why? [SERGIUS *turns away in silence, and goes to the stove, where he stands watching her as she continues, to* BLUNTSCHLI] What about?

BLUNTSCHLI. I dont know: he hasnt told me. Better not interfere, dear young lady. No harm will be done: Ive often acted as sword instructor. He wont be able to touch me; and I'll not hurt him. It will save explanations. In the morning I shall be off home; and youll never see me or hear of me again. You and he will then make it up and live happily ever after.

RAINA [*turning away deeply hurt, almost with a sob in her voice*] I never said I wanted to see you again.

SERGIUS [*striding forward*] Ha! That is a confession.

RAINA [*haughtily*] What do you mean?

SERGIUS. You love that man!

RAINA [*scandalized*] Sergius!

SERGIUS. You allow him to make love to you behind my back, just as you treat me as your affianced husband behind his. Bluntschli: you knew our relations; and you deceived me. It is for that that I call you to account, not for having received favors *I* never enjoyed.

BLUNTSCHLI [*jumping up indignantly*] Stuff! Rubbish! I have received no favors. Why, the young lady doesnt even know whether I'm married or not.

RAINA [*forgetting herself*] Oh! [*Collapsing on the ottoman*] Are you?

SERGIUS. You see the young lady's concern, Captain Bluntschli. Denial is useless. You have enjoyed the privilege of being received in her own room, late at night—

BLUNTSCHLI [*interrupting him pepperily*] Yes, you blockhead! she received me with a pistol at her head. Your cavalry were at my heels. I'd have blown out her brains if she'd uttered a cry.

SERGIUS [*taken aback*] Bluntschli! Raina: is this true?

RAINA [*rising in wrathful majesty*] Oh, how dare you, how dare you?

BLUNTSCHLI. Apologize, man: apologize. [*He resumes his seat at the table*].

SERGIUS [*with the old measured emphasis, folding his arms*] I never apologize!

RAINA [*passionately*] This is the doing of that friend of yours, Captain Bluntschli. It is he who is spreading this horrible story about me. [*She walks about excitedly*].

BLUNTSCHLI. No: he's dead. Burnt alive.

RAINA [*stopping, shocked*] Burnt alive!

BLUNTSCHLI. Shot in the hip in a woodyard. Couldnt drag himself out. Your fellows' shells set the timber on fire and burnt him, with half a dozen other poor devils in the same predicament.

RAINA. How horrible!

SERGIUS. And how ridiculous! Oh, war! war! the dream of patriots and heroes! A fraud, Bluntschli. A hollow sham, like love.

RAINA [*outraged*] Like love! You say that before me!

BLUNTSCHLI. Come, Saranoff: that matter is explained.

SERGIUS. A hollow sham, I say. Would you have come back here if nothing had passed between you except at the muzzle of your pistol? Raina is mistaken about your friend who was burnt. He was not my informant.

RAINA. Who then? [*Suddenly guessing the truth*] Ah, Louka! my maid! my servant! You were with her this morning all that time after— after—Oh, what sort of god is this I have been worshipping! [*He meets her gaze with sardonic enjoyment of her disenchantment. Angered all the more, she goes closer to him, and says, in a lower, intenser tone*] Do you know that I looked out of the window as I went upstairs, to have another sight of my hero; and I saw something I did not understand then. I know now that you were making love to her.

SERGIUS [*with grim humor*] You saw that?

RAINA. Only too well. [*She turns away, and throws herself on the divan under the centre window, quite overcome*].

SERGIUS [*cynically*] Raina: our romance is shattered. Life's a farce.

BLUNTSCHLI [*to RAINA, whimsically*] You see: he's found himself out now.

SERGIUS [*going to him*] Bluntschli: I have allowed you to call me a blockhead. You may now call me a coward as well. I refuse to fight you. Do you know why?

BLUNTSCHLI. No; but it doesnt matter. I didnt ask the reason when you cried on; and I dont ask the reason now that you cry off. I'm a professional soldier: I fight when I have to, and am very glad to get out of it when I havnt to. Youre only an amateur: you think fighting's an amusement.

SERGIUS [*sitting down at the table, nose to nose with him*] You shall hear the reason all the same, my professional. The reason is that it takes two men—real men—men of heart, blood and honor—to make a genuine combat. I could no more fight with you than I could make love to an ugly woman. Youve no magnetism: youre not a man: youre a machine.

BLUNTSCHLI [*apologetically*] Quite true, quite true. I always was that sort of chap. I'm very sorry.

SERGIUS. Psha!

BLUNTSCHLI. But now that youve found that life isnt a farce, but something quite sensible and serious, what further obstacle is there to your happiness?

RAINA [*rising*] You are very solicitous about my happiness and his. Do you forget his new love—Louka? It is not you that he must fight now, but his rival, Nicola.

SERGIUS. Rival!! [*bounding half across the room*].

RAINA. Dont you know that theyre engaged?

SERGIUS. Nicola! Are fresh abysses opening? Nicola!

RAINA [*sarcastically*] A shocking sacrifice, isnt it? Such beauty! such intellect! such modesty! wasted on a middle-aged servant man. Really, Sergius, you cannot stand by and allow such a thing. It would be unworthy of your chivalry.

SERGIUS [*losing all self-control*] Viper! Viper! [*He rushes to and fro, raging*].

BLUNTSCHLI. Look here, Saranoff: youre getting the worst of this.

RAINA [*getting angrier*] Do you realize what he has done, Captain Bluntschli? He has set this girl as a spy on us; and her reward is that he makes love to her.

SERGIUS. False! Monstrous!

RAINA. Monstrous! [*Confronting him*] Do you deny that she told you about Captain Bluntschli being in my room?

SERGIUS. No; but—

RAINA [*interrupting*] Do you deny that you were making love to her when she told you?

SERGIUS. No; but I tell you—

RAINA [*cutting him short contemptuously*] It is unnecessary to tell us anything more. That is quite enough for us. [*She turns away from him and sweeps majestically back to the window*].

BLUNTSCHLI [*quietly, as* SERGIUS, *in an agony of mortification, sinks on the ottoman, clutching his averted head between his fists*] I told you you were getting the worst of it, Saranoff.

SERGIUS. Tiger cat!

RAINA [*running excitedly to* BLUNTSCHLI] You hear this man calling me names, Captain Bluntschli?

BLUNTSCHLI. What else can he do, dear lady? He must defend himself somehow. Come

[*very persuasively*]: dont quarrel. What good does it do?

RAINA, *with a gasp, sits down on the ottoman, and after a vain effort to look vexedly at* BLUNTSCHLI, *falls a victim to her sense of humor, and actually leans back babyishly against the writhing shoulder of* SERGIUS.

SERGIUS. Engaged to Nicola! Ha! ha! Ah well, Bluntschli, you are right to take this huge imposture of a world coolly.

RAINA [*quaintly to* BLUNTSCHLI, *with an intuitive guess at his state of mind*] I daresay you think us a couple of grown-up babies, dont you?

SERGIUS [*grinning savagely*] He does: he does. Swiss civilization nursetending Bulgarian barbarism, eh?

BLUNTSCHLI [*blushing*] Not at all, I assure you. I'm only very glad to get you two quieted. There! there! let's be pleasant and talk it over in a friendly way. Where is this other young lady?

RAINA. Listening at the door, probably.

SERGIUS [*shivering as if a bullet had struck him, and speaking with quiet but deep indignation*] I will prove that that, at least, is a calumny. [*He goes with dignity to the door and opens it. A yell of fury bursts from him as he looks out. He darts into the passage, and returns dragging in* LOUKA, *whom he flings violently against the table, exclaiming*] Judge her, Bluntschli. You, the cool impartial man: judge the eavesdropper.

LOUKA *stands her ground, proud and silent.*

BLUNTSCHLI [*shaking his head*] I mustnt judge her. I once listened myself outside a tent when there was a mutiny brewing. It's all a question of the degree of provocation. My life was at stake.

LOUKA. My love was at stake. I am not ashamed.

RAINA [*contemptuously*] Your love! Your curiosity, you mean.

LOUKA [*facing her and returning her contempt with interest*] My love, stronger than anything you can feel, even for your chocolate cream soldier.

SERGIUS [*with quick suspicion, to* LOUKA] What does that mean?

LOUKA [*fiercely*] It means—

SERGIUS [*interrupting her slightingly*] Oh, I remember: the ice pudding. A paltry taunt, girl!

MAJOR PETKOFF *enters, in his shirtsleeves.*

PETKOFF. Excuse my shirtsleeves, gentlemen. Raina: somebody has been wearing that coat of mine: I'll swear it. Somebody with a differently shaped back. It's all burst open at the sleeve. Your mother is mending it. I wish she'd make haste: I shall catch cold. [*He looks more attentively at them*]. Is anything the matter?

RAINA. No. [*She sits down at the stove, with a tranquil air*].

SERGIUS. Oh no. [*He sits down at the end of the table, as at first*].

BLUNTSCHLI [*who is already seated*] Nothing. Nothing.

PETKOFF [*sitting down on the ottoman in his old place*] Thats all right. [*He notices* LOUKA]. Anything the matter, Louka?

LOUKA. No, sir.

PETKOFF [*genially*] Thats all right. [*He sneezes*] Go and ask your mistress for my coat, like a good girl, will you?

NICOLA *enters with the coat.* LOUKA *makes a pretence of having business in the room by taking the little table with the hookah away to the wall near the windows.*

RAINA [*rising quickly as she sees the coat on* NICOLA*'s arm*] Here it is, papa. Give it to me, Nicola; and do you put some more wood on the fire. [*She takes the coat, and brings it to the* MAJOR, *who stands up to put it on.* NICOLA *attends to the fire*].

PETKOFF [*to* RAINA, *teasing her affectionately*] Aha! Going to be very good to poor old papa just for one day after his return from the wars, eh?

RAINA [*with solemn reproach*] Ah, how can you say that to me, father?

PETKOFF. Well, well, only a joke, little one. Come: give me a kiss. [*She kisses him*]. Now give me the coat.

RAINA. No: I am going to put it on for you. Turn your back. [*He turns his back and feels behind him with his arms for the sleeves. She dexterously takes the photograph from the pocket and throws it on the table before* BLUNTSCHLI, *who covers it with a sheet of paper under the very nose of* SERGIUS, *who looks on amazed, with his suspicions roused in the highest degree. She then helps* PETKOFF *on with his coat*]. There, dear! Now are you comfortable?

PETKOFF. Quite, little love. Thanks [*He sits down; and* RAINA *returns to her seat near the stove*]. Oh, by the bye, Ive found something funny. Whats the meaning of this? [*He puts his hand into the picked pocket*]. Eh? Hallo! [*He tries the other pocket*]. Well, I could have sworn—! [*Much puzzled, he tries the breast pocket*]. I wonder—[*trying the original pocket*]. Where can it—? [*He rises, exclaiming*] Your mother's taken it!

RAINA [*very red*] Taken what?

PETKOFF. Your photograph, with the inscription: "Raina, to her Chocolate Cream Soldier: a Souvenir." Now you know theres something more in this than meets the eye; and I'm going to find it out. [*Shouting*] Nicola!

NICOLA [*coming to him*] Sir!

PETKOFF. Did you spoil any pastry of Miss Raina's this morning?

NICOLA. You heard Miss Raina say that I did, sir.

PETKOFF. I know that, you idiot. Was it true?

NICOLA. I am sure Miss Raina is incapable of saying anything that is not true, sir.

PETKOFF. Are you? Then I'm not. [*Turning to the others*] Come: do you think I dont see it all? [*He goes to* SERGIUS, *and slaps him on the shoulder*]. Sergius: youre the chocolate cream soldier, arnt you?

SERGIUS [*starting up*] I! A chocolate cream soldier! Certainly not.

PETKOFF. Not! [*He looks at them. They are all very serious and very conscious*]. Do you mean to tell me that Raina sends things like that to other men?

SERGIUS [*enigmatically*] The world is not such an innocent place as we used to think, Petkoff.

BLUNTSCHLI [*rising*] It's all right, Major. I'm the chocolate cream soldier. [PETKOFF *and* SERGIUS *are equally astonished*]. The gracious young lady saved my life by giving me chocolate creams when I was starving: shall I ever forget their flavor! My late friend Stolz told you the story at Pirot. I was the fugitive.

PETKOFF. You! [*He gasps*]. Sergius: do you remember how those two women went on this morning when we mentioned it? [SERGIUS *smiles cynically.* PETKOFF *confronts* RAINA *severely*]. Youre a nice young woman, arnt you?

RAINA [*bitterly*] Major Saranoff has changed his mind. And when I wrote that on the photograph, I did not know that Captain Bluntschli was married.

BLUNTSCHLI [*startled into vehement protest*] I'm not married.

RAINA [*with deep reproach*] You said you were.

BLUNTSCHLI. I did not. I positively did not. I never was married in my life.

PETKOFF [*exasperated*] Raina: will you kindly inform me, if I am not asking too much, which of these gentlemen you are engaged to?

RAINA. To neither of them. This young lady [*introducing* LOUKA, *who faces them all proudly*] is the object of Major Saranoff's affections at present.

PETKOFF. Louka! Are you mad, Sergius? Why, this girl's engaged to Nicola.

NICOLA. I beg your pardon, sir. There is a mistake. Louka is not engaged to me.

PETKOFF. Not engaged to you, you scoundrel! Why, you had twenty-five levas from me on the day of your betrothal; and she had that gilt bracelet from Miss Raina.

NICOLA [*with cool unction*] We gave it out so, sir. But it was only to give Louka protection. She had a soul above her station; and I have been no more than her confidential servant. I intend, as you know, sir, to set up a shop later on in Sofia; and I look forward to her custom and recommendation should she marry into the nobility. [*He goes out with impressive discretion, leaving them all staring after him*].

PETKOFF [*breaking the silence*] Well, I am —hm!

SERGIUS. This is either the finest heroism or the most crawling baseness. Which is it, Bluntschli?

BLUNTSCHLI. Never mind whether it's heroism or baseness. Nicola's the ablest man Ive met in Bulgaria. I'll make him manager of a hotel if he can speak French and German.

LOUKA [*suddenly breaking out at* SERGIUS] I have been insulted by everyone here. You set them the example. You owe me an apology.

SERGIUS, *like a repeating clock of which the spring has been touched, immediately begins to fold his arms.*

BLUNTSCHLI [*before he can speak*] It's no use. He never apologizes.

LOUKA. Not to you, his equal and his enemy. To me, his poor servant, he will not refuse to apologize.

SERGIUS [*approvingly*] You are right. [*He*

*bends his knee in his grandest manner*] Forgive me.

LOUKA. I forgive you. [*She timidly gives him her hand, which he kisses*]. That touch makes me your affianced wife.

SERGIUS [*springing up*] Ah! I forgot that.

LOUKA [*coldly*] You can withdraw if you like.

SERGIUS. Withdraw! Never! You belong to me. [*He puts his arm about her*].

CATHERINE *comes in and finds* LOUKA *in* SERGIUS's *arms with all the rest gazing at them in bewildered astonishment.*

CATHERINE. What does this mean?

SERGIUS *releases* LOUKA.

PETKOFF. Well, my dear, it appears that Sergius is going to marry Louka instead of Raina. [*She is about to break out indignantly at him: he stops her by exclaiming testily*] Dont blame me: Ive nothing to do with it. [*He retreats to the stove*].

CATHERINE. Marry Louka! Sergius: you are bound by your word to us!

SERGIUS [*folding his arms*] Nothing binds me.

BLUNTSCHLI [*much pleased by this piece of common sense*] Saranoff: your hand. My congratulations. These heroics of yours have their practical side after all. [*To* LOUKA] Gracious young lady: the best wishes of a good Republican! [*He kisses her hand, to* RAINA's *great disgust, and returns to his seat*].

CATHERINE. Louka: you have been telling stories.

LOUKA. I have done Raina no harm.

CATHERINE [*haughtily*] Raina!

RAINA, *equally indignant, almost snorts at the liberty.*

LOUKA. I have a right to call her Raina: she calls me Louka. I told Major Saranoff she would never marry him if the Swiss gentleman came back.

BLUNTSCHLI [*rising, much surprised*] Hallo!

LOUKA [*turning to* RAINA] I thought you were fonder of him than of Sergius. You know best whether I was right.

BLUNTSCHLI. What nonsense! I assure you, my dear Major, my dear Madame, the gracious young lady simply saved my life, nothing else. She never cared two straws for me. Why, bless my heart and soul, look at the young lady and look at me. She, rich, young, beautiful, with her imagination full of fairy princes and noble natures and cavalry charges and goodness knows what! And I, a commonplace Swiss soldier who hardly knows what a decent life is after fifteen years of barracks and battles: a vagabond, a man who has spoiled all his chances in life through an incurably romantic disposition, a man—

SERGIUS [*starting as if a needle had pricked him and interrupting* BLUNTSCHLI *in incredulous amazement*] Excuse me, Bluntschli: what did you say had spoiled your chances in life?

BLUNTSCHLI [*promptly*] An incurably romantic disposition. I ran away from home twice when I was a boy. I went into the army instead of into my father's business. I climbed the balcony of this house when a man of sense would have dived into the nearest cellar. I came sneaking back here to have another look at the young lady when any other man of my age would have sent the coat back—

PETKOFF. My coat!

BLUNTSCHLI.—yes: thats the coat I mean—would have sent it back and gone quietly home. Do you suppose I am the sort of fellow a young girl falls in love with? Why, look at our ages! I'm thirty-four: I dont suppose the young lady is much over seventeen. [*This estimate produces a marked sensation, all the rest turning and staring at one another. He proceeds innocently*] All that adventure which was life or death to me, was only a schoolgirl's game to her—chocolate creams and hide and seek. Heres the proof! [*He takes the photograph from the table*]. Now, I ask you, would a woman who took the affair seriously have sent me this and written on it "Raina, to her Chocolate Cream Soldier: a Souvenir"? [*He exhibits the photograph triumphantly, as if it settled the matter beyond all possibility of refutation*].

PETKOFF. Thats what I was looking for. How the deuce did it get there? [*He comes from the stove to look at it, and sits down on the ottoman*].

BLUNTSCHLI [*to* RAINA, *complacently*] I have put everything right, I hope, gracious young lady.

RAINA [*going to the table to face him*] I quite agree with your account of yourself. You are a romantic idiot. [BLUNTSCHLI *is unspeakably taken aback*]. Next time, I hope you will know the difference between a schoolgirl of seventeen and a woman of twenty-three.

BLUNTSCHLI [*stupefied*] Twenty-three!

RAINA *snaps the photograph contemptuously from his hand; tears it up; throws the pieces in*

his face; and sweeps back to her former place.

SERGIUS [*with grim enjoyment of his rival's discomfiture*] Bluntschli: my one last belief is gone. Your sagacity is a fraud, like everything else. You have less sense than even I!

BLUNTSCHLI [*overwhelmed*] Twenty-three! twenty-three!! [*He considers*]. Hm! [*Swiftly making up his mind and coming to his host*] In that case, Major Petkoff. I beg to propose formally to become a suitor for your daughter's hand, in place of Major Saranoff retired.

RAINA. You dare!

BLUNTSCHLI. If you were twenty-three when you said those things to me this afternoon, I shall take them seriously.

CATHERINE [*loftily polite*] I doubt, sir, whether you quite realize either my daughter's position or that of Major Sergius Saranoff, whose place you propose to take. The Petkoffs and the Saranoffs are known as the richest and most important families in the country. Our position is almost historical: we can go back for twenty years.

PETKOFF. Oh, never mind that, Catherine. [*To* BLUNTSCHLI] We should be most happy, Bluntschli, if it were only a question of your position; but hang it, you know, Raina is accustomed to a very comfortable establishment. Sergius keeps twenty horses.

BLUNTSCHLI. But who wants twenty horses? We're not going to keep a circus.

CATHERINE [*severely*] My daughter, sir, is accustomed to a first-rate stable.

RAINA. Hush, mother: youre making me ridiculous.

BLUNTSCHLI. Oh well, if it comes to a question of an establishment, here goes! [*He darts impetuously to the table; seizes the papers in the blue envelope; and turns to* SERGIUS]. How many horses did you say?

SERGIUS. Twenty, noble Switzer.

BLUNTSCHLI. I have two hundred horses. [*They are amazed*]. How many carriages?

SERGIUS. Three.

BLUNTSCHLI. I have seventy. Twenty-four of them will hold twelve inside, besides two on the box, without counting the driver and conductor. How many tablecloths have you?

SERGIUS. How the deuce do I know?

BLUNTSCHLI. Have you four thousand?

SERGIUS. No.

BLUNTSCHLI. I have. I have nine thousand six hundred pairs of sheets and blankets, with two thousand four hundred eider-down quilts. I have ten thousand knives and forks, and the same quantity of dessert spoons. I have three hundred servants. I have six palatial establishments, besides two livery stables, a tea garden, and a private house. I have four medals for distinguished services; I have the rank of an officer and the standing of a gentleman; and I have three native languages. Shew me any man in Bulgaria that can offer as much!

PETKOFF [*with childish awe*] Are you Emperor of Switzerland?

BLUNTSCHLI. My rank is the highest known in Switzerland: I am a free citizen.

CATHERINE. Then, Captain Bluntschli, since you are my daughter's choice—

RAINA [*mutinously*] He's not.

CATHERINE [*ignoring her*]—I shall not stand in the way of her happiness. [PETKOFF *is about to speak*] That is Major Petkoff's feeling also.

PETKOFF. Oh, I shall be only too glad. Two hundred horses! Whew!

SERGIUS. What says the lady?

RAINA [*pretending to sulk*] The lady says that he can keep his tablecloths and his omnibuses. I am not here to be sold to the highest bidder. [*She turns her back on him*].

BLUNTSCHLI. I wont take that answer. I appealed to you as a fugitive, a beggar, and a starving man. You accepted me. You gave me your hand to kiss, your bed to sleep in, and your roof to shelter me.

RAINA. I did not give them to the Emperor of Switzerland.

BLUNTSCHLI. Thats just what I say. [*He catches her by the shoulders and turns her face-to-face with him*]. Now tell us whom you did give them to.

RAINA [*succumbing with a shy smile*] To my chocolate cream soldier.

BLUNTSCHLI [*with a boyish laugh of delight*] Thatll do. Thank you. [*He looks at his watch and suddenly becomes businesslike*]. Time's up, Major. Youve managed those regiments so well that youre sure to be asked to get rid of some of the infantry of the Timok division. Send them home by way of Lom Palanka. Saranoff: dont get married until I come back: I shall be here punctually at five in the evening on Tuesday fortnight. Gracious ladies [*his heels click*] good evening. [*He makes them a military bow, and goes*].

SERGIUS. What a man! Is he a man?

# C H A P T E R   F I V E.

# INDIVIDUAL AND SOCIETY

$S$OME CHARACTERS in literature interest us primarily because they work out their destinies in the midst of uncomprehending or hostile environments. Such works dramatize a conflict, not between individuals, but between an individual and the society that contains him. He may be a misfit because, like Eliot's Prufrock, he cannot live up to the society— but sometimes, it appears, the society cannot live up to him: for example, John Brown, as Thoreau describes him, and Jean Valjean in *Les Misérables*. In other works the responsibility is distributed, the forces more ambiguous, as in "The Secret Life of Walter Mitty," "A Rose For Emily," and *The Doctor and The Devils*.

We are seldom of one mind in contemplating collisions of this sort. We can see in society, the immovable body, something that was there before the individual and will be there after he is gone, something that is essential for the realization of the highest human life. At the same time, though, we can see in the drives and talents of the individual some integrity, initiative, or rebelliousness that stands for the irresistible forces of change and progress. In the paradox of this human situation writers have found limitless varieties of material. We see in what different terms human beings can respond to the pressures of their groups— resisting, overcoming, being engulfed, running away: compare, for example, Wordsworth's leech-gatherer, the Scholar-Gipsy, Fra Lippo Lippi, the characters in Robinson's poems, Conradin in "Sredni Vashtar," and Whittaker Chambers.

Some of these works, it is true, appear to be concerned with a struggle between persons. Even in these, however, it will be seen that the antagonist embodies the standards of the group to which he belongs. And the fate of the protagonist, whether he ends in victory or

223

defeat, is made understandable by the pressures to which that group subjects him. Such conflicts often mirror large and pervasive points of view, sometimes profound and half-realized, that themselves reach into all departments of human life, and demand reflective thought if the full power of the literary work is to be felt. In the collision of Socrates and his Athenian contemporaries or that between Captain John Brown and his half-slave, half-free society—and, in different ways, in the situations of Whittaker Chambers, Emily Grierson, and the Hunger-Artist—there is implicit a collision of ethical and religious convictions, of two ways of life, of two philosophies.

*Victor Hugo*

# JEAN VALJEAN AND THE BISHOP

As the cathedral clock was striking two, Jean Valjean woke up. The bed was too good; it was this that had waked him. He had not slept in a bed for nearly twenty years, and the experience, even though he had not undressed, was such a novel one that it disturbed his sleep.

He had been asleep for over four hours. He was no longer tired. He was not in the habit of devoting many hours to rest.

Opening his eyes, he stared for a moment into the darkness around him. Then he shut them again, so as to go back to sleep.

When a man has been troubled during the day by many and various sensations, when things weigh upon his mind, he may go to sleep but be unable to get back to sleep. Sleep comes more readily than it returns. So it was with Jean Valjean: not being able to fall asleep again, he began to think.

He was in one of those periods when the mind is in a turmoil. There was a kind of dark ebbing and flowing in his brain. Old memories and new ones bobbed up and mingled in confusion, losing their shapes, getting big and suddenly vanishing: as though in roiling, murky water. Of the many thoughts that occurred to him, one continually presented itself and drove out all the rest. What it was shall straightway be told: his attention had been caught by the six sets of silver knives, forks, and spoons, and

JEAN VALJEAN AND THE BISHOP: From *Les Misérables*, Part One, Book II. Translated by Robert Daniel.

the big ladle with which Mme. Magloire had set the table.

The thought of this silver obsessed him. There it was . . . a few steps away. As he had passed through the next room to get to the one where he lay, the old servant had been putting the silver up in a little cupboard at the head of the bed. He had noticed that cupboard . . . on the right as you came from the dining-room. The silver was very heavy . . . antique. With the big ladle it would bring two hundred francs at least—twice what he had earned in nineteen years. . . . True, he would have had more if *"the government* had not *robbed* him."

For a long hour his mind vacillated in an indecision of which struggle formed some part. Three o'clock sounded. He opened his eyes again, sat up abruptly, put out his arm, and felt the knapsack that he had thrown into a corner of the alcove. Then, lowering his legs and setting his feet on the floor, he found himself seated on the bed, almost without knowing how.

Lost in thought, he remained for a while in this position, which would have seemed somewhat sinister to anyone who had seen him thus in the darkness, the only one awake in the sleeping house. All at once he stooped over, took off his shoes, and placed them softly on the mat by the bed; then he resumed his posture of reverie and was again motionless.

In that frightful meditation, the ideas that have been mentioned troubled his mind without relief—came in, went out, returned, made a kind of weight upon him; and in addition, without his knowing why, with the mechanical stubbornness of reverie, he thought of a convict named Brevet whom he had known in the galley, and whose pants had been held up by a single suspender of knitted cotton. The checked pattern of that suspender kept coming back to his mind.

He would perhaps have remained in this state until daybreak if the clock had not struck one note, the quarter- or the half-hour. It was as if that note had said to him: Let's go!

Getting up, he hesitated a moment longer, listening. The house was quiet. Then he went on tiptoe straight towards the outline of the window, which he could see. The night was not very dark; there was a full moon, before which the wind was driving large clouds. This made shadow alternate with brightness outside— eclipses, then illuminations—and inside, a kind of twilight. Varying with the clouds, this twilight, which was enough to find one's way by, resembled the pale gleams admitted by the air-hole of a cellar beyond which passersby are coming and going. Having reached the window, Jean Valjean examined it. It was unbarred, opened on the garden, and was fastened, after the custom of the region, only by a small peg. He opened it, but as a sharp, cold draft abruptly blew into the room, he shut it again directly. He looked at the garden with that attentive stare which scrutinizes rather than looks. The garden was enclosed by a white wall, fairly low and easy to climb. Farther on, at the end, he could make out the tops of trees set at equal distances, showing that this wall separated the garden from an avenue or small street.

Having taken all this in, he moved as though his mind were made up: went to his alcove, picked up his knapsack, reached in, took out something that he laid on the bed, put his shoes in one of his pockets, closed the knapsack, shouldered it, pulled the vizor of his cap over his eyes, groped for his staff, and went and placed it in the corner of the window. Then he returned to the bed and resolutely grasped the thing that he had left there. This appeared to be a short iron bar, sharpened at one end like a spear.

In the darkness it would have been hard to tell for what purpose this piece of iron had been made. Was it a lever, perhaps? or a club? By daylight it could have been identified as nothing other than a miner's crowbar. In those days convicts were sometimes used to quarry stone from the high hills that surround Toulon, and it was not unusual for them to have access to miners' tools. Miners' crowbars are solid iron, pointed at the end so that they can be driven into the rock.

He took the crowbar in his right hand and, holding his breath, crept to the door of the next room, which, as we know, was the Bishop's. When he reached the door, he found it ajar. The Bishop had not shut it.

Jean Valjean listened. Silence.

He pushed the door.

He pushed it gently at the end of his finger, with the stealthy, nervous smoothness of a cat who wants to get in. The door yielded to the pressure and moved, silently and imperceptibly, so that the opening grew a little larger. He waited a moment, then gave the door a second, bolder push. It yielded again without a sound. The opening was now big enough for him to get through. But near the door there was a small table that formed an awkward angle with it and barred the entrance.

Jean Valjean saw the difficulty. It was imperative that the opening should be enlarged even more. Having made up his mind, he pushed the door a third time, more strongly than before. This time a hinge which needed oiling suddenly sent out a hoarse, prolonged screech into the darkness.

Jean Valjean started. To his ears the noise of the hinge sounded as clear and frightful as the Last Trumpet.

In the fantastic exaggerations of the first moment, he almost imagined that the hinge had suddenly taken on a terrible life, and that it was baying like a dog to warn everyone and wake up those who were asleep.

Shuddering, he stopped aghast and sank back on his heels. He heard the pulses in his temples beating like two blacksmiths' hammers, and it seemed to him that his breath was issuing from his chest as noisily as wind from a cave. Surely it was impossible that the horrible outcry of that exasperated hinge had not shaken the whole house like a tremor of an earthquake; the door that he had pushed had taken fright and called out; the old man would get up, the two old women would shriek, help would come; in fifteen minutes the town would be in an uproar and the police astir. For a moment he thought he was done for.

He remained where he was, motionless as the pillar of salt, not daring to move a muscle. Some minutes went by. The door had opened wide. He risked a look into the room. Nothing in it had moved. He listened. In the house nothing was stirring. The noise of the rusty hinge had not aroused anyone.

This first danger had passed, but inside him there was still a fearful tumult. Yet he did not draw back. Even when he had believed himself lost he had not drawn back. He thought only of finishing quickly. He stepped forward and entered the room.

The room was perfectly quiet. Here and there could be discerned confused, vague shapes that by daylight were papers scattered on a table, open folio volumes, books piled on a stool, an armchair covered with clothes, a kneeling-desk—and at this hour were only shadowy corners and whitish spots. Jean Valjean advanced, taking care to avoid the furniture. Across the room he heard the regular, tranquil breathing of the sleeping Bishop.

Suddenly he stopped. He was near the bed. He had reached it sooner than he had expected to.

Sometimes, with a sort of dark, intelligent appropriateness Nature blends her effects and shows with our actions, as though wishing to make us ponder. For nearly half an hour a great cloud had been covering the sky. Just as Jean Valjean stopped before the bed, this cloud parted as though on purpose, and all at once a moonbeam, passing through the deep window, illuminated the pale countenance of the Bishop. He was sleeping peacefully. On account of the cold nights of the Lower Alps, he lay in bed almost fully dressed, in a brown woolen robe that covered his arms to the wrists. His head was turned on the pillow in the careless attitude of sleep; adorned with the pastoral ring, the hand from which had proceeded so many good works and saintly actions hung down outside the covers. His whole face was lighted by an indistinct expression of contentment, hope, and blessedness. More than a smile, it was almost a radiance. On his forehead there was the indescribable reflection of an unseen light. In sleep the souls of the just look upon a mysterious heaven.

A ray from this heaven rested upon the Bishop.

It was a luminous transparency also, for this heaven was within him. It was his conscience.

At the moment when the moonbeam super-imposed itself (as it were) on this inner brightness, the sleeping Bishop appeared to be invested with a halo. But the effect was mild and veiled by an ineffable twilight. The moon in the sky, Nature drowsing, the garden where nothing stirred, the quiet house, the time, the moment, the silence—these added an inexpressible solemnity to the saintly repose of this man, and surrounded with a sort of august, serene nimbus this white hair, these closed eyes, this countenance where all was hope and all was confidence, this old man's head and this childlike slumber.

There was almost divinity in this man, who was thus unknowingly majestic.

As for Jean Valjean, he was in shadow, his iron crowbar in his hand, upright, unmoving, bewildered by this luminous old man. He had never seen anything like it. That serenity appalled him. The moral world affords no grander spectacle than this: a conscience troubled and uneasy, on the brink of a wicked deed, gazing upon the sleep of a righteous man.

There was something sublime about this sleep, in such solitude and with a neighbor like himself, which he felt faintly yet commandingly. No one, not even he himself, could have said what was taking place within him. To try to get an idea of it, one must visualize the utmost in violence face to face with the utmost in mildness. On his face nothing could have been made out with certainty. There was a sort of wild astonishment. He was gazing on the scene. That was all. But what was he thinking about? No one could have guessed. Plainly he was affected and upset. But what was the nature of this emotion?

His eyes did not leave the old man. The only thing that stood forth clearly from his posture and his features was an extraordinary lack of decision. One would have said that he hesitated between two chasms, the one in which one is lost and the one in which one is saved. He seemed ready either to crush that skull or to kiss that hand.

After some moments his left hand rose slowly to his forehead, and he took off his cap; then his arm sank back with the same slowness, and Jean Valjean returned to his watching, his cap in his left hand, his club in his right, his hair bristling on his savage head.

Under this frightful gaze the Bishop went on sleeping in profound peace.

Reflected moonlight made the crucifix above

the mantelpiece indistinctly visible. It seemed to be opening its arms to both of them, with a blessing for one and a pardon for the other.

Suddenly Jean Valjean put on his cap again and quickly walked alongside the bed, without looking at the Bishop, straight to the cupboard which he could just see at the head of the bed. He raised the crowbar as though to force the lock: the key was in it. He opened it; the first thing he saw was the basket of silverware; he took it, crossed the room in long steps without caution and without bothering about the noise, reached the door, re-entered the chapel, opened the window, grasped his stick, threw his leg over the ground-floor windowsill, put the silver in his bag, threw the basket away, ran across the garden, leapt over the wall like a tiger, and fled.

The next morning at sunrise Monseigneur Bienvenu was walking in his garden. Mme. Magloire ran to him in great agitation.

"Monseigneur, Monseigneur," she cried, "does Your Lordship know where the silver-basket is?"

"Yes," said the Bishop.

"The Lord Jesus be thanked!" she responded. "I didn't know what had become of it."

The Bishop had just picked up the basket in a flower-bed. He gave it to Mme. Magloire. "Here it is."

"What?" said she. "Nothing in it? What about the silver?"

"Ah," returned the Bishop, "so it is the silver you are concerned about. I do not know where that is."

"Mercy on us—it is stolen! The man who was here yesterday evening has taken it!"

In a twinkling, with the liveliness of a spry old woman, Mme. Magloire ran to the chapel, entered the alcove, and returned to the Bishop. The Bishop had stooped down and with a sigh was contemplating a cochlearia plant that the basket had broken when it fell across the flower-bed. He straightened up again at Mme. Magloire's outcry.

"Monseigneur, the man is gone! The silver is stolen!"

While she was uttering this exclamation, her eyes lit upon a corner of the garden where it was evident that the wall had been scaled. The coping of the wall was damaged.

"Look! There's where he got away. He jumped into Cochefilet Lane! Oh, the villain! He has stolen our silver!"

For a moment the Bishop was silent; then he lifted his grave eyes and gently said to Mme. Magloire: "First of all, did this silver belong to us?"

Mme. Magloire was dumbfounded. After another silence the Bishop continued: "For a long time, Mme. Magloire, I have been wrongfully keeping possession of this silver. It belonged to the poor. What was that man? Plainly one of the poor."

"Dear Lord!" returned Mme. Magloire. "It's not on account of me or Mademoiselle; surely it is all the same to us. It's for the sake of Monseigneur. How is Monseigneur going to eat his dinner now?"

The Bishop looked at her in surprise. "Why, are there no tin knives and forks?"

Mme. Magloire shrugged. "Tin has a smell."

"Iron ones, then."

Mme. Magloire made an eloquent gesture. "Iron has a taste."

"Well, then," said the Bishop, "wooden knives and forks."

Some moments later he was having breakfast at the very table at which Jean Valjean had been seated the previous evening. As he breakfasted, Monseigneur Bienvenu humorously remarked to his sister, who was silent, and to Mme. Magloire, who was indistinctly muttering, that for dipping a piece of bread into a cup of milk neither a spoon nor a fork, even of wood, was necessary.

While Mme. Magloire was moving about, she said to herself: "Imagine letting in a man of that sort! And putting him in the room next to you! How lucky that stealing was all he did! Good heavens, it makes one shudder to think about it!"

As the brother and sister were getting up from the table, there was a knock at the door.

"Come in," said the Bishop.

The door opened. A strange, violent group of men were seen in the entrance. Three of them were holding the fourth by the collar. The three were policemen, the other was Jean Valjean.

A police-sergeant, who seemed to be in command, was near the door. He entered and, giving a military salute, came up to the Bishop.

"Monseigneur—," said he.

At this word Jean Valjean, who was dejected and looked crestfallen, raised his head as though thunderstruck.

"Monseigneur!" he muttered. "Then he is not the parish priest. . . ."

"Be silent," said one of the policemen. "He is the Bishop."

Monseigneur Bienvenu, however, had come forward as quickly as his age would allow.

"Oh, there you are!" he exclaimed, looking at Jean Valjean. "I am pleased to see you. Well, but I also gave you the candlesticks, which are silver like the rest and for which you could have easily gotten two hundred francs. Why did you not take them along with your knives and forks?"

Jean Valjean opened his eyes and looked at the venerable Bishop with an expression that no human tongue could describe.

"Monseigneur," said the police-sergeant, "this man was telling the truth, then? We met him; he was going like a man who is running away. We stopped him to investigate. He had this silver."

"And he told you," interrupted the Bishop smiling, "that it had been given to him by a nice old priest at whose house he spent the night? I understand the whole thing. And you brought him back here? It is all a mistake."

"In that case," returned the sergeant, "we can let him go?"

"Of course," replied the Bishop.

The policemen released Jean Valjean, who shrank away from them.

"Have they really let me go?" he said almost inarticulately, as though he were talking in his sleep.

"Yes, you are free," said a policeman; "don't you hear?"

"Friend," said the Bishop, "before you leave here are your candlesticks. Take them."

He went to the mantelpiece, picked up the two silver candlesticks, and brought them to Jean Valjean. The two women were watching his actions without a word, a gesture, or a look that could disturb the Bishop.

Jean Valjean was shaking in every limb. He took the two candlesticks mechanically, as though bewildered.

"Now," said the Bishop, "go in peace. By the way, my friend, when you come back there is no need to use the garden. You can always come and go by the street door. It is on the latch, day and night." Then, turning to the policemen: "Gentlemen, you may go." The policemen withdrew.

Jean Valjean was like a man who is about to faint.

The Bishop approached and said to him in a low voice: "Don't forget, don't ever forget that you have promised me to use this money to become an honest man."

Jean Valjean, who had no recollection of having promised anything, was stupefied. The Bishop had laid emphasis on those words as he spoke them. He continued gravely: "Jean Valjean, my brother, you belong no more to evil, but to good. It is your soul that I am buying for you; I redeem it from black thoughts and the spirit of perdition, and I give it to God."

## Whittaker Chambers
# LES MISÉRABLES

About two hundred of my grandfather Whittaker's books lay in barrels in our attic, just beyond the incubator where we hatched our chicks. One day, when I was eight or nine, my reading curiosity took me up there. I lifted from the top of one barrel a big book whose pages were dog-eared, evidently from much turning by my grandfather. It was an old-fashioned book. The text was set in parallel columns, two columns to a page. There were more than a thousand pages. The type was small. I took the book to the little diamond-shaped attic window to read the small type in the light. I opened to the first page and read the brief foreword:

"So long as there shall exist, by reason of law and custom, a social damnation, which, in the face of civilization, creates hells on earth, and complicates a destiny which is divine with human fatality—

"So long as the three problems of the age— the degradation of man by poverty, the ruin of woman by hunger, and the stunting of childhood by physical and spiritual night—are not solved;—

"So long as, in certain areas, social asphyxia shall be possible—

"So long as ignorance and misery remain on earth, books like this cannot be useless."

I did not understand half the words. How should I know what "human fatality" meant, or "social asphyxia"? But when I read those lines, there moved through my mind a solemn music that is the overtone of justice and compassion. A spirit moved upon the page and through my ignorance I sensed that spirit.

The book, of course, was Victor Hugo's *Les Misérables—The Wretched of the Earth*. In its pages can be found the play of forces that carried me into the Communist Party, and in the same pages can be found the play of forces that carried me out of the Communist Party. The roots of both influences are in the same book, which I read devotedly for almost a decade before I ever opened a Bible, and which was, in many respects, the Bible of my boyhood. I think I can hear a derisive question: "How can anyone take seriously a man who says flatly that his life has been influenced by Victor Hugo's *Les Misérables?*" I understand. I can only answer that, behind its colossal failings, its melodrama, its windy philosophizing, its clots of useless knowledge, its overblown rhetoric and repellent posturings, which offend me, like everybody else, on almost every page, *Les Misérables* is a great act of the human spirit. And it is a fact that books which fall short of greatness sometimes have a power to move us greatly, especially in childhood when we are least critical and most forgiving, for their very failures confess their humanity. As a boy, I did not know that *Les Misérables* is a *Summa* of the revolt of the mind and soul of modern man against the materialism that was closing over them with the close of the Middle Ages and the rise of industrial civilization—or, as Karl Marx would later teach me to call it: capitalism.

I took the book downstairs and read for the first time the first line of its story: "In 1815, Charles Francois Bienvenu Myriel was Bishop of Digne." I do not know how many times I have since read that simplest of leads, which has for me, like many greater first lines, the quality of throwing open a door upon man's fate.

I read and reread *Les Misérables* many times in its entirety. It taught me two seemingly irreconcilable things—Christianity and revolution. It taught me first of all that the basic virtue of life is humility, that before humility, ambition, arrogance, pride and power are seen for what they are, the stigmata of littleness, the betrayal by the mind of the soul, a betrayal which continually fails against a humility that is authentic and consistent. It taught me justice and compassion, not a justice of the law, or, as we say, human justice, but a justice that transcends human justice whenever humanity transcends itself to reach that summit where justice and compassion are one. It taught me that, in a world of force, the least act of humility and compassion requires the utmost exertion of all the powers of mind and soul, that nothing is so difficult, that there can be no true humility and no true compassion where there is no courage. That was the gist of its Christian teaching. It taught me revolution, not as others were to teach me—as a political or historical fact—but as a reflex of human suffering and desperation, a perpetual insurgence of that instinct for justice and truth that lay within the human soul, from which a new vision of truth and justice was continually issuing to meet the new needs of the soul in new ages of the world.

I scarcely knew that *Les Misérables* was teaching me Christianity, and never thought of it that way, for it showed it to me, not as a doctrine of the mind, but in action in the world, in prisons, in slums, among the poor, the sick, the dying, thieves, murderers, harlots and outcast, lonely children, in the sewers of Paris and on the barricades of revolution. Its operation did not correspond to anything I knew as Christian in the world about me. But it corresponded exactly to a need I felt within myself.

*Les Misérables* gave me my first full-length picture of the modern world—a vast, complex, scarcely human structure, built over a social abyss of which the sewers of Paris was the symbol, and resting with crushing weight upon the wretched of the earth. Dickens' novels showed me much the same thing, in a series of glimpses rather than in one appalling view of the human pit. But Dickens' novels, when they did not merely bore me, left me completely unmoved. His tear-jerking scenes jerked no tears from me, though I sometimes resented their efforts to. I knew that the unfortunate hero would always come into a legacy, or a kindly eccentric would intervene to snatch the good outcast or the lost child from the engulfing evil which was, after all, rather quaint. And though I did not know that there was such a thing as a problem of evil, I recognized that Dickens' way was too easy a way out, and no more an answer to the problem that he had raised than life insurance is an answer to the problem of death. Moreover, Dickens was entirely secular. Again, while I did not know the difference between secular and spiritual, I felt it. I brushed Dickens aside and plunged into Hugo.

It was, above all, the character of the Bishop of Digne and the stories about him that I cherished in *Les Misérables*. As a boy I read them somewhat as other people read the legends of the saints. Perhaps it is necessary to have read them as a child to be able to feel the full force of those stories, which are in many ways childish, and appeal instantly to the child mind, just as today they appeal to what is most childlike in me as a man.

That first day, when I sat in our living room and read how the Bishop came to Digne, I knew that I had found a book that had been written for me. I read how the Bishop moved into his palace with its vast salons and noticed next door a tiny hospital with its sick crowded into a few small rooms. The Bishop called in the director of the hospital and questioned him: How many rooms are there in the hospital; how many sick; how many beds in each room? "Look," he said at last, "there is evidently some mistake here. You have my house and I have yours. Give me back my house and move into yours." The next day the Bishop was in the hospital and the patients were in the palace. "He is showing off," said the solid citizens.

The Bishop's views on human fallibility fixed mine and made it impossible for me ever to be a puritan. "To be a saint," he sometimes preached to the "ferociously virtuous," "is the exception; to be upright is the rule. Err, falter, sin, but be upright. To commit the least possible sin is the law for man. . . . Sin is a gravitation."

He first raised in my mind the question of relative human guilt. Everybody was praising the cleverness of a public prosecutor. A man and woman had been arrested for some mischief. There was no evidence against the man. By a trick, the prosecutor convinced the woman falsely that the man had been unfaithful to her.

She testified against him. "Where are the man and woman to be tried?" asked the Bishop. "At the assizes." "And where," asked the Bishop, "is the prosecutor to be tried?"

The Bishop lodged in my mind a permanent suspicion of worldly success and pride of place that never changed in all the changes of my life. He was not one of the "rich mitres." In Paris he did not "catch on." He was not considered "to have any future." For, said Hugo, "We live in a sad society. Succeed—that is the advice that falls, drop by drop, from the overhanging corruption."

The story about the Bishop that I liked best also involved the question of worldly appearances. One day the Bishop had to visit a parish in the steep mountains, where no horse could go. Few bishops would have gone there, either. The Bishop of Digne went, riding on a surefooted donkey. The solid citizens of the town turned out to greet him. When they saw the Bishop climbing down from his donkey, some of them could not hide their smiles. "My bourgeois friends," said the Bishop pleasantly, "I know why you are smiling. You think that it is pretty presumptuous of a poor priest to use the same conveyance that was used by Jesus Christ." Thus I first learned the meaning of the word bourgeois, so that, unlike most Americans, I was quite familiar with it when I came across it later in the writings of Marx and Lenin.

Finally, the Bishop's view of the world left a permanent, indelible impress on me: "He inclined toward the distressed and the repentant. The universe appeared to him like a vast disease; he perceived fever everywhere; he auscultated suffering everywhere. And without trying to solve the enigma, he sought to staunch the wound. The formidable spectacle of created things developed a tenderness in him. . . ."

My life failed at the moment when I began to try to "solve the enigma" and "staunch the wound," for Marx and Lenin did little more for me than give me a modern diagnosis and a clinical ways and means to deal with that "vast disease" which the Bishop of Digne felt and that "social damnation" which his author first made me conscious of. Even as a Communist, I never quite escaped the Bishop. I put him out of my mind, but I could not put him out of my life.

One night, in the Union Station, in Washington, I stood in line with J. Peters, the head of the underground section of the American Communist Party, to buy a ticket for New York. I noticed a man watching me closely. As I left the line, he came up to me and explained that he had some kind of special ticket to New York. It was good only for the week-end. It was Sunday night. He wanted to stay over in Washington. Would I exchange my regular ticket for his special ticket? His ticket seemed to be in order. I gave him mine. Peters, who had walked away so as not to be observed, asked me what had happened. I told him. "Bob," he said, "you're a fool." He must have been pondering on the matter, for as we walked out to the train, he suddenly put his hand on my arm and said gently: "The party needs more fools." I would have been surprised if someone had then suggested to me that the Bishop of Digne had handed my ticket to the stranger. J. Peters would have been horrified to think that it was still the invisible Bishop who made him touch my arm and say: "The party needs more fools."

No doubt, the Bishop was invisibly present still when I broke from the Communist Party, though by then I had strayed so far from him that I could no longer hear him saying: "Jean Valjean, my brother, you belong no longer to evil, but to good. It is your soul that I am buying for you. I withdraw it from dark thoughts and the spirit of perdition, and I give it to God."

## Plato
# THE DEATH OF SOCRATES

*The first selection is from Socrates' speech to the Athenian Court when he was brought before it on the charge of impiety and corrupting the youth of Athens by his teaching. The second selection is from Plato's account of Socrates' last conversation with his friends, in prison, after he has been condemned to drink the hemlock.*

THE DEATH OF SOCRATES: From the *Apology* and the *Phaedo*, fourth edition, Clarendon Press. Translated by Benjamin Jowett. Used by permission of the Clarendon Press.

I

How you, O Athenians, have been affected by my accusers, I cannot tell; but I know that they almost made me forget who I was—so persuasively did they speak; and yet they have hardly uttered a word of truth. But of the many falsehoods told by them, there was one which quite amazed me;—I mean when they said that you should be upon your guard and not allow yourselves to be deceived by the force of my eloquence. To say this, when they were certain to be detected as soon as I opened my lips and proved myself to be anything but a great speaker, did indeed appear to me most shameless—unless by the force of eloquence they mean the force of truth; for if such is their meaning, I admit that I am eloquent. But in how different a way from theirs! Well, as I was saying, they have scarcely spoken the truth at all; but from me you shall hear the whole truth: not, however, delivered after their manner in a set oration duly ornamented with words and phrases. No, by heaven! but I shall use the words and arguments which occur to me at the moment; for I am confident in the justice of my cause: at my time of life I ought not to be appearing before you, O men of Athens, in the character of a juvenile orator—let no one expect it of me. And I must beg of you to grant me a favour:—If I defend myself in my accustomed manner, and you hear me using the words which I have been in the habit of using in the agora, at the tables of the money-changers, or anywhere else, I would ask you not to be surprised, and not to interrupt me on this account. For I am more than seventy years of age, and appearing now for the first time in a court of law, I am quite a stranger to the language of the place; and therefore I would have you regard me as if I were really a stranger, whom you would excuse if he spoke in his native tongue, and after the fashion of his country:—Am I making an unfair request of you? Never mind the manner, which may or may not be good; but think only of the truth of my words, and give heed to that: let the speaker speak truly and the judge decide justly. . . .

I will begin at the beginning, and ask what is the accusation which has given rise to the slander of me, and in fact has encouraged Meletus to prefer this charge against me. Well, what do the slanderers say? They shall be my prosecutors, and I will sum up their words in an affidavit: "Socrates is an evildoer, and a curious person, who searches into things under the earth and in heaven, and he makes the worse appear the better cause; and he teaches the aforesaid doctrines to others." Such is the nature of the accusation: it is just what you have yourselves seen in the comedy of Aristophanes,[1] who has introduced a man whom he calls Socrates, going about and saying that he walks in air, and talking a deal of nonsense concerning matters of which I do not pretend to know either much or little—not that I mean to speak disparagingly of any one who is a student of natural philosophy. I should be very sorry if Meletus could bring so grave a charge against me. But the simple truth is, O Athenians, that I have nothing to do with physical speculations. Very many of those here present are witnesses to the truth of this, and to them I appeal. Speak then, you who have heard me, and tell your neighbours whether any of you have ever known me hold forth in few words or in many upon such matters. . . . You hear their answer. And from what they say of this part of the charge you will be able to judge of the truth of the rest.

As little foundation is there for the report that I am a teacher, and take money; this accusation has no more truth in it than the other. Although, if a man were really able to instruct mankind, to receive money for giving instruction would, in my opinion, be an honour to him. There is Gorgias of Leontium, and Prodicus of Ceos, and Hippias of Elis, who go the round of the cities, and are able to persuade the young men to leave their own citizens by whom they might be taught for nothing, and come to them whom they not only pay, but are thankful if they may be allowed to pay them. There is at this time a Parian philosopher residing in Athens, of whom I have heard; and I came to hear of him in this way:—I came across a man who has spent a world of money on the Sophists, Callias, the son of Hipponicus, and knowing that he had sons, I asked him: "Callias," I said, "if your two sons were foals or calves, there would be no difficulty in finding some one to put over them; we should hire a trainer of

horses, or a farmer, probably, who would improve and perfect them in their own proper virtue and excellence; but as they are human beings, whom are you thinking of placing over them? Is there any one who understands human and political virtue? You must have thought about the matter, for you have sons; is there any one?" "There is," he said. "Who is he?" said I; "and of what country? and what does he charge?" "Evenus the Parian," he replied; "he is the man, and his charge is five minae." Happy is Evenus, I said to myself, if he really has this wisdom, and teaches at such a moderate charge. Had I the same, I should have been very proud and conceited; but the truth is that I have no knowledge of the kind.

I dare say, Athenians, that some one among you will reply, "Yes, Socrates, but what is the origin of these accusations which are brought against you; there must have been something strange which you have been doing? All these rumours and this talk about you would never have arisen if you had been like other men: tell us, then, what is the cause of them, for we should be sorry to judge hastily of you." Now, I regard this as a fair challenge, and I will endeavour to explain to you the reason why I am called wise and have such an evil fame. Please to attend then. And although some of you may think that I am joking, I declare that I will tell you the entire truth. Men of Athens, this reputation of mine has come of a certain sort of wisdom which I possess. If you ask me what kind of wisdom, I reply, wisdom such as may perhaps be attained by man, for to that extent I am inclined to believe that I am wise; whereas the persons of whom I was speaking have a super-human wisdom, which I may fail to describe, because I have it not myself; and he who says that I have, speaks falsely, and is taking away my character. And here, O men of Athens, I must beg you not to interrupt me, even if I seem to say something extravagant. For the word which I will speak is not mine. I will refer you to a witness who is worthy of credit; that witness shall be the god of Delphi—he will tell you about my wisdom, if I have any, and of what sort it is. You must have known Chaerephon; he was early a friend of mine, and also a friend of yours, for he shared in the recent exile of the people, and returned with you. Well, Chaerephon, as you know, was very impetuous in all his doings, and he went to

---

[1] *The Clouds,* in which Aristophanes made fun of Socrates.

Delphi and boldly asked the oracle to tell him whether—as I was saying, I must beg you not to interrupt—he asked the oracle to tell him whether any one was wiser than I was, and the Pythian prophetess answered, that there was no man wiser. Chaerephon is dead himself; but his brother, who is in court, will confirm the truth of what I am saying.

Why do I mention this? Because I am going to explain to you why I have such an evil name. When I heard the answer, I said to myself, What can the god mean? and what is the interpretation of his riddle? for I know that I have no wisdom, small or great. What then can he mean when he says that I am the wisest of men? And yet he is a god, and cannot lie; that would be against his nature. After long consideration, I thought of a method of trying the question. I reflected that if I could only find a man wiser than myself, then I might go to the god with a refutation in my hand. I should say to him, "Here is a man who is wiser than I am; but you said that I was the wisest." Accordingly I went to one who had the reputation of wisdom, and observed him—his name I need not mention; he was a politician whom I selected for examination—and the result was as follows: When I began to talk with him, I could not help thinking that he was not really wise, although he was thought wise by many, and still wiser by himself; and thereupon I tried to explain to him that he thought himself wise, but was not really wise; and the consequence was that he hated me, and his enmity was shared by several who were present and heard me. So I left him, saying to myself, as I went away: Well, although I do not suppose that either of us knows anything really beautiful and good, I am better off than he is,—for he knows nothing, and thinks that he knows; I neither know nor think that I know. In this latter particular, then, I seem to have slightly the advantage of him. Then I went to another who had still higher pretensions to wisdom, and my conclusion was exactly the same. Whereupon I made another enemy of him, and of many others besides him.

Then I went to one man after another, being not unconscious of the enmity which I provoked, and I lamented and feared this: but necessity was laid upon me,—the word of God, I thought, ought to be considered first. And I said to myself, Go I must to all who appear to know, and find out the meaning of the oracle.

And I swear to you, Athenians, by the dog I swear!—for I must tell you the truth—the result of my mission was just this: I found that the men most in repute were all but the most foolish; and that others less esteemed were really wiser and better. I will tell you the tale of my wanderings and of the "Herculean" labours, as I may call them, which I endured only to find at last the oracle irrefutable. After the politicians, I went to the poets; tragic, dithyrambic, and all sorts. And there, I said to myself, you will be instantly detected; now you will find out that you are more ignorant than they are. Accordingly I took them some of the most elaborate passages in their own writings, and asked what was the meaning of them—thinking that they would teach me something. Will you believe me? I am almost ashamed to confess the truth, but I must say that there is hardly a person present who would not have talked better about their poetry than they did themselves. Then I knew that not by wisdom do poets write poetry, but by a sort of genius and inspiration; they are like diviners or soothsayers who also say many fine things, but do not understand the meaning of them. The poets appeared to me to be much in the same case; and I further observed that upon the strength of their poetry they believed themselves to be the wisest of men in other things in which they were not wise. So I departed, conceiving myself to be superior to them for the same reason that I was superior to the politicians.

At last I went to the artisans. I was conscious that I knew nothing at all, as I may say, and I was sure that they knew many fine things; and here I was not mistaken, for they did know many things of which I was ignorant, and in this they certainly were wiser than I was. But I observed that even the good artisans fell into the same error as the poets;—because they were good workmen they thought that they also knew all sorts of high matters, and this defect in them overshadowed their wisdom; and therefore I asked myself on behalf of the oracle, whether I would like to be as I was, neither having their knowledge nor their ignorance, or like them in both; and I made answer to myself and to the oracle that I was better off as I was.

This inquisition has led to my having many enemies of the worst and most dangerous kind, and has given occasion also to many calumnies. And I am called wise, for my hearers always imagine that I myself possess the wisdom which I find wanting in others: but the truth is, O men of Athens, that God only is wise; and by his answer he intends to show that the wisdom of men is worth little or nothing; he is not speaking of Socrates, he is only using my name by way of illustration, as if he said, He, O men, is the wisest, who, like Socrates, knows that his wisdom is in truth worth nothing. And so I go about the world obedient to the god, and search and make enquiry into the wisdom of any one, whether citizen or stranger, who appears to be wise; and if he is not wise, then in vindication of the oracle I show him that he is not wise; and my occupation quite absorbs me, and I have no time to give either to any public matter of interest or to any concern of my own, but I am in utter poverty by reason of my devotion to the god. . . .

Some one will say: And are you not ashamed, Socrates, of a course of life which is likely to bring you to an untimely end? To him I may fairly answer: There you are mistaken: a man who is good for anything ought not to calculate the chance of living or dying; he ought only to consider whether in doing anything he is doing right or wrong—acting the part of a good man or of a bad. Whereas, upon your view, the heroes who fell at Troy were not good for much, and the son of Thetis [2] above all, who altogether despised danger in comparison with disgrace; and when he was so eager to slay Hector, his goddess mother said to him, that if he avenged his companion Patroclus, and slew Hector, he would die himself—"Fate," she said, in these or the like words, "waits for you next after Hector"; he, receiving this warning, utterly despised danger and death, and instead of fearing them, feared rather to live in dishonour, and not to avenge his friend. "Let me die forthwith," he replies, "and be avenged of my enemy, rather than abide here by the beaked ships, a laughing stock and a burden of the earth." Had Achilles any thought of death and danger? For wherever a man's place is, whether the place which he has chosen or that in which he has been placed by a commander, there he ought to remain in the hour of danger; he should not think of death or of anything but of disgrace. And this, O men of Athens, is a true saying.

---

[2] Achilles.

Strange, indeed, would be my conduct, O men of Athens, if I, who, when I was ordered by the generals whom you chose to command me at Potidaea and Amphipolis and Delium, remained where they placed me, like any other man, facing death—if now, when, as I conceive and imagine, God orders me to fulfil the philosopher's mission of searching into myself and other men, I were to desert my post through fear of death, or any other fear; that would indeed be strange, and I might justly be arraigned in court for denying the existence of the gods, if I disobeyed the oracle because I was afraid of death, fancying that I was wise when I was not wise. For the fear of death is indeed the pretence of wisdom, and not real wisdom, being a pretence of knowing the unknown; and no one knows whether death, which men in their fear apprehend to be the greatest evil, may not be the greatest good. Is not this ignorance of a disgraceful sort, the ignorance which is the conceit that a man knows what he does not know? And in this respect only I believe myself to differ from men in general, and may perhaps claim to be wiser than they are:—that whereas I know but little of the world below, I do not suppose that I know: but I do know that injustice and disobedience to a better, whether God or man, is evil and dishonourable, and I will never fear or avoid a possible good rather than a certain evil. And therefore if you let me go now, and are not convinced by Anytus, who said that since I had been prosecuted I must be put to death; (or if not that I ought never to have been prosecuted at all); and that if I escape now, your sons will all be utterly ruined by listening to my words—if you say to me, Socrates, this time we will not mind Anytus, and you shall be let off, but upon one condition, that you are not to enquire and speculate in this way any more, and that if you are caught doing so again you shall die;—if this was the condition on which you let me go, I should reply: Men of Athens, I honour and love you; but I shall obey God rather than you, and while I have life and strength I shall never cease from the practice and teaching of philosophy, exhorting any one whom I meet and saying to him after my manner: You, my friend,—a citizen of the great and mighty and wise city of Athens,—are you not ashamed of heaping up the greatest amount of money and honour and reputation, and caring so little about wisdom and truth and the greatest improvement of the soul, which you never regard or heed at all? And if the person with whom I am arguing, says: Yes, but I do care; then I do not leave him or let him go at once; but I proceed to interrogate and examine and cross-examine him, and if I think that he has no virtue in him, but only says that he has, I reproach him with undervaluing the greater, and overvaluing the less. And I shall repeat the same words to every one whom I meet, young and old, citizen and alien, but especially to the citizens, inasmuch as they are my brethren. For know that this is the command of God; and I believe that no greater good has ever happened in the State than my service to the God. For I do nothing but go about persuading you all, old and young alike, not to take thought for your persons or your properties, but first and chiefly to care about the greatest improvement of the soul. I tell you that virtue is not given by money, but that from virtue comes money and every other good of man, public as well as private. This is my teaching, and if this is the doctrine which corrupts the youth, I am a mischievous person. But if any one says that this is not my teaching, he is speaking an untruth. Wherefore, O men of Athens, I say to you, do as Anytus bids or not as Anytus bids, and either acquit me or not; but whichever you do, understand that I shall never alter my ways, not even if I have to die many times.

## II

When he had done speaking, Crito said: And have you any commands for us, Socrates—anything to say about your children, or any other matter in which we can serve you?

Nothing particular, Crito, he replied: only, as I have always told you, take care of yourselves; that is a service which you may be ever rendering to me and mine and to all of us, whether you promise to do so or not. But if you have no thought for yourselves, and care not to walk according to the rule which I have prescribed for you, not now for the first time, however much you may profess or promise at the moment, it will be of no avail.

We will do our best, said Crito: And in what way shall we bury you?

In any way that you like; but you must get hold of me, and take care that I do not run away from you. Then he turned to us, and added with a smile:—I cannot make Crito believe that I am the same Socrates who have been talking and conducting the argument; he fancies that I am the other Socrates whom he will soon see, a dead body—and he asks, How shall he bury me? And though I have spoken many words in the endeavour to show that when I have drunk the poison I shall leave you and go to the joys of the blessed,—these words of mine, with which I was comforting you and myself, have had, as I perceive, no effect upon Crito. And therefore I want you to be surety for me to him now, as at the trial he was surety to the judges for me: but let the promise be of another sort; for he was surety for me to the judges that I would remain, and you must be my surety to him that I shall not remain, but go away and depart; and then he will suffer less at my death, and not be grieved when he sees my body being burned or buried. I would not have him sorrow at my hard lot, or say at the burial, Thus we lay out Socrates, or, Thus we follow him to the grave or bury him; for false words are not only evil in themselves, but they inflict the soul with evil. Be of good cheer then, my dear Crito, and say that you are burying my body only, and do with that whatever is usual, and what you think best.

When he had spoken these words, he arose and went into a chamber to bathe; Crito followed him and told us to wait. So we remained behind, talking and thinking of the subject of discourse, and also of the greatness of our sorrow; he was like a father of whom we were being bereaved, and we were about to pass the rest of our lives as orphans. When he had taken the bath his children were brought to him (he had two young sons and an elder one); and the women of his family also came, and he talked to them and gave them a few directions in the presence of Crito; then he dismissed them and returned to us.

Now the hour of sunset was near, for a good deal of time had passed while he was within. When he came out, he sat down with us again after his bath, but not much was said. Soon the jailer, who was the servant of the Eleven,[3] entered and stood by him, saying:—To you, Socrates, whom I know to be the noblest and gentlest and best of all who ever came to this place, I will not impute the angry feeling of

---

[3] The administrative government of Athens.

other men, who rage and swear at me, when, in obedience to the authorities, I bid them drink the poison—indeed, I am sure that you will not be angry with me; for others, as you are aware, and not I, are to blame. And so fare you well, and try to bear lightly what must needs be—you know my errand. Then bursting into tears he turned away and went out.

Socrates looked at him and said: I return your good wishes, and will do as you bid. Then turning to us, he said, How charming the man is: since I have been in prison he has always been coming to see me, and at times he would talk to me, and was as good to me as could be, and now see how generously he sorrows on my account. We must do as he says, Crito; and therefore let the cup be brought, if the poison is prepared: if not, let the attendant prepare some.

Yet, said Crito, the sun is still upon the hilltops, and I know that many a one has taken the draught late, and after the announcement has been made to him, he has eaten and drunk, and enjoyed the society of his beloved: do not hurry—there is time enough.

Socrates said: Yes, Crito, and they of whom you speak are right in so acting, for they think that they will be gainers by the delay; but I am right in not following their example, for I do not think that I should gain anything by drinking the poison a little later; I should only be ridiculous in my own eyes for sparing and saving a life which is already forfeit. Please then to do as I say, and not to refuse me.

Crito made a sign to the servant, who was standing by; and he went out, and having been absent for some time, returned with the jailer carrying the cup of poison. Socrates said: You, my good friend, who are experienced in these matters, shall give me directions how I am to proceed. The man answered: You have only to walk about until your legs are heavy, and then to lie down, and the poison will act. At the same time he handed the cup to Socrates, who in the easiest and gentlest manner, without the least fear or change of colour or feature, looking at the man with all his eyes, Echecrates,[4] as his manner was, took the cup and said: What do you say about making a libation out of this cup to any god? May I, or not? The man answered: We only prepare, Socrates, just so

much as we deem enough. I understand, he said: but I may and must ask the gods to prosper my journey from this to the other world —even so—and so be it according to my prayer. Then raising the cup to his lips, quite readily and cheerfully he drank off the poison. And hitherto most of us had been able to control our sorrow; but now when we saw him drinking, and saw too that he had finished the draught, we could no longer forbear, and in spite of myself my own tears were flowing fast; so that I covered my face and wept, not for him, but at the thought of my own calamity in having to part from such a friend. Nor was I the first; for Crito, when he found himself unable to restrain his tears, had got up, and I followed; and at that moment, Apollodorus, who had been weeping all the time, broke out in a loud and passionate cry which made cowards of us all. Socrates alone retained his calmness: What is this strange outcry? he said. I sent away the women mainly in order that they might not misbehave in this way, for I have been told that a man should die in peace. Be quiet then, and have patience. When we heard his words we were ashamed, and refrained our tears; and he walked about until, as he said, his legs began to fail, and then he lay on his back, according to directions, and the man who gave him the poison now and then looked at his feet and legs; and after a while he pressed his foot hard, and asked him if he could feel; and he said, No; and then his leg, and so upwards and upwards, and showed us that he was cold and stiff. And he felt them himself, and said: When the poison reaches the heart, that will be the end. He was beginning to grow cold about the groin, when he uncovered his face, for he had covered himself up, and said—they were his last words—he said: Crito, I owe a cock to Asclepius;[5] will you remember to pay the debt? The debt shall be paid, said Crito; is there anything else? There was no answer to this question; but in a minute or two a movement was heard, and the attendants uncovered him; his eyes were set, and Crito closed his eyes and mouth.

Such was the end, Echecrates, of our friend; concerning whom I may truly say, that of all men of his time whom I have known, he was the wisest and justest and best.

---

[4] The speaker is describing the event to Echecrates.

[5] The god of health.

*Henry David Thoreau*

# A PLEA FOR
# CAPTAIN JOHN BROWN

[*John Brown and a small band of followers dedicated to the abolition of slavery
attacked and captured the government ordnance factory at Harper's Ferry, Virginia, on
October 16, 1859, to set free the slaves who
were there. Two days later, after they had been
surrounded in the Engine House, the raiders
were captured, in a fight in which several were
killed and their leader badly wounded. While
John Brown was in prison, on a charge of
treason, Thoreau went to his neighbors in Concord, Massachusetts, and invited them to meet
together to hear what he had to say about the
attack. On October 30, 1859 he read "A Plea
for Captain John Brown" to the citizens of
Concord.*]

I trust that you will pardon me for being
here. I do not wish to force my thoughts upon
you, but I feel forced myself. Little as I know
of Captain Brown, I would fain do my part to
correct the tone and the statements of the newspapers, and of my countrymen generally, respecting his character and actions. It costs us
nothing to be just. We can at least express our
sympathy with, and admiration of, him and his
companions, and that is what I now propose
to do.

First, as to his history. I will endeavor to
omit, as much as possible, what you have already read. I need not describe his person to
you, for probably most of you have seen and
will not soon forget him. I am told that his
grandfather, John Brown, was an officer in the
Revolution; that he himself was born in Connecticut about the beginning of this century, but
early went with his father to Ohio. I heard him
say that his father was a contractor who furnished beef to the army there, in the war of
1812; that he accompanied him to the camp,
and assisted him in that employment, seeing a
good deal of military life,—more, perhaps, than
if he had been a soldier; for he was often present at the councils of the officers. Especially, he
learned by experience how armies are supplied
and maintained in the field,—a work which, he
observed, requires at least as much experience
and skill as to lead them in battle. He said that
few persons had any conception of the cost,
even the pecuniary cost, of firing a single bullet
in war. He saw enough, at any rate, to disgust
him with a military life; indeed, to excite in him
a great abhorrence of it; so much so, that
though he was tempted by the offer of some
petty officer in the army, when he was about
eighteen, he not only declined that, but he also
refused to train when warned, and was fined
for it. He then resolved that he would never
have anything to do with any war, unless it
were a war for liberty.

When the troubles in Kansas [6] began, he sent
several of his sons thither to strengthen the
party of the Free State men, fitting them out
with such weapons as he had; telling them that
if the troubles should increase, and there should
be any need of him, he would follow, to assist
them with his hand and his counsel. This, as
you all know, he soon after did; and it was
through his agency, far more than any other's,
that Kansas was made free.

For a part of his life he was a surveyor, and
at one time he was engaged in wool-growing,
and he went to Europe as an agent about that
business. There, as everywhere, he had his eyes
about him, and made many original observations. He said, for instance, that he saw why the
soil of England was so rich, and that of Germany (I think it was) so poor, and he thought
of writing to some of the crowned heads about
it. It was because in England the peasantry live
on the soil which they cultivate, but in Germany they are gathered into villages at night.
It is a pity that he did not make a book of
his observations.

I should say that he was an old-fashioned
man in his respect for the Constitution, and his
faith in the permanence of this Union. Slavery
he deemed to be wholly opposed to these, and
he was its determined foe.

He was by descent and birth a New England
farmer, a man of great common sense, deliberate and practical as that class is, and tenfold
more so. He was like the best of those who
stood at Concord Bridge once, on Lexington

---

[6] The agitation and fighting over the question of introducing slavery to the Kansas-Nebraska Territory.

Common, and on Bunker Hill, only he was firmer and higher principled than any that I have chanced to hear of as there. It was no abolition lecturer that converted him. Ethan Allen and Stark, with whom he may in some respects be compared, were rangers in a lower and less important field. They could bravely face their country's foes, but he had the courage to face his country herself when she was in the wrong. A Western writer says, to account for his escape from so many perils, that he was concealed under a "rural exterior"; as if, in that prairie land, a hero should, by good rights, wear a citizen's dress only.

He did not go to the college called Harvard, good old Alma Mater as she is. He was not fed on the pap that is there furnished. As he phrased it, "I know no more of grammar than one of your calves." But he went to the great university of the West, where he sedulously pursued the study of Liberty, for which he had early betrayed a fondness, and having taken many degrees, he finally commenced the public practice of Humanity in Kansas, as you all know. Such were *his humanities,* and not any study of grammar. He would have left a Greek accent slanting the wrong way, and righted up a falling man.

He was one of that class of whom we hear a great deal, but, for the most part, see nothing at all,—the Puritans. It would be in vain to kill him. He died lately in the time of Cromwell, but he reappeared here. Why should he not? Some of the Puritan stock are said to have come over and settled in New England. They were a class that did something else than celebrate their forefathers' day, and eat parched corn in remembrance of that time. They were neither Democrats nor Republicans, but men of simple habits, straightforward, prayerful; not thinking much of rulers who did not fear God, not making many compromises, nor seeking after available candidates. . . .

A man of rare common sense and directness of speech, as of action; a transcendentalist above all, a man of ideas and principles,—that was what distinguished him. Not yielding to a whim or transient impulse, but carrying out the purpose of a life. I noticed that he did not overstate anything, but spoke within bounds. I remember, particularly, how, in his speech here, he referred to what his family had suffered in Kansas, without ever giving the least vent to his pent-up fire. It was a volcano with an ordinary chimney-flue. Also referring to the deeds of certain Border Ruffians, he said, rapidly paring away his speech, like an experienced soldier, keeping a reserve of force and meaning, "They had a perfect right to be hung." He was not in the least a rhetorician, was not talking to Buncombe or his constituents anywhere, had no need to invent anything but to tell the simple truth, and communicate his own resolution; therefore he appeared incomparably strong, and eloquence in Congress and elsewhere seemed to me at a discount. It was like the speeches of Cromwell compared with those of an ordinary king.

As for his tact and prudence, I will merely say, that at a time when scarcely a man from the Free States was able to reach Kansas by any direct route, at least without having his arms taken from him, he, carrying what imperfect guns and other weapons he could collect, openly and slowly drove an ox-cart through Missouri, apparently in the capacity of a surveyor, with his surveying compass exposed in it, and so passed unsuspected, and had ample opportunity to learn the designs of the enemy. For some time after his arrival he still followed the same profession. When, for instance, he saw a knot of the ruffians on the prairie, discussing, of course, the single topic which then occupied their minds, he would, perhaps, take his compass and one of his sons, and proceed to run an imaginary line right through the very spot on which that conclave had assembled, and when he came up to them, he would naturally pause and have some talk with them, learning their news, and, at last, all their plans perfectly; and having thus completed his real survey he would resume his imaginary one, and run on his line till he was out of sight.

When I expressed surprise that he could live in Kansas at all, with a price set upon his head, and so large a number, including the authorities, exasperated against him, he accounted for it by saying, "It is perfectly well understood that I will not be taken." Much of the time for some years he has had to skulk in swamps, suffering from poverty and from sickness, which was the consequence of exposure, befriended only by Indians and a few whites. But though it might be known that he was lurking in a particular swamp, his foes commonly did not care to go in after him. He could even come out into a town where there were more Border Ruffians than Free State men, and transact some business, without delaying long, and yet not be molested; for, said he, "no little handful of men were willing to undertake it, and a large body could not be got together in season."

As for his recent failure, we do not know the facts about it. It was evidently far from being a wild and desperate attempt. His enemy, Mr. Vallandigham,[7] is compelled to say that "it was among the best planned and executed conspiracies that ever failed."

Not to mention his other successes, was it a failure, or did it show a want of good management, to deliver from bondage a dozen human beings, and walk off with them by broad daylight, for weeks if not months, at a leisurely pace, through one State after another, for half the length of the North, conspicuous to all parties, with a price set upon his head, going into a court-room on his way and telling what he had done, thus convincing Missouri that it was not profitable to try to hold slaves in his neighborhood?—and this, not because the government menials were lenient, but because they were afraid of him.

Yet he did not attribute his success, foolishly, to "his star," or to any magic. He said, truly, that the reason why such greatly superior numbers quailed before him was, as one of his prisoners confessed, because they *lacked a cause,*— a kind of armor which he and his party never lacked. When the time came, few men were found willing to lay down their lives in defense of what they knew to be wrong; they did not like that this should be their last act in this world. . . .

On the whole, my respect for my fellow-men, except as one may outweigh a million, is not being increased these days. I have noticed the cold-blooded way in which newspaper writers and men generally speak of this event, as if an ordinary malefactor, though one of unusual "pluck,"—as the Governor of Virginia is reported to have said, using the language of the cock-pit, "the gamest man he ever saw,"—had been caught, and were about to be hung. He was not dreaming of his foes when the governor thought he looked so brave. It turns what

sweetness I have to gall, to hear, or hear of, the remarks of some of my neighbors. When we heard at first that he was dead, one of my townsmen observed that "he died as the fool dieth"; which, pardon me, for an instant suggested a likeness in him dying to my neighbor living. Others, craven-hearted, said disparagingly, that "he threw his life away," because he resisted the government. Which way have they thrown *their* lives, pray?—such as would praise a man for attacking singly an ordinary band of thieves or murderers. I hear another ask, Yankee-like, "What will he gain by it?" as if he expected to fill his pockets by this enterprise. Such a one has no idea of gain but in this worldly sense. If it does not lead to a "surprise" party, if he does not get a new pair of boots, or a vote of thanks, it must be a failure. "But he won't gain anything by it." Well, no, I don't suppose he could get four-and-sixpence a day for being hung, take the year round; but then he stands a chance to save a considerable part of his soul,—and *such* a soul!—when *you* do not. No doubt you can get more in your market for a quart of milk than for a quart of blood, but that is not the market that heroes carry their blood to.

Such do not know that like the seed is the fruit, and that, in the moral world, when good seed is planted, good fruit is inevitable, and does not depend on our watering and cultivating; that when you plant, or bury, a hero in his field, a crop of heroes is sure to spring up. This is a seed of such force and vitality, that it does not ask our leave to germinate.

The momentary charge at Balaklava, in obedience to a blundering command, proving what a perfect machine the soldier is, has, properly enough, been celebrated by a poet laureate; but the steady, and for the most part successful, charge of this man, for some years, against the legions of Slavery, in obedience to an infinitely higher command, is as much more memorable than that as an intelligent and conscientious man is superior to a machine. Do you think that that will go unsung? . . .

Our foes are in our midst and all about us. There is hardly a house but is divided against itself, for our foe is the all but universal woodenness of both head and heart, the want of vitality in man, which is the effect of our vice; and hence are begotten fear, superstition, bigotry, persecution, and slavery of all kinds. We are

---

[7] Clement Laird Vallandigham, 1820–1871, an Ohio Congressman who urged appeasement of the South on the slavery question.

mere figure-heads upon a hulk, with livers in the place of hearts. The curse is the worship of idols, which at length changes the worshiper into a stone image himself; and the New Englander is just as much an idolater as the Hindoo. This man was an exception, for he did not set up even a political graven image between him and his God.

A church that can never have done with excommunicating Christ while it exists! Away with your broad and flat churches, and your narrow and tall churches! Take a step forward, and invent a new style of out-houses. Invent a salt that will save you, and defend our nostrils.

The modern Christian is a man who has consented to say all the prayers in the liturgy, provided you will let him go straight to bed and sleep quietly afterward. All his prayers begin with "Now I lay me down to sleep," and he is forever looking forward to the time when he shall go to his "*long* rest." He has consented to perform certain old-established charities, too, after a fashion, but he does not wish to hear of any newfangled ones; he doesn't wish to have any supplementary articles added to the contract, to fit it to the present time. He shows the whites of his eyes on the Sabbath, and the blacks all the rest of the week. The evil is not merely a stagnation of blood, but a stagnation of spirit. Many, no doubt, are well disposed, but sluggish by constitution and by habit, and they cannot conceive of a man who is actuated by higher motives than they are. Accordingly they pronounce this man insane, for they know that *they* could never act as he does, as long as they are themselves.

We dream of foreign countries, of other times and races of men, placing them at a distance in history or space; but let some significant event like the present occur in our midst, and we discover, often, this distance and this strangeness between us and our nearest neighbors. *They* are our Austrias, and Chinas, and South Sea Islands. Our crowded society becomes well spaced all at once, clean and handsome to the eye,—a city of magnificent distances. We discover why it was that we never got beyond compliments and surfaces with them before; we become aware of as many versts between us and them as there are between a wandering Tartar and a Chinese town. The thoughtful man becomes a hermit in the thoroughfares of the market-place. Impassable seas suddenly find

their level between us, or dumb steppes stretch themselves out there. It is the difference of constitution, of intelligence, and faith, and not streams and mountains, that make the true and impassable boundaries between individuals and between states. None but the like-minded can come plenipotentiary to our court.

I read all the newspapers I could get within a week after this event, and I do not remember in them a single expression of sympathy for these men. I have since seen one noble statement, in a Boston paper, not editorial. Some voluminous sheets decided not to print the full report of Brown's words to the exclusion of other matter. It was as if a publisher should reject the manuscript of the New Testament, and print Wilson's [8] last speech. The same journal which contained this pregnant news was chiefly filled, in parallel columns, with the reports of the political conventions that were being held. But the descent to them was too steep. They should have been spared this contrast,—been printed in an extra, at least. To turn from the voices and deeds of earnest men to the *cackling* of political conventions! Office-seekers and speech-makers, who do not so much as lay an honest egg, but wear their breasts bare upon an egg of chalk! Their great game is the game of straws, or rather that universal aboriginal game of the platter, at which the Indians cried *hub, hub!* Exclude the reports of religious and political conventions, and publish the words of a living man.

But I object not so much to what they have omitted as to what they have inserted. Even the *Liberator* called it "a misguided, wild, and apparently insane—effort." As for the herd of newspapers and magazines, I do not chance to know an editor in the country who will deliberately print anything which he knows will ultimately and permanently reduce the number of his subscribers. They do not believe that it would be expedient. How then can they print truth? If we do not say pleasant things, they argue, nobody will attend to us. And so they do like some traveling auctioneers, who sing an obscene song, in order to draw a crowd around them. Republican editors, obliged to get their sentences ready for the morning edi-

---

8 Henry Wilson, 1812–1875, United States Senator from Massachusetts. He was a strong opponent of slavery, but Thoreau had little use for politicians.

tion, and accustomed to look at everything by the twilight of politics, express no admiration, nor true sorrow even, but call these men "deluded fanatics,"—"mistaken men,"—"insane," or "crazed." It suggests what a *sane* set of editors we are blessed with, *not* "mistaken men"; who know very well on which side their bread is buttered, at least.

A man does a brave and humane deed, and at once, on all sides, we hear people and parties declaring, "I didn't do it, nor countenance *him* to do it, in any conceivable way. It can't be fairly inferred from my past career." I, for one, am not interested to hear you define your position. I don't know that I ever was or ever shall be. I think it is mere egotism, or impertinent at this time. Ye needn't take so much pains to wash your skirts of him. No intelligent man will ever be convinced that he was any creature of yours. He went and came, as he himself informs us, "under the auspices of John Brown and nobody else." The Republican party does not perceive how many his *failure* will make to vote more correctly than they would have them. They have counted the votes of Pennsylvania & Co., but they have not correctly counted Captain Brown's vote. He has taken the wind out of their sails,—the little wind they had,— and they may as well lie to and repair.

What though he did not belong to your clique! Though you may not approve of his method or his principles, recognize his magnanimity. Would you not like to claim kindredship with him in that, though in no other thing he is like, or likely, to you? Do you think that you would lose your reputation so? What you lost at the spile, you would gain at the bung.

If they do not mean all this, then they do not speak the truth, and say what they mean. They are simply at their old tricks still.

"It was always conceded to him," *says one who calls him crazy,* "that he was a conscientious man, very modest in his demeanor, apparently inoffensive, until the subject of Slavery was introduced, when he would exhibit a feeling of indignation unparalleled."

The slave-ship is on her way, crowded with its dying victims; new cargoes are being added in mid-ocean; a small crew of slaveholders, countenanced by a large body of passengers, is smothering four millions under the hatches, and yet the politician asserts that the only proper way by which deliverance is to be obtained is by "the quiet diffusion of the sentiments of humanity," without any "outbreak." As if the sentiments of humanity were ever found unaccompanied by its deeds, and you could disperse them, all finished to order, the pure article, as easily as water with a watering-pot, and so lay the dust. What is that that I hear cast over-board? The bodies of the dead that have found deliverance. That is the way we are "diffusing" humanity, and its sentiments with it.

Prominent and influential editors, accustomed to deal with politicians, men of an infinitely lower grade, say, in their ignorance, that he acted "on the principle of revenge." They do not know the man. They must enlarge themselves to conceive of him. I have no doubt that the time will come when they will begin to see him as he was. They have got to conceive of a man of faith and of religious principle, and not a politician or an Indian; of a man who did not wait till he was personally interfered with or thwarted in some harmless business before he gave his life to the cause of the oppressed.

If Walker [9] may be considered the representative of the South, I wish I could say that Brown was the representative of the North. He was a superior man. He did not value his bodily life in comparison with ideal things. He did not recognize unjust human laws, but resisted them as he was bid. For once we are lifted out of the trivialness and dust of politics into the region of truth and manhood. No man in America has ever stood up so persistently and effectively for the dignity of human nature, knowing himself for a man, and the equal of any and all governments. In that sense he was the most American of us all. He needed no babbling lawyer, making false issues, to defend him. He was more than a match for all the judges that American voters, or office-holders of whatever grade, can create. He could not have been tried by a jury of his peers, because his peers did not exist. When a man stands up serenely against the condemnation and vengeance of mankind, rising above them literally *by a whole body,*—even though he were of late the vilest murderer, who has settled that matter with himself,—the spectacle is a sublime one,—didn't ye know it, ye *Liber-*

---

[9] Robert J. Walker, 1801–1869, who had been a United States Senator from Mississippi and Governor of the Kansas Territory, 1857–1858.

*ators,* ye *Tribunes,* ye *Republicans?*—and we become criminal in comparison. Do yourselves the honor to recognize him. He needs none of your respect.

As for the Democratic journals, they are not human enough to affect me at all. I do not feel indignation at anything they may say.

I am aware that I anticipate a little,—that he was still, at the last accounts, alive in the hands of his foes; but that being the case, I have all along found myself thinking and speaking of him as physically dead.

I do not believe in erecting statues to those who still live in our hearts, whose bones have not yet crumbled in the earth around us, but I would rather see the statue of Captain Brown in the Massachusetts State-House yard than that of any other man whom I know. I rejoice that I live in this age, that I am his contemporary. . . .

What have Massachusetts and the North sent a few *sane* representatives to Congress for, of late years?—to declare with effect what kind of sentiments? All their speeches put together and boiled down—and probably they themselves will confess it—do not match for manly directness and force, and for simple truth, the few casual remarks of crazy John Brown on the floor of the Harper's Ferry engine-house,— that man whom you are about to hang, to send to the other world, though not to represent *you* there. No, he was not our representative in any sense. He was too fair a specimen of a man to represent the like of us. Who, then, *were* his constituents? If you read his words understandingly you will find out. In his case there is no idle eloquence, no made, nor maiden speech, no compliments to the oppressor. Truth is his inspirer, and earnestness the polisher of his sentences. He could afford to lose his Sharp's rifles, while he retained his faculty of speech,— a Sharp's rifle of infinitely surer and longer range.

And the New York *Herald* reports the conversation *verbatim!* It does not know of what undying words it is made the vehicle.

I have no respect for the penetration of any man who can read the report of that conversation and still call the principal in it insane. It has the ring of a saner sanity than ordinary discipline and habits of life, than an ordinary organization, secure. Take any sentence of it,— "Any questions that I can honorably answer,

I will; not otherwise. So far as I am myself concerned, I have told everything truthfully. I value my word, sir." The few who talk about his vindictive spirit, while they really admire his heroism, have no test by which to detect a noble man, no amalgam to combine with his pure gold. They mix their own dross with it.

It is a relief to turn from these slanders to the testimony of his more truthful, but frightened jailers and hangmen. Governor Wise [10] speaks far more justly and appreciatingly of him than any Northern editor, or politician, or public personage, that I chance to have heard from. I know that you can afford to hear him again on this subject. He says: "They are themselves mistaken who take him to be a madman. . . . He is cool, collected, and indomitable, and it is but just to him to say that he was humane to his prisoners. . . . And he inspired me with great trust in his integrity as a man of truth. He is a fanatic, vain and garrulous" (I leave that part to Mr. Wise), "but firm, truthful, and intelligent. His men, too, who survive, are like him. . . . Colonel Washington [11] says that he was the coolest and firmest man he ever saw in defying danger and death. With one son dead by his side, and another shot through, he felt the pulse of his dying son with one hand, and held his rifle with the other, and commanded his men with the utmost composure, encouraging them to be firm, and to sell their lives as dear as they could. Of the three white prisoners, Brown, Stevens, and Coppoc, it was hard to say which was most firm."

Almost the first Northern men whom the slaveholder has learned to respect!

The testimony of Mr. Vallandigham, though less valuable, is of the same purport, that "it is vain to underrate either the man or his conspiracy. . . . He is the farthest possible removed from the ordinary ruffian, fanatic, or madman."

"All is quiet at Harper's Ferry," say the journals. What is the character of that calm which follows when the law and the slaveholder prevail? I regard this event as a touchstone designed to bring out, with glaring distinctness, the character of this government. We needed to be thus assisted to see it by the light of history. It needed to see itself. When a govern-

---

[10] Henry Wise, Governor of Virginia, 1856–1860.

[11] Lewis W. Washington, who lived near Harper's Ferry and was one of the men taken prisoner by Brown's men on the night of October 16.

ment puts forth its strength on the side of injustice, as ours to maintain slavery and kill the liberators of the slave, it reveals itself a merely brute force, or worse, a demoniacal force. It is the head of the Plug-Uglies. It is more manifest than ever that tyranny rules. I see this government to be effectually allied with France and Austria in oppressing mankind. There sits a tyrant holding fettered four millions of slaves; here comes their heroic liberator. This most hypocritical and diabolical government looks up from its seat on the gasping four millions, and inquires with an assumption of innocence: "What do you assault me for? Am I not an honest man? Cease agitation on this subject, or I will make a slave of you, too, or else hang you."

We talk about a *representative* government; but what a monster of a government is that where the noblest faculties of the mind, and the *whole* heart, are not *represented*. A semi-human tiger or ox, stalking over the earth, with its heart taken out and the top of its brain shot away. Heroes have fought well on their stumps when their legs were shot off, but I never heard of any good done by such a government as that.

The only government that I recognize—and it matters not how few are at the head of it, or how small its army—is that power that establishes justice in the land, never that which establishes injustice. What shall we think of a government to which all the truly brave and just men in the land are enemies, standing between it and those whom it oppresses? A government that pretends to be Christian and crucifies a million Christs every day!

Treason! Where does such treason take its rise? I cannot help thinking of you as you deserve, ye governments. Can you dry up the fountains of thought? High treason, when it is resistance to tyranny here below, has its origin in, and is first committed by, the power that makes and forever recreates man. When you have caught and hung all these human rebels, you have accomplished nothing but your own guilt, for you have not struck at the fountainhead. You presume to contend with a foe against whom West Point cadets and rifled cannon *point* not. Can all the art of the cannon-founder tempt matter to turn against its maker? Is the form in which the founder thinks he casts it more essential than the constitution of it and of himself?

The United States have a coffle of four millions of slaves. They are determined to keep them in this condition; and Massachusetts is one of the confederated overseers to prevent their escape. Such are not all the inhabitants of Massachusetts, but such are they who rule and are obeyed here. It was Massachusetts, as well as Virginia, that put down this insurrection at Harper's Ferry. She sent the marines there, and she will have *to pay the penalty of her sin.* . . .

I hear many condemn these men because they were so few. When were the good and the brave ever in a majority? Would you have had him wait till that time came?—till you and I came over to him? The very fact that he had no rabble or troop of hirelings about him would alone distinguish him from ordinary heroes. His company was small indeed, because few could be found worthy to pass muster. Each one who there laid down his life for the poor and oppressed was a picked man, culled out of many thousands, if not millions; apparently a man of principle, of rare courage, and devoted humanity; ready to sacrifice his life at any moment for the benefit of his fellow-man. It may be doubted if there were as many more their equals in these respects in all the country,—I speak of his followers only,—for their leader, no doubt, scoured the land far and wide, seeking to swell his troop. These alone were ready to step between the oppressor and the oppressed. Surely they were the very best men you could select to be hung. That was the greatest compliment which this country could pay them. They were ripe for her gallows. She has tried a long time, she has hung a good many, but never found the right one before.

When I think of him, and his six sons, and his son-in-law, not to enumerate the others, enlisted for this fight, proceeding coolly, reverently, humanely to work, for months if not years, sleeping and waking upon it, summering and wintering the thought, without expecting any reward but a good conscience, while almost all America stood ranked on the other side,—I say again that it affects me as a sublime spectacle. If he had had any journal advocating *"his cause,"* any organ, as the phrase is, monotonously and wearisomely playing the same old tune, and then passing round the hat, it would have been fatal to his efficiency. If he had acted in any way so as to be let alone by the government, he might have been suspected. It was the fact that the tyrant must give place to him, or he to the tyrant, that distinguished him from all the reformers of the day that I know.

It was his peculiar doctrine that a man has a perfect right to interfere by force with the slave-holder, in order to rescue the slave. I agree with him. They who are continually shocked by slavery have some right to be shocked by the violent death of the slaveholder, but no others. Such will be more shocked by his life than by his death. I shall not be forward to think him mistaken in his method who quickest succeeds to liberate the slave. I speak for the slave when I say that I prefer the philanthropy of Captain Brown to that philanthropy which neither shoots me nor liberates me. At any rate, I do not think it is quite sane for one to spend his whole life in talking or writing about this mat-ter, unless he is continuously inspired, and I have not done so. A man may have other affairs to attend to. I do not wish to kill nor to be killed, but I can foresee circumstances in which both these things would be by me unavoidable. We preserve the so-called peace of our com-munity by deeds of petty violence every day. Look at the policeman's billy and handcuffs! Look at the jail! Look at the gallows! Look at the chaplain of the regiment! We are hoping only to live safely on the outskirts of *this* pro-visional army. So we defend ourselves and our hen-roosts, and maintain slavery. I know that the mass of my countrymen think that the only righteous use that can be made of Sharp's rifles and revolvers is to fight duels with them, when we are insulted by other nations, or to hunt Indians, or shoot fugitive slaves with them, or the like. I think that for once the Sharp's rifles and the revolvers were employed in a righteous cause. The tools were in the hands of one who could use them.

The same indignation that is said to have cleared the temple once will clear it again. The question is not about the weapon, but the spirit in which you use it. No man has appeared in America, as yet, who loved his fellow-man so well, and treated him so tenderly. He lived for him. He took up his life and he laid it down for him. What sort of violence is that which is encouraged, not by soldiers, but by peaceable citizens, not so much by the fighting sects as by the Quakers, and not so much by Quaker men as by Quaker women?

This event advertises me that there is such a fact as death,—the possibility of a man's dying. It seems as if no man had ever died in America before; for in order to die you must first have lived. I don't believe in the hearses, and palls, and funerals that they have had. There was no death in the case, because there had been no life; they merely rotted or sloughed off, pretty much as they had rotted or sloughed along. No temple's veil was rent, only a hole dug somewhere. Let the dead bury their dead. The best of them fairly ran down like a clock. Franklin,—Washington,—they were let off without dying; they were merely missing one day. I hear a good many pretend that they are going to die; or that they have died, for aught that I know. Nonsense! I'll defy them to do it. They haven't got life enough in them. They'll deliquesce like fungi, and keep a hundred eulo-gists mopping the spot where they left off. Only half a dozen or so have died since the world began. Do you think that you are going to die, sir? No! there's no hope of you. You haven't got your lesson yet. You've got to stay after school. We make a needless ado about capital punishment,—taking lives, when there is no life to take. *Memento mori!* We don't understand that sublime sentence which some worthy got sculptured on his grave-stone once. We've in-terpreted it in a groveling and sniveling sense; we've wholly forgotten how to die.

But be sure you do die nevertheless. Do your work, and finish it. If you know how to begin, you will know when to end.

These men, in teaching us how to die, have at the same time taught us how to live. If this man's acts and words do not create a revival, it will be the severest possible satire on the acts and words that do. It is the best news that America has ever heard. It has already quick-ened the feeble pulse of the North, and infused more and more generous blood into her veins and heart than any number of years of what is called commercial and political prosperity could. How many a man who was lately con-templating suicide has now something to live for! . . .

Newspaper editors argue also that it is a proof of his *insanity* that he thought he was appointed to do this work which he did,—that he did not suspect himself for a moment! They talk as if it were impossible that a man could be "divinely appointed" in these days to do any work whatever; as if vows and religion were out of date as connected with any man's daily work; as if the agent to abolish slavery could only be somebody appointed by the President, or by some political party. They talk as if a man's death were a failure, and his continued life, be it of whatever character, were a success. . . .

Any man knows when he is justified, and all the wits in the world cannot enlighten him on that point. The murderer always knows that he is justly punished; but when a government takes the life of a man without the consent of his conscience, it is an audacious government, and is taking a step towards its own dissolution. Is it not possible that an individual may be right and a government wrong? Are laws to be enforced simply because they were made? or declared by any number of men to be good, if they are *not* good? Is there any necessity for a man's being a tool to perform a deed of which his better nature disapproves? Is it the intention of law-makers that *good* men shall be hung ever? Are judges to interpret the law according to the letter, and not the spirit? What right have *you* to enter into a compact with yourself that you *will* do thus or so, against the light within you? Is it for *you* to *make up* your mind,—to form any resolution whatever,—and not accept the convictions that are forced upon you, and which never pass your understanding? I do not believe in lawyers, in that mode of attacking or defending a man, because you descend to meet the judge on his own ground, and, in cases of the highest importance, it is of no consequence whether a man breaks a human law or not. Let lawyers decide trivial cases. Business men may arrange that among themselves. If they were the interpreters of the everlasting laws which rightfully bind man, that would be another thing. A counterfeiting law-factory, standing half in a slave land and half in a free! What kind of laws for free men can you expect from that?

I am here to plead his cause with you. I plead not for his life, but for his character,—his immortal life; and so it becomes your cause wholly, and is not his in the least. Some eighteen hundred years ago Christ was crucified; this morning, perchance, Captain Brown was hung. These are the two ends of a chain which is not without its links. He is not Old Brown any longer; he is an angel of light.

I see now that it was necessary that the bravest and humanest man in all the country should be hung. Perhaps he saw it himself. I *almost fear* that I may yet hear of his deliverance, doubting if a prolonged life, if *any* life, can do as much good as his death.

"Misguided!" "Garrulous!" "Insane!" "Vindictive!" So ye write in your easy-chairs, and thus he wounded responds from the floor of the Armory, clear as a cloudless sky, true as the voice of nature is: "No man sent me here; it was my own prompting and that of my Maker. I acknowledge no master in human form."

And in what a sweet and noble strain he proceeds, addressing his captors, who stand over him: "I think, my friends, you are guilty of a great wrong against God and humanity, and it would be perfectly right for any one to interfere with you so far as to free those you willfully and wickedly hold in bondage."

And, referring to his movement: "It is, in my opinion, the greatest service a man can render to God."

"I pity the poor in bondage that have none to help them; that is why I am here; not to gratify any personal animosity, revenge, or vindictive spirit. It is my sympathy with the oppressed and the wronged, that are as good as you, and as precious in the sight of God."

You don't know your testament when you see it.

"I want you to understand that I respect the rights of the poorest and weakest of colored people, oppressed by the slave power, just as much as I do those of the most wealthy and powerful."

"I wish to say, furthermore, that you had better, all you people at the South, prepare yourselves for a settlement of that question, that must come up for settlement sooner than you are prepared for it. The sooner you are prepared the better. You may dispose of me very easily. I am nearly disposed of now; but this question is still to be settled,—this negro question, I mean; the end of that is not yet."

I foresee the time when the painter will paint that scene, no longer going to Rome for a subject; the poet will sing it; the historian record it; and, with the Landing of the Pilgrims and the Declaration of Independence, it will be the ornament of some future national gallery, when at least the present form of slavery shall be no more here. We shall then be at liberty to weep for Captain Brown. Then, and not till then, we will take our revenge.

*Saki*

# SREDNI VASHTAR

Conradin was ten years old, and the doctor had pronounced his professional opinion that the boy would not live another five years. The doctor was silky and effete, and counted for little, but his opinion was endorsed by Mrs. De Ropp, who counted for nearly everything. Mrs. De Ropp was Conradin's cousin and guardian, and in his eyes she represented those three-fifths of the world that are necessary and disagreeable and real; the other two-fifths, in perpetual antagonism to the foregoing, were summed up in himself and his imagination. One of these days Conradin supposed he would succumb to the mastering pressure of wearisome necessary things—such as illnesses and coddling restrictions and drawn-out dulness. Without his imagination, which was rampant under the spur of loneliness, he would have succumbed long ago.

Mrs. De Ropp would never, in her honestest moments, have confessed to herself that she disliked Conradin, though she might have been dimly aware that thwarting him "for his good" was a duty which she did not find particularly irksome. Conradin hated her with a desperate sincerity which he was perfectly able to mask. Such few pleasures as he could contrive for himself gained an added relish from the likelihood that they would be displeasing to his guardian, and from the realm of his imagination she was locked out—an unclean thing, which should find no entrance.

In the dull, cheerless garden, overlooked by so many windows that were ready to open with a message not to do this or that, or a reminder that medicines were due, he found little attraction. The few fruit-trees that it contained were set jealously apart from his plucking, as though they were rare specimens of their kind blooming in an arid waste; it would probably have

been difficult to find a market-gardener who would have offered ten shillings for their entire yearly produce. In a forgotten corner, however, almost hidden behind a dismal shrubbery, was a disused tool-shed of respectable proportions, and within its walls Conradin found a haven, something that took on the varying aspects of a playroom and a cathedral. He had peopled it with a legion of familiar phantoms, evoked partly from fragments of history and partly from his own brain, but it also boasted two inmates of flesh and blood. In one corner lived a ragged-plumaged hen, on which the boy lavished an affection that had scarcely another outlet. Further back in the gloom stood a large hutch, divided into two compartments, one of which was fronted with close iron bars. This was the abode of a large polecat-ferret, which a friendly butcher-boy had once smuggled, cage and all, into its present quarters, in exchange for a long-secreted hoard of small silver. Conradin was dreadfully afraid of the lithe, sharp-fanged beast, but it was his most treasured possession. Its very presence in the tool-shed was a secret and fearful joy, to be kept scrupulously from the knowledge of the Woman, as he privately dubbed his cousin. And one day, out of Heaven knows what material, he spun the beast a wonderful name, and from that moment it grew into a god and a religion. The Woman indulged in religion once a week at a church near by, and took Conradin with her, but to him the church service was an alien rite in the House of Rimmon. Every Thursday, in the dim and musty silence of the tool-shed, he worshipped with mystic and elaborate ceremonial before the wooden hutch where dwelt Sredni Vashtar, the great ferret. Red flowers in their season and scarlet berries in the wintertime were offered at his shrine, for he was a god who laid some special stress on the fierce impatient side of things, as opposed to the Woman's religion, which, as far as Conradin could observe, went to great lengths in the contrary direction. And on great festivals powdered nutmeg was strewn in front of his hutch, an important feature of the offering being that the nutmeg had to be stolen. These festivals were of irregular occurrence, and were chiefly appointed to celebrate some passing event. On one occasion, when Mrs. De Ropp suffered from acute toothache for three days, Conradin kept up the festival during the entire three days, and almost succeeded in persuading himself that Sredni Vashtar was personally responsible for the toothache. If the malady had lasted for another day the supply of nutmeg would have given out.

The Houdan hen was never drawn into the cult of Sredni Vashtar. Conradin had long ago settled that she was an Anabaptist. He did not pretend to have the remotest knowledge as to what an Anabaptist was, but he privately hoped that it was dashing and not very respectable. Mrs. De Ropp was the ground plan on which he based and detested all respectability.

After a while Conradin's absorption in the tool-shed began to attract the notice of his guardian. "It is not good for him to be pottering down there in all weathers," she promptly decided, and at breakfast one morning she announced that the Houdan hen had been sold and taken away overnight. With her short-sighted eyes she peered at Conradin, waiting for an outbreak of rage and sorrow, which she was ready to rebuke with a flow of excellent precepts and reasoning. But Conradin said nothing: there was nothing to be said. Something perhaps in his white set face gave her a momentary qualm, for at tea that afternoon there was toast on the table, a delicacy which she usually banned on the ground that it was bad for him; also because the making of it "gave trouble," a deadly offence in the middle-class feminine eye.

"I thought you liked toast," she exclaimed, with an injured air, observing that he did not touch it.

"Sometimes," said Conradin.

In the shed that evening there was an innovation in the worship of the hutch-god. Conradin had been wont to chant his praises, tonight he asked a boon.

"Do one thing for me, Sredni Vashtar."

The thing was not specified. As Sredni Vashtar was a god he must be supposed to know. And choking back a sob as he looked at that other empty corner, Conradin went back to the world he so hated.

And every night, in the welcome darkness of his bedroom, and every evening in the dusk of the tool-shed, Conradin's bitter litany went up: "Do one thing for me, Sredni Vashtar."

Mrs. De Ropp noticed that the visits to the shed did not cease, and one day she made a further journey of inspection.

"What are you keeping in that locked hutch?" she asked. "I believe it's guinea-pigs. I'll have them all cleared away."

Conradin shut his lips tight, but the Woman ransacked his bedroom till she found the carefully hidden key, and forthwith marched down to the shed to complete her discovery. It was a cold afternoon, and Conradin had been bidden to keep to the house. From the furthest window of the dining-room the door of the shed could just be seen beyond the corner of the shrubbery, and there Conradin stationed himself. He saw the Woman enter, and then he imagined her opening the door of the sacred hutch and peering down with her short-sighted eyes into the thick straw bed where his god lay hidden. Perhaps she would prod at the straw in her clumsy impatience. And Conradin fervently breathed his prayer for the last time. But he knew as he prayed that he did not believe. He knew that the Woman would come out presently with that pursed smile he loathed so well on her face, and that in an hour or two the gardener would carry away his wonderful god, a god no longer, but a simple brown ferret in a hutch. And he knew that the Woman would triumph always as she triumphed now, and that he would grow ever more sickly under her pestering and domineering and superior wisdom, till one day nothing would matter much more with him, and the doctor would be proved right. And in the sting and misery of his defeat, he began to chant loudly and defiantly the hymn of his threatened idol:

Sredni Vashtar went forth,
His thoughts were red thoughts and his teeth
    were white.
His enemies called for peace, but he brought
    them death.
Sredni Vashtar the Beautiful.

And then of a sudden he stopped his chanting and drew closer to the window-pane. The door of the shed still stood ajar as it had been left, and the minutes were slipping by. They were long minutes, but they slipped by nevertheless. He watched the starlings running and flying in little parties across the lawn; he counted them over and over again, with one eye always on that swinging door. A sour-faced maid came in to lay the table for tea, and still Conradin stood and waited and watched. Hope had crept by inches into his heart, and now a look of triumph began to blaze in his eyes that had only known the wistful patience of defeat. Under his breath, with a furtive exultation, he began once again the paean of victory and devastation. And presently his eyes were rewarded: out through that doorway came a long, low, yellow-and-brown beast, with eyes a-blink at the waning daylight, and dark wet stains around the fur of jaws and throat. Conradin dropped on his knees. The great polecat-ferret made its way down to a small brook at the foot of the garden, drank for a moment, then crossed a little plank bridge and was lost to sight in the bushes. Such was the passing of Sredni Vashtar.

"Tea is ready," said the sour-faced maid; "where is the mistress?"

"She went down to the shed some time ago," said Conradin.

And while the maid went to summon her mistress to tea, Conradin fished a toasting-fork out of the sideboard drawer and proceeded to toast himself a piece of bread. And during the toasting of it and the buttering of it with much butter and the slow enjoyment of eating it, Conradin listened to the noises and silences which fell in quick spasms beyond the dining-room door. The loud foolish screaming of the maid, the answering chorus of wondering ejaculations from the kitchen region, the scuttering footsteps and hurried embassies for outside help, and then, after a lull, the scared sobbings and the shuffling tread of those who bore a heavy burden into the house.

"Whoever will break it to the poor child? I couldn't for the life of me!" exclaimed a shrill voice. And while they debated the matter among themselves, Conradin made himself another piece of toast.

*James Thurber*

# THE SECRET LIFE OF WALTER MITTY

"We're going through!" The Commander's voice was like thin ice breaking. He wore his full-dress uniform, with the heavily

THE SECRET LIFE OF WALTER MITTY: By permission of the author. Copyright, 1944, by James Thurber. Originally published in *The New Yorker*.

braided white cap pulled down rakishly over one cold gray eye. "We can't make it, sir. It's spoiling for a hurricane, if you ask me." "I'm not asking you, Lieutenant Berg," said the Commander. "Throw on the power lights! Rev her up to 8,500! We're going through!" The pounding of the cylinders increased: ta-pocketa-pocketa-pocketa-*pocketa-pocketa*. The Commander stared at the ice forming on the pilot window. He walked over and twisted a row of complicated dials. "Switch on No. 8 auxiliary!" he shouted. "Switch on No. 8 auxiliary!" repeated Lieutenant Berg. "Full strength in No. 3 turret!" shouted the Commander. "Full strength in No. 3 turret!" The crew, bending to their various tasks in the huge, hurtling eight-engined Navy hydroplane, looked at each other and grinned. "The Old Man'll get us through," they said to one another. "The Old Man ain't afraid of Hell!". . .

"Not so fast! You're driving too fast!" said Mrs. Mitty. "What are you driving so fast for?"

"Hmm?" said Walter Mitty. He looked at his wife, in the seat beside him, with shocked astonishment. She seemed grossly unfamiliar, like a strange woman who had yelled at him in a crowd. "You were up to fifty-five," she said. "You know I don't like to go more than forty. You were up to fifty-five." Walter Mitty drove on toward Waterbury in silence, the roaring of the SN202 through the worst storm in twenty years of Navy flying fading in the remote, intimate airways of his mind. "You're tensed up again," said Mrs. Mitty. "It's one of your days. I wish you'd let Dr. Renshaw look you over."

Walter Mitty stopped the car in front of the building where his wife went to have her hair done. "Remember to get those overshoes while I'm having my hair done," she said. "I don't need overshoes," said Mitty. She put her mirror back into her bag. "We've been all through that," she said, getting out of the car. "You're not a young man any longer." He raced the engine a little. "Why don't you wear your gloves? Have you lost your gloves?" Walter Mitty reached in a pocket and brought out the gloves. He put them on, but after she had turned and gone into the building and he had driven on to a red light, he took them off again. "Pick it up, brother!" snapped a cop as the light changed, and Mitty hastily pulled on his gloves and lurched ahead. He drove around the streets aimlessly for a time, and then he drove past the hospital on his way to the parking lot.

... "It's the millionaire banker, Wellington McMillan," said the pretty nurse. "Yes?" said Walter Mitty, removing his gloves slowly. "Who has the case?" "Dr. Renshaw and Dr. Benbow, but there are two specialists here, Dr. Remington from New York and Mr. Pritchard-Mitford from London. He flew over." A door opened down a long, cool corridor and Dr. Renshaw came out. He looked distraught and haggard. "Hello, Mitty," he said. "We're having the devil's own time with McMillan, the millionaire banker and close personal friend of Roosevelt. Obstreosis of the ductal tract. Tertiary. Wish you'd take a look at him." "Glad to," said Mitty.

In the operating room there were whispered introductions: "Dr. Remington, Dr. Mitty. Mr. Pritchard-Mitford, Dr. Mitty." "I've read your book on streptothricosis," said Pritchard-Mitford, shaking hands. "A brilliant performance, sir." "Thank you," said Walter Mitty. "Didn't know you were in the States, Mitty," grumbled Remington. "Coals to Newcastle, bringing Mitford and me here for a tertiary." "You are very kind," said Mitty. A huge, complicated machine, connected to the operating table, with many tubes and wires, began at this moment to go pocketa-pocketa-pocketa. "The new anesthetizer is giving way!" shouted an interne. "There is no one in the East who knows how to fix it!" "Quiet, man!" said Mitty, in a low, cool voice. He sprang to the machine, which was now going pocketa-pocketa-queep-pocketa-queep. He began fingering delicately a row of glistening dials. "Give me a fountain pen!" he snapped. Someone handed him a fountain pen. He pulled a faulty piston out of the machine and inserted the pen in its place. "That will hold for ten minutes," he said. "Get on with the operation." A nurse hurried over and whispered to Renshaw, and Mitty saw the man turn pale. "Coreopsis has set in," said Renshaw nervously. "If you would take over, Mitty?" Mitty looked at him and at the craven figure of Benbow, who drank, and at the grave, uncertain faces of the two great specialists. "If you wish," he said. They slipped a white gown on him; he adjusted a mask and drew on thin gloves; nurses handed him shining ...

"Back it up, Mac! Look out for that Buick!" Walter Mitty jammed on the brakes. "Wrong lane, Mac," said the parking-lot attendant, looking at Mitty closely. "Gee. Yeh," muttered Mitty. He began cautiously to back out of the lane marked "Exit Only." "Leave her sit there," said the attendant. "I'll put her away." Mitty got out of the car. "Hey, better leave the key." "Oh," said Mitty, handing the man the ignition key. The attendant vaulted into the car, backed it up with insolent skill, and put it where it belonged.

They're so damn cocky, thought Walter Mitty, walking along Main Street; they think they know everything. Once he had tried to take his chains off, outside New Milford, and he had got them wound around the axles. A man had had to come out in a wrecking car and unwind them, a young, grinning garageman. Since then Mrs. Mitty always made him drive to a garage to have the chains taken off. The next time, he thought, I'll wear my right arm in a sling; they won't grin at me then. I'll have my right arm in a sling and they'll see I couldn't possibly take the chains off myself. He kicked at the slush on the sidewalk. "Overshoes," he said to himself, and he began looking for a shoe store.

When he came out into the street again, with the overshoes in a box under his arm, Walter Mitty began to wonder what the other thing was his wife had told him to get. She had told him twice, before they set out from their house for Waterbury. In a way he hated these weekly trips to town—he was always getting something wrong. Kleenex, he thought, Squibb's, razor blades? No. Toothpaste, toothbrush, bicarbonate, carborundum, initiative and referendum? He gave it up. But she would remember it. "Where's the what's-its-name?" she would ask. "Don't tell me you forgot the what's-its-name?" A newsboy went by shouting something about the Waterbury trial.

... "Perhaps this will refresh your memory." The District Attorney suddenly thrust a heavy automatic at the quiet figure on the witness stand. "Have you ever seen this before?" Walter Mitty took the gun and examined it expertly. "This is my Webley-Vickers 50.80," he said calmly. An excited buzz ran around the courtroom. The judge rapped for order. "You are a crack shot with any sort of firearms, I believe?" said the District Attorney, insinuatingly. "Objection!" shouted Mitty's attorney. "We have shown that the defendant could not have fired the shot. We have shown that he wore his right arm in a sling on the night of the fourteenth of July." Walter Mitty raised his hand briefly and the bickering attorneys were stilled. "With any known make of gun," he said evenly, "I could have killed Gregory Fitzhurst at three hundred feet *with my left hand*." Pandemonium broke loose in the courtroom. A woman's scream rose above the bedlam and suddenly a lovely, dark-haired girl was in Walter Mitty's arms. The District Attorney struck at her savagely. Without rising from his chair, Mitty let the man have it on the point of the chin. "You miserable cur!". . .

"Puppy biscuit," said Walter Mitty. He stopped walking and the buildings of Waterbury rose up out of the misty courtroom and surrounded him again. A woman who was passing laughed. "He said 'Puppy biscuit,' " she said to her companion. "That man said 'Puppy biscuit' to himself." Walter Mitty hurried on. He went into an A. & P., not the first one he came to but a smaller one farther up the street. "I want some biscuit for small, young dogs," he said to the clerk. "Any special brand, sir?" The greatest pistol shot in the world thought a moment. "It says 'Puppies Bark for It' on the box," said Walter Mitty.

His wife would be through at the hairdresser's in fifteen minutes, Mitty saw in looking at his watch, unless they had trouble drying it; sometimes they had trouble drying it. She didn't like to get to the hotel first; she would want him to be there waiting for her as usual. He found a big leather chair in the lobby, facing a window, and he put the overshoes and the puppy biscuit on the floor beside it. He picked up an old copy of *Liberty* and sank down into the chair. "Can Germany Conquer the World Through the Air?" Walter Mitty looked at the pictures of bombing planes and of ruined streets.

. . . "The cannonading has got the wind up in young Raleigh, sir," said the sergeant. Captain Mitty looked up at him through tousled hair. "Get him to bed," he said wearily. "With the others. I'll fly alone." "But you can't, sir," said the sergeant anxiously. "It takes two men to handle that bomber and the Archies are pounding hell out of the air. Von Richtman's circus is between here and Saulier." "Somebody's got to get that ammunition dump," said Mitty. "I'm

going over. Spot of brandy?" He poured a drink for the sergeant and one for himself. War thundered and whined around the dugout and battered at the door. There was a rending of wood and splinters flew through the room. "A bit of a near thing," said Captain Mitty carelessly. "The box barrage is closing in," said the sergeant. "We only live once, Sergeant," said Mitty, with his faint, fleeting smile. "Or do we?" He poured another brandy and tossed it off. "I never see a man could hold his brandy like you, sir," said the sergeant. "Begging your pardon, sir." Captain Mitty stood up and strapped on his huge Webley-Vickers automatic. "It's forty kilometers through hell, sir," said the sergeant. Mitty finished one last brandy. "After all," he said softly, "what isn't?" The pounding of the cannon increased; there was the rat-tat-tatting of machine guns, and from somewhere came the menacing pocketa-pocketa-pocketa of the new flame-throwers. Walter Mitty walked to the door of the dugout humming "Auprès de Ma Blonde." He turned and waved to the sergeant. "Cheerio!" he said. . . .

Something struck his shoulder. "I've been looking all over this hotel for you," said Mrs. Mitty. "Why do you have to hide in this old chair? How did you expect me to find you?" "Things close in," said Walter Mitty vaguely. "What?" Mrs. Mitty said. "Did you get the what's-its-name? The puppy biscuit? What's in that box?" "Overshoes," said Mitty. "Couldn't you have put them on in the store?" "I was thinking," said Walter Mitty. "Does it ever occur to you that I am sometimes thinking?" She looked at him. "I'm going to take your temperature when I get you home," she said.

They went out through the revolving doors that made a faintly derisive whistling sound when you pushed them. It was two blocks to the parking lot. At the drugstore on the corner she said, "Wait here for me. I forgot something. I won't be a minute." She was more than a minute. Walter Mitty lighted a cigarette. It began to rain, rain with sleet in it. He stood up against the wall of the drugstore, smoking. . . . He put his shoulders back and his heels together. "To hell with the handkerchief," said Walter Mitty scornfully. He took one last drag on his cigarette and snapped it away. Then, with that faint, fleeting smile playing about his lips, he faced the firing squad; erect and motionless, proud and disdainful, Walter Mitty the Undefeated, inscrutable to the last.

*William Faulkner*

# A ROSE FOR EMILY

## I

When Miss Emily Grierson died, our whole town went to her funeral: the men through a sort of respectful affection for a fallen monument, the women mostly out of curiosity to see the inside of her house, which no one save an old manservant—a combined gardener and cook—had seen in at least ten years.

It was a big, squarish frame house that had once been white, decorated with cupolas and spires and scrolled balconies in the heavily lightsome style of the Seventies, set on what had once been our most select street. But garages and cotton gins had encroached and obliterated even the august names of that neighborhood; only Miss Emily's house was left, lifting its stubborn and coquettish decay above the cotton wagons and the gasoline pumps—an eyesore among eyesores. And now Miss Emily had gone to join the representatives of those august names where they lay in the cedar-bemused cemetery among the ranked and anonymous graves of Union and Confederate soldiers who fell at the battle of Jefferson.

Alive, Miss Emily had been a tradition, a duty, and a care; a sort of hereditary obligation upon the town, dating from that day in 1894 when Colonel Sartoris, the mayor—he who fathered the edict that no Negro woman should appear on the streets without an apron—remitted her taxes, the dispensation dating from the death of her father on into perpetuity. Not that Miss Emily would have accepted charity. Colonel Sartoris invented an involved tale to the effect that Miss Emily's father had loaned money to the town, which the town, as a matter of business, preferred this way of repaying. Only a man of Colonel Sartoris' generation and thought could have invented it, and only a woman could have believed it.

When the next generation, with its more modern ideas, became mayors and aldermen, this arrangement created some little dissatisfaction. On the first of the year they mailed her a tax notice. February came, and there was no reply. They wrote her a formal letter, asking her to call at the sheriff's office at her convenience. A week later the mayor wrote her himself, offering to call or to send his car for her, and received in reply a note on paper of an archaic shape, in a thin, flowing calligraphy in faded ink, to the effect that she no longer went out at all. The tax notice was also enclosed, without comment.

They called a special meeting of the Board of Aldermen. A deputation waited upon her, knocked at the door through which no visitor had passed since she ceased giving china-painting lessons eight or ten years earlier. They were admitted by the old Negro into a dim hall from which a stairway mounted into still more shadow. It smelled of dust and disuse—a close, dank smell. The Negro led them into the parlor. It was furnished in heavy, leather-covered furniture. When the Negro opened the blinds of one window, they could see that the leather was cracked; and when they sat down, a faint dust rose sluggishly about their thighs, spinning with slow motes in the single sun-ray. On a tarnished gilt easel before the fireplace stood a crayon portrait of Miss Emily's father.

They rose when she entered—a small, fat woman in black, with a thin gold chain descending to her waist and vanishing into her belt, leaning on an ebony cane with a tarnished gold head. Her skeleton was small and spare; perhaps that was why what would have been merely plumpness in another was obesity in her. She looked bloated, like a body long submerged in motionless water, and of that pallid hue. Her eyes, lost in the fatty ridges of her face, looked like two small pieces of coal pressed into a lump of dough as they moved from one face to another while the visitors stated their errand.

She did not ask them to sit. She just stood in the door and listened quietly until the spokesman came to a stumbling halt. Then they could hear the invisible watch ticking at the end of the gold chain.

Her voice was dry and cold. "I have no taxes in Jefferson. Colonel Sartoris explained it to me. Perhaps one of you can gain access to the city records and satisfy yourselves."

"But we have. We are the city authorities, Miss Emily. Didn't you get a notice from the sheriff, signed by him?"

"I received a paper, yes," Miss Emily said. "Perhaps he considers himself the sheriff . . . I have no taxes in Jefferson."

"But there is nothing on the books to show that, you see. We must go by the—"

"See Colonel Sartoris. I have no taxes in Jefferson."

"But, Miss Emily—"

"See Colonel Sartoris." (Colonel Sartoris had been dead almost ten years.) "I have no taxes in Jefferson. Tobe!" The Negro appeared. "Show these gentlemen out."

## II

So she vanquished them, horse and foot, just as she had vanquished their fathers thirty years before about the smell. That was two years after her father's death and a short time after her sweetheart—the one we believed would marry her—had deserted her. After her father's death she went out very little; after her sweetheart went away, people hardly saw her at all. A few of the ladies had the temerity to call, but were not received, and the only sign of life about the place was the Negro man—a young man then—going in and out with a market basket.

"Just as if a man—any man—could keep a kitchen properly," the ladies said; so they were not surprised when the smell developed. It was another link between the gross, teeming world and the high and mighty Griersons.

A neighbor, a woman, complained to the mayor, Judge Stevens, eighty years old.

"But what will you have me do about it, madam?" he said.

"Why, send her word to stop it," the woman said. "Isn't there a law?"

"I'm sure that won't be necessary," Judge Stevens said. "It's probably just a snake or a rat that nigger of hers killed in the yard. I'll speak to him about it."

The next day he received two more complaints, one from a man who came in diffident deprecation. "We really must do something about it, Judge. I'd be the last one in the world to bother Miss Emily, but we've got to do something." That night the Board of Aldermen met—three graybeards and one younger man, a member of the rising generation.

"It's simple enough," he said. "Send her word to have her place cleaned up. Give her a certain time to do it in, and if she don't . . ."

"Dammit, sir," Judge Stevens said, "will you accuse a lady to her face of smelling bad?"

So the next night, after midnight, four men crossed Miss Emily's lawn and slunk about the house like burglars, sniffing along the base of the brickwork and at the cellar openings while one of them performed a regular sowing motion with his hand out of a sack slung from his shoulder. They broke open the cellar door and sprinkled lime there, and in all the outbuildings. As they recrossed the lawn, a window that had been dark was lighted and Miss Emily sat in it, the light behind her, and her upright torso motionless as that of an idol. They crept quietly across the lawn and into the shadow of the locusts that lined the street. After a week or two the smell went away.

That was when people had begun to feel really sorry for her. People in our town, remembering how Old Lady Wyatt, her great-aunt, had gone completely crazy at last, believed that the Griersons held themselves a little too high for what they really were. None of the young men were quite good enough for Miss Emily and such. We had long thought of them as a tableau: Miss Emily a slender figure in white in the background, her father a spraddled silhouette in the foreground, his back to her and clutching a horse-whip, the two of them framed by the back-flung front door. So when she got to be thirty and was still single, we were not pleased exactly, but vindicated; even with insanity in the family she wouldn't have turned down all of her chances if they had really materialized.

When her father died, it got about that the house was all that was left to her; and in a way, people were glad. At last they could pity Miss Emily. Being left alone, and a pauper, she had become humanized. Now she too would know the old thrill and the old despair of a penny more or less.

The day after his death all the ladies prepared to call at the house and offer condolence and aid, as is our custom. Miss Emily met them at the door, dressed as usual and with no trace of grief on her face. She told them that her father was not dead. She did that for three days, with the ministers calling on her, and the doctors, trying to persuade her to let them dispose of the body. Just as they were about to resort to law and force, she broke down, and they buried her father quickly.

We did not say she was crazy then. We believed she had to do that. We remembered all the young men her father had driven away, and we knew that with nothing left, she would have to cling to that which had robbed her, as people will.

## III

She was sick for a long time. When we saw her again, her hair was cut short, making her look like a girl, with a vague resemblance to those angels in colored church windows—sort of tragic and serene.

The town had just let the contracts for paving the sidewalks, and in the summer after her father's death they began the work. The construction company came with niggers and mules and machinery, and a foreman named Homer Barron, a Yankee—a big, dark, ready man, with a big voice and eyes lighter than his face. The little boys would follow in groups to hear him cuss the niggers, and the niggers singing in time to the rise and fall of picks. Pretty soon he knew everybody in town. Whenever you heard a lot of laughing anywhere about the square, Homer Barron would be in the center of the group. Presently we began to see him and Miss Emily on Sunday afternoons driving in the yellow-wheeled buggy and the matched team of bays from the livery stable.

At first we were glad that Miss Emily would have an interest, because the ladies all said, "Of course a Grierson would not think seriously of a Northerner, a day laborer." But there were still others, older people, who said that even grief could not cause a real lady to forget *noblesse oblige*—without calling it *noblesse oblige*. They just said, "Poor Emily. Her kinsfolk should come to her." She had some kin in Alabama; but years ago her father had fallen out with them over the estate of Old Lady Wyatt, the crazy woman, and there was no communication between the two families. They had not even been represented at the funeral.

And as soon as the old people said, "Poor Emily," the whispering began. "Do you suppose it's really so?" they said to one another. "Of course it is. What else could . . ." This behind their hands; rustling of craned silk and satin behind jalousies closed upon the sun of Sunday

afternoon as the thin, swift clop-clop-clop of the matched team passed: "Poor Emily."

She carried her head high enough—even when we believed that she was fallen. It was as if she demanded more than ever the recognition of her dignity as the last Grierson; as if it had wanted that touch of earthiness to reaffirm her imperviousness. Like when she bought the rat poison, the arsenic. That was over a year after they had begun to say "Poor Emily," and while the two female cousins were visiting her.

"I want some poison," she said to the druggist. She was over thirty then, still a slight woman, though thinner than usual, with cold, haughty black eyes in a face the flesh of which was strained across the temples and about the eye-sockets as you imagine a lighthouse-keeper's face ought to look. "I want some poison," she said.

"Yes, Miss Emily. What kind? For rats and such? I'd recom—"

"I want the best you have. I don't care what kind."

The druggist named several. "They'll kill anything up to an elephant. But what you want is—"

"Arsenic," Miss Emily said. "Is that a good one?"

"Is . . . arsenic? Yes, ma'am. But what you want—"

"I want arsenic."

The druggist looked down at her. She looked back at him, erect, her face like a strained flag. "Why, of course," the druggist said. "If that's what you want. But the law requires you to tell what you are going to use it for."

Miss Emily just stared at him, her head tilted back in order to look him eye for eye, until he looked away and went and got the arsenic and wrapped it up. The Negro delivery boy brought her the package; the druggist didn't come back. When she opened the package at home there was written on the box, under the skull and bones: "For rats."

## IV

So the next day we all said, "She will kill herself"; and we said it would be the best thing. When she had first begun to be seen with Homer Barron, we had said, "She will marry him." Then we said, "She will persuade him yet," because Homer himself had remarked—

he liked men, and it was known that he drank with the younger men in the Elks' Club—that he was not a marrying man. Later we said, "Poor Emily" behind the jalousies as they passed on Sunday afternoon in the glittering buggy, Miss Emily with her head high and Homer Barron with his hat cocked and a cigar in his teeth, reins and whip in a yellow glove.

Then some of the ladies began to say that it was a disgrace to the town and a bad example to the young people. The men did not want to interfere, but at last the ladies forced the Baptist minister—Miss Emily's people were Episcopal—to call upon her. He would never divulge what happened during that interview, but he refused to go back again. The next Sunday they again drove about the streets, and the following day the minister's wife wrote to Miss Emily's relations in Alabama.

So she had blood-kin under her roof again and we sat back to watch developments. At first nothing happened. Then we were sure that they were to be married. We learned that Miss Emily had been to the jeweler's and ordered a man's toilet set in silver, with the letter H. B. on each piece. Two days later we learned that she had bought a complete outfit of men's clothing, including a nightshirt, and we said, "They are married." We were really glad. We were glad because the two female cousins were even more Grierson than Miss Emily had ever been.

So we were not surprised when Homer Barron—the streets had been finished some time since—was gone. We were a little disappointed that there was not a public blowing-off, but we believed that he had gone on to prepare for Miss Emily's coming, or to give her a chance to get rid of the cousins. (By that time it was a cabal, and we were all Miss Emily's allies to help circumvent the cousins.) Sure enough, after another week they departed. And, as we had expected all along, within three days Homer Barron was back in town. A neighbor saw the Negro man admit him at the kitchen door at dusk one evening.

And that was the last we saw of Homer Barron. And of Miss Emily for some time. The Negro man went in and out with the market basket, but the front door remained closed. Now and then we would see her at a window for a moment, as the men did that night when they sprinkled the lime, but for almost six months she did not appear on the streets. Then we knew that this was to be expected too; as if that quality of her father which had thwarted her woman's life so many times had been too virulent and too furious to die.

When we next saw Miss Emily, she had grown fat and her hair was turning gray. During the next few years it grew grayer and grayer until it attained an even pepper-and-salt iron-gray, when it ceased turning. Up to the day of her death at seventy-four it was still that vigorous iron-gray, like the hair of an active man.

From that time on her front door remained closed, save for a period of six or seven years, when she was about forty, during which she gave lessons in china-painting. She fitted up a studio in one of the downstairs rooms, where the daughters and granddaughters of Colonel Sartoris' contemporaries were sent to her with the same regularity and in the same spirit that they were sent to church on Sundays with a twenty-five-cent piece for the collection plate. Meanwhile her taxes had been remitted.

Then the newer generation became the backbone and the spirit of the town, and the painting pupils grew up and fell away and did not send their children to her with boxes of color and tedious brushes and pictures cut from the ladies' magazines. The front door closed upon the last one and remained closed for good. When the town got free postal delivery, Miss Emily alone refused to let them fasten the metal numbers above her door and attach a mailbox to it. She would not listen to them.

Daily, monthly, yearly we watched the Negro grow grayer and more stooped, going in and out with the market basket. Each December we sent her a tax notice, which would be returned by the post office a week later, unclaimed. Now and then we would see her in one of the downstairs windows—she had evidently shut up the top floor of the house—like the carven torso of an idol in a niche, looking or not looking at us, we could never tell which. Thus she passed from generation to generation—dear, inescapable, impervious, tranquil, and perverse.

And so she died. Fell ill in the house filled with dust and shadows, with only a doddering Negro man to wait on her. We did not even know she was sick; we had long since given up trying to get any information from the Negro. He talked to no one, probably not even to her, for his voice had grown harsh and rusty, as if from disuse.

She died in one of the downstairs rooms, in a heavy walnut bed with a curtain, her gray head propped on a pillow yellow and moldy with age and lack of sunlight.

## V

The Negro met the first of the ladies at the front door and let them in, with their hushed, sibilant voices and their quick, curious glances, and then he disappeared. He walked right through the house and out the back and was not seen again.

The two female cousins came at once. They held the funeral on the second day, with the town coming to look at Miss Emily beneath a mass of bought flowers, with the crayon face of her father musing profoundly above the bier and the ladies sibilant and macabre; and the very old men—some in their brushed Confederate uniforms—on the porch and the lawn, talking of Miss Emily as if she had been a contemporary of theirs, believing that they had danced with her and courted her perhaps, confusing time with its mathematical progression, as the old do, to whom all the past is not a diminishing road but, instead, a huge meadow which no winter ever quite touches, divided from them now by the narrow bottle-neck of the most recent decade of years.

Already we knew that there was one room in that region above stairs which no one had seen in forty years, and which would have to be forced. They waited until Miss Emily was decently in the ground before they opened it.

The violence of breaking down the door seemed to fill this room with pervading dust. A thin, acrid pall as of the tomb seemed to lie everywhere upon this room decked and furnished as for a bridal: upon the valence curtains of faded rose color, upon the rose-shaded lights, upon the dressing table, upon the delicate array of crystal and the man's toilet things backed with tarnished silver, silver so tarnished that the monogram was obscured. Among them lay a collar and tie, as if they had just been removed, which, lifted, left upon the surface a pale crescent in the dust. Upon a chair hung the suit, carefully folded; beneath it the two mute shoes and the discarded socks.

The man himself lay in the bed.

For a long while we just stood there, looking down at the profound and fleshless grin. The body had apparently once lain in the attitude of an embrace, but now the long sleep that outlasts love, that conquers even the grimace of love, had cuckolded him. What was left of him, rotted beneath what was left of the nightshirt, had become inextricable from the bed in which he lay; and upon him and upon the pillow beside him lay that even coating of the patient and biding dust.

Then we noticed that in the second pillow was the indentation of a head. One of us lifted something from it, and leaning forward, that faint and invisible dust dry and acrid in the nostrils, we saw a long strand of iron-gray hair.

## *Franz Kafka*

# A HUNGER ARTIST

In recent decades there has been a distinct falling-off in the interest shown in hunger-artists. Whereas in earlier times one could stage such exhibitions at one's own expense and be quite sure of success, today such a thing is utterly impossible. Those were other times. In those days the entire city occupied itself with the hunger-artist; the interest in him grew from fast day to fast day; every one wanted to see the hunger-artist at least once a day, and in the latter stages there were regular subscribers who sat before the small latticed cage for days on end. Performances were given at night too, in order to heighten the effect by torchlight. On sunny days the cage was carried out into the open, and on these occasions it was especially the children to whom the hunger-artist was exhibited. But whereas for the adults he was often no more than a source of amusement, of which they partook only because it was the stylish thing to do, the children would gaze upon him open-mouthed, holding one another by the hand for safety's sake, as he sat there on his straw, scorning even so much as a chair, deathly pale, dressed in black tights, his ribs protruding powerfully, sometimes nodding politely and answering questions with a forced smile, even thrusting his arm through the bars

A HUNGER ARTIST: From the *Rocky Mountain Review*, 1946. Used with permission of the translator, Marion L. Neilsen, and *Western Review*.

to let them feel his emaciation, then lapsing once more into complete self-absorption and paying attention to no one, ignoring even the striking of the clock which was the cage's sole decoration, looking straight before him with eyes almost closed, and sipping occasionally from a tiny glass of water to wet his lips.

Besides the spectators who merely came and went, there were also regular guards chosen by the public—usually butchers, for some remarkable reason, and always by threes—to whom was assigned the task of watching the hunger-artist day and night, lest he might succeed after all in surreptitiously partaking of nourishment. But that was no more than a formality, introduced to satisfy the masses, because the initiated were well aware that the hunger-artist would never under any circumstances, not even under compulsion, partake of any nourishment during the period of fasting. His honor as an artist forbade such a thing. Of course not every guard could comprehend this. Sometimes there were groups of watchers who were very lax in their guard duty, who would purposely sit down together in a distant corner and absorb themselves in a game of cards with the obvious intention of allowing the hunger-artist a little refreshment which they seemed to believe he could produce from some secret supply. To the hunger-artist nothing was more painful than such guards; they filled him with unspeakable sadness; they made fasting terribly difficult for him. Sometimes he would overcome his weakness and sing during such a watch as this, sing as long as his strength held out, just to show the people how unjust were their suspicions. But it availed him little; in such cases they would simply marvel at the cleverness which enabled him to eat even while singing. Much more to his liking were the guards who sat down close to the cage, and not satisfied with the gloomy illumination of the hall, turned upon him the pocket torches with which they had been provided by the impresario. The bright light bothered him not at all. Sleep was impossible in any case, and he could always drowse a little, under any illumination and at any hour, even when the hall was noisy and overcrowded. He was only too willing to pass the night with such watchers entirely without sleep; he would put himself out to joke with them, to tell them tales of his wanderings or

on the other hand to listen to their stories: anything to stay awake, to be able to show them again and again that he had nothing edible in his cage and that he was fasting as none of them could possibly do. But his happiest moment was when morning came and a sumptuous breakfast was brought to them at his expense, and he saw them fall upon it with the appetite of healthy men who had spent a tiresome night in wakeful watching. To be sure there were people who pretended to see in this breakfast an unseemly attempt to influence the guards, but that was going too far, and when they were asked whether they would be willing to take upon themselves the task of watching through the night for the sake of the thing itself and without the breakfast, they made a wry face, though they continued to harbor their suspicions just the same.

After all, this was simply one of the suspicions unavoidably connected with fasting. Obviously no one was in a position to spend every day and night as a watchman at the side of the hunger-artist, and no one could be sure from his own observation that the fasting was really uninterrupted and complete; only the hunger-artist himself could know that, and so only he who was the faster could be at the same time a completely satisfied spectator of his fasting. And yet for another reason he never was satisfied. Perhaps it wasn't fasting at all which made him so emaciated that some people to their great regret had to stay away because they couldn't bear the sight of him; perhaps his emaciation came solely from his dissatisfaction with himself. For the fact was that only he and no one else, not even the initiated, knew how easy a thing it was to fast. It was the easiest thing in the world. He didn't keep it a secret either, but no one would believe him. At best people said he was modest, but usually he was accused of being a publicity hound or even an out-and-out fraud for whom fasting was easy because he knew how to make it easy, and who had the cheek on top of that practically to admit as much. All this he was forced to accept; he had become accustomed to it in the course of years; but inside him was the constant gnawing of dissatisfaction.

And yet never, never once at the end of any hunger period—this all were forced to admit— had he left his cage willingly. The impresario had set forty days as the maximum period for fasting, beyond that he would never let the fasting go, not even in the great world centers—and for a very good reason. Experience had shown that for about forty days, through the use of gradually intensified publicity, the interest of a city could be brought to an ever higher pitch, but that at the end of that time public enthusiasm began to wane and a marked decrease in patronage became apparent. There were of course minor differences in this respect from city to city and country to country, but the rule was that forty days was the maximum time. And so on the fortieth day the door of the flower-bedecked cage was opened, an enthusiastic audience filled the amphitheater, a military band played, two doctors entered the cage to carry out the necessary measurements on the body of the hunger-artist, the results were announced to the hall through a megaphone, and finally there came two young ladies, happy in the knowledge that they and no one else had been chosen for the task, whose duty it was to lead the hunger-artist from his cage and down a few steps at the bottom of which stood a tiny table set with a carefully-chosen invalid's repast. And at this moment the hunger-artist invariably rebelled. He was willing enough to place his bony arms into the helping hands which the young ladies extended as they bent over him, but he didn't want to stand up. Why stop just now, at the end of forty days? He could have borne it much longer, immeasurably longer; why stop just now, at the point when his fasting was at its best—no, not even yet at its best. Why did they want to rob him of the honor of fasting on, of becoming not only the greatest hunger-artist of all time, which he probably was already, but of surpassing himself beyond measure, for he sensed that there was no limit to his capacity for fasting. Why did this throng, which pretended to marvel so at his feat, have so little patience with him? If he could bear to go on fasting, why could they not bear with him? Besides he was weary, his seat in the straw was comfortable, and now they wanted him to rouse himself, stand up, and go to the meal, the very thought of which induced in him a nausea which he was barely able to suppress out of respect for the women. And he looked into the eyes of the women who appeared so friendly but were in reality so cruel

and wearily shook the head which was so much too heavy for the fragile neck. But now there happened the thing which always happened at this point. The impresario would come, and silently—for the music rendered speech impossible—he would raise his arms over the hunger-artist as if inviting heaven to look down upon its work here upon the straw, this pitiful martyr —and martyr the hunger-artist was, to be sure, though in an entirely different sense. Then he would grasp the hunger-artist about his frail waist, trying as he did to make it obvious by his exaggerated caution with what a fragile object he was dealing, and, after surreptitiously shaking him a little and causing his legs to wobble and his body to sway uncontrollably, would turn him over to the ladies, who had meanwhile turned as pale as death. Now the hunger-artist offered no further resistance. His head lay on his chest, as if it had rolled there and somehow inexplicably stuck fast; his torso was cavernous; his legs, impelled by the urge to self-preservation, were pressed tightly together at the knees, and yet his feet scraped the earth as if it were not real, as if they were seeking the real one. And the entire weight of his body, light though it was, rested upon one of the ladies, who, breathless and looking about imploringly for help (she had not pictured this post of honor thus), first tried to avoid contact with the hunger-artist by stretching her neck as far as possible, and then—since this availed her nothing and her more fortunate companion did nothing to help her, but simply contented herself with carrying the hand of the hunger-artist, a mere bundle of bones, in her own trembling hand—she broke into tears to the accompaniment of delighted laughter from the audience, and had to be relieved at her post by an attendant who had long been held in readiness. Then came the meal, a little of which the impresario managed to force down the half-unconscious hunger-artist, the while he chattered amiably to divert attention from his condition; then a toast was spoken to the public, which the impresario pretended had been whispered to him by the hunger-artist; the orchestra provided a mighty climax with a flourish of trumpets; the crowd broke up, and no one had the right to be dissatisfied with what he had seen, no one but the hunger-artist, always only he.

And so it went on for many years, with only

brief intervals of recuperation. He lived in apparent glory, honored by the world, but for the most part filled with a gloomy melancholy which was deepened by the fact that no one understood it. And indeed what comfort could one offer him? What else could he wish for? And when sometimes a good-natured person appeared who felt sorry for him and tried to explain to him that his sadness was caused by the lack of food, it was quite likely—especially if the fasting period was far advanced—that the hunger-artist would answer by flying into a rage and terrifying all those around him by shaking the bars of his cage like a wild animal. But for such outbreaks the impresario had a method of punishment which he was very fond of employing. He would apologize to the assembled public on behalf of the hunger-artist and admit that his conduct could be pardoned only by understanding the irritability caused by fasting, an irritability which would be less easy to understand in a well-fed person; then he would lead logically to the hunger-artist's claim—also to be explained by his over-wrought state—that he could fast much longer, and would praise the lofty endeavor, worthy determination and great self-denial which were evidenced by this claim. But then he would attempt to refute this claim simply by passing around photographs—which at the same time were offered for sale —in which one could see the hunger-artist on the fortieth day of fasting, lying in bed and so weak that he was on the point of expiring. This perversion of the truth, so well known to the hunger-artist, and yet so unnerving when applied, was more than he could bear. That which was the effect of the premature ending of the fasting was here being set forth as its cause! Against this lack of understanding, this universal lack of understanding, it was impossible to fight. Each time he would stand at the bars and listen eagerly to what the impresario was saying, but always when the photographs were brought forth he would relax his hold on the bars and sink back onto the straw, and once more the reassured public could come near and view him undisturbed.

When the witnesses of such scenes thought back on them a few years later, they found it hard to understand themselves. For meanwhile the aforementioned transformation had taken place. Perhaps there were deep-lying reasons for it; but who was interested in seeking them

out? At any rate, the pampered hunger-artist one day found himself abandoned by the pleasure-seeking multitude, which preferred to flock to other spectacles. Once again the impresario raced through half of Europe with him to see whether the old interest would not here and there manifest itself. But in vain; as if by some secret agreement a genuine dislike for fasting exhibitions had everywhere developed. In reality of course it couldn't have come as suddenly as all that, and now one tardily remembered certain warning signs which at the time, in the intoxication of success, had not been sufficiently heeded or sufficiently combatted— but it was too late now to do anything about it. To be sure it was certain that one day the time for fasting would come again, but for the living that was no comfort. What was the hunger-artist to do now?—He whom thousands had acclaimed couldn't put himself on display in the exhibition booths at small annual fairs, and as for going into some other profession he was not only too old but above all too fanatically devoted to fasting. And so he dismissed the impresario, the companion of a brilliant career, and hired himself out to a great circus. In order to spare his feelings, he did not even examine the terms of his contract.

A great circus with its huge throng of contrasting yet complementary men and animals and its masses of equipment can always find a place for another attraction, even a hunger-artist—that is, if his claims are modest enough. But in this case it was not only the hunger-artist who was engaged, but also his old and well-known name itself. Indeed it wasn't even possible to say, in view of the peculiar nature of this art which showed no flagging with increasing age, that a superannuated artist no longer at the height of his powers had taken refuge in a quiet position with a circus. On the contrary: the hunger-artist gave assurance that he could fast as well as he ever could—a thoroughly credible claim—indeed, he even maintained that, if allowed to go his own way (a privilege immediately granted to him), he would only now for the first time set the world in justifiable astonishment, a claim which, in view of the temper of the times, forgotten by the hunger-artist in his zeal, evoked no more than a smile from those who were in the know.

Actually, however, even the hunger-artist did not lose sight of the true state of affairs, and he was not at all surprised when he saw that his cage was stationed not in the middle of the circus as a feature attraction but out in the vicinity of the menagerie, a place which in its own way certainly was accessible enough. Large, gaily-colored signs surrounded the cage and proclaimed what was to be seen there. During the intermissions in the performances, when the crowds thronged to see the animals fed, it was almost unavoidable that they should pass by the hunger-artist and pause there for a little. Perhaps they would have stayed there longer had it not been for the fact that the people who were pushing impatiently from the rear in the narrow alley way, not understanding the reason for the delay on the way to the eagerly-awaited stalls, made a longer and more leisurely view impossible. This explained too why the hunger-artist, though longing impatiently for these visits, which he naturally saw as his reason for existence, couldn't help feeling at the same time a certain apprehension. At first he could scarcely wait for the intermissions; he would note the approach of the throng with charmed anticipation; but only too soon he became convinced of the fact that again and again, without exception, they were on their way to the animals, and his experience in this matter overcame even the most stubborn, almost conscious self-deception. And this view of the throng from a distance continued to be the most agreeable one. For once they had reached his cage, he was immediately submerged in a sea of shouting, cursing people who formed ever-changing groups, one made up of those who wanted to view him at their leisure—not because they had any understanding for him, but simply impelled by a whim or out of sheer willfulness (and these soon became for the hunger-artist the more unpleasant)—and the other consisting of those who were bent on getting immediately to the stalls. Once the great crowd had passed by, there would come the stragglers, and these of course, for whom there was no obstacle to stopping had they only felt the desire, strode by with hurried steps in order not to be late at the stalls. And it was no more than a fortunate but infrequent stroke of luck when the father of a family would come by with his children, point to the hunger-artist, and explain in detail what it was all about; and he would tell about earlier times when he had been present at similar but incomparably finer ex-

hibitions. But naturally the children, on account of inadequate preparation in the schools and in life, always remained without any understanding. What did fasting mean to them? And yet in the sparkling of their penetrating eyes they gave a hint of new and more merciful days to come. Perhaps, the hunger-artist would say to himself on such occasions, everything would be better if his station were not quite so close to the animals. It made the choice too easy for the people, to say nothing of the fact that the evil odors from the stalls, the restlessness of the animals at night, the sight of pieces of raw meat for the beasts of prey being carried by, and the screams of the animals at feeding time offended him and kept him in a constant state of depression. But he didn't venture to complain to the management; after all he owed to the animals the fact that he had so many visitors, among whom there might be now and then one destined for him. And who knew to what spot they might banish him if he reminded them of his existence, and of the fact that, when seen aright, he served only as a hindrance on the way to the animals.

A minor hindrance, to be sure, and one that was constantly growing smaller. People came to take for granted the novelty of having anyone demand attention for a hunger-artist in modern times, and this taking-for-granted spelled his doom. Let him fast with all the skill of which he was capable—and he did—but nothing could save him now, people simply passed him by. Just try to explain the art of fasting to some one! He who has no feeling for it simply cannot comprehend it. The beautiful signs grew dirty and illegible; they were torn down, and it occurred to no one to replace them. The little board showing the number of days of fasting achieved, which at first had been conscientiously changed, had remained the same for weeks on end, for the attendants had grown weary even of this little task. And so the hunger-artist fasted on without hindrance, as he had once dreamed of doing, and was able to do it without difficulty, just as he had once predicted, but no one counted the days; no one, not even the hunger-artist himself, knew how great his achievement actually was, and his heart grew heavy. And if on occasion some idler stopped, ridiculed the old numbers on the board, and spoke of fraud, it was the most stupid lie which indifference and inborn malice could possibly invent, because it was not the hunger-artist who was cheating; he was doing his duty honorably, but the world was cheating him of his reward.

And yet more days passed, but that too had its end. Once one of the managers happened to notice the cage, and he asked the attendants why such a good serviceable cage with its putrid straw should be left standing unused. No one could say, until one of them, with the help of the numbered board, remembered the hunger-artist. The straw was probed with poles, and inside they found the hunger-artist. "You're still fasting?" asked the manager. "When in heaven's name will you be done?" "Forgive me, all of you," whispered the hunger-artist. "Certainly," said the manager, and he pointed to his head with his finger to indicate the hunger-artist's condition to the attendants, "we forgive you." "I always wanted you to admire my fasting," said the hunger-artist. "And we do admire it," replied the manager obligingly. "But you shouldn't admire it," said the hunger-artist. "Well, then, we don't admire it," said the manager, "but why shouldn't we admire it?" "Because I have to fast, I can't help myself," said the hunger-artist. "Just listen to that," said the manager; "and why can't you help yourself?" "Because," said the hunger-artist, and he lifted his dainty head a little, and, thrusting his lips forward as if for a kiss, spoke directly into the manager's ear so that no word would be lost, "because I could find no food to my liking. If I had found it, believe me, I should have caused no stir, I should have eaten my fill just as you do, and all others." Those were his last words, but in his glazed eyes there remained the firm, though no longer proud, conviction that he was still fasting.

"Well, now clean things up!" said the manager, and they buried the hunger-artist together with the straw. And into the cage they put a young panther. It was perceptibly refreshing even to the dullest temperament to see this wild animal hurl itself about in this cage which so long had been desolate. He lacked for nothing. Without any delay, the keepers brought him just the kind of food he craved. And he appeared not even to miss his freedom. This noble body, healthy to the point of bursting, seemed in fact to carry its own freedom around with it (a freedom which appeared to reside somewhere in the region of its teeth); and its joy in

living issued forth from its throat with such fierceness that it wasn't easy for those who watched it to stand firm. But they overcame their hesitation, crowded about the cage, and just couldn't tear themselves away.

*William Wordsworth*

# RESOLUTION AND INDEPENDENCE

### I

There was a roaring in the wind all night:
The rain came heavily and fell in floods;
But now the sun is rising calm and bright;
The birds are singing in the distant woods;
Over his own sweet voice the Stock-dove broods;
The Jay makes answer as the Magpie chatters;
And all the air is filled with pleasant noise of
  waters.

### II

All things that love the sun are out of doors;
The sky rejoices in the morning's birth;
The grass is bright with rain-drops;—on the
  moors               10
The hare is running races in her mirth;
And with her feet she from the plashy earth
Raises a mist; that, glittering in the sun,
Runs with her all the way, wherever she doth run.

### III

I was a Traveller then upon the moor;
I saw the hare that raced about with joy;
I heard the woods and distant waters roar;
Or heard them not, as happy as a boy:
The pleasant season did my heart employ:
My old remembrances went from me wholly;  20
And all the ways of men, so vain and melancholy.

### IV

But, as it sometimes chanceth, from the might
Of joy in minds that can no further go,
As high as we have mounted in delight
In our dejection do we sink as low;
To me that morning did it happen so;
And fears and fancies thick upon me came;
Dim sadness—and blind thoughts, I knew not, nor
  could name.

### V

I heard the skylark warbling in the sky;
And I bethought me of the playful hare:                    30
Even such a happy child of earth am I;
Even as these blissful creatures do I fare;
Far from the world I walk, and from all care;
But there may come another day to me—
Solitude, pain of heart, distress, and poverty.

### VI

My whole life I have lived in pleasant thought,
As if life's business were a summer mood;
As if all needful things would come unsought
To genial faith, still rich in genial good;
But how can He expect that others should       40
Build for him, sow for him, and at his call
Love him, who for himself will take no heed at all?

### VII

I thought of Chatterton, the marvellous Boy,
The sleepless Soul that perished in his pride;
Of Him [12] who walked in glory and in joy
Following his plough, along the mountainside:
By our own spirits are we deified:
We Poets in our youth begin in gladness;
But thereof come in the end despondency and
    madness.

### VIII

Now, whether it were by peculiar grace,       50
A leading from above, a something given,
Yet it befell that, in this lonely place,
When I with these untoward thoughts had striven,
Beside a pool bare to the eye of heaven
I saw a Man before me unawares:
The oldest man he seemed that ever wore grey
    hairs.

### IX

As a huge stone is sometimes seen to lie
Couched on the bald top of an eminence;
Wonder to all who do the same espy,
By what means it could thither come, and
    whence;                                               60
So that it seems a thing endued with sense:
Like a sea-beast crawled forth, that on a shelf
Of rock or sand reposeth, there to sun itself;

### X

Such seemed this Man, not all alive nor dead,
Nor all asleep—in his extreme old age:

---

[12] Robert Burns.

His body was bent double, feet and head
Coming together in life's pilgrimage;
As if some dire constraint of pain, or rage
Of sickness felt by him in times long past,
A more than human weight upon his frame had
    cast.                                                 70

### XI

Himself he propped, limbs, body, and pale face,
Upon a long grey staff of shaven wood:
And, still as I drew near with gentle pace,
Upon the margin of that moorish flood
Motionless as a cloud the old Man stood,
That heareth not the loud winds when they call;
And moveth all together, if it move at all.

### XII

At length, himself unsettling, he 'the pond
Stirred with his staff, and fixedly did look
Upon the muddy water, which he conned,       80
As if he had been reading in a book:
And now a stranger's privilege I took;
And, drawing to his side, to him did say,
"This morning gives us promise of a glorious day."

### XIII

A gentle answer did the old Man make,
In courteous speech which forth he slowly drew:
And him with further words I thus bespake,
"What occupation do you there pursue?
This is a lonesome place for one like you."
Ere he replied, a flash of mild surprise       90
Broke from the sable orbs of his yet-vivid eyes.

### XIV

His words came feebly, from a feeble chest,
But each in solemn order followed each,
With something of a lofty utterance drest—
Choice word and measured phrase, above the
    reach
Of ordinary men; a stately speech;
Such as grave Livers do in Scotland use,
Religious men, who give to God and man their
    dues.

### XV

He told, that to these waters he had come
To gather leeches, being old and poor:       100
Employment hazardous and wearisome!
And he had many hardships to endure:
From pond to pond he roamed, from moor to
    moor;

Housing, with God's good help, by choice or
    chance;
And in this way he gained an honest maintenance.

### XVI

The old Man still stood talking by my side;
But now *his* voice to me was like a stream
Scarce heard; nor word from word could I divide;
And the whole body of the Man did seem
Like one whom I had met with in a dream;    110
Or like a man from some far region sent,
To give me human strength, by apt admonishment.

### XVII

My former thoughts returned: the fear that kills;
And hope that is unwilling to be fed;
Cold, pain, and labour, and all fleshly ills;
And mighty Poets in their misery dead.
—Perplexed, and longing to be comforted,
My question eagerly did I renew,
"How is it that you live, and what is it you do?"

### XVIII

He with a smile did then his words repeat;    120
And said that, gathering leeches, far and wide
He travelled; stirring thus about his feet
The waters of the pools where they abide.
"Once I could meet with them on every side;
But they have dwindled long by slow decay;
Yet still I persevere, and find them where I may."

### XIX

While he was talking thus, the lonely place,
The old Man's shape, and speech—all troubled
    me:
In my mind's eye I seemed to see him pace
About the weary moors continually,    130
Wandering about alone and silently.
While I these thoughts within myself pursued,
He, having made a pause, the same discourse
    renewed.

### XX

And soon with this he other matter blended,
Cheerfully uttered, with demeanour kind,
But stately in the main; and, when he ended,
I could have laughed myself to scorn to find
In that decrepit Man so firm a mind.
"God," said I, "be my help and stay secure;
I'll think of the Leech-gatherer on the lonely
    moor!"    140

*Percy Bysshe Shelley*
# ODE TO THE WEST WIND

### I

O wild West Wind, thou breath of Autumn's being,
Thou, from whose unseen presence the leaves dead
Are driven, like ghosts from an enchanter fleeing,

Yellow, and black, and pale, and hectic red,
Pestilence-stricken multitudes: O thou,
Who chariotest to their dark wintry bed

The wingèd seeds, where they lie cold and low,
Each like a corpse within its grave, until
Thine azure sister of the Spring shall blow

Her clarion o'er the dreaming earth, and fill    10
(Driving sweet buds like flocks to feed in air)
With living hues and odours plain and hill:

Wild Spirit, which art moving everywhere;
Destroyer and preserver; hear, oh, hear!

### II

Thou on whose stream, mid the steep sky's
    commotion,
Loose clouds like earth's decaying leaves are shed,
Shook from the tangled boughs of Heaven and
    Ocean,

Angels of rain and lightning: there are spread
On the blue surface of thine aëry surge,
Like the bright hair uplifted from the head    20

Of some fierce Maenad,[13] even from the dim verge
Of the horizon to the zenith's height,
The locks of the approaching storm. Thou dirge

Of the dying year, to which this closing night
Will be the dome of a vast sepulchre,
Vaulted with all thy congregated might

Of vapours, from whose solid atmosphere
Black rain, and fire, and hail will burst: oh, hear!

---

[13] Female worshipper of Bacchus or Dionysus.

III

Thou who didst waken from his summer dreams
The blue Mediterranean, where he lay,          30
Lulled by the coil of his crystàlline streams,

Beside a pumice isle in Baiae's [14] bay,
And saw in sleep old palaces and towers
Quivering within the wave's intenser day,

All overgrown with azure moss and flowers
So sweet, the sense faints picturing them! Thou
For whose path the Atlantic's level powers

Cleave themselves into chasms, while far below
The sea-blooms and the oozy woods which wear
The sapless foliage of the ocean, know          40

Thy voice, and suddenly grow gray with fear,
And tremble and despoil themselves: oh, hear!

IV

If I were a dead leaf thou mightest bear;
If I were a swift cloud to fly with thee;
A wave to pant beneath thy power, and share

The impulse of thy strength, only less free
Than thou, O uncontrollable! If even
I were as in my boyhood, and could be

The comrade of thy wanderings over Heaven,
As then, when to outstrip thy skiey speed          50
Scarce seemed a vision; I would ne'er have striven

As thus with thee in prayer in my sore need.
Oh, lift me as a wave, a leaf, a cloud!
I fall upon the thorns of life! I bleed!

A heavy weight of hours has chained and bowed
One too like thee: tameless, and swift, and proud.

V

Make me thy lyre, even as the forest is:
What if my leaves are falling like its own!
The tumult of thy mighty harmonies

Will take from both a deep, autumnal tone,          60
Sweet though in sadness. Be thou, Spirit fierce,
My spirit! Be thou me, impetuous one!

Drive my dead thoughts over the universe
Like withered leaves to quicken a new birth!
And, by the incantation of this verse,

[14] Small bay near Naples.

Scatter, as from an unextinguished hearth
Ashes and sparks, my words among mankind!
Be through my lips to unawakened earth

The trumpet of a prophecy! O, Wind,
If Winter comes, can Spring be far behind?          70

## Edwin Arlington Robinson
# RICHARD CORY

Whenever Richard Cory went down town,
    We people on the pavement looked at him:
He was a gentleman from sole to crown,
    Clean favored, and imperially slim.

And he was always quietly arrayed,
    And he was always human when he talked;
But still he fluttered pulses when he said,
    "Good-morning," and he glittered when he
        walked.

And he was rich—yes, richer than a king,
    And admirably schooled in every grace:          10
In fine, we thought that he was everything
    To make us wish that we were in his place.

So on we worked, and waited for the light,
    And went without the meat, and cursed the
        bread;
And Richard Cory, one calm summer night,
    Went home and put a bullet through his head.

RICHARD CORY: From *The Children of the Night,*
1897, by Edwin Arlington Robinson. Used by permission of Charles Scribner's Sons.

## Edwin Arlington Robinson
# THE MILL

The miller's wife had waited long,
    The tea was cold, the fire was dead;
And there might yet be nothing wrong

THE MILL: From *Collected Poems,* by Edwin
Arlington Robinson. Copyright, 1935, 1937, by The
Macmillan Company. Used by permission of the
publishers.

In how he went and what he said:
"There are no millers any more,"
    Was all that she had heard him say;
And he had lingered at the door
    So long that it seemed yesterday.

Sick with a fear that had no form
    She knew that she was there at last;          10
And in the mill there was a warm
    And mealy fragrance of the past.
What else there was would only seem
    To say again what he had meant;
And what was hanging from a beam
    Would not have heeded where she went.

And if she thought it followed her,
    She may have reasoned in the dark
That one way of the few there were
    Would hide her and would leave no mark:     20
Black water, smooth above the weir
    Like starry velvet in the night,
Though ruffled once, would soon appear
    The same as ever to the sight.

# A. E. Housman
# BE STILL, MY SOUL

Be still, my soul, be still; the arms you bear are
    brittle,
    Earth and high heaven are fixt of old and
    founded strong.
Think rather,—call to thought, if now you grieve
    a little,
    The days when we had rest, O soul, for they
    were long.

Men loved unkindness then, but lightless in the
    quarry
    I slept and saw not; tears fell down, I did not
    mourn;

Sweat ran and blood sprang out and I was never
    sorry:
    Then it was well with me, in days ere I was born.

Now, and I muse for why and never find the
    reason,
    I pace the earth, and drink the air, and feel the
    sun.                                          10
Be still, be still, my soul; it is but for a season:
    Let us endure an hour and see injustice done.

Ay, look: high heaven and earth ail from the prime
    foundation;
    All thoughts to rive the heart are here, and all
    are vain:
Horror and scorn and hate and fear and indigna-
    tion—
    Oh why did I awake? when shall I sleep again?

# John Milton
# SAMSON

*The Scene, before the Prison in Gaza.*

SAMSON. A little onward lend thy guiding hand
To these dark steps, a little further on;
For yonder bank hath choice of sun or shade.
There I am wont to sit, when any chance
Relieves me from my task of servile toil,
Daily in the common prison else enjoined me,
Where I, a prisoner chained, scarce freely draw
The air, imprisoned also, close and damp,
Unwholesome draught. But here I feel amends—
The breath of heaven fresh blowing, pure and
    sweet,                                        10
With day-spring born; here leave me to respire.
This day a solemn feast the people hold
To Dagon, their sea-idol, and forbid
Laborious works. Unwillingly this rest
Their superstition yields me; hence, with leave
Retiring from the popular noise, I seek
This unfrequented place to find some ease—
Ease to the body some, none to the mind
From restless thoughts, that, like a deadly swarm
Of hornets armed, no sooner found alone           20
But rush upon me thronging, and present
Times past, what once I was, and what am now.
Oh, wherefore was my birth from heaven foretold
Twice by an angel, who at last, in sight

Of both my parents, all in flames ascended
From off the altar where an offering burned,
As in a fiery column charioting
His godlike presence, and from some great act
Or benefit revealed to Abraham's race?
Why was my breeding ordered and prescribed    30
As of a person separate to God,
Designed for great exploits, if I must die
Betrayed, captived, and both my eyes put out,
Made of my enemies the scorn and gaze,
To grind in brazen fetters under task
With this heaven-gifted strength? O glorious
   strength,
Put to the labor of a beast, debased
Lower than bond-slave! Promise was that I
Should Israel from Philistian yoke deliver!
Ask for this great deliverer now, and find him    40
Eyeless in Gaza, at the mill with slaves,
Himself in bonds under Philistian yoke.
Yet stay; let me not rashly call in doubt
Divine prediction. What if all foretold
Had been fulfilled but through mine own default?
Whom have I to complain of but myself,
Who this high gift of strength committed to me,
In what part lodged, how easily bereft me,
Under the seal of silence could not keep,
But weakly to a woman must reveal it,    50
O'ercome with importunity and tears?
O impotence of mind in body strong!
But what is strength without a double share
Of wisdom? Vast, unwieldy, burdensome,
Proudly secure, yet liable to fall
By weakest subtleties; not made to rule,
But to subserve where wisdom bears command.
God, when he gave me strength, to show withal
How slight the gift was, hung it in my hair.
But peace! I must not quarrel with the will    60
Of highest dispensation, which herein
Haply had ends above my reach to know.
Suffices that to me strength is my bane,
And proves the source of all my miseries—
So many, and so huge, that each apart
Would ask a life to wail. But, chief of all,
O loss of sight, of thee I most complain!
Blind among enemies! O worse than chains,
Dungeon, or beggary, or decrepit age!
Light, the prime work of God, to me is extinct,    70
And all her various objects of delight
Annulled, which might in part my grief have eased.
Inferior to the vilest now become
Of man or worm, the vilest here excel me:
They creep, yet see; I, dark in light, exposed
To daily fraud, contempt, abuse, and wrong,

Within doors, or without, still as a fool,
In power of others, never in my own—
Scarce half I seem to live, dead more than half.
O dark, dark, dark, amid the blaze of noon,    80
Irrecoverably dark, total eclipse
Without all hope of day!
O first-created beam, and thou great Word,
"Let there be light, and light was over all,"
Why am I thus bereaved thy prime decree?
The sun to me is dark
And silent as the moon,
When she deserts the night,
Hid in her vacant interlunar cave.
Since light so necessary is to life,    90
And almost life itself, if it be true
That light is in the soul,
She all in every part, why was the sight
To such a tender ball as the eye confined,
So obvious and so easy to be quenched,
And not, as feeling, through all parts diffused,
That she might look at will through every pore?
Then had I not been thus exiled from light,
As in the land of darkness, yet in light,
To live a life half dead, a living death,    100
And buried; but, O yet more miserable!
Myself my sepulchre, a moving grave:
Buried, yet not exempt
By privilege of death and burial
From worst of other evils, pains, and wrongs;
But made hereby obnoxious more
To all the miseries of life,
Life in captivity
Among inhuman foes.

# Robert Browning
# FRA LIPPO LIPPI

I am poor brother Lippo, by your leave!
You need not clap your torches to my face.
Zooks, what's to blame? you think you see a monk!
What, it's past midnight, and you go the rounds,
And here you catch me at an alley's end
Where sportive ladies leave their doors ajar?
The Carmine's [15] my cloister: hunt it up,
Do,—harry out, if you must show your zeal,
Whatever rat, there, haps on his wrong hole,
And nip each softling of a wee white mouse,    10

--------

[15] A monastery of Del Carmine Friars.

*Weke, weke,* that's crept to keep him company!
Aha, you know your betters! Then, you'll take
Your hand away that's fiddling on my throat,
And please to know me likewise. Who am I?
Why, one, sir, who is lodging with a friend
Three streets off—he's a certain . . . how d'ye call?
Master—a . . . Cosimo of the Medici,[16]
In the house that caps the corner. Boh! you were
   best!
Remember and tell me, the day you're hanged,
How you affected such a gullet's-gripe!          20
But you, sir, it concerns you that your knaves
Pick up a manner nor discredit you:
Zooks, are we pilchards,[17] that they sweep the
   streets
And count fair prize what comes into their net?
He's Judas to a tittle, that man is!
Just such a face! why, sir, you make amends.
Lord, I'm not angry! Bid your hang-dogs go
Drink out this quarter-florin to the health
Of the munificent House that harbours me
(And many more beside, lads! more beside!)     30
And all's come square again. I'd like his face—
His, elbowing on his comrade in the door
With the pike and lantern,—for the slave that
   holds
John Baptist's head a-dangle by the hair
With one hand ("Look you, now," as who should
   say)
And his weapon in the other, yet unwiped!
It's not your chance to have a bit of chalk,
A wood-coal or the like? or you should see!
Yes, I'm the painter, since you style me so.
What, brother Lippo's doings, up and down,     40
You know them and they take you? like enough!
I saw the proper twinkle in your eye—
'Tell you, I liked your looks at very first.
Let's sit and set things straight now, hip to haunch.
Here's spring come, and the nights one makes up
   bands
To roam the town and sing out carnival,
And I've been three weeks shut within my mew,
A-painting for the great man, saints and saints
And saints again. I could not paint all night—
Ouf! I leaned out of window for fresh air.      50
There came a hurry of feet and little feet,
A sweep of lute-strings, laughs, and whiffs of
   song,—
*Flower o' the broom,*

Take away love, and our earth is a tomb!
*Flower o' the quince,*
*I let Lisa go, and what good in life since?*
*Flower o' the thyme*—and so on. Round they
   went.
Scarce had they turned the corner when a titter
Like the skipping of rabbits by moonlight,—three
   slim shapes—
And a face that looked up . . . zooks, sir, flesh and
   blood,                                        60
That's all I'm made of! Into shreds it went,
Curtain and counterpane and coverlet,
All the bed-furniture—a dozen knots,
There was a ladder! Down I let myself,
Hands and feet, scrambling somehow, and so
   dropped,
And after them. I came up with the fun
Hard by Saint Laurence,[18] hail fellow, well met,—
*Flower o' the rose,*
*If I've been merry, what matter who knows?*
And so as I was stealing back again            70
To get to bed and have a bit of sleep
Ere I rise up to-morrow and go work
On Jerome [19] knocking at his poor old breast
With his great round stone to subdue the flesh,
You snap me of the sudden. Ah, I see!
Though your eye twinkles still, you shake your
   head—
Mine's shaved,—a monk, you say—the sting's in
   that!
If Master Cosimo announced himself,
Mum's the word naturally; but a monk!
Come, what am I a beast for? tell us, now!       80
I was a baby when my mother died
And father died and left me in the street.
I starved there, God knows how, a year or two
On fig-skins, melon-parings, rinds and shucks,
Refuse and rubbish. One fine frosty day
My stomach being empty as your hat,
The wind doubled me up and down I went.
Old Aunt Lapaccia trussed me with one hand,
(Its fellow was a stinger as I knew)
And so along the wall, over the bridge,          90
By the straight cut to the convent. Six words there,
While I stood munching my first bread that month:
"So, boy, you're minded," quoth the good fat
   father
Wiping his own mouth, 'twas refection-time,—
"To quit this very miserable world?

---

[16] Banker and patron of the arts, the real ruler of
Florence.
[17] Sardines.

[18] Church of San Lorenzo.
[19] St. Jerome, who translated the Bible into Latin.

Will you renounce" ... The mouthful of bread?
  thought I;
By no means! Brief, they made a monk of me;
I did renounce the world, its pride and greed,
Palace, farm, villa, shop and banking-house,
Trash, such as these poor devils of Medici        100
Have given their hearts to—all at eight years old.
Well, sir, I found in time, you may be sure,
'Twas not for nothing—the good bellyful,
The warm serge and the rope that goes all round,
And day-long blessed idleness beside!
"Let's see what the urchin's fit for"—that came
  next.
Not overmuch their way, I must confess.
Such a to-do! they tried me with their books:
Lord, they'd have taught me Latin in pure waste!
*Flower o' the clove,*                                    110
*All the Latin I construe is, "amo" I love!*
But, mind you, when a boy starves in the streets
Eight years together, as my fortune was,
Watching folk's faces to know who will fling
The bit of half-stripped grape-bunch he desires,
And who will curse or kick him for his pains,—
Which gentleman processional and fine,
Holding a candle to the Sacrament
Will wink and let him lift a plate and catch
The droppings of the wax to sell again,         120
Or holla for the Eight [20] and have him whipped,—
How say I?—nay, which dog bites, which lets drop
His bone from the heap of offal in the street,—
Why, soul and sense of him grow sharp alike,
He learns the look of things, and none the less
For admonition from the hunger-pinch.
I had a store of such remarks, be sure,
Which, after I found leisure, turned to use.
I drew men's faces on my copy-books,
Scrawled them within the antiphonary's marge,[21]
Joined legs and arms to the long music-notes,    130
Found eyes and nose and chin for A's and B's,
And made a string of pictures of the world
Betwixt the ins and outs of verb and noun,
On the wall, the bench, the door. The monks
  looked black.
"Nay," quoth the Prior, "turn him out, d'ye say?
In no wise. Lose a crow and catch a lark.
What if at last we get our man of parts,
We Carmelites, like those Camaldolese
And Preaching Friars, to do our church up
  fine                                                    140
And put the front on it that ought to be!"

And hereupon they bade me daub away.
Thank you! my head being crammed, the walls a
  blank,
Never was such prompt disemburdening.
First, every sort of monk, the black and white,
I drew them, fat and lean: then, folk at church,
From good old gossips waiting to confess
Their cribs [22] of barrel-droppings, candle-ends,—
To the breathless fellow at the altar-foot,
Fresh from his murder, safe and sitting there    150
With the little children round him in a row
Of admiration, half for his beard and half
For that white anger of his victim's son
Shaking a fist at him with one fierce arm,
Signing himself with the other because of Christ
(Whose sad face on the cross sees only this
After the passion of a thousand years)
Till some poor girl, her apron o'er her head,
(Which the intense eyes looked through) came at
  eve
On tiptoe, said a word, dropped in a loaf,       160
Her pair of earrings and a bunch of flowers
(The brute took growling), prayed, and so was
  gone.
I painted all, then cried " 'T is ask and have;
Choose, for more's ready!"—laid the ladder flat,
And showed my covered bit of cloister-wall.
The monks closed in a circle and praised loud
Till checked, taught what to see and not to see,
Being simple bodies,—"That's the very man!
Look at the boy who stoops to pat the dog!
That woman's like the Prior's niece who comes   170
To care about his asthma: it's the life!"
But there my triumph's straw-fire flared and
  funked;
Their betters took their turn to see and say:
The Prior and the learned pulled a face
And stopped all that in no time. "How? what's
  here?
Quite from the mark of painting, bless us all!
Faces, arms, legs and bodies like the true
As much as pea and pea! it's devil's-game!
Your business is not to catch men with show,
With homage to the perishable clay,              180
But lift them over it, ignore it all,
Make them forget there's such a thing as flesh.
Your business is to paint the souls of men—
Man's soul, and it's a fire, smoke ... no, it's not ...
It's vapour done up like a new-born babe—
(In that shape when you die it leaves your mouth)
It's ... well, what matters talking, it's the soul!

---

[20] The governing magistrates of Florence.
[21] Margin of the choir book.

[22] Petty thefts.

Give us no more of body than shows soul!
Here's Giotto,[23] with his Saint a-praising God,
That sets us praising,—why not stop with him? 190
Why put all thoughts of praise out of our heads
With wonder at lines, colours, and what not?
Paint the soul, never mind the legs and arms!
Rub all out, try at it a second time.
Oh, that white smallish female with the breasts,
She's just my niece . . . Herodias,[24] I would say,—
Who went and danced and got men's heads cut off!
Have it all out!" Now, is this sense, I ask?
A fine way to paint soul, by painting body
So ill, the eye can't stop there, must go
    further                                          200
And can't fare worse! Thus, yellow does for white
When what you put for yellow's simply black,
And any sort of meaning looks intense
When all beside itself means and looks nought.
Why can't a painter lift each foot in turn,
Left foot and right foot, go a double step,
Make his flesh liker and his soul more like,
Both in their order? Take the prettiest face,
The Prior's niece . . . patron-saint—is it so pretty
You can't discover if it means hope, fear,    210
Sorrow or joy? won't beauty go with these?
Suppose I've made her eyes all right and blue,
Can't I take breath and try to add life's flash,
And then add soul and heighten them threefold?
Or say there's beauty with no soul at all—
(I never saw it—put the case the same—)
If you get simple beauty and nought else,
You get about the best thing God invents:
That's somewhat: and you'll find the soul you have
    missed,
Within yourself, when you return him thanks. 220
"Rub all out!" Well, well, there's my life, in short,
And so the thing has gone on ever since.
I'm grown a man no doubt, I've broken bounds:
You should not take a fellow eight years old
And make him swear to never kiss the girls.
I'm my own master, paint now as I please—
Having a friend, you see, in the Cornerhouse!
Lord, it's fast holding by the rings in front—
Those great rings serve more purposes than just
To plant a flag in, or tie up a horse!          230
And yet the old schooling sticks, the old grave eyes
Are peeping o'er my shoulders as I work,
The heads shake still—"It's art's decline, my son!
You're not of the true painters, great and old;

Brother Angelico's [25] the man, you'll find;
Brother Lorenzo [26] stands his single peer:
Fag on at flesh, you'll never make the third!"
*Flower o' the pine,*
*You keep your mistr . . . manners, and I'll stick to*
*mine!*
I'm not the third, then: bless us, they must
    know!                                           240
Don't you think they're the likeliest to know,
They with their Latin? So, I swallow my rage,
Clench my teeth, suck my lips in tight, and paint
To please them—sometimes do, and sometimes
    don't;
For, doing most, there's pretty sure to come
A turn, some warm eve finds me at my saints—
A laugh, a cry, the business of the world—
(*Flower o' the peach,*
*Death for us all, and his own life for each!*)
And my whole soul revolves, the cup runs
    over,                                            250
The world and life's too big to pass for a dream,
And I do these wild things in sheer despite,
And play the fooleries you catch me at,
In pure rage! The old mill-horse, out at grass
After hard years, throws up his stiff heels so,
Although the miller does not preach to him
The only good of grass is to make chaff.
What would men have? Do they like grass or no—
May they or mayn't they? all I want's the thing
Settled for ever one way. As it is,            260
You tell too many lies and hurt yourself:
You don't like what you only like too much,
You do like what, if given you at your word,
You find abundantly detestable.
For me, I think I speak as I was taught;
I always see the garden and God there
A-making man's wife: and, my lesson learned,
The value and significance of flesh,
I can't unlearn ten minutes afterwards.

You understand me: I'm a beast, I know.    270
But see, now—why, I see as certainly
As that the morning-star's about to shine,
What will hap some day. We've a youngster here
Comes to our convent, studies what I do,
Slouches and stares and lets no atom drop—
His name is Guidi [27]—he'll not mind the monks—
They call him Hulking Tom, he lets them talk—
He picks my practice up—he'll paint apace,

---

[23] Giotto di Bondone (1276?–1337), Florentine
painter.
[24] Mother of Salome.

[25] Fra Angelico, 1387–1455, Florentine painter.
[26] Lorenzo Monaco, painter and Lippi's teacher.
[27] Tommaso Guidi, 1401–1428.

I hope so—though I never live so long,
I know what's sure to follow. You be judge!     280
You speak no Latin more than I, belike;
However, you're my man, you've seen the world
—The beauty and the wonder and the power,
The shapes of things, their colours, lights and
    shades,
Changes, surprises,—and God made it all!
—For what? do you feel thankful, ay or no,
For this fair town's face, yonder river's line,
The mountain round it and the sky above,
Much more the figures of man, woman, child,
These are the frame to? What's it all about?     290
To be passed over, despised? or dwelt upon,
Wondered at? oh, this last of course!—you say.
But why not do as well as say,—paint these
Just as they are, careless what comes of it?
God's works—paint any one, and count it crime
To let a truth slip. Don't object, "His works
Are here already; nature is complete:
Suppose you reproduce her—(which you can't)
There's no advantage! you must beat her, then."
For, don't you mark? we're made so that we
    love                                         300
First when we see them painted, things we have
    passed
Perhaps a hundred times nor cared to see;
And so they are better, painted—better to us,
Which is the same thing. Art was given for that;
God uses us to help each other so,
Lending our minds out. Have you noticed, now,
Your cullion's [28] hanging face? A bit of chalk,
And trust me but you should, though! How much
    more,
If I drew higher things with the same truth!
That were to take the Prior's pulpit-place,     310
Interpret God to all of you! Oh, oh,
It makes me mad to see what men shall do
And we in our graves! This world's no blot for us,
Nor blank; it means intensely, and means good:
To find its meaning is my meat and drink.
"Ay, but you don't so instigate to prayer!"
Strikes in the Prior: "when your meaning's plain
It does not say to folk—remember matins,
Or, mind you fast next Friday!" Why, for this
What need of art at all? A skull and bones,     320
Two bits of stick nailed crosswise, or, what's best,
A bell to chime the hour with, does as well.
I painted a Saint Laurence [29] six months since
At Prato,[30] splashed the fresco in fine style:

"How looks my painting, now the scaffold's
    down?"
I ask a brother: "Hugely," he returns—
"Already not one phiz [31] of your three slaves
Who turn the Deacon off his toasted side,
But's scratched and prodded to our heart's content,
The pious people have so eased their own     330
When coming to say prayers there in a rage:
We get on fast to see the bricks beneath.
Expect another job this time next year,
For pity and religion grow i' the crowd—
Your painting serves its purpose!" Hang the fools!

—That is—you'll not mistake an idle word
Spoke in a huff by a poor monk, God wot,
Tasting the air this spicy night which turns
The unaccustomed head like Chianti wine!
Oh, the church knows! don't misreport me,
    now!                                         340
It's natural a poor monk out of bounds
Should have his apt word to excuse himself:
And hearken how I plot to make amends.
I have bethought me: I shall paint a piece
. . . There's for you! Give me six months, then go,
    see
Something in Sant' Ambrogio's! [32] Bless the nuns!
They want a cast o' my office. I shall paint
God in the midst, Madonna and her babe,
Ringed by a bowery flowery angel-brood,
Lilies and vestments and white faces, sweet     350
As puff on puff of grated orris-root
When ladies crowd to church at midsummer.
And then i' the front, of course a saint or two—
Saint John, because he saves the Florentines,
Saint Ambrose, who puts down in black and white
The convent's friends and gives them a long day,
And Job, I must have him there past mistake,
The man of Uz (and Us without the z,
Painters who need his patience). Well, all these
Secured at their devotions, up shall come     360
Out of a corner when you least expect,
As one by a dark stair into a great light,
Music and talking, who but Lippo! I!—
Mazed, motionless and moon-struck—I'm the
    man!
Back I shrink—what is this I see and hear?
I, caught up with my monk's-things by mistake,
My old serge gown and rope that goes all round,
I, in this presence, this pure company!
Where's a hole, where's a corner for escape?

---

[28] A vulgar fellow.
[29] St. Laurence, martyred by being burned alive.
[30] Town near Florence.

[31] Face (from *physiognomy*).
[32] Convent in Florence.

Then steps a sweet angelic slip of a thing      370
Forward, puts out a soft palm—"Not so fast!"
—Addresses the celestial presence, "nay—
He made you and devised you, after all,
Though he's none of you! Could Saint John there
    draw—
His camel-hair make up a painting-brush?
We come to brother Lippo for all that,
*Iste perfect opus!*" [33] So, all smile—
I shuffle sideways with my blushing face
Under the cover of a hundred wings
Thrown like a spread of kirtles when you're
    gay                                           380

And play hot cockles, all the doors being shut,
Till, wholly unexpected, in there pops
The hothead husband! Thus I scuttle off
To some safe bench behind, not letting go
The palm of her, the little lily thing
That spoke the good word for me in the nick,
Like the Prior's niece . . . Saint Lucy, I would say.
And so all's saved for me, and for the church
A pretty picture gained. Go, six months hence!
Your hand, sir, and good-bye: no lights, no
    lights!                                       390
The street's hushed, and I know my own way back,
Don't fear me! There's the grey beginning. Zooks!

[33] "This person executed the work."

## T. S. Eliot

# THE LOVE SONG OF
# J. ALFRED PRUFROCK

*S'io credesse che mia risposta fosse
A persona che mai tornasse al mondo,
Questa fiamma staria senza piu scosse.
Ma perciocche giammai di questo fondo
Non torno vivo alcun, s'i'odo il vero,
Senza tema d'infamia ti rispondo.* [34]

Let us go then, you and I,
When the evening is spread out against the sky
Like a patient etherized upon a table;
Let us go, through certain half-deserted streets,
The muttering retreats
Of restless nights in one-night cheap hotels
And sawdust restaurants with oyster-shells:
Streets that follow like a tedious argument
Of insidious intent
To lead you to an overwhelming question . . .      10
Oh, do not ask, "What is it?"
Let us go and make our visit.

[34] From Dante's *Inferno,* XXVII, 61-6: As Dante is being conducted through the Inferno by Virgil, the spirit (*i.e.,* the flame) of Count Guido da Montefeltro approaches and inquires about the people of his country. Dante then requests Guido to relate why he is condemned to torment and Guido, who had broken his oath, replies: "If I thought I were answering someone who would ever return to the [upper] world, this flame would shake no more, but since no one ever did return alive from this depth (if what I hear be true), I answer you without fear of infamy."

In the room the women come and go
Talking of Michelangelo.[35]

The yellow fog that rubs its back upon the window-panes,
The yellow smoke that rubs its muzzle on the window-panes
Licked its tongue into the corners of the evening,
Lingered upon the pools that stand in drains,
Let fall upon its back the soot that falls from chimneys,
Slipped by the terrace, made a sudden leap,                                    20
And seeing that it was a soft October night,
Curled once about the house, and fell asleep.

And indeed there will be time
For the yellow smoke that slides along the street,
Rubbing its back upon the window-panes;
There will be time, there will be time
To prepare a face to meet the faces that you meet;
There will be time to murder and create,
And time for all the works and days of hands
That lift and drop a question on your plate;                                    30
Time for you and time for me,
And time yet for a hundred indecisions,
And for a hundred visions and revisions,
Before the taking of a toast and tea.

In the room the women come and go
Talking of Michelangelo.

And indeed there will be time
To wonder, "Do I dare?" and, "Do I dare?"
Time to turn back and descend the stair,
With a bald spot in the middle of my hair—                                     40
(They will say: "How his hair is growing thin!")
My morning coat, my collar mounting firmly to the chin,
My necktie rich and modest, but asserted by a simple pin—
(They will say: "But how his arms and legs are thin!")
Do I dare
Disturb the universe?
In a minute there is time
For decisions and revisions which a minute will reverse.

For I have known them all already, known them all:—
Have known the evenings, mornings, afternoons,                                 50
I have measured out my life with coffee spoons;
I know the voices dying with a dying fall
Beneath the music from a farther room.
  So how should I presume?

And I have known the eyes already, known them all—
The eyes that fix you in a formulated phrase,
And when I am formulated, sprawling on a pin,

---

[35] 1475–1564, the great Florentine painter and sculptor.

When I am pinned and wriggling on the wall,
Then how should I begin
To spit out all the butt-ends of my days and ways?                    60
   And how should I presume?

And I have known the arms already, known them all—
Arms that are braceleted and white and bare
(But in the lamplight, downed with light brown hair!)
Is it perfume from a dress
That makes me so digress?
Arms that lie along a table, or wrap about a shawl.
   And should I then presume?
   And how should I begin?

     .     .     .     .     .

Shall I say, I have gone at dusk through narrow streets             70
And watched the smoke that rises from the pipes
Of lonely men in shirt-sleeves, leaning out of windows? . . .

I should have been a pair of ragged claws
Scuttling across the floors of silent seas.

     .     .     .     .     .

And the afternoon, the evening, sleeps so peacefully!
Smoothed by long fingers,
Asleep . . . tired . . . or it malingers,
Stretched on the floor, here beside you and me.
Should I, after tea and cakes and ices,
Have the strength to force the moment to its crisis?                80
But though I have wept and fasted, wept and prayed,
Though I have seen my head (grown slightly bald) brought in upon a platter,[36]
I am no prophet—and here's no great matter;
I have seen the moment of my greatness flicker,
And I have seen the eternal Footman hold my coat, and snicker,
And in short, I was afraid.

And would it have been worth it, after all,
After the cups, the marmalade, the tea,
Among the porcelain, among some talk of you and me,
Would it have been worth while,                                    90
To have bitten off the matter with a smile,
To have squeezed the universe into a ball
To roll it toward some overwhelming question,
To say: "I am Lazarus,[37] come from the dead,
Come back to tell you all, I shall tell you all"—
If one, settling a pillow by her head,
   Should say: "That is not what I meant at all,
   That is not it, at all."

     .     .     .     .     .

And would it have been worth it, after all,
Would it have been worth while,                                    100

---

[36] Reference is to the murder of John the Baptist.
[37] The brother of Mary and Martha who was raised from the dead by Jesus.

After the sunsets and the dooryards and the sprinkled streets,
After the novels, after the teacups, after the skirts that trail along the floor—
And this, and so much more?—
It is impossible to say just what I mean!
But as if a magic lantern threw the nerves in patterns on a screen:
Would it have been worth while
If one, settling a pillow or throwing off a shawl,
And turning toward the window, should say:
   "That is not it at all,
   That is not what I meant, at all."                                    110

     .     .     .     .     .

No! I am not Prince Hamlet, nor was meant to be;
Am an attendant lord, one that will do
To swell a progress,[38] start a scene or two,
Advise the prince; no doubt, an easy tool,
Deferential, glad to be of use,
Politic, cautious, and meticulous;
Full of high sentence,[39] but a bit obtuse;
At times, indeed, almost ridiculous—
Almost, at times, the Fool.

I grow old . . . I grow old . . .                                          120
I shall wear the bottoms of my trousers rolled.

Shall I part my hair behind? Do I dare to eat a peach?
I shall wear white flannel trousers, and walk upon the beach.
I have heard the mermaids singing, each to each.

I do not think that they will sing to me.

I have seen them riding seaward on the waves
Combing the white hair of the waves blown back
When the wind blows the water white and black.

We have lingered in the chambers of the sea
By sea-girls wreathed with seaweed red and brown                           130
Till human voices wake us, and we drown.

---

[38] Take a minor part in a royal march or promenade.
[39] Noble-sounding but empty statements.

## Matthew Arnold
# THE SCHOLAR-GIPSY

Go, for they call you, shepherd, from the hill;
  Go, shepherd, and untie the wattled cotes! [40]
   No longer leave thy wistful flock unfed,

[40] Shed for sheep.

Nor let thy bawling fellows rack their throats,
  Nor the cropped herbage shoot another head.
   But when the fields are still,
And the tired men and dogs all gone to rest,
  And only the white sheep are sometimes seen
  Cross and recross the strips of moon-blanched green,
   Come, shepherd, and again begin the quest! [41]

[41] i.e., the search for the "scholar-gipsy." In his
Vanity of Dogmatizing (1661), Joseph Glanvil had
told the anecdote of the scholar who went to live with
the gipsies (see lines 31 ff).

Here, where the reaper was at work of late—   10
In this high field's dark corner, where he leaves
His coat, his basket, and his earthen cruse,[42]
And in the sun all morning binds the sheaves,
Then here, at noon, comes back his stores to
use—
Here will I sit and wait,
While to my ear from uplands far away
The bleating of the folded flocks is borne,
With distant cries of reapers in the corn—
All the live murmur of a summer's day.   20

Screened is this nook o'er the high, half-reaped
field,
And here till sun-down, shepherd! will I be.
Through the thick corn the scarlet poppies
peep,
And round green roots and yellowing stalks I
see
Pale pink convolvulus[43] in tendrils creep;
And air-swept lindens yield
Their scent, and rustle down their perfumed
showers
Of bloom on the bent grass where I am laid,
And bower me from the August sun with
shade;
And the eye travels down to Oxford's towers.  30

And near me on the grass lies Glanvil's book—
Come, let me read the oft-read tale again!
The story of the Oxford scholar poor,
Of pregnant parts and quick inventive brain,
Who, tired of knocking at preferment's door,
One summer-morn forsook
His friends, and went to learn the gipsy-lore,
And roamed the world with that wild brother-
hood,
And came, as most men deemed, to little
good,
But came to Oxford and his friends no more.  40

But once, years after, in the country-lanes,
Two scholars, whom at college erst he knew,
Met him, and of his way of life enquired;
Whereat he answered, that the gipsy-crew,
His mates, had arts to rule as they desired
The workings of men's brains,
And they can bind them to what thoughts they
will.
"And I," he said, "the secret of their art,
When fully learned, will to the world impart;

But it needs heaven-sent moments for   this
skill."                                        50

This said, he left them, and returned no more.—
But rumours hung about the countryside,
That the lost Scholar long was seen to stray,
Seen by rare glimpses, pensive and tongue-tied,
In hat of antique shape, and cloak of grey,
The same the gipsies wore.
Shepherds had met him on the Hurst[44] in
spring;
At some lone alehouse in the Berkshire moors,
On the warm ingle-bench,[45] the smock-
frocked boors
Had found him seated at their entering,        60

But, 'mid their drink and clatter, he would fly.
And I myself seem half to know thy looks,
And put the shepherds, wanderer! on thy
trace;
And boys who in lone wheatfields scare the
rooks
I ask if thou hast passed their quiet place;
Or in my boat I lie
Moored to the cool bank in the summer-heats,
'Mid wide grass meadows which the sunshine
fills,
And watch the warm, green-muffled Cumner
hills,[46]
And wonder if thou haunt'st their   shy
retreats.                                      70

For most, I know, thou lov'st retired ground!
Thee at the ferry Oxford riders blithe,
Returning home on summer-nights, have met
Crossing the stripling Thames at Bablock-
hithe,[47]
Trailing in the cool stream thy fingers wet,
As the punt's rope chops round;
And leaning backward in a pensive dream,
And fostering in thy lap a heap of flowers
Plucked in shy fields and distant Wych-
wood[48] bowers,
And thine eyes resting on the moonlit stream.  80

And then they land, and thou art seen no more!—
Maidens, who from the distant hamlets come

---

[42] Water jug.
[43] The morning glory.

[44] Cumner Hurst, a hill southwest of Oxford.
[45] A chimney-corner bench.
[46] Hills southwest of Oxford.
[47] Where the river may be crossed by a ferry-boat
operated on a cable.
[48] Wychwood Forest, northwest of Oxford.

To dance around the Fyfield [49] elm in May,
Oft through the darkening fields have seen thee
    roam,
    Or cross a stile into the public way.
    Oft thou hast given them store
Of flowers—the frail-leafed, white anemony,
    Dark bluebells drenched with dews of summer
        eves,
    And purple orchises [50] with spotted leaves—
But none hath words she can report of thee.   90

And, above Godstow Bridge,[51] when haytime's
    here
In June, and many a scythe in sunshine flames,
    Men who through those wide fields of breezy
        grass
    Where black-winged swallows haunt the glitter-
        ing Thames,
    To bathe in the abandoned lasher [52] pass,
        Have often passed thee near
Sitting upon the river bank o'ergrown;
    Marked thine outlandish garb, thy figure
        spare,
    Thy dark vague eyes, and soft abstracted
        air—
But, when they came from bathing, thou wast
    gone!                                      100

At some lone homestead in the Cumner hills,
    Where at her open door the housewife darns,
    Thou hast been seen, or hanging on a gate
To watch the threshers in the mossy barns.
    Children, who early range these slopes and
        late
        For cresses from the rills,
Have known thee eying, all an April-day,
    The springing pastures and the feeding
        kine;
    And marked thee, when the stars come out
        and shine,
Through the long dewy grass move slow
    away.                                      110

In autumn, on the skirts of Bagley wood [53]
Where most the gipsies by the turf-edged way
    Pitch their smoked tents, and every bush you
        see
With scarlet patches tagged and shreds of grey,
    Above the forest-ground called Thessaly—
        The blackbird, picking food,

Sees thee, nor stops his meal, nor fears at all;
    So often has he known thee past him stray,
    Rapt, twirling in thy hand a withered spray,
And waiting for the spark from heaven to
    fall.                                      120

And once, in winter, on the causeway chill
    Where home through flooded fields foot-
        travellers go,
    Have I not passed thee on the wooden bridge,
Wrapt in thy cloak and battling with the snow,
    Thy face towards Hinksey [54] and its wintry
        ridge?
    And thou hast climbed the hill,
And gained the white brow of the Cumner
    range;
    Turned once to watch, while thick the snow-
        flakes fall,
    The line of festal light in Christ-Church
        hall [55]—
Then sought thy straw in some sequestered
    grange.[56]                               130

But what—I dream! Two hundred years are flown
    Since first thy story ran through Oxford halls,
    And the grave Glanvil did the tale inscribe
That thou wert wandered from the studious
    walls
    To learn strange arts, and join a gipsy-tribe;
        And thou from earth art gone
Long since, and in some quiet churchyard laid—
    Some country-nook, where o'er thy unknown
        grave
    Tall grasses and white flowering nettles wave,
Under a dark, red-fruited yew-tree's shade.  140

—No, no, thou hast not felt the lapse of hours!
    For what wears out the life of mortal men?
    'Tis that from change to change their being
        rolls;
    'Tis that repeated shocks, again, again,
        Exhaust the energy of strongest souls
            And numb the elastic powers.
Till having used our nerves with bliss and teen,[57]
    And tired upon a thousand schemes our wit,
    To the just-pausing Genius [58] we remit
Our worn-out life, and are—what we have
    been.                                      150

---

[49] Village southwest of Oxford.
[50] Wild orchids, lady's-slippers.
[51] Bridge over Thames, southwest of Oxford.
[52] Pool below a dam.
[53] Forest southwest of Oxford.

[54] Village south of Oxford.
[55] Dining hall of Christ Church, an Oxford college.
[56] Farm.
[57] Sorrow.
[58] One's attendant spirit, according to ancient
Roman belief.

Thou hast not lived, why should'st thou perish, so?
   Thou hadst *one* aim, *one* business, *one* desire;
      Else wert thou long since numbered with the
         dead!
   Else hadst thou spent, like other men, thy fire!
      The generations of thy peers are fled,
         And we ourselves shall go;
   But thou possessest an immortal lot,
      And we imagine thee exempt from age
      And living as thou liv'st on Glanvil's page,
   Because thou hadst—what we, alas! have
      not.                                                160

For early didst thou leave the world, with powers
   Fresh, undiverted to the world without,
      Firm to their mark, not spent on other things;
   Free from the sick fatigue, the languid doubt,
      Which much to have tried, in much been
         baffled, brings.
      O life unlike to ours!
Who fluctuate idly without term or scope,
   Of whom each strives, nor knows for what
      he strives,
   And each half lives a hundred different lives;
Who wait like thee, but not, like thee, in
      hope.                                               170

Thou waitest for the spark from heaven! and we,
   Light half-believers of our casual creeds,
      Who never deeply felt, nor clearly willed,
   Whose insight never has borne fruit in deeds,
      Whose vague resolves never have been
         fulfilled;
      For whom each year we see
Breeds new beginnings, disappointments new;
   Who hesitate and falter life away,
   And lose to-morrow the ground won to-day—
Ah! do not we, wanderer! await it too?        180

Yes, we await it!—but it still delays,
   And then we suffer! and amongst us one,[59]
      Who most has suffered, takes dejectedly
   His seat upon the intellectual throne;
      And all his store of sad experience he
         Lays bare of wretched days;
Tells us his misery's birth and growth and signs,
   And how the dying spark of hope was fed,
   And how the breast was soothed, and how the
      head,
And all his hourly varied anodynes.[60]        190

This for our wisest! and we others pine,
   And wish the long unhappy dream would end,
      And waive all claim to bliss, and try to bear;
   With close-lipped patience for our only friend,
      Sad patience, too near neighbour to despair—
         But none has hope like thine!
Thou through the fields and through the woods
      dost stray,
   Roaming the country-side, a truant boy,
   Nursing thy project in unclouded joy,
And every doubt long blown by time away.   200

O born in days when wits were fresh and clear,
   And life ran gaily as the sparkling Thames;
      Before this strange disease of modern life,
   With its sick hurry, its divided aims,
      Its heads o'ertaxed, its palsied hearts, was
         rife—
      Fly hence, our contact fear!
Still fly, plunge deeper in the bowering wood!
   Averse, as Dido [61] did with gesture stern
   From her false friend's approach in Hades
      turn,
Wave us away, and keep thy solitude!        210

Still nursing the unconquerable hope,
   Still clutching the inviolable shade,
      With a free, onward impulse brushing
         through,
   By night, the silvered branches of the glade—
      Far on the forest-skirts, where none pursue,
         On some mild pastoral slope
Emerge, and resting on the moonlit pales
   Freshen thy flowers as in former years
   With dew, or listen with enchanted ears,
From the dark dingles,[62] to the night-
      ingales!                                           220

But fly our paths, our feverish contact fly!
   For strong the infection of our mental strife,
      Which, though it gives no bliss, yet spoils for
         rest;
   And we should win thee from thy own fair life,
      Like us distracted, and like us unblest.
      Soon, soon thy cheer would die,
Thy hopes grow timorous, and unfixed thy
      powers,
      And thy clear aims be cross and shifting
      made;

---

[59] Probably Goethe; some think Carlyle or Tennyson.
[60] Pain-relieving drug.

[61] Queen of Carthage, deserted by Aeneas.
[62] Wooded valleys.

And then thy glad perennial youth would
    fade,
Fade, and grow old at last, and die like
    ours.                                              230

Then fly our greetings, fly our speech and smiles!
—As some grave Tyrian [63] trader, from the sea,
Descried at sunrise an emerging prow
Lifting the cool-haired creepers stealthily,
    The fringes of a southward-facing brow
        Among the Ægæan isles;
And saw the merry Grecian coaster [64] come,
    Freighted with amber grapes, and Chian [65]
    wine,
    Green, bursting figs, and tunnies [66] steeped in
    brine—
And knew the intruders on his ancient
    home,                                              240
The young light-hearted masters of the waves—
    And snatched his rudder, and shook out more
    sail;
    And day and night held on indignantly
O'er the blue Midland waters with the gale,
    Betwixt the Syrtes [67] and soft Sicily,
        To where the Atlantic raves
Outside the western straits; and unbent sails
    There, where down cloudy cliffs, through
    sheets of foam,
    Shy traffickers, the dark Iberians [68] come;
And on the beach undid his corded bales.     250

[63] From Tyre, Phoenician.
[64] Ship engaged in coastal trade.
[65] From island of Chios, in Aegean Sea.
[66] Tuna fish.
[67] Gulf on north coast of Africa.
[68] Ancient inhabitants of Spanish peninsula.

## Dylan Thomas
# THE DOCTOR
# AND THE DEVILS

## 1

MORNING

*Music.*
*From a long way off, we see a deserted road
winding downwards from a hill-top.*
*Huge sky, slow clouds.*

*A small black figure appears at the top of
the road, and moves downhill. A small black
figure with another darkness billowing around
it.*
*Now we see the downhill-approaching figure
as a top-hatted man in the wind. From our distance he is still the mystery of a man, alone in
a blowing morning on a lonely hill-top; still the
shadow, not the recognizably featured substance, of a man.*
*Closer now, we see that he is a youngish man
in severe professional black; and his long cloak
is the other darkness around him.*
*Closer still, we see his body and face as he
strides down towards us. He wields his stick
like a prophet's staff. We see the deep-set eyes
behind the large spectacles; the wide sensual
mouth tightened into its own denial; the wild
fringes of hair blowing from under the sides of
the stiff hat-rim; the coffin-shaped forehead;
the insatiable, and even predatory, curiosity of
the bent-forward head.*
*Suddenly he stops, looks down.*
*Now, with his eyes, we see the City that lies
below him. An early nineteenth-century City,
its crossing, twisting patterns of roofs at so
many different levels, its streets and houses
dangerously clambering, scaling, falling down
from the steep hill, its patchwork of threading
alleys, its compact wilderness of little arch-
wayed courts and closes, sunless dead ends,
market spaces surrounded by tumbling top-
heavy tenements, hovels, cottages, pigsties . . .*
*And now, from behind him, we see him
stride on, top-hat and stick, towards the City;
towards the rising sigh of city sounds, the
mingling and slowly loudening voices of people
and bells, the noise of hooves and wheels on
cobble stones, and street cries unintelligibly
distant.*

*DISSOLVE to*

## 2

CITY MARKET-PLACE

*And up come the City sounds.*
*The straw-strewn cobbles of the Market are
crowded with stalls. Stalls that sell rags and
bones, kept by rags and bones. Stalls that sell
odds and ends of every odd kind, odd boots,
bits of old meat, fish heads, trinkets, hats with
feathers, broadsheets, hammers. Stalls with*

*shawls. Stalls like ash bins. Anything that is marketable, to the very poor.*

*Pigs and chickens grunt, root, cluck, and peck among the straw heaps and the refuse, getting in every one's way though no one notices or cares.*

*A heaped high hay-cart rumbles over the cobbles.*

*The doors of the shops and the public-houses are open on to the Market, and singing comes from inside some of them, and outside some of them stand men and women drinking.*

*And men and women lean, drinking, against the stalls.*

*There are many, many children, some very old.*

*Among the children, the butt of their noise, is a humpback with the smile of an idiot.*

*And across the Market the man in cloak and top-hat is walking: black and purposeful among all the turbulent laziness, among the talkers, the hawkers, the old leaners, the drinkers, the shrill children.*

*We move with him.*

*Two men whom we see we will remember later. With earthenware tankards in their hands, they are standing almost in the middle of the Market. One is tall and very thin; the other squat, barrel-chested. The tall one is hollow-cheeked, corpse-pale, with jerky, inconsequent gestures; the short one full and ruddy-faced, knob-nosed, surly, slow-moving.*

*We see that the tall one is laughing: at nothing. We hear his laugh: a high-pitched snarl, an animal noise. The squat one pays no attention, but curses the whole Market with his scowling eyes.*

*We see a woman pushing a barrow heaped with rags and hucksters' scraps, and another woman trailing behind her.*

*We hear the first woman's cry as she turns into a side alley:*

Rags and bones . . . rags and bones . . . *she cries.*

*And then the cry of the second woman:*

. . . Cat-skin . . . human hair . . .

*The faces of the two women also we shall remember.*

Rags, rags . . . rags and bones . . .

Cat-skin . . . human hair . . .

*The tall man mimics the cries.*

*A hawker passes, crying her cry of:*

Fresh herrings . . . fresh herrings . . .

*We hear behind her cry the high yelping mimicry of the tall drinker.*

*The man in cloak and top-hat moves on.*

*And the noises of the Market fade as we*

DISSOLVE *to*

### 3

CITY SQUARE

*The man in cloak and top-hat is walking through the trimly treed garden in the Square towards a large building.*

*We follow him into the building.*

### 4

HALLWAY OF ROCK'S ACADEMY

*As he walks through the Hallway, a* PORTER, *in black coat, black trousers, and brass-buttoned waistcoat, approaches him. He is a little man with a very pale face.*

PORTER. They're here, Doctor Rock.

ROCK *stops.*

ROCK. Indeed, Mr. Forsythe? Who or what are "they," and where is "here"?

PORTER. The specimens for the Anatomical Museum, sir, are in the Museum.

ROCK. How fortunate they are not in the gentlemen's cloak-room. I should hate skeletons in all my cupboards. Thank you.

ROCK *walks to the end of the Hallway, opens a door, goes through.*

### 5

SMALL CLOAK-ROOM

ROCK *hangs up his hat and cloak, very neatly, puts his stick in a stand, and turns to look at himself in a full-length mirror.*

*We see, in the mirror, that he is wearing a long, dark coat, immaculately tailored, an ornate, embroidered waistcoat across which gold chains hang in festoons, a high cravat, higher than is the fashion of the gentlemen we shall see in future scenes, with its folds passed through a diamond ring, a prominent shirt-collar, delicately plaited cambrics, watch-seals and pendants, dark trousers, shining boots, a gay waist-band.*

*At all this excellence he looks with approval; he preens himself, he flicks off invisible dust.*

*Softly he says to his reflection:*

Rock. Well, Thomas. To work!

*And he crosses the Cloak-room to another door, and opens it, and walks through.*

*From the Cloak-room door we see into:*

## 6

THE ANATOMICAL MUSEUM

*It is a very large room.*

*Around the walls are anatomical specimens mounted and labelled.*

*There are specimens in glass cases, many unmounted specimens, and a great number of packing-cases of all sizes.*

*Assistants are unpacking the cases.*

*All over the floor are bones; the skeletons of birds, beasts, reptiles, fishes; odd fish; fossils; osteological curiosities; pickled monsters; brains in jars; the scattered treasures of a static, silent zoo.*

Rock, *some distance from his assistants, is opening a case and throwing aside the top layers of straw.*

*We TRACK TOWARDS him.*

*He takes a little skeleton from the case: the skeleton of a baby or a monkey.*

*A man's voice is heard.*

Man's Voice. Good Morning, Thomas.

Rock *looks round.*

*PAN ROUND to door through which a heavily built, elderly man is entering. His hair is close clipped and iron grey, his demeanour severe, his face unaccustomed to smiling.*

*Now, from the door, we see him cross over to* Rock.

*They shake hands.*

Rock *still holds the little skeleton under one arm.*

Rock. Doctor Manson! You see me to-day, sir, with one foot in the grave. Now, where is a chair?

*He looks around the Museum room.*

Rock. Perhaps you could make yourself comfortable on this case of . . .

*He glances at a label on a packing-case near him.*

Rock. . . . stomachs of cetacea. I am *sure* there was a chair here yesterday. I remember it distinctly . . .

Manson. You probably talked its hind legs off. Don't fuss around me, Thomas. I shall sit here on your stomachs.

Manson *sits on the near case.*

Rock *puts the little skeleton carefully down. He goes on unpacking specimens throughout the conversation.*

Manson. You look well. Odd, but well. How is your wife?

Rock. Well, and not at all odd, thank you, sir. Oh, the doctors' wives still cut her in the street, but fortunately they resemble their husbands at an operation: they cannot cut anything properly. And you, sir?

Manson. I am an old man. You should not ask old men how they feel, or they will tell you. I am old, like Doctor Hocking.

Rock. Doctor Hocking was in his second childhood before he was adolescent. When he is your age, sir—a good age—he'll be old as the grandfather of a tortoise, take a week to put his boots on, a fortnight to suck his bread and milk, and a month to make up his absence of mind.

Manson. You still do not approve of the distinguished Professor of Anatomy in our University.

Rock. I still do not approve of stupidity and inefficiency, and sycophantic compromise, and pretentious, intolerable airs and graces.

Manson. [*Unsmiling, as throughout*]. You speak too highly of him.

Rock. He has become a professor on no wits at all. If he were a half-wit, with *his* self-assertion he would be known as a Scotch Sophocles.

Manson. I am thinking of retiring, Thomas.

Rock. If you leave your School of Anatomy, sir, you consign the medical reputation of the City to a man who reads his grandfather's lectures for his own and dissects like a labourer with a pick.

Manson. I have no intention of leaving my students to *Doctor Hocking*. I would rather continue lecturing myself, toothless, on crutches, with my beard to my boots. I founded *my* School to keep the teaching of Anatomy away from hacks and drudges and medical impostors, crammers, and quacks. [*Slowly, emphatically.*] My successor must be a person of precision, method, vigilance, and expertness.

Rock. In this City?

Manson. I have found him.

Rock. Oh, in heaven, sir, not here.

Manson. In a museum.

Rock. In a mummy-case?

Manson. No, standing like a fool in front of me, with a leg under his arm.

MANSON *looks at* ROCK. *And from his eyes we see* ROCK *standing, a plaster leg under his arm, among the specimens he has unpacked from the cases;* ROCK *staring back at* MANSON.

*And we TRACK BACK to see* ROCK *and* MANSON *still, silent, in the great room surrounded by bones and bodies, like men in a spilt graveyard.*

*DISSOLVE to*

7

A ROOM IN ROCK'S HOUSE (*henceforward to be known as* ELIZABETH'S ROOM)

*It is an intimate, comfortable room.*
*A fire is blazing in the deep fire-place.*
*There is a table with sewing upon it.*
*And another small table with books.*
ROCK *stands at the long window of the room, looking out.*
*Coming closer to him, we see, through the window, the roofs of the City.*
*It is dusk in autumn.*
*A woman comes in. She is young, small, fair, with a candid, tranquil face.*
*She is carrying a tray with biscuits and a glass of milk on it.*
*She stands for a moment, looking at* ROCK.
*Then he turns.*
ROCK. I never heard you come in, Elizabeth. You're a witch in a white apron. Downstairs you keep a little instrument, no bigger than a baby mouse, that can hear my brain ticking and my heart beating.
ELIZABETH *puts the tray down on a table.*
ROCK. [*Gently.*] Shall I tell you my news now? Or shall I kiss you first . . .
ELIZABETH *smiles calmly up at him.*
ELIZABETH. Yes.
*He kisses her.*
ROCK. . . . and ask you what you have been doing all day . . .
ELIZABETH. Oh, the ordinary things.
ROCK. . . . and how our little boy behaved . . .
ELIZABETH. He's asleep now. He said his prayers, and then he said there was a tiger in his bed.
*She smiles.*
ELIZABETH. Tell me your news now.
ROCK. Do you remember Doctor Manson? Stern as a judge and solid as a mountain. When I was a student, he had the bearing and the

voice of a god surrounded by the angels of logic.
Now he's old, and ill. He knows death. He can hear it growling and scratching around him now, like a dog after a bone.
He wants me to take his place. Do you know what that means? A whole School of Anatomy outside any influence but Manson's and my own. All the work I have ever wanted to do, I can do there. Can you see me as another St. Hilaire, my dear, another Cuvier? . . . Another old stick-in-the-mud, maybe, with bees in his bald head . . .
*The room is growing slowly darker.*
ROCK. I said "Yes" to Manson. Are you glad?
ELIZABETH *nods.*
ROCK. When one burns one's boats, what a very nice fire it makes.
*He looks out of the window, over the roofs in the gathering darkness,* ELIZABETH *near him. He speaks almost as though to himself alone.*
ROCK. What can spoil or hurt us now? Nothing, nothing, nothing. Nothing out there. . . .
*He makes a gesture towards the dusky City.*
ROCK. My future's here.
*He raises his hands, palms upwards, then draws them back towards him, inviting* ELIZABETH.
*She moves to him, and he takes her hands.*
ROCK. And some of it is in your hands. Oh, I am happy to-day, Elizabeth, happy and tired. I am tired of the dead! . . .
*He puts his arm around her, draws her close. Together they stand at the window. His hand moves along her bare arm.*

*FADE OUT*

*FADE IN*

8

LECTURE HALL OF ROCK'S ACADEMY

ROCK *is on the platform, lecturing.*
*Another younger man sits at a small table on the other side of the platform.*
*The amphitheatre is crowded with students.*
ROCK, *as a lecturer, shows a rare felicity of movement, now reminding us of the slow and graceful minuet, then the quiet pose or soldierly attention; and these again are succeeded by the rapid gesture. After each diversion of his sub-*

ject he readjusts his spectacles, draws up his
gay waist-band and then, presenting a steady
front to his class, resumes his prelection.

ROCK. I stand before you, gentlemen, as a
lecturer in Anatomy, a scientist, a specialist,
a *material* man to whom the heart, for instance,
is an elaborate physical organ and not the "seat
of love," a man to whom the "soul," because
it has no shape, does not exist.

But paradox is inherent in all dogma, and so
I stand before you also as a man of sentiment,
of spiritual aspirations, intellectually creative
impulses, social convictions, moral passions.
And it is in my dual capacity of scientist and
sociologist, materialist and moralist, anatomist
and artist, that I shall attempt to conduct my
lectures, to expound, inform, illustrate, entertain, and edify.

Our aim for ever must be the pursuit of the
knowledge of Man in his entirety. To study the
flesh, the skin, the bones, the organs, the nerves
of Man, is to equip our minds with a knowledge that will enable us to search *beyond* the
body. The noble profession at whose threshold
you stand as neophytes is not an end in itself.
The science of Anatomy contributes to the great
sum of all Knowledge, which is the Truth: the
whole Truth of the Life of Man upon this turning earth. And so: Observe precisely. Record
exactly. Neglect nothing. Fear no foe. Never
swerve from your purpose. Pay no heed to
Safety.

For I believe that all men can be happy and
that the good life can be led upon this earth.

I believe that all men must work towards
that end.

*And I believe that that end justifies any*
*means. . . .*

*Let no scruples stand in the way of the*
*progress of medical science!*

ROCK *bows: a curt, but studied bow.*

*The students rise.*

*And* ROCK *walks off the platform.*

*The other man on the platform makes a ges-*
*ture of dismissal to the students, then follows*
ROCK.

*And all the students suddenly begin talking*
*as they move down the Lecture Hall.*

## 9

HALLWAY OF ROCK'S ACADEMY

ROCK *and his companion on the platform*

*are walking through the Hallway towards a*
*door under the stairs. They open the door and*
*go through. We follow them, through the open*
*door, into a*

## 10

SMALL  CLOAK-ROOM

*It is a bare, dark room. A few pegs on the*
*wall*—ROCK's *cloak and top-hat hang from one*
—*and a table with a water jug and a basin on it.*

ROCK *rolls up his sleeves, very circumspectly,*
*as his companion pours water into the basin.*

*We hear, from outside, the noise of the stu-*
*dents.*

ROCK. [*With a nod towards the noise.*] What
do they talk about afterwards, I wonder? Do
they repeat one's words of golden guidance?
Or make disparaging remarks about one's
waistcoat? I think when I was a student we
used to tell one another stories: they were anatomical, too. Ah, thank you, Murray. . . .

ROCK *begins to wash his hands in the basin.*
MURRAY *takes off his coat.*

MURRAY. You agree with all you said?

ROCK. But naturally.

MURRAY. "The end justifies *any* means"?
That is—to say the least of it—unscrupulous.

ROCK. Then do not say "the least of it." Say
"the most": that it is *honest.*

*And* MURRAY *begins to wash his hands.*

ROCK. You're coming to my dinner, of
course? I can guarantee the cooking. Only the
conversation will be half-baked and only the
politeness overdone.

MURRAY. [*Smiling.*] Of course . . .

ROCK. . . . Do not trust an elder sister to
choose one's company for one. Annabella will
never believe I am properly grown up and so
sits me down next to an elderly lady whose conversational ability would disgrace a defective
three-year-old, or else closets me with a deaf
historian so far advanced into the next world
that he can only dribble and splutter in this.

MURRAY. [*With a kind of tolerant affection.*]
Dinner will be a monologue, as usual, Thomas.
I can't think how you ever manage to eat or
drink anything at all on those occasions. . . .

ROCK. I eat during the yawns.

*Now he has finished washing. He adjusts his*
*coat-sleeves. And* MURRAY *helps him on with*
*his cloak.*

ROCK. I *loathe* all Dinners with a capital

"D." Why can't I have a *quiet* meal with a small "m" and a large port?

MURRAY. Oh, but Thomas! A Dinner to Celebrate the Opening of the New Session of Doctor Rock's Academy!

ROCK. I wish it were still Rock's and Manson's Academy . . .

*He puts on his top-hat.* MURRAY *passes him his stick.*

ROCK. [*As though to himself.*] . . . Poor Manson . . . [*Suddenly in a different mood.*] If Annabella hasn't invited at least one Duke I shall be so surprised that I shall have to ask one myself. And throw in a drunk baronet for bad measure.

Good night, Murray.

*He walks to the door of the small, dark room.*

MURRAY. Good night. Sleep well.

ROCK. Don't be a dam' fool. . . .

MURRAY *smiles after him as* ROCK *goes out. And from* MURRAY'S *eyes we see* ROCK *walk down the Hallway towards the main door, which is opened for him by the Porter,* TOM.

## 11

DINING-ROOM OF ROCK'S HOUSE

*On the large, shining table of the large and handsome room the candles are lit in their heavy silver candlesticks.*

*The curtains are drawn.*

*The furniture of the room is good and solid. There is little ornamentation.*

*At the table sits a woman, writing. There are coffee-things near her.*

*We TRACK TOWARDS her, from the door.*

*And, close, we see that she is a woman of about forty, with black hair combed sternly back, strong features, straight unrelenting mouth: a woman of determination, who knows her own mind and, though she may not like it, will always speak it.*

*She is writing, with severe, upright pen strokes, on large white cards.*

*There is the sound of a door opening.*

*She looks up from her writing, and says:*

ANNABELLA. Oh, Thomas. Can you spare me a moment?

*And now, from a little way behind her, we look at* ROCK *standing in the doorway. hesitant, top-hat in hand.*

ROCK. A hundred, my dear Annabella. All my time is at your disposal, except when I am working or eating or drinking or sleeping. And so on.

ANNABELLA. Then come in and close the door.

ROCK. I *was* going upstairs to work. I had thought of completing my Observations on the Structure of the Stomach of the Peruvian Llama to-night.

ANNABELLA. I doubt if such a creature exists. I think you invented it as an excuse. And besides, if it does exist, it probably has no stomach.

*Reluctantly* ROCK *comes in and closes the door behind him. He approaches the table.*

ANNABELLA. I want you to look at the invitations, that is all. I may have forgotten someone.

ROCK. Oh, fortunate someone!

ANNABELLA *hands the little pile of cards to* ROCK. *He looks through them, idly.*

ANNABELLA. There is no need to be contemptuous of a celebration in your own honour. It may well be the last if you continue to go around the City capriciously insulting every one, and writing absurd letters to the papers about every subject from salmon-fishing to astronomy, and preaching perverted nonsense to a lot of credulous youths and calling it the new philosophy.

ROCK. I smell vinegar in the air to-night.

*But now he is looking through the cards again, and this time not idly. He speaks in a changed voice.*

ROCK. Why are not Doctor and Mrs. Gregory invited?

ANNABELLA. Mrs. Gregory will not sit at table with *her.*

*She makes a little gesture of her head towards the door.* ROCK *gives no sign of having heard or understood.*

ROCK. And the Nicolsons?

ANNABELLA. No self-respecting body would sit down at dinner in the presence of . . .

ROCK. [*Interrupting, quickly, but in an expressionless voice.*] . . . my wife.

ANNABELLA. You can't think that you can outrage every convention and not suffer for it. You married her for better or for worse; and it's worse. I have never understood why you didn't keep the girl as your mistress in some other part of the town.

But no, you have to bring your shabby amours back into the house and *legalize* them.

People have long memories. They don't forget that you disgraced your name, *and* mine, and defied every social decency when you married . . .

*But* ROCK, *silent, is walking to the door, opening it, and going out. He pays no attention to* ANNABELLA. *She is left standing at the table, her sentence unfinished.*

## 12

STAIRWAY OF ROCK'S HOUSE

ROCK *is climbing the stairs. As he climbs we hear the voice of his mind.*

ROCK'S VOICE. . . . When I married Elizabeth. When I said, cool as ice, one morning—cool as fire!—"Elizabeth and I are married." Oh, the shame and horror on the faces of all the puritanical hyenas, prudery ready to pounce and bite, snobbery braying in all the drawing-rooms and breeding-boxes, false pride and prejudice coming out of their holes, hissing and spitting because a man married for love and not for property or position or for any of the dirty devices of the world . . .

*We see him, from below, climbing up, disappearing round one winding corner, then appearing again out of shadow. And the voice of his mind grows softer and, slowly, fades.*

## 13

ELIZABETH'S ROOM

ELIZABETH *is sitting near the fire, nursing a young child, as* ROCK *comes in. She looks up. She sees the controlled fury on his face.*

ELIZABETH. Thomas. You have been losing your temper again.

*He crosses to her, and looks down at her and the child.*

ROCK. Not this time. No, my dear, society has been losing its temper with *me*. And you.

ELIZABETH. Society. That's a lot of people.

ROCK. Oh, Annabella is the priestess of the whole genteel rabble. She speaks for all the slanderers and backbiters from here to hell.

ELIZABETH. [*Gentle, as throughout.*] Was it you and me again?

ROCK. Again.

ELIZABETH. It makes people so angry, still. They think that if they don't *show* they're angry *all* the doctors and lawyers will be marrying market girls and housemaids . . .

ROCK. It would do them good. I wish all the mummified lawyers would marry women of the streets and breed howling families of thieves and vagabonds. I wish the professors would marry their cooks and breed *proper* children, not more little scholars in diapers.

ELIZABETH. Oh no, that wouldn't work at all. You are famous. People want to look up to you. They can't do that if you insult them by marrying below you.

ROCK. Below me! Love is not below me! What am I? An insensible pedagogue, cold-blooded as a herring, with my nose permanently buried in a body? A mincing old maid of a man with . . .

ELIZABETH. No, dear. Which of your friends have been refusing to meet me now? I've only met a few of them. I thought they were very nice and they got up when I came in and called me ma'am . . .

ROCK. I do not need any friends. I prefer enemies. They are better company and their feelings towards you are always genuine. No, it is only that some overweening and underbred women, the wives and tormentors of unlucky doctors, have contrived to tell Annabella that they would not accept our invitation to dinner.

ELIZABETH. Oh, but they *must*. It's very important. You must be at your best. I want them to respect you. You must tell your sister to send off all the invitations, and at the foot of the ones to the ladies who won't accept because of me you must tell her to write, very nicely, that I won't be able to be present at dinner because I am indisposed.

ROCK. I shall cancel the dinner.

ELIZABETH. You'll do nothing of the sort, Thomas.

ROCK. Then I shall write to tell them that their inability to accept our invitation is obviously due to the fact that they suffer from swine-fever, and that I appreciate their delicacy in not wishing to spread it.

ELIZABETH. You'll tell Annabella exactly what I've told you. And now that subject is all over. You haven't asked anything about your son. He couldn't go to sleep to-night. He cried and cried. He was frightened. I've had to nurse him to sleep.

ROCK *kisses* ELIZABETH. *He touches on the forehead the child in her arms.*

ROCK. Good night, little boy.

*And we TRACK PAST* ROCK *towards the window, out of the window and into darkness.*

## 14

*Music.*
*Night.*
*A graveyard.*
*Three muffled figures skulk down the grave-yard path. One carries a lantern. By the lantern-light we see the shapes of the grave-stones on either side; some of the graves are thickly spiked and railinged round. And by this light we make out the appearances of the silent, shadowy figures.*

*One is very tall and thin; he wears a top-hat. One, also top-hatted, carries some heavy im-plements; the lantern, for a moment, flickers his way, and we see the shape of a spade, the coils of a heavy chain. The lantern-carrier is a very short man.*

*Now the lantern-carrier stops at a new grave, and lowers his light. The grave is only a tidy heap of newly turned earth; no stone stands at its head.*

*We hear the whisper of the lantern-carrier:*
Here it is. This is the one.
*The spade-bearer puts down his implements. We hear his whisper:*
Hallelujah.
*And the tall, top-hatted man whispers:*
Go to it, Mole.
*The short man begins to dig at the end of the grave earth.*
*And the tall one, looking carefully, slyly, around, whispers again:*
Quiet as death to-night.
*And the one who carried the spade whispers in return:*
Praise be the Lord.
*The short man digs on. Then, putting down the spade, he whispers:*
The chain!
*The tall man hands it to him. We see that the chain has a large hook at the end. We see it thrust into the hole the spade has dug. And we hear the noise of steel knocking on wood.*
*The chain, in the hands of the short man, wriggles above the earth like a snake.*
*Steel! grates against steel.*
*The short man whispers:*
It's a hard clasp they've put on the coffin.

*His companion whispers:*
... The unbelievers.
*And the tall man whispers:*
Break it with the spade, then. Hurry. The cold's got into my bones.
*The short man pushes his spade through the earth. Spade against steel. The ripping of wood.*
*The tall man whispers:*
Careful.
*And the chain is lowered again.*
*And slowly, out of the earth, comes the head of a man, and then the shrouded shoulders, hauled up by the hook of the chain.*
*The tall man whispers:*
Easy, easy. Don't wake him.
*Slowly the three men raise up the fourth.*
*The arm of the dead man drops, stiff, against the lantern.*
*The lantern goes out.*
*And suddenly, to loud gay music, we DIS-SOLVE to:*

## 15

INTERIOR OF TAVERN A

*On a bench in a corner sit three men. No one sits quite next to them, though the tavern is crowded. We recognize them as the three men of the graveyard. All three are drunk, though solemnly as befits men whose business is death.*

*The very tall top-hatted man* (ANDREW MERRY-LEES) *is a cadaverous clown; a deacon of the drinking-cellar, a pillar of unrespect-ability.*

*The other top-hatted man* (PRAYING HOW-ARD) *has an almost benevolent, almost sweet and saintly, appearance run to seed and whisky.*

*The short man* (MOLE) *is very hairy; almost furry, like a mole.*

*They raise their tankards to each other.*
ANDREW MERRY-LEES. To the dead!
PRAYING HOWARD. To the Surgeons of our City!
*They drink.*
*Now we see, sitting quite close to them, the two men of the Marketplace. They are listening hard, but cautiously, to the other three.*
MOLE. It's been a good month. I'm thirsty.
PRAYING HOWARD. A blessed month.
ANDREW MERRY-LEES. Subjects like penny pies. Plenty of 'em. I'm thirsty too, Mole. I've

drunk three pints o' gin. And I'm goin' to drink *three pints more . . .*

PRAYING HOWARD. Careful, careful, Andrew, you'll get the taste for it.

*And the three of them croak and laugh, without smiling, like three carrion-crows.*

*And the two men of the Market are listening all the time.*

*The short, squat man beckons, secretly, with a stubby black finger, to an old woman, all rags and bones, standing drinking near them.*

*Coming closer, we hear his whisper:*

Who would they be with all that money for the drink?

*The woman looks, with frightened eyes, at the croakers in the corner. Then she whispers:*

Andrew Merry-Lees, and Praying Howard, and . . . [*her voice goes softer*] . . . the Mole.

*And the squat man questions her again, in a rough, Irish whisper:*

And what do they do for a living, my lovely?

*She answers, in a sharp whisper full of fear:*

Body-snatchers.

*He makes a movement as though to cross himself, then lets his hand fall, and looks at his companion.*

*We see the thin side-twisted lips of his companion frame the syllables:*

Body-snatchers.

*They look at each other as the camera TRACKS BACK to show the whole tavern and the three solemnly croaking, laughing men in the corner.*

*DISSOLVE to*

### 16

DINING-ROOM OF ROCK'S HOUSE

*There are eight gentlemen at table.*

*The port is being passed.*

*Through the general conversation we hear:*

GREEN. I was sorry to hear that Mrs. Rock was indisposed, Thomas. Only once I had the honour . . .

FIRST GENTLEMAN. Nothing, I hope? . . .

ROCK. [*Shaking his head.*] . . . Serious. . . . The child. . . . The weather . . .

SECOND GENTLEMAN. [*Nodding in the direction of* MURRAY *across the table.*] I was asking Mr. Murray, purely out of academic interest, why body-snatchers are known as Resurrec-

tionists. He was polite enough to excuse my morbidity so soon after dinner, but . . .

MURRAY. I'm afraid I was rather uncertain myself. Thomas can tell you.

GREEN. Thomas knows *every* answer. I sometimes suspect him of prearranging the questions so that his encyclopaedic information can come rolling "spontaneously" out.

ROCK. You overestimate me, Doctor Green. I can answer every question only *after dinner* when people are usually not in a position to verify my facts. But Mr. Sinclair's question is too simple. The removal of a body from the walled precincts of God's Acre was viewed by the superstitious and the credulous as nothing less than an interference with the plans of Providence and the Great Resurrection. So the poor ghoul of a body-snatcher became a "Resurrectionist."

THIRD GENTLEMAN. If by the superstitious and the credulous you mean believers in Christianity, Doctor Rock . . .

ROCK. Sir, I did not say a superstitious and credulous Christian any more than Brahmin or Buddhist or Worshipper of Elephants. If I say, in conversation, that I know a woman who is opinionated, vicious, and ugly, I *do* distrust the man who immediately says: "Sir, you are talking about my mother!"

THIRD GENTLEMAN. If Logic itself came to dine with you, you would give it an excellent dinner and then try to strangle it. All I wanted to say was that as a Christian I deplore the sacrilege of digging up the dead for anatomists to dissect.

FIRST GENTLEMAN. [*To no one in particular.*] I wish I had retired with the ladies.

ROCK. I am no platform drummer, no hawker of slogans, but I say that the Resurrectionists who dig up the dead and sell them to the Anatomical Schools are a direct result of the wrongness of the Law. The Law says that surgeons must possess a high degree of skill. And a surgeon cannot acquire that skill without working upon dead human beings. But the Law also says that the only dead human beings we *can* work upon must come from the public gallows; a very uncertain, and meagre, supply. Legally, the hangman is our one provider. But he would have to hang all the *liars* in the City or all the men who are unfaithful to their wives, before there would be sufficient subjects for us.

Therefore, we have to obtain our bodies illegally.

I myself, last term, had to pay out five hundred guineas to the Resurrectionists.

ROCK *drinks.*

MURRAY *passes the port to the* SECOND GENTLEMAN. *The* SECOND GENTLEMAN *fills his glass.*

SECOND GENTLEMAN. [*Aside.*] What very good port they provide in a mortuary these days . . .

*But* ROCK *now has the attention of the whole table.*

ROCK. Do not suppose for a moment that, even after dinner and in one of those mellow, argumentative moods in which one would try to prove that black is white or that politicians are incorruptible, I regard the Resurrectionists as anything but the vicious human vermin of the gutters of the city; in fact, a pack of devils.

But as the Law says "No" to our need, to the need of progressive science, so up crawl these creatures to satisfy that need *against* the Law. The same applies to every city, though *ours* is rather more fortunate than most; it is *full* of perverted blackguards.

GREEN. [*Provokingly.*] If you dislike so much the Law that applies to your own science, Thomas, why did you become an anatomist rather than anything else?

ROCK. There was more body to it.

FIRST GENTLEMAN. You would make our City sound to a stranger like Sodom or Gomorrah. . . .

GREEN. It *is* a seat of learning, after all, Thomas . . .

ROCK. And the bowels of squalor. Look any night at the streets of this "cultured city." Observe, with academic calm, the homeless and the hopeless and the insane and the wretchedly drunken lying in their rags on the stinking cobbles. Look for yourselves, sirs, at the beggars, and the cripples, and the tainted children, and the pitiful, doomed girls. Write a scholastic pamphlet on the things that prowl in the alleys, afraid to see the light; they were men and women once. Be proud of *that* if you can.

*In the silence that follows,* MURRAY *rises to his feet.*

MURRAY. If you'll excuse me, gentlemen, I must try to brave this—"*terrible* city at night." You'll excuse me?

*At a smiling nod—for* ROCK *has again, suddenly, changed mood—*MURRAY *bows and goes out of the room.*

ROCK. [*At his most jocularly donnish.*] And now, gentlemen, no more such talk from me.

SECOND GENTLEMAN. Oh, surely, not a little entertaining gossip about cannibalism, for a change?

ROCK. No, no, no, not another word. Or, as my friend Murray would say, "Let us change the subject."

*LONG SHOT of the dinner table,* ROCK *at the head, waggishly professional.*

## 17

CITY STREET

*Music.*

*Night.*

MURRAY *is walking along the middle of the street. On both sides of the street are many ragged bodies, of men, women, and children. Some are stretched out asleep; some are sprawled drunk, their hands still clutching a bottle; some are huddled together, like large, dishevelled birds, for company and warmth. A few have not managed to reach the comparative shelter of the sides of the street, but lie, ungainly outcasts, snoring scarecrows and men of garbage, across the cobbled middle. Over these bodies* MURRAY *steps quickly, carelessly.*

*CUT to*

## 18

*Another humanity-littered* CITY STREET, *with* MURRAY *walking along it.*

*CUT to*

## 19

DOORWAY OF ROCK'S ACADEMY

MURRAY *is knocking at the door.*

*The door opens slowly, only a few inches at first, then we hear a husky voice from within.*

VOICE. Och, it's you, Mr. Murray.

MURRAY. Open up, Tom.

*And the door is quickly opened wide.* MURRAY *goes in.*

## 20

HALLWAY OF ROCK'S ACADEMY

MURRAY *stands waiting in the gloom of the Hallway while* TOM *closes the door.*

TOM *has a candle in his hand. He moves hurriedly in front of* MURRAY *and leads the way through the darkness down the Hall.*

TOM. I thought it might be another *subject*, sir, at this time of night. There was one brought in only an hour ago... [*In a whisper.*] By you know who. Andrew and...

MURRAY. Shut your mouth.

*They reach a door at the end of the Hall.*
MURRAY *opens the door.* TOM, *with his candle, scuttles back into the darkness.*

## 21

DISSECTING ROOM OF ROCK'S ACADEMY

*Night.*
*A large room, cold, clean, and echoing.*
*Tables and slabs.*
*Anatomical diagrams on the walls.*
*On one of the tables we see an array of shining instruments: knives, saws, choppers, and long sharp steel tools.*
*The room is lit by one flickering gas-jet.*
*Two young men stand at one of the tables.*
*On it we see, half in shadow, a shrouded body wrapped in sacking.* MURRAY *is coming into the room.*

MURRAY. [*Brusquely.*] Evening, Brown... 'ning, Harding.

MURRAY *crosses to the table. He unwraps the sacking, flings aside a few soiled white cloths, lowers his hand in between them.*

*For a moment there is silence.*

MURRAY. Stand out of the light, will you?

*Suddenly he flings back the cloths, and straightens up.*

MURRAY. [*In angry undertone.*] Ugh! This is a week old! Why can't the fools bring something fresh? Don't they get paid enough? Might as well dissect a dog dragged out of the river after the fishes have been at it. Come on, let's go and have a drink in the market. *That*'s not worth pickling. Come on.

*He walks towards the door, opens it, stands waiting.*

HARDING *lowers the gas.*

*And out of the dim room the three of them walk into darkness.*

*And out of the darkness comes loud, gay music, and we are in:*

## 22

INTERIOR OF TAVERN B

*Shouts and laughter, and a wet dribble of singing.*

*The benches are packed tight with beggars, hawkers, cheap-jacks, drunks, street women, rogues, and slummers.*

*The rough tables are crowded with tankards and bottles, stained with spilt drink.*

*At the open doorway, children rabble together.*

*Moving slowly down the room, we pass the two women whom last we saw crying "Rags and bones" and "Cat-skin" through the Market.*

*In their bedraggled shawls and cock-eyed bonnets they look as though they might have been made out of their own wares.*

*Moving slowly down, we pass, near the two women, a beautiful girl of about twenty years who has spent nearly half of them trying to defeat her beauty. She is giggling, half tipsy, at some unpleasantry.*

*Moving slowly down we pass* ANDREW MERRY-LEES *and* PRAYING HOWARD. *Sober as churchyard worms, in their corpse-dusty top-hats, they are trying to cure the hiccups of* MOLE—*who sits, small and furry, between them—by pouring drink from a tankard down his throat.*

*Moving slowly down, we reach* MURRAY *and the two young students,* BROWN *and* HARDING, *with tankards before them. They are, all three, a little tight and talkative.*

BROWN. Refined gathering to-night.

HARDING. Too refined for old Murray after his hurly-burly with the great. How did the dinner go?

MURRAY. Thomas was on top of the world.

BROWN. Gracious, loquacious, insulting, exulting...

HARDING. [*Overtopping him.*] ... drastic, bombastic, charming, disarming...

BROWN. [*Not to be outdone, with extravagant gestures.*] ... avuncular, carbuncular.

HARDING. What did he talk about at dinner, apart from sex and religion and politics?

MURRAY. Body-snatchers.

HARDING, *with a "Sh!" of warning, gives* MURRAY *a dig with his elbow, and nods up the room to where* MERRY-LEES *and the* MOLE *are now solemnly pouring whisky down* PRAYING HOWARD.

*As* MURRAY *looks in their direction, so he sees the beautiful girl and beckons her over to him.*

*Beautifully unsteady, she approaches.* BROWN *and* HARDING *squeeze up to make room for her beside* MURRAY.

MURRAY. Sit down and drink with us, sweet Jennie Bailey, my lovely charmer. . . .

*CUT to the two Market women looking with undisguised dislike at* JENNIE BAILEY, MURRAY, *and the two students, who are now drinking and laughing together.*

*The first of the women, she who cried the cry of "Rags and bones," is soddenly morose, a coarse slattern and drab.*

*The second woman, she who cried the cry of "Cat-skin," is a bawd and virago.*

*The first woman says:*

Look at Jennie Bailey, the lady. Drinking with the doctors. Look at her, Kate.

KATE. I'd like to be putting my nails in her eyes. . . . I saw that Bob Fallon looking at her yesterday. Mind your step, Nelly.

NELLY. She won't be young for long. Another year and the men won't look at her. She's the sort that grows old in a night.

I seen your Mr. Broom looking at her, too. Showing all his teeth.

KATE. She wouldn't go with Fallon or Broom, not she. Look at her. Not when there's money.

*CUT to CLOSE SHOT of* MURRAY *and* JENNIE. *They are sitting close together.* BROWN *and* HARDING *have moved away from them, further down the table.*

MURRAY. Why can't we meet in another place, sometimes, Jennie? Anywhere else, not always in this damned tavern, with all the sluts and drunks staring at us.

JENNIE. Where else *could* you take me, sweetheart, except for a walk in the field—and in winter too! Kissing in a hedge in the snow like two robins.

MURRAY. We could find somewhere to be together.

JENNIE. Loving in the lanes, with all the trees dripping down your back and the thorns tearing your petticoats, and little insects wrig-

gling all over you—oh no! Or sitting holding hands in your lodgings all the evening, and your brother studying books in the other corner! [*Softly.*] You know you could come home with me.

MURRAY. And you know that I won't. I *can't*! Don't you understand that I couldn't go back with you there. Not there, in that house. I don't want to think of you in that house, ever. I don't want to think of the others, and your smiling at them and letting them . . .

JENNIE. Oh, the "others" don't mean a thing in the wide world. They're *different*. I'm for *you*. Come back; now. I'll tell Rosie you're staying and . . .

MURRAY. No. No, Jennie. Please. You're beautiful. Come away. Come away from everything here. Are you never going to say "Yes" to me, even if I ask you a thousand thousand times! I'm asking you again, Jennie . . .

JENNIE. [*Gaily.*] Oh, a fine young doctor's wife I'd make. Wouldn't the ladies love me? "And from what part do you come, Mrs. Murray?" "Number 23 Pigs' Yard. Your husband used to call on Wednesdays.". . .

*CUT to the door of the tavern, where the two men of the Grassmarket, the tall, thin, always half-dancing one, and the squat one, are standing.*

*They look round the room.*

*They see* KATE *and* NELLY, *and make their way across the crowded, swirling bar towards them.*

*The tall one crackles his way through the crowd, jumping and finger-snapping, a long damp leer stuck on the side of his face.*

*The squat one elbows his way through, now sullenly truculent, now oily and almost bowing.*

*They stand over their women.*

*And the squat man says, ingratiatingly and yet with an under-menace:*

Can you buy a little drink for us, Nelly darling? We're thirsty, love.

*And the thin man says, in his high, mad voice:*

Can you buy a little drink for Fallon and Broom, Fallon and Broom. . . .

*He makes the grotesque movements of drinking, still finger-snapping, one shoulder higher than the other.*

NELLY. There's money for two more and that's all. Here, buy 'em yourself, Bob Fallon.

*She tosses* FALLON *a coin. And as he catches the coin and shoulders the few steps to the bar,* BROOM *reaches for* NELLY'S *drink.* NELLY *makes as if to snatch the tankard back, but* BROOM *suddenly shows his teeth and pretends to snap at her.*

KATE. Ach, leave him be. Broom's got the devil in him to-night. He'd bite your hand through. I know him.

*By this time* FALLON *has returned with two drinks, and hands one to* BROOM, *who attacks it hungrily again.*

FALLON, *from under his heavy, hanging eyebrows, stares around the bar. Suddenly he sees* MERRY-LEES *and the two others.*

FALLON. [*To the women.*] There's the three ... [*His voice lowers.*] ... snatchers we see in the "Old Bull." They're swillin' the drink again. Must've digged up another to-night.

*He turns to look at* BROOM, *who is staring at the three Resurrectionists with glinting, unseeing eyes.*

FALLON. Fourteen pounds for a corpse they get when it's digged up new. . . . Fourteen pounds! . . .

BROOM. [*In his high, loud voice.*] Fourteen pounds for gin and pies . . .

KATE. Hush! you mad dog. . . .

NELLY. There's no more left.

*She gets up and goes towards the door.* FALLON *follows her,* BROOM *and* KATE *behind him. As they move through the bar to the door, we hear* FALLON *whine:*

FALLON. Come on, Nelly darlin', scrape up a penny or two for a drop for us . . . There's plenty of ways, lovey . . .

## 23

THE MARKET-PLACE, OUTSIDE TAVERN B

*Moonlight.*

*The noise of the tavern swirls in a hiccuping gust out into the street.*

*The Market stalls are shrouded like deadcarts.*

*And the doors of other pubs and houses are open, staining light out on to the cobbles.*

*People stand at doorways, up to no good.*

*People and other pigs flop on the strawed cobbles.*

NELLY *walks to a barrow just outside the pub and takes the handles. The barrow is heaped with rags.*

FALLON, BROOM, *and* KATE *follow her as she begins to push the barrow through the moonlit Market.*

*Suddenly, with a yelp,* BROOM *leaps on to the barrow, sitting bolt upright among the rags.*

BROOM. [*In a high, gay snarl.*]
    Broom
    In his carriage and pair . . .

NELLY *takes no notice but doggedly pushes the barrow on.*

*And sullenly* FALLON *walks at the side,* KATE *trailing after him.*

FALLON. Fourteen pounds for a corpse! . . .

*They move out of the Market, through the alleyways.*

NELLY. [*In a harsh grumble as she trundles the barrow on with its load of rags and one cackling man.*] Why don't you dig one up yourself? You're frightened of the dark.

*Over the cobbles of lonely alleys the barrow rattles, and the finger-snapping, dog-haired man squatting on the rags points his finger at one dark doorway, then at another.*

BROOM. They're dead in there. . . . Dig 'em up, Fallon. . . . In there. . . . In there. . . .

*Round a corner they come into Rag-and-Bone Alley.*

## 24

RAG-AND-BONE ALLEY

*They stop at the door of a tenement.*

*In a first-floor window hangs a sign:*
    CLEAN BEDS

KATE *opens the door and goes through.* FALLON *follows her.* BROOM *leaps from the barrow and is inside the dark doorway like a weasel into a hole.*

## 25

LARGE LODGING-ROOM

*The four of them are moving through the room.*

*Around the walls of the room are many narrow beds.*

*Some of these beds are occupied. By men, or by women, or by human beings at all, we cannot see, but we can hear the noises of unhappy sleep, the sodden snore, the broken sigh, the whimpering of breath.*

*The four move through the room towards a small open door.*

*The two women go through the door into the darkness of the adjoining room.*

FALLON *stops at the last two beds against the wall. He looks down upon them.*

*In each of them sleeps an old man covered with rags.*

*One old man is mumbling in his sleep the almost inaudible scraps and ends of prayer.*

*And as* FALLON *looks down upon him,* BROOM *tiptoes to his side.*

*Silently* FALLON *and* BROOM *look down upon the two old sleeping men, whose hideously haggard faces for a moment we see close.*

### 26

LECTURE HALL OF ROCK'S ACADEMY

*CLOSE-UP of* ROCK *lecturing. He has a large volume in his hand.*

ROCK. This, gentlemen, is a volume by Vesalius, the acknowledged father of our art. Look at its size, and bear in mind that its thousand folio pages . . .

*From* ROCK'S *angle we look down at the densely packed auditorium of his Lecture Hall. Among the faces of the students we recognize those of* BROWN *and* HARDING.

ROCK. [*Continuing throughout.*] . . . embrace only a special part of the human anatomy. . . . Now, gentlemen . . .

*From the auditorium we look up at* ROCK *as, with a very small volume in his other hand, he continues:*

ROCK. . . . behold the advance of the age, the progress of science to-day, the *Pocket Anatomist,* said to contain the *whole* of Anatomy within the compass of three inches by two.

*Reverently he lays down the large volume on his lecturing table.*

*With the greatest contempt he casts the small volume across the platform.*

*Laughter of the students.*

### 27

PRIVATE SMOKEROOM IN AN INN

*A snug little box of a room that could not hold more than four.*

*Two small oak settles facing each other.*

*A fire-place. A blazing wood fire.*

*A mantelpiece. A shining ebony clock. On either side of the clock, a tall silver candlestick. Candles burning.*

*A little counter. Behind the counter, bottles gleaming in candlelight.*

*Two old gentlemen are seated in the room. They have an air of judicious, contented permanency. They seem part of the furniture; their baldness gleams like the silver, like the mellow bottles. Each holds a silver tankard.*

FIRST GENTLEMAN. Now if I had a boy . . .

SECOND GENTLEMAN. . . . He'd be no boy now, John . . .

FIRST GENTLEMAN. . . . If I had a boy and he decided to enter the medical profession— against my wishes, needless to say; the legal profession has always been good enough for us—I would no more send him to Thomas Rock than I'd lay down the law to my wife. Your health!

SECOND GENTLEMAN. Health!

FIRST GENTLEMAN. They tell me, for example, that he openly condones the activities of the Resurrectionists. . . .

SECOND GENTLEMAN. He married a young person who was in domestic employment, too, I believe. . . .

FIRST GENTLEMAN. No, Richard, my wife tells me that she sold fish. . . .

SECOND GENTLEMAN. It is all the same—fish or dish-clouts.

FIRST GENTLEMAN. And I have heard that he has a most scurrilous tongue. . . . Preaches Anarchy. . . . Ridicules the Law. . . . Has all his young men *laughing,* and spouting revolutionary doctrine. . . . Interpolates violent criticisms of the Constitution in the very middle of his supposedly scientific lectures. . . . He does not even try to live like a gentleman. . . . My wife says that they keep only *one* maid in the whole house. . . .

SECOND GENTLEMAN. Mrs. Rock can do the rest of the work, I suppose. She is used to it.

FIRST GENTLEMAN. No, no, Richard, she sold fish. . . .

SECOND GENTLEMAN. Another, John?

FIRST GENTLEMAN. Thank you. . . . No more than a double. . . .

*The* FIRST GENTLEMAN *raises his hand in a restraining gesture.*

*DISSOLVE to*

### 28

*Bright sunshine.*

*Students rushing pell-mell across* THE SQUARE *towards* ROCK'S *Academy.*

*A baker, carrying a big wooden tray of loaves across the Square, only just manages to avoid them.*

*We see the students race up the steps.*

### 29

*We see the students in the* LECTURE HALL OF ROCK'S ACADEMY.

ROCK *enters.*

*He enters like a great actor; he acknowledges the ovation of his audience; he bows; he steps to the platform table; he adjusts his spectacles and his cuffs; every movement is studied.*

ROCK. Gentlemen . . .

*DISSOLVE to*

### 30

LECTURE HALL AT NIGHT

*The hall is dimly lit.*

ROCK, *in shirt-sleeves, is rehearsing a lecture to an audience of one solitary skeleton.*

ROCK. . . . And are we to be told that the Kafir is a savage because he lives in the wilds, and that John Bull is the happy creature of civilization because he wears breeches, learns catechism, and cheats his neighbours? I say that . . .

*During this rehearsal, the door of the Lecture Hall opens slowly, and two very young students poke their heads around to watch the master in uncomprehension and awe.*

### 31

*CLOSE-UP of two elderly professors, in mortar-boards and gowns, standing against the background of a very large, ornately gold-framed portrait of another old professor.*

FIRST PROFESSOR. I knew him when he was a boy. He was clever as a monkey, and he looked like one, too. But he was never *really young.*

SECOND PROFESSOR. Or sound.

FIRST PROFESSOR. No, one cannot say one likes him, or approves of him. But that is not the question. We·must disregard personal prejudice.

SECOND PROFESSOR. Difficult, when *he* re-

fuses to disregard it. He called me "insipid booby" in the *Scientific Journal.* . . .

FIRST PROFESSOR. [*With a side glance at his companion.*] Most uncalled for. No, my point is that one cannot look upon him as an insignificant opponent. His medical history is, unfortunately, brilliant. And they *do* think very highly of him on the Continent. Add to that, that he has five hundred students attending his classes, and that his nearest rival, our old friend Hocking, has less than a dozen. . . .

SECOND PROFESSOR. Nine, to be exact, and that includes three nephews. . . .

FIRST PROFESSOR. . . . and we begin to see what a pernicious influence the fellow might have upon the whole scholastic life of the City; indeed, upon the trend of scholastic thought everywhere. . . .

SECOND PROFESSOR. A menace. A menace. So rude, too. . . .

### 32

ROCK LECTURING

*He holds a human skull high in his hands.*

### 33

*CLOSE SHOT, from above, of an Old Man lying in his coffin.*

*We recognize him as one of the two old men who were sleeping when* FALLON *and* BROOM *looked down at them in Sequence 25.*

*The lid of the coffin comes down.*

*TRACK BACK to show that we are in the Large Lodging-room of* FALLON *and* BROOM'S *house.*

*A Coffin Carpenter is nailing the coffin which lies at the foot of a bed. The straw of the bed lies scattered round it.*

*In the next bed, the other* OLD MAN, *wrapped in his rags, is staring at the coffin, at the Carpenter, and at* FALLON *and* BROOM, *who stand at the entrance to the small adjoining room.*

*The rest of the beds in the Lodging-room are empty.*

BROOM. Hammer him in, hammer him in. Four pounds rent all dead in a box.

FALLON. Now who would've thought old Daniel could be so mean. Dying without a word, and owing us four pounds. He didn't even have a penny piece hidden under the straw. . . .

BROOM. If only he was alive again so that I could kill him with my hands. . . .

FALLON. And all he left was a bit of a broken pipe. . . . And livin' here all these months on the fat of the land. . . . Many's the night I've beaten the rats off him myself. . . .

FALLON *is slouched against the doorway in a kind of self-pitying gloom, but* BROOM *is half dancing with rage. . . .*

*The* CARPENTER *goes on hammering.*

BROOM. Four pounds gone! Whisky and gin and bonnets gone! No more money for Broom! Hammer him in—hammer him in!

COFFIN CARPENTER. [*Without looking up.*] And what do you think I'm doing? Pullin' him out?

*The beating of the hammer on the nails of the coffin.*

*And slowly* BROOM'S *dancing fury dies; he swivels his eyes towards* FALLON.

FALLON *looks back at him, and slowly through his mulish blood-shot stupidity he seems to understand.*

*Now the* CARPENTER *rises, collects his tools, goes out through the far door.*

FALLON. [*In a heavy whisper.*] Hammer him in, hammer him in . . .

BROOM. [*Softly.*] . . . and what do you think I'm doing . . . [*More loudly.*] . . . pullin' him out?

BROOM *runs swiftly to the far door, looks out, turns back, slams the door, bolts it, runs back. . . .*

BROOM. Four pounds he owes us and ten pounds they'll give us for him. . . .

FALLON. [*With a kind of sodden horror.*] Body-snatchers!

*But* BROOM *is calling through the other door:*

BROOM. Kate, Kate, come here!

NELLY *and* KATE *come in.*

BROOM. Here, take one end. Take his head.

*Without understanding, the women obey, take hold of the top of the coffin while* BROOM *takes the other. Together they drag the coffin through the door into the other room. Still* FALLON *does not move.*

*Then, suddenly, he draws back his heavy, muscle-bound shoulders, and follows them.*

*And the eyes of the* OLD MAN *in the bed follow him.*

*We hear whispering from the other room.*

*Then a scraping, screwing noise.*
*Then the door is shut.*

## 34

CITY STREET

*Late evening.*

*We see, in LONG SHOT,* FALLON *and* BROOM *moving up the street away from camera.*

FALLON *is carrying a tea-chest on his back.*

*By his side, at a zany trot, goes* BROOM.

*We see two policemen coming slowly down the street towards them and towards us.*

*And* FALLON *and* BROOM *move quickly and suddenly down a side street.*

## 35

ANOTHER CITY STREET

*Late evening.*

FALLON *and* BROOM *walking along with the tea-chest.*

*Two students pass them.*

BROOM *nudges* FALLON, *who puts down the tea-chest and follows them a few steps.*

FALLON. [*In his whining voice.*] Beg your pardon me askin', sirs, if it's not too much trouble for you, could you be telling me where the Academy is? We've a little matter of business . . .

*The students have paused and turned round.*

FIRST STUDENT. What Academy do you want?

SECOND STUDENT. . . . And what's the little business? Oh!

*The* SECOND STUDENT *has seen the tea-chest a little way off, with* BROOM, *its attendant, winking and leering.*

*He draws the* FIRST STUDENT'S *attention to the tea-chest.*

FIRST STUDENT. If it's a subject . . .

FALLON *cringes, and nods, and nods again.*

FIRST STUDENT. . . . take it along to Doctor Rock's. That's over there. Round that corner. It's the second house in the square. He'll pay you a better price than Hocking.

FALLON. Oh yes, that was the name, sirs, Hocking, sirs, Hocking. . . .

FIRST STUDENT. You take it to Doctor Rock. . . .

FALLON. Oh, thank you, sirs, thank you, my humblest thanks to you, sirs. . . .

*But the two students have walked off.*
*And* FALLON *rejoins the tea-chest and* BROOM, *and lifts the tea-chest on his back and moves on. . . .*

## 36
### DOORWAY OF ROCK'S ACADEMY

BROOM *raps at the door, then quickly steps back, ready to run.*

FALLON, *with the tea-chest, stands, bowed, near the door, stubbornly servile.*

*The grille in the door opens, and the face of* TOM *stares through: a face through a spider-web.*

*Through the grille, through* TOM'S *eyes, we see the two men: the barrel-bulk of* FALLON *in the foreground, the lean lank* BROOM *craning a little way behind him.*

FALLON. [*Ingratiatingly.*] Two young gentle-men told us we could sell an article here. . . . We got it in the tea-chest. . . .

*Now, from* FALLON'S *eyes, we see the face of* TOM *at the grille.*

TOM. [*With a grunt.*] Wait.

*The grille closes. Bolts rattle. The door opens slowly.*

*We hear* TOM'S *voice from the darkness within the door, but we do not see him.*

TOM'S VOICE. Come in. Walk quiet.

*From behind them we see* FALLON *and* BROOM *walk into the darkness. The door closes.*

## 37
### HALLWAY OF ROCK'S ACADEMY

*In the gloom, what stands within the tall, glass-fronted cases that line the Hallway can-not clearly be seen. But* FALLON *and* BROOM *glance quickly, fearfully, at them, and we catch for a moment the glint of a bone, the shape of a stripped head.*

TOM *beckons, and walks down the Hall towards the door under the stairs.*

TOM. Follow. Walk quiet.

FALLON *and* BROOM *follow him into the small, dark, bare Cloak-room.*

TOM. Put it down there. Wait. Don't move now.

TOM *goes out, leaving* FALLON *and* BROOM *standing one at each side of the tea-chest in the dark room.*

TOM *walks into the Hall, climbs the stairs.*

## 38
### CORRIDOR IN ROCK'S ACADEMY

TOM *walks along the Corridor. He stops at a door.*

*From within we hear the voice of* ROCK:

ROCK'S VOICE. . . . It was Herophilus who first traced the arachnoid membrane into the ventricles of the brain and . . .

TOM *knocks three times on the door, and we hear* ROCK *interrupt his sentence to say:*

ROCK'S VOICE. Come in.

*And* TOM *enters.*

*From the open door we see into:*

## 39
### REFERENCE LIBRARY IN ROCK'S ACADEMY

*It is a smallish book-lined room, in which* ROCK *is talking, informally, to a small group of seated students. He is walking up and down before them, his arms behind his back, but he stops at sight of* TOM *and raises his eyebrows questioningly.*

TOM. [*In a confidential voice.*] There's a couple of new hands downstairs, sir, they've brought . . .

*But* ROCK, *turning to the students, interrupts him.*

ROCK. Excuse me, gentlemen, you and Hero-philus must wait a few moments.

*And he walks out of the room,* TOM *stepping back to allow him passage.*

*Then* TOM *follows him.*

## 40
### CORRIDOR IN ROCK'S ACADEMY

*We follow* ROCK *and* TOM *along the Corri-dor, down the stairs, and into the Hallway.*

*They go into the Cloak-room under the stairs.*

## 41
### SMALL CLOAK-ROOM

FALLON *and* BROOM *move aside nervously into the shadows as* ROCK, *taking no notice of them at all, goes straight to the tea-chest.*

TOM *hurries to his side, cuts the ropes around the chest, drags away the straw and rags.*

ROCK *looks inside.*

*Then he straightens up, takes out a purse, hands it to* TOM.

ROCK. Give them seven pounds ten.

*As* TOM *opens the purse and counts out the money from it,* ROCK, *for the first time, looks at* FALLON *and* BROOM.

ROCK. What are your names?

FALLON *steps, toadying, out of the shadows.*

FALLON. Bob Fallon, sir.

ROCK *nods towards the shadows.*

ROCK. And the other?

BROOM *comes out, like a ghost, smiling his long side smile, but he does not speak. His long fingers rap-rap-rap on his elbow.*

FALLON. Broom, sir.

ROCK. If you have any more, let us have them.

ROCK *turns away and walks out of the room. And* TOM *hands over the money to* FALLON.

## 42

CITY SQUARE

*Music.*

FALLON *and* BROOM *are moving through the moonlit Square towards us,* ROCK'S *Academy behind them.*

BROOM *is half dancing, finger-snapping, his whole body one long lean grin.*

FALLON, *at his side clinking coins in his hand, is shambling an accompanying dance.*

*Nearer, nearer, they dance towards us until their faces fill the screen; until all we can see is the thick snout-mouth and the thin fox-lips, the little glinting eyes and the slant slits.*

## 43

INTERIOR OF TAVERN B

*Closely we see, at a table, the faces of* FAL-LON, BROOM, NELLY, *and* KATE.

*Coming closer, at the level of the table, we move past mugs and bottle to a pile of coins and* FALLON'S *hands around them. The hands move, pushing some of the coins across the table.*

FALLON'S VOICE. For you, Nelly love. All for yourself. For you, Kate.

*Now, still closely, we see the four at the table.*

FALLON. Broom and I share the rest.

*And* FALLON *divides, in one movement of his broad fingers like big toes, the remaining coins.*

BROOM *snatches his coins up.*

BROOM. A bottle, a bottle, another bottle!

*And he darts away from the table and brings a bottle back and pours whisky into each mug.*

NELLY. [*Softly, in a kind of drunken, lumpish amazement.*] Seven pounds ten for an *old* man. . . .

*And they all drink.*

FALLON. Oh, the shame that he wasn't a *young* man. . . .

*And, with their own kinds of laughter, they drink again.*

## 44

MARKET-PLACE

*Day.*

FALLON *and* BROOM *are looking at the wares on a clothes-stall.*

*They plough and scatter through the clothes, while the stall-keeper, a fat woman smoking a pipe, looks on expressionlessly.*

FALLON *pulls out a shawl from a heap of oddments and tosses a coin to the woman who, still expressionlessly but with the deftness of a trained seal, catches it.*

FALLON. I'll have this . . .

*He pulls out another shawl, and a skirt, and a petticoat.*

FALLON. . . . and   this . . . and   this . . . and this . . .

*And* BROOM *has decked himself with lace from the stall and is mincing around in the parody of a drunken woman.*

FALLON, *with a wide, extravagant gesture, piles all his presents under his arm, and tosses the woman another coin. She catches it.*

*And* BROOM *still prances, now with a bonnet on his head.*

BROOM. Look at me. . . . look at me. My *mother* wouldn't know me. . . .

*And* FALLON *and* BROOM *link arms and move away through the Market,* BROOM *in his fineries,* FALLON *trailing a shawl behind him in the mud of the cobbles.*

*Arm in arm they move on through the Market, to the distant playing of a fiddle.*

## 45

CITY PARK

*Music.*

*A windy afternoon.*

ROCK *and* ELIZABETH *are walking down a*

*path under the trees.* ANNABELLA *walks a little way apart from them, stiffly, primly.*

*Some way in front of them two little children are running along and playing.*

*Through the music we hear the voice of* ROCK's *mind.*

ROCK's VOICE. Oh, such a cold day for walking abroad, and the wind like a drunk beggar with his fiddle. Well, I suppose it does us good. It does *me* good to feel the family man again, walking through the respectable, gusty park with Elizabeth on my arm.... Oh, the years fly! Time with his wingèd chariot, hurrying near, and my life going true and even, and my children growing, and Elizabeth with me for ever, and books to write, and work to do.... Lord, but it's a happy time ... even in the unhappy times....

*Slowly, sedately, they move on through the cold afternoon.*

## 46

RAG-AND-BONE ALLEY

*Slowly, disconsolately,* FALLON *and* BROOM *walk down the Alley towards the Lodging-house.*

BROOM *is no longer dancing, finger-snapping, pirouetting, but walks like a wraith, holding his shabby thinness against the cold; and* FALLON, *head down, shambles without seeing or caring.*

*They reach the Lodging-house.*

## 47

LARGE LODGING-ROOM

*All the beds are empty, the earth-coloured blankets flung half off them.*

*All the beds except one: that bed nearest to the door of the small adjoining room, in which the second* OLD MAN *lies still under his filth and rags.*

FALLON *and* BROOM *walk past the* OLD MAN, *open the door of the small room.*

*His eyes follow them.*

*The door closes.*

## 48

SMALL ROOM IN LODGING-HOUSE

*In one corner a straw bed.*

*In another, heaps of rags.*

*There is a table, a few broken chairs.*

*Straw and broken glass litter the foul floor.*

FALLON *throws himself on to the straw bed.*

BROOM *walks about the room, caged, his eyes darting sharply at every squalor.*

FALLON. And what d'you think you'll find? Prowling like a cat. D'you think there's money in the old straw?

BROOM *has stopped at the cobwebbed window and is looking out.*

BROOM. There's fat pigs in the yard outside.

FALLON. [*Not listening.*] Drain the dry bottles, lick the floor, scrabble in the muck for a farthing. There's nothing, nothing.

BROOM. [*Still at the window.*] Fat, juicy porkers waiting for the knife to cut them ear to ear. Squeeeel!

FALLON. Shut your squeal. Ach, if old Daniel was here, dying again!

BROOM. [*In a quiet voice, still looking out of the window.*] Geordie's dying.

*Without turning from the window,* BROOM *nods back at the door between the small room and the large room.*

*We move towards* BROOM.

BROOM. Geordie coughs all night. Krawf! Krawf!

*We move closer to* BROOM.

BROOM. [*Softly, but clearly.*] It's awful tedious waiting for Geordie to die....

*We are right up to* BROOM's *face.*

*There is complete silence.*

*Then there is the sound of the rustle of straw. Then the sound of a door opening.*

*Still* BROOM *does not look round.*

*Only when a cry comes from the next room, a cry like an old sheep's, half moan and half bleat, does* BROOM *spin round like a dancer at a cue.*

*We see him, in* CLOSE-UP, *staring towards the other room. Staring. And smiling.*

*DISSOLVE.*

## 49

CITY STREET

*Music.*

*Late evening.*

*LONG SHOT of* FALLON *and* BROOM *walking away from camera.*

FALLON *carries the tea-chest on his back.*

BROOM *capers at his side.*

## 50

LARGE LODGING-ROOM

KATE and NELLY walking through the room.
They stop at the OLD MAN's bed.

NELLY leans down to look at the empty bed.
Then she straightens up with a little shudder.
And KATE looks.

Silently they pull up the rags and bits of
blanket from where they have been pulled on
to the floor, and cover the straw bed with them,
carefully, like two housewives.

Suddenly, from outside, there is a loud
knocking on the door.

The women start, look at each other.

NELLY. [Whispering.] Perhaps that's the ...

KATE. [Whispering.] Perhaps it's ... lodgers.

And straightening her dirty shawls about her,
she walks down the room to see.

## 51

HALLWAY OF ROCK'S ACADEMY

TOM is climbing the stairs. From the foot of
the stairs we see him climb.

He is half-way up when ROCK, with top-hat
and stick, comes down.

TOM stops.

As ROCK approaches him, TOM speaks:

TOM. It's Bob Fallon and Broom again, sir.
They've brought a new subject. It's an old man.
He's not ... very long dead. They want ten
pounds, sir.

ROCK. Give it to them.

He walks downstairs, down towards us. His
face is expressionless, his attire immaculate.

## 52

CITY CHURCH

Organ music as the worshippers come out
into the street.

Among the worshippers, distinguished by his
loose-flowing cloak and his florid clothing, is
ROCK.

With him are four of his students, including
BROWN whom last we saw in Tavern B with
MURRAY and JENNIE BAILEY. Other of the
faces we recognize, too, as having been among
those in the lecture classes.

Many of the worshippers stop outside the
church, bow, raise their hats, gather in groups.

But ROCK and his four disciples stride on
down the street.

From outside the church we see how the eyes
of many worshippers follow them; and a few
black-apparelled heads come whispering together.

The organ music fades.

## 53

HILL ABOVE THE CITY

ROCK and the students are walking up the
Hill.

They stop. They look down at the City.

ROCK sits on the grass, and the students sit
at his feet.

BROWN. Did you ever hear such a mealy-
mouthed sermon, sir? It made me ...

ROCK. Indeed? In my student days I fancied
myself as something of a sermon-taster, but I
cannot say that I was ever actually ill from it.
I grew accustomed to the taste: a not too unpleasant mixture of boiled brimstone and the
day before yesterday's sprouts....

FIRST STUDENT. What was the sermon
about? The Sanctity of Human Life, was it?
I went to sleep.

ROCK. To sleep, Mr. Duncan? I would not
have known. You seemed to me to be wearing
the same expression of studious concentration
that you wear in my Anatomy classes. How
strange and beautiful the City looks to-day.
A city where good men walk in dignity and
peace, and children play in green places, and
girls are both pure and merry, and the hearts
of young men are lifted with the aspirations of
love, and scholars labour diligently with no
other motive than the advancement of the
knowledge and happiness of mankind. Dear
me! Who would think that that lovely City
below us is a Gibraltar of propriety and mediocrity, where the good men starve or are
hounded into the dark, and the worthless
thrive, and the scholars think only of material
rewards, and the girls are born with their noses
snobbed in the air and their eyes searching for
a marriage bargain, and the young men's hearts
are lifted only by the thought of easy success.
And who would think, too, that within that
Gibraltar lies an inner island of active evil....

BENNET. [Slowly.] Yes. The Sanctity of the
Human Body and the Human Soul. That's what

the sermon was about, sir. It's my opinion that . . .

ROCK. Ah! An opinion! Gentlemen, what priceless treasure is to be revealed to us now. . . .

BENNET. [*Blushing, and very confused.*] I was only going to say, sir, that I haven't got much of an opinion about it anyway. . . .

ROCK. [*To the others.*] What did I tell you? A treasure! "My opinion is that I have no opinion." Excellent! . . . But let us talk about other things. . . .

That Rabelaisian *raconteur,* Mr. Bennet, shall tell us some disreputable stories of his early youth.

*And the very young* MR. BENNET *is confused again.*

*DISSOLVE to*

ROCK *and students walking downhill.*
*Music.*
*Gathering darkness.*

*At the foot of the hill,* BROWN *and* STUDENTS ONE *and* TWO *part from* ROCK *and* BENNET.

*We see them in LONG SHOT.*

*We hear none of their words, but only the evening music.*

*CUT to*

54

MARKET-PLACE

*Music.*
*Darkness gathering deeper.*

*The lights are coming on. Lights in the windows of the taverns, and tallow-sticks flaring at the alley corners and outside a few of the Market houses.*

*But the ordinary life of the Market does not cease with the dark and the coming on of the lights. Children still play on the cobbles; and from the alleys behind them, in the unseen courts and closes, come the voices of other children. And men and women stand about in shop and house and tavern doorways, drinking, talking, quarrelling. And a horse and cart rumble out of darkness, over the cobbles, and into darkness again.*

*We see* ROCK *and* BENNET *walking through the Market, towards us.*

*And we see, too, the crippled boy with the idiot smile (whom we first saw in Sequence 2) playing among a little crowd of children.*

*He runs away from the children, over to* ROCK.

*And* ROCK *stops, and smiles at him.*

ROCK. Good evening, Billy.

BILLY *smiles back delightedly, and bobs his head up and down.*

ROCK. It's a cold night to be running about in the streets. . . .

BILLY. Not for Billy Bedlam. . . . Not cold. . . . [*And, like a taught parrot, he gabbles.*] He's never cold in September or November or December. . . .

ROCK. [*Patiently.*] Why, Billy?

BILLY. Because there's an ember in the month. . . .

ROCK *puts money gently into* BILLY'S *hand.*

ROCK. Here's a present for you, boy. Hold it in your hand. Don't lose it.

ROCK *and* BENNET *walk on.*

*We hear, from behind them,* BILLY'S *voice crying:*

BILLY'S VOICE. Night . . . night . . . Doctor Rock. . . .

*And we move with* ROCK *and* BENNET *through the night-time Market.*

ROCK. Now he'll hurry as fast as he can on his bent bones to the nearest tavern, and fuddle his few poor wits, and crack his crazed little jokes half remembered from the cradle. . . . Oh, how the pious would lift their hands to heaven to think of a man giving money to an idiot so that he could get drunk and be warm and happy for an hour or two. Let him rather die a sober frozen idiot in the gutter! . . . Would you care to join me at dinner, sir? . . .

BENNET. Thank you, Doctor. . . .

ROCK. Don't call me Doctor. Do I call you Student? Come on, sir. . . .

*And they walk out of the Market into:*

55

ALLEYWAY

ROCK *and* BENNET *walk on down the Alley, away from us, into darkness.*

*And we TRACK UP the Alley towards a doorway with a tallow-stick burning above it.*

*Two figures stand in the doorway: a man and a woman.*

*And coming closer to them, we see that they are* MURRAY *and* JENNIE BAILEY.

*They are very close together.*

*They stand, their faces half illuminated and half shadowed by the burning tallow-stick, as though in a little island surrounded by a sea of darkness.*

*And from that sea come the cries of children at play in the dark; though far off now.*

JENNIE. It's good night. . . . good night at the door again. Parting like strangers. . . .

MURRAY. You're close to me for a moment. . . .

JENNIE. Is a moment enough for you, then, my dear, my dear? And all the long night to go. . . . You're a sad, strange boy, saying you love me and leaving me all alone. . . .

MURRAY. It's I'll be all alone. . . .

JENNIE. Draw a pretty picture of me, then, to carry about with you so that you'll never be alone, and put it under your pillow at nights like a girl puts a lock of hair or a bit of weddin' cake to wish her sweetheart will come to her. . . .

MURRAY. I couldn't draw *your* picture, Jennie. You're never the same for a single minute. [*Softly.*] But you're always beautiful. I *know* you now; but sometimes I don't know you at all—when you're gay and *hard* and drinking and dancing. . . . And not caring. . . . It's the others that know you then. . . .

JENNIE. Oh, my sweet, you and your silly— others. . . . Come inside with me now. . . .

*And* JENNIE *opens the dark door beneath the burning tallow-stick.*

*And we see a little passage-way, lit by a gas-jet. And a curtain at the end of the passage-way.*

*And from behind the curtain we hear the voices of men and women.*

JENNIE *stands against the passage light, with the other light bright about her head.*

MURRAY. No. No, Jennie. Good night.

*And he kisses her, and turns away quickly.*

*And she steps into the passage-way, and closes the door as the voices behind the curtain rise. . . .*

## 56

DINING-ROOM OF ROCK'S HOUSE

*From the angle of the door we see that under the light of the high, many-branched candlesticks sit* ROCK, BENNET, ANNABELLA, *and* ELIZABETH.

*We TRACK UP to the table.*

*They are drinking coffee, but there is a decanter at* ROCK'S *elbow.* ANNABELLA *is frigidly angry.*

ANNABELLA. . . . And that is what I *believe,* and that is what is right. . . .

ROCK. [*Pointedly to* BENNET.] Have some brandy. . . .

ANNABELLA. There can be, and there always has been, only *one* path of virtue.

ROCK. Surprisingly I agree with you, Annabella.

ANNABELLA. Then it is only for the second time in your life.

ROCK. I can't remember the first. But I agree with what you say, not with what you *mean.* *I believe in the virtue of following no path but your own, wherever it leads. . . .*

ANNABELLA. And that is precisely the sort of statement that antagonizes you to the whole of the profession. . . .

For all your great successes and your famous friends, you do not know how many people there are who would be delighted to see you ruined. . . .

ELIZABETH. [*To* BENNET.] Do you like this City, Mr. Bennet, after the Continent? I think you were very fortunate to have travelled around so much with your parents in the holidays. . . .

BENNET. I like France, ma'am, very much indeed. Of course, I like this City, too. . . .

ANNABELLA. Mr. Bennet, do you, as a student, find that my brother's language and attitude are congenial to the other students?

ROCK. How d'you find the brandy, Bennet? Not mellow enough for you?

BENNET. No, sir . . . it's . . . excellent. Yes, Miss Rock, we all find Doctor Rock's language and . . . er . . . attitude . . . most . . . congenial and, and . . . and *stimulating.*

ANNABELLA. Like brandy on persons of weak health, physical or mental.

ELIZABETH. I should very much like to see Paris, Mr. Bennet. . . .

ANNABELLA. My dear Elizabeth, is this a geographical conversazione? I merely wanted to know . . .

ROCK. [*To* BENNET.] Without embarrassing you further, and allowing you no opportunity of savouring, let alone swallowing, the brandy you were kind enough to call excellent, may I explain to you that what my sister really wishes to know is whether you agree with her that the medical profession, with some notable exceptions, consider me a seducer of youth and an atheist? [*In another tone.*] You have no need to answer, of course.... [*Gently.*] Has he, Elizabeth, my dear? I would far prefer to talk about Paris....

BENNET. [*In an agony of embarrassment, but still determined to defend his master.*] I can't pretend to know what the medical profession thinks of Doctor Rock, Miss Rock, but *we* all think that most of the other doctors and professors are enormously *jealous* of him. [*To* ELIZABETH.] Jealous because he's a great anatomist, ma'am, and a great—[*He breaks off.*]

ROCK. H'm! I know Paris well, especially the cafés. I always used to wear a yachting cap in France, I can't think why.... I wish you'd been there with me, my dear....

*DISSOLVE to*

57

SMALL ROOM IN LODGING-HOUSE

NELLY, *at the fire, is stirring a wooden spoon in a black pot, and something is being fried. We hear the sizzling.*

KATE, *with an almost bristleless broom, is brushing the broken glass into a corner.*

*The broken table has been laid: there are four pewter mugs on it.*

*Suddenly there is a noise of singing and stamping from outside.*

*The door is crashed open and* BROOM *dances in, a bottle under each arm.*

*He winks and leers at the women, nods and jerks his fingers at the open door.*

*And in through the door* FALLON *staggers, singing, with a little old woman hanging, half falling, on his arm. She too is trying to sing.*

FALLON. And look what I've brought home, my doves. A pretty old woman with nowhere to sleep... have you, Granny? Nowhere to sleep but with us. Shall we give her a bed?

NELLY. Where d'you find her?

BROOM *is opening a bottle and pouring whisky into the mugs. He gives the* OLD WOMAN *one.*

BROOM. Drink with Broom!

FALLON. She was lying in the gutter like an old cabbage, weren't you, Granny? Her poor grey hairs dragging in the mud. And who should pick her up but kind Bob?

FALLON *lifts the* OLD WOMAN *up and places her on the bed.*

FALLON. There. The place of honour. Nothing's too good for her.

KATE. What you're going to do?

BROOM. Do? Drink!

FALLON. Do? Drink with Granny. All night long.

*The* OLD WOMAN *titters and drinks. She nearly falls off the bed, but* FALLON *catches her and lays her down gently.*

FALLON. [*Softly.*] No harm must come to you now. You might have bumped your head. Then what'd the doctors think?

BROOM *skips over and takes the* OLD WOMAN'S *mug from her hand and pours whisky down her throat.*

*She coughs and gasps.*

FALLON. [*In a different voice, to the women.*] You two be running off on an errand.

BROOM *points at the* OLD WOMAN *who is now almost unconscious, spread on her back, her black mouth open.*

BROOM. You needn't be long.

FALLON. [*Slowly.*] Go now.

*And the women, without a word, and without looking at the* OLD WOMAN, *fasten their shawls and go out.*

FALLON. [*To the* OLD WOMAN, *as though to a child.*] Up you get, dear. Don't you want no more whisky? [*Into her ear.*] Whisky, whisky!

*And, trembling, the* OLD WOMAN *manages to regain some consciousness. As soon as she does,* BROOM, *ready all the time, pours more whisky down her throat.*

*She falls back.*

FALLON. Give me the bottle.

BROOM *hands it to him.* FALLON *drinks from it. He passes the bottle back. He rubs off the sweat from his forehead. He moves, unsteadily, but heavily, to the head of the bed.*

*And* BROOM *crouches at the foot.*

*From above, we look down on to the* OLD WOMAN'S *face.*

*Her eyes open.*

*Suddenly her face is frightened.*

58

CITY SQUARE

*We see* FALLON *and* BROOM *through the grille in the door of* ROCK'S *Academy, as through prison bars.*

FALLON *carries the tea-chest.*

*Now, from behind* FALLON *and* BROOM, *we see the door opened by* TOM.

*We follow* FALLON *and* BROOM *as they enter the Hallway.*

### 59

HALLWAY OF ROCK'S ACADEMY

*Without any need for instruction from* TOM, FALLON *and* BROOM *move with the tea-chest into the Cloak-room under the stairs.*

*As they go in, so* MURRAY, *in evening dress, comes down the stairs and sees them.*

*In the Hallway he beckons* TOM *over to him.*

MURRAY. Who are the dapper gentlemen?

TOM. Bob Fallon and Broom, sir. They're new hands . . . but they're getting pretty regular. They ask for tèn pounds.

MURRAY *goes into the Cloak-room and comes out a moment later.*

*He nods his head.*

MURRAY. That'll do.

*Now, from the back of the Hallway, at the foot of the stairs, we see* TOM *opening the door wide to* MURRAY.

*In the street outside we see a stationary coach.*

MURRAY. [*At the door.*] If any more bodies call, tell them I'm at the theatre with Doctor Rock. Good evening, Tom.

*And we see him, in* LONG SHOT *from the back of the Hallway, walk out, down the steps, and into the coach.*

### 60

VESTIBULE OF THEATRE

*At the door leans* JENNIE BAILEY, *with a gay shawl round her shoulders.*

*We see, outside the Theatre, coaches waiting.*

*There is a great burst of applause, and she turns round to look towards the door of the auditorium.*

*The audience pours out.*

*Down the stairs at the side come* ROCK, ELIZ-ABETH, GREEN, MURRAY, *and* ANNABELLA.

*From* JENNIE'S *angle we see them stop to talk to other members of the audience.*

*We see* MURRAY *looking round him.*

*We see* HOCKING.

TRACK UP *close to* ROCK'S *party.*

HOCKING. Good evening, Doctor Rock.

ROCK. Good evening, Doctor Hocking.

HOCKING. I do not often see you at the play . . .

ROCK. No, sir. I am able to find my entertainment elsewhere. The City is full of low comedians: it is a pity that the lowest of them all should also be a surgeon. Good night.

*And* ROCK *takes* ELIZABETH'S *arm, and leads his guests out.*

*The last of the party is* MURRAY. *He sees* JENNIE BAILEY, *and stops as the others walk out to the waiting coaches.*

*He looks round him quickly, then whispers to her, and hurries after the others.*

*Coaches drive off.*

*And* JENNIE *goes out, too.*

*We follow her through the darkness until the Theatre lights behind us fade.*

*DISSOLVE to*

### 61

MARKET-PLACE

*Night.*

*We see the entrance to Tavern B from which light and voices pour on to the cobbles.*

JENNIE BAILEY *comes out of darkness into the light and into the tavern.*

### 62

INTERIOR OF TAVERN B

*The tavern is crowded.*

*Many of the faces are familiar to us now: That old bag of female bones over there, she was the one who described to* FALLON *and* BROOM *the profession of* ANDREW MERRY-LEES; *that fat woman with a pipe there, who tosses down her drink as a tamed seal swallows a fish, she was the one who kept the stall where* FALLON *and* BROOM *bought clothes for their women; that humpback there, looking at everything with an idiot smile, he is the one called* BILLY BEDLAM; *one of those two very young men over there, being wise and waggish to a pretty girl of sixteen, is the student* BENNET; *that tall man in a scarecrow's top-hat, hiccuping solemnly, he is the one called* ANDREW MERRY-LEES; *and there are others we have seen before, in the tavern, in the street, in the Market, all of them, in their way, vice-residents of the tavern; and among them a few honest, very poor people.*

*We see all this through* JENNIE BAILEY'S *eyes.*

*A dark, pretty young woman with a sulky expression, seated at the far end of the room, waves her hand.*

*And from her view we see* JENNIE BAILEY, *in her gay shawl, charming her way down the room, being familiar with every one (including* BILLY BEDLAM*) and over-familiar with some.*

,*Now we see that* JENNIE BAILEY *is sitting next to the dark young woman.*

*And now we see them very close.*

JENNIE *drinks from the dark girl's drink.*

JENNIE. I been to see the play in the theatre, Alice.

ALICE. You didn't see no play, dear. You been up High Street.

JENNIE. I did. From the outside. Who shall we get to buy us a drink?

*She roves her eye round the pub. She nods towards* BILLY BEDLAM.

JENNIE. Him?

*She nods towards* ANDREW MERRY-LEES.

JENNIE. Him? Oooh, no!

*She nods towards* BENNET. *He catches her glance, is about to blush, then, remembering his age, winks back.*

JENNIE. Him!

*She smiles at* BENNET, *beckons him over. He comes over.*

JENNIE. Going to buy us some medicine, Doctor?

BENNET. Oh, of course I am, Jennie. . . .

JENNIE. Some for Alice and some for me? It's a cold night for poor working girls like us. . . .

BENNET *goes off.*

JENNIE. I saw my Doctor at the theatre. In my box.

ALICE. John Murray?

JENNIE *nods.*

ALICE. Why d'you treat the poor creature so badly, Jennie?

JENNIE. Oh, but Alice darling, I'm so very very fond of him. I like him better than any man in the whole world. . . .

ALICE. Then why d'you carry on in front of his eyes and . . .

JENNIE. Oh, but I don't, I don't. . . .

ALICE. . . . and teasing him that he's a par-son's son, and letting him see you walk out with any Tom, Dick, and Harry. . . .

JENNIE. . . . I don't know any Harry. . . .

ALICE. . . . No one could know you loved him, you're so *brazen,* dear. . . .

JENNIE. Oh, I want some fun before I die. . . . You're a parson's daughter yourself. . . . He must love me for what I am, that's all there is. . . .

BENNET *comes back with two mugs.*

JENNIE. There, you can always tell, he's got a sweet face. . . . I *do* like students and doctors and . . .

ALICE. . . . butchers and bakers and candle-stick-makers. . . .

*We hear a high yelping laugh, and then* FALLON'S *voice.*

FALLON'S VOICE. And there's my darling Jennie. . . .

BROOM'S VOICE. And mine, and mine!

*And* FALLON *and* BROOM *stagger to the table, pushing* BENNET *aside.* FALLON *pulls a bottle out of his pocket.*

FALLON. Who's going to share a bottle with two county gentlemen?

FALLON *and* BROOM *sit themselves next to* ALICE *and* JENNIE, FALLON *next to* JENNIE, BROOM *to* ALICE. FALLON *pulls two mugs across the table, and fills them.*

JENNIE. I never drink with strangers except on Mondays. . . .

FALLON. And it's *Monday* to-night.

O the stars are shining, the bells are chiming, we'll drink to Monday and Tuesday and . . .

FALLON *pours out another drink.*

JENNIE. And I never drink twice with strangers before twelve o'clock. . . .

FALLON. And Lord, it's *after twelve.*

O the moon is singing, the grass is growing. We'll drink to twelve o'clock . . . and one o'clock . . . and two o'clock. . . .

*QUICK DISSOLVE to the same table with more mugs and bottles on it.*

FALLON *and* JENNIE *are now very tipsy.*

BROOM *is smiling, leering, giggling, and clowning to* JENNIE.

ALICE *still remains comparatively sober, and still sulky.*

FALLON. [*Wheedling.*] I got two more bottles in my little room, Miss Pretty Bailey. Two great bottles of dancin' dew that'll make you think the sun's shining in the middle of the night . . . and satiny shining couches for all the kings and queens to be lying on.... And ...

ALICE. We're not going.

JENNIE. Will you give me a diamond ring and a golden bracelet and ...

FALLON. I'll give you a bucketful of pearls. We'll sing and dance. We'll be merry as crickets in Rag-and-Bone Alley....

JENNIE. [*Half laughing, half singing.*] We'll be merry as crickets in Rag-and-Bone Alley....

ALICE. [*In an angry whisper to* JENNIE.] You're not going with these two creatures.... You must wait for John Murray.... Don't drink any more with that Bob Fallon....

BROOM. And I'll cook you liver and lights....

JENNIE. Will you cook a partridge for me? ...

FALLON. And I'll put a peacock's feathers in your hair....

JENNIE. Oh, listen to them both.... You'd think they were great rich men with crowns and palaces, not a couple of naughty tinkers....

ALICE. We're not going....

*QUICK DISSOLVE to*

### 63

MARKET-PLACE *in the dim moonlight*

*Four figures move through the Market:* FALLON, JENNIE, BROOM, ALICE.

FALLON *and* JENNIE *are singing*.

FALLON AND JENNIE. We'll be merry as crickets in ...

*And* BROOM *accompanies their singing, like a dog baying at the moon. Now they are moving through:*

### 64

RAG-AND-BONE ALLEY

*Their singing wakes up a shape that is lying in a dark doorway.*

*Slowly, awkwardly, it rises to its feet. It is* BILLY BEDLAM.

*He follows the four, with his eyes, down the Alley, and sees them enter the Lodging-house.*

### 65

*Darkness.*

FALLON, JENNIE, *and* BROOM *singing and baying in the darkness.*

*A door is flung open.*

*We see, for a moment, the small room of the Lodging-house.* NELLY *stands there at the dead fire.*

*Then* FALLON *and* JENNIE *and* BROOM *and* ALICE *stumble into the light of the room.*

FALLON *lurches over to the table, opens a bottle with his teeth.*

*He makes an unsteady bow, offers the bottle to* JENNIE....

FALLON. You first, my Jennie, my merry, my cricket....

JENNIE *drinks.*

ALICE *looks round the room with fear and revulsion.*

BROOM *leaps on to the bed.*

NELLY *stands, drab and cross, before* FALLON.

NELLY. Who told you you could bring your women here, you and that mad dog....

FALLON. Now, now, Nelly macushla, we've come to sing and drink....

*But* NELLY *rushes across to* JENNIE *and pulls the bottle from her lips.*

ALICE. [*Urgently.*] I told you not to come, Jennie Bailey.... Let's go, let's go!

FALLON. My Jennie's not going, she's not going, any one else in the wide world can go, not Jennie.

ALICE. Come on, Jennie, come on.

*But* JENNIE *is sitting, swinging her legs, on the table, and is trying to open the other bottle.*

FALLON. If you don't like it here, go to your own pigsty.

ALICE *looks at* JENNIE, *but* JENNIE *has opened the bottle and is pouring from it into a glass.*

*And* ALICE *goes. She slams the door behind her.*

NELLY. And *she* goes, too.

NELLY, *still with the one bottle in her hand, tries to tear the other bottle from* JENNIE.

FALLON *suddenly lifts a glass and throws it in* NELLY'S *face.*

*As she staggers, he takes the bottle from her. She puts her hand up slowly to her face, and feels the running blood.*

*And she goes out of the room like an old woman whipped.*

FALLON *takes* JENNIE'S *glass, drinks from it, puts it back in her hand.*

*And* JENNIE *drinks, swinging her legs.*

*And* BROOM *is dog-creeping on the floor. As*

FALLON and JENNIE *drink he slips off the buckles from her shoes and leaps, lightly and silently, to his feet, and is out of the room, closing the door with no sound.*

*And* FALLON'S *hand, as he looks at* JENNIE, *slowly drops, and the drink from the bottle he is holding runs over her dress and down her legs.*

### 66

DOORWAY IN ALLEY (*as in Sequence 55*)

ALICE *is talking excitedly to a woman in the doorway.*

*The woman nearly fills the doorway. She is dressed in a long, loose shift. Her huge arms are bare.*

ALICE. And I tried to tell her, Rosie, but she wouldn't listen, she was laughing and drinking with him. . . . Oh, I didn't like the looks of him, Rosie. . . .

ROSIE. Go and fetch her back.

ROSIE *has a voice deep as a man's, and heavy, and slow.*

ALICE. But I'm telling you, Rosie, he's no good, he's like an *animal;* won't you send someone back with me? . . .

ROSIE. Go and fetch her back. There's persons waiting for her here. . . .

ALICE *turns away.*

### 67

*Darkness.*
*The pattering of footsteps in the darkness.*
*A door is flung open.*
*We see into the small room of the Lodging-house.*
*But we see no one there.*
*Then* ALICE *runs in, looks round. She sees* FALLON *lying stretched on his back on the straw bed in the corner.*

ALICE. Where's Jennie?

FALLON. [*In a dulled voice.*] Jennie? She went a long time ago.

ALICE. Where did she go?

FALLON. She went out.

*And* ALICE *runs out of the room, leaving the door open.*

### 68

ALICE *is running down Rag-and-Bone Alley in the moonlight.*

*A dark shape leans against a doorway.*
ALICE *stops.*

ALICE. Which way did Jennie go?

BILLY BEDLAM *shakes his head.*

ALICE *points up the Alley.*

ALICE. Did she go that way?

*He shakes his head, and stretches out his hand.*

BILLY. Have some snuff. . . .

*But* ALICE *runs on up Rag-and-Bone Alley.*

### 69

SMALL ROOM IN LODGING-HOUSE

FALLON *is still lying on the straw bed.*
*The door is still open.*

NELLY *comes in. The blood has dried on her cheek. She looks round the room.*

NELLY. Where's Jennie?

*He puts his hand down at his side, the side nearest the wall, and drags up* JENNIE'S *gay shawl, and holds it up to* NELLY.

*His face is hot and wet.*

*FADE OUT*


*FADE IN*

### 70

CITY STREET

*Broad daylight.*
*Music and the ringing of church bells.*
FALLON *and* BROOM *walking up street away from camera.*

FALLON *is carrying a sack on his back.* BROOM *is holding the end of the sack mock-solemnly like a man at the end of a coffin.*

*We see, as they move, children coming out of the doorways, children scampering away from their play to sing and cry together:*

CHILDREN'S VOICES. You've got a body in the sack!

Body-snatchers!

Dead!

Dead!

Dead!

Body-snatchers!

*And they dance around the sack.*

*And* BROOM *snaps his teeth at them.*

FALLON *and* BROOM *walk on. The voices fade behind them.*

*DISSOLVE to*

### 71

CLOSE SHOT *of the sack on a table.*
*TRACK BACK to see that the table is in the Dissecting Room of* ROCK'S *Academy.*
*There are many students. Some, with their backs to us, are bent over the tables, cutting, probing, snipping. We see their movements but not the objects upon which they are working. Some of the students are talking together. None of them takes any notice of the sack.*
MURRAY *comes in and walks up to the sack.*
MURRAY. [*Casually.*] Let's see what we've got to-day.
*He begins to untie the thick ropes about the sack.*
*Several students gather around him.*
MURRAY. An old trull of eighty with bow legs and a belly like a Lord Mayor's, eh? A tramp from the gutter with cirrhosis of the liver and three teeth? What's your guess? . . . An old . . .
*He opens the neck of the sack, and begins to draw the sack down from the head.*
*Suddenly he stops talking. We see what he sees:* JENNIE'S *long fair hair. Slowly he draws the sack down from the face, but we do not see it. The students, silent now, gather around it, and we see only their backs and the profile of* MURRAY. *We see that his face has hardened and become grim, his lips are held very tightly together, as though he were forcing himself not to utter a word.*
BENNET. [*In a long-drawn-out half-sighing whisper.*] God!
FIRST STUDENT. Here, let me look.
*The* FIRST STUDENT *bends closer over the table.*
FIRST STUDENT. It's Jennie Bailey.
SECOND STUDENT. Sweet Jennie Bailey.
BENNET. [*Softly.*] Yes, it's Jennie! I saw her last night in the Market. . . . She was *singing. . . .*
*But* MURRAY *does not utter a word.*
THIRD STUDENT. How did she die? . . .
BENNET. She was *singing* . . . and *dancing. . . .*
*Suddenly* MURRAY *turns away and strides out of the room.*
*The students still stand around the body that we do not see.*

### 72

*Out in the* HALLWAY MURRAY *strides across to the door of the small Cloak-room.*
*The door is open. Beyond it is darkness.* MURRAY *calls into the darkness.*
MURRAY. Tom!
*And from the darkness we hear* TOM'S *voice:*
TOM'S VOICE. Coming, sir.
TOM *comes out of the darkness like an underground animal. He blinks at the light.*
TOM. Yes, sir? I was . . . cleaning up.
MURRAY. Who brought the subject in?
TOM. In the sack, sir? That was Bob Fallon and Broom. . . . Wasn't it fresh, sir?
MURRAY *turns away abruptly and, without a word, goes upstairs.*
*Now we see* MURRAY *walking along the Corridor.*
*He opens a door and strides in.*

### 73

*We see* MURRAY *stride into the* REFERENCE LIBRARY.
ROCK *is standing at a bookshelf at the far end of the room, his back to us and to* MURRAY.
*He turns round as* MURRAY *comes in.*
ROCK. You knock at the door very softly, Mr. Murray.
MURRAY *closes the door, and stands with his back to it.*
ROCK *stands with his back to the bookcase.*
MURRAY *speaks slowly, deliberately, like a man with a passionate temper who is afraid to lose control of it.*
MURRAY. They've got Jennie Bailey downstairs.
ROCK. Indeed? Jennie Bailey? Oh yes, I think I remember the name. A beautiful slut with a bold eye and a tongue like a drunken horse-thief's.
And what might she be doing downstairs? I am sure, Mr. Murray, that she is an expert in Anatomy, but her knowledge would be too specialized. . . . Or has she come merely to entertain?
MURRAY. She has come, sir, to be dissected.
ROCK. How very generous of her. I did not think that science was so near her heart. Does she wish to be dissected *alive?*
MURRAY. She is dead.

ROCK. That is carrying scientific generosity to its furthest limit.

MURRAY. She was murdered.

ROCK. [*Sharply.*] Who says so?

MURRAY. She was murdered.

ROCK. Are there signs of violence upon the body?

MURRAY. She was murdered by two paid thugs of yours: Fallon and Broom. I saw her last night after the theatre. She was well and gay. There are no signs of violence upon her body.

ROCK. Thugs of *mine,* Mr. Murray? Do you remember that you yourself paid them for the last *three* subjects?

MURRAY. She was murdered. I saw her. [*Slowly, rememberingly.*] She had a red shawl on.

ROCK. Indisputable evidence that she was murdered. She should have worn a white shawl, for purity. And what if she *was* murdered, Mr. Murray? We are anatomists, not policemen; we are scientists, not moralists. Do *I, I,* care if every lewd and sottish woman of the streets has her throat slit from ear to ear? She served no purpose in life save the cheapening of physical passion and the petty traffics of lust. Let her serve her purpose in death.

MURRAY. You hired Fallon and Broom to murder her as you hired them to murder the others.

ROCK. I need bodies. They brought bodies. I pay for what I need. I do not hire murderers. . . .

ROCK *walks over to the door.* MURRAY *still has his back to it.* ROCK *stops. Their eyes meet. Then* MURRAY *moves aside.* ROCK *opens the door and walks out. We see him walking down the Corridor.*

## 74

CUT. DISSECTING ROOM OF ROCK'S ACADEMY

ROCK *walks in.*

*Students are gathered round the table where* JENNIE'S *body lies. We do not see the body.*

*The students move aside as* ROCK *enters.*

*He stands in the middle of the group. For a moment he is silent, his head held a little to one side, looking down at the unseen body.*

*Then* ROCK *turns away from the table.*

MURRAY *stands at the door.*

ROCK. Oh, Mr. Murray. I think that before the body is put into the brine bath, a drawing should be made of it. Shall we not allow posterity to share our exhilaration at the sight of such perfect physical beauty?

I should be much obliged if you yourself would perpetuate on paper the loveliness of this poor clay, Mr. Murray. We know your skill with the pencil. God should have made you an artist. He did the next best thing: he gave you a very vivid imagination.

*And* ROCK *walks out of the Dissecting Room.*

MURRAY *does not move.*

*The eyes of the students are upon him.*

## 75

A CITY STREET IN THE FASHIONABLE AREA

*Daylight.*

*Music.*

FALLON *and* BROOM *are walking slowly up the middle of the street towards us, looking all around them with a nudging delight.*

BROOM *wears a new extravagant cravat, but still keeps to his ruffian's coat.*

FALLON *has tied a gipsy-coloured kerchief round his neck.*

*We do not hear any of the street noises. This is a brief, silent scene, to music.*

*People are walking past them, up and down the street. An elegant old lady goes by.* BROOM *side grins, points his finger after her.*

*A nursemaid with two children passes on their other side. And* FALLON *wags his head in their direction. For their own enjoyment, with winks and nudges, they point out in dumb show various of the passers-by, especially the elderly and the very young.*

*DISSOLVE to*

## 76

MURRAY *sitting, alone, in the* DISSECTING ROOM.

*Night.*

*A drawing block is on his knees.*

*We see, over his shoulder, the drawing on the block.*

*It is a half-finished drawing of* JENNIE BAILEY, *lying as though asleep.* MURRAY *goes on drawing. Now, on the paper, we see take shape one arm that hangs over the edge of the table, over the edge of her last bed.*

*Now* MURRAY *is drawing the clenched hand of the hanging arm.*

*And from the picture we* TRACK UP *towards the real hand.*

*And suddenly the hand unclenches itself: an after-death jerk of the nerves.*

*And two pennies fall out of the now open hand, and drop on to the floor. We see them roll along the floor.*

## 77

LARGE LODGING-ROOM

NELLY *and* KATE *are tidying the room, sweeping dirt into corners, covering up tousled beds with mud-coloured blankets, stopping to drink from a bottle on the broken table in the centre of the room.*

*We hear, from outside, the sound of a knock on the door.*

KATE *wipes her lips on her shawl and tucks the bottle inside her cabby-like layers of clothes.*

KATE. More lodgers!

*She goes out of the room by the far door.*

NELLY *tipsily tidies herself, spits in her hand to help straighten a hanging lock of stiff hair.*

*And* KATE *comes back with a big, old, ragged beggar-man shuffling behind her, all dirt and hair, like a tame, tired, time- and whip- and weather-beaten bear.*

KATE. You can sleep in any bed you like dad, for twopence a night. Clean and comfy.

NELLY. Are you alone?

*The* OLD MAN *nods his head.*

KATE. All alone in the world? Nobody to care about you at all?

*The* OLD MAN *shakes his head.*

KATE. Ach, isn't it a shame.... Nobody to care if you're alive or dead....

KATE *looks at* NELLY.

NELLY. Let the old man have his bed for a penny, Kate.

*And* KATE *takes the* OLD MAN'S *luggage— which is wrapped up in a handkerchief—and they each hold an arm and lead him over to the bed near the small-room door: the bed where the other* OLD MAN *died.*

## 78

DINING-ROOM OF ROCK'S HOUSE

*Day.*

ELIZABETH, *in dust-cap and apron, is cleaning the silver.*

*Suddenly there is the long pealing ring of a door bell. And* ELIZABETH *puts down her cleaning cloth, hurriedly takes off her cap and apron, and goes out of the room, leaving the door open.*

*We hear the opening of the street door, and then the voices of* ELIZABETH *and* MURRAY.

MURRAY. I hope I am not disturbing you, Mrs. Rock.

ELIZABETH. Come in, please, Mr. Murray. Do you want to see Thomas? He's lecturing. Oh, you'd know that, of course. My sister-in-law's upstairs....

MURRAY. I want to see *you,* if I may.

*And* MURRAY *follows* ELIZABETH *into the room.*

ELIZABETH. You shall see me cleaning the silver, then....

*She puts on her cap and apron again, and begins to polish the candlesticks on the table.*

ELIZABETH. I thought it might be a stranger at the door.... That's why I had to take my cap and apron off. Miss Annabella would never forgive me if I went to the door dressed like this.... But it's only you. I needn't have worried, need I?...

MURRAY. I'm afraid that after I tell you what I have to tell you, you will never want to see me again....

ELIZABETH. [*Smiling.*] Oh no, no, nothing could be as bad as that.... What has Thomas been doing now? Writing terrible letters to the papers, or telling all the young men to put gunpowder under the City Hall?

MURRAY. No, ma'am.

ELIZABETH. *I* don't mind, you know.... It's only—some other people mind. Thomas can write or say anything he likes: I don't *understand* very much of it.... What have you got to tell me?

MURRAY. [*Slowly, deliberately.*] I believe that Thomas has instructed two men called Fallon and Broom to commit murder and to sell him the bodies.

*There is a silence.* ELIZABETH *stands still, half turned away from* MURRAY. *Then:*

ELIZABETH. That is a—*horrible* lie. If Thomas hears it...

MURRAY. He *has* heard it.

ELIZABETH *begins again to polish the candlesticks. She still does not look at* MURRAY.

MURRAY. Yesterday the body of a young woman called Jennie Bailey was delivered to the Academy by Fallon and Broom. Less than twelve hours before, I had seen her outside the theatre, alive and well. It is not possible that she could have died a natural death.

ELIZABETH. Can't people die a "natural death" in twelve hours?

*And under* ELIZABETH'S *calm voice there is a new hardness. There is a tenseness in all her smallest movements as she cleans and polishes, not turning round. She is, quite suddenly, not a sweet and mild young woman but a protectress and an enemy.*

MURRAY. She did not die a natural death.

ELIZABETH. Was this "young woman" strangled, or stabbed, or shot, or poisoned, or beaten to death?

MURRAY. [*In a slow, low voice, as though he had said the words over and over to himself.*] There were no marks of violence upon the body. . . .

*We see* ELIZABETH'S *relief expressed in the relaxing of the tenseness of the muscles of her shoulders. And now she turns round to face* MURRAY.

ELIZABETH. And so you have no proof at all. . . . How could you? Why did you come to me with such a story? You should go to the police. . . .

MURRAY. I believe that she was smothered to death in such a way as to leave no signs. . . . I came to you first, because I want you to tell Thomas that he must go away. At once. Out of the country. I owe him a great deal. I would not care to see him hanged.

ELIZABETH. You are very kind. . . . Have you thought about yourself? Run out now and shout your lies in the streets, and they will lock you up because you are a madman. Or run to all the lawyers and justices, and they'll ask you for proof and you won't have any: and they'll lock you up because you bear false witness against your neighbour. Or go around in the dark, whispering all the foul things in your own mind to everybody that will listen, and you'll make such a panic and scare that Thomas's school will have to close and all the people who had anything to do with it will be stoned and spat upon and driven out. And you'll never, never, never again be allowed to work in any hospital or any school or anywhere. And nobody will ever speak to you again, or touch you, or be seen anywhere in the world with you. . . .

MURRAY. I have thought of that. I have thought of everything.

ELIZABETH. And if you call Thomas a murderer, everybody will call you murderer, too. They will call you murderer and butcher. . . .

MURRAY. All I know is that if Thomas did not *tell* these men to murder, he bought the bodies *knowing* that they were murdered.

ELIZABETH. I thought Thomas told me that it was one of *your* duties to buy the bodies. Will *that* help you very much when you accuse him? Will you go to the police now? Will you tell people what you've told me? It will be quite easy for you to wreck your life, and his, and mine! I shan't try to stop you.

MURRAY. What shall I do?

ELIZABETH. Keep quiet. You knew the girl—Jennie Bailey?

MURRAY. Yes.

ELIZABETH. What was she?

MURRAY. She was a girl from the market. . . .

ELIZABETH. Was she pretty?

MURRAY *nods, slowly.*

ELIZABETH. I think I remember her if she was the girl outside the theatre. She was—*beautiful.* You liked her very much?

MURRAY. Yes.

ELIZABETH. I think you liked her so much that when she died you—lost your head. You didn't know what you were doing or what you were saying. Do you understand? You *imagined things.* Do you understand?

ANNABELLA *comes in.*

ANNABELLA. Good afternoon, Mr. Murray. I didn't know any one had called. I see my sister-in-law is entertaining you. . . .

ELIZABETH. Mr. Murray called to see if Thomas was here. He had something to discuss with him. But now he says it doesn't matter. . . . Does it, Mr. Murray?

*And* MURRAY *looks, without speaking, at the faces of the two women.*

## 79

INTERIOR OF TAVERN B, FROM THE ANGLE OF THE DOOR

BROOM *is standing in the middle of the room, looking around him. There are few customers.*

*In one corner, alone, wrapped up as though against the cold, we recognize* ALICE. *She raises her head, sees* BROOM, *clutches her shawl more tightly round her, and turns her head away to the wall.*

*And we see* BILLY BEDLAM *sitting, also alone, staring at an empty mug before him.*

BROOM *flicks a coin in the air, catches it in the palm of his hand, looks down into his palm. Then he crosses to* BILLY.

*CLOSE SHOT of* BILLY *and* BROOM.

BROOM. Would you be having a little drink, Billy?

BILLY *smiles up, trustfully, delighted.*

BROOM. [*Without turning from* BILLY, *in a high, loud voice.*] Two gins. [*Then ingratiatingly.*] It's you and me could drink the sea dry, Billy, and eat the fishes and cuddle the mermaids and dance a jig and play the penny whistle and . . .

*The potman comes up with the drinks.* BROOM *pays as he talks, and the potman goes off.*

*They drink them off in a gulp.*

BILLY. I've seen a shark. . . .

BROOM. [*Loudly.*] Two gins. [*Softly.*] You could wrestle the shark and toss him over your head like a pound of cat's-meat. . . . *You're* strong, Billy. . . .

*The potman comes up with the drinks.* BROOM *pays as he talks, and the potman goes off.*

*They drink them off in a gulp.*

BILLY. I know a riddle. . . .

BROOM. Tell Broom your riddle. . . . Two drinks!

BILLY. In what month of the year do the ladies talk least?

BROOM. Oh, that's a good one. And what month *would* it be, Billy?

BILLY. The month of February, because there wiz least days in it.

*And* BROOM *raises his head and yelps with laughter; and slaps his thigh, and cracks his fingers.*

*Delighted,* BILLY *splutters and crows.*

BROOM. Tell Broom a riddle, Billy . . . another riddle. . . .

BROOM *beckons over his shoulder in the direction of the bar, then leans close to* BILLY *again.*

BILLY. I can tell you a riddle that nobody knows and nobody can guess it. . . .

BROOM. What is it, Billy?

BILLY. Though I black an' dirty am,

An' black as black can be,
There's many a lady that will come
And by the hand tak' me.

Now you can't guess that. . . .

BROOM. Ah no, Billy, I can't guess that fickly one. Who learned you all those fickly guesses?

BILLY. It wiz my half step-mither. Oh, she's a cunning old body! Oh, she's cunning as a kitten when we're all sitting beside her round the fireside. She tells us a million million million funny stories, but I don't remember them all. . . .

Though I am black an' dirty an' . . .

BROOM. It's a tea-kettle. . . .

BILLY. [*Almost in tears.*] Somebody told you.

BROOM. Well, tell us another, *Royal* Billy. . . .

*And he beckons over his shoulder, towards the counter, for more drink, and leans again across the table to listen to* BILLY.

BROOM. And we'll drink . . . and we'll drink . . . and we'll . . .

*And his voice softens and softens until it fades.*

## 80

SMALL ROOM IN LODGING-HOUSE

*Candles in bottles on the table.*

*We see, in a corner, the pile of old rags and bones. It is far higher than when we last saw it.*

KATE *lies half on, half off the straw bed near the wall.*

NELLY *is looking out of the window. The window is open. From outside we hear the squealing of pigs.*

*The door is flung open.*

BROOM *and* BILLY *lurch in.*

NELLY *turns from the window.*

*We hear her whisper:*

NELLY. Not Billy Bedlam!

BROOM. [*To Nelly.*] Shut the window. The pigs is too loud. It sounds like a killing. . . .

NELLY *shuts the window.*

BROOM. And bring out a bottle for Billy. . . .

BILLY *staggers to a chair in a corner, sits on it, tilts it back on two legs and smiles at* NELLY, *who is staring at him as she brings out a bottle from a cupboard near the window.*

BILLY. He bought me snuff. . . .

BILLY *opens his box of snuff. Half of it spills over him. He scrabbles it off his clothes.*

*And* BROOM *takes the bottle from Nelly and carries it over to* BILLY *and gives it to him and watches him drink.*

*We see* BILLY'S *face as he drinks: drunkenly made beautiful.*

*But we see only the back of the watching* BROOM, *and he does not turn round as he speaks:*

BROOM. Go round the shebeens and find Fallon. Tell him there's business.

NELLY *goes to the door; she looks over her shoulder at* BILLY.

*From her angle we see* BILLY *and* BROOM'S *back.*

BILLY. He gave me snuff. . . .
He gave me snuff and whisky. . . .
He promised me a shilling. . . .

BROOM. [*Still not looking round.*] And a sleep. . . .

*And, looking at* BROOM'S *back and at* BILLY, *we hear the door close.*

### 81

SMALL ROOM IN LODGING-HOUSE

INTERIOR OF TAVERN A

*CLOSE SHOT of* FALLON *sitting at a table, a mug before him.*

*His face is covered with sweat.*

*And terror looks out of his eyes.*

*He raises his hands before him, palms upward. They are trembling.*

*His lips are moving, but no words come.*

*TRACK BACK to see* NELLY *sitting down next to him.*

NELLY. Broom says you're to come.

FALLON *stares in front of him.*

NELLY. He says there's . . . work.

FALLON. [*Without turning to her.*] My hands have worked enough. There's devils in my hands.

NELLY. It's . . . somebody we know Broom's got there. . . .

FALLON. I've known them all, all of them. They were my brothers . . . and my sisters . . . and my mother. . . . [*In a horrified whisper.*] . . . All dead . . . dead. . . .

NELLY. Hurry up with you. . . . Broom's waiting. . . .

FALLON *does not move.*

NELLY. You've drunk yourself daft again . . . like when you went on your knees in the street, praying and shouting. . . .

FALLON. I wish I was workin' again, on the roads, on the canals, anywhere. . . .

NELLY. D'you want us all to starve while you blather and weep your eyes out. . . .

FALLON. Starving's better than these . . .

*And he raises his hands again . . . and suddenly tautens them.*

*And* NELLY *pulls roughly, violently, at his sleeve, and drags him up, and pushes him out of the door into the darkness.*

### 82

SMALL ROOM IN LODGING-HOUSE

*We see the room from the angle of the window.*

BILLY *is still sprawling on the tilted chair in the corner.*

BROOM *leans against the table, arms folded, watching* BILLY. *He leans with his head a little to one side, enjoying the spectacle: a freak admiring a freak show.*

KATE *is still lying half on, half off the bed, her hand trailed in a puddle on the floor.*

BROOM. [*Softly.*] And when Mr. Fallon comes back, oh, we'll have fun and singing. . . . It's he's got a voice that'll send you to sleep like your mother's. . . . And oh, the joking and riddles!

*PAN ROUND to the door as* BROOM *speaks.* FALLON *is standing there. Behind him, almost in darkness, we see* NELLY.

FALLON *stands there at the door with his shoulders back and his head high. There is something almost of dignity about him: something that might suggest he is about to make a sacrifice.*

*And when he speaks, it is without the usual blarneying whine; a horror that has reached him has deepened the tone of his voice.*

FALLON. [*Slowly.*] Make Kate go.

*Now, from* NELLY'S *angle, behind* FALLON, *we see* BROOM *move across to the bed in two cat-padded jumps and pinch* KATE *awake.*

*She looks round the room, thick with sleep. She sees* BILLY *smiling at every one and no one; she sees the malicious face of* BROOM *above her; she sees* FALLON *grim in the doorway. And, sober in a second, and frightened, she scrambles to the door.*

FALLON *does not move; she has to squeeze herself past him, keeping her body as far away from his as she can.*

FALLON. Close the door.

*CUT to shot, from behind* BILLY, *over his crippled shoulders, of* FALLON *at the door and* BROOM *by the bed.*

FALLON's *eyes are staring straight at us.*

FALLON. [*Slowly.*] You mustn't be frightened, Billy.

FALLON *takes a step forward.*

FALLON. [*Slowly.*] It'll all be over soon. No more bein' hungry. . . .

*Now* FALLON, *slow as a priest, is moving towards us and* BILLY.

*CUT to shot, from door, of* FALLON *moving towards* BILLY, *and of* BILLY'S *bewildered, but still smiling, face. . . .*

FALLON. [*Slowly.*] No more . . . cold. . . .

*CUT to shot, from* BILLY'S *angle, of* FALLON *moving, as though in procession, down the room.*

*And behind him, on tiptoes, comes* BROOM. *Now they are almost upon us.*

*And suddenly we hear the voice of* BILLY: *screaming.*

### 83

OUTSIDE THE DOOR OF THE SMALL ROOM

NELLY *and* KATE *are standing close to the door.*

*A little light, as though from one candle, falls on their faces.*

*Around them, darkness.*

*The women stand tensed, waiting, close together. And from beyond the door comes* BILLY'S *scream.*

*The scream mounts, breaks, and bursts out again. The crash of a falling chair.*

*And now it is not a scream that comes from beyond the door but a terrified howling; and with it the sound of a deeper voice:* FALLON'S *voice—the voice of the damned inarticulately praying. And with it the smashing of wood, and glass breaking.*

*Then one scream destroys all other sounds. The women put their hands over their ears, press their hands hard.*

*And the women are rocking slowly to and fro, as though at the side of a death-bed, as though at a wailing-wall.*

*Then the scream goes out.*

*Slowly the women grow still, and they move their hands down.*

*The door opens.*

*Light falls upon the white-faced women.*

FALLON *stands at the door with his back to the room, so that we cannot see his face or the room behind him.*

FALLON *raises his hand to beckon the women in.*

*He turns around, goes into the light.*

*The women go after him, so that the doorway is never unoccupied and so that we do not see into the room.*

*Then the door closes.*

*FADE OUT*


*FADE IN*

### 84

*Birds flying over the City roofs.*
*Morning.*
*Music.*
*PAN DOWN from the roofs to the* MARKET-PLACE.

*As we PAN, we hear the voices of* CHILDREN *rising.*

*And* CHILDREN *are playing in the middle of the Market.*

*Then there is the clop-clop of hooves on cobbles. And down the Market comes a horse and cart.*

*As the horse and cart approach us, we see that* FALLON *is driving.*

*There is a large barrel in the back of the cart.*

BROOM *is thumping the barrel in time to the hoof-beats on the cobbles.*

*The* CHILDREN *scatter as the cart drives down.*

*And then the horse stops.*

FALLON *raises a stick and beats the horse. The horse will not move.*

BROOM *stops his rhythmic thumping on the barrel and stands up.*

*He shouts at* FALLON *and the horse in his piercing voice, and the scampering* CHILDREN *gather round the cart.*

BROOM. Beat the hide off his back, skin the divil alive. . . .

FALLON *beats the horse methodically, as though it were a carpet.*

THE CHILDREN. Skin the divil alive.

BROOM. Oh, the mule of hell, the stinkin' gob of the knackers' yard, I'll tear off its tail. . . .

THE CHILDREN. Tear off its tail, tear off its tail. . . .

FALLON *climbs off the cart and tries to drag the horse along by its bridle.*

*The horse will not move. And as* FALLON

*drags and pulls, so* BROOM *in the cart capers and cries, and so the* CHILDREN *in delight caper and cry with* BROOM.

*The people of the Market look on with little interest.*

BROOM. I'll tear the bit out its mouth. . . . Give me a red-hot poker. . . .

THE CHILDREN. Red-hot poker, red-hot poker. . . .

FALLON. [*Solemnly.*] You'd think the old mare had risen in judgment against us. . . .

*A* PORTER *passes the horse and cart, pushing an empty barrow. He pays no heed to the cater-wauling of* BROOM *and the* CHILDREN.

FALLON *sees the* PORTER.

FALLON. Hi, there!

*The* PORTER *stops.*

BROOM. I'll kick it in the kyte. . . .

FALLON. Would you take a barrel with you for two shillings? It's only a little barrel. . . .

PORTER. Where to? It's a great big barrel. . . .

FALLON. My friend'll show you where.

FALLON *beckons* BROOM, *who has now stopped cursing the horse and is snapping like a dog at the* CHILDREN.

FALLON. Here's the shillings.

*And* FALLON, BROOM, *and the* PORTER *lift the barrel down and put it on the barrow. As they carry it the* PORTER *says:*

PORTER. What you got in the barrel?

BROOM. Potatoes.

FALLON. Keep your talk in your mouth. You've got your money. . . .

*And* BROOM *and the* PORTER *go off with the barrow.*

*And suddenly the horse, as soon as the barrow has gone, goes off himself down the Market, to the cries of the* CHILDREN, *at a brisk trot.*

FALLON *shouts after it, but it trots on.*

THE CHILDREN. Skin the divil alive. . . . Tear off its tail, tear off its tail . . . Kick it in the kyte. . . .

FALLON, *after one shout, makes no attempt to follow the horse but walks back in the direction from which he had come; walks off heavy-shouldered and heavy-footed, his head sunken.*

*The voices of the* CHILDREN *fade.*

### 85

RAG-AND-BONE ALLEY

*TRACK UP to where a middle-aged* MAN

*and* WOMAN *are standing outside the door of the Lodging-house. The* WOMAN *carries a baby in a shawl. The* MAN *holds a little child by the hand. They are dressed like beggars. The* MAN *is carrying a bundle in a stick over his shoulder. He knocks at the door.*

WOMAN. It's a poor, dirty place.

MAN. It's got a roof. . . .

WOMAN. I think I'd rather be on the roads, sleeping in the hedge in the cold. . . .

*The door opens.*

KATE *stands in the doorway.*

*She wears a new shawl.*

KATE. You'll be wanting a bed? They're twopence.

MAN. Bed.

*The man unwraps a piece of cloth from his pocket, and brings out a coin.*

KATE. There's nobody sleeping at all here now. . . . You can take your fancy where you sleep. . . .

*The* MAN *and the* WOMAN *follow her into the house and into:*

*The Lodging-Room.*

*Even in daylight it is half dark. . . .*

KATE *walks down the room, and the* MAN *and the* WOMAN *follow her.*

KATE. You're strangers here. . . .

MAN. Strangers everywhere. . . .

KATE. You're from the roads?

*The* MAN *nods.*

WOMAN. I think we won't be troubling you for a bed. . . . It's *dark* here. . . .

KATE. It's darker on the roads. With no one you know in the world, and no one to take care of you. . . . I'll make the beds a penny each. What names d'you go by?

MAN. Mr. and Mrs. Webb.

WOMAN. We're respectable people. . . .

KATE. We're all respectable here. Just my husband and me. He's in the way of a merchant. . . .

*The* MAN *flings his bundle on a bed. And* KATE *looks at* MR. *and* MRS. WEBB.

### 86

CITY STREET

*The* PORTER *is pushing his barrow along,* BROOM *at his side.*

PORTER. You're sure you said it was potatoes in your—*little* barrel?

BROOM *winks.*

PORTER. They're very heavy potatoes. Where do we go with them?

BROOM. Up the City square. Doctor Rock's Academy.

PORTER. [*With a sideways glance at* BROOM.] He must be very fond of vegetables. . . .

## 87

HALLWAY OF ROCK'S ACADEMY

*Night.*

*The Hallway is deserted.*

*The door to the small Cloak-room under the stairs stands open.*

MURRAY *comes out of the Cloak-room.*

*He looks around him, like a man slowly coming out of a nightmare and trying to grow accustomed again to the familiar things of the daytime world.*

MURRAY. Tom! Tom! Where are you, Tom?

*But it is only a whisper.*

*And now he walks up the Hallway past the glass cases slowly.*

*He opens the door, and walks out through the colonnade into the moonlit garden of City Square. And as he moves through the garden so we hear the voice of his mind, and the remembered voices of others.*

MURRAY'S VOICE. Who brought the subject in, Tom? There's no need to ask.

TOM'S VOICE. Fallon and Broom, sir; Fallon and Broom. . . .

MURRAY'S VOICE. What can I do?

ELIZABETH'S VOICE. Keep quiet. . . .

MURRAY'S VOICE. Keep quiet about Jennie or they'll lock you up. . . .

ELIZABETH'S VOICE. Keep quiet. . . .

MURRAY'S VOICE. Keep quiet about Billy Bedlam in the little room, or they'll call you a murderer and a butcher. . . .

ELIZABETH'S VOICE. . . . stabbed or strangled, or beaten to death, or . . .

MURRAY'S VOICE. There are no marks of violence upon the body.

ELIZABETH'S VOICE. . . . You bear false witness. . . .

MURRAY'S VOICE. I swear that Jennie and Billy are murdered. . . .

ELIZABETH'S VOICE. It is quite easy for you to wreck your life. . . .

*And he turns and walks back through the garden towards the Academy. Now his step is quicker and more purposeful.*

## 88

ELIZABETH'S ROOM

ROCK, *his coat off, but still immaculately dressed, is seated in a deep chair with his head against the back of it.*

ELIZABETH *is curling what remains of his hair with curling-tongs.*

ROCK *has an air of indolent luxury.*

ROCK. [*Complacently.*] The sensual apotheosis of the intellectual animal. . . .

ELIZABETH. If you say so, my dear.

ROCK. The mind is relaxed, the body is pleasured and pampered, rancour has taken a holiday, and I am full of bliss, like a cat on the tiles of heaven. . . .

ELIZABETH. It must be very nice to talk. . . .

ROCK. It is comparable only to the pleasure of not having to think *as* you talk. . . . [*Sighing.*] I am a fool to-day.

ELIZABETH. Yes. Thomas . . .

ROCK. [*With a change of voice.*] But not so much of a fool as some I know. That rumour-breeder of a Murray! Falls in love with a pretty face and then won't cut it up once the little trollop's dead. Says she's murdered. Says, in effect, I murdered her myself.

ELIZABETH. [*Mildly.*] Oh, Thomas.

ROCK. When *I* take up assassination, I shall start with the surgeons in this city and work *up* to the gutter. . . . And now, to-day, along he comes with some fantastic rigmarole about a crippled idiot. Billy Bedlam. Says *he's* murdered, too. Poor Billy's bed was the cobbles, rain or snow, and he ate like a rat from the garbage heaps, and swallowed all the rot-gut he could buy or beg. He was a consumptive and an epileptic. A wonder he hadn't been found dead years ago. . . .

ELIZABETH. What did you tell Mr. Murray?

ROCK. I said: "Mr. Murray, go down and cut up the body and put it in the brine baths. Be careful you don't fall in yourself—you're wearing a good suit!"

ELIZABETH. [*Casually.*] And what did he do?

ROCK. What did he do? Why, what I told him to do, of course. No vicious-minded little prig with emotional adenoids is going to intimidate *me* with his whine and wail of "Murder! Murder!" He suffers from hallucinations. My hands, to him, are red as Macbeth's. . . .

ROCK *raises his very white hands in an ele-*

gant gesture, and smoothes the palm of one hand along the back of the other. . . .

## 89

*Music.*

*Pitch darkness.*

*Through the darkness, the laughter of* BROOM.

*Then sudden light, and* FALLON'S *hands, palms downwards, fingers stretched and tautened, murdering down the screen.*

*As the hands move we hear* FALLON'S *voice, blurred in a distorting mirror of sound.*

FALLON'S VOICE. There's devils in my hands. Let me go, my hands!

*Then, close, from above, the upward-staring faces of old women and children, their eyes wide, their mouths open.*

FALLON'S VOICE. Don't be frightened. . . . There's nothing to lose. . . .

*Then* FALLON'S *hands, palms upwards, fingers damp and limp, trembling up the screen.*

FALLON'S VOICE. It's all lost. . . .

*Then CLOSE-UP of* FALLON'S *face, drunk, arrogant, grinning. And we hear a voice questioning the face.*

VOICE. And where d'you get all the money so quick? You're rich, you're *rich,* you're . . .

FALLON'S VOICE. Ach, I done a little smuggling; a little bit o' drink on the sly. . . .

*The questioning* VOICE *continues through a CLOSE-UP of* NELLY *in a new feathered bonnet.* NELLY *drunk, secretive. . . .*

VOICE. And where d'you get all the money so quick? You're *rich,* you're . . .

NELLY'S VOICE. Oh, I've been left a property in the country.

*CLOSE-UP of* KATE *in a new bonnet.*

VOICE. And where d'you get all the money . . . [*The* VOICE *fades.*]

KATE'S VOICE. Oh, Fallon's the favourite of a great lady. . . . *Twenty* pounds a visit she gives him. . . .

*Then CLOSE-UP of* CHILDREN'S *faces.*

VOICE. Where's Billy? Billy Bedlam?

*And the voices of the* CHILDREN *answer as we see a CLOSE-UP of* ALICE.

VOICES OF CHILDREN. Gone, gone . . .

VOICE. Where's Jennie? Jennie Bailey?

*And* ALICE'S *voice answers as we see a CLOSE SHOT of a sack put down and hands undoing the sack.*

ALICE'S VOICE. Gone, gone . . .

*And out of the undone sack comes a human arm, and we hear the voice of the* PORTER.

PORTER'S VOICE. Doctor Rock is very fond of vegetables. . . .

*CLOSE SHOT of an* OLD MAN, *drooling drunk, his head capsized on one shoulder.*

BROOM'S VOICE. Drink with Broom. . . . Drink. . . .

*A hand with a bottle in it stretches across the screen towards him.*

*CUT to CLOSE-UP of the face of an* OLD WOMAN *looking up at the bottle held across the screen.*

BROOM'S VOICE. Drink . . . drink. . . .

*And, loudly, there is the noise of the pigs squealing.*

*DISSOLVE the picture to*

## 90

INTERIOR OF GROCER'S SHOP

*From the end of the shop, opposite the door, we can see a section of the Market-place in daylight.*

*The* GROCER, *behind the counter, is a truculent man in a dirty apron, who seems to have given up hope a long time ago: a man always at the end of his patience.*

*And before the counter an* OLD WOMAN *is standing, wrapped in pieces of the discarded clothing of the other poor.*

GROCER. For the last time, I don't know a Flynn. . . .

OLD WOMAN. Timothy Boylan Flynn. . . .

GROCER. I don't know a Flynn, I've never known a Flynn, I never want to . . .

OLD WOMAN. From County Donegal. . . . He came over two years ago and a half. . . . He's a tall, dark boy. . . . The lobes of his ears is pointed. . . .

FALLON *comes in at the shop door. He stands, framed against the Market, listening.*

GROCER. "What's the time of the day?" "Can you give me a wooden box?" "My sister's fallen under a hay cart—can you lend me a penn'orth of brandy?" "Have you seen a Flynn?" Will nobody ever *buy* anything? . . .

OLD WOMAN. Could you spare me a bite o' bread, then?

*The* GROCER *controls himself as* FALLON, *with a winning smile, comes to the counter.*

FALLON. [*To the* OLD WOMAN.] Did I hear you say "Flynn"? That was my mother's name.

OLD WOMAN. From Ardara, Donegal?

FALLON. [*Amazed.*] Ardara, Donegal! My mother's town! And would *your* name be—Flynn, too?

GROCER. *Her* name's Flynn, she's *looking* for a Flynn, and now your *mother's* name is Flynn. . . .

FALLON, *still looking at the* OLD WOMAN, *hands an earthenware jug over the counter to the* GROCER.

FALLON. Fill it up with dew.

*The* GROCER *disappears behind the counter.*

FALLON. [*Affectionately to the* OLD WOMAN.] Then you're my little cousin. . . .

*He kisses her forehead.* . . .

FALLON. Cousin Flynn. . . .

Faith, what a day of all days! I'm walking along gay as a thrush, I'm fragrant with the sweet smell of money, to-night's Hallowe'en when the witches fly and the whisky pours like rain, and who should I meet on top of it all but a Flynn from Ardara!

*The* GROCER *returns to his place behind the counter; he hands over the earthenware jug to* FALLON. FALLON, *tossing coins carelessly on the counter, pays for it; but he does not take his eyes off* MRS. FLYNN. . . .

MRS. FLYNN. It's my son for I'm looking all over, sir. . . .

FALLON. [*Emphatically.*] . . . Cousin. . . .

MRS. FLYNN. [*Hesitatingly.*] . . . Cousin. . . .

FALLON. And we'll find your son for you if we have to pull the town down and scramble among the cobbles. . . .

You come with me, cousin . . . you're welcome as sunlight. . . . I'll buy you a present for Hallowe'en, and I'll take you back to my fine house and we'll kick up a din like all Donegal drunk. . . .

FALLON, *with the jug and* MRS. FLYNN, *moves towards the door of the shop, towards the darkening Market.*

*As they go out we see a* CLOSE SHOT *of the* GROCER.

GROCER. [*With an awful resignation.*] Hallowe'en! . . .

## 91

RAG-AND-BONE ALLEY

*Late evening.*
*Music.*

*The Close is desolate.*

*We hear the dark noise of the wind blowing.*

*The noise grows, but the Close is emptily still.*

*The wind rises, to the rise of music.*

*And out of the gutters float the wind-driven shapes of witches and demons:*

*Waste paper flying out of the gutter, eddying into the air, fluttering, as though winged, past the shadowy houses:*

*Paper and rubbish gusted suddenly from the cobbles to flap and float about the street, to beat against the windows and scrabble there, to rise on the screaming breath of a wind and drift before the Lodging-house:*

*Straw blown in a squall, straw shapes and garbage shapes puffed through the growing, blowing dark:*

*Hay wisps and knotted straw, dust clouds and cloth shreds, small crumpled nameless shapes, light as paper and string, scudding through the narrowness:*

*All the inanimate furies of the Close alive suddenly, crying like the wind through telegraph wires, grotesque dancers from the dirt.* . . .

## 92

*Now we are standing at the end of the* LARGE LODGING-ROOM.

*We are looking down the mostly dark long room and through the open door into the small room.*

*We hear laughter, and snatches of singing, and a jig tune played on a penny whistle.*

BROOM *and* KATE, *arm in arm, come dancing out of the small room, turn in the narrow aisle between the beds, and dance, singing, back. We* TRACK UP *slowly to the open door.*

*As we track we see that one of the beds is occupied: by a* BABY *and a young* CHILD. *They are the children of* MR. *and* MRS. WEBB. *They are asleep. The* CHILD'S *arm is held protectingly around the* BABY.

*Now we are near the open door.*

*We see, in the small room,* FALLON *leaning against the table, playing a whistle. There are cups and mugs on the table, bottles, and the earthenware jug.*

*Behind* FALLON *are a* MAN *and a* WOMAN: *a squat and hairy* MAN *not unlike* FALLON, *and a slatternly young* WOMAN *with wayward hair and smile.*

*And* BROOM *and* MRS. FLYNN, *arm in arm, come dancing out of the small room, towards us.*

*We see them close as they turn in the narrow aisle between the beds.*

MRS. FLYNN *is gay as an old cat.*

BROOM *is smiling and possessive.*

*They dance, singing, back into the small room.*

*We TRACK right up to the open door.*

*In the small room we see that there are nine people:* FALLON, *penny-whistling at the table; the two strangers behind him singing the words of a jig;* KATE *and* NELLY *on the straw bed, beating jig-time on the littered floor;* BROOM *and* MRS. FLYNN *dancing between the table and the bed, dancing around the table; and* MR. *and* MRS. WEBB. MR. WEBB, *with a look of bemused contentment, is soaking pieces of bread in the earthenware jug and eating them;* MRS. WEBB, *disapproving, sits on the edge of the one sound chair in the room.*

MRS. WEBB *complains, through the singing, the dancing, the floor-beating, and the whistling.*

MRS. WEBB. Oh, the noise, it'll wake all the neighbours. . . .

THE MAN. They wouldn't wake to-night if you set their clothes on fire. . . . All the city's drunk. . . .

MRS. WEBB. [*To* MR. WEBB.] And stop eatin' bread and gin; it's bad for the stomach.

BROOM. It's Hallowe'en. . . .

THE MAN. It isn't us who's only making the din, you listen now. . . . Shh!

*The* MAN *raises his hand. For a moment the room is quiet. The dancers pause. From outside we hear the noise of drunken singing, and voices bawling and brawling.*

*Then* FALLON *begins to play again, and* BROOM *and* MRS. FLYNN *dance again, and the* MAN *and the* WOMAN *sing, and* KATE *and* NELLY, *speechless on the bed, go on thumping.*

MR. WEBB. Bread and gin's good for the stomach.

MRS. WEBB. You'll be waking the children, that's what'll happen next, with your caterwauling and your bang-bangs and your . . .

FALLON *stops playing.*

FALLON. And can't a man have a party now in honour of his cousin?

MR. WEBB. And rum and spuds is good.

FALLON. [*To* MRS. WEBB.] You're an auld spoil-sport, Mrs. Webb, you'd stop the dead dancin' on Judgment Day. . . .

*The* BABY, *from the next room, begins to scream.*

MRS. WEBB *jumps up and goes out.*

*But the screaming continues.*

FALLON. Now that's a baby that likes good music. . . .

*And he raises his penny whistle and plays again.*

MRS. WEBB *puts her head round the door.*

MRS. WEBB. For the Lord's sake now, is this a lodging house or a wake?

FALLON *nods to* NELLY.

*And* NELLY *totters to her feet and goes out of the room.*

## 93

*In the* LARGE LODGING-ROOM *we see* NELLY *and* MRS. WEBB *at the bed of the screaming* BABY.

*Through the open door we see the singers and dancers.*

NELLY. Oh, the poor creature. It screams like it swallowed a pin. . . . And Fallon'll be playing his whistle all night . . .

*Through the open door we see* FALLON *whistling and dancing a lonely jig.*

NELLY. . . . and there'll not be a breath of peace. . . . [*Wheedling.*] Now why don't you take the children away for the night. . . . Fallon's brother there will give you a bed and a plate of food. . . . And Fallon and us'll stay singing with old Mrs. Flynn till we a' fall down. . . .

*The* BABY *screams louder than ever.*

MRS. WEBB. [*Calling through the door.*] Come on with ye, Mr. Webb.

MRS. WEBB *begins to lift the children out of bed and wrap clothes around them.*

## 94

*Through darkness we see a shivering candle move, and moving figures. The* BABY *is still screaming.*

MR. WEBB. I don't want to go out in the cold. . . .

MRS. WEBB. You and your bread and gin! . . .

THE MAN. Only a couple of steps from here, Mrs. Webb. . . .

MR. WEBB. It's Hallowe'en! . . .

NELLY. I think you're very wise to go, my dear. There's no knowing what pranks Mr. Fallon'll be up to to-night. . . .

*A door is opened.*

*We see Rag-and-Bone Alley in the moonlight.*

*And the* MAN *and the* WOMAN, *and* MR. *and* MRS. WEBB *and the* BABY *and the* CHILD, *go out into the moonlight.*

*And* NELLY *closes the door.*

*Pitch darkness. From the darkness a sudden swell of sound: the squealing and squeaking of the tin whistle, and the singing of* BROOM.

*Then momentary quiet.*

*Then* BROOM'S *singing again, and, suddenly through it, a long, high, distant cry dwindling into silence again.*

### 95

*Snow falling in hard, bright morning light. Nothing on the screen but the falling snow. We hear a cock crow.*

*We CUT to a cock, on a wall, crowing in the middle of the snow, defiantly crying the morning up to the thick, falling flakes.*

*And now, as the snow drifts and drives past our eyes, we are looking, from the outside, through the Lodging-house window into the small room.*

*Isolated, behind the shifting wall of snow, sit* FALLON *and* BROOM, NELLY *and* KATE, *at the table in the middle of the room. Only* FALLON *is not eating.*

*We move through the snow and through the window into the room and towards the table.*

*We see the details of the room very clearly now in the merciless morning snow-light: no shadows, no twisted shapes in half-darkness, but only the bed with its straw guts straggling out, and the fouled straw-heap on the floor at the foot of the bed, and the thrown-away bottles and the flung scraps of clothes, and the broken glass and the drying pools of drink, and the last and the snippets of leather, and the tin whistle cast near the straw, and the piled boots in the corner, and the iron pot near the smoking fire.*

*Then* FALLON *rises from the table and crosses to the window.*

*From behind him, looking over his tensed shoulders, we see the falling snow.*

FALLON. The snow won't ever stop. It's like the last day.

*And his voice, and his measured movements, and the concentrated stillness of the others, suggest the anticlimax after death.*

*And now, from the end of the room opposite the door, we see the door open and* MR. *and* MRS. WEBB *come in. Their clothes are white with snow.*

BROOM *leaps to his feet.* FALLON *turns, with a measured, deliberate movement from the window.*

NELLY *and* KATE *sit still at the table, looking up at* MRS. WEBB.

BROOM. [*With a frightening smile.*] You frightened us.

*And he goes out of the room, followed by* KATE.

NELLY. You're early.

MRS. WEBB. I been up and about since dawn; the baby wouldn't fall to sleep at all—it screamed like things were after it. . . .

FALLON *stands still at the window, looking at* MRS. WEBB.

NELLY. What have you come for so early?

MRS. WEBB. I come to look for the little boy's stockings. I left them here last night drying by the fire; and I come for our bits and pieces. . . . It's time we're moving. . . .

MRS. WEBB *is looking round the room.*

*She pulls out a clay pipe from her wrappings and lights it at the fire.*

*With the blackened pipe burning like a little hayrick in her mouth, she bends down and searches among the scraps of clothes on the floor near the straw.*

FALLON. Get away from that straw with your old pipe. . . . You'll have the room blazing. . . .

FALLON *speaks so harshly that* MRS. WEBB *takes an involuntary step backward and sits on the end of the bed.*

MR. WEBB. Where's Mrs. Flynn? [*Appreciatively.*] She was a very gay old woman, dancin' like a nanny-goat. . . .

NELLY. She was ow'r gay with Fallon. I tumbled her out of the house in the middle o' the night. . . .

MR. WEBB. [*With a side look at his wife.*] I like a gay old woman. . . .

FALLON. Get out o' my room. . . . Take your reeky scraps of rubbish and your yelpin' children and get out. . . .

FALLON *does not move from the window, but*

*his stillness is more menacing than movement.*

*And* MR. *and* MRS. WEBB *go out. As they go* MRS. WEBB *whines:*

MRS. WEBB. I want my little boy's stockings. . . .

FALLON *is alone with* NELLY.

FALLON. The snow's falling heavier. The world's cold.

*He shivers, pulls his coat closer about him.*

FALLON. It's cold in hell to-day. The fires are out.

NELLY *looks at him in uncomprehending silence.*

FALLON. Nothing can burn me any more. I'm a cold man, Nelly. I'm numb all over, like an old dead finger-nail. No more dancing. No more drinking and singing.

*He shivers again, standing against the window and the snow.*

FALLON. I got work to do.

*And he goes out, followed by the strangely silent* NELLY.

*The door closes.*

*The room is empty.*

*Then the door opens, very slowly, and* MRS. WEBB *puts her head round and looks at the emptiness.*

*She comes in, whispering over her shoulder.*

MRS. WEBB. They've gone.

*And* MR. WEBB *comes in, nervously glancing behind him and on every side.*

MR. WEBB. Find the stockings and let's be out of the house.

MRS. WEBB *is down on her knees now by the pile of old clothes; she rummages through them.*

MRS. WEBB. Who wanted to come to this house? I said it was bad. I could smell the badness as I come in. It's nothing but drinking and howling all night. . . .

*Suddenly she stops in her scrabbling search through the clothes and lifts up a crumpled dress.*

MRS. WEBB. It's the old woman's dress.

MR. WEBB. How'd she be walking in the streets in the snow without her dress?

MRS. WEBB. It's the old woman's dress. I mind the colour.

*She starts to search among the clothes again, her hands nearing the straw.*

MR. WEBB. A body doesna walk in the streets without her . . .

MRS. WEBB *lifts up a ragged shawl.*

MRS. WEBB. And here's her little patchy shawl. . . .

*Now she is worrying the straw, like a dog on a scent.*

MRS. WEBB. And here's her . . .

*And* MRS. WEBB *screams.*

*A human arm lies naked in the parted straw.*

MRS. WEBB *springs up and stands, with her back to us, looking down at the straw and the arm.*

*The scream stops.*

MR. WEBB *bends down; facing us, he flings the rest of the straw aside.*

*We do not see what he reveals, for* MRS. WEBB *stands between us and it.*

MR. WEBB. The gay old woman! Her face is a' slimy.

*Music.*

MRS. WEBB *rushes out of the room.*

*And, as* MR. WEBB *follows her, we see, for a flash, the dead white face among the straw.*

## 96

*In the* LARGE LODGING-ROOM MR. *and* MRS. WEBB *are frenziedly packing their bits and pieces into a sheet.*

*The music rises.*

*They rush, he with the sheet sacked over his shoulder, to the far door.*

*And suddenly* NELLY *is standing there, in the doorway.*

*The music stops.*

NELLY. Where are you going? What have you seen?

MRS. WEBB. Let me out, she's dead. . . .

NELLY. She died in her sleep. . . .

MR. WEBB. Her mouth's blood. . . .

MRS. WEBB. For the love o' Mary . . .

NELLY. *She died in her sleep.* . . .

MRS. WEBB. . . . Let me out. . . .

NELLY *tears inside her apron, pulls out a purse, opens it. She pushes a handful of coins towards* MRS. WEBB.

NELLY. Nobody knows her, nobody'll claim her, you mustn't tell a word . . .

MR. WEBB. Stand away . . .

NELLY. . . . she died like a baby. . . .

MRS. WEBB. You killed her in there last night. . . .

NELLY. You mustn't tell a word, mercy, quiet, quiet. . . . Fallon'll give you ten pounds, ten pounds a week . . .

MR. WEBB *thrusts* NELLY *aside.*

MRS. WEBB *runs through the door,* MR. WEBB *after her.*

NELLY, *at the door, cries out after them* ...

NELLY. Ten pounds ...

## 97

RAG-AND-BONE ALLEY

*Music.*

*Snow falling heavily.*

MR. *and* MRS. WEBB *rush out of the Lodging-house.*

*The* WEBB'S *boy, with the* BABY *in his arms, stands, waiting, like a little snow man near the door.*

MRS. WEBB *snatches the* BABY *from his arms, hugs it to her shawls, and hurries on up the Alley.*

MR. WEBB *takes the* BOY'S *hand and follows. They keep to the right of the Alley.*

*And down the left of the Alley, coming towards the Lodging-house, we see* FALLON *and* BROOM *and a* PORTER.

*But, with the fierce snow driving upon them, upon their faces and their eyes, they do not see the wrapped-up figures of the hurrying* WEBBS.

*And the* WEBBS *do not see them.*

## 98

SMALL ROOM IN LODGING-HOUSE

*In the middle of the room is a tea-chest.*

FALLON, BROOM, *and the* PORTER *stand, snowy-coated, around the chest.*

*The* PORTER *is the one we saw taking the barrel in his barrow.*

*He is pressing down the lid with all his weight.*

*And* FALLON *helps him.*

BROOM *points a finger at the top of the lid.*

*A bunch of grey hair hangs out.*

FALLON *crosses to the last and the leather pieces and brings back a pair of cobbler's scissors.*

*The* PORTER *cuts off the hair with the scissors.*

## 99

INTERIOR OF POLICE STATION

MR. *and* MRS. WEBB *are talking to a* POLICEMAN.

MR. WEBB. And there was blood all over her face. . . .

POLICEMAN. Aye.

MRS. WEBB. And her poor lips were blue and her eyes were staring out as though somebody'd pressed 'em with his thumbs. . . .

*The* POLICEMAN *nods.*

MR. WEBB. She said she came from Donegal. . . .

POLICEMAN. The "dead woman" told ye she'd come from Donegal?

## 100

CITY STREET

*We see* FALLON *and* BROOM *walking, in the slanting snowstorm, by the side of the* PORTER *and his barrow with the tea-chest on it.*

## 101

INTERIOR OF POLICE STATION

MR. *and* MRS. WEBB *are still pleading to the* POLICEMAN.

MR. WEBB. No, no, sir, she said she'd come from Donegal when we was all drinkin' together last night. . . .

POLICEMAN. Drinkin'!

MRS. WEBB. Mrs. Flynn her name was, I've told you twenty times. . . .

MR. WEBB, *with hesitant, frightened fingers touches his own mouth.*

MR. WEBB. And now there's blood all over here. . . .

POLICEMAN. [*Placatingly.*] You sit down now. I'll come with you by and by. . . .

*He turns away from them and moves towards the back of the room.*

MRS. WEBB. [*Dully, as though repeating a lesson.*] Mrs. Flynn her name was. . . . They killed her. . . . Fallon and Broom. . . .

## 102

*The always shadowy* HALL IN ROCK'S ACADEMY, *with its white secret witnesses staring from the glass cases.*

ROCK *is mounting the stairs.*

*We follow him as he climbs, and hear the voice of his mind.*

ROCK'S VOICE. Gentlemen. . . . Gentlemen, let us to-day dissect the human conscience. Lay it on the slab. Open it up.

You see? The liver of the conscience is knobbled by emotional excesses.

The veins of the conscience are full of bad blood.

The heart of the conscience palpitates like a snared rabbit's. . . .

*Now he is walking along the Corridor, opening a door, to the small Reference Library.*

## 103

REFERENCE LIBRARY IN ROCK'S ACADEMY

ROCK'S VOICE. In short, gentlemen, the conscience is a *very* unhealthy subject. . . .

*And, at the end of these words, he is sitting in a chair behind a desk, facing us.*

*The room is empty.*

*And* ROCK, *at the desk, addresses the empty room as though there were a gathering of students in it, turning from one invisible listener to another.*

ROCK. There is right and wrong, gentlemen, just as there is right and left. Mine is the *right* direction. The fact that the majority would consider it the *wrong* direction, only substantiates my opinion that I am right. . . .

*There is a knock on the door.*

ROCK. Stay out.

TOM *comes in.*

ROCK. I see, sir, that to keep you out I should have said, "Come in."

TOM. Fallon and Broom, sir.

ROCK. Indeed? Must I laugh, weep, tear my hair, swoon for ecstasy!

TOM. They've brought a body, sir.

ROCK. I did not expect that they would bring a soul.

TOM. [*Suggestively.*] They bring so many subjects, sir . . . sixteen or more up till to-day . . . and always fresh. . . .

ROCK. They are corpse-diviners. Or, as some have green fingers for gardening, so they have black fingers for death. Do you expect the dead to walk here, Tom? They need assistance. Fallon and Broom provide that assistance. Have Mr. Murray pay them.

TOM. Yes, sir.

TOM, *with a side glance at* ROCK, *goes out.*

*And* ROCK, *alone, again speaks in a soft voice to his unseen audience.*

ROCK. You see, gentlemen?

## 104

SMALL ROOM IN LODGING-HOUSE

*We look at the room from above.*

*In the centre of the room stands the* POLICE-MAN. *Behind him, standing close together for protection, are* MR. *and* MRS. WEBB.

FALLON *leans against the table, facing the* POLICEMAN.

*And behind him are* KATE, NELLY, *and* BROOM.

*They are frozen.*

*As, from above, we move down closer to them, they unfreeze.*

FALLON. [*Smiling.*] And where did the old fools tell ye they saw the body, sir?

MRS. WEBB *points to the straw.*

*The* POLICEMAN *kicks the straw aside.* BROOM *laughs.*

FALLON. Maybe the mice, they dragged it down their little hole. . . .

*The* POLICEMAN *bends down, to stare at the floor-boards.*

POLICEMAN. Blood on the boards.

*A moment's silence.*

FALLON. And has there ever been, for the love o' God, a Hallowe'en party with no blood spilt? We was all convivial; there was fightin' in every room of the house.

NELLY. And the old woman Flynn, she was so fashous I told her go with the toe of my boot. . . .

KATE. [*Pointing to the* WEBBS.] And it's they were picking the pockets of the poor innocent persons that couldn't get up from the floor. . . .

NELLY. It's all lies, lies they said. . . .

*The* POLICEMAN *picks up the dress that* MRS. WEBB *had found.*

KATE. Don't you trust them, they're beggars, sir. . . .

BROOM. They eat dead cats. . . .

MRS. WEBB. That's Mrs. Flynn's dress. . . . I mind the colour. . . .

BROOM. Fur and all. . . .

NELLY. That's not hers, it's mine. . . .

POLICEMAN. Blood on the front.

NELLY. Fallon hit me with a glass in the face and the cut ran. . . .

MR. WEBB. The old woman's face was a' slimy. . . .

*And as* MR. WEBB *speaks, so we hear the ringing of church bells. . . .*

*DISSOLVE.*

## 105

POLICEMAN *and* MR. *and* MRS. WEBB *with their two children walking up snow-thick* STREET. *Snow is no longer falling.*

*The sound of Sunday church bells rises.*

*And, black for Sunday, people hurry by over the white snow.*

## 106

CITY SQUARE

*Outside Hocking's Academy* MR. *and* MRS. WEBB *stand shivering and waiting, the* BABY *huddled in* MRS. WEBB'S *shawls, the little* BOY *with his hands dug deep in* MR. WEBB'S *coat pocket.*

*The door of Hocking's Academy opens.*

*The* POLICEMAN *comes out.*

*A* PORTER *stands at the door.*

POLICEMAN. If there's a new subject comes in to-day, let me know.

*He walks towards Rock's Academy, beckoning the* WEBBS *to follow him.*

*He knocks on the door of Rock's Academy.*

*The grille opens.*

*From the* POLICEMAN'S *angle we see* TOM'S *face through the bars.*

POLICEMAN'S VOICE. Have you had a new subject to-day?

TOM. Aye.

POLICEMAN'S VOICE. Open the door.

*The door opens.*

*The* POLICEMAN *walks in.*

## 107

SMALL DARK ROOM off the HALL in ROCK'S ACADEMY

*We see the figures of* TOM *and the* POLICEMAN, *and the shape of the tea-chest.*

POLICEMAN. Open the chest.

TOM *opens the tea-chest.*

*The* POLICEMAN *looks down into it.*

POLICEMAN. When was it brought?

TOM. An hour ago.

POLICEMAN. Who brought it?

*CUT to CLOSE-UP of* MRS. FLYNN'S *face. With a sudden after-death jerk of the muscles, her mouth drops open, as though she were speaking.*

*And* TOM *speaks as the mouth opens.*

TOM'S VOICE. Fallon and Broom.

*CUT BACK to the small dark room, the* POLICEMAN, *and* TOM.

POLICEMAN. Fetch in the old couple. They're waiting outside.

TOM *goes out.*

*The* POLICEMAN *looks round the dark room. We follow his eyes: we see, in a corner, what might be a body covered with a sheet: in another corner, what might be a cupboard or an upright coffin.*

POLICEMAN. [*In a whisper.*] Cold!

MR. *and* MRS. WEBB *come into the room.*

*The* POLICEMAN *nods towards the open tea-chest.*

*Timidly they move towards it and look down.*

MR. WEBB. The old woman.

MRS. WEBB *nods and crosses herself.*

POLICEMAN. What was her name?

*CUT again to CLOSE-UP of* MRS. FLYNN'S *face.*

MRS. WEBB'S VOICE. Mrs. Flynn....

## 108

REFERENCE LIBRARY IN ROCK'S ACADEMY

ROCK, *a sheet of paper in his hand, is walking up and down, in a characteristic lecture manner, behind his desk.*

*Some distance away, the other side of the desk, sits* MURRAY.

ROCK. [*Gesturing with the paper in his hand.*] If this does not upset some apple-carts, I shall believe that the apples have been glued on like the coco-nuts in coco-nut shies; if this does not help to change the idiotic laws that apply to our profession, I shall run amok; I shall send Doctor Hocking a Christmas Greeting and sign it "Yours in Homage"; I shall place my spiritual welfare in the hands of the Reverend Doctor Lever and have my seat *reserved* in hell.

MURRAY. I tell you, this isn't the time to attack.

ROCK. The national anthem of the rabbit world.

MURRAY. If you publish that letter now, attacking the system by which the medical schools get their bodies, you'll be raising a question you might have some difficulty in answering *yourself.*

ROCK. Am I still a Doctor Bluebeard to you, then, you terrified old lady? Do I spend my nights a-murdering?

MURRAY. I do not know, sir, what you do

with your nights. I do not imagine that you can *sleep*. But I do know that *Fallon* and *Broom* are murderers. It is only my respect for you, and my great obligations, and my *cowardice*, that have stopped me from running out of this murder school and telling the whole city what I know and what I guess.... Even so, there are rumours. *I* have not spread them. But Jennie's death, and Billy's, have not passed *quite* unnoticed. Rumours are contagious.

ROCK. So are scabies. To destroy them you do not wear the armour of defence, you wield the weapon of sulphur ointment. And, by God, there's sulphur in this letter....

TOM *comes in.*

TOM. The police have been here.

ROCK. What is yours, sir? A rum and bitters?

TOM. [*Bewildered.*] Sir?

ROCK. Since you do not knock before you come in, I must assume that this is a public-house....

TOM. I beg your pardon, sir, but the police came about the new subject. Fallon and Broom, sir.

ROCK. Am I never to hear the end of those men's names?

MURRAY. [*Softly.*] Never, perhaps....

TOM. And they're taking the subject away....

ROCK. Why didn't you call the police? ...

TOM. [*More bewildered.*] Sir, I ...

ROCK. Go away and lock up the silver. If there isn't any silver, lock up Mr. Mattheson: he has a gold tooth.

*And* TOM *goes out.*

MURRAY. Must you antagonize every one?

ROCK. Yes.

MURRAY. You heard? The police.

ROCK. Outside the gates of hell are not the words "Abandon Hope All Ye Who Enter Here," but "I Told You So."

MURRAY. And if the police ask me questions, as they are bound to do, what shall I say?

ROCK. Say nothing. Squeak. They will recognize the voice of a rat.

MURRAY *goes to the door. As he opens it* ROCK *speaks.*

ROCK. You will find cheese in the larder. Leave some for Tom.

*The door slams.*

CLOSE-UP *of* ROCK. *The sardonicism, the mockery, have vanished from his face.*

*DISSOLVE.*

## 109

*LONG SHOT of* LONG CORRIDOR IN ROCK'S ACADEMY

*We see* TOM *coming up towards us from the end of the Corridor.*

*We see him open a door, put his head round the door. We hear him speak into the room behind the door, but are too far away to catch the words.*

*He comes on up the Corridor, opens another door, puts his head round the door. We hear him speak into the room behind the door, but though his voice is louder now, we still cannot catch the words.*

*He comes on up the Corridor, opens the door of the Reference Library, puts his head round the door. And now we are close enough to hear the words.*

TOM. Fallon and Broom. They've arrested Fallon and Broom. Murder.

*He withdraws his head.*

*From the opposite end of the Corridor we now see, in LONG SHOT,* TOM *padding on, away from camera....*

*DISSOLVE.*

## 110

*To another* CORRIDOR

*TRACK UP the empty Corridor.*

*As we track we hear a mumble of voices growing louder. We reach a door marked "Board Room."*

*The noise rises.*

## 111

INTERIOR OF BOARD ROOM

*Around the long table are* ATTORNEYS, COUNSEL, POLICE OFFICIALS, HOCKING, *and* GREEN.

FIRST POLICE OFFICIAL.... and if Doctor Rock did not know that these bodies were murdered, he's a far less canny gentleman than I supposed....

FIRST ATTORNEY. He knew. One corpse might pass him by, but Fallon and Broom were in the wholesale trade....

SECOND POLICE OFFICIAL. Indict him as accessory after the fact....

HOCKING. I do not exonerate Doctor Rock,

but I will not have the whole medical profession of the City put on trial.

GREEN. Accuse Rock, you accuse the integrity of all the surgeons in the City.

*The* CHAIRMAN (*the* LORD CHIEF JUSTICE) *nods in agreement.*

HOCKING. Oh, more than that. The whole aristocracy of learning that has been so carefully built up would be tumbled to the ground. The stain upon his character would spread across the whole of our culture. There could be no more respect for us. Indictment of Rock would mean *the death of a class....*

### 112

PRIVATE SMOKEROOM IN AN INN (*as in Sequence 27*)

*The two old* GENTLEMEN *are seated there with silver tankards in their hands.*

FIRST GENTLEMAN. A great pity his letter appeared in all the newspapers....

SECOND GENTLEMAN. On the very day of the arrest. Your health!

FIRST GENTLEMAN. Health!

SECOND GENTLEMAN. It was so very untactful.

*There is a silence during which they drink. They gaze at their tankards.*

FIRST GENTLEMAN. "We must have more bodies," he said. Dear, dear.

SECOND GENTLEMAN. We must have more *murders.*

FIRST GENTLEMAN. An ugly word, Richard.

SECOND GENTLEMAN. Doctor Rock has endangered the dignity of the higher professions. ... If he is indicted as accessory after the fact ...

FIRST GENTLEMAN. No, no, Richard, that must never be. Guilty or not guilty, his part in this affair must be kept in a decent obscurity, or Anarchy will be walking abroad in the land....

SECOND GENTLEMAN. They should all be shot against the wall....

FIRST GENTLEMAN. Who, Richard?

*The* SECOND GENTLEMAN *makes a vague, sweeping gesture.*

SECOND GENTLEMAN. All of 'em....

### 113

*CLOSE SHOT of two elderly* PROFESSORS *in mortar-boards and gowns, against the back-*

*ground of a very large, ornately gold-framed portrait of another old professor.*

FIRST PROFESSOR. I agree with you entirely. His whole attitude to society spelt ruin from the first. Attack Tradition, it always bites back; and its teeth are well grounded.

SECOND PROFESSOR. A man who could be so persistently and obnoxiously rude to his elders and intellectual betters would think *nothing* of murdering his *own children* for a penny piece.

FIRST PROFESSOR. That is, perhaps, a little extravagant. We *must* disregard personal prejudice, though I agree that to be called "anaemic buffoon" could not predispose him in your favour. But Rock is a *symbol....*

SECOND PROFESSOR. I agree. A symbol of scholarship. In a manner of speaking, we could regard ourselves as "the royal family of the intellect," and ...

FIRST PROFESSOR. My dear Fraser! ...

SECOND PROFESSOR. ... and if a member of the royal family is accused of a commoner's crime, then it is the *whole family* that is accused. An elaborate simile—but you see my point?

*And the two professors wag their chins in complete agreement.*

### 114

INTERIOR OF BOARD ROOM

*Around the table the* ATTORNEYS, COUNSEL, POLICE OFFICIALS, HOCKING, *and* GREEN.

FIRST ATTORNEY. Perhaps we are forgetting the murder of children and old women in our concern for our sacred society of autocratic schoolmen....

CHAIRMAN. It is a very grave position....

SECOND POLICE OFFICIAL. Rock is guilty of connivance....

FIRST POLICE OFFICIAL. I am afraid we *will* have to use him as a witness, gentlemen....

CHAIRMAN. Oh, certainly, certainly....

*The* POLICE OFFICIALS *rise.*

CHAIRMAN. [*In an undertone to* HOCKING *next to him.*] But we won't call him, of course.

### 115

CORRIDOR IN ROCK'S ACADEMY

TOM *padding up the Corridor.*

*He stops outside the Reference Library, opens the door.*

*From behind him we see into the library.*

Rock *is seated at his desk.*

Tom. Broom has turned king's evidence, sir.

Rock. [*Without looking up.*] The king will be pleased. . . .

Tom *closes the door, pads on up the long Corridor again, and turns a corner, leaving the Corridor empty.*

*We hear the very distant noise of a crowd. . . .*

### 116

*LONG SHOT of narrow* CITY STREET

*Early morning.*

*The street is empty.*

*We hear, kept very low, the noise of a great* • *crowd: the grumbling of a sea far off.*

### 117

*LONG SHOT of another narrow, empty* STREET

*The noise of a great crowd rising, slowly.*

### 118

*LONG SHOT of another narrow, empty* STREET

*Then, across the far end of the desolate tunnel of the street, we see the crowd surging.*

*And the noise increases.*

*The camera moves down the narrow street towards the surge of the crowd and the increasing noise.*

*It moves past empty doorways.*

*And out of the empty doorways, through the clamour of the nearing crowd, we hear chanted:*

First Voice. Up the alley and down the street . . .

*On, on, past another doorway.*

Second Voice. Fallon and Broom sell bones and meat. . . .

*Past another doorway.*

Third Voice. Fallon's the butcher, Broom's the thief . . .

*Now we are nearly among the crowd pouring past the narrow street end, but we hear a fourth voice through the noise. . . .*

Fourth Voice. And Rock's the boy who buys the beef. . . .

*And now, through and under the loud noise of the crowd, we hear many voices together taking up the chant.*

*The camera cranes with and over the heads*

*of the crowd and up to the windows of the court-room, and into the court-room.*

### 119

COURT-ROOM

*We see the backs of the* JUDGES.

*We move past them, across the court, towards the dock.*

*As we move we hear the droning voice of the* CLERK *of the Court. . . .*

CLERK. Robert Fallon and Nelly Connor, you are both and each of you indicted and accused . . .

*In the dock, facing us, are* FALLON *and* NELLY. *They are both more neatly dressed than usual.* NELLY *is in black.* FALLON *is cleanshaven.*

*We move past them.*

*Now from behind them, we look down at the* CLERK *of the Court, who is seated beneath the* JUDGES' *bench.*

*The* CLERK *has not stopped speaking. Now the sound of his voice rises.*

CLERK. . . . that albeit by the laws of this and every other well-governed realm, murder is a crime of an heinous nature, and severely punishable, yet true it is and of verity that you the said Robert Fallon and Nelly Connor are both and each, or one or other of you, guilty of the said crime. . . .

*The sound of the* CLERK'S *voice is lowered. Now it is a drone the words of which we cannot catch.*

*And, through the droning, we hear the muffled noise of the crowd outside.*

*We move, past* FALLON *and* NELLY, *towards the judges.*

*PAN ALONG the* JUDGES' *bench.*

*PAN DOWN to the* CLERK. *The* CLERK'S *voice rises.*

CLERK. . . . when she the said Jennie Bailey was lying in the said house in a state of intoxication, and did, by the pressure thereof, and by covering her mouth and nose with your body or person, and forcibly compressing her throat with your hands, and forcibly keeping her down, notwithstanding her resistance, or in some other way to the prosecutor unknown . . .

*CUT to CLOSE-UP of* FALLON.

CLERK. . . . preventing her from breathing, did suffocate or strangle her. . . .

*The noise of the crowd rises, then is dimmed into a background.*

*DISSOLVE to*

### 120

ROCK'S LECTURE HALL

*Evening.*
*The background of the crowd noise.*
ROCK *is on the platform.*
*The candles are lit on the platform table.*
*The auditorium is crowded with students.*
*The noise of the crowd rises violently.*
*Through the noise of the crowd, we hear the percussive voice-beat of "Rock! Rock! Rock!"*
*And, like a cymbal clashing, the sharp crash of smashed glass.*
*Stones hurl through the shattered window at one side of the Lecture Hall.*
*The students stampede to their feet.*
*And a heavy stone crashes at* ROCK'S *foot.*
*The students begin to rush down the gallery steps towards the doors and the platform, shouting.*
ROCK *stands rigid.*
*He pales with temper, glaring at the rushing students as though they were his enemies.*
*In its intensity, his dignity is malevolent.*
ROCK. Gentlemen!
*Cold, controlled fury stops the rush.*
*The students stand frozen.*
*The noise of the crowd is still loud.*
ROCK. I have attempted to teach you the dignity of man; I have succeeded in producing the degradation of a *mob*. Because the verminous gutter-snipes of the City snarl and gibber in the street, because the scum from the brothels and the rot-gut shops howl for blood outside my window, must *you* conduct yourselves, in return, as though you were born in a quagmire and nurtured on hog-wash?

Take your seats. Pay no attention to *the mob*. The mob can never win. Remember that the louder a man shouts, the emptier is his argument.

Remember that you are here to study osteology, syndesmology, myology, angiology, neurology, splanchnology: not bar-room pugilism or the morals of the crapulous bog-trotter and the tosspot.

[*In his usual lecturing voice.*] The heart,

gentlemen, is a four-chambered muscular bag which lies in the cavity of the thorax . . .

*DISSOLVE to*

### 121

CITY STREET

*Night.*
*The noise of the crowd is a distant, insistent background. We see, striding in front of us, the black-cloaked top-hatted figure of* ROCK *with his heavy stick.*
*We follow him along the street.*
*Two figures, muffled against the cold, come out of a side-street.*
*They stumble into* ROCK.
*He pushes them aside.*
*And suddenly one of them cries out:*
FIRST MAN. Rock! Rock! Doctor Rock!
ROCK *strides on.*
*The men cry after him, and follow him down the street, though keeping a safe distance from him.*
SECOND MAN. Doctor Rock! Rock!
*And, from some way off, we hear the crowd take up the percussive noise of "Rock! Rock! Rock!"*

### 122

*DISSOLVE to* ROCK, *hatless, but still in his cloak, entering* ELIZABETH'S ROOM.

ELIZABETH, *by the fire, is sewing.*
ELIZABETH *looks up as he comes in, and puts her sewing down.*
*He crosses to her; kisses her; stands still then, looking down at her.*
*CLOSE-UP of* ROCK *and* ELIZABETH.
ROCK. Oh, there's peace in here.
ELIZABETH. You didn't come home *alone* through the streets? I've been hearing the crowd everywhere, all the evening.
ROCK. Alone.
ELIZABETH. They might have hurt you. . . .
ROCK. Hurt *me*?
*With a flourish he opens his cloak. Stuck in a belt around his waist are two pistols and a long dagger.*
ROCK. I'd fell them to the ground. I'd flood the gutters with their . . .
ELIZABETH *begins to laugh, though quite gently.*

ELIZABETH. Take off your cloak. And put your silly knives and guns away. You're like a boy pretending to be a highwayman. "Stand and deliver." Oh, Thomas, my dear . . .

*He takes off his cloak and flings it over a chair and places the belt, the knife, and the guns on a table near the fire: a small table covered with sewing and bales of wool and cotton reels.*

ELIZABETH. Why do you have to go out alone at night, *now?* Why do you *always* have to be alone?

ROCK. If the crowd wants me, it can have me. I am not going to hide. I am not going to surround myself by a company of paid protectors. . . .

ELIZABETH. [*Softly.*] I've always wanted to see another country. Couldn't we go away? Every one is against us here, now.

*The distant noise of the crowd.*

ELIZABETH. The women in the street didn't nod to me this morning. Not because I'm your wife—that's why they used to have nothing to do with me—but because *you're* my husband.

ROCK. We won't go away.

ELIZABETH. [*Gently, as throughout.*] I know why. You want to show them that they can't hurt you by calling you names. You want to show them that you don't *mind* when they say that you told those men to murder people. But they *do* hurt you.

ROCK. *Time's a wilderness.* [*Then, in a changed voice.*] Do you remember walking in the park? Oh, not so long ago. It was very, very, very cold and windy, people were scudding along like ships in a gale, and I remember thinking: "Here's my life going true and even, and my children growing, and Elizabeth with me for ever, and books to write, and work to do. . . . Lord, but it's a happy time . . . even in the unhappy times."

ELIZABETH. I'm with you for ever, that's true. And there's books to write, and work to do.

*Noise of the crowd nearer.*

ROCK. [*Suddenly in another mood.*] I was successful, I was established, I was standing in the light. . . . Then out of the mud of the darkness come two ignorant animals, and slowly, quite unknown to themselves, they set about the task of bringing my life and my work down, down, into the slime that bred them. . . . Perhaps from the very moment of their monstrous births, it was decreed, by some sadistic jack-in-office of the universe, that they should befoul and ruin a fellow creature they had never heard of: a garrulous, over-credulous, conceited little anatomist, in a city they had never seen. . . .

*From outside the noise of the crowd rises. And as the noise rises, so the voices of* ELIZABETH *and* ROCK *become quieter and more intimate.*

ELIZABETH. Let us go away.

ROCK. No, we must stay for ever.

ELIZABETH. I have never asked you before, Thomas, because I love you. Did you know that the bodies that those men brought you had been murdered?

*The noise of the crowd rises. Now it is very loud.*

*And the night sky beyond the window is glowing.*

ELIZABETH *and* ROCK *turn sharply to look towards the window.*

VOICES OF THE CROWD. Rock! Rock! Hang Rock! Burn him! Burn! Burn! Rock's the boy who buys the beef. . . .

ANNABELLA *comes in. She is palely, composedly angry.*

ANNABELLA. Do you know what those hooligans are *doing,* Thomas?

*She crosses to the window.*

ROCK. I gather that they are not subscribing to a testimonial to me. . . .

ANNABELLA. Look! Look!

*She points accusingly out of the window.*

*And* ROCK *and* ELIZABETH, *he with his arm around her shoulder, cross to* ANNABELLA'S *side and look, through the window, down on to the street.*

## 123

STREET OUTSIDE ROCK'S HOUSE

*We see, from the window, the crowd straining against the iron railings of the house; the crowd, in the middle of the street, dancing with torches in their hands; the crowd carrying an effigy of* ROCK, *an absurdly top-hatted scarecrow; the crowd waving their torches, stamping, howling, making a witches' Sabbath in the decorous, graciously façaded street.*

*And then the effigy, the guy carried on a*

*pole, is held in a position directly opposite the window.*

*And a young woman with wild hair thrusts her blazing torch into the belly of the effigy.*

*In the torchlight, in the light of the burning* ROCK, *we see that the young woman is* ALICE.

*And another torch is thrust into the burning body; and another; and another.*

*Soon the effigy is writhing on fire. And the crowd waves it, crying in a high, hysterical triumph.*

*And they carry it along the street; and the dark figures of the crowd, their torches above them like long streams of fiery hair, follow it down the street.*

## 124

CITY SQUARE

*Night.*

*Outside* ROCK'S *Academy stand* MURRAY *and* TOM.

*Crowd noise, in the not so far distance.*

MURRAY. What's the light over there?

*The sky beyond the Square is glowing.*

TOM. They're burning an auld scarecrow of the Doctor in the streets.

*CLOSE SHOT of* MURRAY. *He says, softly:*

MURRAY. Can that children's magic bring back the dead?

*The crowd noise rises on the wind.*

MURRAY. Here we are, Tom, the two of us: the two "rats"! the two "deserters"!

TOM. Aye, the Doctor was wrong again. We're no "rats" or "deserters." He should have known we didna want to lose our jobs, eh, Mr. Murray?

MURRAY *draws a little way apart from* TOM, *then asks abruptly:*

MURRAY. What's the time?

TOM. One after midnight. The trial's been nearly twelve hours now. . . .

*CLOSE SHOT of* MURRAY.

MURRAY. It took a few short minutes to stop her breath. . . .

## 125

COURT-ROOM

BROOM *in the witness-box.*

*We see him very close.*

*We hear the* PROSECUTOR, *but do not see him.*

PROSECUTOR'S VOICE. What did he do then?

BROOM. He got on her with his breast on her head, and kept in her breath; she gave a kind of cry and moaned a little after the first cry. . . .

*CUT to CLOSE-UP of* FALLON *in the dock.*

PROSECUTOR'S VOICE. Did he say anything while this was going on?

BROOM'S VOICE. No, he got up then and put his hand across her mouth and kept it there three or four minutes. She appeared quite dead then.

PROSECUTOR'S VOICE. Were you looking on all this while?

*CUT to CLOSE-UP of* BROOM.

BROOM. I was sittin' on the chair.

PROSECUTOR'S VOICE. Did you sit in that chair and see Fallon for ten minutes killing the woman, and offer her no assistance?

BROOM. Aye.

BROOM *smiles.*

## 126

NEWSPAPER OFFICE

*Crowd noise from outside.*

*A room with a long, large window.*

*The* FIRST REPORTER *is writing at a table.*

*The* SECOND REPORTER *is walking up and down the room and glancing, every few moments, out of the window.*

SECOND REPORTER. Was he smiling when he said *that?*

FIRST REPORTER. [*Without looking up.*] If you call it smiling.

SECOND REPORTER. What did he look like?

FIRST REPORTER. [*Briefly, as he writes.*] Devil.

SECOND REPORTER. Fallon?

FIRST REPORTER. Quite quiet. Vurry polite.

SECOND REPORTER. And the woman?

FIRST REPORTER. Sober.

*The crowd noise rises.*

SECOND REPORTER. What are you calling the article? [*At the window.*] They're running down the street now. . . Thousands of them. . . .

FIRST REPORTER. "Justice."

SECOND REPORTER. "Broom! Broom! Broom!" . . . D'you hear them?

FIRST REPORTER. Broom'll go free.

SECOND REPORTER. [*Still looking out of the window.*] There's another fire over Newington way . . . somewhere near Rock's place. . . . D' you hear them?

FIRST REPORTER. [*Writing, not looking up.*]

They won't call Rock as a witness. That'll be taken care of. . . .

*A great cry from the crowd outside. . . .*

SECOND REPORTER. D'you hear that? . . .

FIRST REPORTER. I'm not deaf. They're nearing the end now. . . .

### 127

COURT-ROOM

*CLOSE SHOT of* LORD MEADOWBANK. *Camera PANS ALONG judges' faces.*

LORD MEADOWBANK. My Lords, I am confident that, although speaking in the presence of your Lordships, so much better instructed than myself, and so able to correct me were I in error, there is no chance of my being contradicted when I say that in the history of this country— nay, in the whole history of civilized society— there has never been exhibited such a system of barbarous and savage iniquity, or anything at all corresponding in atrocity, to what this trial has brought to light. . . .

### 128

NEWSPAPER OFFICE

*Night.*

*The two reporters.*

*The* FIRST REPORTER *flings down his pen.*

FIRST REPORTER. Fallon guilty. The rest— innocent! And my title is *"Justice."* I wrote the verdict *myself,* hours ago. Only the sentence now: I've written that, too.

### 129

COURT-ROOM

LORD CHIEF JUSTICE. The Lord Justice Clerk and Lord Commissioners of Justiciary in respect of the verdict before recorded, determine and adjudge the said Robert Fallon, to be carried from the bar, and to be fed upon bread and water only until Wednesday, the 28th January, and upon that day to be taken forth to the common place of execution and then and there between the hours of eight and ten o'clock to be hanged by the neck until he be dead. And may Almighty God have mercy on your soul.

*DISSOLVE to*

### 130

*Large CLOSE-UP of* ROCK.

ROCK. I have no need of your sympathy. When I see a tear, I smell a crocodile.

*TRACK BACK to show that* ROCK *is standing on the platform of the empty Lecture Hall.* MURRAY, *a good distance from* ROCK, *stands at the window, looking out.*

*Their voices echo in the Hall.*

MURRAY. [*Turning round*] For God's sake, Thomas, can you do nothing but—stand still and gibe?

ROCK. Would you have me death-dance and *moan,* like a Gaelic dipsomaniac at a distillery fire? Must tragedy go immediately to the feet and the tongue? Because I can observe my history *calmly* as it burns and topples around me, you emotional gluttons think yourselves cheated. "Oh, he can't *feel* anything," you say. "When we told him his life was over, he did not tear the relics of his hair or address the travelling moon in blank verse. He blew his nose and called for Burgundy."

MURRAY. [*Deliberately.*] Fallon is to hang.

ROCK. A quick end. If they wished his death to be longer and infinitely more painful, they should marry him to Doctor Hocking's daughter.

MURRAY. Fallon is to hang. Nelly Connor is "not guilty"! Broom and his woman are free to murder again! And *you?*

ROCK. I shall stay here.

I shall listen to the voices of the crowd outside my window, *inside my head;* it will not be long before they forget me; I shall never forget them.

I shall stay here. The whispers of the slanderer and the backbiter will always be with me: mice behind the wall.

I shall stay here. I shall count my friends on the fingers of one hand, then on one finger, then on none.

*CAMERA CRANES BACK, looking down at* ROCK *and* MURRAY *all the time, over the empty tiers of the classroom.*

*Although* ROCK *becomes further and further off, in LONG SHOT, the sound, booming hollowly through the empty classroom, remains in full close-up.*

ROCK. My lectures will be very well attended, at the beginning. I shall possess a sinister attraction to the young: dangerous and exciting, like dining with a vampire. But the attendance will diminish.

I shall stay here to see in the eyes of the passing stranger in the street cruelty and contempt; in the eyes of the poor the terrible accusation: "You killed the lost, the weak, the homeless, the hopeless, the helpless. Murderer of the poor!"

God help me, life will go on. . . .

## 131

CONDEMNED CELL

FALLON *on a chair in the middle of the cell. His hair is shaven.*

*A* PHRENOLOGIST *is measuring his head. He speaks the measurements aloud to an assistant, who writes them down in a book.*

FALLON *submits, with interest, to the examination.*

PHRENOLOGIST. From the ear to lower Individuality: 5 inches. From the ear to the centre of philo-progenitiveness: 4.8. From the ear to Benevolence: 5.7. From the ear to Destructiveness: 6.125.

Let us see:
Acquisitiveness: large.
Secretiveness: large.
Wit: deficient.
Cautiousness: h'm, rather large.
Sense of Tune: moderate.
Self-esteem: rather large.
*Hope: small.*

## 132

EXTERIOR OF PRISON

*Night.*

*A coach draws up.*

*The driver is heavily shawled about, and his hat is pulled down over his eyes.*

*And two cloaked, muffled figures hurry* BROOM *towards the coach.*

BROOM *is wrapped in a thick coat, and hooded. It is hard to recognize him.*

*But suddenly, at the door of the coach, he pulls back his hood, looks up at the sky.*

*He shakes his shaven head, like a monstrous dog coming out of the water.*

*And he begins to laugh his high, clear, yelping laugh as the two cloaked figures smuggle him into the coach.*

*The coach moves off, out of picture.*

## 133

MARKET-PLACE

*Late evening.*

*The stalls closed down.*

*And a woman's scream, a scream of hate and anger, is coming from a Market tavern.*

*And with her scream are mingled the voices of men and women: voices shouting, cursing, and threatening.*

*Then a knot of people tangles inside the open door of the tavern.*

*A whirl of arms and a squall of voices.*

*And we see* KATE *thrown out of the tavern on to the cobble stones of the Market.*

*She stumbles to her feet, runs, squawking like a chased hen, down the Market.*

*But only the voices chase her.*

*People pour from the tavern, stand outside it, throw stones after her, manure, rubbish.*

KATE *runs on, huddled.*

*And windows, high up in the tenements around the Market, open.*

*And the contents of buckets are thrown upon her as she runs.*

## 134

ROAD ON THE OUTSKIRTS OF THE CITY

*Night.*

*The road is long and winding.*

*We see* NELLY CONNOR, *with a bundle on her back, coming towards us, along the road, out of the distance.*

*She is pushing a hurly: a hurly with old boots upon it, and remnants of clothing, and odds and ends from the room in Rag-and-Bone Alley, and shapes one cannot identify in the night.*

*And we hear her voice as she pushes her barrow through darkness up the desolate road that leads out of the City.*

NELLY'S VOICE. [*Softly.*] Old boots to sell! . . . Cat-skin! . . . *Human hair! . . .*

## 135

NEWSPAPER OFFICE

*Daylight.*

*We see the street through the tall window.*

*The* SECOND REPORTER *stands at the window, looking out, his back towards us.*

*The* FIRST REPORTER *sits at the other side of the window, a pad on his knee. Through the window we see, at the end of the street, in LONG SHOT, a scaffold.*

*The platform of the scaffold is raised above the heads of the crowd. On the platform we see*

*the gibbet; it is shaped like a T with one addi-
tional vertical on the right.*

*On the platform are several figures: clergy-
men, magistrates, hangman, and* FALLON.

*And we hear the crowd noise rise.*

*And looking through the window at the
scene of execution, and hearing the cries of the
crowd, we hear, too, the voices of the two men
at the window.*

SECOND REPORTER. Do you hear? "Hang
Broom! Hang Rock!"

FIRST REPORTER. Fallon's on his knees. He's
praying.

*The noise of the crowd rises. Then:*

SECOND REPORTER. The rope's round his
neck. They've put a cotton nightcap on his
head.

FIRST REPORTER. Good night.

*The noise of the crowd rises again.*

CRIES OF THE CROWD. You'll see Billy Bedlam in a minute.

FIRST REPORTER. What are they shouting?

SECOND REPORTER. "You'll see Billy Bedlam
in a minute!" He's on the drop.

*A great cheer from the crowd.*

FIRST REPORTER. He was always one for
dancing. He's dancing now.


### 136

*CLOSE SHOT of* ALICE *and* MURRAY *at a
table in a* TAVERN. *Around them the noise of
the Market-place drinking. And pipes in the
distance.*

ALICE. Fallon's dead—why isn't the Doctor
dead? Nobody remembers Jennie now.

MURRAY. Oh, there's lots of ways of dying.
*I* remember.


### 137

*CLOSE SHOT of* ANNABELLA *and* ELIZA-
BETH; *behind them, the window of* ELIZABETH'S
ROOM *looking out on the wintry trees in the
garden.*

ANNABELLA. Do you *know* what it is to be
lonely? I've always been lonely. I wanted to be
mistress of my brother's house, I wanted to give
dinner parties and dances and be charming and
admired. I wanted to marry. But people
wouldn't visit us because *you* married *him.* It
doesn't matter now. Now nobody'll come....

ELIZABETH. I married him because I loved
him. But we're only a very little part of his life,
Bella. I've been lonely, too.


### 138

*CLOSE SHOT of* HOCKING *and the* CHAIR-
MAN (*the* LORD CHIEF JUSTICE, *whom we saw
in Sequences 111 and 114) against the background of imposing bookcases.*

CHAIRMAN. So, officially speaking, he's innocent as a lamb, the wolf.

HOCKING. We saved him from a criminal
prosecution.

CHAIRMAN. Of course, of course. In order to
save the good name of society. Fallon and
Broom could have brought their bodies to *you,*
of course. It just happened it was Rock they
chose.

HOCKING. I would have none of their bodies.

CHAIRMAN. No?

HOCKING. But now it's all over. All over. We
can speak our minds now.

CHAIRMAN. We save him from public ruin,
so that we can ruin him privately. H'm, I'm sure
he's grateful....


### 139

LECTURE HALL OF ROCK'S ACADEMY

ROCK *is on the platform.*

*The auditorium is densely packed.*

*We see* ROCK *from the back of the Hall, over
the heads of the students.*

*And we move, slowly, over the heads towards
him as he speaks.*

ROCK. To think, then, is to enter into a perilous country, colder of welcome than the polar
wastes, darker than a Scottish Sunday, where
the hand of the unthinker is always raised
against you, where the wild animals, who go by
such names as Envy, Hypocrisy, and Tradition,
are notoriously carnivorous, and *where the
parasites rule.*

To *think* is dangerous. The majority of men
have found it easier to writhe their way into the
parasitical bureaucracy, or to *droop* into the
slack ranks of the ruled. I beg you all to devote
your lives to danger; I pledge you to adventure;
I command you to experiment. [*Slowly.*] Remember that the practice of Anatomy is absolutely vital to the *progress* of medicine. Remember that the progress of medicine is vital to the
progress of mankind. And mankind is worth
fighting for: killing and lying and dying for. For-

get what you like. Forget all I have ever told you. But remember that. . . .

*Now we see* ROCK *in CLOSE-UP.*

*DISSOLVE to*

### 140

CITY STREET

*Gathering dusk.*

*We hear the thin, high singing of the wind in the street.*

*And, in the background, the sound of the voices of children drifting through the dusk.*

ROCK, *from a grey distance, is walking towards us along the street. He is cloaked, top-hatted.*

*And as he comes closer to us a little* GIRL *runs out of the shadows of a side-street, runs barefoot through the wind, her black hair leaping.*

*She is grimed from the gutters of the city; her dress is thin and ragged; one shoulder is naked.*

*And she runs at* ROCK'S *side, crying out:*

GIRL. Give us a penny, mister, give us a penny. . . .

*The camera TRACKS BACK as* ROCK, *and the little girl running at his side, move on down the street.*

*Then* ROCK *stops, at a corner.*

*And the little* GIRL *stops; she stands still in a shadow at the mouth of a narrow tunnel-like street. She is almost lost in the shadow, her hair is mixed into the darkness, but we see her white face and white, naked shoulder.*

ROCK *stands just outside the shadow.*

*He puts a penny in her hand.*

*He looks down at her, and is silent for a moment.*

ROCK. It's a bitter cold night to be running about in the streets. You should go home.

*The child in the shadows shakes her head.*

CHILD. Granny says I can't come home till I got fourpence. . . .

ROCK *fumbles in his pocket for another coin.*

*The child holds out her hand from the shadow around her.*

ROCK. What's your name, lassie?

CHILD. I'm Maggie Bell.

ROCK. [*Almost as though to himself.*] I'm Doctor Rock.

*And the child runs screaming into the darkness.*

*And* ROCK *walks on, away from us.*

### 141

HILL ABOVE THE CITY

*The dusk is deeper. . . .*

*The wind is blowing wilder. . . .*

*We look down the hill.*

*Out of the dusk, a long way off,* ROCK *is climbing up towards us.*

*And as he climbs, we hear his voice. But it is only the little, wind-blown whisper of a voice, and we cannot hear a word of it.*

*And as he climbs on and up, so the windy whisper loudens and we begin to hear the words.*

*We begin to hear the fragments of sentences.*

*We hear some words and then the wind rises for a second and blows them away.*

*Then we hear more words, from the voice of his mind; the wind again will not let the words finish but blows them away.*

*And again; and again; and again.*

*Always the voice is the voice of* ROCK, *but it is never twice on the same level: it is the voice of* ROCK *young, then old, then gay, then sad; a high voice, a low voice.*

*And the sound of it rises as he climbs.*

ROCK'S VOICE. And the child in the cold runs away from my name. . . .

My name is a ghost to frighten children. . . .

Will *my* children cry *"Murder"* and *"Blood"* when I touch them . . . as if my hands were Fallon's hands? . . .

"Be good, be good, or the terrible Doctor will come with his knife."

Poor Billy! I came to you with my knife.

Did I *know,* did I *know* from the very beginning?

Never answer, never answer, even to yourself alone in the night. . . .

All's over now. . . .

Oh, Elizabeth, hold my hand. . . .

"Oh, it isn't a hand, it's a pair of scissors! . . ."

Did I set myself up as a little god over death? Over death. . . .

All over . . . over . . . over . . .

Did I set myself above pity? . . .

*Oh, my God, I knew what I was doing!*

*And he passes us and climbs up the long hill, and his voice climbs with him into darkness, into a whisper, into silence, into the climax of MUSIC.*

C H A P T E R   S I X

# ARTS AND THE MAN

W<small>E SHOULD</small> expect the writer occasionally to wonder about the meaning and purpose of his art. And since his vocation is words, we might expect him to be more articulate than, say, a painter, musician, or dancer. Yet, as some of the selections in this chapter show, creators in the other arts can sometimes write well and illuminatingly about their work.

The experience that is central to this chapter is the aesthetic experience. Sometimes it is described in terms of beauty: one of the greatest blessings of the human condition is that we are able to find and create beauty, though the pursuit of this good, where the goal is conceived so highly that the pursuit cannot succeed, brings about one of man's tragic experiences. Hawthorne's story, "The Birthmark," is a comment upon this sort of aesthetic perfectionism.

The experiences of art, although having common elements, may be divided into two sorts: the creative and the appreciative. Hawthorne, Greenough, Bishop, Marianne Moore, and Menotti are intent upon the problems of the creative artist himself: the demands of his medium, the obstacles placed in his path by a hostile or indifferent society, the difficulties of working out his own conception of what art should be and how it should be made. Other selections, such as "The Figure in the Carpet," and those by Copland, Brooks, Yeats, and Housman, address themselves to the understanding of art, the duties and obligations of the consumer rather than the producer. Naturally, however, each of these groups of writers throws light upon the problems of the other.

The most vital question that recurs in these selections concerns the ultimate value of art.

331

What is it for? What is the final use of paintings, poems, musical compositions? Partly this question arises when the difference between art and life is ignored, which is the theme of several works reprinted here. Ovid's story of Pygmalion is the classic myth about the relationship of the imagined to the actual. Nevertheless, the valid question remains: why would the destruction of all art leave the world poorer? No writer, neither those represented in this book nor those left out, has answered this question to everyone's satisfaction. At the same time, it is improbable that most students of the arts can long ignore it. The reading of literature about the arts will help the reader to formulate his own answer, tentative and incomplete as it may have to be.

*Gian-Carlo Menotti*

# A PLEA FOR THE CREATIVE ARTIST

Perhaps the only tiresome thing about being an American is that one is continually being told by foreigners what is wrong with this country. Fortunately, most Americans seem rather to enjoy this type of criticism and wisely so because, after all, criticism is a form of homage. One criticizes only that which seems potentially perfect.

In most European countries, national faults are so fatally integrated into their historical background that by now these faults are considered not only part of the present and past, but also of an inevitable future. Criticism is defeated a priori. To create an ideal Italy, for example, one would almost have to destroy it first.

But as flattering and constructive as criticism can often be, it is, on the other hand, rather annoying to be paternally advised and sanctimoniously chastised by people who are hardly acquainted with one's problems.

Plutarch tells how the ancient Romans exposed the ailing on public thoroughfares so that passers-by who had suffered from the same illness or fancied themselves as possessing therapeutic powers could give advice to the sufferers. This example of unparalleled stoicism on the part of the patient could easily be compared to that of an American accepting without protest the criticism of the European who has spent

two weeks in New York and therefore feels entitled to dissect the heart of America for him.

Unhappily, not all these judgments that come from abroad, more often than not in the form of accusations, are to be dismissed with amusement. Some of the more persistent ones contain more than a grain of truth. Without a doubt, the oldest and most persistent of these accusations is directed toward American culture. It is a known fact to the American that the European, in both friendly and unfriendly countries, has a tendency to consider him culturally inferior. This high-handed attitude of the European must often puzzle the average American citizen. After all, doesn't America have the best symphonic orchestras in the world, some of the largest libraries, some of the richest museums? Where else is there such an abundance of lectures, symposiums, concerts, and university courses in all branches of the arts?

Having lived more than twenty years in this country and being considered even by my compatriots as an American composer, I hope it will not appear too arrogant if I attempt to explain why this attitude toward America still exists abroad and what to a great extent justifies it.

I am afraid that America has not yet realized, except in a small elite circle, that art is essentially a creative process. No matter how much and how long a nation may absorb art, it still will not be considered an artistic country unless it *produces* art. (The same principle applies to culture in general, but I shall limit myself in discussing the one aspect that most concerns me—art, particularly as represented by music.) I am not denying that art is being produced in America. Actually, few countries in the world can boast such creative activity, and I would even like to add that its quality is in my opinion not inferior to that of most European countries. But how are Europeans supposed to recognize the importance of creative life in America, or for that matter to even know of its existence, if Americans themselves ignore or minimize it?

Americans have always concerned themselves more with the possession and display of art rather than with the production of it. In music, especially, they take great pride in their orchestras and in the men who interpret music for them, but they have always relegated the composer to a secondary place. A symphony concert presented by a celebrated conductor is often described by the press as having made "musical history," although no new work has been presented. Actually, no concert that I know of has ever made musical history unless it was by the creation of new music. Americans live under a delusion if they believe that musical history is made by simply performing old tired-out works, no matter how brilliantly interpreted.

It is pathetic to see the timidity and apologetic air with which Americans introduce their creative artists to Europe. (I insist on the distinction between creative and interpretive artists.) Who can ever forget the shabby concerts of American music half-heartedly organized all through an expectant Europe by well-meaning souls in the State Department shortly after the War? At one of the Lucerne festivals, while England sent an orchestra conducted by Sir Adrian Boult to represent its composers, and France, an orchestra conducted by Münch, American composers were embarrassingly represented by a concert of records—the kind of concert one might expect in a summer camp. (After the concert, however, cocktails served by the American Embassy to the stunned body of international critics were by far the best served by any embassy.) Who will not feel sorry for the young American painter who gives his first exhibit in a French gallery and who already knows that regardless of how successful his exhibit may be, no one—but no one—in his home town will know about it unless he himself sends a little news item to the local paper so that his mother may see it?

It is my contention that the average American has little or no respect for the creative artist and is apt to consider him as an almost useless member of the community. The average American father still views with dismay the fact that one of his sons may choose to become a composer, writer, or painter. He will consider any such pursuit a sign of "softness," an unmanly and, I venture to say, an un-American choice.

I must add in all frankness that this hostility toward the arts is not uncommon in Europe within a certain class of society. But it exists only in a very small percentage of the population, mostly among the *nouveaux riches* and the very orthodox members of the aristocracy who still feel that it is more noble to patronize than to create. Moreover, even in this latter small and moribund class, artistic activity is at least looked upon as an essential element of gracious living rather than the adornment of uneventful Sunday afternoons.

Curiously enough, Americans accept as a perfectly normal phenomenon that a foreigner should choose art as his profession. While an American artist often is subtly ostracized by his own community, a foreign one in that same milieu is apt to be honored. It is almost as if one should have no respect for Mohammedanism unless it is practiced by a Hindu.

No wonder that the young American artist is perhaps the most neurotic in the world, and for generations has sought in Europe his spiritual home. There he knows he will not be considered as an exotic member of civilization but as a valuable citizen of the world.

I have remarked before that I insist on the separation between creative and interpretive artists, not only because the roles are scarcely related, but also because curiously enough the interpretive artist, although his role is of minor importance, is more readily tolerated by the American community. This may be due to the fact that the nature of his contribution, ephemeral as it is, is easier to appraise and consequently has greater commercial value than that of the creator. The singer who finally is accepted by the Metropolitan and is heard regularly on radio programs, or the violinist who can ask his own local music club for a two-thousand-dollar concert fee, becomes a highly respectable member of his home town and consequently a hero to his own family. But the struggling composer who may or may not succeed in having his symphony performed by a well-known symphony orchestra (a recognition that will earn him a one-hundred-dollar fee out of which he must pay for the copying of the parts), or the painter who slowly and painfully works for months on a single canvas which may never be bought, will be considered an incorrigible eccentric. He will never be asked to preside over any of the town committees, and will be invited to dinner almost exclusively by the one "arty" family in town—the family whose children seem to have difficulty in making friends.

This perhaps explains the uncommon anxiety of the young American artist toward the problem of financial success. Artists all over the world have to face the dilemma of finding freedom to work and earn a living at the same time; but for most of them, money represents only the necessary means of acquiring this freedom. For the American artist, financial success stands for much more than that. It usually represents the unconscious desire to rehabilitate himself in front of the family and the community to show them that he is worth more than they thought him to be, and that he not only *can* earn a living, but actually a *better* living than many of the members of more respected professions. The mature artist will disclaim any such thought of self-vindication, but the younger one will be secretly delighted at the thought of the devastating effect that his success will have upon "friends of the family" or the Eumenides-like group of relatives whose silent commiseration he had to bear throughout his youth.

Except for this anxiety toward financial success, I cannot otherwise explain the tragic fate of so many promising young writers who, having achieved or rather, let us say, fallen by chance into the category of "best seller," repeat themselves into sterility for fear of losing their buying public or their commercially minded publishers, or the even worse fate of the talented young painter who finally succumbs to the lure of commercial advertising and by cheapening himself eventually destroys the freshness of his creative powers.

I strongly feel that American parents, fathers in particular, are frequently to blame for the feeling of insecurity which often leads their artistic sons to the betrayal of their ideals and thence to mediocrity or failure. Being a teacher in a well-known American school, I am again and again confronted by the case of the young composer whose well-to-do father will stubbornly refuse him any financial help after he is twenty-one years of age. This all-too-prevalent type of father is unable to accept the fact that art is a long and painful process. He will

inevitably suspect of emasculation the son who at the age of twenty-one (which American custom has consecrated as the age of financial independence) still requires the help of his family. Consequently, to avoid contempt, the young American artist, long before his coming of age, begins to seek feverishly for any kind of grant or prize which will save him from the humiliation of financial dependence. (The case of Ravel, whose family provided him an income all through his life, is not an uncommon one in Europe.)

In a certain sense, the Messrs. Guggenheim and Pulitzer are playing the part of the ideal father to these American outcasts. Without them, I really do not know what many young American artists would do. But, generous and commendable as these grants are, they still are not enough. What the young artist longs for most and needs as vital sustenance is not only money but the faith and love of people around him. How often, when I describe to some of my pupils the atmosphere surrounding my youth, I hear them exclaim with envy, "Oh, if only I had a family like yours!"

All of this rather puzzles me. Why is it that the American father must feel apologetic for—if not thoroughly ashamed by—the fact that his son may want to pursue a nonmoney-making profession, and concentrate on spiritual values rather than material ones? What is the use of making money if we deny ourselves the rare privilege of helping those within our own family who are destined to enrich the culture of our nation? Why, may I ask, is a father to be more proud of the son who can earn his living at twenty-one rather than of the struggling son who one day may be the pride of his country and whose work may be remembered for generations to come?

How well I remember as a child watching the profound sorrow of all Milan as the funeral of Puccini passed through the streets! It was a loss for each of us as well as for our country. No wonder that a young Italian boy's wanting to be a composer could only be a source of satisfaction and pride to his family and friends. But the family's regard for music was only a reflection of the general public's esteem in which the composer was held in Italy.

The indifference of the American public toward creative life is even reflected in its cultural institutions. Except for a few philanthropic organizations who do their utmost to meet the problem, most American institutions, artistic ones included, are apt to ignore it completely. It is shocking to observe how seldom a well-known painter, composer, or writer is singled out by American universities as worthy of an honorary degree. It is much easier for a singer who can hardly read music to be academically cited than for a composer whose symphonies have been performed all over the country. The few times that composers are offered a doctorate of music, it is more often than not for their academic standing (either as teachers or directors of schools) rather than for their creative achievements.

Although most artists may tend to refuse academic recognition, relatively few have ever been granted such recognition by a first-rank university. I believe that a composer of such standing as Aaron Copland has only been honored once by a university—Samuel Barber, never—and William Schuman only since he has become the Director of the Juilliard School. I happen to know that the only time Virgil Thomson was offered an honorary degree by a college, he found himself on the same platform as Elizabeth Arden, the cosmetician, also a recipient. For that matter, composers are not even taken into consideration by those same institutions that apparently devote themselves to music. At the reception given by the New York Philharmonic for its one-hundredth anniversary, to which practically every Tom, Dick, and Harry of the music world was invited, I don't know of one single composer of note who received an invitation. Nor is a composer ever asked to be a member of orchestra or opera boards. Businessmen are considered better judges, even in the direction of artistic matters.

This reluctance to appoint an American artist to a responsible position may be the outcome of the current fallacy that an artist is inevitably an unreliable person, devoid of any executive abilities whatsoever. Obviously, artists have little interest in becoming financial wizards or brilliant executives, but whenever they do assume such roles, they often prove themselves to be perceptive and outstanding. It is no mystery that Strauss was an admirable businessman and Verdi a shrewd landowner. Creative artists in Europe are sought, as a matter of course, to hold important positions in the direction of institutions concerned with art; and it is not uncommon to find them holding high diplomatic positions in their government. Among innumerable examples I mention the poet, T. S. Eliot, who certainly has been largely responsible for the policy of his publishing house; the composer, Ibert, for the direction of the French Academy in Rome; the writers, Claudel and Giraudoux, who both held positions as French Ambassadors; and the philosopher, Benedetto Croce, who was asked to honor the new free government of Italy with his presence.

As for the notion that all artists are eccentric, and thus incapable of holding a responsible position, all one has to do is read the biography of some of the most celebrated American millionaires. I know few artists who, in the matter of eccentricity, could hold a candle to these financial acrobats!

Most flagrant of all is the indifferent attitude of the American government toward creative art. Possessing the most formidable means and material for cultural propaganda, it stubbornly insists upon ignoring the only facet of American culture that would really impress Europe—the arts. France has always been a master in exploiting her creative sons. Its tourism, its fashion, its incredible prestige as a leader in cultural and intellectual matters are the outcome of centuries of national pride in its art. The arrival of, let us say, Sartre in a foreign country is greeted by the French Embassy with lavish receptions worthy of royalty. (It is an extravagant dream to imagine that someone like Faulkner would receive such honors from his own government. Has a composer ever been asked to perform at the White House? Has a painter's exhibit ever been graced by the presence of an American President?) The recent deaths in France of Gide and of Bérard were almost considered as national disasters. Sibelius in Finland is already a national monument; Benjamin Britten of England is rapidly becoming one; and George Bernard Shaw, of course, was immortalized long before his death. But who knows or cares to know in America what is happening to its greatest dramatist, Eugene O'Neill, sick and lonely somewhere in this country?

I find the general American press equally guilty in its stress upon what is only the cheaper and more ephemeral aspect of American culture. Occasionally some of the weekly magazines have rather lavishly publicized the work of younger painters, but does the press of America actually care where its composers, writers, and painters live and what they are doing? Will it ever consider it "news" that a new American symphony receives its première in Vienna or Paris, or that a young American painter has won recognition in Rome? Journalists will faithfully quote what Rita Hayworth has to say about Truth and Beauty, will take pride in the success of Judy Garland in England, and report with meticulous accuracy the debut of an American singer at La Scala. But that is as far as the general press of America dares to go in covering the art field. Will creative art ever be *"news"*?

It is a rather sad panorama. America must finally realize that its present civilization will be crystallized and remembered in the future only as portrayed by its contemporary creative artists. It is the Germany of Bach, Beethoven, and Goethe that we love and forgive. It is the Italy of Leonardo and Michelangelo and of the countless architects who have been asked to enrich it with their monuments that is portrayed in every schoolboy's textbook. It is the France of Utrillo and Rimbaud that the American tourist unconsciously seeks in his eternal pilgrimage to Paris.

Most Americans are apt to excuse themselves by answering that, after all, there are no Beethovens and Michelangelos in this country. This argument reminds me of the proverbial young man who, after having murdered his father and mother, asks the judge to be lenient because he is an orphan. A nation is directly responsible for preparing the kind of soil that will produce art. I agree with Emerson who said, "The fine arts have nothing casual, but spring from the instincts of the nations that created them."

## *Aaron Copland*
# HOW WE LISTEN

We all listen to music according to our separate capacities. But, for the sake of analy-

sis, the whole listening process may become clearer if we break it up into its component parts, so to speak. In a certain sense we all listen to music on three separate planes. For lack of a better terminology, one might name these: (1) the sensuous plane, (2) the expressive plane, (3) the sheerly musical plane. The only advantage to be gained from mechanically splitting up the listening process into these hypothetical planes is the clearer view to be had of the way in which we listen.

The simplest way of listening to music is to listen for the sheer pleasure of the musical sound itself. That is the sensuous plane. It is the plane on which we hear music without thinking, without considering it in any way. One turns on the radio while doing something else and absent-mindedly bathes in the sound. A kind of brainless but attractive state of mind is engendered by the mere sound appeal of the music.

You may be sitting in a room reading this book. Imagine one note struck on the piano. Immediately that one note is enough to change the atmosphere of the room—proving that the sound element in music is a powerful and mysterious agent, which it would be foolish to deride or belittle.

The surprising thing is that many people who consider themselves qualified music lovers abuse that plane in listening. They go to concerts in order to lose themselves. They use music as a consolation or an escape. They enter an ideal world where one doesn't have to think of the realities of everyday life. Of course they aren't thinking about the music either. Music allows them to leave it, and they go off to a place to dream, dreaming because of and apropos of the music yet never quite listening to it.

Yes, the sound appeal of music is a potent and primitive force, but you must not allow it to usurp a disproportionate share of your interest. The sensuous plane is an important one in music, a very important one, but it does not constitute the whole story.

There is no need to digress further on the sensuous plane. Its appeal to every normal human being is self-evident. There is, however, such a thing as becoming more sensitive to the different kinds of sound stuff as used by various composers. For all composers do not use that sound stuff in the same way. Don't get the idea that the value of music is commensurate with its sensuous appeal or that the loveliest sound-ing music is made by the greatest composer. If that were so, Ravel would be a greater creator than Beethoven. The point is that the sound element varies with each composer, that his usage of sound forms an integral part of his style and must be taken into account when listening. The reader can see, therefore, that a more conscious approach is valuable even on this primary plane of music listening.

The second plane on which music exists is what I have called the expressive one. Here, immediately, we tread on controversial ground. Composers have a way of shying away from any discussion of music's expressive side. Did not Stravinsky himself proclaim that his music was an "object," a "thing," with a life of its own, and with no other meaning than its own purely musical existence? This intransigent atti-tude of Stravinsky's may be due to the fact that so many people have tried to read different meanings into so many pieces. Heaven knows it is difficult enough to say precisely what it is that a piece of music means, to say it definitely, to say it finally so that everyone is satisfied with your explanation. But that should not lead one to the other extreme of denying to music the right to be "expressive."

My own belief is that all music has an expres-sive power, some more and some less, but that all music has a certain meaning behind the notes and that that meaning behind the notes constitutes, after all, what the piece is saying, what the piece is about. This whole problem can be stated quite simply by asking, "Is there a meaning to music?" My answer to that would be, "Yes." And "Can you state in so many words what the meaning is?" My answer to that would be, "No." Therein lies the difficulty.

Simple-minded souls will never be satisfied with the answer to the second of these ques-tions. They always want music to have a mean-ing, and the more concrete it is the better they like it. The more the music reminds them of a train, a storm, a funeral, or any other familiar conception the more expressive it appears to be to them. This popular idea of music's meaning —stimulated and abetted by the usual run of musical commentator—should be discouraged wherever and whenever it is met. One timid lady once confessed to me that she suspected something seriously lacking in her appreciation of music because of her inability to connect it

with anything definite. That is getting the whole thing backward, of course.

Still, the question remains, How close should the intelligent music lover wish to come to pin-ning a definite meaning to any particular work? No closer than a general concept, I should say. Music expresses, at different moments, serenity or exuberance, regret or triumph, fury or de-light. It expresses each of these moods, and many others, in a numberless variety of subtle shadings and differences. It may even express a state of meaning for which there exists no adequate word in any language. In that case, musicians often like to say that it has only a purely musical meaning. They sometimes go farther and say that *all* music has only a purely musical meaning. What they really mean is that no appropriate word can be found to express the music's meaning and that, even if it could they do not feel the need of finding it.

But whatever the professional musician may hold, most musical novices still search for spe-cific words with which to pin down their musical reactions. That is why they always find Tschai-kovsky easier to "understand" than Beethoven. In the first place, it is easier to pin a meaning-word on a Tschaikovsky piece than on a Bee-thoven one. Much easier. Moreover, with the Russian composer, every time you come back to a piece of his it almost always says the same thing to you, whereas with Beethoven it is often quite difficult to put your finger right on what he is saying. And any musician will tell you that that is why Beethoven is the greater composer. Because music which always says the same thing to you will necessarily soon become dull music, but music whose meaning is slightly dif-ferent with each hearing has a greater chance of remaining alive.

Listen, if you can, to the forty-eight fugue themes of Bach's *Well-Tempered Clavichord*. Listen to each theme, one after another. You will soon realize that each theme mirrors a dif-ferent world of feeling. You will also soon real-ize that the more beautiful a theme seems to you the harder it is to find any word that will describe it to your complete satisfaction. Yes, you will certainly know whether it is a gay theme or a sad one. You will be able, in other words, in your own mind, to draw a frame of emotional feeling around your theme. Now study the sad one a little closer. Try to pin down the exact quality of its sadness. Is it pessimistically sad or resignedly sad; is it fatefully sad or smilingly sad?

Let us suppose that you are fortunate and can describe to your own satisfaction in so many words the exact meaning of your chosen theme. There is still no guarantee that anyone else will be satisfied. Nor need they be. The important thing is that each one feel for himself the specific expressive quality of a theme or, similarly, an entire piece of music. And if it is a great work of art, don't expect it to mean exactly the same thing to you each time you return to it.

Themes or pieces need not express only one emotion, of course. Take such a theme as the first main one of the *Ninth Symphony,* for example. It is clearly made up of different elements. It does not say only one thing. Yet anyone hearing it immediately gets a feeling of strength, a feeling of power. It isn't a power that comes simply because the theme is played loudly. It is a power inherent in the theme itself. The extraordinary strength and vigor of the theme results in the listener's receiving an impression that a forceful statement has been made. But one should never try to boil it down to "the fateful hammer of life," etc. That is where the trouble begins. The musician, in his exasperation, says it means nothing but the notes themselves, whereas the nonprofessional is only too anxious to hang on to any explanation that gives him the illusion of getting closer to the music's meaning.

Now, perhaps, the reader will know better what I mean when I say that music does have an expressive meaning but that we cannot say in so many words what that meaning is.

The third plane on which music exists is the sheerly musical plane. Besides the pleasurable sound of music and the expressive feeling that it gives off, music does exist in terms of the notes themselves and of their manipulation. Most listeners are not sufficiently conscious of this third plane. . . .

Professional musicians, on the other hand, are, if anything, too conscious of the mere notes themselves. They often fall into the error of becoming so engrossed with their arpeggios and staccatos that they forget the deeper aspects of the music they are performing. But from the layman's standpoint, it is not so much a matter of getting over bad habits on the sheerly musical plane as of increasing one's awareness of what is going on, in so far as the notes are concerned.

When the man in the street listens to the "notes themselves" with any degree of concentration, he is most likely to make some mention of the melody. Either he hears a pretty melody or he does not, and he generally lets it go at that. Rhythm is likely to gain his attention next, particuiarly if it seems exciting. But harmony and tone color are generally taken for granted, if they are thought of consciously at all. As for music's having a definite form of some kind, that idea seems never to have occurred to him.

It is very important for all of us to become more alive to music on its sheerly musical plane. After all, an actual musical material is being used. The intelligent listener must be prepared to increase his awareness of the musical material and what happens to it. He must hear the melodies, the rhythms, the harmonies, the tone colors in a more conscious fashion. But above all he must, in order to follow the line of the composer's thought, know something of the principles of musical form. Listening to all of these elements is listening on the sheerly musical plane.

Let me repeat that I have split up mechanically the three separate planes on which we listen merely for the sake of greater clarity. Actually, we never listen on one or the other of these planes. What we do is to correlate them—listening in all three ways at the same time. It takes no mental effort, for we do it instinctively.

Perhaps an analogy with what happens to us when we visit the theater will make this instinctive correlation clearer. In the theater, you are aware of the actors and actresses, costumes and sets, sounds and movements. All these give one the sense that the theater is a pleasant place to be in. They constitute the sensuous plane in our theatrical reactions.

The expressive plane in the theater would be derived from the feeling that you get from what is happening on the stage. You are moved to pity, excitement, or gaiety. It is this general feeling, generated aside from the particular words being spoken, a certain emotional something which exists on the stage, that is analogous to the expressive quality in music.

The plot and plot development is equivalent to our sheerly musical plane. The playwright creates and develops a character in just the same way that a composer creates and develops a theme. According to the degree of your awareness of the way in which the artist in either field handles his material will you become a more intelligent listener.

It is easy enough to see that the theatergoer never is conscious of any of these elements separately. He is aware of them all at the same time. The same is true of music listening. We simultaneously and without thinking listen on all three planes.

In a sense, the ideal listener is both inside and outside the music at the same moment, judging it and enjoying it, wishing it would go one way and watching it go another—almost like the composer at the moment he composes it; because in order to write his music, the composer must also be inside and outside his music, carried away by it and yet coldly critical of it. A subjective and objective attitude is implied in both creating and listening to music.

What the reader should strive for, then, is a more *active* kind of listening. Whether you listen to Mozart or Duke Ellington, you can deepen your understanding of music only by being a more conscious and aware listener—not someone who is just listening, but someone who is listening *for* something.

## José Limon
# ON DANCE

The Dance is all things to all men. Parents are delighted and amazed at the instinctive response of their infant to music. "Look, he's dancing." Children do not walk to school. They run, skip, hop, leap: they dance to school, or into the dining room, or up the stairs to bed. The adolescent is notorious for his nervous, jittery dances. And love's young dream: imagine our early romances without a waltz by moonlight! We discover the rapture and intoxication of love during the dance. And even maturity finds a new dimension to the weary business of existence during the sedate

ON DANCE: Reprinted from *7 Arts, #1,* a Permabook published by Doubleday and Company, Inc., edited by Fernando Puma. Used by permission of the editor.

ritual of the ballroom: a suspension, a surcease, an inexplicable lifting of the spirit, when even the corns cease to hurt. The dance is an atavism. It has been with us since we became humans, and no doubt even before that. It will be with us to the end. It is a human necessity, profound and not to be denied. Puritans have banned and proscribed it at various times as the work of the Devil, happily without success. I believe that we are never more truly and profoundly human than when we dance.

It is religion. In primitive societies it solemnizes birth, puberty, marriage, and death, the seasons, the sowing and the harvest, war and peace, and to this day in our western world, young boys dance to the Virgin before the high altar in the Cathedral in Seville, and the Indians in Mexico and the Southwest dance their religion.

It is joy. I have seen sober, middle-aged people lose themselves utterly in congas and square dances. Young people would not be young without their dances, those rituals which celebrate the ineffable joy of being alive.

It is pleasure. Think only what musicals would be if you were to leave out the dances, and can you imagine a circus without the dances of the clowns and the acrobats? For certainly the buffoons are dancing. And what the performers on the trapezes and tight ropes do is a very exciting sort of dance.

It is art. Some of the most sublime and creative works of man in the twentieth century have been accomplished by dancers. It is an inspiring panorama, both in Europe, with the traditional dance, and here in this country with the so-called Modern Dance. This latter aspect of the art of the dance, which is the one that I serve, has been referred to by various names, such as the "Serious Dance," the "Concert Dance," the "Creative Dance," etc. It has made some very great contributions to the art. It has influenced greatly the traditional dance. But I think that its greatest contribution lies in giving the dance to the individual. It has broken with the great orthodoxy of the traditional Ballet, and given validity to personal expression. Since one human being differs from another, this has often led to painful results. But in the case of the disciplined artist, this liberation has given us, in this country, certainly, the most exalted art.

The dancer is fortunate indeed, for he has for

his instrument the most eloquent and miraculous of all instruments, the human body. My teacher, Doris Humphrey, when I first came to her studio as an unpromising but dedicated beginner, told us something I have never forgotten. She said, "The human body is the most powerfully expressive medium there is. It is quite possible to hide behind words, or to mask facial expression. It is conceivable that one can dissimulate and deceive with paints, clay, stone, print, sounds. But the body reveals. Movement and gesture are the oldest languages known to man. They are still the most revealing. When you move you stand revealed for what you are."

This great power of expression is ours from the day we are born to the hour of our death. With most human beings it remains largely unconscious. We dancers use this faculty consciously. But it is subjected to long and arduous discipline. The body must be made strong and supple. It is subjected to the exercises of the traditional Ballet and the modern dance techniques to train it in balance, control, elevation, speed, coordination, and exactitude of execution. But to me the most fascinating part of our craft lies in a great search. We explore the possibilities and potentialities for movement inherent in every part of the body. I like to compare it to the symphony orchestra, with its tremendous range and variety of sound, from the robust and percussive to the delicate and subtle. I like to devise exercises and studies which focus on a certain part of the anatomy. This section is isolated, so to speak, and made to move in as many conceivable ways as possible, so that one may become aware of its complete range and capacity, in the same manner that a musical composer must know what each instrument in the orchestra can do. There are exercises, first and foremost, for that great source of movement, the breath center. Then there are others for the shoulders, the ribs, pelvis, knees, feet, elbows, hands, and the head. Each of these regions of the body possesses its own special qualities of movement, and has great possibilities.

Take the head. Leave aside such important means of expression as the eyes and the mouth. The head, from the perpendicular, can be made to hang forward on the chest, or fall backwards as far as the cords of the neck will permit. It can rest sidewise on either shoulder. It can describe a complete circumference, touching the four points just mentioned. Beginning with these simple and rudimentary directions one can devise such complex and endless variations to the movement of the head that, given creativeness and imagination, entire dances can be based on these. The head can be an erect proud symbol, or droop abjectly, or roll in drunken ecstasy and abandonment. It is capable of great pendular convolutions, or infinitely contained, minute gestures. Within its orbit it can move in tilted diagonals, tangents, and obliques, which give it a great expressive range.

The chest can be made empty, to fall inwards and downwards to an utter inversion, a defeat. It can rise with the breath, like a plant growing up and out from the pelvis, and there be suspended, noble and affirmative and aspiring. It can extend beyond this to attitudes of pride and arrogance, and overextend further to the comic, the pompous, the absurd. This region of the chest, the breath, is the fecund source of movement, and its range is limited only by one's inventiveness and imagination.

The shoulder closes forward, and opens backward, and can be lifted or lowered, and made to rotate to describe a full circle. This part of the "orchestra" is capable of small and delicate movement. It can describe with subtlety and nuance.

The area of the ribs can expand and contract, giving the torso great flexibility and fluidity. The ability to bend, to fall away from the balance and poise of the perpendicular into the excitement of the unbalance, the oblique, the wild Dionysian regions, is centered in this part of the body.

The pelvis has a great potency. When it is held in centered discipline it polarizes the body into a powerful and beautiful column, in perfect harmony with the earth's gravity, serene and Apollonian. From this axis, the pelvis can thrust forward, pull backwards, move from side to side, and describe a complete circumference, and in so doing generate a labyrinth of movement and gesture which can make the body into a graceful object of poetry and lyricism, or break it into crude and violent shapes, discordant and brutal.

In the dramatic language of the dance the use of the knees offers a great paradox. They can project the body into the air, and propel it through space. When locked into a stretched tautness, they raise and suspend the body where it seems to float and deny the pull of gravity. On the other hand, by bending they lower the body to the earth, to a surrender and a death. The inward rotations of the knees create primitive or grotesque attitudes. The outward manipulations lend elegance and expansiveness. The use of the knee-level in the Modern Dance has opened a remarkable new territory. I have seen some stunning passages executed on the knees in the works of Martha Graham and Charles Weidman.

Our contact with the earth with and through the foot gives this part of the dancer a special significance. It is the "radix," and like the roots of plants, it gives the dancer the substance and sustenance of the earth. The use of the foot reveals the entire philosophy of the dance. Surely there is no greater contrast than that between the dance on the points, which seems to etherealize completely the human form, and the use of the bare foot in the contemporary dance. The first came into being through the poetic imagination of the Romantic period, when the dancer was not human, but a supernatural creature borne by the zephyrs. The bare foot came to us through the great rebel, Isadora Duncan. It is a very expressive part of our instrument, supple and beautiful in itself, capable of many more things than being brought to an elegant point. It can be, in the right hands, so to speak, almost as eloquent and expressive as those hands themselves. When emphasis is placed on the heel of the foot a strength and robustness is attained. It can articulate, twist, roll, rotate. It can speak with tenderness or violence. It has grown to be symbolic of the revolt against the academic dance. Duncan, in her search for a new language for the dance of our time, discarded not only the corsets but the slippers. Her successors in post-World War I Germany and the United States followed in her bare footsteps. In a stricken and turbulent century they created a new language of the dance which could say something about the present world and its tragic realities. The use of the foot in its naked and unfettered beauty was as necessary to the new dance as was the toe-slipper to that of a less disillusioned, less harassed age.

The elbow can articulate in the same fashion as the knee, with the exception that it cannot project the body into the air. It can, however, play an important part in supporting it when the dancer uses the floor level, in falls. This flexible joint gives the arms a rich, flowing quality. The stretching of the joint gives the arm an extended power. The acute bend, with the resultant angularity, opens an entire region of expression, very much related to the cubistic in painting and the dissonant in music. The inward rotations of the flexed or rounded elbow create an inverted, minor tonality in movement, while the opposite, or outward manipulations suggest an open, major one.

One of the most eloquent of the voices of the body is the hand. It is its function to give completion to movement and gesture. The hand is the seal upon the deed. A powerful gesture with the body cannot fully convince unless the hand is in accord with it, nor can a subtle, restrained one be completely so without having the hand in full consonance. The hand can be said to breathe like the lungs. It expands and contracts. It can project movements seemingly to infinity, or gather them back to their source within the body. It is a mouthpiece, a moderator. It has a brilliant range, capable of complexities and subtleties unequalled by other regions of the dancer's "orchestra." It is the abettor of all that the dancer intends. It is unthinkable, a dance without hands.

These are the rich resources of the body. These are the voices. They must be disciplined and developed so that they can speak with truth and power. This necessitates the study of the quality of movement. A single gesture can be phrased in different ways: smoothly, sharply, slowly, rapidly. It can be performed in its entirety, or broken into its component parts. The basic and all-important principle is never forgotten, that movement, in order to have power and eloquence and beauty must spring from the organic center of the body. It must have its source and impulse from the breathing of the lungs and the beating of the heart. It must be intensely and completely human, or it will be gymnastics, and be mechanical and empty. It is this quality, this inflection in the movement that creates that magic in the theater which dance alone can create. Complete mastery of the nuance and color in gesture and movement is the goal toward which the dancer works continually, for this command is what gives his utterance import and validity.

This highly trained, responsible instrument we dedicate to a single idea: that the dance is a serious, adult art, every bit as serious and adult as serious music, painting, literature, and poetry. The oldest of the arts need not exist only as entertainment. It has a great tradition to uphold and by which to be guided and inspired. The American Dance has an imposing gallery of the illustrious. The entire artistic life of the West has felt the impact of Isadora Duncan, the Inceptor. Ruth St. Denis and Ted Shawn pioneered the Wilderness, and took the magic of the dance to the remotest corners of the earth. Their organization was the womb which brought forth Martha Graham, Doris Humphrey, and Charles Weidman. The accomplishments of these children of Denishawn rank with the highest in the cultural story of America. Each has made Art and Civilization in his own very special way. Graham the dark flame, the personifier, the dithyrambic. Humphrey the symphonist, the molder, author of mighty works. Weidman the inspired clown, the Harlequin from the prairie.

These artists have given us something priceless. They have restored the dance to its ancient function, and proven to the modern world that it can reveal, instruct, and ennoble. It can exalt. It can ritualize the great tragedies and ecstasies of man. It is in its power and province to reaffirm the dignity of man in an age that desperately needs this affirmation. Never have the arts been so much needed, nor so challenged, as in these times of mechanized bestiality, when the human species seems possessed by a suicidal frenzy. Surely the Dance can remind us of the greatness of man's spirit, and of his creativeness, not his destructiveness. The Dance is many things. It is a Power. It can help stem the putrefaction and decay gnawing at the heart of human courage, and withstand the philosophies of doom and surrender. The dancer can use his voice to call for reason out of unreason, and order out of disorder. That has always been the high task of the artist. The great Goethe, as death engulfed him, cried "Light, more light." The contemporary artist can do no less than to dedicate the power of his spirit and the flame of his art to bring light to the dark places.

## Bernard Shaw
# DUSE AND BERNHARDT

This week began with the relapse of Sarah Bernhardt into her old profession of serious actress. She played Magda in Sudermann's *Heimat,* and was promptly challenged by Duse in the same part at Drury Lane on Wednesday. The contrast between the two Magdas is as extreme as any contrast could possibly be between artists who have finished their twenty years apprenticeship to the same profession under closely similar conditions. Madame Bernhardt has the charm of a jolly maturity, rather spoilt and petulant, perhaps, but always ready with a sunshine-through-the-clouds smile if only she is made much of. Her dresses and diamonds, if not exactly splendid, are at least splendacious; her figure, far too scantily upholstered in the old days, is at its best; and her complexion shews that she has not studied modern art in vain. Those charming roseate effects which French painters produce by giving flesh the pretty color of strawberries and cream, and painting the shadows pink and crimson, are cunningly reproduced by Madame Bernhardt in the living picture. She paints her ears crimson and allows them to peep enchantingly through a few loose braids of her auburn hair. Every dimple has its dab of pink; and her fingertips are so delicately incarnadined that you fancy they are transparent like her ears, and that the light is shining through their delicate blood-vessels. Her lips are like a newly-painted pillar box; her cheeks, right up to the languid lashes, have the bloom and surface of a peach; she is beautiful with the beauty of her school, and entirely inhuman and incredible. But the incredibility is pardonable, because, though it is all the greatest nonsense, nobody believing in it, the actress herself least of all, it is so artful, so clever, so well recognized a part of the business, and carried off with such a genial air, that it is impossible not to accept it with good-humor. One feels, when the heroine bursts on the scene, a dazzling vision of beauty, that instead of impos-

DUSE AND BERNHARDT: From the *Saturday Review,* 1895. Used by permission of The Public Trustee and The Society of Authors.

ing on you, she adds to her own piquancy by looking you straight in the face, and saying, in effect: "Now who would ever suppose that I am a grandmother?" That, of course, is irresistible; and one is not sorry to have been coaxed to relax one's notions of the dignity of art when she gets to serious business and shews how ably she does her work. The coaxing suits well with the childishly egotistical character of her acting, which is not the art of making you think more highly or feel more deeply, but the art of making you admire her, pity her, champion her, weep with her, laugh at her jokes, follow her fortunes breathlessly, and applaud her wildly when the curtain falls. It is the art of finding out all your weaknesses and practising on them—cajoling you, harrowing you, exciting you—on the whole, fooling you. And it is always Sarah Bernhardt in her own capacity who does this to you. The dress, the title of the play, the order of the words may vary; but the woman is always the same. She does not enter into the leading character: she substitutes herself for it.

All this is precisely what does not happen in the case of Duse, whose every part is a separate creation. When she comes on the stage, you are quite welcome to take your opera-glass and count whatever lines time and care have so far traced on her. They are the credentials of her humanity; and she knows better than to obliterate that significant handwriting beneath a layer of peach-bloom from the chemist's. The shadows on her face are grey, not crimson; her lips are sometimes nearly grey also; there are neither dabs nor dimples; her charm could never be imitated by a barmaid with unlimited pin money and a row of footlights before her instead of the handles of a beer-engine. The result is not so discouraging as the patrons of the bar might suppose. Wilkes, who squinted atrociously, boasted that he was only quarter of an hour behind the handsomest man in Europe: Duse is not in action five minutes before she is quarter of a century ahead of the handsomest woman in the world. I grant that Sarah's elaborate Monna Lisa smile, with the conscious droop of the eyelashes and the long carmined lips coyly disclosing the brilliant row of teeth, is effective of its kind—that it not only appeals to your susceptibilities, but positively jogs them. And it lasts quite a minute, sometimes longer. But Duse, with a tremor of the lip which you feel rather than see, and which lasts half an instant, touches you straight on the very heart; and there is not a line in the face, or a cold tone in the grey shadow that does not give poignancy to that tremor. As to youth and age, who can associate purity and delicacy of emotion, and simplicity of expression, with the sordid craft that repels us in age; or voluptuous appeal and egotistical self-insistence with the candor and generosity that attract us in youth? Who ever thinks of Potiphar's wife as a young woman, or St. Elizabeth of Hungary as an old one? These associations are horribly unjust to age, and undeserved by youth: they belong of right to differences of character, not of years; but they rule our imaginations; and the great artist profits by them to appear eternally young. However, it would be a critical blunder as well as a personal folly on my part to suggest that Duse, any more than Sarah Bernhardt, neglects any art that could heighten the effect of her acting when she is impersonating young and pretty women. The truth is that in the art of being beautiful, Madame Bernhardt is a child beside her. The French artist's stock of attitudes and facial effects could be catalogued as easily as her stock of dramatic ideas: the counting would hardly go beyond the fingers of both hands. Duse produces the illusion of being infinite in variety of beautiful pose and motion. Every idea, every shade of thought and mood, expresses itself delicately but vividly to the eye; and yet, in an apparent million of changes and inflexions, it is impossible to catch any line at an awkward angle, or any strain interfering with the perfect abandonment of all the limbs to what appears to be their natural gravitation towards the finest grace. She is ambidextrous and supple, like a gymnast or a panther; only the multitude of ideas which find physical expression in her movements are all of that high quality which marks off humanity from the animals, and, I fear I must add, from a good many gymnasts. When it is remembered that the majority of tragic actors excel only in explosions of those passions which are common to man and brute, there will be no difficulty in understanding the indescribable distinction which Duse's acting acquires from the fact that behind every stroke of it is a distinctively human idea. In nothing is this more apparent than in the vigilance in her of that high human instinct which seeks to awaken the deepest responsive feeling without giving pain. In *La Dame aux Camélias,* for instance, it is easy for an intense actress to harrow us with her sorrows and paroxysms of phthisis, leaving us with a liberal pennyworth of sensation, not fundamentally distinguishable from that offered by a public execution, or any other evil in which we still take a hideous delight. As different from this as light from darkness is the method of the actress who shews us how human sorrow can express itself only in its appeal for the sympathy it needs, whilst striving by strong endurance to shield others from the infection of its torment. That is the charm of Duse's interpretation of the stage poem of Marguerite Gauthier. It is unspeakably touching because it is exquisitely considerate: that is, exquisitely sympathetic. No physical charm is noble as well as beautiful unless it is the expression of a moral charm; and it is because Duse's range includes these moral high notes, if I may so express myself, that her compass, extending from the depths of a mere predatory creature like Claude's wife up to Marguerite Gauthier at her kindest or Magda at her bravest, so immeasurably dwarfs the poor little octave and a half on which Sarah Bernhardt plays such pretty canzonets and stirring marches.

Obvious as the disparity of the two famous artists has been to many of us since we first saw Duse, I doubt whether any of us realized, after Madame Bernhardt's very clever performance as Magda on Monday night, that there was room in the nature of things for its annihilation within forty-eight hours by so comparatively quiet a talent as Duse's. And yet annihilation is the only word for it. Sarah was very charming, very jolly when the sun shone, very petulant when the clouds covered it, and positively angry when they wanted to take her child away from her. And she did not trouble us with any fuss about the main theme of Sudermann's play, the revolt of the modern woman against that ideal of home which exacts the sacrifice of her whole life to its care, not by her grace, and as its own sole help and refuge, but as a right which it has to the services of all females as abject slaves. In fact, there is not the slightest reason to suspect Madame Bernhardt of having discovered any such theme in the play; though Duse, with one look at Schwartze, the father, nailed it to the stage as the subject of the impending dramatic struggle

before she had been five minutes on the scene. Before long, there came a stroke of acting which will probably never be forgotten by those who saw it, and which explained at once why those artifices of the dressing-table which help Madame Bernhardt would hinder Duse almost as much as a screen placed in front of her. I should explain, first, that the real name of the play is not *Magda* but *Home.* Magda is a daughter who has been turned out of doors for defying her father, one of those outrageous persons who mistake their desire to have everything their own way in the house for a sacred principle of home life. She has a hard time of it, but at last makes a success as an opera singer, though not until her lonely struggles have thrown her for sympathy on a fellow student, who in due time goes his way, and leaves her to face motherhood as best she can. In the fullness of her fame she returns to her native town, and in an attack of homesickness makes advances to her father, who consents to receive her again. No sooner is she installed in the house than she finds that one of the most intimate friends of the family is the father of her child. In the third act of the play she is on the stage when he is announced as a visitor. It must be admitted that Sarah Bernhardt played this scene very lightly and pleasantly: there was genuine good fellowship in the way in which she reassured the embarrassed gallant and made him understand that she was not going to play off the sorrows of Gretchen on him after all those years, and that she felt that she owed him the priceless experience of maternity, even if she did not particularly respect him for it. Her self-possession at this point was immense: the peach-bloom never altered by a shade. Not so with Duse. The moment she read the card handed her by the servant, you realized what it was to have to face a meeting with the man. It was interesting to watch how she got through it when he came in, and how, on the whole, she got through it pretty well. He paid his compliments and offered his flowers; they sat down; and she evidently felt that she had got it safely over and might allow herself to think at her ease, and to look at him to see how much he had altered. Then a terrible thing happened to her. She began to blush; and in another moment she was conscious of it, and the blush was slowly spreading and deepening until, after a few vain efforts to avert her face or to obstruct his view of it without seeming to do so, she gave up and hid the blush in her hands. After that feat of acting I did not need to be told why Duse does not paint an inch thick. I could detect no trick in it: it seemed to me a perfectly genuine effect of the dramatic imagination. In the third act of *La Dame aux Camélias,* where she produces a touching effect by throwing herself down, and presently rises with her face changed and flushed with weeping, the flush is secured by the preliminary plunge to a stooping attitude, imagination or no imagination; but Magda's blush did not admit of that explanation; and I must confess to an intense professional curiosity as to whether it always comes spontaneously.

I shall make no attempt to describe the rest of that unforgettable act. To say that it left the house not only frantically applauding, but actually roaring, is to say nothing; for had we not applauded Sarah as Gismonda and roared at Mrs Patrick Campbell as Fedora? But there really was something to roar at this time. There was a real play, and an actress who understood the author and was a greater artist than he. And for me, at least, there was a confirmation of my sometimes flagging faith that a dramatic critic is really the servant of a high art, and not a mere advertiser of entertainments of questionable respectability of motive.

*Cleanth Brooks*

# THE MOTIVATION OF TENNYSON'S WEEPER

Tennyson is perhaps the last English poet one would think of associating with the subtleties of paradox and ambiguity. He is not the thoughtless poet, to be sure: he grapples—particularly in his later period—with the "big" questions which were up for his day; and he struggles manfully with them. But the struggle, as Tennyson conducted it, was usually kept out of the grammar and symbolism of the poetry

For the text of "Tears, Idle Tears," see Chapter 9.

itself. Like his own protagonist in "In Memoriam," Tennyson "fought his doubts"—he does not typically build them into the structure of the poetry itself as enriching ambiguities.

Yet substantially true as this generalization is, Tennyson was not always successful in avoiding the ambiguous and the paradoxical; and indeed, in some of his poems his failure to avoid them becomes a saving grace. The lyric "Tears, Idle Tears" is a very good instance. It is a poem which, from a strictly logical point of view, Tennyson may be thought to have blundered into. But, whether he blundered into it or not, the poem gains from the fact that it finds its unity in a principle of organization higher than that which seems to be operative in many of Tennyson's more "thoughtful" poems.

Any account of the poem may very well begin with a consideration of the nature of the tears. Are they *idle* tears? Or are they not rather the most meaningful of tears? Does not the very fact that they are "idle" (that is, tears occasioned by no immediate grief) become in itself a guarantee of the fact that they spring from a deeper, more universal cause?

It would seem so, and that the poet is thus beginning his poem with a paradox. For the third line of the poem indicates that there is no doubt in the speaker's mind about the origin of the tears in some divine despair. They "rise in the heart"—for all that they have been first announced as "idle."

But the question of whether Tennyson is guilty of (or to be complimented upon) a use of paradox may well wait upon further discussion. At this point in our commentary, it is enough to observe that Tennyson has chosen to open his poem with some dramatic boldness—if not with the bold step of equating "idle" with "from the depth of some divine despair," then at least with a bold and violent reversal of the speaker's first characterization of his tears.

The tears "rise in the heart" as the speaker looks upon a scene of beauty and tranquillity. Does looking on the "happy Autumn-fields" bring to mind the days that are no more? The poet does not say so. The tears rise to the eyes in looking on the "happy Autumn-fields" *and* thinking of the days that are no more. The poet himself does not stand responsible for any closer linkage between these actions, though, as a matter of fact, most of us will want to make a closer linkage here. For, if we change "happy Autumn-fields," say, to "happy April-fields," the two terms tend to draw apart. The fact that the fields are autumn-fields which, though happy, point back to something which is over—which is finished—*does* connect them with the past and therefore properly suggests to the observer thoughts about that past.

To sum up: The first stanza has a unity, but it is not a unity which finds its sanctions in the ordinary logic of language. Its sanctions are to be found in the dramatic context, and, to my mind, there alone. Indeed, the stanza suggests the play of the speaker's mind as the tears unexpectedly start, tears for which there is no apparent occasion, and as he searches for an explanation of them. He calls them "idle," but, even as he says "I know not what they mean," he realizes that they must spring from the depths of his being—is willing, with his very next words, to associate them with "some divine despair." Moreover, the real occasion of the tears, though the speaker himself comes to realize it only as he approaches the end of the stanza, is the thought about the past. It is psychologically and dramatically right, therefore, that the real occasion should be stated explicitly only with the last line of the stanza.

This first stanza, then, recapitulates the surprise and bewilderment in the speaker's own mind, and sets the problem which the succeeding stanzas are to analyze. The dramatic effect may be described as follows: the stanza seems, not a meditated observation, but a speech begun impulsively—a statement which the speaker has begun before he knows how he will end it.

In the second stanza we are not surprised to have the poet characterize the days that are no more as "sad," but there is some shock in hearing him apply to them the adjective "fresh." Again, the speaker does not pause to explain: the word "fresh" actually begins the stanza. Yet the adjective justifies itself.

The past is fresh as with a dawn freshness—as fresh as the first beam glittering on the sail of an incoming ship. The ship is evidently expected; it brings friends, friends "up from the underworld." On the surface, the comparison is innocent: the "underworld" is merely the antipodes, the world which lies below the horizon—an underworld in the sense displayed in old-fashioned geographies with their sketches illustrating the effects of the curvature of the earth. The sails, which catch the light and glitter, will necessarily be the part first seen of any ship which is coming "up" over the curve of the earth.

But the word "underworld" will necessarily suggest the underworld of Greek mythology, the realm of the shades, the abode of the dead. The attempt to characterize the freshness of the days that are no more has, thus, developed, almost imperceptibly, into a further characterization of the days themselves as belonging, not to our daylight world, but to an "underworld." This suggestion is, of course, strengthened in the lines that follow in which the ship metaphor is reversed so as to give us a picture of sadness: evening, the last glint of sunset light on the sail of a ship

That sinks with all we love below the verge . . .

The conjunction of the qualities of sadness and freshness is reinforced by the fact that the same basic symbol—the light on the sails of a ship hull down—has been employed to suggest both qualities. With the third stanza, the process is carried one stage further: the two qualities (with the variant of "strange" for "fresh") are explicitly linked together:

Ah, sad and strange as in dark summer dawns . .

And here the poet is not content to suggest the qualities of sadness and strangeness by means of two different, even if closely related, figures. In this third stanza the special kind of sadness and strangeness is suggested by one and the same figure.

It is a figure developed in some detail. It, too, involves a dawn scene, though ironically so, for the beginning of the new day is to be the beginning of the long night for the dying man. The dying eyes, the poem suggests, have been for some time awake—long enough to have had time to watch the

. . . casement slowly [grow] a glimmering
   square. . . .

The dying man, soon to sleep the lasting sleep, is more fully awake than the "half-awaken'd birds" whose earliest pipings come to his dying ears. We know why these pipings are sad; but why are they *strange?* Because to the person hearing a bird's song for the last time, it will seem that he has never before really heard one.

The familiar sound will take on a quality of unreality—of strangeness.

If this poem were merely a gently melancholy reverie on the sweet sadness of the past, Stanzas II and III would have no place in the poem. But the poem is no such reverie: the images from the past rise up with a strange clarity and sharpness that shock the speaker. Their sharpness and freshness account for the sudden tears and for the psychological problem with which the speaker wrestles in the poem. If the past would only remain melancholy but dimmed, sad but worn and familiar, we should have no problem and no poem. At least, we should not have *this* poem; we should certainly not have the intensity of the last stanza.

That intensity, if justified, must grow out of a sense of the apparent nearness and intimate presence of what is irrevocably beyond reach: the days that are no more must be more than the conventional "dear, dead days beyond recall." They must be beyond recall, yet alive— tantalizingly vivid and near. It is only thus that we can feel the speaker justified in calling them

Dear as remember'd kisses after death,
And sweet as those by hopeless fancy feign'd
On lips that are for others. . . .

It is only thus that we can accept the culminating paradox of

O Death in Life, the days that are no more.

We have already observed, in the third stanza, how the speaker compares the strangeness and sadness of the past to the sadness of the birds' piping as it sounds to dying ears. There is a rather brilliant ironic contrast involved in the comparison. The speaker, a living man, in attempting to indicate how sad and strange to him are the days of the past, says that they are as sad and strange as is the natural activity of the awakening world to the man who is dying: the dead past seems to the living man as unfamiliar and fresh in its sadness as the living present seems to the dying man. There is more here, however, than a mere, ironic reversal of roles; in each case there is the sense of being irrevocably barred out from the known world.

This ironic contrast, too, accounts for the sense of desperation which runs through the concluding lines of the poem. The kisses feigned by "hopeless fancy" are made the more precious because of the very hopelessness; but memory takes on the quality of fancy. It is equally hopeless—the kisses can as little be renewed as those "feign'd / On lips that are for others" can be obtained. The realized past has become as fabulous as the unrealizable future. The days that are no more are as dear as the one, as sweet as the other, the speaker says; and it does not matter whether we compare them to the one or to the other or to both: it comes to the same thing.

But the days that are no more are not merely "dear" and "sweet"; they are "deep" and "wild." Something has happened to the grammar here. How can the *days* be "deep as love" or "wild with all regret"? And what is the status of the exclamation "O Death in Life"? Is it merely a tortured cry like "O God! the days that are no more"? Or is it a loose appositive: "the days that are no more are a kind of death in life?"

The questions are not asked in a censorious spirit, as if there were no justification for Tennyson's license here. But it is important to see how much license the poem requires, and the terms on which the reader decides to accord it justification. What one finds on closer examination is not muddlement but richness. But it is a richness achieved through principles of organization which many an admirer of the poet has difficulty in allowing to the "obscure" modern poet.

For example, how can the days of the past be *deep?* Here, of course, the problem is not very difficult. The past is buried within one: the days that are no more constitute the deepest level of one's being, and the tears that arise from thinking on them may be said to come from the "depth of some divine despair." But how can the days be "wild with all regret"? The extension demanded here is more ambitious. In matter of fact, it is the speaker, the man, who is made wild with regret by thinking on the days.

One can, of course, justify the adjective as a transferred epithet on the model of Vergil's *maestum timorem;* [1] and perhaps this was Tennyson's own conscious justification (if, indeed, the need to justify it ever occurred to him). But one can make a better case than a mere

---

[1] "Sad fear"; *Aeneid* I. 202.

appeal to the authority of an established literary convention. There is a sense in which the man and the remembered days are one and the same. A man is the sum of his memories. The adjective which applies to the man made wild with regret can apply to those memories which make him wild with regret. For, does the man charge the memories with his own passion, or is it the memories that give the emotion to him? If we pursue the matter far enough, we come to a point where the distinction lapses. Perhaps I should say, more accurately, adopting the metaphor of the poem itself, we *descend* to a depth where the distinction lapses. The days that are no more are *deep* and *wild,* buried but not dead—below the surface and unthought of, yet at the deepest core of being, secretly alive.

The past *should* be tame, fettered, brought to heel; it is not. It is capable of breaking forth and coming to the surface. The word "wild" is bold, therefore, but justified. It reasserts the line of development which has been maintained throughout the earlier stanzas: "fresh," "strange," and now "wild"—all adjectives which suggest passionate, irrational life. The word "wild," thus, not only pulls into focus the earlier paradoxes, but is the final stage in the preparation for the culminating paradox, "O Death in Life."

The last stanza evokes an intense emotional response from the reader. The claim could hardly be made good by the stanza taken in isolation. The stanza leans heavily upon the foregoing stanzas, and the final paradox draws heavily upon the great metaphors in Stanzas II and III. This is as it should be. The justification for emphasizing the fact here is this: the poem, for all its illusion of impassioned speech—with the looseness and *apparent* confusion of unpremeditated speech—is very tightly organized. It represents an organic structure; and the intensity of the total effect is a reflection of the total structure.

The reader, I take it, will hardly be disposed to quarrel with the general statement of the theme of the poem as it is given in the foregoing account; and he will probably find himself in accord with this general estimate of the poem's value. But the reader may well feel that the amount of attention given to the structure of the poem is irrelevant, if not positively bad. In particular, he may find the emphasis on

paradox, ambiguity, and ironic contrast displeasing. He has not been taught to expect these in Tennyson, and he has had the general impression that the presence of these qualities represents the intrusion of alien, "unpoetic" matter.

I have no wish to intellectualize the poem—to make conscious and artful what was actually spontaneous and simple. Nevertheless, the qualities of ironic contrast and paradox *do* exist in the poem; and they *do* have a relation to the poem's dramatic power.

Those who still feel that "simple eloquence" is enough might compare "Tears, Idle Tears" with another of Tennyson's poems which has somewhat the same subject matter and hints of the same imagery, the lyric "Break, Break, Break."

> Break, break, break.
>   On thy cold grey stones, O sea!
> And I would that my tongue could utter
>   The thoughts that arise in me.
>
> O, well for the fisherman's boy,
>   That he shouts with his sister at play!
> O well for the sailor lad,
>   That he sings in his boat on the bay!
>
> And the stately ships go on
>   To their haven under the hill;
> But O for the touch of a vanished hand,
>   And the sound of a voice that is still!
>
> Break, break, break,
>   At the foot of thy crags, O sea!
> But the tender grace of a day that is dead
>   Will never come back to me.

It is an easier poem than "Tears," and, in one sense, a less confusing poem. But it is also a much thinner poem, and unless we yield comfortably and easily to the strain of gentle melancholy, actually a coarser and a more confused poem. For example, the ships are said to be "stately," but this observation is idle and finally irrelevant. What relation has their stateliness to the experience of grief? (Perhaps one may argue that the term suggests that they go on to fulfill their missions, unperturbed and with no regard for the speaker's mood. But this interpretation is forced, and even under forcing, the yield of relevance is small.)

Again, consider the status of the past as it appears in this poem: the hand is vanished, the voice is still. It is true, as the poem itself indicates, that there is a sense in which the hand has not vanished and the voice is yet heard; otherwise we should not have the poem at all. But the poet makes no effort to connect this activity, still alive in memory, with its former "actual" life. He is content to keep close to the conventional prose account of such matters. Memory in this poem does not become a kind of life: it is just "memory"—whatever that is— and, in reading the poem, we are not forced beyond the bounds of our conventional thinking on the subject.

In the same way, the elements of the line, "the tender grace of a day that is dead," remain frozen at the conventional prose level. The day is "dead"; the "tender grace" of it will never "come back" to him. We are not encouraged to take the poignance of his present memory of it as a ghost from the tomb. The poet does not recognize that his experience represents such an ironical resurrection; nor does he allow the metaphors buried in "dead" and "come back" to suffer a resurrection into vigorous poetic life. With such phenomena the poet is not concerned.

Of course, the poet *need* not be concerned with them; I should agree that we have no right to demand that this poem should explore the nature of memory as "Tears, Idle Tears" explores it. At moments, men are unaccountably saddened by scenes which are in themselves placid and even happy. The poet is certainly entitled, if he chooses, to let it go at that. Yet, it should be observed that in avoiding the psychological exploration of the experience, the poet risks losing dramatic force.

Mere psychological analysis is, of course, not enough to insure dramatic force; and such analysis, moreover, carries its own risks: the poem may become unnatural and coldly rhetorical. But when the poet is able, as in "Tears, Idle Tears," to analyze his experience, and in the full light of the disparity and even apparent contradiction of the various elements, bring them into a new unity, he secures not only richness and depth but dramatic power as well. Our conventional accounts of poetry which oppose emotion to intellect, "lyric simplicity" to "thoughtful meditation," have done no service to the cause of poetry. The opposition is not only merely superficial: it falsifies the real relationships. For the lyric quality, if it be genuine, is not the result of some transparent and "simple" redaction of a theme or a situation which is somehow poetic in itself; it is, rather, the result of an imaginative grasp of diverse materials—but an imaginative grasp so sure that it may show itself to the reader as unstudied and unpredictable without for a moment relaxing its hold on the intricate and complex stuff which it carries.

## *Horatio Greenough*
# AMERICAN ARCHITECTURE

[*The following remarks by a nineteenth-century American sculptor represent one of the earliest American pleas (1843) for "functionalism" in art and architecture.*]

We have heard the learned in matters relating to art express the opinion that these United States are destined to form a new style of architecture. Remembering that a vast population, rich in material and guided by the experience, the precepts, and the models of the Old World, was about to erect durable structures for every function of civilized life, we also cherished the hope that such a combination would speedily be formed.

We forgot that, though the country was young, yet the people were old; that as Americans we have no childhood, no half-fabulous, legendary wealth, no misty, cloud-enveloped background. We forgot that we had not unity of religious belief, nor unity of origin; that our territory, extending from the white bear to the alligator, made our occupations dissimilar, our character and tastes various. We forgot that the Republic had leaped full-grown and armed to the teeth from the brain of her parent, and that a hammer had been the instrument of delivery. We forgot that reason had been the dry nurse of the giant offspring, and had fed her from the beginning with the strong bread and meat of fact; that every wry face the bantling ever made had been daguerreotyped, and all her words and deeds printed and labeled away in the pigeonholes of official bureaus.

AMERICAN ARCHITECTURE: From *Form and Function,* ed. Harold A. Small. University of California Press, 1947.

Reason can dissect, but cannot originate; she can adopt, but cannot create; she can modify, but cannot find. Give her but a cock-boat, and she will elaborate a line-of-battle ship; give her but a beam with its wooden tooth, and she turns out the patent plow. She is not young; and when her friends insist upon the phenomena of youth, then is she least attractive. She can imitate the flush of the young cheek, but where is the flash of the young eye? She buys the teeth—alas! she cannot buy the breath of childhood. The puny cathedral of Broadway,[2] like an elephant dwindled to the size of a dog, measures her yearning for Gothic sublimity, while the roar of the Astor House, and the mammoth vase of the great reservoir, shows how she works when she feels at home and is in earnest.

The mind of this country has never been seriously applied to the subject of building. Intently engaged in matters of more pressing importance, we have been content to receive our notions of architecture as we have received the fashion of our garments and the form of our entertainments, from Europe. In our eagerness to appropriate, we have neglected to adapt, to distinguish,—nay, to understand. We have built small Gothic temples of wood and have omitted all ornaments for economy, unmindful that size, material, and ornament are the elements of effect in that style of building. Captivated by the classic symmetry of the Athenian models, we have sought to bring the Parthenon into our streets, to make the temple of Theseus work in our towns. We have shorn them of their lateral colonnades, let them down from their dignified platform, pierced their walls for light, and, instead of the storied relief and the eloquent statue which enriched the frieze and graced the pediment, we have made our chimneytops to peer over the broken profile and tell, by their rising smoke, of the traffic and desecration of the interior. Still the model may be recognized, some of the architectural features are entire; like the captive king, stripped alike of arms and purple and drudging amid the Helots of a capital, the Greek temple, as seen among us, claims pity for its degraded majesty, and attests the barbarian force which has abused its nature and been blind to its qualities.

If we trace architecture from its perfection in the days of Pericles to its manifest decay in the reign of Constantine,[3] we shall find that one of the surest symptoms of decline was the adoption of admired forms and models for purposes not contemplated in their invention. The forum became a temple; the tribunal became a temple; the theater was turned into a church; nay, the column, that organized member, that subordinate part, set up for itself, usurped unity, and was a monument! The great principles of architecture being once abandoned, correctness gave way to novelty, economy and vainglory associated produced meanness and pretension. Sculpture, too, had waned. The degenerate workmen could no longer match the fragments they sought to mingle, nor copy the originals they only hoped to repeat. The moldering remains of better days frowned contempt upon such impotent efforts, till, in the gradual coming of darkness, ignorance became contempt, and insensibility ceased to compare.

We say that the mind of this country has never been seriously applied to architecture. True it is that the commonwealth, with that desire of public magnificence which has ever been a leading feature of democracy, has called from the vasty deep of the past the spirits of the Greek, the Roman, and the Gothic styles; but they would not come when she did call to them! The vast cathedral, with its ever-open portals, towering high above the courts of kings, inviting all men to its cool and fragrant twilight, where the voice of the organ stirs the blood, and the dim-seen visions of saints and martyrs bleed and die upon the canvas amid the echoes of hymning voices and the clouds of frankincense—this architectural embodying of the divine and blessed words, "Come to me, ye who labor and are heavy laden, and I will give you rest!" demands a sacrifice of what we hold dearest. Its cornerstone must be laid upon the right to judge the claims of the church. The style of Greek architecture, as seen in the Greek temple, demands the aid of sculpture, insists upon every feature of its original organization, loses its harmony if a note be dropped in the execution, and when so modified as to

[2] Apparently a reference to Trinity Church, completed in 1846.

[3] Pericles (d. 429 B.C.) ruled Athens in its greatest age, when the Parthenon and the "Temple of Theseus" were built; Constantine (280?-337) enlarged Byzantium, or Constantinople, and made it the eastern capital of the Roman Empire.

serve for a custom-house or bank, departs from its original beauty and propriety as widely as the crippled gelding of a hackney coach differs from the bounding and neighing wild horse of the desert. Even where, in the fervor of our faith in shapes, we have sternly adhered to the dictum of another age, and have actually succeeded in securing the entire exterior which echoes the forms of Athens, the pile stands a stranger among us, and receives a respect akin to what we should feel for a fellow citizen in the garb of Greece. It is a make-believe. It is not the real thing. We see the marble capitals; we trace the acanthus leaves of a celebrated model—incredulous; it is not a temple.

The number and variety of our experiments in building show the dissatisfaction of the public taste with what has been hitherto achieved; the expense at which they have been made proves how strong is the yearning after excellence; the talents and acquirements of the artists whose services have been engaged in them are such as to convince us that the fault lies in the system, not in the men. Is it possible that out of this chaos order can arise?—that of these conflicting dialects and jargons a language can be born? When shall we have done with experiments? What refuge is there from the absurdities that have successively usurped the name and functions of architecture? Is it not better to go on with consistency and uniformity, in imitation of an admired model, than incur the disgrace of other failures? In answering these questions let us remember with humility that all salutary changes are the work of many and of time; but let us encourage experiment at the risk of license, rather than submit to an iron rule that begins by sacrificing reason, dignity, and comfort. Let us consult nature, and in the assurance that she will disclose a mine richer than was ever dreamed of by the Greeks, in art as well as in philosophy. Let us regard as ingratitude to the author of nature the despondent idleness that sits down while one want is unprovided for, one worthy object unattained.

If, as the first step in our search after the great principles of construction, we but observe the skeletons and skins of animals, through all the varieties of beast and bird, of fish and insect, are we not as forcibly struck by their variety as by their beauty? There is no arbitrary law of proportion, no unbending model of form. There is scarce a part of the animal organization which we do not find elongated or shortened, increased, diminished, or suppressed, as the wants of the genus or species dictate, as their exposure or their work may require. The neck of the swan and that of the eagle, however different in character and proportion, equally charm the eye and satisfy the reason. We approve the length of the same member in grazing animals, its shortness in beasts of prey. The horse's shanks are thin, and we admire them; the greyhound's chest is deep, and we cry, beautiful! It is neither the presence nor the absence of this or that part, or shape, or color, that wins our eye in natural objects; it is the consistency and harmony of the parts juxtaposed, the subordination of details to masses, and of the masses to the whole.

The law of adaptation is the fundamental law of nature in all structure. So unflinchingly does she modify a type in accordance with a new position, that some philosophers have declared a variety of appearance to be the object aimed at; so entirely does she limit the modification to the demands of necessity, that adherence to one original plan seems, to limited intelligence, to be carried to the very verge of caprice. The domination of arbitrary rules of taste has produced the very counterpart of the wisdom thus displayed in every object around us; we tie up the camelopard to the rack; we shave the lion, and call him a dog; we strive to bind the unicorn with his band in the furrow, and make him harrow the valleys after us!

When the savage of the South Sea islands shapes his war club, his first thought is of its use. His first efforts pare the long shaft, and mold the convenient handle; then the heavier end takes gradually the edge that cuts, while it retains the weight that stuns. His idler hour divides its surface by lines and curves, or embosses it with figures that have pleased his eye or are linked with his superstition. We admire its effective shape, its Etruscan-like quaintness, its graceful form and subtle outline, yet we neglect the lesson it might teach. If we compare the form of a newly invented machine with the perfected type of the same instrument, we observe, as we trace it through the phases of improvement, how weight is shaken off where strength is less needed, how functions are made to approach without impeding each other, how straight becomes curved, and the curve is straightened, till the straggling and cumbersome machine becomes the compact, effective, and beautiful engine.

So instinctive is the perception of organic beauty in the human eye, that we cannot withhold our admiration even from the organs of destruction. There is majesty in the royal paw of the lion, music in the motion of the brindled tiger; we accord our praise to the sword and the dagger, and shudder our approval of the frightful aptitude of the ghastly guillotine.

Conceiving destruction to be a normal element of the system of nature equally with production, we have used the word beauty in connection with it. We have no objection to exchange it for the word character, as indicating the mere adaptation of forms to functions, and would gladly substitute the actual pretensions of our architecture to the former, could we hope to secure the latter.

Let us now turn to a structure of our own, one which, from its nature and uses, commands us to reject authority, and we shall find the result of the manly use of plain good sense, so like that of taste, and genius too, as scarce to require a distinctive title. Observe a ship at sea! Mark the majestic form of her hull as she rushes through the water, observe the graceful bend of her body, the gentle transition from round to flat, the grasp of her keel, the leap of her bows, the symmetry and rich tracery of her spars and rigging, and those grand wind muscles, her sails. Behold an organization second only to that of an animal, obedient as the horse, swift as the stag, and bearing the burden of a thousand camels from pole to pole! What academy of design, what research of connoisseurship, what imitation of the Greeks produced this marvel of construction? Here is the result of the study of man upon the great deep, where Nature spake of the laws of building, not in the feather and in the flower, but in winds and waves, and he bent all his mind to hear and to obey. Could we carry into our civil architecture the responsibilities that weigh upon our shipbuilding, we should ere long have edifices as superior to the Parthenon, for the purposes that we require, as the *Constitution* or the *Pennsylvania* is to the galley of the Argonauts. Could our blunders on terra firma be put to the same dread test that those of shipbuilders are, little would be now left to say on this subject.

Instead of forcing the functions of every sort of building into one general form, adopting an outward shape for the sake of the eye or of association, without reference to the inner distribution, let us begin from the heart as the nucleus, and work outward. The most convenient size and arrangement of the rooms that are to constitute the building being fixed, the access of the light that may, of the air that must be wanted, being provided for, we have the skeleton of our building. Nay, we have all excepting the dress. The connection and order of parts, juxtaposed for convenience, cannot fail to speak of their relation and uses. As a group of idlers on the quay, if they grasp a rope to haul a vessel to the pier, are united in harmonious action by the cord they seize, as the slowly yielding mass forms a thorough-bass to their livelier movement, so the unflinching adaptation of a building to its position and use gives, as a sure product of that adaptation, character and expression.

What a field of study would be opened by the adoption in civil architecture of those laws of apportionment, distribution, and connection which we have thus hinted at? No longer could the mere tyro huddle together a crowd of ill-arranged, ill-lighted, and stifled rooms and, masking the chaos with the sneaking copy of a Greek façade, usurp the name of architect. If this anatomic connection and proportion has been attained in ships, in machines, and, in spite of false principles, in such buildings as made a departure from it fatal, as in bridges and in scaffolding, why should we fear its immediate use in all construction? As its first result, the bank would have the physiognomy of a bank, the church would be recognized as such, nor would the billiard room and the chapel wear the same uniform of columns and pediment. The African king, standing in mock majesty with his legs and feet bare, and his body clothed in a cast coat of the Prince Regent, is an object whose ridiculous effect defies all power of face. Is not the Greek temple jammed in between the brick shops of Wall Street or Cornhill, covered with lettered signs, and occupied by groups of money-changers and applewomen, a parallel even for his African majesty?

We have before us a letter in which Mr. Jefferson recommends the model of the Maison

Carrée [4] for the State House at Richmond. Was he aware that the Maison Carrée is but a fragment, and that, too, of a Roman temple? He was; it is beautiful—is the answer. An English society erected in Hyde Park a cast in bronze of the colossal Achilles of the Quirinal, and, changing the head, transformed it into a monument to Wellington. But where is the distinction between the personal prowess, the invulnerable body, the heaven-shielded safety of the hero of the Iliad and the complex of qualities which makes the modern general? The statue is beautiful—is the answer. If such reasoning is to hold, why not translate one of Pindar's [5] odes in memory of Washington, or set up in Carolina a colossal Osiris [6] in honor of General Greene?

The monuments of Egypt and of Greece are sublime as expressions of their power and their feeling. The modern nation that appropriates them displays only wealth in so doing. The possession of means, not accompanied by the sense of propriety or feeling for the true, can do no more for a nation than it can do for an individual. The want of an illustrious ancestry may be compensated, fully compensated; but the purloining of the coat-of-arms of a defunct family is intolerable. That such a monument as we have described should have been erected in London while Chantrey flourished, when Flaxman's [7] fame was cherished by the few, and Baily and Behnes [8] were already known, is an instructive fact. That the illustrator of the Greek poets and of the Lord's Prayer should in the meanwhile have been preparing designs for George the Fourth's silversmiths, is not less so.

The edifices in whose construction the principles of architecture are developed may be classed as organic, formed to meet the wants of their occupants, or monumental, addressed to the sympathies, the faith, or the taste of a people. These two great classes of buildings, embracing almost every variety of structure, though occasionally joined and mixed in the same edifice, have their separate rules, as they have a distinct abstract nature. In the former class the laws of structure and apportionment, depending on definite wants, obey a demonstrable rule. They may be called machines each individual of which must be formed with reference to the abstract type of its species. The individuals of the latter class, bound by no other laws than those of the sentiment which inspired them, and the sympathies to which they are addressed, occupy the positions and assume the forms best calculated to render their parent feeling. No limits can be put to their variety; their size and richness have always been proportioned to the means of the people who have erected them.

If, from what has been thus far said, it shall have appeared that we regard the Greek masters as aught less than the true apostles of correct taste in building, we have been misunderstood. We believe firmly and fully that they can teach us; but let us learn principles, not copy shapes; let us imitate them like men, and not ape them like monkeys. Remembering what a school of art it was that perfected their system of ornament, let us rather adhere to that system in enriching what we invent than substitute novelty for propriety. After observing the innovations of the ancient Romans, and of the modern Italian masters in this department, we cannot but recur to the Horatian precept—

"exemplaria Graeca
Nocturna versate manu, versate diurna!" [9]

To conclude: The fundamental laws of building found at the basis of every style of architecture must be the basis of ours. The adaptation of the forms and magnitude of structures to the climate they are exposed to, and the offices for which they are intended, teaches us to study our own varied wants in these respects. The harmony of their ornaments with the nature that they embellished, and the institutions from which they sprang, calls on us to do the like justice to our country, our government, and our faith. As a Christian preacher may give weight to truth, and add persuasion to proof, by studying the models of pagan writers, so the American builder by

---

4 Roman ruin in Nîmes, France.

5 Greek poet, 522?-443 B.C.

6 *i.e.,* a statue of the Egyptian god of the underworld.

7 Sir Francis Chantrey, 1781–1841, and John Flaxman, 1755–1826, British sculptors.

8 Edward Baily, 1788–1867, was a student of Flaxman. Henry Behnes, died 1837, was a British sculptor who worked under the name of Burlowe.

9 "Occupy your mind with the examples of the Greeks, both day and night"; *Ars Poetica,* ll. 268-9.

a truly philosophic investigation of ancient art will learn of the Greeks to be American.

The system of building we have hinted at cannot be formed in a day. It requires all the science of any country to ascertain and fix the proportions and arrangements of the members of a great building, to plant it safely on the soil, to defend it from the elements, to add the grace and poetry of ornament to its frame. Each of these requisites to a good building requires a special study and a lifetime. Whether we are destined soon to see so noble a fruit may be doubtful; but we can, at least, break the ground and throw in the seed.

*Lewis Mumford*
# CRYSTAL LANTERN

The Manufacturers Trust Company's new Fifth Avenue office, at the southwest corner of Forty-third Street, revives the dream of building a whole city of glass that haunted the Victorian imagination. Most of the big cities of Europe perpetuated that dream to the extent of building at least one glass-covered shopping arcade; George Pullman, in projecting his ill-fated town of Pullman, Illinois, built a great glass-covered market and community hall; even Ebenezer Howard, most practical of idealists, conceived an enormous under-glass shopping avenue as one of the spectacular features of his proposed Garden City near London; and the dream of sparkling crystalline cities, all glass and metal, figured in more than one of H. G. Wells' many utopias. But only in our time has this dream begun to come nearer to general realization, and among the architects who have done most to put the idea to practical use—Philip Johnson in his own house, in New Canaan; Mies van der Rohe in the Lake Shore Drive Apartments, in Chicago; Frank Lloyd Wright in the S. C. Johnson & Son's Laboratory, in Racine, Wisconsin—none has done more (in New York, anyway) than the firm of Skidmore, Owings & Merrill. In the Manufacturers Trust, they have followed up

CRYSTAL LANTERN: Used by permission of the author. Copyright, 1954, by The New Yorker Magazine, Inc.

their Lever House with a quite different mode of design, and in the course of executing it they have pointed up many of the possibilities of glass, both structurally and aesthetically.

While Lever House is, at most times of the day and the night, a dark-green, almost opaque building, in which the glass sheath seems stretched taut, like a film, over the frame it conceals, this new bank is a paradoxical combination of transparence and solidity—crystalline, yes, but not in the slightest frail or film-like, for, if anything, it is both rugged and monumental. Lacking any vestige of classic Greek or Roman form, or anything to remind one of the conventional banking temple except its low, four-square form, it nevertheless expresses the classic qualities of dignity, serenity, and order. To the observer approaching it along Fifth Avenue, this structure, with its heavy vertical aluminum ribs and its massive glass wall panels, conveys the feeling that it is there to stay. The over-all treatment of the façade actually says aloud what the engineers' calculations had indicated—that these glass walls could withstand a wind of up to a hundred miles an hour, a velocity that, because of its sheltered position, the building would never be subjected to.

The notion of designing a bank with an all-glass façade was first broached, I believe, in these columns in the nineteen-thirties, the theory being that exposure to public view was a much greater protection against assault and robbery than any number of stately Corinthian columns and bronze grille cages. As a matter of fact, the classic column, once the pat symbol of conservatism and financial solvency, did not, as a symbol, survive the awful financial revelations of the great depression, yet it was a long time after that before banks began to free themselves of this antique image. The move toward modern design in banks first manifested itself only in the interiors; the cold, chilly, railroad-station atmosphere was gradually warmed up with "homey" touches of the sticky kind associated with Georgian revivalism, and later with equally dubious attempts at mural painting in the genteel tradition of the eighteen-nineties. During the past ten years, though, many banks —there is a whole nest of them around Rockefeller Center—have adopted modern decoration of the sort one might expect to find in a fancy club. But nowhere have both interior and exterior been conceived more effectively as a whole, or treated in a more forthright manner, at once businesslike and elegant, than in this new structure. The great merit of the Manufacturers Trust's new quarters is that, being all of one piece, every part tells the same story, and to perfection. This is true of the little things as well as of the big ones; thus, the clock on the second floor, ignoring the foolish modern convention that requires blank dials and small, stubby hands that don't indicate more than a vague approximation of the time of day, actually tells the hour with pointed precision. Admittedly, part of the building's success is due to the very special advantages of its site, which I will more fully touch on later, but the fact that the architects made use of these advantages is no little part of their achievement.

Viewed from outside, this building is essentially a glass lantern, and, like a lantern, it is even more striking by dark than by daylight. The main shell contains four floors, counting the street-level one, and it is topped by a fifth floor, a penthouse that is set back to provide a terrace, which, like the Fifth Avenue frontage, is planted with trees, thus suggesting the natural landscape so many of us leave behind when we must do business in the Plutonian underworld of megalopolis. This landscaping makes the building an urban equivalent of Poe's "Domain of Arnheim." Indeed, the bank is as prodigal in the luxuriance of its vegetation as in the luxury of its working equipment, for the extensive greenery, planned and installed by Clarke & Rapuano, landscape architects, requires the services of a gardener two full days a week. The glass walls of this building—there are no windows—are set between tall, vertical ribs of aluminum that rise from a scuffle base of black granite. These walls are interrupted only by three emphatic spandrels of dark-grey glass that girdle the upper floors, while the second story, a mezzanine, is fringed by a thinner band of leafy plants, which offer a contrasting touch of green. The crystalline quality of the structure is further brought out by sheathing the ceilings in opaque plastic panels, ribbed like a washboard, behind which cold-cathode lamps evenly diffuse a pale-yellow light throughout every floor. The only screen of any kind against sunlight is provided by spun-glass curtains of neutral color and texture, which are probably more useful for in-

sulation than for visual protection. The glass panels are really curtains themselves, for although they are firmly fixed in place, their crushing weight is actually suspended from the roof, which, like the floors, is cantilevered out from the columns that support the entire building. The suspending of these walls eliminates the need for heavy, clumsy supporting beams, and thus adds to the feeling of lightness in the structure. This is but one of the many costly technical feats that make this whole audacious enclosure of space seem so simple and so effortless. Another trick is using only eight of these columns, all of them freestanding and all of them set well back from the outer walls of glass, to support the building. This device, which opens up the interior space by eliminating the once mandatory row upon row of supporting columns, is one of the positive contributions of modern engineering to the luminous, lantern-like effect of this building.

To the passing spectator, there are two features that become striking only when he nears the building. One is the great horizontal banks of foliage in the huge boxes that serve as pedestals for the pair of rapidly moving escalators that rise from the main floor to the mezzanine on the Fifth Avenue side. The other is the vast round entrance, also on the Avenue side, to the vaults of the bank, with its massive door of shiny metal—the most impressive possible symbol of security. This thirty-ton door holds the eyes of a constant crowd on the sidewalk, as once upon a time the white-capped chef making hot cakes held people in front of Childs. (Customers with business in the safe-deposit vaults enter them through a series of less ostentatious but well-guarded portals from a small side door at the western end of the Forty-third Street façade.) By raising the most dramatic physical object in a bank from the cellar to the ground floor, the architects have made the most of a natural advertisement. This is what one might call inherent symbolism; it contrasts sharply with the more traditional kind, as old as Assyria—a symbolism that might be represented by two ferocious granite lions. This use of the bank's vaults as an expressive and visible feature was truly an inspiration.

The main entrance to the bank is on the Forty-third Street side, near the corner, and it is clearly indicated by a vertical slab of black granite in the middle of it and a horizontal siding of the same stone, with the bank's name, above it. There are two even more modest legends, in stainless-steel letters, at eye level on the glass of the Fifth Avenue façade. Remembering how one of Louis Sullivan's little banks in Iowa was bedevilled by no less than seven signs, all frantically proclaiming the name of the bank, one is grateful to the Manufacturers Trust for believing that this is enough; after all, the building has already become self-identifying.

At last we are ready to enter the building. On the ground floor, the main aesthetic ingredients of the whole composition are on display—the ceiling of corrugated plastic exuding that even yellow light; the pale terrazzo floor; the open tellers' counters, minus the old grilles and cages, forming an ell against the back walls; i.e., the south and west ones. The first of these walls, which also serves as an outer wall of the bank vault, is of black granite up to the mezzanine, and then white, light-green, and blue plaster on successive floors; the other is of sky-blue plaster up as far as the mezzanine, and then gray marble. (The walls of the fifth, or penthouse, floor are all of glass.) Since the escalators go no higher than the mezzanine, there is a bank of elevators, with handsome red-lacquered doors, in this wall. The bases of the tellers' counters are of ebony wood set between vertical ribs of stainless steel. The tops of the counters are done in a beautiful, creamy Italian marble, with a light-tan figure weaving through it. The ebony of the counters is repeated in the long, bowed table in the directors' room on the top floor, and the marble of the counters is used again for the floor of the president's room, and as a wall panel on the fifth floor. This flow of materials and colors from one floor to another, now for one purpose, now for another, contributes powerfully to the unity of the building, while the basic palette used by the design consultant, Eleanor Le Maire, is sufficiently comprehensive—white, light yellow, tan, brown, blue, and black are her principal colors—to be capable of endless variations and combinations. Radically contrasting colors are introduced only in the powder room, on the fifth floor—where all sorts of lipstick pinks and reds dominate—and in the employees' lounge, in

the basement, where, doubtless in an attempt to be gay and to put banking associations aside, the color scheme is somewhat distracting, if not incongruous. Apart from this lapse, and the fact that the sky blue of various wall spaces is not merely cold but is at odds with the indigo blue in some of the textiles and leathers, Miss Le Maire's decoration seems in admirable accord with the spirit of the whole structure, including its directness—one might also say its masculinity.

Aesthetically, the topmost floor and the main banking floor are almost without reproach. The first of these is the final word in quiet luxury, though it utilizes no materials or motifs that are not already at work on the other floors. The most notable part of its decoration is the perilously artful arrangement of potted tropical plants (such as philodendrons) whose waxen perfection rouses a suspicion of complete artificiality, and the series of modern prints, paintings, and sculptures that bring into this highly rationalized interior some of the more subjective emotional elements that are usually absent from the surface operations of a banker's mind, and certainly absent from the kind of art that banks have in general patronized. But the second floor, dedicated to the senior officers of this branch of the bank, and to the Trust and Foreign Departments, is the crown of the architects' and decorator's aesthetic achievement. The noble height of this story, the tallest of the five, emphasizes its almost unbroken space, and the cold pallor of the white walls and the white marble-sheathed columns is softened by a splatter of vermilion chairs, in a reception area near the escalators, and the brilliance of a huge golden screen that is placed near the west end of this floor to separate the counter in front of it from the elevators behind. This screen is a feature that I gravely doubted when I saw the preliminary illustrations, but the truth is that it lifts the whole composition to a higher plane. It is a mass of loosely assembled and variously twisted oblong steel plaques, plated with bronze and gold and welded together, and it has just enough minor variations in texture and color, plus an occasional break into abstract shapes, to make it stand out from the glossy mechanical refinement of the rest of the structure. The screen is the work of Harry Bertoia, the Pennsylvania sculptor. Though it is purely abstract, making no effort at symbolic significance, it humanizes these quarters even more effectively than the living plants, mainly because it suggests something frail, incomplete, yet unexpected and defiant of rational statement, and thus lovable, a note that is not audible in most of the representative architectural expressions of our time. On this ground, one might also defend the tangled hair-net of wire that floats in the air above the escalators as they end, on the second floor, and that was meant to cast a complicated shadow on the south wall, but, frankly, this creation does not seem worthy of the sculptor and craftsmen who executed the screen. And the shadow has evaporated in the diffused glare of the overhead lights, since the spotlights that were to produce it were too strong for the tellers' eyes. (This problem, however, is being given further study.)

All in all, then, the Manufacturers Trust Building is perhaps as complete a fusion of rational thinking and humane imagination as we are capable of producing today. If you reject it, you reject many of the notable excellences of our age. As a symbol of the modern world, this structure is almost an ideal expression. The interpenetration of inner space and outer space, the fact that the principal functions of the building are as visible from the outside as those of a supermarket, that the same freedom of space and light has been provided in every part of the structure, thus giving the executive officers, the staff, the clients the same architectural background—this surely reflects the economic, the social, and the aesthetic principles of the modern business world at their best. This architecture is a formal expression of the culture that has explored the innermost recesses of the atom, that knows that visible boundaries and solid objects are only figments of the intellect, that looks with the aid of X-rays and radioactive isotopes at the innerness of any sort of object, from armor plate to human bodies. That architects and sculptors should seek to express this world of transparent forms and dynamic processes, that they should actually revel in this exposure, is natural, since it is the eternal business of the artist to express in new forms what would otherwise remain at the commonplace levels of daily perception.

But there is a catch to this method of symbolic interpretation that some of our best architects have too often overlooked. Achieving effective symbolic expression frequently demands a surrender of practical convenience to expressiveness, a sacrifice acceptable only for religious ends. An all-glass building, fully exposed to sunlight, is a hotbox in our climate, and then the penalty one usually must pay for symbolism is to cower a large part of the time behind a Venetian blind, which robs the form of its aesthetic significance. Happily for the architects of this bank, its location and its purpose greatly reduced the practical objections to an all-glass structure. Because it is surrounded by taller buildings, there is no need for screens or blinds or green heat-ray-resistant glass. In addition, the architects, instead of treating all the functions of the bank as public ones, because of a theoretic commitment to the open plan, have provided a series of snug rooms, with doors, on the third floor to insure privacy where privacy is desirable. In other words, the functional requirements of this building coincide remarkably well with the symbolic or expressive functions, and the result is a bold, straightforward design, consistent in every detail without being arbitrary or formalistic. But let novices take warning! An attempt to imitate this design under different physical conditions might easily result in lamentable sacrifices of pleasure and comfort.

And this brings me to the last factor that insured the excellence of this structure: no expense was spared in its conception and execution. By making this building just large enough for its own uses, instead of pushing it up to a height of ten or fifteen stories to provide pigeonholes for other tenants, the bank not only refrained from adding to the congested population of Fifth Avenue but enabled the architects to conceive a completely articulated and unified structure. Some of the best features of its design would have been forfeited if it had been necessary to build the usual steel skeleton with the usual number of columns. Again, the system of ceiling and cove lighting chosen was an expensive installation, but it may be that because of its unity, efficiency, and pleasantness it will turn out much cheaper in the long run. In other words, the richness and perfection of the interior are due largely to the fact that there was no penny-pinching about first costs. Perhaps the bank's president, Mr. H. C. Flanigan, took to heart the lesson of this bank's only architectural rival, the handsome P.S.F.S. Building, in Philadelphia, done by Howe & Lescaze in 1932. For there the costly materials and meticulous craftsmanship have, in the course of a quarter century, paid off in utility, low upkeep costs, and undatable beauty. What matters, really, is not first costs but final costs. Possibly the cheapest quarters in the world, as regards *total* cost, and the most profitable in the long run, are the group of buildings—originally residences—that frame the Place Vendôme in Paris. They are still spacious and sound enough to be serviceable (and bring high rents as offices) after two and a half centuries. By thinking in such long-range terms, more New York enterprises might produce buildings and even whole districts of comparable excellence.

## *Roger Fry*
# THE ARTIST'S VISION

Biologically speaking, art is a blasphemy. We were given our eyes to see things, not to look at them. Life takes care that we all learn the lesson thoroughly, so that at a very early age we have acquired a very considerable ignorance of visual appearances. We have learned the meaning for life of appearances so well that we understand them, as it were, in shorthand. The subtlest differences of appearance that have a utility value still continue to be appreciated, while large and important visual characters, provided they are useless for life, will pass unnoticed. With all the ingenuity and resource which manufacturers put into their business, they can scarcely prevent the ordinary eye from seizing on the minute visual characteristics that distinguish margarine from butter. Some of us can tell Canadian cheddar at a glance, and no one was ever taken in by sham suède gloves.

THE ARTIST'S VISION: From *Vision and Design*, 1920. Used by permission of Chatto & Windus, Ltd., publishers.

The sense of sight supplies prophetic knowledge of what may affect the inner fortifications, the more intimate senses of taste and touch, where it may already be too late to avert disaster. So we learn to read the prophetic message, and, for the sake of economy, to neglect all else. Children have not learned it fully, and so they look at things with some passion. Even the grown man keeps something of his unbiological, disinterested vision with regard to a few things. He still looks at flowers, and does not merely see them. He also keeps objects which have some marked peculiarity of appearance that catches his eye. These may be natural, like precious stones, fossils, incrustations and such like; or they may be manufactured entirely with a view to pleasing by peculiarities of colour or shape, and these are called ornaments. Such articles, whether natural or artificial, are called by those who sell them "curios," and the name is not an unhappy one to denote the kind of interest which they arouse. As I showed in a previous article, such objects get attached to them a secondary interest, arising from the kind of social milieu that they were made for, so that they become not merely curious for the eye, but stimulating to our social-historical imagination.

The vision with which we regard such objects is quite distinct from the practical vision of our instinctive life. In the practical vision we have no more concern after we have read the label on the object; vision ceases the moment it has served its biological function. But the curiosity vision does contemplate the object disinterestedly; the object *ex hypothesi* has no significance for actual life; it is a play or fancy object, and our vision dwells much more consciously and deliberately upon it. We notice to some extent its forms and colours, especially when it is new to us.

But human perversity goes further even than this in its misapplication of the gift of sight. We may look at objects not even for their curiosity or oddity, but for their harmony of form and colour. To arouse such a vision the object must be more than a "curio": it has to be a work of art. I suspect that such an object must be made by some one in whom the impulse was not to please others, but to express a feeling of his own. It is probably this fundamental difference of origin between the "curio" or ornament and the work of art that makes it impossible for any commercial system, with its eye necessarily on the customer, ever to produce works of art, whatever the ingenuity with which it is attempted.

But we are concerned here not with the origin, but with the vision. This is at once more intense and more detached from the passions of the instinctive life than either of the kinds of vision hitherto discussed. Those who indulge in this vision are entirely absorbed in apprehending the relation of forms and colour to one another, as they cohere within the object. Suppose, for example, that we are looking at a Sung bowl; we apprehend gradually the shape of the outside contour, the perfect sequence of the curves, and the subtle modifications of a certain type of curve which it shows; we also feel the relation of the concave curves to the outside contour; we realise that the precise thickness of the walls is consistent with the particular kind of matter of which it is made, its appearance of density and resistance; and finally we recognise, perhaps, how satisfactory for the display of all these plastic qualities are the colour and the dull lustre of the glaze. Now while we are thus occupied there comes to us, I think, a feeling of purpose; we feel that all these sensually logical conformities are the outcome of a particular feeling, or of what, for want of a better word, we call an idea; and we may even say that the pot is the expression of an idea in the artist's mind. Whether we are right or not in making this deduction, I believe it nearly always occurs in such aesthetic apprehension of an object of art. But in all this no element of curiosity, no reference to actual life, comes in; our apprehension is unconditioned by considerations of space or time; it is irrelevant to us to know whether the bowl was made seven hundred years ago in China, or in New York yesterday. We may, of course, at any moment switch off from the aesthetic vision, and become interested in all sorts of quasi-biological feelings; we may inquire whether it is genuine or not, whether it is worth the sum given for it, and so forth; but in proportion as we do this we change the focus of our vision; we are more likely to examine the bottom of the bowl for traces of marks than to look at the bowl itself.

Such, then, is the nature of the aesthetic vision, the vision with which we contemplate works of art. It is to such a vision, if to anything outside himself, that the artist appeals, and the artist in his spare hours may himself indulge in the aesthetic vision; and if one can get him to do so, his verdict is likely to be as good as any one's.

The artist's main business in life, however, is carried on by means of yet a fourth kind of vision, which I will call the creative vision. This, I think, is the furthest perversion of the gifts of nature of which man is guilty. It demands the most complete detachment from any of the meanings and implications of appearances. Almost any turn of the kaleidoscope of nature may set up in the artist this detached and impassioned vision, and, as he contemplates the particular field of vision, the (aesthetically) chaotic and accidental conjunction of forms and colours begins to crystallise into a harmony; and as this harmony becomes clear to the artist, his actual vision becomes distorted by the emphasis of the rhythm which has been set up within him. Certain relations of directions of line become for him full of meaning; he apprehends them no longer casually or merely curiously, but passionately, and these lines begin to be so stressed and stand out so clearly from the rest that he sees them far more distinctly than he did at first. Similarly colours, which in nature have almost always a certain vagueness and elusiveness, become so definite and clear to him, owing to their now necessary relation to other colours, that if he chooses to paint his vision he can state them positively and definitely. In such a creative vision the objects as such tend to disappear, to lose their separate unities, and to take their places as so many bits in the whole mosaic of vision. The texture of the whole field of vision becomes so close that the coherence of the separate patches of tone and colour within each object is no stronger than the coherence with every other tone and colour throughout the field.

In such circumstances the greatest object of art becomes of no more significance than any casual piece of matter; a man's head is no more and no less important than a pumpkin, or, rather, these things may be so or not according to the rhythm that obsesses the artist and crystallises his vision. Since it is the habitual practice of the artist to be on the look out for

these peculiar arrangements of objects that
arouse the creative vision, and become material
for creative contemplation, he is liable to look
at all objects from this point of view. In so far
as the artist looks at objects only as part of
a whole field of vision which is his own potential picture, he can give no account of their
aesthetic value. Every solid object is subject to
the play of light and shade, and becomes a
mosaic of visual patches, each of which for the
artist is related to other visual patches in the
surroundings. It is irrelevant to ask him, while
he is looking with this generalised and all-
embracing vision, about the nature of the objects which compose it. He is likely even to
turn away from works of art in which he may
be tempted to relapse into an aesthetic vision,
and so see them as unities apart from their
surroundings. By preference he turns to objects
which make no strong aesthetic appeal in themselves. But he may like objects which attract
by some oddity or peculiarity of form or colour,
and thereby suggest to him new and intriguing
rhythms. In his continual and restless preoccupation with appearance he is capable of looking at objects from which both aesthetic and
even curious vision may turn instinctively, or
which they may never notice, so little prospect
of satisfaction do they hold out. But the artist
may always find his satisfaction, the material
for his picture, in the most unexpected quarters. Objects of the most despised periods, or
objects saturated for the ordinary man with the
most vulgar and repulsive associations, may be
grist to his mill. . . .

The artist is of all men the most constantly
observant of his surroundings, and the least
affected by their intrinsic aesthetic value. He is
more likely on the whole to paint a slum in
Soho than St. Paul's, and more likely to do a
lodging-house interior than a room at Hampton
Court. He may, of course, do either, but his
necessary detachment comes more easily in one
case than the other. The artist is, I believe, a
very good critic if you can make him drop his
own job for a minute, and really attend to
some one else's work of art; but do not go to
him when he is on duty as an artist if you want
a sound judgment about objects of art. The
different visions I have discussed are like the
different gears of a motor-car, only that we
sometimes step from one gear into another

without knowing it, and the artist may be on
the wrong gear for answering us truly.

*Nathaniel Hawthorne*

# THE BIRTHMARK

In the latter part of the last century
there lived a man of science, an eminent pro-
ficient in every branch of natural philosophy,
who not long before our story opens had made
experience of a spiritual affinity more attractive
than any chemical one. He had left his laboratory to the care of an assistant, cleared his fine
countenance from the furnace smoke, washed
the stain of acids from his fingers, and persuaded a beautiful woman to become his wife.
In those days when the comparatively recent
discovery of electricity and other kindred mysteries of Nature seemed to open paths into the
region of miracle, it was not unusual for the
love of science to rival the love of woman in
its depth and absorbing energy. The higher intellect, the imagination, the spirit, and even the
heart might all find their congenial aliment in
pursuits which, as some of their ardent votaries
believed, would ascend from one step of powerful intelligence to another, until the philosopher
should lay his hand on the secret of creative
force and perhaps make new worlds for himself. We know not whether Aylmer possessed
this degree of faith in man's ultimate control
over Nature. He had devoted himself, however, too unreservedly to scientific studies ever
to be weaned from them by any second passion.
His love for his young wife might prove the
stronger of the two; but it could only be by
intertwining itself with his love of science, and
uniting the strength of the latter to his own.

Such a union accordingly took place, and
was attended with truly remarkable consequences and a deeply impressive moral. One
day, very soon after their marriage, Aylmer
sat gazing at his wife with a trouble in his
countenance that grew stronger as he spoke.

"Georgiana," said he, "has it never occurred
to you that the mark upon your cheek might
be removed?"

"No, indeed," said she, smiling; but perceiv-
ing the seriousness of his manner, she blushed
deeply. "To tell you the truth, it has been so

often called a charm that I was simple enough to imagine it might be so."

"Ah, upon another face perhaps it might," replied her husband; "but never on yours. No, dearest Georgiana, you came so nearly perfect from the hand of Nature that this slightest possible defect, which we hesitate whether to term a defect or a beauty, shocks me, as being the visible mark of earthly imperfection."

"Shocks you, my husband!" cried Georgiana, deeply hurt; at first reddening with momentary anger, but then bursting into tears. "Then why did you take me from my mother's side? You cannot love what shocks you!"

To explain this conversation it must be mentioned that in the center of Georgiana's left cheek there was a singular mark, deeply interwoven, as it were, with the texture and substance of her face. In the usual state of her complexion—a healthy though delicate bloom —the mark wore a tint of deeper crimson, which imperfectly defined its shape amid the surrounding rosiness. When she blushed it gradually became more indistinct, and finally vanished amid the triumphant rush of blood that bathed the whole cheek with its brilliant glow. But if any shifting motion caused her to turn pale there was the mark again, a crimson stain upon the snow, in what Aylmer sometimes deemed an almost fearful distinctness. Its shape bore not a little similarity to the human hand, though of the smallest pygmy size. Georgiana's lovers were wont to say that some fairy at her birth hour had laid her tiny hand upon the infant's cheek, and left this impress there in token of the magic endowments that were to give her such sway over all hearts. Many a desperate swain would have risked life for the privilege of pressing his lips to the mysterious hand. It must not be concealed, however, that the impression wrought by this fairy sign manual varied exceedingly, according to the difference of temperament in the beholders. Some fastidious persons—but they were exclusively of her own sex—affirmed that the bloody hand, as they chose to call it, quite destroyed the effect of Georgiana's beauty, and rendered her countenance even hideous. But it would be as reasonable to say that one of those small blue stains which sometimes occur in the purest statuary marble would convert the Eve of Powers to a monster. Masculine observers, if the birthmark did not heighten their admira-

tion, contented themselves with wishing it away, that the world might possess one living specimen of ideal loveliness without the semblance of a flaw. After his marriage—for he thought little or nothing of the matter before— Aylmer discovered that this was the case with himself.

Had she been less beautiful—if Envy's self could have found aught else to sneer at—he might have felt his affection heightened by the prettiness of this mimic hand, now vaguely portrayed, now lost, now stealing forth again and glimmering to and fro with every pulse of emotion that throbbed within her heart; but seeing her otherwise so perfect, he found this one defect grow more and more intolerable with every moment of their united lives. It was the fatal flaw of humanity which Nature, in one shape or another, stamps ineffaceably on all her productions, either to imply that they are temporary and finite, or that their perfection must be wrought by toil and pain. The crimson hand expressed the ineludible gripe in which mortality clutches the highest and purest of earthly mold, degrading them into kindred with the lowest, and even with the very brutes, like whom their visible frames return to dust. In this manner, selecting it as the symbol of his wife's liability to sin, sorrow, decay, and death, Aylmer's somber imagination was not long in rendering the birthmark a frightful object, causing him more trouble and horror than ever Georgiana's beauty, whether of soul or sense, had given him delight.

At all the seasons which should have been their happiest, he invariably and without intending it, nay, in spite of a purpose to the contrary, reverted to this one disastrous topic. Trifling as it at first appeared, it so connected itself with innumerable trains of thought and modes of feeling that it became the central point of all. With the morning twilight Aylmer opened his eyes upon his wife's face and recognized the symbol of imperfection; and when they sat together at the evening hearth his eyes wandered stealthily to her cheek, and beheld, flickering with the blaze of the wood fire, the spectral hand that wrote mortality where he would fain have worshiped. Georgiana soon learned to shudder at his gaze. It needed but a glance with the peculiar expression that his face often wore to change the roses of her cheek into a deathlike paleness, amid which the crimson hand was brought strongly out, like a bas-relief of ruby on the whitest marble.

Late one night when the lights were growing dim, so as hardly to betray the stain on the poor wife's cheek, she herself, for the first time, voluntarily took up the subject.

"Do you remember, my dear Aylmer," said she, with a feeble attempt at a smile, "have you any recollection of a dream last night about this odious hand?"

"None! none whatever!" replied Aylmer, starting; but then he added, in a dry, cold tone, affected for the sake of concealing the real depth of his emotion, "I might well dream of it; for before I fell asleep it had taken a pretty firm hold of my fancy."

"And you did dream of it!" continued Georgiana, hastily; for she dreaded lest a gush of tears should interrupt what she had to say. "A terrible dream! I wonder that you can forget it. Is it possible to forget this one expression?— 'It is in her heart now; we must have it out!' Reflect, my husband; for by all means I would have you recall that dream."

The mind is in a sad state when Sleep, the all-involving, cannot confine her specters within the dim region of her sway, but suffers them to break forth, affrighting this actual life with secrets that perchance belong to a deeper one. Aylmer now remembered his dream. He had fancied himself with his servant Aminadab, attempting an operation for the removal of the birthmark; but the deeper went the knife, the deeper sank the hand, until at length its tiny grasp appeared to have caught hold of Georgiana's heart; whence, however, her husband was inexorably resolved to cut or wrench it away.

When the dream had shaped itself perfectly in his memory, Aylmer sat in his wife's presence with a guilty feeling. Truth often finds its way to the mind close muffled in robes of sleep, and then speaks with uncompromising directness of matters in regard to which we practice an unconscious self-deception during our waking moments. Until now he had not been aware of the tyrannizing influence acquired by one idea over his mind, and of the lengths which he might find in his heart to go for the sake of giving himself peace.

"Aylmer," resumed Georgiana, solemnly, "I know not what may be the cost to both of us to rid me of this fatal birthmark. Perhaps its removal may cause cureless deformity; or it

may be the stain goes as deep as life itself. Again: do we know that there is a possibility, on any terms, of unclasping the firm gripe of this little hand which was laid upon me before I came into the world?"

"Dearest Georgiana, I have spent much thought upon the subject," hastily interrupted Aylmer. "I am convinced of the perfect practicability of its removal."

"If there be the remotest possibility of it," continued Georgiana, "let the attempt be made at whatever risk. Danger is nothing to me; for life, while this hateful mark makes me the object of your horror and disgust—life is a burden which I would fling down with joy. Either remove this dreadful hand, or take my wretched life! You have deep science. All the world bears witness of it. You have achieved great wonders. Cannot you remove this little, little mark, which I cover with the tips of two small fingers? Is this beyond your power, for the sake of your own peace, and to save your poor wife from madness?"

"Noblest, dearest, tenderest wife," cried Aylmer, rapturously, "doubt not my power. I have already given this matter the deepest thought—thought which might almost have enlightened me to create a being less perfect than yourself. Georgiana, you have led me deeper than ever into the heart of science. I feel myself fully competent to render this dear cheek as faultless as its fellow; and then, most beloved, what will be my triumph when I shall have corrected what Nature left imperfect in her fairest work! Even Pygmalion, when his sculptured woman assumed life, felt not greater ecstasy than mine will be."

"It is resolved, then," said Georgiana, faintly smiling. "And, Aylmer, spare me not, though you should find the birthmark take refuge in my heart at last."

Her husband tenderly kissed her cheek—her right cheek—not that which bore the impress of the crimson hand.

The next day Aylmer apprised his wife of a plan that he had formed whereby he might have opportunity for the intense thought and constant watchfulness which the proposed operation would require; while Georgiana, likewise, would enjoy the perfect repose essential to its success. They were to seclude themselves in the extensive apartments occupied by Aylmer as a laboratory, and where, during his toilsome youth, he had made discoveries in the elemental powers of Nature that had roused the admiration of all the learned societies in Europe. Seated calmly in this laboratory, the pale philosopher had investigated the secrets of the highest cloud region and of the profoundest mines; he had satisfied himself of the causes that kindled and kept alive the fires of the volcano; and had explained the mysteries of fountains, and how it is that they gush forth, some so bright and pure, and others with such rich medicinal virtues, from the dark bosom of the earth. Here, too, at an earlier period, he had studied the wonders of the human frame, and attempted to fathom the very process by which Nature assimilates all her precious influences from earth and air, and from the spiritual world, to create and foster man, her masterpiece. The latter pursuit, however, Aylmer had long laid aside in unwilling recognition of the truth—against which all seekers sooner or later stumble—that our great creative Mother, while she amuses us with apparently working in the broadest sunshine, is yet severely careful to keep her own secrets, and, in spite of her pretended openness, shows us nothing but results. She permits us, indeed, to mar, but seldom to mend, and, like a jealous patentee, on no account to make. Now, however, Aylmer resumed these half-forgotten investigations; not, of course, with such hopes or wishes as first suggested them; but because they involved much physiological truth and lay in the path of his proposed scheme for the treatment of Georgiana.

As he led her over the threshold of the laboratory, Georgiana was cold and tremulous. Aylmer looked cheerfully into her face, with intent to reassure her, but was so startled with the intense glow of the birthmark upon the whiteness of her cheek that he could not restrain a strong convulsive shudder. His wife fainted.

"Aminadab! Aminadab!" shouted Aylmer, stamping violently on the floor.

Forthwith there issued from an inner apartment a man of low stature, but bulky frame, with shaggy hair hanging about his visage, which was grimed with the vapors of the furnace. This personage had been Aylmer's underworker during his whole scientific career, and was admirably fitted for that office by his great mechanical readiness, and the skill with which,

while incapable of comprehending a single principle, he executed all the details of his master's experiments. With his vast strength, his shaggy hair, his smoky aspect, and the indescribable earthiness that incrusted him, he seemed to represent man's physical nature; while Aylmer's slender figure and pale, intellectual face, were no less apt a type of the spiritual element.

"Throw open the door of the boudoir, Aminadab," said Aylmer, "and burn a pastille."

"Yes, master," answered Aminadab, looking intently at the lifeless form of Georgiana; and then he muttered to himself, "If she were my wife, I'd never part with that birthmark."

When Georgiana recovered consciousness she found herself breathing an atmosphere of penetrating fragrance, the gentle potency of which had recalled her from her deathlike faintness. The scene around her looked like enchantment. Aylmer had converted those smoky, dingy somber rooms, where he had spent his brightest years in recondite pursuits, into a series of beautiful apartments not unfit to be the secluded abode of a lovely woman. The walls were hung with gorgeous curtains, which imparted the combination of grandeur and grace that no other species of adornment can achieve; and as they fell from the ceiling to the floor, their rich and ponderous folds, concealing all angles and straight lines, appeared to shut in the scene from infinite space. For aught Georgiana knew, it might be a pavilion among the clouds. And Aylmer, excluding the sunshine, which would have interfered with his chemical processes, had supplied its place with perfumed lamps, emitting flames of various hue, but all uniting in a soft, impurpled radiance. He now knelt by his wife's side, watching her earnestly, but without alarm; for he was confident in his science, and felt that he could draw a magic circle round her within which no evil might intrude.

"Where am I? Ah, I remember," said Georgiana, faintly; and she placed her hand over her cheek to hide the terrible mark from her husband's eyes.

"Fear not, dearest!" exclaimed he. "Do not shrink from me! Believe me, Georgiana, I even rejoice in this single imperfection, since it will be such a rapture to remove it."

"Oh, spare me!" sadly replied his wife.

"Pray do not look at it again. I never can forget that convulsive shudder."

In order to soothe Georgiana, and, as it were, to release her mind from the burden of actual things, Aylmer now put in practice some of the light and playful secrets which science had taught him among its profounder lore. Airy figures, absolutely bodiless ideas, and forms of unsubstantial beauty came and danced before her, imprinting their momentary footsteps on beams of light. Though she had some indistinct idea of the method of these optical phenomena, still the illusion was almost perfect enough to warrant the belief that her husband possessed sway over the spiritual world. Then again, when she felt a wish to look forth from her seclusion, immediately, as if her thoughts were answered, the procession of external existence flitted across a screen. The scenery and the figures of actual life were perfectly represented, but with that bewitching, yet indescribable difference which always makes a picture, an image, or a shadow so much more attractive than the original. When wearied of this, Aylmer bade her cast her eyes upon a vessel containing a quantity of earth. She did so, with little interest at first; but was soon startled to perceive the germ of a plant shooting upward from the soil. Then came the slender stalk; the leaves gradually unfolded themselves; and amid them was a perfect and lovely flower.

"It is magical!" cried Georgiana. "I dare not touch it."

"Nay, pluck it," answered Aylmer—"pluck it, and inhale its brief perfume while you may. The flower will wither in a few moments and leave nothing save its brown seed vessels; but thence may be perpetuated a race as ephemeral as itself."

But Georgiana had no sooner touched the flower than the whole plant suffered a blight, its leaves turning coal-black as if by the agency of fire.

"There was too powerful a stimulus," said Aylmer, thoughtfully.

To make up for this abortive experiment, he proposed to take her portrait by a scientific process of his own invention. It was to be effected by rays of light striking upon a polished plate of metal. Georgiana assented; but, on looking at the result, was affrighted to find the features of the portrait blurred and indefinable; while the minute figure of a hand ap- peared where the cheek should have been. Aylmer snatched the metallic plate and threw it into a jar of corrosive acid.

Soon, however, he forgot these mortifying failures. In the intervals of study and chemical experiment he came to her flushed and exhausted, but seemed invigorated by her presence, and spoke in glowing language of the resources of his art. He gave a history of the long dynasty of the alchemists, who spent so many ages in quest of the universal solvent by which the golden principle might be elicited from all things vile and base. Aylmer appeared to believe that, by the plainest scientific logic, it was altogether within the limits of possibility to discover this long-sought medium; "but," he added, "a philosopher who should go deep enough to acquire the power would attain too lofty a wisdom to stoop to the exercise of it." Not less singular were his opinions in regard to the *elixir vitae*.[10] He more than intimated that it was at his option to concoct a liquor that should prolong life for years, perhaps interminably; but that it would produce a discord in Nature which all the world, and chiefly the quaffer of the immortal nostrum, would find cause to curse.

"Aylmer, are you in earnest?" asked Georgiana, looking at him with amazement and fear. "It is terrible to possess such power, or even to dream of possessing it."

"Oh, do not tremble, my love," said her husband. "I would not wrong either you or myself by working such inharmonious effects upon our lives; but I would have you consider how trifling, in comparison, is the skill requisite to remove this little hand."

At the mention of the birthmark, Georgiana, as usual, shrank as if a red-hot iron had touched her cheek.

Again Aylmer applied himself to his labors. She could hear his voice in the distant furnace room giving directions to Aminadab, whose harsh, uncouth, misshapen tones were audible in response, more like the grunt or growl of a brute than human speech. After hours of absence, Aylmer reappeared and proposed that she should now examine his cabinet of chemical products and natural treasures of the earth. Among the former he showed her a small vial, in which, he remarked, was contained a gentle

---

[10] Elixir of life.

yet most powerful fragrance, capable of impregnating all the breezes that blow across a kingdom. They were of inestimable value, the contents of that little vial; and, as he said so, he threw some of the perfume into the air and filled the room with piercing and invigorating delight.

"And what is this?" asked Georgiana, pointing to a small crystal globe containing a gold-colored liquid. "It is so beautiful to the eyes that I could imagine it the elixir of life."

"In one sense it is," replied Aylmer; "or, rather, the elixir of immortality. It is the most precious poison that ever was concocted in this world. By its aid I could apportion the lifetime of any mortal at whom you might point your finger. The strength of the dose would determine whether he were to linger out years, or drop dead in the midst of a breath. No king on his guarded throne could keep his life if I, in my private station, should deem that the welfare of millions justified me in depriving him of it."

"Why do you keep such a terrific drug?" inquired Georgiana in horror.

"Do not mistrust me, dearest," said her husband, smiling; "its virtuous potency is yet greater than its harmful one. But see! here is a powerful cosmetic. With a few drops of this in a vase of water, freckles may be washed away as easily as the hands are cleansed. A stronger infusion would take the blood out of the cheek, and leave the rosiest beauty a pale ghost."

"Is it with this lotion that you intend to bathe my cheek?" asked Georgiana, anxiously.

"Oh, no," hastily replied her husband; "this is merely superficial. Your case demands a remedy that shall go deeper."

In his interviews with Georgiana, Aylmer generally made minute inquiries as to her sensations and whether the confinement of the rooms and the temperature of the atmosphere agreed with her. These questions had such a particular drift that Georgiana began to conjecture that she was already subjected to certain physical influences, either breathed in with the fragrant air or taken with her food. She fancied likewise, but it might be altogether fancy, that there was a stirring up of her system—a strange, indefinite sensation creeping through her veins, and tingling, half painfully, half pleasurably, at her heart. Still, whenever she dared to look into the mirror, there she beheld herself pale as a white rose and with the crimson birthmark stamped upon her cheek. Not even Aylmer now hated it so much as she.

To dispel the tedium of the hours which her husband found it necessary to devote to the processes of combination and analysis, Georgiana turned over the volumes of his scientific library. In many dark old tomes she met with chapters full of romance and poetry. They were works of philosophers of the middle ages, such as Albertus Magnus, Cornelius Agrippa, Paracelsus, and the famous friar who created the prophetic Brazen Head. All these antique naturalists stood in advance of their centuries, yet were imbued with some of their credulity, and therefore were believed, and perhaps imagined themselves to have acquired from the investigation of Nature a power above Nature, and from physics a sway over the spiritual world. Hardly less curious and imaginative were the early volumes of the *Transactions of the Royal Society* in which the members, knowing little of the limits of natural possibility, were continually recording wonders or proposing methods whereby wonders might be wrought.

But to Georgiana the most engrossing volume was a large folio from her husband's own hand, in which he recorded every experiment of his scientific career, its original aim, the methods adopted for its development, and its final success or failure, with the circumstances to which either event was attributable. The book, in truth, was both the history and emblem of his ardent, ambitious, imaginative, yet practical and laborious life. He handled physical details as if there were nothing beyond them; yet spiritualized them all, and redeemed himself from materialism by his strong and eager aspiration towards the infinite. In his grasp the veriest clod of earth assumed a soul. Georgiana, as she read, reverenced Aylmer and loved him more profoundly than ever, but with a less entire dependence on his judgment than heretofore. Much as he had accomplished, she could not but observe that his most splendid successes were almost invariably failures, if compared with the ideal at which he aimed. His brightest diamonds were the merest pebbles, and felt to be so by himself, in comparison with the inestimable gems which lay hidden beyond his reach. The volume, rich with achievements that had won renown for its author, was yet as melanchoiy a record as ever mortal hand had penned. It was the sad confession and continual exemplification of the shortcomings of the composite man, the spirit burdened with clay and working in matter, and of the despair that assails the higher nature at finding itself so miserably thwarted by the earthly part. Perhaps every man of genius in whatever sphere might recognize the image of his own experience in Aylmer's journal.

So deeply did these reflections affect Georgiana that she laid her face upon the open volume and burst into tears. In this situation she was found by her husband.

"It is dangerous to read in a sorcerer's books," said he with a smile, though his countenance was uneasy and displeased. "Georgiana, there are pages in that volume which I can scarcely glance over and keep my senses. Take heed lest it prove as detrimental to you."

"It has made me worship you more than ever," said she.

"Ah, wait for this one success," rejoined he, "then worship me if you will. I shall deem myself hardly unworthy of it. But come, I have sought you for the luxury of your voice. Sing to me, dearest."

So she poured out the liquid music of her voice to quench the thirst of his spirit. He then took his leave with a boyish exuberance of gayety, assuring her that her seclusion would endure but a little longer, and that the result was already certain. Scarcely had he departed when Georgiana felt irresistibly impelled to follow him. She had forgotten to inform Aylmer of a symptom which for two or three hours past had begun to excite her attention. It was a sensation in the fatal birthmark, not painful, but which induced a restlessness throughout her system. Hastening after her husband, she intruded for the first time into the laboratory.

The first thing that struck her eye was the furnace, that hot and feverish worker, with the intense glow of its fire, which by the quantities of soot clustered above it seemed to have been burning for ages. There was a distilling apparatus in full operation. Around the room were retorts, tubes, cylinders, crucibles, and other apparatus of chemical research. An electrical machine stood ready for immediate use. The atmosphere felt oppressively close, and was tainted with gaseous odors which had been tor-

mented forth by the processes of science. The severe and homely simplicity of the apartment, with its naked walls and brick pavement, looked strange, accustomed as Georgiana had become to the fantastic elegance of her boudoir. But what chiefly, indeed almost solely, drew her attention, was the aspect of Aylmer himself.

He was pale as death, anxious and absorbed, and hung over the furnace as if it depended upon his utmost watchfulness whether the liquid which it was distilling should be the draught of immortal happiness or misery. How different from the sanguine and joyous mien that he had assumed for Georgiana's encouragement!

"Carefully now, Aminadab; carefully, thou human machine; carefully, thou man of clay!" muttered Aylmer, more to himself than his assistant. "Now, if there be a thought too much or too little, it is all over."

"Ho! ho!" mumbled Aminadab. "Look, master! look!"

Aylmer raised his eyes hastily, and at first reddened, then grew paler than ever, on beholding Georgiana. He rushed towards her and seized her arm with a gripe that left the print of his fingers upon it.

"Why do you come hither? Have you no trust in your husband?" cried he, impetuously. "Would you throw the blight of that fatal birthmark over my labors? It is not well done. Go, prying woman, go!"

"Nay, Aylmer," said Georgiana with the firmness of which she possessed no stinted endowment, "it is not you that have a right to complain. You mistrust your wife; you have concealed the anxiety with which you watch the development of this experiment. Think not so unworthily of me, my husband. Tell me all the risk we run, and fear not that I shall shrink; for my share in it is far less than your own."

"No, no, Georgiana!" said Aylmer, impatiently; "it must not be."

"I submit," replied she calmly. "And, Aylmer, I shall quaff whatever draught you bring me; but it will be on the same principle that would induce me to take a dose of poison if offered by your hand."

"My noble wife," said Aylmer, deeply moved, "I knew not the height and depth of your nature until now. Nothing shall be concealed. Know, then, that this crimson hand, superficial as it seems, has clutched its grasp into your being with a strength of which I had no previous conception. I have already administered agents powerful enough to do aught except to change your entire physical system. Only one thing remains to be tried. If that fail us we are ruined."

"Why did you hesitate to tell me this?" asked she.

"Because, Georgiana," said Aylmer, in a low voice, "there is danger."

"Danger? There is but one danger—that this horrible stigma shall be left upon my cheek!" cried Georgiana. "Remove it, remove it, whatever be the cost, or we shall both go mad!"

"Heaven knows your words are too true," said Aylmer, sadly. "And now, dearest, return to your boudoir. In a little while all will be tested."

He conducted her back and took leave of her with a solemn tenderness which spoke far more than his words how much was now at stake. After his departure Georgiana became rapt in musings. She considered the character of Aylmer, and did it completer justice than at any previous moment. Her heart exulted, while it trembled, at his honorable love—so pure and lofty that it would accept nothing less than perfection nor miserably make itself contented with an earthlier nature than he had dreamed of. She felt how much more precious was such a sentiment than that meaner kind which would have borne with the imperfection for her sake, and have been guilty of treason to holy love by degrading its perfect ideal to the level of the actual; and with her whole spirit she prayed that, for a single moment, she might satisfy his highest and deepest conception. Longer than one moment she well knew it could not be; for his spirit was ever on the march, ever ascending, and each instant required something that was beyond the scope of the instant before.

The sound of her husband's footsteps aroused her. He bore a crystal goblet containing a liquor colorless as water, but bright enough to be the draught of immortality. Aylmer was pale; but it seemed rather the consequence of a highly wrought state of mind and tension of spirit than of fear or doubt.

"The concoction of the draught has been perfect," said he, in answer to Georgiana's look. "Unless all my science have deceived me, it cannot fail."

"Save on your account, my dearest Aylmer," observed his wife, "I might wish to put off this birthmark of mortality by relinquishing mortality itself in preference to any other mode. Life is but a sad possession to those who have attained precisely the degree of moral advancement at which I stand. Were I weaker and blinder it might be happiness. Were I stronger, it might be endured hopefully. But, being what I find myself, methinks I am of all mortals the most fit to die."

"You are fit for heaven without tasting death!" replied her husband. "But why do you speak of dying? The draught cannot fail. Behold its effect upon this plant."

On the window seat there stood a geranium diseased with yellow blotches, which had overspread all its leaves. Aylmer poured a small quantity of the liquid upon the soil in which it grew. In a little time, when the roots of the plant had taken up the moisture, the unsightly blotches began to be extinguished in a living verdure.

"There needed no proof," said Georgiana, quietly. "Give me the goblet. I joyfully stake all upon your word."

"Drink, then, thou lofty creature!" exclaimed Aylmer with fervid admiration. "There is no taint of imperfection on thy spirit. Thy sensible frame, too, shall soon be all perfect."

She quaffed the liquid and returned the goblet to his hand.

"It is grateful," said she with a placid smile. "Methinks it is like water from a heavenly fountain; for it contains I know not what of unobtrusive fragrance and deliciousness. It allays a feverish thirst that had parched me for many days. Now, dearest, let me sleep. My earthly senses are closing over my spirit like the leaves around the heart of a rose at sunset."

She spoke the last words with a gentle reluctance, as if it required almost more energy than she could command to pronounce the faint and lingering syllables. Scarcely had they loitered through her lips ere she was lost in slumber. Aylmer sat by her side, watching her aspect with the emotions proper to a man the whole value of whose existence was involved in the process now to be tested. Mingled with this mood, however, was the philosophic investigation characteristic of the man of science. Not the minutest symptom escaped him. A heightened flush of the cheek, a slight irregularity of

breath, a quiver of the eyelid, a hardly perceptible tremor through the frame—such were the
details which, as the moments passed, he wrote
down in his folio volume. Intense thought had
set its stamp upon every previous page of that
volume, but the thoughts of years were all
concentrated upon the last.

While thus employed, he failed not to gaze
often at the fatal hand, and not without a
shudder. Yet once, by a strange and unaccountable impulse, he pressed it with his lips. His
spirit recoiled, however, in the very act; and
Georgiana, out of the midst of her deep sleep,
moved uneasily and murmured as if in remon-
strance. Again Aylmer resumed his watch. Nor
was it without avail. The crimson hand, which
at first had been strongly visible upon the
marble paleness of Georgiana's cheek, now
grew more faintly outlined. She remained not
less pale than ever; but the birthmark, with
every breath that came and went, lost somewhat of its former distinctness. Its presence had
been awful; its departure was more awful still.
Watch the stain of the rainbow fading out of the
sky, and you will know how that mysterious
symbol passed away.

"By Heaven! it is well-nigh gone!" said Aylmer to himself, in almost irrepressible ecstasy.
"I can scarcely trace it now. Success! success!
And now it is like the faintest rose color. The
lightest flush of blood across her cheek would
overcome it. But she is so pale!"

He drew aside the window curtain and suffered the light of natural day to fall into the
room and rest upon her cheek. At the same
time he heard a gross, hoarse chuckle, which
he had long known as his servant Aminadab's
expression of delight.

"Ah, clod! ah, earthly mass!" cried Aylmer,
laughing in a sort of frenzy, "you have served
me well! Matter and spirit—earth and heaven
—have both done their part in this! Laugh,
thing of the senses! You have earned the right
to laugh."

These exclamations broke Georgiana's sleep.
She slowly unclosed her eyes and gazed into
the mirror which her husband had arranged
for that purpose. A faint smile flitted over her
lips when she recognized how barely perceptible was now that crimson hand which had
once blazed forth with such disastrous brilliancy as to scare away all their happiness. But
then her eyes sought Aylmer's face with a

trouble and anxiety that he could by no means
account for.

"My poor Aylmer!" murmured she.

"Poor? Nay, richest, happiest, most fa-
vored!" exclaimed he. "My peerless bride, it
is successful! You are perfect!"

"My poor Aylmer," she repeated with a
more than human tenderness, "you have aimed
loftily; you have done nobly. Do not repent
that with so high and pure a feeling, you have
rejected the best the earth could offer. Aylmer,
dearest Aylmer, I am dying!"

Alas! it was too true! The fatal hand had
grappled with the mystery of life, and was the
bond by which an angelic spirit kept itself in
union with a mortal frame. As the last crimson
tint of the birthmark—that sole token of human
imperfection—faded from her cheek, the parting breath of the now perfect woman passed
into the atmosphere, and her soul, lingering a
moment near her husband, took its heavenward flight. Then a hoarse, chuckling laugh was
heard again! Thus ever does the gross fatality
of earth exult in its invariable triumph over the
immortal essence which, in this dim sphere of
half development, demands the completeness
of a higher state. Yet, had Aylmer reached a
profounder wisdom, he need not thus have
flung away the happiness which would have
woven his mortal life of the selfsame texture
with the celestial. The momentary circumstance
was too strong for him; he failed to look beyond the shadowy scope of time, and, living
once for all in eternity, to find the perfect
future in the present.

*Henry James*

# THE FIGURE IN
# THE CARPET

### I

I had done a few things and earned a
few pence—I had perhaps even had time to
begin to think I was finer than was perceived
by the patronising; but when I take the little

THE FIGURE IN THE CARPET: From *Embarrassments*,
1896, by Henry James. Used by permission of The
Macmillan Company, and William Heinemann,
Ltd.

measure of my course (a fidgety habit, for it's none of the longest yet) I count my real start from the evening George Corvick, breathless and worried, came in to ask me a service. He had done more things than I, and earned more pence, though there were chances for cleverness I thought he sometimes missed. I could only, however, that evening declare to him that he never missed one for kindness. There was almost rapture in hearing it proposed to me to prepare for *The Middle,* the organ of our lucubrations, so called from the position in the week of its day of appearance, an article for which he had made himself responsible and of which, tied up with a stout string, he laid on my table the subject. I pounced upon my opportunity—that is on the first volume of it—and paid scant attention to my friend's explanation of his appeal. What explanation could be more to the point than my obvious fitness for the task? I had written on Hugh Vereker, but never a word in *The Middle,* where my dealings were mainly with the ladies and the minor poets. This was his new novel, an advance copy, and whatever much or little it should do for his reputation I was clear on the spot as to what it should do for mine. Moreover if I always read him as soon as I could get hold of him I had a particular reason for wishing to read him now: I had accepted an invitation to Bridges for the following Sunday, and it had been mentioned in Lady Jane's note that Mr. Vereker was to be there. I was young enough for a flutter at meeting a man of his renown, and innocent enough to believe the occasion would demand the display of an acquaintance with his "last."

Corvick, who had promised a review of it, had not even had time to read it; he had gone to pieces in consequence of news requiring— as on precipitate reflexion he judged—that he should catch the night-mail to Paris. He had had a telegram from Gwendolen Erme in answer to his letter offering to fly to her aid. I knew already about Gwendolen Erme; I had never seen her, but I had my ideas, which were mainly to the effect that Corvick would marry her if her mother would only die. That lady seemed now in a fair way to oblige him; after some dreadful mistake about a climate or a "cure" she had suddenly collapsed on the return from abroad. Her daughter, unsupported and alarmed, desiring to make a rush for home

but hesitating at the risk, had accepted our friend's assistance, and it was my secret belief that at sight of him Mrs. Erme would pull round. His own belief was scarcely to be called secret; it discernibly at any rate differed from mine. He had showed me Gwendolen's photograph with the remark that she wasn't pretty but was awfully interesting; she had published at the age of nineteen a novel in three volumes, "Deep Down," about which, in *The Middle,* he had been really splendid. He appreciated my present eagerness and undertook that the periodical in question should do no less; then at the last, with his hand on the door, he said to me: "Of course you'll be all right, you know." Seeing I was a trifle vague he added: "I mean you won't be silly."

"Silly—about Vereker! Why what do I ever find him but awfully clever?"

"Well, what's that but silly? What on earth does 'awfully clever' mean? For God's sake try to get *at* him. Don't let him suffer by our arrangement. Speak of him, you know, if you can, as *I* should have spoken of him."

I wondered an instant. "You mean as far and away the biggest of the lot—that sort of thing?"

Corvick almost groaned. "Oh you know, I don't put them back to back that way; it's the infancy of art! But he gives me a pleasure so rare; the sense of"—he mused a little—"something or other."

I wondered again. "The sense, pray, of what?"

"My dear man, that's just what I want *you* to say!"

Even before he had banged the door I had begun, book in hand, to prepare myself to say it. I sat up with Vereker half the night; Corvick couldn't have done more than that. He was awfully clever—I stuck to that, but he wasn't a bit the biggest of the lot. I didn't allude to the lot, however; I flattered myself that I emerged on this occasion from the infancy of art. "It's all right," they declared vividly at the office; and when the number appeared I felt there was a basis on which I could meet the great man. It gave me confidence for a day or two—then that confidence dropped. I had fancied him reading it with relish, but if Corvick wasn't satisfied how could Vereker himself be? I reflected indeed that the heat of the admirer was sometimes grosser even than the appetite of the scribe. Corvick at all events wrote me from Paris a little ill-humouredly. Mrs. Erme was pulling round, and I hadn't at all said what Vereker gave him the sense of.

## II

The effect of my visit to Bridges was to turn me out for more profundity. Hugh Vereker, as I saw him there, was of a contact so void of angles that I blushed for the poverty of imagination involved in my small precautions. If he was in spirits it wasn't because he had read my review; in fact on the Sunday morning I felt sure he hadn't read it, though *The Middle* had been out three days and bloomed, I assured myself, in the stiff garden of periodicals which gave one of the ormolu tables the air of a stand at a station. The impression he made on me personally was such that I wished him to read it, and I corrected to this end with a surreptitious hand what might be wanting in the careless conspicuity of the sheet. I'm afraid I even watched the result of my manoeuvre, but up to luncheon I watched in vain.

When afterwards, in the course of our gregarious walk, I found myself for half an hour, not perhaps without another manoeuvre, at the great man's side, the result of his affability was a still livelier desire that he shouldn't remain in ignorance of the peculiar justice I had done him. It wasn't that he seemed to thirst for justice; on the contrary I hadn't yet caught in his talk the faintest grunt of a grudge—a note for which my young experience had already given me an ear. Of late he had had more recognition, and it was pleasant, as we used to say in *The Middle,* to see how it drew him out. He wasn't of course popular, but I judged one of the sources of his good humour to be precisely that his success was independent of that. He had none the less become in a manner the fashion; the critics at least had put on a spurt and caught up with him. We had found out at last how clever he was, and he had had to make the best of the loss of his mystery. I was strongly tempted, as I walked beside him, to let him know how much of that unveiling was my act; and there was a moment when I probably should have done so had not one of the ladies of our party, snatching a place at his other elbow, just then appealed to him in a spirit comparatively selfish. It was very discouraging: I almost felt the liberty had been taken with myself.

I had had on my tongue's end, for my own part, a phrase or two about the right word at the right time; but later on I was glad not to have spoken, for when on our return we clustered at tea I perceived Lady Jane, who had not been out with us, brandishing *The Middle* with her longest arm. She had taken it up at her leisure; she was delighted with what she had found, and I saw that, as a mistake in a man may often be a felicity in a woman, she would practically do for me what I hadn't been able to do for myself. "Some sweet little truths that needed to be spoken," I heard her declare, thrusting the paper at rather a bewildered couple by the fireplace. She grabbed it away from them again on the reappearance of Hugh Vereker, who after our walk had been upstairs to change something. "I know you don't in general look at this kind of thing, but it's an occasion really for doing so. You *haven't* seen it? Then you must. The man has actually got *at* you, at what *I* always feel, you know." Lady Jane threw into her eyes a look evidently intended to give an idea of what she always felt; but she added that she couldn't have expressed it. The man in the paper expressed it in a striking manner. "Just see there, and there, where I've dashed it, how he brings it out." She had literally marked for him the brightest patches of my prose, and if I was a little amused Vereker himself may well have been. He showed how much he was when before us all Lady Jane wanted to read something aloud. I liked at any rate the way he defeated her purpose by jerking the paper affectionately out of her clutch. He'd take it upstairs with him and look at it on going to dress. He did this half an hour later—I saw it in his hand when he repaired to his room. That was the moment at which, thinking to give her pleasure, I mentioned to Lady Jane that I was the author of the review. I did give her pleasure, I judged, but perhaps not quite so much as I had expected. If the author was "only me" the thing didn't seem quite so remarkable. Hadn't I had the effect rather of diminishing the lustre of the article than of adding to my own? Her ladyship was subject to the most extraordinary drops. It didn't matter; the only effect I cared about was the one it would have on Vereker up there by his bedroom fire.

At dinner I watched for the signs of this impression, tried to fancy some happier light in his eyes; but to my disappointment Lady Jane gave me no chance to make sure. I had hoped she'd call triumphantly down the table, publicly demand if she hadn't been right. The party was large—there were people from outside as well, but I had never seen a table long enough to deprive Lady Jane of a triumph. I was just reflecting in truth that this interminable board would deprive *me* of one when the guest next me, dear woman—she was Miss Poyle, the vicar's sister, a robust unmodulated person—had the happy inspiration and the unusual courage to address herself across it to Vereker, who was opposite, but not directly, so that when he replied they were both leaning forward. She inquired, artless body, what he thought of Lady Jane's "panegyric," which she had read—not connecting it however with her right-hand neighbour; and while I strained my ear for his reply I heard him, to my stupefaction, call back gaily, his mouth full of bread: "Oh it's all right—the usual twaddle!"

I had caught Vereker's glance as he spoke, but Miss Poyle's surprise was a fortunate cover for my own. "You mean he doesn't do you justice?" said the excellent woman.

Vereker laughed out, and I was happy to be able to do the same. "It's a charming article," he tossed us.

Miss Poyle thrust her chin half across the cloth. "Oh you're so deep!" she drove home.

"As deep as the ocean! All I pretend is that the author doesn't see—" But a dish was at this point passed over his shoulder, and we had to wait while he helped himself.

"Doesn't see what?" my neighbour continued.

"Doesn't see anything."

"Dear me—how very stupid!"

"Not a bit," Vereker laughed again. "Nobody does."

The lady on his further side appealed to him and Miss Poyle sank back to myself. "Nobody sees anything!" she cheerfully announced; to which I replied that I had often thought so too, but had somehow taken the thought for a proof on my own part of a tremendous eye. I didn't tell her the article was mine; and I observed that Lady Jane, occupied at the end of the table, had not caught Vereker's words.

I rather avoided him after dinner, for I confess he struck me as cruelly conceited, and the revelation was a pain. "The usual twaddle"—

my acute little study! That one's admiration should have had a reserve or two could gall him to that point? I had thought him placid, and he was placid enough; such a surface was the hard polished glass that encased the bauble of his vanity. I was really ruffled, and the only comfort was that if nobody saw anything George Corvick was quite as much out of it as I. This comfort however was not sufficient, after the ladies had dispersed, to carry me in the proper manner—I mean in a spotted jacket and humming an air—into the smoking-room. I took my way in some dejection to bed; but in the passage I encountered Mr. Vereker, who had been up once more to change, coming out of his room. *He* was humming an air and had on a spotted jacket, and as soon as he saw me his gaiety gave a start.

"My dear young man," he exclaimed, "I'm so glad to lay hands on you! I'm afraid I most unwittingly wounded you by those words of mine at dinner to Miss Poyle. I learned but half an hour ago from Lady Jane that you're the author of the little notice in *The Middle*."

I protested that no bones were broken; but he moved with me to my own door, his hand on my shoulder, kindly feeling for a fracture; and on hearing that I had come up to bed he asked leave to cross my threshold and just tell me in three words what his qualification of my remarks had represented. It was plain he really feared I was hurt, and the sense of his solicitude suddenly made all the difference to me. My cheap review fluttered off into space, and the best things I had said in it became flat enough beside the brilliancy of his being there. I can see him there still, on my rug, in the firelight and his spotted jacket, his fine clear face all bright with the desire to be tender to my youth. I don't know what he had at first meant to say, but I think the sight of my relief touched him, excited him, brought up words to his lips from far within. It was so these words presently conveyed to me something that, as I afterwards knew, he had never uttered to any one. I've always done justice to the generous impulse that made him speak; it was simply compunction for a snub unconsciously administered to a man of letters in a position inferior to his own, a man of letters moreover in the very act of praising him. To make the thing right he talked to me exactly as an equal and on the ground of what we both loved best. The hour, the place, the unexpectedness deepened the impression: he couldn't have done anything more intensely effective.

## III

"I don't quite know how to explain it to you," he said, "but it was the very fact that your notice of my book had a spice of intelligence, it was just your exceptional sharpness, that produced the feeling—a very old story with me, I beg you to believe—under the momentary influence of which I used in speaking to that good lady the words you so naturally resent. I don't read the things in the newspapers unless they're thrust upon me as that one was—it's always one's best friend who does it! But I used to read them sometimes—ten years ago. I dare say they were in general rather stupider then; at any rate it always struck me they missed my little point with a perfection exactly as admirable when they patted me on the back as when they kicked me in the shins. Whenever since I've happened to have a glimpse of them they were still blazing away—still missing it, I mean, deliciously. *You* miss it, my dear fellow, with inimitable assurance; the fact of your being awfully clever and your article's being awfully nice doesn't make a hair's breadth of difference. It's quite with you rising young men," Vereker laughed, "that I feel most what a failure I am!"

I listened with keen interest; it grew keener as he talked. *"You* a failure—heavens! What then may your 'little point' happen to be?"

"Have I got to *tell* you, after all these years and labours?" There was something in the friendly reproach of this—jocosely exaggerated—that made me, as an ardent young seeker for truth, blush to the roots of my hair. I'm as much in the dark as ever, though I've grown used in a sense to my obtuseness; at that moment, however, Vereker's happy accent made me appear to myself, and probably to him, a rare dunce. I was on the point of exclaiming "Ah yes, don't tell me: for my honour, for that of the craft, don't!" when he went on in a manner that showed he had read my thought and had his own idea of the probability of our some day redeeming ourselves. "By my little point I mean—what shall I call it?—the particular thing I've written my books most *for*. Isn't there for every writer a particular thing of that sort, the thing that most makes him apply him-

self, the thing without the effort to achieve which he wouldn't write at all, the very passion of his passion, the part of the business in which, for him, the flame of art burns most intensely? Well, it's *that!"*

I considered a moment—that is I followed at a respectful distance, rather gasping. I was fascinated—easily, you'll say; but I wasn't going after all to be put off my guard. "Your description's certainly beautiful, but it doesn't make what you describe very distinct."

"I promise you it would be distinct if it should dawn on you at all." I saw that the charm of our topic overflowed for my companion into an emotion as lively as my own. "At any rate," he went on, "I can speak for myself: there's an idea in my work without which I wouldn't have given a straw for the whole job. It's the finest fullest intention of the lot, and the application of it has been, I think, a triumph of patience, of ingenuity. I ought to leave that to somebody else to say; but that nobody does say it is precisely what we're talking about. It stretches, this little trick of mine, from book to book, and everything else, comparatively, plays over the surface of it. The order, the form, the texture of my books will perhaps someday constitute for the initiated a complete representation of it. So it's naturally the thing for the critic to look for. It strikes me," my visitor added, smiling, "even as the thing for the critic to find."

This seemed a responsibility indeed. "You call it a little trick?"

"That's only my little modesty. It's really an exquisite scheme."

"And you hold that you've carried the scheme out?"

"The way I've carried it out is the thing in life I think a bit well of myself for."

I had a pause. "Don't you think you ought—just a trifle—to assist the critic?"

"Assist him? What else have I done with every stroke of my pen? I've shouted my intention in his great blank face!" At this, laughing out again, Vereker laid his hand on my shoulder to show the allusion wasn't to my personal appearance.

"But you talk about the initiated. There must therefore, you see, *be* initiation."

"What else in heaven's name is criticism supposed to be?" I'm afraid I coloured at this too; but I took refuge in repeating that his account of his silver lining was poor in something or other that a plain man knows things by. "That's only because you've never had a glimpse of it," he returned. "If you had had one the element in question would soon have become practically all you'd see. To me it's exactly as palpable as the marble of this chimney. Besides, the critic just *isn't* a plain man: if he were, pray, what would he be doing in his neighbour's garden? You're anything but a plain man yourself, and the very *raison d'être* of you all is that you're little demons of subtlety. If my great affair's a secret, that's only because it's a secret in spite of itself—the amazing event has made it one. I not only never took the smallest precaution to keep it so, but never dreamed of any such accident. If I had I shouldn't in advance have had the heart to go on. As it was, I only became aware little by little, and meanwhile I had done my work."

"And now you quite like it?" I risked.

"My work?"

"Your secret. It's the same thing."

"Your guessing that," Vereker replied, "is a proof that you're as clever as I say!" I was encouraged by this to remark that he would clearly be pained to part with it, and he confessed that it was indeed with him now the great amusement of life. "I live almost to see if it will ever be detected." He looked at me for a jesting challenge; something far within his eyes seemed to peep out. "But I needn't worry—it won't!"

"You fire me as I've never been fired," I declared; "you make me determined to do or die." Then I asked: "Is it a kind of esoteric message?"

His countenance fell at this—he put out his hand as if to bid me good-night. "Ah my dear fellow, it can't be described in cheap journalese!"

I knew of course he'd be awfully fastidious, but our talk had made me feel how much his nerves were exposed. I was unsatisfied—I kept hold of his hand. "I won't make use of the expression then," I said, "in the article in which I shall eventually announce my discovery, though I dare say I shall have hard work to do without it. But meanwhile, just to hasten that difficult birth, can't you give a fellow a clue?" I felt much more at my ease.

"My whole lucid effort gives him the clue—every page and line and letter. The thing's as

concrete there as a bird in a cage, a bait on a hook, a piece of cheese in a mouse-trap. It's stuck into every volume as your foot is stuck into your shoe. It governs every line, it chooses every word, it dots every i, it places every comma."

I scratched my head. "Is it something in the style or something in the thought? An element of form or an element of feeling?"

He indulgently shook my hand again, and I felt my questions to be crude and my distinctions pitiful. "Good-night, my dear boy—don't bother about it. After all, you do like a fellow."

"And a little intelligence might spoil it?" I still detained him.

He hesitated. "Well, you've got a heart in your body. Is that an element of form or an element of feeling? What I contend that nobody has ever mentioned in my work is the organ of life."

"I see—it's some idea *about* life, some sort of philosophy. Unless it be," I added with the eagerness of a thought perhaps still happier, "some kind of game you're up to with your style, something you're after in the language. Perhaps it's a preference for the letter P!" I ventured profanely to break out. "Papa, potatoes, prunes—that sort of thing?" He was suitably indulgent: he only said I hadn't got the right letter. But his amusement was over; I could see he was bored. There was nevertheless something else I had absolutely to learn. "Should you be able, pen in hand, to state it clearly yourself—to name it, phrase it, formulate it?"

"Oh," he almost passionately sighed, "if I were only, pen in hand, one of *you* chaps!"

"That would be a great chance for you of course. But why should you despise us chaps for not doing what you can't do yourself?"

"Can't do?" He opened his eyes. "Haven't I done it in twenty volumes? I do it in my way," he continued. "Go *you* and do it in yours."

"Ours is so devilish difficult," I weakly observed.

"So's mine! We each choose our own. There's no compulsion. You won't come down and smoke?"

"No. I want to think this thing out."

"You'll tell me then in the morning that you've laid me bare?"

"I'll see what I can do; I'll sleep on it. But just one word more," I added. We had left the room—I walked again with him a few steps along the passage. "This extraordinary 'general intention,' as you call it—for that's the most vivid description I can induce you to make of it—is then, generally, a sort of buried treasure?"

His face lighted. "Yes, call it that, though it's perhaps not for me to do so."

"Nonsense!" I laughed. "You know you're hugely proud of it."

"Well, I didn't propose to tell you so; but it *is* the joy of my soul!"

"You mean it's a beauty so rare, so great?"

He waited a little again. "The loveliest thing in the world!" We had stopped, and on these words he left me; but at the end of the corridor, while I looked after him rather yearningly, he turned and caught sight of my puzzled face. It made him earnestly, indeed I thought quite anxiously, shake his head and wave his finger. "Give it up—give it up!"

This wasn't a challenge—it was fatherly advice. If I had had one of his books at hand I'd have repeated my recent act of faith—I'd have spent half the night with him. At three o'clock in the morning, not sleeping, remembering moreover how indispensable he was to Lady Jane, I stole down to the library with a candle. There wasn't, so far as I could discover, a line of his writing in the house.

## IV

Returning to town I feverishly collected them all; I picked out each in its order and held it up to the light. This gave me a maddening month, in the course of which several things took place. One of these, the last, I may as well immediately mention, was that I acted on Vereker's advice: I renounced my ridiculous attempt. I could really make nothing of the business; it proved a dead loss. After all I had always, as he had himself noted, liked him; and what now occurred was simply that my new intelligence and vain preoccupation damaged my liking. I not only failed to run a general intention to earth, I found myself missing the subordinate intentions I had formerly enjoyed. His books didn't even remain the charming things they had been for me; the exasperation of my search put me out of conceit of them. Instead of being a pleasure the more they became a resource the less; for from the moment I was unable to follow up the author's hint I of course felt it a point of honour not to make use professionally of my knowledge of them. I *had* no knowledge—nobody had any. It was humiliating, but I could bear it—they only annoyed me now. At last they even bored me, and I accounted for my confusion—perversely, I allow—by the idea that Vereker had made a fool of me. The buried treasure was a bad joke, the general intention a monstrous *pose*.

The great point of it all is, however, that I told George Corvick what had befallen me and that my information had an immense effect on him. He had at last come back, but so, unfortunately, had Mrs. Erme, and there was as yet, I could see, no question of his nuptials. He was immensely stirred up by the anecdote I had brought from Bridges; it fell in so completely with the sense he had had from the first that there was more in Vereker than met the eye. When I remarked that the eye seemed what the printed page had been expressly invented to meet he immediately accused me of being spiteful because I had been foiled. Our commerce had always that pleasant latitude. The thing Vereker had mentioned to me was exactly the thing he, Corvick, had wanted me to speak of in my review. On my suggesting at last that with the assistance I had now given him he would doubtless be prepared to speak of it himself he admitted freely that before doing this there was more he must understand. What he would have said, had he reviewed the new book, was that there was evidently in the writer's inmost art something to *be* understood. I hadn't so much as hinted at that: no wonder the writer hadn't been flattered! I asked Corvick what he really considered he meant by his own supersubtlety, and, unmistakably kindled, he replied: "It isn't for the vulgar—it isn't for the vulgar!" He had hold of the tail of something: he would pull hard, pull it right out. He pumped me dry on Vereker's strange confidence and, pronouncing me the luckiest of mortals, mentioned half-a-dozen questions he wished to goodness I had had the gumption to put. Yet on the other hand he didn't want to be told too much—it would spoil the fun of seeing what would come. The failure of *my* fun was at the moment of our meeting not complete, but I saw it ahead, and Corvick saw that I saw it. I, on my side, saw likewise that one of the first things he would do would be to rush off with my story to Gwendolen.

On the very day after my talk with him I was surprised by the receipt of a note from Hugh Vereker, to whom our encounter at Bridges had been recalled, as he mentioned, by his falling, in a magazine, on some article to which my signature was attached. "I read it with great pleasure," he wrote, "and remembered under its influence our lively conversation by your bedroom fire. The consequence of this has been that I begin to measure the temerity of my having saddled you with a knowledge that you may find something of a burden. Now that the fit's over I can't imagine how I came to be moved so much beyond my wont. I had never before mentioned, no matter in what state of expansion, the fact of my little secret, and I shall never speak of that mystery again. I was accidentally so much more explicit with you than it had ever entered into my game to be, that I find this game—I mean the pleasure of playing it—suffers considerably. In short, if you can understand it, I've rather spoiled my sport. I really don't want to give anybody what I believe you clever young men call the tip. That's of course a selfish solicitude, and I name it to you for what it may be worth to you. If you're disposed to humour me don't repeat my revelation. Think me demented—it's your right; but don't tell anybody why."

The sequel to this communication was that as early on the morrow as I dared I drove straight to Mr. Vereker's door. He occupied in those years one of the honest old houses in Kensington Square. He received me immediately, and as soon as I came in I saw I hadn't lost my power to minister to his mirth. He laughed out at sight of my face, which doubtless expressed my perturbation. I had been indiscreet—my compunction was great. "I *have* told somebody," I panted, "and I'm sure that person will by this time have told somebody else! It's a woman, into the bargain."

"The person you've told?"

"No, the other person. I'm quite sure he must have told her."

"For all the good it will do her—or do *me!* A woman will never find out."

"No, but she'll talk all over the place: she'll do just what you don't want."

Vereker thought a moment, but wasn't so disconcerted as I had feared: he felt that if the harm was done it only served him right. "It doesn't matter—don't worry."

"I'll do my best, I promise you, that your talk with me shall go no further."

"Very good; do what you can."

"In the meantime," I pursued, "George Corvick's possession of the tip may, on his part, really lead to something."

"That will be a brave day."

I told him about Corvick's cleverness, his admiration, the intensity of his interest in my anecdote; and without making too much of the divergence of our respective estimates mentioned that my friend was already of opinion that he saw much further into a certain affair than most people. He was quite as fired as I had been at Bridges. He was moreover in love with the young lady: perhaps the two together would puzzle something out.

Vereker seemed struck with this. "Do you mean they're to be married?"

"I dare say that's what it will come to."

"That may help them," he conceded, "but we must give them time!"

I spoke of my own renewed assault and confessed my difficulties; whereupon he repeated his former advice: "Give it up, give it up!" He evidently didn't think me intellectually equipped for the adventure. I stayed half an hour, and he was most good-natured, but I couldn't help pronouncing him a man of unstable moods. He had been free with me in a mood, he had repented in a mood, and now in a mood he had turned indifferent. This general levity helped me to believe that, so far as the subject of the tip went, there wasn't much in it. I contrived however to make him answer a few more questions about it, though he did so with visible impatience. For himself, beyond doubt, the thing we were all so blank about was vividly there. It was something, I guessed, in the primal plan; something like a complex figure in a Persian carpet. He highly approved of this image when I used it, and he used another himself. "It's the very string," he said, "that my pearls are strung on!" The reason of his note to me had been that he really didn't want to give us a grain of succour—our density was a thing too perfect in its way to touch. He had formed the habit of depending on it, and if the spell was to break it must break by some force of its own. He comes back to me from that last occasion—for I was never to speak to him again—as a man with some safe preserve for sport. I wondered as I walked away where he had got *his* tip.

## V

When I spoke to George Corvick of the caution I had received he made me feel that any doubt of his delicacy would be almost an insult. He had instantly told Gwendolen, but Gwendolen's ardent response was in itself a pledge of discretion. The question would now absorb them and would offer them a pastime too precious to be shared with the crowd. They appeared to have caught instinctively at Vereker's high idea of enjoyment. Their intellectual pride, however, was not such as to make them indifferent to any further light I might throw on the affair they had in hand. They were indeed of the "artistic temperament," and I was freshly struck with my colleague's power to excite himself over a question of art. He'd call it letters, he'd call it life, but it was all one thing. In what he said I now seemed to understand that he spoke equally for Gwendolen, to whom, as soon as Mrs. Erme was sufficiently better to allow her a little leisure, he made a point of introducing me. I remember our going together one Sunday in August to a huddled house in Chelsea, and my renewed envy of Corvick's possession of a friend who had some light to mingle with his own. He could say things to her that I could never say to him. She had indeed no sense of humour and, with her pretty way of holding her head on one side, was one of those persons whom you want, as the phrase is, to shake, but who have learnt Hungarian by themselves. She conversed perhaps in Hungarian with Corvick; she had remarkably little English for his friend. Corvick afterwards told me that I had chilled her by my apparent indisposition to oblige them with the detail of what Vereker had said to me. I allowed that I felt I had given thought enough to that indication: hadn't I even made up my mind that it was vain and would lead nowhere? The importance they attached to it was irritating and quite envenomed my doubts.

That statement looks unamiable, and what probably happened was that I felt humiliated at seeing other persons deeply beguiled by an experiment that had brought me only chagrin. I was out in the cold while, by the evening fire, under the lamp, they followed the chase for which I myself had sounded the horn. They did

as I had done, only more deliberately and sociably—they went over their author from the beginning. There was no hurry, Corvick said— the future was before them and the fascination could only grow; they would take him page by page, as they would take one of the classics, inhale him in slow draughts and let him sink all the way in. They would scarce have got so wound up, I think, if they hadn't been in love: poor Vereker's inner meaning gave them endless occasion to put and to keep their young heads together. None the less it represented the kind of problem for which Corvick had a special aptitude, drew out the particular pointed patience of which, had he lived, he would have given more striking and, it is to be hoped, more fruitful examples. He at least was, in Vereker's words, a little demon of subtlety. We had begun by disputing, but I soon saw that without my stirring a finger his infatuation would have its bad hours. He would bound off on false scents as I had done—he would clap his hands over new lights and see them blown out by the wind of the turned page. He was like nothing, I told him, but the maniacs who embrace some bedlamical theory of the cryptic character of Shakespeare. To this he replied that if we had had Shakespeare's own word for his being cryptic he would at once have accepted it. The case there was altogether different—we had nothing but the word of Mr. Snooks. I returned that I was stupefied to see him attach such importance even to the word of Mr. Vereker. He wanted thereupon to know if I treated Mr. Vereker's word as a lie. I wasn't perhaps prepared, in my unhappy rebound, to go so far as that, but I insisted that till the contrary was proved I should view it as too fond an imagination. I didn't, I confess, say—I didn't at that time quite know—all I felt. Deep down, as Miss Erme would have said, I was uneasy, I was expectant. At the core of my disconcerted state—for my wonted curiosity lived in its ashes—was the sharpness of a sense that Corvick would at last probably come out somewhere. He made, in defence of his credulity, a great point of the fact that from of old, in his study of this genius, he had caught whiffs and hints of he didn't know what, faint wandering notes of a hidden music. That was just the rarity, that was the charm: it fitted so perfectly into what I reported.

If I returned on several occasions to the little

house in Chelsea I dare say it was as much for news of Vereker as for news of Miss Erme's ailing parent. The hours spent there by Corvick were present to my fancy as those of a chess-player bent with a silent scowl, all the lamplit winter, over his board and his moves. As my imagination filled it out the picture held me fast. On the other side of the table was a ghost-lier form, the faint figure of an antagonist good-humouredly but a little wearily secure—an antagonist who leaned back in his chair with his hands in his pockets and a smile on his fine clear face. Close to Corvick, behind him, was a girl who had begun to strike me as pale and wasted and even, on more familiar view, as rather handsome, and who rested on his shoulder and hung on his moves. He would take up a chessman and hold it poised a while over one of the little squares, and then would put it back in its place with a long sigh of disappointment. The young lady, at this, would slightly but uneasily shift her position and look across, very hard, very long, very strangely, at their dim participant. I had asked them at an early stage of the business if it mightn't contribute to their success to have some closer communication with him. The special circumstances would surely be held to have given me a right to introduce them. Corvick immediately replied that he had no wish to approach the altar be-fore he had prepared the sacrifice. He quite agreed with our friend both as to the delight and as to the honour of the chase—he would bring down the animal with his own rifle. When I asked him if Miss Erme were as keen a shot he said after thinking: "No, I'm ashamed to say she wants to set a trap. She'd give anything to see him; she says she requires another tip. She's really quite morbid about it. But she must play fair—she *shan't* see him!" he emphatically added. I wondered if they hadn't even quar-relled a little on the subject—a suspicion not corrected by the way he more than once ex-claimed to me: "She's quite incredibly literary, you know—quite fantastically!" I remember his saying of her that she felt in italics and thought in capitals. "Oh when I've run him to earth," he also said, "then, you know, I shall knock at his door. Rather—I beg you to be-lieve. I'll have it from his own lips: 'Right you are, my boy; you've done it this time!' He shall crown me victor—with the critical laurel."

Meanwhile he really avoided the chances London life might have given him of meeting the distinguished novelist; a danger, however, that disappeared with Vereker's leaving Eng-land for an indefinite absence, as the news-papers announced—going to the south for mo-tives connected with the health of his wife, which had long kept her in retirement. A year —more than a year—had elapsed since the incident at Bridges, but I had had no further sight of him. I think I was at bottom rather ashamed—I hated to remind him that, though I had irremediably missed his point, a reputa-tion for acuteness was rapidly overtaking me. This scruple led me a dance; kept me out of Lady Jane's house, made me even decline, when in spite of my bad manners she was a second time so good as to make me a sign, an invitation to her beautiful seat. I once became aware of her under Vereker's escort at a con-cert, and was sure I was seen by them, but I slipped out without being caught. I felt, as on that occasion I splashed along in the rain, that I couldn't have done anything else; and yet I remember saying to myself that it was hard, was even cruel. Not only had I lost the books, but I had lost the man himself: they and their author had been alike spoiled for me. I knew too which was the loss I most regretted. I had taken to the man still more than I had ever taken to the books.

## VI

Six months after our friend had left England George Corvick, who made his living by his pen, contracted for a piece of work which im-posed on him an absence of some length and a journey of some difficulty, and his under-taking of which was much of a surprise to me. His brother-in-law had become editor of a great provincial paper, and the great provincial paper, in a fine flight of fancy, had conceived the idea of sending a "special commissioner" to India. Special commissioners had begun, in the "metropolitan press," to be the fashion, and the journal in question must have felt it had passed too long for a mere country cousin. Corvick had no hand, I knew, for the big brush of the correspondent, but that was his brother-in-law's affair, and the fact that a particular task was not in his line was apt to be with him-self exactly a reason for accepting it. He was prepared to out-Herod the metropolitan press; he took solemn precautions against priggishness, he exquisitely outraged taste. Nobody ever knew it—that offended principle was all his own. In addition to his expenses he was to be conveniently paid, and I found myself able to help him, for the usual fat book, to a plausible arrangement with the usual fat publisher. I naturally inferred that his obvious desire to make a little money was not unconnected with the prospect of a union with Gwendolen Erme. I was aware that her mother's opposition was largely addressed to his want of means and of lucrative abilities, but it so happened that, on my saying the last time I saw him something that bore on the question of his separation from our young lady, he brought out with an emphasis that startled me: "Ah I'm not a bit engaged to her, you know!"

"Not overtly," I answered, "because her mother doesn't like you. But I've always taken for granted a private understanding."

"Well, there *was* one. But there isn't now." That was all he said save something about Mrs. Erme's having got on her feet again in the most extraordinary way—a remark pointing, as I supposed, the moral that private understandings were of little use when the doctor didn't share them. What I took the liberty of more closely inferring was that the girl might in some way have estranged him. Well, if he had taken the turn of jealousy, for instance, it could scarcely be jealousy of me. In that case—over and above the absurdity of it—he wouldn't have gone away just to leave us together. For some time before his going we had indulged in no allusion to the buried treasure, and from his silence, which my reserve simply emulated, I had drawn a sharp conclusion. His courage had dropped, his ardour had gone the way of mine—this appearance at least he left me to scan. More than that he couldn't do; he couldn't face the triumph with which I might have greeted an explicit admission. He needn't have been afraid, poor dear, for I had by this time lost all need to triumph. In fact I considered I showed magnanimity in not reproaching him with his collapse, for the sense of his having thrown up the game made me feel more than ever how much I at last depended on him. If Corvick had broken down I should never know; no one would be of any use if *he* wasn't. It wasn't a bit true I had ceased to care for knowledge; little by little my curiosity not only had begun to ache again, but had become the

familiar torment of my days and my nights. There are doubtless people to whom torments of such an order appear hardly more natural than the contortions of disease; but I don't after all know why I should in this connexion so much as mention them. For the few persons, at any rate, abnormal or not, with whom my anecdote is concerned, literature was a game of skill, and skill meant courage, and courage meant honour, and honour meant passion, meant life. The stake on the table was a special substance and our roulette the revolving mind, but we sat round the green board as intently as the grim gamblers at Monte Carlo. Gwendolen Erme, for that matter, with her white face and her fixed eyes, was of the very type of the lean ladies one had met in the temples of chance. I recognised in Corvick's absence that she made this analogy vivid. It was extravagant, I admit, the way she lived for the art of the pen. Her passion visibly preyed on her, and in her presence I felt almost tepid. I got hold of "Deep Down" again: it was a desert in which she had lost herself, but in which too she had dug a wonderful hole in the sand—a cavity out of which Corvick had still more remarkably pulled her.

Early in March I had a telegram from her, in consequence of which I repaired immediately to Chelsea, where the first thing she said to me was: "He has got it, he has got it!"

She was moved, as I could see, to such depths that she must mean the great thing. "Vereker's idea?"

"His general intention. George has cabled from Bombay."

She had the missive open there; it was emphatic though concise. "Eureka. Immense." That was all—he had saved the cost of the signature. I shared her emotion, but I was disappointed. "He doesn't say what it is."

"How could he—in a telegram? He'll write it."

"But how does he know?"

"Know it's the real thing? Oh I'm sure that when you see it you do know. *Vera incessu patuit dea!*" [11]

"It's you, Miss Erme, who are a 'dear' for bringing me such news!"—I went all lengths

----

[11] "She shows by her walk that she is really a goddess"; said of Venus appearing to Aeneas, in Virgil's *Aeneid* I. 405.

in my high spirits. "But fancy finding our goddess in the temple of Vishnu! How strange of George to have been able to go into the thing again in the midst of such different and such powerful solicitations!"

"He hasn't gone into it, I know; it's the thing itself, let severely alone for six months, that has simply sprung out at him like a tigress out of the jungle. He didn't take a book with him—on purpose; indeed he wouldn't have needed to—he knows every page, as I do, by heart. They all worked in him together, and some day somewhere, when he wasn't thinking, they fell, in all their superb intricacy, into the one right combination. The figure in the carpet came out. That's the way he knew it would come and the real reason—you didn't in the least understand, but I suppose I may tell you now—why he went and why I consented to his going. We knew the change would do it—that the difference of thought, of scene, would give the needed touch, the magic shake. We had perfectly, we had admirably calculated. The elements were all in his mind, and in the *secousse* of a new and intense experience they just struck light." She positively struck light herself—she was literally, facially luminous. I stammered something about unconscious cerebration, and she continued: "He'll come right home—this will bring him."

"To see Vereker, you mean?"

"To see Vereker—and to see *me*. Think what he'll have to tell me!"

I hesitated. "About India?"

"About fiddlesticks! About Vereker—about the figure in the carpet."

"But, as you say, we shall surely have that in a letter."

She thought like one inspired, and I remembered how Corvick had told me long before that her face was interesting. "Perhaps it can't be got into a letter if it's 'immense.'"

"Perhaps not if it's immense bosh. If he has hold of something that can't be got into a letter he hasn't hold of *the* thing. Vereker's own statement to me was exactly that the 'figure' *would* fit into a letter."

"Well, I cabled to George an hour ago—two words," said Gwendolen.

"Is it indiscreet of me to ask what they were?"

She hung fire, but at last brought them out. " 'Angel, write.' "

"Good!" I cried. "I'll make it sure—I'll send him the same."

## VII

My words however were not absolutely the same—I put something instead of "angel"; and in the sequel my epithet seemed the more apt, for when eventually we heard from our traveller it was merely, it was thoroughly to be tantalised. He was magnificent in his triumph, he described his discovery as stupendous; but his ecstasy only obscured it—there were to be no particulars till he should have submitted his conception to the supreme authority. He had thrown up his commission, he had thrown up his book, he had thrown up everything but the instant need to hurry to Rapallo, on the Genoese shore, where Vereker was making a stay. I wrote him a letter which was to await him at Aden—I besought him to relieve my suspense. That he had found my letter was indicated by a telegram which, reaching me after weary days and in the absence of any answer to my laconic dispatch to him at Bombay, was evidently intended as a reply to both communications. Those few words were in familiar French, the French of the day, which Corvick often made use of to show he wasn't a prig. It had for some persons the opposite effect, but his message may fairly be paraphrased. "Have patience; I want to see, as it breaks on you, the face you'll make!" *"Tellement envie de voir ta tête!"*—that was what I had to sit down with. I can certainly not be said to have sat down, for I seem to remember myself at this time as rattling constantly between the little house in Chelsea and my own. Our impatience, Gwendolen's and mine, was equal, but I kept hoping her light would be greater. We all spent during this episode, for people of our means, a great deal of money in telegrams and cabs, and I counted on the receipt of news from Rapallo immediately after the junction of the discoverer with the discovered. The interval seemed an age, but late one day I heard a hansom precipitated to my door with the crash engendered by a hint of liberality. I lived with my heart in my mouth and accordingly bounded to the window—a movement which gave me a view of a young lady erect on the footboard of the vehicle and eagerly looking up at my house. At sight of me she flourished a paper with a movement that brought me straight down, the movement with which, in melodramas, handkerchiefs and reprieves are flourished at the foot of the scaffold.

"Just seen Vereker—not a note wrong. Pressed me to bosom—keeps me a month." So much I read on her paper while the cabby dropped a grin from his perch. In my excitement I paid him profusely and in hers she suffered it; then as he drove away we started to walk about and talk. We had talked, heaven knows, enough before, but this was a wondrous lift. We pictured the whole scene at Rapallo, where he would have written, mentioning my name, for permission to call; that is *I* pictured it, having more material than my companion, whom I felt hang on my lips as we stopped on purpose before shop-windows we didn't look into. About one thing we were clear: if he was staying on for fuller communication we should at least have a letter from him that would help us through the dregs of delay. We understood his staying on, and yet each of us saw, I think, that the other hated it. The letter we were clear about arrived; it was for Gwendolen, and I called on her in time to save her the trouble of bringing it to me. She didn't read it out, as was natural enough; but she repeated to me what it chiefly embodied. This consisted of the remarkable statement that he'd tell her after they were married exactly what she wanted to know.

"Only *then,* when I'm his wife—not before," she explained. "It's tantamount to saying—isn't it?—that I must marry him straight off!" She smiled at me while I flushed with disappointment, a vision of fresh delay that made me at first unconscious of my surprise. It seemed more than a hint that on me as well he would impose some tiresome condition. Suddenly, while she reported several more things from his letter, I remembered what he had told me before going away. He had found Mr. Vereker deliriously interesting and his own possession of the secret a real intoxication. The buried treasure was all gold and gems. Now that it was there it seemed to grow and grow before him; it would have been, through all time and taking all tongues, one of the most wonderful flowers of literary art. Nothing, in especial, once you were face to face with it, could show for more consummately *done.* When once it came out it came out, was there with a splendour that made you ashamed; and there hadn't been, save in

the bottomless vulgarity of the age, with every one tasteless and tainted, every sense stopped, the smallest reason why it should have been overlooked. It was great, yet so simple, was simple, yet so great, and the final knowledge of it was an experience quite apart. He intimated that the charm of such an experience, the desire to drain it, in its freshness, to the last drop, was what kept him there close to the source. Gwendolen, frankly radiant as she tossed me these fragments, showed the elation of a prospect more assured than my own. That brought me back to the question of her marriage, prompted me to ask if what she meant by what she had just surprised me with was that she was under an engagement.

"Of course I am!" she answered. "Didn't you know it?" She seemed astonished, but I was still more so, for Corvick had told me the exact contrary. I didn't mention this, however; I only reminded her how little I had been on that score in her confidence, or even in Corvick's, and that moreover I wasn't in ignorance of her mother's interdict. At bottom I was troubled by the disparity of the two accounts; but after a little I felt Corvick's to be the one I least doubted. This simply reduced me to asking myself if the girl had on the spot improvised an engagement—vamped up an old one or dashed off a new—in order to arrive at the satisfaction she desired. She must have had resources of which I was destitute, but she made her case slightly more intelligible by returning presently: "What the state of things has been is that we felt of course bound to do nothing in mamma's lifetime."

"But now you think you'll just dispense with mamma's consent?"

"Ah it mayn't come to that!" I wondered what it might come to, and she went on: "Poor dear, she may swallow the dose. In fact, you know," she added with a laugh, "she really *must!*"—a proposition of which, on behalf of everyone concerned, I fully acknowledged the force.

## VIII

Nothing more vexatious had ever happened to me than to become aware before Corvick's arrival in England that I shouldn't be there to put him through. I found myself abruptly called to Germany by the alarming illness of my younger brother, who, against my advice, had gone to Munich to study, at the feet indeed of a great master, the art of portraiture in oils. The near relative who made him an allowance had threatened to withdraw it if he should, under specious pretexts, turn for superior truth to Paris—Paris being somehow, for a Chelten-ham aunt, the school of evil, the abyss. I de-plored this prejudice at the time, and the deep injury of it was now visible—first in the fact that it hadn't saved the poor boy, who was clever frail and foolish, from congestion of the lungs, and second in the greater break with London to which the event condemned me. I'm afraid that what was uppermost in my mind during several anxious weeks was the sense that if we had only been in Paris I might have run over to see Corvick. This was actually out of the question from every point of view: my brother, whose recovery gave us both plenty to do, was ill for three months, during which I never left him and at the end of which we had to face the absolute prohibition of a return to England. The consideration of climate imposed itself, and he was in no state to meet it alone. I took him to Meran and there spent the sum-mer with him, trying to show him by example how to get back to work and nursing a rage of another sort that I tried *not* to show him.

The whole business proved the first of a series of phenomena so strangely interlaced that, taken all together—which was how I had to take them—they form as good an illustration as I can recall of the manner in which, for the good of his soul doubtless, fate sometimes deals with a man's avidity. These incidents certainly had larger bearings than the comparatively meagre consequence we are here concerned with—though I feel that consequence also a thing to speak of with some respect. It's mainly in such a light, I confess, at any rate, that the ugly fruit of my exile is at this hour present to me. Even at first indeed the spirit in which my avidity, as I have called it, made me regard that term owed no element of ease to the fact that before coming back from Rapallo George Corvick addressed me in a way I objected to. His letter had none of the sedative action I must to-day profess myself sure he had wished to give it, and the march of occurrences was not so ordered as to make up for what it lacked. He had begun on the spot, for one of the quar-terlies, a great last word on Vereker's writings, and this exhaustive study, the only one that

would have counted, have existed, was to turn on the new light, to utter—oh so quietly!—the unimagined truth. It was in other words to trace the figure in the carpet through every convolution, to reproduce it in every tint. The result, according to my friend, would be the greatest literary portrait ever painted, and what he asked of me was just to be so good as not to trouble him with questions till he should hang up his masterpiece before me. He did me the honour to declare that, putting aside the great sitter himself, all aloft in his indifference, I was individually the connoisseur he was most working for. I was therefore to be a good boy and not try to peep under the curtain before the show was ready: I should enjoy it all the more if I sat very still.

I did my best to sit very still, but I couldn't help giving a jump on seeing in *The Times*, after I had been a week or two in Munich and before, as I knew, Corvick had reached Lon-don, the announcement of the sudden death of poor Mrs. Erme. I instantly, by letter, appealed to Gwendolen for particulars, and she wrote me that her mother had yielded to long-threatened failure of the heart. She didn't say, but I took the liberty of reading into her words, that from the point of view of her marriage and also of her eagerness, which was quite a match for mine, this was a solution more prompt than could have been expected and more radical than waiting for the old lady to swallow the dose. I candidly admit indeed that at the time —for I heard from her repeatedly—I read some singular things into Gwendolen's words and some still more extraordinary ones into her silences. Pen in hand, this way, I live the time over, and it brings back the oddest sense of my having been, both for months and in spite of myself, a kind of coerced spectator. All my life had taken refuge in my eyes, which the procession of events appeared to have com-mitted itself to keep astare. There were days when I thought of writing to Hugh Vereker and simply throwing myself on his charity. But I felt more deeply that I hadn't fallen quite so low—besides which, quite properly, he would send me about my business. Mrs. Erme's death brought Corvick straight home, and within the month he was united "very quietly"—as quietly, I seemed to make out, as he meant in his article to bring out his *trouvaille*—to the young lady he had loved and quitted. I use this last term, I may parenthetically say, because I subsequently grew sure that at the time he went to India, at the time of his great news from Bombay, there had been no positive pledge between them whatever. There had been none at the moment she was affirming to me the very opposite. On the other hand he had certainly become engaged the day he returned. The happy pair went down to Torquay for their honeymoon, and there, in a reckless hour, it occurred to poor Corvick to take his young bride a drive. He had no command of that business: this had been brought home to me of old in a little tour we had once made together in a dogcart. In a dogcart he perched his companion for a rattle over Devonshire hills, on one of the likeliest of which he brought his horse, who, it was true, had bolted, down with such violence that the occupants of the cart were hurled forward and that he fell horribly on his head. He was killed on the spot; Gwendolen escaped unhurt.

I pass rapidly over the question of this unmitigated tragedy, of what the loss of my best friend meant for me, and I complete my little history of my patience and my pain by the frank statement of my having, in a postscript to my very first letter to her after the receipt of the hideous news, asked Mrs. Corvick whether her husband mightn't at least have finished the great article on Vereker. Her answer was as prompt as my question: the article, which had been barely begun, was a mere heartbreaking scrap. She explained that our friend, abroad, had just settled down to it when interrupted by her mother's death, and that then, on his return, he had been kept from work by the engrossments into which that calamity was to plunge them. The opening pages were all that existed; they were striking, they were promising, but they didn't unveil the idol. That great intellectual feat was obviously to have formed his climax. She said nothing more, nothing to enlighten me as to the state of her own knowledge—the knowledge for the acquisition of which I had fancied her prodigiously acting. This was above all what I wanted to know: had *she* seen the idol unveiled? Had there been a private ceremony for a palpitating audience of one? For what else but that ceremony had the nuptials taken place? I didn't like as yet to press her, though

when I thought of what had passed between us on the subject in Corvick's absence her reticence surprised me. It was therefore not till much later, from Meran, that I risked another appeal, risked it in some trepidation, for she continued to tell me nothing. "Did you hear in those few days of your blighted bliss," I wrote, "what we desired so to hear?" I said "we" as a little hint; and she showed me she could take a little hint. "I heard everything," she replied, "and I mean to keep it to myself!"

## IX

It was impossible not to be moved with the strongest sympathy for her, and on my return to England I showed her every kindness in my power. Her mother's death had made her means sufficient, and she had gone to live in a more convenient quarter. But her loss had been great and her visitation cruel; it never would have occurred to me, moreover, to suppose she could come to feel the possession of a technical tip, of a piece of literary experience, a counterpoise to her grief. Strange to say, none the less, I couldn't help believing after I had seen her a few times that I caught a glimpse of some such oddity. I hasten to add that there had been other things I couldn't help believing, or at least imagining; and as I never felt I was really clear about these, so, as to the point I here touch on, I give her memory the benefit of the doubt. Stricken and solitary, highly accomplished and now, in her deep mourning, her maturer grace and her uncomplaining sorrow, incontestably handsome, she presented herself as leading a life of singular dignity and beauty. I had at first found a way to persuade myself that I should soon get the better of the reserve formulated, the week after the catastrophe, in her reply to an appeal as to which I was not unconscious that it might strike her as mistimed. Certainly that reserve was something of a shock to me—certainly it puzzled me the more I thought of it and even though I tried to explain it (with moments of success) by an imputation of exalted sentiments, of superstitious scruples, of a refinement of loyalty. Certainly it added at the same time hugely to the price of Vereker's secret, precious as this mystery already appeared. I may as well confess abjectly that Mrs. Corvick's unexpected attitude was the final tap on the nail that was to fix fast my luckless idea, convert it into the obsession of which I'm for ever conscious.

But this only helped me the more to be artful, to be adroit, to allow time to elapse before renewing my suit. There were plenty of speculations for the interval, and one of them was deeply absorbing. Corvick had kept his information from his young friend till after the removal of the last barrier to their intimacy—then only had he let the cat out of the bag. Was it Gwendolen's idea, taking a hint from him, to liberate this animal only on the basis of the renewal of such a relation? Was the figure in the carpet traceable or describable only for husbands and wives—for lovers supremely united? It came back to me in a mystifying manner that in Kensington Square, when I mentioned that Corvick would have told the girl he loved, some word had dropped from Vereker that gave colour to this possibility. There might be little in it, but there was enough to make me wonder if I should have to marry Mrs. Corvick to get what I wanted. Was I prepared to offer her this price for the blessing of her knowledge? Ah that way madness lay!—so I at least said to myself in bewildered hours. I could see meanwhile the torch she refused to pass on flame away in her chamber of memory —pour through her eyes a light that shone in her lonely house. At the end of six months I was fully sure of what this warm presence made up to her for. We had talked again and again of the man who had brought us together—of his talent, his character, his personal charm, his certain career, his dreadful doom, and even of his clear purpose in that great study which was to have been a supreme literary portrait, a kind of critical Vandyke or Velasquez. She had conveyed to me in abundance that she was tongue-tied by her perversity, by her piety, that she would never break the silence it had not been given to the "right person," as she said, to break. The hour, however, finally arrived. One evening when I had been sitting with her longer than usual I laid my hand firmly on her arm. "Now at last what *is* it?"

She had been expecting me and was ready. She gave a long slow soundless headshake, merciful only in being inarticulate. This mercy didn't prevent its hurling at me the largest finest coldest "Never!" I had yet, in the course of a life that had known denials, had to take full in the face. I took it and was aware that with the hard blow the tears had come into my eyes. So for a while we sat and looked at each other; after which I slowly rose. I was wondering if some day she would accept me; but this was not what I brought out. I said as I smoothed down my hat: "I know what to think then. It's nothing!"

A remote disdainful pity for me gathered in her dim smile; then she spoke in a voice that I hear at this hour. "It's my *life!*" As I stood at the door she added: "You've insulted him!"

"Do you mean Vereker?"

"I mean the Dead!"

I recognised when I reached the street the justice of her charge. Yes, it was her life—I recognised that too; but her life none the less made room with the lapse of time for another interest. A year and a half after Corvick's death she published in a single volume her second novel, "Overmastered," which I pounced on in the hope of finding in it some tell-tale echo or some peeping face. All I found was a much better book than her younger performance, showing I thought the better company she had kept. As a tissue tolerably intricate it was a carpet with a figure of its own; but the figure was not the figure I was looking for. On sending a review of it to *The Middle* I was surprised to learn from the office that a notice was already in type. When the paper came out I had no hesitation in attributing this article, which I thought rather vulgarly overdone, to Drayton Deane, who in the old days had been something of a friend of Corvick's, yet had only within a few weeks made the acquaintance of his widow. I had had an early copy of the book, but Deane had evidently had an earlier. He lacked all the same the light hand with which Corvick had gilded the gingerbread—he laid on the tinsel in splotches.

## X

Six months later appeared "The Right of Way," the last chance, though we didn't know it, that we were to have to redeem ourselves. Written wholly during Vereker's sojourn abroad, the book had been heralded, in a hundred paragraphs, by the usual ineptitudes. I carried it, as early a copy as any, I this time flattered myself, straightway to Mrs. Corvick.

This was the only use I had for it; I left the inevitable tribute of *The Middle* to some more ingenious mind and some less irritated temper. "But I already have it," Gwendolen said. "Drayton Deane was so good as to bring it to me yesterday, and I've just finished it."

"Yesterday? How did he get it so soon?"

"He gets everything so soon! He's to review it in *The Middle*."

"He—Drayton Deane—review Vereker?" I couldn't believe my ears.

"Why not? One fine ignorance is as good as another."

I winced but I presently said: "You ought to review him yourself!"

"I don't 'review,'" she laughed. "I'm reviewed!"

Just then the door was thrown open. "Ah yes, here's your reviewer!" Drayton Deane was there with his long legs and his tall forehead: he had come to see what she thought of "The Right of Way," and to bring news that was singularly relevant. The evening papers were just out with a telegram on the author of that work, who, in Rome, had been ill for some days with an attack of malarial fever. It had at first not been thought grave, but had taken, in consequence of complications, a turn that might give rise to anxiety. Anxiety had indeed at the latest hour begun to be felt.

I was struck in the presence of these tidings with the fundamental detachment that Mrs. Corvick's overt concern quite failed to hide: it gave me the measure of her consummate independence. That independence rested on her knowledge, the knowledge which nothing now could destroy and which nothing could make different. The figure in the carpet might take on another twist or two, but the sentence had virtually been written. The writer might go down to his grave: she was the person in the world to whom—as if she had been his favoured heir—his continued existence was least of a need. This reminded me how I had observed at a particular moment—after Corvick's death—the drop of her desire to see him face to face. She had got what she wanted without that. I had been sure that if she hadn't got it she wouldn't have been restrained from the endeavour to sound him personally by those superior reflexions, more conceivable on a man's part than on a woman's, which in my

case had served as a deterrent. It wasn't however, I hasten to add, that my case, in spite of this invidious comparison, wasn't ambiguous enough. At the thought that Vereker was perhaps at that moment dying there rolled over me a wave of anguish—a poignant sense of how inconsistently I still depended on him. A delicacy that it was my one compensation to suffer to rule me had left the Alps and the Apennines between us, but the sense of the waning occasion suggested that I might in my despair at last have gone to him. Of course I should really have done nothing of the sort. I remained five minutes, while my companions talked of the new book, and when Drayton Deane appealed to me for my opinion of it I made answer, getting up, that I detested Hugh Vereker and simply couldn't read him. I departed with the moral certainty that as the door closed behind me Deane would brand me for awfully superficial. His hostess wouldn't contradict *that* at least.

I continue to trace with a briefer touch our intensely odd successions. Three weeks after this came Vereker's death, and before the year was out the death of his wife. That poor lady I had never seen, but I had had a futile theory that, should she survive him long enough to be decorously accessible, I might approach her with the feeble flicker of my plea. Did she know and if she knew would she speak? It was much to be presumed that for more reasons than one she would have nothing to say; but when she passed out of all reach I felt renouncement indeed my appointed lot. I was shut up in my obsession for ever—my gaolers had gone off with the key. I find myself quite as vague as a captive in a dungeon about the time that further elapsed before Mrs. Corvick became the wife of Drayton Deane. I had foreseen, through my bars, this end of the business, though there was no indecent haste and our friendship had rather fallen off. They were both so "awfully intellectual" that it struck people as a suitable match, but I had measured better than any one the wealth of understanding the bride would contribute to the union. Never, for a marriage in literary circles—so the newspapers described the alliance—had a lady been so bravely dowered. I began with due promptness to look for the fruit of the affair—that fruit, I mean, of which the premonitory symptoms would be peculiarly visible in the husband. Taking for granted the splendour of the other party's nuptial gift, I expected to see him make a show commensurate with his increase of means. I knew what his means had been—his article on "The Right of Way" had distinctly given one the figure. As he was now exactly in the position in which still more exactly I was not I watched from month to month, in the likely periodicals, for the heavy message poor Corvick had been unable to deliver and the responsibility of which would have fallen on his successor. The widow and wife would have broken by the rekindled hearth the silence that only a widow and wife might break, and Deane would be as aflame with the knowledge as Corvick in his own hour, as Gwendolen in hers, had been. Well, he was aflame doubtless, but the fire was apparently not to become a public blaze. I scanned the periodicals in vain: Drayton Deane filled them with exuberant pages, but he withheld the page I most feverishly sought. He wrote on a thousand subjects, but never on the subject of Vereker. His special line was to tell truths that other people either "funked," as he said, or overlooked, but he never told the only truth that seemed to me in these days to signify. I met the couple in those literary circles referred to in the papers: I have sufficiently intimated that it was only in such circles we were all constructed to revolve. Gwendolen was more than ever committed to them by the publication of her third novel, and I myself definitely classed by holding the opinion that this work was inferior to its immediate predecessor. Was it worse because she had been keeping worse company? If her secret was, as she had told me, her life—a fact discernible in her increasing bloom, an air of conscious privilege that, cleverly corrected by pretty charities, gave distinction to her appearance—it had yet not a direct influence on her work. That only made one—everything only made one—yearn the more for it; only rounded it off with a mystery finer and subtler.

## XI

It was therefore from her husband I could never remove my eyes: I beset him in a manner that might have made him uneasy. I went even so far as to engage him in conversation. *Didn't he know*, hadn't he come into it as a matter of course?—that question hummed in my brain. Of course he knew; otherwise he wouldn't return my stare so queerly. His wife had told him what I wanted and he was amiably amused at my impotence. He didn't laugh—he wasn't a laugher: his system was to present to my irritation, so that I should crudely expose myself, a conversational blank as vast as his big bare brow. It always happened that I turned away with a settled conviction from these unpeopled expanses, which seemed to complete each other geographically and to symbolise together Drayton Deane's want of voice, want of form. He simply hadn't the art to use what he knew; he literally was incompetent to take up the duty where Corvick had left it. I went still further—it was the only glimpse of happiness I had. I made up my mind that the duty didn't appeal to him. He wasn't interested, he didn't care. Yes, it quite comforted me to believe him too stupid to have joy of the thing I lacked. He was as stupid after as he had been before, and that deepened for me the golden glory in which the mystery was wrapped. I had of course none the less to recollect that his wife might have imposed her conditions and exactions. I had above all to remind myself that with Vereker's death the major incentive dropped. He was still there to be honoured by what might be done—he was no longer there to give it his sanction. Who alas but he had the authority?

Two children were born to the pair, but the second cost the mother her life. After this stroke I seemed to see another ghost of a chance. I jumped at it in thought, but I waited a certain time for manners, and at last my opportunity arrived in a remunerative way. His wife had been dead a year when I met Drayton Deane in the smoking-room of a small club of which we both were members, but where for months—perhaps because I rarely entered it—I hadn't seen him. The room was empty and the occasion propitious. I deliberately offered him, to have done with the matter for ever, that advantage for which I felt he had long been looking.

"As an older acquaintance of your late wife's than even you were," I began, "you must let me say to you something I have on my mind. I shall be glad to make any terms with you that you see fit to name for the information she must have had from George Corvick—the information, you know, that had come to *him,* poor chap, in one of the happiest hours of his life, straight from Hugh Vereker."

He looked at me like a dim phrenological bust. "The information—?"

"Vereker's secret, my dear man—the general intention of his books: the string the pearls were strung on, the buried treasure, the figure in the carpet."

He began to flush—the numbers on his bumps to come out. "Vereker's books had a general intention?"

I stared in my turn. "You don't mean to say you don't know it?" I thought for a moment he was playing with me. "Mrs. Deane knew it; she had it, as I say, straight from Corvick, who had, after infinite search and to Vereker's own delight, found the very mouth of the cave. Where *is* the mouth? He told after their marriage—and told alone—the person who, when the circumstances were reproduced, must have told *you.* Have I been wrong in taking for granted that she admitted you, as one of the highest privileges of the relation in which you stood to her, to the knowledge of which she was after Corvick's death the sole depository? All *I* know is that that knowledge is infinitely precious, and what I want you to understand is that if you'll in your turn admit me to it you'll do me a kindness for which I shall be lastingly grateful."

He had turned at last very red; I dare say he had begun by thinking I had lost my wits. Little by little he followed me; on my own side I stared with a livelier surprise. Then he spoke. "I don't know what you're talking about."

He wasn't acting—it was the absurd truth. "She *didn't* tell you—?"

"Nothing about Hugh Vereker."

I was stupefied; the room went round. It had been too good even for that! "Upon your honour?"

"Upon my honour. What the devil's the matter with you?" he growled.

"I'm astounded—I'm disappointed. I wanted to get it out of you."

"It isn't *in* me!" he awkwardly laughed. "And even if it were—"

"If it were you'd let me have it—oh yes, in

common humanity. But I believe you. I see—I see!" I went on, conscious, with the full turn of the wheel, of my great delusion, my false view of the poor man's attitude. What I saw, though I couldn't say it, was that his wife hadn't thought him worth enlightening. This struck me as strange for a woman who had thought him worth marrying. At last I explained it by the reflexion that she couldn't possibly have married him for his understanding. She had married him for something else.

He was to some extent enlightened now, but he was even more astonished, more disconcerted: he took a moment to compare my story with his quickened memories. The result of his meditation was his presently saying with a good deal of rather feeble form: "This is the first I hear of what you allude to. I think you must be mistaken as to Mrs. Drayton Deane's having had any unmentioned, and still less any unmentionable, knowledge of Hugh Vereker. She'd certainly have wished it—should it have borne on his literary character—to be used."

"It *was* used. She used it herself. She told me with her own lips that she 'lived' on it."

I had no sooner spoken than I repented of my words; he grew so pale that I felt as if I had struck him. "Ah 'lived'—!" he murmured, turning short away from me.

My compunction was real; I laid my hand on his shoulder. "I beg you to forgive me—I've made a mistake. You *don't* know what I thought you knew. You could, if I had been right, have rendered me a service; and I had my reasons for assuming that you'd be in a position to meet me."

"Your reasons?" he echoed. "What were your reasons?"

I looked at him well; I hesitated; I considered. "Come and sit down with me here and I'll tell you." I drew him to a sofa, I lighted another cigar and, beginning with the anecdote of Vereker's one descent from the clouds, I recited to him the extraordinary chain of accidents that had, in spite of the original gleam, kept me till that hour in the dark. I told him in a word just what I've written out here. He listened with deepening attention, and I became aware, to my surprise, by his ejaculations, by his questions, that he would have been after all not unworthy to be trusted by his wife. So abrupt an experience of her want of trust had now a disturbing effect on him; but I saw the immediate shock throb away little by little and then gather again into waves of wonder and curiosity—waves that promised, I could perfectly judge, to break in the end with the fury of my own highest tides. I may say that to-day as victims of unappeased desire there isn't a pin to choose between us. The poor man's state is almost my consolation; there are really moments when I feel it to be quite my revenge.

## Percy Bysshe Shelley
## OZYMANDIAS

I met a traveller from an antique land
Who said: Two vast and trunkless legs of stone
Stand in the desert ... Near them, on the sand,
Half sunk, a shattered visage lies, whose frown,
And wrinkled lip, and sneer of cold command,
Tell that its sculptor well those passions read
Which yet survive, stamped on these lifeless
    things,
The hand that mocked them, and the heart that
    fed:
And on the pedestal these words appear:
"My name is Ozymandias, king of kings:        10
Look on my works, ye Mighty, and despair!"
Nothing beside remains. Round the decay
Of that colossal wreck, boundless and bare
The lone and level sands stretch far away.

## John Keats
## ON FIRST LOOKING INTO CHAPMAN'S HOMER [12]

Much have I travelled in the realms of gold,
    And many goodly states and kingdoms seen;
    Round many western islands have I been
Which bards in fealty to Apollo hold.
Oft of one wide expanse had I been told
    That deep-browed Homer ruled as his
        demesne; [13]

---

[12] George Chapman, about 1559 to 1634, was the Elizabethan translator of Homer.
[13] Domain.

Yet did I never breathe its pure serene
Till I heard Chapman speak out loud and bold:
Then felt I like some watcher of the skies
    When a new planet swims into his ken;        10
Or like stout Cortez [14] when with eagle eyes
    He stared at the Pacific—and all his men
Looked at each other with a wild surmise—
    Silent, upon a peak in Darien. [15]

---

[14] Keats' history is at fault. It was not Cortez but Balboa who was the first European to look upon the Pacific Ocean.
[15] Panama.

## A. E. Housman
## TERENCE, THIS IS STUPID STUFF

"Terence, this is stupid stuff:
You eat your victuals fast enough;
There can't be much amiss, 'tis clear,
To see the rate you drink your beer.
But oh, good Lord, the verse you make,
It gives a chap the belly-ache.
The cow, the old cow, she is dead;
It sleeps well, the hornèd head:
We poor lads, 'tis our turn now
To hear such tunes as killed the cow.        10
Pretty friendship 'tis to rhyme
Your friends to death before their time
Moping melancholy mad:
Come, pipe a tune to dance to, lad."

Why, if 'tis dancing you would be,
There's brisker pipes than poetry.
Say, for what were hop-yards meant,
Or why was Burton built on Trent?
Oh, many a peer of England brews
Livelier liquor than the Muse,        20
And malt does more than Milton can
To justify God's ways to man.

---

Ale, man, ale's the stuff to drink
For fellows whom it hurts to think:
Look into the pewter pot
To see the world as the world's not.
And faith, 'tis pleasant till 'tis past:
The mischief is that 'twill not last.
Oh, I have been to Ludlow fair
And left my necktie God knows where,                30
And carried half-way home, or near,
Pints and quarts of Ludlow beer:
Then the world seemed none so bad,
And I myself a sterling lad;
And down in lovely muck I've lain,
Happy till I woke again.
Then I saw the morning sky:
Heigho, the tale was all a lie;
The world, it was the old world yet,
I was I, my things were wet,                        40
And nothing now remained to do
But begin the game anew.

Therefore, since the world has still
Much good, but much less good than ill,
And while the sun and moon endure
Luck's a chance, but trouble's sure,
I'd face it as a wise man would,
And train for ill and not for good.
'Tis true, the stuff I bring for sale
Is not so brisk a brew as ale:                      50
Out of a stem that scored the hand
I wrung it in a weary land.
But take it: if the smack is sour,
The better for the embittered hour;
It should do good to heart and head
When your soul is in my soul's stead;
And I will friend you, if I may,
In the dark and cloudy day.

There was a king reigned in the East:
There, when kings will sit to feast,                60
They get their fill before they think
With poisoned meat and poisoned drink.
He gathered all that springs to birth
From the many-venomed earth;
First a little, thence to more,
He sampled all her killing store;
And easy, smiling, seasoned sound,
Sate the king when healths went round.
They put arsenic in his meat
And stared aghast to watch him eat;                 70
They poured strychnine in his cup
And shook to see him drink it up:

They shook, they stared as white's their shirt:
Them it was their poison hurt.
—I tell the tale that I heard told.
Mithridates, he died old.

## W. H. Auden
# MUSÉE DES BEAUX ARTS [16]

About suffering they were never wrong,
The Old Masters: how well they understood
Its human position; how it takes place
While someone else is eating or opening a window
    or just walking dully along;
How, when the aged are reverently, passionately
    waiting
For the miraculous birth, there always must be
Children who did not specially want it to happen,
    skating
On a pond at the edge of the wood:
They never forgot
That even the dreadful martyrdom must run its
    course                                          10
Anyhow in a corner, some untidy spot
Where the dogs go on with their doggy life and the
    torturer's horse
Scratches its innocent behind on a tree.

In Brueghel's *Icarus,* for instance: how everything
    turns away
Quite leisurely from the disaster; the ploughman
    may
Have heard the splash, the forsaken cry,
But for him it was not an important failure; the
    sun shone
As it had to on the white legs disappearing into the
    green
Water; and the expensive delicate ship that must
    have seen
Something amazing, a boy falling out of the sky, 20
Had somewhere to get to and sailed calmly on.

------

    [16] Museum of Fine Arts; the name of the gallery in
Brussels which owns *The Fall of Icarus,* by Pieter
Brueghel the Elder (1520?–1569).

*Publius Ovidius Naso*

# PYGMALION

Pygmalion, loathing their lascivious life,
Abhorred all womankind, but most a wife;
So single chose to live, and shunned to wed,
Well pleased to want a consort of his bed;
Yet fearing idleness, the nurse of ill,
In sculpture exercised his happy skill,
And carved in ivory such a maid, so fair,
As Nature could not with his art compare,
Were she to work; but, in her own defence,
Must take her pattern here, and copy hence.     10
Pleased with his idol, he commends, admires,
Adores, and last, the thing adored desires:
A very virgin in her face was seen,
And had she moved, a living maid had been:
One would have thought she could have stirred,
     but strove
With modesty, and was ashamed to move:
Art hid with art, so well performed the cheat,
It caught the carver with his own deceit:
He knows 'tis madness, yet he must adore,
And still the more he knows it, loves the more.    20
The flesh, or what so seems, he touches oft,
Which feels so smooth that he believes it soft;
Fired with this thought, at once he strained the
     breast,
And on the lips a burning kiss impressed.
'Tis true, the hardened breast resists the gripe,
And the cold lips return a kiss unripe:
But when, retiring back, he looked again,
To think it ivory was a thought too mean;
With flattery now he seeks her mind to move,
And now with gifts (the powerful bribes of
     love):                                                      30
He furnishes her closet first, and fills
The crowded shelves with rarities of shells;
Adds orient pearls, which from the conchs he
     drew,
And all the sparkling stones of various hue;
And parrots, imitating human tongue,
And singing birds, in silver cages hung;
And every fragrant flower and odorous green
Were sorted well, with lumps of amber laid
     between:

---

Rich fashionable robes her person deck,
Pendants her ears, and pearls adorn her neck:    40
Her tapered fingers too with rings are graced,
And an embroidered zone surrounds her slender
     waist.
Thus like a queen arrayed, so richly dressed,
Beauteous she showed, but unadorned the best.
Then from the floor he raised a royal bed,
With coverings of Sidonian purple spread.
     The feast of Venus came, a solemn day,
To which the Cypriots due devotion pay;
With gilded horns the milk white heifers led,
Slaughtered before the sacred altars bled.       50
     Pygmalion offering, first approached the shrine,
And then with prayers implored the powers divine:
Almighty gods, if all we mortals want,
If all we can require, be yours to grant,
Make this fair statue mine, he would have said,
But changed his words for shame, and only prayed,
"Give me the likeness of my ivory maid."
     The golden goddess, present at the prayer,
Well knew he meant the inanimated fair,
And gave the sign of granting his desire;         60
For thrice in cheerful flames ascends the fire.
The youth, returning to his mistress hies,
And, impudent in hope, with ardent eyes,
And beating breast, by the dear statue lies.
He kisses her white lips, renews the bliss,
And looks, and thinks they redden at the kiss;
He thought them warm before, nor longer stays,
But next his hand on the hard substance lays;
Hard as it was, beginning to relent,
It seemed the block beneath his fingers bent:     70
He felt again—his fingers made a print,
'Twas flesh, but flesh so firm, it rose against the
     dint:
The pleasing task he fails not to renew—
Soft, and more soft, at every touch it grew;
Like pliant wax, when chafing hands reduce
The former mass to form, and frame for use.
He would believe, but yet is still in pain,
And tries his argument of sense again—
Presses the pulse, and feels the leaping vein:
Convinced, o'erjoyed, his studied thanks and
     praise,                                                    80
To her who made the miracle, he pays:
Then lips to lips he joined; now freed from fear,
He found the savor of the kiss sincere.
At this the wakened image oped her eyes,
And viewed at once the light and lover with
     surprise.
The goddess, present at the match she made,

---

PYGMALION: From *Metamorphoses,* Book X; translated by John Dryden.

So blessed the bed, such fruitfulness conveyed,
That ere ten months had sharpened either horn,
To crown their bliss, a lovely boy was born:
Paphos his name, who, grown to manhood, walled          90
The city Paphos, from the founder called.

## Archibald MacLeish
# ARS POETICA [17]

A poem should be palpable and mute
As a globed fruit

Dumb
As old medallions to the thumb

Silent as the sleeve-worn stone
Of casement ledges where the moss has grown—

A poem should be wordless
As the flight of birds

A poem should be motionless in time
As the moon climbs          10

Leaving, as the moon releases
Twig by twig the night-entangled trees,

Leaving, as the moon behind the winter leaves,
Memory by memory the mind—

A poem should be motionless in time
As the moon climbs

A poem should be equal to:
Not true

For all the history of grief
An empty doorway and a maple leaf          20

For love
The leaning grasses and two lights above the sea—

A poem should not mean
But be.

ARS POETICA: From *Poems 1924–1935*, by Archibald MacLeish. Copyright, 1925, 1926, 1928, 1932, 1933, by Archibald MacLeish. Used by permission of Houghton Mifflin Company.

[17] An allusion to the *Ars Poetica* ("Art of Poetry") of Horace (65–8 B.C.), which asserts that poems should instruct the reader as well as delighting him.

## John Peale Bishop
# SPEAKING OF POETRY

The ceremony must be found
That will wed Desdemona to the huge Moor.[18]

                              It is not enough—
To win the approval of the Senator
Or to outwit his disapproval; honest Iago
Can manage that: it is not enough. For then,
Though she may pant again in his black arms
(His weight resilient as a Barbary stallion's)
She will be found
When the ambassadors of the Venetian state arrive          10
Again smothered. These things have not been changed,
Not in three hundred years

                    (Tupping is still tupping
Though that particular word is obsolete.
Naturally, the ritual would not be in Latin.)

For though Othello had his blood from kings
His ancestry was barbarous, his ways African,
His speech uncouth. It must be remembered
That though he valued an embroidery—
Three mulberries proper on a silk like silver—          20
It was not for the subtlety of the stitches,
But for the magic in it. Whereas, Desdemona
Once contrived to imitate in needlework
Her father's shield, and plucked it out
Three times, to begin again, each time
With diminished colors. This is a small point
But indicative.

                    Desdemona was small and fair,
Delicate as a grasshopper
At the tag-end of summer: a Venetian          30
To her noble finger-tips.

                    O, it is not enough
That they should meet, naked, at dead of night

SPEAKING OF POETRY: Reprinted from *Now with His Love*, by John Peale Bishop. Copyright, 1933, by Charles Scribner's Sons. Used by permission of the publishers.

[18] For Shakespeare's *Othello*, see chapter 7.

In a small inn on a dark canal. Procurers
Less expert than Iago can arrange as much.

The ceremony must be found

Traditional, with all its symbols
Ancient as the metaphors in dreams;
Strange, with never before heard music; continuous
Until the torches deaden at the bedroom door.   40


### Marianne Moore
# POETRY

I, too, dislike it: there are things that are important beyond all this fiddle.
  Reading it, however, with a perfect contempt for it, one discovers in
  it after all, a place for the genuine.
      Hands that can grasp, eyes
      that can dilate, hair that can rise
          if it must, these things are important not because a

high-sounding interpretation can be put upon them but because they are
  useful. When they become so derivative as to become unintelligible,
  the same thing may be said for all of us, that we
      do not admire what                                                              10
      we cannot understand: the bat
          holding on upside down or in quest of something to

eat, elephants pushing, a wild horse taking a roll, a tireless wolf under
  a tree, the immovable critic twitching his skin like a horse that feels a flea, the baseball fan, the statistician—
      nor is it valid
          to discriminate against "business documents and

school-books"; all these phenomena are important. One must make a distinction
  however: when dragged into prominence by half poets, the result is not poetry,
  nor till the poets among us can be                                                  20
      "literalists of
      the imagination"—above
          insolence and triviality and can present

for inspection, imaginary gardens with real toads in them, shall we have
  it. In the meantime, if you demand on the one hand,
  the raw material of poetry in
      all its rawness and
      that which is on the other hand
          genuine, then you are interested in poetry.

---

# THE NATURE OF EVIL

P HILOSOPHERS and theologians sometimes question whether the evil that we seem to find in the world and in ourselves is a reality or an illusion. Those who agree with our common everyday experience that it is real enough, have pointed out profound problems raised by the existence of evil; for example, the problem of reconciling it with the assumed benevolence and omnipotence of God. Some of the works in this chapter view evil as a problem; some do not. All of them concern human beings who come face to face with the fact of evil in one form or another. They recognize it for the first time, in themselves or others; they wonder about its meaning in the universe or in human life.

Because conflict is essential to dramatic narrative, and a narrator can seldom withhold or balance his moral judgment perfectly, most stories and plays treat of good and evil in some form. One side in the conflict is regarded as wrong, or as less right than the other. In the simplest plots, as in a conflict between cowboys and Indians or cops and robbers, the good is all on one side, the evil on the other. Such works present the matter in very primitive terms. In more complicated works, the rights and wrongs are mixed, and the claims of justice may be more baffling.

Thus we see that an interest in ethics characterizes virtually all narratives. The writings in this chapter, however, concern evil in a more specific and exclusive sense. First, they show various kinds of evil that human beings have encountered: the defiance of a divine command, in Genesis and St. Augustine's *Confessions;* social injustice, in Blake's poem and "Act of Faith"; the inescapable fact of time and change, in "Spring and Fall"; the poison of pride and selfishness in the human will that is analyzed by Niebuhr and brought out in dif-

392

ferent ways in "Spotted Horses," "Crisis," and perhaps most of all in *Othello*. Second, these works show various ways in which human beings may react to the discovery of evil: Milton's resignation, Blake's passionate protest, Lewis Mumford's careful and wide-ranging attempt to work out a reasoned view of the place of evil in human life. These reactions, whether intellectual and abstract or immediate and emotional, are often embodied in symbols: for example, the snake, the tree of Eden, the black cat, the spotted horses, the beast in Robert Penn Warren's poem, and the "blond boy" in Auden's poem.

## From the Bible
## THE FALL OF MANKIND

### CHAPTER 1

In the beginning God created the heaven and the earth. And the earth was without form and void; and darkness was upon the face of the deep. And the Spirit of God moved upon the face of the waters.

And God said, Let there be light: and there was light. And God saw the light, that it was good: and God divided the light from the darkness. And God called the light Day, and the darkness he called Night. And the evening and the morning were the first day.

And God said, Let there be a firmament in the midst of the waters, and let it divide the waters from the waters. And God made the firmament, and divided the waters which were under the firmament from the waters which were above the firmament: and it was so. And God called the firmament Heaven. And the evening and the morning were the second day.

And God said, Let the waters under the heaven be gathered together unto one place, and let the dry land appear: and it was so. And God called the dry land Earth; and the gathering together of the waters called he Seas: and God saw that it was good. And God said, Let the earth bring forth grass, the herb yielding seed, and the fruit tree yielding fruit after his kind, whose seed is in itself, upon the earth: and it was so. And the earth brought forth grass, and herb yielding seed after his kind, and the tree yielding fruit, whose seed was in itself, after his kind: and God saw that it was good. And the evening and the morning were the third day.

THE FALL OF MANKIND: From *The Book of Genesis,* chapters 1-3.

And God said, Let there be lights in the firmament of the heaven to divide the day from the night; and let them be for signs, and for seasons, and for days, and years: and let them be for lights in the firmament of the heaven to give light upon the earth: and it was so. And God made two great lights; the greater light to rule the day, and the lesser light to rule the night: he made the stars also. And God set them in the firmament of the heaven to give light upon the earth, and to rule over the day and over the night and to divide the light from the darkness: and God saw that it was good. And the evening and morning were the fourth day. And God said, Let the waters bring forth abundantly the moving creature that hath life, and fowl that may fly above the earth in the open firmament of heaven. And God created great whales and every living creature that moveth, which the waters brought forth abundantly after their kind, and every winged fowl after his kind: and God saw that it was good. And God blessed them saying, Be fruitful, and multiply, and fill the waters in the seas, and let fowl multiply in the earth. And the evening and the morning were the fifth day.

And God said, Let the earth bring forth the living creature after his kind, cattle, and creeping thing, and beast of the earth after his kind: and it was so. And God made the beast of the earth after his kind, and cattle after their kind, and every thing that creepeth upon the earth after his kind: and God saw that it was good.

And God said, Let us make man in our image, after our likeness: and let them have dominion over the fish of the sea, and over the fowl of the air, and over the cattle, and over all the earth, and over every creeping thing that creepeth upon the earth. So God created man in his own image, in the image of God created he him; male and female created he them. And God blessed them, and God said unto them,

Be fruitful, and multiply, and replenish the earth, and subdue it: and have dominion over the fish of the sea, and over the fowl of the air, and over every living thing that moveth upon the earth.

And God said, Behold, I have given you every herb bearing seed, which is upon the face of all the earth, and every tree in which is the fruit of a tree yielding seed; to you it shall be for meat. And to every beast of the earth, and to every fowl of the air, and to every thing that creepeth upon the earth, wherein there is life, I have given every green herb for meat: and it was so. And God saw every thing that he had made, and behold, it was very good. And the evening and the morning were the sixth day.

## CHAPTER 2

Thus the heavens and the earth were finished, and all the host of them. And on the seventh day God ended his work which he had made; and he rested on the seventh day from all his work which he had made. And God blessed the seventh day, and sanctified it: because that in it he had rested from all his work which God created and made.

These are the generations of the heavens and of the earth when they were created, in the day that the Lord God made the earth and the heavens, and every plant of the field before it was in the earth, and every herb of the field before it grew: for the Lord God had not caused it to rain upon the earth, and there was not a man to till the ground. But there went up a mist from the earth, and watered the whole face of the ground. And the Lord God formed man of the dust of the ground, and breathed into his nostrils the breath of life; and man became a living soul.

And the Lord God planted a garden eastward in Eden; and there he put the man whom he had formed. And out of the ground made the Lord God to grow every tree that is pleasant to the sight, and good for food; the tree of life also in the midst of the garden, and the tree of knowledge of good and evil. And a river went out of Eden to water the garden; and from thence it was parted, and became into four heads. The name of the first is Pison: that is it which compasseth the whole land of Havilah, where there is gold; and the gold of that land is good: there is bdellium and the onyx stone. And the name of the second river is Gihon: the same is it that compasseth the whole land of Ethiopia. And the name of the third river is Hiddekel: that is it which goeth toward the east of Assyria. And the fourth river is Euphrates. And the Lord God took the man, and put him into the garden of Eden to dress it and to keep it. And the Lord God commanded the man, saying, Of every tree of the garden thou mayest freely eat: but of the tree of knowledge of good and evil, thou shalt not eat of it; for in the day that thou eatest thereof thou shalt surely die.

And the Lord God said, It is not good that the man should be alone; I will make him an help meet for him. And out of the ground the Lord God formed every beast of the field, and every fowl of the air; and brought them unto Adam to see what he would call them: and whatsoever Adam called every living creature, that was the name thereof. And Adam gave names to all cattle, and to the fowl of the air, and to every beast of the field; but for Adam there was not found an help meet for him. And the Lord God caused a deep sleep to fall upon Adam, and he slept: and he took one of his ribs, and closed up the flesh instead thereof; and the rib, which the Lord God had taken from man, made he a woman, and brought her unto the man. And Adam said, This is now bone of my bones, and flesh of my flesh; she shall be called Woman, because she was taken out of Man. Therefore shall a man leave his father and his mother, and shall cleave unto his wife: and they shall be one flesh. And they were both naked, the man and his wife, and were not ashamed.

## CHAPTER 3

Now the serpent was more subtil than any beast of the field which the Lord God had made. And he said unto the woman, Yea, hath God said, Ye shall not eat of every tree of the garden? And the woman said unto the serpent, We may eat of the fruit of the trees of the garden: but of the fruit of the tree which is in the midst of the garden, God hath said, Ye shall not eat of it, neither shall ye touch it, lest ye die. And the serpent said unto the woman, Ye shall not surely die: for God doth know that in the day ye eat thereof, then your eyes shall be opened, and ye shall be as gods, knowing good and evil. And when the woman saw that the tree was good for food, and that it was pleasant to the eyes, and a tree to be desired to make one wise, she took of the fruit thereof, and did eat, and gave also unto her husband with her; and he did eat. And the eyes of them both were opened, and they knew that they were naked; and they sewed fig leaves together, and made themselves aprons. And they heard the voice of the Lord God walking in the garden in the cool of the day: and Adam and his wife hid themselves from the presence of the Lord God amongst the trees of the garden. And the Lord God called unto Adam, and said unto him, Where art thou? And he said, I heard thy voice in the garden, and I was afraid, because I was naked; and I hid myself. And he said, Who told thee that thou wast naked? Hast thou eaten of the tree, whereof I commanded thee that thou shouldest not eat? And the man said, The woman whom thou gavest to be with me, she gave me of the tree, and I did eat. And the Lord God said unto the woman, What is this that thou hast done? And the woman said, The serpent beguiled me, and I did eat. And the Lord God said unto the serpent, Because thou hast done this thou art cursed above all cattle, and above every beast of the field; upon thy belly shalt thou go and dust shalt thou eat all the days of thy life: and I will put enmity between thee and the woman, and between thy seed and her seed; it shall bruise thy head, and thou shalt bruise his heel. Unto the woman he said, I will greatly multiply thy sorrow and thy conception; in sorrow thou shalt bring forth children; and thy desire shall be to thy husband, and he shall rule over thee. And unto Adam he said, Because thou hast hearkened unto the voice of thy wife, and hast eaten of the tree, of which I commanded thee, saying, Thou shalt not eat of it: cursed is the ground for thy sake; in sorrow shalt thou eat of it all the days of thy life; thorns also and thistles shall it bring forth to thee; and thou shalt eat the herb of the field; in the sweat of thy face shalt thou eat bread, till thou return unto the ground; for out of it wast thou taken; for dust thou art, and unto dust shalt thou return. And Adam called his wife's name Eve; because she was the mother of all living. Unto Adam also and to his wife did the Lord God make coats of skins, and clothed them.

And the Lord God said, Behold, the man is become as one of us, to know good and evil: and now, lest he put forth his hand, and take also of the tree of life, and eat, and live for ever: therefore the Lord God sent him forth from the garden of Eden, to till the ground from whence he was taken. So he drove out the man; and he placed at the east of the garden of Eden Cherubims, and a flaming sword which turned every way, to keep the way of the tree of life.

## *St. Augustine*
# WHY I STOLE

Theft is punished by Thy Law, O Lord, and the law written in the hearts of men, which iniquity itself effaces not. For what thief will abide a thief? not even a rich thief, one stealing through want. Yet I lusted to thieve, and did it, compelled by no hunger, nor poverty, but through a cloyedness of well-doing, and a pamperedness of iniquity. For I stole that, of which I had enough, and much better. Nor cared I to enjoy what I stole, but joyed in the theft and sin itself. A pear tree there was near our vineyard, laden with fruit, tempting neither for colour nor taste. To shake and rob this, some lewd young fellows of us went, late one night (having according to our pestilent custom prolonged our sports in the streets till then), and took huge loads, not for our eating, but to fling to the very hogs, having only tasted them. And this, but to do what we liked only, because it was misliked. Behold my heart, O God, behold my heart, which Thou hadst pity upon in the bottom of the bottomless pit. Now, behold let my heart tell Thee what it sought there, that I should be gratuitously evil, having no temptation to ill, but the ill itself. It was foul, and I loved it; I loved to perish, I loved mine own fault, not that for which I was faulty, but my fault itself. Foul soul, falling from Thy firmament to utter destruction: not seeking aught through the shame, but the shame itself!

For there is an attractiveness in beautiful bodies, in gold and silver, and all things; and

WHY I STOLE: From *Confessions,* Book II. Translated by Edward B. Pusey for the *Harvard Classics.* Used by permission of P. F. Collier & Son Corporation.

in bodily touch, sympathy hath much influence, and each other sense hath his proper object answerably tempered. Worldly honour hath also its grace, and the power of overcoming, and of mastery; whence springs also the thirst for revenge. But yet, to obtain all these, we may not depart from Thee, O Lord, nor decline from Thy law. The life also which here we live hath its own enchantment, through a certain proportion of its own, and a correspondence with all things beautiful here below. Human friendship also is endeared with a sweet tie by reason of the unity formed of many souls. Upon occasion of all these, and the like, is sin committed, while through an immoderate inclination towards these goods of the lowest order, the better and higher are forsaken,— Thou, our Lord God, Thy truth, and Thy law. For these lower things have their delights, but not like my God, who made all things; for *in Him doth the righteous delight, and He is the joy of the upright in heart.*[1]

When, then, we ask why a crime was done, we believe it not, unless it appear that there might have been some desire of obtaining some of those which we called lower goods, or a fear of losing them. For they are beautiful and comely; although compared with those higher and beatific goods, they be abject and low. A man hath murdered another; why? he loved his wife or his estate; or would rob for his own livelihood; or feared to lose some such things by him; or, wronged, was on fire to be revenged. Would any commit murder upon no cause, delighted simply in murdering? who would believe it? for as for that furious and savage man, of whom it is said that he was gratuitously evil and cruel, yet is the cause assigned; "lest" (saith he) "through idleness hand or heart should grow inactive." And to what end? that, through that practice of guilt, he might, having taken the city, attain to honours, empire, riches, and be freed from fear of the laws, and his embarrassments from domestic needs, and consciousness of villainies. So then, not even Catiline himself loved his own villainies, but something else, for whose sake he did them.

What then did wretched I so love in thee, thou theft of mine, thou deed of darkness, in that sixteenth year of my age? Lovely thou wert

not, because thou wert theft. But art thou any thing, that thus I speak to thee? Fair were the pears we stole, because they were Thy creation, Thou fairest of all, Creator of all, Thou good God; God, the sovereign good and my true good. Fair were those pears, but not them did my wretched soul desire; for I had store of better, and those I gathered, only that I might steal. For, when gathered, I flung them away, my only feast therein being my own sin, which I was pleased to enjoy. For if aught of those pears came within my mouth, what sweetened it was the sin. And now, O Lord my God, I enquire what in that theft delighted me; and behold it hath no loveliness; I mean not such loveliness as in justice and wisdom; nor such as is in the mind and memory, and senses, and animal life of man; nor yet as the stars are glorious and beautiful in their orbs; or the earth, or sea, full of embryo-life, replacing by its birth that which decayeth; nay, nor even that false and shadowy beauty which belongeth to deceiving vices.

For so doth pride imitate exaltedness; whereas Thou alone art God exalted over all. Ambition, what seeks it, but honours and glory? whereas Thou alone art to be honoured above all, and glorious for evermore. The cruelty of the great would fain be feared; but who is to be feared but God alone, out of whose power what can be wrested or withdrawn? when, or where, or whither, or by whom? The tenderness of the wanton would fain be counted love: yet is nothing more tender than Thy charity; nor is aught loved more healthfully than that Thy truth, bright and beautiful above all. Curiosity makes semblance of a desire of knowledge; whereas Thou supremely knowest all. Yea, ignorance and foolishness itself is cloaked under the name of simplicity and uninjuriousness; because nothing is found more single than Thee: and what less injurious, since they are his own works which injure the sinner? Yea, sloth would fain be at rest; but what stable rest besides the Lord? Luxury affects to be called plenty and abundance; but Thou art the fulness and never-failing plenteousness of incorruptible pleasures. Prodigality presents a shadow of liberality; but Thou art the most overflowing Giver of all good. Covetousness would possess many things: and Thou possesseth all things. Envy disputes for excellency; what more excellent

---

[1] Psalms 64.10.

than Thou? Anger seeks revenge: who revenges more justly than Thou? Fear startles at things unwonted and sudden, which endanger things beloved, and takes forethought for their safety; but to Thee what unwonted or sudden, or who separateth from Thee what Thou lovest? [2] Or where but with Thee is unshaken safety? Grief pines away for things lost, the delight of its desires; because it would have nothing taken from it, as nothing can from Thee.

Thus doth the soul commit fornication, when she turns from Thee, seeking without Thee, what she findeth not pure and untainted, till she returns to Thee. Thus all pervertedly imitate Thee, who remove far from Thee, and lift themselves up against Thee. But even by thus imitating Thee, they imply Thee to be the Creator of all nature; whence there is no place whither altogether to retire from Thee. What then did I love in that theft? and wherein did I even corruptly and pervertedly imitate my Lord? Did I wish even by stealth to do contrary to Thy law, because by power I could not, so that being a prisoner, I might mimic a maimed liberty by doing with impunity things unpermitted me, a darkened likeness of Thy Omnipotency? Behold, Thy servant, fleeing from his Lord, and obtaining a shadow.[3] O rottenness, O monstrousness of life, and depth of death! could I like what I might not, only because I might not?

*What shall I render unto the Lord,*[4] that, whilst my memory recalls these things, my soul is not affrighted at them? *I will love Thee, O Lord, and thank Thee, and confess unto Thy name;* because Thou hast forgiven me these so great and heinous deeds of mine. To Thy grace I ascribe it, and to Thy mercy, that Thou hast melted away my sins as it were ice. To Thy grace I ascribe also whatsoever I have not done of evil; for what might I not have done, who even loved a sin for its own sake? Yea, all I confess to have been forgiven me; both what evils I committed by own wilfulness, and what by Thy guidance I committed not. What man is he, who, weighing his own infirmity, dares to ascribe his purity and innocency to his own strength; that so he should love Thee the less, as if he had less needed Thy mercy, whereby

Thou remittest sins to those that turn to Thee? For whosoever, called by Thee, followed Thy voice, and avoided those things which he reads me recalling and confessing of myself, let him not scorn me, who being sick was cured by that Physician, through whose aid it was that he was not, or rather was less, sick: and for this let him love Thee as much, yea and more; since by whom he sees me to have been recovered from such deep consumption of sin, by Him he sees himself to have been from the like consumption of sin preserved.

*What fruit had I then* (wretched man!) *in those things, of the remembrance whereof I am now ashamed?* [5] Especially, in that theft which I loved for the theft's sake; and it too was nothing, and therefore the more miserable I, who loved it. Yet alone I had not done it: such was I then, I remember, alone I had never done it. I loved then in it also the company of the accomplices, with whom I did it? I did not then love nothing else but the theft, yea rather I did love nothing else; for that circumstance of the company was also nothing. What is, in truth? who can teach me, save He that enlighteneth my heart, and discovereth its dark corners? What is it which hath come into my mind to enquire, and discuss, and consider? For had I then loved the pears I stole, and wished to enjoy them, I might have done it alone, had the bare commission of the theft sufficed to attain my pleasure; nor needed I have inflamed the itching of my desires by the excitement of accomplices. But since my pleasure was not in those pears, it was in the offence itself, which the company of fellow-sinners occasioned.

What then was this feeling? For of a truth it was too foul: and woe was me, who had it. But yet what was it? *Who can understand his errors?* [6] It was the sport, which as it were tickled our hearts, that we beguiled those who little thought what we were doing, and much disliked it. Why then was my delight of such sort that I did it not alone? Because none doth ordinarily laugh alone? ordinarily no one; yet laughter sometimes masters men alone and singly when no one whatever is with them, if any thing very ludicrous presents itself to their senses or mind. Yet I had not done this alone; alone I had never done it. Behold my God,

[2] Romans 8.9.
[3] Jonah 1.4.
[4] Psalms 116.12.

[5] Romans 6.21.
[6] Psalms 19.12.

before Thee, the vivid remembrance of my soul; alone, I had never committed that theft wherein what I stole pleased me not, but that I stole; nor had it alone liked me to do it, nor had I done it. O friendship too unfriendly! thou incomprehensible inveigler of the soul, thou greediness to do mischief out of mirth and wantonness, thou thirst of others' loss, without lust of my own gain or revenge: but when it is said, "Let's go, let's do it," we are ashamed not to be shameless.

Who can disentangle that twisted and intricate knottiness? Foul is it: I hate to think on it, to look on it. But Thee I long for, O Righteousness and Innocency, beautiful and comely to all pure eyes, and of a satisfaction unsating. With Thee is rest entire, and life imperturbable. Whoso enters into Thee, *enters into the joy of his Lord:* [7] and shall not fear, and shall do excellently in the All-Excellent. I sank away from Thee, and I wandered, O my God, too much astray from Thee my stay, in these days of my youth, and I became to myself a barren land.

-------

[7] Matthew 25.21.

*Reinhold Niebuhr*
# THE NEMESIS OF NATIONS

"*And it came to pass in the eleventh year, in the third month, in the first day of the month, that the word of the Lord came unto me, saying, Son of man, say unto Pharaoh king of Egypt, and to his multitude; Whom art thou like in thy greatness? Behold, the Assyrian was a cedar in Lebanon with fair branches, and with a shadowing shroud, and of high stature; and his top was among the thick boughs. The waters made him great, the deep set him up on high with her rivers running round about his plants; and sent out her little rivers unto all the trees of the field. Therefore his height was exalted above all the trees of the field, and his boughs were multiplied, and his branches be-*

-------

THE NEMESIS OF NATIONS: Reprinted from *Discerning the Signs of the Times,* by Reinhold Niebuhr. Copyright, 1946, by Charles Scribner's Sons. Used by permission of the publishers.

*came long because of the multitude of waters, when he shot forth. All the fowls of heaven made their nests in his boughs, and under his branches did all the beasts of the field bring forth their young; and under his shadow dwelt all great nations. Thus was he fair in his greatness, in the length of his branches: for his root was by great waters. The cedars in the garden of God could not hide him: the fir trees were not like his boughs, and the chestnut trees were like his branches; nor any tree in the garden of God was like unto him in his beauty. I have made him fair by the multitude of his branches: so that all the trees of Eden, that were in the garden of God, envied him.*

"*Therefore thus said the Lord God; Because thou hast lifted up thyself in height, and he hath shot up his top among the thick boughs, and his heart is lifted up in his height: I have therefore delivered him into the hand of the mighty one of the heathen; he shall surely deal with him; I have driven him out for his wickedness. And strangers, the terrible of the nations, have cut him off, and have left him: upon the mountains and in all the valleys his branches are broken, and his boughs are broken by all the rivers of the land; and all the people of the earth are gone down from his shadow, and have left him. Upon his ruin shall all the fowls of the heaven remain, and all the beasts of the field shall be upon his branches: To the end that none of all the trees by the waters exalt themselves for their height, neither shoot up their top among the thick boughs, neither their trees stand up in their height, all that drink water: for they are all delivered unto death, to the nether parts of the earth, in the midst of the children of men, with them that go down to the pit.*" Ezek. 31:1-14.

## I

This parable of the trees is one of a series of judgments upon the nations which the prophet Ezekiel proclaimed in the name of God. It was one of the distinctive aspects of Hebraic prophecy that it did not think of the judgment of God as resting primarily upon the enemies and competitors of Israel. For the prophets the divine judgment fell first of all upon Israel, the chosen nation. "You only have I known of all the families of the earth," declares the prophet Amos in the name of the Lord, "therefore I will punish you for all your iniquities." But the prophetic idea of judgment became more and more universal and the whole of history was regarded as moving under God's providence. Under this providence each of the nations could, upon occasion, become the instrument of God's designs in history, even if, as in the case of Persia under Cyrus, it was not consciously seeking to perform God's will.

However, each of the nations would also, in turn, fall under the divine condemnation. The cause of this condemnation was always the same. They exalted themselves above measure, and engaged in pretensions which exceeded the bounds of human mortality. Thus Ezekiel proclaims the judgment of God upon Tyre, "Because thine heart is lifted up, and thou hast said, I am a God, I sit in the seat of God, in the midst of the seas; yet thou art a man, and not God;—thine heart is lifted up because of thy riches,—behold, therefore, I will bring strangers upon thee, the terrible of the nations: and they shall draw their swords against the beauty of thy wisdom, and they shall defile thy brightness. They shall bring thee down to the pit. . . . Wilt thou yet say before him that slayeth thee, I am God? but thou shalt be a man, and no God, in the hand of him that slayeth thee." [8]

The prophetic judgments against the nations are always prompted by their pride, which seeks to hide the common human frailty of all achievements and constructions of men, or which denies the divine source of their power and pretends that their position among the nations is due altogether to their own achievements. Thus in the parable of our text, Assyria is compared to a tree which grows by the waters and "the waters made him great, the deep set him up on high"; but the nation forgot that it was the providence of God which made him "fair in his greatness, in the length of his branches." The nation will therefore be delivered to judgment "To the end that none of all the trees by the waters exalt themselves for their height"—nor that the mighty ones "stand up in their height—for they are all delivered unto death."

In the case of Egypt, a civilization which rested upon the fecundity produced by the Nile's periodic overflow, the pride takes the form of assuming that what has been given it as a special gift of grace is really its own achievement, and therefore belongs completely to itself. The divine judgment runs: "Behold, I am against thee, Pharaoh king of Egypt, the great dragon that lieth in the midst of his rivers, which hath said, My river is mine own, and I have made it for myself. But I will put hooks in thy jaws . . . And I will leave thee thrown into the wilderness." [9]

The theme which underlies the prophetic judgment upon the nations is thus the idea that "nemesis" overtakes the nations because mortal men contend against God. They seek to make themselves stronger than mortal men have a right to be; and they pretend to be wiser than mortal men are. They come thus in conflict with the divine prerogatives. It may take a long while, but in the end the Divine Avenger humbles these human pretensions and brings all false majesties of history "into the pit" "to the end that none of all the trees by the waters exalt themselves for their height."

This theme is not confined to the prophets. It is one of the basic themes of the Bible. In the Genesis myth of the Fall it is suggested that false pride lies at the foundation of human sin. Man sought to penetrate to the final mystery of the "tree of the knowledge of good and evil," which, alone among the trees of the garden, was forbidden to him. That was the cause of his Fall. In the profound parable of the Tower of Babel, we are told that men sought to build a structure "whose top may reach unto heaven," and "make us a name." God is pictured as jealous of this human effort, declaring "now nothing will be restrained from them, which they have imagined to do." Therefore he confounded their language and "scattered them abroad from thence upon the face of all the earth." [10]

Nor does the New Testament lack the same interpretation of the ultimate issue between man and God. St. Paul defines sin as man's effort to change "the glory of the uncorruptible God into an image made like to corruptible man" [11] and in his second letter to the Corinthians he defines the warfare of Christians as "casting down imaginations, and every high thing that exalteth itself against the knowledge

---

[8] Ezekiel 28.2,5,7,8,9.

[9] Ezekiel 29.3–5.
[10] Genesis 11.4,6,8.
[11] Romans 1.23.

of God, and bringing into captivity every thought to the obedience of Christ." [12] There is thus in biblical thought in general a perpetual theme of warning to men and nations "not to think of themselves more highly than they ought to think." These warnings express the uneasiness of the human soul, when informed by a profound faith, over the tendency of man to hide his weakness with a false show of strength; or to forget his limitations in the knowledge of his real, yet always limited, strength. This uneasiness is accomplished by a sense of judgment and doom. It is felt that ultimately any man or nation who seeks to usurp the place of God will be brought low. The ultimate majesty which rules the world will be able to subdue all false majesties. God, who is the Creator and Judge of the whole of life, has the power to put down any rebellion of the various parts of life which make themselves into the whole. In the judgments of the prophet Ezekiel, of which our text is one, the justification for the various judgments upon the various proud nations is always that in "that day" of judgment "they may know that I am the Lord."

## II

This theme of the contest between a jealous God and the pride and pretension of men is not limited to biblical thought. It is a recurring motif in Greek tragedy. The very word NEMESIS, which is generally used to describe the fate of arrogance, is derived from Greek thought. Nemesis is the consequence of pride (HYBRIS). The theme is most explicitly presented in the Promethean myth, though not confined to it. Prometheus was, it will be remembered, the demi-god who aroused the jealousy of Zeus by teaching men the use of fire. In Greek tragedy the heroes are warned again and again (frequently by words spoken by the chorus) not to arouse the anger of Zeus by attempting feats which are beyond the limit of mortal men, or by making pretensions which are in conflict with the pride of Zeus.

There is one significant difference between the manner in which this theme is handled in Greek tragedy and its development in biblical thought. In Greek drama we are never quite certain whether Zeus's jealousy is an unwar-

ranted divine egotism, seeking to prevent men from developing their full capacities for the sake of preserving the unchallenged character of the divine power, or whether it is the justified anger of the guardian of the whole against the anarchic pretensions of the various parts of life. Sophocles seems to come nearest to the perception of the biblical idea that the jealousy of Zeus is not some unwarranted divine caprice, but the expression of the power of ultimate order against those vitalities of life which seek to make themselves the false center of that order.

This ambivalence of Greek tragedy would seem at first blush to take the complexity of the human situation into account more adequately than the biblical account. It would seem particularly to do justice to the fact that all human powers and all extensions of these powers are creative, as well as destructive. The taming of fire was a necessary step in human civilization; and Zeus's anger against Prometheus would therefore seem to be unjustified. The "knowledge of good and evil" is a necessary expression of the final "freedom of the human spirit" and the building of towers "whose top may reach into heaven" is a necessary expression of the human skill which has raised man from complete dependence upon nature to a relative mastery of nature.

The extension of human powers is the basis of the progressive character of human history. Every new conquest of nature and every new elaboration of human skills means that human actions and responsibilities are set in the context of a wider field. This is the creative side of human history. Yet every new mastery of nature and every enlargement of human powers is also the new occasion for pride and a fresh temptation to human arrogance. If biblical thought seems to neglect the creative aspect of the extension of human powers in its prophecies of doom upon proud nations, this is due only to the fact that it is more certain than is Greek thought that, whatever the creative nature of human achievements, there is always a destructive element in human power. The Bible is so certain of this because it is more certain of the majesty of God and more sure of the justice of His jealousy. It is certain that there is one God, and that "it is he that hath made us and not we ourselves," and that His majesty transcends all human majesties. It is

---

[12] II Corinthians 10.5.

also certain that all human majesties and powers claim a more central position in the scheme of things than is their rightful due. It understands, in other words, the tragedy of sin without denying the creative character of human achievements. It knows that jealousy of God is not the caprice of one life in competition with other life. It is rather the justice of the Lord of life against the pretentious attempts of little forms of life "To the end that none of all the trees by the waters exalt themselves for their height,"—nor that the mighty ones "stand up in their height—for they are all delivered unto death."

## III

Living in an age of atomic energy and of total wars, it seems almost fantastic to think that men of any other age should have considered the perils of human pride and the temptations of human power. There were, to be sure, great empires in those days; and their rulers claimed divine majesty. But these ancient civilizations, resting upon a simple agrarian economy, were infantile in their strength compared to the power which modern men and nations have achieved through the technics of modern civilization. If the human situation warranted the warnings of the prophets in those days, how much more are those warnings justified in our day! There is in fact no greater proof of the perennial relevance of the biblical analysis of the meaning of life than that the course of history seems to make it ever more true. While our modern culture rested upon the assumption that the elaboration of human powers would be almost exclusively creative and would guarantee the achievement of ever wider and more inclusive human communities, our modern civilization produced an atomic bomb—the first effect of which can only be to sharpen the conflict of nations and to tempt nations to new forms of pride and arrogance. The atomic bomb is the most telling proof of the perpetual relevance of the biblical warnings; and even of their ever-increasing relevance as human powers increase, while the essential finiteness of the agents who wield these powers does not change.

The most immediate relevance of the prophetic promise of doom upon the trees that "exalt themselves for their height" is, of course, the ignominious end of proud dictators and "master" races, who sought only yesterday to enthrall the world and who are today completely humiliated and defeated. In one fateful week of the year 1945, one dictator died an obscene death in expiation for an obscenely ambitious life; and another died in the violence which his life had breathed. Whatever the sins of other nations, those nations were still good enough to be executors of divine judgment upon the impossible pretensions of power of these dictators and of the nations who had followed their beguilements. We are not wrong if we sense, beyond and above the purely political dimensions of the drama of these years, a deeper and more divine dimension. One can almost hear God speaking through Ezekiel to these nations: "Wilt thou yet say before him that slayeth thee, I am God? but thou shalt be a man, and no God, in the hand of him that slayeth thee."

The most obvious relevance of the biblical conception of the contest between God and man is thus the explicit doom which has descended upon nations which have most explicitly defied the proper limits of all human agencies which "are all delivered unto death," and which have tried most idolatrously to usurp the place of the divine. Yet it would be very superficial to apply this prophecy of judgment only to our enemies. We do well to remember how great the power of the victorious nations is, and what temptations lurk in the possession of this power.

We did not contrive, as the Nazis did, to bring other nations completely in our power; but we do well to consider that the defeated nations are, in fact, in our power; and that the possession of absolute power is a peril to justice.

No man or nation is wise or good enough to hold the power which the great nations in the victorious alliance hold without being tempted to both pride and injustice. Pride is the religious dimension of the sin which flows from absolute power; and injustice is its social dimension. The great nations speak so glibly of their passion for justice and peace; and so obviously betray interests which contradict justice and peace. This is precisely the kind of spiritual pride which the prophets had in mind when they pronounced divine judgment upon the nations which said, "I am god, I sit in the seat of God." Consider how blandly the victorious nations draw plans for destroying the economic and political life of defeated nations in the hope of rebuilding them as democracies "from the ground up." This lack of consideration for the organic aspects of the social existence of other nations, this confidence in our ability to create something better by our fiat, is a perfect illustration of the pride of power. It is not made any more sufferable by the idea that we are doing all this for the sake of "purging" the defeated nations of their evil and bestowing our "democracy" upon them. The very absurdity of bestowing democracy by the will of the conqueror contains the pretension against which the prophets inveighed.

## IV

But neither the doom which has already fallen upon the pride of dictators, nor the impending doom which must fall upon the pride of the victors, is the most obvious point of relevance between the biblical theme of the contest between God and man and the experience of our own day. The most obvious point of relevance lies in the fact that several centuries of technical achievement have been crowned with the discovery of methods for releasing atomic energy. This new discovery crowns the creative achievements of a technical society which has increased man's mastery of nature immeasurably and which has enhanced the power of all human vitalities. But the new discovery also crowns the pretensions of modern civilization; it gives man a power which obscures his weakness. And it is a dangerous new power precisely because it is given to some men and some nations who are actually in competition with other nations; but who will seek by this power to place themselves above this competition.

The contradiction between the greatness of the power in the hands of modern men and nations, and the weakness and mortality of the agencies which wield the power, is commonly interpreted as a contradiction between the perfection of the natural sciences and the imperfection of the social sciences; or as a contrast between the scientific and the moral achievements of men. But these contrasts are due to something more than a cultural lag. They reach down to the very paradox of human existence: the greatness and the weakness of man. This paradox becomes progressively more dangerous because man's powers are continually increasing and yet man's essential weakness remains the same.

A nation which has the power to annihilate other nations does not achieve, as a concomitant of that power, the transcendent wisdom which would make it the safe custodian of such power. The possession of this power by a group of nations has the immediate prospects of peace because it will make other nations reluctant to challenge the possessors. Yet there are no ultimate promises of peace in the possession of such power by a nation or a group of nations; because other nations will resent this exclusive possession; will rightly or wrongly question the justice of the policies which are dictated by it; and will seek to come into the possession of the same power or of some other secret equally potent and dangerous.

Ultimately, of course, the increase in the power of human destructiveness must make for the organization of the world community. The destructive power has become so great that it threatens the nations with mutual annihilation. It may be, therefore, that the fear of such annihilation will persuade them to moderate their pride and their inclination to cling to the momentary advantages of the possession of disproportionate power. Whether this will be accomplished before men taste, even more than they have done, the terror of modern warfare; whether they must be brought to the very brink of disaster before they will seek to bring great power under the agency of the most impartial instruments of government which human ingenuity can devise, depends upon the degree to which they sense and anticipate the NEMESIS which threatens all human pretensions.

The point of the prophetic anticipations of doom was always partly to avoid the doom by inducing a humble and contrite anticipation of it. There are always possibilities of "fleeing the wrath which is to come." Our generation has been given such a possibility even as it is confronted with a kind of wrath more terrible than that faced by previous generations.

The kind of humility which is required of the nations to meet the possession of the new powers in their possession may be partly achieved by a shrewd political intelligence, which is able to measure the probable effect of certain policies upon attitudes of other nations. It is possible, for instance, for a shrewd political observer to know in advance that the display of power by a single nation or group of nations can not permanently secure the acquiescence of other nations. But ultimately this humility is a religious achievement. Rather it is not so much an achievement as it is a gift of grace, a by-product of the faith which discerns life in its total dimension and senses the divine judgment which stands above and against all human judgments; and of the divine majesty which is justifiably jealous of human pretensions. The more men and nations fear the wrath of God, the more can they be brought under the sway of the divine mercy. The more they anticipate doom, the more can they avoid it.

*Lewis Mumford*

# MORAL AMBIGUITIES

### THE CHALLENGE OF EVIL

In most historic definitions of the good there is a tendency to affirm as a conclusion the very question one has asked. The old Stoic dictum, "Nothing but goodness is good," is only a caricature of every other definition: not excluding, of course, that which I have attempted to give. For the good, as Thomas Aquinas observed and as Aristotle taught before him, is in one sense the very property of life itself: "The good is being as an object of appetite." Life itself is its own blessing and when man appeared matter at last laughed. Taking life as the very core of goodness, the Greeks before Socrates naturally rated health as the supreme good of life, and after health, beauty. But this youthful over-emphasis on bodily delight unfortunately is too innocent to provide for all of life's occasions. Are no goods left when youth has disappeared and energy dwindled? When one follows the full trajectory of life one must face the fact that human beings, even before life reaches the downward curve, often

face painful crises and suffer penalties: we may encounter crippling accidents and fatal diseases, as well as consummations, gains, and fulfillments. An optimistic ethics, which makes health and prosperity the central, or even the supreme goods, becomes childishly bewildered and helpless when overtaken by bodily disaster. By contrast, a pessimistic ethics, deliberately embracing the bad in order to fend off something worse, partly fortifies the spirit, as Mithridates did his body, by taking a daily dose of poison. But by its own logic such an ethic is forced to assert that love is a snare, that joys are worthless because they vanish, and that prosperity is only a more subtle kind of misfortune.

Now, no matter how bad life may prove, we need an ethics that will do justice to its benign moments; and no matter how good it may become, we must still reckon with life's final undoing. With wise teaching and provident laws and improved technics we may abolish poverty, crime, and disease, or reduce them to minimal amounts, as Robert Owen [13] once preached: that hope is a wholly legitimate one. But in some form, deviously if not directly, the forces of evil will still beset life, if only because there is a widening discrepancy, as man advances upward in the scale of being, between his own purposes and the lower order of nature.

These extraneous forces will threaten man's plans sometimes with the appearance of concentrated malice, such as enraged the soul of Captain Ahab, [14] sometimes with the drooling inconsequence of an idiot giant whose fumbling hands may strangle a baby as easily as a mouse. An earthquake, a bolt of lightning, a raging fire, a falling meteor, a plague, a plane wreck, though they be events in an orderly and purposeful world, nevertheless cut across the path of some living creature's growth and development. From the standpoint of life, such happenings are senseless and evil: yet this not-goodness that overpowers goodness is closely bound up, at every stage, with man's existence. One can recognize all these facts without, like the

---

MORAL AMBIGUITIES: From *The Conduct of Life,* by Lewis Mumford. Copyright, 1951, by Lewis Mumford. Used by permission of Harcourt, Brace and Company, Inc.

[13] Robert Owen, 1771–1858, socialist and philanthropist, owner of successful cotton mills in Manchester, England, did much to improve the lot of English laborers.

[14] In *Moby Dick,* by Herman Melville, the captain of the *Pequod,* whose leg has been bitten off by a whale.

fashionable existentialists, making a religion of that recognition. Evil, by its constant threat, introduces an element of tragic struggle into a world that would otherwise be in a state of effortless enjoyment, like some smiling Polynesian island; but by the very fact that it rouses life to fuller effort, it may be essential to human growth and renewal.

Are evil and good polar opposites, then, so intimately related that one could not exist without the other? Or are they, as Augustine thought, substance and shadow, so that evil is only the absence and dearth of the good; or are they each positive but not necessarily interdependent aspects of life? Or finally, is there something ambiguous in their character, which neither the doctrine of absolutism nor the doctrine of relativism sufficiently acknowledges? I put off this question for later discussion in order to deal with still another doctrine widely held today, that evil is merely a projection of fears and anxieties, and that, by proper psychological therapy, it may be removed from the mind and will therefore have no objective existence. This view was put forward, with no little acumen, by Mary Baker Eddy, who with psychosomatic insight even applied her philosophy to such bodily evils as disease. Since then it has been taken over, on a materialistic rather than a transcendental basis, by many psychiatrists, who would be somewhat embarrassed by this underlying association with Christian Science.

There is no doubt whatever that evils may have a subjective or psychal origin: but this fact in no wise lessens their reality; nor does it in the least prove that extirpation of a sense of guilt solves the problem of evil in any case except a neurosis. Evils that are of human origin require constant rectification; and the doctrine that "modern man can do no wrong," which so easily absolves him of all sense of self-condemnation, has the effect of increasing the social burden of evil by lifting responsibility from the shoulders of the evildoer. By that fact, it removes the impulse to repentance and self-correction, both essential for moral development.

Recently, an intelligent and earnest group of people in Texas resolved to come to grips with the cause of the domestic and international tensions that are visible today: they formed a cooperative group and enlisted aid from the outside, in their search for a method which would banish the fear and anxiety which, following current psychological fashion, they took to be the only source of positive evil.

The general premises of the Behavior Research Project can be summed up, in their own words, as follows: "If we are to reduce human fears in order to eliminate evil, we can no longer use the devices of blame and reprisal in our social action in community life. Blaming the other fellow (or ourselves) is further punishing the already insecure personality. This creates greater fear and generates more 'evil' counteractions. . . . If the problem of evil is the problem of fear, we must find the causes of fears, ease them, and thus triumph over evil." These premises are highly characteristic of the general attitude toward evil in our civilization: one which reduces life to a sequence of external causes and effects, and has no place for human reason and purpose; for, on these popular terms, reasons are merely rationalizations that cover brute impulses, and in a non-purposeful world, the means generate their own ends: "the going is the goal." The issues raised by this group were so general, that I will illustrate my point further by giving with slight amplifications my own comments on their inability to overcome their own inertia.

"The dilemma in which you find yourselves reveals, from my standpoint, what was wrong in your original approach and what, I fear, will vitiate your further work, unless you can bring yourselves to re–examine your original assumptions.

"The unexamined premise is, as you must know, the chief source of radical errors. Your unexamined premise is the belief, which seems to you axiomatic and unquestionable, that evil has only one source, fear, and therefore the simple, indeed the only way, to eliminate evil is to reduce fear. This for you, following many latter-day psychiatrists, means banishing any sense of guilt; and to do this effectively you must nullify the tendency to blame other people or even to blame oneself.

"I question this whole set of assumptions, including your notion that any evil that does not derive from fear is 'mystical,' that is, unreal or without objective foundation. You have closed your eyes to a large body of evidence when you define fear and evil in such narrow terms: you forget that both Greek and Christian culture, with a far longer experience of life than modern psychiatry, have attributed the chief source of sin, not to fear but to pride and self-love, which are only exaggerations of the constructive virtues of dignity and self-respect.

"Now even fear has a proper function in the organism, if it is fear of a real danger, not of an imaginary one; and similarly, blame has an effective part in the human economy, if he who is blamed has in fact committed a wrong action that greater conscientiousness or wakefulness might have avoided. In the extreme case you will of course acknowledge this: you will admit that no amount of love and fellow-feeling and psychological understanding should lead one to withhold reproach from, say, a locomotive engineer who has fallen asleep on the job and caused a wreck. Because all of us wish social approval in some degree, blame becomes a means of re-enforcing the super-ego, when it might flag in its supervision; or when, to protect himself from undue pain, a person might seek to anesthetize his conscience.

"An honest ethics, it seems to me, cannot attempt to lift the burden of guilt from one who has sinned or committed a crime. What it will seek to do, rather, is to appraise the evil that has been done, sensitively and understandingly; it will discourage excessive neurotic reactions to the normal errors, and be lenient or merciful to the extent that others have been implicated or must bear some of the burden of the guilt. Thus if the engineer fell asleep because he had been overworked by his superiors, the latter would share a large portion of the responsibility. But avoid fixing blame altogether? No. The truth is that people in our culture have a morbid tendency to avoid blame, because they do not wish to take the trouble to change their conduct in any way: blame-avoidance and blame-transference are therefore endemic amongst us. These are substitutes for repentance and renewal.

"In fine, the way to neutralize evil tendencies is not to deny the objective existence of evil or to avoid hating what is hateful and blaming what is blameworthy, but to accept the fact that we have in our own conduct the very tendencies we dislike and see so plainly in those who oppose us; and without abating our legitimate responsibilities to correct acts in others that need correction, to call upon our fellows in turn to help correct them in us. An ethics which seeks to promote good without recognizing any evil but that derived from fear, and which offers rewards without daring to inflict penalties, will prove a much more formidable obstacle to human co-operation than the systems it seeks to replace.

"Let us grant that some forms of evil must be treated as a remediable disease, as Samuel Butler first satirically suggested in *Erewhon*. But if all evils were of a purely neurotic origin, the psychotic's gifts for murder or torture would be indistinguishable from acts of love since they leave him with no sense of guilt or remorse. That is the *reductio ad absurdum* of your attempt to reduce evil to fear and to banish all blame and guilt: 'goodness,' on those terms, would merely be a name covering large areas of unacknowledged evil."

### THE SALT OF LIFE

In practice, evil offers a dramatic contrast to good and heightens its quality, as vinegar or salt bring out the taste of food: the fact that life turns out to be a dramatic struggle, rather than a pageant, is due precisely to this constant clash of impulses and forces, within and without. But let us not repeat the common mistake of an exclusively dialectical analysis of this struggle: the value of the good is not positively increased by its negation. Food would be nourishing even if starvation never threatened one, and friendship would be rewarding even if enemies did not exist. Theoretically, then, one may easily conceive a world in which there would be only a choice of lesser or greater goods.

The dream of such a world of innocence and plenty, health and joy, has haunted man from the beginnings of his consciousness of pain and evil; and one finds it expressed in all the great literatures: in Hesiod's picture of the Golden Age, in Chuang-Chou's description of a similar state, and of course in the Biblical account of the Garden of Eden. Even now, this is the world that our more naive contemporaries believe we are on the point of establishing through the advances of medical science, mass production, and an "economy of abundance." A world in which every disease will be cured by magic drugs, every pain effaced by anesthetics, a world where no inordinate desire will exist that the industrial mechanism cannot gratify, since by sedulous training human beings will be conditioned to express no desires that cannot so be met.

So man might mature as the trees grow:

self-contained, filling out his shape, never experiencing disharmonies, never encountering
crises, wholly at one with himself and with his
environment. William Morris, in *News from
Nowhere,* conceived such a two-dimensional
wallpaper world, without strong highlights and
without depths; but he was honest enough to
admit that the possibility of murder would remain. Indeed, in a letter written in 1874, his
insight into the nature of evil in the human
economy went even farther: "Years ago," he
wrote, "men's minds were full of art and the
dignified shows of life, and they had but little
time for justice and peace; and the vengeance
on them was not increase of the violence they
did not heed, but destruction of the art they
heeded. So perhaps the gods are preparing
troubles and terrors for the world (or our small
corner of it) again, that it may once again become beautiful and dramatic withal."

Even were the equable self-fulfillment of a
Golden Age actually achieved, it would in its
very perfection bring about a new kind of evil:
it would arrest life and stultify it; for it would
no longer produce the kind of disruption and
conflict out of which higher forms of life become possible. The fact is that temporary chaos,
if it does not harden into a pattern of disorder,
may be more helpful to man's development than
a regularity too easily accepted, a happiness and
equilibrium too effortlessly achieved: it is not
in the hothouse, under "ideal" conditions, that
one grows life's most perfect fruit. If life is to
escape the cycle of repetition and mere survival
on a dull animal level, some measure of disintegration, as Lloyd Morgan pointed out, is
essential to its higher emergence. The seed must
be buried, the husk of the seed must rot, the
body must die to its old habits and constraints,
if a higher order of growth is to come forth.

In some sense pain and organic disharmony
and psychological conflict, so far from being
wholly deplorable accidents, are among the
requisites for development: for growth is a state
of unbalance on the way to a higher equilibrium. In this sense, crises are normal events in
growth. Childbirth, teething, the first coitus,
not merely painfully punctuate the successive
phases of bodily maturity but have their parallels in the spirit. Graham Wallas collected a
long list of biographies of exceptionally gifted
people, whose opportunity for a more intense
and fruitful development was furthered by ill-

nesses or disabling accidents. Many of the experiences of life which one would avoid as evil,
or at very least as damnably unpleasant, if one
had the possibility of rejecting them, often turn
out to be conditions for adequate growth. That
is why those who have been able to assimilate
their experiences in war usually have a far
higher degree of maturity than those who never
faced extreme hardship and terrifying danger.
If one had life completely on one's own terms
and lived it solely according to the pleasure
principle, as people so often dream, it would
probably turn out to be as vapid and empty as
the historic lives of the ruling classes: lives so
flavorless that the aristocracy, in their boredom,
must provide themselves danger and difficulty
in the form of polo or mountain climbing or
duels of honor in order not to lose their appetites entirely.

This does not mean, however, that good and
evil are everywhere quantitatively equal; or that
they are the right and the wrong sides of the
same coin, inseparable by nature. And it does
not necessarily lead to the conclusion, to which
Dr. Reinhold Niebuhr comes in his *Interpretation of Christian Ethics,* that the possibilities
of evil inevitably grow with the possibilities of
good, so that "human history is therefore not
so much a chronicle of the progressive victory
of good over evil, of cosmos over chaos, as the
story of an ever-increasing cosmos, creating
ever-increasing possibilities of chaos." These
are, no doubt, theoretic possibilities, and sometimes they have had historic existence: indeed,
they would fit very closely in a "diagnosis of
our own time." But there is no ground for
thinking that such possibilities are constant
necessities. On the contrary, viewing life as a
whole, one may say that within its realm order
has been on the increase and the realm of the
good has widened. The complex symphonic order that life seeks is of a more unstable kind
than the order of the physical universe; and precisely because it is so complex and so delicately
balanced and timed, it carries with it the
constant possibility of retrogression and complete disruption. So far Niebuhr is right.

But many communities that have freed themselves from leprosy and typhus have not merely
decreased the quantity of evil from that particular source: they have at the same time lowered
the general death rate. If the processes of improvement were as self-negating as Niebuhr

makes them out to be, even such a temporary gain could hardly be expected. The whole case for ethical guidance, indeed, rests on the fact that both relatively and absolutely the quantity of good can be increased and the quantity of evil reduced. As I have said elsewhere, evil, like arsenic, is a tonic in grains and a poison in ounces: hence its decrease is a major goal of human effort. But all goods are perishable, and evils, like weeds, continue to spring up: so that every generation must continue its discriminations and persist in its efforts.

If there were not this difference in favor of the good, if, speaking mythically, the devil were fully the equal of God, and not an inferior power who schemes to overthrow his lord but never quite succeeds, there would be hardly any sense in preferring good to evil, since any gain in the first would only make the second more formidable. On those terms, life would be doomed to inescapable frustration. But that is like saying that the better a city is planned and built, the more slums it will show, or the more law-abiding citizens there are in a country the more criminals they will have to fight: propositions contrary to both reason and observed fact. (Thanks to good laws and vigilant moral discipline, it was once possible for Daniel Webster in all honesty to boast, so low was the rate of crime in mid-nineteenth century Massachusetts, that no householder had to lock his door at night.) Every assumption that the proportion of good and evil is unalterable must lead, as it has constantly led in Christian thought, to a doctrine of quietism: a false creed which, incidentally, is fatal to the pursuit of justice and the exercise of civic virtue.

Our second problem is whether moral principles are absolute or relative. That is an ancient theme in ethics; but the modern displacement of positive standards began in the eighteenth century with that representative philosopher, Denis Diderot: in some ways the first and the most admirable of the "moderns." In his annotated edition of Shaftesbury he noted that "there is no moral principle, no rule of virtue whatever," that could not be contradicted by customs and conditions in some other race or climate of the world. The observation was true; but the implied conclusion was unsound.

This devaluation was founded on a romantic exaggeration of the importance of the surviving primitives; and it failed to distinguish between forms of life that are repetitive, stultifying, infantile, and the forms produced by the higher civilizations which, for all their sins and lapses, have tended toward development, maturation, emergence. Civilized man has indeed much to learn from primitive peoples; but those tribes and communities that differ most widely in moral values from the universal standards of civilization have contributed few important values to the rest of mankind. Against many minor departures from the common norm, which back up Diderot's dictum, one must place the much more significant fact that the majority of civilized people for the last three thousand years— billions as compared to a few poor millions— have lived by progressively universal principles, whose similarities are far more significant than their differences.

Within the great circle of the historic civilizations the main directions of morality have been well set: to follow customs and frame laws that regulate social relations, in order to make conduct predictable, instead of wholly erratic and self-willed; to respect symbols and conserve values; to refrain from murder, violence, and theft; to respect organized and sanctioned forms of sexual relationship; to nurture the young and stand by them as long as they are helpless; to tell the truth and to refrain from falsehood— though as to lies, violence, and thefts the Greeks of the Homeric poems were still a little shaky. This basic morality is in fact common to all human society: what distinguishes civilization is a heightened consciousness of the occasions for moral choice and a positive effort to extend the benefits of the moral code outside the community where it originated.

These, and many similar precepts and regulations, are deeply ingrained in the human tradition: they remain operative as long as that tradition is deliberately passed on from parent to child, from teacher to student, from master to disciple or apprentice. Customs and choices may, in minor respects, differ; but to have no customs and to make no choices—on the ground that obvious historic and natural differences make them all meaningless—is to be demoralized. So, too, to make any "original" departures from the common norm, such as Nietzsche made when he extolled torture, is to open the way for such psychopathic conduct as Hitler and his followers practiced.

Plainly, some norms of conduct are better

established than others: some are still reserved for in-groups and denied to the out-groups. But except in times of social disintegration (when they are widely rejected) these norms help to establish an essential part of man's humanness.

Now, none of mankind's present "absolutes" in morals existed from the beginning: man was not born, in his primitive state, with a special moral sense that enabled him to distinguish at once these universal principles. Each is the result of long-continued efforts, experiments, appraisals: trials that must still go on. By now, however, certain questions, like cannibalism or incest, are no longer open ones. The fate of the human race today depends largely upon our moral decision to place torture, war, and genocide under the same inviolable rule. Relativism, by its indifference to the universal, by its insistence that all goods are equally valuable expressions of local taste or ephemeral impulse, actually places itself on the side of the tribal, the static, the unprogressive: processes and states that obstruct human growth. Even the most hidebound ethical system is still more favorable to life than a relativism that denies the possibility of universal principles and stable standards, or whose one form of obligation is conformity to external change.

Good and evil nonetheless remain in an ambiguous relationship; and in interpreting their operation further we shall, incidentally, do justice to the element of truth in the relativist's position.

CHRONOMETRICALS AND HOROLOGICALS

Perhaps the classic statement of this two-faced role of good and evil is to be found in the novel, *Pierre,* by Herman Melville: a novel whose sub-title, *The Ambiguities,* underlines the discoveries that Melville himself made in the very course of writing it, and embodied in the paper attributed to the Transcendental philosopher, Plotinus Plinlimmon, a curious spiritual caricature of Hawthorne and Emerson.

The title of the paper, "Chronometricals and Horologicals," points to the relationship between the absolute and the relative. Here Melville shows that in the modern world absolute time, as reckoned by the planetary movements, is set by the observatory at Greenwich; and every vessel setting out from London checks its ship's chronometer by Greenwich time. But by the time the ship reached, say, China, its cap-

tain would discover a startling discrepancy between his own accurate chronometer and the local clocks or sundials. If the captain tried to conduct the day's business by a schedule that kept to his own Greenwich time, he would be sleeping by daylight and making sociable calls when his Chinese neighbors were in bed.

So with the highest principles of conduct. Each generation, Melville observes, produces a few rare souls who try to guide their lives by heavenly time, and seek to make that absolute and universal: they are ready to sell all that they have and give to the poor, or to turn their right cheek when their left is slapped. But men in the mass live their lives by local time; they desire to reach heaven before giving all they have to the poor; although, as Melville ironically remarks, they will find it easier to practice this virtue in heaven, since there are no poor in that place. From the smug standpoint of the local time-observers, it is heavenly time that is wrong.

All this brings out a fact that Niebuhr has skillfully, indeed brilliantly, developed: that our ideals, however imperative and absolute, must nevertheless reckon with the fact that we live in the realm of the historically conditioned, subject to pressures and environmental limitations that cannot be entirely put aside. In other words, the moral ideal is a compass point, not a destination: while a fixed orientation to north and south is essential in order to find one's way to port, one may have to tack one's ship, now to the east, now to the west, in order to move in the general direction one has chosen; while if one sets one's course unconditionally to north or south, one will find oneself at last only in a polar waste. One steers by the fixed North Star, not in order to reach an ideal north, but in order to find a fair haven.

Pierre makes some of these discoveries for himself; but unfortunately neither he nor Herman Melville drew the correct conclusions. In his endeavor to confound the morality of prudence, exemplified by Pierre's worldly mother and her spiritual counselor, the Reverend Mr. Folsgrave, Pierre brings disorder and disaster into the lives of all those around him: his "noble" unconditioned conduct, released from all traditional guidance, penetrates the patched garments of convention like an X-ray, only to attack the living flesh beneath. His mother, his new-found half-sister, his wife, and finally himself pay the penalty for his proud intransigence. In pursuing the absolute, with his eyes fixed only on the distant horizon, Pierre stumbles into deeper sloughs than he would have encountered if he had never raised his eyes from the ground and attempted merely to leap over the mudholes that blocked his path, or pursued a circumspect course around them.

Wherein lay Pierre's radical error? Mainly in the fact that he forgot it is only at Greenwich—at an ideal point—that absolute and local time coincide. Worse, he forgot that once the Astronomer Royal leaves his observatory, he must keep time by an ordinary watch, an imperfect instrument which gains or loses time or flatly stops and must be wound up: such time will no longer coincide with astronomical observation, if he moves east or west of the meridian line.

Melville may be right in saying that the saints are those who live closest to this zero meridian; but that does not make them infallible in their daily living, nor does it condemn as untrue to Greenwich time the timekeepers that are followed in other lands, provided they have made their own corrections with reference to astronomical time. In other words, there is no abstract formula for virtue that yields an unconditioned result. What do Pierre's unconditional idealism or his sexual purity profit if they lead to frigidity and impotence, to hate and anguish, to misery and suicide? Melville was as wrongheaded as Pierre in his conclusions; and the black disaster that finally envelops his hero and those whom he loves was the natural climax to his error: repeated once more, in effect, in his personal life.

There is no virtue that may not, at any moment, turn into its opposite. Humility, pursued too steadfastly, may give rise to pride over its very achievement: Pierre's absolute integrity produces disintegration. "The good in goodness often find an enemy to dread," as an ancient Hindu scripture observes. By the same token, there is no vice so desperate, no impulse so depraved, that man may not out of his depths, by reaction, create an otherwise unattainable good. This explains Jesus's preference for the sinner to the Pharisee: it was not only that the sinner needed more urgently to be saved, but that, once saved, he would perhaps be a better man than his more studiously virtuous rival.

As essences, good and evil are poles apart:

fixed poles. But in existence, they are the algebraic signs that indicate positive or negative quantities; and they change values as the symbols of life shift from one side of the equation to the other. Was not this the meaning of Emerson's Uriel: "Evil will bless and ice will burn"? These paradoxes and ambiguities in the moral life are well illustrated by two contrasting historic occasions: at Athens in the time of Demosthenes and in England in the days of Churchill. The Athenians, unable to depart from their beloved way of life, doomed themselves to defeat; whereas the moral readiness to face danger and death brought life to the British and reversed a long series of disasters, occasioned by their earlier unwillingness to encounter positive evil.

That change, as we know, brought compensations that other countries, which shrank collectively from making the same choice, did not share. The high morale of Britain after the war, with its equable system of rationing, "fair shares for all"; the resolute effort to cope with economic difficulties through the exacting discipline of the austerity program; the statesmanlike surrender of its rule in India—all these positive moral gains were made possible by the original decision to accept death and destruction. As long as Britain sought safety and peace, its very life was in danger: as soon as Britain dared to face insecurity and even extinction, it was saved. That algebraic shift is a constant factor in the moral life: hence the need for unremitting watchfulness.

If fullness of life fits the positive definition of the good, this plenitude does not belong to life in its primeval innocence, overflowing with fresh animal spirits and radiant health: it comes only with knowledge of good *and* evil, with action on behalf of one and against the other. Ambiguously, though evil itself must be combated, diminished, forced into retreat, it enters the human situation as one of the conditions for life's highest fulfillment. Evil and good are both phases in the process of growth and self-realization: who shall say which is the better teacher? In other words, the very forces which, if triumphant, would destroy life are needful to ripen experience and deepen understanding.

Those who aim at a particular good, are often carried to their destination by the very path they consciously seek to avoid. In achieving a life abundant, accordingly, success lies not in altogether escaping evil, but in being able to turn the negative forces to the account of the personality itself. For those unprepared to cope with evil, life's injurious moments count only as a dead loss. But once evil is accepted, as an element as much in the run of vital processes as waste and fatigue, the law of compensation may operate; and in energizing the spirit evil may—as Helen Keller's life reminds us—sometimes give back more than it has taken.

The good, then, is that which furthers growth, integration, transcendence, and renewal. Evil, by contrast, is that which brings about disintegration and de-building, arrests growth, creates a permanent unbalance, dissipates energy, degrades life, baffles and frustrates the spirit, and prevents the emergence of the divine. Not sin but indifference, not erroneous knowledge, but skepticism, are the chief aids of the destroyer.

The concepts of growth, emergence, and transcendence take us far in the interpretation of human life: but they provide no terminus for human effort; and in that sense, even if life went well at every stage, they would leave each of us with a tantalizing sense of incompleteness and non-fulfillment, an endless stirring and striving, without any goal except a provisional one: a continued ascent of pinnacles that revealed only further peaks to climb. But actually, at least in human life, a provisional stopping place is provided, in the sense that one may have momentary glimpses of the end of the journey and of all that one could accomplish if one had endless days to command. The need for some such finality undoubtedly has led to the conjuring up of eternal heavens: mirages of unqualified beatitude, enjoyed forever; but there is a more functional interpretation of this idea of heaven which places it, not in a period after death, but in the midst of life itself.

Mary Boole remarked that "anything which seems to you worth doing you will never be allowed to do long: *'pour vous empêcher de routiner.'* " [15] This is true of all man's most intense or highest experiences: from the delight of a common orgasm with one's beloved to the joys of intellectual illumination. But it is in such moments that life seems irradiated in every direction: moments detached from all preparatory activity or further result, moments so intensely

---

[15] "To keep you from falling into a routine."

good in themselves, so complete, so all-satisfying that neither further emergence nor transcendence seem needed, since they are present in the experience itself. These are the moments when art seems poignantly to encompass all of life's possibilities, or, by the same token, when life reveals the significances of art.

Without such consummations, without such precious moments, man would be but the traditional donkey, flayed by a stick behind, lured by a deceptive carrot in front of him. To be alert to seize such moments of high insight, unconditioned action, and perfect fulfillment is one of the main lessons of life: endless activity, without this detachment and contemplation and ultimate delight, cannot bring life's fullest satisfaction. What man creates in art and thought justifies itself, not only by contributing to life's development and the emergence of new values, but by the production of significant moments. Those who have encountered these moments, who have held them close, can never be altogether cheated or frustrated, even by life's worst misfortunes or by its untimely curtailment. An education or a general mode of life that does not lead—though by indirection—to such moments and heighten their savor, falls short of man's needs.

### REPENTANCE AND RE-AFFIRMATION

We are now prepared to understand the significance of the Jewish-Christian insight into the nature of evil: in particular, its perception of the fact that the assumptions that man is naturally good or that he may, by trusting entirely to scientific thought and technical invention, avoid any contamination of evil, are both illusions. Evil is as much a part of human existence as entropy, or the running down of energy: in one sense, it is the human counterpart of entropy and chance, breaking down organization, direction, and purpose. In this respect, Greek philosophers, who took pride in their own goodness even when they denied the certainty of truth or the usefulness of positive science, and humanistic philosophers of the eighteenth century type, who believed that man was born good and was corrupted only by external institutions and wily authorities, both failed to take in the facts of existence.

Unfortunately, the illusion that man is naturally good and can at will avoid evil is almost as much an obstacle to human development as the philosophy that man is naturally bad and cannot, by any efforts of his own, attain to the good: both of them leave human nature in a static condition, incapable of achieving wisdom through trial and error or reflective insight into its own actual nature. In a time of social disintegration, both these interpretations of the dynamic interaction of good and evil not merely share the field: they impede the necessary transformation of personal conduct and social plans. For the fact that evil is a constant element in life does not mean that one must submit to it; but it means that, if one is to get the better of it, one must acknowledge it, and above all, one must repent of it—repent in the literal sense of changing one's attitude and turning away.

As a protection against altering their ways, modern people tend to recoil from the very word sin: they will not admit, first of all, that they are capable of sinning, and they regard a sense of guilt as an unfortunate mental disturbance that should be removed, as promptly as possible, by a psychoanalyst. These blameless people, in their massive serenity and self-complacence, are probably a greater block to the renewal of life today than the most brutal dictators, whose nefarious designs often awaken the very opposition and struggle that produce change. It was the blameless statesmen, too rational to entertain a conviction of sin—the Blums, the Benešes, the Chamberlains—who led their contemporaries into appeasement and surrender: it was a good and upright man, an exemplary citizen, Henry L. Stimson, sure that his own decisions were untainted by evil, who not merely sanctioned the use of extermination bombing but even after there was time for reflection continued to justify that infamous policy.

These blameless ones do not repent: in a mood of fervid self-justification they continue their follies and magnify them. That rigid sense of self-righteousness, with its inability to confess the evils it commits and bring them to an end, is perhaps the chief mark of a dying civilization. If it could admit the possibility that it was on the wrong course, and that every extra effort only hastened the moment of destruction, it would be able to change its direction. Not wishing to be other than they are, the blameless ones, in their self-love, cannot conceive the real alternative: another self, cleansed of guilt and freed from folly, capable of renewal.

This general sense of blamelessness has been abetted, in our time, by the fact that our most extravagant sins, perhaps, are less sins of violence than sins of inertia. There have perhaps never before been such a large number of people in the world who live blameless lives: people who work regularly at their jobs, support their families decently, show a reasonable degree of kindness to those about them, endure colorless days, and go to the grave at last without having done active wrong to a single living creature, except the god within themselves. The very colorlessness of the existence of such people—like the colorlessness of sea water in small quantities—conceals the collective blackness of their conduct. For this kind of sin consists in the withdrawal from more exacting opportunities, in a denial of one's higher capacities: in a slothfulness, an indifference, a complacence, a passivity more fatal to life than more outrageous sins and crimes. The passionate murderer may repent: the disloyal friend may regret his faithlessness and fulfill his obligations of friendship: but the mean sensual man, who has obeyed the rules and meticulously filled out all the legal papers, may glory in what he is—and that is a deeper misfortune; for it is in his name, and by his connivance, precisely because he sees no need for changing his mind or rectifying his ways, that our society slips from misfortune to crisis and from crisis to catastrophe. No wonder that Dante consigned these blameless ones to the Inferno—those who were neither for nor against the good. The hell of our times is in no small part of their making.

On this matter, Christian theology has perhaps shown a more profound insight than any other religion or philosophy; and though the essential doctrines relating to evil, sin, repentance, and renewal are too often set aside in the Churches today on the ground that they affront modern man, proud of his neutral, scientific, sinless world, these insights constitute the living core of Christianity, which every fuller synthesis must make use of. The fact is we must admit the constant possibility of sin, at every stage of life, indeed at every moment: partiality, narrowness of vision, self-seekingness, rigidity, miscalculation, stiff-necked pride, involuntary involvement with evils that carry one along in their surge, as an innocent man may be caught in the midst of a homicidal mob —all these have us in their grip. In our civilization, the very impersonal forces that preside over so much of our destiny implicate each of us, almost automatically, in sinful acts. Whether we are conscious of it or not, prisoners are mistreated, insane people are neglected, poor people are allowed to starve, beastly weapons of genocide are manufactured, and a thousand other evil acts are committed, not without our connivance. We are involved in these sins and can correct them only if we confess our involvement and take upon ourselves personally the burden of correcting them.

If the men who misguided France during the fatal decade that ended with the surrender of France to Hitler could have had the courage publicly to confess and repent, they might have brought back the general capacity to think and act in a more heroic mold. If the men who misguided America since 1945, giving away the fatal secret of the atomic bomb by exploding it, full of misplaced confidence in atomic and bacterial weapons of genocide, failing to place our full force and authority behind the United Nations, following the wholly negative policy of "containment" toward Soviet Russia, could have confessed their sins, at any moment we might have made a new start, on a basis that might have brought the world into measures of co-operation still unthinkable. Instead, they magnified the enormity of their military errors and their moral guilt—their lack of even a self-preservative life-sense—by commissioning the manufacture of the hydrogen bomb.

If resistance to such an inner transformation continues, our whole civilization will harden further in the very mold that will paralyze what benign forces remain and prevent us from escaping a worldwide catastrophe. Only people strong enough to admit their constant tendency to err and sin will be capable of finding new paths: only those who confess their sins will be re-activated sufficiently to attempt the transformation that must now take place in every institution, in every group, in every person.

But the negative side of this change is not enough; for no one can really turn aside from evil unless he has some positive vision of the good. Alongside repentance goes a process too often overlooked: the re-affirmation of virtues and goods. No more than evil can goodness be taken for granted. One cannot hold fast to any good and hope that it will remain intact, like a buried treasure: the best tradition, the happiest state, will dry up and disappear unless one constantly reviews it, replenishes it, and re-affirms it. Nothing that we do by routine and habit is safe from corruption. In order to keep old truths alive, we must re-think them, every year and every generation, testing them in the light of further experience, altering the very terms and words with which we express them in order to be sure that our thought is still active and dealing with realities. In order to keep good institutions in operation, we must re-dedicate ourselves to them, correct the errors time constantly discloses in their workings, even deliberately break up regulations and conventions that are about to crystallize to a point where they resist human intervention.

Without a poignant consciousness of the goods of life, in all their freshness and intensity, without some daily glimpse of beauty, some expression of tenderness, some stir of passion, some release in gaiety and laughter, some quickening of rhythm and music, our very humanity is not safe. To summon up the courage to go through our daily tasks, above all in a Time of Troubles, where no goals can be reached without sacrifice, we must remind ourselves, by conscious daily dedication, of the goods we desire and value. This dedication is perhaps the psychological core of prayer; and every concrete expression of the good, in a song or a symphony, a poem or a loving embrace, has some of the quality of prayer. There is no creation, in the end, except in the mood of love; and if we are impotent to love, the mere recounting of our sins will leave ashes in our mouths and cinders in our eyes.

Indeed, in the process of making over our lives, so that a new pattern, more favorable to growth and renewal, may be designed, we shall not merely re-appraise but re-savor all life's multifarious goods: making the most of them, no longer snatching and filching them with a sore conscience or a sense of personal inadequacy and positive shirking. For the final effect of repentance and affirmation is a fresh appetite for life, all the keener for the fastings, abstentions, renunciations that must necessarily precede it. The pain of rebirth will turn, on delivery, into a shout of joy. The fellowship of those who have experienced renewal will be written on their faces: in a good-humored patience, and tenderness, in an outer resolution tempered by an inner mirth.

## Edgar Allan Poe
# THE BLACK CAT

For the most wild, yet most homely narrative which I am about to pen, I neither expect nor solicit belief. Mad indeed would I be to expect it, in a case where my very senses reject their own evidence. Yet, mad am I not— and very surely do I not dream. But to-morrow I die, and to-day I would unburthen my soul. My immediate purpose is to place before the world, plainly, succinctly, and without comment, a series of mere household events. In their consequences, these events have terrified —have tortured—have destroyed me. Yet I will not attempt to expound them. To me, they have presented little but Horror—to many they will seem less terrible than *baroques*. Hereafter, perhaps, some intellect may be found which will reduce my phantasm to the common-place —some intellect more calm, more logical, and far less excitable than my own, which will perceive, in the circumstances I detail with awe, nothing more than an ordinary succession of very natural causes and effects.

From my infancy I was noted for the docility and humanity of my disposition. My tenderness of heart was even so conspicuous as to make me the jest of my companions. I was especially fond of animals, and was indulged by my parents with a great variety of pets. With these I spent most of my time, and never was so happy as when feeding and caressing them. This peculiarity of character grew with my growth, and, in my manhood, I derived from it one of my principal sources of pleasure. To those who have cherished an affection for a faithful and sagacious dog, I need hardly be at the trouble of explaining the nature or the intensity of the gratification thus derivable. There is something in the unselfish and self-sacrificing love of a brute, which goes directly to the heart of him who has had frequent occasion to test the paltry friendship and gossamer fidelity of mere *Man*.

I married early, and was happy to find in my wife a disposition not uncongenial with my own. Observing my partiality for domestic pets, she lost no opportunity of procuring those of the most agreeable kind. We had birds, gold fish, a fine dog, rabbits, a small monkey, and *a cat*.

This latter was a remarkably large and beautiful animal, entirely black, and sagacious to an astonishing degree. In speaking of his intelligence, my wife, who at heart was not a little tinctured with superstition, made frequent allusion to the ancient popular notion, which regarded all black cats as witches in disguise. Not that she was ever *serious* upon this point— and I mention the matter at all for no better reason than that it happens, just now, to be remembered.

Pluto—this was the cat's name—was my favorite pet and playmate. I alone fed him, and he attended me wherever I went about the house. It was even with difficulty that I could prevent him from following me through the streets.

Our friendship lasted, in this manner, for several years, during which my general temperament and character—through the instrumentality of the Fiend Intemperance—had (I blush to confess it) experienced a radical alteration for the worse. I grew, day by day, more moody, more irritable, more regardless of the feelings of others. I suffered myself to use intemperate language to my wife. At length, I even offered her personal violence. My pets, of course, were made to feel the change in my disposition. I not only neglected, but ill-used them. For Pluto, however, I still retained sufficient regard to restrain me from maltreating him, as I made no scruple of maltreating the rabbits, the monkey, or even the dog, when by accident, or through affection, they came in my way. But my disease grew upon me—for what disease is like Alcohol!—and at length even Pluto, who was now becoming old, and consequently somewhat peevish—even Pluto began to experience the effects of my ill temper.

One night, returning home, much intoxicated, from one of my haunts about town, I fancied that the cat avoided my presence. I seized him; when, in his fright at my violence, he inflicted a slight wound upon my hand with his teeth. The fury of a demon instantly possessed me. I knew myself no longer. My original soul seemed, at once, to take its flight from my body; and a more than fiendish malevolence, gin-nurtured, thrilled every fibre of my frame. I took from my waistcoat-pocket a penknife, opened it, grasped the poor beast by the throat, and deliberately cut one of its eyes from the socket! I blush, I burn, I shudder, while I pen the damnable atrocity.

When reason returned with the morning—when I had slept off the fumes of the night's debauch—I experienced a sentiment half of horror, half of remorse, for the crime of which I had been guilty; but it was, at best, a feeble and equivocal feeling, and the soul remained untouched. I again plunged into excess, and soon drowned in wine all memory of the deed.

In the meantime the cat slowly recovered. The socket of the lost eye presented, it is true, a frightful appearance, but he no longer appeared to suffer any pain. He went about the house as usual, but, as might be expected, fled in extreme terror at my approach. I had so much of my old heart left, as to be at first grieved by this evident dislike on the part of a creature which had once so loved me. But this feeling soon gave place to irritation. And then came, as if to my final and irrevocable overthrow, the spirit of PERVERSENESS. Of this spirit philosophy takes no account. Yet I am not more sure that my soul lives, than I am that perverseness is one of the primitive impulses of the human heart—one of the indivisible primary faculties, or sentiments, which give direction to the character of Man. Who has not, a hundred times, found himself committing a vile or a silly action, for no other reason than because he knows he should *not?* Have we not a perpetual inclination, in the teeth of our best judgment, to violate that which is *Law,* merely because we understand it to be such? This spirit of perverseness, I say, came to my final overthrow. It was this unfathomable longing of the soul *to vex itself*—to offer violence to its own nature—to do wrong for the wrong's sake only—that urged me to continue and finally to consummate the injury I had inflicted upon the unoffending brute. One morning, in cool blood, I slipped a noose about its neck and hung it to the limb of a tree;—hung it with the tears streaming from my eyes, and with the bitterest remorse at my heart;—hung it *because* I knew that it had loved me, and *because* I felt it had given me no reason

of offence;—hung it *because* I knew that in so doing I was committing a sin—a deadly sin that would so jeopardize my immortal soul as to place it—if such a thing were possible—even beyond the reach of the infinite mercy of the Most Merciful and Most Terrible God.

On the night of the day on which this cruel deed was done, I was aroused from sleep by the cry of fire. The curtains of my bed were in flames. The whole house was blazing. It was with great difficulty that my wife, a servant, and myself, made our escape from the conflagration. The destruction was complete. My entire worldly wealth was swallowed up, and I resigned myself thenceforward to despair.

I am above the weakness of seeking to establish a sequence of cause and effect, between the disaster and the atrocity. But I am detailing a chain of facts—and wish not to leave even a possible link imperfect. On the day succeeding the fire, I visited the ruins. The walls, with one exception, had fallen in. This exception was found in a compartment wall, not very thick, which stood about the middle of the house, and against which had rested the head of my bed. The plastering had here, in great measure, resisted the action of the fire—a fact which I attributed to its having been recently spread. About this wall a dense crowd were collected, and many persons seemed to be examining a particular portion of it with very minute and eager attention. The words "strange!" "singular!" and other similar expressions, excited my curiosity. I approached and saw, as if graven in *bas relief* upon the white surface, the figure of a gigantic *cat*. The impression was given with an accuracy truly marvellous. There was a rope about the animal's neck.

When I first beheld this apparition—for I could scarcely regard it as less—my wonder and my terror were extreme. But at length reflection came to my aid. The cat, I remembered, had been hung in a garden adjacent to the house. Upon the alarm of fire, this garden had been immediately filled by the crowd—by some one of whom the animal must have been cut from the tree and thrown, through an open window, into my chamber. This had probably been done with the view of arousing me from sleep. The falling of other walls had compressed the victim of my cruelty into the substance of the freshly-spread plaster; the lime of which, with the flames, and the *ammonia* from the carcass, had then accomplished the portraiture as I saw it.

Although I thus readily accounted to my reason, if not altogether to my conscience, for the startling fact just detailed, it did not the less fail to make a deep impression upon my fancy. For months I could not rid myself of the phantasm of the cat; and, during this period, there came back into my spirit a half-sentiment that seemed, but was not, remorse. I went so far as to regret the loss of the animal, and to look about me, among the vile haunts which I now habitually frequented, for another pet of the same species, and of somewhat similar appearance, with which to supply its place.

One night as I sat, half stupefied, in a den of more than infamy, my attention was suddenly drawn to some black object, reposing upon the head of one of the immense hogsheads of Gin, or of Rum, which constituted the chief furniture of the apartment. I had been looking steadily at the top of this hogshead for some minutes, and what now caused me surprise was the fact that I had not sooner perceived the object thereupon. I approached it, and touched it with my hand. It was a black cat—a very large one—fully as large as Pluto, and closely resembling him in every respect but one. Pluto had not a white hair upon any portion of his body; but this cat had a large, although indefinite splotch of white, covering nearly the whole region of the breast.

Upon my touching him, he immediately arose, purred loudly, rubbed against my hand, and appeared delighted with my notice. This, then, was the very creature of which I was in search. I at once offered to purchase it of the landlord; but this person made no claim to it— knew nothing of it—had never seen it before.

I continued my caresses, and, when I prepared to go home, the animal evinced a disposition to accompany me. I permitted it to do so; occasionally stooping and patting it as I proceeded. When it reached the house it domesticated itself at once, and became immediately a great favorite with my wife.

For my own part, I soon found a dislike to it arising within me. This was just the reverse of what I had anticipated; but I know not how or why it was—its evident fondness for myself rather disgusted and annoyed. By slow degrees, these feelings of disgust and annoyance rose into the bitterness of hatred. I avoided the creature; a certain sense of shame, and the remembrance of my former deed of cruelty, preventing me from physically abusing it. I did not, for some weeks, strike, or otherwise violently ill use it; but gradually—very gradually —I came to look upon it with unutterable loathing, and to flee silently from its odious presence, as from the breath of a pestilence.

What added, no doubt, to my hatred of the beast, was the discovery, on the morning after I brought it home, that, like Pluto, it also had been deprived of one of its eyes. This circumstance, however, only endeared it to my wife, who, as I have already said, possessed, in a high degree, that humanity of feeling which had once been my distinguishing trait, and the source of many of my simplest and purest pleasures.

With my aversion to this cat, however, its partiality for myself seemed to increase. It followed my footsteps with a pertinacity which it would be difficult to make the reader comprehend. Whenever I sat, it would crouch beneath my chair, or spring upon my knees, covering me with its loathsome caresses. If I arose to walk it would get between my feet and thus nearly throw me down, or, fastening its long and sharp claws in my dress, clamber, in this manner, to my breast. At such times, although I longed to destroy it with a blow, I was yet withheld from so doing, partly by a memory of my former crime, but chiefly—let me confess it at once—by absolute *dread* of the beast.

This dread was not exactly a dread of physical evil—and yet I should be at a loss how otherwise to define it. I am almost ashamed to own—yes, even in this felon's cell, I am almost ashamed to own—that the terror and horror with which the animal inspired me, had been heightened by one of the merest chimæras it would be possible to conceive. My wife had called my attention, more than once, to the character of the mark of white hair, of which I have spoken, and which constituted the sole visible difference between the strange beast and the one I had destroyed. The reader will remember that this mark, although large, had been originally very indefinite; but, by slow degrees—degrees nearly imperceptible, and which for a long time my Reason struggled to reject as fanciful—it had, at length, assumed a rigorous distinctness of outline. It was now the representation of an object that I shudder to name—and for this, above all, I loathed, and dreaded, and would have rid myself of the monster *had I dared*—it was now, I say, the image of a hideous—of a ghastly thing—of the GALLOWS!—oh, mournful and terrible engine of Horror and of Crime—of Agony and of Death!

And now was I indeed wretched beyond the wretchedness of mere Humanity. And *a brute beast*—whose fellow I had contemptuously destroyed—*a brute beast* to work out for *me*—for me a man, fashioned in the image of the High God—so much of insufferable wo! Alas! neither by day nor by night knew I the blessing of Rest any more! During the former the creature left me no moment alone; and, in the latter, I started, hourly, from dreams of unutterable fear, to find the hot breath of *the thing* upon my face, and its vast weight—an incarnate Night-Mare that I had no power to shake off—incumbent eternally upon my *heart!*

Beneath the pressure of torments such as these, the feeble remnant of the good within me succumbed. Evil thoughts became my sole intimates—the darkest and most evil of thoughts. The moodiness of my usual temper increased to hatred of all things and of all mankind; while, from the sudden, frequent, and ungovernable outbursts of a fury to which I now blindly abandoned myself, my uncomplaining wife, alas! was the most usual and the most patient of sufferers.

One day she accompanied me, upon some household errand, into the cellar of the old building which our poverty compelled us to inhabit. The cat followed me down the steep stairs, and, nearly throwing me headlong, exasperated me to madness. Uplifting an axe, and forgetting, in my wrath, the childish dread which had hitherto stayed my hand, I aimed a blow at the animal which, of course, would have proved instantly fatal had it descended as I wished. But this blow was arrested by the hand of my wife. Goaded, by the interference, into a rage more than demoniacal, I withdrew my arm from her grasp and buried the axe in her brain. She fell dead upon the spot, without a groan.

This hideous murder accomplished, I set myself forthwith, and with entire deliberation, to the task of concealing the body. I knew that I could not remove it from the house, either by day or by night, without the risk of being observed by the neighbors. Many projects entered my mind. At one period I thought of cutting the corpse into minute fragments, and destroying them by fire. At another, I resolved to dig a grave for it in the floor of the cellar. Again, I deliberated about casting it in the well in the yard—about packing it in a box, as if merchandize, with the usual arrangements, and so getting a porter to take it from the house. Finally I hit upon what I considered a far better expedient than either of these. I determined to wall it up in the cellar—as the monks of the middle ages are recorded to have walled up their victims.

For a purpose such as this the cellar was well adapted. Its walls were loosely constructed, and had lately been plastered throughout with a rough plaster, which the dampness of the atmosphere had prevented from hardening. Moreover, in one of the walls was a projection, caused by a false chimney, or fireplace, that had been filled up, and made to resemble the rest of the cellar. I made no doubt that I could readily displace the bricks at this point, insert the corpse, and wall the whole up as before, so that no eye could detect anything suspicious.

And in this calculation I was not deceived. By means of a crow-bar I easily dislodged the bricks, and, having carefully deposited the body against the inner wall, I propped it in that position, while, with little trouble, I re-laid the whole structure as it originally stood. Having procured mortar, sand, and hair, with every possible precaution, I prepared a plaster which could not be distinguished from the old, and with this I very carefully went over the new brick-work. When I had finished, I felt satisfied that all was right. The wall did not present the slightest appearance of having been disturbed. The rubbish on the floor was picked up with the minutest care. I looked around triumphantly, and said to myself—"Here at least, then, my labor has not been in vain."

My next step was to look for the beast which had been the cause of so much wretchedness; for I had, at length, firmly resolved to put it to death. Had I been able to meet with it, at the moment, there could have been no doubt of its fate; but it appeared that the crafty animal had been alarmed at the violence of my previous anger, and forebore to present itself in my present mood. It is impossible to describe, or to imagine, the deep, the blissful sense of relief which the absence of the detested creature occasioned in my bosom. It did not make its appearance during the night—and thus for one night at least, since its introduction into the house, I soundly and tranquilly slept; aye, *slept* even with the burden of murder upon my soul!

The second and the third day passed, and still my tormentor came not. Once again I breathed as a freeman. The monster, in terror, had fled the premises forever! I should behold it no more! My happiness was supreme! The guilt of my dark deed disturbed me but little. Some few inquiries had been made, but these had been readily answered. Even a search had been instituted—but of course nothing was to be discovered. I looked upon my future felicity as secured.

Upon the fourth day of the assassination, a party of the police came, very unexpectedly, into the house, and proceeded again to make rigorous investigation of the premises. Secure, however, in the inscrutability of my place of concealment, I felt no embarrassment whatever. The officers bade me accompany them in their search. They left no nook or corner unexplored. At length, for the third or fourth time, they descended into the cellar. I quivered not in a muscle. My heart beat calmly as that of one who slumbers in innocence. I walked the cellar from end to end. I folded my arms upon my bosom, and roamed easily to and fro. The police were thoroughly satisfied and prepared to depart. The glee at my heart was too strong to be restrained. I burned to say if but one word, by way of triumph, and to render doubly sure their assurance of my guiltlessness.

"Gentlemen," I said at last, as the party ascended the steps, "I delight to have allayed your suspicions. I wish you all health, and a little more courtesy. By the bye, gentlemen, this—this is a very well constructed house." [In the rabid desire to say something easily, I scarcely knew what I uttered at all.]—"I may say an *excellently* well constructed house. These walls—are you going, gentlemen?— these walls are solidly put together"; and here, through the mere phrenzy of bravado, I rapped heavily, with a cane which I held in my hand, upon that very portion of the brick-work behind which stood the corpse of the wife of my bosom.

But may God shield and deliver me from the fangs of the Arch-Fiend! No sooner had the reverberation of my blows sunk into silence, than I was answered by a voice from within the tomb!—by a cry, at first muffled and broken, like the sobbing of a child, and then quickly swelling into one long, loud, and continuous scream, utterly anomalous and inhuman—a howl—a wailing shriek, half of horror and half of triumph, such as might have arisen only out of hell, conjointly from the throats of the damned in their agony and of the demons that exult in the damnation.

Of my own thoughts it is folly to speak. Swooning, I staggered to the opposite wall. For one instant the party upon the stairs remained motionless, through extremity of terror and of awe. In the next, a dozen stout arms were toiling at the wall. It fell bodily. The corpse, already greatly decayed and clotted with gore, stood erect before the eyes of the spectators. Upon its head, with red extended mouth and solitary eye of fire, sat the hideous beast whose craft had seduced me into murder, and whose informing voice had consigned me to the hangman. I had walled the monster up within the tomb!

## *Irwin Shaw*
## ACT OF FAITH

"Present it in a pitiful light," Olson was saying, as they picked their way through the mud toward the orderly room tent. "Three combat-scarred veterans, who fought their way from Omaha Beach to—what was the name of the town we fought our way to?"

"Konigstein," Seeger said.

"Konigstein." Olson lifted his right foot heavily out of a puddle and stared admiringly at the three pounds of mud clinging to his overshoe. "The backbone of the army. The noncommissioned officer. We deserve better of our country. Mention our decorations in passing."

"What decorations should I mention?" Seeger asked. "The marksman's medal?"

"Never quite made it," Olson said. "I had a cross-eyed scorer at the butts. Mention the bronze star, the silver star, the Croix de Guerre, with palms, the unit citation, the Congressional Medal of Honor."

"I'll mention them all." Seeger grinned. "You don't think the CO'll notice that we haven't won most of them, do you?"

"Gad, sir," Olson said with dignity, "do you think that one Southern military gentleman will dare doubt the word of another Southern military gentleman in the hour of victory?"

"I come from Ohio," Seeger said.

"Welch comes from Kansas," Olson said, coolly staring down a second lieutenant who was passing. The lieutenant made a nervous little jerk with his hand as though he expected a salute, then kept it rigid, as a slight superior smile of scorn twisted at the corner of Olson's mouth. The lieutenant dropped his eyes and splashed on through the mud. "You've heard of Kansas," Olson said. "Magnolia-scented Kansas."

"Of course," said Seeger. "I'm no fool."

"Do your duty by your men, Sergeant." Olson stopped to wipe the rain off his face and lectured him. "Highest ranking noncom present took the initiative and saved his comrades, at great personal risk, above and beyond the call of you-know-what, in the best traditions of the American army."

"I will throw myself in the breach," Seeger said.

"Welch and I can't ask more," said Olson, approvingly.

They walked heavily through the mud on the streets between the rows of tents. The camp stretched drearily over the Rheims plain, with the rain beating on the sagging tents. The division had been there over three weeks by now, waiting to be shipped home, and all the meager diversions of the neighborhood had been sampled and exhausted, and there was an air of watchful suspicion and impatience with the military life hanging over the camp now, and there was even reputed to be a staff sergeant in C Company who was laying odds they would not get back to America before July Fourth.

"I'm redeployable," Olson sang. "It's so en-joyable ..." It was a jingle he had composed to no recognizable melody in the early days after the victory in Europe, when he had added up his points and found they only came to 63. "Tokyo, wait for me ..."

They were going to be discharged as soon as they got back to the States, but Olson persisted in singing the song, occasionally adding a mournful stanza about dengue fever and brown girls with venereal disease. He was a short, round boy who had been flunked out of air cadets' school and transferred to the infantry, but whose spirits had not been damaged in the process. He had a high, childish voice and a pretty baby face. He was very good-natured, and had a girl waiting for him at the University of California, where he intended to finish his course at government expense when he got out of the army, and he was just the type who is killed off early and predictably and sadly in motion pictures about the war, but he had gone through four campaigns and six major battles without a scratch.

Seeger was a large, lanky boy, with a big nose, who had been wounded at Saint Lô, but had come back to his outfit in the Siegfried Line, quite unchanged. He was cheerful and dependable, and he knew his business and had broken in five or six second lieutenants who had been killed or wounded and the CO had tried to get him commissioned in the field, but the war had ended while the paperwork was being fumbled over at headquarters.

They reached the door of the orderly tent and stopped. "Be brave, Sergeant," Olson said. "Welch and I are depending on you."

"O.K.," Seeger said, and went in.

The tent had the dank, army-canvas smell that had been so much a part of Seeger's life in the past three years. The company clerk was reading a July, 1945, issue of the *Buffalo Courier-Express*, which had just reached him, and Captain Taney, the company CO, was seated at a sawbuck table he used as a desk, writing a letter to his wife, his lips pursed with effort. He was a small, fussy man, with sandy hair that was falling out. While the fighting had been going on, he had been lean and tense and his small voice had been cold and full of authority. But now he had relaxed, and a little pot belly was creeping up under his belt and he kept the top button of his trousers open when he could do it without too public loss of dignity. During the war Seeger had thought of him as a natural soldier, tireless, fanatic about detail, aggressive, severely anxious to kill Germans. But in the past few months Seeger had seen him relapsing gradually and pleasantly into a small-town wholesale hardware merchant, which he had been before the war, sedentary and a little shy, and, as he had once told Seeger, worried, here in the bleak champagne fields of France, about his daughter, who had just turned twelve and had a tendency to go after the boys and had been caught by her mother kissing a fifteen-year-old neighbor in the hammock after school.

"Hello, Seeger," he said, returning the salute in a mild, offhand gesture. "What's on your mind?"

"Am I disturbing you, sir?"

"Oh, no. Just writing a letter to my wife. You married, Seeger?" He peered at the tall boy standing before him.

"No, sir."

"It's very difficult," Taney sighed, pushing dissatisfiedly at the letter before him. "My wife complains I don't tell her I love her often enough. Been married fifteen years. You'd think she'd know by now." He smiled at Seeger. "I thought you were going to Paris," he said. "I signed the passes yesterday."

"That's what I came to see you about, sir."

"I suppose something's wrong with the passes." Taney spoke resignedly, like a man who has never quite got the hang of army regulations and has had requisitions, furloughs, requests for court-martial returned for correction in a baffling flood.

"No, sir," Seeger said. "The passes're fine. They start tomorrow. Well, it's just . . ." He looked around at the company clerk, who was on the sports page.

"This confidential?" Taney asked.

"If you don't mind, sir."

"Johnny," Taney said to the clerk, "go stand in the rain some place."

"Yes, sir," the clerk said, and slowly got up and walked out.

Taney looked shrewdly at Seeger, spoke in a secret whisper. "You pick up anything?" he asked.

Seeger grinned. "No, sir, haven't had my hands on a girl since Strasbourg."

"Ah, that's good." Taney leaned back, relieved, happy he didn't have to cope with the disapproval of the Medical Corps.

"It's—well," said Seeger, embarrassed, "it's hard to say—but it's money."

Taney shook his head sadly. "I know."

"We haven't been paid for three months, sir, and . . ."

"Damn it!" Taney stood up and shouted furiously. "I would like to take every bloody chair-warming old lady in the Finance Department and wring their necks."

The clerk stuck his head into the tent. "Anything wrong? You call for me, sir?"

"No," Taney shouted. "Get out of here."

The clerk ducked out.

Taney sat down again. "I suppose," he said, in a more normal voice, "they have their problems. Outfits being broken up, being moved all over the place. But it is rugged."

"It wouldn't be so bad," Seeger said. "But we're going to Paris tomorrow. Olson, Welch and myself. And you need money in Paris."

"Don't I know it." Taney wagged his head. "Do you know what I paid for a bottle of champagne on the Place Pigalle in September . . . ?" He paused significantly. "I won't tell you. You won't have any respect for me the rest of your life."

Seeger laughed. "Hanging," he said, "is too good for the guy who thought up the rate of exchange."

"I don't care if I never see another franc as long as I live." Taney waved his letter in the air, although it had been dry for a long time.

There was silence in the tent and Seeger swallowed a little embarrassedly, watching the CO wave the flimsy sheet of paper in regular sweeping movements. "Sir," he said, "the truth is, I've come to borrow some money for Welch, Olson and myself. We'll pay it back out of the first pay we get, and that can't be too long from now. If you don't want to give it to us, just tell me and I'll understand and get the hell out of here. We don't like to ask, but you might just as well be dead as be in Paris broke."

Taney stopped waving his letter and put it down thoughtfully. He peered at it, wrinkling his brow, looking like an aged bookkeeper in the single gloomy light that hung in the middle of the tent.

"Just say the word, Captain," Seeger said, "and I'll blow . . ."

"Stay where you are, son," said Taney. He

dug in his shirt pocket and took out a worn, sweat-stained wallet. He looked at it for a moment. "Alligator," he said, with automatic, absent pride. "My wife sent it to me when we were in England. Pounds don't fit in it. However . . ." He opened it and took out all the contents. There was a small pile of francs on the table in front of him. He counted them. "Four hundred francs," he said. "Eight bucks."

"Excuse me," Seeger said humbly. "I shouldn't have asked."

"Delighted," Taney said vigorously. "Absolutely delighted." He started dividing the francs into two piles. "Truth is, Seeger, most of my money goes home in allotments. And the truth is, I lost eleven hundred francs in a poker game three nights ago, and I ought to be ashamed of myself. Here . . ." he shoved one pile toward Seeger. "Two hundred francs."

Seeger looked down at the frayed, meretricious paper, which always seemed to him like stage money, anyway. "No, sir," he said, "I can't take it."

"Take it," Taney said. "That's a direct order."

Seeger slowly picked up the money, not looking at Taney. "Some time, sir," he said, "after we get out, you have to come over to my house and you and my father and my brother and I'll go on a real drunk."

"I regard that," Taney said, gravely, "as a solemn commitment."

They smiled at each other and Seeger started out.

"Have a drink for me," said Taney, "at the Café de la Paix. A small drink." He was sitting down to write his wife he loved her when Seeger went out of the tent.

Olson fell into step with Seeger and they walked silently through the mud between the tents.

"Well, *mon vieux?*" Olson said finally.

"Two hundred francs," said Seeger.

Olson groaned. "Two hundred francs! We won't be able to pinch a whore's behind on the Boulevard des Capucines for two hundred francs. That miserable, penny-loving Yankee!"

"He only had four hundred," Seeger said.

"I revise my opinion," said Olson.

They walked disconsolately and heavily back toward their tent.

Olson spoke only once before they got there. "These raincoats," he said, patting his. "Most

ingenious invention of the war. Highest saturation point of any modern fabric. Collect more water per square inch, and hold it, than any material known to man. All hail the quartermaster!"

Welch was waiting at the entrance of their tent. He was standing there peering excitedly and short-sightedly out at the rain through his glasses, looking angry and tough, like a big-city hack-driver, individual and incorruptible even in the ten-million colored uniform. Every time Seeger came upon Welch unexpectedly, he couldn't help smiling at the belligerent stance, the harsh stare through the steel-rimmed GI glasses, which had nothing at all to do with the way Welch really was. "It's a family inheritance," Welch had once explained. "My whole family stands as though we were getting ready to rap a drunk with a beer glass. Even my old lady." Welch had six brothers, all devout, according to Welch, and Seeger from time to time idly pictured them standing in a row, on Sunday mornings in church, seemingly on the verge of general violence, amid the hushed Latin and Sabbath millinery.

"How much?" Welch asked loudly.

"Don't make us laugh," Olson said, pushing past him into the tent.

"What do you think I could get from the French for my combat jacket?" Seeger said. He went into the tent and lay down on his cot.

Welch followed them in and stood between the two of them, a superior smile on his face. "Boys," he said, "on a man's errand."

"I can just see us now," Olson murmured, lying on his cot with his hands clasped behind his head, "painting Montmartre red. Please bring on the naked dancing girls. Four bucks worth."

"I am not worried," Welch announced.

"Get out of here." Olson turned over on his stomach.

"I know where we can put our hands on sixty-five bucks." Welch looked triumphantly first at Olson, then at Seeger.

Olson turned over slowly and sat up. "I'll kill you," he said, "if you're kidding."

"While you guys are wasting your time," Welch said, "fooling around with the infantry, I used my head. I went into Reems and used my head."

"Rance," Olson said automatically. He had had two years of French in college and he felt, now that the war was over, that he had to introduce his friends to some of his culture.

"I got to talking to a captain in the air force," Welch said eagerly. "A little fat old paddle-footed captain that never got higher off the ground than the second floor of Com Z headquarters, and he told me that what he would admire to do more than anything else is take a nice shiny German Luger pistol with him to show to the boys back in Pacific Grove, California."

Silence fell on the tent and Welch and Olson looked tentatively at Seeger.

"Sixty-five bucks for a Luger, these days," Olson said, "is a very good figure."

"They've been sellin' for as low as thirty-five," said Welch hesitantly. "I'll bet," he said to Seeger, "you could sell yours now and buy another one back when you get some dough, and make a clear twenty-five on the deal."

Seeger didn't say anything. He had killed the owner of the Luger, an enormous SS major, in Coblenz, behind some paper bales in a warehouse, and the major had fired at Seeger three times with it, once nicking his helmet, before Seeger hit him in the face at twenty feet. Seeger had kept the Luger, a long, heavy, well-balanced gun, very carefully since then, lugging it with him, hiding it at the bottom of his bedroll, oiling it three times a week, avoiding all opportunities of selling it, although he had been offered as much as a hundred dollars for it and several times eighty and ninety, while the war was still on, before German weapons became a glut on the market.

"Well," said Welch, "there's no hurry. I told the captain I'd see him tonight around 8 o'clock in front of the Lion D'Or Hotel. You got five hours to make up your mind. Plenty of time."

"Me," said Olson, after a pause. "I won't say anything."

Seeger looked reflectively at his feet and the other two men avoided looking at him. Welch dug in his pocket. "I forgot," he said. "I picked up a letter for you." He handed it to Seeger.

"Thanks," Seeger said. He opened it absently, thinking about the Luger.

"Me," said Olson, "I won't say a bloody word. I'm just going to lie here and think about that nice fat air force captain."

Seeger grinned a little at him and went to the tent opening to read the letter in the light. The letter was from his father, and even from one glance at the handwriting, scrawly and hurried and spotted, so different from his father's usual steady, handsome, professorial script, he knew that something was wrong.

"Dear Norman," it read, "sometime in the future, you must forgive me for writing this letter. But I have been holding this in so long, and there is no one here I can talk to, and because of your brother's condition I must pretend to be cheerful and optimistic all the time at home, both with him and your mother, who has never been the same since Leonard was killed. You're the oldest now, and although I know we've never talked very seriously about anything before, you have been through a great deal by now, and I imagine you must have matured considerably, and you've seen so many different places and people. . . . Norman, I need help. While the war was on and you were fighting, I kept this to myself. It wouldn't have been fair to burden you with this. But now the war is over, and I no longer feel I can stand up under this alone. And you will have to face it some time when you get home, if you haven't faced it already, and perhaps we can help each other by facing it together. . . ."

"I'm redeployable," Olson was singing softly, on his cot. "It's so enjoyable, In the Pelilu mud, With the tropical crud . . ." He fell silent after his burst of song.

Seeger blinked his eyes, at the entrance of the tent, in the wan rainy light, and went on reading his father's letter, on the stiff white stationery with the University letterhead in polite engraving at the top of each page.

"I've been feeling this coming on for a long time," the letter continued, "but it wasn't until last Sunday morning that something happened to make me feel it in its full force. I don't know how much you've guessed about the reason for Jacob's discharge from the Army. It's true he was pretty badly wounded in the leg at Metz, but I've asked around, and I know that men with worse wounds were returned to duty after hospitalization. Jacob got a medical discharge, but I don't think it was for the shrapnel wound in his thigh. He is suffering now from what I suppose you call combat fatigue, and he is subject to fits of depression and hallucinations. Your mother and I thought that as time went by and the war and the army receded, he would grow better. Instead, he is growing worse. Last Sunday morning when I came down into the living room from upstairs he was crouched in his old uniform, next to the window, peering out . . ."

"What the hell," Olson was saying, "if we don't get the sixty-five bucks we can always go to the Louvre. I understand the Mona Lisa is back."

"I asked Jacob what he was doing," the letter went on. "He didn't turn around. 'I'm observing,' he said. 'V-1's and V-2's. Buzz-bombs and rockets. They're coming in by the hundreds.' I tried to reason with him and he told me to crouch and save myself from flying glass. To humor him I got down on the floor beside him and tried to tell him the war was over, that we were in Ohio, 4,000 miles away from the nearest spot where bombs had fallen, that America had never been touched. He wouldn't listen. 'These're the new rocket bombs,' he said, 'for the Jews.' "

"Did you ever hear of the Pantheon?" Olson asked loudly.

"No," said Welch.

"It's free."

"I'll go," said Welch.

Seeger shook his head a little and blinked his eyes before he went back to the letter.

"After that," his father went on, "Jacob seemed to forget about the bombs from time to time, but he kept saying that the mobs were coming up the street armed with bazookas and Browning automatic rifles. He mumbled incoherently a good deal of the time and kept walking back and forth saying, 'What's the situation? Do you know what the situation is?' And he told me he wasn't worried about himself, he was a soldier and he expected to be killed, but he was worried about Mother and myself and Leonard and you. He seemed to forget that Leonard was dead. I tried to calm him and get him back to bed before your mother came down, but he refused and wanted to set out immediately to rejoin his division. It was all terribly disjointed and at one time he took the ribbon he got for winning the Bronze star and threw it in the fireplace, then he got down on his hands and knees and picked it out of the ashes and made me pin it on him again, and he kept repeating, 'This is when they are coming for the Jews.' "

"The next war I'm in," said Olson, "they don't get me under the rank of colonel."

It had stopped raining by now and Seeger

folded the unfinished letter and went outside. He walked slowly down to the end of the company street, and facing out across the empty, soaked French fields, scarred and neglected by various armies, he stopped and opened the letter again.

"I don't know what Jacob went through in the army," his father wrote, "that has done this to him. He never talks to me about the war and he refuses to go to a psychoanalyst, and from time to time he is his own bouncing, cheerful self, playing in tennis tournaments, and going around with a large group of girls. But he has devoured all the concentration camp reports, and I have found him weeping when the newspapers reported that a hundred Jews were killed in Tripoli some time ago.

"The terrible thing is, Norman, that I find myself coming to believe that it is not neurotic for a Jew to behave like this today. Perhaps Jacob is the normal one, and I, going about my business, teaching economics in a quiet classroom, pretending to understand that the world is comprehensible and orderly, am really the mad one. I ask you once more to forgive me for writing you a letter like this, so different from any letter or any conversation I've ever had with you. But it is crowding me, too. I do not see rockets and bombs, but I see other things.

"Wherever you go these days—restaurants, hotels, clubs, trains—you seem to hear talk about the Jews, mean, hateful, murderous talk. Whatever page you turn to in the newspapers you seem to find an article about Jews being killed somewhere on the face of the globe. And there are large, influential newspapers and well-known columnists who each day are growing more and more outspoken and more popular. The day that Roosevelt died I heard a drunken man yelling outside a bar, 'Finally, they got the Jew out of the White House.' And some of the people who heard him merely laughed and nobody stopped him. And on V-E Day, in celebration, hoodlums in Los Angeles savagely beat a Jewish writer. It's difficult to know what to do, whom to fight, where to look for allies.

"Three months ago, for example, I stopped my Thursday night poker game, after playing with the same men for over ten years. John Reilly happened to say that the Jews were getting rich out of this war, and when I demanded an apology, he refused, and when I looked around at the faces of the men who had been my friends for so long, I could see they were not with me. And when I left the house no one said good night to me. I know the poison was spreading from Germany before the war and during it, but I had not realized it had come so close.

"And in my economics class, I find myself idiotically hedging in my lectures. I discover that I am loath to praise any liberal writer or any liberal act and find myself somehow annoyed and frightened to see an article of criticism of existing abuses signed by a Jewish name. And I hate to see Jewish names on important committees, and hate to read of Jews fighting for the poor, the oppressed, the cheated and hungry. Somehow, even in a country where my family has lived a hundred years, the enemy has won this subtle victory over me—he has made me disfranchise myself from honest causes by calling them foreign, Communist, using Jewish names connected with them as ammunition against them.

"And, most hateful of all, I find myself looking for Jewish names in the casualty lists and secretly being glad when I discover them there, to prove that there at least, among the dead and wounded, we belong. Three times, thanks to you and your brothers, I have found our name there, and, may God forgive me, at the expense of your blood and your brother's life, through my tears, I have felt that same twitch of satisfaction. . . .

"When I read the newspapers and see another story that Jews are still being killed in Poland, or Jews are requesting that they be given back their homes in France, or that they be allowed to enter some country where they will not be murdered, I am annoyed with them, I feel they are boring the rest of the world with their problems, they are making demands upon the rest of the world by being killed, they are disturbing everyone by being hungry and asking for the return of their property. If we could all fall through the crust of the earth and vanish in one hour, with our heroes and poets and prophets and martyrs, perhaps we would be doing the memory of the Jewish race a service. . . .

"This is how I feel today, son. I need some help. You've been to the war, you've fought and killed men, you've seen the people of other countries. Maybe you understand things that

I don't understand. Maybe you see some hope somewhere. Help me. Your loving father."

Seeger folded the letter slowly, not seeing what he was doing because the tears were burning his eyes. He walked slowly and aimlessly across the dead autumn grass of the empty field, away from the camp.

He tried to wipe away his tears, because with his eyes full and dark, he kept seeing his father and brother crouched in the old-fashioned living room in Ohio and hearing his brother, dressed in the old, discarded uniform, saying, "These're the new rocket bombs. For the Jews."

He sighed, looking out over the bleak, wasted land. Now, he thought, now I have to think about it. He felt a slight, unreasonable twinge of anger at his father for presenting him with the necessity of thinking about it. The army was good about serious problems. While you were fighting, you were too busy and frightened and weary to think about anything, and at other times you were relaxing, putting your brain on a shelf, postponing everything to that impossible time of clarity and beauty after the war. Well, now, here was the impossible, clear, beautiful time, and here was his father, demanding that he think. There are all sorts of Jews, he thought, there are the sort whose every waking moment is ridden by the knowledge of Jewishness, who see signs against the Jew in every smile on a streetcar, every whisper, who see pogroms in every newspaper article, threats in every change of the weather, scorn in every handshake, death behind each closed door. He had not been like that. He was young, he was big and healthy and easy-going and people of all kinds had seemed to like him all his life, in the army and out. In America, especially, what was going on in Europe had seemed remote, unreal, unrelated to him. The chanting, bearded old men burning in the Nazi furnaces, and the dark-eyed women screaming prayers in Polish and Russian and German as they were pushed naked into the gas chambers had seemed as shadowy and almost as unrelated to him as he trotted out onto the Stadium field for a football game, as they must have been to the men named O'Dwyer and Wickersham and Poole who played in the line beside him.

They had seemed more related in Europe. Again and again in the towns that had been taken back from the Germans, gaunt, gray-faced men had stopped him humbly, looking searchingly at him, and had asked, peering at his long, lined, grimy face, under the anonymous helmet, "Are you a Jew?" Sometimes they asked it in English, sometimes French, or Yiddish. He didn't know French or Yiddish, but he learned to recognize the phrase. He had never understood exactly why they had asked the question, since they never demanded anything from him, rarely even could speak to him, until, one day in Strasbourg, a little bent old man and a small, shapeless woman had stopped him, and asked, in English, if he was Jewish.

"Yes," he said, smiling at them.

The two old people had smiled widely, like children. "Look," the old man had said to his wife. "A young American soldier. A Jew. And so large and strong." He had touched Seeger's arm reverently with the tips of his fingers, then had touched the Garand he was carrying. "And such a beautiful rifle . . ."

And there, for a moment, although he was not particularly sensitive, Seeger got an inkling of why he had been stopped and questioned by so many before. Here, to these bent, exhausted old people, ravaged of their families, familiar with flight and death for so many years, was a symbol of continuing life. A large young man in the uniform of the liberator, blood, as they thought, of their blood, but not in hiding, not quivering in fear and helplessness, but striding secure and victorious down the street, armed and capable of inflicting terrible destruction on his enemies.

Seeger had kissed the old lady on the cheek and she had wept and the old man had scolded her for it, while shaking Seeger's hand fervently and thankfully before saying good-bye.

And, thinking back on it, it was silly to pretend that, even before his father's letter, he had been like any other American soldier going through the war. When he had stood over the huge dead SS major with the face blown in by his bullets in the warehouse in Coblenz, and taken the pistol from the dead hand, he had tasted a strange little extra flavor of triumph. How many Jews, he'd thought, has this man killed, how fitting it is that I've killed him. Neither Olson nor Welch, who were like his brothers, would have felt that in picking up the Luger, its barrel still hot from the last shots

its owner had fired before dying. And he had resolved that he was going to make sure to take this gun back with him to America, and plug it and keep it on his desk at home, as a kind of vague, half-understood sign to himself that justice had once been done and he had been its instrument.

Maybe, he thought, maybe I'd better take it back with me, but not as a memento. Not plugged, but loaded. America by now was a strange country for him. He had been away a long time and he wasn't sure what was waiting for him when he got home. If the mobs were coming down the street toward his house, he was not going to die singing and praying.

When he was taking basic training he'd heard a scrawny, clerklike-looking soldier from Boston talking at the other end of the PX bar, over the watered beer. "The boys at the office," the scratchy voice was saying, "gave me a party before I left. And they told me one thing. 'Charlie,' they said, 'hold onto your bayonet. We're going to be able to use it when you get back. On the Yids.' "

He hadn't said anything then, because he'd felt it was neither possible nor desirable to fight against every random overheard voice raised against the Jews from one end of the world to another. But again and again, at odd moments, lying on a barracks cot, or stretched out trying to sleep on the floor of a ruined French farmhouse, he had heard that voice, harsh, satisfied, heavy with hate and ignorance, saying above the beery grumble of apprentice soldiers at the bar, "Hold onto your bayonet. . . ."

And the other stories—Jews collected stories of hatred and injustice and inklings of doom like a special, lunatic kind of miser. The story of the naval officer, commander of a small vessel off the Aleutians, who, in the officers' wardroom, had complained that he hated the Jews because it was the Jews who had demanded that the Germans be beaten first and the forces in the Pacific had been starved in consequence. And when one of his junior officers, who had just come aboard, had objected and told the commander that he was a Jew, the commander had risen from the table and said, "Mister, the Constitution of the United States says I have to serve in the same navy with Jews, but it doesn't say I have to eat at the same table with them." In the fogs and the cold, swelling Arctic seas off the Aleutians, in a small boat, subject to sudden, mortal attack at any moment . . .

And the two young combat engineers in an attached company on D Day, when they were lying off the coast right before climbing down into the landing barges. "There's France," one of them had said.

"What's it like?" the second one had asked, peering out across the miles of water toward the smoking coast.

"Like every place else," the first one had answered. "The Jews've made all the dough during the war."

"Shut up!" Seeger had said, helplessly thinking of the dead, destroyed, wandering, starving Jews of France. The engineers had shut up, and they'd climbed down together into the heaving boat, and gone into the beach together.

And the million other stories. Jews, even the most normal and best adjusted of them, became living treasuries of them, scraps of malice and bloodthirstiness, clever and confusing and cunningly twisted so that every act by every Jew became suspect and blameworthy and hateful. Seeger had heard the stories, and had made an almost conscious effort to forget them. Now, holding his father's letter in his hand, he remembered them all.

He stared unseeingly out in front of him. Maybe, he thought, maybe it would've been better to have been killed in the war, like Leonard. Simpler. Leonard would never have to face a crowd coming for his mother and father. Leonard would not have to listen and collect these hideous, fascinating little stories that made of every Jew a stranger in any town, on any field, on the face of the earth. He had come so close to being killed so many times, it would have been so easy, so neat and final.

Seeger shook his head. It was ridiculous to feel like that, and he was ashamed of himself for the weak moment. At the age of twenty-one, death was not an answer.

"Seeger!" It was Olson's voice. He and Welch had sloshed silently up behind Seeger, standing in the open field. "Seeger, *mon vieux,* what're you doing—grazing?"

Seeger turned slowly to them. "I wanted to read my letter," he said.

Olson looked closely at him. They had been together so long, through so many things, that flickers and hints of expression on each other's faces were recognized and acted upon. "Anything wrong?" Olson asked.

"No," said Seeger. "Nothing much."

"Norman," Welch said, his voice young and solemn. "Norman, we've been talking, Olson and me. We decided—you're pretty attached to that Luger, and maybe—if you—well . . ."

"What he's trying to say," said Olson, "is we withdraw the request. If you want to sell it, O.K. If you don't, don't do it for our sake. Honest."

Seeger looked at them, standing there, disreputable and tough and familiar. "I haven't made up my mind yet," he said.

"Anything you decide," Welch said oratorically, "is perfectly all right with us. Perfectly."

They walked aimlessly and silently across the field, away from camp. As they walked, their shoes making a wet, sliding sound in the damp, dead grass, Seeger thought of the time Olson had covered him in the little town outside Cherbourg, when Seeger had been caught going down the side of a street by four Germans with a machine gun on the second story of a house on the corner and Olson had had to stand out in the middle of the street with no cover at all for more than a minute, firing continuously, so that Seeger could get away alive. And he thought of the time outside Saint Lô when he had been wounded and had lain in a minefield for three hours and Welch and Captain Taney had come looking for him in the darkness and had found him and picked him up and run for it, all of them expecting to get blown up any second.

And he thought of all the drinks they'd had together and the long marches and the cold winter together, and all the girls they'd gone out with together, and he thought of his father and brother crouching behind the window in Ohio waiting for the rockets and the crowds armed with Browning automatic rifles.

"Say," he stopped and stood facing them. "Say, what do you guys think of the Jews?"

Welch and Olson looked at each other, and Olson glanced down at the letter in Seeger's hand.

"Jews?" Olson said finally. "What're they? Welch, you ever hear of the Jews?"

Welch looked thoughtfully at the gray sky. "No," he said. "But remember, I'm an uneducated fellow."

"Sorry, Bud," Olson said, turning to Seeger.

"We can't help you. Ask us another question. Maybe we'll do better."

Seeger peered at the faces of his friends. He would have to rely upon them, later on, out of uniform, on their native streets, more than he had ever relied on them on the bullet-swept street and in the dark minefield in France. Welch and Olson stared back at him, troubled, their faces candid and tough and dependable.

"What time," Seeger asked, "did you tell that captain you'd meet him?"

"Eight o'clock," Welch said. "But we don't have to go. If you have any feeling about that gun . . ."

"We'll meet him," Seeger said. "We can use that sixty-five bucks."

"Listen," Olson said, "I know how much you like that gun and I'll feel like a heel if you sell it."

"Forget it," Seeger said, starting to walk again. "What could I use it for in America?"

## William Faulkner
# SPOTTED HORSES

Yes sir. Flem Snopes has filled that whole country full of spotted horses. You can hear folks running them all day and all night, whooping and hollering, and the horses running back and forth across them little wooden bridges ever now and then kind of like thunder. Here I was this morning pretty near halfway to town, with the team ambling along and me setting in the buckboard about half asleep, when all of a sudden something come swurging up outen the bushes and jumped the road clean, without touching hoof to it. It flew right over my team big as a billboard and flying through the air like a hawk. It taken me thirty minutes to stop my team and untangle the harness and the buckboard and hitch them up again.

That Flem Snopes. I be dog if he ain't a case, now. One morning about ten years ago the boys was just getting settled down on Varner's

SPOTTED HORSES: From *The Hamlet*, by William Faulkner. Copyright, 1931, by Random House, Inc. Used by permission of the publishers.

porch for a little talk and tobacco, when here come Flem out from behind the counter, with his coat off and his hair all parted, like he might have been clerking for Varner for ten years already. Folks all knowed him; it was a big family of them about five miles down the bottom. That year, at least. Share-cropping. They never stayed on any place over a year. Then they would move on to another place, with the chap or maybe the twins of that year's litter. It was a regular nest of them. But Flem. The rest of them stayed tenant farmers, moving ever year, but here come Flem one day, walking out from behind Jody Varner's counter like he owned it. And he wasn't there but a year or two before folks knowed that if him and Jody was both still in that store in ten years more it would be Jody clerking for Flem Snopes. Why, that fellow could make a nickel where it wasn't but four cents to begin with. He skun me in two trades myself, and the fellow that can do that, I just hope he'll get rich before I do; that's all.

All right. So here Flem was, clerking at Varner's, making a nickel here and there and not telling nobody about it. No, sir. Folks never knowed when Flem got the better of somebody lessen the fellow he beat told it. He'd just set there in the store-chair, chewing his tobacco and keeping his own business to hisself, until about a week later we'd find out it was somebody else's business he was keeping to hisself— provided the fellow he trimmed was mad enough to tell it. That's Flem.

We give him ten years to own ever thing Jody Varner had. But he never waited no ten years. I reckon you-all know that gal of Uncle Billy Varner's, the youngest one, Eula. Jody's sister. Ever Sunday ever yellow-wheeled buggy and curried riding horse in that country would be hitched to Bill Varner's fence, and the young bucks setting on the porch, swarming around Eula like bees around a honey pot. One of these here kind of big, soft-looking gals that could giggle richer than plowed new-ground. Wouldn't none of them leave before the others, and so they would set there on the porch until time to go home, with some of them with nine and ten miles to ride and then get up tomorrow and go back to the field. So they would all leave together and they would ride in a clump down to the creek ford and hitch them curried horses and yellow-wheeled buggies and get out and fight one another. Then they would get in the buggies again and go on home.

Well, one day about a year ago, one of them yellow-wheeled buggies and one of them curried saddle-horses quit this country. We heard they was heading for Texas. The next day Uncle Billy and Eula and Flem come in to town in Uncle Bill's surrey, and when they come back, Flem and Eula was married. And on the next day we heard that two more of them yellow-wheeled buggies had left the country. They mought have gone to Texas, too. It's a big place.

Anyway, about a month after the wedding, Flem and Eula went to Texas, too. They was gone pretty near a year. Then one day last month, Eula come back, with a baby. We figgered up, and we decided that it was as well-growed a three-months-old baby as we ever see. It can already pull up on a chair. I reckon Texas makes big men quick, being a big place. Anyway, if it keeps on like it started, it'll be chewing tobacco and voting time it's eight years old.

And so last Friday here come Flem himself. He was on a wagon with another fellow. The other fellow had one of these two-gallon hats and a ivory-handled pistol and a box of gingersnaps sticking out of his hind pocket, and tied to the tail-gate of the wagon was about two dozen of them Texas ponies, hitched to one another with barbed wire. They was colored like parrots and they was quiet as doves, and ere a one of them would kill you quick as a rattlesnake. Nere a one of them had two eyes the same color, and nere a one of them had ever see a bridle, I reckon; and when that Texas man got down offen the wagon and walked up to them to show how gentle they was, one of them cut his vest clean offen him, same as with a razor.

Flem had done already disappeared; he had went on to see his wife, I reckon, and to see if that ere baby had done gone on to the field to help Uncle Billy plow, maybe. It was the Texas man that taken the horses on to Mrs. Littlejohn's lot. He had a little trouble at first, when they come to the gate, because they hadn't never see a fence before, and when he finally got them in and taken a pair of wire cutters and unhitched them and got them into

the barn and poured some shell corn into the trough, they durn nigh tore down the barn. I reckon they thought that shell corn was bugs, maybe. So he left them in the lot and he announced that the auction would begin at sunup tomorrow.

That night we was setting on Mrs. Littlejohn's porch. You-all mind the moon was nigh full that night, and we could watch them spotted varmints swirling along the fence and back and forth across the lot same as minnows in a pond. And then now and then they would all kind of huddle up against the barn and rest themselves by biting and kicking one another. We would hear a squeal, and then a set of hoofs would go Bam! against the barn, like a pistol. It sounded just like a fellow with a pistol, in a nest of cattymounts, taking his time.

II

It wasn't ere a man knowed yet if Flem owned them things or not. They just knowed one thing: that they wasn't never going to know for sho if Flem did or not, or if maybe he didn't just get on that wagon at the edge of town, for the ride or not. Even Eck Snopes didn't know, Flem's own cousin. But wasn't nobody surprised at that. We knowed that Flem would skin Eck quick as he would ere a one of us.

They was there by sunup next morning, some of them come twelve and sixteen miles, with seed-money tied up in tobacco sacks in their overalls, standing along the fence, when the Texas man come out of Mrs. Littlejohn's after breakfast and clumb onto the gate post with that ere white pistol butt sticking outen his hind pocket. He taken a new box of gingersnaps outen his pocket and bit the end offen it like a cigar and spit out the paper, and said the auction was open. And still they was coming up in wagons and a horse- and mule-back and hitching the teams across the road and coming to the fence. Flem wasn't nowhere in sight.

But he couldn't get them started. He begun to work on Eck, because Eck holp him last night to get them into the barn and feed them that shell corn. Eck got out just in time. He come outen that barn like a chip on the crest of a busted dam of water, and clumb into the wagon just in time.

He was working on Eck when Henry Armstid come up in his wagon. Eck was saying he was skeered to bid on one of them, because he might get it, and the Texas man says, "Them ponies? Them little horses?" He clumb down offen the gate post and went toward the horses. They broke and run, and him following them, kind of chirping to them, with his hand out like he was fixing to catch a fly, until he got three or four of them cornered. Then he jumped into them, and then we couldn't see nothing for a while because of the dust. It was a big cloud of it, and them blare-eyed, spotted things swoaring outen it twenty foot to a jump, in forty directions without counting up. Then the dust settled and there they was, that Texas man and the horse. He had its head twisted clean around like a owl's head. Its legs was braced and it was trembling like a new bride and groaning like a sawmill, and him holding its head wrung clean around on its neck so it was snuffing sky. "Look it over," he says, with his heels dug too and that white pistol sticking outen his pocket and his neck swole up like a spreading adder's until you could just tell what he was saying, cussing the horse and talking to us all at once: "Look him over, the fiddle-headed son of fourteen fathers. Try him, buy him; you will get the best—" Then it was all dust again, and we couldn't see nothing but spotted hide and mane, and that ere Texas man's boot-heels like a couple of walnuts on two strings, and after a while that two-gallon hat come sailing out like a fat old hen crossing a fence.

When the dust settled again, he was just getting outen the far fence corner, brushing himself off. He come and got his hat and brushed it off and come and clumb onto the gate post again. He was breathing hard. The hammer-head horse was still running round and round the lot like a merry-go-round at a fair. That was when Henry Armstid come shoving up to the gate in them patched overalls and one of them dangle-armed shirts of hisn. Hadn't nobody noticed him until then. We was all watching the Texas man and the horses. Even Mrs. Littlejohn; she had done come out and built a fire under the wash-pot in her back yard, and she would stand at the fence a while and then go back into the house and come out again with a arm full of wash and stand at the fence again.

Well, here come Henry shoving up, and then we see Mrs. Armstid right behind him, in that ere faded wrapper and sunbonnet and them tennis shoes. "Git on back to that wagon," Henry says.

"Henry," she says.

"Here, boys," the Texas man says; "make room for missus to git up and see. Come on Henry," he says; "here's your chance to buy that saddle-horse missus has been wanting. What about ten dollars, Henry?"

"Henry," Mrs. Armstid says. She put her hand on Henry's arm. Henry knocked her hand down.

"Git on back to that wagon, like I told you," he says.

Mrs. Armstid never moved. She stood behind Henry, with her hands rolled into her dress, not looking at nothing. "He hain't no more despair than to buy one of them things," she says. "And us not five dollars ahead of the pore house, he hain't no more despair." It was the truth, too. They ain't never made more than a bare living offen that place of theirs, and them with four chaps and the very clothes they wears she earns by weaving by the firelight at night while Henry's asleep.

"Shut your mouth and git on back to that wagon," Henry says. "Do you want I taken a wagon stake to you here in the big road?"

Well, that Texas man taken one look at her. Then he begun on Eck again, like Henry wasn't even there. But Eck was skeered. "I can git me a snapping turtle or a water moccasin for nothing. I ain't going to buy none."

So the Texas man said he would give Eck a horse. "To start the auction, and because you holp me last night. If you'll start the bidding on the next horse," he says, "I'll give you that fiddle-head horse."

I wish you could have seen them, standing there with their seed-money in their pockets, watching that Texas man give Eck Snopes a live horse, all fixed to call him a fool if he taken it or not. Finally Eck says he'll take it. "Only I just starts the bidding," he says. "I don't have to buy the next one lessen I ain't overtopped." The Texas man said all right, and Eck bid a dollar on the next one, with Henry Armstid standing there with his mouth already open, watching Eck and the Texas man like a mad-dog or something. "A dollar," Eck says.

The Texas man looked at Eck. His mouth was already open too, like he had started to say something and what he was going to say had up and died on him. "A dollar? You mean, *one* dollar, Eck?"

"Durn it," Eck says; "two dollars, then."

Well, sir, I wish you could a seen that Texas man. He taken out that gingersnap box and held it up and looked into it, careful, like it might have been a diamond ring in it, or a spider. Then he throwed it away and wiped his face with a bandanna. "Well," he says. "Well. Two dollars. Two dollars. Is your pulse all right, Eck?" he says. "Do you have ager-sweats at night, maybe?" he says. "Well," he says, "I got to take it. But are you boys going to stand there and see Eck get two horses at a dollar a head?"

That done it. I be dog if he wasn't nigh as smart as Flem Snopes. He hadn't no more than got the words outen his mouth before here was Henry Armstid, waving his hand. "Three dollars," Henry says. Mrs. Armstid tried to hold him again. He knocked her hand off, shoving up to the gate post.

"Mister," Mrs. Armstid says, "we got chaps in the house and not corn to feed the stock. We got five dollars I earned my chaps a-weaving after dark, and him snoring in the bed. And he hain't no more despair."

"Henry bid three dollars," the Texas man says. "Raise him a dollar, Eck, and the horse is yours."

"Henry," Mrs. Armstid says.

"Raise him, Eck," the Texas man says.

"Four dollars," Eck says.

"Five dollars," Henry says, shaking his fist. He shoved up right under the gate post. Mrs. Armstid was looking at the Texas man too.

"Mister," she says, "if you take that five dollars I earned my chaps a-weaving for one of them things, it'll be a curse onto you and yourn during all the time of man."

But it wasn't no stopping Henry. He had shoved up, waving his fist at the Texas man. He opened it; the money was in nickels and quarters, and one dollar bill that looked like a cow's cud. "Five dollars," he says. "And the man that raises it'll have to beat my head off, or I'll beat hisn."

"All right," the Texas man says. "Five dollars is bid. But don't you shake your hand at me."

## III

It taken till nigh sundown before the last one was sold. He got them hotted up once and the bidding got up to seven dollars and a quarter, but most of them went around three or four dollars, him setting on the gate post and picking the horses out one at a time by mouth-word, and Mrs. Littlejohn pumping up and down at the tub and stopping and coming to the fence for a while and going back to the tub again. She had done got done too, and the wash was hung on the line in the back yard, and we could smell supper cooking. Finally they was all sold; he swapped the last two and the wagon for a buckboard.

We was all kind of tired, but Henry Armstid looked more like a mad-dog than ever. When he bought, Mrs. Armstid had went back to the wagon, setting in it behind them two rabbit-sized, bone-pore mules, and the wagon itself looking like it would fall all to pieces soon as the mules moved. Henry hadn't even waited to pull it outen the road; it was still in the middle of the road and her setting in it, not looking at nothing, ever since this morning.

Henry was right up against the gate. He went up to the Texas man. "I bought a horse and I paid cash," Henry says. "And yet you expect me to stand around here until they are all sold before I can get my horse. I'm going to take my horse outen that lot."

The Texas man looked at Henry. He talked like he might have been asking for a cup of coffee at the table. "Take your horse," he says.

Then Henry quit looking at the Texas man. He begun to swallow, holding onto the gate. "Ain't you going to help me?" he says.

"It ain't my horse," the Texas man says.

Henry never looked at the Texas man again, he never looked at nobody. "Who'll help me catch my horse?" he says. Never nobody said nothing. "Bring the plowline," Henry says. Mrs. Armstid got outen the wagon and brought the plowline. The Texas man got down offen the post. The woman made to pass him, carrying the rope.

"Don't you go in there, missus," the Texas man says.

Henry opened the gate. He didn't look back. "Come on here," he says.

"Don't you go in there, missus," the Texas man says.

Mrs. Armstid wasn't looking at nobody, neither, with her hands across her middle, holding the rope. "I reckon I better," she says. Her and Henry went into the lot. The horses broke and run. Henry and Mrs. Armstid followed.

"Get him into the corner," Henry says. They got Henry's horse cornered finally, and Henry taken the rope, but Mrs. Armstid let the horse get out. They hemmed it up again, but Mrs. Armstid let it get out again, and Henry turned and hit her with the rope. "Why didn't you head him back?" Henry says. He hit her again. "Why didn't you?" It was about that time I looked around and see Flem Snopes standing there.

It was the Texas man that done something. He moved fast for a big man. He caught the rope before Henry could hit the third time, and Henry whirled and made like he would jump at the Texas man. But he never jumped. The Texas man went and taken Henry's arm and led him outen the lot. Mrs. Armstid come behind them and the Texas man taken some money outen his pocket and he give it into Mrs. Armstid's hand. "Get him into the wagon and take him on home," the Texas man says, like he might have been telling them he enjoyed his supper.

Then here come Flem. "What's that for, Buck?" Flem says.

"Thinks he bought one of them ponies," the Texas man says. "Get him on away, missus."

But Henry wouldn't go. "Give him back that money," he says. "I bought that horse and I aim to have him if I have to shoot him."

And there was Flem, standing there with his hands in his pockets, chewing, like he had just happened to be passing.

"You take your money and I take my horse," Henry says. "Give it back to him," he says to Mrs. Armstid.

"You don't own no horse of mine," the Texas man says. "Get him on home, missus."

Then Henry seen Flem. "You got something to do with these horses," he says. "I bought one. Here's the money for it." He taken the bill outen Mrs. Armstid's hand. He offered it to Flem. "I bought one. Ask him. Here. Here's the money," he says, giving the bill to Flem.

When Flem taken the money, the Texas man dropped the rope he had snatched outen Henry's hand. He had done sent Eck Snopes's boy up to the store for another box of gingersnaps, and he taken the box outen his pocket and looked into it. It was empty and he dropped it on the ground. "Mr. Snopes will have your money for you tomorrow," he says to Mrs. Armstid. "You can get it from him tomorrow. He don't own no horse. You get him into the wagon and get him on home." Mrs. Armstid went back to the wagon and got in. "Where's that ere buckboard I bought?" the Texas man says. It was after sundown then. And then Mrs. Littlejohn come out on the porch and rung the supper bell.

IV

I come on in and et supper. Mrs. Littlejohn would bring in a pan of bread or something, then she would go out to the porch a minute and come back and tell us. The Texas man had hitched his team to the buckboard he had swapped them last two horses for, and him and Flem had gone, and then she told that the rest of them that never had ropes had went back to the store with I. O. Snopes to get some ropes, and wasn't nobody at the gate but Henry Armstid, and Mrs. Armstid setting in the wagon in the road, and Eck Snopes and that boy of hisn. "I don't care how many of them fool men gets killed by them things," Mrs. Littlejohn says, "but I ain't going to let Eck Snopes take that boy into that lot again." So she went down to the gate, but she come back without the boy or Eck neither.

"It ain't no need to worry about that boy," I says. "He's charmed." He was right behind Eck last night when Eck went to help feed them. The whole drove of them jumped clean over that boy's head and never touched him. It was Eck that touched him. Eck snatched him into the wagon and taken a rope and frailed the tar outen him.

So I had done et and went to my room and was undressing, long as I had a long trip to make next day; I was trying to sell a machine to Mrs. Bundren up past Whiteleaf; when Henry Armstid opened that gate and went in by hisself. They couldn't make him wait for the balance of them to get back with their ropes. Eck Snopes said he tried to make Henry wait, but Henry wouldn't do it. Eck said Henry walked right up to them and that when they broke, they run clean over Henry like a haymow breaking down. Eck said he snatched that boy of hisn out of the way just in time and that them things went through that gate like a creek flood and into the wagons and teams hitched side the road, busting wagon tongues and snapping harness like it was fishing-line, with Mrs. Armstid still setting in their wagon in the middle of it like something carved outen wood. Then they scattered, wild horses and tame mules with pieces of harness and singletrees dangling offen them, both ways up and down the road.

"There goes ourn, paw!" Eck said his boy said. "There it goes, into Mrs. Littlejohn's house." Eck says it run right up the steps and into the house like a boarder late for supper. I reckon so. Anyway, I was in my room, in my underclothes, with one sock on and one sock in my hand, leaning out the window when the commotion busted out, when I heard something run into the melodeon in the hall; it sounded like a railroad engine. Then the door to my room come sailing in like when you throw a tin bucket top into the wind and I looked over my shoulder and see something that looked like a fourteen-foot pinwheel a-blaring its eyes at me. It had to blare them fast, because I was already done jumped out the window.

I reckon it was anxious, too. I reckon it hadn't never seen barbed wire or shell corn before, but I know it hadn't never seen underclothes before, or maybe it was a sewing-machine agent it hadn't never seen. Anyway, it whirled and turned to run back up the hall and outen the house, when it met Eck Snopes and that boy just coming in, carrying a rope. It swirled again and run down the hall and out the back door just in time to meet Mrs. Littlejohn. She had just gathered up the clothes she had washed, and she was coming onto the back porch with a armful of washing in one hand and a scrubbing-board in the other, when the horse skidded up to her, trying to stop and swirl again. It never taken Mrs. Littlejohn no time a-tall.

"Git outen here, you son," she says. She hit it across the face with the scrubbing-board; that ere scrubbing-board split as neat as ere a axe could have done it, and when the horse swirled to run back up the hall, she hit it again with what was left of the scrubbing-board, not on the head this time. "And stay out," she says.

Eck and that boy was halfway down the hall by this time. I reckon that horse looked like a pinwheel to Eck too. "Git to hell outen here, Ad!" Eck says. Only there wasn't time. Eck dropped flat on his face, but the boy never moved. The boy was about a yard tall maybe, in overalls just like Eck's; that horse swoared over his head without touching a hair. I saw that, because I was just coming back up the front steps, still carrying that ere sock and still in my underclothes, when the horse come onto the porch again. It taken one look at me and swirled again and run to the end of the porch and jumped the banisters and the lot fence like a hen-hawk and lit in the lot running and went out the gate again and jumped eight or ten upside-down wagons and went on down the road. It was a full moon then. Mrs. Armstid was still setting in the wagon like she had done been carved outen wood and left there and forgot.

That horse. It ain't never missed a lick. It was going about forty miles a hour when it come to the bridge over the creek. It would have had a clear road, but it so happened that Vernon Tull was already using the bridge when it got there. He was coming back from town; he hadn't heard about the auction; him and his wife and three daughters and Mrs. Tull's aunt, all setting in chairs in the wagon bed, and all asleep, including the mules. They waked up when the horse hit the bridge one time, but Tull said the first he knew was when the mules tried to turn the wagon around in the middle of the bridge and he seen that spotted varmint run right twixt the mules and run up the wagon tongue like a squirrel. He said he just had time to hit it across the face with his whip-stock, because about that time the mules turned the wagon around on that ere one-way bridge and that horse clumb across onto the bridge again and went on, with Vernon standing up in the wagon and kicking at it.

Tull said the mules turned in the harness and clumb back into the wagon too, with Tull trying to beat them out again, with the reins wrapped around his wrist. After that he says all he seen was overturned chairs and women-folks' legs and white drawers shining in the moonlight, and his mules and that spotted horse going on up the road like a ghost.

The mules jerked Tull outen the wagon and drug him a spell on the bridge before the reins broke. They thought at first that he was dead, and while they was kneeling around him, picking the bridge splinters outen him, here come Eck and that boy, still carrying the rope. They was running and breathing a little hard. "Where'd he go?" Eck said.

## V

I went back and got my pants and shirt and shoes on just in time to go and help get Henry Armstid outen the trash in the lot. I be dog if he didn't look like he was dead, with his head hanging back and his teeth showing in the moonlight, and a little rim of white under his eye-lids. We could still hear them horses, here and there; hadn't none of them got more than four-five miles away yet, not knowing the country, I reckon. So we could hear them and folks yelling now and then: "Whooey. Head him!"

We toted Henry into Mrs. Littlejohn's. She was in the hall; she hadn't put down the armful of clothes. She taken one look at us, and she laid down the busted scrubbing-board and taken up the lamp and opened a empty door. "Bring him in here," she says.

We toted him in and laid him on the bed. Mrs. Littlejohn set the lamp on the dresser, still carrying the clothes. "I'll declare, you men," she says. Our shadows was way up the wall, tiptoeing too; we could hear ourselves breathing. "Better get his wife," Mrs. Littlejohn says. She went out, carrying the clothes.

"I reckon we had," Quick says. "Go get her, somebody."

"Whyn't you go?" Winterbottom says.

"Let Ernest git her," Durley says. "He lives neighbors with them."

Ernest went to fetch her. I be dog if Henry didn't look like he was dead. Mrs. Littlejohn come back, with a kettle and some towels. She went to work on Henry, and then Mrs. Armstid and Ernest come in. Mrs. Armstid come to the foot of the bed and stood there, with her hands rolled into her apron, watching what Mrs. Littlejohn was doing, I reckon.

"You men get outen the way," Mrs. Littlejohn says. "Git outside," she says. "See if you can't find something else to play with that will kill some more of you."

"Is he dead?" Winterbottom says.

"It ain't your fault if he ain't," Mrs. Little-

john says. "Go tell Will Varner to come up here. I reckon a man ain't so different from a mule, come long come short. Except maybe a mule's got more sense."

We went to get Uncle Billy. It was a full moon. We could hear them, now and then, four miles away: "Whooey. Head him." The country was full of them, one on ever wooden bridge in the land, running across it like thunder: "Whooey. There he goes. Head him."

We hadn't got far before Henry begun to scream. I reckon Mrs. Littlejohn's water had brung him to; anyway, he wasn't dead. We went on to Uncle Billy's. The house was dark. We called to him, and after a while the window opened and Uncle Billy put his head out, peart as a peckerwood, listening. "Are they still trying to catch them durn rabbits?" he says.

He come down, with his britches on over his night-shirt and his suspenders dangling, carrying his horse-doctoring grip. "Yes, sir," he says, cocking his head like a woodpecker; "they're still a-trying."

We could hear Henry before we reached Mrs. Littlejohn's. He was going Ah-Ah-Ah. We stopped in the yard. Uncle Billy went on in. We could hear Henry. We stood in the yard, hearing them on the bridges, this-a-way and that: "Whooey. Whooey."

"Eck Snopes ought to caught hisn," Ernest says.

"Looks like he ought," Winterbottom said.

Henry was going Ah-Ah-Ah steady in the house; then he begun to scream. "Uncle Billy's started," Quick says. We looked into the hall. We could see the light where the door was. Then Mrs. Littlejohn come out.

"Will needs some help," she says. "You, Ernest. You'll do." Ernest went into the house.

"Hear them?" Quick said. "That one was on Four Mile bridge." We could hear them; it sounded like thunder a long way off; it didn't last long:

"Whooey."

We could hear Henry: "Ah-Ah-Ah-Ah-Ah."

"They are both started now," Winterbottom says. "Ernest too."

That was early in the night. Which was a good thing, because it taken a long night for folks to chase them things right and for Henry to lay there and holler, being as Uncle Billy never had none of this here chloryfoam to set Henry's leg with. So it was considerate in Flem to get them started early. And what do you reckon Flem's com-ment was?

That's right. Nothing. Because he wasn't there. Hadn't nobody see him since that Texas man left.

## VI

That was Saturday night. I reckon Mrs. Armstid got home about daylight, to see about the chaps. I don't know where they thought her and Henry was. But lucky the oldest one was a gal, about twelve, big enough to take care of the little ones. Which she did for the next two days. Mrs. Armstid would nurse Henry all night and work in the kitchen for hern and Henry's keep, and in the afternoon she would drive home (it was about four miles) to see to the chaps. She would cook up a pot of victuals and leave it on the stove, and the gal would bar the house and keep the little ones quiet. I would hear Mrs. Littlejohn and Mrs. Armstid talking in the kitchen. "How are the chaps making out?" Mrs. Littlejohn says.

"All right," Mrs. Armstid says.

"Don't they git skeered at night?" Mrs. Littlejohn says.

"Ina May bars the door when I leave," Mrs. Armstid says. "She's got the axe in bed with her. I reckon she can make out."

I reckon they did. And I reckon Mrs. Armstid was waiting for Flem to come back to town; hadn't nobody seen him until this morning; to get her money the Texas man said Flem was keeping for her. Sho. I reckon she was.

Anyway, I heard Mrs. Armstid and Mrs. Littlejohn talking in the kitchen this morning while I was eating breakfast. Mrs. Littlejohn had just told Mrs. Armstid that Flem was in town. "You can ask him for that five dollars," Mrs. Littlejohn says.

"You reckon he'll give it to me?" Mrs. Armstid says.

Mrs. Littlejohn was washing dishes, washing them like a man, like they was made out of iron. "No," she says. "But asking him won't do no hurt. It might shame him. I don't reckon it will, but it might."

"If he wouldn't give it back, it ain't no use to ask," Mrs. Armstid says.

"Suit yourself," Mrs. Littlejohn says. "It's your money."

I could hear the dishes.

"Do you reckon he might give it back to me?" Mrs. Armstid says. "That Texas man said he would. He said I could get it from Mr. Snopes later."

"Then go and ask him for it," Mrs. Littlejohn says.

I could hear the dishes.

"He won't give it back to me," Mrs. Armstid says.

"All right," Mrs. Littlejohn says. "Don't ask him for it, then."

I could hear the dishes; Mrs. Armstid was helping. "You don't reckon he would, do you?" she says. Mrs. Littlejohn never said nothing. It sounded like she was throwing the dishes at one another. "Maybe I better go and talk to Henry about it," Mrs. Armstid says.

"I would," Mrs. Littlejohn says. I be dog if it didn't sound like she had two plates in her hands, beating them together. "Then Henry can buy another five-dollar horse with it. Maybe he'll buy one next time that will out and out kill him. If I thought that, I'd give you back the money, myself."

"I reckon I better talk to him first," Mrs. Armstid said. Then it sounded like Mrs. Littlejohn taken up all the dishes and throwed them at the cook-stove, and I come away.

That was this morning. I had been up to Bundren's and back, and I thought that things would have kind of settled down. So after breakfast, I went up to the store. And there was Flem, setting in the store chair and whittling, like he might not have ever moved since he come to clerk for Jody Varner. I. O. was leaning in the door, in his shirt sleeves and with his hair parted too, same as Flem was before he turned the clerking job over to I. O. It's a funny thing about them Snopes: they all looks alike, yet there ain't ere a two of them that claims brothers. They're always just cousins, like Flem and Eck and Flem and I. O. Eck was there too, squatting against the wall, him and that boy, eating cheese and crackers outen a sack; they told me that Eck hadn't been home a-tall. And that Lon Quick hadn't got back to town, even. He followed his horse clean down to Samson's Bridge, with a wagon and a camp outfit. Eck finally caught one of hisn. It run into a blind lane at Freeman's and Eck and the boy taken and tied their rope across the end of the lane, about three foot high. The horse come to the end of the lane and whirled and run back without ever stopping. Eck says it never seen the rope a-tall. He says it looked just like one of these here Christmas pinwheels. "Didn't it try to run again?" I says.

"No," Eck says, eating a bite of cheese offen his knife blade. "Just kicked some."

"Kicked some?" I says.

"It broke its neck," Eck says.

Well, they was squatting there, about six of them, talking, talking at Flem; never nobody knowed yet if Flem had ere a interest in them horses or not. So finally I come right out and asked him. "Flem's done skun all of us so much," I says, "that we're proud of him. Come on, Flem," I says, "how much did you and that Texas man make offen them horses? You can tell us. Ain't nobody here but Eck that bought one of them; the others ain't got back to town yet, and Eck's your own cousin; he'll be proud to hear, too. How much did you-all make?"

They was all whittling, not looking at Flem, making like they was studying. But you could a heard a pin drop. And I. O. He had been rubbing his back up and down on the door, but he stopped now, watching Flem like a pointing dog. Flem finished cutting the sliver offen his stick. He spit across the porch, into the road. "Twarn't none of my horses," he said.

I. O. cackled, like a hen, slapping his legs with both hands. "You boys might just as well quit trying to get ahead of Flem," he said.

Well, about that time I see Mrs. Armstid come outen Mrs. Littlejohn's gate, coming up the road. I never said nothing. I says, "Well, if a man can't take care of himself in a trade, he can't blame the man that trims him."

Flem never said nothing, trimming at the stick. He hadn't seen Mrs. Armstid. "Yes, sir," I says. "A fellow like Henry Armstid ain't got nobody but hisself to blame."

"Course he ain't," I. O. says. He ain't seen her, either. "Henry Armstid's a born fool. Always is been. If Flem hadn't a got his money, somebody else would."

We looked at Flem. He never moved. Mrs. Armstid come on up the road.

"That's right," I says. "But come to think of it, Henry never bought no horse." We looked at Flem; you could a heard a match drop. "That Texas man told her to get that five dollars back from Flem next day. I reckon Flem's done already taken that money to Mrs. Littlejohn's and give it to Mrs. Armstid."

We watched Flem. I. O. quit rubbing his back against the door again. After a while Flem raised his head and spit across the porch, into the dust. I. O. cackled, just like a hen. "Ain't he a beating fellow, now?" I. O. says.

Mrs. Armstid was getting closer, so I kept on talking, watching to see if Flem would look up and see her. But he never looked up. I went on talking about Tull, about how he was going to sue Flem, and Flem setting there, whittling his stick, not saying nothing else after he said they wasn't none of his horses.

Then I. O. happened to look around. He seen Mrs. Armstid. "Psssst!" he says. Flem looked up. "Here she comes!" I. O. says. "Go out the back. I'll tell her you done went in to town today."

But Flem never moved. He just set there, whittling, and we watched Mrs. Armstid come up onto the porch, in that ere faded sunbonnet and wrapper and them tennis shoes that make a kind of hissing noise on the porch. She come onto the porch and stopped, her hands rolled into her dress in front, not looking at nothing.

"He said Saturday," she says, "that he wouldn't sell Henry no horse. He said I could get the money from you."

Flem looked up. The knife never stopped. It went on trimming off a sliver same as if he was watching it. "He taken that money off with him when he left," Flem says.

Mrs. Armstid never looked at nothing. We never looked at her, neither, except that boy of Eck's. He had a half-et cracker in his hand, watching her, chewing.

"He said Henry hadn't bought no horse," Mrs. Armstid says. "He said for me to get the money from you today."

"I reckon he forgot about it," Flem said. "He taken that money off with him Saturday." He whittled again. I. O. kept on rubbing his back, slow. He licked his lips. After a while the woman looked up the road, where it went on up the hill, toward the graveyard. She looked up that way for a while, with that boy of Eck's watching her and I. O. rubbing his back slow against the door. Then she turned back toward the steps.

"I reckon it's time to get dinner started," she says.

"How's Henry this morning, Mrs. Armstid?" Winterbottom says.

She looked at Winterbottom; she almost stopped. "He's resting, I thank you kindly," she says.

Flem got up, outen the chair, putting his knife away. He spit across the porch. "Wait a minute, Mrs. Armstid," he says. She stopped again. She didn't look at him. Flem went on into the store, with I. O. done quit rubbing his back now, with his head craned after Flem, and Mrs. Armstid standing there with her hands rolled into her dress, not looking at nothing. A wagon come up the road and passed; it was Freeman, on the way to town. Then Flem come out again, with I. O. still watching him. Flem had one of these little striped sacks of Jody Varner's candy; I bet he still owes Jody that nickel, too. He put the sack into Mrs. Armstid's hand, like he would have put it into a hollow stump. He spit again across the porch. "A little sweetening for the chaps," he says.

"You're right kind," Mrs. Armstid says. She held the sack of candy in her hand, not looking at nothing. Eck's boy was watching the sack, the half-et cracker in his hand; he wasn't chewing now. He watched Mrs. Armstid roll the sack into her apron. "I reckon I better get on back and help with dinner," she says. She turned and went back across the porch. Flem set down in the chair again and opened his knife. He spit across the porch again, past Mrs. Armstid where she hadn't went down the steps yet. Then she went on, in that ere sunbonnet and wrapper all the same color, back down the road toward Mrs. Littlejohn's. You couldn't see her dress move, like a natural woman walking. She looked like a old snag still standing up and moving along on a high water. We watched her turn in at Mrs. Littlejohn's and go outen sight. Flem was whittling. I. O. begun to rub his back on the door. Then he begun to cackle, just like a durn hen.

"You boys might just as well quit trying," I. O. says. "You can't git ahead of Flem. You can't touch him. Ain't he a sight, now?"

I be dog if he ain't. If I had brung a herd of wild cattymounts into town and sold them to my neighbors and kinfolks, they would have lynched me. Yes, sir.

## John Milton
## ON HIS BLINDNESS

When I consider how my light is spent
Ere half my days in this dark world and wide,
And that one talent which is death to hide
Lodged with me useless, though my soul more bent
To serve therewith my Maker, and present
My true account, lest He returning chide;
"Doth God exact day-labor, light denied?"
I fondly ask. But Patience, to prevent
That murmur, soon replies, "God doth not need
Either man's work or his own gifts. Who best    10
Bear his mild yoke, they serve him best. His state
Is kingly: thousands at his bidding speed,
And post o'er land and ocean without rest;
They also serve who only stand and wait."

## William Blake
## LONDON

I wander through each chartered street,
Near where the chartered Thames does flow,
And mark in every face I meet
Marks of weakness, marks of woe.

In every cry of every man,
In every infant's cry of fear,
In every voice, in every ban,
The mind-forged manacles I hear:

How the chimney-sweeper's cry
Every blackening church appalls,        10
And the hapless soldier's sigh
Runs in blood down palace walls.

But most, through midnight streets I hear
How the youthful harlot's curse
Blasts the new-born infant's tear,
And blights with plagues the marriage hearse.

*Emily Dickinson*
# A NARROW FELLOW IN THE GRASS

A narrow fellow in the grass
Occasionally rides;
You may have met him—did you not?
His notice sudden is.

The grass divides as with a comb,
A spotted shaft is seen;
And then it closes at your feet
And opens further on.

He likes a boggy acre,
A floor too cool for corn.                          10
Yet when a child, and barefoot,
I more than once, at morn,

Have passed, I thought, a whip-lash
Unbraiding in the sun—
When, stooping to secure it,
It wrinkled, and was gone.

Several of nature's people
I know, and they know me;
I feel for them a transport
Of cordiality;                                      20

But never met this fellow,
Attended or alone,
Without a tighter breathing,
And zero at the bone.

A NARROW FELLOW IN THE GRASS: From *Poems by
Emily Dickinson,* edited by Martha Dickinson Bianchi.
Used by permission of Little, Brown and Company.

*Gerard Manley Hopkins*
# SPRING AND FALL:
*to a young child*

Márgarét, are you grieving
Over Goldengrove unleaving?
Leáves, líke the things of man, you
With your fresh thoughts care for, can you?

SPRING AND FALL: TO A YOUNG CHILD: From *Collected Poems,* by Gerard Manley Hopkins. Used by
permission of the Oxford University Press.

Áh! ás the heart grows older
It will come to such sights colder
By and by, nor spare a sigh
Though worlds of wanwood leafmeal lie.
And yet you wíll weep and know why.
Now no matter, child, the name:                     10
Sórrow's springs áre the same.
Nor mouth had, no nor mind, expressed
What heart heard of, ghost guessed:
It ís the blight man was born for,
It is Margaret you mourn for.

*George Meredith*
# LUCIFER IN STARLIGHT

On a starred night Prince Lucifer uprose.
Tired of his dark dominion swung the fiend
Above the rolling ball in cloud part screened,
Where sinners hugged their specter of repose.
Poor prey to his hot fit of pride were those.
And now upon his western wing he leaned,
Now his huge bulk o'er Afric's sands careened,
Now the black planet shadowed Arctic snows.
Soaring through wider zones that pricked his scars
With memory of the old revolt from Awe,            10
He reached a middle height, and at the stars,
Which are the brain of heaven, he looked, and
    sank.
Around the ancient track marched, rank on rank,
The army of unalterable law.

*William Butler Yeats*
# THE SECOND COMING

Turning and turning in the widening gyre
The falcon cannot hear the falconer;
Things fall apart; the centre cannot hold;
Mere anarchy is loosed upon the world,

THE SECOND COMING: From *Collected Poems,* by
William Butler Yeats. Copyright, 1903, 1906, 1907,
1912, 1916, 1918, 1919, 1924, 1928, 1931, 1933,
1934, 1935, 1940, 1944, 1945, 1946, 1950, by The
Macmillan Company. Copyright, 1940, by Georgie
Yeats. Used by permission of The Macmillan Com-
pany. Canadian rights granted by Mrs. Yeats, The
Macmillan Company of Canada, and A. P. Watt &
Son, Ltd.

The blood-dimmed tide is loosed, and everywhere
The ceremony of innocence is drowned;
The best lack all conviction, while the worst
Are full of passionate intensity.

Surely some revelation is at hand;
Surely the Second Coming is at hand.                    10
The Second Coming! Hardly are those words out
When a vast image out of *Spiritus Mundi* [16]
Troubles my sight: somewhere in sands of the
    desert
A shape with lion body and the head of a man,
A gaze blank and pitiless as the sun,
Is moving its slow thighs, while all about it
Reel shadows of the indignant desert birds.
The darkness drops again; but now I know
That twenty centuries of stony sleep
Were vexed to nightmare by a rocking cradle,   20
And what rough beast, its hour come round at last,
Slouches towards Bethlehem to be born?

---

[16] *i.e.*, the world's collective spirit or memory.

## W. H. Auden
# THE CRISIS

Where do They come from? Those whom we so
    much dread
As on our dearest location falls the chill
    Of their crooked wing and endangers
    The melting friend, the aqueduct, the flower.

Terrible Presences that the ponds reflect
Back at the famous, and when the blond boy
    Bites eagerly into the shining
    Apple, emerge in their shocking fury.

And we realise the woods are deaf and the sky
Nurses no one, and we are awake and these     10
    Like farmers have purpose and knowledge,
    And towards us their hate is directed.

We are the barren pastures to which they bring
The resentment of outcasts; on us they work
    Out their despair; they wear our weeping
    As the disgraceful badge of their exile.

---

O we conjured them here like a lying map;
Desiring the extravagant joy of life
    We lured with a mirage of orchards
    Fat in the lazy climate of refuge.          20

Our money sang like streams on the aloof peaks
Of our thinking that beckoned them on like girls;
    Our culture like a West of wonder
    Shone a solemn promise in their faces.

We expected the beautiful or the wise
Ready to see a charm in our childish fib,
    Pleased to find nothing but stones and
    Able at once to create a garden.

But those who come are not even children with
The big indiscriminate eyes we had lost,      30
    Occupying our narrow spaces
    With their anarchist vivid abandon.

They arrive, already adroit, having learned
Restraint at the table of a father's rage;
    In a mother's distorting mirror
    They discovered the Meaning of Knowing.

These pioneers have long adapted themselves
To the night and the nightmare; they come
    equipped
    To reply to terror with terror,
    With lies to unmask the least deception.   40

For a future of marriage nevertheless
The bed is prepared; though all our whiteness
    shrinks
    From the hairy and clumsy bridegroom,
    We conceive in the shuddering instant.

For the barren must wish to bear though the Spring
Punish; and the crooked that dreads to be straight
    Cannot alter its prayer but summons
    Out of the dark a horrible rector.

O the striped and vigorous tiger can move
With style through the borough of murder; the
    ape                                          50
    Is really at home in the parish
    Of grimacing and licking: but we have

Failed as their pupils. Our tears well from a love
We have never outgrown; our cities predict
    More than we hope; even our armies
    Have to express our need of forgiveness.

*Robert Penn Warren*

# ORIGINAL SIN:
# A SHORT STORY

Nodding, its great head rattling like a gourd,
And locks like seaweed strung on the stinking stone,
The nightmare stumbles past, and you have heard
It fumble your door before it whimpers and is gone:
It acts like the old hound that used to snuffle your door and moan.

You thought you had lost it when you left Omaha,
For it seemed connected then with your grandpa, who
Had a wen on his forehead and sat on the veranda
To finger the precious protuberance, as was his habit to do,
Which glinted in sun like rough garnet or the rich old brain bulging through.          10

But you met it in Harvard Yard as the historic steeple
Was confirming the midnight with its hideous racket,
And you wondered how it had come, for it stood so imbecile,
With empty hands, humble, and surely nothing in pocket:
Riding the rods, perhaps—or grandpa's will paid the ticket.

You were almost kindly then, in your first homesickness,
As it tortured its stiff face to speak, but scarcely mewed;
Since then you have outlived all your homesickness,
But have met it in many another distempered latitude:
Oh, nothing is lost, ever lost! at last you understood.          20

But it never came in the quantum glare of sun
To shame you before your friends, and had nothing to do
With your public experience or private reformation:
But it thought no bed too narrow—it stood with lips askew
And shook its great head sadly like the abstract Jew.

Never met you in the lyric arsenical meadows
When children call and your heart goes stone in the bosom;
At the orchard anguish never, nor ovoid horror,
Which is furred like a peach or avid like the delicious plum.
It takes no part in your classic prudence or fondled axiom.          30

Not there when you exclaimed: "Hope is betrayed by
Disastrous glory of sea-capes, sun-torment of whitecaps
—There must be a new innocence for us to be stayed by."
But there it stood, after all the timetables, all the maps,
In the crepuscular clutter of *always, always,* or *perhaps.*

---

You have moved often and rarely left an address,
And hear of the deaths of friends with a sly pleasure,
A sense of cleansing and hope, which blooms from distress;
But it has not died, it comes, its hand childish, unsure,
Clutching the bribe of chocolate or a toy you used to treasure.          40

It tries the lock; you hear, but simply drowse:
There is nothing remarkable in that sound at the door.
Later you may hear it wander the dark house
Like a mother who rises at night to seek a childhood picture;
Or it goes to the backyard and stands like an old horse cold in the pasture.

---

*William Shakespeare*

# OTHELLO
# THE MOOR OF VENICE

## CHARACTERS

*in order of their appearance*

RODERIGO, *a Venetian of good family*

IAGO, *an army officer*

BRABANTIO, *a wealthy Senator*

OTHELLO, *a Moor; commander of a Venetian army*

CASSIO, *a Florentine;* OTHELLO'S *second-in-command*

*Other* OFFICERS *of the Venetian army*

*The* DUKE, *ruler of Venice*

SENATORS

A SAILOR

A MESSENGER

DESDEMONA, BRABANTIO'S *daughter*

MONTANO, *Venetian governor of Cyprus*

GENTLEMEN *in the government of Cyprus*

EMILIA, IAGO'S *wife*

A HERALD

PEOPLE *of Cyprus*

MUSICIANS

A CLOWN

BIANCA, *a loose woman of Cyprus*

LODOVICO, DESDEMONA'S *cousin*

GRATIANO, DESDEMONA'S *uncle*

ATTENDANTS

*Historic period: May, 1565*

## ACT 1. *Venice.*

SCENE 1. *The street on which stands the house of* BRABANTIO; *about midnight.*

RODERIGO, *a Venetian of good family, and* IAGO, *an army officer.*

RODERIGO. Tush! never tell me; I take it much unkindly
That thou, Iago, who hast had my purse
As if the strings were thine, shouldst know of this.

IAGO. 'Sblood, but you will not hear me:
If ever I did dream of such a matter
Abhor me.

RODERIGO. Thou toldest me thou didst hold him in thy hate.

IAGO. Despise me, if I do not. Three great ones of the city,
In personal suit to make me his lieutenant,
Off-capped to him: and, by the faith of man,          10
I know my price, I am worth no worse a place:
But he, as loving his own pride and purposes,
Evades them, with a bombast circumstance
Horribly stuffed with epithets of war;
And, in conclusion,
Nonsuits my mediators: for, "Certes," says he,
"I have already chose my officer."
And what was he?
Forsooth, a great arithmetician,
One Michael Cassio, a Florentine,          20
A fellow almost damned in a fair wife;
That never set a squadron in the field,

---

4 *'Sblood:* by God's blood. 9 *lieutenant:* second-in-command. 10 *Off-capped:* uncovered their heads. 13 *bombast circumstance:* wordy rigmarole. 16 *Nonsuits my mediators:* refuses my pleaders. 19 *arithmetician: i.e.,* since bookkeeping was developed at Florence. 21 *damned, etc.:* ruined by his liking for pretty women (?).

Nor the division of a battle knows
More than a spinster; unless the bookish theoric
Wherein the togèd consuls can propose
As masterly as he: mere prattle, without prac-
    tice,
In all his soldiership. But he, sir, had the elec-
    tion:
And I, of whom his eyes had seen the proof
At Rhodes, at Cyprus, and on other grounds
Christian and heathen, must be be-leed and
    calmed                      30
By debitor and creditor: this counter-caster,
He, in good time, must his lieutenant be,
And I—God bless the mark!—his Moorship's
    ancient.
    RODERIGO. By heaven, I rather would have
      been his hangman.
    IAGO. Why, there's no remedy; 't is the curse
      of service,
Preferment goes by letter and affection,
And not by old gradation, where each second
Stood heir to the first. Now, sir, be judge your-
    self,
Whether I in any just term am affined
To love the Moor.
    RODERIGO.  I would not follow him then. 40
    IAGO. O, sir, content you;
I follow him to serve my turn upon him:
We cannot all be masters, nor all masters
Cannot be truly followed. You shall mark
Many a duteous and knee-crooking knave,
That, doting on his own obsequious bondage,
Wears out his time, much like his master's ass,
For nought but provender, and when he's old,
    cashiered:
Whip me such honest knaves. Others there are
Who, trimmed in forms and visages of duty, 50
Keep yet their hearts attending on themselves,
And, throwing but shows of service on their
    lords,
Do well thrive by them, and when they have
    lined their coats
Do themselves homage: these fellows have
    some soul;
And such a one do I profess myself. For, sir,

It is as sure as you are Roderigo,
Were I the Moor, I would not be Iago:
In following him, I follow but myself;
Heaven is my judge, not I for love and duty,
But seeming so, for my peculiar end:        60
For when my outward action doth demonstrate
The native act and figure of my heart   ·
In compliment extern, 't is not long after
But I will wear my heart upon my sleeve
For daws to peck at; I am not what I am.
    RODERIGO. What a full fortune does the
      thick-lips owe,
If he can carry't thus!
    IAGO.               Call up her father;
Rouse him, make after him, poison his delight,
Proclaim him in the streets; incense her kins-
    men,
And, though he in a fertile climate dwell, 70
Plague him with flies: though that his joy be
    joy,
Yet throw such changes of vexation on 't,
As it may lose some color.
    RODERIGO. Here is her father's house; I'll
      call aloud.
    IAGO. Do; with like timorous accent and dire
      yell
As when, by night and negligence, the fire
Is spied in populous cities.
    RODERIGO. What, ho, Brabantio! Signior
      Brabantio, ho!
    IAGO. Awake! what, ho, Brabantio! thieves!
      thieves! thieves!
Look to your house, your daughter, and your
    bags!                              80
Thieves! thieves!

BRABANTIO, *a Senator, appears at an upper*
*window of his house.*

    BRABANTIO. What is the reason of this
      terrible summons?
What is the matter there?
    RODERIGO. Signior, is all your family within?
    IAGO. Are your doors locked?
    BRABANTIO.  Why, wherefore ask you this?
    IAGO. 'Zounds, sir, you're robbed; for shame,
      put on your gown;
Your heart is burst, you have lost half your
    soul;

---

23 *division:* arrangement.  24 *unless:* except for; *theoric:* theory. 25 *togèd consuls:* senators in civilian dress. 27 *had the election:* was chosen. 28 *his:* Othello's. 30 *be-leed:* made to stagnate. 31 *debitor and creditor: i.e.,* the "bookkeeper" Cassio; *counter-caster:* accountant. 33 *ancient:* ensign, the next rank. 36 *letter: i.e.,* of recommendation. 37 *gradation:* right of advancement. 39 *term:* terms; *affined:* compelled. 42 *turn:* interests. 50 *trimmed .in:* disguised by; *visages:* facial expressions.

---

60 *peculiar:* private. 63 *compliment extern:* outward appearance. 65 *daws:* crows. 66 *owe:* possess. 67 *carry't:* be successful. 68 *Rouse ... him: i.e.,* rouse Othello like game and pursue him. 75 *timorous:* terrifying. 80 *bags:* money-bags. 86 *'Zounds:* by God's wounds.

Even now, now, very now, an old black ram
Is tupping your white ewe. Arise, arise!
Awake the snorting citizens with the bell,     90
Or else the devil will make a grandsire of you:
Arise, I say.

> BRABANTIO.          What, have you lost your
> wits?
> RODERIGO. Most reverend signior, do you
> know my voice?
> BRABANTIO. Not I: what are you?
> RODERIGO. My name is Roderigo.
> BRABANTIO.          The worser welcome:

I have charged thee not to haunt about my
doors:
In honest plainness thou hast heard me say
My daughter is not for thee; and now, in
madness,
Being full of supper and distempering draughts,
Upon malicious bravery, dost thou come     100
To start my quiet.

> RODERIGO.          Sir, sir, sir!
> BRABANTIO.          But thou must
> needs be sure

My spirit and my place have in them power
To make this bitter to thee.

> RODERIGO.          Patience, good sir.
> BRABANTIO. What tellest thou me of
> robbing? This is Venice;

My house is not a grange.

> RODERIGO.          Most grave Brabantio,

In simple and pure soul I come to you.

> IAGO. 'Zounds, sir, you are one of those that
> will not serve God, if the devil bid you.
> Because we come to do you service and
> you think we are ruffians, you'll have     110
> your daughter covered with a Barbary
> horse; you'll have your nephews neigh to
> you; you'll have coursers for cousins and
> gennets for germans.
> BRABANTIO. What profane wretch art thou?
> IAGO. I am one, sir, that comes to tell you
> your daughter and the Moor are now
> making the beast with two backs.
> BRABANTIO. Thou art a villain.
> IAGO.          You are—a senator.
> BRABANTIO. This thou shalt answer; I know
> thee, Roderigo.          120

> RODERIGO. Sir, I will answer anything. But, I
> beseech you,

If't be your pleasure and most wise consent,
As partly I find it is, that your fair daughter,
At this odd-even and dull watch o' the night,
Transported, with no worse nor better guard
But with a knave of common hire, a gòndolier,
To the gross clasps of a lascivious Moor,—
If this be known to you and your allowance,
We then have done you bold and saucy wrongs;
But if you know not this, my manners tell
me                                          130
We have your wrong rebuke. Do not believe
That, from the sense of all civility,
I thus would play and trifle with your reverence:
Your daughter, if you have not given her leave,
I say again, hath made a gross revolt;
Tying her duty, beauty, wit and fortunes
In an extravagant and wheeling stranger
Of here and everywhere. Straight satisfy
yourself:
If she be in her chamber or your house,
Let loose on me the justice of the state     140
For thus deluding you.

> BRABANTIO.          Strike on the tinder, ho!

Give me a taper! Call up all my people!
This accident is not unlike my dream:
Belief of it oppresses me already.
Light, I say! light!

>          [BRABANTIO *disappears from the window.*
> IAGO.          Farewell, for I must leave you:

It seems not meet, nor wholesome to my
place,
To be produced—as, if I stay, I shall—
Against the Moor. For I do know, the state,
However this may gall him with some check,
Cannot with safety cast him, for he's
embarked                                     150
With such loud reason to the Cyprus wars,
Which even now stand in act, that, for their
souls,
Another of his fathom they have none,
To lead their business: in which regard,
Though I do hate him as I do hell-pains,
Yet for necessity of present life
I must show out a flag and sign of love,
Which is indeed but sign. That you shall surely
find him,

---

89 *tupping:* mounting.  90 *snorting:* snoring.  94 *what:*
who.  99 *distempering draughts:* intoxicants.  100 *Upon
. . . bravery:* with malicious intent to defy me.  101 *start:*
disturb.  102 *place:* high position.  105 *grange:* farm.
112 *nephews:* grandsons.  113 *coursers:* race-horses.
114 *gennets:* Spanish ponies; *germans:* relations.

124 *odd-even, etc.:* about midnight.  128 *allowance:* consent.  132 *from:* in spite of.  137 *In an extravagant, etc.:*
to a vagabond.  142 *people:* servants.  147 *produced:*
made a witness.  149 *check:* rebuke.  150 *cast:* dismiss.
151 *With such, etc.:* on such urgent need.  153 *fathom:*
ability.

Lead to the Sagittary the raisèd search;
And there will I be with him. So, farewell.    160

[IAGO *goes out.*

BRABANTIO, *wearing a dressing-gown and followed by* ATTENDANTS *with torches, comes out
his front door.*

BRABANTIO. It is too true an evil: gone she is;
And what's to come of my despisèd time
Is nought but bitterness. Now, Roderigo,
Where didst thou see her? O unhappy girl!
With the Moor, sayest thou? Who would be a
father!
How didst thou know't was she? O, she deceives
me
Past thought! What said she to you? Get more
tapers;
Raise all my kindred. Are they married, think
you?

RODERIGO. Truly, I think they are.

BRABANTIO. O heaven! How got she out? O
treason of the blood!                          170
Fathers, from hence trust not your daughters'
minds
By what you see them act. Is there not charms
By which the property of youth and maidhood
May be abused? Have you not read, Roderigo,
Of some such thing?

RODERIGO.                Yes, sir, I have indeed.

BRABANTIO. Call up my brother. O, that you
had had her!
Some one way, some another. Do you know
Where we may apprehend her and the Moor?

RODERIGO. I think I can discover him, if you
please
To get good guard and go along with me.    180

BRABANTIO. Pray you, lead on. At every
house I'll call;
I may command at most. Get weapons, ho!
And raise some special officers of night.
On, good Roderigo; I'll deserve your pains.

SCENE 2. *A street near the Sagittary Inn, a few
minutes later.*

IAGO; OTHELLO, *the Moorish general; and*
ATTENDANTS *with torches.*

IAGO. Though in the trade of war I have slain
men,
Yet do I hold it very stuff o' the conscience

To do no còntrived murder: I lack iniquity
Sometimes to do me service: nine or ten times
I had thought to have yerked him here under
the ribs.

OTHELLO. 'T is better as it is.

IAGO.                        Nay, but he prated,
And spoke such scurvy and provoking terms
Against your honor
That, with the little godliness I have,
I did full hard forbear him. But, I pray you,
sir,                                            10
Are you fast married? Be assured of this,
That the magnifico is much beloved,
And hath in his effect a voice potential
As double as the Duke's: he will divorce you,
Or put upon you what restraint and grievance
The law, with all his might to enforce it on,
Will give him cable.

OTHELLO.              Let him do his spite:
My services which I have done the signiory
Shall out-tongue his complaints. 'Tis yet to
know,—
Which when I know that boasting is an
honor                                          20
I shall promulgate—I fetch my life and being
From men of royal siege, and my demerits
May speak unbonneted to as proud a fortune
As this that I have reached: for know, Iago,
But that I love the gentle Desdemona,
I would not my unhousèd free condition
Put into circumscription and confine
For the sea's worth. But, look! what lights
come yond?

IAGO. Those are the raisèd father and his
friends:
You were best go in.

OTHELLO.        Not I; I must be found:    30
My parts, my title and my perfect soul
Shall manifest me rightly. Is it they?

IAGO. By Janus, I think no.

CASSIO, *Othello's second-in-command, comes
in, followed by* OFFICERS *with torches.*

OTHELLO. The servants of the Duke, and my
lieutenant.
The goodness of the night upon you, friends!
What is the news?

---

159 *Sagittary:* an inn; *raisèd:* aroused. 162 *despisèd
time:* disgraced old age. 170 *blood:* sexual passion.
173 *property:* nature. 174 *abused:* corrupted. 176 *Call:*
wake. 184 *deserve:* reward.

5 *yerked him:* stabbed Roderigo. 10 *did, etc.:* could
scarcely put up with. 12 *magnifico:* nobleman. 13–14 *hath,
etc.:* i.e., his influence is as powerful as the Duke's double
vote. 17 *give him cable:* permit him to do. 18 *signiory:*
governing body. 22 *siege:* rank; *demerits:* merit. 23 *unbonneted:* on equal terms. 26 *unhousèd:* without household ties. 31 *parts:* abilities; *perfect:* innocent.

CASSIO. The Duke does greet you, general,
And he requires your haste-post-haste
appearance,
Even on the instant.
    OTHELLO. What is the matter, think you?
    CASSIO. Something from Cyprus, as I may
divine:
It is a business of some heat. The galleys   40
Have sent a dozen sequent messengers
This very night at one another's heels,
And many of the consuls, raised and met,
Are at the Duke's already: you have been hotly
called for;
When, being not at your lodging to be found,
The senate hath sent about three several quests
To search you out.
    OTHELLO.     'T is well I am found by you.
I will but spend a word here in the house,
And go with you. [OTHELLO *goes into the inn.*
    CASSIO.     Ancient, what makes he here?
    IAGO. 'Faith, he tonight hath boarded a
land carack:     50
If it prove lawful prize, he's made for ever.
    CASSIO. I do not understand.
    IAGO.     He's married.
    CASSIO.     To who?
    IAGO. Marry, to—

*OTHELLO comes out.*

Come, captain, will you go?
    OTHELLO.     Have with you.
    CASSIO. Here comes another troop to seek
for you.
    IAGO. It is Brabantio. General, be advised;
He comes to bad intent.

*BRABANTIO and RODERIGO arrive, followed by
OFFICERS with torches and drawn swords.*

    OTHELLO.     Holla! stand there!
    RODERIGO. Signior, it is the Moor.
    BRABANTIO.     Down with him, thief!

*BRABANTIO, RODERIGO, and IAGO draw their
swords.*

    IAGO. You, Roderigo! come, sir, I am for
you.
    OTHELLO. Keep up your bright swords, for
the dew will rust them.

Good signior, you shall more command with
years     60
Than with your weapons.
    BRABANTIO. O thou foul thief, where hast
thou stowed my daughter?
Damned as thou art, thou hast enchanted her;
For I'll refer me to all things of sense,
If she in chains of magic were not bound,
Whether a maid so tender, fair and happy,
So opposite to marriage that she shunned
The wealthy curlèd darlings of our nation,
Would ever have, to incur a general mock,
Run from her guardage to the sooty bosom   70
Of such a thing as thou, to fear, not to delight.
Judge me the world, if 't is not gross in sense
That thou hast practised on her with foul
charms,
Abused her delicate youth with drugs or
minerals
That weaken motion: I'll have't disputed on;
'T is probable and palpable to thinking.
I therefore apprehend and do attach thee
For an abuser of the world, a practiser
Of arts inhibited and out of warrant.
Lay hold upon him: if he do resist,     80
Subdue him at his peril.
    OTHELLO.     Hold your hands,
Both you of my inclining, and the rest:
Were it my cue to fight, I should have known it
Without a prompter. Where will you that I go
To answer this your charge?
    BRABANTIO.     To prison, till fit time
Of law and course of direct session
Call thee to answer.
    OTHELLO.     What if I do obey?
How may the Duke be therewith satisfied,
Whose messengers are here about my side,
Upon some present business of the state   90
To bring me to him?
    FIRST OFFICER.     'T is true, most worthy
signior;
The Duke's in council, and your noble self,
I am sure, is sent for.
    BRABANTIO.     How! the Duke in council!
In this time of the night! Bring him away:
Mine's not an idle cause: the Duke himself,
Or any of my brothers of the state,
Cannot but feel this wrong as 't were their own;

---

41 *sequent:* successive. 48 *spend:* speak. 50 *carack:* cargo-ship. 53 *Marry:* By St. Mary (with a pun); *Have:* I'll go. 56 *to:* with. 58 *am for:* challenge.

62 *stowed:* hidden. 64 *refer me:* appeal; *of sense:* capable of judgment. 67 *opposite:* opposed. 70 *guardage:* father's protection. 72 *gross in sense:* obvious. 75 *motion:* understanding; *disputed on:* analyzed by learned men. 79 *out of warrant:* illegal. 82 *inclining:* side. 86 *direct session:* regular law-court. 94 *him away:* Othello along.

For if such actions may have passage free,
Bond-slaves and pagans shall our statesmen be.

SCENE 3. *A council-chamber, shortly afterward.*

*The* DUKE *and* SENATORS *sitting at a table;*
OFFICERS *attending.*

DUKE. There is no composition in these news
That gives them credit.
FIRST SENATOR.          Indeed, they are dis-
     proportioned;
My letters say a hundred and seven galleys.
DUKE. And mine, a hundred and forty.
SECOND SENATOR.   And mine, two hundred:
But though they jump not on a just account,—
As in these cases, where the aim reports,
'T is oft with difference—yet do they all
     confirm
A Turkish fleet, and bearing up to Cyprus.
DUKE. Nay, it is possible enough to
     judgment:
I do not so secure me in the error,          10
But the main article I do approve
In fearful sense.
SAILOR, *off-stage.* What, ho! what, ho! what,
     ho!
FIRST OFFICER. A messenger from the
     galleys.

*A* SAILOR *enters.*

DUKE.               Now, what's the business?
SAILOR. The Turkish preparation makes for
     Rhodes;
So was I bid report here to the state
By Signior Angelo.
DUKE. How say you by this change?
FIRST SENATOR.               This cannot be,
By no assay of reason: 't is a pageant,
To keep us in false gaze. When we consider
The importancy of Cyprus to the Turk,          20
And let ourselves again but understand
That as it more concerns the Turk than Rhodes,
So may he with more facile question bear it,
For that it stands not in such warlike brace,
But altogether lacks the abilities
That Rhodes is dressed in: if we make thought
     of this,
We must not think the Turk is so unskilful

To leave that latest which concerns him first,
Neglecting an attempt of ease and gain,
To wake and wage a danger profitless.          30
DUKE. Nay, in all confidence, he's not for
     Rhodes.
FIRST OFFICER. Here is more news.

*A* MESSENGER *enters.*

MESSENGER. The Ottomites, reverend and
     gracious,
Steering with due course towards the isle of
     Rhodes,
Have there injointed them with an after fleet.
FIRST SENATOR. Ay, so I thought. How
     many, as you guess?
MESSENGER. Of thirty sail: and now they
     do re-stem
Their backward course, bearing with ' frank
     appearance
Their purposes toward Cyprus. Signior
     Montano,
Your trusty and most valiant servitor,          40
With his free duty recommends you thus,
And prays you to believe him.
DUKE. 'T is certain, then, for Cyprus.
Marcus Luccicos, is not he in town?
FIRST SENATOR. He's now in Florence.
DUKE. Write from us to him; post-post-haste
     dispatch.

BRABANTIO, OTHELLO, IAGO, RODERIGO, *and*
OFFICERS *enter.*

FIRST SENATOR. Here comes Brabantio and
     the valiant Moor.
DUKE. Valiant Othello, we must straight
     employ you
Against the general enemy Ottoman.
[*To* BRABANTIO] I did not see you; welcome,
     gentle signior;          50
We lacked your counsel and your help tonight.
BRABANTIO. So did I yours. Good your
     grace, pardon me;
Neither my place nor aught I heard of business
Hath raised me from my bed, nor doth the
     general care
Take hold on me, for my particular grief
Is of so flood-gate and o'erbearing nature
That it engluts and swallows other sorrows
And it is still itself.

---

1 *composition:* consistency.  5 *jump:* agree; *just:* exact.
6 *the aim:* guesswork.  10 *secure me in:* feel reassured by.
11 *approve:* believe.  18 *no assay:* any test; *pageant:* pretense.  23 *facile question:* easy contest; *bear:* storm.
24 *brace:* defensive posture.  26 *dressed in:* defended by.

28 *latest:* till last.  33 *Ottomites:* Turks.  35 *injointed:*
combined; *after:* second.  37 *re-stem:* reverse.  40 *servitor:*
retainer.  41 *free duty:* sincere respects; *recommends:*
informs.  49 *general:* national.  51 *lacked:* missed.  57 *engluts:* eats up.

DUKE.                  Why, what's the matter?
BRABANTIO. My daughter! O, my daughter!
DUKE *and* SENATORS.                  Dead?
BRABANTIO.                           Ay, to me;
She is abused, stolen from me, and
   corrupted                                    60
By spells and medicines bought of
   mountebanks;
For nature so preposterously to err,
Being not deficient, blind, or lame of sense,
Sans witchcraft could not.
   DUKE. Whoe'er he be that in this foul
      proceeding
Hath thus beguiled your daughter of herself
And you of her, the bloody book of law
You shall yourself read in the bitter letter
After your own sense, yea, though our proper
   son
Stood in your action.
   BRABANTIO. Humbly I thank your grace. 70
Here is the man, this Moor, whom now, it
   seems,
Your special mandate for the state-affairs
Hath hither brought.
   DUKE *and* SENATORS. We are very sorry
      for 't.
   DUKE, *to* OTHELLO. What, in your own part,
      can you say to this?
   BRABANTIO. Nothing, but this is so.
   OTHELLO. Most potent, grave, and reverend
      signiors,
My very noble and approved good masters,
That I have ta'en away this old man's daughter,
It is most true; true, I have married her:
The very head and front of my offending    80
Hath this extent, no more. Rude am I in my
   speech,
And little blessed with the soft phrase of peace:
For since these arms of mine had seven years'
   pith,
Till now some nine moons wasted, they have
   used
Their dearest action in the tented field;
And little of this great world can I speak,
More than pertains to feats of broil and battle,
And therefore little shall I grace my cause
In speaking for myself. Yet, by your gracious
   patience,
I will a round unvarnished tale deliver       90

Of my whole course of love; what drugs, what
   charms,
What conjuration and what mighty magic—
For such proceeding I am charged withal—
I won his daughter.
   BRABANTIO.            A maiden never bold;
Of spirit so still and quiet, that her motion
Blushed at herself; and she—in spite of nature,
Of years, of country, credit, everything—
To fall in love with what she feared to look on!
It is a judgment maimed and most imperfect
That will confess perfection so could err   100
Against all rules of nature; and must be driven
To find out practices of cunning hell,
Why this should be. I therefore vouch again
That with some mixtures powerful o'er the
   blood,
Or with some dram conjured to this effect,
He wrought upon her.
   DUKE.             To vouch this, is no proof,
Without more wider and more overt test
Than these thin habits and poor likelihoods
Of modern seeming do prefer against him.
   FIRST SENATOR. But, Othello, speak:    110
Did you by indirect and forcèd courses
Subdue and poison this young maid's affections?
Or came it by request and such fair question
As soul to soul affordeth!
   OTHELLO.               I do beseech you
Send for the lady to the Sagittary,
And let her speak of me before her father:
If you do find me foul in her report,
The trust, the office I do hold of you,
Not only take away, but let your sentence
Even fall upon my life.
   DUKE.          Fetch Desdemona hither.   120
   OTHELLO. Ancient, conduct them: you best
      know the place.
                  [IAGO *and* ATTENDANTS *go out.*
And, till she come, as truly as to heaven
I do confess the vices of my blood,
So justly to your grave ears I'll present
How I did thrive in this fair lady's love,
And she in mine.
   DUKE. Say it, Othello.
   OTHELLO. Her father loved me, oft invited
      me,
Still questioned me the story of my life,

---

61 *mountebanks:* quacks.  64 *sans:* without.  68–9 *read,
etc.:* apply as harshly as you please; *our proper:* my own.
70 *Stood, etc.:* were the defendant.  81 *Rude:* unpolished.
84 *moons wasted:* months ago.  85 *dearest:* most intense.
90 *round unvarnished:* direct and truthful.

95–6 *that her motion, etc.:* that any emotion in that
serene spirit was embarrassed by its own daring and
blushed.  97 *credit:* reputation.  108–9 *thin, etc.:* un-
convincing appearances of guilt.  129 *Still:* continually.

From year to year, the battles, sieges,
    fortunes,                                                   130
That I have passed.
I ran it through, even from my boyish days,
To the very moment that he bade me tell it;
Wherein I spake of most disastrous chances,
Of moving accidents by flood and field,
Of hair-breadth scapes i' the imminent deadly
    breach,
Of being taken by the insolent foe
And sold to slavery, of my redemption thence
And portance in my travels' history;
Wherein of antres vast and deserts idle,      140
Rough quarries, rocks and hills whose heads
    touch heaven,
It was my hint to speak,—such was the process;
And of the cannibals that each other eat,
The Anthropophagi, and men whose heads
Do grow beneath their shoulders. This to hear
Would Desdemona seriously incline;
But still the house-affairs would draw her
    thence,
Which ever as she could with haste dispatch,
She'd come again, and with a greedy ear
Devour up my discourse. Which I
    observing,                                                 150
Took once a pliant hour, and found good means
To draw from her a prayer of earnest heart
That I would all my pilgrimage dilate,
Whereof by parcels she had something heard,
But not intentively. I did consent,
And often did beguile her of her tears,
When I did speak of some distressful stroke
That my youth suffered. My story being done,
She gave me for my pains a world of sighs;
She swore, in faith, 't was strange, 't was
    passing strange,                                           160
'T was pitiful, 't was wondrous pitiful:
She wished she had not heard it, yet she wished
That heaven had made her such a man; she
    thanked me,
And bade me, if I had a friend that loved her,
I should but teach him how to tell my story,
And that would woo her. Upon this hint I
    spake:
She loved me for the dangers I had passed,
And I loved her that she did pity them.
This only is the witchcraft I have used.

DESDEMONA, IAGO, *and* ATTENDANTS *enter.*

Here comes the lady; let her witness it.   170
  DUKE. I think this tale would win my
    daughter too.
Good Brabantio,
Take up this mangled matter at the best:
Men do their broken weapons rather use
Than their bare hands.
  BRABANTIO.        I pray you, hear her speak:
If she confess that she was half the wooer,
Destruction on my head, if my bad blame
Light on the man! Come hither, gentle mistress:
Do you perceive in all this noble company
Where most you owe obedience?
  DESDEMONA.              My noble father,   180
I do perceive here a divided duty:
To you I am bound for life and education;
My life and education both do learn me
How to respect you; you are the lord of duty;
I am hitherto your daughter. But here's my
    husband,
And so much duty as my mother showed
To you, preferring you before her father,
So much I challenge that I may profess
Due to the Moor my lord.
  BRABANTIO.    God be with you! I have done.
Please it your grace, on to the state-affairs: 190
I had rather to adopt a child than get it.
Come hither, Moor:
    [BRABANTIO *puts* DESDEMONA'S *hand in*
                                    OTHELLO'S.
I here do give thee that with all my heart
Which, but thou hast already, with all my heart
I would keep from thee. For your sake, jewel,
I am glad at soul I have no other child;
For thy escape would teach me tyranny,
To hang clogs on them. I have done, my lord.
  DUKE. Let me speak like yourself, and lay a
    sentence,
Which, as a grise or step, may help these
    lovers                                                     200
Into your favor.
When remedies are past, the griefs are ended
By seeing the worst, which late on hopes
    depended.
To mourn a mischief that is past and gone
Is the next way to draw new mischief on.
What cannot be preserved when fortune takes,
Patience her injury a mockery makes.

---

136 *Imminent deadly:* threatening death; *breach:* i.e.,
in the wall of a besieged town. 139 *portance:* behavior.
140 *antres:* caves. 142 *hint:* chance. 153 *dilate:* describe
fully. 155 *intentively:* intently.

173 *Take, etc.:* i.e., make the best of it. 178 *mistress:*
madam. 195 *For your sake:* Because of you. 199 *like
yourself:* as you should.

The robbed that smiles steals something from
    the thief;
He robs himself that spends a bootless grief.
    BRABANTIO. So let the Turk of Cyprus us
      beguile;                                      210
We lose it not, so long as we can smile.
He bears the sentence well that nothing bears
But the free comfort which from thence he
    hears,
But he bears both the sentence and the sorrow
That, to pay grief, must of poor patience
    borrow.
These sentences, to sugar, or to gall,
Being strong on both sides, are equivocal:
But words are words; I never yet did hear
That the bruisèd heart was piercèd through
    the ear.
I humbly beseech you, proceed to the affairs
    of state.                                      220
    DUKE. The Turk with a most mighty prepara-
tion makes for Cyprus. Othello, the fortitude of the place is best known to you; and
though we have there a substitute of most
allowed sufficiency, yet opinion, a sover-
eign mistress of effects, throws a more safer
voice on you: you must therefore be con-
tent to slubber the gloss of your new for-
tunes with this more stubborn and boister-
ous expedition.                                      230
    OTHELLO. The tyrant custom, most grave
    senators,
Hath made the flinty and steel couch of war
My thrice-driven bed of down: I do agnize
A natural and prompt alacrity
I find in hardness, and do undertake
These present wars against the Ottomites.
Most humbly therefore bending to your state,
I crave fit disposition for my wife,
Due reference of place and exhibition,
With such accommodation and besort          240
As levels with her breeding.
    DUKE.              If you please,
Be 't at her father's.
    BRABANTIO.        I'll not have it so.
    OTHELLO. Nor I.
    DESDEMONA. Nor I; I would not there reside,

To put my father in impatient thoughts
By being in his eye. Most gracious duke,
To my unfolding lend your prosperous ear,
And let me find a charter in your voice,
To assist my simpleness.
    DUKE.          What would you, Desdemona?
    DESDEMONA. That I did love the Moor to
    live with him,
My downright violence and storm of for-
    tunes             ·                250
May trumpet to the world; my heart's
    subdued
Even to the very quality of my lord;
I saw Othello's visage in his mind,
And to his honors and his valiant parts
Did I my soul and fortunes consecrate.
So that, dear lords, if I be left behind,
A moth of peace, and he go to the war,
The rights for which I love him are bereft me,
And I a heavy interim shall support
By his dear absence. Let me go with him.     260
    OTHELLO. Let her have your voices.
Vouch with me, heaven, I therefore beg it not
To please the palate of my appetite
Nor to comply with heat—the young affects
In me defunct—and proper satisfaction,
But to be free and bounteous to her mind;
And heaven defend your good souls, that you
    think
I will your serious and great business scant
For she is with me. No, when light-winged toys
Of feathered Cupid seel with wanton dull-
    ness                               270
My speculative and officed instruments,
That my disports corrupt and taint my business,
Let housewives make a skillet of my helm,
And all indign and base adversities
Make head against my estimation!
    DUKE. Be it as you shall privately determine,
Either for her stay or going. The affair cries
    haste,
And speed must answer it.
    FIRST SENATOR. You must away tonight.
    OTHELLO.           With all my heart.
    DUKE. At nine i' the morning here we'll
    meet again.                                      280

---

209 *spends:* indulges; *bootless:* useless. 217 *equivocal:* inclined equally. 219 *piercèd:* entered (to be soothed). 222 *fortitude:* strength. 225 *allowed sufficiency:* recognized ability. 225–6 *sovereign, etc.:* potent influence on the outcome of anything. 228 *slubber:* tarnish. 233 *driven:* sifted; *agnize:* recognize. 239 *reference:* assignment; *exhibition:* living allowance. 240 *besort:* companions. 241 *levels with:* suits.

246 *prosperous:* favorable. 250 *storm of fortunes:* taking my destiny into my own hands. 252 *quality:* profession. 260 *dear:* painful. 261 *voices:* consent. 264 *affects:* desires. 267 *defend, etc.:* keep you from supposing. 270–71 *seel, etc.:* blind with passion my intelligence, which is in your service. 272 *that:* so that; *disports:* amusements. 274 *indign:* undignified. 275 *Make, etc.:* take away my honor.

Othello, leave some officer behind,
And he shall our commission bring to you;
With such things else of quality and respect
As doth import you.

    OTHELLO. So please your grace, my ancient;
A man he is of honesty and trust:
To his conveyance I assign my wife,
With what else needful your good grace shall
    think
To be sent after me.

    DUKE.           Let it be so.
Good night to every one. [*To* BRABANTIO.
    And, noble signior,
If virtue no delighted beauty lack,      290
Your son-in-law is far more fair than black.

    FIRST SENATOR. Adieu, brave Moor; use
    Desdemona well.

    BRABANTIO. Look to her, Moor, if thou hast
    eyes to see:
She has deceived her father, and may thee.

    OTHELLO. My life upon her faith!
[*All go out except* OTHELLO, DESDEMONA,
    IAGO, *and* RODERIGO.] Honest Iago,
My Desdemona must I leave to thee:
I prithee, let thy wife attend on her;
And bring them after in the best advantage.
Come, Desdemona; I have but an hour
Of love, of worldly matters and direction,    300
To spend with thee: we must obey the time.

            [OTHELLO *and* DESDEMONA *go out.*

    RODERIGO. Iago.

    IAGO. What sayest thou, noble heart?

    RODERIGO. What will I do, thinkest thou?

    IAGO. Why, go to bed, and sleep.

    RODERIGO. I will incontinently drown myself.

    IAGO. If thou dost, I shall never love thee
    after. Why, thou silly gentleman!

    RODERIGO. It is silliness to live when to live
    is torment; and then have we a pre-  310
    scription to die when death is our physician.

    IAGO. O villanous! I have looked upon the
    world for four times seven years; and since
    I could distinguish betwixt a benefit and
    an injury, I never found man that knew
    how to love himself. Ere I would say I
    would drown myself for the love of a
    guinea-hen, I would change my humanity
    with a baboon.

    RODERIGO. What should I do? I con-  320

fess it is my shame to be so fond; but it is
not in my virtue to amend it.

    IAGO. Virtue? a fig! 't is in ourselves that we
are thus or thus. Our bodies are gardens,
to the which our wills are gardeners; so
that if we will plant nettles or sow lettuce,
set hyssop and weed up thyme, supply it
with one gender of herbs or distract it with
many, either to have it sterile with idleness or manured with industry, why,    330
the power and corrigible authority of
this lies in our wills. If the balance of our
lives had not one scale of reason to poise
another of sensuality, the blood and baseness of our natures would conduct us to
most preposterous conclusions; but we
have reason to cool our raging motions,
our carnal stings, our unbitted lusts;
whereof I take this that you call love to
be a sect or scion.    340

    RODERIGO. It cannot be.

    IAGO. It is merely a lust of the blood and a
permission of the will. Come, be a man.
Drown thyself! Drown cats and blind
puppies. I have professed me thy friend,
and I confess me knit to thy deserving
with cables of perdurable toughness; I
could never better stead thee than now.
Put money in thy purse; follow thou the
wars; defeat thy favor with an  350
usurped beard; I say, put money in thy
purse. It cannot be that Desdemona
should long continue her love to the
Moor—put money in thy purse—nor he
his to her. It was a violent commencement, and thou shalt see an answerable
sequestration;—put but money in thy
purse. These Moors are changeable in
their wills:—fill thy purse with money—
the food that to him now is as lus-  360
cious as locusts, shall be to him shortly as
bitter as coloquintida. She must change
for youth: when she is sated with his body,
she will find the error of her choice; she
must have change, she must; therefore put
money in thy purse. If thou wilt needs
damn thyself, do it a more delicate way

---

    283 *such things, etc.*: other things befitting your high
rank. 290 *virtue*: valor; *delighted*: pleasing. 298 *in* . . .
*advantage*: at . . . opportunity. 306 *incontinently*: at once.

    328 *gender*: species. 331 *corrigible*: corrective. 337 *mo-
tions*: impulses. 338 *unbitted*: uncontrolled. 340 *sect or
scion*: sprout or twig. 346 *knit, etc.*: allied to the furtherance of your aims. 348 *stead*: be useful to. 350 *defeat,
etc.*: disguise your face; *usurped*: false. 356–7 *answerable
sequestration*: corresponding separation. 361 *locusts*: a
sweet fruit. 362 *coloquintida*: a bitter drug.

than drowning. Make all the money thou
canst: if sanctimony and a frail vow
betwixt an erring barbarian and a    370
super-subtle Venetian be not too hard for
my wits and all the tribe of hell, thou shalt
enjoy her; therefore make money. A pox
of drowning thyself! It is clean out of the
way: seek thou rather to be hanged in
compassing thy joy than to be drowned
and go without her.

RODERIGO. Wilt thou be fast to my hopes if
I depend on the issue?

IAGO. Thou art sure of me: go, make    380
money; I have told thee often, and I re-tell
thee again and again, I hate the Moor. My
cause is hearted; thine hath no less reason.
Let us be conjunctive in our revenge
against him. If thou canst cuckold him,
thou dost thyself a pleasure, me a sport.
There are many events in the womb of
time which will be delivered. Traverse;
go; provide thy money. We will have more
of this tomorrow. Adieu.    390

RODERIGO. Where shall we meet i' the
morning?

IAGO. At my lodging.

RODERIGO. I'll be with thee betimes.

IAGO. Go to; farewell. Do you hear, Roderigo?

RODERIGO. What say you?

IAGO. No more of drowning, do you hear?

RODERIGO. I am changed: I'll go sell all my
land.    [RODERIGO *goes out.*    400

IAGO. Thus do I ever make my fool my
purse;
For I mine own gained knowledge should
profane,
If I would time expend with such a snipe,
But for my sport and profit. I hate the
Moor;
And it is thought abroad that 'twixt my sheets
He has done my office: I know not if't be true;
But I, for mere suspicion in that kind,
Will do as if for surety. He holds me well;
The better shall my purpose work on him.
Cassio's a proper man; let me see now:    410
To get his place and to plume up my will

In double knavery—how, how? Let's see:
After some time, to abuse Othello's ear
That he is too familiar with his wife.
He hath a person and a smooth dispose
To be suspected, framed to make women false.
The Moor is of a free and open nature,
That thinks men honest that but seem to be so,
And will as tenderly be led by the nose
As asses are.    420
I have 't. It is engendered. Hell and night
Must bring this monstrous birth to the world's
light.

## ACT II. *Cyprus.*

SCENE 1. *An open place near the quay of a
seaport, several days later.*

MONTANO, *Venetian governor of Cyprus, and
two* GENTLEMEN *in the government.*

MONTANO. What from the cape can you
discern at sea?

FIRST GENTLEMAN. Nothing at all: it is a
high-wrought flood;
I cannot, 'twixt the heaven and the main
Descry a sail.

MONTANO. Methinks the wind hath spoke
aloud at land;
A fuller blast ne'er shook our battlements;
If it hath ruffianed so upon the sea,
What ribs of oak, when mountains melt on
them,
Can hold the mortise? What shall we hear of
this?

SECOND GENTLEMAN. A segregation of the
Turkish fleet:    10
For do but stand upon the foaming shore,
The chidden billow seems to pelt the clouds;
The wind-shaked surge, with high and mon-
strous mane,
Seems to cast water on the burning Bear
And quench the guards of the ever-fixèd pole:
I never did like molestation view
On the enchafèd flood.

MONTANO.    If that the Turkish fleet
Be not ensheltered and embayed, they are
drowned;
It is impossible they bear it out.

---

369 *sanctimony:* the sanctity of marriage.    370 *erring:*
wandering. 373–4: *pox of:* plague on. 378 *fast:* steadfast. 383 *hearted:* heartfelt. 384 *conjunctive:* united.
385 *cuckold him:* seduce his wife. 388 *Traverse:* march.
394 *betimes:* early. 405 *abroad:* everywhere. 408 *holds,
etc.:* thinks highly of me. 410 *proper:* handsome.
411 *plume up:* make triumph.

---

414 *he:* Cassio. 415 *dispose:* manner.
ACT II. SCENE 1. 3 *main:* sea. 6 *fuller:* stronger.
9 *hold. etc.:* keep their joints together. 10 *segregation:*
dispersal.    14 *Bear:* the constellation. 15 *guards:* two stars
in the Little Dipper; *pole:* polestar.

*A* THIRD GENTLEMAN *enters.*

THIRD GENTLEMAN. News, lads! Our wars
  are done.                                       20
That desperate tempest hath so banged the
  Turks,
That their designment halts: a noble ship of
  Venice
Hath seen a grievous wreck and sufferance
On most part of their fleet.
  MONTANO. How! is this true?
  THIRD GENTLEMAN.          The ship is here
  put in,
A Veronesa; Michael Cassio,
Lieutenant to the warlike Moor Othello,
Is come on shore: the Moor himself at sea,
And is in full commission here for Cyprus.
  MONTANO. I am glad on 't; 't is a worthy
  governor.                                       30
  THIRD GENTLEMAN. But this same Cassio,
  though he speak of comfort
Touching the Turkish loss, yet he looks sadly,
And prays the Moor be safe; for they were
  parted
With foul and violent tempest.
  MONTANO.                  Pray heavens he be;
For I have served him, and the man commands
Like a full soldier. Let's to the seaside, ho!
As well to see the vessel that's come in
As to throw out our eyes for brave Othello,
Even till we make the main and the aerial blue
An indistinct regard.
  THIRD GENTLEMAN. Come, let's do so;   40
For every minute is expectancy
Of more arrivance.

CASSIO *enters.*

CASSIO. Thanks, you the valiant of this
  warlike isle,
That so approve the Moor! O, let the heavens
Give him defence against the elements,
For I have lost him on a dangerous sea.
  MONTANO. Is he well shipped?
  CASSIO. His bark is stoutly timbered, and his
  pilot
Of very expert and approved allowance;
Therefore my hopes, not surfeited to death,   50

Stand in bold cure.
      [*Shouts off-stage:* "A sail, a sail, a sail!"

*A* FOURTH GENTLEMAN *enters.*

  CASSIO. What noise?
  FOURTH GENTLEMAN. The town is empty;
  on the brow o' the sea
Stand ranks of people, and they cry "A sail!"
  CASSIO. My hopes do shape him for the
  governor.        [*Noise of cannon off-stage.*
  SECOND GENTLEMAN. They do discharge
  their shot of courtesy:
Our friends at least.
  CASSIO.          I pray you, sir, go forth
And give us truth who 't is that is arrived.
  SECOND GENTLEMAN. I shall.
          [SECOND GENTLEMAN *goes out.*
  MONTANO. But, good lieutenant, is your
  general wived?                                  60
  CASSIO. Most fortunately: he hath achieved
  a maid
That paragons description and wild fame;
One that excels the quirks of blazoning pens
And in the essential vesture of creation
Does tire the ingener.

SECOND GENTLEMAN *returns.*

                  How now! who has put in?
  SECOND GENTLEMAN. 'T is one Iago, ancient
  to the general.
  CASSIO. He's had most favorable and happy
  speed:
Tempests themselves, high seas and howling
  winds,
The guttered rocks and congregated sands,
Traitors ensteeped to clog the guiltless keel,   70
As having sense of beauty, do omit
Their mortal natures, letting go safely by
The divine Desdemona.
  MONTANO.             What is she?
  CASSIO. She that I spake of, our great
  captain's captain,
Left in the conduct of the bold Iago,
Whose footing here anticipates our thoughts

---

22 *designment:* undertaking. 23 *sufferance:* damage.
26 *Veronesa:* a ship of Verona, then subject to Venice.
39–40 *till, etc.:* until our eyes confuse the colors of the sea
and sky. 49 *expert, etc.:* known by much experience to
be expert. 50–51 *my hopes, etc.: i.e.,* though I am not
overconfident (?), my hopes may with luck be fulfilled.

53 *brow o':* height overlooking. 55 *My, etc.: i.e.,* I
hope the ship is the new governor's. 56 *of:* out of.
57 *Our friends: i.e.,* the ship is a friendly one. 62 *paragons:* surpasses. 63 *quirks, etc.:* metaphors of writers'
praises. 64–5 *in, etc.:* by her real endowments causes the
romancer to despair (?). 69 *guttered:* hollowed out,
jagged; *congregated:* heaped up. 70 *ensteeped:* hidden
under water. 72 *mortal:* deadly. 76–7 *footing, etc.:* arrival is a week earlier than expected.

A se'nnight's speed. Great Jove, Othello guard
And swell his sail with thine own powerful
  breath,
That he may bless this bay with his tall ship,
Make love's quick pants in Desdemona's
  arms,                                          80
Give renewed fire to our extinced spirits,
And bring all Cyprus comfort!

DESDEMONA, IAGO, RODERIGO, *and* EMILIA,
  IAGO'S *wife, enter with* ATTENDANTS.
                              O, behold,
The riches of the ship is come on shore!
Ye men of Cyprus, let her have your knees.
Hail to thee, lady! and the grace of heaven,
Before, behind thee, and on every hand,
Enwheel thee round!
  DESDEMONA.    I thank you, valiant Cassio.
What tidings can you tell me of my lord?
  CASSIO. He is not yet arrived, nor know I
    aught
But that he's well and will be shortly here.  90
  DESDEMONA. O, but I fear—How lost you
    company?
  CASSIO. The great contention of the sea and
    skies
Parted our fellowship—
[*Shouts off-stage:* "A sail, a sail!"; *then noise
                                of cannon.*
                      But, hark! a sail.
  SECOND GENTLEMAN. They give their greet-
    ing to the citadel:
This likewise is a friend.
  CASSIO.              See for the news.
            [SECOND GENTLEMAN *goes out.*
Good ancient, you are welcome. [*To* EMILIA]
    Welcome, mistress:
Let it not gall your patience, good Iago,
That I extend my manners; 't is my breeding
That gives me this bold show of courtesy.   100
                    [CASSIO *kisses* EMILIA.
  IAGO. Sir, would she give you so much of her
    lips
As of her tongue she oft bestows on me,
You'd have enough.
  DESDEMONA.      Alas, she has no speech.
  IAGO. In faith, too much;
I find it still, when I have list to sleep:
Marry, before your ladyship, I grant,
She puts her tongue a little in her heart,

And chides with thinking.
  EMILIA.       You have little cause to say so.
  IAGO. Come on, come on; you are pictures
    out of doors,
Bells in your parlors, wild-cats in your
    kitchens,                                   110
Saints in your injuries, devils being offended,
Players in your housewifery, and housewives
    in your beds.
  DESDEMONA. O, fie upon thee, slanderer!
  IAGO. Nay, it is true, or else I am a Turk:
You rise to play and go to bed to work.
  EMILIA. You shall not write my praise.
  IAGO.                      No, let me not.
  DESDEMONA. What wouldst thou write of
    me, if thou shouldst praise me?
  IAGO. O gentle lady, do not put me to 't;
For I am nothing if not critical.
  DESDEMONA. Come on, assay.—There's one
    gone to the harbor?                         120
  IAGO. Ay, madam.
  DESDEMONA. I am not merry; but I do
    beguile
The thing I am by seeming otherwise.
Come, how wouldst thou praise me?
  IAGO. I am about it, but indeed my invention
Comes from my pate as birdlime does from
    frize:
It plucks out brains and all. But my Muse
    labors,
And thus she is delivered.
If she be fair and wise, fairness and wit,
The one's for use, the other useth it.         130
  DESDEMONA. Well praised! How if she be
    black and witty?
  IAGO. If she be black, and thereto have a wit,
She'll find a white that shall her blackness fit.
  DESDEMONA. Worse and worse.
  EMILIA. How if fair and foolish?
  IAGO. She never yet was foolish that was fair;
For even her folly helped her to an heir.
  DESDEMONA. These are old fond paradoxes
    to make fools laugh i' the alehouse. What
    miserable praise hast thou for her      140
    that's foul and foolish?

---

84 *knees:* bows.  87 *enwheel:* encircle.  99 *extend:* employ.  105 *have list:* desire.

109 *pictures: i.e.,* painted faces.  110 *Bells: i.e.,* noisy.
111 *Saints, etc.: i.e.,* saintly in manner when doing injuries.
112 *Players:* triflers; *housewifery:* housekeeping; *housewives* (pronounced "hussifs"): *i.e.,* economical, with a
pun on "hussies."  120 *assay:* try.  122 *beguile:* relieve.
126 *frize:* coarse cloth with a nap, which birdlime would
pull off.  131 *black:* brunette.  133 *white:* blonde (with
pun on "wight"; *cf.,* 160).  137 *folly:* lewdness.  138 *fond:*
silly.

IAGO. There's none so foul and foolish there-
 unto,
But does foul pranks which fair and wise ones
 do.
DESDEMONA. O heavy ignorance! thou prais-
 est the worst best. But what praise couldst
 thou bestow on a deserving woman in-
 deed, one that, in the authority of her
 merit, did justly put on the vouch of very
 malice itself? ·
IAGO. She that was ever fair and never
 proud,         150
Had tongue at will and yet was never loud,
Never lacked gold and yet went never gay,
Fled from her wish and yet said "Now I
 may,"
She that being angered, her revenge being nigh,
Bade her wrong stay and her displeasure fly,
She that in wisdom never was so frail
To change the cod's head for the salmon's tail,
She that could think and ne'er disclose her
 mind,
See suitors following and not look behind,
She was a wight, if ever such wight were— 160
DESDEMONA. To do what?
IAGO. To suckle fools and chronicle small
 beer.
DESDEMONA. O most lame and impotent
 conclusion! Do not learn of him, Emilia,
 though he be thy husband. How say you,
 Cassio? Is he not a most profane and
 liberal counsellor?
CASSIO. He speaks home, madam; you may
 relish him more in the soldier than in the
 scholar.         170
IAGO, to himself. He takes her by the palm;
 ay, well said, whisper; with as little a web
 as this will I ensnare as great a fly as
 Cassio. Ay, smile upon her, do; I will gyve
 thee in thine own courtship. You say true;
 't is so, indeed: if such tricks as these
 strip you out of your lieutenantry, it had
 been better you had not kissed your three
 fingers so oft, which now again you are
 most apt to play the sir in. Very 180
 good; well kissed! an excellent courtesy!
 't is so, indeed. Yet again your fingers to

your lips? Would they were clyster-pipes
 for your sake!
     [A trumpet sounds off-stage.
IAGO, to CASSIO etc. The Moor! I know his
 trumpet.
CASSIO. 'T is truly so.
DESDEMONA. Let's meet him and receive
 him.
CASSIO. Lo, where he comes!

  OTHELLO and ATTENDANTS enter.

OTHELLO. O my fair warrior!
DESDEMONA.     My dear Othello!
OTHELLO. It gives me wonder great as my
 content        190
To see you here before me. O my soul's joy!
If after every tempest come such calms,
May the winds blow till they have wakened
 death!
And let the laboring bark climb hills of seas
Olympus-high and duck again as low
As hell's from heaven! If it were now to die,
'T were now to be most happy; for I fear
My soul hath her content so absolute
That not another comfort like to this
Succeeds in unknown fate.    200
 DESDEMONA.    The heavens forbid
But that our loves and comforts should increase,
Even as our days do grow!
 OTHELLO.  Amen to that, sweet powers!
I cannot speak enough of this content;
It stops me here—[OTHELLO touches his lips,
 then kisses DESDEMONA twice.] it is too
 much of joy:
And this, and this, the greatest discords be
That e'er our hearts shall make!
 IAGO, to himself. O, you are well tuned now!
But I'll set down the pegs that make this music,
As honest as I am.
 OTHELLO.   Come, let us to the castle.
News, friends; our wars are done, the Turks
 are drowned.     210
How does my old acquaintance of this isle?
Honey, you shall be well desired in Cyprus;
I have found great love amongst them. O my
 sweet,
I prattle out of fashion, and I dote
In mine own comforts. I prithee, good Iago,
Go to the bay and disembark my coffers.

---

141 foul: ugly. 147 put, etc.: secure the approval.
156 in wisdom, etc.: i.e., never was so unwise as to exchange better for worse. 160 wight: person. 162 small
beer: weak beer, i.e., trifles. 167 liberal: licentious.
168 home: bluntly. 169 in the: as a. 174 gyve: fetter.
180 apt, etc.: adept at being the courtier in.

---

183 clyster-pipes: enema-tubes. 200 succeeds: will follow. 208 set down: turn, so as to untune. ·212 desired:
welcome. 216 coffers: trunks.

Bring thou the master to the citadel;
He is a good one, and his worthiness
Does challenge much respect. Come, Desdemona,
Once more, well met at Cyprus.          220
    [*All go out except* IAGO *and* RODERIGO.
IAGO. Do thou meet me presently at the
harbor. Come hither. If thou be'st valiant
—as, they say, base men being in love
have then a nobility in their natures more
than is native to them—list me. The
lieutenant tonight watches on the court of
guard. First, I must tell thee this: Desdemona is directly in love with him.
RODERIGO. With him! why, 't is not possible.
IAGO. Lay thy finger thus, and let thy     230
soul be instructed. Mark me with what
violence she first loved the Moor, but for
bragging and telling her fantastical lies:
and will she love him still for prating? Let
not thy discreet heart think it. Her eye
must be fed; and what delight shall she
have to look on the devil? When the blood
is made dull with the act of sport, there
should be, again to inflame it and to give
satiety a fresh appetite, loveliness     240
in favor, sympathy in years, manners, and
beauties; all which the Moor is defective
in. Now, for want of these required
conveniences, her delicate tenderness will
find itself abused, begin to heave the
gorge, disrelish and abhor the Moor; very
nature will instruct her in it and compel
her to some second choice. Now, sir, this
granted,—as it is a most pregnant and
unforced position—who stands so     250
eminent in the degree of this fortune as
Cassio does? a knave very voluble; no
further conscionable than in putting on
the mere form of civil and humane seeming, for the better compassing of his salt
and most hidden loose affection? Why,
none; why, none: a slipper and subtle
knave, a finder of occasions, that has an
eye can stamp and counterfeit advantages,
though true advantage never present     260
itself; a devilish knave. Besides, the knave
is handsome, young, and hath all those
requisites in him that folly and green

minds look after: a pestilent complete
knave; and the woman hath found him
already.
RODERIGO. I cannot believe that in her; she's
full of most blessed condition.
IAGO. Blessed fig's-end! the wine she drinks
is made of grapes; if she had been     270
blessed, she would never have loved the
Moor. Blessed pudding! Didst thou not
see her paddle with the palm of his hand?
Didst not mark that?
RODERIGO. Yes, that I did; but that was but
courtesy.
IAGO. Lechery, by this hand; an index and
obscure prologue to the history of lust and
foul thoughts. They met so near with their
lips that their breaths embraced     280
together. Villanous thoughts, Roderigo!
When these mutualities so marshal the
way, hard at hand comes the master and
main exercise, the incorporate conclusion.
Pish! But, sir, be you ruled by me: I have
brought you from Venice. Watch you
tonight; for the command, I'll lay 't upon
you. Cassio knows you not. I'll not be far
from you: do you find some occasion to
anger Cassio, either by speaking too     290
loud, or tainting his discipline; or from
what other course you please, which the
time shall more favorably minister.
RODERIGO. Well.
IAGO. Sir, he is rash and very sudden in
choler, and haply may strike at you:
provoke him, that he may; for even out of
that will I cause these of Cyprus to
mutiny, whose qualification shall come
into no true taste again but by the     300
displanting of Cassio. So shall you have
a shorter journey to your desires by the
means I shall then have to prefer them;
and the impediment most profitably removed, without the which there were no
expectation of our prosperity.
RODERIGO. I will do this, if you can bring
it to any opportunity.
IAGO. I warrant thee. Meet me by and by
at the citadel: I must fetch his     310
necessaries ashore. Farewell.

---

217 *master:* ship-captain. 221 *presently:* at once.
225 *list:* listen to. 230 *thus:* i.e., on the lips. 241 *favor:*
face. 253 *conscionable:* conscientious. 254 *humane:* courteous. 255 *salt:* lecherous. 257 *slipper:* slippery.

268 *condition:* character. 282 *mutualities:* intimacies;
*marshal:* lead. 284 *incorporate:* carnally united.
291 *tainting:* insulting. 293 *minister:* supply. 296 *choler:*
anger. 299–301 *whose, etc.:* who will be pacified only by
Cassio's dismissal. 303 *prefer:* further.

RODERIGO. Adieu.        [RODERIGO *goes out.*
IAGO. That Cassio loves her, I do well
    believe it;
That she loves him, 't is apt and of great credit.
The Moor, howbeit that I endure him not,
Is of a constant, loving, noble nature,
And I dare think he'll prove to Desdemona
A most dear husband. Now, I do love her too;
Not out of absolute lust, though peradventure
I stand accountant for as great a sin,        320
But partly led to diet my revenge,
For that I do suspect the lusty Moor
Hath leaped into my seat; the thought whereof
Doth, like a poisonous mineral, gnaw my
    inwards;
And nothing can or shall content my soul
Till I am evened with him, wife for wife,
Or failing so, yet that I put the Moor
At least into a jealousy so strong
That judgment cannot cure. Which thing to do,
If this poor trash of Venice, whom I trash   330
For his quick hunting, stand the putting-on,
I'll have our Michael Cassio on the hip,
Abuse him to the Moor in the rank garb—
For I fear Cassio with my night-cap too—
Make the Moor thank me, love me, and reward
    me
For making him egregiously an ass
And practising upon his peace and quiet
Even to madness. 'T is here, but yet confused:
Knavery's plain face is never seen till used.

SCENE 2. *A street, later that day.*

*A* HERALD *with a proclamation;* PEOPLE
    *listening.*

HERALD. It is Othello's pleasure, our noble
    and valiant general, that, upon certain
    tidings now arrived, importing the mere
    perdition of the Turkish fleet, every man
    put himself into triumph; some to dance,
    some to make bonfires, each man to what
    sport and revels his addiction leads him:
    for, besides these beneficial news, it is the
    celebration of his nuptial. So much was
    his pleasure should be proclaimed.    10
    All offices are open, and there is full

liberty of feasting from this present hour
of five till the bell have told eleven.
Heaven bless the isle of Cyprus and our
noble general Othello!

SCENE 3. *A hall in the castle, that night.*

OTHELLO, DESDEMONA, CASSIO, *and*
    ATTENDANTS.

OTHELLO. Good Michael, look you to the
    guard tonight:
Let's teach ourselves that honorable stop,
Not to outsport discretion.
    CASSIO. Iago hath direction what to do;
But, notwithstanding, with my personal eye
Will I look to 't.
    OTHELLO.        Iago is most honest.
Michael, good night: tomorrow with your
    earliest
Let me have speech with you. [*To* DESDEMONA]
    Come, my dear love,
The purchase made, the fruits are to ensue;
That profit's yet to come 'tween me and
    you.                                10
Good night.

IAGO *returns as* OTHELLO, DESDEMONA, *and*
    ATTENDANTS *go out.*

CASSIO. Welcome, Iago; we must to the
    watch.
IAGO. Not this hour, lieutenant; 't is not yet
    ten o' the clock. Our general cast us thus
    early for the love of his Desdemona, who
    let us not therefore blame: he hath not
    yet made wanton the night with her, and
    she is sport for Jove.
CASSIO. She's a most exquisite lady.    20
IAGO. And, I'll warrant her, full of game.
CASSIO. Indeed, she's a most fresh and
    delicate creature.
IAGO. What an eye she has! Methinks it
    sounds a parley of provocation.
CASSIO. An inviting eye; and yet methinks
    right modest.
IAGO. And when she speaks, is it not an
    alarum to love?
CASSIO. She is indeed perfection.    30
IAGO. Well, happiness to their sheets! Come,
    lieutenant, I have a stoup of wine; and
    here without are a brace of Cyprus

---

314 *apt, etc.*: likely and easily believed.  320 *accountant:*
answerable.  321 *diet:* feed.  323 *Hath, etc.*: has seduced
my wife.  330–31 *I trash, etc.*: i.e., restrain from pursuing
Desdemona directly.  331 *putting-on:* incitement, *i.e.,*
against Cassio.  333 *in, etc.*: as a seducer.  334 *with, etc.*:
*i.e.,* for the same reason.
    SCENE 2. 3–4 *mere perdition:* complete destruction.
11 *offices:* stores of food.

---

3 *outsport:* enjoy ourselves beyond.  21 *game:* amorous
play.  29 *alarum:* call to arms.  32 *stoup:* two-quart con-
tainer.

gallants that would fain have a measure to the health of black Othello.

CASSIO. Not tonight, good Iago: I have very poor and unhappy brains for drinking: I could well wish courtesy would invent some other custom of entertainment.

IAGO. O, they are our friends; but one    40 cup: I'll drink for you.

CASSIO. I have drunk but one cup tonight, and that was craftily qualified too, and, behold, what innovation it makes here [CASSIO *touches his head*]. I am unfortunate in the infirmity, and dare not task my weakness with any more.

IAGO. What, man! 't is a night of revels: the gallants desire it.

CASSIO. Where are they?    50

IAGO. Here at the door; I pray you, call them in.

CASSIO. I'll do 't; but it dislikes me.

[CASSIO *goes out.*

IAGO. If I can fasten but one cup upon him,
With that which he hath drunk tonight already,
He'll be as full of quarrel and offence
As my young mistress' dog. Now, my sick fool Roderigo,
Whom love hath turned almost the wrong side out,
To Desdemona hath tonight caroused
Potations pottle-deep; and he's to watch.    60
Three lads of Cyprus, noble swelling spirits,
That hold their honors in a wary distance,
The very elements of this warlike isle,
Have I tonight flustered with flowing cups,
And they watch too. Now, 'mongst this flock of drunkards,
Am I to put our Cassio in some action
That may offend the isle. But here they come:
If consequence do but approve my dream,
My boat sails freely, both with wind and stream.

CASSIO *returns with* MONTANO *and* GENTLEMEN; SERVANTS *follow with wine.*

CASSIO. 'Fore God, they have given me    70 a rouse already.

MONTANO. Good faith, a little one; not past a pint, as I am a soldier.

IAGO. Some wine, ho!
[*Sings*]
"And let me the canakin clink, clink,
    And let me the canakin clink:
        A soldier's a man;
        A life's but a span;
    Why, then, let a soldier drink."
Some wine, boys!    80

CASSIO. 'Fore God, an excellent song.

IAGO. I learned it in England, where, indeed, they are most potent in potting: your Dane, your German, and your swag-bellied Hollander—[*To a* SERVANT] Drink, ho!—are nothing to your English.

CASSIO. Is your Englishman so expert in his drinking?

IAGO. Why, he drinks you with facility your Dane dead drunk; he sweats not to overthrow your Almain; he gives your    90 Hollander a vomit, ere the next pottle can be filled.

CASSIO. To the health of our general!

MONTANO. I am for it, lieutenant; and I'll do you justice.

IAGO. O sweet England!
[*Sings*]
"King Stephen was a worthy peer,
    His breeches cost him but a crown;
He held them sixpence all too dear,
    With that he called the tailor lown.    100
He was a wight of high renown,
    And thou art but of low degree:
'T is pride that pulls the country down;
    Then take thine auld cloak about thee."
Some wine, ho!

CASSIO. Why, this is a more exquisite song than the other.

IAGO. Will you hear 't again?

CASSIO. No, for I hold him to be unworthy of his place that does those things.    110 Well, God's above all; and there be souls must be saved, and there be souls must not be saved.

IAGO. It's true, good lieutenant.

CASSIO. For mine own part—no offence to the general, nor any man of quality—I hope to be saved.

IAGO. And so do I too, lieutenant.

CASSIO. Ay, but, by your leave, not before me; the lieutenant is to be saved    120

---

34 *measure:* i.e., of wine. 43 *craftily qualified:* carefully diluted. 44 *innovation:* change for the worse. 60 *pottle-deep:* to the bottom of the cup. 62 *hold, etc.:* are touchy about their honor. 63 *elements:* epitomes. 68 *consequence:* results; *approve:* make real. 70 *rouse:* big drink.

84 *swag-:* sagging.    90 *Almain:* German.    100 *lown:* stupid.    104 *auld:* old.

before the ancient. Let's have no more of this; let's to our affairs. God forgive us our sins! Gentlemen, let's look to our business. Do not think, gentlemen, I am drunk: this is my ancient; this is my right hand, and this is my left. I am not drunk now; I can stand well enough, and speak well enough.

ALL. Excellent well.

CASSIO. Why, very well then; you must     130
not think then that I am drunk.

                    [CASSIO *goes out.*

MONTANO. To the platform, masters; come, let's set the watch.

IAGO. You see this fellow that is gone before;
He is a soldier fit to stand by Cæsar
And give direction: and do but see his vice;
'T is to his virtue a just equinox,
The one as long as the other: 't is pity of him.
I fear the trust Othello puts him in,
On some odd time of his infirmity,
Will shake this island.

MONTANO.              But is he often thus?     140

IAGO. 'T is evermore the prologue to his sleep:
He'll watch the horologe a double set,
If drink rock not his cradle.

MONTANO.                    It were well
The general were put in mind of it.
Perhaps he sees it not, or his good nature
Prizes the virtue that appears in Cassio,
And looks not on his evils: is not this true?

RODERIGO *enters, unseen by* MONTANO.

IAGO, *softly, while* MONTANO *drinks.* How now, Roderigo!

I pray you, after the lieutenant; go.

                    [RODERIGO *leaves.*

MONTANO. And 't is great pity that the noble
Moor                                       150
Should hazard such a place as his own second
With one of an ingraft infirmity:
It were an honest action to say
So to the Moor.

IAGO.              Not I, for this fair island:
I do love Cassio well, and would do much
To cure him of this evil.

[*Shouts of* "Help!" *and noise of running off-stage.*

            But, hark! what noise?

RODERIGO *runs in, followed by* CASSIO *with his sword drawn.*

CASSIO. You rogue! you rascal!

MONTANO.      What's the matter, lieutenant?

CASSIO. A knave teach me my duty!
I'll beat the knave into a twiggen bottle.     160

RODERIGO. Beat me!

CASSIO, *striking* RODERIGO. Dost thou prate, rogue?

MONTANO, *seizing* CASSIO's *arm.* Nay, good lieutenant; I pray you, sir, hold your hand.

CASSIO. Let me go, sir, or I'll knock you o'er the mazzard.

MONTANO. Come, come, you're drunk.

CASSIO. Drunk!

[CASSIO *lunges at* MONTANO, *who draws his sword and defends himself.*

IAGO, *softly to* RODERIGO. Away, I say; go out, and cry a mutiny.     170

                    [RODERIGO *runs out.*

Nay, good lieutenant! God's will, gentlemen;—
Help, ho!—Lieutenant! Sir! Montano! Sir!
Help, masters! Here's a goodly watch indeed!

                [*A bell rings off-stage.*

Who's that which rings the bell? Diablo, ho!
The town will rise. [CASSIO *wounds* MONTANO.
            God's will, lieutenant, hold!
You will be shamed for ever.

OTHELLO *enters with* ATTENDANTS *as the fighting stops.*

OTHELLO.              What is the matter here?

MONTANO. 'Zounds! I bleed still; I am hurt to the death.

            [MONTANO *and* CASSIO *fight again.*

OTHELLO. Hold, for your lives!

IAGO. Hold, ho! Lieutenant! Sir! Montano, gentlemen!
Have you forgot all sense of place and duty?     180
Hold! the general speaks to you; hold, hold, for shame!              [*The fighting ends.*

OTHELLO. Why, how now, ho! from whence ariseth this?
Are we turned Turks, and to ourselves do that
Which heaven hath forbid the Ottomites?
For Christian shame, put by this barbarous brawl;

---

136 *equinox:* counterpoise.  142 *watch, etc.:* stay awake while the hour hand revolves twice, *i.e.,* twenty-four hours. 151 *second: i.e.,* in command.  152 *ingraft:* deep-rooted.

167 *mazzard:* head.     174 *Diablo:* Devil.     177 *still:* steadily.

He that stirs next to carve for his own rage
Holds his soul light; he dies upon his motion.
Silence that dreadful bell: it frights the isle
From her propriety. What is the matter,
    masters?
Honest Iago, that lookest dead with griev-
    ing,                          190
Speak, who began this? On thy love, I charge
    thee.
    IAGO. I do not know; friends all but now,
    even now,
In quarter, and in terms like bride and groom
Devesting them for bed; and then, but now,
As if some planet had unwitted men,
Swords out, and tilting one at other's breast,
In opposition bloody. I cannot speak
Any beginning to this peevish odds,
And would in action glorious I had lost
Those legs that brought me to a part of it!   200
    OTHELLO. How comes it, Michael, you are
    thus forgot?
    CASSIO. I pray you, pardon me; I cannot
    speak.
    OTHELLO. Worthy Montano, you were wont
    be civil;
In mouths of wisest censure: what's the matter,
The gravity and stillness of your youth
The world hath noted, and your name is great
That you unlace your reputation thus
And spend your rich opinion for the name
Of a night-brawler? Give me answer to it.
    MONTANO. Worthy Othello, I am hurt to
    danger;                        210
Your officer, Iago, can inform you—
While I spare speech, which something now
    offends me—
Of all that I do know; nor know I aught
By me that 's said or done amiss this night,
Unless self-charity be sometimes a vice,
And to defend ourselves it be a sin
When violence assails us.
    OTHELLO.            Now, by heaven,
My blood begins my safer guides to rule;
And passion, having my best judgment collied,
Assays to lead the way. If I once stir,    220
Or do but lift this arm, the best of you
Shall sink in my rebuke. Give me to know
How this foul rout began, who set it on;

And he that is approved in this offence,
Though he had twinned with me, both at a
    birth,
Shall lose me. What! in a town of war,
Yet wild, the people's hearts brimful of fear,
To manage private and domestic quarrel,
In night, and on the court and guard of safety!
'T is monstrous. Iago, who began 't?    230
    MONTANO. If partially affined, or leagued in
    office,
Thou dost deliver more or less than truth,
Thou art no soldier.
    IAGO.             Touch me not so near.
I had rather have this tongue cut from my
    mouth
Than it should do offence to Michael Cassio;
Yet, I persuade myself, to speak the truth
Shall nothing wrong him. Thus it is, general.
Montano and myself being in speech,
There comes a fellow crying out for help;
And Cassio following him with determined
    sword,                        240
To execute upon him. Sir, this gentleman
Steps in to Cassio and entreats his pause;
Myself the crying fellow did pursue,
Lest by his clamor—as it so fell out—
The town might fall in fright; he, swift of foot,
Outran my purpose, and I returned the rather
For that I heard the clink and fall of swords,
And Cassio high in oath; which till tonight
I ne'er might say before. When I came back—
For this was brief—I found them close
    together,                        250
At blow and thrust, even as again they were
When you yourself did part them.
More of this matter cannot I report:
But men are men; the best sometimes forget:
Though Cassio did some little wrong to him,
As men in rage strike those that wish them
    best,
Yet surely Cassio, I believe, received
From him that fled some strange indignity,
Which patience could not pass.
    OTHELLO.            I know, Iago,
Thy honesty and love doth mince this
    matter,                        260
Making it light to Cassio. Cassio, I love thee;
But never more be officer of mine.

---

193 *In . . . like:* as amicable as. 198 *odds:* strife.
204 *stillness:* steadiness. 206 *censure:* judgment. 207 *unlace:* undo. 208 *rich opinion:* good character. 212 *offends:* pains. 215 *self-charity:* caring for oneself.
218 *blood:* anger. 219 *collied:* darkened. 223 *rout:* uproar.

224 *approved in:* convicted of. 229 *on . . . safety:* in the
very headquarters of the watch entrusted with our
security. 231 *partially, etc.:* influenced by being a brother
officer.

DESDEMONA *enters with* ATTENDANTS

Look, if my gentle love be not raised up!

[*To* CASSIO] I'll make thee an example.

    DESDEMONA.            What's the matter?

    OTHELLO. All's well now, sweeting; come
away to bed.

[*To* MONTANO] Sir, for your hurts, myself will
be your surgeon:

Lead him off. [MONTANO *is assisted from the
room.*]

Iago, look with care about the town,

And silence those whom this vile brawl
distracted.

Come, Desdemona: 't is the soldiers' life   270

To have their balmy slumbers waked with
strife.

        [*All go out except* IAGO *and* CASSIO.

IAGO. What, are you hurt, lieutenant?

CASSIO. Ay, past all surgery.

IAGO. Marry, heaven forbid!

CASSIO. Reputation, reputation, reputation!
O, I have lost my reputation! I have lost
the immortal part of myself, and what remains is bestial. My reputation, Iago, my
reputation!

IAGO. As I am an honest man, I   280
thought you had received some bodily
wound; there is more sense in that than in
reputation. Reputation is an idle and most
false imposition: oft got without merit,
and lost without deserving; you have lost
no reputation at all, unless you repute
yourself such a loser. What, man! there
are ways to recover the general again;
you are but now cast in his mood, a punishment more in policy than in   290
malice; even so as one would beat his
offenceless dog to affright an imperious
lion. Sue to him again, and he's yours.

CASSIO. I will rather sue to be despised than
to deceive so good a commander with so
slight, so drunken, and so indiscreet an
officer. Drunk? and speak parrot? and
squabble? swagger? swear? and discourse
fustian with one's own shadow? O thou
invisible spirit of wine, if thou hast   300
no name to be known by, let us call thee
devil!

IAGO. What was he that you followed with
your sword? What had he done to you?

CASSIO. I know not.

IAGO. Is 't possible?

CASSIO. I remember a mass of things, but
nothing distinctly; a quarrel, but nothing
wherefore. O God, that men should put
an enemy in their mouths to steal   310
away their brains! that we should, with
joy, pleasance, revel, and applause, trans-
form ourselves into beasts!

IAGO. Why, but you are now well enough;
how came you thus recovered?

CASSIO. It hath pleased the devil drunkenness
to give place to the devil wrath; one unper-
fectness shows me another, to make me
frankly despise myself.

IAGO. Come, you are too severe a mor-   320
aler. As the time, the place, and the condition of this country stands, I could heartily wish this had not befallen; but, since it
is as it is, mend it for your own good.

CASSIO. I will ask him for my place again; he
shall tell me I am a drunkard! Had I as
many mouths as Hydra, such an answer
would stop them all. To be now a sensible
man, by and by a fool, and presently a
beast! O strange! Every inordinate cup 330
is unblessed and the ingredient is a devil.

IAGO. Come, come, good wine is a good
familiar creature, if it be well used; exclaim no more against it. And, good lieutenant, I think you think I love you.

CASSIO. I have well approved it, sir. I drunk!

IAGO. You or any man living may be drunk
at some time, man. I'll tell you what you
shall do. Our general's wife is now the general: I may say so in this respect, for   340
that he hath devoted and given up himself
to the contemplation, mark, and denote-
ment of her parts and graces: confess
yourself freely to her; importune her help
to put you in your place again. She is of so
free, so kind, so apt, so blessed a disposition, she holds it a vice in her goodness
not to do more than she is requested. This
broken joint between you and her husband
entreat her to splinter; and, my for-   350
tunes against any lay worth naming, this

---

289 *cast, etc.*: discharged on an impulse.  290 *in policy*:
for the sake of policy.  293 *sue*: appeal.  298 *discourse
fustian*: rave, bluster.

crack of your love shall grow stronger than it was before.

CASSIO. You advise me well.

IAGO. I protest, in the sincerity of love and honest kindness.

CASSIO. I think it freely; and betimes in the morning I will beseech the virtuous Desdemona to undertake for me. I am desperate of my fortunes if they check    360 me here.

IAGO. You are in the right. Good night, lieutenant; I must to the watch.

CASSIO. Good night, honest Iago.

[CASSIO *goes out.*

IAGO. And what's he then that says I play the villain?

When this advice is free I give and honest,
Probal to thinking, and indeed the course
To win the Moor again? For 't is most easy
The inclining Desdemona to subdue
In any honest suit: she's framed as fruitful    370
As the free elements. And then for her
To win the Moor, were 't to renounce his baptism,
All seals and symbols of redeemèd sin,
His soul is so enfettered to her love,
That she may make, unmake, do what she list,
Even as her appetite shall play the god
With his weak function. How am I then a villain
To counsel Cassio to this parallel course,
Directly to his good? Divinity of hell!
When devils will the blackest sins put on,    380
They do suggest at first with heavenly shows,
As I do now; for whiles this honest fool
Plies Desdemona to repair his fortunes
And she for him pleads strongly to the Moor,
I'll pour this pestilence into his ear,
That she repeals him for her body's lust;
And by how much she strives to do him good,
She shall undo her credit with the Moor.
So will I turn her virtue into pitch,
And out of her own goodness make the net    390
That shall enmesh them all.

---

367 *Probal, etc.:* seeming likely to succeed.  369 *subdue:* win over.  370 *framed, etc.:* as generous by nature. 372 *were't: i.e.,* even if she asked him.  375 *list:* wishes. 377 *function:* reason.  378 *parallel:* corresponding (to Iago's plan).  380 *put on:* bring about.  386 *repeals him:* urges his reinstatement.

RODERIGO *comes back.*

How now, Roderigo!

RODERIGO. I do follow here in the chase, not like a hound that hunts, but one that fills up the cry. My money is almost spent; I have been tonight exceedingly well cudgeled; and I think the issue will be, I shall have so much experience for my pains, and so, with no money at all and a little more wit, return again to Venice.

IAGO. How poor are they that have not patience!    400
What wound did ever heal but by degrees?
Thou knowest we work by wit, and not by witchcraft;
And wit depends on dilatory time.
Does't not go well? Cassio hath beaten thee,
And thou by that small hurt hast cashiered Cassio.
Though other things grow fair against the sun,
Yet fruits that blossom first will first be ripe.
Content thyself awhile. By the mass, 't is morning;
Pleasure and action make the hours seem short.
Retire thee; go where thou art billeted:    410
Away, I say; thou shalt know more hereafter:
Nay, get thee gone. [RODERIGO *goes out.*] Two things are to be done:
My wife must move for Cassio to her mistress;
I'll set her on;
Myself the while to draw the Moor apart,
And bring him jump when he may Cassio find
Soliciting his wife: ay, that's the way;
Dull not device by coldness and delay.

## ACT III. *Cyprus.*

SCENE 1. *The open place before the castle; morning.*

CASSIO *and* MUSICIANS.

CASSIO. Masters, play here; I will content your pains;
Something that's brief; and bid "Good morrow, general."

*While* MUSICIANS *are playing, a* CLOWN *enters.*

CLOWN. Why, masters, have your instruments been in Naples, that they speak i' the nose thus?

---

393-4 *fills . . . cry: i.e.,* follows only to bay.  399 *wit:* brains.  416 *jump:* precisely.  418 *device:* a plan.

FIRST MUSICIAN. How, sir, how!

CLOWN. Are these, I pray you, wind-instruments?

FIRST MUSICIAN. Ay, marry, are they, sir.

CLOWN. O, thereby hangs a tail.          10

FIRST MUSICIAN. Whereby hangs a tale, sir?

CLOWN. Marry, sir, by many a wind-instrument that I know. But, masters, here's money for you: and the general so likes your music, that he desires you, for love's sake, to make no more noise with it.

FIRST MUSICIAN. Well, sir, we will not.

CLOWN. If you have any music that may          20 not be heard, to 't again; but, as they say, to hear music the general does not greatly care.

FIRST MUSICIAN. We have none such, sir.

CLOWN. Then put up your pipes in your bag, for I'll away. Go; vanish into air; away!
                              [MUSICIANS go out.

CASSIO. Dost thou hear, my honest friend?

CLOWN. No, I hear not your honest friend; I hear you.

CASSIO. Prithee, keep up thy quillets.          30 There's a poor piece of gold for thee: if the gentlewoman that attends the general's wife be stirring, tell her there's one Cassio entreats her a little favor of speech; wilt thou do this?

CLOWN. She is stirring, sir; if she will stir hither, I shall seem to notify unto her.

CASSIO. Do, good my friend.

*As* CLOWN *leaves,* IAGO *enters.*

                              In happy time, Iago.

IAGO. You have not been a-bed, then?

CASSIO. Why, no; the day had broke          40 Before we parted. I have made bold, Iago, To send in to your wife; my suit to her Is that she will to virtuous Desdemona Procure me some access.

IAGO.                    I'll send her to you presently; And I'll devise a mean to draw the Moor Out of the way, that your converse and business May be more free.

CASSIO. I humbly thank you for't. [IAGO *goes out.*] I never knew A Florentine more kind and honest.

EMILIA *enters.*

EMILIA. Good morrow, good lieutenant: I am sorry          50 For your displeasure; but all will sure be well. The general and his wife are talking of it, And she speaks for you stoutly: the Moor replies That he you hurt is of great fame in Cyprus And great affinity, and that in wholesome wisdom He might not but refuse you; but he protests he loves you, And needs no other suitor but his likings To take the safest occasion by the front To bring you in again.

CASSIO.                    Yet, I beseech you, If you think fit, or that it may be done,          60 Give me advantage of some brief discourse With Desdemona alone.

EMILIA.                    Pray you, come in. I will bestow you where you shall have time To speak your bosom freely.

CASSIO.                    I am much bound to you.

SCENE 2. *A room in the castle.*
OTHELLO, IAGO, *and* GENTLEMEN.

OTHELLO. These letters give, Iago, to the pilot, And by him do my duties to the senate; That done, I will be walking on the works; Repair there to me.

IAGO.                    Well, my good lord, I'll do 't.

OTHELLO. This fortification, gentlemen, shall we see 't?

GENTLEMEN. We 'll wait upon your lordship.

SCENE 3. *The garden of the castle.*
DESDEMONA, CASSIO, *and* EMILIA.

DESDEMONA. Be thou assured, good Cassio, I will do All my abilities in thy behalf.

EMILIA. Good madam, do: I warrant it grieves my husband. As if the case were his.

DESDEMONA. O, that's an honest fellow. Do not doubt, Cassio,

---

51 *your displeasure:* i.e., Othello's anger at you.  55 [*is of*] *great affinity:* has important connections.  56 *might not but:* could only.  58 *take, etc.:* seize the first safe opportunity.  64 *bound:* obliged.
    SCENE 2. 2 *do my duties:* send my respects.  3 *works:* ramparts.

---

30 *keep, etc.:* stop your jokes.  44 *presently:* at once.

But I will have my lord and you again
As friendly as you were.

CASSIO.                     Bounteous madam,
Whatever shall become of Michael Cassio,
He's never anything but your true servant.

DESDEMONA. I know't; I thank you. You do
   love my lord;                                     10
You have known him long; and be you well
   assured
He shall in strangeness stand no further off
Than in a politic distance.

CASSIO.                        Ay, but, lady,
That policy may either last so long,
Or feed upon such nice and waterish diet,
Or breed itself so out of circumstance,
That, I being absent and my place supplied,
My general will forget my love and service.

DESDEMONA. Do not doubt that; before
   Emilia here
I give thee warrant of thy place. Assure
   thee,                                          20
If I do vow a friendship, I'll perform it
To the last article: my lord shall never rest;
I'll watch him tame and talk him out of
   patience;
His bed shall seem a school, his board a shrift;
I'll intermingle everything he does
With Cassio's suit. Therefore be merry, Cassio;
For thy solicitor shall rather die
Than give thy cause away.

OTHELLO *and* IAGO *enter at the far side of the*
*stage.*

EMILIA. Madam, here comes my lord.
CASSIO. Madam, I'll take my leave.          30
DESDEMONA. Nay, stay, and hear me speak.
CASSIO. Madam, not now: I am very ill at
   ease,
Unfit for mine own purposes.
DESDEMONA. Well, do your discretion.
                [CASSIO *goes out.*
IAGO. Ha! I like not that.
OTHELLO.               What dost thou say?
IAGO. Nothing, my lord: or if—I know not
   what.
OTHELLO. Was not that Cassio parted from
   my wife?

IAGO. Cassio, my lord! No, sure, I cannot
   think it,
That he would steal away so guilty-like,
Seeing you coming.
OTHELLO.            I do believe 't was he.   40
DESDEMONA. How now, my lord!
I have been talking with a suitor here,
A man that languishes in your displeasure.
OTHELLO. Who is't you mean?
DESDEMONA. Why, your lieutenant, Cassio.
   Good my lord,
If I have any grace or power to move you,
His present reconciliation take;
For if he be not one that truly loves you,
That errs in ignorance and not in cunning,
I have no judgment in an honest face.        50
I prithee, call him back.
OTHELLO.                 Went he hence now?
DESDEMONA. Ay, sooth; so humbled
That he hath left part of his grief with me,
To suffer with him. Good love, call him back.
OTHELLO. Not now, sweet Desdemona; some
   other time.
DESDEMONA. But shall 't be shortly?
OTHELLO.              The sooner, sweet, for you.
DESDEMONA. Shall't be tonight at supper?
OTHELLO.                       No, not tonight.
DESDEMONA. Tomorrow dinner, then?
OTHELLO.                 I shall not dine at home;
I meet the captains at the citadel.
DESDEMONA. Why then tomorrow night; or
   Tuesday morn;                                  60
On Tuesday noon, or night; on Wednesday
   morn:
I prithee, name the time; but let it not
Exceed three days: in faith he's penitent;
And yet his trespass, in our common reason—
Save that, they say, the wars must make
   examples
Out of their best—is not almost a fault
To incur a private check. When shall he come?
Tell me, Othello. I wonder in my soul,
What you would ask me that I should deny,
Or stand so mammering on. What! Michael
   Cassio,                                        70
That came a-wooing with you, and so many a
   time,
When I have spoke of you dispraisingly,
Hath ta'en your part; to have so much to do

---

12 *strangeness:* unfriendliness. 13 *Than in, etc.:* i.e.,
than political considerations make necessary. 15 *nice:*
delicate. 16 *Or, etc.:* or be so often renewed by circumstances. 17 *supplied:* filled by someone else. 19 *doubt:*
fear. 23 *watch him tame:* tame him by keeping him
awake. 24 *board:* dining-table; *shrift:* confessional.
34 *do:* follow.

47 *present:* immediate; *take:* make. 51 *call him back:*
reinstate him. 64 *our common reason:* the commonsense
view. 66 *Out of their best:* of the best fighters. 66-7 *is
not, etc.:* hardly deserves even a private rebuke. 70 *mammering:* hesitating.

To bring him in! Trust me, I could do much—
  OTHELLO. Prithee, no more; let him come
    when he will.
I will deny thee nothing.
  DESDEMONA.      Why, this is not a boon;
'T is as I should entreat you wear your gloves,
Or feed on nourishing dishes, or keep you
    warm,
Or sue to you to do a peculiar profit
To your own person: nay, when I have a
    suit          80
Wherein I mean to touch your love indeed,
It shall be full of poise and difficult weight,
And fearful to be granted.
  OTHELLO.      I will deny thee nothing:
Whereon, I do beseech thee, grant me this,
To leave me but a little to myself.
  DESDEMONA. Shall I deny you? no: farewell,
    my lord.
  OTHELLO. Farewell, my Desdemona: I'll
    come to thee straight.
  DESDEMONA. Emilia, come. Be as your
    fancies teach you;
Whate'er you be, I am obedient.
    [DESDEMONA *and* EMILIA *go into the castle.*
  OTHELLO. Excellent wretch! Perdition catch
    my soul,      90
But I do love thee! and when I love thee not,
Chaos is come again.
  IAGO. My noble lord,—
  OTHELLO.      What dost thou say, Iago?
  IAGO. Did Michael Cassio, when you wooed
    my lady,
Know of your love?
  OTHELLO. He did, from first to last: why
    dost thou ask?
  IAGO. But for a satisfaction of my thought;
No further harm.
  OTHELLO.      Why of thy thought, Iago?
  IAGO. I did not think he had been acquainted
    with her.
  OTHELLO. O, yes; and went between us
    very oft.      100
  IAGO. Indeed!
  OTHELLO. Indeed! ay, indeed: discernest
    thou aught in that?
Is he not honest?
  IAGO.      Honest, my lord!
  OTHELLO.      Honest! ay, honest.
  IAGO. My lord, for aught I know.
  OTHELLO. What dost thou think?

  IAGO.          Think, my lord!
  OTHELLO. Think, my lord!
          By heaven, he echoes me,
As if there were some monster in his thought
Too hideous to be shown. Thou dost mean
    something:
I heard thee say even now, thou likedst not that,
When Cassio left my wife: what didst not
    like?      110
And when I told thee he was of my counsel
In my whole course of wooing, thou criedst
    "Indeed!"
And didst contract and purse thy brow
    together,
As if thou then hadst shut up in thy brain
Some horrible conceit. If thou dost love me,
Show me thy thought.
  IAGO. My lord, you know I love you.
  OTHELLO.      I think thou dost;
And, for I know thou'rt full of love and
    honesty,
And weighest thy words before thou givest
    them breath,
Therefore these stops of thine fright me the
    more;      120
For such things in a false disloyal knave
Are tricks of custom, but in a man that's just
They are close delations, working from the
    heart
That passion cannot rule.
  IAGO.      For Michael Cassio,
I dare be sworn I think that he is honest.
  OTHELLO. I think so too.
  IAGO.    Men should be what they seem;
Or those that be not, would they might seem
    none!
  OTHELLO. Certain, men should be what they
    seem.
  IAGO. Why then I think Cassio's an honest
    man.
  OTHELLO. Nay, yet there's more in this. 130
I prithee, speak to me as to thy thinkings,
As thou dost ruminate, and give thy worst of
    thoughts
The worst of words.
  IAGO.      Good my lord, pardon me:
Though I am bound to every act of duty,
I am not bound to that all slaves are free to.
Utter my thoughts? Why, say they are vile and
    false;

---

79 *peculiar:* particular. 82 *poise:* weight. 83 *fearful:*
dangerous. 90 *wretch:* (an endearment).

115 *conceit:* conception. 122 *tricks of custom:* mere
habits. 123 *close delations:* carefully considered accusations. 124 *passion:* emotion. 135 *that:* what; *to:* from.

As where's that palace whereinto foul things
Sometimes intrude not? Who has a breast so
    pure,
But some uncleanly apprehensions
Keep leets and law-days and in session sit  140
With meditations lawful?
    OTHELLO. Thou dost conspire against thy
    friend, Iago,
If thou but thinkest him wronged and makest
    his ear
A stranger to thy thoughts.
  · IAGO.              I do beseech you—
Though I perchance am vicious in my guess,
As, I confess, it is my nature's plague
To spy into abuses, and oft my jealousy
Shapes faults that are not—that your wisdom
    yet,
From one that so imperfectly conceits,
Would take no notice, nor build yourself a
    trouble                    150
Out of his scattering and unsure observance.
It were not for your quiet nor your good,
Nor for my manhood, honesty, or wisdom,
To let you know my thoughts.
    OTHELLO.        What dost thou mean?
    IAGO. Good name in man and woman, dear
    my lord,
Is the immediate jewel of their souls:
Who steals my purse steals trash; 't is
    something, nothing;
'T was mine, 't is his, and has been slave to
    thousands;
But he that filches from me my good name
Robs me of that which not enriches him,  160
And makes me poor indeed.
    OTHELLO. By heaven, I'll know thy thoughts.
    IAGO. You cannot, if my heart were in your
    hand;
Nor shall not, whilst 't is in my custody.
    OTHELLO. Ha!
    IAGO.        O! beware, my lord, of jealousy;
It is the green-eyed monster which doth mock
The meat it feeds on: that cuckold lives in
    bliss
Who, certain of his fate, loves not his wronger;
But O! what damnèd minutes tells he o'er
Who dotes, yet doubts, suspects, yet strongly
    loves!                    170
    OTHELLO. O misery!

IAGO. Poor and content is rich, and rich
    enough,
But riches fineless is as poor as winter
To him that ever fears he shall be poor.
Good heaven, the souls of all my tribe defend
From jealousy!
    OTHELLO.     Why, why is this?
Thinkest thou I'd make a life of jealousy,
To follow still the changes of the moon
With fresh suspicions? No; to be once in doubt
Is once to be resolved. Exchange me for a
    goat,                   180
When I shall turn the business of my soul
To such exsufflicate and blown surmises,
Matching thy inference. 'T is not to make me
    jealous
To say my wife is fair, feeds well, loves
    company,
Is free of speech, sings, plays, and dances well;
Where virtue is, these are more virtuous:
Nor from mine own weak merits will I draw
The smallest fear or doubt of her revolt;
For she had eyes, and chose me. No, Iago;
I'll see before I doubt; when I doubt, prove; 190
And on the proof, there is no more but this,
Away at once with love or jealousy!
    IAGO. I am glad of it; for now I shall have
    reason
To show the love and duty that I bear you
With franker spirit; therefore, as I am bound,
Receive it from me. I speak not yet of proof.
Look to your wife; observe her well with
    Cassio;
Wear your eye thus, not jealous nor secure:
I would not have your free and noble nature,
Out of self-bounty, be abused; look to 't.   200
I know our country disposition well;
In Venice they do let heaven see the pranks
They dare not show their husbands; their best
    conscience
Is not to leave 't undone, but keep 't unknown.
    OTHELLO. Dost thou say so?
    IAGO. She did deceive her father, marrying
    you;
And when she seemed to shake and fear your
    looks,
She loved them most.
    OTHELLO.        And so she did.
    IAGO.             Why, go to, then;

---

140 *leets:* district courts. 149 *conceits:* perceives.
151 *scattering:* random.  168 *wronger:* i.e., his unfaithful
wife.

---

173 *fineless:* unlimited.  180 *once:* at once.  182 *ex-*
*sufflicate:* swollen; *blown:* blown up. 200 *self-bounty:*
goodness.  201 *country:* national.  208 *go to: i.e.,* "wake
up."

She that so young could give out such a
    seeming,
To seel her father's eyes up close as oak— 210
He thought 't was witchcraft; but I am much
    to blame;
I humbly do beseech you of your pardon
For too much loving you.
    OTHELLO.       I am bound to thee for ever.
    IAGO. I see this hath a little dashed your
    spirits.
    OTHELLO. Not a jot, not a jot.
    IAGO.           I' faith, I fear it has.
I hope you will consider what is spoke
Comes from my love. But I do see you're
    moved;
I am to pray you not to strain my speech
To grosser issues nor to larger reach
Than to suspicion.                 220
    OTHELLO. I will not.
    IAGO.        Should you do so, my lord,
My speech should fall into such vile success
As my thoughts aim not at. Cassio's my worthy
    friend—
My lord, I see you're moved.
    OTHELLO.        No, not much moved:
I do not think but Desdemona's honest.
    IAGO. Long live she so! And long live you
    to think so!
    OTHELLO. And yet, how nature erring from
    itself—
    IAGO. Ay, there's the point: as—to be bold
    with you—
Not to affect many proposèd matches
Of her own clime, complexion, and degree, 230
Whereto we see in all things nature tends—
Foh! one may smell in such a will most rank,
Foul disproportion, thoughts unnatural.
But pardon me; I do not in position
Distinctly speak of her; though I may fear
Her will, recoiling to her better judgment,
May fall to match you with her country forms
And happily repent.
    OTHELLO.        Farewell, farewell:
If more thou dost perceive, let me know more;
Set on thy wife to observe. Leave me, Iago. 240
    IAGO, *going.* My lord, I take my leave.
    OTHELLO. Why did I marry? This honest
    creature doubtless

Sees and knows more, much more, than he
    unfolds.
    IAGO, *returning.* My lord, I would I might
    entreat your honor
To scan this thing no further; leave it to time.
Though it be fit that Cassio have his place,
For, sure, he fills it up with great ability,
Yet, if you please to hold him off awhile,
You shall by that perceive him and his means:
Note, if your lady strain his entertainment 250
With any strong or vehement importunity;
Much will be seen in that. In the mean time
Let me be thought too busy in my fears—
As worthy cause I have to fear I am—
And hold her free, I do beseech your honor.
    OTHELLO. Fear not my government.
    IAGO. I once more take my leave.
                     [IAGO *goes out.*
    OTHELLO. This fellow 's of exceeding
    honesty,
And knows all qualities, with a learnèd spirit,
Of human dealings. If I do prove her
    haggard,                  260
Though that her jesses were my dear heart-
    strings
I'd whistle her off and let her down the wind,
To prey at fortune. Haply, for I am black
And have not those soft parts of conversation
That chamberers have, or for I am declined
Into the vale of years—yet that's not much—
She's gone. I am abused; and my relief
Must be to loathe her. O curse of marriage,
That we can call these delicate creatures ours,
And not their appetites! I had rather be a
    toad,                  270
And live upon the vapor of a dungeon,
Than keep a corner in the thing I love
For others' uses. Yet, 't is the plague of great
    ones;
Prerogatived are they less than the base;
'T is destiny unshunnable, like death:
Even then this forkèd plague is fated to us
When we do quicken.

---

210 *seel:* sew.  219 *grosser issues:* worse conclusions;
*reach:* meaning.    229 *affect:* like.    230 *degree:* class.
233 *disproportion:* unsuitableness.  234 *in position:* in my
hypothesis.  237–8 *fall, etc.:* happen to compare you with
young Venetians, and so perhaps regret her marriage.

249 *means:* methods.  250 *strain, etc.:* insist on his
reinstatement.  256 *Fear:* doubt; *government:* self-control.  260 *haggard:* unmanageable.  261 *jesses:* bonds.
262–3 *whistle, etc.:* i.e., cast her off like an unmanageable hawk to live as she may.  263 *haply:* it may be.
265 *chamberers:* ladies' men.  267 *abused:* deceived.
274 *Prerogatived:* exempted; *base:* common people.
276 *this forkèd plague:* the cuckold's symbolic horns.
277 *do quicken:* are conceived.

DESDEMONA *and* EMILIA *come out of the castle.*

Desdemona comes:
If she be false, O, then heaven mocks itself!
I'll not believe 't.

DESDEMONA.    How now, my dear Othello!
Your dinner, and the generous islanders    280
By you invited, do attend your presence.

OTHELLO, *in a low voice.* I am to blame.

DESDEMONA.    Why do you speak so faintly?
Are you not well?

OTHELLO. I have a pain upon my forehead
here.

DESDEMONA. Faith, that's with watching;
't will away again:
Let me but bind it hard, within this hour
It will be well. [DESDEMONA *ties a handkerchief
round* OTHELLO's *head.*

OTHELLO.            Your napkin is too little.
[*The handkerchief falls;* DESDEMONA *starts to
pick it up.*
Let it alone. Come, I'll go in with you.

DESDEMONA. I am very sorry that you are
not well.

[OTHELLO *and* DESDEMONA *go into the castle.*

EMILIA. I am glad I have found this
napkin.    290
This was her first remembrance from the Moor;
My wayward husband hath a hundred times
Wooed me to steal it; but she so loves the token,
For he conjured her she should ever keep it,
That she reserves it evermore about her
To kiss and talk to. I'll have the work ta'en out,
And give 't Iago: what he will do with it
Heaven knows, not I;
I nothing but to please his fantasy.

IAGO *returns.*

IAGO. How now! what do you here
alone?    300

EMILIA. Do not you chide; I have a thing
for you.

IAGO. A thing for me? it is a common thing—

EMILIA. Ha!

IAGO. To have a foolish wife.

EMILIA. O, is that all? What will you give me
now
For that same handkerchief?

IAGO.            What handkerchief?

EMILIA. What handkerchief!

Why, that the Moor first gave to Desdemona,
That which so often you did bid me steal.

IAGO. Hast stolen it from her?    310

EMILIA. No, 'faith; she let it drop by
negligence,
And, to the advantage, I, being here, took 't up.
Look, here it is.

IAGO.            A good wench; give it me.

EMILIA. What will you do with 't, that you
have been so earnest
To have me filch it?

IAGO, *snatching it.* Why, what's that to you?

EMILIA. If 't be not for some purpose of
import
Give 't me again; poor lady, she'll run mad
When she shall lack it.

IAGO. Be not acknown on 't; I have use for it.
Go, leave me.            [EMILIA *goes in.*    320
I will in Cassio's lodging lose this napkin,
And let him find it. Trifles light as air
Are to the jealous confirmations strong
As proofs of holy writ; this may do something.
The Moor already changes with my poison:
Dangerous conceits are in their natures poisons,
Which at the first are scarce found to distaste,
But with a little act upon the blood,
Burn like the mines of sulphur.

OTHELLO *comes out, his expression agonized.*

I did say so:
Look, where he comes! Not poppy, nor
mandragora,    330
Nor all the drowsy syrups of the world,
Shall ever medicine thee to that sweet sleep
Which thou owedst yesterday.

OTHELLO.            Ha! ha! false to me?

IAGO. Why, how now, general! no more of
that.

OTHELLO. Avaunt! be gone! Thou hast set
me on the rack;
I swear 't is better to be much abused
Than but to know 't a little.

IAGO.            How now, my lord!

OTHELLO. What sense had I of her stolen
hours of lust?
I saw 't not, thought it not, it harmed not me;
I slept the next night well, was free and
merry;    340
I found not Cassio's kisses on her lips;

---

281 *attend:* await.   284 *a pain: i.e.,* the "forkèd plague."
285 *with watching:* from staying awake. 287 *napkin:*
handkerchief. 296 *ta'en out:* copied. 299 *I:* I know;
*fantasy:* whim.

312 *to the advantage:* seeing my chance. 319 *Be not
acknown:* admit no knowledge. 326 *conceits:* conceptions.
330 *mandragora:* mandrake, an opiate. 331 *drowsy:*
sleep-producing. 333 *owedst:* possessed. 335 *Avaunt:* get
out.

He that is robbed, not wanting what is stolen,
Let him not know 't, and he's not robbed at all.
   IAGO. I am sorry to hear this.
    OTHELLO. I had been happy, if the general
      camp,
Pioners and all, had tasted her sweet body,
So I had nothing known. O, now forever
Farewell the tranquil mind! Farewell content!
Farewell the plumèd troop and the big wars
That make ambition virtue! O, farewell!   350
Farewell the neighing steed and the shrill
     trump,
The spirit-stirring drum, the ear-piercing fife,
The royal banner, and all quality,
Pride, pomp, and circumstance of glorious war!
And, O you mortal engines, whose rude throats
The immortal Jove's dread clamors counterfeit,
Farewell! Othello's occupation 's gone!
   IAGO. Is 't possible, my lord?
    OTHELLO. Villain, be sure thou prove my
     love a whore,
Be sure of it; give me the ocular proof;   360
Or, by the worth of man's eternal soul,
Thou hadst been better have been born a dog
Than answer my waked wrath!
   IAGO.               Is 't come to this?
    OTHELLO. Make me to see 't; or, at the least,
     so prove it,
That the probation bear no hinge nor loop
To hang a doubt on; or woe upon thy life!
   IAGO. My noble lord—
    OTHELLO. If thou dost slander her and
     torture me,
Never pray more; abandon all remorse;
On horror's head horrors accumulate;   370
Do deeds to make heaven weep, all earth
    amazed;
For nothing canst thou to damnation add
Greater than that.
   IAGO.        O grace! O heaven forgive me!
Are you a man? Have you a soul or sense?
God be wi' you; take mine office. O wretched
    fool,
That livest to make thine honesty a vice!
O monstrous world! Take note, take note, O
    world,
To be direct and honest is not safe.
I thank you for this profit, and from hence

I'll love no friend, sith love breeds such
   offence.   380
   OTHELLO. Nay, stay; thou shouldst be
   honest.
   IAGO. I should be wise, for honesty 's a fool
And loses that it works for.
   OTHELLO.           By the world,
I think my wife be honest, and think she is not;
I think that thou art just, and think thou art
   not.
I'll have some proof. Her name, that was as
   fresh
As Dian's visage, is now begrimed and black
As mine own face. If there be cords, or knives,
Poison, or fire, or suffocating streams,
I'll not endure it. Would I were satisfied!   390
   IAGO. I see, sir, you are eaten up with
   passion.
I do repent me that I put it to you.
You would be satisfied?
   OTHELLO.          Would! nay, I will.
   IAGO. And may; but how? how satisfied, my
   lord?
Would you, the supervisor, grossly gape on—
Behold her topped?
   OTHELLO.       Death and damnation! O!
   IAGO. It were a tedious difficulty, I think,
To bring them to that prospect; damn them
   then
If ever mortal eyes do see them bolster
More than their own! What then? how
   then?   400
What shall I say? Where's satisfaction?
It is impossible you should see this,
Were they as prime as goats, as hot as monkeys,
As salt as wolves in pride, and fools as gross
As ignorance made drunk. But yet, I say,
If imputation and strong circumstances,
Which lead directly to the door of truth,
Will give you satisfaction, you may have 't.
   OTHELLO. Give me a living reason she's
   disloyal.
   IAGO. I do not like the office;   410
But, sith I am entered in this cause so far,
Pricked to 't by foolish honesty and love,
I will go on. I lay with Cassio lately;
And, being troubled with a raging tooth,
I could not sleep.
There are a kind of men so loose of soul
That in their sleeps will mutter their affairs:

---

346 *Pioners:* ditchdiggers.  350 *ambition:* eagerness to
outshine others, ordinarily considered a vice.  355 *mortal
engines:* deadly cannon.  365 *probation:* proof.  375 *fool:*
i.e., himself.  379 *profit:* knowledge.

387 *Dian's:* that of the moon, as goddess of chastity.  395 *supervisor:* spectator.  399 *boister:* copulate.
403 *prime:* ruttish.  404 *salt:* lascivious.

One of this kind is Cassio.
In sleep I heard him say, "Sweet Desdemona,
Let us be wary, let us hide our loves";        420
And then, sir, would he gripe and wring my
   hand,
Cry, "O sweet creature!" and then kiss me
   hard,
As if he plucked up kisses by the roots,
That grew upon my lips; then laid his leg
Over my thigh, and sighed and kissed, and then
Cried, "Cursèd fate that gave thee to the
   Moor!"

OTHELLO. O monstrous! monstrous!

IAGO.              Nay, this was but his dream.

OTHELLO. But this denoted a foregone conclusion:
'T is a shrewd doubt, though it be but a dream.

IAGO. And this may help to thicken other
   proofs                                      430
That do demonstrate thinly.

OTHELLO.            I'll tear her all to pieces.

IAGO. Nay, but be wise: yet we see nothing
   done;
She may be honest yet. Tell me but this,
Have you not sometimes seen a handkerchief
Spotted with strawberries in your wife's hand?

OTHELLO. I gave her such a one; 't was my
   first gift.

IAGO. I know not that: but such a handker-
   chief—
I am sure it was your wife's—did I today
See Cassio wipe his beard with.

OTHELLO.                     If it be that,—

IAGO. If it be that, or any that was hers, 440
It speaks against her with the other proofs.

OTHELLO. O, that the slave had forty thou-
   sand lives!
One is too poor, too weak for my revenge.
Now do I see 't is true. Look here, Iago;
        [OTHELLO *blows out his breath.*
All my fond love thus do I blow to heaven:
'T is gone.
Arise, black vengeance, from thy hollow cell!
Yield up, O love, thy crown and hearted throne
To tyrannous hate! Swell, bosom, with thy
   fraught,
For 't is of aspics' tongues!

IAGO.               Yet be content.    450

OTHELLO. O, blood, blood, blood!

IAGO. Patience, I say; your mind perhaps
   may change.

OTHELLO. Never, Iago. Like to the Pontic
   sea,
Whose icy current and compulsive course
Ne'er feels retiring ebb, but keeps due on
To the Propontic and the Hellespont,
Even so my bloody thoughts, with violent pace,
Shall ne'er look back, ne'er ebb to humble love,
Till that a capable and wide revenge
Swallow them up.              [OTHELLO *kneels.*
        Now, by yond marble heaven,    460
In the due reverence of a sacred vow
I here engage my words.

IAGO, *kneeling.*         Do not rise yet.
Witness, you ever-burning lights above,
You elements that clip us round about,
Witness that here Iago doth give up
The execution of his wit, hands, heart,
To wronged Othello's service! Let him com-
   mand,
And to obey shall be in me remorse,
What bloody business ever.        [*They rise.*

OTHELLO.              I greet thy love,
Not with vain thanks, but with acceptance
   bounteous,                                  470
And will upon the instant put thee to 't:
Within these three days let me hear thee say
That Cassio's not alive.

IAGO. My friend is dead; 't is done at your
   request.
But let her live.

OTHELLO.       Damn her, lewd minx! O,
   damn her!
Come, go with me apart; I will withdraw
To furnish me with some swift means of death
For the fair devil. Now art thou my lieutenant.

IAGO. I am your own for ever.


SCENE 4. *Before the castle.*

DESDEMONA, EMILIA, *and* CLOWN.

DESDEMONA. Do you know, sirrah, where
   Lieutenant Cassio lies?

CLOWN. I dare not say he lies anywhere.

DESDEMONA. Why, man?

CLOWN. He's a soldier, and for one to say
   a soldier lies, is stabbing.

DESDEMONA. Go to: where lodges he?

CLOWN. To tell you where he lodges is to
   tell you where I lie.

---

421 *gripe:* grasp.   428 *foregone conclusion:* previous act.
429 *shrewd doubt:* strong evidence.   442 *slave:* wretch.
449 *fraught:* burden.   450 *aspics':* poisonous snakes'; *content:* calm.

459 *capable:* complete.   463 *lights:* stars.   464 *clip:* embrace.   466 *execution:* action.   468 *remorse:* conscience.
SCENE 4. 2. *lies:* is living.

DESDEMONA. Can anything be made of   10
this?

CLOWN. I know not where he lodges, and for
me to devise a lodging and say he lies here
or he lies there, were to lie in mine own
throat.

DESDEMONA. Can you inquire him out and
be edified by report?

CLOWN. I will catechize the world for him;
that is, make questions, and by them
answer.                              20

DESDEMONA. Seek him, bid him come hither;
tell him I have moved my lord on his behalf and hope all will be well.

CLOWN. To do this is within the compass of
man's wit; and therefore I will attempt the
doing it.                   [CLOWN goes out.

DESDEMONA. Where should I lose that handkerchief, Emilia?

EMILIA. I know not, madam.

DESDEMONA. Believe me, I had rather have
lost my purse                        30
Full of crusadoes; and, but my noble Moor
Is true of mind and made of no such baseness
As jealous creatures are, it were enough
To put him to ill thinking.

EMILIA.                    Is he not jealous?

DESDEMONA. Who, he? I think the sun where
he was born
Drew all such humors from him.

OTHELLO comes out of the castle.

EMILIA.              Look, where he comes.

DESDEMONA. I will not leave him now till
Cassio
Be called to him. How is 't with you, my lord?

OTHELLO. Well, my good lady. [To himself]
O, hardness to dissemble!
How do you, Desdemona?

DESDEMONA.      Well, my good lord.   40

OTHELLO. Give me your hand: this hand is
moist, my lady.

DESDEMONA. It yet hath felt no age nor
known no sorrow.

OTHELLO. This argues fruitfulness and lib-
eral heart;
Hot, hot, and moist; this hand of yours requires
A sequester from liberty, fasting and prayer,
Much castigation, exercise devout;

For here's a young and sweating devil here,
That commonly rebels. 'T is a good hand,
A frank one.

DESDEMONA. You may, indeed, say so;
For 't was that hand that gave away my
heart.                               50

OTHELLO. A liberal hand; the hearts of old
gave hands,
But our new heraldry is hands, not hearts.

DESDEMONA. I cannot speak of this. Come
now, your promise.

OTHELLO. What promise, chuck?

DESDEMONA. I have sent to bid Cassio come
speak with you.

OTHELLO. I have a salt and sorry rheum
offends me;
Lend me thy handkerchief.

DESDEMONA.              Here, my lord.

OTHELLO. That which I gave you.

DESDEMONA.          I have it not about me.

OTHELLO. Not?

DESDEMONA.      No, indeed, my lord.

OTHELLO.                    That is a fault.
That handkerchief                    60
Did an Egyptian to my mother give;
She was a charmer, and could almost read
The thoughts of people; she told her, while she
kept it,
'T would make her amiable and subdue my
father
Entirely to her love, but if she lost it
Or made a gift of it, my father's eye
Should hold her loathèd and his spirits should
hunt
After new fancies. She dying gave it me
And bid me, when my fate would have me
wive,
To give it her. I did so: and take heed on 't;  70
Make it a darling like your precious eye;
To lose 't or give 't away were such perdition
As nothing else could match.

DESDEMONA.              Is 't possible?

OTHELLO. 'T is true; there's magic in the web
of it.
A sibyl, that had numbered in the world
The sun to course two hundred compasses,
In her prophetic fury sewed the work;
The worms were hallowed that did breed the
silk,

---

17 be edified by: learn from the.  27 should I lose:
could I have lost.  31 crusadoes: gold coins.  36 humors:
moods.  43 liberal: generous, licentious.  45 sequester:
removal.

51–2 the hearts, etc.: i.e., formerly hearts joined when
hands did (in marriage); nowadays only the hands join.
56 salt: teary; rheum: cold.  75 sybil: woman supposed to
have powers of prophecy.  76 compasses: annual circuits.

And it was dyed in mummy which the skilful
Conserved of maidens' hearts.

DESDEMONA.              Indeed! is 't true?    80

OTHELLO. Most veritable; therefore look to
't well.

DESDEMONA. Then would to God that I had
never seen 't!

OTHELLO. Ha! wherefore?

DESDEMONA. Why do you speak so startingly
and rash?

OTHELLO. Is 't lost? Is 't gone? Speak, is it
out o' the way?

DESDEMONA. Heaven bless us!

OTHELLO. Say you?

DESDEMONA. It is not lost, but what an if it
were?

OTHELLO. How!

DESDEMONA. I say, it is not lost.

OTHELLO.              Fetch 't, let me see 't.    90

DESDEMONA. Why, so I can, sir, but I will
not now.
This is a trick to put me from my suit:
Pray you, let Cassio be received again.

OTHELLO. Fetch me the handkerchief; my
mind misgives.

DESDEMONA. Come, come;
You'll never meet a more sufficient man.

OTHELLO. The handkerchief!

DESDEMONA.              I pray, talk me of Cassio.

OTHELLO. The handkerchief!

DESDEMONA.              A man that all his time
Hath founded his good fortunes on your love,
Shared dangers with you—              100

OTHELLO. The handkerchief!

DESDEMONA. In sooth, you are to blame.

OTHELLO. Away!        [OTHELLO *rushes out.*

EMILIA. Is not this man jealous?

DESDEMONA. I ne'er saw this before.
Sure, there's some wonder in this handkerchief;
I am most unhappy in the loss of it.

EMILIA. 'T is not a year or two shows us a
man:
They are all but stomachs, and we all but food.
They eat us hungerly, and when they are
full,              110
They belch us.

CASSIO *and* IAGO *enter.*

              Look you, Cassio and my husband!

IAGO. There is no other way; 't is she must
do 't,

And, lo, the happiness! Go, and importune her.

DESDEMONA. How now, good Cassio! What's
the news with you?

CASSIO. Madam, my former suit: I do
beseech you
That by your virtuous means I may again
Exist, and be a member of his love
Whom I with all the office of my heart
Entirely honor; I would not be delayed.
If my offence be of such mortal kind        120
That nor my service past, nor present sorrows,
Nor purposed merit in futurity,
Can ransom me into his love again,
But to know so must be my benefit;
So shall I clothe me in a forced content,
And shut myself up in some other course
To fortune's alms.

DESDEMONA.              Alas, thrice-gentle Cassio!
My advocation is not now in tune;
My lord is not my lord; nor should I know him
Were he in favor as in humor altered.        130
So help me every spirit sanctified,
As I have spoken for you all my best
And stood within the blank of his displeasure
For my free speech. You must awhile be
patient;
What I can do I will, and more I will
Than for myself I dare; let that suffice you.

IAGO. Is my lord angry?

EMILIA.              He went hence but now,
And certainly in strange unquietness.

IAGO. Can he be angry? I have seen the
cannon,
When it hath blown his ranks into the air,    140
And, like the devil, from his very arm
Puffed his own brother—and can he be angry?
Something of moment then; I will go meet him.
There's matter in 't indeed if he be angry.

DESDEMONA. I prithee, do so.

                                    [IAGO *goes out.*
              Something, sure, of state,
Either from Venice, or some unhatched practice
Made demonstrable here in Cyprus to him,
Hath puddled his clear spirit; and in such cases
Men's natures wrangle with inferior things,
Though great ones are their object. 'T is even
so;              150
For let our finger ache, and it indues
Our other healthful members even to that sense

---

79 *mummy:* mummy-juice.    88 *an if:* if.

121 *nor . . . nor:* neither . . . nor.    124 *But:* merely.
128 *advocation:* power as an advocate.    130 *favor:* face.
133 *blank:* center (of a target).    146 *practice:* plot.
151 *indues:* brings.

Of pain. Nay, we must think men are not gods,
Nor of them look for such observancy
As fits the bridal. Beshrew me much, Emilia,
I was, unhandsome warrior as I am,
Arraigning his unkindness with my soul;
But now I find I had suborned the witness,
And he 's indicted falsely.

EMILIA. Pray heaven it be state-matters, as
    you think,                                        160
And no conception nor no jealous toy
Concerning you.

DESDEMONA. Alas the day, I never gave him
    cause!

EMILIA. But jealous souls will not be
    answered so;
They are not ever jealous for the cause,
But jealous for they are jealous: 't is a monster
Begot upon itself, born on itself.

DESDEMONA. Heaven keep that monster
    from Othello's mind!

EMILIA. Lady, amen.

DESDEMONA. I will go seek him. Cassio,
    walk hereabout:                                   170
If I do find him fit, I'll move your suit,
And seek to effect it to my uttermost.

CASSIO. I humbly thank your ladyship.

        [DESDEMONA and EMILIA go out.

BIANCA, *a loose woman, enters at other side of*
    *stage.*

BIANCA. Save you, friend Cassio!

CASSIO.              What make you from home?
How is it with you, my most fair Bianca?
I' faith, sweet love, I was coming to your house.

BIANCA. And I was going to your lodging,
    Cassio.
What, keep a week away? seven days and
    nights?
Eight score eight hours? and lovers' absent
    hours,
More tedious than the dial eight score
    times?                                            180
O weary reckoning!

CASSIO.              Pardon me, Bianca;
I have this while with leaden thoughts been
    pressed;
But I shall, in a more continuate time,
Strike off this score of absence. Sweet Bianca,

    [*Giving her* DESDEMONA's *handkerchief.*
Take me this work out.

BIANCA.              O Cassio, whence came this?

This is some token from a newer friend;
To the felt absence now I feel a cause:
Is 't come to this? Well, well.

CASSIO.                          Go to, woman!
Throw your vile guesses in the devil's teeth,
From whence you have them. You are jealous
    now                                               190
That this is from some mistress, some remem-
    brance.
No, in good troth, Bianca.

BIANCA.                      Why, whose is it?

CASSIO. I know not, sweet; I found it in my
    chamber.
I like the work well; ere it be demanded,
As like enough it will, I'd have it copied;
Take it and do 't, and leave me for this time.

BIANCA. Leave you! wherefore?

CASSIO. I do attend here on the general;
And think it no addition, nor my wish,
To have him see me womaned.

BIANCA.              Why, I pray you?   200

CASSIO. Not that I love you not.

BIANCA.              But that you do not love me.
I pray you, bring me on the way a little,
And say if I shall see you soon at night.

CASSIO. 'T is but a little way that I can bring
    you,
For I attend here; but I'll see you soon.

BIANCA. 'T is very good; I must be circum-
    stanced.

## ACT IV. *Cyprus.*

SCENE 1. *Before the castle, later that day.*

OTHELLO *and* IAGO.

IAGO. Will you think so?

OTHELLO.              Think so, Iago!

IAGO.                                  What,
To kiss in private?

OTHELLO.              An unauthorized kiss.

IAGO. Or to be naked with her friend in bed
An hour or more, not meaning any harm?

OTHELLO. Naked in bed, Iago, and not mean
    harm!
It is hypocrisy against the devil:
They that mean virtuously, and yet do so,
The devil their virtue tempts, and they tempt
    heaven.

IAGO. So they do nothing, 't is a venial slip;

---

154 *observancy:* courtesy.   155 *Beshrew:* curse.   161 *toy:*
whim.   183 *continuate:* uninterrupted.

199 *addition:* honor.   202 *bring:* go with.   206 *be cir-*
*cumstanced:* put up with the circumstances.
ACT IV. SCENE 1. 6 *hypocrisy against:* an effort to cheat.

But if I give my wife a handkerchief—     10
OTHELLO. What then?
IAGO. Why, then, 't is hers, my lord; and, being hers,
She may, I think, bestow 't on any man.
OTHELLO. She is protectress of her honor too:
May she give that?
IAGO. Her honor is an essence that's not seen;
They have it very oft that have it not:
But, for the handkerchief—
OTHELLO. By heaven, I would most gladly have forgot it.
Thou saidst—O, it comes o'er my memory   20
As doth the raven o'er the infected house,
Boding to all—he had my handkerchief.
IAGO. Ay, what of that?
OTHELLO.          That's not so good now.
IAGO.                                    What
If I had said I had seen him do you wrong?
Or heard him say—as knaves be such abroad,
Who having, by their own importunate suit
Or voluntary dotage of some mistress,
Convincèd or supplied them, cannot choose
But they must blab—
OTHELLO.          Hath he said anything?
IAGO. He hath, my lord; but be you well assured,                              30
No more than he 'll unswear.
OTHELLO.          What hath he said?
IAGO. 'Faith, that he did—I know not what he did.
OTHELLO. What? what?
IAGO. Lie—
OTHELLO.    With her?
IAGO.          With her, on her; what you will.
OTHELLO. Lie with her! lie on her! We say lie on her when they belie her. Lie with her! That's fulsome. Handkerchief—confessions—handkerchief! To confess, and be hanged for his labor; first to be hanged, and then to confess: I tremble at it.   40
Nature would not invest herself in such shadowing passion without some instruction. It is not words that shake me thus. Pish! Noses, ears, and lips. Is 't possible? Confess—handkerchief—O devil!
          [OTHELLO *falls in a fit.*

IAGO. Work on,
My medicine, work! Thus credulous fools are caught;
And many a worthy and chaste dames even thus,
All guiltless, meet reproach. What, ho! my lord!
My lord, I say! Othello!

          CASSIO *enters.*

                    How now, Cassio!   50
CASSIO. What's the matter?
IAGO. My lord is fallen into an epilepsy.
This is his second fit; he had one yesterday.
CASSIO. Rub him about the temples.
IAGO.                         No, forbear;
The lethargy must have his quiet course:
If not, he foams at mouth and by and by
Breaks out to savage madness. Look, he stirs.
Do you withdraw yourself a little while,
He will recover straight; when he is gone,
I would on great occasion speak with you.   60
                    [CASSIO *goes out.*
How is it, general? Have you not hurt your head?
OTHELLO. Dost thou mock me?
IAGO.          I mock you! no, by heaven.
Would you would bear your fortune like a man!
OTHELLO. A hornèd man's a monster and a beast.
IAGO. There's many a beast then in a populous city,
And many a civil monster.
OTHELLO. Did he confess it?
IAGO.                    Good sir, be a man;
Think every bearded fellow that's but yoked
May draw with you; there's millions now alive
That nightly lie in those unproper beds   70
Which they dare swear peculiar: your case is better.
O, 't is the spite of hell, the fiend's arch-mock,
To lip a wanton in a secure couch,
And to suppose her chaste! No, let me know;
And knowing what I am, I know what she shall be.
OTHELLO. O, thou art wise; 't is certain.
IAGO.          Stand you awhile apart;
Confine yourself but in a patient list.
Whilst you were here o'erwhelmèd with your grief—
A passion most unsuiting such a man—

---

22 *boding:* foretelling evil. 25 *knaves, etc. i.e.,* such knaves do exist. 28 *Convincèd or supplied:* overcome the objections of a reluctant mistress, or satisfied the desires of a willing one. 41–3 *Nature, etc.: i.e.,* my anger is so strong that it must be based on facts.

55 *his:* its. 62 *mock: i.e.,* by a joke about horns. 68 *yoked:* married. 69 *with you: i.e.,* the same burden as you. 70 *unproper:* not theirs only. 71 *peculiar:* private. 73 *secure: i.e.,* supposedly secure. 77 *Confine, etc.:* only be patient.

Cassio came hither; I shifted him away          80
And laid good 'scuse upon your ecstasy,
Bade him anon return and here speak with me;
The which he promised. Do but encave yourself,
And mark the fleers, the gibes, and notable
      scorns,
That dwell in every region of his face;
For I will make him tell the tale anew,
Where, how, how oft, how long ago, and when
He hath, and is again to cope your wife:
I say, but mark his gesture. Marry, patience;
Or I shall say you are all in all in spleen,        90
And nothing of a man.
      OTHELLO.            Dost thou hear, Iago?
I will be found most cunning in my patience;
But—dost thou hear?—most bloody.
      IAGO.                    That's not amiss;
But yet keep time in all. Will you withdraw?
[OTHELLO *conceals himself at the side of stage.*
Now will I question Cassio of Bianca,
A housewife that by selling her desires
Buys herself bread and clothes; it is a creature
That dotes on Cassio; as 't is the strumpet's
      plague
To beguile many and be beguiled by one.
He, when he hears of her, cannot refrain          100
From the excess of laughter.

CASSIO *returns.*

                        Here he comes:
As he shall smile, Othello shall go mad;
And his unbookish jealousy must construe
Poor Cassio's smiles, gestures, and light be-
      havior
Quite in the wrong. How do you now, lieu-
      tenant?
      CASSIO. The worser that you give me the
addition
Whose want even kills me.
      IAGO. Ply Desdemona well, and you are sure
on 't.
[*Speaking lower*] Now, if this suit lay in
Bianca's power,
How quickly should you speed!              110
      CASSIO, *laughing.*          Alas, poor caitiff!
      OTHELLO. Look, how he laughs already!
      IAGO. I never knew woman love man so.
      CASSIO. Alas, poor rogue! I think, i' faith,
she loves me.

OTHELLO. Now he denies it faintly, and
    laughs it out.
IAGO. Do you hear, Cassio?
OTHELLO.              Now he importunes him
To tell it o'er. Go to; well said, well said.
IAGO. She gives it out that you shall marry
    her:
Do you intend it?
    CASSIO. Ha, ha, ha!
OTHELLO. Do you triumph, Roman? Do you
    triumph?                              120
CASSIO. I marry her! what, a customer?
    Prithee, bear some charity to my wit; do
    not think it so unwholesome. Ha, ha, ha!
OTHELLO. So, so, so, so: they laugh that win.
IAGO. 'Faith, the cry goes that you shall
    marry her.
CASSIO. Prithee, say true.
IAGO. I am a very villain else.
OTHELLO. Have you scored me? Well.
CASSIO. This is the monkey's own giv-    130
    ing out; she is persuaded I will marry her,
    out of her own love and flattery, not out
    of my promise.
OTHELLO. Iago beckons me; now he begins
    the story.
CASSIO. She was here even now; she haunts
    me in every place. I was the other day
    talking on the sea-bank with certain
    Venetians; and thither comes the bauble,
    and, by this hand, she falls me thus    140
    about my neck— [CASSIO *embraces* IAGO.
OTHELLO. Crying "O dear Cassio!" as it
    were; his gesture imports it.
CASSIO, *acting it out.* So hangs and lolls and
    weeps upon me; so hales and pulls me; ha,
    ha, ha!
OTHELLO. Now he tells how she plucked him
    to my chamber. O, I see that nose of
    yours, but not that dog I shall throw it to!
CASSIO. Well, I must leave her company.  150
IAGO. Before me! look, where she comes.
CASSIO. 'T is such another fitchew! marry,
    a perfumed one.

BIANCA *enters.*

What do you mean by this haunting of me?
    BIANCA. Let the devil and his dam haunt
    you! What did you mean by that same

---

81 *ecstasy:* fit. 83 *encave:* conceal. 84 *fleers:* sneers.
88 *cope:* meet (in amorous contest). 94 *keep, etc.:* let
each thing have its proper time. 103 *unbookish:* ignorant.
106 *addition:* title. 110 *caitiff:* wretch.

120 *Roman: i.e.,* like a Roman emperor. 121 *customer:*
whore. 122 *wit:* intellect. 129 *scored:* settled accounts
with. 145 *hales:* hauls. 151 *Before me:* (an exclamation). 152 *fitchew:* polecat.

handkerchief you gave me even now? I was a fine fool to take it. I must take out the work? A likely piece of work, that you should find it in your chamber, and 160 not know who left it there! This is some minx's token, and I must take out the work? There; give it your hobby horse; wheresoever you had it, I'll take out no work on 't.

CASSIO. How now, my sweet Bianca! how now! how now!

OTHELLO. By heaven, that should be my handkerchief!

BIANCA. An you'll come to supper to- 170 night, you may; an you will not, come when you are next prepared for.

[BIANCA *goes out.*

IAGO. After her, after her.

CASSIO. 'Faith, I must; she'll rail in the street else.

IAGO. Will you sup there?

CASSIO. 'Faith, I intend so.

IAGO. Well, I may chance to see you; for I would very fain speak with you.

CASSIO. Prithee, come; will you?        180

[CASSIO *runs after* BIANCA.

IAGO. Go to; say no more.

OTHELLO, *coming to* IAGO. How shall I murder him, Iago?

IAGO. Did you perceive how he laughed at his vice?

OTHELLO. O Iago!

IAGO. And did you see the handkerchief?

OTHELLO. Was that mine?

IAGO. Yours, by this hand; and to see how he prizes the foolish woman your 190 wife! She gave it him, and he hath given it his whore.

OTHELLO. I would have him nine years a-killing. A fine woman! a fair woman! a sweet woman!

IAGO. Nay, you must forget that.

OTHELLO. Ay, let her rot, and perish, and be damned tonight; for she shall not live. No, my heart is turned to stone; I strike it, and it hurts my hand. O, the 200 world hath not a sweeter creature; she might lie by an emperor's side and command him tasks.

IAGO. Nay, that's not your way.

OTHELLO. Hang her! I do but say what she

is: so delicate with her needle! an admirable musician! O! she will sing the savageness out of a bear; of so high and plenteous wit and invention—

IAGO. She's the worse for all this.        210

OTHELLO. O, a thousand thousand times. And then, of so gentle a condition!

IAGO. Ay, too gentle.

OTHELLO. Nay, that's certain; but yet the pity of it, Iago! O Iago, the pity of it, Iago!

IAGO. If you are so fond over her iniquity, give her patent to offend; for if it touch not you it comes near nobody.

OTHELLO. I will chop her into messes:        220 cuckold me!

IAGO. O, 't is foul in her.

OTHELLO. With mine officer!

IAGO. That's fouler.

OTHELLO. Get me some poison, Iago, this night. I'll not expostulate with her, lest her body and beauty unprovide my mind again. This night, Iago.

IAGO. Do it not with poison; strangle her in her bed, even the bed she hath 230 contaminated.

OTHELLO. Good, good; the justice of it pleases; very good.

IAGO. And for Cassio, let me be his undertaker; you shall hear more by midnight.

OTHELLO. Excellent good. [*A trumpet sounds off-stage.*] What trumpet is that same?

IAGO. Something from Venice, sure.

DESDEMONA, *her cousin* LODOVICO, *and* ATTENDANTS *enter.*

                         'T is Lodovico

Come from the duke; and, see, your wife is with him.

LODOVICO. Save you, worthy general!

OTHELLO.                 With all my heart, sir.

LODOVICO. The duke and senators of Venice greet you.                         240

[LODOVICO *gives a letter to* OTHELLO.

OTHELLO. I kiss the instrument of their pleasures.

[OTHELLO *kisses the letter, then opens and reads it.*

DESDEMONA. And what's the news, good cousin Lodovico?

IAGO. I am very glad to see you, signior;

---

170 *an:* if.

218 *patent:* permission.    227 *unprovide:* confuse.

Welcome to Cyprus.

LODOVICO. I thank you. How does Lieutenant Cassio?

IAGO. Lives, sir.

DESDEMONA. Cousin, there's fallen between
him and my lord

An unkind breach; but you shall make all well.

OTHELLO. Are you sure of that?

DESDEMONA. My lord?                              250

OTHELLO, reading. "This fail you not
to do, as you will—"

LODOVICO. He did not call; he's busy in the
paper.

Is there division 'twixt my lord and Cassio?

DESDEMONA. A most unhappy one; I would
do much

To atone them, for the love I bear to Cassio.

OTHELLO. Fire and brimstone!

DESDEMONA.                      My lord?

OTHELLO.                               Are you wise?

DESDEMONA. What, is he angry?

LODOVICO.    May be the letter moved him;
For, as I think, they do command him home,
Deputing Cassio in his government.

DESDEMONA. Trust me, I am glad on 't.

OTHELLO.                      Indeed!

DESDEMONA.                      My lord?   260

OTHELLO. I am glad to see you mad.

DESDEMONA.              Why, sweet Othello—

OTHELLO, striking her. Devil!

DESDEMONA. I have not deserved this.

LODOVICO. My lord, this would not be believed in Venice,

Though I should swear I saw 't. 'T is very
much:

Make her amends; she weeps.

OTHELLO.              O devil, devil!

If that the earth could teem with woman's tears,
Each drop she falls would prove a crocodile.
Out of my sight!

DESDEMONA, leaving. I will not stay to
offend you.

LODOVICO. Truly, an obedient lady:     270
I do beseech your lordship, call her back.

OTHELLO. Mistress!

DESDEMONA.      My lord?

OTHELLO.    What would you with her, sir?

LODOVICO. Who, I, my lord?

OTHELLO. Ay; you did wish that I would
make her turn:

Sir, she can turn, and turn, and yet go on,

And turn again; and she can weep, sir, weep;
And she's obedient, as you say, obedient,
Very obedient. Proceed you in your tears.
Concerning this, sir,—O well-painted pas-
sion!—
I am commanded home. Get you away;     280
I'll send for you anon. Sir, I obey the mandate.
And will return to Venice. Hence, avaunt!

[DESDEMONA goes out.

Cassio shall have my place. And, sir, tonight
I do entreat that we may sup together;
You are welcome, sir, to Cyprus.—Goats and
monkeys!            [OTHELLO goes out.

LODOVICO. Is this the noble Moor whom our
full senate

Call all in all sufficient? Is this the nature
Whom passion could not shake? whose solid
virtue

The shot of accident, nor dart of chance,
Could neither graze nor pierce?

IAGO.            He is much changed.   290

LODOVICO. Are his wits safe? Is he not light
of brain?

IAGO. He 's that he is; I may not breathe my
censure.

What he might be, if what he might he is not,
I would to heaven he were!

LODOVICO.            What, strike his wife!

IAGO. 'Faith, that was not so well; yet would
I knew

That stroke would prove the worst!

LODOVICO.                      Is it his use?

Or did the letters work upon his blood,
And new-create this fault?

IAGO.            Alas, alas!

It is not honesty in me to speak
What I have seen and known. You shall
observe him,                            300

And his own courses will denote him so
That I may save my speech. Do but go after
And mark how he continues.

LODOVICO. I am sorry that I am deceived in
him.

SCENE 2. A room in the castle.

OTHELLO and EMILIA

OTHELLO. You have seen nothing then?

EMILIA. Nor ever heard, nor ever did
suspect.

OTHELLO. Yes, you have seen Cassio and
she together.

---

255 atone: reconcile.  259 Deputing: appointing; government: governorship.  267 teem: become pregnant.

279 passion: grief.  296 use: custom.

EMILIA. But then I saw no harm, and then
   I heard
Each syllable that breath made up between
   them.
OTHELLO. What, did they never whisper?
EMILIA.                Never, my lord.
OTHELLO. Nor send you out o' the way?
EMILIA. Never.
OTHELLO. To fetch her fan, her gloves, her
   mask, nor nothing?
EMILIA. Never, my lord.             10
OTHELLO. That's strange.
EMILIA. I durst, my lord, to wager she is
   honest,
Lay down my soul at stake. If you think other,
Remove your thought; it doth abuse your
   bosom.
If any wretch have put this in your head,
Let heaven requite it with the serpent's curse!
For if she be not honest, chaste, and true,
There's no man happy; the purest of their wives
Is foul as slander.
OTHELLO.          Bid her come hither: go.
                  [EMILIA *goes out.*
She says enough; yet she's a simple bawd    20
That cannot say as much. This is a subtle
   whore,
A closet lock and key of villanous secrets;
And yet she'll kneel and pray; I have seen her
   do 't.

      DESDEMONA *and* EMILIA *enter.*

DESDEMONA. My lord, what is your will?
OTHELLO.         Pray, chuck, come hither.
DESDEMONA. What is your pleasure?
OTHELLO.            Let me see your eyes;
Look in my face.
DESDEMONA.      What horrible fancy's this?
OTHELLO, *to* EMILIA. Some of your function,
   mistress;
Leave procreants alone and shut the door;
Cough, or cry "hem" if anybody come:
Your mystery, your mystery; nay, dispatch.   30
                  [EMILIA *goes out.*
DESDEMONA. Upon my knees, what doth
   your speech import?
I understand a fury in your words,
But not the words.
OTHELLO. Why, what art thou?

DESDEMONA. Your wife, my lord; your true
And loyal wife.
OTHELLO.      Come, swear it, damn thyself;
Lest, being like one of heaven, the devils
   themselves
Should fear to seize thee: therefore be double
   damned;
Swear thou art honest.
DESDEMONA.      Heaven doth truly know it.
OTHELLO. Heaven truly knows that thou art
   false as hell.
DESDEMONA. To whom, my lord? with
   whom? How am I false?         40
OTHELLO. O Desdemona! Away! away!
   away!
DESDEMONA. Alas, the heavy day! Why do
   you weep?
Am I the motive of these tears, my lord?
If haply you my father do suspect
An instrument of this your calling back,
Lay not your blame on me: if you have lost
   him,
Why, I have lost him too.
OTHELLO.             Had it pleased heaven
To try me with affliction; had they rained
All kinds of sores and shames on my bare head,
Steeped me in poverty to the very lips,     50
Given to captivity me and my utmost hopes,
I should have found in some place of my soul
A drop of patience; but, alas, to make me
A fixèd figure for the time of scorn
To point his slow unmoving finger at!
Yet could I bear that too; well, very well:
But there, where I have garnered up my heart,
Where either I must live, or bear no life;
The fountain from the which my current runs,
Or else dries up; to be discarded thence!    60
Or keep it as a cistern for foul toads
To knot and gender in! Turn thy complexion
   there,
Patience, thou young and rose-lipped cherubim;
Ay, there, look grim as hell!
DESDEMONA. I hope my noble lord esteems
   me honest.
OTHELLO. O, ay; as summer flies are in the
   shambles,
That quicken even with blowing. O thou weed,
Who art so lovely fair and smellest so sweet

---

20 *she's:* any woman is.   21 *This:* Emilia.   27 *function,*
*i.e.,* as a bawd.   28 *procreants:* love-makers.   30 *mystery:*
vocation; *dispatch:* do it.

44 *haply:* perhaps.   46 *him:* his friendship.   57 *there:*
*i.e.,* Desdemona's breast.   62 *gender:* breed; *Turn, etc.:*
*i.e.,* Desdemona is blushing (?).   66 *shambles:* slaughter-
house.   67 *That . . . blowing:* which breed as fast as they
lay their eggs.

That the sense aches at thee, would thou hadst
 ne'er been born!
 DESDEMONA. Alas, what ignorant sin have I
  committed?          70
 OTHELLO. Was this fair paper, this most
  goodly book,
Made to write "whore" upon? What committed!
Committed! O thou public commoner!
I should make very forges of my cheeks,
That would to cinders burn up modesty,
Did I but speak thy deeds. What committed!
Heaven stops the nose at it and the moon
 winks,
The bawdy wind that kisses all it meets
Is hushed within the hollow mine of earth,
And will not hear it. What committed! 80
Impudent strumpet!
 DESDEMONA. By heaven, you do me wrong.
 OTHELLO. Are you not a strumpet?
 DESDEMONA.   No, as I am a Christian.
If to preserve this vessel for my lord
From any other foul unlawful touch
Be not to be a strumpet, I am none.
 OTHELLO. What, not a whore?
 DESDEMONA.  No, as I shall be saved.
 OTHELLO. Is 't possible?
 DESDEMONA. O, heaven forgive us!
 OTHELLO.   I cry you mercy, then;
I took you for that cunning whore of Venice
That married with Othello.
[*Calling to* EMILIA.]  You, mistress, 90
That have the office opposite to Saint Peter,
And keep the gate of hell!

EMILIA *comes in.*

      You, you, ay, you!
We have done our course; there's money for
 your pains:
I pray you, turn the key and keep our counsel.
      [OTHELLO *goes out.*
 EMILIA. Alas, what does this gentleman
  conceive?
How do you, madam? How do you, my good
 lady?
 DESDEMONA. Faith, half asleep.
 EMILIA. Good madam, what's the matter
  with my lord?
 DESDEMONA. With who?
 EMILIA. Why, with my lord, madam. 100
 DESDEMONA. Who is thy lord?
 EMILIA.  He that is yours, sweet lady.

---

73 *commoner:* prostitute.

 DESDEMONA. I have none; do not talk to me,
  Emilia;
I cannot weep, nor answer have I none,
But what should go by water. Prithee, tonight
Lay on my bed my wedding sheets: remember;
And call thy husband hither.
 EMILIA.   Here's a change indeed!
        [EMILIA *goes out.*
 DESDEMONA. 'T is meet I should be used so,
  very meet.
How have I been behaved, that he might stick
The smallest opinion on my least misuse?

EMILIA *returns with* IAGO.

 IAGO. What is your pleasure, madam? How
  is 't with you?       110
 DESDEMONA. I cannot tell. Those that do
  teach young babes
Do it with gentle means and easy tasks;
He might have chid me so, for in good faith
I am a child to chiding.
 IAGO.    What's the matter, lady?
 EMILIA. Alas, Iago, my lord hath so
  bewhored her,
Thrown such despite and heavy terms upon her,
As true hearts cannot bear.
 DESDEMONA. Am I that name, Iago?
 IAGO.    What name, fair lady?
 DESDEMONA. Such as she says my lord did
  say I was.
 EMILIA. He called her whore; a beggar in his
  drink         120
Could not have laid such terms upon his callet.
 IAGO. Why did he so?
 DESDEMONA. I do not know; I am sure I am
  none such.
 IAGO. Do not weep, do not weep. Alas the
  day!
 EMILIA. Hath she forsook so many noble
  matches,
Her father and her country and her friends,
To be called whore? Would it not make one
 weep?
 DESDEMONA. It is my wretched fortune.
 IAGO.    Beshrew him for 't!
How comes this trick upon him?
 DESDEMONA.  Nay, heaven doth know.
 EMILIA. I will be hanged, if some eternal
  villain,        130

---

104 *by water:* with tears. 107 *meet:* right. 108–9 *How, etc.:* what slightest wrong have I done that would justify the least suspicion? 116 *despite:* scorn. 121 *callet:* wench. 128 *Beshrew:* curse. 129 *trick:* mood.

Some busy and insinuating rogue,
Some cogging, cozening slave, to get some
    office,
Have not devised this slander; I'll be hanged
    else.
　　IAGO. Fie, there is no such man; it is
    impossible.
　　DESDEMONA. If any such there be, heaven
    pardon him!
　　EMILIA. A halter pardon him and hell gnaw
    his bones!
Why should he call her whore? Who keeps her
    company?
What place? what time? what form? what likeli-
    hood?
The Moor's abused by some most villanous
    knave,
Some base notorious knave, some scurvy fel-
    low.                                        140
O heaven, that such companions thou 'dst
    unfold,
And put in every honest hand a whip
To lash the rascals naked through the world
Even from the east to the west!
　　IAGO.　　　　　　　Speak within door.
　　EMILIA. O, fie upon them! Some such squire
    he was
That turned your wit the seamy side without
And made you to suspect me with the Moor.
　　IAGO. You are a fool; go to.
　　DESDEMONA.　　　　　O good Iago,
What shall I do to win my lord again?
Good friend, go to him; for, by this light of
    heaven,                                     150
I know not how I lost him. Here I kneel:
If e'er my will did trespass 'gainst his love,
Either in discourse of thought or actual deed,
Or that mine eyes, mine ears, or any sense,
Delighted them in any other form;
Or that I do not yet, and ever did,
And ever will—though he do shake me off
To beggarly divorcement—love him dearly,
Comfort forswear me! Unkindness may do
    much,
And his unkindness may defeat my life     160
But never taint my love. I cannot say "whore":
It doth abhor me now I speak the word;
To do the act that might the addition earn

Not the world's mass of vanity could make me.
　　IAGO. I pray you, be content; 't is but his
    humor;
The business of the state does him offence,
And he does chide with you.
　　DESDEMONA. If 't were no other—
　　IAGO.　　　　　　　'T is but so, I warrant.
　　　　　　　　　　　[*Trumpets sound off-stage.*
Hark, how those instruments summon to
    supper!
The messengers of Venice stay the meat.   170
Go in, and weep not; all things shall be well.
　　　　　　[DESDEMONA *and* EMILIA *go out.*

　　　　　　　　RODERIGO *enters.*

How now, Roderigo!
　　RODERIGO. I do not find that thou dealest
    justly with me.
　　IAGO. What in the contrary?
　　RODERIGO. Every day thou daffest me with
    some device, Iago; and rather, as it seems
    to me now, keepest from me all con-
    veniency than suppliest me with the least
    advantage of hope. I will indeed   180
    no longer endure it, nor am I yet per-
    suaded to put up in peace what already
    I have foolishly suffered.
　　IAGO. Will you hear me, Roderigo?
　　RODERIGO. 'Faith, I have heard too much,
    for your words and performances are no
    kin together.
　　IAGO. You charge me most unjustly.
　　RODERIGO. With nought but truth. I have
    wasted myself out of my means.   190
    The jewels you have had from me to
    deliver to Desdemona would half have
    corrupted a votarist; you have told me she
    hath received them and returned me
    expectations and comforts of sudden re-
    spect and acquaintance, but I find none.
　　IAGO. Well; go to; very well.
　　RODERIGO. Very well! go to! I cannot go
    to, man; nor 't is not very well: nay, I
    think it is scurvy, and begin to find   200
    myself fopped in it.
　　IAGO. Very well.
　　RODERIGO. I tell you 't is not very well. I
    will make myself known to Desdemona;
    if she will return me my jewels, I will
    give over my suit and repent my unlawful

---

132 *cogging:* cheating; *cozening:* deceiving.　141 *unfold:*
reveal.　144 *within door: i.e.,* not so loud as to be heard
outside the house.　145 *squire:* low fellow.　155 *them in:*
themselves with.

170 *stay:* await.　176 *daffest:* put off.　193 *votarist:* nun.
201 *fopped:* made to look silly.

solicitation; if not, assure yourself I will seek satisfaction of you.

IAGO. You have said now.

RODERIGO. Ay, and said nothing but 210 what I protest intendment of doing.

IAGO. Why, now I see there's mettle in thee, and even from this instant do build on thee a better opinion than ever before. Give me thy hand, Roderigo; thou hast taken against me a most just exception; but yet I protest I have dealt most directly in thy affair.

RODERIGO. It hath not appeared.

IAGO. I grant indeed it hath not ap- 220 peared, and your suspicion is not without wit and judgment. But, Roderigo, if thou hast that in thee indeed, which I have greater reason to believe now than ever, I mean purpose, courage, and valor, this night show it: if thou the next night following enjoy not Desdemona, take me from this world with treachery and devise engines for my life.

RODERIGO. Well, what is it? Is it within 230 reason and compass?

IAGO. Sir, there is especial commission come from Venice to depute Cassio in Othello's place.

RODERIGO. Is that true? Why, then Othello and Desdemona return again to Venice.

IAGO. O, no; he goes into Mauritania and takes away with him the fair Desdemona, unless his abode be lingered here by some accident: wherein none can be so 240 determinate as the removing of Cassio.

RODERIGO. How do you mean, removing of him?

IAGO. Why, by making him uncapable of Othello's place; knocking out his brains.

RODERIGO. And that you would have me to do?

IAGO. Ay, if you dare do yourself a profit and a right. He sups tonight with a har-lotry, and thither will I go to him; he 250 knows not yet of his honorable fortune. If you will watch his going thence, which I will fashion to fall out between twelve and one, you may take him at your pleas-ure; I will be near to second your attempt, and he shall fall between us. Come, stand

not amazed at it, but go along with me; I will show you such a necessity in his death that you shall think yourself bound to put it on him. It is now high 260 supper-time, and the night grows to waste: about it.

RODERIGO. I will hear further reason for this.

IAGO. And you shall be satisfied.

SCENE 3. *Another room in the castle.*

OTHELLO, LODOVICO, DESDEMONA,
EMILIA, and ATTENDANTS

LODOVICO. I do beseech you, sir, trouble yourself no further.

OTHELLO. O, pardon me; 't will do me good to walk.

LODOVICO. Madam, good night; I humbly thank your ladyship.

DESDEMONA. Your honor is most welcome.

OTHELLO.                          Will you walk, sir?
O! Desdemona.

DESDEMONA. My lord?

OTHELLO. Get you to bed on the instant; I will be returned forthwith; dismiss your attendant there: look it be done.

DESDEMONA. I will, my lord. 10
[OTHELLO, LODOVICO, *and* ATTENDANTS
                                          *go out.*

EMILIA. How goes it now? He looks gentler than he did.

DESDEMONA. He says he will return incontinent;
He hath commanded me to go to bed
And bade me to dismiss you.

EMILIA.                          Dismiss me!

DESDEMONA. It was his bidding; therefore, good Emilia,
Give me my nightly wearing, and adieu.
We must not now displease him.

EMILIA. I would you had never seen him!

DESDEMONA. So would not I; my love doth so approve him
That even his stubbornness, his checks, his frowns— 20
Prithee, unpin me—have grace and favor in them.

EMILIA. I have laid those sheets you bade me on the bed.

DESDEMONA. All's one. Good faith, how foolish are our minds!

---

209 *said:* finished speaking. 228 *engines for:* plots against. 240–41 *determinate:* effectual.

12 *incontinent:* at once. 20 *checks:* reproofs.

If I do die before thee, prithee shroud me
In one of those same sheets.
 EMILIA.     Come, come, you talk.
 DESDEMONA. My mother had a maid called
  Barbara;
She was in love, and he she loved proved mad
And did forsake her; she had a song of
 "willow";
An old thing 't was, but it expressed her
 fortune,
And she died singing it; that song tonight 30
Will not go from my mind; I have much to do
But to go hang my head all at one side,
And sing it like poor Barbara. Prithee,
 dispatch.
 EMILIA. Shall I go fetch your night-gown?
 DESDEMONA.    No, unpin me here.
This Lodovico is a proper man.
 EMILIA. A very handsome man.
 DESDEMONA. He speaks well.
 EMILIA. I know a lady in Venice would have
 walked barefoot to Palestine for a touch
 of his nether lip.      40
 DESDEMONA, *singing.* "The poor soul sat
  sighing by a sycamore tree,
 Sing all a green willow;
 Her hand on her bosom, her head on her
  knee,
 Sing willow, willow, willow:
 The fresh streams ran by her, and murmured
  her moans;
 Sing willow, willow, willow;
 Her salt tears fell from her, and softened
  the stones;—"
Lay by these.
[*Singing*] "Sing willow, willow, willow;"
Prithee, hie thee; he'll come anon.  50
[*Singing*] "Sing all a green willow must be my
 garland.
 Let nobody blame him; his scorn I
  approve—"
Nay, that's not next. Hark! who is 't that
 knocks?
 EMILIA. It 's the wind.
 DESDEMONA, *singing.* "I called my love false
 love; but what said he then?
  Sing willow, willow, willow:
 If I court moe women, you'll couch with
  moe men."
So, get thee gone; good night. Mine eyes do
 itch;

Doth that bode weeping?
 EMILIA.    'T is neither here nor there.
 DESDEMONA. I have heard it said so. O, these
 men, these men!      60
Dost thou in conscience think—tell me,
 Emilia—
That there be women do abuse their husbands
In such gross kind?
 EMILIA.  There be some such, no question.
 DESDEMONA. Wouldst thou do such a deed
 for all the world?
 EMILIA. Why, would not you?
 DESDEMONA.   No, by this heavenly light!
 EMILIA. Nor I neither by this heavenly light;
I might do 't as well i' the dark.
 DESDEMONA. Wouldst thou do such a deed
 for all the world?
 EMILIA. The world's a huge thing; it is a
 great price
For a small vice.
 DESDEMONA.  In troth, I think thou wouldst
 not.         70
 EMILIA. In troth, I think I should; and undo
 't when I had done. Marry, I would not
 do such a thing for a joint-ring, nor for
 measures of lawn, nor for gowns, petticoats, nor caps, nor any petty exhibition;
 but, for the whole world, why who would
 not make her husband a cuckold to make
 him a monarch? I should venture purgatory for 't.
 DESDEMONA. Beshrew me, if I would do
 such a wrong      80
For the whole world.
 EMILIA. Why, the wrong is but a wrong i' the
 world; and having the world for your
 labor, 't is a wrong in your own
 world, and you might quickly make it
 right.
 DESDEMONA. I do not think there is any
 such woman.
 EMILIA. Yes, a dozen; and as many to the
 vantage as would store the world they 90
 played for.
But I do think it is their husbands' faults
If wives do fall. Say that they slack their duties
And pour our treasures into foreign laps,
Or else break out in peevish jealousies,

---

31–2 *I have, etc.:* It is hard for me not to. 57 *moe:* more.

63 *kind:* manner. 73 *joint-ring:* finger-ring with interlocking halves. 74 *lawn:* linen. 75 *exhibition:* pay. 89–90 *to the vantage:* in addition. 90 *store:* stock. 93 *they:* husbands.

Throwing restraint upon us; or say they strike
    us,
Or scant our former having in despite;
Why, we have galls, and though we have some
    grace,
Yet have we some revenge. Let husbands know
Their wives have sense like them; they see and
    smell                                        100
And have their palates both for sweet and sour,
As husbands have. What is it that they do
When they change us for others? Is it sport?
I think it is; and doth affection breed it?
I think it doth; is 't frailty that thus errs?
It is so too; and have not we affections,
Desires for sport, and frailty, as men have?
Then let them use us well; else let them know,
The ills we do, their ills instruct us so.
    DESDEMONA. Good night, good night;
        heaven me such uses send,              110
Not to pick bad from bad, but by bad mend!


## ACT V. *Cyprus.*

SCENE 1. *A dark street, that night.*

IAGO *and* RODERIGO.

IAGO. Here, stand behind this bulk; straight
    will he come:
Wear thy good rapier bare, and put it home:
Quick, quick; fear nothing; I'll be at thy elbow.
It makes us or it mars us; think on that,
And fix most firm thy resolution.
    RODERIGO. Be near at hand; I may miscarry
        in 't.
    IAGO. Here, at thy hand: be bold, and take
        thy stand.                    [IAGO *hides.*
    RODERIGO. I have no great devotion to the
        deed,
And yet he hath given me satisfying reasons;
'T is but a man gone.    [RODERIGO *draws.*  10
                    Forth, my sword: he dies.
    IAGO. I have rubbed this young quat almost
        to the sense,
And he grows angry. Now, whether he kill
    Cassio,
Or Cassio him, or each do kill the other,
Every way makes my gain: live Roderigo,
He calls me to a restitution large
Of gold and jewels that I bobbed from him

---

97 *scant, etc.*: cut down our allowance through spite.
98 *galls*: capacities for resenting injury.
    ACT V. SCENE 1. 1 *bulk*: projecting part of building.
11 *quat*: pimple; *sense*: quick. 16 *bobbed*: cheated.

As gifts to Desdemona;
It must not be: if Cassio do remain,
He hath a daily beauty in his life
That makes me ugly; and, besides, the
    Moor                                        20
May unfold me to him; there stand I in much
    peril.
No, he must die. But so: I hear him coming.

CASSIO *enters.*

    RODERIGO. I know his gait; 't is he.—Villain,
        thou diest!
        [RODERIGO *makes a pass at* CASSIO.
    CASSIO. That thrust had been mine enemy
        indeed,
But that my coat is better than thou knowest.
I will make proof of thine.
        [CASSIO *draws his sword and wounds*
                                        RODERIGO.
    RODERIGO.          O, I am slain!
    [IAGO *from behind wounds* CASSIO *in the
                        leg, and runs out.*
    CASSIO. I am maimed for ever. Help, ho!
        murder! murder!            [CASSIO *falls.*

OTHELLO *enters.*

    OTHELLO. The voice of Cassio: Iago keeps
        his word.
    RODERIGO. O, villain that I am!
    OTHELLO.                    It is even so.
    CASSIO. O, help, ho! light! a surgeon!      30
    OTHELLO. 'T is he. O brave Iago, honest and
        just,
That hast such noble sense of thy friend's
    wrong,
Thou teachest me. Minion, your dear lies dead,
And your unblest fate hies; strumpet, I come.
Forth of my heart those charms, thine eyes,
    are blotted;
Thy bed, lust-stained, shall with lust's blood
    be spotted.            [OTHELLO *goes out.*

LODOVICO *and* GRATIANO, DESDEMONA'S *uncle,
        enter at other side.*

    CASSIO. What, ho! no watch? no passage?
        murder! murder!
    GRATIANO. 'T is some mischance; the cry
        is very direful.
    CASSIO. O, help!
    LODOVICO. Hark!                             40
    RODERIGO. O wretched villain!

---

33 *Minion*: darling.  34 *hies*: draws near.  37 *passage*:
passers-by.

LODOVICO. Two or three groan; it is a heavy
night:
These may be counterfeits; let's think 't unsafe
To come in to the cry without more help.
  RODERIGO. Nobody come? Then shall I bleed
to death.
  LODOVICO. Hark!

      IAGO *returns with a light.*

  GRATIANO. Here 's one comes in his shirt,
with light and weapons.
  IAGO. Who 's there? Whose noise is this that
cries on murder?
  LODOVICO. We do not know.
  IAGO.           Did not you hear a cry?
  CASSIO. Here, here! For heaven's sake, help
me!
  IAGO.  What's the matter?       50
  GRATIANO. This is Othello's ancient, as I
take it.
  LODOVICO. The same indeed; a very valiant
fellow.
  IAGO. What are you here that cry so griev-
ously?
  CASSIO. Iago? O, I am spoiled, undone by
villains!
Give me some help.
  IAGO. O me, lieutenant! What villains have
done this?
  CASSIO. I think that one of them is here-
about,
And cannot make away.
  IAGO.         O treacherous villains!
[*To* LODOVICO *and* GRATIANO] What are you
there? Come in and give some help.
  RODERIGO. O, help me here!     60
  CASSIO. That's one of them.
  IAGO, *stabbing* RODERIGO.   O murderous
slave! O villain!
  RODERIGO. O damned Iago! O inhuman dog!
  IAGO. Kill men i' the dark! Where be these
bloody thieves?
How silent is this town! Ho! murder! murder!
What may you be? Are you of good or evil?
  LODOVICO. As you shall prove us, praise us.
  IAGO. Signior Lodovico?
  LODOVICO. He, sir.
  IAGO. I cry you mercy. Here's Cassio hurt by
villains.
  GRATIANO. Cassio!         70

  IAGO. How is 't, brother?
  CASSIO. My leg is cut in two.
  IAGO.          Marry, heaven forbid!
Light, gentlemen; I'll bind it with my shirt.

      BIANCA *enters.*

  BIANCA. What is the matter, ho? Who is 't
that cried?
  IAGO. Who is 't that cried!
  BIANCA. O my dear Cassio! my sweet Cassio!
O Cassio, Cassio, Cassio!
  IAGO. O notable strumpet! Cassio, may you
suspect
Who they should be that have thus mangled
you?
  CASSIO. No.           80
  GRATIANO. I am sorry to find you thus; I
have been to seek you.
  IAGO. Lend me a garter. So. O, for a chair,
To bear him easily hence!
  BIANCA. Alas, he faints! O Cassio, Cassio,
Cassio!
  IAGO. Gentlemen all, I do suspect this trash
To be a party in this injury.
Patience awhile, good Cassio. Come, come;
Lend me a light. Know we this face or no?
Alas, my friend and my dear countryman
Roderigo! No—yes, sure—O heaven! Rod-
erigo.         90
  GRATIANO. What, of Venice?
  IAGO. Even he, sir; did you know him?
  GRATIANO.         Know him! ay.
  IAGO. Signior Gratiano? I cry you gentle
pardon;
These bloody accidents must excuse my
manners,
That so neglected you.
  GRATIANO.       I am glad to see you.
  IAGO. How do you, Cassio? O, a chair, a
chair!
  GRATIANO. Roderigo!
  IAGO. He, he, 't is he.
        [ATTENDANTS *bring in a chair.*
      O, that's well said; the chair.
Some good man bear him carefully from hence;
I'll fetch the general's surgeon. [*To* BIANCA]
  For you, mistress,     100
Save you your labor. He that lies slain here,
Cassio,
Was my dear friend. What malice was between
you?
  CASSIO. None in the world; nor do I know
the man.

---

42 *heavy:* dark. 66 *prove us:* find us to be; *praise:*
appraise.

IAGO, *to* BIANCA. What, look you pale? O,
bear him out o' the air.

      [CASSIO *and* RODERIGO *are borne off.*
Stay you, good gentlemen. Look you pale,
mistress?
Do you perceive the gastness of her eye?
Nay, if you stare, we shall hear more anon.
Behold her well; I pray you, look upon her:
Do you see, gentlemen? Nay, guiltiness will
speak,
Though tongues were out of use.     110

           EMILIA *enters.*

EMILIA. 'Las, what's the matter? What's the
    matter, husband?
IAGO. Cassio hath here been set on in the
    dark
By Roderigo and fellows that are scaped.
He's almost slain, and Roderigo dead.
EMILIA. Alas, good gentleman! alas, good
    Cassio!
IAGO. This is the fruit of whoring. Prithee,
    Emilia,
Go know of Cassio where he supped tonight.
[*To* BIANCA] What, do you shake at that?
BIANCA. He supped at my house; but I there-
    fore shake not.
IAGO. O, did he so? I charge you, go with
    me.     120
EMILIA. Fie, fie upon thee, strumpet!
BIANCA. I am no strumpet, but of life as
    honest
As you that thus abuse me.
EMILIA.         As I! foh! fie upon thee!
IAGO. Kind gentlemen, let's go see poor
    Cassio dressed.
Come, mistress, you must tell 's another tale.
Emilia, run you to the citadel,
And tell my lord and lady what hath happed.
Will you go on afore? [*To himself*] This is the
    night
That either makes me or fordoes me quite.

     SCENE 2. *A bedchamber in the castle;*
     DESDEMONA *is in bed asleep.*

OTHELLO *comes in with a light, which he sets*
        *on a table.*

OTHELLO. It is the cause, it is the cause, my
    soul.

Let me not name it to you, you chaste stars!
It is the cause. Yet I'll not shed her blood,
Nor scar that whiter skin of hers than snow,
And smooth as monumental alabaster.
Yet she must die, else she'll betray more men.
Put out the light, and then put out the light:
If I quench thee, thou flaming minister,
I can again thy former light restore,
Should I repent me; but once put out thy
    light,    10
Thou cunningest pattern of excelling nature,
I know not where is that Promethean heat
That can thy light relume. When I have plucked
    the rose
I cannot give it vital growth again;
It must needs wither: I'll smell it on the tree.
        [OTHELLO *kisses* DESDEMONA.
Ah, balmy breath, that dost almost persuade
Justice to break her sword! One more, one
    more.     [*He kisses her.*
Be thus when thou art dead, and I will kill thee
And love thee after. One more, and this the
    last.     [*He kisses her.*
So sweet was ne'er so fatal. I must weep,    20
But they are cruel tears; this sorrow's heavenly:
It strikes where it doth love. She wakes.
DESDEMONA. Who's there? Othello?
OTHELLO.            Ay, Desdemona.
DESDEMONA. Will you come to bed, my lord?
OTHELLO. Have you prayed tonight, Desde-
    mona?
DESDEMONA.    Ay, my lord.
OTHELLO. If you bethink yourself of any
    crime
Unreconciled as yet to heaven and grace,
Solicit for it straight.
DESDEMONA. Alas, my lord, what do you
    mean by that?
OTHELLO. Well, do it, and be brief; I will
    walk by.    30
I would not kill thy unprepared spirit;
No, heaven forfend! I would not kill thy soul.
DESDEMONA. Talk you of killing?
OTHELLO.         Ay, I do.
DESDEMONA.             Then heaven
Have mercy on me!
OTHELLO.      Amen, with all my heart!
DESDEMONA. If you say so, I hope you will
    not kill me.
OTHELLO. Hum!

---

106 *gastness:* terror. 124 *Cassio:* i.e., his wound.
129 *fordoes:* ruins.

8 *minister:* servant. 12 *Promethean heat:* divine fire.
13 *relume:* rekindle. 18 *I will, etc.:* i.e., though I shall
have killed thee, I'll .... 28 *Solicit:* ask forgiveness.

DESDEMONA. And yet I fear you, for you are
fatal then
When your eyes roll so. Why I should fear I
know not,
Since guiltiness I know not; but yet I feel I fear.
OTHELLO. Think on thy sins.
DESDEMONA.                        They are loves
I bear to you.                                            40
OTHELLO. Ay, and for that thou diest.
DESDEMONA. That death 's unnatural that
kills for loving.
Alas, why gnaw you so your nether lip?
Some bloody passion shakes your very frame.
These are portents; but yet I hope, I hope,
They do not point on me.
OTHELLO.                    Peace, and be still!
DESDEMONA. I will so. What's the matter?
OTHELLO. That handkerchief which I so
loved and gave thee
Thou gavest to Cassio.
DESDEMONA.            No, by my life and soul!
Send for the man, and ask him.
OTHELLO.            Sweet soul, take heed,   50
Take heed of perjury; thou art on thy death-
bed.
DESDEMONA. Ay, but not yet to die.
OTHELLO.                        Yes, presently:
Therefore confess thee freely of thy sin;
For to deny each article with oath
Cannot remove nor choke the strong conception
That I do groan withal. Thou art to die.
DESDEMONA. Then Lord have mercy on me!
OTHELLO.                        I say, amen.
DESDEMONA. And have you mercy too! I
never did
Offend you in my life, never loved Cassio
But with such general warranty of heaven   60
As I might love; I never gave him token.
OTHELLO. By heaven, I saw my handker-
chief in 's hand.
O perjured woman! thou dost stone my heart
And makest me call what I intend to do
A murder, which I thought a sacrifice:
I saw the handkerchief.
DESDEMONA.            He found it then;
I never gave it him. Send for him hither;
Let him confess a truth.
OTHELLO.            He hath confessed.
DESDEMONA. What, my lord?
OTHELLO. That he hath used thee.
DESDEMONA.            How? unlawfully?

OTHELLO.                                    Ay.   70
DESDEMONA. He will not say so.
OTHELLO.            No, his mouth is stopped;
Honest Iago hath ta'en order for 't.
DESDEMONA. O, my fear interprets! What, is
he dead?
OTHELLO. Had all his hairs been lives, my
great revenge
Had stomach for them all.
DESDEMONA, *weeping*. Alas! he is betrayed
and I undone.
OTHELLO. Out, strumpet! Weepest thou for
him to my face?
DESDEMONA. O, banish me, my lord, but kill
me not!
OTHELLO. Down, strumpet!
DESDEMONA. Kill me tomorrow; let me live
tonight!                                               80
OTHELLO. Nay, if you strive—
DESDEMONA. But half an hour!
OTHELLO.        Being done, there is no pause.
DESDEMONA. But while I say one prayer!
OTHELLO.                        It is too late.
      [OTHELLO *smothers* DESDEMONA.
EMILIA, *off-stage*. My lord, my lord! what,
ho! my lord, my lord!
OTHELLO. What noise is this? Not dead? not
yet quite dead?
I that am cruel am yet merciful;
I would not have thee linger in thy pain.
So, so.                    [*He again smothers her.*
EMILIA, *off-stage*. What, ho! my lord, my
lord!
OTHELLO. Who's there?
EMILIA, *off-stage*. O, good my lord, I would
speak a word with you!                         90
OTHELLO. Yes: 't is Emilia. By and by.
She 's dead.
'T is like she comes to speak of Cassio's death.
The noise was here. Ha! no more moving?
Still as the grave. Shall she come in? Were 't
good?
I think she stirs again: no. What 's best to do?
If she come in, she 'll sure speak to my wife:
My wife! my wife! what wife? I have no wife.
O, insupportable! O heavy hour!
Methinks it should be now a huge eclipse
Of sun and moon, and that the affrighted
globe                                               100

---

37 *fatal*: deadly. 52 *presently*: immediately. 60 *warranty*: approval.

72 *ta'en order for*: undertaken. 75 *stomach*: appetite.
82 *Being done*: everything being settled.

Should yawn at alteration.

EMILIA, *off-stage.*          I do beseech you
That I may speak with you, O, good my lord!

OTHELLO. I had forgot thee. O, come in,
    Emilia.                [EMILIA *rattles the door.*
Soft; by and by. Let me the curtains draw.
Where art thou?

*Closing the bed-curtains,* OTHELLO *unlocks the
          door.* EMILIA *enters.*

                    What's the matter with thee now?

EMILIA. O, my good lord, yonder 's foul
    murders done!

OTHELLO. What, now?

EMILIA. But now, my lord.

OTHELLO. It is the very error of the moon;
She comes more nearer earth than she was
    wont                                                    110
And makes men mad.

EMILIA. Cassio, my lord, hath killed a young
    Venetian
Called Roderigo.

OTHELLO.          Roderigo killed!
And Cassio killed!

EMILIA.          No, Cassio is not killed.

OTHELLO. Not Cassio killed! Then murder 's
    out of tune,
And sweet revenge grows harsh.

DESDEMONA. O, falsely, falsely murdered!

EMILIA.                Alas, what cry is that?

OTHELLO. That! what?

EMILIA, *running to the bed.* Out, and alas!
    that was my lady's voice.
Help! help, ho! help! O lady, speak again!    120
Sweet Desdemona! O sweet mistress, speak!

DESDEMONA. A guiltless death I die.

EMILIA. O, who hath done this deed?

DESDEMONA. Nobody; I myself. Farewell:
Commend me to my kind lord: O, farewell!
                                        [DESDEMONA *dies.*

OTHELLO. Why, how should she be mur-
    dered?

EMILIA.   Alas, who knows?

OTHELLO. You heard her say herself, it was
    not I.

EMILIA. She said so; I must needs report the
    truth.

OTHELLO. She 's like a liar gone to burning
    hell:
'T was I that killed her.

EMILIA.          O, the more angel she,    130

And you the blacker devil!

OTHELLO. She turned to folly, and she was
    a whore.

EMILIA. Thou dost belie her, and thou art
    a devil.

OTHELLO. She was false as water.

EMILIA.                Thou art rash as fire to say
That she was false: O, she was heavenly true!

OTHELLO. Cassio did top her; ask thy hus-
    band else.
O, I were damned beneath all depth in hell,
But that I did proceed upon just grounds
To this extremity. Thy husband knew it all.

EMILIA. My husband!                              140

OTHELLO. Thy husband.

EMILIA. That she was false to wedlock?

OTHELLO. Ay, with Cassio. Nay, had she
    been true,
If heaven would make me such another world
Of one entire and perfect chrysolite,
I'd not have sold her for it.

EMILIA. My husband!

OTHELLO.          Ay, 't was he that told me first.
An honest man he is, and hates the slime
That sticks on filthy deeds.

EMILIA.                          My husband!

OTHELLO. What needs this iteration, woman?
    I say thy husband.                            150

EMILIA. O mistress, villany hath made
    mocks with love!
My husband say that she was false!

OTHELLO.                              He, woman;
I say thy husband: dost understand the word?
My friend, thy husband, honest honest Iago.

EMILIA. If he say so, may his pernicious soul
Rot half a grain a day! He lies to the heart:
She was too fond of her most filthy bargain.

OTHELLO. Ha!

EMILIA. Do thy worst;
This deed of thine is no more worthy heav-
    en                                                  160
Than thou wast worthy her.

OTHELLO.                    Peace, you were best!

EMILIA. Thou hast not half that power to do
    me harm
As I have to be hurt. O gull! O dolt!
As ignorant as dirt! Thou hast done a deed—
          [OTHELLO *draws his sword and threatens her.*
I care not for thy sword; I'll make thee known
Though I lost twenty lives. Help! help, ho!
    help!

---

101 *yawn at alteration:* split open because of the change.
104 *Soft:* be patient.

---

145 *chrysolite:* precious stone.   161 *Peace:* hush.

The Moor hath killed my mistress! Murder!
murder!

MONTANO, GRATIANO, IAGO, *and* ATTENDANTS
*enter.*

MONTANO. What is the matter? How now,
general!

EMILIA. O, are you come, Iago? You have
done well,

That men must lay their murders on your
neck.                                        170

GRATIANO. What is the matter?

EMILIA. Disprove this villain if thou beest a
man:

He says thou toldest him that his wife was false.

I know thou didst not, thou 'rt not such a
villain.

Speak, for my heart is full.

IAGO. I told him what I thought, and told
no more

Than what he found himself was apt and true.

EMILIA. But did you ever tell him she was
false?

IAGO. I did.

EMILIA. You told a lie; an odious, damnèd
lie;                                         180

Upon my soul, a lie, a wicked lie.

She false with Cassio! Did you say with Cassio?

IAGO. With Cassio, mistress. Go to, charm
your tongue.

EMILIA. I will not charm my tongue; I am
bound to speak:

My mistress here lies murdered in her bed.

ALL. O heavens forfend!

EMILIA. And your reports have set the murder on.

OTHELLO. Nay, stare not, masters; it is true,
indeed.

GRATIANO. 'T is a strange truth.

MONTANO. O monstrous act!

EMILIA.        Villany, villany, villany!   190

I think upon 't, I think, I smell 't: O villany!

I thought so then: I 'll kill myself for grief.

O villany, villany!

IAGO. What, are you mad? I charge you, get
you home.

EMILIA. Good gentlemen, let me have leave
to speak.

'T is proper I obey him, but not now.

Perchance, Iago, I will ne'er go home.

OTHELLO, *falling on the bed.* O! O! O!

EMILIA.        Nay, lay thee down and roar;

For thou hast killed the sweetest innocent

That e'er did lift up eye.

OTHELLO, *rising.* O, she was foul!         200

I scarce did know you, uncle. There lies your
niece,

Whose breath, indeed, these hands have newly
stopped;

I know this act shows horrible and grim.

GRATIANO. Poor Desdemona! I am glad thy
father's dead.

Thy match was mortal to him, and pure grief

Shore his old thread in twain: did he live now,

This sight would make him do a desperate turn,

Yea, curse his better angel from his side,

And fall to reprobation.

OTHELLO. 'T is pitiful; but yet Iago
knows                                        210

That she with Cassio hath the act of shame

A thousand times committed; Cassio confessed
it;

And she did gratify his amorous works

With that recognizance and pledge of love

Which I first gave her. I saw it in his hand:

It was a handkerchief, an antique token

My father gave my mother.

EMILIA. O heaven! O heavenly powers!

IAGO. Come, hold your peace.

EMILIA.        'T will out, 't will out; I peace!

No, I will speak as liberal as the north.      220

Let heaven and men and devils, let them all,

All, all, cry shame against me, yet I'll speak.

IAGO. Be wise, and get you home.

EMILIA.                           I will not.

[IAGO *tries to stab* EMILIA, *but* GRATIANO *prevents him.*

GRATIANO.                          Fie!

Your sword upon a woman?

EMILIA. O thou dull Moor! That handkerchief thou speakest of

I found by fortune and did give my husband;

For often with a solemn earnestness,

More than indeed belonged to such a trifle,

He begged o' me to steal it.

IAGO.                        Villanous whore!

EMILIA. She give it Cassio! No, alas! I found
it,                                          230

And I did give 't my husband.

IAGO.                        Filth, thou liest!

---

186 *forfend:* forbid.

203 *shows:* appears. 205 *mortal:* fatal. 209 *reprobation:* sinfulness. 214 *recognizance:* token. 220 *liberal:*
unrestrainedly.

EMILIA. By heaven, I do not, I do not,
  gentlemen.
O murderous coxcomb! What should such a
  fool
Do with so good a wife?
  OTHELLO.      Are there no stones in heaven
But what serve for the thunder? Precious vil-
  lain!
[OTHELLO *runs at* IAGO; IAGO, *from behind,
              stabs* EMILIA *and runs out.*
  GRATIANO. The woman falls; sure, he hath
  killed his wife.
  EMILIA. Ay, ay: O, lay me by my mistress'
  side.
  GRATIANO. He's gone, but his wife 's killed.
  MONTANO, *taking* OTHELLO's *sword.* 'T is a
  notorious villain. Take you this weapon,
Which I have here recovered from the
  Moor.                                        240
Come, guard the door without; let him not
  pass,
But kill him rather. I'll after that same villain,
For 't is a damnèd slave.
                  [MONTANO *and* GRATIANO *go out.*
  OTHELLO.          I am not valiant neither,
But every puny whipster gets my sword.
But why should honor outlive honesty?
Let it go all.
  EMILIA.      What did thy song bode, lady?
Hark, canst thou hear me? I will play the swan,
And die in music. [*Singing*] "Willow, willow,
  willow."
Moor, she was chaste; she loved thee, cruel
  Moor;
So come my soul to bliss, as I speak true,   250
So speaking as I think, I die, I die.
                              [EMILIA *dies.*
  OTHELLO. I have another weapon in this
  chamber;
It is a sword of Spain, the ice-brook's temper.
O, here it is. Uncle, I must come forth.
  GRATIANO, *off-stage.* If thou attempt it, it
  will cost thee dear:
Thou hast no weapon, and perforce must
  suffer.
  OTHELLO. Look in upon me then and speak
  with me.
Or, naked as I am, I will assault thee.

GRATIANO *comes in.*
  GRATIANO. What is the matter?
  OTHELLO.          Behold, I have a weapon;
A better never did itself sustain            260
Upon a soldier's thigh: I have seen the day,
That, with this little arm and this good sword,
I have made my way through more impedi-
  ments
Than twenty times your stop: but, O vain
  boast!
Who can control his fate? 'T is not so now.
Be not afraid, though you do see me weaponed;
Here is my journey's end, here is my butt,
And very sea-mark of my utmost sail.
Do you go back dismayed? 'T is a lost fear;
Man but a rush against Othello's breast,     270
And he retires. Where should Othello go?
                  [OTHELLO *opens the bed-curtains.*
Now, how dost thou look now? O ill-starred
  wench!
Pale as thy smock! When we shall meet at
  compt,
This look of thine will hurl my soul from
  heaven,
And fiends will snatch at it. Cold, cold, my
  girl!
Even like thy chastity. O cursed slave!
Whip me, ye devils,
From the possession of this heavenly sight!
Blow me about in winds! Roast me in sulphur!
Wash me in steep-down gulfs of liquid
  fire!                                       280
O Desdemona! Desdemona! dead!
Oh! Oh! Oh!

LODOVICO *and* MONTANO *enter with* CASSIO
  *carried in a chair and* OFFICERS *holding*
              IAGO *prisoner.*

  LODOVICO. Where is this rash and most
  unfortunate man?
  OTHELLO. That's he that was Othello: here
  I am.
  LODOVICO. Where is that viper? Bring the
  villain forth.
  OTHELLO. I look down towards his feet; but
  that's a fable.
If that thou beest a devil, I cannot kill thee.
                          [OTHELLO *wounds* IAGO.

---

233 *coxcomb:* fool. 234 *stones:* i.e., that Jove might
hurl at Iago. 239 *notorious:* conspicuous. 244 *whipster:*
youth. 253 *the ice-brook's temper:* tempered in an icy
brook. 258 *naked:* unarmed.

264 *stop:* attempt to stop me. 267 *butt:* target, where
arrows stop. 268 *sea-mark:* beacon, goal; *utmost:* last.
270 *Man but a rush:* wave a mere reed. 273 *compt:* the
Last Judgment. 286 *I look,* etc.: i.e., to see his cloven
hoofs.

LODOVICO. Wrench his sword from him.
        [*An* OFFICER *disarms* OTHELLO.
IAGO.          I bleed, sir; but not killed.
OTHELLO. I am not sorry neither: I'd have
    thee live;
For, in my sense, 't is happiness to die.   290
LODOVICO. O thou Othello, that wert once
    so good,
Fallen in the practice of a damnèd slave,
What shall be said to thee?
OTHELLO.          Why, anything:
An honorable murderer, if you will;
For nought I did in hate, but all in honor.
LODOVICO. This wretch hath part confessed
    his villany:
Did you and he consent in Cassio's death?
OTHELLO. Ay.
CASSIO. Dear general, I never gave you
    cause.
OTHELLO. I do believe it, and I ask your
    pardon.   300
Will you, I pray, demand that demi-devil
Why he hath thus ensnared my soul and body?
IAGO. Demand me nothing: what you know,
    you know.
From this time forth I never will speak word.
LODOVICO. What, not to pray?
GRATIANO.      Torments will ope your lips.
OTHELLO. Well, thou dost best.
LODOVICO. Sir, you shall understand what
    hath befallen,
Which, as I think, you know not. Here is a
    letter
Found in the pocket of the slain Roderigo,
And here another: the one of them im-
    ports   310
The death of Cassio to be undertook
By Roderigo.
OTHELLO. O villain!
CASSIO.     Most heathenish and most gross!
LODOVICO. Now here's another discontented
    paper,
Found in his pocket too; and this, it seems,
Roderigo meant to have sent this damnèd
    villain;
But that belike Iago in the interim
Came in and satisfied him.
OTHELLO.        O the pernicious caitiff!
How came you, Cassio, by that handkerchief
That was my wife's?

CASSIO.      I found it in my chamber;   320
And he himself confessed but even now
That there he dropped it for a special purpose
Which wrought to his desire.
OTHELLO.          O fool! fool! fool!
CASSIO. There is besides in Roderigo's letter
How he upbraids Iago, that he made him
Brave me upon the watch; whereon it came
That I was cast; and even but now he spake,
After long seeming dead, Iago hurt him,
Iago set him on.
LODOVICO. You must forsake this room, and
    go with us.   330
Your power and your command is taken off,
And Cassio rules in Cyprus. For this slave,
If there be any cunning cruelty
That can torment him much and hold him long,
It shall be his. You shall close prisoner rest
Till that the nature of your fault be known
To the Venetian state. Come, bring him away.
OTHELLO. Soft you; a word or two before
    you go.
I have done the state some service, and they
    know 't.
No more of that. I pray you, in your let-
    ters,   340
When you shall these unlucky deeds relate,
Speak of me as I am; nothing extenuate,
Nor set down aught in malice: then must you
    speak
Of one that loved not wisely but too well;
Of one not easily jealous, but, being wrought,
Perplexed in the extreme; of one whose hand,
Like the base Indian, threw a pearl away
Richer than all his tribe; of one whose subdued
    eyes,
Albeit unusèd to the melting mood,
Drop tears as fast as the Arabian trees   350
Their medicinal gum. Set you down this;
And say besides, that in Aleppo once,
Where a malignant and a turbaned Turk
Beat a Venetian and traduced the state,
I took by the throat the circumcisèd dog,
And smote him, thus.
    [*Drawing a dagger from under his coat,*
                 OTHELLO *stabs himself.*
LODOVICO. O bloody period!
GRATIANO.       All that's spoke is marred.
OTHELLO. I kissed thee ere I killed thee; no
    way but this,

---

290 *sense:* opinion.  292 *in the practice:* in the snare.
297 *consent:* conspire.  317 *belike:* probably.

326 *brave:* provoke.  327 *cast:* dismissed.  345 *wrought:* worked on.

Killing myself, to die upon a kiss.
[OTHELLO *falls on* DESDEMONA'S *body and*
                                                                        *dies.*
     CASSIO. This did I fear, but thought he had
          no weapon;                                              360
For he was great of heart.
     LODOVICO, *to* IAGO.       O Spartan dog,
More fell than anguish, hunger, or the sea!
Look on the tragic loading of this bed;
This is thy work; the object poisons sight;

———————

361 *Spartan dog:* bloodhound.   362 *fell:* cruel.

Let it be hid. Gratiano, keep the house,
And seize upon the fortunes of the Moor,
For they succeed on you. To you, lord gov-
     ernor,
Remains the censure of this hellish villain,
The time, the place, the torture: O, enforce it!
Myself will straight aboard; and to the
     state                                                          370
This heavy act with heavy heart relate.

———————

367 *succeed:* i.e., you inherit as Desdemona's cousin.
371 *heavy act:* tragic action.

# SKEPTICISM AND FAITH

THE TERM *religious* can be applied to an organization of people; a set of ritual practices, a special kind of experience in which something holy or awe-inspiring is encountered, a belief in a power transcending nature, or a way of living that expresses spiritual qualities. Literature may be called religious if it encompasses any of these with some explicitness, and the present chapter contains a variety of religious literature. Despite their great range of religious experience, all these works show human beings, nobly or ignobly, intelligently or unintelligently, successfully or vainly, reaching out toward a great and beneficent superhuman power that could sustain and explain man, and give meaning to his life.

Some of these works, like the Sermon on the Mount, are of practical import; others, like Russell's "Dreams and Facts," are polemic and philosophical. But when we consider them as literature, it is not their theses, their arguments, or their devotional usefulness that we are primarily concerned with: it is the dramatization of the conflict between skepticism and faith, or the concrete embodiment of the experience of worship or of doubt. Religious literature, to be sure, provides material that one can reflect upon abstractly, but it is the whole experience, not the inference that may be drawn from it, that counts here. One of the qualifications of a good reader is that when he reads such works as these, which come to grips with ultimate questions, he can share the experiences of all sorts of writers who deal with these questions, even when he utterly disagrees with their answers.

The contrasts of belief and feeling about various aspects of religion make these selections particularly rewarding to analyze and compare. The scientific humanism and naturalism of Russell and Morris Cohen contrast with the theism of C. S. Lewis and Graham Greene,

489

Hardy's skepticism about Nature's being the product of a divine design with Addison's clear perception of the hand of God in Nature. The calm, firm faith of Herbert and the mystic rapture of Hopkins are opposed by the troubled and complex faiths of Donne and Young Goodman Brown. But these contrasts are not merely to be extracted for inspection: it is also important to see how they are given precise shape in the structure and texture of the works themselves.

*St. Matthew*

# THE SERMON ON THE MOUNT

And seeing the multitudes, he went up into a mountain; and when he was set, his disciples came unto him: and he opened his mouth, and taught them, saying, Blessed are the poor in spirit: for theirs is the kingdom of heaven. Blessed are they that mourn: for they shall be comforted. Blessed are the meek: for they shall inherit the earth. Blessed are they which do hunger and thirst after righteousness: for they shall be filled. Blessed are the merciful: for they shall obtain mercy. Blessed are the pure in heart: for they shall see God. Blessed are the peacemakers: for they shall be called the children of God. Blessed are they which are persecuted for righteousness' sake: for theirs is the kingdom of heaven. Blessed are ye, when men shall revile you, and persecute you, and shall say all manner of evil against you falsely, for my sake. Rejoice, and be exceeding glad: for great is your reward in heaven: for so persecuted they the prophets which were before you.

Ye are the salt of the earth: but if the salt have lost his savour, wherewith shall it be salted? it is thenceforth good for nothing, but to be cast out, and to be trodden under foot of men. Ye are the light of the world. A city that is set on an hill cannot be hid. Neither do men light a candle, and put it under a bushel, but on a candlestick; and it giveth light unto all that are in the house. Let your light so shine before men, that they may see your good works, and glorify your Father which is in

heaven. Think not that I am come to destroy the law, or the prophets; I am not come to destroy, but to fulfil. For verily I say unto you, Till heaven and earth pass, one jot or one tittle shall in no wise pass from the law, till all be fulfilled. Whosoever therefore shall break one of these least commandments, and shall teach men so, he shall be called the least in the kingdom of heaven: but whosoever shall do and teach them, the same shall be called great in the kingdom of heaven. For I say unto you, That except your righteousness shall exceed the righteousness of the scribes and Pharisees, ye shall in no case enter into the kingdom of heaven.

Ye have heard that it was said by them of old time, Thou shalt not kill; and whosoever shall kill shall be in danger of the judgment: but I say unto you, That whosoever is angry with his brother without a cause shall be in danger of the judgment: and whosoever shall say to his brother, Raca,[1] shall be in danger of the council: but whosoever shall say, Thou fool, shall be in danger of hell fire. Therefore if thou bring thy gift to the altar, and there rememberest that thy brother hath ought against thee; leave there thy gift before the altar, and go thy way; first be reconciled to thy brother, and then come and offer thy gift. Agree with thine adversary quickly, whiles thou art in the way with him; lest at any time the adversary deliver thee to the judge, and the judge deliver thee to the officer, and thou be cast into prison. Verily I say unto thee, Thou shalt by no means come out thence, till thou hast paid the uttermost farthing.

Ye have heard that it was said by them of old time, Thou shalt not commit adultery; but I say unto you, That whosoever looketh on a woman to lust after her hath committed adultery with her already in his heart. And if thy

THE SERMON ON THE MOUNT: From *The Gospel According to St. Matthew,* Chapters 5–7.

[1] Vain fellow.

right eye offend thee, pluck it out, and cast it from thee: for it is profitable for thee that one of thy members should perish, and not that thy whole body should be cast into hell. And if thy right hand offend thee, cut it off, and cast it from thee: for it is profitable for thee that one of thy members should perish, and not that thy whole body should be cast into hell. It hath been said, Whosoever shall put away his wife, let him give her a writing of divorcement: but I say unto you, That whosoever shall put away his wife, saving for the cause of fornication, causeth her to commit adultery: and whosoever shall marry her that is divorced committeth adultery.

Again, ye have heard that it hath been said by them of old time, Thou shalt not forswear thyself, but shalt perform to the Lord thine oaths: but I say unto you, Swear not at all; neither by heaven; for it is God's throne: nor by the earth; for it is his footstool: neither by Jerusalem; for it is the city of the great King. Neither shalt thou swear by thy head, because thou canst not make one hair white or black. But let your communication be, Yea, yea; Nay, nay: for whatsoever is more than these cometh of evil.

Ye have heard that it hath been said, An eye for an eye, and a tooth for a tooth: but I say unto you, That ye resist not evil: but whosoever shall smite thee on thy right cheek, turn to him the other also. And if any man will sue thee at the law, and take away thy coat, let him have thy cloke also. And whosoever shall compel thee to go a mile, go with him twain. Give to him that asketh thee, and from him that would borrow of thee turn not thou away.

Ye have heard that it hath been said, Thou shalt love thy neighbor, and hate thine enemy. But I say unto you, Love your enemies, bless them that curse you, do good to them that hate you, and pray for them which despitefully use you, and persecute you; that ye may be the children of your Father which is in heaven; for he maketh his sun to rise on the evil and on the good, and sendeth rain on the just and on the unjust. For if ye love them which love you, what reward have ye? do not even the publicans the same? And if ye salute your brethren only, what do ye more than others? do not even the publicans so? Be ye therefore perfect, even as your Father which is in heaven is perfect.

Take heed that ye do not your alms before men, to be seen of them: otherwise ye have no reward of your Father which is in heaven. Therefore when thou doest thine alms, do not sound a trumpet before thee, as the hypocrites do in the synagogues and in the streets, that they may have glory of men. Verily I say unto you, They have their reward. But when thou doest alms, let not thy left hand know what thy right hand doeth: that thine alms may be in secret: and thy Father which seeth in secret himself shall reward thee openly. And when thou prayest, thou shalt not be as the hypocrites are: for they love to pray standing in the synagogues and in the corners of the streets, that they may be seen of men. Verily I say unto you, They have their reward. But thou, when thou prayest, enter into thy closet, and when thou hast shut thy door, pray to thy Father which is in secret; and thy Father which seeth in secret shall reward thee openly. But when ye pray, use not vain repetitions, as the heathen do: for they think that they shall be heard for their much speaking. Be not ye therefore like unto them: for your Father knoweth what things ye have need of, before ye ask him. After this manner therefore pray ye: Our Father which art in heaven, Hallowed be thy name. Thy kingdom come. Thy will be done in earth, as it is in heaven. Give us this day our daily bread. And forgive us our debts, as we forgive our debtors. And lead us not into temptation, but deliver us from evil: for thine is the kingdom, and the power, and the glory, for ever. Amen. For if ye forgive men their trespasses, your heavenly Father will also forgive you: but if ye forgive not men their trespasses, neither will your Father forgive your trespasses.

Moreover when ye fast, be not, as the hypocrites, of a sad countenance: for they disfigure their faces, that they may appear unto men to fast. Verily I say unto you, They have their reward. But thou, when thou fastest, anoint thine head, and wash thy face; that thou appear not unto men to fast, but unto thy Father which is in secret; and thy Father, which seeth in secret, shall reward thee openly.

Lay not up for yourselves treasures upon earth, where moth and rust doth corrupt, and where thieves break through and steal: but lay up for yourselves treasures in heaven, where neither moth nor rust doth corrupt, and where thieves do not break through nor steal: for where your treasure is, there will your heart be also. The light of the body is the eye: if therefore thine eye be single, thy whole body shall be full of light. But if thine eye be evil, thy whole body shall be full of darkness. If therefore the light that is in thee be darkness, how great is that darkness! No man can serve two masters: for either he will hate the one, and love the other; or else he will hold to the one, and despise the other. Ye cannot serve God and mammon. Therefore I say unto you, Take no thought for your life, what ye shall eat, or what ye shall drink; nor yet for your body, what ye shall put on. Is not the life more than meat, and the body than raiment? Behold the fowls of the air: for they sow not, neither do they reap, nor gather into barns; yet your Father feedeth them. Are ye not much better than they? Which of you by taking thought can add one cubit unto his stature? And why take ye thought for raiment? Consider the lilies of the field, how they grow; they toil not, neither do they spin: and yet I say unto you, That even Solomon in all his glory was not arrayed like one of these. Wherefore, if God so clothe the grass of the field, which today is, and tomorrow is cast into the oven, shall he not much more clothe you, O ye of little faith? Therefore take no thought, saying, What shall we eat? or, What shall we drink? or, Wherewithal shall we be clothed? (For after all these things do the Gentiles seek:) for your heavenly Father knoweth that ye have need of all these things. But seek ye first the kingdom of God, and his righteousness; and all these things shall be added unto you. Take therefore no thought for the morrow: for the morrow shall take thought for the things of itself. Sufficient unto the day is the evil thereof.

Judge not, that ye be not judged. For with what judgment ye judge, ye shall be judged: and with what measure ye mete, it shall be measured to you again. And why beholdest thou the mote that is in thy brother's eye, but considerest not the beam that is in thine own eye? Or how wilt thou say to thy brother, Let me pull out the mote out of thine eye; and, behold, a beam is in thine own eye? Thou hypocrite, first cast out the beam out of thine own eye; and then shalt thou see clearly to cast out the mote out of thy brother's eye.

Give not that which is holy unto the dogs, neither cast ye your pearls before swine, lest they trample them under their feet, and turn again and rend you. Ask, and it shall be given you; seek, and ye shall find; knock, and it shall be opened unto you: for every one that asketh receiveth; and he that seeketh findeth; and to him that knocketh it shall be opened. Or what man is there of you, whom if his son ask bread, will he give him a stone? Or if he ask a fish, will he give him a serpent? If ye then, being evil, know how to give good gifts unto your children, how much more shall your Father which is in heaven give good things to them that ask him? Therefore all things whatsoever ye would that men should do to you, do ye even so to them: for this is the law and the prophets.

Enter ye in at the strait gate: for wide is the gate, and broad is the way, that leadeth to destruction, and many there be which go in thereat: because strait is the gate, and narrow is the way, which leadeth unto life, and few there be that find it. Beware of false prophets, which come to you in sheep's clothing, but inwardly they are ravening wolves. Ye shall know them by their fruits. Do men gather grapes of thorns, or figs of thistles? Even so every good tree bringeth forth good fruit; but a corrupt tree bringeth forth evil fruit. A good tree cannot bring forth evil fruit, neither can a corrupt tree bring forth good fruit. Every tree that bringeth not forth good fruit is hewn down, and cast into the fire. Wherefore by their fruits ye shall know them. Not every one that saith unto me, Lord, Lord, shall enter into the kingdom of heaven; but he that doeth the will of my Father which is in heaven. Many will say to me in that day, Lord, Lord, have we not prophesied in thy name? And in thy name have cast out devils? and in thy name done many wonderful works? And then will I profess unto them, I never knew you: depart from me, ye that work iniquity. Therefore whosoever heareth these sayings of mine, and doeth them, I will liken him unto a wise man, which built his house upon a rock: and the rain descended, and the floods came, and the winds blew, and beat upon that house; and it fell not: for it was founded upon a rock. And every one that heareth these sayings of mine, and doeth them not, shall be likened unto a foolish man, which built his house upon the sand: and the rain descended, and the floods came, and the winds blew, and beat upon that house; and it fell: and great was the fall of it.

And it came to pass, when Jesus had ended these sayings, the people were astonished at his doctrine: For he taught them as one having authority, and not as the scribes.

*Bertrand Russell*
# DREAMS AND FACTS

### I

The influence of our wishes upon our beliefs is a matter of common knowledge and observation, yet the nature of this influence is very generally misconceived. It is customary to suppose that the bulk of our beliefs are derived from some rational ground, and that desire is only an occasional disturbing force. The exact opposite of this would be nearer the truth: the great mass of beliefs by which we are supported in our daily life is merely the bodying forth of desire, corrected here and there, at isolated points, by the rude shock of fact. Man is essentially a dreamer, wakened sometimes for a moment by some peculiarly obtrusive element in the outer world, but lapsing again quickly into the happy somnolence of imagination. Freud has shown how largely our dreams at night are the pictured fulfillment of our wishes; he has, with an equal measure of truth, said the same of day-dreams; and he might have included the day-dreams which we call beliefs.

There are three ways by which this non-rational origin of our convictions can be demonstrated: there is the way of psycho-analysis, which, starting from an understanding of the insane and the hysterical, gradually makes it plain how little, in essence, these victims of malady differ from ordinary healthy people; then there is the way of the sceptical philosopher, showing how feeble is the rational evidence for even our most cherished beliefs; and finally there is the way of common observation of men. It is only the last of these three that I propose to consider.

The lowest savages, as they have become known through the labors of anthropologists,

are not found groping in conscious ignorance amid phenomena that they are aware of not understanding. On the contrary, they have innumerable beliefs, so firmly held as to control all their more important actions. They believe that by eating the flesh of an animal or a warrior it is possible to acquire the virtues possessed by the victim when alive. Many of them believe that to pronounce the name of their chief is such sacrilege as to bring instant death; they even go so far as to alter all words in which his name occurs as one of the syllables; for example, if we had a king named John, we should speak of a jonquil as (say) a George-quil, and of a dungeon as a dun-george. When they advance to agriculture, and weather becomes important for the food supply, they believe that magical incantations or the kindling of small fires will cause rain to come or the sun to burn brightly. They believe that when a man is slain his blood, or ghost, pursues the slayer to obtain vengeance, but can be misled by a simple disguise such as painting the face red or putting on mourning. The first half of this belief has obviously originated from those who feared murder, the second from those who had committed it.

Nor are irrational beliefs confined to savages. A great majority of the human race have religious opinions different from our own, and therefore groundless. People interested in politics, with the exception of politicians, have passionate convictions upon innumerable questions which must appear incapable of rational decision to any unprejudiced person. Voluntary workers in a contested election always believe that their side will win, no matter what reason there may be for expecting defeat. There can be no doubt that, in the autumn of 1914, the immense majority of the German nation felt absolutely certain of victory for Germany. In this case fact has intruded and dispelled the dream. But if, by some means, all non-German historians could be prevented from writing during the next hundred years, the dream would reinstate itself: the early triumphs would be remembered, while the ultimate disaster would be forgotten.

Politeness is the practice of respecting that part of a man's beliefs which is specially concerned with his own merits or those of his group. Every man, wherever he goes, is encompassed by a cloud of comforting convictions, which move with him like flies on a summer day. Some of these convictions are personal to himself: they tell him of his virtues and excellencies, the affection of his friends and the respect of his acquaintances, the rosy prospects of his career, and his unflagging energy in spite of delicate health. Next come convictions of the superior excellence of his family: how his father had that unbending rectitude which is now so rare, and brought up his children with a strictness beyond what is to be found among modern parents; how his sons are carrying all before them in school games, and his daughter is not the sort of girl to make an imprudent marriage. Then there are beliefs about his class, which, according to his station, is the best socially, or the most intelligent, or the most deserving morally, of the classes in the community—though all are agreed that the first of these merits is more desirable than the second, and the second than the third. Concerning his nation, also, almost every man cherishes comfortable delusions. "Foreign nations, I am sorry to say, do as they do do." So said Mr. Podsnap,[2] giving expression, in these words, to one of the deepest sentiments of the human heart. Finally we come to the theories that exalt mankind in general, either absolutely or in comparison with the "brute creation." Men have souls, though animals have not; Man is the "rational animal"; any peculiarly cruel or unnatural action is called "brutal" or "bestial" (although such actions are in fact distinctively human); God made Man in His own image, and the welfare of Man is the ultimate purpose of the universe.

We have thus a hierarchy of comforting beliefs: those private to the individual, those which he shares with his family, those common to his class or his nation, and finally those that are equally delightful to all mankind. If we desire good relations with a man, we must respect these beliefs; we do not, therefore, speak of a man to his face as we should behind his back. The difference increases as his remoteness from ourselves grows greater. In speaking to a brother, we have no need of conscious politeness as regards his parents. The need of politeness is at its maximum in speaking with foreigners, and is so irksome as to be paralyzing to those who are only accustomed to

compatriots. I remember once suggesting to an untraveled American that possibly there were a few small points in which the British Constitution compared favorably with that of the United States. He instantly fell into a towering passion; having never heard such an opinion before, he could not imagine that any one seriously entertained it. We had both failed in politeness, and the result was disaster.

But the results of failure in politeness, however bad from the point of view of a social occasion, are admirable from the point of view of dispelling myths. There are two ways in which our natural beliefs are corrected: one the contact with fact, as when we mistake a poisonous fungus for a mushroom and suffer pain in consequence; the other, when our beliefs conflict, not directly with objective fact, but with the opposite beliefs of other men. One man thinks it lawful to eat pork, but not beef; another, beef but not pork. The usual result of this difference of opinion has been bloodshed; but gradually there is beginning to be a rationalist opinion that perhaps neither is really sinful. Modesty, the correlative of politeness, consists in pretending not to think better of ourselves and our belongings than of the man we are speaking to and his belongings. It is only in China that this art is thoroughly understood. I am told that, if you ask a Chinese mandarin after the health of his wife and children, he will reply: "That contemptible slut and her verminous brood are, as your Magnificence deigns to be informed, in the enjoyment of rude health."[3]

But such elaboration demands a dignified and leisurely existence; it is impossible in the swift but important contacts of business or politics. Step by step, relations with other human beings dispel the myths of all but the most successful. Personal conceit is dispelled by brothers, family conceit by schoolfellows, class conceit by politics, national conceit by defeat in war or commerce. But human conceit remains, and in this region, so far as the effect of social intercourse is concerned, the myth-making faculty has free play. Against this form of delusion, a partial corrective is found in Science; but the corrective can never be more than partial, for without some credulity Science itself would crumble and collapse.

---

[2] Self-satisfied character in *Our Mutual Friend,* by Charles Dickens.

[3] Russell's note: "This was written before I came to know China. It would not be true of the China that I saw."

## II

Men's personal and group dreams may be ludicrous but their collective human dreams, to us who cannot pass outside the circle of humanity, are pathetic. The universe as astronomy reveals it is very vast. How much there may be beyond what our telescopes show we cannot tell; but what we can know is of unimaginable immensity. In the visible world, the Milky Way is a tiny fragment; within this fragment, the solar system is an infinitesimal speck, and of this speck our planet is a microscopic dot. On this dot tiny lumps of impure carbon and water, of complicated structure, with somewhat unusual physical and chemical properties, crawl about for a few years, until they are dissolved again into the elements of which they are compounded. They divide their time between labor designed to postpone the moment of dissolution for themselves and frantic struggles to hasten it for others of their kind. Natural convulsions periodically destroy some thousands or millions of them, and disease prematurely sweeps away many more. These events are considered to be misfortunes; but when men succeed in inflicting similar destruction by their own efforts, they rejoice, and give thanks to God. In the life of the solar system the period during which the existence of man will have been physically possible is a minute portion of the whole; but there is some reason to hope that even before this period is ended man will have set a term to his own existence by his efforts at mutual annihilation. Such is man's life viewed from the outside.

But such a view of life, we are told, is intolerable, and would destroy the instinctive energy by which men persist. The way of escape that they have found is through religion and philosophy. However alien and indifferent the outer world may seem, we are assured by our comforters that there is harmony beneath the apparent conflict. All the long development from the original nebula is supposed to lead up to man as the culmination of the process. *Hamlet* is a very well-known play, yet few readers would have any recollection of the part of the "First Sailor," which consists of the four words: "God bless you, sir." But suppose a society of men whose sole business in life was to act this part; suppose them isolated from contact with the Hamlets, Horatios, and even

Guildensterns: would they not invent systems of literary criticism according to which the four words of the "First Sailor" were the kernel of the whole drama? Would they not punish with ignominy or exile any one of their number who should suggest that other parts were possibly of equal importance? And the life of mankind takes up a much smaller proportion of the universe than the "First Sailor's" speech does of *Hamlet,* but we cannot listen behind the scenes to the rest of the play, and we know very little of its characters or plot.

When we think of mankind, we think primarily of ourself as its representative; we therefore think well of mankind, and consider its preservation important. Mr. Jones, the Nonconformist grocer, is sure that he deserves eternal life, and that a universe which refused it to him would be intolerably bad. But when he thinks of Mr. Robinson, his Anglican competitor, who mixes sand with his sugar and is lax about Sunday, he feels that the universe might well carry charity too far. To complete his happiness, there is need of hell-fire for Mr. Robinson; in this way the cosmic importance of man is preserved, but the vital distinction between friends and enemies is not obliterated by a weak universal benevolence. Mr. Robinson holds the same view with the parts inverted, and general happiness results.

In the days before Copernicus there was no need of philosophic subtlety to maintain the anthropocentric view of the world. The heavens visibly revolved about the earth, and on the earth man had dominion over all the beasts of the field. But when the earth lost its central position, man, too, was deposed from his eminence, and it became necessary to invent a metaphysic to correct the "crudities" of science. This task was achieved by those who are called "idealists," who maintain that the world of matter is unreal appearance, while the reality is Mind or Spirit—transcending the mind or spirit of the philosopher as he transcends common men. So far from there being no place like home, these thinkers assure us that every place is like home. In all our best, that is, in all those tasks which we share with the philosopher in question, we are at one with the universe. Hegel [4] assures us that the universe resembles the Prus-

---

[4] Georg Wilhelm Friedrich Hegel, 1770–1831, German philosopher, who taught the Idealist theory that reality is one Absolute Mind or Spirit.

sian State of his day; his English followers consider it more analogous to a bi-cameral plutocratic democracy. The reasons offered for these views are carefully camouflaged so as to conceal even from their authors the connection with human wishes: they are derived, nominally, from such dry sources as logic and the analysis of propositions. But the influence of wishes is shown by the fallacies committed, which all tend in one direction. When a man adds up an account, he is much more likely to make a mistake in his favor than to his detriment; and when a man reasons, he is more apt to incur fallacies which favor his wishes than such as thwart them. And so it comes that, in the study of nominally abstract thinkers, it is their mistakes that give the key to their personality.

Many may contend that, even if the systems men have invented are untrue, they are harmless and comforting, and should be left undisturbed. But they are in fact not harmless, and the comfort they bring is dearly bought by the preventable misery which they lead men to tolerate. The evils of life spring partly from natural causes, partly from men's hostility to each other. In former times, competition and war were necessary for the securing of food, which could only be obtained by the victors. Now, owing to the mastery of natural forces which science has begun to give, there would be more comfort and happiness for all if all devoted themselves to the conquest of Nature rather than of each other. The representation of Nature as a friend, and sometimes as even an ally in our struggles with other men, obscures the true position of man in the world, and diverts his energies from the pursuit of scientific power, which is the only fight that can bring long-continued well-being to the human race.

Apart from all utilitarian arguments, the search for a happiness based upon untrue beliefs is neither very noble nor very glorious. There is a stark joy in the unflinching perception of our true place in the world, and a more vivid drama than any that is possible to those who hide behind the enclosing walls of myth. There are "perilous seas" in the world of thought, which can only be sailed by those who are willing to face their own physical powerlessness. And, above all, there is liberation from the tyranny of Fear, which blots out the light of day and keeps men groveling and cruel. No man is liberated from fear who dare not see his place in the world as it is; no man can achieve the greatness of which he is capable until he has allowed himself to see his own littleness.

## Morris R. Cohen
# RELIGION

In the winter of 1890 there had been some question as to whether my mother, my sister and myself should go to join the rest of the family in America, and I wrote a letter to my father expressing my fear of the irreligious surroundings to which I should thus be subject and my hope that he would allow me to continue my pious studies where I was. But my father's efforts to establish a livelihood for himself and his family in the following months in Minsk were doomed to failure. And when my mother, my sister and I traveled to America two years later, my youthful fears of what would happen to my religion in the irreligious atmosphere of America were borne out by events. It was only a few months after we had arrived that my childhood faith was broken on the sharp edge of Mr. Tunick's skepticism. The questions our old neighbor asked of my father and my father's inability to give a rational answer shocked me to the quick. The angels that guard us, recited in every prayer, had been very real to me. I had lived in strict conformity to the tenets of Jewish Orthodoxy. But I could not forget Mr. Tunick's questions: "What proof have you that there is a God and that he told anything to Moses? And why should I believe that Jews are the only ones that have the truth? And are there not other people just as intelligent as we, and can we prove the Jewish religion is superior to all others?"

After some soul-searching I came to the conclusion that I had no evidence that could effectively answer these questions. I have not since that day ever seen any reason to change that conclusion.

The loss of the religion of my childhood brought no suffering in its train. It seemed to me that the restraints from which I was freed outbalanced the consolations that were lost. Perhaps that is because not all of the consolations were lost. Rational argument could never wholly efface a natural clinging to the joys of Friday night. Much less could it efface the larger spiritual patterns and values of my childhood religion. Indeed, in my youthful rejection of the Orthodox Jewish observances, I did not feel that I was cutting myself off from religion. I knew that the rejection of ritual is itself deeply rooted in the Hebraic tradition. I could not forget that the Hebrew Prophets, from Amos to Jeremiah, the founders of spiritual monotheism, all made Jahveh despise the ritual with which Israel believed it served Him. Says the God of Amos—and his command is repeated by Micah, Isaiah and Jeremiah:

> I hate, I despise your feast days,
> And will not delight in the day of your solemn assemblies—
> Put thou away from me the noise of thy songs—
> But let justice run down as waters,
> And righteousness as a mighty stream.

If I was a heretic, at least I felt that I was erring in good company. As with ritual, so, I felt, with creed. The essence of religion, it seemed to me, was not in the words uttered with the lips but rather in the faith which shows itself in our moral life. I could not bring myself to think that a just God would condemn the upright and spiritual-minded men I knew in all churches, and outside of all churches, merely because they did not pronounce the right formulas. Beyond any divinity of creed, it seemed to me, there was a God of morality, but even beyond this there was a God of nature. Or to put it in other words, man is a spiritual being in relation not only to his equals, other men, but also in relation to the whole universe. Here again I found myself in company with the Hebrew prophet Micah who strikes at the root of the matter when he says:

> And what doth the Lord require of thee,
> But to do justice and to love mercy,
> And to walk humbly with thy God.

Something more than mercy and justice are required, for one may be just and merciful and still be an intolerable prig. What is needed beyond these in a character that we can revere is humility. This does not mean that we are to bow down before God as we do before a petty tyrant. It means that we need to recognize that we are in a universe which contains a reality which is and always will be beyond all our knowledge and power; with that reality the spiritual faculty seeks communion. It means, too, that we must all be prepared to suffer and be punished for the sins of others; otherwise we are not entitled to the benefits which we all do derive from the virtues of others.

My youthful rejection of the claims of the Jewish religion to absolute truth was subsequently reinforced by philosophical reflections which led me to reject all forms of absolutism, the source of all fanaticism, and all forms of monism—including monotheism. The essence of monotheism is an emphasis upon the harmony of the universe, which seems to me to be most unfortunate in that it tends to dull the sense of resentment against the injustices of the world. I have never been able to reconcile the reality of evil and of the struggle against injustice with the idea of a benevolent and all-powerful deity.

If evil is real, and I am as persuaded of that as of anything else in this world, then God is either the author of evil or else He is defeated by other forces. However comforting the thought of an all-good and all-powerful deity may be in cultivating a wise resignation in the face of evils we cannot surmount, I found myself unable to follow my revered teacher, William James,[5] in considering the comfort that flows from a doctrine any sign of its truth. And making a God in man's image has seemed to me the height of arrogance.

On the other hand I have hesitated to violate ordinary understanding by using the word "God" to refer to an ideal of holiness that enables us to distinguish between the good and evil in men and thus saves us from the idolatrous worship of a humanity that is full of imperfections. Such a conception of God has seemed to me valid, but since I do not generally know what other people have in mind when they ask whether I believe in God, I have generally replied, "That depends upon what you mean by God." This usually brings forth a denunciation of metaphysical quibbling.

---

[5] William James, 1842–1910, American philosopher and psychologist, who taught the Pragmatist theory that a belief is true if it "works."

There have, of course, been many attempts by rabbis who are not complete strangers to science to formulate a concept of Judaism that may free the Orthodox creed from its incrustations of superstition. But these efforts to rationalize the Jewish faith, and similar attempts to rationalize other historic faiths, have not impressed me. I do not believe that there is any such thing as Judaism as an abstract doctrine—which is what an "ism" is—upon which all Jews can agree. I have heard many definitions of Judaism and they all seem hollow. I know of no religious belief that is common to all Jews, and I know of no belief held by any substantial number of Jews which is not to be found also, in some measure, among other people. Jews are people first, and only Jews incidentally. I have never believed that the Jews, as a people, have to justify their existence. Jews exist because they are human beings, and human beings have a right to exist.

I do not know of any religious doctrine which I share with any large number of my fellow Jews, and certainly there is no political or economic doctrine which unites all Jews. I have always been a Jew because I was born and brought up in a Jewish family. When, in 1899, I was in a position to order my own life, I ceased to observe the traditional Jewish code of ritual practices. This, however, did not carry with it any loss of respect for those who maintained the old observances where such observances represented the expression of an inner conviction. I have always had the highest reverence for those who, like my sainted parents, have a genuine and abiding faith that God listens to their prayers and that His actions are influenced by their petitions and oaths. I have never had any missionary zeal to convert anyone from his own views on religion, or to engage in any polemics with those among whom I was brought up. But I must, in the interest of truth, record my observation that the number of those who outwardly profess Orthodoxy is much greater than of those who really let it influence their lives.

I remember as a boy having a talk with the late Joseph Jacobs. He asked, "Why do your young people on the East Side keep away from the synagogue? Don't they believe in religion?" I replied, "Going to synagogue or not going is a minor matter, Mr. Jacobs. We take religion more seriously than you do." I think that was

the truth. True religion must be an expression of the inner soul and cannot be forced on anyone merely because he happens to have been born of a certain ancestry. It seemed to me that in the friction between the older generation and the younger generation which the religious question brought to the fore in the days of my youth, both sides were at fault. The older generation was at fault in not distinguishing between ritual forms and true religious faith. It was lacking in human sympathy with the honest views of the younger generation. It could not learn that the real vitality of a religion does not show itself in the power to resist the advance of new truth but rather in the capacity to adapt itself to whatever new light it can get.

On the other hand there was a certain superficiality in the attitude that many of my generation took towards religion. We used to read accounts of a conflict between science and religion in which, we were told, science had gradually conquered. This, however, seemed to me to leave out of consideration the realm where science cannot rule, where neither the telescope nor the microscope can penetrate, the realm of ideal expression. Appropriation or rejection of science thus did not solve the problem of religion. Those who called themselves atheists seemed to be singularly blind, as a rule, to the limitations of our knowledge and to the infinite possibilities beyond us. And those who called themselves materialists appeared to me to be shutting themselves off from philosophy, wisdom, and the life of the spirit, which are certainly not material things. Those of my circle who rejected religion *in toto* seemed to me to be casting away the ideals that had sustained our people through so many generations before we had fashioned guideposts to our own lives that could stand up against the sort of buffeting that the old guideposts had withstood. In this some of us lost sight of the larger view that Thomas Davidson had taught, that we have no right to break away from the past until we have appropriated all its experience and wisdom, and that reverence for the past may go hand in hand with loyalty to the future, "to the Kingdom which doth not yet appear."

The ideal of intellectual integrity compelled me and many others of my generation to reject superstitions that had been bound up with the practices of our Orthodox parents, but it did not prevent us from cherishing the spiritual values which they had found in those practices, and which many others have found in the practices of other older and younger religions. The struggle between Orthodoxy and active opposition to all religion seemed to me, like so many of the passionate struggles of life, to overlook possibilities and values which a more tolerant and rational outlook could find.

Indeed I marveled then, and have never ceased to marvel, at the fact that on matters where knowledge is readily demonstrable—such as cooking or chemistry—discussions show little of the heated mood of the zealot and fanatic, whereas, in matters on which it is much more difficult to arrive at the truth, such as questions of religion, we are inclined to be very sure of ourselves. Perhaps we try to make up by our vehemence for the lack of demonstrative evidence.

Of course, if you claim to be in possession of a special revelation, then you have a mortgage on the truth of the universe, the other fellow can have nothing true to tell you, and the thing to do is to hold on to your revealed truth with all the ardor that is in you. But then the other fellow is just as certain that he alone has all the truth and there is no use in any argumentation. But if you take your stand on human history and human reason, and recognize, for example, that the claim to the possession of a special revelation of the Jew is, as such, not a bit better than that of the Christian or the Mohammedan, or any of the ten thousand other claims, then, it seemed to me, you must grant that each possesses both truth and error.

Having once made up my mind that the whole truth of the matter did not lie with either side, I saw the religious problem of my own intellectual generation as a problem calling for creative thought rather than simple loyalty. "Before we can appropriate the religion of our ancestors," I wrote in an article on the religious question on the East Side, in June, 1902, "we must build it over again in our own hearts. This holds good not only of religion but of all the products of civilization. Whatever thou hast inherited from thy ancestors, earn in order to possess. Only that which we have worked out ourselves is truly ours."

Twenty years later I was still seeking for a way of uniting naturalism in science with piety towards that which has been revered as noble and sacred in the spiritual history of man. Of all philosophers, it seemed to me that Spinoza [6] had most clearly developed the rational and tolerant attitude to the values of religion for which I had been searching. In my addresses before the American Philosophical Association in 1922 on "The Intellectual Love of God," I undertook to defend the validity of the Spinozistic ideal, "amor Dei intellectualis," as a beacon that may illumine the problems of modern life and thought. Naturalism, for Spinoza, did not import that worldliness which wise men in all generations have recognized as a state of spiritual death. Nor did he conceive of love as a passive emotion. The quest for understanding, Spinoza saw, is an activity, often a breathless activity, that even apart from its practical consequences, is the most divine of human enterprises.

It is true that Spinoza rejects the idea of an anthropomorphic God who will respond to our flattering prayers, reward us for our unsuccessful efforts, and in general compensate us for the harshness of the natural order and the weaknesses of our reason. If, however, religion consists in humility (as a sense of infinite powers beyond our scope), charity or love (as a sense of the mystic potency in our fellow human beings), and spirituality (as a sense of the limitations of all that is merely material, actual or even attainable), then no one was more deeply religious than Spinoza.

And while Spinoza has little regard for the immortality which means the postponement of certain human gratifications to a period beyond our natural life, he does believe in the immortality which we achieve when we live in the eternal present or identify ourselves with those human values that the process of time can never adequately realize or destroy. He thus showed me the path to that serenity which follows a view of life fixed on those things that go on despite all the tragedies and depressions which frighten hysterical people. Above all, Spinoza made clear to me the vision that saves us from the worldliness that drowns out life. We are all like the waves tossed high up by the ocean and breaking on the sands of actuality. If we are to attain true human dignity, we need some sense of our continuity with the past and the future, a consciousness of ourselves not as temporary

---

[6] Baruch Spinoza, 1632–1677, Dutch Jewish philosopher, who taught the Pantheist theory that God and Nature are identical.

flies but as waves of a human ocean larger than our own lives and efforts.

Spinoza, like the other great religious teachers and the morally wise men of science, teaches the great lesson of humility—that there are always vast realms beyond our ken or control, and that the great blessing of inner peace is unattainable without a sense of the mystery of creation about us and a wisely cultivated resignation to our mortal but inevitable limitations.

These limitations men surmount only as they learn to subordinate their separate individualities to the interest of families, social or religious groups, nations, races, or that humanity whose life is the whole cosmic drama of which, as thinkers, we are spectators.

In the days of my first youthful revolt against the Jewish observances, I was inclined to regard cultus, prayer and ritual as of little importance in comparison with belief or faith. This was certainly the view that my teacher William James took of the matter. The conclusion he drew from this was that the religious experience of the great mass of people, who follow in the steps of great masters, is of little significance. My own studies of the great historic religions led me, however, to see that ritual, what men do on certain occasions, is a primary fact in human religious experience, and that the beliefs and emotions associated with ritual are more variable than ritual itself, as is shown by the diverse explanations and justifications of the Hebrew Sabbath and the Easter ceremonies. Indeed the character of the founders of the great religions, as we know it, is largely a product of tradition.

Men cling to sanctified phrases not only because of the insights they contain but even more because, through ritual and repetition, they have become redolent with the wine of human experience. For each of us the symbolism of our childhood offers paths to peace and understanding that can never be wholly replaced by other symbolisms. For me the ancient ceremonies that celebrate the coming and going of life, the wedding ceremony, the b'rith, and the funeral service, give an expression to the continuity of the spiritual tradition that is more eloquent than any phrases of my own creation. The ritual may be diluted by English and by modernisms, but the Hebraic God is still a potent symbol of the continuous life of which

we individuals are waves. So it is, too, with the celebration of the eternal struggle for freedom, in the family service of the Passover.

Like vivid illustrations in the book of my life are the prayers of my parents, the services at their graves, the memory of an old man chanting funeral songs at the *Jahrzeit* of my dear friend Dr. Himwich, the unveiling of the monument to the beloved comrade of my life's journeys, and the celebration of the continuity of generations in the Passover services in the home of my parents and in the homes of my children. And though I have never gone back to theologic supernaturalism, I have come to appreciate more than I once did the symbolism in which is celebrated the human need of trusting to the larger vision, according to which calamities come and go but the continuity of life and faith in its better possibilities survive.

## C. S. Lewis
# CHRISTIANITY AND "RELIGION"

*Those who make religion their god will not have God for their religion.*
THOMAS ERSKINE OF LINLATHEN.

The Christians say that God has done miracles. The modern world, even when it believes in God, and even when it has seen the defencelessness of Nature, does not. It thinks God would not do that sort of thing. Have we any reason for supposing that the modern world is right? I agree that the sort of God conceived by the popular "religion" of our own times would almost certainly work no miracles. The question is whether that popular religion is at all likely to be true.

I call it "religion" advisedly. We who defend Christianity find ourselves constantly opposed not by the irreligion of our hearers but by their real religion. Speak about beauty, truth and goodness, or about a God who is simply the indwelling principle of these three, speak about

CHRISTIANITY AND "RELIGION": From *Miracles*, by C. S. Lewis. Copyright, 1947, by The Macmillan Company. Used by permission of the publishers. Canadian rights granted by Geoffrey Bles, Ltd.

a great spiritual force pervading all things, a common mind of which we are all parts, a pool of generalised spirituality to which we can all flow, and you will command friendly interest. But the temperature drops as soon as you mention a God who has purposes and performs particular actions, who does one thing and not another, a concrete, choosing, commanding, prohibiting God with a determinate character. People become embarrassed or angry. Such a conception seems to them primitive and crude and even irreverent. The popular "religion" excludes miracles because it excludes the "living God" of Christianity and believes instead in a kind of God who obviously would not do miracles, or indeed anything else. This popular "religion" may roughly be called Pantheism, and we must now examine its credentials.

In the first place it is usually based on a quite fanciful picture of the history of religion. According to this picture, Man starts by inventing "spirits" to explain natural phenomena; and at first he imagines these spirits to be exactly like himself. As he gets more enlightened they become less manlike, less "anthropomorphic" as the scholars call it. Their anthropomorphic attributes drop off one by one—first the human shape, then human passions, then personality, will, activity—in the end every concrete or positive attribute whatever. There is left in the end a pure abstraction—mind as such, spirituality as such. God, instead of being a particular entity with a real character of its own, becomes simply "the whole show" looked at in a particular way or the theoretical point at which all the lines of human aspiration would meet if produced to infinity. And since, on the modern view, the final stage of anything is the most refined and civilised stage, this "religion" is held to be a more profound, more spiritual, and more enlightened belief than Christianity.

Now this imagined history of religion is not true. Pantheism certainly is (as its advocates would say) congenial to the modern mind; but the fact that a shoe slips on easily does not prove that it is a new shoe—much less that it will keep your feet dry. Pantheism is congenial to our minds not because it is the final stage in a slow process of enlightenment, but because it is almost as old as we are. It may even be the most primitive of all religions, and the *orenda* of a savage tribe has been interpreted by some to be an "all-pervasive spirit." It is immemorial

in India. The Greeks rose above it only at their peak, in the thought of Plato and Aristotle; their successors relapsed into the great Pantheistic system of the Stoics. Modern Europe escaped it only while she remained predominantly Christian; with Giordano Bruno and Spinoza it returned. With Hegel it became almost the agreed philosophy of highly educated people, while the more popular Pantheism of Wordsworth, Carlyle and Emerson conveyed the same doctrine to those on a slightly lower cultural level. So far from being the final religious refinement, Pantheism is in fact the permanent natural bent of the human mind; the permanent ordinary level below which man sometimes sinks, under the influence of priestcraft and superstition, but above which his own unaided efforts can never raise him for very long. Platonism and Judaism, and Christianity (which has incorporated both) have proved the only things capable of resisting it. It is the attitude into which the human mind automatically falls when left to itself. No wonder we find it congenial. If "religion" means simply what man says about God, and not what God does about man, then Pantheism almost *is* religion. And "religion" in that sense has, in the long run, only one really formidable opponent—namely Christianity. Modern philosophy has rejected Hegel and modern science started out with no bias in favour of religion; but they have both proved quite powerless to curb the human impulse towards Pantheism. It is nearly as strong to-day as it was in ancient India or in ancient Rome. Theosophy and the worship of the life-force are both forms of it: even the German worship of a racial spirit is only Pantheism truncated or whittled down to suit barbarians. Yet, by a strange irony, each new relapse into this immemorial "religion" is hailed as the last word in novelty and emancipation.

This native bent of the mind can be paralleled in quite a different field of thought. Men believed in atoms centuries before they had any experimental evidence of their existence. It was apparently natural to do so. And the sort of atoms we naturally believe in are little hard pellets—just like the hard substances we meet in experience, but too small to see. The mind reaches this conception by an easy analogy from grains of sand or of salt. It explains a number of phenomena; and we feel at home with atoms of that sort—we can picture them. The belief would have lasted forever if later science had not been so troublesome as to find out what atoms are *really* like. The moment it does that, all our mental comfort, all the immediate plausibility and obviousness of the old atomic theory, is destroyed. The real atoms turn out to be quite alien from our natural mode of thought. They are not even made of hard "stuff" or "matter" (as the imagination understands "matter") at all: they are not simple, but have a structure: they are not all the same: and they are unpicturable. The old atomic theory is in physics what Pantheism is in religion—the normal, instinctive guess of the human mind, not utterly wrong, but needing correction. Christian theology, and quantum physics, are both, by comparison with the first guess, hard, complex, dry and repellent. The first shock of the object's real nature, breaking in on our spontaneous dreams of what that object ought to be, always has these characteristics. You must not expect Schrödinger [7] to be as plausible as Democritus; [8] he knows too much. You must not expect St. Athanasius [9] to be as plausible as Mr. Bernard Shaw: he also knows too much.

The true state of the question is often misunderstood because people compare an adult knowledge of Pantheism with a knowledge of Christianity which they acquired in their childhood. They thus get the impression that Christianity gives the "obvious" account of God, the one that is too easy to be true, while Pantheism offers something sublime and mysterious. In reality, it is the other way round. The apparent profundity of Pantheism thinly veils a mass of spontaneous picture-thinking and owes its plausibility to that fact. Pantheists and Christians agree that God is present everywhere. Pantheists conclude that He is "diffused" or "concealed" in all things and therefore a universal medium rather than a concrete entity, because their minds are really dominated by the picture of a gas, or fluid, or space itself. The Christian, on the other hand, deliberately rules out such images by saying that God is totally present at every point of space and time, and

locally present in none. Again the Pantheist and Christian agree that we are all dependent on God and intimately related to Him. But the Christian defines this relation in terms of Maker and made, whereas the Pantheist (at least of the popular kind) says, we are "parts" of Him, or are contained in Him. Once more, the picture of a vast extended something which can be divided into areas has crept in. Because of this fatal picture Pantheism concludes that God must be equally present in what we call evil and what we call good and therefore indifferent to both (ether permeates the mud and the marble impartially). The Christian has to reply that this is far too simple; God is present in a great many different modes: not present in matter as He is present in man, not present in all men as in some, not present in any other man as in Jesus. Pantheist and Christian also agree that God is super-personal. The Christian means by this that God has a positive structure which we could never have guessed in advance, any more than a knowledge of squares would have enabled us to guess at a cube. He contains "persons" (three of them) while remaining one God, as a cube combines six squares while remaining one solid body. We cannot comprehend such a structure any more than the Flatlanders [10] could comprehend a cube. But we can at least comprehend our incomprehension, and see that if there is something beyond personality it *ought* to be incomprehensible in that sort of way. The Pantheist, on the other hand, though he may say "super personal" really conceives God in terms of what is sub personal—as though the Flatlanders thought a cube existed in *fewer* dimensions than a square.

At every point Christianity has to correct the natural expectations of the Pantheist and offer something more difficult, just as Schrödinger has to correct Democritus. At every moment he has to multiply distinctions and rule out false analogies. He has to substitute the mappings of something that has a positive, concrete, and highly articulated character for the formless generalities in which Pantheism is at home. Indeed, after the discussion has been going on for some time the Pantheist is apt to change his ground and where he before accused us of childish naivety now to blame us for the pedan-

[7] Erwin Schrödinger, 1887–    , Austrian physicist whose contributions to atomic theory and quantum mechanics won him a Nobel prize in 1933.

[8] Greek philosopher, 460?–362? B.C., who taught that matter is made up of small, hard particles.

[9] Theologian, 296?–373, after whom is named the Athanasian Creed.

[10] Characters in *Flatland,* a fantasy of a two-dimensional world, by Edwin A. Abbott.

tic complexity of our "cold Christs and tangled Trinities." And we may well sympathise with him. Christianity, faced with popular "religion" is continuously troublesome. To the large well-meant statements of "religion" it finds itself forced to reply again and again, "Well, not quite like that," or, "I should hardly put it that way." This troublesomeness does not of course prove it to be true; but if it were true it would be bound to have this troublesomeness. The real musician is similarly troublesome to a man who wishes to indulge in untaught "musical appreciation"; the real historian is similarly a nuisance when we want to romance about "the old days" or "the ancient Greeks and Romans." The ascertained nature of any real thing is always at first a nuisance to our natural fantasies—a wretched, pedantic, logic-chopping intruder upon a conversation which was getting on famously without it.

But "religion" also claims to base itself on experience. The experiences of the mystics (that ill-defined but popular class) are held to indicate that God is the God of "religion" rather than of Christianity; that He—or It—is not a concrete Being but "being in general" about which nothing can be truly asserted. To everything which we try to say about Him, the mystics tend to reply, "Not thus." What all these negatives of the mystics really mean I shall consider in a moment: but I must first point out why it seems to me impossible that they should be true in the sense popularly understood.

It will be agreed that, however they came there, concrete, individual, determinate things do now exist: things like flamingoes, German generals, lovers, sandwiches, pineapples, comets and kangaroos. These are not mere principles or generalities or theorems, but things—facts—real, resistent existences. One might even say *opaque* existences, in the sense that each contains something which our intelligence cannot completely digest. In so far as they illustrate general laws it can digest them: but then they are never mere illustrations. Above and beyond that there is in each of them the "opaque" brute fact of existence, the fact that it is actually there and is itself. Now this opaque fact, this concreteness, is not in the least accounted for by the laws of Nature or even by the laws of thought. Every law can be reduced to the form "If A, then B." Laws give us only a universe of "Ifs and Ands": not this universe which

actually exists. What we know through laws and general principles is a series of connexions. But in order for there to be a real universe the connexions must be given something to connect; a torrent of opaque actualities must be fed into the pattern. If God created the world, then He is precisely the source of this torrent, and it alone gives our truest principles anything to be true *about*. But if God is the ultimate source of all concrete, individual things and events, then God Himself must be concrete, and individual in the highest degree. Unless the origin of all other things were itself concrete and individual, nothing else could be so; for there is no conceivable means whereby what is abstract or general could itself produce concrete reality. Book-keeping, continued to all eternity, could never produce one farthing. Metre, of itself, could never produce a poem. Book-keeping needs something else (namely, real money put into the account) and metre needs something else (real words, fed into it by a poet) before any income or any poem can exist. If anything is to exist at all, then the Original Thing must be, not a principle nor a generality, much less an "ideal" or a "value," but an utterly concrete fact.

Probably no thinking person would, in so many words, deny that God is concrete and individual. But not all thinking people, and certainly not all who believe in "religion," keep this truth steadily before their minds. We must beware, as Professor Whitehead says, of paying God ill-judged "metaphysical compliments." We say that God is "infinite." In the sense that His knowledge and power extend not to some things but to all, this is true. But if by using the word "infinite" we encourage ourselves to think of Him as a formless "everything" about whom nothing in particular and everything in general is true, then it would be better to drop that word altogether. Let us dare to say that God is a particular Thing. Once He was the only Thing: but He is creative, He made other things to be. He is not those other things. He is not "universal being": if He were there would be no creatures, for a generality can make nothing. He is "absolute being"—or rather *the* Absolute Being—in the sense that He alone exists in His own right. But there are things which God is not. In that sense He has a determinate character. Thus He is righteous, not a-moral; creative, not inert. The Hebrew writings here observe an admirable balance. Once God says simply I AM, proclaiming the mystery of self-existence. But times without number He says, "I am the Lord"—I, the ultimate Fact, have *this* determinate character, and not *that*. And men are exhorted to "know the Lord," to discover and experience this particular character.

The error which I am here trying to correct is one of the most sincere and respectable errors in the world; I have sympathy enough with it to feel shocked at the language I have been driven to use in stating the opposite view, which I believe to be the true one. To say that God "is a particular Thing" does seem to obliterate the immeasurable difference not only between what He is and what all other things are but between the very mode of His existence and theirs. I must at once restore the balance by insisting that derivative things, from atoms to archangels, hardly attain to existence at all in comparison with their Creator. Their principle of existence is not in themselves. You can distinguish *what* they are from the fact *that* they are. The definition of them can be understood and a clear idea of them formed without even knowing *whether* they are. Existence is an "opaque" addition to the idea of them. But with God it is not so: if we fully understood *what* God is we should see that there is no question *whether* He is. It would always have been impossible that He should not exist. He is the opaque centre of all existences, the thing that simply and entirely *is,* the fountain of facthood. And yet, now that He has created, there is a sense in which we must say that He is a particular Thing and even one Thing among others. To say this is not to lessen the immeasurable difference between Him and them. On the contrary, it is to recognise in Him a positive perfection which Pantheism has obscured; the perfection of being creative. He is so brim-full of existence that He can give existence away, can cause things to be, and to be really other than Himself, can make it untrue to say that He is everything.

It is clear that there never was a time when nothing existed; otherwise nothing would exist now. But to exist means to be a positive Something, to have (metaphorically) a certain shape or structure, to be this and not that. The Thing which always existed, namely God, has therefore always had His own positive character.

Throughout all eternity certain statements about Him would have been true and others false. And from the mere fact of our own existence and Nature's we already know to some extent which are which. We know that He invents, acts, creates. After that there can be no ground for assuming in advance that He does not do miracles.

Why, then, do the mystics talk of Him as they do, and why are many people prepared in advance to maintain that, whatever else God may be, He is not the concrete, living, willing, and acting God of Christian theology? I think the reason is as follows. Let us suppose a mystical limpet, a sage among limpets, who (rapt in vision) catches a glimpse of what Man is like. In reporting it to his disciples, who have some vision themselves (though less than he) he will have to use many negatives. He will have to tell them that Man has no shell, is not attached to a rock, is not surrounded by water. And his disciples, having a little vision of their own to help them, do get some idea of Man. But then there come erudite limpets, limpets who write histories of philosophy and give lectures on comparative religion, and who have never had any vision of their own. What they get out of the prophetic limpet's words is simply and solely the negatives. From these, uncorrected by any positive insight, they build up a picture of Man as a sort of amorphous jelly (he has no shell) existing nowhere in particular (he is not attached to a rock) and never taking nourishment (there is no water to drift it towards him). And having a traditional reverence for Man they conclude that to be a famished jelly in a dimensionless void is the supreme mode of existence, and reject as crude, materialistic superstition any doctrine which would attribute to Man a definite shape, a structure, and organs.

Our own situation is much like that of the erudite limpets. Great prophets and saints have an intuition of God which is positive and concrete in the highest degree. Because, just touching the fringes of His being, they have seen that He is plenitude of life and energy and joy, therefore (and for no other reason) they have to pronounce that He transcends those limitations which we call personality, passion, change, materiality, and the like. The positive quality in Him which repels these limitations is their only ground for all the negatives. But when we come limping after and try to construct an intellectual or "enlightened" religion, we take over these negatives (infinite, immaterial, impassible, immutable, etc.) and use them unchecked by any positive intuition. At each step we have to strip off from our idea of God some human attribute. But the only real reason for stripping off the human attribute is to make room for putting on some positive divine attribute. In St. Paul's language, the purpose of all this unclothing is not that our idea of God should reach nakedness but that it should be re-clothed. But unhappily we have no means of doing the re-clothing. When we have removed from our idea of God some puny human characteristic, we (as merely erudite or intelligent enquirers) have no resources from which to supply that blindingly real and concrete attribute of Deity which ought to replace it. Thus at each step in the process of refinement our idea of God contains less, and the fatal pictures come in (an endless, silent sea, an empty sky beyond all stars, a dome of white radiance) and we reach at last mere zero and worship a nonentity. And the understanding, left to itself, can hardly help following this path. That is why the Christian statement that only He who does the will of the Father will ever know the true doctrine is philosophically accurate. Imagination may help a little: but in the moral life, and (still more) in the devotional life we touch something concrete which will at once begin to correct the growing emptiness of our idea of God. One moment even of feeble contrition or blurred thankfulness will, at least in some degree, head us off from the abyss of abstraction. It is Reason herself which teaches us not to rely on Reason only in this matter. For Reason knows that she cannot work without materials. When it becomes clear that you cannot find out by reasoning whether the cat is in the linen-cupboard, it is Reason herself who whispers, "Go and look. This is not my job: it is a matter for the senses." So here. The materials for correcting our abstract conception of God cannot be supplied by Reason: she will be the first to tell you to go and try experience—"Oh, taste and see!" For of course she will have already pointed out that your present position is absurd. As long as we remain Erudite Limpets we are forgetting that if no-one had ever seen more of God than we, we should have no

reason even to believe Him immaterial, immutable, impassible and all the rest of it. Even that negative knowledge which seems to us so enlightened is only a relic left over from the positive knowledge of better men—only the pattern which that heavenly wave left on the sand when it retreated.

"A Spirit and a Vision," said Blake, "are not, as the modern philosophy supposes, a cloudy vapour, or a nothing. They are organised and minutely articulated beyond all that the mortal and perishing nature can produce." [11] He is speaking only of how to draw pictures of apparitions which may well have been illusory, but his words suggest a truth on the metaphysical level also. God is basic Fact or Actuality, the source of all other facthood. At all costs therefore He must not be thought of as a featureless generality. If He exists at all, He is the most concrete thing there is, the most individual, "organised and minutely articulated." He is unspeakable not by being indefinite but by being too definite for the unavoidable vagueness of language. The words *incorporeal* and *impersonal* are misleading, because they suggest that He lacks some reality which we possess. It would be safer to call Him *trans-corporeal, trans-personal*. Body and personality as we know them are the real negatives —they are what is left of positive being when it is sufficiently diluted to appear in temporal or finite forms. Even our sexuality should be regarded as the transposition into a minor key of that creative joy which in Him is unceasing and irresistible. Grammatically the things we say of Him are "metaphorical": but in a deeper sense it is our physical and psychic energies that are mere "metaphors" of the real Life which is God. Divine Sonship is, so to speak, the solid of which biological sonship is merely a diagrammatic representation on the flat.

And here the subject of imagery, which crossed our path in the last chapter, can be seen in a new light. For it is just the recognition of God's positive and concrete reality which the religious imagery preserves. The crudest Old Testament picture of Jahweh thundering and lightning out of dense smoke, making mountains skip like rams, threatening, promising, pleading, even changing His mind, transmits that sense of *living* Deity which

---

[11] *A Descriptive Catalogue*, No. 4.

evaporates in abstract thought. Even sub-Christian images—even a Hindoo idol with a hundred hands—gets in *something* which mere "religion" in our own days has left out. We rightly reject it, for by itself it would encourage the most blackguardly of superstitions, the adoration of mere power. Perhaps we may rightly reject much of the Old Testament imagery. But we must be clear why we are doing so: not because the images are too strong but because they are too weak. The ultimate spiritual reality is not vaguer, more inert, more transparent than the images, but more positive, more dynamic, more opaque. Confusion between Spirit and soul (or "ghost") has here done much harm. Ghosts must be pictured, if we are to picture them at all, as shadowy and tenuous, for ghosts are half-men, one element abstracted from a creature that ought to have flesh. But Spirit, if pictured at all, must be pictured in the very opposite way. Neither God nor even the gods are "shadowy" in traditional imagination: even the human dead, when glorified in Christ, cease to be "ghosts" and become "saints." The difference of atmosphere which even now surrounds the words "I saw a ghost" and the words "I saw a saint"—all the pallor and insubstantiality of the one, all the gold and blue of the other—contains more wisdom than whole libraries of "religion." If we must have a mental picture to symbolise Spirit, we should represent it as something *heavier* than matter.

And if we say that we are rejecting the old images in order to do more justice to the moral attributes of God, we must again be careful of what we are really meaning. When we wish to learn of the love and goodness of God by *analogy*—by imagining parallels to them in the realm of human relations—we turn of course to the parables of Christ. But when we try to conceive the reality as it may be in itself, we must beware lest we interpret "moral attributes" in terms of mere conscientiousness or abstract benevolence. The mistake is easily made because we (correctly) deny that God has passions; and with us a love that is not passionate means a love that is something less. But the reason why God has no passions is that passions imply passivity and intermission. The passion of love is something that happens to us, as "getting wet" happens to a body: and God is exempt from that "passion" in the same way that water is exempt from "getting wet." He

cannot be affected with love, because He *is* love. To imagine that love as something less torrential or less sharp than our own temporary and derivative "passions" is a most disastrous fantasy.

Again, we may find a violence in some of the traditional imagery which tends to obscure the changelessness of God, the peace, which nearly all who approach Him have reported—the "still, small voice." And it is here, I think, that the pre-Christian imagery is least suggestive. Yet even here, there is a danger lest the half conscious picture of some huge thing at rest—a clear, still ocean, a dome of "white radiance"—should smuggle in ideas of inertia or vacuity. The stillness in which the mystics approach Him is intent and alert—at the opposite pole from sleep or reverie. They are becoming like Him. Silences in the physical world occur in empty places: but the ultimate Peace is silent through very density of life. Saying is swallowed up in being. There is no movement because His action (which is Himself) is timeless. You might, if you wished, call it movement at an infinite speed, which is the same thing as rest, but reached by a different—perhaps a less misleading—way of approach.

Men are reluctant to pass over from the notion of an abstract and negative deity to the living God. I do not wonder. Here lies the deepest tap-root of Pantheism and of the objection to traditional imagery. It was hated not, at bottom, because it pictured Him as man but because it pictured Him as king, or even as warrior. The Pantheist's God does nothing, demands nothing. He is there if you wish for Him, like a book on a shelf. He will not pursue you. There is no danger that at any time heaven and earth should flee away at His glance. If He were the truth, then we could really say that all the Christian images of kingship were a historical accident of which our religion ought to be cleansed. It is with a shock that we discover them to be indispensable. You have had a shock like that before, in connection with smaller matters—when the line pulls at your hand, when something breathes beside you in the darkness. So here; the shock comes at the precise moment when the thrill of *life* is communicated to us along the clue we have been following. It is always shocking to meet life where we thought we were alone. "Look out!"

we cry, "it's *alive.*" And therefore this is the very point at which so many draw back—I would have done so myself if I could—and proceed no further with Christianity. An "impersonal God"—well and good. A subjective God of beauty, truth and goodness, inside our own heads—better still. A formless life-force surging through us, a vast power which we can tap—best of all. But God Himself, alive, pulling at the other end of the cord, perhaps approaching at an infinite speed, the hunter, king, husband—that is quite another matter. There comes a moment when the children who have been playing at burglars hush suddenly: was that a *real* footstep in the hall? There comes a moment when people who have been dabbling in religion ("Man's search for God!") suddenly draw back. Supposing we really found Him? We never meant it to come to *that!* Worse still, supposing He had found us?

So it is a sort of Rubicon. One goes across; or not. But if one does, there is no manner of security against miracles. One may be in for *anything.*

## *Graham Greene*
## THE HINT OF AN EXPLANATION

A long train journey on a late December evening, in this new version of peace, is a dreary experience. I suppose that my fellow traveller and I could consider ourselves lucky to have a compartment to ourselves, even though the heating apparatus was not working, even though the lights went out entirely in the frequent Pennine tunnels and were too dim anyway for us to read our books without straining our eyes, and though there was no restaurant car to give at least a change of scene. It was when we were trying simultaneously to chew the same kind of dry bun bought at the same station buffet that my companion and I

came together. Before that we had sat at opposite ends of the carriage, both muffled to the chin in overcoats, both bent low over type we could barely make out, but as I threw the remains of my cake under the seat our eyes met, and he laid his book down.

By the time we were half-way to Bedwell Junction we had found an enormous range of subjects for discussion; starting with buns and the weather, we had gone on to politics, the government, foreign affairs, the atom bomb, and, by an inevitable progression, God. We had not, however, become either shrill or acid. My companion, who now sat opposite me, leaning a little forward, so that our knees nearly touched, gave such an impression of serenity that it would have been impossible to quarrel with him, however much our views differed, and differ they did profoundly.

I had soon realized I was speaking to a Catholic, to someone who believed—how do they put it?—in an omnipotent and omniscient Deity, while I was what is loosely called an Agnostic. I have a certain intuition (which I do not trust, founded as it may well be on childish experiences and needs) that a God exists, and I am surprised occasionally into belief by the extraordinary coincidences that beset our path like the traps set for leopards in the jungle, but intellectually I am revolted at the whole notion of such a God who can so abandon his creatures to the enormities of Free Will. I found myself expressing this view to my companion, who listened quietly and with respect. He made no attempt to interrupt: he showed none of the impatience or the intellectual arrogance I have grown to expect from Catholics; when the lights of a wayside station flashed across his face that had escaped hitherto the rays of the one globe working in the compartment, I caught a glimpse suddenly of—what? I stopped speaking, so strong was the impression. I was carried back ten years, to the other side of the great useless conflict, to a small town, Gisors in Normandy. I was again, for a moment, walking on the ancient battlements and looking down across the grey roofs, until my eyes for some reason lit on one grey stony "back" out of the many, where the face of a middle-aged man was pressed against a windowpane (I suppose that face has ceased to exist now, just as I believe the whole town with its medieval memories has been reduced to rubble). I remembered saying to myself with astonishment, "That man is happy—completely happy." I looked across the compartment at my fellow traveller, but his face was already again in shadow. I said weakly, "When you think what God—if there is a God—allows. It's not merely the physical agonies, but think of the corruption, even of children. . . ."

He said, "Our view is so limited," and I was disappointed at the conventionality of his reply. He must have been aware of my disappointment (it was as though our thoughts were huddled as closely as ourselves for warmth), for he went on, "Of course there is no answer here. We catch hints . . ." and then the train roared into another tunnel and the lights again went out. It was the longest tunnel yet; we went rocking down it, and the cold seemed to become more intense with the darkness like an icy fog (perhaps when one sense—of sight—is robbed of sensation, the others grow more sensitive). When we emerged into the mere grey of night and the globe lit up once more, I could see that my companion was leaning back on his seat.

I repeated his last words as a question, "Hints?"

"Oh, they mean very little in cold print—or cold speech," he said, shivering in his overcoat. "And they mean nothing at all to a human being other than the man who catches them. They are not scientific evidence—or evidence at all for that matter. Events that don't, somehow, turn out as they were intended—by the human actors I mean, or by the thing behind the human actors."

"The thing?"

"The word Satan is so anthropomorphic."

I had to lean forward now: I wanted to hear what he had to say. I am—I really am, God knows—open to conviction.

He said, "One's words are so crude, but I sometimes feel pity for that thing. It is so continually finding the right weapon to use against its Enemy and the weapon breaks in its own breast. It sometimes seems to me so—powerless. You said something just now about the corruption of children. It reminded me of something in my own childhood. You are the first person—except for one—that I have thought of telling it to, perhaps because you are anonymous. It's not a very long story, and in a way it's relevant."

I said, "I'd like to hear it."

"You mustn't expect too much meaning. But to me there seems to be a hint. That's all. A hint."

He went slowly on, turning his face to the pane, though he could have seen nothing real in the whirling world outside except an occasional signal lamp, a light in a window, a small country station torn backwards by our rush, picking his words with precision. He said, "When I was a child they taught me to serve at Mass. The church was a small one, for there were very few Catholics where I lived. It was a market town in East Anglia, surrounded by flat, chalky fields and ditches—so many ditches. I don't suppose there were fifty Catholics all told, and for some reason there was a tradition of hostility to us. Perhaps it went back to the burning of a Protestant martyr in the sixteenth century—there was a stone marking the place near where the meat stalls stood on Wednesdays. I was only half aware of the enmity, though I knew that my school nickname of Popey Martin had something to do with my religion, and I had heard that my father was nearly excluded from the Constitutional Club when he first came to the town.

"Every Sunday I had to dress up in my surplice and serve Mass. I hated it—I have always hated dressing up in any way (which is funny when you come to think of it), and I never ceased to be afraid of losing my place in the service and doing something which would put me to ridicule. Our services were at a different hour from the Anglican, and as our small, far-from-select band trudged out of the hideous chapel the whole of the townsfolk seemed to be on the way past to the proper church—I always thought of it as the proper church. We had to pass the parade of their eyes, indifferent, supercilious, mocking; you can't imagine how seriously religion can be taken in a small town, if only for social reasons.

"There was one man in particular; he was one of the two bakers in the town, the one my family did not patronize. I don't think any of the Catholics patronized him because he was called a free-thinker—an odd title, for, poor man, no one's thoughts were less free than his. He was hemmed in by his hatred—his hatred of us. He was very ugly to look at, with one wall-eye and a head the shape of a turnip, with the hair gone on the crown, and he was unmarried. He had no interests, apparently, but his baking and his hatred, though now that I am older I begin to see other sides to his nature —it did contain, perhaps, a certain furtive love. One would come across him suddenly sometimes on a country walk, especially if one were alone and it was Sunday. It was as if he rose from the ditches, and the smear of chalk on his clothes reminded one of the flour on his working overalls. He would have a stick in his hand and stab at the hedges, and if his mood were very black he would call out after one strange abrupt words like a foreign tongue—I know the meaning of those words, of course, now. Once the police went to his house because of what a boy said he'd seen, but nothing came of it except that the hate shackled him closer. His name was Blacker and he terrified me.

"I think he had a particular hatred of my father—I don't know why. My father was manager of the Midland Bank, and it's possible that at some time Blacker may have had unsatisfactory dealings with the bank; my father was a very cautious man who suffered all his life from anxiety about money—his own and other people's. If I try and picture Blacker now I see him walking along a narrowing path between high windowless walls, and at the end of the path stands a small boy of ten—me. I don't know whether it's a symbolic picture or the memory of one of our encounters—our encounters somehow got more and more frequent. You talked just now about the corruption of children. That poor man was preparing to revenge himself on everything he hated—my father, the Catholics, the God whom people persisted in crediting—and that by corrupting me. He had evolved a horrible and ingenious plan.

"I remember the first time I had a friendly word from him. I was passing his shop as rapidly as I could when I heard his voice call out with a kind of sly subservience as though he were an under servant. 'Master David,' he called, 'Master David,' and I hurried on. But the next time I passed that way he was at his door (he must have seen me coming) with one of those curly cakes in his hand that we called Chelsea buns. I didn't want to take it, but he made me, and then I couldn't be other than polite when he asked me to come into his parlour behind the shop and see something very special.

"It was a small electric railway—a rare sight in those days, and he insisted on showing me how it worked. He made me turn the switches and stop and start it, and he told me that I could come in any morning and have a game with it. He used the word 'game' as though it were something secret, and it's true that I never told my family of this invitation and of how, perhaps twice a week those holidays, the desire to control that little railway became overpowering, and looking up and down the street to see if I were observed, I would dive into the shop."

Our larger, dirtier, adult train drove into a tunnel and the light went out. We sat in darkness and silence, with the noise of the train blocking our ears like wax. When we were through we didn't speak at once and I had to prick him into continuing. "An elaborate seduction," I said.

"Don't think his plans were as simple as that," my companion said, "or as crude. There was much more hate than love, poor man, in his make-up. Can you hate something you don't believe in? And yet he called himself a free-thinker. What an impossible paradox, to be free and to be so obsessed. Day by day all through those holidays his obsession must have grown, but he kept a grip; he bided his time. Perhaps that thing I spoke of gave him the strength and the wisdom. It was only a week from the end of the holidays that he spoke to me on what concerned him so deeply.

"I heard him behind me as I knelt on the floor, coupling two coaches. He said, 'You won't be able to do this, Master David, when school starts.' It wasn't a sentence that needed any comment from me any more than the one that followed. 'You ought to have it for your own, you ought,' but how skilfully and unemphatically he had sowed the longing, the idea of a possibility. . . . I was coming to his parlour every day now; you see, I had to cram every opportunity in before the hated term started again, and I suppose I was becoming accustomed to Blacker, to that wall-eye, that turnip head, that nauseating subservience. The Pope, you know, describes himself as 'the servant of the servants of God,' and Blacker— I sometimes think that Blacker was 'the servant of the servants of . . . ,' well, let it be.

"The very next day, standing in the doorway watching me play, he began to talk to me about religion. He said, with what untruth even I recognized, how much he admired the Catholics; he wished he could believe like that, but how could a baker believe? He accented 'a baker' as one might say a biologist, and the tiny train spun round the gauge 0 track. He said, 'I can bake the things you eat just as well as any Catholic can,' and disappeared into his shop. I hadn't the faintest idea what he meant. Presently he emerged again, holding in his hand a little wafer. 'Here,' he said, 'eat that and tell me. . . .' When I put it in my mouth I could tell that it was made in the same way as our wafers for communion—he had got the shape a little wrong, that was all—and I felt guilty and irrationally scared. 'Tell me,' he said, 'what's the difference?'

" 'Difference?' I asked.

" 'Isn't that just the same as you eat in church?'

"I said smugly, 'It hasn't been consecrated.'

"He said, 'Do you think, if I put the two of them under a microscope, you could tell the difference?'

"But even at ten I had the answer to that question. 'No.' I said, 'the—accidents don't change,' stumbling a little on the word 'accidents' which had suddenly conveyed to me the idea of death and wounds.

"Blacker said with sudden intensity, 'How I'd like to get one of your ones in my mouth—just to see. . . .'

"It may seem odd to you, but this was the first time that the idea of transsubstantiation really lodged in my mind. I had learned it all by rote; I had grown up with the idea. The Mass was as lifeless to me as the sentences in De Bello Gallico; [12] communion a routine like drill in the school-yard, but here suddenly I was in the presence of a man who took it seriously, as seriously as the priest whom naturally one didn't count—it was his job. I felt more scared than ever.

"He said, 'It's all nonsense, but I'd just like to have it in my mouth.'

" 'You could if you were a Catholic,' I said naïvely.

"He gazed at me with his one good eye, like /a Cyclops. He said, 'You serve at Mass, don't

---

[12] Caesar's *Gallic War,* usually studied in second-year Latin.

you? It would be easy for you to get at one of those things. I tell you what I'd do—I'd swap this electric train for one of your wafers—consecrated, mind. It's got to be consecrated.'

" 'I could get you one out of the box,' I said. I think I still imagined that his interest was a baker's interest—to see how they were made.

" 'Oh, no,' he said, 'I want to see what your God tastes like.'

" 'I couldn't do that.'

" 'Not for a whole electric train, just for yourself? You wouldn't have any trouble at home. I'd pack it up and put a label inside that your dad could see: "For my bank manager's little boy from a grateful client." He'd be pleased as punch with that.'

"Now that we are grown men it seems a trivial temptation, doesn't it? But try to think back to your own childhood. There was a whole circuit of rails there on the floor at our feet, straight rails and curved, and a little station with porters and passengers, a tunnel, a footbridge, a level crossing, two signals, buffers, of course—and, above all, a turntable. The tears of longing came into my eyes when I looked at the turntable. It was my favorite piece—it looked so ugly and practical and true. I said weakly, 'I wouldn't know how.'

"How carefully he had been studying the ground! He must have slipped several times into Mass at the back of the church. It would have been no good, you understand, in a little town like that, presenting himself for communion. Everybody there knew him for what he was. He said to me, 'When you've been given communion you could just put it under your tongue a moment. He serves you and the other boy first, and I saw you once go out behind the curtain straight afterwards. You'd forgotten one of those little bottles.'

" 'The cruet,' I said.

" 'Pepper and salt.' He grinned at me jovially, and I—well, I looked at the little railway which I could no longer come and play with when term started. I said, 'You'd just swallow it, wouldn't you?'

" 'Oh, yes,' he said. 'I'd just swallow it.'

"Somehow I didn't want to play with the train any more that day. I got up and made for the door, but he detained me, gripping my lapel. He said, 'This will be a secret between you and me. Tomorrow's Sunday. You come along here in the afternoon. Put it in an envelope and post it me. Monday morning the train will be delivered bright and early.'

" 'Not tomorrow,' I implored him.

" 'I'm not interested in any other Sunday,' he said. 'It's your only chance.' He shook me gently backwards and forwards. 'It will always have to be a secret between you and me,' he said. 'Why, if anyone knew they'd take away the train and there'd be me to reckon with. I'd bleed you something awful. You know how I'm always about on Sunday walks. You can't avoid a man like me. I crop up. You wouldn't ever be safe in your own house. I know ways to get into houses when people are asleep.' He pulled me into the shop after him and opened a drawer. In the drawer was an odd looking key and a cut-throat razor. He said, 'That's a master key that opens all locks and that—that's what I bleed people with.' Then he patted my cheek with his plump floury fingers and said, 'Forget it. You and me are friends.'

"That Sunday Mass stays in my head, every detail of it, as though it had happened only a week ago. From the moment of the Confession to the moment of Consecration it had a terrible importance; only one other Mass has ever been so important to me—perhaps not even one, for this was a solitary Mass which would never happen again. It seemed as final as the last Sacrament when the priest bent down and put the wafer in my mouth where I knelt before the altar with my fellow server.

"I suppose I had made up my mind to commit this awful act—for, you know, to us it must always seem an awful act—from the moment when I saw Blacker watching from the back of the church. He had put on his best black Sunday clothes and, as though he could never quite escape the smear of his profession, he had a dab of dried talcum on his cheek, which he had presumably applied after using that cut-throat of his. He was watching me closely all the time, and I think it was fear—fear of that terrible undefined thing called bleeding—as much as covetousness that drove me to carry out my instructions.

"My fellow server got briskly up and, taking the paten, preceded Father Carey to the altar rail where the other communicants knelt. I had the Host lodged under my tongue: it felt like a blister. I got up and made for the curtain to get the cruet that I had purposely left in the sacristy. When I was there I looked quickly round for a hiding place and saw an old copy of the *Universe* lying on a chair. I took the Host from my mouth and inserted it between two sheets—a little damp mess of pulp. Then I thought: perhaps Father Carey has put out the paper for a particular purpose and he will find the Host before I have time to remove it, and the enormity of my act began to come home to me when I tried to imagine what punishment I should incur. Murder is sufficiently trivial to have its appropriate punishment, but for this act the mind boggled at the thought of any retribution at all. I tried to remove the Host, but it stuck clammily between the pages, and in desperation I tore out a piece of the newspaper and, screwing the whole thing up, stuck it in my trousers pocket. When I came back through the curtain carrying the cruet my eyes met Blacker's. He gave me a grin of encouragement and unhappiness —yes, I am sure, unhappiness. Was it perhaps that the poor man was all the time seeking something incorruptible?

"I can remember little more of that day. I think my mind was shocked and stunned, and I was caught up too in the family bustle of Sunday. Sunday in a provincial town is the day for relations. All the family are at home, and unfamiliar cousins and uncles are apt to arrive, packed in the back seats of other people's cars. I remember that some crowd of the kind descended on us and pushed Blacker temporarily out of the foreground of my mind. There was somebody called Aunt Lucy, with a loud hollow laugh that filled the house with mechanical merriment like the sound of recorded laughter from inside a hall of mirrors, and I had no opportunity to go out alone even if I had wished to. When six o'clock came and Aunt Lucy and the cousins departed and peace returned, it was too late to go to Blacker's, and at eight it was my own bed-time.

"I think I had half forgotten what I had in my pocket. As I emptied my pocket the little screw of newspaper brought quickly back the Mass, the priest bending over me, Blacker's grin. I laid the packet on the chair by my bed and tried to go to sleep, but I was haunted by the shadows on the wall where the curtains blew, the squeak of furniture, the rustle in the chimney, haunted by the presence of God there on the chair. The Host had always been to me —well, the Host. I knew theoretically, as I have said, what I had to believe, but suddenly, as someone whistled in the road outside, whistled secretively, knowingly, to me, I knew that this which I had beside my bed was something of infinite value—something a man would pay for with his whole peace of mind, something that was so hated one could love it as one loves an outcast or a bullied child. These are adult words, and it was a child of ten who lay scared in bed, listening to the whistle from the road, Blacker's whistle, but I think he felt fairly clearly what I am describing now. That is what I meant when I said this Thing, whatever it is, that seizes every possible weapon against God, is always, everywhere, disappointed at the moment of success. It must have felt as certain of me as Blacker did. It must have felt certain too of Blacker. But I wonder, if one knew what happened later to that poor man, whether one would not find again that the weapon had been turned against its own breast.

"At last I couldn't bear that whistle any more and got out of bed. I opened the curtains a little way, and there right under my window, the moonlight on his face, was Blacker. If I had stretched my hand down, his fingers reaching up could almost have touched mine. He looked up at me, flashing the one good eye, with hunger—I realize now that near-success must have developed his obsession almost to the point of madness. Desperation had driven him to the house. He whispered up at me. 'David, where is it?'

"I jerked my head back at the room. 'Give it me,' he said. 'Quick. You shall have the train in the morning.'

"I shook my head. He said, 'I've got the bleeder here, and the key. You'd better toss it down.'

" 'Go away,' I said, but I could hardly speak for fear.

" 'I'll bleed you first and then I'll have it just the same.'

" 'Oh, no, you won't,' I said. I went to the chair and picked it—Him—up. There was only one place where He was safe. I couldn't separate the Host from the paper, so I swallowed both. The newsprint stuck like a prune skin

to the back of my throat, but I rinsed it down with water from the ewer. Then I went back to the window and looked down at Blacker. He began to wheedle me. 'What have you done with it, David? What's the fuss? It's only a bit of bread,' looking so longingly and pleadingly up at me that even as a child I wondered whether he could really think that, and yet desire it so much.

" 'I swallowed it,' I said.

" 'Swallowed it?'

" 'Yes,' I said. 'Go away.'

"Then something happened which seems to me now more terrible than his desire to corrupt or my thoughtless act: he began to weep—the tears ran lopsidedly out of the one good eye and his shoulders shook. I only saw his face for a moment before he bent his head and strode off, the bald turnip head shaking, into the dark. When I think of it now, it's almost as if I had seen that Thing weeping for its inevitable defeat. It had tried to use me as a weapon, and now I had broken in its hands and it wept its hopeless tears through one of Blacker's eyes."

The black furnaces of Bedwell Junction gathered around the line. The points switched and we were tossed from one set of rails to another. A spray of sparks, a signal light changing to red, tall chimneys jetting into the grey night sky, the fumes of steam from stationary engines—half the cold journey was over, and now remained the long wait for the slow cross-country train. I said, "It's an interesting story. I think I should have given Blacker what he wanted. I wonder what he would have done with it."

"I really believe," my companion said, "that he would first of all have put it under his microscope—before he did all the other things I expect he had planned."

"And the hints," I said. "I don't quite see what you mean by that."

"Oh, well," he said vaguely, "you know for me it was an odd beginning, that affair, when you come to think of it," but I never should have known what he meant had not his coat, when he rose to take his bag from the rack, come open and disclosed the collar of a priest.

I said, "I suppose you think you owe a lot to Blacker."

"Yes," he said, "you see, I am a very happy man."

*Nathaniel Hawthorne*

# YOUNG GOODMAN BROWN

Young Goodman Brown came forth at sunset into the street at Salem village; but put his head back, after crossing the threshold, to exchange a parting kiss with his young wife. And Faith, as the wife was aptly named, thrust her own pretty head into the street, letting the wind play with the pink ribbons of her cap while she called to Goodman Brown.

"Dearest heart," whispered she, softly and rather sadly, when her lips were close to his ear, "prithee put off your journey until sunrise and sleep in your own bed to–night. A lone woman is troubled with such dreams and such thoughts that she's afeard of herself sometimes. Pray tarry with me this night, dear husband, of all nights in the year."

"My love and my Faith," replied young Goodman Brown, "of all nights in the year, this one night must I tarry away from thee. My journey, as thou callest it, forth and back again, must needs be done 'twixt now and sunrise. What, my sweet, pretty wife, dost thou doubt me already, and we but three months married?"

"Then God bless you!" said Faith, with the pink ribbons; "and may you find all well when you come back."

"Amen!" cried Goodman Brown. "Say thy prayers, dear Faith, and go to bed at dusk, and no harm will come to thee."

So they parted; and the young man pursued his way until, being about to turn the corner by the meeting-house, he looked back and saw the head of Faith still peeping after him with a melancholy air, in spite of her pink ribbons.

"Poor little Faith!" thought he, for his heart smote him. "What a wretch am I to leave her on such an errand! She talks of dreams, too. Methought as she spoke there was trouble in her face, as if a dream had warned her what work is to be done tonight. But no, no; 't would kill her to think it. Well, she's a blessed angel on earth; and after this one night I'll cling to her skirts and follow her to heaven."

With this excellent resolve for the future, Goodman Brown felt himself justified in making more haste on his present evil purpose. He had taken a dreary road, darkened by all the gloomiest trees of the forest, which barely stood aside to let the narrow path creep through, and closed immediately behind. It was all as lonely as could be; and there is this peculiarity in such a solitude, that the traveller knows not who may be concealed by the innumerable trunks and the thick boughs overhead; so that with lonely footsteps he may yet be passing through an unseen multitude.

"There may be a devilish Indian behind every tree," said Goodman Brown to himself; and he glanced fearfully behind him as he added, "What if the devil himself should be at my very elbow!"

His head being turned back, he passed a crook of the road, and, looking forward again, beheld the figure of a man, in grave and decent attire, seated at the foot of an old tree. He arose at Goodman Brown's approach and walked onward side by side with him.

"You are late, Goodman Brown," said he. "The clock of the Old South was striking as I came through Boston, and that is full fifteen minutes agone."

"Faith kept me back a while," replied the young man, with a tremor in his voice, caused by the sudden appearance of his companion, though not wholly unexpected.

It was now deep dusk in the forest, and deepest in that part of it where these two were journeying. As nearly as could be discerned, the second traveller was about fifty years old, apparently in the same rank of life as Goodman Brown, and bearing a considerable resemblance to him, though perhaps more in expression than features. Still they might have been taken for father and son. And yet, though the elder person was as simply clad as the younger, and as simple in manner too, he had an indescribable air of one who knew the world, and who would not have felt abashed at the governor's dinner table or in King William's court, were it possible that his affairs should call him thither. But the only thing about him that could be fixed upon as remarkable was his staff, which bore the likeness of a great black snake, so curiously wrought that it might almost be seen to twist and wriggle itself like a living serpent. This, of course, must have been an ocular deception, assisted by the uncertain light.

"Come, Goodman Brown," cried his fellow-traveller, "this is a dull pace for the beginning of a journey. Take my staff, if you are so soon weary."

"Friend," said the other, exchanging his slow pace for a full stop, "having kept covenant by meeting thee here, it is my purpose now to return whence I came. I have scruples touching the matter thou wot'st of."

"Sayest thou so?" replied he of the serpent, smiling apart. "Let us walk on, nevertheless, reasoning as we go; and if I convince thee not thou shalt turn back. We are but a little way in the forest yet."

"Too far! too far!" exclaimed the goodman, unconsciously resuming his walk. "My father never went into the woods on such an errand, nor his father before him. We have been a race of honest men and good Christians since the days of the martyrs; and shall I be the first of the name of Brown that ever took this path and kept"—

"Such company, thou wouldst say," observed the elder person, interpreting his pause. "Well said, Goodman Brown! I have been as well acquainted with your family as with ever a one among the Puritans; and that's no trifle to say. I helped your grandfather, the constable, when he lashed the Quaker woman so smartly through the streets of Salem; and it was I that brought your father a pitch-pine knot, kindled at my own hearth, to set fire to an Indian village, in King Philip's war. They were my good friends, both; and many a pleasant walk have we had along this path, and returned merrily after midnight. I would fain be friends with you for their sake."

"If it be as thou sayest," replied Goodman Brown, "I marvel they never spoke of these matters; or, verily, I marvel not, seeing that the least rumor of the sort would have driven them from New England. We are a people of prayer, and good works to boot, and abide no such wickedness."

"Wickedness or not," said the traveller with the twisted staff, "I have a very general acquaintance here in New England. The deacons of many a church have drunk the communion wine with me; the selectmen of divers towns make me their chairman; and a majority of the Great and General Court are firm supporters of my interest. The governor and I, too—But these are state secrets."

"Can this be so?" cried Goodman Brown, with a stare of amazement at his undisturbed companion. "Howbeit, I have nothing to do with the governor and council; they have their own ways, and are no rule for a simple husbandman like me. But, were I to go on with thee, how should I meet the eye of that good old man, our minister, at Salem village? Oh, his voice would make me tremble both Sabbath day and lecture day."

Thus far the elder traveller had listened with due gravity; but now burst into a fit of irrepressible mirth, shaking himself so violently that his snake-like staff actually seemed to wriggle in sympathy.

"Ha! ha! ha!" shouted he again and again; then composing himself, "Well, go on, Goodman Brown, go on; but, prithee, don't kill me with laughing."

"Well, then, to end the matter at once," said Goodman Brown, considerably nettled, "there is my wife, Faith. It would break her dear little heart; and I'd rather break my own."

"Nay, if that be the case," answered the other, "e'en go thy ways, Goodman Brown. I would not for twenty old women like the one hobbling before us that Faith should come to any harm."

As he spoke he pointed his staff at a female figure on the path, in whom Goodman Brown recognized a very pious and exemplary dame, who had taught him his catechism in youth, and was still his moral and spiritual adviser, jointly with the minister and Deacon Gookin.

"A marvel, truly, that Goody Cloyse should be so far in the wilderness at nightfall," said he. "But with your leave, friend, I shall take a cut through the woods until we have left this Christian woman behind. Being a stranger to you, she might ask whom I was consorting with and whither I was going."

"Be it so," said his fellow-traveller. "Betake you to the woods, and let me keep the path."

Accordingly the young man turned aside, but took care to watch his companion, who advanced softly along the road until he had come within a staff's length of the old dame. She, meanwhile, was making the best of her way, with singular speed for so aged a woman, and mumbling some indistinct words—a prayer, doubtless—as she went. The traveller put forth his staff and touched her withered neck with what seemed the serpent's tail.

"The devil!" screamed the pious old lady.

"Then Goody Cloyse knows her old friend?" observed the traveller, confronting her and leaning on his writhing stick.

"Ah, forsooth, and is it your worship indeed?" cried the good dame. "Yea, truly is it, and in the very image of my old gossip, Goodman Brown, the grandfather of the silly fellow that now is. But—would your worship believe it?—my broomstick hath strangely disappeared, stolen, as I suspect, by that unhanged witch, Goody Cory, and that, too, when I was all anointed with the juice of smallage, and cinquefoil, and wolf's bane"—

"Mingled with fine wheat and the fat of a new-born babe," said the shape of old Goodman Brown.

"Ah, your worship knows the recipe," cried the old lady, cackling aloud. "So, as I was saying, being all ready for the meeting, and no horse to ride on, I made up my mind to foot it; for they tell me there is a nice young man to be taken into communion to-night. But now your good worship will lend me your arm, and we shall be there in a twinkling."

"That can hardly be," answered her friend. "I may not spare you my arm, Goody Cloyse; but here is my staff, if you will."

So saying, he threw it down at her feet, where, perhaps, it assumed life, being one of the rods which its owner had formerly lent to the Egyptian magi. Of this fact, however, Goodman Brown could not take cognizance. He had cast up his eyes in astonishment, and, looking down again, beheld neither Goody Cloyse nor the serpentine staff, but his fellow-traveller alone, who waited for him as calmly as if nothing had happened.

"That old woman taught me my catechism," said the young man; and there was a world of meaning in this simple comment.

They continued to walk onward, while the elder traveller exhorted his companion to make good speed and persevere in the path, discoursing so aptly that his arguments seemed rather to spring up in the bosom of his auditor than to be suggested by himself. As they went, he plucked a branch of maple to serve for a walking stick, and began to strip it of the twigs and little boughs, which were wet with evening dew. The moment his fingers touched them they became strangely withered and dried up as with a week's sunshine. Thus the pair proceeded, at a good free pace, until suddenly, in a gloomy

hollow of the road, Goodman Brown sat himself down on the stump of a tree and refused to go any farther.

"Friend," said he, stubbornly, "my mind is made up. Not another step will I budge on this errand. What if a wretched old woman do choose to go to the devil when I thought she was going to heaven: is that any reason why I should quit my dear Faith and go after her?"

"You will think better of this by and by," said his acquaintance, composedly. "Sit here and rest yourself a while; and when you feel like moving again, there is my staff to help you along."

Without more words, he threw his companion the maple stick, and was as speedily out of sight as if he had vanished into the deepening gloom. The young man sat a few moments by the roadside, applauding himself greatly, and thinking with how clear a conscience he should meet the minister in his morning walk, nor shrink from the eye of good old Deacon Gookin. And what calm sleep would be his that very night, which was to have been spent so wickedly, but so purely and sweetly now, in the arms of Faith! Amidst these pleasant and praiseworthy meditations, Goodman Brown heard the tramp of horses along the road, and deemed it advisable to conceal himself within the verge of the forest, conscious of the guilty purpose that had brought him thither, though now so happily turned from it.

On came the hoof tramps and the voices of the riders, two grave old voices, conversing soberly as they drew near. These mingled sounds appeared to pass along the road, within a few yards of the young man's hiding-place; but, owing doubtless to the depth of the gloom at that particular spot, neither the travellers nor their steeds were visible. Though their figures brushed the small boughs by the wayside, it could not be seen that they intercepted, even for a moment, the faint gleam from the strip of bright sky athwart which they must have passed. Goodman Brown alternately crouched and stood on tiptoe, pulling aside the branches and thrusting forth his head as far as he durst without discerning so much as a shadow. It vexed him the more, because he could have sworn, were such a thing possible, that he recognized the voices of the minister and Deacon Gookin, jogging along quietly, as they were wont to do, when bound to some ordination or ecclesiastical council. While yet within hearing, one of the riders stopped to pluck a switch.

"Of the two, reverend sir," said the voice like the deacon's, "I had rather miss an ordination dinner than to-night's meeting. They tell me that some of our community are to be here from Falmouth and beyond, and others from Connecticut and Rhode Island, besides several of the Indian powwows, who, after their fashion, know almost as much deviltry as the best of us. Moreover, there is a goodly young woman to be taken into communion."

"Mighty well, Deacon Gookin!" replied the solemn old tones of the minister. "Spur up, or we shall be late. Nothing can be done, you know, until I get on the ground."

The hoofs clattered again; and the voices, talking so strangely in the empty air, passed on through the forest, where no church had ever been gathered or solitary Christian prayed. Whither, then, could these holy men be journeying so deep into the heathen wilderness? Young Goodman Brown caught hold of a tree for support, being ready to sink down on the ground, faint and overburdened with the heavy sickness of his heart. He looked up to the sky, doubting whether there really was a heaven above him. Yet there was the blue arch, and the stars brightening in it.

"With heaven above and Faith below, I will yet stand firm against the devil!" cried Goodman Brown.

While he still gazed upward into the deep arch of the firmament and had lifted his hands to pray, a cloud, though no wind was stirring, hurried across the zenith and hid the brightening stars. The blue sky was still visible, except directly overhead, where this black mass of cloud was sweeping swiftly northward. Aloft in the air, as if from the depths of the cloud, came a confused and doubtful sound of voices. Once the listener fancied that he could distinguish the accents of towns-people of his own, men and women, both pious and ungodly, many of whom he had met at the communion table, and had seen others rioting at the tavern. The next moment, so indistinct were the sounds, he doubted whether he had heard aught but the murmur of the old forest, whispering without a wind. Then came a stronger swell of those familiar tones, heard daily in the sunshine at Salem village, but never until now from a cloud

of night. There was one voice of a young woman, uttering lamentations, yet with an uncertain sorrow, and entreating for some favor, which, perhaps, it would grieve her to obtain; and all the unseen multitude, both saints and sinners, seemed to encourage her onward.

"Faith!" shouted Goodman Brown, in a voice of agony and desperation; and the echoes of the forest mocked him, crying, "Faith! Faith!" as if bewildered wretches were seeking her all through the wilderness.

The cry of grief, rage, and terror was yet piercing the night, when the unhappy husband held his breath for a response. There was a scream, drowned immediately in a louder murmur of voices, fading into far-off laughter, as the dark cloud swept away, leaving the clear and silent sky above Goodman Brown. But something fluttered lightly down through the air and caught on the branch of a tree. The young man seized it, and beheld a pink ribbon.

"My Faith is gone!" cried he, after one stupefied moment. "There is no good on earth; and sin is but a name. Come, devil; for to thee is this world given."

And, maddened with despair, so that he laughed loud and long, did Goodman Brown grasp his staff and set forth again, at such a rate that he seemed to fly along the forest path rather than to walk or run. The road grew wilder and drearier and more faintly traced, and vanished at length, leaving him in the heart of the dark wilderness, still rushing onward with the instinct that guides mortal men to evil. The whole forest was peopled with frightful sounds —the creaking of the trees, the howling of wild beasts, and the yell of Indians; while sometimes the wind tolled like a distant church bell, and sometimes gave a broad roar around the traveller, as if all Nature were laughing him to scorn. But he was himself the chief horror of the scene, and shrank not from its other horrors.

"Ha! ha! ha!" roared Goodman Brown when the wind laughed at him. "Let us hear which will laugh loudest. Think not to frighten me with your deviltry. Come witch, come wizard, come Indian powwow, come devil himself, and here comes Goodman Brown. You may as well fear him as he fear you."

In truth, all through the haunted forest there could be nothing more frightful than the figure of Goodman Brown. On he flew among the black pines, brandishing his staff with frenzied gestures, now giving vent to an inspiration of horrid blasphemy, and now shouting forth such laughter as set all the echoes of the forest laughing like demons around him. The fiend in his own shape is less hideous than when he rages in the breast of man. Thus sped the demoniac on his course, until, quivering among the trees, he saw a red light before him, as when the felled trunks and branches of a clearing have been set on fire, and throw up their lurid blaze against the sky, at the hour of midnight. He paused, in a lull of the tempest that had driven him onward, and heard the swell of what seemed a hymn, rolling solemnly from a distance with the weight of many voices. He knew the tune; it was a familiar one in the choir of the village meeting-house. The verse died heavily away, and was lengthened by a chorus, not of human voices, but of all the sounds of the benighted wilderness pealing in awful harmony together. Goodman Brown cried out, and his cry was lost to his own ear by its unison with the cry of the desert.

In the interval of silence he stole forward until the light glared full upon his eyes. At one extremity of an open space, hemmed in by the dark wall of the forest, arose a rock, bearing some rude, natural resemblance either to an altar or a pulpit, and surrounded by four blazing pines, their tops aflame, their stems untouched, like candles at an evening meeting. The mass of foliage that had overgrown the summit of the rock was all on fire, blazing high into the night and fitfully illuminating the whole field. Each pendent twig and leafy festoon was in a blaze. As the red light arose and fell, a numerous congregation alternately shone forth, then disappeared in shadow, and again grew, as it were, out of the darkness, peopling the heart of the solitary woods at once.

"A grave and dark-clad company," quoth Goodman Brown.

In truth they were such. Among them, quivering to and fro between gloom and splendor, appeared faces that would be seen next day at the council board of the province, and others which, Sabbath after Sabbath, looked devoutly heavenward, and benignantly over the crowded pews, from the holiest pulpits in the land. Some affirm that the lady of the governor was there. At least there were high dames well known to her, and wives of honored husbands, and widows, a great multitude, and ancient maidens, all of excellent repute, and fair young girls, who trembled lest their mothers should espy them. Either the sudden gleams of light flashing over the obscure field bedazzled Goodman Brown, or he recognized a score of the church members of Salem village famous for their especial sanctity. Good old Deacon Gookin had arrived, and waited at the skirts of that venerable saint, his revered pastor. But, irreverently consorting with these grave, reputable, and pious people, these elders of the church, these chaste dames and dewy virgins, there were men of dissolute lives and women of spotted fame, wretches given over to all mean and filthy vice, and suspected even of horrid crimes. It was strange to see that the good shrank not from the wicked, nor were the sinners abashed by the saints. Scattered also among their pale-faced enemies were the Indian priests, or powwows, who had often scared their native forest with more hideous incantations than any known to English witchcraft.

"But where is Faith?" thought Goodman Brown; and, as hope came into his heart, he trembled.

Another verse of the hymn arose, a slow and mournful strain, such as the pious love, but joined to words which expressed all that our nature can conceive of sin, and darkly hinted at far more. Unfathomable to mere mortals is the lore of fiends. Verse after verse was sung; and still the chorus of the desert swelled between like the deepest tone of a mighty organ; and with the final peal of that dreadful anthem there came a sound, as if the roaring wind, the rushing streams, the howling beasts, and every other voice of the unconcerted wilderness were mingling and according with the voice of guilty man in homage to the prince of all. The four blazing pines threw up a loftier flame, and obscurely discovered shapes and visages of horror on the smoke wreaths above the impious assembly. At the same moment the fire on the rock shot redly forth and formed a glowing arch above its base, where now appeared a figure. With reverence be it spoken, the figure bore no slight similitude, both in garb and manner, to some grave divine of the New England churches.

"Bring forth the converts!" cried a voice that

echoed through the field and rolled into the forest.

At the word, Goodman Brown stepped forth from the shadow of the trees and approached the congregation, with whom he felt a loathful brotherhood by the sympathy of all that was wicked in his heart. He could have well-nigh sworn that the shape of his own dead father beckoned him to advance, looking downward from a smoke wreath, while a woman, with dim features of despair, threw out her hand to warn him back. Was it his mother? But he had no power to retreat one step, nor to resist, even in thought, when the minister and good old Deacon Gookin seized his arms and led him to the blazing rock. Thither came also the slender form of a veiled female, led between Goody Cloyse, that pious teacher of the catechism, and Martha Carrier, who had received the devil's promise to be queen of hell. A rampant hag was she. And there stood the proselytes beneath the canopy of fire.

"Welcome, my children," said the dark figure, "to the communion of your race. Ye have found thus young your nature and your destiny. My children, look behind you!"

They turned; and flashing forth, as it were, in a sheet of flame, the fiend worshippers were seen; the smile of welcome gleamed darkly on every visage.

"There," resumed the sable form, "are all whom ye have reverenced from youth. Ye deemed them holier than yourselves, and shrank from your own sin, contrasting it with their lives of righteousness and prayerful aspirations heavenward. Yet here are they all in my worshipping assembly. This night it shall be granted you to know their secret deeds: how hoary-bearded elders of the church have whispered wanton words to the young maids of their households; how many a woman, eager for widows' weeds, has given her husband a drink at bedtime and let him sleep his last sleep in her bosom; how beardless youths have made haste to inherit their fathers' wealth; and how fair damsels—blush not, sweet ones—have dug little graves in the garden, and bidden me, the sole guest, to an infant's funeral. By the sympathy of your human hearts for sin ye shall scent out all the places—whether in church, bedchamber, street, field, or forest—where crime has been committed, and shall exult to behold the whole earth one stain of guilt, one mighty blood spot. Far

more than this. It shall be yours to penetrate, in every bosom, the deep mystery of sin, the fountain of all wicked arts, and which inexhaustibly supplies more evil impulses than human power—than my power at its utmost—can make manifest in deeds. And now, my children, look upon each other."

They did so; and, by the blaze of the hell-kindled torches, the wretched man beheld his Faith, and the wife her husband, trembling before that unhallowed altar.

"Lo, there ye stand, my children," said the figure, in a deep and solemn tone, almost sad with its despairing awfulness, as if his once angelic nature could yet mourn for our miserable race. "Depending upon one another's hearts, ye had still hoped that virtue were not all a dream. Now are ye undeceived. Evil is the nature of mankind. Evil must be your only happiness. Welcome again, my children, to the communion of your race."

"Welcome," repeated the fiend worshippers, in one cry of despair and triumph.

And there they stood, the only pair, as it seemed, who were yet hesitating on the verge of wickedness in this dark world. A basin was hollowed, naturally, in the rock. Did it contain water, reddened by the lurid light? or was it blood? or, perchance, a liquid flame? Herein did the shape of evil dip his hand and prepare to lay the mark of baptism upon their foreheads, that they might be partakers of the mystery of sin, more conscious of the secret guilt of others, both in deed and thought, than they could now be of their own. The husband cast one look at his pale wife, and Faith at him. What polluted wretches would the next glance show them to each other, shuddering alike at what they disclosed and what they saw!

"Faith! Faith!" cried the husband, "look up to heaven, and resist the wicked one."

Whether Faith obeyed he knew not. Hardly had he spoken when he found himself amid calm night and solitude, listening to a roar of the wind which died heavily away through the forest. He staggered against the rock, and felt it chill and damp; while a hanging twig, that had been all on fire, besprinkled his cheek with the coldest dew.

The next morning young Goodman Brown came slowly into the street of Salem village, staring around him like a bewildered man. The good old minister was taking a walk along the graveyard to get an appetite for breakfast and meditate his sermon, and bestowed a blessing, as he passed, on Goodman Brown. He shrank from the venerable saint as if to avoid an anathema. Old Deacon Gookin was at domestic worship, and the holy words of his prayer were heard through the open window. "What God doth the wizard pray to?" quoth Goodman Brown. Goody Cloyse, that excellent old Christian, stood in the early sunshine at her own lattice, catechizing a little girl who had brought her a pint of morning's milk. Goodman Brown snatched away the child as from the grasp of the fiend himself. Turning the corner by the meeting-house, he spied the head of Faith, with the pink ribbons, gazing anxiously forth, and bursting into such joy at sight of him that she skipped along the street and almost kissed her husband before the whole village. But Goodman Brown looked sternly and sadly into her face, and passed on without a greeting.

Had Goodman Brown fallen asleep in the forest and only dreamed a wild dream of a witch-meeting?

Be it so if you will; but, alas! it was a dream of evil omen for young Goodman Brown. A stern, a sad, a darkly meditative, a distrustful, if not a desperate man did he become from the night of that fearful dream. On the Sabbath day, when the congregation were singing a holy psalm, he could not listen because an anthem of sin rushed loudly upon his ear and drowned all the blessed strain. When the minister spoke from the pulpit with power and fervid eloquence, and, with his hand on the open Bible, of the sacred truths of our religion, and of saint-like lives and triumphant deaths, and of future bliss or misery unutterable, then did Goodman Brown turn pale, dreading lest the roof should thunder down upon the gray blasphemer and his hearers. Often, waking suddenly at midnight, he shrank from the bosom of Faith; and at morning or eventide, when the family knelt down at prayer, he scowled and muttered to himself, and gazed sternly at his wife, and turned away. And when he had lived long, and was borne to his grave a hoary corpse, followed by Faith, an aged woman, and children and grandchildren, a goodly procession, besides neighbors not a few, they carved no hopeful verse upon his tombstone, for his dying hour was gloom.

## *Joseph Addison*
# THE SPACIOUS FIRMAMENT ON HIGH

The spacious firmament on high,
With all the blue ethereal sky,
And spangled heavens, a shining frame,
Their great Original proclaim.
Th' unwearied Sun from day to day
Does his Creator's power display;
And publishes to every land
The work of an Almighty hand.

Soon as the evening shades prevail,
The Moon takes up the wondrous tale;      10
And nightly to the listening Earth
Repeats the story of her birth:
Whilst all the stars that round her burn,
And all the planets in their turn,
Confirm the tidings as they roll,
And spread the truth from pole to pole.

What though in solemn silence all
Move round the dark terrestrial ball;
What though no real voice nor sound
Amidst their radiant orbs be found?      20
In Reason's ear they all rejoice,
And utter forth a glorious voice;
Forever singing as they shine,
"The Hand that made us is divine."

## *Thomas Hardy*
# NATURE'S QUESTIONING

When I look forth at dawning, pool,
    Field, flock, and lonely tree,
    All seem to gaze at me
Like chastened children sitting silent in a school;

Their faces dulled, constrained, and worn,
  As though the master's ways
  Through the long teaching days
Had cowed them till their early zest was overborne.

  Upon them stirs in lippings mere
    (As if once clear in call,          10
    But now scarce breathed at all)—
"We wonder, ever wonder, why we find us here!

  "Has some Vast Imbecility,
    Mighty to build and blend,
    But impotent to tend,
Framed us in jest, and left us now to hazardry?

  "Or come we of an Automaton
    Unconscious of our pains? . . .
    Or are we live remains
Of Godhead dying downwards, brain and eye now
    gone?                20

  "Or is it that some high Plan betides,
    As yet not understood,
    Of Evil stormed by Good,
We the Forlorn Hope over which Achievement
    strides?"

  Thus things around. No answerer I . . .
    Meanwhile the winds, and rains,
    And Earth's old glooms and pains
Are still the same, and Life and Death are
    neighbors nigh.

## Archibald MacLeish
# THE END OF THE WORLD

Quite unexpectedly as Vasserot
The armless ambidextrian was lighting
A match between his great and second toe
And Ralph the lion was engaged in biting
The neck of Madame Sossman while the drum
Pointed, and Teeny was about to cough
In waltz-time swinging Jocko by the thumb—
Quite unexpectedly the top blew off:

And there, there overhead, there, there, hung over
Those thousands of white faces, those dazed
  eyes,                 10
There in the starless dark the poise, the hover,
There with vast wings across the canceled skies,
There in the sudden blackness the black pall
Of nothing, nothing, nothing—nothing at all.

## John Betjeman
# IN WESTMINSTER ABBEY

Let me take this other glove off
  As the *vox humana* swells,
And the beauteous fields of Eden
  Bask beneath the Abbey bells.
Here, where England's statesmen lie,
Listen to a lady's cry.

Gracious Lord, oh bomb the Germans.
  Spare their women for Thy sake,
And if that is not too easy
  We will pardon Thy Mistake.      10
But, gracious Lord, whate'er shall be,
Don't let anyone bomb me.

Keep our Empire undismembered
  Guide our Forces by Thy Hand,
Gallant blacks from far Jamaica,
  Honduras and Togoland;
Protect them Lord in all their fights,
And, even more, protect the whites.

Think of what our Nation stands for,
  Books from Boots' and country lanes,    20
Free speech, free passes, class distinction,
  Democracy and proper drains.
Lord, put beneath Thy special care
One-eighty-nine Cadogan Square.

Although dear Lord I am a sinner,
  I have done no major crime;
Now I'll come to Evening Service
  Whensoever I have time.
So, Lord, reserve for me a crown,
And do not let my shares go down.    30

I will labour for Thy Kingdom,
  Help our lads to win the war,
Send white feathers to the cowards
  Join the Women's Army Corps,
Then wash the Steps around Thy Throne
In the Eternal Safety Zone.

Now I feel a little better,
  What a treat to hear Thy Word,
Where the bones of leading statesmen,
  Have so often been interr'd.                                        40
And now, dear Lord, I cannot wait
Because I have a luncheon date.

## *Robert Burns*
## HOLY WILLIE'S PRAYER

O Thou, wha [13] in the Heavens dost dwell,
Wha, as it pleases best thysel',
Sends ane [14] to heaven and ten to hell,
    A' [15] for thy glory,
And no for ony guid [16] or ill
    They've done afore thee!

I bless and praise thy matchless might,
Whan thousands thou hast left in night,
That I am here afore thy sight,
    For gifts an' grace                         10
A burnin' an' a shinin' light,
    To a' this place.

What was I, or my generation,[17]
That I should get sic [18] exaltation?
I, wha deserve most just damnation,
    For broken laws,
Sax [19] thousand years 'fore my creation,
    Thro' Adam's cause.

When frae [20] my mither's womb I fell,
Thou might hae [21] plungèd me in hell,     20
To gnash my gums, to weep and wail,
    In burnin' lakes,
Where damnèd devils roar and yell,
    Chained to their stakes;

Yet I am here a chosen sample,
To show thy grace is great and ample:
I'm here a pillar in thy temple,
    Strong as a rock,
A guide, a buckler,[22] an example
    To a' thy flock.                                      30

O Lord, thou kens [23] what zeal I bear,
When drinkers drink, and swearers swear,
And singin' there and dancin' here,
    Wi' great an' sma': [24]
For I am keepit by thy fear
    Free frae them a'.

But yet, O Lord! confess I must
At times I'm fashed [25] wi' fleshy lust;
An' sometimes too, in warldly trust,
    Vile self gets in;                                     40
But thou remembers we are dust,
    Defiled wi' sin.

O Lord! yestreen,[26] thou kens, wi' Meg—
Thy pardon I sincerely beg;
O! may 't ne'er be a livin' plague
    To my dishonour,
An' I'll ne'er lift a lawless leg
    Again upon her.

Besides, I farther maun [27] avow,
Wi' Leezie's lass, three times, I trow [28]—     50
But Lord, that Friday I was fou,[29]
    When I cam near her;
Or else, Thou kens, Thy servant true
    Wad [30] never steer [31] her.

Maybe Thou lets this fleshy thorn
Buffet Thy servant e'en and morn,
Lest he owre [32] proud and high should turn,
    That he's sae gifted: [33]
If sae, Thy han' [34] maun e'en be borne,
    Until Thou lift it.                                      60

Lord, bless Thy chosen in this place,
For here Thou has a chosen race:
But God confound their stubborn face,
    An' blast their name,
Wha bring Thy elders [35] to disgrace
    An' public shame.

---

[13] Who.      [14] One.      [15] All.
[16] Good.     [17] Beginning.     [18] Such.
[19] Six (an allusion to the traditional date of creation, 4004 b.c.).
[20] From.     [21] Have.

[22] Shield.        [23] Knowest.        [24] Small.
[25] Bothered by.   [26] Last night.     [27] Must.
[28] Believe.       [29] Full (of drink).   [30] Would.
[31] Molest.        [32] Overly.
[33] *i.e.,* by the grace of God.
[34] Hand.     [35] Church governors.

Lord, mind Gaw'n Hamilton's [36] deserts;
He drinks, an' swears, an' plays at cartes,[37]
Yet has sae mony [38] takin arts,
      Wi' great and sma',      70
Frae God's ain [39] priest the people's hearts
      He steals awa.[40]


An' when we chastened him therefor,
Thou kens how he bred sic a splore, [41]
An' set the warld in a roar
      O' laughin' at us;—
Curse Thou his basket and his store,
      Kail [42] an' potatoes.


Lord, hear my earnest cry and pray'r,
Against that Presbyt'ry o' Ayr; [43]      80
Thy strong right hand, Lord, make it bare
      Upo' their heads;
Lord, visit them, an' dinna [44] spare,
      For their misdeeds.


O Lord my God, that glib-tongu'd Aiken, [45]
My very heart and soul are quakin',
To think how we stood sweatin', shakin',
      An' pissed wi' dread,
While he, wi' hingin' [46] lips and snakin',[47]
      Held up his head.      90


Lord, in the day of vengeance try him;
Lord, visit him wha did employ him,
And pass not in thy mercy by them,
      Nor hear their pray'r:
But, for thy people's sake, destroy them,
      And dinna spare.


But, Lord, remember me and mine
Wi' mercies temp'ral and divine,
That I for gear [48] and grace may shine
      Excelled by nane,      100
And a' the glory shall be thine,
      Amen, Amen!

---

[36] A friend of Burns.    [37] Cards.
[38] Many.    [39] Own.
[40] Away.    [41] Bred such amusement.
[42] Greens.
[43] The church body that tried the case when Holy
Willie charged Hamilton with immorality.
[44] Do not.    [45] Hamilton's lawyer.
[46] Hanging.    [47] Sneering.
[48] Worldly goods.

## T. S. Eliot
# THE HOLLOW MEN

*Mistah Kurtz—he dead.*

*A penny for the Old Guy.*[49]

### I

We are the hollow men
We are the stuffed men
Leaning together
Headpiece filled with straw. Alas!
Our dried voices, when
We whisper together
Are quiet and meaningless
As wind in dry grass
Or rats' feet over broken glass
In our dry cellar      10


Shape without form, shade without colour,
Paralysed force, gesture without motion;


Those who have crossed
With direct eyes, to death's other Kingdom
Remember us—if at all—not as lost
Violent souls, but only
As the hollow men
The stuffed men.


### II

Eyes I dare not meet in dreams
In death's dream kingdom      20
These do not appear:
There, the eyes are
Sunlight on a broken column
There, is a tree swinging
And voices are
In the wind's singing
More distant and more solemn
Than a fading star.

---

THE HOLLOW MEN: From *Collected Poems 1909–1935,* by T. S. Eliot. Copyright, 1936, by Harcourt, Brace and Company, Inc. Used by permission of Harcourt, Brace and Company, Inc., and Faber and Faber, Ltd.

[49] The first phrase is quoted from *Heart of Darkness,* by Joseph Conrad; the second is the cry with which English children beg for pennies on Guy Fawkes Day, November 5.

Let me be no nearer
In death's dream kingdom                                    30
Let me also wear
Such deliberate disguises
Rat's coat, crowskin, crossed staves
In a field
Behaving as the wind behaves
No nearer—

Not that final meeting
In the twilight kingdom

### III

This is the dead land
This is cactus land                                              40
Here the stone images
Are raised, here they receive
The supplication of a dead man's hand
Under the twinkle of a fading star.

Is it like this
In death's other kingdom
Waking alone
At the hour when we are
Trembling with tenderness
Lips that would kiss                                            50
Form prayers to broken stone.

### IV

The eyes are not here
There are no eyes here
In this valley of dying stars
In this hollow valley
This broken jaw of our lost kingdoms

In this last of meeting places
We grope together
And avoid speech
Gathered on this beach of the tumid river        60

Sightless, unless
The eyes reappear
As the perpetual star
Multifoliate rose
Of death's twilight kingdom
The hope only
Of empty men.

### V

*Here we go round the prickly pear*
*Prickly pear prickly pear*
*Here we go round the prickly pear*                     70
*At five o'clock in the morning.*

Between the idea
And the reality
Between the motion
And the act
Falls the shadow
    *For Thine is the Kingdom*

Between the conception
And the creation
Between the emotion                                            80
And the response
Falls the Shadow
    *Life is very long*

Between the desire
And the spasm
Between the potency
And the existence
Between the essence
And the descent
Falls the Shadow                                                90
    *For Thine is the Kingdom*

For Thine is
Life is
For Thine is the

*This is the way the world ends*
*This is the way the world ends*
*This is the way the world ends*
*Not with a bang but a whimper.*

*George Herbert*

# EASTER WINGS

Lord, who createdst man in wealth and store,
    Though foolishly he lost the same,
        Decaying more and more
            Till he became
                Most poor;
                With Thee
            O let me rise
        As larks, harmoniously,
    And sing this day Thy victories;
Then shall the fall further the flight in me.   10

My tender age in sorrow did begin;
  And still with sickness and shame
    Thou didst so punish sin,
      That I became
        Most thin.
        With Thee
      Let me combine,
    And feel this day Thy victory;
  For if I imp [50] my wing on Thine,
Affliction shall advance the flight in me. 20

---

[50] Graft.

## John Donne
# HOLY SONNET 7

At the round earth's imagined corners, blow
Your trumpets, angels; and arise, arise
From death, you numberless infinities
Of souls, and to your scattered bodies go;
All whom the flood did, and fire shall, o'erthrow,
All whom war, dearth, age, agues, tyrannies,
Despair, law, chance hath slain, and you whose
  eyes
Shall behold God, and never taste death's woe.
But let them sleep, Lord, and me mourn a space;
For, if above all these, my sins abound,          10
'Tis late to ask abundance of Thy grace
When we are there. Here on this lowly ground,
Teach me how to repent; for that's as good
As if Thou hadst sealed my pardon with Thy blood.

## John Donne
# HOLY SONNET 10

Death, be not proud, though some have callèd thee
Mighty and dreadful, for thou art not so;
For those whom thou think'st thou dost overthrow

Die not, poor Death, nor yet canst thou kill me.
From rest and sleep, which but thy pictures be,
Much pleasure; then from thee much more must
  flow,
And soonest our best men with thee do go,
Rest of their bones, and souls' delivery.
Thou art slave to fate, chance, kings, and desperate
  men,
And dost with poison, war, and sickness dwell,  10
And poppy [51] or charms can make us sleep as well
And better than thy stroke; why swell'st thou,
  then?
One short sleep past, we wake eternally,
And Death shall be no more; Death, thou shalt die.

---

[51] Opium.

## John Donne
# HOLY SONNET 14

Batter my heart, three-personed [52] God; for You
As yet but knock, breathe, shine, and seek to
  mend;
That I may rise, and stand, o'erthrow me, and bend
Your force, to break, blow, burn, and make me
  new.
I, like an usurped town to another due,
Labor to admit You, but oh! to no end;
Reason, Your viceroy in me, me should defend,
But is captived and proves weak or untrue.
Yet dearly I love You, and would be loved fain,
But am betrothed unto Your enemy.              10
Divorce me, untie, or break that knot again,
Take me to You, imprison me, for I
Except You enthrall me, never shall be free;
Nor ever chaste, except You ravish me.

---

[52] *i.e.,* the Trinity: Father, Son, and Holy Ghost.

## Gerard Manley Hopkins
# THE WINDHOVER

TO CHRIST OUR LORD

I caught this morning morning's minion, king-
    dom of daylight's dauphin, dapple-dawn-drawn Falcon, in his riding
    Of the rolling level underneath him steady air, and striding
High there, how he rung upon the rein of a wimpling wing
In his ecstasy! then off, off forth on swing,
    As a skate's heel sweeps smooth on a bow-bend: the hurl and gliding
    Rebuffed the big wind. My heart in hiding
Stirred for a bird,—the achieve of, the mastery of the thing!

Brute beauty and valour and act, oh, air, pride, plume, here
    Buckle! AND the fire that breaks from thee then, a billion    10
Times told lovelier, more dangerous, O my chevalier!

    No wonder of it: shéer plód makes plough down sillion
Shine, and blue-bleak embers, ah my dear,
    Fall, gall themselves, and gash gold-vermilion.

THE WINDHOVER: From *The Poems of Gerard Manley Hopkins.* Used by permission of the Oxford University Press.

## Karl Shapiro
# THE LEG

Among the iodoform, in twilight-sleep,
*What have I lost?* he first inquires,
Peers in the middle distance where a pain,
Ghost of a nurse, hastily moves, and day,
Her blinding presence pressing in his eyes
And now his ears. They are handling him
With rubber hands. He wants to get up.

One day beside some flowers near his nose
He will be thinking, *When will I look at it?*
And pain, still in the middle distance, will reply, 10
*At what?* and he will know it's gone,
O where! and begin to tremble and cry.
He will begin to cry as a child cries
Whose puppy is mangled under a screaming wheel.

Later, as if deliberately, his fingers
Begin to explore the stump. He learns a shape

THE LEG: From *Poems 1940–1953,* by Karl Shapiro. Copyright, 1944, by Karl Shapiro. Used by permission of Random House, Inc.

That is comfortable and tucked in like a sock.
This has a sense of humor, this can despise
The finest surgical limb, the dignity of limping,
The nonsense of wheel-chairs. Now he smiles to
    the wall:    20
The amputation becomes an acquisition.

For the leg is wondering where he is (all is not
    lost)
And surely he has a duty to the leg;
He is its injury, the leg is his orphan,
He must cultivate the mind of the leg,
Pray for the part that is missing, pray for peace
In the image of man, pray, pray for its safety,
And after a little it will die quietly.

The body, what is it, Father, but a sign
To love the force that grows us, to give back    30
What in Thy palm is senselessness and mud?
Knead, knead the substance of our understanding
Which must be beautiful in flesh to walk,
That if Thou take me angrily in hand
And hurl me to the shark, I shall not die!

# LAST DAYS

ONE OF the oldest uses of literature is that it holds up to man his own images of death, along with its harbinger, old age, and objectifies his feelings about them for contemplation. When we are young we are little given, doubtless, to brooding about the end of life; nor do we then feel the need of inoculating ourselves against the terrors of death by facing up to them in small doses, vicariously, through literary experience. But this is one way of testing one's skill as a reader: to see whether the imagination can be stretched to share the feelings of those who are dying or bereaved. The literature of this subject leads to some profoundly interesting questions, for as Stevenson says in "Aes Triplex," death "stands alone in man's experience."

The common element of the works in this chapter is that each concerns someone who, coming into immediate contact with death, is brought into a new relation with himself through his awareness of death's possible meanings. Some of these works show us a person faced with the death of someone else. He may be indifferent, like the drivers in Tolstoy's "Three Deaths"; or ironically detached, like the speaker in Ransom's "Dead Boy"; or saddened, like the speaker in the poems by Tennyson; or brought half-comprehendingly closer to maturity, as are the two children in "The Grave." In other works, the chief character is faced with the nearness of his own death, and the range of possible emotions extends from the terror of Claudio in *Measure for Measure* to the hope of eternal blessedness evinced by Donne and Jeremy Taylor. Other attitudes complicate the possibilities, as appears in the willingness of Stevenson, Hazlitt, and the old man in "The Last Day in the Field" to make

526

the most of life whatever threatens. From another point of view, death may provide a symbolic meaning for the higher goods of life itself, as is suggested in "Ode to a Nightingale" and "Sailing to Byzantium."

Among the subjects of literature, that of death has a special place. It has generally been considered essential to one literary mode, namely tragedy, though of course not every death is a tragic one. In the broad sense, *The Doctor and the Devils* may be called a tragedy, though the hero does not die, but is merely ruined; Antigone and Othello end their stories with their lives, their deaths seeming both inevitable dramatically and right symbolically, for in them the characters and achievements of the tragic figures are crystallized. This chapter leads directly into the next, and some of its meaning may be brought out by a comparison of *Antigone* and *Othello,* and by further consideration of the nature of tragedy and the reasons for its pre-eminence among literary forms.

## *Sir Francis Bacon*
## OF YOUTH AND AGE

A man that is young in years may be old in hours, if he have lost no time. But that happeneth rarely. Generally youth is like the first cogitations, not so wise as the second. For there is a youth in thoughts as well as in ages. And yet the invention of young men is more lively than that of old; and imaginations stream into their minds better, and, as it were, more divinely.

Natures that have much heat, and great and violent desires and perturbations, are not ripe for action till they have passed the meridian of their years; as it was with Julius Caesar and Septimius Severus, of the latter of whom it is said, *Juventutem egit erroribus, imo furoribus, plenam.*[1] And yet he was the ablest emperor, almost, of all the list. But reposed natures may do well in youth, as it is seen in Augustus Caesar, Cosmus[2] Duke of Florence, Gaston de Fois,[3] and others.

On the other side, heat and vivacity in age is an excellent composition for business. Young men are fitter to invent than to judge, fitter for execution than for counsel, and fitter for new projects than for settled business. For the experience of age, in things that fall within the compass of it, directeth them, but in new things abuseth[4] them.

The errors of young men are the ruin of business; but the errors of aged men amount but to this,—that more might have been done, or sooner. Young men, in the conduct and manage of actions, embrace more than they can hold; stir more than they can quiet; fly to the end, without consideration of the means and degrees; pursue some few principles, which they have chanced upon, absurdly; care not to innovate,[5] which draws unknown inconveniences; use extreme remedies at first; and, that which doubleth all errors, will not acknowledge or retract them; like an unready horse, that will neither stop nor turn.

Men of age object too much, consult too long, adventure too little, repent too soon, and seldom drive business home to the full period, but content themselves with a mediocrity of success.

Certainly it is good to compound employments of both:[6] for that will be good for the present, because the virtues of either age may correct the defects of both; and good for succession, that young men may be learners, while men in age are actors; and, lastly, good for extern accidents,[7] because authority followeth old men, and favour and popularity, youth.

But, for the moral part, perhaps, youth will have the pre-eminence, as age hath for the

---

[1] "His youth was full of errors, even acts of madness." Severus was a Roman emperor, 193–211.

[2] Cosimo de Medici, 1389–1464.

[3] French general, 1489–1512.

[4] Misleads.

[5] Are not cautious about introducing new plans.

[6] *i.e.,* to employ both young and old.

[7] External attributes.

politic. A certain Rabbin[8] upon the text, "Your young men shall see visions, and your old men shall dream dreams," inferreth that young men are admitted nearer to God than old, because vision is a clearer revelation than a dream. And certainly the more a man drinketh of the world, the more it intoxicateth; and age doth profit rather in the powers of understanding, than in the virtues of the will and affections.

There be some have an over-early ripeness in their years, which fadeth betimes. These are, first, such as have brittle wits, the edge whereof is soon turned; such as was Hermogenes,[9] the rhetorician, whose books are exceedingly subtile, who afterwards waxed stupid. A second sort is of those that have some natural dispositions which have better grace in youth than in age; such as is a fluent and luxuriant speech, which becomes youth well, but not age. So Tully[10] saith of Hortensius, *Idem manebat, neque idem decebat.* The third is of such as take too high a strain at the first, and are magnanimous more than tract of years can uphold. As was Scipio Africanus, of whom Livy saith in effect, *Ultima primis cedebant.*[11]

---

[8] Rabbi Isaac Abrabanel.

[9] A Greek rhetorician, said to have lost his memory at the age of twenty-three.

[10] Cicero, who said of the orator Hortensius, "He remained the same, and it was not becoming."

[11] "His final actions did not come up to his first ones"; *i.e.,* his victories over Hannibal and the Carthaginians in 202 B.C.

*William Hazlitt*

## ON THE FEAR OF DEATH

And our little life is rounded with a sleep.

Perhaps the best cure for the fear of death is to reflect that life has a beginning as well as an end. There was a time when we were not: this gives us no concern—why then should it trouble us that a time will come when we shall cease to be? I have no wish to have been alive a hundred years ago, or in the reign of Queen Anne: why should I regret and lay it so much to heart that I shall not be alive a hundred years hence, in the reign of I cannot tell whom?

When Bickerstaff[12] wrote his Essays, I knew nothing of the subjects of them: nay, much later, and but the other day, as it were, in the beginning of the reign of George III,[13] when Goldsmith, Johnson, Burke used to meet at the Globe, when Garrick was in his glory, and Reynolds was over head and ears with his portraits, and Sterne brought out the volumes of *Tristram Shandy* year by year, it was without consulting me: I had not the slightest intimation of what was going on: the debates in the House of Commons on the American war, or the firing at Bunker's Hill, disturbed not me: yet I thought this no evil—I neither ate, drank, nor was merry, yet I did not complain: I had not then looked out into this breathing world, yet I was well; and the world did quite as well without me as I did without it! Why then should I make all this outcry about parting with it, and being no worse off than I was before? There is nothing in the recollection that at a certain time we were not come into the world, that "the gorge rises at"—why should we revolt at the idea that we must one day go out of it? To die is only to be as we were before we were born; yet no one feels any remorse, or regret, or repugnance, in contemplating this last idea. It is rather a relief and disburthening of the mind: it seems to have been holiday-time with us then: we were not called to appear upon the stage of life, to wear robes or tatters, to laugh or cry, be hooted or applauded; we had lain *perdus*[14] all this while, snug, out of harm's way; and had slept out our thousands of centuries without wanting to be waked up; at peace and free from care, in a long nonage, in a sleep deeper and calmer than that of infancy, wrapped in the softest and finest dust. And the worst that we dread is, after a short, fretful, feverish being, after vain hopes, and idle fears, to sink to final repose again, and forget the troubled dream of life! . . . Ye armed men, knights templars, that sleep in the stone aisles of that old Temple Church, where all is silent above, and where a deeper silence reigns below (not broken by the pealing organ), are ye not contented where ye lie? Or would you come out of your long homes to go to the Holy War? Or do ye complain that

---

[12] Pseudonym used by Richard Steele for his *Tatler* essays, begun in 1709.

[13] *i.e.,* about 1760–1774.

[14] Hidden.

pain no longer visits you, that sickness has done its worst, that you have paid the last debt to nature, that you hear no more of the thickening phalanx of the foe, or your lady's waning love; and that while this ball of earth rolls its eternal round, no sound shall ever pierce through to disturb your lasting repose, fixed as the marble over your tombs, breathless as the grave that holds you! And thou, oh! thou, to whom my heart turns, and will turn while it has feeling left, who didst love in vain, and whose first was thy last sigh, wilt not thou too rest in peace (or wilt thou cry to me complaining from thy clay-cold bed) when that sad heart is no longer sad, and that sorrow is dead which thou wert only called into the world to feel!

It is certain that there is nothing in the idea of a pre-existent state that excites our longing like the prospect of a posthumous existence. We are satisfied to have begun life when we did; we have no ambition to have set out on our journey sooner; and feel that we have had quite enough to do to battle our way through since. We cannot say,

The wars we well remember of King Nine,
Of old Assaracus and Inachus divine.

Neither have we any wish: we are contented to read of them in story, and to stand and gaze at the vast sea of time that separates us from them. It was early days then: the world was not well-aired enough for us: we have no inclination to have been up and stirring. We do not consider the six thousand years of the world before we were born as so much time lost to us: we are perfectly indifferent about the matter. We do not grieve and lament that we did not happen to be in time to see the grand mask and pageant of human life going on in all that period; though we are mortified at being obliged to quit our station before the rest of the procession passes.

It may be suggested in explanation of this difference, that we know from various records and traditions what happened in the time of Queen Anne, or even in the reigns of the Assyrian monarchs: but that we have no means of ascertaining what is to happen hereafter but by awaiting the event, and that our eagerness and curiosity are sharpened in proportion as we are in the dark about it. This is not at all the case; for at that rate we should be constantly wishing to make a voyage of discovery to Greenland

or to the Moon, neither of which we have, in general, the least desire to do. Neither, in truth, have we any particular solicitude to pry into the secrets of futurity, but as a pretext for prolonging our own existence. It is not so much that we care to be alive a hundred or a thousand years hence, any more than to have been alive a hundred or a thousand years ago: but the thing lies here, that we would all of us wish the present moment to last for ever. We would be as we are, and would have the world remain just as it is, to please us.

The present eye catches the present object—

to have and to hold while it may; and we abhor, on any terms, to have it torn from us, and nothing left in its room. It is the pang of parting, the unloosing our grasp, the breaking asunder some strong tie, the leaving some cherished purpose unfulfilled, that creates the repugnance to go, and "makes calamity of so long life," as it often is.

                                —Oh! thou strong heart!
There's such a covenant 'twixt the world and thee,
Ye're loth to break!

The love of life, then, is an habitual attachment, not an abstract principle. Simply *to be* does not "content man's natural desire": we long to be in a certain time, place, and circumstance. We would much rather be now, "on this bank and shoal of time," than have our choice of any future period, than take a slice of fifty or sixty years out of the Millennium, for instance. This shows that our attachment is not confined either to *being* or to *well-being;* but that we have an inveterate prejudice in favour of our immediate existence, such as it is. The mountaineer will not leave his rock; nor the savage his hut; neither are we willing to give up our present mode of life, with all its advantages and disadvantages, for any other that could be substituted for it. No man would, I think, exchange his existence with any other man, however fortunate. We had as lief *not be, as not be ourselves.* There are some persons of that reach of soul that they would like to live two hundred and fifty years hence, to see to what height of empire America will have grown up in that period, or whether the English constitution will last so long. These are points beyond me. But I confess I should like to live to see the downfall of the Bourbons.[15] That is a vital question with me; and I shall like it the better, the sooner it happens!

No young man ever thinks he shall die. He may believe that others will, or assent to the doctrine that "all men are mortal" as an abstract proposition, but he is far enough from bringing it home to himself individually. Youth, buoyant activity, and animal spirits, hold absolute antipathy with old age as well as with death; nor have we, in the hey-day of life, any more than in the thoughtlessness of childhood, the remotest conception how

> This sensible warm motion can become
> A kneaded clod—

nor how sanguine, florid health and vigour, shall "turn to withered, weak, and grey." Or if in a moment of idle speculation we indulge in this notion of the close of life as a theory, it is amazing at what a distance it seems; what a long, leisurely interval there is between; what a contrast its slow and solemn approach affords to our present gay dreams of existence! We eye the farthest verge of the horizon, and think what a way we shall have to look back upon, ere we arrive at our journey's end; and without our in the least suspecting it, the mists are at our feet, and the shadows of age encompass us. The two divisions of our lives have melted into each other: the extreme points close and meet with none of that romantic interval stretching out between them, that we had reckoned upon; and for the rich, melancholy, solemn hues of age, "the sear, the yellow leaf," the deepening shadows of an autumnal evening, we only feel a dank, cold mist encircling all objects, after the spirit of youth is fled. There is no inducement to look forward; and what is worse, little interest in looking back to what has become so trite and common. The pleasures of our existence have worn themselves out, are "gone into the wastes of time," or have turned their indifferent side to us: the pains by their repeated blows have worn us out, and have left us neither spirit nor inclination to encounter them again in retrospect. We do not want to rip up old grievances, nor to renew our youth like the phœnix, nor to live our lives twice over. Once is enough. As the tree falls, so let it lie. We shut up the book and close the account once for all!

It has been thought by some that life is like the exploring of a passage that grows narrower and darker the farther we advance, without a possibility of ever turning back, and where we are stifled for want of breath at last. For myself, I do not complain of the greater thickness of the atmosphere as I approach the *narrow house*. I felt it more formerly, when the idea alone seemed to suppress a thousand rising hopes, and weighed upon the pulses of the blood. At present I rather feel a thinness and want of support, I stretch out my hand to some object and find none, I am too much in a world of abstraction; the naked map of life is spread out before me, and in the emptiness and desolation I see Death coming to meet me. In my youth I could not behold him for the crowd of objects and feelings, and Hope stood always between us, saying—"Never mind that old fellow!" If I had lived *indeed,* I should not care to die. But I do not like a contract of pleasure broken off unfulfilled, a marriage with joy unconsummated, a promise of happiness rescinded. My public and private hopes have been left a ruin, or remain only to mock me. I would wish them to be re-edified. I should like to see some prospect of good to mankind, such as my life began with. I should like to leave some sterling work behind me. I should like to have some friendly hand to consign me to the grave. On these conditions I am ready, if not willing, to depart. I could then write on my tomb—GRATEFUL AND CONTENTED! But I have thought and suffered too much to be willing to have thought and suffered in vain.—In looking back, it sometimes appears to me as if I had in a manner slept out my life in a dream or trance on the side of the hill of knowledge, where I have fed on books, on thoughts, on pictures, and only heard in half-murmurs the trampling of busy feet, or the noises of the throng below. Waked out of this dim, twilight existence, and startled with the passing scene, I have felt a wish to descend to the world of realities, and join in the chase. But I fear too late, and that I had better return to my bookish chimeras and indolence once more! *Zanetto, lascia le donne, et studia la matematica.*[16] I will think of it.

---

[15] The dynasty which again ruled France after the restoration of Louis XVIII in 1815.

[16] "Leave women alone, Zanetto. and study mathematics."

It is not wonderful that the contemplation and fear of death become more familiar to us as we approach nearer to it: that life seems to ebb with the decay of blood and youthful spirits; and that as we find every thing about us subject to chance and change, as our strength and beauty die, as our hopes and passions, our friends and our affections leave us, we begin by degrees to feel ourselves mortal!

I have never seen death but once, and that was in an infant. It is years ago. The look was calm and placid, and the face was fair and firm. It was as if a waxen image had been laid out in the coffin, and strewed with innocent flowers. It was not like death, but more like an image of life! No breath moved the lips, no pulse stirred, no sight or sound would enter those eyes or ears more. While I looked at it, I saw no pain was there; it seemed to smile at the short pang of life which was over: but I could not bear the coffin-lid to be closed—it almost stifled me; and still as the nettles wave in a corner of the church-yard over his little grave, the welcome breeze helps to refresh me and ease the tightness at my breast!

An ivory or marble image, like Chantry's monument of the two children, is contemplated with pure delight. Why do we not grieve and fret that the marble is not alive, or fancy that it has a shortness of breath? It never was alive; and it is the difficulty of making the transition from life to death, the struggle between the two in our imagination, that confounds their properties painfully together, and makes us conceive that the infant that is but just dead, still wants to breathe, to enjoy, and look about it, and is prevented by the icy hand of death, locking up its faculties and benumbing its senses; so that, if it could, it would complain of its own hard state. Perhaps religious considerations reconcile the mind to this change sooner than any others, by representing the spirit as fled to another sphere, and leaving the body behind it. But in reflecting on death generally, we mix up the idea of life with it, and thus make it the ghastly monster it is. We think how we should feel, not how the dead feel.

Still from the tomb the voice of nature cries;
Even in our ashes live their wonted fires!

There is an admirable passage on this subject in Tucker's *Light of Nature Pursued,* which I shall transcribe, as by much the best illustration I can offer of it.

"The melancholy appearance of a lifeless body, the mansion provided for it to inhabit, dark, cold, close and solitary, are shocking to the imagination; but it is to the imagination only, not the understanding; for whoever consults this faculty will see at first glance, that there is nothing dismal in all these circumstances: if the corpse were kept wrapped up in a warm bed, with a roasting fire in the chamber, it would feel no comfortable warmth therefrom; were store of tapers lighted up as soon as day shuts in, it would see no objects to divert it; were it left at large it would have no liberty, nor if surrounded with company would be cheered thereby; neither are the distorted features expressions of pain, uneasiness, or distress. This every one knows, and will readily allow upon being suggested, yet still cannot behold, nor even cast a thought upon those objects without shuddering; for knowing that a living person must suffer grievously under such appearances, they become habitually formidable to the mind, and strike a mechanical horror, which is increased by the customs of the world around us."

There is usually one pang added voluntarily and unnecessarily to the fear of death, by our affecting to compassionate the loss which others will have in us. If that were all, we might reasonably set our minds at rest. The pathetic exhortation on country tombstones, "Grieve not for me, my wife and children dear," &c. is for the most part speedily followed to the letter. We do not leave so great a void in society as we are inclined to imagine, partly to magnify our own importance, and partly to console ourselves by sympathy. Even in the same family the gap is not so great; the wound closes up sooner than we should expect. Nay, *our room* is not unfrequently thought better than *our company.* People walk along the streets the day after our deaths just as they did before, and the crowd is not diminished. While we were living, the world seemed in a manner to exist only for us, for our delight and amusement, because it contributed to them. But our hearts cease to beat, and it goes on as usual, and thinks no more about us than it did in our life-time. The million are devoid of sentiment, and care as little for you or me as if we belonged to the moon. We live the week over in the Sunday's newspaper, or are decently interred in some obituary at the month's end. It is not surprising that we are forgotten so soon after we quit this mortal stage: we are scarcely noticed, while we are on it. It is not merely that our names are not known in China—they have hardly been heard of in the next street. We are hand and glove with the universe, and think the obligation is mutual. This is an evident fallacy. If this, however, does not trouble us now, it will not hereafter. A handful of dust can have no quarrel to pick with its neighbours, or complaint to make against Providence, and might well exclaim, if it had but an understanding and a tongue, "Go thy ways, old world, swing round in blue ether, voluble to every age, you and I shall no more jostle!"

It is amazing how soon the rich and titled, and even some of those who have wielded great political power, are forgotten:

> A little rule, a little sway,
> Is all the great and mighty have
> Betwixt the cradle and the grave—

and, after its short date, they hardly leave a name behind them. "A great man's memory may, at the common rate, survive him half a year." His heirs and successors take his titles, his power, and his wealth—all that made him considerable or courted by others; and he has left nothing else behind him either to flatter or benefit the world. Posterity are not by any means so disinterested as they are supposed to be. They give their gratitude and admiration only in return for benefits conferred. They cherish the memory of those to whom they are indebted for instruction and delight; and they cherish it just in proportion to the instruction and delight they are conscious of receiving. The sentiment of admiration springs immediately from this ground; and cannot be otherwise than well founded.

The effeminate clinging to life as such, as a general or abstract idea, is the effect of a highly civilised and artificial state of society. Men formerly plunged into all the vicissitudes and dangers of war, or staked their all upon a single die, or some one passion, which if they could not have gratified, life became a burthen to them—now our strongest passion is to think, our chief amusement is to read new plays, new poems, new novels, and this we may do at our leisure, in perfect security, *ad infinitum*. If we

look into the old histories and romances, before the *belles-lettres* neutralised human affairs and reduced passion to a state of mental equivocation, we find the heroes and heroines not setting their lives "at a pin's fee," but rather courting opportunities of throwing them away in very wantonness of spirit. They raise their fondness for some favourite pursuit to its height, to a pitch of madness, and think no price too dear to pay for its full gratification. Every thing else is dross. They go to death as to a bridal bed, and sacrifice themselves or others without remorse at the shrine of love, of honour, of religion, or any other prevailing feeling. Romeo runs his "sea-sick, weary bark upon the rocks" of death, the instant he finds himself deprived of his Juliet; and she clasps his neck in their last agonies, and follows him to the same fatal shore. One strong idea takes possession of the mind and overrules every other; and even life itself, joyless without that, becomes an object of indifference or loathing. There is at least more of imagination in such a state of things, more vigour of feeling and promptitude to act than in our lingering, languid, protracted attachment to life for its own poor sake. It is, perhaps, also better, as well as more heroical, to strike at some daring or darling object, and if we fail in that, to take the consequences manfully, than to renew the lease of a tedious, spiritless, charmless existence, merely (as Pierre [17] says) "to lose it afterwards in some vile brawl" for some worthless object. Was there not a spirit of martyrdom as well as a spice of the reckless energy of barbarism in this bold defiance of death? Had not religion something to do with it; the implicit belief in another state of being, which rendered this of less value, and embodied something beyond it to the imagination; so that the rough soldier, the infatuated lover, the valorous knight, &c. could afford to throw away the present venture, and take a leap into the arms of futurity, which the modern sceptic shrinks back from, with all his boasted reason and vain philosophy, weaker than a woman! I cannot help thinking so myself; but I have endeavoured to explain this point before, and will not enlarge farther on it here.

A life of action and danger moderates the

---

[17] In *Venice Preserved,* by Thomas Otway, Act IV, Sc. 2, Pierre says, "To lose it, may be, at last in a lewd quarrel."

dread of death. It not only gives us fortitude to bear pain, but teaches us at every step the precarious tenure on which we hold our present being. Sedentary and studious men are the most apprehensive on this score. Dr. Johnson was an instance in point. A few years seemed to him soon over, compared with those sweeping contemplations on time and infinity with which he had been used to pose himself. In the *still-life* of a man of letters, there was no obvious reason for a change. He might sit in an arm-chair and pour out cups of tea to all eternity. Would it had been possible for him to do so! The most rational cure after all for the inordinate fear of death is to set a just value on life. If we merely wish to continue on the scene to indulge our headstrong humours and tormenting passions, we had better begone at once: and if we only cherish a fondness for existence according to the benefits we reap from it, the pang we feel at parting with it will not be very severe!

## James Boswell
# THE DEATH OF JOHNSON

It is not my intention to give a very minute detail of the particulars of Johnson's remaining days, of whom it was now evident that the crisis was fast approaching when he must *die like men, and fall like one of the Princes.*[18] Yet it will be instructive, as well as gratifying to the curiosity of my readers, to record a few circumstances, on the authenticity of which they may perfectly rely, as I have been at the utmost pains to obtain an accurate account of his last illness, from the best authority.

Dr. Heberden, Dr. Brocklesby, Dr. Warren, and Dr. Butter, physicians, generously attended him, without accepting of any fees, as did Mr. Cruikshank, surgeon; and all that could be done from professional skill and ability was tried, to prolong a life so truly valuable. He himself, indeed, having, on account of his very bad constitution, been perpetually applying himself to medical inquiries, united his own efforts with those of the gentlemen who attended him; and imagining that the dropsical collection of water which oppressed him might

be drawn off by making incisions in his body, he, with his usual resolute defiance of pain, cut deep, when he thought that his surgeon had done it too tenderly.

About eight or ten days before his death, when Dr. Brocklesby paid him his morning visit, he seemed very low and desponding, and said, "I have been as a dying man all night." He then emphatically broke out in the words of Shakespeare,

Canst thou not minister to a mind diseased;
Pluck from the memory a rooted sorrow;
Raze out the written troubles of the brain;
And, with some sweet oblivious antidote,
Cleanse the stuffed bosom of that perilous stuff,
Which weighs upon the heart?

To which Dr. Brocklesby readily answered, from the same great poet:

————————therein the patient
Must minister to himself.[19]

Having no near relations, it had been for some time Johnson's intention to make a liberal provision for his faithful servant, Mr. Francis Barber, whom he looked upon as particularly under his protection, and whom he had all along treated truly as an humble friend. Having asked Dr. Brocklesby what would be a proper annuity to bequeath to a favorite servant, and being answered that it must depend on the circumstances of the master; and, that in the case of a nobleman, fifty pounds a year was considered as an adequate reward for many years' faithful service, "Then, (said Johnson,) shall I be *nobilissimus*,[20] for I mean to leave Frank seventy pounds a year, and I desire you to tell him so." It is strange, however, to think that Johnson was not free from that general weakness of being averse to execute a will, so that he delayed it from time to time; and had it not been for Sir John Hawkins's repeatedly urging it, I think it is probable that his kind resolution would not have been fulfilled.

Two very valuable articles, I am sure, we have lost, which were two quarto volumes containing a full, fair, and most particular account of his own life, from his earliest recollection. I owned to him, that having accidentally seen them, I had read a great deal in them; and

---

THE DEATH OF JOHNSON: From *The Life of Samuel Johnson, LL.D.,* A.D. *1784—Aetat. 75.*
[18] Psalm LXXXII, 7.

---

[19] *Macbeth,* Act V, Scene 3.
[20] "Very noble."

apologizing for the liberty I had taken, asked him if I could help it. He placidly answered, "Why, Sir, I do not think you could have helped it." I said that I had, for once in my life, felt half an inclination to commit theft. It had come into my mind to carry off those two volumes, and never see him more. Upon my inquiring how this would have affected him, "Sir, (said he,) I believe I should have gone mad. . . ."

Amidst the melancholy clouds which hung over the dying Johnson, his characteristical manner showed itself on different occasions.

When Dr. Warren, in the usual style, hoped that he was better, his answer was, "No, Sir; you cannot conceive with what acceleration I advance towards death."

Mr. Windham having placed a pillow conveniently to support him, he thanked him for his kindness and said, "That will do,—all that a pillow can do."

As he opened a note which his servant brought to him, he said, "An odd thought strikes me:—we shall receive no letters in the grave."

He requested three things of Sir Joshua Reynolds: [21]—To forgive him thirty pounds which he had borrowed of him;—to read the Bible;—and never to use his pencil on a Sunday. Sir Joshua readily acquiesced.

Indeed he showed the greatest anxiety for the religious improvement of his friends, to whom he discoursed of its infinite consequence. He begged of Mr. Hoole to think of what he had said, and to commit it to writing: and, upon being afterwards assured that this was done, pressed his hands, and in an earnest tone thanked him. Dr. Brocklesby having attended him with the utmost assiduity and kindness as his physician and friend, he was peculiarly desirous that this gentleman should not entertain any loose speculative notions, but be confirmed in the truths of Christianity, and insisted on his writing down in his presence, as nearly as he could collect it, the import of what passed on the subject: and Dr. Brocklesby having complied with the request, he made him sign the paper, and urged him to keep it in his own custody as long as he lived.

Johnson, with that native fortitude, which, amidst all his bodily distress and mental sufferings, never forsook him, asked Dr. Brocklesby, as a man in whom he had confidence, to tell him plainly whether he could recover. "Give me (said he) a direct answer." The Doctor having first asked him if he could bear the whole truth, which way soever it might lead, and being answered that he could, declared that, in his opinion, he could not recover without a miracle. "Then, (said Johnson,) I will take no more physic,[22] not even my opiates; for I have prayed that I may render up my soul to God unclouded." In this resolution he persevered, and, at the same time, used only the weakest kinds of sustenance. Being pressed by Mr. Windham to take somewhat more generous nourishment, lest too low a diet should have the very effect which he dreaded, by debilitating his mind, he said, "I will take anything but inebriating sustenance."

Having, as has been already mentioned, made his will on the 8th and 9th of December, and settled all his worldly affairs, he languished till Monday, the 13th of that month, when he expired, about seven o'clock in the evening, with so little apparent pain that his attendants hardly perceived when his dissolution took place.

About two days after his death, the following very agreeable account was communicated to Mr. Malone, in a letter by the Honorable John Byng, to whom I am much obliged for granting me permission to introduce it in my work.

Dear Sir,
    SINCE I saw you, I have had a long conversation with Cawston, who sat up with Dr. Johnson from nine o'clock on Sunday evening till ten o'clock on Monday morning. And, from what I can gather from him, it should seem that Dr. Johnson was perfectly composed, steady in hope, and resigned to death. At the interval of each hour, they assisted him to sit up in his bed and move his legs, which were in much pain; when he regularly addressed himself to fervent prayer; and though, sometimes, his voice failed him, his senses never did, during that time. The only sustenance he received was cider and water. He said his mind was prepared, and the time to his dissolution seemed long. At six in the morning, he enquired the hour, and, on being informed, said that all went on regularly, and he felt he had but a few hours to live.

---

[21] Landscape and portrait painter (1723-1792); close friend of Johnson. *The Life of Samuel Johnson* is dedicated to him.

[22] Medicine.

This account has given us the satisfaction of thinking that that great man died as he lived, full of resignation, strengthened in faith, and joyful in hope.

A few days before his death, he had asked Sir John Hawkins, as one of his executors, where he should be buried; and on being answered, "Doubtless, in Westminster Abbey," seemed to feel a satisfaction very natural to a poet; and indeed, in my opinion, very natural to every man of any imagination, who has no family sepulchre in which he can be laid with his fathers. Accordingly, upon Monday, December 20, his remains were deposited in that noble and renowned edifice; and over his grave was placed a large blue flagstone, with this inscription:

SAMUEL JOHNSON, LL.D.
*Obiit* XIII *die Decembris,*
*Anno Domini*
M. DCC. LXXXIV.
*Ætatis suæ* LXXV.[23]

## John Donne
# MEDITATION XVI

We have a convenient [24] author who writ a discourse of bells, when he was prisoner in Turkey. How would he have enlarged himself if he had been my fellow-prisoner in this sick bed, so near to that steeple, which never ceases, no more than the harmony of the spheres, but is more heard. When the Turks took Constantinople, they melted the bells into ordnance; I have heard both bells and ordnance, but never been so much affected with those, as with these bells. I have lien [25] near a steeple, in which there are said to be more than thirty bells; and near another, where there is one so big as that the clapper is said to weigh more than six hundred pound, yet never so affected as here. Here the bells can scarce solemnize the funeral of any person,

but that I knew him, or knew that he was my neighbor: we dwelt in houses near to one another before, but now he is gone into that house, into which I must follow him. There is a way of correcting the children of great persons, that other children are corrected in their behalf, and in their names, and this works upon them, who indeed had more deserved it. And when these bells tell me that now one and now another is buried, must not I acknowledge that they have the correction due to me, and paid the debt that I owe? There is a story of a bell in a monastery which, when any of the house was sick to death, rung always voluntarily, and they knew the inevitableness of the danger by that. It rung once, when no man was sick; but the next day one of the house fell from the steeple and died, and the bell held the reputation of a prophet still. If these bells that warn to a funeral now, were appropriated to none, may not I, by the hour of the funeral, supply? How many men that stand at an execution, if they would ask, for what dies that man, should hear their own faults condemned, and see themselves executed, by attorney? We scarce hear of any man preferred, but we think of ourselves, that we might very well have been that man; why might not I have been that man that is carried to his grave now? Could I fit myself to stand or sit in any man's place, and not to lie in any man's grave? I may lack much of the good parts of the meanest, but I lack nothing of the mortality of the weakest; they may have acquired better abilities than I, but I was born to as many infirmities as they. To be an incumbent by lying down in a grave, to be a doctor by teaching mortification by example, by dying, though I may have seniors, others may be elder than I, yet I have proceeded apace in a good university, and gone a great way in a little time, by the furtherance of a vehement fever; and whomsoever these bells bring to the ground today, if he and I had been compared yesterday, perchance I should have been thought likelier to come to this preferment, then, than he. God hath kept the power of death in his own hands, lest any man should bribe death. If man knew the gain of death, the ease of death, he would solicit, he would provoke death to assist him, by any hand which he might use. But as when men see many of their own professions preferred, it ministers a hope that that may light

---

[23] "He died the 13th day of December, A.D. 1784, at the age of seventy-five."
[24] Near at hand.
[25] Mortgaged property.

upon them; so when these hourly bells tell me of so many funerals of men like me, it presents, if not a desire that it may, yet a comfort whensoever mine shall come.

## John Donne
# MEDITATION XVII

Perchance he for whom this bell tolls may be so ill as that he knows not it tolls for him; and perchance I may think myself so much better than I am as that they who are about me and see my state may have caused it to toll for me, and I know not that. The church is catholic, universal, so are all her actions; all that she does belongs to all. When she baptizes a child, that action concerns me; for that child is thereby connected to that body which is my head too and ingrafted into that body whereof I am a member. And when she buries a man, that action concerns me. All mankind is of one author, and is one volume; when one man dies, one chapter is not torn out of the book, but transplanted into a better language; and every chapter must be so translated. God employs several translators; some pieces are translated by age, some by sickness, some by war, some by justice; but God's hand is in every translation, and his hand shall bind up all our scattered leaves again for that library where every book shall lie open to one another. As therefore the bell that rings to a sermon calls not upon the preacher only but upon the congregation to come, so this bell calls us all; but how much more me who am brought so near the door by this sickness! There was a contention as far as a suit—in which piety and dignity, religion and estimation, were mingled—which of the religious orders should ring to prayers first in the morning; and it was determined that they should ring first that rose earliest. If we understand aright the dignity of this bell that tolls for our evening prayer, we would be glad to make it ours by rising early, in that application, that it might be ours as well as his, whose indeed it is. The bell doth toll for him that thinks it doth; and though it intermit again, yet from that minute that that occasion wrought upon him he is united to God. Who casts not up his eye to the sun when it rises? but who takes off his eye from a comet when that breaks out? Who bends not his ear to any bell which upon any occasion rings? but who can remove it from that bell which is passing a piece of himself out of this world? No man is an island entire of itself; every man is a piece of the continent, a part of the main. If a clod be washed away by the sea, Europe is the less, as well as if a promontory were, as well as if a manor of thy friend's or of thine own were. Any man's death diminishes me, because I am involved in mankind, and therefore never send to know for whom the bell tolls; it tolls for thee. Neither can we call this a begging of misery or a borrowing of misery, as though we were not miserable enough of ourselves but must fetch in more from the next house, in taking upon us the misery of our neighbors. Truly it were an excusable covetousness if we did, for affliction is a treasure, and scarce any man hath enough that is not matured and ripened by it and made fit for God by that affliction. If a man carry treasure in bullion or in a wedge of gold and have none coined into current money, his treasure will not defray him as he travels. Tribulation is treasure in the nature of it, but it is not current money in the use of it, except we get nearer and nearer our home, heaven, by it. Another man may be sick too, and sick to death, and this affliction may lie in his bowels as gold in a mine and be of no use to him; but this bell that tells me of his affliction digs out and applies that gold to me, if by this consideration of another's danger I take mine own into contemplation and so secure myself by making my recourse to my God, who is our only security.

## Jeremy Taylor
# THE VANITY AND SHORTNESS OF LIFE

A man is a bubble, said the Greek proverb; which Lucian [26] represents with advantages and its proper circumstances, to this

THE VANITY AND SHORTNESS OF LIFE: From *The Rule and Exercises of Holy Dying*, 1651, chapter 1, section 1.

[26] Greek satirist, *c.* 125–*c.* 190.

purpose; saying, that all the world is a storm, etc., and men rise up in their several generations, like bubbles descending *a Jove pluvio*,[27] from God and the dew of heaven, from a tear and drop of man, from nature and providence: and some of these instantly sink into the deluge of their first parent, and are hidden in a sheet of water, having had no other business in the world but to be born that they might be able to die: others float up and down two or three turns, and suddenly disappear, and give their place to others: and they that live longest upon the face of the waters, are in perpetual motion, restless and uneasy; and, being crushed with the great drop of a cloud, sink into flatness and a froth; the change not being great, it being hardly possible it should be more a nothing than it was before. So is every man: he is born in vanity and sin; he comes into the world like morning mushrooms, soon thrusting up their heads into the air, and conversing with their kindred of the same production, and as soon they turn into dust and forgetfulness: some of them without any other interest in the affairs of the world but that they made their parents a little glad, and very sorrowful: others ride longer in the storm; it may be until seven years of vanity be expired, and then peradventure the sun shines hot upon their heads, and they fall into the shades below, into the cover of death and darkness of the grave to hide them. But if the bubble stands the shock of a bigger drop, and outlives the chances of a child, of a careless nurse, of drowning in a pail of water, of being overlaid by a sleepy servant, or such little accidents, then the young man dances like a bubble, empty and gay, and shines like a dove's neck, or the image of a rainbow, which hath no substance, and whose very imagery and colors are fantastical; and so he dances out the gaiety of his youth, and is all the while in a storm, and endures only because he is not knocked on the head by a drop of bigger rain, or crushed by the pressure of a load of indigested meat, or quenched by the disorder of an ill-placed humor: and to preserve a man alive in the midst of so many chances and hostilities, is as great a miracle as to create him; to preserve him from rushing into nothing, and at first to draw him up from nothing, were equally the issues of an almighty

---

[27] "From Jupiter, giver of rain."

power. And therefore the wise men of the world have contended who shall best fit man's condition with words signifying his vanity and short abode. Homer calls a man "a leaf," the smallest, the weakest piece of a short-lived, unsteady plant: Pindar [28] calls him "the dream of a shadow": another, "the dream of the shadow of smoke": but St. James spake by a more excellent spirit, saying, "our life is but a vapor," *viz.*, drawn from the earth by a celestial influence; made of smoke, or the lighter parts of water, tossed with every wind, moved by the motion of a superior body, without virtue in itself, lifted up on high or left below, according as it pleases the sun its foster-father. But it is lighter yet; it is but "appearing"; a fantastic vapor, an apparition, nothing real: it is not so much as a mist, not the matter of a shower, nor substantial enough to make a cloud; but it is like Cassiopeia's chair, or Pelops' shoulder, or the circles of heaven, φαινόμενα, than which you cannot have a word that can signify a verier nothing. [29] And yet the expression is one degree more made diminutive: a "vapor," and "fantastical," or a "mere appearance," and this but for a little while neither; the very dream, the phantasm disappears in a small time, "like the shadow that departeth"; or "like a tale that is told"; or "as a dream when one awaketh." A man is so vain, so unfixed, so perishing a creature, that he cannot long last in the scene of fancy: a man goes off, and is forgotten, like the dream of a distracted person. The sum of all is this: that thou art a man, than whom there is not in the world any greater instance of heights and declensions, of lights and shadows, of misery and folly, of laughter and tears, of groans and death.

And because this consideration is of great usefulness and great necessity to many purposes of wisdom and the spirit, all the succession of time, all the changes in nature, all the varieties of light and darkness, the thousand thousands of accidents in the world, and every contingency to every man, and to every crea-

---

[28] Greek poet, 522?–433 B.C., writer of odes.

[29] The five stars resembling a chair in the constellation of Cassiopeia, the ivory shoulder which the gods gave Pelops when they restored him to life and could not find his real shoulder, the crystal spheres that were supposed to support the heavenly bodies— these are mere φαινόμενα, "appearances."

ture, doth preach our funeral sermon, and calls us to look and see how the sexton Time throws up the earth, and digs a grave where we must lay our sins or our sorrows, and sow our bodies, till they rise again in a fair or in an intolerable eternity. Every revolution which the sun makes about the world, divides between life and death; and death possesses both those portions by the next morrow; and we are dead to all those months which we have already lived, and we shall never live them over again: and still God makes little periods of our age. First we change our world, when we come from the womb to feel the warmth of the sun. Then we sleep and enter into the image of death, in which state we are unconcerned in all the changes of the world: and if our mothers or our nurses die, or a wild boar destroy our vineyards, or our king be sick, we regard it not, but during that state are as disinterested as if our eyes were closed with the clay that weeps in the bowels of the earth. At the end of seven years our teeth fall and die before us, representing a formal prologue to the tragedy; and still every seven years it is odds but we shall finish the last scene: and when nature, or chance, or vice, takes our body in pieces, weakening some parts and loosing others, we taste the grave and the solemnities of our own funerals, first in those parts that ministered to vice, and next in them that served for ornament, and in a short time even they that served for necessity become useless, and entangled like the wheels of a broken clock. Baldness is but a dressing to our funerals, the proper ornament of mourning, and of a person entered very far into the regions and possession of death: and we have many more of the same signification; gray hairs, rotten teeth, dim eyes, trembling joints, short breath, stiff limbs, wrinkled skin, short memory, decayed appetite. Every day's necessity calls for a reparation of that portion which death fed on all night, when we lay in his lap, and slept in his outer chambers. The very spirits of a man prey upon the daily portion of bread and flesh, and every meal is a rescue from one death, and lays up for another; and while we think a thought, we die; and the clock strikes, and reckons on our portion of eternity: we form our words with the breath of our nostrils, we have the less to live upon for every word we speak.

Thus nature calls us to meditate of death by those things which are the instruments of acting it: and God by all the variety of circumstances, and dressed up for all the fancies and the expectation of every single person. Nature hath given us one harvest every year, but death hath two, and the spring and the autumn send throngs of men and women to charnel-houses; and all the summer long men are recovering from their evils of the spring, till the dog-days come, and then the Sirian [30] star makes the summer deadly; and the fruits of autumn are laid up for all the year's provision, and the man that gathers them eats and surfeits, and dies and needs them not, and himself is laid up for eternity; and he that escapes till winter only stays for another opportunity which the distempers of that quarter minister to him with great variety. Thus death reigns in all the portions of our time; the autumn with its fruits provides disorders for us, and the winter's cold turns them into sharp diseases, and the spring brings flowers to strew our hearse, and the summer gives green turf and brambles to bind upon our graves. Calentures and surfeit, cold and agues, are the four quarters of the year, and all minister to death; and you can go no whither but you tread upon a dead man's bones.

The wild fellow in Petronius [31] that escaped upon a broken table from the furies of a shipwreck, as he was sunning himself upon the rocky shore espied a man rolled upon his floating bed of waves, ballasted with sand in the folds of his garment, and carried by his civil enemy, the sea, towards the shore to find a grave: and it cast him into some sad thoughts: that peradventure this man's wife in some part of the continent, safe and warm, looks next month for the good man's return; or, it may be, his son knows nothing of the tempest; or his father thinks of that affectionate kiss, which still is warm upon the good old man's cheek, ever since he took a kind farewell; and he weeps with joy to think how blessed he shall be when his beloved boy returns into the circle of his father's arms. These are the thoughts of mortals, this is the end and sum of all their designs: a dark night and an ill guide, a bois-

---

[30] Sirius, the dog star.
[31] Latin satirist of the first century.

terous sea and a broken cable, a hard rock and a rough wind, dashed in pieces the fortune of a whole family, and they that shall weep loudest for the accident are not yet entered into the storm, and yet have suffered shipwreck. Then looking upon the carcase, he knew it, and found it to be the master of the ship, who the day before cast up the accounts of his patrimony and his trade, and named the day when he thought to be at home: see how the man swims who was so angry two days since; his passions are becalmed with the storm, his accounts cast up, his cares at an end, his voyage done, and his gains are the strange events of death, which whether they be good or evil, the men that are alive seldom trouble themselves concerning the interest of the dead.

But seas alone do not break our vessel in pieces: everywhere we may be shipwrecked. A valiant general, when he is to reap the harvest of his crowns and triumphs, fights unprosperously; or falls into a fever with joy and wine, and changes his laurel into cypress, his triumphal chariot to a hearse, dying the night before he was appointed to perish in the drunkenness of his festival joys. It was a sad arrest of the loosenesses and wilder feasts of the French court, when their King Henry the Second was killed really by the sportive image of a fight. And many brides have died under the hands of paranymphs [32] and maidens, dressing them for uneasy joy, the new and undiscerned chains of marriage, according to the saying of Bensirah, the wise Jew, "the bride went into her chamber, and knew not what should befall her there." Some have been paying their vows, and giving thanks for a prosperous return to their own house, and the roof hath descended upon their heads, and turned their loud religion into the deeper silence of a grave. And how many teeming mothers have rejoiced over their swelling wombs, and pleased themselves in becoming the channels of blessing to a family, and the midwife hath quickly bound their heads and feet, and carried them forth to burial! Or else the birthday of an heir hath seen the coffin of the father brought into the house, and the divided mother hath been forced to travail twice, with a painful birth, and a sadder death.

There is no state, no accident, no circumstance of our life, but it hath been soured by some sad instance of a dying friend: a friendly meeting often ends in some sad mischance, and makes an eternal parting: and when the poet Æschylus was sitting under the walls of his house, an eagle hovering over his bald head mistook it for a stone, and let fall his oyster, hoping there to break the shell, but pierced the poor man's skull.

Death meets us everywhere, and is procured by every instrument and in all chances, and enters in at many doors; by violence and secret influence, by the aspect of a star and the stink of a mist, by the emissions of a cloud and the meeting of a vapor, the fall of a chariot and the stumbling at a stone, by a full meal or an empty stomach, by watching at the wine or by watching at prayers, by the sun or the moon, by a heat or a cold, by sleepless nights or sleeping days, by water frozen into the hardness and sharpness of a dagger, or water thawed into the floods of a river, by a hair or a raisin, by violent motion or sitting still, by severity or dissolution, by God's mercy or God's anger; by everything in providence and everything in manners, by everything in nature and everything in chance;—*eripitur persona, manet res,*[33] we take pains to heap up things useful to our life, and get our death in the purchase; and the person is snatched away, and the goods remain. And all this is the law and constitution of nature; it is a punishment to our sins, the unalterable event of providence, and the decree of heaven: the chains that confine us to this condition are strong as destiny, and immutable as the eternal laws of God.

I have conversed with some men who rejoiced in the death or calamity of others, and accounted it as a judgment upon them for being on the other side, and against them in the contention: but within the revolution of a few months, the same man met with a more uneasy and unhandsome death: which when I saw, I wept, and was afraid; for I knew that it must be so with all men; for we also shall die, and end our quarrels and contentions by passing to a final sentence.

---

[32] Bridesmaids.

[33] "The individual is snatched away; things remain."

*Robert Louis Stevenson*

# ÆS TRIPLEX [34]

The changes wrought by death are in themselves so sharp and final, and so terrible and melancholy in their consequences, that the thing stands alone in man's experience, and has no parallel upon earth. It outdoes all other accidents because it is the last of them. Sometimes it leaps suddenly upon its victims like a Thug,[35] sometimes it lays a regular siege and creeps upon their citadel during a score of years. And when the business is done, there is sore havoc made in other people's lives, and a pin knocked out by which many subsidiary friendships hung together. There are empty chairs, solitary walks, and single beds at night. Again, in taking away our friends, death does not take them away utterly, but leaves behind a mocking, tragical, and soon intolerable residue, which must be hurriedly concealed. Hence a whole chapter of sights and customs striking to the mind, from the pyramids of Egypt to the gibbets and dule trees of mediæval Europe. The poorest persons have a bit of pageant going toward the tomb; memorial stones are set up over the least memorable; and, in order to preserve some show of respect for what remains of our old loves and friendships, we must accompany it with much grimly ludicrous ceremonial, and the hired undertaker parades before the door. All this, and much more of the same sort, accompanied by the eloquence of poets, has gone a great way to put humanity in error; nay, in many philosophies the error has been embodied and laid down with every circumstance of logic; although in real life the bustle and swiftness, in leaving people little time to think, have not left them enough to go dangerously wrong in practice.

As a matter of fact, although few things are spoken of with more fearful whisperings than this prospect of death, few have less influence on conduct under healthy circumstances. We have all heard of cities in South America built upon the side of fiery mountains, and how, even in this tremendous neighborhood, the inhabitants are not a jot more impressed by the solemnity of mortal conditions than if they were delving gardens in the greenest corner of England. There are serenades and suppers and much gallantry among the myrtles overhead; and meanwhile the foundation shudders underfoot, the bowels of the mountain growl, and at any moment living ruin may leap sky-high into the moonlight, and tumble man and his merrymaking in the dust. In the eyes of very young people, and very dull old ones, there is something indescribably reckless and desperate in such a picture. It seems not credible that respectable married people, with umbrellas, should find appetite for a bit of supper within quite a long distance of a fiery mountain; ordinary life begins to smell of high-handed *debauch* when it is carried on so close to a catastrophe; and even cheese and salad, it seems, could hardly be relished in such circumstances without something like a defiance of the Creator. It should be a place for nobody but hermits dwelling in prayer and *maceration,* or mere born-devils drowning care in a perpetual carouse.

And yet, when one comes to think upon it calmly, the situation of these South American citizens forms only a very pale figure for the state of ordinary mankind. This world itself, travelling blindly and swiftly in overcrowded space, among a million other worlds travelling blindly and swiftly in contrary directions, may very well come by a knock that would set it into explosion like a penny squib. And what, *pathologically* looked at, is the human body with all its organs, but a mere bagful of *petards?* The least of these is as dangerous to the whole economy as the ship's powder-magazine to the ship; and with every breath we breathe, and every meal we eat, we are putting one or more of them in peril. If we clung as devotedly as some philosophers pretend we do to the abstract idea of life, or were half as frightened as they make out we are, for the subversive accident that ends it all, the trumpets might sound by the hour and no one would follow them into battle—the blue peter might fly at the truck, but who would climb into a seagoing ship? Think (if these philosophers were right) with what a preparation of spirit we should affront the daily peril of the dinner-table: a deadlier spot than any battle-field in history, where the far greater proportion of our ances-

[34] "Triple brass."

[35] A member of a fanatic group in India dedicated to murder.

tors have miserably left their bones! What woman would ever be lured into marriage, so much more dangerous than the wildest sea? And what would it be to grow old? For, after a certain distance, every step we take in life we find the ice growing thinner below our feet, and all around us and behind us we see our contemporaries going through. By the time a man gets well into the seventies, his continued existence is a mere miracle; and when he lays his old bones in bed for the night, there is an overwhelming probability that he will never see the day. Do the old men mind it, as a matter of fact? Why, no. They were never merrier; they have their grog at night, and tell the raciest stories; they hear of the death of people about their own age, or even younger, not as if it was a grisly warning, but with a simple childlike pleasure at having outlived some one else; and when a draught might puff them out like a guttering candle, or a bit of a stumble shatter them like so much glass, their old hearts keep sound and unaffrighted, and they go on, bubbling with laughter, through years of man's age compared to which the valley of Balaclava was as safe and peaceful as a village cricket-green on Sunday. It may fairly be questioned (if we look to the peril only) whether it was a much more daring feat for Curtius [36] to plunge into the gulf, than for any old gentleman of ninety to doff his clothes and clamber into bed.

Indeed, it is a memorable subject for consideration, with what unconcern and gaiety mankind pricks on along the Valley of the Shadow of Death. The whole way is one wilderness of snares, and the end of it, for those who fear the last pinch, is irrevocable ruin. And yet we go spinning through it all, like a party for the Derby. Perhaps the reader remembers one of the humorous devices of the deified Caligula: [37] how he encouraged a vast concourse of holiday-makers on to his bridge over Baiæ bay; and when they were in the height of their enjoyment, turned loose the Prætorian guards among the company, and had them tossed into the sea. This is no bad miniature of the dealings of nature with the transitory race of man. Only, what a checkered picnic we have of it, even while it lasts! and into what great waters, not to be crossed by any swimmer, God's pale Prætorian throws us over in the end!

We live the time that a match flickers; we pop the cork of a ginger-beer bottle, and the earthquake swallows us on the instant. Is it not odd, is it not incongruous, is it not, in the highest sense of human speech, incredible, that we should think so highly of the ginger-beer, and regard so little the devouring earthquake? The love of Life and the fear of Death are two famous phrases that grow harder to understand the more we think about them. It is a well-known fact that an immense proportion of boat accidents would never happen if people held the sheet in their hands instead of making it fast; and yet, unless it be some martinet of a professional mariner or some landsman with shattered nerves, every one of God's creatures makes it fast. A strange instance of man's unconcern and brazen boldness in the face of death!

We confound ourselves with metaphysical phrases, which we import into daily talk with noble inappropriateness. We have no idea of what death is, apart from its circumstances and some of its consequences to others; and although we have some experience of living, there is not a man on earth who has flown so high into abstraction as to have any practical guess at the meaning of the word *life*. All literature, from Job and Omar Khayyam to Thomas Carlyle or Walt Whitman, is but an attempt to look upon the human state with such largeness of view as shall enable us to rise from the consideration of living to the Definition of Life. And our sages give us about the best satisfaction in their power when they say that it is a vapor, or a show, or made of the same stuff with dreams. Philosophy, in its more rigid sense, has been at the same work for ages; and after a myriad bald heads have wagged over the problem, and piles of words have been heaped one upon another into dry and cloudy volumes without end, philosophy has the honor of laying before us, with modest pride, her contribution toward the subject: that life is a Permanent Possibility of Sensation. Truly a fine result! A man may very well love beef, or

---

[36] A Roman citizen who sacrificed himself to save the state. According to legend, a chasm appeared in the Roman forum in 362 B.C., which could be filled only if Rome's greatest treasure were thrown into it. Curtius, saying that Rome could have no greater treasure than a brave citizen, mounted his horse and leaped into the chasm, which closed over him.

[37] Roman emperor, 37–41 A.D.

hunting, or a woman; but surely, surely, not a Permanent Possibility of Sensation! He may be afraid of a precipice, or a dentist, or a large enemy with a club, or even an undertaker's man; but not certainly of abstract death. We may trick with the word life in its dozen senses until we are weary of tricking; we may argue in terms of all the philosophies on earth, but one fact remains true throughout—that we do not love life, in the sense that we are greatly preoccupied about its conservation—that we do not, properly speaking, love life at all, but living. Into the views of the least careful there will enter some degree of providence; no man's eyes are fixed entirely on the passing hour; but although we have some anticipation of good health, good weather, wine, active employment, love, and self-approval, the sum of these anticipations does not amount to anything like a general view of life's possibilities and issues; nor are those who cherish them most vividly, at all the most scrupulous of their personal safety. To be deeply interested in the accidents of our existence, to enjoy keenly the mixed texture of human experience, rather leads a man to disregard precautions, and risk his neck against a straw. For surely the love of living is stronger in an Alpine climber roping over a peril, or a hunter riding merrily at a stiff fence, than in a creature who lives upon a diet and walks a measured distance in the interest of his constitution.

There is a great deal of very vile nonsense talked upon both sides of the matter: tearing divines reducing life to the dimensions of a mere funeral procession, so short as to be hardly decent; and melancholy unbelievers yearning for the tomb as if it were a world too far away. Both sides must feel a little ashamed of their performances now and again when they draw in their chairs to dinner. Indeed, a good meal and a bottle of wine is an answer to most standard works upon the question. When a man's heart warms to his viands, he forgets a great deal of sophistry, and soars into a rosy zone of contemplation. Death may be knocking at the door, like the Commander's statue; we have something else in hand, thank God, and let him knock. Passing bells are ringing all the world over. All the world over, and every hour, some one is parting company with all his aches and ecstasies. For us also the trap is laid. But we are so fond of life that we have

no leisure to entertain the terror of death. It is a honeymoon with us all through, and none of the longest. Small blame to us if we give our whole hearts to this glowing bride of ours, to the appetites, to honor, to the hungry curiosity of the mind, to the pleasure of the eyes in nature, and the pride of our own nimble bodies.

We all of us appreciate the sensations; but as for caring about the Permanence of the Possibility, a man's head is generally very bald, and his senses very dull, before he comes to that. Whether we regard life as a lane leading to a dead wall—a mere bag's end, as the French say—or whether we think of it as a vestibule or gymnasium, where we wait our turn and prepare our faculties for some more noble destiny; whether we thunder in a pulpit, or pule in little atheistic poetry-books, about its vanity and brevity; whether we look justly for years of health and vigor, or are about to mount into a Bath chair, as a step toward the hearse; in each and all of these views and situations there is but one conclusion possible: that a man should stop his ears against paralyzing terror, and run the race that is set before him with a single mind. No one surely could have recoiled with more heartache and terror from the thought of death than our respected lexicographer;[38] and yet we know how little it affected his conduct, how wisely and boldly he walked, and in what a fresh and lively vein he spoke of life. Already an old man, he ventured on his Highland tour; and his heart, bound with triple brass, did not recoil before twenty-seven individual cups of tea. As courage and intelligence are the two qualities best worth a good man's cultivation, so it is the first part of intelligence to recognize our precarious estate in life, and the first part of courage to be not at all abashed before the fact. A frank and somewhat headlong carriage, not looking too anxiously before, not dallying in maudlin regret over the past, stamps the man who is well armored for this world.

And not only well armored for himself, but a good friend and a good citizen to boot. We do not go to cowards for tender dealing; there is nothing so cruel as panic; the man who has least fear for his own carcass, has most time to

---

[38] Samuel Johnson, who published the first English dictionary in 1755, journeyed on horseback through the mountains of Scotland at the age of sixty-four.

consider others. That eminent chemist who took his walks abroad in tin shoes, and subsisted wholly upon tepid milk, had all his work cut out for him in considerate dealings with his own digestion. So soon as prudence has begun to grow up in the brain, like a dismal fungus, it finds its first expression in a paralysis of generous acts. The victim begins to shrink spiritually; he develops a fancy for parlors with a regulated temperature, and takes his morality on the principle of tin shoes and tepid milk. The care of one important body or soul becomes so engrossing, that all the noises of the outer world begin to come thin and faint into the parlor with the regulated temperature; and the tin shoes go equally forward over blood and rain. To be overwise is to ossify; and the scruple-monger ends by standing stock-still. Now the man who has his heart on his sleeve, and a good whirling weathercock of a brain, who reckons his life as a thing to be dashingly used and cheerfully hazarded, makes a very different acquaintance of the world, keeps all his pulses going true and fast, and gathers impetus as he runs, until, if he be running toward anything better than wildfire, he may shoot up and become a constellation in the end. Lord, look after his health; Lord, have a care of his soul, says he; and he has at the key of the position, and swashes through incongruity and peril toward his aim. Death is on all sides of him with pointed batteries, as he is on all sides of all of us; unfortunate surprises gird him round; mimmouthed friends and relations hold up their hands in quite a little elegiacal synod about his path: and what cares he for all this? Being a true lover of living, a fellow with something pushing and spontaneous in his inside, he must, like any other soldier, in any other stirring, deadly warfare, push on at his best pace until he touch the goal. "A peerage or Westminster Abbey!" cried Nelson in his bright, boyish, heroic manner. These are great incentives; not for any of these, but for the plain satisfaction of living, of being about their business in some sort or other, do the brave, serviceable men of every nation tread down the nettle danger, and pass flyingly over all the stumbling-blocks of prudence. Think of the heroism of Johnson, think of that superb indifference to mortal limitation that set him upon his dictionary, and carried through triumphantly until the end! Who, if he were wisely considerate of things at large, would ever embark upon any work much more considerable than a halfpenny post card? Who would project a serial novel, after Thackeray and Dickens had each fallen in mid-course? Who would find heart enough to begin to live, if he dallied with the consideration of death?

And, after all, what sorry and pitiful quibbling all this is! To forego all the issues of living in a parlor with the regulated temperature—as if that were not to die a hundred times over, and for ten years at a stretch! As if it were not to die in one's own lifetime, and without even the sad immunities of death! As if it were not to die, and yet be the patient spectators of our own pitiable change! The Permanent Possibility is preserved, but the sensations carefully held at arm's length, as if one kept a photographic plate in a dark chamber. It is better to lose health like a spendthrift than to waste it like a miser. It is better to live and be done with it, than to die daily in the sickroom. By all means begin your folio; even if the doctor does not give you a year, even if he hesitates about a month, make one brave push and see what can be accomplished in a week. It is not only in finished undertakings that we ought to honor useful labor. A spirit goes out of the man who means execution, which outlives the most untimely ending. All who have meant good work with their whole hearts, have done good work, although they may die before they have the time to sign it. Every heart that has beat strong and cheerfully has left a hopeful impulse behind it in the world, and bettered the tradition of mankind. And even if death catch people, like an open pitfall, and in mid-career, laying out vast projects, and planning monstrous foundations, flushed with hope, and their mouths full of boastful languages, they should be at once tripped up and silenced: is there not something brave and spirited in such a termination? and does not life go down with a better grace, foaming in full body over a precipice, than miserably straggling to an end in sandy deltas? When the Greeks made their fine saying that those whom the gods love die young, I cannot help believing they had this sort of death also in their eye. For surely at whatever age it overtake the man, this is to die young. Death has not been suffered to take so much as an illusion from his heart. In the hot-fit of life, a-tiptoe on the highest point of being, he passes at a bound on to the other side. The noise of the mallet and chisel is scarcely quenched, the trumpets are hardly done blowing, when, trailing with him clouds of glory, this happy-starred, full-blooded spirit shoots into the spiritual land.

## Caroline Gordon
# THE LAST DAY IN THE FIELD

That was the fall when the leaves stayed green so long. We had a drouth in August and the ponds everywhere were dry and the water-courses shrunken. Then in September heavy rains came. Things greened up. It looked like winter was never coming.

"You aren't going to hunt this year, Aleck," Molly said. "Remember how you stayed awake nights last fall with that pain in your leg."

In October light frosts came. In the afternoons when I sat on the back porch going over my fishing tackle I marked their progress on the elderberry bushes that were left standing against the stable fence. The lower, spreading branches had turned yellow and were already sinking to the ground but the leaves in the top clusters still stood up stiff and straight.

"Ah-h, it'll get you yet!" I said, thinking how frost creeps higher and higher out of the ground each night of fall.

The dogs next door felt it and would thrust their noses through the wire fence scenting the wind from the north. When I walked in the back yard they would bound twice their height and whine, for meat scraps Molly said, but it was because they smelled blood on my old hunting coat.

They were almost matched liver-and-white pointers. The big dog had a beautiful, square muzzle and was deep-chested and rangy. The bitch, Judy, had a smaller head and not so good a muzzle but she was springy loined too and had one of the merriest tails I've ever watched. When Joe Thomas, the boy that owned them,

THE LAST DAY IN THE FIELD: Reprinted from *The Forest of the South*, by Caroline Gordon. Copyright, 1945, by Caroline Gordon. Used by permission of the publishers, Charles Scribner's Sons.

came home from the hardware store he would change his clothes and then come down the back way into the wired enclosure and we would stand there watching the dogs and wondering how they would work. Joe said they were keen as mustard. He was going to take them out the first good Saturday and wanted me to come along.

"I can't make it," I said, "my leg's worse this year than it was last."

The fifteenth of November was clear and so warm that we sat out on the porch till nine o'clock. It was still warm when we went to bed towards eleven. The change must have come in the middle of the night. I woke once, hearing the clock strike two, and felt the air cold on my face and thought before I went back to sleep that the weather had broken at last. When I woke again at dawn the cold air was slapping my face hard. I came wide awake, turned over in bed and looked out of the window.

There was a scaly-bark hickory tree growing on the east side of the house. You could see its upper branches from the bedroom window. The leaves had turned yellow a week ago. But yesterday evening when I walked out there in the yard they had still been flat with green streaks showing in them. Now they were curled up tight and a lot of leaves had fallen on to the ground.

I got out of bed quietly so as not to wake Molly, dressed and went down the back way over to the Thomas house. There was no one stirring but I knew which room Joe's was. The window was open and I could hear him snoring. I went up and stuck my head in.

"Hey," I said, "killing frost."

He opened his eyes and looked at me and then his eyes went shut. I reached my arm through the window and shook him. "Get up," I said, "we got to start right away."

He was awake now and out on the floor stretching. I told him to dress and be over at the house as quick as he could. I'd have breakfast ready for us both.

Aunt Martha had a way of leaving fire in the kitchen stove at night. There were red embers there now. I poked the ashes out and piled kindling on top of them. When the flames came up I put some heavier wood on, filled the coffee pot, and put some grease on in a skillet. By the time Joe got there I had coffee ready and some hoe cakes to go with our fried eggs. Joe had brought a thermos bottle. We put the rest of the coffee in it and I found a ham in the pantry and made some sandwiches.

While I was fixing the lunch Joe went down to the lot to hitch up. He was just driving Old Dick out of the stable when I came down the back steps. The dogs knew what was up, all right. They were whining and surging against the fence and Bob, the big dog, thrust his paw through and into the pocket of my hunting coat as I passed. While Joe was snapping on the leashes I got a few handfuls of straw from the rack and put it in the foot of the buggy. It was twelve miles where we were going; the dogs would need to ride warm coming back late.

Joe said he would drive. We got in the buggy and started out, up Seventh Street and on over to College and out through Scufftown. When we got into the nigger section we could see what a killing frost it had been. A light shimmer over all the ground still and the weeds around the cabins dark and matted the way they are when the frost hits them hard and twists them.

We drove on over the Red River bridge and up into the open country. At Jim Gill's place the cows had come up and were standing waiting to be milked but nobody was stirring yet from the house. I looked back from the top of the hill and saw that the frost mists still hung heavy in the bottom and thought it was a good sign. A day like this when the earth is warmer than the air currents is good for the hunter. Scent particles are borne on the warm air and birds will forage far on such a day.

It took us over an hour to get from Gloversville to Spring Creek. Joe wanted to get out as soon as we hit the big bottom there but I held him down and we drove on to the top of the ridge. We got out there, unhitched Old Dick and turned him into one of Rob Fayerlee's pastures—I thought how surprised Rob would be when he saw him grazing there—put our guns together, and started out, the dogs still on leash.

It was rough, broken ground, scrub oak, with a few gum trees and lots of buckberry bushes. One place a patch of corn ran clear up to the top of the ridge. As we passed along between the rows I could see the frost glistening on the north side of the stalks. I knew it was going to be a good day.

I walked over to the brow of the hill. From here you can see off over the whole valley— I've hunted every foot of it in my time— tobacco land, mostly. One or two patches of corn there on the side of the ridge. I thought we might start there and then I knew that wouldn't do. Quail will linger on the roost a cold day and feed in shelter during the morning. It is only in the afternoon that they will work out to the open.

The dogs were whining. Joe bent down and was about to slip their leashes. "Hey, boy," I said, "don't do that."

I turned around and looked down the other side of the ridge. It was better that way. The corn land of the bottoms ran high up on to the hill in several places there and where the corn stopped there were big patches of ironweed and buckberry. I knocked my pipe out on a stump.

"Let's go that way," I said.

Joe was looking at my old buckhorn whistle that I had slung around my neck. "I forgot to bring mine."

"All right," I said, "I'll handle 'em."

He unfastened their collars and cast off. They broke away, racing for the first hundred yards and barking, then suddenly swerved. The big dog took off to the right along the hillside. The bitch, Judy, skirted a belt of corn along the upper bottomlands. I kept my eye on the big dog. A dog that has bird sense will know cover when he sees it. This big Bob was an independent hunter, all right. I could see him moving fast through the scrub oaks, working his way down toward a patch of ironweed. He caught first scent just on the edge of the weed patch and froze with every indication of class, head up, nose stuck out, and tail straight in air. Judy, meanwhile, had been following the line of the corn field. A hundred yards away she caught sight of Bob's point and backed him.

We went up and flushed the birds. They got up in two bunches. I heard Joe's shot while I was in the act of raising my gun and I saw his bird fall not thirty paces from where I stood. I had covered the middle bird of the larger bunch—that's the one led by the boss cock—the way I usually do. He fell, whirling head over heels, driven a little forward by the impact. A well-centered shot. I could tell by the way the feathers fluffed as he tumbled.

The dogs were off through the grass. They had retrieved both birds. Joe stuck his in his pocket. He laughed. "I thought there for a minute you were going to let him get away."

I looked at him but I didn't say anything. It's a wonderful thing to be twenty years old.

The majority of the singles had flown straight ahead to settle in the rank grass that jutted out from the bottomland. Judy got down to work at once but the big dog broke off to the left, wanting to get footloose to find another covey. I thought of how Trecho, the best dog I ever had—the best dog any man ever had—used always to be wanting to do the same thing and I laughed.

"Naw, you don't," I said, "come back here, you scoundrel, and hunt these singles."

He stopped on the edge of a briar patch, looked at me and heeled up promptly. I clucked him out again. He gave me another look. I thought we were beginning to understand each other better. We got some nice points among those singles but we followed that valley along the creek bed and through two or three more corn fields without finding another covey. Joe was disappointed but I wasn't beginning to worry yet; you always make your bag in the afternoon.

It was twelve o'clock by this time, no sign of frost anywhere and the sun beating down steady on the curled-up leaves.

"Come on," I said, "let's go up to Buck's spring and eat."

We walked up the ravine whose bed was still moist with the fall rains and came out at the head of the hollow. They had cleared out some of the trees on the side of the ravine but the spring itself was the same: a deep pool welling up between the roots of an old sycamore. I unwrapped the sandwiches and the piece of cake and laid them on a stump. Joe got the thermos bottle out of his pocket. Something had gone wrong with it and the coffee was stone cold. We were about to drink it that way when Joe saw a good tin can flung down beside the spring. He made a trash fire and we put the coffee in the can and heated it to boiling.

It was warm in the ravine, sheltered from the wind, with the little fire burning. I turned my game leg so that the heat fell full on my knee. Joe had finished his last sandwich and was reaching for the cake.

"Good ham," he said.

"It's John Ferguson's," I told him.

He had got up and was standing over the spring. "Wonder how long this wood'll last, under water this way."

I looked at the sycamore root, green and slick where the thin stream of water poured over it, then my eyes went back to the dogs. They were tired, all right. Judy had gone off to lie down in a cool place at the side of the spring, but the big dog, Bob, lay there, his forepaws stretched out in front of him, never taking his eyes off our faces. I looked at him and thought how different he was from his mate and like some dogs I had known—and men too—who lived only for hunting and could never get enough no matter how long the day. There was something about his head and his markings that reminded me of another dog I used to hunt with a long time ago and I asked the boy who had trained him. He said the old fellow he bought the dogs from had been killed last spring, over in Trigg—Charley Morrison.

Charley Morrison! I remembered how he died, out hunting by himself and the gun had gone off, accidentally they said. Charley had called his dog to him, got blood over him and sent him home. The dog went, all right, but when they got there Charley was dead. Two years ago that was and now I was hunting the last dogs he'd ever trained. . . .

Joe lifted the thermos bottle. "Another cup?"

I held my cup out and he filled it. The coffee was still good and hot. I drank it, standing up, running my eye over the country in front of us. Afternoon is different from morning, more exciting. It isn't only as I say that you'll make your bag in the afternoon, but it takes more figuring. They're fed and rested and when they start out again they'll work in the open and over a wider range.

Joe was stamping out his cigarette: "Let's go."

The dogs were already out of sight but I could see the sedge grass ahead moving and I knew they'd be making for the same thing that took my eye: a spearhead of thicket that ran far out into this open field. We came up over a little rise. There they were, Bob on a point and Judy backing him not fifty feet from the thicket. I saw it was going to be tough shooting. No way to tell whether the birds were between the dog and the thicket or in the thicket itself. Then I saw that the cover was more open along the side of the thicket and I thought that that was the way they'd go if they were in the thicket. But Joe had already broken away to the left. He got too far to the side. The birds flushed to the right and left him standing, flat-footed, without a shot.

He looked sort of foolish and grinned.

I thought I wouldn't say anything and then I found myself speaking: "Trouble with you, you try to out-think the dog."

There was nothing to do about it, though. The chances were that the singles had pitched in the trees below. We went down there. It was hard hunting. The woods were open, the ground everywhere heavily carpeted with leaves. Dead leaves make a tremendous rustle when the dogs surge through them. It takes a good nose to cut scent keenly in such noisy cover. I kept my eye on Bob. He never faltered, getting over the ground in big, springy strides but combing every inch of it. We came to an open place in the woods. Nothing but hickory trees and bramble thickets overhung with trailing vines. Bob passed the first thicket and came to a beautiful point. We went up. He stood perfectly steady but the bird flushed out fifteen or twenty steps ahead of him. I saw it swing to the right, gaining altitude very quickly— woods birds will always cut back to known territory—and it came to me how it would be.

I called to Joe: "Don't shoot yet."

He nodded and raised his gun, following the bird with the barrel. It was directly over the treetops when I gave the word and he shot, scoring a clean kill.

He laughed excitedly as he stuck the bird in his pocket. "My God, man, I didn't know you could take that much time!"

We went on through the open woods. I was thinking about a day I'd had years ago in the woods at Grassdale, with my uncle, James Morris, and his son, Julian. Uncle James had given Julian and me hell for missing just such a shot. I can see him now standing up against a big pine tree, his face red from liquor and his gray hair ruffling in the wind: *Let him alone! Let him alone!* And establish your lead as he climbs."

Joe was still talking about the shot he'd made. "Lord, I wish I could get another one like that."

"You won't," I said, "we're getting out of the woods now."

We struck a path that led due west and followed it for half a mile. My leg was stiff from the hip down now and every time I brought it over, the pain would start in my knee, Zing! and travel up and settle in the small of my back. I walked with my head down, watching the light catch on the ridges of Joe's brown corduroy trousers and then shift and catch again. Sometimes he would get on ahead and then there would be nothing but the black tree trunks coming up out of the dead leaves.

Joe was talking about some wild land up on the Cumberland. We could get up there on an early train. Have a good day. Might even spend the night. When I didn't answer he turned around: "Man, you're sweating."

I pulled my handkerchief out and wiped my face. "Hot work," I said.

He had stopped and was looking about him. "Used to be a spring somewhere around here."

He had found the path and was off. I sat down on a stump and mopped my face some more. The sun was halfway down through the trees now, the whole west woods ablaze with the light. I sat there and thought that in another hour it would be good and dark and I wished that the day could go on and not end so soon and yet I didn't see how I could make it much farther with my leg the way it was.

Joe was coming up the path with his folding cup full of water. I hadn't thought I was thirsty but the cold water tasted good. We sat there awhile and smoked, then Joe said that we ought to be starting back, that we must be a good piece from the rig by this time.

We set out, working north through the edge of the woods. It was rough going and I was thinking that it would be all I could do to make it back to the rig when we climbed a fence and came out at one end of a long field that sloped down to a wooded ravine. Broken ground, badly gullied and covered with sedge everywhere except where sumac thickets had sprung up—as birdy a place as ever I saw. I looked it over and knew I had to hunt it, leg or no leg, but it would be close work, for me and the dogs too.

I blew them in a bit and we stood there watching them cut up the cover. The sun was down now; there was just enough light left to see the dogs work. The big dog circled the far wall of the basin and came up wind just off the drain, then stiffened to a point. We walked down to it. The birds had obviously run a bit into the scraggly sumac stalks that bordered the ditch. My mind was so much on the dogs I forgot Joe. He took one step too many. The fullest blown bevy of the day roared up through the tangle. It had to be fast work. I raised my gun and scored with the only barrel I had time to peg. Joe shouted; I knew he had got one too.

We stood there trying to figure out which way the singles had gone but they had fanned out too quick for us, excited as we were, and after beating around awhile we gave up and went on.

We came to the rim of the swale, eased over it, crossed the dry creek that was drifted thick with leaves, and started up the other side. I had blown in the dogs, thinking there was no use for them to run their heads off now we'd started home, but they didn't come. I walked on a little farther, then I looked back and saw Bob's white shoulders through a tangle of cinnamon vine.

Joe had turned around too. "They've pinned a single out of that last covey," he said.

I looked over at him quick. "Your shot."

He shook his head. "No, you take it."

I limped back and flushed the bird. It went skimming along the buckberry bushes that covered that side of the swale. In the fading light I could hardly make it out and I shot too quick. It swerved over the thicket and I let go with the second barrel. It staggered, then zoomed up. Up, up, up, over the rim of the hill and above the tallest hickories. It hung there for a second, its wings black against the gold light, before, wings still spread, it came whirling down, like an autumn leaf, like the leaves that were everywhere about us, all over the ground.

## *Katherine Anne Porter*
# THE GRAVE

The grandfather, dead for more than thirty years, had been twice disturbed in his long repose by the constancy and possessiveness of his widow. She removed his bones first

THE GRAVE: From *The Leaning Tower and Other Stories*, by Katherine Anne Porter. Copyright, 1944, by Katherine Anne Porter. Reprinted by permission of Harcourt, Brace and Company, Inc.

to Louisiana and then to Texas as if she had set out to find her own burial place, knowing well she would never return to the places she had left. In Texas she set up a small cemetery in a corner of her first farm, and as the family connection grew, and oddments of relations came over from Kentucky to settle, it contained at last about twenty graves. After the grandmother's death, part of her land was to be sold for the benefit of certain of her children, and the cemetery happened to lie in the part set aside for sale. It was necessary to take up the bodies and bury them again in the family plot in the big new public cemetery, where the grandmother had been buried. At last her husband was to lie beside her for eternity, as she had planned.

The family cemetery had been a pleasant small neglected garden of tangled rose bushes and ragged cedar trees and cypress, the simple flat stones rising out of uncropped sweet-smelling wild grass. The graves were lying open and empty one burning day when Miranda and her brother Paul, who often went together to hunt rabbits and doves, propped their twenty-two Winchester rifles carefully against the rail fence, climbed over and explored among the graves. She was nine years old and he was twelve.

They peered into the pits all shaped alike with such purposeful accuracy, and looking at each other with pleased adventurous eyes, they said in solemn tones: "These were graves!" trying by words to shape a special, suitable emotion in their minds, but they felt nothing except an agreeable thrill of wonder: they were seeing a new sight, doing something they had not done before. In them both there was also a small disappointment at the entire commonplaceness of the actual spectacle. Even if it had once contained a coffin for years upon years, when the coffin was gone a grave was just a hole in the ground. Miranda leaped into the pit that had held her grandfather's bones. Scratching around aimlessly and pleasurably as any young animal, she scooped up a lump of earth and weighed it in her palm. It had a pleasantly sweet, corrupt smell, being mixed with cedar needles and small leaves, and as the crumbs fell apart, she saw a silver dove no larger than a hazel nut, with spread wings and a neat fan-shaped tail. The breast had a deep round hollow in it. Turning it up to the fierce sunlight, she saw that the inside of the hollow was cut in little whorls. She scrambled out, over the pile of loose earth that had fallen back into one end of the grave, calling to Paul that she had found something, he must guess what . . . His head appeared smiling over the rim of another grave. He waved a closed hand at her. "I've got something too!" They ran to compare treasures, making a game of it, so many guesses each, all wrong, and a final showdown with opened palms. Paul had found a thin wide gold ring carved with intricate flowers and leaves. Miranda was smitten at sight of the ring and wished to have it. Paul seemed more impressed by the dove. They made a trade, with some little bickering. After he had got the dove in his hand, Paul said, "Don't you know what this is? This is a screw head for a *coffin!* . . . I'll bet nobody else in the world has one like this!"

Miranda glanced at it without covetousness. She had the gold ring on her thumb; it fitted perfectly. "Maybe we ought to go now," she said, "maybe one of the niggers 'll see us and tell somebody." They knew the land had been sold, the cemetery was no longer theirs, and they felt like trespassers. They climbed back over the fence, slung their rifles loosely under their arms—they had been shooting at targets with various kinds of firearms since they were seven years old—and set out to look for the rabbits and doves or whatever small game might happen along. On these expeditions Miranda always followed at Paul's heels along the path, obeying instructions about handling her gun when going through fences; learning how to stand it up properly so it would not slip and fire unexpectedly; how to wait her time for a shot and not just bang away in the air without looking, spoiling shots for Paul, who really could hit things if given a chance. Now and then, in her excitement at seeing birds whizz up suddenly before her face, or a rabbit leap across her very toes, she lost her head, and almost without sighting she flung her rifle up and pulled the trigger. She hardly ever hit any sort of mark. She had no proper sense of hunting at all. Her brother would be often completely disgusted with her. "You don't care whether you get your bird or not," he said. "That's no way to hunt." Miranda could not understand his indignation. She had seen him smash his hat and yell with fury when he had

missed his aim. "What I like about shooting," said Miranda, with exasperating inconsequence, "is pulling the trigger and hearing the noise."

"Then, by golly," said Paul, "whyn't you go back to the range and shoot at bulls-eyes?"

"I'd just as soon," said Miranda, "only like this, we walk around more."

"Well, you just stay behind and stop spoiling my shots," said Paul, who, when he made a kill, wanted to be certain he had made it. Miranda, who alone brought down a bird once in twenty rounds, always claimed as her own any game they got when they fired at the same moment. It was tiresome and unfair and her brother was sick of it.

"Now, the first dove we see, or the first rabbit, is mine," he told her. "And the next will be yours. Remember that and don't get smarty."

"What about snakes?" asked Miranda idly. "Can I have the first snake?"

Waving her thumb gently and watching her gold ring glitter, Miranda lost interest in shooting. She was wearing her summer roughing outfit: dark blue overalls, a light blue shirt, a hired-man's straw hat, and thick brown sandals. Her brother had the same outfit except his was a sober hickory-nut color. Ordinarily Miranda preferred her overalls to any other dress, though it was making rather a scandal in the countryside, for the year was 1903, and in the back country the law of female decorum had teeth in it. Her father had been criticized for letting his girls dress like boys and go careering around astride barebacked horses. Big sister Maria, the really independent and fearless one, in spite of her rather affected ways, rode at a dead run with only a rope knotted around her horse's nose. It was said the motherless family was running down, with the Grandmother no longer there to hold it together. It was known that she had discriminated against her son Harry in her will, and that he was in straits about money. Some of his old neighbors reflected with vicious satisfaction that now he would probably not be so stiffnecked, nor have any more high-stepping horses either. Miranda knew this, though she could not say how. She had met along the road old women of the kind who smoked corn-cob pipes, who had treated her grandmother with most sincere respect. They slanted their gummy old eyes side-ways at the granddaughter and said, "Ain't you ashamed of yoself, Missy? It's against the Scriptures to dress like that. Whut yo Pappy thinkin about?" Miranda, with her powerful social sense, which was like a fine set of antennae radiating from every pore of her skin, would feel ashamed because she knew well it was rude and ill-bred to shock anybody, even bad-tempered old crones, though she had faith in her father's judgment and was perfectly comfortable in the clothes. Her father had said, "They're just what you need, and they'll save your dresses for school . . ." This sounded quite simple and natural to her. She had been brought up in rigorous economy. Wastefulness was vulgar. It was also a sin. These were truths; she had heard them repeated many times and never once disputed.

Now the ring, shining with the serene purity of fine gold on her rather grubby thumb, turned her feelings against her overalls and sockless feet, toes sticking through the thick brown leather straps. She wanted to go back to the farmhouse, take a good cold bath, dust herself with plenty of Maria's violet talcum powder—provided Maria was not present to object, of course—put on the thinnest, most becoming dress she owned, with a big sash, and sit in a wicker chair under the trees . . . These things were not all she wanted, of course; she had vague stirrings of desire for luxury and a grand way of living which could not take precise form in her imagination but were founded on family legend of past wealth and leisure. These immediate comforts were what she could have, and she wanted them at once. She lagged rather far behind Paul, and once she thought of just turning back without a word and going home. She stopped, thinking that Paul would never do that to her, and so she would have to tell him. When a rabbit leaped, she let Paul have it without dispute. He killed it with one shot.

When she came up with him, he was already kneeling, examining the wound, the rabbit trailing from his hands. "Right through the head," he said complacently, as if he had aimed for it. He took out his sharp, competent bowie knife and started to skin the body. He did it very cleanly and quickly. Uncle Jimbilly knew how to prepare the skins so that Miranda always had fur coats for her dolls, for though she never cared much for her dolls she liked seeing them in fur coats. The children knelt facing

each other over the dead animal. Miranda watched admiringly while her brother stripped the skin away as if he were taking off a glove. The flayed flesh emerged dark scarlet, sleek, firm; Miranda with thumb and finger felt the long fine muscles with the silvery flat strips binding them to the joints. Brother lifted the oddly bloated belly. "Look," he said, in a low amazed voice. "It was going to have young ones."

Very carefully he slit the thin flesh from the center ribs to the flanks, and a scarlet bag appeared. He slit again and pulled the bag open, and there lay a bundle of tiny rabbits, each wrapped in a thin scarlet veil. The brother pulled these off and there they were, dark gray, their sleek wet down lying in minute even ripples, like a baby's head just washed, their unbelievably small delicate ears folded close, their little blind faces almost featureless.

Miranda said, "Oh, I want to *see*," under her breath. She looked and looked—excited but not frightened, for she was accustomed to the sight of animals killed in hunting—filled with pity and astonishment and a kind of shocked delight in the wonderful little creatures for their own sakes, they were so pretty. She touched one of them ever so carefully, "Ah, there's blood running over them," she said and began to tremble without knowing why. Yet she wanted most deeply to see and to know. Having seen, she felt at once as if she had known all along. The very memory of her former ignorance faded, she had always known just this. No one had ever told her anything outright, she had been rather unobservant of the animal life around her because she was so accustomed to animals. They seemed simply disorderly and unaccountably rude in their habits, but altogether natural and not very interesting. Her brother had spoken as if he had known about everything all along. He may have seen all this before. He had never said a word to her, but she knew now a part at least of what he knew. She understood a little of the secret, formless intuitions in her own mind and body, which had been clearing up, taking form, so gradually and so steadily she had not realized that she was learning what she had to know. Paul said cautiously, as if he were talking about something forbidden: "They were just about ready to be born." His voice dropped on the last word. "I know," said Miranda, "like kittens. I know, like babies." She was quietly and terribly agitated, standing again with her rifle under her arm, looking down at the bloody heap. "I don't want the skin," she said, "I won't have it." Paul buried the young rabbits again in their mother's body, wrapped the skin around her, carried her to a clump of sage bushes, and hid her away. He came out again at once and said to Miranda, with an eager friendliness, a confidential tone quite unusual in him, as if he were taking her into an important secret on equal terms: "Listen now. Now you listen to me, and don't ever forget. Don't you ever tell a living soul that you saw this. Don't tell a soul. Don't tell Dad because I'll get into trouble. He'll say I'm leading you into things you ought not to do. He's always saying that. So now don't you go and forget and blab out sometime the way you're always doing . . . Now, that's a secret. Don't you tell."

Miranda never told, she did not even wish to tell anybody. She thought about the whole worrisome affair with confused unhappiness for a few days. Then it sank quietly into her mind and was heaped over by accumulated thousands of impressions, for nearly twenty years. One day she was picking her path among the puddles and crushed refuse of a market street in a strange city of a strange country, when without warning, plain and clear in its true colors as if she looked through a frame upon a scene that had not stirred nor changed since the moment it happened, the episode of that far-off day leaped from its burial place before her mind's eye. She was so reasonlessly horrified she halted suddenly staring, the scene before her eyes dimmed by the vision back of them. An Indian vendor had held up before her a tray of dyed sugar sweets, in the shapes of all kinds of small creatures: birds, baby chicks, baby rabbits, lambs, baby pigs. They were in gay colors and smelled of vanilla, maybe. . . . It was a very hot day and the smell in the market, with its piles of raw flesh and wilting flowers, was like the mingled sweetness and corruption she had smelled that other day in the empty cemetery at home: the day she had remembered always until now vaguely as the time she and her brother had found treasure in the opened graves. Instantly upon this thought the dreadful vision faded, and she saw clearly her brother, whose childhood face she had forgotten, standing again in the blazing sunshine, again twelve years old, a pleased sober smile in his eyes, turning the silver dove over and over in his hands.

## Leo Tolstoy
# THREE DEATHS

### I

It was autumn. Two vehicles were rolling briskly along the wide road. In the coach in front were two women: one a lady, thin and pale, the other a plump maidservant with a ruddy, shining face. The maid's short, dry hair kept poking out from under a faded bonnet, and her red hand in its torn glove kept rearranging it jerkily. Health emanated with every breath from her full bosom, which was covered with a heavy shawl; her darting black eyes now followed the moving fields outside the window, now glanced timidly at her mistress, and now nervously scanned the corners of the coach. The lady's hat, hung on the baggage rack, swayed in front of her nose, and a puppy was lying on her knees. Her feet. raised on top of the boxes on the floor, were lightly tapping on them to the jolting of the springs and the rattling of the windows.

Eyes closed and hands folded in her lap, the lady was swaying gently upon the pillows placed behind her and, frowning slightly, coughed inwardly. She wore a white nightcap, and a baby-blue kerchief was tied around her pale, delicate throat. Dividing her fair, overly pomaded flat hair, a straight, wide part with a dry and deathly look to its white skin, receded under the cap. Her faded, yellowish skin was drawn loosely over the fine and handsome lines of her face, and her cheeks were flushed. Her lips were dry and restless, her sparse eyelashes had no curl to them, and her cloth traveling robe made straight pleats on her sunken chest. Even though her eyes were closed, the lady's face showed weariness, irritation, and habitual suffering.

THREE DEATHS: Translated by Anna Vakar and used with her permission. ©–Copyright, 1956, by Anna Vakar.

The footman, leaning on his elbows, dozed in his seat; the coach driver, shouting lustily to urge the four big, sweating horses, glanced every once in a while at the driver who was shouting in the calèche behind. The wide parallel marks of the tires spread evenly and rapidly on the limy dirt of the road. The sky was cold and gray, and a damp mist hung over the fields and the road. Inside the coach the air was stuffy and smelled of dust and Eau de Cologne. The sick woman drew her head back and slowly opened her large, brilliant, beautifully dark eyes.

"Again!" said she, nervously pushing aside with her beautiful, very thin hand the edge of the maid's coat which was barely touching her leg. And her lips curved painfully. Matryósha picked up the coat with both hands, raised herself on her sturdy legs, and sat down further away, her fresh face a bright scarlet. The invalid's beautiful dark eyes avidly followed the maid's movements. She leaned heavily with both hands on the seat and tried likewise to raise herself, in order to sit up higher; but her strength failed her. Her mouth twisted and her whole face became distorted by a look of impotent, spiteful irony. "You might at least help me! . . . Oh, never mind! I can do it myself. If only you'd be kind enough not to put your bags or whatever behind me! No! . . . don't even touch them, since you can't do it properly!" The lady closed her eyes, then quickly raising her eyelids again, glared at the maid. Matryósha, looking at her, was biting her red lower lip. A deep sigh arose from the invalid's chest but, incompleted, it turned into a cough. She turned aside, puckered her face, and clutched her chest with both hands. When the coughing stopped she again closed her eyes and sat still.

The two vehicles drove into a village. Matryósha put her plump hand out from under the shawl and crossed herself.

"What's that?" asked the lady.

"The post-station, madam."

"I am asking why you are crossing yourself!"

"There's a church, madam."

The sick woman turned to the window and began to cross herself slowly, staring intently at the big wooden church which the coach was passing.

The coach and the calèche both stopped at the post-station. The lady's husband and the doctor stepped from the calèche and went up to the coach.

"How are you feeling?" asked the doctor, testing her pulse.

"Well, my dear, how are you? Not too tired?" asked her husband in French. "Would you like to come out?"

Matryósha, having picked up her bundles, shrank back in the corner so as not to disturb the conversation.

"Oh, all right. Always the same," answered the sick lady. "No, I shan't come out."

Her husband, after standing there a moment, went into the station-house. Matryósha jumped out of the coach and ran on tiptoe across the mud to the gates.

"That I am ill is no reason for you not to have lunch," said the invalid, forcing a slight smile, to the doctor, who was standing at the window.

"None of them care about me," she added to herself as soon as the doctor, having moved away from her slowly, quickly ran up the steps of the station-house. "They feel fine, so they don't care. Oh, my God!"

"Well, Eduárd Ivánovich," said the husband, rubbing his hands together and smiling gaily as he met the doctor, "I've ordered our food-basket to be brought. How does that strike you?"

"Fine idea," answered the doctor.

"Well, how is she?" asked the husband with a sigh, lowering his voice and raising his eyebrows.

"As I've told you, she can't possibly get to Italy. God grant she even gets to Moscow, especially on these roads."

"But what can we do? Oh, my God! My God!" and the husband covered his eyes with his hand. "Set it there," he added to the man who had brought the food-basket.

"She should never have left," answered the doctor, shrugging his shoulders.

"But what could I do?" objected the husband. "I tried everything to hold her back: I spoke about the cost, about the children we would have to leave behind, about my business —she wouldn't listen to anything. She's planning her life in Italy as if she were in good health, and to tell her of her condition would be the same as to kill her."

"But she's already dead; you must realize that, Vasíli Dmítrich. A person can't live without lungs, and lungs don't grow in again. It is sad and tragic, but what can we do? My business and yours consists only in seeing that her end comes as peacefully as possible. What she needs is a priest."

"Oh, God! Try to understand my position—reminding her of her last will. Come what may, I won't tell her that. You know how good she is . . ."

"Still, try to persuade her to wait until winter when the roads are fit for sleighing," said the doctor shaking his head significantly, "or it might go ill on these roads."

"Aksyúsha, hey Aksyúsha!" yelled the station-master's daughter, throwing her jacket on over her head and stamping her feet on the muddy back porch. "Let's go look at the Shirkin [39] lady. I hear they're taking her abroad because of chest trouble. I've never seen yet what consumptives look like!"

Aksyúsha jumped down the steps, and the two girls grabbed hands and ran through the gate. Slowing their pace, they passed by the coach and peeked through the lowered window. The invalid turned her head toward them but, noticing their curiosity, frowned and turned away.

"Hea—ven sakes!" said the station-master's daughter, quickly turning her head away. "What a beauty she must have been, and now look at her! It's terrible. Did you see her, Aksyúsha? Did you see?"

"Yes, how thin!" Aksyúsha agreed. "Let's pretend we're going to the well and take another look. She turned her head away, but I caught a glimpse just the same. What a pity, Másha!"

"Yes, but look at that mud!" answered Másha, and both ran back through the gate.

"Apparently I look frightful," thought the sick woman. "If only I could get abroad sooner, sooner, I should quickly get well there."

"Well, how are you, my dear?" said her husband, coming up to the coach, still chewing.

"Always the same question," thought the invalid. "How can he eat?"

"I'm all right," she muttered through her teeth.

"You know, my dear, I'm afraid you'll get worse traveling in this weather, and Eduárd

Ivánovich says so too. Don't you think we'd better turn back?"

She remained angrily silent.

"The weather will perhaps improve and the roads be better fit for travel; you would feel better and then we could all go together."

"I'm sorry. Had I stopped listening to you a long time ago I would by now be in Berlin and completely well."

"What could we do, my angel? You know it was impossible. But now, if you stayed another month your health would improve nicely, I would wind up my business affairs, and we could take the children with us."

"The children are well, and I am not."

"But try to understand, my dear. In this weather, if you should get worse on the road . . . well, at least you would be home."

"What's so good about being at home?" answered the invalid, flaring up. "To die at home?"

But apparently the word *die* frightened her. She looked at her husband imploringly and questioningly. He lowered his eyes and was silent. Her mouth suddenly curved like a petulant child's, and tears rolled down her cheeks. Her husband hid his face in a handkerchief and silently walked away from the coach.

"No, I will go on," said the sick woman, and lifting her eyes to heaven, she folded her hands and began whispering incoherently. "Oh God! Why should this happen?" said she, and the tears flowed faster. She prayed long and fervently. But the ache in her chest was just as painful and tight; the sky, the fields, and the road were just as gray and gloomy, and the autumnal mist, neither thickening nor lifting, kept settling on the muddy road, the roofs, the coach, and the sheepskin coats of the drivers, who were talking in powerful, merry voices as they greased the wheels and harnessed the horses.

## II

The coach was ready, but the driver tarried. He went into the drivers' room in the post-station. It was hot, stuffy, and dark there, with an oppressive smell of people, baked bread, cabbage, and sheepskin. There were several drivers in the room, and the cook was busy at the oven, on top of which lay a sick man covered with sheepskins.

"Uncle Fyódor! I say, uncle Fyódor!" said

---

[39] From the name of the place where the lady lived.

the young driver to the sick man as he entered the room, his whip stuck in the belt of his sheepskin coat.

"What do you want Fédka for, you loafer?" asked one of the drivers; "they're waiting for you in the coach!"

"I want to ask for his boots; I've worn mine out," answered the fellow, tossing back his hair and straightening the mittens tucked in his belt. "Is he asleep? Hey, uncle Fyódor!" he called again, going up to the oven.

"What do you want?" said a weak voice, and a lean, red-bearded face looked down from the top of the oven. A broad, pale, and emaciated hand, covered with hair, pulled a coat over a sharp shoulder in a dirty shirt. "Give me a drink, lad. What do you want?"

The young fellow handed up a dipper of water.

"Well, you see, Fédya," he said, shifting from one foot to the other, "I don't suppose you need your boots now; will you give them to me? You probably won't be doing any walking."

The sick man, having lowered his weary head to the shiny dipper, drank weakly but avidly, wetting his sparse, drooping mustache in the muddled water. His matted beard was dirty. It was hard for him to lift his sunken, lusterless eyes to the young man's face. Having finished drinking he wanted to raise his hand to wipe his wet lips but couldn't, and wiped his mouth on his coat sleeve. Saying nothing and breathing heavily through his nose, he looked straight into the young fellow's eyes, gathering his strength.

"Maybe you've promised them to somebody else," said the young man, "then forget it. You see, it's wet outside and I have to do my work; so I thought to myself: why not ask Fédka for his boots? I don't imagine he needs them. But if you still need them for yourself— just say so."

Something began to rumble and gurgle in the sick man's chest. He doubled up and started to choke from an abortive, throaty cough.

"Need them indeed!" the cook suddenly blurted out, so loudly she was heard throughout the room. "The second month now that he hasn't come down from the oven. Look at him choking! It makes me ache inside just to hear him. What should he need boots for? They won't bury him with new ones on. And

it was time long ago—God forgive me. Look how he chokes! He should be moved to some other place or somewhere. And there are hospitals in the town. This way he just takes up a lot of room, and is good for nothing. There's no room to turn around in, and still they want me to keep the place clean!"

"Hey Sergéi! Come on! The people are waiting!" yelled the drivers' overseer through the door.

Sergéi wanted to leave without awaiting his reply, but the sick man, while coughing, looked at him and said with his eyes that he wished to answer.

"You take the boots, Sergéi," he said, having stifled his cough and rested a bit. "But listen," he added hoarsely, "buy a stone for me when I die."

"Thank you, uncle. I'll take them, and I'll buy a stone for sure."

"There, lads, you heard that?" The sick man just managed to utter it and then again doubled over and started choking.

"All right, we heard," said one of the drivers. "Go on, Sergéi, take your place; there's the overseer running back. The Shirkin lady is ill, you know."

Quickly Sergéi pulled off his torn, ill-fitting boots, and flung them under a bench. Uncle Fyódor's new boots fitted perfectly and Sergéi walked out toward the coach constantly glancing down at them.

"What fancy boots! Let me grease them," said a driver, axle-grease in hand, as Sergéi was climbing to his seat and taking hold of the reins. "Did he give them to you for nothing?"

"Why, are you jealous?" answered Sergéi, rising and wrapping the skirts of the coat about his legs.

"Off you go! Giddap, my beauties!" he shouted to the horses, cracking his whip. And the two carriages with their occupants, boxes, and trunks rolled swiftly along the muddy road and vanished in the gray autumnal mist.

The sick driver remained on the oven in the stuffy room and, feeling no relief from coughing, turned with great effort to his other side and was quiet.

Until late in the evening people came and went and ate in the room. The sick man made no sound. When night came, the cook climbed on the oven and reached over his legs to get her sheepskin coat.

"Don't be cross with me, Nastásia," mumbled the sick man. "I'll leave your space empty soon."

"All right, all right. It doesn't matter," muttered Nastásia. "But tell me, uncle, what hurts you?"

"My whole inside is wasted away. God knows what it is."

"Your throat hurts too, when you cough?"

"It hurts all over. My end has come, that's what. Oh-h-h-h," moaned the sick man.

"Here, cover up your legs like this," said Nastásia, drawing his coat over him as she got down from the oven.

A night light burned dimly in the room. Nastásia and about ten drivers were sleeping on the floor and on the benches, snoring loudly. The sick man groaned feebly and coughed restlessly on the oven. By morning he was completely quiet.

"I had a queer dream last night," said the cook the next morning, stretching herself in the dim light. "I dreamt that uncle Fyódor came down off the oven and went out to chop wood. 'Here, Nástya,' he says, 'I'll help you.' So I say to him: 'How can you possibly chop wood?' But he just seizes the axe and starts chopping so quickly, quickly, that the chips fly all over. 'Why,' I say, 'you were very sick!' 'No,' he says, 'I am well,' and the way he swings the axe, I was quite scared. I cried out, and woke up. Do you think he's dead yet? Uncle Fyódor! Hey, uncle!"

Fyódor did not answer.

"He may be dead at that. I'll go see," said one of the drivers who was awake.

The lean hand, covered with hair, that hung down from the oven was pale and cold. "I'll go tell the station-master," said the driver. "Looks like he's dead."

Fyódor had no relatives: he came from some distant place. The following day they buried him in the new cemetery beyond the woods, and for several days Nastásia told everybody about the dream she had had, and the fact that she was the first to discover that Uncle Fyódor was dead.

### III

Spring came. On the wet streets of the city rapidly flowing rivulets gurgled between lumps of frozen manure. As the people moved along, the colors of their clothes were gay and the sound of their voices cheerful. The buds swelled on the trees behind the garden walls, and the branches swayed with a faint whisper in the fresh breeze. Everywhere transparent drops were forming and falling. The sparrows chirped and fluttered awkwardly with their little wings. On the sunny side of the street, on the garden walls, on the houses and the trees, everything was in sparkling motion. There was joy and youth in the sky, and on the earth, and in the hearts of men.

On one of the main streets fresh straw had been strewn in front of an imposing house where that same sick lady who had been hurrying abroad lay dying.

Her husband and an elderly woman were standing by the closed door to her room. On the sofa sat the priest, eyes lowered, holding something wrapped in his vestment. In the corner, the invalid's old mother was lying in a large Voltairian easy-chair, weeping bitterly. Beside her one maidservant stood holding a clean handkerchief in her hand, waiting for the old lady to ask for it, and another was rubbing her temples with something and blowing under her cap on her gray head.

"Well, Christ be with you, dear friend," the husband was saying to the elderly woman standing at the door with him. "She has such confidence in you, and you know so well how to talk to her—persuade her as well as you can, the darling—go to her." He was about to open the door, but her cousin stopped him, applied her handkerchief to her eyes several times, and gave a shake to her head.

"Now," she said, "I don't think it looks as if I had been crying," and she opened the door herself and went in.

The husband was in a state of great anxiety and appeared completely distracted. He started to go toward the old lady, but several steps away from her he turned and walked across the room to the priest. The priest looked at him, raised his eyebrows to heaven, and sighed. His thick, grayish beard also rose and then came down.

"Oh, God! Oh, God!" said the husband.

"What can you do?" said the priest with a sigh; and again his eyebrows and his beard rose and fell.

"And her mother here!" said the husband almost in despair. "She won't be able to bear it. Loving her as she does . . . she loves her so, how will she . . . I don't know. Father, if you would only try to calm her and persuade her to leave the room."

The priest stood up and went to the old lady.

"It is true, no one can appreciate a mother's love," he said, "but God is merciful."

The old lady's face suddenly twitched all over and she began to hiccough hysterically.

"God is merciful," continued the priest when she had calmed down a little. "I can tell you about a patient in my parish whose condition was much worse than Mária Dmítrevna's—and what do you know, a simple tradesman cured him with herbs in a short time. And that very same tradesman is now in Moscow. I've told Vasíli Dmítrich . . . maybe we can try him. It would be a comfort to her at least. To God, all is possible."

"No, she will not live," said the old lady. "God should be taking me, but He's taking her instead." And the hysterical hiccoughing became so violent that she fainted.

The sick woman's husband covered his face with his hands and rushed out of the room.

The first person he met in the corridor was his six-year-old boy who was running full speed after his little sister.

"Aren't you going to order the children to be taken to their mamma?" asked the nurse.

"No, she doesn't wish to see them. It would upset her."

The boy stopped a moment, looked intently into his father's face, then gave a kick and ran on, shouting merrily.

"She's pretending to be a black horse, papa!" he shouted, pointing to his sister.

Meanwhile, the cousin sat beside the sick woman in the other room, and with carefully selected words tried to prepare her for the thought of death. By the other window the doctor was mixing some medicine.

The invalid, in a white dressing gown, was sitting up amid supporting pillows, and looked silently at her cousin.

"Ah, dear," she said, interrupting her unexpectedly, "don't prepare me. Don't treat me like a child. I am a Christian; I know all about it. I know that I have not much longer to live, I know that if my husband had only listened to me earlier I would now be in Italy and perhaps—no, I am certain—I would now be well. Everyone told him so. But what can be done now? Apparently God wished it this way. We have all committed many sins—I know that. But I trust that in God's mercy everyone will be forgiven, probably all of us will be forgiven. I am trying to understand myself—I too have committed many sins, dear. But then how much I have suffered! I have tried to bear my sufferings bravely . . ."

"Then shall I call the priest, my dear? It will make it even easier when you've received communion," said her cousin.

The invalid nodded her head in assent.

"God forgive me, sinner that I am!" she whispered.

Her cousin stepped out and signaled to the priest with her eyes.

"She's an angel!" she said to the husband with tears in her eyes. The husband began to weep, the priest left the room, the old lady remained unconscious, and everything was completely quiet. Five minutes later the priest came out, took off his vestment, and straightened his hair.

"Thank God, she is calmer now," he said. "She wishes to see you."

The cousin and the husband went into the sick-room. The invalid was weeping quietly, her eyes on the ikon.

"I congratulate you, my dear," said her husband.[40]

"Thank you! How well I feel now! What inexplicable joy I feel!" And a slight smile played on her thin lips. "How merciful God is! Is He not? Merciful and all-powerful?" And again, her eyes full of tears, she looked at the ikon with eager entreaty.

Then she seemed suddenly to remember something. She beckoned to her husband to come closer.

"You never want to do what I ask," said she in a weak and pouting voice.

Her husband, craning his neck, listened to her humbly.

"What is it, my dear?"

"How often have I said that these doctors know nothing . . . but there are some plain people . . . they know how to cure. The priest told me . . . there's a tradesman . . . send for him."

---

[40] He congratulates her for receiving communion, as was the Russian custom.

"For whom, my dear?"

"Oh, God! He won't understand anything!" And the invalid puckered up her face and closed her eyes.

The doctor came up and took her hand. Her pulse was beating more and more feebly. He glanced at the husband. The invalid noticed the glance and looked round, frightened. Her cousin turned away and began to weep.

"Don't cry! Don't torture yourself and me," said the sick woman. "You take away my last moments of tranquility."

"You are an angel!" said her cousin, kissing her hand.

"No, kiss me here! Only the dead are kissed on the hand. Oh, God! Oh, God!"

That same evening the invalid was dead, and the body lay in a coffin in the ballroom of the big house. A deacon, sitting alone in the large room with closed doors, was reading the Psalms of David in a monotonous, nasal voice. A bright light from the high silver candlesticks fell upon the pale forehead of the dead lady, on her heavy, wax-like hands, and on the still folds of the shroud which brought out the knees and the toes in awful relief. The deacon, not understanding the words, read on monotonously, and in the quiet room the words sounded oddly and died away. From a distant room came the occasional sound of children's voices and the patter of their feet.

" 'Thou hidest thy face, they are troubled,' " intoned the psalm-reader. " 'Thou takest away their breath, they die, and return to their dust. Thou sendest forth thy spirit, they are created: and thou renewest the face of the earth. The glory of the Lord shall endure forever.' "

The dead woman's face looked stern and calmly majestic. Neither on her clear, cold forehead nor on her firmly closed lips was there any movement. She was all attention. But did she even. now understand those august words?

## IV

A month later a stone chapel was standing over the grave of the dead woman. Over the driver's grave there still was no stone: only light green grass sprouted on a little mound which served as the only token of the past life of a man.

"There'll be sin on your soul, Sergéi," the cook at the post-station said one day, "if you don't buy a stone for Fyódor. You've been saying: 'It's winter, it's winter!'—but why don't you keep your word now? I was here then, you know. He's already come back once to ask you for it. If you don't buy it he'll come to haunt you again."

"Well, I'm not backing out, am I?" answered Sergéi. "I'll buy a stone, like I said I would. A nice one for a ruble and a half. I haven't forgotten, it's just that it has to be fetched. Next time I happen to be in town, then I'll get one."

"You ought to put up a cross at least, that's what," interposed an old driver. "It's really a shame. You're wearing his boots, aren't you?"

"Where can I get a cross? I can't carve it out of a log, can I?"

"What are you talking about? You can't carve it out of a log, but you can take your axe and go to the woods early, and then you can make one. Chop down a young ash or something. That's all. And you won't even have to treat the forester to vodka: if you spilled vodka for every trifle there'd never be enough. Just the other day I broke the splinter-bar, went and cut myself an even better one, and no one said a word."

Early in the morning, almost before dawn, Sergéi took his axe and went to the woods.

Everything was covered with the still falling dew. There was no sun to make it glisten and it formed a cold and lusterless blanket. The east was brightening imperceptibly, reflecting a weak glow on the thinly clouded sky. On the ground not a single blade of grass was moving, nor a single leaf on the topmost branches of the trees. An occasional beating of wings in the thickness of a tree or a rustling on the ground was the only sound that marred the silence. Suddenly a strange, unnatural sound rang out and died. But it came again, and soon was repeated rhythmically down below by the trunk of one of the motionless trees on the edge of the woods. The crown of the tree began to tremble, the juicy leaves started whispering something, and a thrush, sitting on a branch, whistled, twice fluttered from place to place, and sat upon another tree, jerking her tail.

Below, the strokes grew heavier and heavier, and sappy white chips flew on the dewy grass. A slight cracking was heard through the blows.

The body of the tree shuddered, bent over, then, as if frightened, quickly straightened up and balanced uncertainly on its roots. For an instant all was quiet, then again the cracking was heard, again the tree bent over, and, bending and breaking its branches, fell top first on the damp earth. The sounds of axe-blows and footsteps died out. The thrush whistled and flew up higher, grazing a branch with its wings. The branch swayed a while and then its leaves were still like all the others. In the newly cleared space the trees spread out their immobile branches with even greater beauty.

The first gleaming rays of the sun broke through a milky cloud and traveled along the earth and heavens. The mist began to roll like waves in the hollows, the dew glistened and played on the verdure, and transparent white cloudlets dispersed hurriedly across the deepening blueness of the sky. The birds bustled aimlessly in the thicket, twittering gaily about something; the healthy leaves whispered quietly and happily in the heights, and the branches of the living trees began to stir slowly and majestically above the dead and fallen tree.

*Edwin Arlington Robinson*

# MR. FLOOD'S PARTY

Old Eben Flood, climbing alone one night
Over the hill between the town below
And the forsaken upland hermitage
That held as much as he should ever know
On earth again of home, paused warily.
The road was his with not a native near;
And Eben, having leisure, said aloud,
For no man else in Tilbury Town to hear:

"Well, Mr. Flood, we have the harvest moon
Again, and we may not have many more;          10
The bird is on the wing, the poet says,
And you and I have said it here before.

---

MR. FLOOD'S PARTY: From *Collected Poems,* by Edwin Arlington Robinson. Copyright, 1935, 1937, by The Macmillan Company. Used by permission of the publishers.

Drink to the bird." He raised up to the light
The jug that he had gone so far to fill,
And answered huskily: "Well, Mr. Flood,
Since you propose it, I believe I will."

Alone, as if enduring to the end
A valiant armor of scarred hopes outworn,
He stood there in the middle of the road
Like Roland's ghost winding a silent horn.     20
Below him, in the town among the trees,
Where friends of other days had honored him,
A phantom salutation of the dead
Rang thinly till old Eben's eyes were dim.

Then, as a mother lays her sleeping child
Down tenderly, fearing it may awake,
He set the jug down slowly at his feet
With trembling care, knowing that most things
      break;
And only when assured that on firm earth
It stood, as the uncertain lives of men        30
Assuredly did not, he paced away,
And with his hand extended paused again:

"Well, Mr. Flood, we have not met like this
In a long time; and many a change has come
To both of us, I fear, since last it was
We had a drop together. Welcome home!"
Convivially returning with himself,
Again he raised the jug up to the light;
And with an acquiescent quaver said:
"Well, Mr. Flood, if you insist, I might.       40

"Only a very little, Mr. Flood—
For auld lang syne. No more, sir; that will do."
So, for the time, apparently it did,
And Eben evidently thought so too;
For soon amid the silver loneliness
Of night he lifted up his voice and sang,
Secure, with only two moons listening,
Until the whole harmonious landscape rang—

"For auld lang syne." The weary throat gave out,
The last word wavered; and the song being
      done,                                      50
He raised again the jug regretfully
And shook his head, and was again alone.
There was not much that was ahead of him,
And there was nothing in the town below—
Where strangers would have shut the many doors
That many friends had opened long ago.

## Alfred, Lord Tennyson
# DARK HOUSE

Dark house, by which once more I stand
    Here in the long unlovely street,
    Doors, where my heart was used to beat
So quickly, waiting for a hand,

A hand that can be clasped no more—
    Behold me, for I cannot sleep,
    And like a guilty thing I creep
At earliest morning to the door.

He is not here; but far away
    The noise of life begins again,        10
    And ghastly thro' the drizzling rain
On the bald street breaks the blank day.

DARK HOUSE: From *In Memoriam*, Part VII.

## Alfred, Lord Tennyson
# TEARS, IDLE TEARS [41]

Tears, idle tears, I know not what they mean,
Tears from the depth of some divine despair
Rise in the heart, and gather to the eyes,
In looking on the happy autumn-fields,
And thinking of the days that are no more.

Fresh as the first beam glittering on a sail,
That brings our friends up from the underworld,
Sad as the last which reddens over one
That sinks with all we love below the verge;
So sad, so fresh, the days that are no more.    10

Ah, sad and strange as in dark summer dawns
The earliest pipe of half-awakened birds
To dying ears, when unto dying eyes
The casement slowly grows a glimmering square;
So sad, so strange, the days that are no more.

Dear as remembered kisses after death,
And sweet as those by hopeless fancy feigned
On lips that are for others; deep as love,
Deep as first love, and wild with all regret;
O Death in Life, the days that are no more.    20

[41] See "The Motivation of Tennyson's Weeper,"
p. 345, an essay on this poem.

## John Crowe Ransom
# DEAD BOY

The little cousin is dead, by foul subtraction,
A green bough from Virginia's aged tree,
And none of the county kin like the transaction,
Nor some of the world of outer dark, like me.

A boy not beautiful, nor good, nor clever,
A black cloud full of storms too hot for keeping,
A sword beneath his mother's heart—yet never
Woman bewept her babe as this is weeping.

A pig with a pasty face, so I had said,
Squealing for cookies, kinned by poor pretense  10
With a noble house. But the little man quite dead,
I see the forebears' antique lineaments.

The elder men have strode by the box of death
To the wide flag porch, and muttering low send
    round
The bruit of the day. O friendly waste of breath!
Their hearts are hurt with a deep dynastic wound.

He was pale and little, the foolish neighbors say;
The first fruits, saith the Preacher, the Lord hath
    taken;
But this was the old tree's late branch wrenched
    away,
Grieving the sapless limbs, the shorn and
    shaken.    20

DEAD BOY: From *Selected Poems*, by John Crowe
Ransom. Copyright, 1927, 1945, by Alfred A. Knopf,
Inc. Reprinted by permission of Alfred A. Knopf, Inc.

## William Shakespeare
# BE ABSOLUTE FOR DEATH

Be absolute for [42] death; either death or life
Shall thereby be the sweeter. Reason thus with life:
If I do lose thee, I do lose a thing
That none but fools would keep: a breath thou art,
Servile to all the skyey influences,[43]

BE ABSOLUTE FOR DEATH: From *Measure for
Measure*, Act III, Scene 1.

[42] Certain of.        [43] Influences of the stars.

That dost this habitation, where thou keep'st,[44]
Hourly afflict: merely,[45] thou art death's fool;
For him thou labour'st by thy flight to shun,
And yet runn'st toward him still. Thou art not
    noble;
For all the accommodations [46] that thou bear'st 10
Are nursed by baseness. Thou'rt by no means
    valiant;
For thou dost fear the soft and tender fork [47]
Of a poor worm. Thy best of rest is sleep,
And that thou oft provok'st; yet grossly fear'st
Thy death, which is no more. Thou art not thyself;
For thou exist'st on many a thousand grains
That issue out of dust. Happy thou art not;
For what thou hast not, still thou striv'st to get,
And what thou hast, forget'st. Thou art not certain;
For thy complexion shifts to strange effects,    20
After the moon.[48] If thou art rich, thou'rt poor;
For, like an ass whose back with ingots bows,
Thou bear'st thy heavy riches but a journey,
And death unloads thee. Friend hast thou none;
For thine own bowels,[49] which do call thee sire,
The mere effusion of thy proper [50] loins,
Do curse the gout, serpigo,[51] and the rheum,
For ending thee no sooner. Thou hast nor youth
    nor age,
But, as it were, an after-dinner's sleep,
Dreaming on both; for all thy blessed youth    30
Becomes as aged, and doth beg the alms
Of palsied eld; [52] and when thou art old and rich,
Thou hast neither heat, affection, limb, nor beauty,
To make thy riches pleasant. What's yet in this
That bears the name of life? Yet in this life
Lie hid moe thousand deaths: yet death we fear,
That makes these odds all even.

---

[44] i.e., the body.    [45] Entirely.    [46] Comforts.
[47] Forked tongue.
[48] i.e., your temperament is as changeable as the moon.
[49] Offspring.    [50] Own.    [51] Skin infection.
[52] Old age.

## William Shakespeare
# AY, BUT TO DIE

Ay, but to die, and go we know not where;
To lie in cold obstruction [53] and to rot;
This sensible warm motion to become

---

AY, BUT TO DIE: From *Measure for Measure*, Act
III, Scene 1.

[53] Stiffness.

A kneaded clod; and the delighted spirit
To bathe in fiery floods, or to reside
In thrilling region of thick-ribbèd ice;
To be imprisoned in the viewless [54] winds,
And blown with restless violence round about
The pendent world; or to be worse than worst
Of those that lawless and uncertain thoughts    10
Imagine howling:—'tis too horrible!
The weariest and most loathèd worldly life
That age, ache, penury, and imprisonment
Can lay on nature is a paradise
To what we fear of death.

---

[54] Invisible.

## Emily Dickinson
# BECAUSE I COULD NOT STOP FOR DEATH

Because I could not stop for Death.
He kindly stopped for me;
The carriage held but just ourselves
And Immortality.

We slowly drove, he knew no haste,
And I had put away
My labor, and my leisure too,
For his civility.

We passed the school where children played
At wrestling in a ring;                            10
We passed the fields of gazing grain,
We passed the setting sun.

We paused before a house that seemed
A swelling of the ground;
The roof was scarcely visible,
The cornice but a mound.

Since then 'tis centuries; but each
Feels shorter than the day
I first surmised the horses' heads
Were toward eternity.                               20

---

BECAUSE I COULD NOT STOP FOR DEATH: From
*Poems by Emily Dickinson,* edited by Martha Dickinson Bianchi. Used by permission of Little, Brown and Company.

## Thomas Nashe

# ADIEU, FAREWELL EARTH'S BLISS

Adieu, farewell earth's bliss,
This world uncertain is;
Fond are life's lustful joys,
Death proves them all but toys,
None from his darts can fly.
I am sick, I must die.
    Lord, have mercy on us!

Rich men, trust not in wealth,
Gold cannot buy you health;
Physic [55] himself must fade,    10
All things to end are made.
The plague full swift goes by;
I am sick, I must die.
    Lord, have mercy on us!

Beauty is but a flower
Which wrinkles will devour:
Brightness falls from the air,
Queens have died young and fair,
Dust has closèd Helen's [56] eye.
I am sick, I must die.    20
    Lord, have mercy on us!

Strength stoops unto the grave,
Worms feed on Hector [57] brave,
Swords may not fight with fate.
Earth still holds ope her gate;
Come! come! the bells do cry.
I am sick, I must die.
    Lord, have mercy on us!

Wit with his wantonness
Tasteth death's bitterness;    30
Hell's executioner
Hath no ears for to hear
What vain art can reply.
I am sick, I must die.
    Lord, have mercy on us!

Haste, therefore, each degree,
To welcome destiny.
Heaven is our heritage,

Earth but a player's stage;
Mount we unto the sky.    40
I am sick, I must die.
    Lord, have mercy on us!

## John Keats

# ODE TO A NIGHTINGALE

My heart aches, and a drowsy numbness pains
    My sense, as though of hemlock [58] I had drunk,
Or emptied some dull opiate to the drains
    One minute past, and Lethe-wards had sunk:
'Tis not through envy of thy happy lot,
    But being too happy in thine happiness,—
        That thou, light-wingèd Dryad of the trees,
        In some melodious plot
    Of beechen green, and shadows numberless,
    Singest of summer in full-throated ease.    10

O, for a draught of vintage! that hath been
    Cooled a long age in the deep-delvèd earth,
Tasting of Flora [59] and the country green,
    Dance, and Provençal song, and sunburnt mirth!
O for a beaker full of the warm South,
    Full of the true, the blushful Hippocrene, [60]
        With beaded bubbles winking at the brim,
        And purple-stainèd mouth;
    That I might drink, and leave the world unseen,
    And with thee fade away into the forest
        dim:    20

Fade far away, dissolve, and quite forget
    What thou among the leaves hast never known,
The weariness, the fever, and the fret
    Here, where men sit and hear each other groan;
Where palsy shakes a few, sad, last gray hairs,
    Where youth grows pale, and spectre-thin, and
        dies;
        Where but to think is to be full of sorrow
        And leaden-eyed despairs,
    Where Beauty cannot keep her lustrous eyes,
        Or new Love pine at them beyond tomor-
        row.    30

---

[55] Medicine.
[56] Helen of Troy.
[57] Bravest of the Trojan warriors, killed by Achilles.

[58] A poison.
[59] Ancient Roman goddess of flowers.
[60] A fountain on Mount Helicon, the waters of which were supposed by the ancient Greeks to impart poetic inspiration.

Away! away! for I will fly to thee,
    Not charioted by Bacchus and his pards,[61]
But on the viewless wings of Poesy,
    Though the dull brain perplexes and retards:
Already with thee! tender is the night,
    And haply the Queen-Moon is on her throne,
        Clustered around by all her starry Fays;
            But here there is no light,
Save what from heaven is with the breezes blown
    Through verdurous glooms and winding
        mossy ways.                                          40

I cannot see what flowers are at my feet,
    Nor what soft incense hangs upon the boughs,
But, in embalmèd darkness, guess each sweet
    Wherewith the seasonable month endows
The grass, the thicket, and the fruit-tree wild;
    White hawthorn, and the pastoral eglantine;
        Fast fading violets covered up in leaves;
            And mid-May's eldest child,
The coming musk-rose, full of dewy wine,
    The murmurous haunt of flies on summer
        eves.                                                50

Darkling I listen; and, for many a time
    I have been half in love with easeful Death,
Called him soft names in many a musèd rhyme,
    To take into the air my quiet breath;
Now more than ever seems it rich to die,
    To cease upon the midnight with no pain,
        While thou art pouring forth thy soul abroad
            In such an ecstasy!
Still wouldst thou sing, and I have ears in vain—
    To thy high requiem become a sod.                       60

Thou wast not born for death, immortal Bird!
    No hungry generations tread thee down;
The voice I hear this passing night was heard
    In ancient days by emperor and clown:
Perhaps the self-same song that found a path
    Through the sad heart of Ruth, when, sick for
        home,
        She stood in tears amid the alien corn;
            The same that oft-times hath
Charmed magic casements, opening on the foam
    Of perilous seas, in faery lands forlorn.               70

Forlorn! the very word is like a bell
    To toll me back from thee to my sole self!
Adieu! the fancy cannot cheat so well
    As she is famed to do, deceiving elf.

---

[61] Leopards, which supposedly drew the chariot of
the god of wine.

Adieu! adieu! thy plaintive anthem fades
    Past the near meadows, over the still stream,
        Up the hill-side; and now 'tis buried deep
            In the next valley-glades:
Was it a vision, or a waking dream?
    Fled is that music:—Do I wake or sleep?   80

## William Butler Yeats
# SAILING TO BYZANTIUM

That is no country for old men. The young
In one another's arms, birds in the trees,
—Those dying generations—at their song,
The salmon-falls, the mackerel-crowded seas,
Fish, flesh, or fowl, commend all summer long
Whatever is begotten, born, and dies.
Caught in that sensual music all neglect
Monuments of unaging intellect.

An aged man is but a paltry thing,
A tattered coat upon a stick, unless         10
Soul clap its hands and sing, and louder sing
For every tatter in its mortal dress,
Nor is there singing school but studying
Monuments of its own magnificence;
And therefore I have sailed the seas and come
To the holy city of Byzantium.

O sages standing in God's holy fire
As in the gold mosaic of a wall,
Come from the holy fire, perne [62] in a gyre,
And be the singing-masters of my soul.       20
Consume my heart away; sick with desire
And fastened to a dying animal
It knows not what it is; and gather me
Into the artifice of eternity.

Once out of nature I shall never take
My bodily form from any natural thing,

---

SAILING TO BYZANTIUM: From *Collected Poems,* by
William Butler Yeats. Copyright, 1903, 1906, 1907,
1912, 1916, 1918, 1919, 1924, 1928, 1931, 1933,
1934, 1935, 1940, 1944, 1945, 1946, 1950, by The
Macmillan Company. Copyright, 1940, by Georgie
Yeats. Used by permission of The Macmillan Com-
pany. Canadian rights granted by Mrs. Yeats, The
Macmillan Company of Canada, and A. P. Watt &
Son, Ltd.

[62] Whirl.

But such a form as Grecian goldsmiths make
Of hammered gold and gold enameling
To keep a drowsy Emperor awake;
Or set upon a golden bough to sing          30
To lords and ladies of Byzantium
Of what is past, or passing, or to come.


*Robert Browning*

# THE BISHOP ORDERS
# HIS TOMB AT
# SAINT PRAXED'S CHURCH


Vanity, saith the preacher, vanity!
Draw round my bed: is Anselm keeping back?
Nephews—sons mine . . . ah God, I know not!
  Well—
She, men would have to be your mother once,
Old Gandolf envied me, so fair she was!
What's done is done, and she is dead beside,
Dead long ago, and I am Bishop since,
And as she died so must we die ourselves,
And thence ye may perceive the world's a dream.
Life, how and what is it? As here I lie          10
In this state-chamber, dying by degrees,
Hours and long hours in the dead night, I ask
"Do I live, am I dead?" Peace, peace seems all.
Saint Praxed's ever was the church for peace;
And so, about this tomb of mine. I fought
With tooth and nail to save my niche, ye know:
—Old Gandolf cozened me, despite my care;
Shrewd was that snatch from out the corner South
He graced his carrion with, God curse the same!
Yet still my niche is not so cramped but thence  20
One sees the pulpit o' the epistle-side,
And somewhat of the choir, those silent seats,
And up into the aery dome where live
The angels, and a sunbeam's sure to lurk:
And I shall fill my slab of basalt there,
And 'neath my tabernacle take my rest,
With those nine columns round me, two and two,
The odd one at my feet where Anselm stands:
Peach-blossom marble all, the rare, the ripe
As fresh-poured red wine of a mighty pulse.     30
—Old Gandolf with his paltry onion-stone,[63]
Put me where I may look at him! True peach,
Rosy and flawless: how I earned the prize!

Draw close: that conflagration of my church
—What then? So much was saved if aught were
  missed!
My sons, ye would not be my death? Go dig
The white-grape vineyard where the oil-press
  stood,
Drop water gently till the surface sink,
And if ye find . . . Ah God, I know not, I! . . .
Bedded in store of rotten fig-leaves soft,       40
And corded up in a tight olive-frail,[64]
Some lump, ah God, of *lapis lazuli*,[65]
Big as a Jew's head cut off at the nape,
Blue as a vein o'er the Madonna's breast . . .
Sons, all have I bequeathed you, villas, all,
That brave Frascati[66] villa with its bath,
So, let the blue lump poise between my knees,
Like God the Father's globe on both his hands
Ye worship in the Jesu Church[67] so gay,
For Gandolf shall not choose but see and burst!  50
Swift as a weaver's shuttle fleet our years:
Man goeth to the grave, and where is he?
Did I say basalt for my slab, sons? Black—
'Twas ever antique-black I meant! How else
Shall ye contrast my frieze to come beneath?
The bas-relief in bronze ye promised me,
Those Pans and Nymphs ye wot of, and perchance
Some tripod, thyrsus,[68] with a vase or so,
The Saviour at his sermon on the mount,
Saint Praxed in a glory, and one Pan            60
Ready to twitch the Nymph's last garment off,
And Moses with the tables[69] . . . but I know
Ye mark me not! What do they whisper thee,
Child of my bowels, Anselm? Ah, ye hope
To revel down my villas while I gasp
Bricked o'er with beggar's mouldy travertine
Which Gandolf from his tomb-top chuckles at!
Nay, boys, ye love me—all of jasper, then!
'Tis jasper ye stand pledged to, lest I grieve.
My bath must needs be left behind, alas!         70
One block, pure green as a pistachio-nut,
There's plenty jasper somewhere in the world—
And have I not Saint Praxed's ear to pray
Horses for ye, and brown Greek manuscripts,
And mistresses with great smooth marbly limbs?
—That's if ye carve my epitaph aright,
Choice Latin, picked phrase, Tully's[70] every word,

---

[63] A poor grade of marble.

[64] Olive basket.
[65] Semi-precious blue stone.
[66] Suburb of Rome.
[67] Jesuit Church in Rome.
[68] Staff carried in festivals honoring the god of wine.
[69] Tablets inscribed with the Ten Commandments.
[70] Cicero, Roman orator.

No gaudy ware like Gandolf's second line—
Tully, my masters? Ulpian [71] serves his need!
And then how I shall lie through centuries,          80
And hear the blessed mutter of the mass,
And see God made and eaten all day long,
And feel the steady candle-flame, and taste
Good strong thick stupefying incense-smoke!
For as I lie here, hours of the dead night,
Dying in state and by such slow degrees,
I fold my arms as if they clasped a crook,
And stretch my feet forth straight as stone can
     point,
And let the bedclothes, for a mortcloth, drop
Into great laps and folds of sculptor's-work:       90
And as yon tapers dwindle, and strange thoughts
Grow, with a certain humming in my ears,
About the life before I lived this life,
And this life too, popes, cardinals and priests,
Saint Praxed at his sermon on the mount,
Your tall pale mother with her talking eyes,
And new-found agate urns as fresh as day,
And marble's language, Latin pure, discreet,
—Aha, ELUCESCEBAT [72] quoth our friend?
No Tully, said I, Ulpian at the best!                 100
Evil and brief hath been my pilgrimage.

---

[71] A Roman jurist whose Latin represented a decline
from the classical purity of Cicero.
   [72] "He was illustrious." The purer form would be
*elucebat.*

All *lapis,* all, sons! Else I give the Pope
My villas! Will ye ever eat my heart?
Ever your eyes were as a lizard's quick,
They glitter like your mother's for my soul,
Or ye would heighten my impoverished frieze,
Piece out its starved design, and fill my vase
With grapes, and add a vizor and a Term, [73]
And to the tripod ye would tie a lynx
That in his struggle throws the thyrsus down,     110
To comfort me on my entablature [74]
Whereon I am to lie till I must ask
"Do I live, am I dead?" There, leave me, there!
For ye have stabbed me with ingratitude
To death—ye wish it—God, ye wish it! Stone—
Gritstone, [75] a-crumble! Clammy squares which
     sweat
As if the corpse they keep were oozing through—
And no more *lapis* to delight the world!
Well, go! I bless ye. Fewer tapers there,
But in a row: and, going, turn your backs          120
—Ay, like departing altar-ministrants,
And leave me in my church, the church for peace,
That I may watch at leisure if he leers—
Old Gandolf, at me, from his onion-stone,
As still he envied me, so fair she was!

---

[73] Bust on a pedestal.
[74] Platform on columns.
[75] Coarse sandstone.

# ACHIEVEMENT AND
# REALIZATION

ERTAIN crucial moments in people's lives bring us to reflect upon the meaning of those lives: their purposes and achievements, their drive or drift. Moreover, whether at crucial moments or not, we frequently ask such questions of ourselves: Am I a success or a failure? What has my life meant up to this point? What have I accomplished? Where am I going? What is the most important thing in my life? And usually our answers are based upon comparisons with the lives of others, either of those we know personally or of those we meet in books.

The impulse toward evaluations of this kind forms the common element of the works collected in this chapter. They are concerned with such fundamental ideas as success, failure, fortune, fame, glory, and ambition—the ideas we use to appraise the quality of a person's life, to decide how far he has accomplished something of worth or become what he had it in him to be. A person's *achievement* is something to be objectively measured by the eyes of others; his *realization* of himself as a person is measured in a relative way—and these two measures may or may not coincide.

The writings in this chapter bear witness to some lives that were eminently worth living, either because they attained greatness and a special nobility, as did Jesus, Lincoln, Cromwell —and, in their own ways, Cortez and the bullfighter in "The Undefeated"—or because in a humbler way they exemplify some common but precious virtue, as do Sir Patrick Spens

565

in his profound sense of duty, or Lawrence's blind man in his vibrant aliveness, or the unnamed folk buried in Gray's country churchyard. "The Secret Sharer" is the story of a man who meets his first great test in life and rises to it; on the other side, "The Beast in the Jungle" presents the classic example of a man who lets life slip through his fingers while waiting for it to begin.

It is one of the values of literature that it helps to reduce that "blindness" of which William James speaks in his essay: the inability to understand sympathetically the goals and ideals that other people set themselves, goals and ideals that, differing as they may from our own, help to define the meaning of those other lives. A. J. Liebling's study of two boxers is a comparison between two ideas of the life worthy of man, just as is the clash between Antigone and Creon. In Tennyson's "Ulysses," Milton's "Lycidas," and the essay on Cortez we see some of the range of purposes that motivate human beings and create the variety of human natures.

## *William James*

# ON A CERTAIN BLINDNESS IN HUMAN BEINGS

Our judgments concerning the worth of things, big or little, depend on the *feelings* the things arouse in us. Where we judge a thing to be precious in consequence of the *idea* we frame of it, this is only because the idea is itself associated already with a feeling. If we were radically feelingless, and if ideas were the only things our mind could entertain, we should lose all our likes and dislikes at a stroke, and be unable to point to any one situation or experience in life more valuable or significant than any other.

Now the blindness in human beings, of which this discourse will treat, is the blindness with which we all are afflicted in regard to the feelings of creatures and people different from ourselves.

We are practical beings, each of us with limited functions and duties to perform. Each is bound to feel intensely the importance of his own duties and the significance of the situations that call these forth. But this feeling is in each of us a vital secret, for sympathy with which we vainly look to others. The others are

too much absorbed in their own vital secrets to take an interest in ours. Hence the stupidity and injustice of our opinions, so far as they deal with the significance of alien lives. Hence the falsity of our judgments, so far as they presume to decide in an absolute way on the value of other persons' conditions or ideals.

Take our dogs and ourselves, connected as we are by a tie more intimate than most ties in this world; and yet, outside of that tie of friendly fondness, how insensible, each of us, to all that makes life significant for the other!— we to the rapture of bones under hedges, or smells of trees and lamp-posts, they to the delights of literature and art. As you sit reading the most moving romance you ever fell upon, what sort of a judge is your fox-terrier of your behavior? With all his good will toward you, the nature of your conduct is absolutely excluded from his comprehension. To sit there like a senseless statue, when you might be taking him to walk and throwing sticks for him to catch! What queer disease is this that comes over you every day, of holding things and staring at them like that for hours together, paralyzed of motion and vacant of all conscious life? The African savages came nearer the truth; but they, too, missed it, when they gathered wonderingly round one of our American travellers who, in the interior, had just come into possession of a stray copy of the New York *Commercial Advertiser,* and was devouring it column by column. When he got through, they offered him a high price for the mysterious object; and, being asked for what they wanted it, they said: "For an eye medicine,"—that being the only reason they could conceive of for the protected bath which he had given his eyes upon its surface.

The spectator's judgment is sure to miss the root of the matter, and to possess no truth. The subject judged knows a part of the world of reality which the judging spectator fails to see, knows more while the spectator knows less; and, wherever there is conflict of opinion and difference of vision, we are bound to believe that the truer side is the side that feels the more, and not the side that feels the less.

Let me take a personal example of the kind that befalls each one of us daily:—

Some years ago, while journeying in the mountains of North Carolina, I passed by a large number of "coves," as they call them there, or heads of small valleys between the hills, which had been newly cleared and planted. The impression on my mind was one of unmitigated squalor. The settler had in every case cut down the more manageable trees, and left their charred stumps standing. The larger trees he had girdled and killed, in order that their foliage should not cast a shade. He had then built a log cabin, plastering its chinks with clay, and had set up a tall zigzag rail fence around the scene of his havoc, to keep the pigs and cattle out. Finally, he had irregularly planted the intervals between the stumps and trees with Indian corn, which grew among the chips; and there he dwelt with his wife and babes—an axe, a gun, a few utensils, and some pigs and chickens feeding in the woods, being the sum total of his possessions.

The forest had been destroyed; and what had "improved" it out of existence was hideous, a sort of ulcer, without a single element of artificial grace to make up for the loss of Nature's beauty. Ugly, indeed, seemed the life of the squatter, scudding, as the sailors say, under bare poles, beginning again away back where our first ancestors started, and by hardly a single item the better off for all the achievements of the intervening generations.

Talk about going back to nature! I said to myself, oppressed by the dreariness, as I drove by. Talk of a country life for one's old age and for one's children! Never thus, with nothing but the bare ground and one's bare hands to fight the battle! Never, without the best spoils of culture woven in! The beauties and com-modities gained by the centuries are sacred. They are our heritage and birthright. No modern person ought to be willing to live a day in such a state of rudimentariness and denudation.

Then I said to the mountaineer who was driving me, "What sort of people are they who have to make these new clearings?" "All of us," he replied. "Why, we ain't happy here, unless we are getting one of these coves under cultivation." I instantly felt that I had been losing the whole inward significance of the situation. Because to me the clearings spoke of naught but denudation, I thought that to those whose sturdy arms and obedient axes had made them they could tell no other story. But, when *they* looked on the hideous stumps, what they thought of was personal victory. The chips, the girdled trees, and the vile split rails spoke of honest sweat, persistent toil, and final reward. The cabin was a warrant of safety for self and wife and babes. In short, the clearing, which to me was a mere ugly picture on the retina, was to them a symbol redolent with moral memories and sang a very paean of duty, struggle, and success.

I had been as blind to the peculiar ideality of their conditions as they certainly would also have been to the ideality of mine, had they had a peep at my strange indoor academic ways of life at Cambridge.

Wherever a process of life communicates an eagerness to him who lives it, there the life becomes genuinely significant. Sometimes the eagerness is more knit up with the motor activities, sometimes with the perceptions, sometimes with the imagination, sometimes with reflective thought. But, wherever it is found, there is the zest, the tingle, the excitement of reality; and there *is* "importance" in the only real and positive sense in which importance ever anywhere can be.

Robert Louis Stevenson has illustrated this by a case, drawn from the sphere of the imagination, in an essay which I really think deserves to become immortal, both for the truth of its matter and the excellence of its form.

"Toward the end of September," Stevenson writes, "when school-time was drawing near, and the nights were already black, we would begin to sally from our respective villas, each equipped with a tin bull's-eye lantern. The thing was so well known that it had worn a rut in the commerce of Great Britain; and the grocers, about the due time, began to garnish their windows with our particular brand of luminary. We wore them buckled to the waist upon a cricket belt, and over them, such was the rigor of the game, a buttoned top-coat. They smelled noisomely of blistered tin. They never burned aright, though they would always burn our fingers. Their use was naught, the pleasure of them merely fanciful, and yet a boy with a bull's-eye under his top-coat asked for nothing more. The fishermen used lanterns about their boats, and it was from them, I suppose, that we had got the hint; but theirs were not bull's-eyes, nor did we ever play at being fishermen. The police carried them at their belts, and we had plainly copied them in that; yet we did not pretend to be policemen. Burglars, indeed, we may have had some haunting thought of; and we had certainly an eye to past ages when lanterns were more common, and to certain story-books in which we had found them to figure very largely. But take it for all in all, the pleasure of the thing was substantive; and to be a boy with a bull's-eye under his top-coat was good enough for us.

"When two of these asses met, there would be an anxious 'Have you got your lantern?' and a gratified 'Yes!' That was the shibboleth, and very needful, too; for, as it was the rule to keep our glory contained, none could recognize a lantern-bearer unless (like the polecat) by the smell. Four or five would sometimes climb into the belly of a ten-man lugger, with nothing but the thwarts above them,—for the cabin was usually locked,—or choose out some hollow of the links where the wind might whistle overhead. Then the coats would be unbuttoned, and the bull's-eyes discovered; and in the chequering glimmer, under the huge, windy hall of the night, and cheered by a rich stream of toasting tinware, these fortunate young gentlemen would crouch together in the cold sand of the links, or on the scaly bilges of the fishing-boat, and delight them with inappropriate talk. Woe is me that I cannot give some specimens! ... But the talk was but a condiment, and these gatherings themselves only accidents in the career of the lantern-bearer. The essence of this bliss was to walk by yourself in the black night, the slide shut, the top-coat buttoned, not a ray escaping, whether to conduct your footsteps or to make your glory public,—a mere pillar of darkness in the dark;

and all the while, deep down in the privacy of your fool's heart, to know you had a bull's-eye at your belt, and to exult and sing over the knowledge.

"It is said that a poet has died young in the breast of the most stolid. It may be contended rather that a (somewhat minor) bard in almost every case survives, and is the spice of life to his possessor. Justice is not done to the versatility and the unplumbed childishness of man's imagination. His life from without may seem but a rude mound of mud: there will be some golden chamber at the heart of it, in which he dwells delighted; and for as dark as his pathway seems to the observer, he will have some kind of bull's-eye at his belt.

... "There is one fable that touches very near the quick of life,—the fable of the monk who passed into the woods, heard a bird break into song, hearkened for a trill or two, and found himself at his return a stranger at his convent gates; for he had been absent fifty years, and of all his comrades there survived but one to recognize him. It is not only in the woods that this enchanter carols, though perhaps he is native there. He sings in the most doleful places. The miser hears him and chuckles, and his days are moments. With no more apparatus than an evil-smelling lantern, I have evoked him on the naked links. All life that is not merely mechanical is spun out of two strands,—seeking for that bird and hearing him. And it is just this that makes life so hard to value, and the delight of each so incommunicable. And it is just a knowledge of this, and a remembrance of those fortunate hours in which the bird *has* sung to *us,* that fills us with such wonder when we turn to the pages of the realist. There, to be sure, we find a picture of life in so far as it consists of mud and of old iron, cheap desires and cheap fears, that which we are ashamed to remember and that which we are careless whether we forget; but of the note of that time-devouring nightingale we hear no news.

... "Say that we came [in such a realistic romance] on some such business as that of my lantern-bearers on the links, and described the boys as very cold, spat upon by flurries of rain, and drearily surrounded, all of which they were; and their talk as silly and indecent, which it certainly was. To the eye of the observer they *are* wet and cold and drearily surrounded; but ask themselves, and they are in the heaven of a recondite pleasure, the ground of which is an ill-smelling lantern.

"For, to repeat, the ground of a man's joy is often hard to hit. It may hinge at times upon a mere accessory, like the lantern; it may reside in the mysterious inwards of psychology. . . It has so little bond with externals . . . that it may even touch them not, and the man's true life, for which he consents to live, lie altogether in the field of fancy. . . In such a case the poetry runs underground. The observer (poor soul, with his documents!) is all abroad. For to look at the man is but to court deception. We shall see the trunk from which he draws his nourishment; but he himself is above and abroad in the green dome of foliage, hummed through by winds and nested in by nightingales. And the true realism were that of the poets, to climb up after him like a squirrel, and catch some glimpse of the heaven for which he lives. And the true realism, always and everywhere, is that of the poets: to find out where joy resides, and give it a voice far beyond singing.

"For to miss the joy is to miss all. In the joy of the actors lies the sense of any action. That is the explanation, that the excuse. To one who has not the secret of the lanterns the scene upon the links is meaningless. And hence the haunting and truly spectral unreality of realistic books. . . In each we miss the personal poetry, the enchanted atmosphere, that rainbow work of fancy that clothes what is naked and seems to ennoble what is base; in each, life falls dead like dough, instead of soaring away like a balloon into the colors of the sunset; each is true, each inconceivable; for no man lives in the external truth, among salts and acids, but in the warm, phantasmagoric chamber of his brain, with the painted windows and the storied walls."

These paragraphs are the best thing I know in all Stevenson. "To miss the joy is to miss all." Indeed, it is. Yet we are but finite, and each one of us has some single specialized vocation of his own. And it seems as if energy in the service of its particular duties might be got only by hardening the heart toward everything unlike them. Our deadness toward all but one particular kind of joy would thus be the price we inevitably have to pay for being practical creatures. Only in some pitiful dreamer, some philosopher, poet, or romancer, or when the common practical man becomes a lover, does the hard externality give way, and a gleam of insight into the ejective world, as Clifford called it, the vast world of inner life beyond us, so different from that of outer seeming, illuminate our mind. Then the whole scheme of our customary values gets confounded, then our self is riven and its narrow interests fly to pieces, then a new centre and a new perspective must be found.

The change is well described by my colleague, Josiah Royce:—

"What, then, is our neighbor? Thou hast regarded his thought, his feeling, as somehow different from thine. Thou hast said, 'A pain in him is not like a pain in me, but something far easier to bear.' He seems to thee a little less living than thou; his life is dim, it is cold, it is a pale fire beside thy own burning desires. . . So, dimly and by instinct hast thou lived with thy neighbor, and hast known him not, being blind. Thou hast made [of him] a thing, no Self at all. Have done with this illusion, and simply try to learn the truth. Pain is pain, joy is joy, everywhere, even as in thee. In all the songs of the forest birds; in all the cries of the wounded and dying, struggling in the captor's power; in the boundless sea where the myriads of water-creatures strive and die; amid all the countless hordes of savage men; in all sickness and sorrow; in all exultation and hope, everywhere, from the lowest to the noblest, the same conscious, burning, wilful life is found, endlessly manifold as the forms of the living creatures, unquenchable as the fires of the sun, real as these impulses that even now throb in thine own little selfish heart. Lift up thy eyes, behold that life, and then turn away, and forget it as thou canst; but, if thou hast *known* that, thou hast begun to know thy duty."

This higher vision of an inner significance in what, until then, we had realized only in the dead external way, often comes over a person suddenly; and, when it does so, it makes an epoch in his history. As Emerson says, there is a depth in those moments that constrains us to ascribe more reality to them than to all other experiences. The passion of love will shake one like an explosion, or some act will awaken a remorseful compunction that hangs like a cloud over all one's later day.

This mystic sense of hidden meaning starts upon us often from non-human natural things.

I take this passage from "Obermann," a French novel that had some vogue in its day: "Paris, March 7.—It was dark and rather cold. I was gloomy, and walked because I had nothing to do. I passed by some flowers placed breast-high upon a wall. A jonquil in bloom was there. It is the strongest expression of desire: it was the first perfume of the year. I felt all the happiness destined for man. This unutterable harmony of souls, the phantom of the ideal world, arose in me complete. I never felt anything so great or so instantaneous. I know not what shape, what analogy, what secret of relation it was that made me see in this flower a limitless beauty. . . I shall never enclose in a conception this power, this immensity that nothing will express; this form that nothing will contain; this ideal of a better world which one feels, but which it would seem that nature has not made."

Wordsworth and Shelley are similarly full of this sense of a limitless significance in natural things. In Wordsworth it was a somewhat austere and moral significance, a "lonely cheer."

To every natural form, rock, fruit, or flower
Even the loose stones that cover the highway,
I gave a moral life: I saw them feel
Or linked them to some feeling: the great mass
Lay bedded in some quickening soul, and all
That I beheld respired with inward meaning.

"Authentic tidings of invisible things!" Just what this hidden presence in nature was, which Wordsworth so rapturously felt, and in the light of which he lived, tramping the hills for days together, the poet never could explain logically or in articulate conceptions. Yet to the reader who may himself have had gleaming moments of a similar sort the verses in which Wordsworth simply proclaims the fact of them come with a heart-satisfying authority:—

Magnificent
The morning rose, in memorable pomp,
Glorious as ere I had beheld. In front
The sea lay laughing at a distance; near
The solid mountains shone, bright as the clouds,
Grain-tinctured, drenched in empyrean light;
And in the meadows and the lower grounds
Was all the sweetness of a common dawn,—
Dews, vapors, and the melody of birds,
And laborers going forth to till the fields.

Ah! need I say, dear Friend, that to the brim
My heart was full; I made no vows, but vows
Were then made for me; bond unknown to me
Was given, that I should be, else sinning greatly,
A dedicated Spirit. On I walked,
In thankful blessedness, which yet survives.

As Wordsworth walked, filled with this strange inner joy, responsive thus to the secret life of nature round about him, his rural neighbors, tightly and narrowly intent upon their own affairs, their crops and lambs and fences, must have thought him a very insignificant and foolish personage. It surely never occurred to any one of them to wonder what was going on inside of *him* or what it might be worth. And yet that inner life of his carried the burden of a significance that has fed the souls of others, and fills them to this day with inner joy.

Richard Jefferies has written a remarkable autobiographic document entitled, *The Story of My Heart*. It tells, in many pages, of the rapture with which in youth the sense of the life of nature filled him. On a certain hill-top he says:—

"I was utterly alone with the sun and the earth. Lying down on the grass, I spoke in my soul to the earth, the sun, the air, and the distant sea, far beyond sight. . . With all the intensity of feeling which exalted me, all the intense communion I held with the earth, the sun and sky, the stars hidden by the light, with the ocean,—in no manner can the thrilling depth of these feelings be written,—with these I prayed as if they were the keys of an instrument. . . The great sun, burning with light, the strong earth,—dear earth,—the warm sky, the pure air, the thought of ocean, the inexpressible beauty of all filled me with a rapture, an ecstasy, an inflatus. With this inflatus, too, I prayed. . . The prayer, this soul-emotion, was in itself, not for an object: it was a passion. I hid my face in the grass. I was wholly prostrated, I lost myself in the wrestle, I was rapt and carried away. . . Had any shepherd accidentally seen me lying on the turf, he would only have thought I was resting a few minutes. I made no outward show. Who could have imagined the whirlwind of passion that was going on in me as I reclined there!"

Surely, a worthless hour of life, when measured by the usual standards of commercial value. Yet in what other *kind* of value can the preciousness of any hour, made precious by any standard, consist, if it consist not in feelings of excited significance like these, engendered in some one, by what the hour contains?

Yet so blind and dead does the clamor of our own practical interests make us to all other things, that it seems almost as if it were necessary to become worthless as a practical being, if one is to hope to attain to any breadth of insight into the impersonal world of worths as such, to have any perception of life's meaning on a large objective scale. Only your mystic, your dreamer, or your insolvent tramp or loafer, can afford so sympathetic an occupation, an occupation which will change the usual standards of human value in the twinkling of an eye, giving to foolishness a place ahead of power, and laying low in a minute the distinctions which it takes a hard-working conventional man a lifetime to build up. You may be a prophet, at this rate; but you cannot be a worldly success.

Walt Whitman, for instance, is accounted by many of us a contemporary prophet. He abolishes the usual human distinctions, brings all conventionalisms into solution, and loves and celebrates hardly any human attributes save those elementary ones common to all members of the race. For this he becomes a sort of ideal tramp, a rider on omnibus-tops and ferryboats, and, considered either practically or academically, a worthless, unproductive being. His verses are but ejaculations—things mostly without subject or verb, a succession of interjections on an immense scale. He felt the human crowd as rapturously as Wordsworth felt the mountains, felt it as an overpoweringly significant presence, simply to absorb one's mind in which should be business sufficient and worthy to fill the days of a serious man. As he crosses Brooklyn ferry, this is what he feels:—

Flood-tide below me! I watch you, face to face;
Clouds of the west! sun there half an hour high!
    I see you also face to face.
Crowds of men and women attired in the usual
    costumes! how curious you are to me!
On the ferry-boats, the hundreds and hundreds that
    cross, returning home, are more curious to me
    than you suppose;
And you that shall cross from shore to shore years
    hence, are more to me, and more in my medi-
    tations, than you might suppose.

Others will enter the gates of the ferry, and cross
    from shore to shore;
Others will watch the run of the flood-tide;
Others will see the shipping of Manhattan north
    and west, and the heights of Brooklyn to the
    south and east;
Others will see the islands large and small;
Fifty years hence, others will see them as they
    cross, the sun half an hour high.
A hundred years hence, or ever so many hundred
    years hence, others will see them,
Will enjoy the sunset, the pouring in of the flood-
    tide, the falling back to the sea of the ebb-tide
It avails not, neither time or place—distance avails
    not.
Just as you feel when you look on the river and
    sky, so I felt;
Just as any of you is one of a living crowd, I was
    one of a crowd;
Just as you are refresh'd by the gladness of the
    river and the bright flow, I was refresh'd;
Just as you stand and lean on the rail, yet hurry
    with the swift current,
    I stood, yet was hurried;
Just as you look on the numberless masts of ships,
    and the thick-stemmed pipes of steamboats, I
    looked.
I too many and many a time cross'd the river, the
    sun half an hour high;
I watched the Twelfth-month sea-gulls—I saw
    them high in the air, with motionless wings,
    oscillating their bodies,
I saw how the glistening yellow lit up parts of their
    bodies, and left the rest in strong shadow,
I saw the slow-wheeling circles, and the gradual
    edging toward the south.
Saw the white sails of schooners and sloops, saw
    the ships at anchor,
The sailors at work in the rigging, or out astride
    the spars;
The scallop-edged waves in the twilight, the ladled
    cups, the frolicsome crests and glistening;
The stretch afar growing dimmer and dimmer, the
    gray walls of the granite store-houses by the
    docks;
On the neighboring shores, the fires from the foun-
    dry chimneys burning high . . . into the night,
Casting their flicker of black . . . into the clefts of
    streets.
These, and all else, were to me the same as they
    are to you.

And so on, through the rest of a divinely beautiful poem. And, if you wish to see what this hoary loafer considered the most worthy way of profiting by life's heaven-sent opportunities, read the delicious volume of his letters to a young car-conductor who had become his friend:—

"New York, Oct. 9, 1868.

*"Dear Pete,*—It is splendid here this forenoon—bright and cool. I was out early taking a short walk by the river only two squares from where I live. . . Shall I tell you about [my life] just to fill up? I generally spend the forenoon in my room writing, etc., then take a bath fix up and go out about twelve and loafe somewhere or call on someone down town or on business, or perhaps if it is very pleasant and I feel like it ride a trip with some driver friend on Broadway from 23rd Street to Bowling Green, three miles each way. (Every day I find I have plenty to do, every hour is occupied with something.) You know it is a never ending amusement and study and recreation for me to ride a couple of hours on a pleasant afternoon on a Broadway stage in this way. You see everything as you pass, a sort of living, endless panorama—shops and splendid buildings and great windows: on the broad sidewalks crowds of women richly dressed continually passing, altogether different, superior in style and looks from any to be seen anywhere else—in fact a perfect stream of people—men too dressed in high style, and plenty of foreigners—and then in the streets the thick crowd of carriages, stages, carts, hotel and private coaches, and in fact all sorts of vehicles and many first class teams, mile after mile, and the splendor of such a great street and so many tall, ornamental, noble buildings many of them of white marble, and the gayety and motion on every side: you will not wonder how much attraction all this is on a fine day, to a great loafer like me, who enjoys so much seeing the busy world move by him, and exhibiting itself for his amusement, while he takes it easy and just looks on and observes."

Truly a futile way of passing the time, some of you may say, and not altogether creditable to a grown-up man. And yet, from the deepest point of view, who knows the more of truth, and who knows the less,—Whitman on his omnibus-top, full of the inner joy with which the spectacle inspires him, or you, full of the

disdain which the futility of his occupation excites?

When your ordinary Brooklynite or New Yorker, leading a life replete with too much luxury, or tired and careworn about his personal affairs, crosses the ferry or goes up Broadway, *his* fancy does not thus "soar away into the colors of the sunset" as did Whitman's, nor does he inwardly realize at all the indisputable fact that this world never did anywhere or at any time contain more of essential divinity, or of eternal meaning, than is embodied in the fields of vision over which his eyes so carelessly pass. There is life; and there, a step away, is death. There is the only kind of beauty there ever was. There is the old human struggle and its fruits together. There is the text and the sermon, the real and the ideal in one. But to the jaded and unquickened eye it is all dead and common, pure vulgarism, flatness, and disgust. "Hech! it is a sad sight!" says Carlyle, walking at night with some one who appeals to him to note the splendor of the stars. And that very repetition of the scene to new generations of men in *secula seculorum,* that eternal recurrence of the common order, which so fills a Whitman with mystic satisfaction, is to a Schopenhauer,[1] with the emotional anæsthesia, the feeling of "awful inner emptiness" from out of which he views it all, the chief ingredient of the tedium it instils. What is life on the largest scale, he asks, but the same recurrent inanities, the same dog barking, the same fly buzzing, forevermore? Yet of the kind of fibre of which such inanities consist is the material woven of all the excitements, joys, and meanings that ever were, or ever shall be, in this world.

To be rapt with satisfied attention, like Whitman, to the mere spectacle of the world's presence, is one way, and the most fundamental way, of confessing one's sense of its unfathomable significance and importance. But how can one attain to the feeling of the vital significance of an experience, if one have it not to begin with? There is no receipt which one can follow. Being a secret and a mystery, it often comes in mysteriously unexpected ways. It blossoms sometimes from out of the very grave wherein we imagined that our happiness was buried. Benvenuto Cellini, after a life all in the outer

---

[1] Arthur Schopenhauer, 1788–1860, German philosopher noted for his pessimistic philosophy.

sunshine, made of adventures and artistic excitements, suddenly finds himself cast into a dungeon in the Castle of San Angelo. The place is horrible. Rats and wet and mould possess it. His leg is broken and his teeth fall out, apparently with scurvy. But his thoughts turn to God as they have never turned before. He gets a Bible, which he reads during the one hour in the twenty-four in which a wandering ray of daylight penetrates his cavern. He has religious visions. He sings psalms to himself, and composes hymns. And thinking, on the last day of July, of the festivities customary on the morrow in Rome, he says to himself: "All these past years I celebrated this holiday with the vanities of the world: from this year henceforth I will do it with the divinity of God. And then I said to myself, 'Oh, how much more happy I am for this present life of mine than for all those things remembered!' "

But the great understander of these mysterious ebbs and flows is Tolstoy. They throb all through his novels. In his *War and Peace,* the hero, Peter, is supposed to be the richest man in the Russian empire. During the French invasion he is taken prisoner, and dragged through much of the retreat. Cold, vermin, hunger, and every form of misery assail him, the result being a revelation to him of the real scale of life's values. "Here only, and for the first time, he appreciated, because he was deprived of it, the happiness of eating when he was hungry, of drinking when he was thirsty, of sleeping when he was sleepy, and of talking when he felt the desire to exchange some words... Later in life he always recurred with joy to this month of captivity, and never failed to speak with enthusiasm of the powerful and ineffaceable sensations, and especially of the moral calm which he had experienced at this epoch. When at daybreak, on the morrow of his imprisonment, he saw [I abridge here Tolstoy's description] the mountains with their wooded slopes disappearing in the grayish mist; when he felt the cool breeze caress him; when he saw the light drive away the vapors, and the sun rise majestically behind the clouds and cupolas, and the crosses, the dew, the distance, the river, sparkle in the splendid, cheerful rays, —his heart overflowed with emotion. This emotion kept continually with him, and increased a hundred-fold as the difficulties of his situation grew graver... He learnt that man is

meant for happiness, and that this happiness is in him, in the satisfaction of the daily needs of existence, and that unhappiness is the fatal result, not of our need, but of our abundance... When calm reigned in the camp, and the embers paled, and little by little went out, the full moon had reached the zenith. The woods and the fields roundabout lay clearly visible; and, beyond the inundation of light which filled them, the view plunged into the limitless horizon. Then Peter cast his eyes upon the firmament, filled at that hour with myriads of stars. 'All that is mine,' he thought. 'All that is in me, is me! And that is what they think they have taken prisoner! That is what they have shut up in a cabin!' So he smiled, and turned in to sleep among his comrades."

The occasion and the experience, then, are nothing. It all depends on the capacity of the soul to be grasped, to have its life-currents absorbed by what is given. "Crossing a bare common," says Emerson, "in snow puddles, at twilight, under a clouded sky, without having in my thoughts any occurrence of special good fortune, I have enjoyed a perfect exhilaration. I am glad to the brink of fear."

Life is always worth living, if one have such responsive sensibilities. But we of the highly educated classes (so called) have most of us got far, far away from Nature. We are trained to seek the choice, the rare, the exquisite exclusively, and to overlook the common. We are stuffed with abstract conceptions, and glib with verbalities and verbosities; and in the culture of these higher functions the peculiar sources of joy connected with our simpler functions often dry up, and we grow stoneblind and insensible to life's more elementary and general goods and joys.

The remedy under such conditions is to descend to a more profound and primitive level. To be imprisoned or shipwrecked or forced into the army would permanently show the good of life to many an over-educated pessimist. Living in the open air and on the ground, the lopsided beam of the balance slowly rises to the level line; and the oversensibilities and insensibilities even themselves out. The good of all the artificial schemes and fevers fades and pales; and that of seeing, smelling, tasting, sleeping, and daring and doing with one's body, grows and grows. The savages and children of nature, to whom we deem ourselves so much superior, certainly are alive where we are often dead, along these lines; and, could they write as glibly as we do, they would read us impressive lectures on our impatience for improvement and on our blindness to the fundamental static goods of life. "Ah! my brother," said a chieftain to his white guest, "thou wilt never know the happiness of both thinking of nothing and doing nothing. This, next to sleep, is the most enchanting of all things. Thus we were before our birth, and thus we shall be after death. Thy people . . . when they have finished reaping one field, they begin to plough another; and, if the day were not enough, I have seen them plough by moonlight. What is their life to ours,—the life that is as naught to them? Blind that they are, they lose it all! But we live in the present."

The intense interest that life can assume when brought down to the non-thinking level, the level of pure sensorial perception, has been beautifully described by a man who *can* write, —Mr. W. H. Hudson, in his volume, *Idle Days in Patagonia.*

"I spent the greater part of one winter," says this admirable author, "at a point on the Rio Negro, seventy or eighty miles from the sea.

. . . "It was my custom to go out every morning on horseback with my gun, and, followed by one dog, to ride away from the valley; and no sooner would I climb the terrace, and plunge into the gray, universal thicket, than I would find myself as completely alone as if five hundred instead of only five miles separated me from the valley and river. So wild and solitary and remote seemed that gray waste, stretching away into infinitude, a waste untrodden by man, and where the wild animals are so few that they have made no discoverable path in the wilderness of thorns. . . Not once nor twice nor thrice, but day after day I returned to this solitude, going to it in the morning as if to attend a festival, and leaving it only when hunger and thirst and the westering sun compelled me. And yet I had no object in going,— no motive which could be put into words; for, although I carried a gun, there was nothing to shoot,—the shooting was all left behind in the valley. . . Sometimes I would pass a whole day without seeing one mammal, and perhaps not more than a dozen birds of any size. The weather at that time was cheerless, generally with a gray film of cloud spread over the sky,

and a bleak wind, often cold enough to make my bridle-hand quite numb. . . At a slow pace, which would have seemed intolerable under other circumstances, I would ride about for hours together at a stretch. On arriving at a hill, I would slowly ride to its summit, and stand there to survey the prospect. On every side it stretched away in great undulations, wild and irregular. How gray it all was! Hardly less so near at hand than on the haze-wrapped horizon where the hills were dim and the outline obscured by distance. Descending from my outlook, I would take up my aimless wanderings again, and visit other elevations to gaze on the same landscape from another point; and so on for hours. And at noon I would dismount, and sit or lie on my folded poncho for an hour or longer. One day in these rambles I discovered a small grove composed of twenty or thirty trees, growing at a convenient distance apart, that had evidently been resorted to by a herd of deer or other wild animals. This grove was on a hill differing in shape from other hills in its neighborhood; and, after a time, I made a point of finding and using it as a resting-place every day at noon. I did not ask myself why I made choice of that one spot, sometimes going out of my way to sit there, instead of sitting down under any one of the millions of trees and bushes on any other hillside. I thought nothing about it, but acted unconsciously. Only afterward it seemed to me that, after having rested there once, each time I wished to rest again, the wish came associated with the image of that particular clump of trees, with polished stems and clean bed of sand beneath; and in a short time I formed a habit of returning, animal like, to repose at that same spot.

"It was, perhaps, a mistake to say that I would sit down and rest, since I was never tired; and yet, without being tired, that noonday pause, during which I sat for an hour without moving, was strangely grateful. All day there would be no sound, not even the rustling of a leaf. One day, while *listening* to the silence, it occurred to my mind to wonder what the effect would be if I were to shout aloud. This seemed at the time a horrible suggestion, which almost made me shudder. But during those solitary days it was a rare thing for any thought to cross my mind. In the state of mind I was in, thought had become impossible. My state was one of *suspense* and *watchfulness;* yet I had no expectation of meeting an adventure, and felt as free from apprehension as I feel now while sitting in a room in London. The state seemed familiar rather than strange, and accompanied by a strong feeling of elation; and I did not know that something had come between me and my intellect until I returned to my former self,—to thinking, and the old insipid existence [again].

"I had undoubtedly *gone back;* and that state of intense watchfulness or alertness, rather, with suspension of the higher intellectual faculties, represented the mental state of the pure savage. He thinks little, reasons little, having a surer guide in his [mere sensory perceptions]. He is in perfect harmony with nature, and is nearly on a level, mentally, with the wild animals he preys on, and which in their turn sometimes prey on him."

For the spectator, such hours as Mr. Hudson writes of form a mere tale of emptiness, in which nothing happens, nothing is gained, and there is nothing to describe. They are meaningless and vacant tracts of time. To him who feels their inner secret, they tingle with an importance that unutterably vouches for itself. I am sorry for the boy or girl, or man or woman, who has never been touched by the spell of this mysterious sensorial life, with its irrationality, if so you like to call it, but its vigilance and its supreme felicity. The holidays of life are its most vitally significant portions, because they are, or at least should be, covered with just this kind of magically irresponsible spell.

And now what is the result of all these considerations and quotations? It is negative in one sense, but positive in another. It absolutely forbids us to be forward in pronouncing on the meaninglessness of forms of existence other than our own; and it commands us to tolerate, respect, and indulge those whom we see harmlessly interested and happy in their own ways, however unintelligible these may be to us. Hands off: neither the whole of truth nor the whole of good is revealed to any single observer, although each observer gains a partial superiority of insight from the peculiar position in which he stands. Even prisons and sick-rooms have their special revelations. It is enough to ask of each of us that he should be faithful to his own opportunities and make the most of his own blessings, without presuming to regulate the rest of the vast field.

## A. J. Liebling
# BROKEN FIGHTER ARRIVES

Last June, I went to Madison Square Garden to see Joe Louis fight a man named Lee Savold, and when Louis knocked him out, I came away singularly revived—as if I, rather than Louis, had demonstrated resistance to the erosion of time. As long as Joe could get by, I felt, I had a link with an era when we were both a lot younger. Only the great champions give their fellow-citizens time to feel that way about them, because only the great ones win the title young and hold on to it. There have been three like that among the heavyweights in this century—Jim Jeffries, Jack Dempsey, and Louis. Jeffries won the championship in 1899, when my father was a footloose young sport, and was beaten, after a period of retirement, by Jack Johnson in 1910, when Father was a solemn burgher with a wife, two children, and three twelve-story loft buildings with second mortgages on them. Dempsey beat Jess Willard in 1919, when I was in short pants. He lost the second decision to Gene Tunney in 1927 (I had believed that the first was an accident, and so I had continued to think of him as champion), and by that time I had written half a novel, spent a year at the Sorbonne, and worked on two newspapers.

Louis was the champion, in the public mind, from 1935, when he slaughtered Primo Carnera and Max Baer, until a couple of weeks ago. Technically, his span was slightly shorter, because he didn't beat Jim Braddock for the title until 1937, but everybody knew from 1935 on that he would beat Braddock whenever he got the match. And he lost the championship by a decision to Ezzard Charles in 1950, but Charles was subsequently knocked out by old Jersey Joe Walcott, whom Louis had flattened a while back. When the three were introduced from the ring before the bout between Sugar Ray Robinson and Randy Turpin last September, the crowd left no doubt that it still considered Louis the leading heavyweight.

At about that same time, I learned that Louis, who was thirty-seven, had been "made" with a new heavyweight, Rocky Marciano, who was twenty-seven and a puncher. I didn't think much about it then, but as October 26th, the date set for the fight, approached, I began to feel uneasy. Marciano, to be sure, had never had a professional fight until shortly after Louis first announced his retirement, in 1948. (Joe had subsequently, of course, recanted.) In addition, Marciano had beaten only two opponents of any note, both young heavyweights like himself, who were rated as no better than promising. He was not big for a heavyweight, and was supposed to be rather crude. What bothered me, though, about the impending affair was that Marciano was, as he still is, steered by a man I know, named Al Weill, who is one of the most realistic fellows in a milieu where illusions are few. Marciano was already a good drawing card and would continue to be as long as he was unbeaten, and Weill, I was sure, would never risk the depreciation of an asset unless he felt he had a good bet.

Weill is at present the matchmaker of the International Boxing Club, which controls boxing here in New York and in a dozen other large cities, and his son, Marty Weill, is Marciano's manager "of record," which means he signs the contracts. The younger Weill has a job-lot commission business in Dayton, Ohio, and isn't properly a boxing man at all. When the elder Weill became matchmaker, he "gave" his son the fighter, much as a lawyer, upon becoming a public official, turns over his private practice to a partner. Marciano is, in effect, a kind of family enterprise, like Rockefeller Center. As the fight date drew near, I decided to go around to the headquarters of the International, above the Iceland Skating Rink in the Madison Square Garden building, and ask the elder Weill what was doing. I could have accomplished this less formally by giving him what he calls a bang on the telephone, but I wished to compare his facial expressions with his asseverations.

The matchmaker is of the build referred to in ready-made-clothing stores as a portly,

which means not quite a stout. There is an implication of at least one kind of recklessness about a fat man; he lets himself go when he eats. A portly man, on the other hand, is a man who would like to be fat but restrains himself —a calculator. Weill has a Roman nose of the short, or budgerigar, variety, and an over-all grayish coloration that is complemented by the suits he generally wears and the cigar ashes he frequently spills on them. On his home block— Eighty-sixth Street between West End Avenue and Riverside Drive—he blends perfectly with the tired 1910 grandeur of the apartment houses; he looks like one more garment manufacturer worried by a swollen inventory. This does not stop him from knowing more about the fight business than any of the flashier types who wear long beige jackets and stay downtown after dark.

Weill is a frugal man, and he likes frugal fighters. Every kind of serious trouble a fighter can get into, he says, has its origin in the disbursement of currency—rich food, liquor, women, horserace betting, and fast automobiles. Once a fighter starts gambling, Weill doesn't want him. "A gambler thinks he can get money without working for it," he says. Weill had a big string of fighters before the war, and used to quarter them all in a lodging house near Central Park West, where the housemaster would issue to each boy a weekly meal ticket with a face value of five dollars and fifty cents, redeemable in trade at a coffeepot on Columbus Avenue. The tickets cost Weill five dollars each, cash. A fighter could get a second ticket before the week was out, but only if he showed that the first one had been punched out to the last nickel. None of those fighters ever suffered a defeat that could be attributed to high living. Mere frugality, however, may prove a boomerang, for the fighter sometimes gets to like it. There was once an old colored heavyweight named Bob Armstrong, who, when asked his utmost ambition, said, "To wake up every morning and find a dollar under my pillow." Naturally, he never got to be champion. Weill wouldn't want a fighter like that. What he really loves is an avaricious fighter.

When I asked Weill about Marciano, he looked happy. "He is a nice boy," he said. "The dollar is his God. That is to say, he is a poor Italian boy from a large, poor family, and he appreciates the buck more than almost anybody else. Them type guys is hard to get outa there. You want to look out for them young broken fighters." By "broken fighter," Weill, who is a purist, meant a fighter who is broke. "He only got two halfway decent purses—with LaStarza and Layne—and it was like a tiger tasting blood," Weill went on. "So you know how confident he is when he will take a fight like this for fifteen per cent of the gate. Louis gets forty-five. Why, Marciano will bring more money into the Garden than Louis. Connecticut, Rhode Island, and half of Massachusetts will be empty that night." Marciano hails from Brockton, Massachusetts.

Having considered the morale factor, which with him always comes first, Weill passed to the tactical level. He said Marciano would never be a clever boxer; he wasn't made for it, anyway, being short for a heavyweight, and wide, with short, thick arms. "But he knows what he has to do," Weill said. "Get in close enough to hit and then keep on hitting. And he don't come walking in straight, like Savold. Anybody would look good punching a punching bag that comes straight to you. This kid will fight out of a crouch. How I got him"—he changed the subject abruptly—"is three years ago a fellow I know used to promote around Boston wrote me there was a hell of an amateur he would like me to take. So I sent up the carfare for them to come down. They come, and we took Rocky to the C.Y.O. gym and put him in with a young heavyweight from Staten Island, a big blond guy belonged to a friend of mine. We had to stop him or he'd killed that Staten Island guy. I seen right then Rocky had the beginning of it. So I sent him up to Manny Almeida, a friend of mine promotes in Providence, which is near where he is out of Brockton, but Brockton is too small to have fights. And I asked Manny to put him in with the same kind he was, but no setups. Because you got a guy knocking over setups, you don't know what you got. He come along good. When I come over here, I give him to Marty. Who should I give him to if not my own flesh and blood?"

A day or two after my talk with Weill, I went out to Louis's training quarters at Pompton Lakes, New Jersey, and it was like going back to the first administration of Franklin D. Roosevelt. There is about all Louis's habits a majestic continuity, as there is about his style

in the ring, which is basically classical. His style has diminished in speed of execution but has never varied in concept. Pompton was his lucky camp; he trained there for his first New York fight, against Carnera, in 1935, when he was twenty-one, and he trained there for all his succeeding fights but four—"way more than twenty," he told me when I talked with him later that day. I hadn't been out there since the summer of 1938, when Louis was preparing for his return fight with Max Schmeling, the only man who had up to that time knocked him out. (That return fight was his happiest victory; he destroyed the German in less than a round.) Incidentally, Louis has knocked out six men who at one time or another held the heavyweight championship—Schmeling, Jack Sharkey, Carnera, Baer, Braddock, and Walcott—a record possible because the championship changed hands so often in the short period between 1930 and 1937, leaving so many mediocre ex-champions simultaneously extant.

The camp, like Louis himself, was essentially the same but much older-looking. Part of the difference, I suppose, was due to the fact that the Schmeling fight had been in the summer, and now the leaves were turning on the sides of the Ramapos, and the air was chill. But that wasn't all of it. Before the war, the camp was operated by a bright and energetic couple named Dr. and Mrs. Bier, who had ambitions about turning it into a health farm for millionaires. On days when Louis was to spar, the grounds were always packed with charabancs from Harlem bringing people to see him work. The money pouring in at the gate, at a dollar a head, made training actually a profitable activity, and the hot-dog concession alone—there was also a bar—brought in enough to pay the sparring partners. The place has since been bought by a man by the name of Baumgartner, and there is no longer a bar, or even a hot dog, on the premises, although I heard that Coca-Cola can be bought on Sundays. The day I was there, there were perhaps a dozen automobiles on the grounds when sparring was scheduled to begin, and no more than twenty-five paying customers, at sixty cents a head, despite the fact that the fight was only a week off. And, except for me, the press was represented only by Colonel John R. Stingo, who writes a column called "Yea Verily" for the New York *Enquirer,* a newspaper always dated

Monday but published only on Sunday afternoon. Colonel Stingo is a small, agile man who helped cover the Corbett-Sullivan fight for the New Orleans *Item* in 1892. A Boston newspaperman named Gilhooley had ridden out with us from New York in a car hired by the International Boxing Club, but had gone on to Marciano's training camp at Greenwood Lake, New York, seventeen miles farther along. The car was to wait there for him, and then pick us up after the workouts were over.

One of the first things I saw on getting out of the car was a familiar sweatered figure sprawled in a lawn chair in front of the red frame building that in livelier days housed the bar. It was Mannie Seamon, Louis's trainer, a white man who stepped into the job after the death of Jack Blackburn, the old colored fighter who formed Louis's style. Seamon is more of a conditioner than a boxing coach— a jovial, rosy-cheeked man who sometimes discourses learnedly on "bone juice" and keeping the air out of his charges' bones. He hadn't changed at all in the intervening years, I noted enviously, but I winced when I thought of how many thousand medicine balls he must have thrown at Louis's and other fighters' stomachs since 1938. All the sparring partners of thirteen years ago were gone—working on the docks, most of them, Seamon said—and so were Louis's managers then, John Roxborough and Julian Black, the two colored sporting men who brought Joe out of the Middle West, and Mike Jacobs, the quondam ticket scalper who once controlled boxing through his control of that great new favorite, Louis. Jacobs lives in Florida now, an invalid.

"Joe's looking the best he has in four years," Mannie said. (It was in 1947, in his first match against Walcott, that Louis first showed he was slipping badly.) We talked awhile about fellows we had known in the thirties, and I asked Mannie if the terrible monotony of training wasn't beginning to tell on Louis. Joe made his pro début in 1934, and he had boxed amateur before that, and the Army meant no letup, for his duty there consisted of boxing exhibitions for other soldiers. So he had been at it for nearly twenty years—light bag, heavy bag, pushups, belly bends, roadwork, and shadow-boxing. It is hard to stay interested in your own shadow for twenty years. Even an old race horse gets so he won't extend himself in works.

"We keep his mind off it as much as we can," Seamon said. "We got a rule here, we never talk fight. Anything but that. We listen to phonograph records, or we play cards, or handicap horses. I tell him funny stories, and the best is different people come in and talk to him."

Seamon walked over to the gymnasium to get the fighter ready for his sparring exhibition, and after a while Colonel Stingo and I followed him. When we got to the dressing room, Louis was sitting on the rubbing table while Seamon prepared his hands—bandages, gauze, and flat sponge-rubber pads over the knuckles, and then adhesive tape to hold the structure in place. Seamon said, "Joe, this is Colonel Stingo. He is seventy-eight years old and he wants to work a couple of rounds with you." Louis looked down at the Colonel and couldn't at the moment think of anything to say except "Glad to meet you." I reminded Louis that he and I had last met in Frisco's, a drinking club on Sackville Street, in London, during the war, and he said, "That man once charged me sixteen dollars for a pint of gin." With us in the dressing room was a slender colored man named Reed, a friend of Louis's who had evidently been a patron of Frisco's at the same time, and he joined in the conversation to say he had once paid a cabby three pounds and six shillings to drive him to Frisco's from a few streets away. " 'Three-and-six,' the man said," Reed recalled. "So I gave him three *pounds* and six shillings, and then I reached in my pocket and all I had left was a ten-shilling note, so I gave it to him for a tip. I didn't know if it was enough. That was my first time on leave in London." Louis began to laugh. "That was a pretty good tip," he said. "Two dollars for a seventy-cent ride that you already paid him nearly fifteen bucks for."

Louis, Reed, and I began telling stories about prices we had paid in London, straining the elastic of credulity with each tale—a kind of auction. Louis stuck closest to plausibility; Reed and I were just trying to be funny. Fruit had been fantastically dear in London by American standards, and Louis said he had once paid thirty shillings for a pound of hot-house grapes, as a present for an English family he knew. "Then I saw just a small apple there for six shillings," he said. "So I bought that, and bit into it outside the store. Man, it was sour! I give the rest of it to an old dog that come along, and he took one bite and took off." Louis also told about going up on a roof to watch an air raid his first night in London. "The tracers was the most beautiful thing I ever saw," he said.

By the time Seamon had finished with his hands, Louis was in high good humor. "I'm sorry we got no boxing shoes to fit you, Colonel," he said to Stingo just before he went into the gymnasium. "So I guess I won't be able to work with you today. You worked with me wearing those shoes, you might step all over my feet and disable me."

There was nothing showy about the workout. Two of Louis's three partners were light heavyweights, much smaller than the old champion, and they worked fast, to speed up his reflexes. He didn't punch hard at either, since the idea wasn't to discourage them. One of them, a brown boy from Bermuda, hit Louis pretty freely, but it was reasonable to suppose the Bermudian was a lot faster than Marciano could possibly be. That's the point of working with a light, fast man. The only partner on hand of the big, rough type that used to staff Louis's camps was a heavyweight named Elkins Brothers, whom I had seen fight in the semifinal on the Robinson-Turpin card. Brothers, a squat, powerful fellow, played the part of Marciano when he sparred with Louis. He came in crouching, and threw overhand rights at Louis's jaw. The overhand right, thrown in a rising arc like an artillery shell, was supposed to be Marciano's best punch. Louis kept jabbing at Brothers' head, trying to hit him just as the right started coming and keep him off balance. When he succeeded, he stepped in with a right uppercut. It was a pattern of battle, but neither man pressed it to its ultimate implication. They were methodical rather than fierce. Louis's body looked good—leaner, if anything, than it had in 1938—and the jab was as sweet as ever.

Stingo and I were sitting out on the lawn after the workout, waiting for the car from Greenwood Lake to pick us up, when Louis came along, on his way from the gym to his living quarters. He looked younger with his snap-brim hat on. It hid the bald spot. And in street clothes, after all, a superbly conditioned man of thirty-seven is still young. It's when he gets into a ring that age comes on

him. Louis hovered over us for a while, but none of us could think of much to say. It was no use asking him how he felt, or whether he thought he could win this one, because clearly he was as good as anybody could get him now, and he had never had a match in his life that he didn't think he was going to win, and sixty-nine times out of seventy-one he had been right. So why would he change his mind this time?

Louis gave a small shiver and said, "Well, I guess I better go in, or I might get a chill." We shook hands all around, and he went along to play cards with the sparring partners who belonged to a younger generation.

The camp at Greenwood Lake, which I visited three days before the fight, was more lively. Marciano looked like the understander in the nine-man pyramid of a troupe of Arab acrobats. He is bull-necked and wide-shouldered, and even when he was merely walking around in the ring, he kept rippling the muscles of his arms and back, as if afraid that if he let them set, they would tie up. He looks as if he should be muscle-bound, but he isn't. He worked with a big, rangy young heavyweight named Jimmy DeLange, who had the Louis role, and they fought as if they wanted to transcend the limitations of the leather head guards and the huge sparring gloves and knock each other out. Marciano moved around briskly on his stubby legs and threw punches well, especially to the body, but DeLange had no trouble reaching his head with left jabs, and the sparmate's right uppercuts to the body came off well in close. Marciano was working in a head guard that was a cross between a gladiatorial helmet and race-horse blinkers, with long leather wings at the sides of his eyes. He wouldn't have that, at any rate, when he fought Louis, I told myself. He finished the third, and last, round with a big burst of punching.

During the workout, I sat alongside the ancient featherweight champion Abe Attell, and after it was over and the trainers had pulled Marciano's gloves off, Abe called up to the fighter, "Take it easy, Rocky! He's only a sparring partner!" The fighter held up three fingers and called back apologetically, "Only tree days!"—signifying that, with but three days to go, he was in too good shape to restrain himself.

"I had five hundred on him," Attell said to

me. "And after what I seen today I'm making it a thousand." Attell, who was himself one of the greatest of boxers, is a knowing man about fights, but he is famous for having an intricate mind. I consoled myself with the thought that he might, in fact, be betting on Louis and speaking favorably of Marciano only to get the odds up.

"Louis is all through," Attell went on, with what I considered a deplorable lack of sentiment in an old champion who had himself felt the sharp tooth of time. But Attell, who looks at you with cold eyes around his huge beak that is like a toucan's with a twisted septum, is not a sentimental man. "If they get a referee who don't let Louis hang on, the kid will knock him out," he said. He then put a handful of BB shot in his mouth and started to pick his teeth. He uses bamboo toothpicks, which he has tailored for him at a novelty shop on Broadway. From time to time, by means of his toothpick, he propels the pellets, one by one, through gaps between his teeth, hitting with perfect accuracy any object up to ten feet away. A nightclub hostess with a plunging neckline is his favorite target, but a busy bartender in a dimly lighted joint will keep him almost equally happy. *En villégiature,*[2] however, he will take targets of opportunity, like the back of a stranger's neck. "I got hit with an automobile a couple years ago and got three new choppers on the right side, with no holes between them," he told me. "So now I developed a curve out the left."

Leaving the unfeeling Mr. Attell, I went over to wait outside the dressing room for Charlie Goldman, Marciano's trainer, an old bantamweight who has coached Weill's fighters for years. Goldman is a fine pedagogue, because of his way of bringing out his pupil's qualities instead of trying to change them. "The great thing about this kid is he's got leverage," he told me when he came out of the dressing room. "He takes a good punch and he's got the equalizers. He had leverage from the start, and when you teach a fellow like that, you have to go slow, because you might change the way he stands or the way he moves, and, by so doing, spoil his hitting. Everything new you show him, you have to ask him, 'Does it feel natural?' 'Can you hit from there?' So naturally

[2] "In the country."

he'll never be a flashy boxer. But he's in the improving phase. He's still six months—maybe a year—away. But whether he beats Louis or not, he's going to be a lot better next summer."

Goldman is a soft-spoken, merry little man with a large head, buffed to a plane surface in front, and a pair of hands that look as if they had been trampled on. "Looka the bum, how many times he broke his hands!" Attell says loftily. His own magnificent fists carried him through three hundred and sixty-five fights with only one break. Goldman's more friable maulies prevented him from knocking out many of the four hundred opponents he fought, but they made him a thoughtful kind of boxer.

"Most fighters at twenty-seven have been boxing eight, nine years, and they are as good as they ever will be," Goldman told me. "But Rocky has only had about the equivalent of one year's experience. So he's still learning. Every time we made a fight for him up in New England, we would bring him down to New York for a week and get him a room at the C.Y.O., and then he would work out four or five afternoons at Stillman's," he said. "But he didn't do as much boxing in the three years as one of the boys who's at Stillman's everyday would do in a year. So he's just beginning to come along. He'll knock them all out."

When I entered Madison Square Garden on the night of the fight, I couldn't help hoping that Marciano was still too far away to demolish Louis. His day was bound to come anyway, if Goldman was right, and I wanted to see Louis get by once more. My seat was about where I had sat when I watched Louis beat Savold, a fight that put him back into a position to challenge for the championship. I was sitting well forward in the mezzanine on the Forty-ninth Street side, midway between the east and west ends of the ring, at a point where I could watch crowd as well as fighters. I got there in time to see the end of the semifinal. The loser, a boxer named Jimmy Gambino, was arrested later that night on a charge of selling narcotics. He had fought in a preoccupied manner.

Then there were the usual introductions from the ring of white and colored men in kneelength jackets with flaring shoulders—rough, tough Paddy DeMarco, Philadelphia's undefeated Gil Turner, Sugar Ray Robinson, former heavyweight champion Ezzard Charles, and, finally, Jersey Joe Walcott, the reigning champion, as old as Louis by his own statement, several years older by popular report. ("I'm not old," he told a sportswriter in 1947. "I'm just ugly.") The names of the judges and referee were announced: Joe Agnello, Harold Barnes, Ruby Goldstein—no surprises. And then the two factions were in the ring—Louis's in the northwest corner, Marciano's in the southeast. Mannie Seamon and a couple of fellows I didn't know were with Louis; Goldman and Marty Weill were with Marciano, together with a fellow New Englander named Al Columbo. Weill, a thin, pale young man with rumpled hair, seemed more awed than his fighter. Marciano was bouncing on his thick legs and punching the air to warm up. A tall, ash-blond woman near me was saying, "I hate him! I hate him! I think he's the most horrible thing I've ever seen." This struck me as being hard on Rocky; he didn't look particularly repulsive. Husky as he was, he looked slight compared to Louis, who was three inches taller and, according to the announced weights, twenty-five pounds heavier. When the fighters were introduced, it was evident that if Connecticut, Rhode Island, and half of Massachusetts were not completely empty, their populations were at least substantially depleted for the evening. The Marciano supporters were cheering him as if he were a high-school football team. But Louis got an even bigger welcome.

And then, as the immortal historian of the British ring, Pierce Egan, wrote of the third fight between Dan Mendoza and Dick Humphries, in 1789, "The awful set-to at length commenced—when every eye beamed with anxiety —the moment was interesting and attractive, and each party was lost in suspense." I had a pair of pocket binoculars, 6 × 15s, and I kept them trained on Louis for the first half minute. His face was impassive, as usual, but his actions showed that he wasn't taking the strong boy lightly. Instead of moving relentlessly forward, as in his great days, he seemed to be waiting to see what he was up against. In the first clinches, it was he who shifted Marciano, and not the other way about; Louis was stronger than the strong boy—at the beginning, anyway. He could outbox him at a distance, and if he could continue to smother him in close, I thought he would get by. Up to the last five seconds of the round, I noted, glancing

at the ringside clock, neither of them had done anything remarkable, and that was all right with me. I had had a feeling that Marciano might rush out of his corner throwing punches and try to take Louis by storm. Then Marciano threw one of those rights, and it landed, it seemed to me, just under Louis's left ear. Louis had dropped his left shoulder after jabbing— an old fault, which brought about most of the bad moments of his career. This was the kind of punch that addles a man's brains, and if it had happened thirty seconds earlier and Marciano had pressed his advantage, he might have knocked Louis out in the first round.

I think that punch was the one that made Joe feel old. Between the rounds, I could see Seamon pressing an ice bag against the back of Louis's neck, and when I turned my binoculars on Charlie Goldman's face, he was grinning. Louis was apparently clearheaded when he came out for the second, but he didn't do much. I thought he won the next three rounds, jabbing Marciano's face and jolting him with rights in close. But the rights didn't sicken Marciano, as they had sickened Louis's opponents from 1935 to 1940; he reacted as if he were being hit by just an ordinary fighter. Marciano was missing almost all his own swings, and Goldman, between the rounds, was looking very serious as he talked to his pupil. Also, he was working on Rocky's brows with cotton-tipped toothpicks that had been steeped in some astringent solution. The jabs had cut. But Rocky came out for each new round very gay, as Egan would say, and went across to Louis as if to ask for a light.

When the fifth round ended, marking the halfway point of the fight, I felt that it would be a long way home but that Louis would make it. He had hardly used his left hook, which was now his best punch. Critics had been saying for years that his right had lost its authority, but the hook had existed in all its pristine glory as recently as the Savold bout, and he had had it in the training camp when I was watching him. ("It would take a Goliath to withstand a couple of those," old Colonel Stingo had said solemnly.) The way I figured it, Louis was being so careful about that crazy Marciano right that he was afraid to pull his own left back to hook. He would just jab and drop his forearm onto Rocky's right biceps, so he couldn't counter. Sooner or later, Joe would throw the hook, I thought, and that would end the fight. It looked like a fight between two men with one good hand apiece.

In the sixth, things started to go sour. It wasn't that Marciano grew better or stronger; it was that Louis seemed to get slower and weaker. The spring was gone from his legs— and it had been only a slight spring in the beginning—and in the clinches Marciano was shoving him around. A man can be as strong for tugging and hauling at thirty-seven, or for that matter at forty-seven, as he was in his twenties, but he can't keep on starting and stopping for as many minutes. And even grazing blows begin to hurt after a while. Near the end of the round, Marciano hit Louis another solid one.

The seventh was bad for Louis. Marciano didn't catch him with one big punch, but he was battering at his body and arms, and shoving him around, and Joe didn't seem to be able to do anything about it. Then, toward the end of the round, he threw the hook. It was beautiful. It hit Marciano flush on the right side of the jaw, but it didn't seem to faze him a bit. I knew then that Joe was beaten, but I thought that it might be only a decision. Three rounds don't seem forever, especially when you're just watching.

Then, in the eighth round, as you probably read in the daily press, Marciano, the right-hand specialist, knocked Louis down with a left hook that Goldman had not previously publicized. When Louis got up, Marciano hit him with two more left hooks, which set him up for the right and the pitiful finish.

Right after Marciano knocked Louis down the first time, Sugar Ray Robinson started working his way toward the ring, as if drawn by some horrid fascination, and by the time Rocky threw the final right, Robinson's hand was on the lowest rope of the ring, as if he meant to jump in. The punch knocked Joe through the ropes and he lay on the ring apron, only one leg inside.

The tall blonde was bawling, and pretty soon she began to boo. The fellow who had brought her was horrified. "Rocky didn't do anything wrong," he said. "He didn't foul him. What you booing?"

The blonde said, "You're so cold. I hate you, too."

Last week, I stopped by the offices of the International Boxing Club to ask Al Weill how he felt about things now. "What did I tell you?" he said. "You want to look out for them broken fighters. The way things look now, the kid could make a fortune of money."

## William H. Prescott
## CORTEZ

*On April 21, 1519, Good Friday, Hernando Cortez, then 33 years old, landed in Mexico at the head of a force consisting of 110 sailors, 553 soldiers, 14 pieces of artillery, and 16 horses. With this force he attacked and overthrew the large, rich, and splendid empire of the Aztec Indians. The Conquest ended on August 13, 1521, after a long siege of the capital city. Prescott concludes his classic history of the Conquest with the following summary of the character and career of Cortez.*

The personal history of Cortez has been so minutely detailed in the preceding narrative, that it will be only necessary to touch on the more prominent features of his character. Indeed, the history of the Conquest, as I have already had occasion to remark, is necessarily that of Cortez, who is, if I may so say, not merely the soul, but the body, of the enterprise, present everywhere in person, in the thick of the fight, or in the building of the works, with his sword or with his musket, sometimes leading his soldiers, and sometimes directing his little navy. The negotiations, intrigues, correspondence, are all conducted by him; and, like Caesar, he wrote his own Commentaries in the heat of the stirring scenes which form the subject of them. His character is marked with the most opposite traits, embracing qualities apparently the most incompatible. He was avaricious, yet liberal; bold to desperation, yet cautious and calculating in his plans; magnanimous, yet very cunning; courteous and affable in his deportment, yet inexorably stern; lax in his notions of morality, yet (not uncommon) a sad bigot. The great feature in his character

---

CORTEZ: From *The Conquest of Mexico*, Book VII, Chapter 5.

was constancy of purpose; a constancy not to be daunted by danger, nor baffled by disappointment, nor wearied out by impediments and delays.

He was a knight-errant, in the literal sense of the word. Of all the band of adventurous cavaliers, whom Spain, in the sixteenth century, sent forth on the career of discovery and conquest, there was none more deeply filled with the spirit of romantic enterprise than Hernando Cortez. Dangers and difficulties, instead of deterring, seemed to have a charm in his eyes. They were necessary to rouse him to a full consciousness of his powers. He grappled with them at the outset, and, if I may so express myself, seemed to prefer to take his enterprises by the most difficult side. He conceived, at the first moment of his landing in Mexico, the design of its conquest. When he saw the strength of its civilization, he was not turned from his purpose. When he was assailed by the superior force of Narvaez,[3] he still persisted in it; and, when he was driven in ruin from the capital, he still cherished his original idea. How successfully he carried it into execution, we have seen. After the few years of repose which succeeded the Conquest, his adventurous spirit impelled him to that dreary march across the marshes of Chiapa; and, after another interval, to seek his fortunes on the stormy Californian Gulf. When he found that no other continent remained for him to conquer, he made serious proposals to the emperor to equip a fleet at his own expense, with which he would sail to the Moluccas, and subdue the Spice-Islands for the Crown of Castile![4]

This spirit of knight-errantry might lead us to undervalue his talents as a general, and to regard him merely in the light of a lucky adventurer. But this would be doing him injustice; for Cortez was certainly a great general, if that man be one, who performs great achievements with the resources which his own genius has created. There is probably no instance in history, where so vast an enterprise has been achieved by means apparently so inadequate. He may be truly said to have effected the Conquest by his own resources. If he was indebted for his success to the co-operation of the Indian

tribes, it was the force of his genius that obtained command of such materials. He arrested the arm that was lifted to smite him, and made it do battle in his behalf. He beat the Tlascalans, and made them his stanch allies. He beat the soldiers of Narvaez, and doubled his effective force by it. When his own men deserted him, he did not desert himself. He drew them back by degrees, and compelled them to act by his will, till they were all as one man. He brought together the most miscellaneous collection of mercenaries who ever fought under one standard; adventurers from Cuba and the Isles, craving for gold; hidalgos, who came from the old country to win laurels; broken-down cavaliers, who hoped to mend their fortunes in the New World; vagabonds flying from justice; the grasping followers of Narvaez, and his own reckless veterans,—men with hardly a common tie, and burning with the spirit of jealousy and faction; wild tribes of the natives from all parts of the country, who had been sworn enemies from their cradles, and who had met only to cut one another's throats, and to procure victims for sacrifice; men, in short, differing in race, in language, and in interests, with scarcely anything in common among them. Yet this motley congregation was assembled in one camp, compelled to bend to the will of one man, to consort together in harmony, to breathe, as it were, one spirit, and to move on a common principle of action! It is in this wonderful power over the discordant masses thus gathered under his banner, that we recognise the genius of the great commander, no less than in the skill of his military operations.

His power over the minds of his soldiers was a natural result of their confidence in his abilities. But it is also to be attributed to his popular manners,—that happy union of authority and companionship, which fitted him for the command of a band of roving adventurers. It would not have done for him to have fenced himself round with the stately reserve of a commander of regular forces. He was embarked with his men in a common adventure, and nearly on terms of equality, since he held his commission by no legal warrant. But, while he indulged this freedom and familiarity with his soldiers, he never allowed it to interfere with their strict obedience, nor to impair the severity of discipline. When he had risen to higher consideration, although he affected

---

[3] Spanish general sent by the Spanish governor of Cuba in March, 1520, to relieve Cortez of his command.

[4] *i.e.,* the Spanish ruling family.

more state, he still admitted his veterans to the same intimacy. "He preferred," says Diaz,[5] "to be called 'Cortez' by us, to being called by any title; and with good reason," continues the enthusiastic old cavalier, "for the name of Cortez is as famous in our day as was that of Caesar among the Romans, or of Hannibal among the Carthaginians." He showed the same kind regard towards his ancient comrades in the very last act of his life. For he appropriated a sum by his will for the celebration of two thousand masses for the souls of those who had fought with him in the campaigns of Mexico. . . .

Cortez was not a vulgar conqueror. He did not conquer from the mere ambition of conquest. If he destroyed the ancient capital of the Aztecs, it was to build up a more magnificent capital on its ruins. If he desolated the land, and broke up its existing institutions, he employed the short period of his administration in digesting schemes for introducing there a more improved culture and a higher civilization. In all his expeditions he was careful to study the resources of the country, its social organization, and its physical capacities. He enjoined it on his captains to attend particularly to these objects. If he was greedy of gold, like most of the Spanish cavaliers in the New World, it was not to hoard it, nor merely to lavish it in the support of a princely establishment, but to secure funds for prosecuting his glorious discoveries. Witness his costly expeditions to the Gulf of California. His enterprises were not undertaken solely for mercenary objects; as is shown by the various expeditions he set on foot for the discovery of a communication between the Atlantic and the Pacific. In his schemes of ambition he showed a respect for the interests of science, to be referred partly to the natural superiority of his mind, but partly, no doubt, to the influence of early education. It is, indeed, hardly possible, that a person of his wayward and mercurial temper should have improved his advantages at the University, but he brought away from it a tincture of scholarship, seldom found among the cavaliers of the period, and which had its influence in enlarging his own conceptions. His celebrated Letters are written with a simple

elegance, that, as I have already had occasion to remark, have caused them to be compared to the military narrative of Caesar. It will not be easy to find in the chronicles of the period a more concise, yet comprehensive, statement, not only of the events of his campaigns, but of the circumstances most worthy of notice in the character of the conquered countries.

Cortez was not cruel; at least, not cruel as compared with most of those who followed his iron trade. The path of the conqueror is necessarily marked with blood. He was not too scrupulous, indeed, in the execution of his plans. He swept away the obstacles which lay in his track; and his fame is darkened by the commission of more than one act which his boldest apologists will find it hard to vindicate. But he was not wantonly cruel. He allowed no outrage on his unresisting foes. This may seem small praise, but it is an exception to the usual conduct of his countrymen in their conquests, and it is something to be in advance of one's time. He was severe, it may be added, in enforcing obedience to his orders for protecting their persons and their property. With his licentious crew, it was, sometimes, not without hazard that he was so. After the Conquest, he sanctioned the system of *repartimientos;*[6] but so did Columbus. He endeavored to regulate it by the most humane laws, and continued to suggest many important changes for ameliorating the condition of the natives. The best commentary on his conduct, in this respect, is the deference that was shown him by the Indians, and the confidence with which they appealed to him for protection in all their subsequent distresses.

In private life he seems to have had the power of attaching to himself, warmly, those who were near his person. The influence of this attachment is shown in every page of Bernal Diaz, though his work was written to vindicate the claims of the soldiers, in opposition to those of the general. He seems to have led a happy life with his first wife, in their humble retirement in Cuba; and regarded the second, to judge from the expressions in his testament, with confidence and love. Yet he cannot be acquitted from the charge of those

---

[5] Bernal Diaz, who was in Cortez's army and who later wrote a first-hand account of the campaigns.

[6] The system of distributing the Indian captives among the conquerors as slaves.

licentious gallantries which entered too generally into the character of the military adventurer of that day. He would seem also, by the frequent suits in which he was involved, to have been of an irritable and contentious spirit. But much allowance must be made for the irritability of a man who had been too long accustomed to independent sway, patiently to endure the checks and control of the petty spirits who were incapable of comprehending the noble character of his enterprises. "He thought," says an eminent writer, "to silence his enemies by the brilliancy of the new career on which he had entered. He did not reflect, that these enemies had been raised by the very grandeur and rapidity of his success." He was rewarded for his efforts by the misinterpretation of his motives; by the calumnious charges of squandering the public revenues and of aspiring to independent sovereignty. But, although we may admit the foundation of many of the grievances alleged by Cortez, yet when we consider the querulous tone of his correspondence and the frequency of his litigation, we may feel a natural suspicion that his proud spirit was too sensitive to petty slights, and too jealous of imaginary wrongs.

One trait more remains to be noticed in the character of this remarkable man; that is, his bigotry, the failing of the age,—for, surely, it should be termed only a failing. When we see the hand, red with the blood of the wretched native, raised to invoke the blessing of Heaven on the cause which it maintains, we experience something like a sensation of disgust at the act, and a doubt of its sincerity. But this is unjust. We should throw ourselves back (it cannot be too often repeated) into the age; the age of the Crusades. For every Spanish cavalier, however sordid and selfish might be his private motives, felt himself to be the soldier of the Cross. Many of them would have died in defence of it. Whoever has read the correspondence of Cortez, or, still more, has attended to the circumstances of his career, will hardly doubt that he would have been among the first to lay down his life for the Faith. He more than once perilled life, and fortune, and the success of his whole enterprise, by the premature and most impolitic manner in which he would have forced conversion on the natives. To the more rational spirit of the present day, enlightened by a purer

Christianity, it may seem difficult to reconcile gross deviations from morals with such devotion to the cause of religion. But the religion taught in that day was one of form and elaborate ceremony. In the punctilious attention to discipline, the spirit of Christianity was permitted to evaporate. The mind, occupied with forms, thinks little of substance. In a worship that is addressed too exclusively to the senses, it is often the case, that morality becomes divorced from religion, and the measure of righteousness is determined by the creed rather than by the conduct.

In the earlier part of the History, I have given a description of the person of Cortez. It may be well to close this review of his character by the account of his manners and personal habits left us by Bernal Diaz, the old chronicler, who has accompanied us through the whole course of our narrative, and who may now fitly furnish the conclusion of it. No man knew his commander better; and, if the avowed object of his work might naturally lead to a disparagement of Cortez, this is more than counterbalanced by the warmth of his personal attachment, and by that *esprit de corps* which leads him to take a pride in the renown of his general.

"In his whole appearance and presence," says Diaz, "in his discourse, his table, his dress, in everything, in short, he had the air of a great lord. His clothes were in the fashion of the time; he set little value on silk, damask, or velvet, but dressed plainly and exceedingly neat; nor did he wear massy chains of gold, but simply a fine one, of exquisite workmanship, from which was suspended a jewel having the figure of our Lady the Virgin and her precious Son, with a Latin motto cut upon it. On his finger he wore a splendid diamond ring; and from his cap which, according to the fashion of that day, was of velvet, hung a medal, the device of which I do not remember. He was magnificently attended, as became a man of his rank, with chamberlains and major-domos and many pages; and the service of his table was splendid, with a quantity of both gold and silver plate. At noon he dined heartily, drinking about a pint of wine mixed with water. He supped well, though he was not dainty in regard to his food, caring little for the delicacies of the table, unless, indeed, on such occasions as made attention to these matters of some consequence.

"He was acquainted with Latin, and, as I have understood, was made Bachelor of Laws; and, when he conversed with learned men who addressed him in Latin, he answered them in the same language. He was also something of a poet; his conversation was agreeable, and he had a pleasant elocution. In his attendance on the services of the Church he was most punctual, devout in his manner, and charitable to the poor.

"When he swore, he used to say, 'On my conscience'; and when he was vexed with any one, 'Evil betide you.' With his men he was very patient; and they were sometimes impertinent and even insolent. When very angry, the veins in his throat and forehead would swell, but he uttered no reproaches against either officer or soldier.

"He was fond of cards and dice, and, when he played, was always in good humor, indulging freely in jests and repartees. He was affable with his followers, especially with those who came over with him from Cuba. In his campaigns he paid strict attention to discipline, frequently going the rounds himself during the night, and seeing that the sentinels did their duty. He entered the quarters of his soldiers without ceremony, and chided those whom he found without their arms and accoutrements, saying, 'It was a bad sheep that could not carry its own wool.' On the expedition to Honduras he acquired the habit of sleeping after his meals, feeling unwell if he omitted it; and, however sultry or stormy the weather, he caused a carpet or his cloak to be thrown under a tree, and slept soundly for some time. He was frank and exceedingly liberal in his disposition, until the last few years of his life, when he was accused of parsimony. But we should consider that his funds were employed on great and costly enterprises; and that none of these, after the Conquest, neither his expedition to Honduras, nor his voyages to California, were crowned with success. It was perhaps intended that he should receive his recompense in a better world; and I fully believe it; for he was a good cavalier, most true in his devotions to the Virgin, to the Apostle St. Peter, and to all the other Saints."

Such is the portrait, which has been left to us by the faithful hand most competent to trace it, of Hernando Cortez, the Conqueror of Mexico.

*St. Matthew*

# THE CRUCIFIXION

And it came to pass, when Jesus had finished all these sayings, he said unto his disciples, Ye know that after two days is the feast of the passover, and the Son of man is betrayed to be crucified. Then assembled together the chief priests, and the scribes, and the elders of the people, unto the palace of the high priest, who was called Caiaphas, and consulted that they might take Jesus by subtilty, and kill him. But they said, Not on the feast day, lest there be an uproar among the people.

Now when Jesus was in Bethany, in the house of Simon the leper, there came unto him a woman having an alabaster box of very precious ointment, and poured it on his head, as he sat at meat. But when his disciples saw it, they had indignation, saying, To what purpose is this waste? For this ointment might have been sold for much, and given to the poor. When Jesus understood it, he said unto them, Why trouble ye the woman? for she hath wrought a good work upon me. For ye have the poor always with you; but me ye have not always. For in that she hath poured this ointment on my body, she did it for my burial. Verily I say unto you, Wheresoever this gospel shall be preached in the whole world, there shall also this, that this woman hath done, be told for a memorial of her.

Then one of the twelve, called Judas Iscariot, went unto the chief priests, and said unto them, What will ye give me, and I will deliver him unto you? And they covenanted with him for thirty pieces of silver. And from that time he sought opportunity to betray him.

Now the first day of the feast of unleavened bread the disciples came to Jesus, saying unto him, Where wilt thou that we prepare for thee

THE CRUCIFIXION: From *The Gospel According to St. Matthew*, Chapters 26–28.

to eat the passover? And he said, Go into the city to such a man, and say unto him, The Master saith, My time is at hand; I will keep the passover at thy house with my disciples. And the disciples did as Jesus had appointed them; and they made ready the passover. Now when the even was come, he sat down with the twelve. And as they did eat, he said, Verily I say unto you, that one of you shall betray me. And they were exceeding sorrowful, and began every one of them to say unto him, Lord, is it I? And he answered and said, He that dippeth his hand with me in the dish, the same shall betray me. The Son of man goeth as it is written of him: but woe unto that man by whom the Son of man is betrayed! it had been good for that man if he had not been born. Then Judas, which betrayed him, answered and said, Master, is it I? He said unto him, Thou hast said.

And as they were eating, Jesus took bread, and blessed it and brake it, and gave it to the disciples, and said, Take, eat; this is my body. And he took the cup, and gave thanks, and gave it to them, saying, Drink ye all of it; for this is my blood of the new testament, which is shed for many for the remission of sins. But I say unto you, I will not drink henceforth of this fruit of the vine, until that day when I drink it new with you in my Father's kingdom. And when they had sung an hymn, they went out into the mount of Olives. Then saith Jesus unto them, All ye shall be offended because of me this night: for it is written I will smite the shepherd, and the sheep of the flock shall be scattered abroad. But after I am risen again, I will go before you into Galilee. Peter answered and said unto him, Though all men shall be offended because of thee, yet will I never be offended. Jesus said unto him, Verily I say unto thee, That this night before the cock crow, thou shalt deny me thrice. Peter said unto him, Though I should die with thee, yet will I not deny thee. Likewise also said all the disciples.

Then cometh Jesus with them unto a place called Gethsemane, and saith unto the disciples, Sit ye here, while I go and pray yonder. And he took with him Peter and the two sons of Zebedee, and began to be sorrowful and very heavy. Then saith he unto them, My soul is exceeding sorrowful, even unto death: tarry ye here, and watch with me. And he went a little farther, and fell on his face, and prayed, saying, O my Father, if it be possible, let this cup pass from me: nevertheless not as I will, but as thou wilt. And he cometh unto the disciples, and findeth them asleep, and saith unto Peter, What, could ye not watch with me one hour? Watch and pray, that ye enter not into temptation: the spirit indeed is willing, but the flesh is weak. He went away the second time, and prayed saying, O my Father, if this cup may not pass away from me, except I drink it, thy will be done. And he came and found them asleep again: for their eyes were heavy. And he left them, and went away again, and prayed the third time, saying the same words. Then cometh he to his disciples, and saith unto them, Sleep on now, and take your rest: behold, the hour is at hand, and the Son of man is betrayed into the hands of sinners. Rise, let us be going: behold, he is at hand that doth betray me.

And while he yet spake, lo, Judas, one of the twelve, came and with him a great multitude with swords and staves, from the chief priests and elders of the people. Now he that betrayed him gave them a sign, saying, Whomsoever I shall kiss, that same is he: hold him fast. And forthwith he came to Jesus, and said, Hail, master; and kissed him. And Jesus said unto him, Friend, wherefore art thou come? Then came they, and laid hands on Jesus, and took him. And behold, one of them which were with Jesus stretched out his hand, and drew his sword, and struck a servant of the high priest's, and smote off his ear. Then said Jesus unto him, Put up again thy sword into his place: for all they that take the sword shall perish with the sword. Thinkest thou that I cannot now pray to my Father, and he shall presently give me more than twelve legions of angels? But how then shall the scriptures be fulfilled, that thus it must be? In that same hour said Jesus to the multitudes, Are ye come out as against a thief with swords and staves for to take me? I sat daily with you teaching in the temple, and ye laid no hold on me. But all this was done, that the scriptures of the prophets might be fulfilled. Then all the disciples forsook him, and fled.

And they that had laid hold on Jesus led him away to Caiaphas the high priest, where the scribes and the elders were assembled. But Peter followed him afar off unto the high priest's palace, and went in, and sat with the servants, to see the end. Now the chief priests, and elders, and all the council, sought false witness against Jesus, to put him to death; but found none: yea, though many false witnesses came, yet found they none. At the last came two false witnesses, and said, This fellow said, I am able to destroy the temple of God, and to build it in three days. And the high priest arose, and said unto him, Answerest thou nothing? What is it which these witness against thee? But Jesus held his peace. And the high priest answered and said unto him, I adjure thee by the living God, that thou tell us whether thou be the Christ, the Son of God. Jesus saith unto him, Thou hast said: nevertheless I say unto you, Hereafter shall ye see the Son of man sitting on the right hand of power, and coming in the clouds of heaven. Then the high priest rent his clothes saying, He hath spoken blasphemy; what further need have we of witnesses? Behold, now ye have heard his blasphemy. What think ye? They answered and said, He is guilty of death. Then did they spit in his face, and buffeted him; and others smote him with the palms of their hands, saying, Prophesy unto us, thou Christ, Who is he that smote thee?

Now Peter sat without in the palace: and a damsel came unto him, saying, Thou also wast with Jesus of Galilee. But he denied before them all, saying, I know not what thou sayest. And when he was gone out into the porch, another maid saw him, and said unto them that were there, This fellow was also with Jesus of Nazareth. And again he denied with an oath, I do not know the man. And after a while came unto him they that stood by, and said to Peter, Surely thou also art one of them, for thy speech bewrayeth thee. Then began he to curse and to swear, saying, I know not the man. And immediately the cock crew. And Peter remembered the word of Jesus, which said unto him, Before the cock crow, thou shalt deny me thrice. And he went out, and wept bitterly.

When the morning was come, all the chief priests and elders of the people took counsel against Jesus to put him to death: and when they had bound him, they led him away, and delivered him to Pontius Pilate the governor.

Then Judas, which had betrayed him, when he saw that he was condemned, repented himself, and brought again the thirty pieces of silver to the chief priests and elders, saying, I have sinned in that I have betrayed the innocent blood. And they said, What is that to us? see thou to that. And he cast down the pieces of silver in the temple, and departed, and went and hanged himself. And the chief priests took the silver pieces, and said, It is not lawful for to put them into the treasury, because it is the price of blood. And they took counsel, and bought with them the potter's field, to bury strangers in. Wherefore the field was called, The field of blood, unto this day. Then was fulfilled that which was spoken by Jeremy the prophet, saying, And they took the thirty pieces of silver, the price of him that was valued, whom they of the children of Israel did value; and gave them for the potter's field, as the Lord appointed me. And Jesus stood before the governor: and the governor asked him, saying, Art thou the King of the Jews? And Jesus said unto him, Thou sayest. And when he was accused of the chief priests and elders, he answered nothing. Then said Pilate unto him, Hearest thou not how many things they witness against thee? And he answered him to never a word; insomuch that the governor marvelled greatly. Now at that feast the governor was wont to release unto the people a prisoner, whom they would. And they had then a notable prisoner, called Barabbas. Therefore when they were gathered together, Pilate said unto them, Whom will ye that I release unto you? Barabbas, or Jesus which is called Christ? For he knew that for envy they had delivered him.

When he was set down on the judgment seat, his wife sent unto him saying, Have thou nothing to do with that just man; for I have suffered many things this day in a dream because of him. But the chief priests and elders persuaded the multitude that they should ask Barabbas, and destroy Jesus. The governor answered and said unto them, Whether of the twain will ye that I release unto you? They said, Barabbas. Pilate saith unto them, What shall I do then with Jesus which is called Christ? They all say unto him, Let him be crucified. And the governor said, Why what evil hath he done? But they cried out the more, saying, Let him be crucified.

When Pilate saw that he could prevail nothing, but that rather a tumult was made, he took water, and washed his hands before the multitude, saying, I am innocent of the blood of this just person: see ye to it. Then answered all the people, and said, His blood be on us, and on our children.

Then released he Barabbas unto them: and when he had scourged Jesus, he delivered him to be crucified. Then the soldiers of the governor took Jesus into the common hall, and gathered unto him the whole band of soldiers. And they stripped him, and put on him a scarlet robe.

And when they had platted a crown of thorns, they put it upon his head, and a reed in his right hand: and they bowed the knee before him, and mocked him, saying, Hail, King of the Jews! And they spit upon him, and took the reed, and smote him on the head. And after that they had mocked him, they took the robe off from him, and put his own raiment on him, and led him away to crucify him. And as they came out, they found a man of Cyrene, Simon by name: him they compelled to bear his cross. And when they were come unto a place called Golgotha, that is to say, a place of a skull, they gave him vinegar to drink mingled with gall: and when he had tasted thereof, he would not drink. And they crucified him, and parted his garments, casting lots: that it might be fulfilled which was spoken by the prophet, They parted my garments among them, and upon my vesture did they cast lots. And sitting down they watched him there; and set up over his head his accusation written, THIS IS JESUS THE KING OF THE JEWS. Then were there two thieves crucified with him, one on the right hand, and another on the left.

And they that passed by reviled him, wagging their heads, and saying, Thou that destroyest the temple, and buildest it in three days, save thyself. If thou be the Son of God, come down from the cross. Likewise also the chief priests mocking him, with the scribes and elders, said, He saved others; himself he cannot save. If he be the King of Israel, let him now come down from the cross, and we will believe him. He trusted in God; let him deliver him now, if he will have him: for he said, I am the Son of God. The thieves also, which were crucified with him, cast the same in his teeth. Now from the sixth hour there was darkness over all the land unto the ninth hour. And about the ninth hour Jesus cried with a loud voice, saying, *Eli, Eli, lama sabachthani?* That is to say, My God, my God, why hast thou forsaken me? Some of them that stood there, when they heard that, said, This man calleth for Elias. And straightway one of them ran, and took a sponge, and filled it with vinegar, and put it on a reed, and gave him to drink. The rest said, Let be, let us see whether Elias will come to save him.

Jesus, when he had cried again with a loud voice, yielded up the ghost. And, behold, the veil of the temple was rent in twain from the top to the bottom; and the earth did quake, and the rocks rent; and the graves were opened; and many bodies of the saints which slept arose, and came out the graves after his resurrection, and went into the holy city, and appeared unto many. Now when the centurion, and they that were with him, watching Jesus, saw the earthquake, and those things that were done, they feared greatly, saying, Truly this was the Son of God. And many women were there beholding afar off, which followed Jesus from Galilee, ministering unto him: among which was Mary Magdalene, and Mary the mother of James and Joses, and the mother of Zebedee's children. When the even was come, there came a rich man of Arimathæa, named Joseph, who also himself was Jesus' disciple: he went to Pilate, and begged the body of Jesus. Then Pilate commanded the body to be delivered. And when Joseph had taken the body, he wrapped it in a clean linen cloth, and laid it in his own new tomb, which he had hewn out in the rock: and he rolled a great stone to the door of the sepulchre, and departed. And there was Mary Magdalene, and the other Mary, sitting over against the sepulchre.

Now the next day, that followed the day of the preparation, the chief priests and Pharisees came together unto Pilate, saying, Sir, we remember that that deceiver said, while he was yet alive, After three days I will rise again. Command therefore that the sepulchre be made sure until the third day, lest his disciples come by night, and steal him away, and say unto the people, He is risen from the dead: so the last error shall be worse than the first. Pilate said unto them, Ye have a watch: go your way, make it as sure as ye can. So they went, and made the sepulchre sure, sealing the stone, and setting a watch.

In the end of the sabbath, as it began to dawn toward the first day of the week, came Mary Magdalene and the other Mary to see the sepulchre. And, behold, there was a great earthquake: for the angel of the Lord descended from heaven, and came and rolled back the stone from the door, and sat upon it. His countenance was like lightning, and his raiment white as snow: and for fear of him the keepers did shake, and became as dead men. And the angel answered and said unto the women, Fear not ye: for I know that ye seek Jesus, which was crucified. He is not here: for he is risen, as he said. Come, see the place where the Lord lay. And go quickly, and tell his disciples that he is risen from the dead; and, behold, he goeth before you into Galilee; there shall ye see him: lo, I have told you. And they departed quickly from the sepulchre with fear and great joy; and did run to bring his disciples word.

And as they went to tell his disciples, behold, Jesus met them, saying, All hail. And they came and held him by the feet, and worshipped him. Then said Jesus unto them, Be not afraid: go tell my brethren that they go into Galilee, and there shall they see me.

Now when they were going, behold, some of the watch came into the city, and shewed unto the chief priests all the things that were done. And when they were assembled with the elders, and had taken counsel, they gave large money unto the soldiers, saying, Say ye, His disciples came by night, and stole him away while we slept. And if this come to the governor's ears, we will persuade him, and secure you. So they took the money, and did as they were taught: and this saying is commonly reported among the Jews until this day.

Then the eleven disciples went away into Galilee, into a mountain where Jesus had appointed them. And when they saw him, they worshipped him: but some doubted. And Jesus came and spake unto them, saying, All power is given unto me in heaven and in earth.

Go ye therefore, and teach all nations, baptizing them in the name of the Father, and of the Son, and of the Holy Ghost: teaching them to observe all things whatsoever I have commanded you: and lo, I am with you alway, even unto the end of the world. Amen.

## *Ernest Hemingway*
# THE UNDEFEATED

Manuel Garcia climbed the stairs to Don Miguel Retana's office. He set down his suitcase and knocked on the door. There was no answer. Manuel, standing in the hallway, felt there was some one in the room. He felt it through the door.

"Retana," he said, listening.

There was no answer.

He's there, all right, Manuel thought.

"Retana," he said and banged the door.

"Who's there?" said some one in the office.

"Me, Manolo," Manuel said.

"What do you want?" asked the voice.

"I want to work," Manuel said.

Something in the door clicked several times and it swung open. Manuel went in, carrying his suitcase.

A little man sat behind a desk at the far side of the room. Over his head was a bull's head, stuffed by a Madrid taxidermist; on the walls were framed photographs and bull-fight posters.

The little man sat looking at Manuel.

"I thought they'd killed you," he said.

Manuel knocked with his knuckles on the desk. The little man sat looking at him across the desk.

"How many corridas [7] you had this year?" Retana asked.

"One," he answered.

"Just that one?" the little man asked.

"That's all."

"I read about it in the papers," Retana said. He leaned back in the chair and looked at Manuel.

Manuel looked up at the stuffed bull. He had seen it often before. He felt a certain family interest in it. It had killed his brother, the promising one, about nine years ago. Manuel remembered the day. There was a brass plate on the oak shield the bull's head was mounted on. Manuel could not read it, but he imagined

---

THE UNDEFEATED: From *Men Without Women*, by Ernest Hemingway. Copyright, 1927, by Charles Scribner's Sons, 1955, by Ernest Hemingway. Reprinted by permission of the publishers.

[7] Bull-fights.

it was in memory of his brother. Well, he had been a good kid.

The plate said: "The Bull 'Mariposa' of the Duke of Veragua, which accepted 9 varas [8] for 7 caballos,[9] and caused the death of Antonio Garcia, Novillero, April 27, 1909."

Retana saw him looking at the stuffed bull's head.

"The lot the Duke sent me for Sunday will make a scandal," he said. "They're all bad in the legs. What do they say about them at the Café?"

"I don't know," Manuel said. "I just got in."

"Yes," Retana said. "You still have your bag."

He looked at Manuel, leaning back behind the big desk.

"Sit down," he said. "Take off your cap."

Manuel sat down; his cap off, his face was changed. He looked pale, and his coleta [10] pinned forward on his head, so that it would not show under the cap, gave him a strange look.

"You don't look well," Retana said.

"I just got out of the hospital," Manuel said.

"I heard they'd cut your leg off," Retana said.

"No," said Manuel. "It got all right."

Retana leaned forward across the desk and pushed a wooden box of cigarettes toward Manuel.

"Have a cigarette," he said.

"Thanks."

Manuel lit it.

"Smoke?" he said, offering the match to Retana.

"No," Retana waved his hand, "I never smoke."

Retana watched him smoking.

"Why don't you get a job and go to work?" he said.

"I don't want to work," Manuel said. "I am a bull-fighter."

"There aren't any bull-fighters any more," Retana said.

"I'm a bull-fighter," Manuel said.

"Yes, while you're in there," Retana said.

Manuel laughed.

Retana sat, saying nothing and looking at Manuel.

"I'll put you in a nocturnal if you want," Retana offered.

"When?" Manuel asked.

"Tomorrow night."

"I don't like to substitute for anybody," Manuel said. That was the way they all got killed. That was the way Salvador got killed. He tapped with his knuckles on the table.

"It's all I've got," Retana said.

"Why don't you put me on next week?" Manuel suggested.

"You wouldn't draw," Retana said. "All they want is Litri and Rubito and La Torre. Those kids are good."

"They'd come to see me get it," Manuel said, hopefully.

"No, they wouldn't. They don't know who you are any more."

"I've got a lot of stuff," Manuel said.

"I'm offering to put you on tomorrow night," Retana said. "You can work with young Hernandez and kill two novillos [11] after the Charlots."

"Whose novillos?" Manuel asked.

"I don't know. Whatever stuff they've got in the corrals. What the veterinaries won't pass in the daytime."

"I don't like to substitute," Manuel said.

"You can take it or leave it," Retana said. He leaned forward over the papers. He was no longer interested. The appeal that Manuel had made to him for a moment when he thought of the old days was gone. He would like to get him to substitute for Larita because he could get him cheaply. He could get others cheaply too. He would like to help him though. Still he had given him the chance. It was up to him.

"How much do I get?" Manuel asked. He was still playing with the idea of refusing. But he knew he could not refuse.

"Two hundred and fifty pesetas," Retana said. He had thought of five hundred, but when he opened his mouth it said two hundred and fifty.

"You pay Villalta seven thousand," Manuel said.

"You're not Villalta," Retana said.

"I know it," Manuel said.

"He draws it, Manolo," Retana said in explanation.

---

[8] Pointed spears used to goad the bull.
[9] Horses.
[10] The bull-fighter's braided pigtail.

[11] Bulls not considered fine enough for a regular bull-fight.

"Sure," said Manuel. He stood up. "Give me three hundred, Retana."

"All right," Retana agreed. He reached in the drawer for a paper.

"Can I have fifty now?" Manuel asked.

"Sure," said Retana. He took a fifty-peseta note out of his pocket-book and laid it, spread out flat, on the table.

Manuel picked it up and put it in his pocket.

"What about a cuadrilla?"[12] he asked.

"There's the boys that always work for me nights," Retana said. "They're all right."

"How about picadors?"[13] Manuel asked.

"They're not much," Retana admitted.

"I've got to have one good pic," Manuel said.

"Get him then," Retana said. "Go and get him."

"Not out of this," Manuel said. "I'm not paying for any cuadrilla out of sixty duros."

Retana said nothing but looked at Manuel across the big desk.

"You know I've got to have one good pic," Manuel said.

Retana said nothing but looked at Manuel from a long way off.

"It isn't right," Manuel said.

Retana was still considering him, leaning back in his chair, considering him from a long way away.

"There're the regular pics," he offered.

"I know," Manuel said. "I know your regular pics."

Retana did not smile. Manuel knew it was over.

"All I want is an even break," Manuel said reasoningly. "When I go out there I want to be able to call my shots on the bull. It only takes one good picador."

He was talking to a man who was no longer listening.

"If you want something extra," Retana said, "go and get it. There will be a regular cuadrilla out there. Bring as many of your own pics as you want. The charlotada is over by 10.30."

"All right," Manuel said. "If that's the way you feel about it."

"That's the way," Retana said.

"I'll see you tomorrow night," Manuel said.

"I'll be out there," Retana said.

Manuel picked up his suitcase and went out.

---

[12] Helper.
[13] Mounted helpers who goad the bull.

"Shut the door," Retana called.

Manuel looked back. Retana was sitting forward looking at some papers. Manuel pulled the door tight until it clicked.

He went down the stairs and out of the door into the hot brightness of the street. It was very hot in the street and the light on the white buildings was sudden and hard on the eyes. He walked down the shady side of the steep street toward the Puerta del Sol. The shade felt solid and cool as running water. The heat came suddenly as he crossed the intersecting streets. Manuel saw no one he knew in all the people he passed.

Just before the Puerta del Sol he turned into a café.

It was quiet in the café. There were a few men sitting at tables against the wall. At one table four men played cards. Most of the men sat against the wall smoking, empty coffee-cups and liqueur-glasses before them on the tables. Manuel went through the long room to a small room in back. A man sat at a table in the corner asleep. Manuel sat down at one of the tables.

A waiter came in and stood beside Manuel's table.

"Have you seen Zurito?" Manuel asked him.

"He was in before lunch," the waiter answered. "He won't be back before five o'clock."

"Bring me some coffee and milk and a shot of the ordinary," Manuel said.

The waiter came back into the room carrying a tray with a big coffee-glass and a liqueur-glass on it. In his left hand he held a bottle of brandy. He swung these down to the table and a boy who had followed him poured coffee and milk into the glass from two shiny, spouted pots with long handles.

Manuel took off his cap and the waiter noticed his pigtail pinned forward on his head. He winked at the coffee-boy as he poured out the brandy into the little glass beside Manuel's coffee. The coffee-boy looked at Manuel's pale face curiously.

"You fighting here?" asked the waiter, corking up the bottle.

"Yes," Manuel said. "Tomorrow."

The waiter stood there, holding the bottle on one hip.

"You in the Charlie Chaplins?" he asked.

The coffee-boy looked away, embarrassed.

"No. In the ordinary."

"I thought they were going to have Chaves and Hernandez," the waiter said.

"No. Me and another."

"Who? Chaves or Hernandez?"

"Hernandez, I think."

"What's the matter with Chaves?"

"He got hurt."

"Where did you hear that?"

"Retana."

"Hey, Looie," the waiter called to the next room, "Chaves got cogida." [14]

Manuel had taken the wrapper off the lumps of sugar and dropped them into his coffee. He stirred it and drank it down, sweet, hot, and warming in his empty stomach. He drank off the brandy.

"Give me another shot of that," he said to the waiter.

The waiter uncorked the bottle and poured the glass full, slopping another drink into the saucer. Another waiter had come up in front of the table. The coffee-boy was gone.

"Is Chaves hurt bad?" the second waiter asked Manuel.

"I don't know," Manuel said, "Retana didn't say."

"A hell of a lot he cares," the tall waiter said. Manuel had not seen him before. He must have just come up.

"If you stand in with Retana in this town, you're a made man," the tall waiter said. "If you aren't in with him, you might just as well go out and shoot yourself."

"You said it," the other waiter who had come in said. "You said it then."

"You're right I said it," said the tall waiter. "I know what I'm talking about when I talk about that bird."

"Look what he's done for Villalta," the first waiter said.

"And that ain't all," the tall waiter said. "Look what he's done for Marcial Lalanda. Look what he's done for Nacional."

"You said it, kid," agreed the short waiter.

Manuel looked at them, standing talking in front of his table. He had drunk his second brandy. They had forgotten about him. They were not interested in him.

"Look at that bunch of camels," the tall waiter went on. "Did you ever see this Nacional II?"

14 Tossed.

"I seen him last Sunday didn't I?" the original waiter said.

"He's a giraffe," the short waiter said.

"What did I tell you?" the tall waiter said. "Those are Retana's boys."

"Say, give me another shot of that," Manuel said. He had poured the brandy the waiter had slopped over in the saucer into his glass and drank it while they were talking.

The original waiter poured his glass full mechanically, and the three of them went out of the room talking.

In the far corner the man was still asleep, snoring slightly on the intaking breath, his head back against the wall.

Manuel drank his brandy. He felt sleepy himself. It was too hot to go out into the town. Besides there was nothing to do. He wanted to see Zurito. He would go to sleep while he waited. He kicked his suitcase under the table to be sure it was there. Perhaps it would be better to put it back under the seat, against the wall. He leaned down and shoved it under. Then he leaned forward on the table and went to sleep.

When he woke there was some one sitting across the table from him. It was a big man with a heavy brown face like an Indian. He had been sitting there some time. He had waved the waiter away and sat reading the paper and occasionally looking down at Manuel, asleep, his head on the table. He read the paper laboriously, forming the words with his lips as he read. When it tired him he looked at Manuel. He sat heavily in the chair, his black Cordoba hat tipped forward

Manuel sat up and looked at him.

"Hello, Zurito," he said.

"Hello, kid," the big man said.

"I've been asleep." Manuel rubbed his forehead with the back of his fist.

"I thought maybe you were."

"How's everything?"

"Good. How is everything with you?"

"Not so good."

They were both silent. Zurito, the picador, looked at Manuel's white face. Manuel looked down at the picador's enormous hands folding the paper to put away in his pocket.

"I got a favor to ask you, Manos," Manuel said.

Manosduros was Zurito's nickname. He never heard it without thinking of his huge hands. He put them forward on the table self-consciously.

"Let's have a drink," he said.

"Sure," said Manuel.

The waiter came and went and came again. He went out of the room looking back at the two men at the table.

"What's the matter, Manolo?" Zurito set down his glass.

"Would you pic two bulls for me tomorrow night?" Manuel asked, looking up at Zurito across the table.

"No," said Zurito. "I'm not pic-ing."

Manuel looked down at his glass. He had expected that answer; now he had it. Well, he had it.

"I'm sorry, Manolo, but I'm not pic-ing." Zurito looked at his hands.

"That's all right," Manuel said.

"I'm too old," Zurito said.

"I just asked you," Manuel said.

"Is it the nocturnal tomorrow?"

"That's it. I figured if I had just one good pic, I could get away with it."

"How much are you getting?"

"Three hundred pesetas."

"I get more than that for pic-ing."

"I know," said Manuel. "I didn't have any right to ask you."

"What do you keep on doing it for?" Zurito asked. "Why don't you cut off your coleta, Manolo?"

"I don't know," Manuel said.

"You're pretty near as old as I am," Zurito said.

"I don't know," Manuel said. "I got to do it. If I can fix it so that I get an even break, that's all I want. I got to stick with it, Manos."

"No, you don't."

"Yes, I do. I've tried keeping away from it."

"I know how you feel. But it isn't right. You ought to get out and stay out."

"I can't do it. Besides, I've been going good lately."

Zurito looked at his face.

"You've been in the hospital."

"But I was going great when I got hurt."

Zurito said nothing. He tipped the cognac out of his saucer into his glass.

"The papers said they never saw a better faena," [15] Manuel said.

---

[15] Show.

Zurito looked at him.

"You know when I get going I'm good," Manuel said.

"You're too old," the picador said.

"No," said Manuel. "You're ten years older than I am."

"With me it's different."

"I'm not too old," Manuel said.

They sat silent, Manuel watching the picador's face.

"I was going great till I got hurt," Manuel offered.

"You ought to have seen me, Manos," Manuel said, reproachfully.

"I don't want to see you," Zurito said. "It makes me nervous."

"You haven't seen me lately."

"I've seen you plenty."

Zurito looked at Manuel, avoiding his eyes.

"You ought to quit it, Manolo."

"I can't," Manuel said. "I'm going good now, I tell you."

Zurito leaned forward, his hands on the table.

"Listen. I'll pic for you and if you don't go big tomorrow night, you'll quit. See? Will you do that?"

"Sure."

Zurito leaned back, relieved.

"You got to quit," he said. "No monkey business. You got to cut the coleta."

"I won't have to quit," Manuel said. "You watch me. I've got the stuff."

Zurito stood up. He felt tired from arguing.

"You got to quit," he said. "I'll cut your coleta myself."

"No, you won't," Manuel said. "You won't have a chance."

Zurito called the waiter.

"Come on," said Zurito. "Come on up to the house."

Manuel reached under the seat for his suitcase. He was happy. He knew Zurito would pic for him. He was the best picador living. It was all simple now.

"Come on up to the house and we'll eat," Zurito said.

Manuel stood in the patio de caballos waiting for the Charlie Chaplins to be over. Zurito stood beside him. Where they stood it was dark. The high door that led into the bull-ring was shut. Above them they heard a shout, then another shout of laughter. Then there was silence. Manuel liked the smell of the stables about the patio de caballos. It smelt good in the dark. There was another roar from the arena and then applause, prolonged applause, going on and on.

"You ever seen these fellows?" Zurito asked, big and looming beside Manuel in the dark.

"No," Manuel said.

"They're pretty funny." Zurito said. He smiled to himself in the dark.

The high, double, tight-fitting door into the bull-ring swung open and Manuel saw the ring in the hard light of the arc-lights, the plaza, dark all the way around, rising high; around the edge of the ring were running and bowing two men dressed like tramps, followed by a third in the uniform of a hotel bell-boy who stooped and picked up the hats and canes thrown down onto the sand and tossed them back up into the darkness.

The electric light went on in the patio.

"I'll climb onto one of those ponies while you collect the kids," Zurito said.

Behind them came the jingle of the mules, coming out to go into the arena and be hitched onto the dead bull.

The members of the cuadrilla, who had been watching the burlesque from the runway between the barrera [16] and the seats, came walking back and stood in a group talking, under the electric light in the patio. A good-looking lad in a silver-and-orange suit came up to Manuel and smiled.

"I'm Hernandez," he said and put out his hand.

Manuel shook it.

"They're regular elephants we've got tonight," the boy said cheerfully.

"They're big ones with horns," Manuel agreed.

"You drew the worst lot," the boy said.

"That's all right," Manuel said. "The bigger they are, the more meat for the poor."

"Where did you get that one?" Hernandez grinned.

"That's an old one," Manuel said. "You line up your cuadrilla, so I can see what I've got."

"You've got some good kids," Hernandez said. He was very cheerful. He had been on twice before in nocturnals and was beginning to get a following in Madrid. He was happy the fight would start in a few minutes.

"Where are the pics?" Manuel asked.

"They're back in the corrals fighting about who gets the beautiful horses," Hernandez grinned.

The mules came through the gate in a rush, the whips snapping, bells jangling and the young bull ploughing a furrow of sand.

They formed up for the paseo [17] as soon as the bull had gone through.

Manuel and Hernandez stood in front. The youths of the cuadrillas were behind, their heavy capes furled over their arms. In back, the four picadors, mounted, holding their steel-tipped push-poles erect in the half-dark of the corral.

"It's a wonder Retana wouldn't give us enough light to see the horses by," one picador said.

"He knows we'll be happier if we don't get too good a look at these skins," another pic answered.

"This thing I'm on barely keeps me off the ground," the first picador said.

"Well, they're horses."

"Sure, they're horses."

They talked, sitting their gaunt horses in the dark.

Zurito said nothing. He had the only steady horse of the lot. He had tried him, wheeling him in the corrals, and he responded to the bit and the spurs. He had taken the bandage off his right eye and cut the strings where they had tied his ears tight shut at the base. He was a good, solid horse, solid on his legs. That was all he needed. He intended to ride him all through the corrida. He had already, since he had mounted, sitting in the half-dark in the big, quilted saddle, waiting for the paseo, pic-ed through the whole corrida in his mind. The other picadors went on talking on both sides of him. He did not hear them.

The two matadors stood together in front of their three peones,[18] their capes furled over their left arms in the same fashion. Manuel was thinking about the three lads in back of him. They were all three Madrilenos, like Hernandez, boys about nineteen. One of them, a gypsy, serious, aloof, and dark-faced, he liked the look of. He turned.

---

16 The fence around the bull-fight ring.

17 The march into the ring.
18 A matador's helper who works on foot.

"What's your name, kid?" he asked the gypsy.

"Fuentes," the gypsy said.

"That's a good name," Manuel said.

The gypsy smiled, showing his teeth.

"You take the bull and give him a little run when he comes out," Manuel said.

"All right," the gypsy said. His face was serious. He began to think about just what he would do.

"Here she goes," Manuel said to Hernandez.

"All right. We'll go."

Heads up, swinging with the music, their right arms swinging free, they stepped out, crossing the sanded arena under the arc-lights, the cuadrillas opening out behind, the picadors riding after; behind came the bull-ring servants and the jingling mules. The crowd applauded Hernandez as they marched across the arena. Arrogant, swinging, they looked straight ahead as they marched.

They bowed before the president, and the procession broke up into its component parts. The bull-fighters went over to the barrera and changed their heavy mantles for the light fighting capes. The mules went out. The picadors galloped jerkily around the ring, and two rode out the gate they had come in by. The servants swept the sand smooth.

Manuel drank a glass of water poured for him by one of Retana's deputies, who was acting as his manager and sword-handler. Hernandez came over from speaking with his own manager.

"You got a good hand, kid," Manuel complimented him.

"They like me," Hernandez said happily.

"How did the paseo go?" Manuel asked Retana's man.

"Like a wedding," said the handler. "Fine. You came out like Joselito and Belmonte."

Zurito rode by, a bulky equestrian statue. He wheeled his horse and faced him toward the toril [19] on the far side of the ring where the bull would come out. It was strange under the arc-light. He pic-ed in the hot afternoon sun for big money. He didn't like this arc-light business. He wished they would get started.

Manuel went up to him.

"Pic him, Manos," he said. "Cut him down to size for me."

"I'll pic him, kid," Zurito spat on the sand. "I'll make him jump out of the ring."

"Lean on him, Manos," Manuel said.

"I'll lean on him," Zurito said. "What's holding it up?"

"He's coming now," Manuel said.

Zurito sat there, his feet in the box-stirrups, his great legs in the buckskin-covered armor gripping the horse, the reins in his left hand, the long pic held in his right hand, his broad hat well down over his eyes to shade them from the lights, watching the distant door of the toril. His horse's ears quivered. Zurito patted him with his left hand.

The red door of the toril swung back and for a moment Zurito looked into the empty passageway far across the arena. Then the bull came out in a rush, skidding on his four legs as he came out under the lights, then charging in a gallop, moving softly in a fast gallop, silent except as he woofed through wide nostrils as he charged, glad to be free after the dark pen.

In the first row of seats, slightly bored, leaning forward to write on the cement wall in front of his knees, the substitute bullfight critic of El Heraldo scribbled: "Campagnero, Negro,[20] 42, came out at 90 miles an hour with plenty of gas ——"

Manuel, leaning against the barrera, watching the bull, waved his hand and the gypsy ran out, trailing his cape. The bull, in full gallop, pivoted and charged the cape, his head down, his tail rising. The gypsy moved in a zigzag, and as he passed, the bull caught sight of him and abandoned the cape to charge the man. The gyp sprinted and vaulted the red fence of the barrera as the bull struck it with his horns. He tossed into it twice with his horns, banging into the wood blindly.

The critic of El Heraldo lit a cigarette and tossed the match at the bull, then wrote in his note-book, "large and with enough horns to satisfy the cash customers, Campagnero showed a tendency to cut into the terrain of the bull-fighters."

Manuel stepped out on the hard sand as the bull banged into the fence. Out of the corner of his eye he saw Zurito sitting the white horse close to the barrera, about a quarter of the way around the ring to the left. Manuel held the cape close in front of him, a fold in each hand,

---

[19] The pen from which the bull enters the ring.

[20] Black; 42 appears to be the bull's number.

and shouted at the bull. "Huh! Huh!" The bull turned, seemed to brace against the fence as he charged in a scramble, driving into the cape as Manuel side-stepped, pivoted on his heels with the charge of the bull, and swung the cape just ahead of the horns. At the end of the swing he was facing the bull again and held the cape in the same position close in front of his body, and pivoted again as the bull re-charged. Each time, as he swung, the crowd shouted.

Four times he swung with the bull, lifting the cape so it billowed full, and each time bringing the bull around to charge again. Then, at the end of the fifth swing, he held the cape against his hip and pivoted, so the cape swung out like a ballet dancer's skirt and wound the bull around himself like a belt, to step clear, leaving the bull facing Zurito on the white horse, come up and planted firm, the horse facing the bull, its ears forward, its lips nervous, Zurito, his hat over his eyes, leaning forward, the long pole sticking out before and behind in a sharp angle under his right arm, held half-way down, the triangular iron point facing the bull.

*El Heraldo's* second-string critic, drawing on his cigarette, his eyes on the bull, wrote: "the veteran Manolo designed a series of acceptable veronicas,[21] ending in a very Belmontistic recorte [22] that earned applause from the regulars, and we entered the tercio of the cavalry."

Zurito sat his horse, measuring the distance between the bull and the end of the pic. As he looked, the bull gathered himself together and charged, his eyes on the horse's chest. As he lowered his head to hook, Zurito sunk the point of the pic in the swelling hump of muscle above the bull's shoulder, leaned all his weight on the shaft, and with his left hand pulled the white horse into the air, front hoofs pawing, and swung him to the right as he pushed the bull under and through so the horns passed safely under the horse's belly and the horse came down, quivering, the bull's tail brushing his chest as he charged the cape Hernandez offered him.

Hernandez ran sideways, taking the bull out and away with the cape, toward the other pic-ador. He fixed him with a swing of the cape, squarely facing the horse and rider, and stepped back. As the bull saw the horse he charged. The picador's lance slid along his back, and as the shock of the charge lifted the horse, the picador was already half-way out of the saddle, lifting his right leg clear as he missed with the lance and falling to the left side to keep the horse between him and the bull. The horse, lifted and gored, crashed over with the bull driving into him, the picador gave a shove with his boots against the horse and lay clear, waiting to be lifted and hauled away and put on his feet.

Manuel let the bull drive into the fallen horse; he was in no hurry, the picador was safe; besides, it did a picador like that good to worry. He'd stay on longer next time. Lousy pics! He looked across the sand at Zurito a little way out from the barrera, his horse rigid, waiting.

"Huh!" he called to the bull, "Tomar!" [23] holding the cape in both hands so it would catch his eye. The bull detached himself from the horse and charged the cape, and Manuel, running sideways and holding the cape spread wide, stopped, swung on his heels, and brought the bull sharply around facing Zurito.

"Campagnero accepted a pair of varas for the death of one rosinante, with Hernandez and Manolo at the quites," [24] *El Heraldo's* critic wrote. "He pressed on the iron and clearly showed he was no horse-lover. The veteran Zurito resurrected some of his old stuff with the pike-pole, notably the suerte [25]————"

"Olé! Olé!" the man sitting beside him shouted. The shout was lost in the roar of the crowd, and he slapped the critic on the back. The critic looked up to see Zurito, directly below him, leaning far out over his horse, the length of the pic rising in a sharp angle under his armpit, holding the pic almost by the point, bearing down with all his weight, holding the bull off, the bull pushing and driving to get at the horse, and Zurito, far out, on top of him, holding him, holding him, and slowly pivoting the horse against the pressure, so that at last he was clear. Zurito felt the moment when the horse was clear and the bull could come past,

---

[21] Movements of the bull-fighter's cape.
[22] A movement that turns the bull.

[23] "Take!"
[24] Movements by which one bull-fighter gets the bull away from another bull-fighter who is in trouble.
[25] A movement by which the picador keeps the bull from hurting his horse.

and relaxed the absolute steel lock of his resistance, and the triangular steel point of the pic ripped in the bull's hump of shoulder muscle as he tore loose to find Hernandez's cape before his muzzle. He charged blindly into the cape and the boy took him out into the open arena.

Zurito sat patting his horse and looking at the bull charging the cape that Hernandez swung for him out under the bright light while the crowd shouted.

"You see that one?" he said to Manuel.

"It was a wonder," Manuel said.

"I got him that time," Zurito said. "Look at him now."

At the conclusion of a closely turned pass of the cape the bull slid to his knees. He was up at once, but far out across the sand Manuel and Zurito saw the shine of the pumping flow of blood, smooth against the black of the bull's shoulder.

"I got him that time," Zurito said.

"He's a good bull," Manuel said.

"If they gave me another shot at him, I'd kill him," Zurito said.

"They'll change the thirds on us," Manuel said.

"Look at him now," Zurito said.

"I got to go over there," Manuel said, and started on a run for the other side of the ring, where the monos [26] were leading a horse out by the bridle toward the bull, whacking him on the legs with rods and all, in a procession, trying to get him toward the bull, who stood, dropping his head, pawing, unable to make up his mind to charge.

Zurito, sitting his horse, walking him toward the scene, not missing any detail, scowled.

Finally the bull charged, the horse leaders ran for the barrera, the picador hit too far back, and the bull got under the horse, lifted him, threw him onto his back.

Zurito watched. The monos, in their red shirts, running out to drag the picador clear. The picador, now on his feet, swearing and flopping his arms. Manuel and Hernandez standing ready with their capes. And the bull, the great, black bull, with a horse on his back, hooves dangling, the bridle caught in the horns. Black bull with a horse on his back, staggering

short-legged, then arching his neck and lifting, thrusting, charging to slide the horse off, horse sliding down. Then the bull into a lunging charge at the cape Manuel spread for him.

The bull was slower now, Manuel felt. He was bleeding badly. There was a sheen of blood all down his flank.

Manuel offered him the cape again. There he came, eyes open, ugly, watching the cape. Manuel stepped to the side and raised his arms, tightening the cape ahead of the bull for the veronica.

Now he was facing the bull. Yes, his head was going down a little. He was carrying it lower. That was Zurito.

Manuel flopped the cape; there he comes; he side-stepped and swung in another veronica. He's shooting awfully accurately, he thought. He's had enough fight, so he's watching now. He's hunting now. Got his eye on me. But I always give him the cape.

He shook the cape at the bull; there he comes; he side-stepped. Awful close that time. I don't want to work that close to him.

The edge of the cape was wet with blood where it had swept along the bull's back as he went by.

All right, here's the last one.

Manuel, facing the bull, having turned with him each charge, offered the cape with his two hands. The bull looked at him. Eyes watching, horns straight forward, the bull looked at him, watching.

"Huh!" Manuel said, "Toro!" [27] and leaning back, swung the cape forward. Here he comes. He side-stepped, swung the cape in back of him, and pivoted, so the bull followed a swirl of cape and then was left with nothing, fixed by the pass, dominated by the cape. Manuel swung the cape under his muzzle with one hand, to show the bull was fixed, and walked away.

There was no applause.

Manuel walked across the sand toward the barrera, while Zurito rode out of the ring. The trumpet had blown to change the act to the planting of the banderillos [28] while Manuel had been working with the bull. He had not consciously noticed it. The monos were spreading

---

[26] Servants.

[27] "Bull!"

[28] Sharp spears that will be "planted" in the bull.

canvas over the two dead horses and sprinkling sawdust around them.

Manuel came up to the barrera for a drink of water. Retana's man handed him the heavy porous jug.

Fuentes, the tall gypsy, was standing holding a pair of banderillos, holding them together, slim, red sticks, fish-hook points out. He looked at Manuel.

"Go on out there," Manuel said.

The gypsy trotted out. Manuel set down the jug and watched. He wiped his face with his handkerchief.

The critic of *El Heraldo* reached for the bottle of warm champagne that stood between his feet, took a drink, and finished his paragraph.

"—— the aged Manolo rated no applause for a vulgar series of lances with the cape and we entered the third of the palings."

Alone in the centre of the ring the bull stood, still fixed. Fuentes, tall, flat-backed, walking toward him arrogantly, his arms spread out, the two slim, red sticks, one in each hand, held by the fingers, points straight forward. Fuentes walked forward. Back of him and to one side was a peon with a cape. The bull looked at him and was no longer fixed.

His eyes watched Fuentes, now standing still. Now he leaned back, calling to him. Fuentes twitched the two banderillos and the light on the steel points caught the bull's eye.

His tail went up and he charged.

He came straight, his eyes on the man. Fuentes stood still, leaning back, the banderillos pointing forward. As the bull lowered his head to hook, Fuentes leaned backward, his arms came together and rose, his two hands touching, the banderillos two descending red lines, and leaning forward drove the points into the bull's shoulder, leaning far in over the bull's horns and pivoting on the two upright sticks, his legs tight together, his body curving to one side to let the bull pass.

"Olé!" from the crowd.

The bull was hooking wildly, jumping like a trout, all four feet off the ground. The red shaft of the banderillos tossed as he jumped.

Manuel, standing at the barrera, noticed that he hooked always to the right.

"Tell him to drop the next pair on the right," he said to the kid who started to run out to Fuentes with the new banderillos.

A heavy hand fell on his shoulder. It was Zurito.

"How do you feel, kid?" he asked.

Manuel was watching the bull.

Zurito leaned forward on the barrera, leaning the weight of his body on his arms. Manuel turned to him.

"You're going good," Zurito said.

Manuel shook his head. He had nothing to do now until the next third.[29] The gypsy was very good with the banderillos. The bull would come to him in the next third in good shape. He was a good bull. It had all been easy up to now. The final stuff with the sword was all he worried over. He did not really worry. He did not even think about it. But standing there he had a heavy sense of apprehension. He looked out at the bull, planning his faena, his work with the red cloth that was to reduce the bull, to make him manageable.

The gypsy was walking out toward the bull again, walking heel-and-toe, insultingly, like a ballroom dancer, the red shafts of the banderillos twitching with his walk. The bull watched him, not fixed now, hunting him, but waiting to get close enough so he could be sure of getting him, getting the horns into him.

As Fuentes walked forward the bull charged. Fuentes ran across the quarter of a circle as the bull charged and, as he passed running backward, stopped, swung forward, rose on his toes, arms straight out, and sunk the banderillos straight down into the tight of the big shoulder muscles as the bull missed him.

The crowd were wild about it.

"That kid won't stay in this night stuff long," Retana's man said to Zurito.

"He's good," Zurito said.

"Watch him now."

They watched.

Fuentes was standing with his back against the barrera. Two of the cuadrilla were back of him, with their capes ready to flop over the fence to distract the bull.

The bull, with his tongue out, his barrel heaving, was watching the gypsy. He thought he had him now. Back against the red planks. Only a short charge away. The bull watched him.

The gypsy bent back, drew back his arms, the banderillos pointing at the bull. He called

---

[29] A bull-fight contains three periods.

to the bull, stamped one foot. The bull was suspicious. He wanted the man. No more barbs in the shoulder.

Fuentes walked a little closer to the bull. Bent back. Called again. Somebody in the crowd shouted a warning.

"He's too damn close," Zurito said.

"Watch him," Retana's man said.

Leaning back, inciting the bull with the banderillos, Fuentes jumped, both feet off the ground. As he jumped the bull's tail rose and he charged. Fuentes came down on his toes, arms straight out, whole body arching forward, and drove the shafts straight down as he swung his body clear of the right horn.

The bull crashed into the barrera where the flopping capes had attracted his eye as he lost the man.

The gypsy came running along the barrera toward Manuel, taking the applause of the crowd. His vest was ripped where he had not quite cleared the point of the horn. He was happy about it, showing it to the spectators. He made the tour of the ring. Zurito saw him go by, smiling, pointing at his vest. He smiled.

Somebody else was planting the last pair of banderillos. Nobody was paying any attention.

Retana's man tucked a baton inside the red cloth of a muleta,[30] folded the cloth over it, and handed it over the barrera to Manuel. He reached in the leather sword-case, took out a sword, and holding it by its leather scabbard, reached it over the fence to Manuel. Manuel pulled the blade out by the red hilt and the scabbard fell limp.

He looked at Zurito. The big man saw he was sweating.

"Now you get him, kid," Zurito said.

Manuel nodded.

"He's in good shape," Zurito said.

"Just like you want him," Retana's man assured him.

Manuel nodded.

The trumpeter, up under the roof, blew for the final act, and Manuel walked across the arena toward where, up in the dark boxes, the president must be.

In the front row of seats the substitute bull-fight critic of *El Heraldo* took a long drink of the warm champagne. He had decided it was not worth while to write a running story and would write up the corrida back in the office. What the hell was it anyway? Only a nocturnal. If he missed anything he would get it out of the morning papers. He took another drink of the champagne. He had a date at Maxim's at twelve. Who were these bull-fighters anyway? Kids and bums. A bunch of bums. He put his pad of paper in his pocket and looked over toward Manuel, standing very much alone in the ring, gesturing with his hat in a salute toward a box he could not see high up in the dark plaza. Out in the ring the bull stood quiet, looking at nothing.

"I dedicate this bull to you, Mr. President, and to the public of Madrid, the most intelligent and generous of the world," was what Manuel was saying. It was a formula. He said it all. It was a little long for nocturnal use.

He bowed at the dark, straightened, tossed his hat over his shoulder, and, carrying the muleta in his left hand and the sword in his right, walked out toward the bull.

Manuel walked toward the bull. The bull looked at him; his eyes were quick. Manuel noticed the way the banderillos hung down on his left shoulder and the steady sheen of blood from Zurito's pic-ing. He noticed the way the bull's feet were. As he walked forward, holding the muleta in his left hand and the sword in his right, he watched the bull's feet. The bull could not charge without gathering his feet together. Now he stood square on them, dully.

Manuel walked toward him, watching his feet. This was all right. He could do this. He must work to get the bull's head down, so he could go in past the horns and kill him. He did not think about the sword, not about killing the bull. He thought about one thing at a time. The coming things oppressed him, though. Walking forward, watching the bull's feet, he saw successively his eyes, his wet muzzle, and the wide, forward-pointing spread of his horns. The bull had light circles about his eyes. His eyes watched Manuel. He felt he was going to get this little one with the white face.

Standing still now and spreading the red cloth of the muleta with the sword, pricking the point into the cloth so that the sword, now held in his left hand, spread the red flannel like the jib of a boat, Manuel noticed the points of the bull's horns. One of them was splintered from banging against the barrera. The other

---

[30] A cloth on a stick, with which the bull-fighter controls the charge of the bull.

was sharp as a porcupine quill. Manuel noticed while spreading the muleta that the white base of the horn was stained red. While he noticed these things he did not lose sight of the bull's feet. The bull watched Manuel steadily.

He's on the defensive now, Manuel thought. He's reserving himself. I've got to bring him out of that and get his head down. Always get his head down. Zurito had his head down once, but he's come back. He'll bleed when I start him going and that will bring it down.

Holding the muleta, with the sword in his left hand widening it in front of him, he called to the bull.

The bull looked at him.

He leaned back insultingly and shook the widespread flannel.

The bull saw the muleta. It was a bright scarlet under the arc-light. The bull's legs tightened.

Here he comes. Whoosh! Manuel turned as the bull came and raised the muleta so that it passed over the bull's horns and swept down his broad back from head to tail. The bull had gone clean up in the air with the charge. Manuel had not moved.

At the end of the pass the bull turned like a cat coming around a corner and faced Manuel.

He was on the offensive again. His heaviness was gone. Manuel noted the fresh blood shining down the black shoulder and dripping down the bull's leg. He drew the sword out of the muleta and held it in his right hand. The muleta held low down in his left hand, leaning toward the left, he called to the bull. The bull's legs tightened, his eyes on the muleta. Here he comes, Manuel thought. Yuh!

He swung with the charge, sweeping the muleta ahead of the bull, his feet firm, the sword following the curve, a point of light under the arcs.

The bull recharged as the pase natural [31] finished and Manuel raised the muleta for a pase de pecho.[31] Firmly planted, the bull came by his chest under the raised muleta. Manuel leaned his head back to avoid the clattering banderillo shafts. The hot, black bull body touched his chest as it passed.

Too damn close, Manuel thought. Zurito, leaning on the barrera, spoke rapidly to the gypsy, who trotted out toward Manuel with a

cape. Zurito pulled his hat down low and looked out across the arena at Manuel.

Manuel was facing the bull again, the muleta held low and to the left. The bull's head was down as he watched the muleta.

"If it was Belmonte doing that stuff, they'd go crazy," Retana's man said.

Zurito said nothing. He was watching Manuel out in the center of the arena.

"Where did the boss dig this fellow up?" Retana's man asked.

"Out of the hospital," Zurito said.

"That's where he's going damn quick," Retana's man said.

Zurito turned on him.

"Knock on that," he said, pointing to the barrera.

"I was just kidding, man," Retana's man said.

"Knock on the wood."

Retana's man leaned forward and knocked three times on the barrera.

"Watch the faena," Zurito said.

Out in the center of the ring, under the lights, Manuel was kneeling, facing the bull, and as he raised the muleta in both hands the bull charged, tail up.

Manuel swung his body clear and, as the bull recharged, brought around the muleta in a half-circle that pulled the bull to his knees.

"Why, that one's a great bull-fighter," Retana's man said.

"No, he's not," said Zurito.

Manuel stood up and, the muleta in his left hand, the sword in his right, acknowledged the applause from the dark plaza.

The bull had humped himself up from his knees and stood waiting, his head hung low.

Zurito spoke to two of the other lads of the cuadrilla and they ran out to stand back of Manuel with their capes. There were four men back of him now. Hernandez had followed him since he first came out with the muleta. Fuentes stood watching, his cape held against his body, tall, in repose, watching lazy-eyed. Now the two came up. Hernandez motioned them to stand one at each side. Manuel stood alone, facing the bull.

Manuel waved back the men with the capes. Stepping back cautiously, they saw his face was white and sweating.

Didn't they know enough to keep back? Did

---

[31] Stylized movements of the muleta.

they want to catch the bull's eye with the capes after he was fixed and ready? He had enough to worry about without that kind of thing.

The bull was standing, his four feet square, looking at the muleta. Manuel furled the muleta in his left hand. The bull's eyes watched it. His body was heavy on his feet. He carried his head low, but not too low.

Manuel lifted the muleta at him. The bull did not move. Only his eyes watched.

He's all lead, Manuel thought. He's all square. He's framed right. He'll take it.

He thought in bullfight terms. Sometimes he had a thought and the particular piece of slang would not come into his mind and he could not realize the thought. His instincts and his knowledge worked automatically, and his brain worked slowly and in words. He knew all about bulls. He did not have to think about them. He just did the right thing. His eyes noted things and his body performed the necessary measures without thought. If he thought about it, he would be gone.

Now, facing the bull, he was conscious of many things at the same time. There were the horns, the one splintered, the other smoothly sharp, the need to profile himself toward the left horn, lance himself short and straight, lower the muleta so the bull would follow it, and, going in over the horns, put the sword all the way into a little spot about as big as a five-peseta piece straight in back of the neck, between the sharp pitch of the bull's shoulders. He must do all this and must then come out from between the horns. He was conscious he must do all this, but his only thought was in words: "Corto y derecho."

"Corto y derecho," he thought, furling the muleta. Short and straight. Corto y derecho, he drew the sword out of the muleta, profiled on the splintered left horn, dropped the muleta across his body, so his right hand with the sword on the level with his eye made the sign of the cross, and, rising on his toes, sighted along the dipping blade of the sword at the spot high up between the bull's shoulders.

Corto y derecho he launched himself on the bull.

There was a shock, and he felt himself go up in the air. He pushed on the sword as he went up and over, and it flew out of his hand. He hit the ground and the bull was on him. Manuel, lying on the ground, kicked at the bull's muzzle with his slippered feet. Kicking, kicking, the bull after him, missing him in his excitement, bumping him with his head, driving the horns into the sand. Kicking like a man keeping a ball in the air, Manuel kept the bull from getting a clean thrust at him.

Manuel felt the wind on his back from the capes flopping at the bull, and then the bull was gone, gone over him in a rush. Dark, as his belly went over. Not even stepped on.

Manuel stood up and picked up the muleta. Fuentes handed him the sword. It was bent where it had struck the shoulder-blade. Manuel straightened it on his knee and ran toward the bull, standing now beside one of the dead horses. As he ran, his jacket flopped where it had been ripped under his armpit.

"Get him out of there," Manuel shouted to the gypsy. The bull had smelled the blood of the dead horse and ripped into the canvas-cover with his horns. He charged Fuentes's cape, with the canvas hanging from his splintered horn, and the crowd laughed. Out in the ring, he tossed his head to rid himself of the canvas. Hernandez, running up from behind him, grabbed the end of the canvas and neatly lifted it off the horn.

The bull followed it in a half-charge and stopped still. He was on the defensive again. Manuel was walking toward him with the sword and muleta. Manuel swung the muleta before him. The bull would not charge.

Manuel profiled toward the bull, sighting along the dipping blade of the sword. The bull was motionless, seemingly dead on his feet, incapable of another charge.

Manuel rose to his toes, sighting along the steel, and charged.

Again there was the shock and he felt himself being borne back in a rush, to strike hard on the sand. There was no chance of kicking this time. The bull was on top of him. Manuel lay as though dead, his head on his arms, and the bull bumped him. Bumped his back, bumped his face in the sand. He felt the horn go into the sand between his folded arms. The bull hit him in the small of the back. His face drove into the sand. The horn drove through one of his sleeves and the bull ripped it off. Manuel was tossed clear and the bull followed the capes.

Manuel got up, found the sword and muleta, tried the point of the sword with his thumb, and then ran toward the barrera for a new sword.

Retana's man handed him the sword over the edge of the barrera.

"Wipe off your face," he said.

Manuel, running again toward the bull, wiped his bloody face with his handkerchief. He had not seen Zurito. Where was Zurito?

The cuadrilla had stepped away from the bull and waited with their capes. The bull stood, heavy and dull again after the action.

Manuel walked toward him with the muleta. He stopped and shook it. The bull did not respond. He passed it right and left, left and right before the bull's muzzle. The bull's eyes watched it and turned with the swing, but he would not charge. He was waiting for Manuel.

Manuel was worried. There was nothing to do but go in. Corto y derecho. He profiled close to the bull, crossed the muleta in front of his body and charged. As he pushed in the sword, he jerked his body to the left to clear the horn. The bull passed him and the sword shot up in the air, twinkling under the arc-lights, to fall red-hilted on the sand.

Manuel ran over and picked it up. It was bent and he straightened it over his knee.

As he came running toward the bull, fixed again now, he passed Hernandez standing with his cape.

"He's all bone," the boy said encouragingly.

Manuel nodded, wiping his face. He put the bloody handkerchief in his pocket.

There was the bull. He was close to the barrera now. Damn him. Maybe he was all bone. Maybe there was not any place for the sword to go in. The hell there wasn't! He'd show them.

He tried a pass with the muleta and the bull did not move. Manuel chopped the muleta back and forth in front of the bull. Nothing doing.

He furled the muleta, drew the sword out, profiled and drove in on the bull. He felt the sword buckle as he shoved it in, leaning his weight on it, and then it shot high in the air, end-over-ending into the crowd. Manuel had jerked clear as the sword jumped.

The first cushions thrown down out of the dark missed him. Then one hit him in the face, his bloody face looking toward the crowd. They were coming down fast. Spotting the sand. Somebody threw an empty champagne-bottle

from close range. It hit Manuel on the foot. He stood there watching the dark, where the things were coming from. Then something whished through the air and struck by him. Manuel leaned over and picked it up. It was his sword. He straightened it over his knee and gestured with it to the crowd.

"Thank you," he said. "Thank you."

Oh, the dirty bastards! Dirty bastards! Oh, the lousy, dirty bastards! He kicked into a cushion as he ran.

There was the bull. The same as ever. All right, you dirty, lousy bastard!

Manuel passed the muleta in front of the bull's black muzzle.

Nothing doing.

You won't! All right. He stepped close and jammed the sharp peak of the muleta into the bull's damp muzzle.

The bull was on him as he jumped back, and as he tripped on a cushion he felt the horn go into him, into his side. He grabbed the horn with his two hands and rode backward, holding tight onto the place. The bull tossed him and he was clear. He lay still. It was all right. The bull was gone.

He got up coughing and feeling broken and gone. The dirty bastards!

"Give me the sword," he shouted. "Give me the stuff."

Fuentes came up with the muleta and the sword.

Hernandez put his arm around him.

"Go on to the infirmary, man," he said. "Don't be a damn fool."

"Get away from me," Manuel said. "Get to hell away from me."

He twisted free. Hernandez shrugged his shoulders. Manuel ran toward the bull.

There was the bull standing, heavy, firmly planted.

All right, you bastard! Manuel drew the sword out of the muleta, sighted with the same movement, and flung himself onto the bull. He felt the sword go in all the way. Right up to the guard. Four fingers and his thumb into the bull. The blood was hot on his knuckles, and he was on top of the bull.

The bull lurched with him as he lay on, and seemed to sink; then he was standing clear. He looked at the bull going down slowly over on his side, then suddenly four feet in the air.

Then he gestured at the crowd, his hand warm from the bull blood.

All right, you bastards! He wanted to say something, but he started to cough. It was hot and choking. He looked down for the muleta. He must go over and salute the president. President hell! He was sitting down looking at something. It was the bull. His four feet up. Thick tongue out. Things crawling around on his belly and under his legs. Crawling where the hair was thin. Dead bull. To hell with the bull! To hell with them all! He started to get to his feet and commenced to cough. He sat down again, coughing. Somebody came and pushed him up.

They carried him across the ring to the infirmary, running with him across the sand, standing blocked at the gate as the mules came in, then around under the dark passageway, men grunting as they took him up the stairway, and then laid him down.

The doctor and two men in white were waiting for him. They laid him out on the table. They were cutting away his shirt. Manuel felt tired. His whole chest felt scalding inside. He started to cough and they held something to his mouth. Everybody was very busy.

There was an electric light in his eyes. He shut his eyes.

He heard some one coming very heavily up the stairs. Then he did not hear it. Then he heard a noise far off. That was the crowd. Well, somebody would have to kill his other bull. They had cut away all his shirt. The doctor smiled at him. There was Retana.

"Hello, Retana!" Manuel said. He could not hear his voice.

Retana smiled at him and said something. Manuel could not hear it.

Zurito stood beside the table, bending over where the doctor was working. He was in his picador clothes, without his hat.

Zurito said something to him. Manuel could not hear it.

Zurito was speaking to Retana. One of the men in white smiled and handed Retana a pair of scissors. Retana gave them to Zurito. Zurito said something to Manuel. He could not hear it.

To hell with this operating-table. He'd been on plenty of operating-tables before. He was not going to die. There would be a priest if he was going to die.

Zurito was saying something to him. Holding up the scissors.

That was it. They were going to cut off his coleta. They were going to cut off his pigtail.

Manuel sat up on the operating-table. The doctor stepped back, angry. Some one grabbed him and held him.

"You couldn't do a thing like that, Manos," he said.

He heard suddenly, clearly, Zurito's voice.

"That's all right," Zurito said. "I won't do it. I was joking."

"I was going good," Manuel said. "I didn't have any luck. That was all."

Manuel lay back. They had put something over his face. It was all familiar. He inhaled deeply. He felt very tired. He was very, very tired. They took the thing away from his face.

"I was going good," Manuel said weakly. "I was going great."

Retana looked at Zurito and started for the door.

"I'll stay here with him," Zurito said.

Retana shrugged his shoulders.

Manuel opened his eyes and looked at Zurito.

"Wasn't I going good, Manos?" he asked, for confirmation.

"Sure," said Zurito. "You were going great."

The doctor's assistant put the cone over Manuel's face and he inhaled deeply. Zurito stood awkwardly, watching.

## D. H. Lawrence

# THE BLIND MAN

Isabel Pervin was listening for two sounds—for the sound of wheels on the drive outside and for the noise of her husband's footsteps in the hall. Her dearest and oldest friend, a man who seemed almost indispensable to her living, would drive up in the rainy dusk of the closing November day. The trap had gone to fetch him from the station. And her husband,

THE BLIND MAN: From *The Portable D. H. Lawrence.* Copyright, 1922, by Thomas Seltzer, Inc., 1950, by Frieda Lawrence. Reprinted by permission of The Viking Press, Inc., New York.

who had been blinded in Flanders, and who had a disfiguring mark on his brow, would be coming in from the outhouses.

He had been home for a year now. He was totally blind. Yet they had been very happy. The Grange was Maurice's own place. The back was a farmstead, and the Wernhams, who occupied the rear premises, acted as farmers. Isabel lived with her husband in the handsome rooms in front. She and he had been almost entirely alone together since he was wounded. They talked and sang and read together in a wonderful and unspeakable intimacy. Then she reviewed books for a Scottish newspaper, carrying on her old interest, and he occupied himself a good deal with the farm. Sightless, he could still discuss everything with Wernham, and he could also do a good deal of work about the place—menial work, it is true, but it gave him satisfaction. He milked the cows, carried in the pails, turned the separator, attended to the pigs and horses. Life was still very full and strangely serene for the blind man, peaceful with the almost incomprehensible peace of immediate contact in darkness. With his wife he had a whole world, rich and real and invisible.

They were newly and remotely happy. He did not even regret the loss of his sight in these times of dark, palpable joy. A certain exultance swelled his soul.

But as time wore on, sometimes the rich glamour would leave them. Sometimes, after months of this intensity, a sense of burden overcame Isabel, a weariness, a terrible ennui, in that silent house approached between a colonnade of tall-shafted pines. Then she felt she would go mad, for she could not bear it. And sometimes he had devastating fits of depression, which seemed to lay waste his whole being. It was worse than depression—a black misery, when his own life was a torture to him, and when his presence was unbearable to his wife. The dread went down to the roots of her soul as these black days recurred. In a kind of panic she tried to wrap herself up still further in her husband. She forced the old spontaneous cheerfulness and joy to continue. But the effort it cost her was almost too much. She knew she could not keep it up. She felt she would scream with the strain, and would give anything, anything, to escape. She longed to possess her husband utterly; it gave her inordinate joy to have him entirely to herself. And yet, when again

he was gone in a black and massive misery, she could not bear him, she could not bear herself; she wished she could be snatched away off the earth altogether, anything rather than live at this cost.

Dazed, she schemed for a way out. She invited friends, she tried to give him some further connection with the outer world. But it was no good. After all their joy and suffering, after their dark, great year of blindness and solitude and unspeakable nearness, other people seemed to them both shallow, rattling, rather impertinent. Shallow prattle seemed presumptuous. He became impatient and irritated, she was wearied. And so they lapsed into their solitude again. For they preferred it.

But now, in a few weeks' time, her second baby would be born. The first had died, an infant, when her husband first went out to France. She looked with joy and relief to the coming of the second. It would be her salvation. But also she felt some anxiety. She was thirty years old, her husband was a year younger. They both wanted the child very much. Yet she could not help feeling afraid. She had her husband on her hands, a terrible joy to her, and a terrifying burden. The child would occupy her love and attention. And then, what of Maurice? What would he do? If only she could feel that he, too, would be at peace and happy when the child came! She did so want to luxuriate in a rich, physical satisfaction of maternity. But the man, what would he do? How could she provide for him, how avert those shattering black moods of his, which destroyed them both?

She sighed with fear. But at this time Bertie Reid wrote to Isabel. He was her old friend, a second or third cousin, a Scotchman, as she was a Scotchwoman. They had been brought up near to one another, and all her life he had been her friend, like a brother, but better than her own brothers. She loved him—though not in the marrying sense. There was a sort of kinship between them, an affinity. They understood one another instinctively. But Isabel would never have thought of marrying Bertie. It would have seemed like marrying in her own family.

Bertie was a barrister and a man of letters, a Scotchman of the intellectual type, quick, ironical, sentimental, and on his knees before the woman he adored but did not want to marry. Maurice Pervin was different. He came of a good old country family—the Grange was not a very great distance from Oxford. He was passionate, sensitive, perhaps over-sensitive, wincing—a big fellow with heavy limbs and a forehead that flushed painfully. For his mind was slow, as if drugged by the strong provincial blood that beat in his veins. He was very sensitive to his own mental slowness, his feelings being quick and acute. So that he was just the opposite to Bertie, whose mind was much quicker than his emotions, which were not so very fine.

From the first the two men did not like each other. Isabel felt that they ought to get on together. But they did not. She felt that if only each could have the clue to the other there would be such a rare understanding between them. It did not come off, however. Bertie adopted a slightly ironical attitude, very offensive to Maurice, who returned the Scotch irony with English resentment, a resentment which deepened sometimes into stupid hatred.

This was a little puzzling to Isabel. However, she accepted it in the course of things. Men were made freakish and unreasonable. Therefore, when Maurice was going out to France for the second time, she felt that, for her husband's sake, she must discontinue her friendship with Bertie. She wrote to the barrister to this effect. Bertram Reid simply replied that in this, as in all other matters, he must obey her wishes, if these were indeed her wishes.

For nearly two years nothing had passed between the two friends. Isabel rather gloried in the fact; she had no compunction. She had one great article of faith, which was, that husband and wife should be so important to one another, that the rest of the world simply did not count. She and Maurice were husband and wife. They loved one another. They would have children. Then let everybody and everything else fade into insignificance outside this connubial felicity. She professed herself quite happy and ready to receive Maurice's friends. She was happy and ready: the happy wife, the ready woman in possession. Without knowing why, the friends retired abashed, and came no more. Maurice, of course, took as much satisfaction in this connubial absorption as Isabel did.

He shared in Isabel's literary activities, she cultivated a real interest in agriculture and cattle-raising. For she, being at heart perhaps an emotional enthusiast, always cultivated the practical side of life and prided herself on her mastery of practical affairs. Thus the husband and wife had spent the five years of their married life. The last had been one of blindness and unspeakable intimacy. And now Isabel felt a great indifference coming over her, a sort of lethargy. She wanted to be allowed to bear her child in peace, to nod by the fire and drift vaguely, physically, from day to day. Maurice was like an ominous thunder-cloud. She had to keep waking up to remember him.

When a little note came from Bertie, asking if he were to put up a tombstone to their dead friendship, and speaking of the real pain he felt on account of her husband's loss of sight, she felt a pang, a fluttering agitation of reawakening. And she read the letter to Maurice.

"Ask him to come down," he said.

"Ask Bertie to come here!" she re-echoed.

"Yes—if he wants to."

Isabel paused for a few moments.

"I know he wants to—he'd only be too glad," she replied. "But what about you, Maurice? How would you like it?"

"I should like it."

"Well—in that case— But I thought you didn't care for him—"

"Oh, I don't know. I might think differently of him now," the blind man replied. It was rather abstruse to Isabel.

"Well, dear," she said, "if you're quite sure—"

"I'm sure enough. Let him come," said Maurice.

So Bertie was coming, coming this evening, in the November rain and darkness. Isabel was agitated, racked with her old restlessness and indecision. She had always suffered from this pain of doubt, just an agonizing sense of uncertainty. It had begun to pass off, in the lethargy of maternity. Now it returned, and she resented it. She struggled as usual to maintain her calm, composed, friendly bearing, a sort of mask she wore over all her body.

A woman had lighted a tall lamp beside the table and spread the cloth. The long dining-room was dim, with its elegant but rather severe pieces of old furniture. Only the round table glowed softly under the light. It had a rich, beautiful effect. The white cloth glistened and dropped its heavy, pointed lace corners almost to the carpet, the china was old and handsome, creamy-yellow, with a blotched pattern of harsh red and deep blue, the cups large and bell-shaped, the teapot gallant. Isabel looked at it with superficial appreciation.

Her nerves were hurting her. She looked automatically again at the high, uncurtained windows. In the last dusk she could just perceive outside a huge fir-tree swaying its boughs: it was as if she thought it rather than saw it. The rain came flying on the window panes. Ah, why had she no peace? These two men, why did they tear at her? Why did they not come—why was there this suspense?

She sat in a lassitude that was really suspense and irritation. Maurice, at least, might come in—there was nothing to keep him out. She rose to her feet. Catching sight of her reflection in a mirror, she glanced at herself with a slight smile of recognition, as if she were an old friend to herself. Her face was oval and calm, her nose a little arched. Her neck made a beautiful line down to her shoulder. With hair knotted loosely behind, she had something of a warm, maternal look. Thinking this of herself, she arched her eyebrows and her rather heavy eyelids, with a little flicker of a smile, and for a moment her grey eyes looked amused and wicked, a little sardonic, out of her transfigured Madonna face.

Then, resuming her air of womanly patience—she was really fatally self-determined—she went with a little jerk towards the door. Her eyes were slightly reddened.

She passed down the wide hall and through a door at the end. Then she was in the farm premises. The scent of dairy, and of farm-kitchen, and of farm-yard and of leather almost overcame her: but particularly the scent of dairy. They had been scalding out the pans. The flagged passage in front of her was dark, puddled, and wet. Light came out from the open kitchen door. She went forward and stood in the doorway. The farm-people were at tea, seated at a little distance from her, round a long, narrow table, in the centre of which stood a white lamp. Ruddy faces, ruddy hands holding food, red mouths working, heads bent over the tea-cups: men, land-girls, boys: it was tea-time, feeding-time. Some faces caught sight of her. Mrs. Wernham, going round behind the chairs with a large black teapot, halting slightly

in her walk, was not aware of her for a moment. Then she turned suddenly.

"Oh, is it Madam!" she exclaimed. "Come in, then, come in! We're at tea." And she dragged forward a chair.

"No, I won't come in," said Isabel. "I'm afraid I interrupt your meal."

"No—no—not likely, Madam, not likely."

"Hasn't Mr. Pervin come in, do you know?"

"I'm sure I couldn't say! Missed him, have you, Madam?"

"No, I only wanted him to come in," laughed Isabel, as if shyly.

"Wanted him, did ye? Get up, boy—get up, now—"

Mrs. Wernham knocked one of the boys on the shoulder. He began to scrape to his feet, chewing largely.

"I believe he's in top stable," said another face from the table.

"Ah! No, don't get up. I'm going myself," said Isabel.

"Don't you go out of a dirty night like this. Let the lad go. Get along wi' ye, boy," said Mrs. Wernham.

"No, no," said Isabel, with a decision that was always obeyed. "Go on with your tea, Tom. I'd like to go across to the stable, Mrs. Wernham."

"Did ever you hear tell!" exclaimed the woman.

"Isn't the trap late?" asked Isabel.

"Why, no," said Mrs. Wernham, peering into the distance at the tall, dim clock. "No, Madam—we can give it another quarter or twenty minutes yet, good—yes, every bit of a quarter."

"Ah! It seems late when darkness falls so early," said Isabel.

"It do, that it do. Bother the days, that they draw in so," answered Mrs. Wernham. "Proper miserable!"

"They are," said Isabel, withdrawing.

She pulled on her overshoes, wrapped a large tartan shawl around her, put on a man's felt hat, and ventured out along the causeways of the first yard. It was very dark. The wind was roaring in the great elms behind the outhouses. When she came to the second yard the darkness seemed deeper. She was unsure of her footing. She wished she had brought a lantern. Rain blew against her. Half she liked it, half she felt unwilling to battle.

She reached at last the just visible door of the stable. There was no sign of a light anywhere. Opening the upper half, she looked in: into a simple well of darkness. The smell of horses and ammonia, and of warmth was startling to her, in that full night. She listened with all her ears but could hear nothing save the night, and the stirring of a horse.

"Maurice!" she called, softly and musically, though she was afraid. "Maurice—are you there?"

Nothing came from the darkness. She knew the rain and wind blew in upon the horses, the hot animal life. Feeling it wrong, she entered the stable and drew the lower half of the door shut, holding the upper part close. She did not stir, because she was aware of the presence of the dark hind-quarters of the horses, though she could not see them, and she was afraid. Something wild stirred in her heart.

She listened intensely. Then she heard a small noise in the distance—far away, it seemed—the chink of a pan, and a man's voice speaking a brief word. It would be Maurice, in the other part of the stable. She stood motionless, waiting for him to come through the partition door. The horses were so terrifyingly near to her, in the invisible.

The loud jarring of the inner door-latch made her start; the door was opened. She could hear and feel her husband entering and invisibly passing among the horses near to her, darkness as they were, actively intermingled. The rather low sound of his voice as he spoke to the horses came velvety to her nerves. How near he was, and how invisible! The darkness seemed to be in a strange swirl of violent life, just upon her. She turned giddy.

Her presence of mind made her call quietly and musically:

"Maurice! Maurice—dear-ar!"

"Yes," he answered. "Isabel?"

She saw nothing, and the sound of his voice seemed to touch her.

"Hello!" she answered cheerfully, straining her eyes to see him. He was still busy, attending to the horses near her, but she saw only darkness. It made her almost desperate.

"Won't you come in, dear?" she said.

"Yes, I'm coming. Just half a minute. Stand over—now! Trap's not come, has it?"

"Not yet," said Isabel.

His voice was pleasant and ordinary, but it had a slight suggestion of the stable to her. She wished he would come away. Whilst he was so utterly invisible, she was afraid of him.

"How's the time?" he asked.

"Not yet six," she replied. She disliked to answer into the dark. Presently he came very near to her, and she retreated out of doors.

"The weather blows in here," he said, coming steadily forward, feeling for the doors. She shrank away. At last she could dimly see him.

"Bertie won't have much of a drive," he said, as he closed the doors.

"He won't indeed!" said Isabel calmly, watching the dark shape at the door.

"Give me your arm, dear," she said.

She pressed his arm close to her, as she went. But she longed to see him, to look at him. She was nervous. He walked erect, with face rather lifted, but with a curious tentative movement of his powerful, muscular legs. She could feel the clever, careful, strong contact of his feet with the earth, as she balanced against him. For a moment he was a tower of darkness to her, as if he rose out of the earth.

In the house-passage he wavered and went cautiously, with a curious look of silence about him as he felt for the bench. Then he sat down heavily. He was a man with rather sloping shoulders, but with heavy limbs, powerful legs that seemed to know the earth. His head was small, usually carried high and light. As he bent down to unfasten his gaiters and boots he did not look blind. His hair was brown and crisp, his hands were large, reddish, intelligent, the veins stood out in the wrists; and his thighs and knees seemed massive. When he stood up his face and neck were surcharged with blood, the veins stood out on his temples. She did not look at his blindness.

Isabel was always glad when they had passed through the dividing door into their own regions of repose and beauty. She was a little afraid of him, out there in the animal grossness of the back. His bearing also changed, as he smelt the familiar indefinable odour that pervaded his wife's surroundings, a delicate, refined scent, very faintly spicy. Perhaps it came from the potpourri bowls.

He stood at the foot of the stairs, arrested, listening. She watched him, and her heart sickened. He seemed to be listening to fate.

"He's not here yet," he said. "I'll go up and change."

"Maurice," she said, "you're not wishing he wouldn't come, are you?"

"I couldn't quite say," he answered. "I feel myself rather on the qui vive."

"I can see you are," she answered. And she reached up and kissed his cheek. She saw his mouth relax into a slow smile.

"What are you laughing at?" she said roguishly.

"You consoling me," he answered.

"Nay," she answered. "Why should I console you? You know we love each other—you know how married we are! What does anything else matter?"

"Nothing at all, my dear."

He felt for her face and touched it, smiling. "You're all right, aren't you?" he asked anxiously.

"I'm wonderfully all right, love," she answered. "It's you I am a little troubled about, at times."

"Why me?" he said, touching her cheeks delicately with the tips of his fingers. The touch had an almost hypnotizing effect on her.

He went away upstairs. She saw him mount into the darkness, unseeing and unchanging. He did not know that the lamps on the upper corridor were unlighted. He went on into the darkness with unchanging step. She heard him in the bath-room.

Pervin moved about almost unconsciously in his familiar surroundings, dark though everything was. He seemed to know the presence of objects before he touched them. It was a pleasure to him to rock thus through a world of things, carried on the flood in a sort of blood-prescience. He did not think much or trouble much. So long as he kept this sheer immediacy of blood-contact with the substantial world he was happy, he wanted no intervention of visual consciousness. In this state there was a certain rich positivity, bordering sometimes on rapture. Life seemed to move in him like a tide lapping, lapping, and advancing, enveloping all things darkly. It was a pleasure to stretch forth the hand and meet the unseen object, clasp it, and possess it in pure contact. He did not try to remember, to visualize. He did not want to. The new way of consciousness substituted itself in him.

The rich suffusion of this state generally kept him happy, reaching its culmination in the consuming passion for his wife. But at times the flow would seem to be checked and thrown back. Then it would beat inside him like a tangled sea, and he was tortured in the shattered chaos of his own blood. He grew to dread this arrest, this throw-back, this chaos inside himself, when he seemed merely at the mercy of his own powerful and conflicting elements. How to get some measure of control or surety, this was the question. And when the question rose maddening in him, he would clench his fists as if he would compel the whole universe to submit to him. But it was in vain. He could not even compel himself.

Tonight, however, he was still serene, though little tremors of unreasonable exasperation ran through him. He had to handle the razor very carefully, as he shaved, for it was not at one with him, he was afraid of it. His hearing also was too much sharpened. He heard the woman lighting the lamps on the corridor, and attending to the fire in the visitors' room. And then, as he went to his room, he heard the trap arrive. Then came Isabel's voice, lifted and calling, like a bell ringing:

"Is it you, Bertie? Have you come?"

And a man's voice answered out of the wind: "Hello, Isabel! There you are."

"Have you had a miserable drive? I'm so sorry we couldn't send a closed carriage. I can't see you at all, you know."

"I'm coming. No, I liked the drive—it was like Perthshire. Well, how are you? You're looking fit as ever, as far as I can see."

"Oh, yes," said Isabel. "I'm wonderfully well. How are you? Rather thin, I think—"

"Worked to death—everybody's old cry. But I'm all right, Ciss. How's Pervin?—isn't he here?"

"Oh, yes, he's upstairs changing. Yes, he's awfully well. Take off your wet things; I'll send them to be dried."

"And how are you both, in spirits? He doesn't fret?"

"No—no, not at all. No, on the contrary, really. We've been wonderfully happy, incredibly. It's more than I can understand—so wonderful: the nearness, and the peace—"

"Ah! Well, that's awfully good news—"

They moved away. Pervin heard no more. But a childish sense of desolation had come over him, as he heard their brisk voices. He seemed shut out—like a child that is left out. He was aimless and excluded, he did not know what to do with himself. The helpless desolation came over him. He fumbled nervously as he dressed himself, in a state almost of childishness. He disliked the Scotch accent in Bertie's speech, and the slight response it found on Isabel's tongue. He disliked the slight purr of complacency in the Scottish speech. He disliked intensely the glib way in which Isabel spoke of their happiness and nearness. It made him recoil. He was fretful and beside himself like a child, he had almost a childish nostalgia to be included in the life circle. And at the same time he was a man, dark and powerful and infuriated by his own weakness. By some fatal flaw, he could not be by himself, he had to depend on the support of another. And this very dependence enraged him. He hated Bertie Reid, and at the same time he knew the hatred was nonsense, he knew it was the outcome of his own weakness.

He went downstairs. Isabel was alone in the dining-room. She watched him enter, head erect, his feet tentative. He looked so strong-blooded and healthy and, at the same time, cancelled. Cancelled—that was the word that flew across her mind. Perhaps it was his scar suggested it.

"You heard Bertie come, Maurice?" she said.

"Yes—isn't he here?"

"He's in his room. He looks very thin and worn."

"I suppose he works himself to death."

A woman came in with a tray—and after a few minutes Bertie came down. He was a little dark man, with a very big forehead, thin, wispy hair, and sad, large eyes. His expression was inordinately sad—almost funny. He had odd, short legs.

Isabel watched him hesitate under the door, and glance nervously at her husband. Pervin heard him and turned.

"Here you are, now," said Isabel. "Come, let us eat."

Bertie went across to Maurice.

"How are you, Pervin?" he said, as he advanced.

The blind man stuck his hand out into space, and Bertie took it.

"Very fit. Glad you've come," said Maurice.

Isabel glanced at them, and glanced away, as if she could not bear to see them.

"Come," she said. "Come to table. Aren't you both awfully hungry? I am, tremendously."

"I'm afraid you waited for me," said Bertie, as they sat down.

Maurice had a curious monolithic way of sitting in a chair, erect and distant. Isabel's heart always beat when she caught sight of him thus.

"No," she replied to Bertie. "We're very little later than usual. We're having a sort of high tea, not dinner. Do you mind? It gives us such a nice long evening, uninterrupted."

"I like it," said Bertie.

Maurice was feeling, with curious little movements, almost like a cat kneading her bed, for his plate, his knife and fork, his napkin. He was getting the whole geography of his cover into his consciousness. He sat erect and inscrutable, remote-seeming. Bertie watched the static figure of the blind man, the delicate tactile discernment of the large, ruddy hands, and the curious mindless silence of the brow, above the scar. With difficulty he looked away, and without knowing what he did, picked up a little crystal bowl of violets from the table, and held them to his nose.

"They are sweet-scented," he said. "Where do they come from?"

"From the garden—under the windows," said Isabel.

"So late in the year—and so fragrant! Do you remember the violets under Aunt Bell's south wall?"

The two friends looked at each other and exchanged a smile, Isabel's eyes lighting up.

"Don't I?" she replied. "Wasn't she queer!"

"A curious old girl," laughed Bertie. "There's a streak of freakishness in the family, Isabel."

"Ah—but not in you and me, Bertie," said Isabel. "Give them to Maurice, will you?" she added, as Bertie was putting down the flowers. "Have you smelled the violets, dear? Do!—they are so scented."

Maurice held out his hand, and Bertie placed the tiny bowl against his large, warm-looking fingers. Maurice's hand closed over the thin white fingers of the barrister. Bertie carefully extricated himself. Then the two watched the blind man smelling the violets. He bent his head and seemed to be thinking. Isabel waited.

"Aren't they sweet, Maurice?" she said at last, anxiously.

"Very," he said. And he held out the bowl. Bertie took it. Both he and Isabel were a little afraid, and deeply disturbed.

The meal continued. Isabel and Bertie

chatted spasmodically. The blind man was silent. He touched his food repeatedly, with quick, delicate touches of his knife-point, then cut irregular bits. He could not bear to be helped. Both Isabel and Bertie suffered: Isabel wondered why. She did not suffer when she was alone with Maurice. Bertie made her conscious of a strangeness.

After the meal the three drew their chairs to the fire, and sat down to talk. The decanters were put on a table near at hand. Isabel knocked the logs on the fire, and clouds of brilliant sparks went up the chimney. Bertie noticed a slight weariness in her bearing.

"You will be glad when your child comes now, Isabel?" he said.

She looked up to him with a quick wan smile.

"Yes, I shall be glad," she answered. "It begins to seem long. Yes, I shall be very glad. So will you, Maurice, won't you?" she added.

"Yes, I shall," replied her husband.

"We are both looking forward so much to having it," she said.

"Yes, of course," said Bertie.

He was a bachelor, three or four years older than Isabel. He lived in beautiful rooms overlooking the river, guarded by a faithful Scottish manservant. And he had his friends among the fair sex—not lovers, friends. So long as he could avoid any danger of courtship or marriage, he adored a few good women with constant and unfailing homage, and he was chivalrously fond of quite a number. But if they seemed to encroach on him, he withdrew and detested them.

Isabel knew him very well, knew his beautiful constancy, and kindness, also his incurable weakness, which made him unable ever to enter into close contact of any sort. He was ashamed of himself because he could not marry, could not approach women physically. He wanted to do so. But he could not. At the centre of him he was afraid, helplessly and even brutally afraid. He had given up hope, had ceased to expect any more that he could escape his own weakness. Hence he was a brilliant and successful barrister, also a litterateur of high repute, a rich man, and a great social success. At the centre he felt himself neuter, nothing.

Isabel knew him well. She despised him even while she admired him. She looked at his sad face, his little short legs, and felt contempt of him. She looked at his dark grey eyes, with their uncanny, almost childlike, intuition, and she loved him. He understood amazingly—but she had no fear of his understanding. As a man she patronized him.

And she turned to the impassive, silent figure of her husband. He sat leaning back, with folded arms, and face a little uptilted. His knees were straight and massive. She sighed, picked up the poker, and again began to prod the fire, to rouse the clouds of soft brilliant sparks.

"Isabel tells me," Bertie began suddenly, "that you have not suffered unbearably from the loss of sight."

Maurice straightened himself to attend but kept his arms folded.

"No," he said, "not unbearably. Now and again one struggles against it, you know. But there are compensations."

"They say it is much worse to be stone deaf," said Isabel.

"I believe it is," said Bertie. "Are there compensations?" he added to Maurice.

"Yes. You cease to bother about a great many things." Again Maurice stretched his figure, stretched the strong muscles of his back, and leaned backwards, with uplifted face.

"And that is a relief," said Bertie. "But what is there in place of the bothering? What replaces the activity?"

There was a pause. At length the blind man replied, as out of a negligent, unattentive thinking:

"Oh, I don't know. There's a good deal when you're not active."

"Is there?" said Bertie. "What, exactly? It always seems to me that when there is no thought and no action, there is nothing."

Again Maurice was slow in replying.

"There is something," he replied. "I couldn't tell you what it is."

And the talk lapsed once more, Isabel and Bertie chatting gossip and reminiscence, the blind man silent.

At length Maurice rose restlessly, a big obtrusive figure. He felt tight and hampered. He wanted to go away.

"Do you mind," he said, "if I go and speak to Wernham?"

"No—go along, dear," said Isabel.

And he went out. A silence came over the two friends. At length Bertie said:

"Nevertheless, it is a great deprivation, Cissie."

"It is, Bertie. I know it is."

"Something lacking all the time," said Bertie.

"Yes, I know. And yet—and yet—Maurice is right. There is something else, something there, which you never knew was there, and which you can't express."

"What is there?" asked Bertie.

"I don't know—it's awfully hard to define it—but something strong and immediate. There's something strange in Maurice's presence—indefinable—but I couldn't do without it. I agree that it seems to put one's mind to sleep. But when we're alone I miss nothing; it seems awfully rich, almost splendid, you know."

"I'm afraid I don't follow," said Bertie.

They talked desultorily. The wind blew loudly outside, rain chattered on the window-panes, making a sharp drum-sound because of the closed, mellow-golden shutters inside. The logs burned slowly, with hot, almost invisible small flames. Bertie seemed uneasy, there were dark circles round his eyes. Isabel, rich with her approaching maternity, leaned looking into the fire. Her hair curled in odd, loose strands, very pleasing to the man. But she had a curious feeling of old woe in her heart, old, timeless night-woe.

"I suppose we're all deficient somewhere," said Bertie.

"I suppose so," said Isabel wearily.

"Damned, sooner or later."

"I don't know," she said, rousing herself. "I feel quite all right, you know. The child coming seems to make me indifferent to everything, just placid. I can't feel that there's anything to trouble about, you know."

"A good thing, I should say," he replied slowly.

"Well, there it is. I suppose it's just Nature. If only I felt I needn't trouble about Maurice, I should be perfectly content—"

"But you feel you must trouble about him?"

"Well—I don't know—" She even resented this much effort.

The night passed slowly. Isabel looked at the clock. "I say," she said. "It's nearly ten o'clock. Where can Maurice be? I'm sure they're all in bed at the back. Excuse me a moment."

She went out, returning almost immediately.

"It's all shut up and in darkness," she said. "I wonder where he is. He must have gone out to the farm—"

Bertie looked at her.

"I suppose he'll come in," he said.

"I suppose so," she said. "But it's unusual for him to be out now."

"Would you like me to go out and see?"

"Well—if you wouldn't mind. I'd go, but—" She did not want to make the physical effort.

Bertie put on an old overcoat and took a lantern. He went out from the side door. He shrank from the wet and roaring night. Such weather had a nervous effect on him: too much moisture everywhere made him feel almost imbecile. Unwilling, he went through it all. A dog barked violently at him. He peered in all the buildings. At last, as he opened the upper door of a sort of intermediate barn, he heard a grinding noise, and looking in, holding up his lantern, saw Maurice, in his shirtsleeves, standing listening, holding the handle of a turnip-pulper. He had been pulping sweet roots, a pile of which lay dimly heaped in a corner behind him.

"That you, Wernham?" said Maurice, listening.

"No, it's me," said Bertie.

A large, half-wild grey cat was rubbing at Maurice's leg. The blind man stooped to rub its sides. Bertie watched the scene, then unconsciously entered and shut the door behind him. He was in a high sort of barn-place, from which, right and left, ran off the corridors in front of the stalled cattle. He watched the slow, stooping motion of the other man, as he caressed the great cat.

Maurice straightened himself.

"You came to look for me?" he said.

"Isabel was a little uneasy," said Bertie.

"I'll come in. I like messing about doing these jobs."

The cat had reared her sinister, feline length against his leg, clawing at his thigh affectionately. He lifted her claws out of his flesh.

"I hope I'm not in your way at all at the Grange here," said Bertie, rather shy and stiff.

"My way? No, not a bit. I'm glad Isabel has somebody to talk to. I'm afraid it's I who am in the way. I know I'm not very lively company. Isabel's all right, don't you think? She's not unhappy, is she?"

"I don't think so."

"What does she say?"

"She says she's very content—only a little troubled about you."

"Why me?"

"Perhaps afraid that you might brood," said Bertie, cautiously.

"She needn't be afraid of that." He continued to caress the flattened grey head of the cat with his fingers. "What I am a bit afraid of," he resumed, "is that she'll find me a dead weight, always alone with me down here."

"I don't think you need think that," said Bertie, though this was what he feared himself.

"I don't know," said Maurice. "Sometimes I feel it isn't fair that she's saddled with me." Then he dropped his voice curiously. "I say," he asked, secretly struggling, "is my face much disfigured? Do you mind telling me?"

"There is the scar," said Bertie, wondering. "Yes, it is a disfigurement. But more pitiable than shocking."

"A pretty bad scar, though," said Maurice.

"Oh, yes."

There was a pause.

"Sometimes I feel I am horrible," said Maurice, in a low voice, talking as if to himself. And Bertie actually felt a quiver of horror.

"That's nonsense," he said.

Maurice again straightened himself, leaving the cat.

"There's no telling," he said. Then again, in an odd tone, he added: "I don't really know you, do I?"

"Probably not," said Bertie.

"Do you mind if I touch you?"

The lawyer shrank away instinctively. And yet, out of very philanthropy, he said, in a small voice: "Not at all."

But he suffered as the blind man stretched out a strong, naked hand to him. Maurice accidently knocked off Bertie's hat.

"I thought you were taller," he said, starting. Then he laid his hand on Bertie Reid's head, closing the dome of the skull in a soft, firm grasp, gathering it, as it were; then, shifting his grasp and softly closing again, with a fine, close pressure, till he had covered the skull and the face of the smaller man, tracing the brows, and touching the full, closed eyes, touching the small nose and the nostrils, the rough, short moustache, the mouth, the rather strong chin. The hand of the blind man grasped the shoulder, the arm, the hand of the other man. He seemed to take him, in the soft, travelling grasp.

"You seem young," he said quietly, at last.

The lawyer stood almost annihilated, unable to answer.

"Your head seems tender, as if you were young," Maurice repeated. "So do your hands. Touch my eyes, will you?—touch my scar."

Now Bertie quivered with revulsion. Yet he was under the power of the blind man, as if hypnotized. He lifted his hand, and laid the fingers on the scar, on the scarred eyes. Maurice suddenly covered them with his own hand, pressed the fingers of the other man upon his disfigured eye-sockets, trembling in every fibre, and rocking slightly, slowly, from side to side. He remained thus for a minute or more, whilst Bertie stood as if in a swoon, unconscious, imprisoned.

Then suddenly Maurice removed the hand of the other man from his brow, and stood holding it in his own.

"Oh, my God," he said, "we shall know each other now, shan't we? We shall know each other now."

Bertie could not answer. He gazed mute and terrorstruck, overcome by his own weakness. He knew he could not answer. He had an unreasonable fear, lest the other man should suddenly destroy him. Whereas Maurice was actually filled with hot, poignant love, the passion of friendship. Perhaps it was this very passion of friendship which Bertie shrank from most.

"We're all right together now, aren't we?" said Maurice. "It's all right now, as long as we live, so far as we're concerned?"

"Yes," said Bertie, trying by any means to escape.

Maurice stood with head lifted, as if listening. The new delicate fulfilment of mortal friendship had come as a revelation and surprise to him, something exquisite and unhoped-for. He seemed to be listening to hear if it were real.

Then he turned for his coat.

"Come," he said, "we'll go to Isabel."

Bertie took the lantern and opened the door. The cat disappeared. The two men went in silence along the causeways. Isabel, as they came, thought their footsteps sounded strange. She looked up pathetically and anxiously for their entrance. There seemed a curious elation about Maurice. Bertie was haggard, with sunken eyes.

"What is it?" she asked.

"We've become friends," said Maurice, standing with his feet apart, like a strange colossus.

"Friends!" re-echoed Isabel. And she looked again at Bertie. He met her eyes with a furtive, haggard look; his eyes were as if glazed with misery.

"I'm so glad," she said, in sheer perplexity.

"Yes," said Maurice.

He was indeed so glad. Isabel took his hand with both hers, and held it fast.

"You'll be happier now, dear," she said.

But she was watching Bertie. She knew that he had one desire—to escape from this intimacy, this friendship, which had been thrust upon him. He could not bear it that he had been touched by the blind man, his insane reserve broken in. He was like a mollusc whose shell is broken.

## *Joseph Conrad*
## THE SECRET SHARER

On my right hand there were lines of fishing stakes resembling a mysterious system of half-submerged bamboo fences, incomprehensible in its division of the domain of tropical fishes, and crazy of aspect as if abandoned forever by some nomad tribe of fishermen now gone to the other end of the ocean; for there was no sign of human habitation as far as the eye could reach. To the left a group of barren islets, suggesting ruins of stone walls, towers, and blockhouses, had its foundations set in a blue sea that itself looked solid, so still and stable did it lie below my feet; even the track of light from the westering sun shone smoothly, without that animated glitter which tells of an imperceptible ripple. And when I turned my head to take a parting glance at the tug which had just left us anchored outside the bar, I saw the straight line of the flat shore joined to the stable sea, edge to edge, with a perfect and unmarked

THE SECRET SHARER: From *'Twixt Land and Sea,* by Joseph Conrad. Copyright, 1912, 1921. Used by permission of J. M. Dent & Sons, Ltd.

closeness, in one levelled floor half brown, half blue under the enormous dome of the sky. Corresponding in their insignificance to the islets of the sea, two small clumps of trees, one on each side of the only fault in the impeccable joint, marked the mouth of the river Meinam we had just left on the first preparatory stage of our homeward journey; and, far back on the inland level, a larger and loftier mass, the grove surrounding the great Paknam pagoda, was the only thing on which the eye could rest from the vain task of exploring the monotonous sweep of the horizon. Here and there gleams as of a few scattered pieces of silver marked the windings of the great river; and on the nearest of them, just within the bar, the tug steaming right into the land became lost to my sight, hull and funnel and masts, as though the impassive earth had swallowed her up without an effort, without a tremor. My eye followed the light cloud of her smoke, now here, now there, above the plain, according to the devious curves of the stream, but always fainter and farther away, till I lost it at last behind the miter-shaped hill of the great pagoda. And then I was left alone with my ship, anchored at the head of the Gulf of Siam.

She floated at the starting point of a long journey, very still in an immense stillness, the shadows of her spars flung far to the eastward by the setting sun. At that moment I was alone on her decks. There was not a sound in her—and around us nothing moved, nothing lived, not a canoe on the water, not a bird in the air, not a cloud in the sky. In this breathless pause at the threshold of a long passage we seemed to be measuring our fitness for a long and arduous enterprise, the appointed task of both our existences to be carried out, far from all human eyes, with only sky and sea for spectators and for judges.

There must have been some glare in the air to interfere with one's sight, because it was only just before the sun left us that my roaming eyes made out beyond the highest ridge of the principal islet of the group something which did away with the solemnity of perfect solitude. The tide of darkness flowed on swiftly; and with tropical suddenness a swarm of stars came out above the shadowy earth, while I lingered yet, my hand resting lightly on my ship's rail as if on the shoulder of a trusted friend. But, with all that multitude of celestial bodies staring down at one, the comfort of quiet communion with her was gone for good. And there were also disturbing sounds by this time—voices, footsteps forward; the steward flitted along the main deck, a busily ministering spirit; a hand bell tinkled urgently under the poop deck. . . .

I found my two officers waiting for me near the supper table, in the lighted cuddy. We sat down at once, and as I helped the chief mate, I said:

"Are you aware that there is a ship anchored inside the islands? I saw her mastheads above the ridge as the sun went down."

He raised sharply his simple face, overcharged by a terrible growth of whisker, and emitted his usual ejaculations: "Bless my soul, sir! You don't say so!"

My second mate was a round-cheeked, silent young man, grave beyond his years, I thought; but as our eyes happened to meet I detected a slight quiver on his lips. I looked down at once. It was not my part to encourage sneering on board my ship. It must be said, too, that I knew very little of my officers. In consequence of certain events of no particular significance, except to myself, I had been appointed to the command only a fortnight before. Neither did I know much of the hands forward. All these people had been together for eighteen months or so, and my position was that of the only stranger on board. I mention this because it has some bearing on what is to follow. But what I felt most was my being a stranger to the ship; and if all the truth must be told, I was somewhat of a stranger to myself. The youngest man on board (barring the second mate), and untried as yet by a position of the fullest responsibility, I was willing to take the adequacy of the others for granted. They had simply to be equal to their tasks; but I wondered how far I should turn out faithful to that ideal conception of one's own personality every man sets up for himself secretly.

Meantime the chief mate, with an almost visible effect of collaboration on the part of his round eyes and frightful whiskers, was trying to evolve a theory of the anchored ship. His dominant trait was to take all things into earnest consideration. He was of a painstaking turn of mind. As he used to say, he "liked to account to himself" for practically everything that came

in his way, down to a miserable scorpion he had found in his cabin a week before. The why and the wherefore of that scorpion—how it got on board and came to select his room rather than the pantry (which was a dark place and more what a scorpion would be partial to), and how on earth it managed to drown itself in the inkwell of his writing desk—had exercised him infinitely. The ship within the islands was much more easily accounted for; and just as we were about to rise from the table he made his pronouncement. She was, he doubted not, a ship from home lately arrived. Probably she drew too much water to cross the bar except at the top of spring tides. Therefore she went into that natural harbor to wait for a few days in preference to remaining in an open roadstead.

"That's so," confirmed the second mate, suddenly, in his slightly hoarse voice. "She draws over twenty feet. She's the Liverpool ship *Sephora* with a cargo of coal. Hundred and twenty-three days from Cardiff."

We looked at him in surprise.

"The tugboat skipper told me when he came on board for your letters, sir," explained the young man. "He expects to take her up the river the day after tomorrow."

After thus overwhelming us with the extent of his information he slipped out of the cabin. The mate observed regretfully that he "could not account for that young fellow's whims." What prevented him telling us about it at once, he wanted to know.

I detained him as he was making a move. For the last two days the crew had had plenty of hard work, and the night before they had very little sleep. I felt painfully that I—a stranger—was doing something unusual when I directed him to let all hands turn in without setting an anchor watch. I proposed to keep on deck myself till one o'clock or thereabouts. I would get the second mate to relieve me at that hour.

"He will turn out the cook and the steward at four," I concluded, "and then give you a call. Of course at the slightest sign of any sort of wind we'll have the hands up and make a start at once."

He concealed his astonishment. "Very well, sir." Outside the cuddy he put his head in the second mate's door to inform him of my unheard-of caprice to take a five hours' anchor watch on myself. I heard the other raise his voice incredulously: "What? The captain himself?" Then a few more murmurs, a door closed, then another. A few moments later I went on deck.

My strangeness, which had made me sleepless, had prompted that unconventional arrangement, as if I had expected in those solitary hours of the night to get on terms with the ship of which I knew nothing, manned by men of whom I knew very little more. Fast alongside a wharf, littered like any ship in port with a tangle of unrelated things, invaded by unrelated shore people, I had hardly seen her yet properly. Now, as she lay cleared for sea, the stretch of her main deck seemed to me very fine under the stars. Very fine, very roomy for her size, and very inviting. I descended the poop and paced the waist, my mind picturing to myself the coming passage through the Malay Archipelago, down the Indian Ocean, and up the Atlantic. All its phases were familiar enough to me, every characteristic, all the alternatives which were likely to face me on the high seas—everything! . . . except the novel responsibility of command. But I took heart from the reasonable thought that the ship was like other ships, the men like other men, and that the sea was not likely to keep any special surprises expressly for my discomfiture.

Arrived at that comforting conclusion, I bethought myself of a cigar and went below to get it. All was still down there. Everybody at the after end of the ship was sleeping profoundly. I came out again on the quarterdeck, agreeably at ease in my sleeping suit on that warm breathless night, barefooted, a glowing cigar in my teeth, and, going forward, I was met by the profound silence of the fore end of the ship. Only as I passed the door of the forecastle I heard a deep, quiet, trustful sigh of some sleeper inside. And suddenly I rejoiced in the great security of the sea as compared with the unrest of the land, in my choice of that untempted life presenting no disquieting problems, invested with an elementary moral beauty by the absolute straightforwardness of its appeal and by the singleness of its purpose.

The riding light in the fore-rigging burned with a clear, untroubled, as if symbolic, flame, confident and bright in the mysterious shades of the night. Passing on my way aft along the other side of the ship, I observed that the rope side ladder, put over, no doubt, for the master of the tug when he came to fetch away our letters, had not been hauled in as it should have been. I became annoyed at this, for exactitude in small matters is the very soul of discipline. Then I reflected that I had myself peremptorily dismissed my officers from duty, and by my own act had prevented the anchor watch being formally set and things properly attended to. I asked myself whether it was wise ever to interfere with the established routine of duties even from the kindest of motives. My action might have made me appear eccentric. Goodness only knew how that absurdly whiskered mate would "account" for my conduct, and what the whole ship thought of that informality of their new captain. I was vexed with myself.

Not from compunction certainly, but, as it were mechanically, I proceeded to get the ladder in myself. Now a side ladder of that sort is a light affair and comes in easily, yet my vigorous tug, which should have brought it flying on board, merely recoiled upon my body in a totally unexpected jerk. What the devil! . . . I was so astounded by the immovableness of that ladder that I remained stock-still, trying to account for it to myself like that imbecile mate of mine. In the end, of course, I put my head over the rail.

The side of the ship made an opaque belt of shadow on the darkling glassy shimmer of the sea. But I saw at once something elongated and pale floating very close to the ladder. Before I could form a guess a faint flash of phosphorescent light, which seemed to issue suddenly from the naked body of a man, flickered in the sleeping water with the elusive, silent play of summer lightning in a night sky. With a gasp I saw revealed to my stare a pair of feet, the long legs, a broad livid back immersed right up to the neck in a greenish cadaverous glow. One hand, awash, clutched the bottom rung of the ladder. He was complete but for the head. A headless corpse! The cigar dropped out of my gaping mouth with a tiny plop and a short hiss quite audible in the absolute stillness of all things under heaven. At that I suppose he raised up his face, a dimly pale oval in the shadow of the ship's side. But even then I could only barely make out down there the shape of his blackhaired head. However, it was enough for the horrid, frost-bound sensation which had gripped me about the chest to pass off. The moment of vain exclamations was past, too. I only climbed on the spare spar and leaned over the rail as far as I could, to bring my eyes nearer to that mystery floating alongside.

As he hung by the ladder, like a resting swimmer, the sea lightning played about his limbs at every stir; and he appeared in it ghastly, silvery, fishlike. He remained as mute as a fish, too. He made no motion to get out of the water, either. It was inconceivable that he should not attempt to come on board, and strangely troubling to suspect that perhaps he did not want to. And my first words were prompted by just that troubled incertitude.

"What's the matter?" I asked in my ordinary tone; speaking down to the face upturned exactly under mine.

"Cramp," it answered, no louder. Then slightly anxious, "I say, no need to call anyone."

"I was not going to," I said.

"Are you alone on deck?"

"Yes."

I had somehow the impression that he was on the point of letting go the ladder to swim away beyond my ken—mysterious as he came. But, for the moment, this being appearing as if he had risen from the bottom of the sea (it was certainly the nearest land to the ship) wanted only to know the time. I told him. And he, down there, tentatively:

"I suppose your captain's turned in?"

"I am sure he isn't," I said.

He seemed to struggle with himself, for I heard something like the low, bitter murmur of doubt. "What's the good?" His next words came out with a hesitating effort.

"Look here, my man. Could you call him out quietly?"

I thought the time had come to declare myself.

"*I* am the captain."

I heard a "By Jove!" whispered at the level of the water. The phosphorescence flashed in the swirl of the water all about his limbs, his other hand seized the ladder.

"My name's Leggatt."

The voice was calm and resolute. A good voice. The self-possession of that man had somehow induced a corresponding state in myself. It was very quietly that I remarked:

"You must be a good swimmer."

"Yes. I've been in the water practically since nine o'clock. The question for me now is whether I am to let go this ladder and go on swimming till I sink from exhaustion, or—to come on board here."

I felt this was no mere formula of desperate speech, but a real alternative in the view of a strong soul. I should have gathered from this that he was young; indeed, it is only the young who are ever confronted by such clear issues. But at the time it was pure intuition on my part. A mysterious communication was established already between us two—in the face of that silent, darkened tropical sea. I was young, too; young enough to make no comment. The man in the water began suddenly to climb up the ladder, and I hastened away from the rail to fetch some clothes.

Before entering the cabin I stood still, listening in the lobby at the foot of the stairs. A faint snore came through the closed door of the chief mate's room. The second mate's door was on the hook, but the darkness in there was absolutely soundless. He, too, was young and could sleep like a stone. Remained the steward, but he was not likely to wake up before he was called. I got a sleeping suit out of my room and, coming back on deck, saw the naked man from the sea sitting on the main hatch, glimmering white in the darkness, his elbows on his knees and his head in his hands. In a moment he had concealed his damp body in a sleeping suit of the same gray-stripe pattern as the one I was wearing and followed me like my double on the poop. Together we moved right aft, barefooted, silent.

"What is it?" I asked in a deadened voice, taking the lighted lamp out of the binnacle, and raising it to his face.

"An ugly business."

He had rather regular features; a good mouth; light eyes under somewhat heavy, dark eyebrows; a smooth, square forehead; no growth on his cheeks; a small, brown mustache, and a well-shaped, round chin. His expression was concentrated, meditative, under the inspecting light of the lamp I held up to his face; such as a man thinking hard in solitude might wear. My sleeping suit was just right for his size. A well-knit young fellow of twenty-five at most. He caught his lower lip with the edge of white, even teeth.

"Yes," I said, replacing the lamp in the binnacle. The warm, heavy tropical night closed upon his head again.

"There's a ship over there," he murmured.

"Yes, I know. The *Sephora*. Did you know of us?"

"Hadn't the slightest idea. I am the mate of her—" He paused and corrected himself. "I should say I *was*."

"Aha! Something wrong?"

"Yes. Very wrong indeed. I've killed a man."

"What do you mean? Just now?"

"No, on the passage. Weeks ago. Thirty-nine south. When I say a man—"

"Fit of temper," I suggested, confidently.

The shadowy, dark head, like mine, seemed to nod imperceptibly above the ghostly gray of my sleeping suit. It was, in the night, as though I had been faced by my own reflection in the depths of a somber and immense mirror.

"A pretty thing to have to own up to for a *Conway* [32] boy," murmured my double, distinctly.

"You're a *Conway* boy?"

"I am," he said, as if startled. Then, slowly . . . "Perhaps you too—"

It was so; but being a couple of years older I had left before he joined. After a quick interchange of dates a silence fell; and I thought suddenly of my absurd mate with his terrific whiskers and the "Bless my soul—you don't say so" type of intellect. My double gave me an inkling of his thoughts by saying:

"My father's a parson in Norfolk. Do you see me before a judge and jury on that charge? For myself I can't see the necessity. There are fellows that an angel from heaven—And I am not that. He was one of those creatures that are just simmering all the time with a silly sort of wickedness. Miserable devils that have no business to live at all. He wouldn't do his duty and wouldn't let anybody else do theirs. But what's the good of talking! You know well enough the sort of ill-conditioned snarling cur—"

He appealed to me as if our experiences had been as identical as our clothes. And I knew well enough the pestiferous danger of such a character where there are no means of legal repression. And I knew well enough also that my double there was no homicidal ruffian. I did not think of asking him for details, and he told me the story roughly in brusque, disconnected sentences. I needed no more. I saw it all going

---

[32] A ship on which officer candidates for the merchant marine were trained.

on as though I were myself inside that other sleeping suit.

"It happened while we were setting a reefed foresail, at dusk. Reefed foresail! You understand the sort of weather. The only sail we had left to keep the ship running; so you may guess what it had been like for days. Anxious sort of job, that. He gave me some of his cursed insolence at the sheet. I tell you I was overdone with this terrific weather that seemed to have no end to it. Terrific, I tell you—and a deep ship. I believe the fellow himself was half crazed with funk. It was no time for gentlemanly reproof, so I turned round and felled him like an ox. He up and at me. We closed just as an awful sea made for the ship. All hands saw it coming and took to the rigging, but I had him by the throat, and went on shaking him like a rat, the men above us yelling, 'Look out! look out!' Then a crash as if the sky had fallen on my head. They say that for over ten minutes hardly anything was to be seen of the ship—just the three masts and a bit of the forecastle head and of the poop all awash driving along in a smother of foam. It was a miracle that they found us, jammed together behind the forebits. It's clear that I meant business, because I was holding him by the throat still when they picked us up. He was black in the face. It was too much for them. It seems they rushed us aft together, gripped as we were, screaming 'Murder!' like a lot of lunatics, and broke into the cuddy. And the ship running for her life, touch and go all the time, any minute her last in a sea fit to turn your hair gray only a-looking at it. I understand that the skipper, too, started raving like the rest of them. The man had been deprived of sleep for more than a week, and to have this sprung on him at the height of a furious gale nearly drove him out of his mind. I wonder they didn't fling me overboard after getting the carcass of their precious shipmate out of my fingers. They had rather a job to separate us, I've been told. A sufficiently fierce story to make an old judge and a respectable jury sit up a bit. The first thing I heard when I came to myself was the maddening howling of that endless gale, and on that the voice of the old man. He was hanging on to my bunk, staring into my face out of his sou'wester.

" 'Mr. Leggatt, you have killed a man. You can act no longer as chief mate of this ship.' "

His care to subdue his voice made it sound

monotonous. He rested a hand on the end of the skylight to steady himself with, and all that time did not stir a limb, so far as I could see. "Nice little tale for a quiet tea party," he concluded in the same tone.

One of my hands, too, rested on the end of the skylight; neither did I stir a limb, so far as I knew. We stood less than a foot from each other. It occurred to me that if old "Bless my soul—you don't say so" were to put his head up the companion and catch sight of us, he would think he was seeing double, or imagine himself come upon a scene of weird witchcraft; the strange captain having a quiet confabulation by the wheel with his own gray ghost. I became very much concerned to prevent anything of the sort. I heard the other's soothing undertone.

"My father's a parson in Norfolk," it said. Evidently he had forgotten he had told me this important fact before. Truly a nice little tale.

"You had better slip down into my stateroom now," I said, moving off stealthily. My double followed my movements; our bare feet made no sound; I let him in, closed the door with care, and, after giving a call to the second mate, returned on deck for my relief.

"Not much sign of any wind yet," I remarked when he approached.

"No, sir. Not much," he assented, sleepily, in his hoarse voice, with just enough deference, no more, and barely suppressing a yawn.

"Well, that's all you have to look out for. You have got your orders."

"Yes, sir."

I paced a turn or two on the poop and saw him take up his position face forward with his elbow in the ratlines of the mizzen-rigging before I went below. The mate's faint snoring was still going on peacefully. The cuddy lamp was burning over the table on which stood a vase with flowers, a polite attention from the ship's provision merchant—the last flowers we should see for the next three months at the very least. Two bunches of bananas hung from the beam symmetrically, one on each side of the rudder casing. Everything was as before in the ship— except that two of her captain's sleeping suits were simultaneously in use, one motionless in the cuddy, the other keeping very still in the captain's stateroom.

It must be explained here that my cabin had the form of the capital letter L, the door being within the angle and opening into the short part

of the letter. A couch was to the left, the bed-place to the right; my writing desk and the chronometers' table faced the door. But anyone opening it, unless he stepped right inside, had no view of what I call the long (or vertical) part of the letter. It contained some lockers surmounted by a book case; and a few clothes, a thick jacket or two, caps, oilskin coat, and such like, hung on hooks. There was at the bottom of that part a door opening into my bathroom, which could be entered also directly from the saloon. But that way was never used.

The mysterious arrival had discovered the advantage of this particular shape. Entering my room, lighted strongly by a big bulkhead lamp swung on gimbals above my writing desk, I did not see him anywhere till he stepped out quietly from behind the coats hung in the recessed part.

"I heard somebody moving about, and went in there at once," he whispered.

I, too, spoke under my breath.

"Nobody is likely to come in here without knocking and getting permission."

He nodded. His face was thin and the sunburn faded, as though he had been ill. And no wonder. He had been, I heard presently, kept under arrest in his cabin for nearly seven weeks. But there was nothing sickly in his eyes or in his expression. He was not a bit like me, really; yet, as we stood leaning over my bed-place, whispering side by side, with our dark heads together and our backs to the door, anybody bold enough to open it stealthily would have been treated to the uncanny sight of a double captain busy talking in whispers with his other self.

"But all this doesn't tell me how you came to hang on to our side ladder," I inquired, in the hardly audible murmurs we used, after he had told me something more of the proceedings on board the *Sephora* once the bad weather was over.

"When we sighted Java Head I had had time to think all those matters out several times over. I had six weeks of doing nothing else, and with only an hour or so every evening for a tramp on the quarter-deck."

He whispered, his arms folded on the side of my bed-place, staring through the open port. And I could imagine perfectly the manner of this thinking out—a stubborn if not a steadfast operation; something of which I should have been perfectly incapable.

"I reckoned it would be dark before we closed with the land," he continued, so low that I had to strain my hearing, near as we were to each other, shoulder touching shoulder almost. "So I asked to speak to the old man. He always seemed very sick when he came to see me—as if he could not look me in the face. You know, that foresail saved the ship. She was too deep to have run long under bare poles. And it was I that managed to set it for him. Anyway, he came. When I had him in my cabin—he stood by the door looking at me as if I had the halter around my neck already—I asked him right away to leave my cabin door unlocked at night while the ship was going through Sunda Straits. There would be the Java coast within two or three miles, off Angier Point. I wanted nothing more. I've had a prize for swimming my second year in the *Conway*."

"I can believe it," I breathed out.

"God only knows why they locked me in every night. To see some of their faces you'd have thought they were afraid I'd go about at night strangling people. Am I a murdering brute? Do I look it? By Jove! if I had been he wouldn't have trusted himself like that into my room. You'll say I might have chucked him aside and bolted out, there and then—it was dark already. Well, no. And for the same reason I wouldn't think of trying to smash the door. There would have been a rush to stop me at the noise, and I did not mean to get into a confounded scrimmage. Somebody else might have got killed—for I would not have broken out only to get chucked back, and I did not want any more of that work. He refused, looking more sick than ever. He was afraid of the men, and also of that old second mate of his who had been sailing with him for years—a gray-headed old humbug; and his steward, too, had been with him devil knows how long—seventeen years or more—a dogmatic sort of loafer who hated me like poison, just because I was the chief mate. No chief mate ever made more than one voyage in the *Sephora*, you know. Those two old chaps ran the ship. Devil only knows what the skipper wasn't afraid of (all his nerve went to pieces altogether in that hellish spell of bad weather we had)—of what the law would do to him—of his wife, perhaps. Oh, yes! she's on board. Though I don't think she would have meddled. She would have been only too glad to have me out of the ship in any way. The 'brand

of Cain' business, don't you see. That's all right. I was ready enough to go off wandering on the face of the earth—and that was price enough to pay for an Abel of that sort. Anyhow, he wouldn't listen to me. 'This thing must take its course. I represent the law here.' He was shaking like a leaf. 'So you won't?' 'No!' 'Then I hope you will be able to sleep on that,' I said, and turned my back on him. 'I wonder that *you* can,' cries he, and locks the door.

"Well, after that, I couldn't. Not very well. That was three weeks ago. We have had a slow passage through the Java Sea; drifted about Carimata for ten days. When we anchored here they thought, I suppose, it was all right. The nearest land (and that's five miles) is the ship's destination; the consul would soon set about catching me; and there would have been no object in bolting to these islets there. I don't suppose there's a drop of water on them. I don't know how it was, but tonight that steward, after bringing me my supper, went out to let me eat it, and left the door unlocked. And I ate it—all there was, too. After I had finished I strolled out on the quarter-deck. I don't know that I meant to do anything. A breath of fresh air was all I wanted, I believe. Then a sudden temptation came over me. I kicked off my slippers and was in the water before I had made up my mind fairly. Somebody heard the splash and they raised an awful hullabaloo. 'He's gone! Lower the boats! He's committed suicide! No, he's swimming.' Certainly I was swimming. It's not so easy for a swimmer like me to commit suicide by drowning. I landed on the nearest islet before the boat left the ship's side. I heard them pulling about in the dark, hailing, and so on, but after a bit they gave up. Everything quieted down and the anchorage became as still as death. I sat down on a stone and began to think. I felt certain they would start searching for me at daylight. There was no place to hide on those stony things—and if there had been, what would have been the good? But now I was clear of that ship, I was not going back. So after a while I took off all my clothes, tied them up in a bundle with a stone inside, and dropped them in the deep water on the outer side of that islet. That was suicide enough for me. Let them think what they liked, but I didn't mean to drown myself. I meant to swim till I sank—but that's not the same thing. I struck out for another of these little islands, and it was from that one that I first saw your riding light. Something to swim for. I went on easily, and on the way I came upon a flat rock a foot or two above water. In the daytime, I dare say, you might make it out with a glass from your poop. I scrambled up on it and rested myself for a bit. Then I made another start. That last spell must have been over a mile."

His whisper was getting fainter and fainter, and all the time he stared straight out through the porthole, in which there was not even a star to be seen. I had not interrupted him. There was something that made comment impossible in his narrative, or perhaps in himself; a sort of feeling, a quality, which I can't find a name for. And when he ceased, all I found was a futile whisper: "So you swam for our light?"

"Yes—straight for it. It was something to swim for. I couldn't see any stars low down because the coast was in the way, and I couldn't see the land, either. The water was like glass. One might have been swimming in a confounded thousand-feet deep cistern with no place for scrambling out anywhere; but what I didn't like was the notion of swimming round and round like a crazed bullock before I gave out; and as I didn't mean to go back . . . No. Do you see me being hauled back, stark naked, off one of these little islands by the scruff of the neck and fighting like a wild beast? Somebody would have got killed for certain, and I did not want any of that. So I went on. Then your ladder—"

"Why didn't you hail the ship?" I asked, a little louder.

He touched my shoulder lightly. Lazy footsteps came right over our heads and stopped. The second mate had crossed from the other side of the poop and might have been hanging over the rail, for all we knew.

"He couldn't hear us talking—could he?" My double breathed into my very ear, anxiously.

His anxiety was an answer, a sufficient answer, to the question I had put to him. An answer containing all the difficulty of that situation. I closed the porthole quietly, to make sure. A louder word might have been overheard.

"Who's that?" he whispered then.

"My second mate. But I don't know much more of the fellow than you do."

And I told him a little about myself. I had been appointed to take charge while I least expected anything of the sort, not quite a fortnight ago. I didn't know either the ship or the people. Hadn't had the time in port to look about me or size anybody up. And as to the crew, all they knew was that I was appointed to take the ship home. For the rest, I was almost as much of a stranger on board as himself, I said. And at the moment I felt it most acutely. I felt that it would take very little to make me a suspect person in the eyes of the ship's company.

He had turned about meantime; and we, the two strangers in the ship, faced each other in identical attitudes.

"Your ladder—" he murmured, after a silence. "Who'd have thought of finding a ladder hanging over at night in a ship anchored out here! I felt just then a very unpleasant faintness. After the life I've been leading for nine weeks, anybody would have got out of condition. I wasn't capable of swimming round as far as your rudder chains. And, lo and behold! there was a ladder to get hold of. After I gripped it I said to myself, 'What's the good?' When I saw a man's head looking over I thought I would swim away presently and leave him shouting—in whatever language it was. I didn't mind being looked at. I—I liked it. And then you speaking to me so quietly—as if you had expected me—made me hold on a little longer. It had been a confounded lonely time—I don't mean while swimming. I was glad to talk a little to somebody that didn't belong to the *Sephora*. As to asking for the captain, that was a mere impulse. It could have been no use, with all the ship knowing about me and the other people pretty certain to be round here in the morning. I don't know—I wanted to be seen, to talk with somebody, before I went on. I don't know what I would have said. . . . 'Fine night, isn't it?' or something of the sort."

"Do you think they will be round here presently?" I asked with some incredulity.

"Quite likely," he said, faintly.

He looked extremely haggard all of a sudden. His head rolled on his shoulders.

"H'm. We shall see then. Meantime get into that bed," I whispered. "Want help? There."

It was a rather high bed-place with a set of drawers underneath. This amazing swimmer really needed the lift I gave him by seizing his leg. He tumbled in, rolled over on his back, and flung one arm across his eyes. And then, with his face nearly hidden, he must have looked exactly as I used to look in that bed. I gazed upon my other self for a while before drawing across carefully the two green serge curtains which ran on a brass rod. I thought for a moment of pinning them together for greater safety, but I sat down on the couch, and once there I felt unwilling to rise and hunt for a pin. I would do it in a moment. I was extremely tired, in a peculiarly intimate way, by the strain of stealthiness, by the effort of whispering and the general secrecy of this excitement. It was three o'clock by now and I had been on my feet since nine, but I was not sleepy; I could not have gone to sleep. I sat there, fagged out, looking at the curtains, trying to clear my mind of the confused sensation of being in two places at once, and greatly bothered by an exasperating knocking in my head. It was a relief to discover suddenly that it was not in my head at all, but on the outside of the door. Before I could collect myself the words "Come in" were out of my mouth, and the steward entered with a tray, bringing in my morning coffee. I had slept, after all, and I was so frightened that I shouted, "This way! I am here, steward," as though he had been miles away. He put down the tray on the table next the couch and only then said, very quietly, "I can see you are here, sir." I felt him give me a keen look, but I dared not meet his eyes just then. He must have wondered why I had drawn the curtains of my bed before going to sleep on the couch. He went out, hooking the door open as usual.

I heard the crew washing decks above me. I knew I would have been told at once if there had been any wind. Calm, I thought, and I was doubly vexed. Indeed, I felt dual more than ever. The steward reappeared suddenly in the doorway. I jumped up from the couch so quickly that he gave a start.

"What do you want here?"

"Close your port, sir—they are washing decks."

"It is closed," I said, reddening.

"Very well, sir." But he did not move from the doorway and returned my stare in an extraordinary, equivocal manner for a time. Then his eyes wavered, all his expression changed, and in a voice unusually gentle, almost coaxingly:

"May I come in to take the empty cup away, sir?"

"Of course!" I turned my back on him while he popped in and out. Then I unhooked and closed the door and even pushed the bolt. This sort of thing could not go on very long. The cabin was as hot as an oven, too. I took a peep at my double, and discovered that he had not moved, his arm was still over his eyes; but his chest heaved; his hair was wet; his chin glistened with perspiration. I reached over him and opened the port.

"I must show myself on deck," I reflected.

Of course, theoretically, I could do what I liked, with no one to say nay to me within the whole circle of the horizon; but to lock my cabin door and take the key away I did not dare. Directly I put my head out of the companion I saw the group of my two officers, the second mate barefooted, the chief mate in long india-rubber boots, near the break of the poop, and the steward halfway down the poop ladder talking to them eagerly. He happened to catch sight of me and dived, the second ran down on the main deck shouting some order or other, and the chief mate came to meet me, touching his cap.

There was a sort of curiosity in his eye that I did not like. I don't know whether the steward had told them that I was "queer" only, or downright drunk, but I know the man meant to have a good look at me. I watched him coming with a smile which, as he got into point-blank range, took effect and froze his very whiskers. I did not give him time to open his lips.

"Square the yards by lifts and braces before the hands go to breakfast."

It was the first particular order I had given on board that ship; and I stayed on deck to see it executed, too. I had felt the need of asserting myself without loss of time. That sneering young cub got taken down a peg or two on that occasion, and I also seized the opportunity of having a good look at the face of every foremast man as they filed past me to go to the after braces. At breakfast time, eating nothing myself, I presided with such frigid dignity that the two mates were only too glad to escape from the cabin as soon as decency permitted and all the time the dual working of my mind distracted me almost to the point of insanity. I was constantly watching myself, my secret self, as dependent on my actions as my own personality, sleeping in that bed, behind that door which faced me as I sat at the head of the table. It was very much like being mad, only it was worse because one was aware of it.

I had to shake him for a solid minute, but when at last he opened his eyes it was in the full possession of his senses, with an inquiring look.

"All's well so far," I whispered. "Now you must vanish into the bathroom."

He did so, as noiseless as a ghost, and I then rang for the steward, and facing him boldly, directed him to tidy up my stateroom while I was having my bath—"and be quick about it." As my tone admitted of no excuses, he said, "Yes, sir," and ran off to fetch his dustpan and brushes. I took a bath and did most of my dressing, splashing, and whistling softly for the steward's edification, while the secret sharer of my life stood drawn up bolt upright in that little space, his face looking very sunken in daylight, his eyelids lowered under the stern, dark line of his eyebrows drawn together by a slight frown.

When I left him there to go back to my room the steward was finishing dusting. I sent for the mate and engaged him in some insignificant conversation. It was, as it were, trifling with the terrific character of his whiskers; but my object was to give him an opportunity for a good look at my cabin. And then I could at last shut, with a clear conscience, the door of my stateroom and get my double back into the recessed part. There was nothing else for it. He had to sit still on a small folding stool, half smothered by the heavy coats hanging there. We listened to the steward going into the bathroom out of the saloon, filling the water bottles there, scrubbing the bath, setting things to rights, whisk, bang, clatter—out again into the saloon—turn the key—click. Such was my scheme for keeping my second self invisible. Nothing better could be contrived under the circumstances. And there we sat; I at my writing desk ready to appear busy with some papers, he behind me, out of sight of the door. It would not have been prudent to talk in daytime; and I could not have stood the excitement of that queer sense of whispering to myself. Now and then, glancing over my shoulder, I saw him far back there, sitting rigidly on the low stool, his bare feet close together, his arms folded, his head hanging on his breast —and perfectly still. Anybody would have taken him for me.

I was fascinated by it myself. Every moment I had to glance over my shoulder. I was looking at him when a voice outside the door said:

"Beg pardon, sir."

"Well!" . . . I kept my eyes on him, and so, when the voice outside the door announced, "There's a ship's boat coming our way, sir," I saw him give a start—the first movement he had made for hours. But he did not raise his bowed head.

"All right. Get the ladder over."

I hesitated. Should I whisper something to him? But what? His immobility seemed to have been never disturbed. What could I tell him he did not know already? . . . Finally I went on deck.

II

The skipper of the *Sephora* had a thin red whisker all round his face, and the sort of complexion that goes with hair of that color; also the particular, rather smeary shade of blue in the eyes. He was not exactly a showy figure; his shoulders were high, his stature but middling—one leg slightly more bandy than the other. He shook hands, looking vaguely around. A spiritless tenacity was his main characteristic, I judged. I behaved with a politeness which seemed to disconcert him. Perhaps he was shy. He mumbled to me as if he were ashamed of what he was saying; gave his name (it was something like Archbold—but at this distance of years I hardly am sure), his ship's name, and a few other particulars of that sort, in the manner of a criminal making a reluctant and doleful confession. He had had terrible weather on the passage out—terrible—terrible —wife aboard, too.

By this time we were seated in the cabin and the steward brought in a tray with a bottle and glasses. "Thanks! No." Never took liquor. Would have some water, though. He drank two tumblerfuls. Terrible thirsty work. Ever since daylight had been exploring the islands round his ship.

"What was that for—fun?" I asked, with an appearance of polite interest.

"No!" He sighed. "Painful duty."

As he persisted in his mumbling and I wanted my double to hear every word, I hit upon the notion of informing him that I regretted to say I was hard of hearing.

"Such a young man, too!" he nodded, keeping his smeary blue, unintelligent eyes fastened upon me. What was the cause of it—some disease? he inquired, without the least sympathy and as if he thought that, if so, I'd got no more than I deserved.

"Yes; disease," I admitted in a cheerful tone which seemed to shock him. But my point was gained, because he had to raise his voice to give me his tale. It is not worth while to record that version. It was just over two months since all this had happened, and he had thought so much about it that he seemed completely muddled as to its bearings, but still immensely impressed.

"What would you think of such a thing happening on board your own ship? I've had the *Sephora* for these fifteen years. I am a well-known shipmaster."

He was densely distressed—and perhaps I should have sympathized with him if I had been able to detach my mental vision from the unsuspected sharer of my cabin as though he were my second self. There he was on the other side of the bulkhead, four or five feet from us, no more, as we sat in the saloon. I looked politely at Captain Archbold (if that was his name), but it was the other I saw, in a gray sleeping suit, seated on a low stool, his bare feet close together, his arms folded, and every word said between us falling into the ears of his dark head bowed on his chest.

"I have been at sea now, man and boy, for seven-and-thirty years, and I've never heard of such a thing happening in an English ship. And that it should be my ship. Wife on board, too."

I was hardly listening to him.

"Don't you think," I said, "that the heavy sea which, you told me, came aboard just then might have killed the man? I have seen the sheer weight of a sea kill a man very neatly, by simply breaking his neck."

"Good God!" he uttered, impressively, fixing his smeary blue eyes on me. "The sea! No man killed by the sea ever looked like that." He seemed positively scandalized at my suggestion. And as I gazed at him, certainly not prepared for anything original on his part, he advanced his head close to mine and thrust his tongue out at me so suddenly that I couldn't help starting back.

After scoring over my calmness in this graphic way he nodded wisely. If I had seen the sight, he assured me, I would never forget it as long as I lived. The weather was too bad to give the corpse a proper sea burial. So next day at dawn they took it up on the poop, covering its face with a bit of bunting; he read a short prayer, and then, just as it was, in its oilskins and long boots, they launched it amongst those mountainous seas that seemed ready every moment to swallow up the ship herself and the terrified lives on board of her.

"That reefed foresail saved you," I threw in.

"Under God—it did," he exclaimed fervently. "It was by a special mercy, I firmly believe, that it stood some of those hurricane squalls."

"It was the setting of that sail which—" I began.

"God's own hand in it," he interrupted me. "Nothing less could have done it. I don't mind telling you that I hardly dared give the order. It seemed impossible that we could touch anything without losing it, and then our last hope would have been gone."

The terror of that gale was on him yet. I let him go on for a bit, then said, casually—as if returning to a minor subject:

"You were very anxious to give up your mate to the shore people, I believe?"

He was. To the law. His obscure tenacity on that point had in it something incomprehensible and a little awful; something, as it were, mystical, quite apart from his anxiety that he should not be suspected of "countenancing any doings of that sort." Seven-and-thirty virtuous years at sea, of which over twenty of immaculate command, and the last fifteen in the *Sephora*, seemed to have laid him under some pitiless obligation.

"And you know," he went on, groping shamefacedly amongst his feelings, "I did not engage that young fellow. His people had some interest with my owners. I was in a way forced to take him on. He looked very smart, very gentlemanly, and all that. But do you know—I never liked him, somehow. I am a plain man. You see, he wasn't exactly the sort for the chief mate of a ship like the *Sephora*."

I had become so connected in thoughts and

impressions with the secret sharer of my cabin that I felt as if I, personally, were being given to understand that I, too, was not the sort that would have done for the chief mate of a ship like the *Sephora*. I had no doubt of it in my mind.

"Not at all the style of man. You understand," he insisted, superfluously, looking hard at me.

I smiled urbanely. He seemed at a loss for a while.

"I suppose I must report a suicide."

"Beg pardon?"

"Sui-cide! That's what I'll have to write to my owners directly I get in."

"Unless you manage to recover him before tomorrow," I assented, dispassionately.... "I mean, alive."

He mumbled something which I really did not catch, and I turned my ear to him in a puzzled manner. He fairly bawled:

"The land—I say, the mainland is at least seven miles off my anchorage."

"About that."

My lack of excitement, of curiosity, of surprise, of any sort of pronounced interest, began to arouse his distrust. But except for the felicitous pretense of deafness I had not tried to pretend anything. I had felt utterly incapable of playing the part of ignorance properly, and therefore was afraid to try. It is also certain that he had brought some ready-made suspicions with him, and that he viewed my politeness as a strange and unnatural phenomenon. And yet how else could I have received him? Not heartily! That was impossible for psychological reasons, which I need not state here. My only object was to keep off his inquiries. Surlily? Yes, but surliness might have provoked a point-blank question. From its novelty to him and from its nature, punctilious courtesy was the manner best calculated to restrain the man. But there was the danger of his breaking through my defense bluntly. I could not, I think, have met him by a direct lie, also for psychological (not moral) reasons. If he had only known how afraid I was of his putting my feeling of identity with the other to the test! But, strangely enough—(I thought of it only afterward)—I believe that he was not a little disconcerted by the reverse side of that weird situation, by something in me that reminded him of the man he was seeking—suggested a mysterious similitude to the young fellow he had distrusted and disliked from the first.

However that might have been, the silence was not very prolonged. He took another oblique step.

"I reckon I had no more than a two-mile pull to your ship. Not a bit more."

"And quite enough, too, in this awful heat," I said.

Another pause full of mistrust followed. Necessity, they say, is mother of invention, but fear, too, is not barren of ingenious suggestions. And I was afraid he would ask me point-blank for news of my other self.

"Nice little saloon, isn't it?" I remarked, as if noticing for the first time the way his eyes roamed from one closed door to the other. "And very well fitted out, too. Here, for instance," I continued, reaching over the back of my seat negligently and flinging the door open, "is my bathroom."

He made an eager movement, but hardly gave it a glance. I got up, shut the door of the bathroom, and invited him to have a look round, as if I were very proud of my accommodation. He had to rise and be shown round, but he went through the business without any raptures whatever.

"And now we'll have a look at my stateroom," I declared, in a voice as loud as I dared to make it, crossing the cabin to the starboard side with purposely heavy steps.

He followed me in and gazed around. My intelligent double had vanished. I played my part.

"Very convenient—isn't it?"

"Very nice. Very comf ...." He didn't finish, and went out brusquely as if to escape from some unrighteous wiles of mine. But it was not to be. I had been too frightened not to feel vengeful; I felt I had him on the run, and I meant to keep him on the run. My polite insistence must have had something menacing in it, because he gave in suddenly. And I did not let him off a single item; mate's room, pantry, storerooms, the very sail locker which was also under the poop—he had to look into them all. When at last I showed him out on the quarter-deck he drew a long, spiritless sigh, and mumbled dismally that he must really be going back to his ship now. I desired my mate, who had joined us, to see to the captain's boat.

The man of whiskers gave a blast on the

whistle which he used to wear hanging round his neck, and yelled, *"Sephora* away!" My double down there in my cabin must have heard, and certainly could not feel more relieved than I. Four fellows came running out from somewhere forward and went over the side, while my own men, appearing on deck too, lined the rail. I escorted my visitor to the gangway ceremoniously, and nearly overdid it. He was a tenacious beast. On the very ladder he lingered, and in that unique, guiltily conscientious manner of sticking to the point:

"I say . . . you . . . you don't think that—"

I covered his voice loudly:

"Certainly not. . . . I am delighted. Goodby."

I had an idea of what he meant to say, and just saved myself by the privilege of defective hearing. He was too shaken generally to insist, but my mate, close witness of that parting, looked mystified and his face took on a thoughtful cast. As I did not want to appear as if I wished to avoid all communication with my officers, he had the opportunity to address me.

"Seems a very nice man. His boat's crew told our chaps a very extraordinary story, if what I am told by the steward is true. I suppose you had it from the captain, sir?"

"Yes. I had a story from the captain."

"A very horrible affair—isn't it, sir?"

"It is."

"Beats all these tales we hear about murders in Yankee ships."

"I don't think it beats them. I don't think it resembles them in the least."

"Bless my soul—you don't say so! But of course I've no acquaintance whatever with American ships, not I, so I couldn't go against your knowledge. It's horrible enough for me. . . . But the queerest part is that those fellows seemed to have some idea the man was hidden aboard here. They had really. Did you ever hear of such a thing?"

"Preposterous—isn't it?"

We were walking to and fro athwart the quarterdeck. No one of the crew forward could be seen (the day was Sunday), and the mate pursued:

"There was some little dispute about it. Our chaps took offense. 'As if we would harbor a thing like that,' they said. 'Wouldn't you like to look for him in our coal hole?' Quite a tiff.

But they made it up in the end. I suppose he did drown himself. Don't you, sir?"

"I don't suppose anything."

"You have no doubt in the matter, sir?"

"None whatever."

I left him suddenly. I felt I was producing a bad impression, but with my double down there it was most trying to be on deck. And it was almost as trying to be below. Altogether a nerve-trying situation. But on the whole I felt less torn in two when I was with him. There was no one in the whole ship whom I dared take into my confidence. Since the hands had got to know his story, it would have been impossible to pass him off for anyone else, and an accidental discovery was to be dreaded now more than ever. . . .

The steward being engaged in laying the table for dinner, we could talk only with our eyes when I first went down. Later in the afternoon we had a cautious try at whispering. The Sunday quietness of the ship was against us; the stillness of air and water around her was against us; the elements, the men were against us—everything was against us in our secret partnership; time itself—for this could not go on forever. The very trust in Providence was, I suppose, denied to his guilt. Shall I confess that this thought cast me down very much? And as to the chapter of accidents which counts for so much in the book of success, I could only hope that it was closed. For what favorable accident could be expected?

"Did you hear everything?" were my first words as soon as we took up our position side by side, leaning over my bed-place.

He had. And the proof of it was his earnest whisper, "The man told you he hardly dared to give the order."

I understood the reference to be to that saving foresail.

"Yes. He was afraid of it being lost in the setting."

"I assure you he never gave the order. He may think he did, but he never gave it. He stood there with me on the break of the poop after the maintopsail blew away, and whimpered about our last hope—positively whimpered about it and nothing else—and the night coming on! To hear one's skipper go on like that in such weather was enough to drive any fellow out of his mind. It worked me up into a sort of desperation. I just took it into my own

hands and went away from him, boiling, and—.
But what's the use telling you? *You* know! . . .
Do you think that if I had not been pretty fierce
with them I should have got the men to do
anything? Not it! The bosun perhaps? Perhaps!
It wasn't a heavy sea—it was a sea gone mad!
I suppose the end of the world will be something like that; and a man may have the heart
to see it coming once and be done with it—but
to have to face it day after day—I don't blame
anybody. I was precious little better than the
rest. Only—I was an officer of that old coal-
wagon, anyhow—"

"I quite understand," I conveyed that sincere assurance into his ear. He was out of
breath with whispering; I could hear him pant
slightly. It was all very simple. The same
strung-up force which had given twenty-four
men a chance, at least, for their lives, had, in
a sort of recoil, crushed an unworthy mutinous
existence.

But I had no leisure to weigh the merits of
the matter—footsteps in the saloon, a heavy
knock. "There's enough wind to get under way
with, sir." Here was the call of a new claim upon
my thoughts and even upon my feelings.

"Turn the hands up," I cried through the
door. "I'll be on deck directly."

I was going out to make the acquaintance
of my ship. Before I left the cabin our eyes
met—the eyes of the only two strangers on
board. I pointed to the recessed part where the
little campstool awaited him and laid my finger
on my lips. He made a gesture—somewhat
vague—a little mysterious, accompanied by a
faint smile, as if of regret.

This is not the place to enlarge upon the
sensations of a man who feels for the first time
a ship move under his feet to his own independent word. In my case they were not un-
alloyed. I was not wholly alone with my
command; for there was that stranger in my
cabin. Or rather, I was not completely and
wholly with her. Part of me was absent. That
mental feeling of being in two places at once
affected me physically as if the mood of secrecy
had penetrated my very soul. Before an hour
had elapsed since the ship had begun to move,
having occasion to ask the mate (he stood by
my side) to take a compass bearing of the
Pagoda, I caught myself reaching up to his
ear in whispers. I say I caught myself, but
enough had escaped to startle the man. I can't

describe it otherwise than by saying that he
shied. A grave, preoccupied manner, as though
he were in possession of some perplexing intelligence, did not leave him henceforth. A little
later I moved away from the rail to look at
the compass with such a stealthy gait that the
helmsman noticed it—and I could not help
noticing the unusual roundness of his eyes.
These are trifling instances, though it's to no
commander's advantage to be suspected of
ludicrous eccentricities. But I was also more
seriously affected. There are to a seaman certain words, gestures, that should in given conditions come as naturally, as instinctively as the
winking of a menaced eye. A certain order
should spring on to his lips without thinking;
a certain sign should get itself made, so to
speak, without reflection. But all unconscious
alertness had abandoned me. I had to make an
effort of will to recall myself back (from the
cabin) to the conditions of the moment. I felt
that I was appearing an irresolute commander
to those people who were watching me more or
less critically.

And, besides, there were the scares. On the
second day out, for instance, coming off the
deck in the afternoon (I had straw slippers on
my bare feet) I stopped at the open pantry
door and spoke to the steward. He was doing
something there with his back to me. At the
sound of my voice he nearly jumped out of his
skin, as the saying is, and incidentally broke
a cup.

"What on earth's the matter with you?" I
asked, astonished.

He was extremely confused. "Beg pardon,
sir. I made sure you were in your cabin."

"You see I wasn't."

"No, sir. I could have sworn I had heard
you moving in there not a moment ago. It's
most extraordinary . . . very sorry, sir."

I passed on with an inward shudder. I was
so identified with my secret double that I did
not even mention the fact in those scanty, fearful whispers we exchanged. I suppose he had
made some slight noise of some kind or other.
It would have been miraculous if he hadn't at
one time or another. And yet, haggard as he
appeared, he looked always perfectly self-con-
trolled, more than calm—almost invulnerable.
On my suggestion he remained almost entirely
in the bathroom, which, upon the whole, was
the safest place. There could be really no

shadow of an excuse for anyone ever wanting to go in there, once the steward had done with it. It was a very tiny place. Sometimes he reclined on the floor, his legs bent, his head sustained on one elbow. At others I would find him on the campstool, sitting in his gray sleeping suit and with his cropped dark hair like a patient, unmoved convict. At night I would smuggle him into my bed-place, and we would whisper together, with the regular footfalls of the officer of the watch passing and repassing over our heads. It was an infinitely miserable time. It was lucky that some tins of fine preserves were stowed in a locker in my stateroom; hard bread I could always get hold of; and so he lived on stewed chicken, paté de foie gras, asparagus, cooked oysters, sardines—on all sorts of abominable sham delicacies out of tins. My early morning coffee he always drank; and it was all I dared do for him in that respect.

Every day there was the horrible maneuvering to go through so that my room and then the bathroom should be done in the usual way. I came to hate the sight of the steward, to abhor the voice of that harmless man. I felt that it was he who would bring on the disaster of discovery. It hung like a sword over our heads.

The fourth day out, I think (we were then working down the east side of the Gulf of Siam, tack for tack, in light winds and smooth water) —the fourth day, I say, of this miserable juggling with the unavoidable, as we sat at our evening meal, that man, whose slightest movement I dreaded, after putting down the dishes ran upon deck busily. This could not be dangerous. Presently he came down again; and then it appeared that he had remembered a coat of mine which I had thrown over a rail to dry after having been wetted in a shower which had passed over the ship in the afternoon. Sitting stolidly at the head of the table I became terrified at the sight of the garment on his arm. Of course he made for my door. There was no time to lose.

"Steward," I thundered. My nerves were so shaken that I could not govern my voice and conceal my agitation. This was the sort of thing that made my terrifically whiskered mate tap his forehead with his forefinger. I had detected him using that gesture while talking on deck with a confidential air to the carpenter. It was too far to hear a word, but I had no doubt that this pantomime could only refer to the strange new captain.

"Yes, sir," the pale-faced steward turned resignedly to me. It was this maddening course of being shouted at, checked without rhyme or reason, arbitrarily chased out of my cabin, suddenly called into it, sent flying out of his pantry on incomprehensible errands, that accounted for the growing wretchedness of his expression.

"Where are you going with that coat?"

"To your room, sir."

"Is there another shower coming?"

"I'm sure I don't know, sir. Shall I go up again and see, sir?"

"No! never mind."

My object was attained, as of course my other self in there would have heard everything that passed. During this interlude my two officers never raised their eyes off their respective plates; but the lip of that confounded cub, the second mate, quivered visibly.

I expected the steward to hook my coat on and come out at once. He was very slow about it; but I dominated my nervousness sufficiently not to shout after him. Suddenly I became aware (it could be heard plainly enough) that the fellow for some reason or other was opening the door of the bathroom. It was the end. The place was literally not big enough to swing a cat in. My voice died in my throat and I went stony all over. I expected to hear a yell of surprise and terror, and made a movement, but had not the strength to get on my legs. Everything remained still. Had my second self taken the poor wretch by the throat? I don't know what I would have done next moment if I had not seen the steward come out of my room, close the door, and then stand quietly by the sideboard.

Saved, I thought. But, no! Lost! Gone! He was gone!

I laid my knife and fork down and leaned back in my chair. My head swam. After a while, when sufficiently recovered to speak in a steady voice, I instructed my mate to put the ship round at eight o'clock himself.

"I won't come on deck," I went on. "I think I'll turn in, and unless the wind shifts I don't want to be disturbed before midnight. I feel a bit seedy."

"You did look middling bad a little while ago," the chief mate remarked without showing any great concern.

They both went out, and I stared at the steward clearing the table. There was nothing to be read on that wretched man's face. But why did he avoid my eyes I asked myself. Then I thought I should like to hear the sound of his voice.

"Steward!"

"Sir!" Startled as usual.

"Where did you hang up that coat?"

"In the bathroom, sir." The usual anxious tone. "It's not quite dry yet, sir."

For some time longer I sat in the cuddy. Had my double vanished as he had come? But of his coming there was an explanation, whereas his disappearance would be inexplicable. . . . I went slowly into my dark room, shut the door, lighted the lamp, and for a time dared not turn round. When at last I did I saw him standing bolt upright in the narrow recessed part. It would not be true to say I had a shock, but an irresistible doubt of his bodily existence flitted through my mind. Can it be, I asked myself, that he is not visible to other eyes than mine? It was like being haunted. Motionless, with a grave face, he raised his hands slightly at me in a gesture which meant clearly, "Heavens! what a narrow escape!" Narrow indeed. I think I had come creeping quietly as near insanity as any man who has not actually gone over the border. That gesture restrained me, so to speak.

The mate with the terrific whiskers was now putting the ship on the other tack. In the moment of profound silence which follows upon the hands going to their stations I heard on the poop his raised voice: "Hard alee!" and the distant shout of the order repeated on the maindeck. The sails, in that light breeze, made but a faint fluttering noise. It ceased. The ship was coming round slowly; I held my breath in the renewed stillness of expectation; one wouldn't have thought that there was a single living soul on her decks. A sudden brisk shout, "Mainsail haul!" broke the spell, and in the noisy cries and rush overhead of the men running away with the main brace we two, down in my cabin, came together in our usual position by the bed-place.

He did not wait for my question. "I heard him fumbling here and just managed to squat myself down in the bath," he whispered to me. "The fellow only opened the door and put his arm in to hang the coat up. All the same—"

"I never thought of that," I whispered back, even more appalled than before at the closeness of the shave, and marveling at that something unyielding in his character which was carrying him through so finely. There was no agitation in his whisper. Whoever was being driven distracted, it was not he. He was sane. And the proof of his sanity was continued when he took up the whispering again.

"It would never do for me to come to life again."

It was something that a ghost might have said. But what he was alluding to was his old captain's reluctant admission of the theory of suicide. It would obviously serve his turn—if I had understood at all the view which seemed to govern the unalterable purpose of his action.

"You must maroon me as soon as ever you can get amongst these islands off the Cambodje shore," he went on.

"Maroon you! We are not living in a boy's adventure tale," I protested. His scornful whispering took me up.

"We aren't indeed! There's nothing of a boy's tale in this. But there's nothing else for it. I want no more. You don't suppose I am afraid of what can be done to me? Prison or gallows or whatever they may please. But you don't see me coming back to explain such things to an old fellow in a wig and twelve respectable tradesmen, do you? What can they know whether I am guilty or not—or of *what* I am guilty, either? That's my affair. What does the Bible say? 'Driven off the face of the earth.' Very well. I am off the face of the earth now. As I came at night so I shall go."

"Impossible!" I murmured. "You can't."

"Can't? . . . Not naked like a soul on the Day of Judgment. I shall freeze on to this sleeping suit. The Last Day is not yet—and . . . you have understood thoroughly. Didn't you?"

I felt suddenly ashamed of myself. I may say truly that I understood—and my hesitation in letting that man swim away from my ship's side had been a mere sham sentiment, a sort of cowardice.

"It can't be done now till next night," I breathed out. "The ship is on the offshore tack and the wind may fail us."

"As long as I know that you understand," he whispered. "But of course you do. It's a great satisfaction to have got somebody to understand. You seem to have been there on purpose." And in the same whisper, as if we two whenever we talked had to say things to each other which were not fit for the world to hear, he added, "It's very wonderful."

We remained side by side talking in our secret way—but sometimes silent or just exchanging a whispered word or two at long intervals. And as usual he stared through the port. A breath of wind came now and again into our faces. The ship might have been moored in dock, so gently and on an even keel she slipped through the water, that did not murmur even at our passage, shadowy and silent like a phantom sea.

At midnight I went on deck, and to my mate's great surprise put the ship round on the other tack. His terrible whiskers flitted round me in silent criticism. I certainly should not have done it if it had been only a question of getting out of that sleepy gulf as quickly as possible. I believe he told the second mate, who relieved him, that it was a great want of judgment. The other only yawned. That intolerable cub shuffled about so sleepily and lolled against the rails in such a slack, improper fashion that I came down on him sharply.

"Aren't you properly awake yet?"

"Yes, sir! I am awake."

"Well, then, be good enough to hold yourself as if you were. And keep a lookout. If there's any current we'll be closing with some islands before daylight."

The east side of the gulf is fringed with islands, some solitary, others in groups. On the blue background of the high coast they seem to float on silvery patches of calm water, arid and gray, or dark green and rounded like clumps of evergreen bushes, with the larger ones, a mile or two long, showing the outlines of ridges, ribs of gray rock under the dark mantle of matted leafage. Unknown to trade, to travel, almost to geography, the manner of life they harbor is an unsolved secret. There must be villages—settlements of fishermen at least—on the largest of them, and some communication with the world is probably kept up by native craft. But all that forenoon, as we headed for them, fanned along by the faintest of breezes, I saw no sign of man or canoe in the field of the telescope I kept on pointing at the scattered group.

At noon I gave no orders for a change of course, and the mate's whiskers became much concerned and seemed to be offering themselves unduly to my notice. At last I said:

"I am going to stand right in. Quite in—as far as I can take her."

The stare of extreme surprise imparted an air of ferocity also to his eyes, and he looked truly terrific for a moment.

"We're not doing well in the middle of the gulf," I continued, casually. "I am going to look for the land breezes tonight."

"Bless my soul! Do you mean, sir, in the dark amongst the lot of all them islands and reefs and shoals?"

"Well—if there are any regular land breezes at all on this coast one must get close inshore to find them, mustn't one?"

"Bless my soul!" he exclaimed again under his breath. All that afternoon he wore a dreamy, contemplative appearance which in him was a mark of perplexity. After dinner I went into my stateroom as if I meant to take some rest. There we two bent our dark heads over a half-unrolled chart lying on my bed.

"There," I said. "It's got to be Koh-ring. I've been looking at it ever since sunrise. It has got two hills and a low point. It must be inhabited. And on the coast opposite there is what looks like the mouth of a biggish river—with some town, no doubt, not far up. It's the best chance for you that I can see."

"Anything. Koh-ring let it be."

He looked thoughtfully at the chart as if surveying chances and distances from a lofty height—and following with his eyes his own figure wandering on the blank land of Cochin-China, and then passing off that piece of paper clean out of sight into uncharted regions. And it was as if the ship had two captains to plan her course for her. I had been so worried and restless running up and down that I had not had the patience to dress that day. I had remained in my sleeping suit, with straw slippers and a soft floppy hat. The closeness of the heat in the gulf had been most oppressive, and the crew were used to see me wandering in that airy attire.

"She will clear the south point as she heads now," I whispered into his ear. "Goodness only knows when, though, but certainly after dark. I'll edge her in to half a mile, as far as I may be able to judge in the dark—"

"Be careful," he murmured, warningly—and I realized suddenly that all my future, the only future for which I was fit, would perhaps go irretrievably to pieces in any mishap to my first command.

I could not stop a moment longer in the room. I motioned him to get out of sight and made my way on the poop. That unplayful cub had the watch. I walked up and down for a while thinking things out, then beckoned him over.

"Send a couple of hands to open the two quarter-deck ports," I said, mildly.

He actually had the impudence, or else so forgot himself in his wonder at such an incomprehensible order, as to repeat:

"Open the quarter-deck ports! What for, sir?"

"The only reason you need concern yourself about is because I tell you to do so. Have them open wide and fastened properly."

He reddened and went off, but I believe made some jeering remark to the carpenter as to the sensible practice of ventilating a ship's quarter-deck. I know he popped into the mate's cabin to impart the fact to him because the whiskers came on deck, as it were by chance, and stole glances at me from below—for signs of lunacy or drunkenness, I suppose.

A little before supper, feeling more restless than ever, I rejoined, for a moment, my second self. And to find him sitting so quietly was surprising, like something against nature, inhuman.

I developed my plan in a hurried whisper.

"I shall stand in as close as I dare and then put her round. I shall presently find means to smuggle you out of here into the sail locker, which communicates with the lobby. But there is an opening, a sort of square for hauling the sails out which gives straight on the quarter-deck and which is never closed in fine weather, so as to give air to the sails. When the ship's way is deadened in stays and all the hands are aft at the main braces you shall have a clear road to slip out and get overboard through the open quarter-deck port. I've had them both fastened up. Use a rope's end to lower yourself into the water so as to avoid a splash—you know. It could be heard and cause some beastly complication."

He kept silent for a while, then whispered, "I understand."

"I won't be there to see you go," I began with an effort. "The rest . . . I only hope I have understood, too."

"You have. From first to last," and for the first time there seemed to be a faltering, something strained in his whisper. He caught hold of my arm, but the ringing of the supper bell made me start. He didn't, though; he only released his grip.

After supper I didn't come below again till well past eight o'clock. The faint, steady breeze was loaded with dew; and the wet, darkened sails held all there was of propelling power in it. The night, clear and starry, sparkled darkly, and the opaque, lightless patches shifting slowly against the low stars were the drifting islets. On the port bow there was a big one more distant and shadowily imposing by the great space of sky it eclipsed.

On opening the door I had a back view of my very own self looking at a chart. He had come out of the recess and was standing near the table.

"Quite dark enough," I whispered.

He stepped back and leaned against my bed with a level, quiet glance. I sat on the couch. We had nothing to say to each other. Over our heads the officer of the watch moved here and there. Then I heard him move quickly. I knew what that meant. He was making for the companion; and presently his voice was outside my door.

"We are drawing in pretty fast, sir. Land looks rather close."

"Very well," I answered. "I am coming on deck directly."

I waited till he was gone out of the cuddy, then rose. My double moved too. The time had come to exchange our last whispers, for neither of us was ever to hear each other's natural voice.

"Look here!" I opened a drawer and took out three sovereigns. "Take this, anyhow. I've got six and I'd give you the lot, only I must keep a little money to buy some fruit and vegetables for the crew from native boats as we go through Sunda Straits."

He shook his head.

"Take it," I urged him, whispering desperately. "No one can tell what—"

He smiled and slapped meaningly the only pocket of the sleeping jacket. It was not safe, certainly. But I produced a large old silk handkerchief of mine, and tying the three pieces of gold in a corner, pressed it on him. He was touched, I suppose, because he took it at last and tied it quickly round his waist under the jacket, on his bare skin.

Our eyes met; several seconds elapsed, till, our glances still mingled, I extended my hand and turned the lamp out. Then I passed through the cuddy, leaving the door of my room wide open. . . . "Steward!"

He was still lingering in the pantry in the greatness of his zeal, giving a rub-up to a plated cruet stand the last thing before going to bed. Being careful not to wake up the mate, whose room was opposite, I spoke in an undertone.

He looked round anxiously. "Sir!"

"Can you get me a little hot water from the galley?"

"I am afraid, sir, the galley fire's been out for some time now."

"Go and see."

He fled up the stairs.

"Now," I whispered, loudly, into the saloon —too loudly, perhaps, but I was afraid I couldn't make a sound. He was by my side in an instant—the double captain slipped past the stairs—through the tiny dark passage . . . a sliding door. We were in the sail locker, scrambling on our knees over the sails. A sudden thought struck me. I saw myself wandering barefooted, bareheaded, the sun beating on my dark poll. I snatched off my floppy hat and tried hurriedly in the dark to ram it on my other self. He dodged and fended off silently. I wonder what he thought had come to me before he understood and suddenly desisted. Our hands met gropingly, lingered united in a steady, motionless clasp for a second. . . . No word was breathed by either of us when they separated.

I was standing quietly by the pantry door when the steward returned.

"Sorry, sir. Kettle barely warm. Shall I light the spirit lamp?"

"Never mind."

I came out on deck slowly. It was now a matter of conscience to shave the land as close as possible—for now he must go overboard whenever the ship was put in stays. Must! There could be no going back for him. After a moment I walked over to leeward and my heart flew into my mouth at the nearness of the land on the bow. Under any other circumstances I would not have held on a minute longer. The second mate had followed me anxiously.

I looked on till I felt I could command my voice.

"She will weather," I said then in a quiet tone.

"Are you going to try that, sir?" he stammered out incredulously.

I took no notice of him and raised my tone just enough to be heard by the helmsman.

"Keep her good full."

"Good full, sir."

The wind fanned my cheek, the sails slept, the world was silent. The strain of watching the dark loom of the land grow bigger and denser was too much for me. I had shut my eyes—because the ship must go closer. She must! The stillness was intolerable. Were we standing still?

When I opened my eyes the second view started my heart with a thump. The black southern hill of Koh-ring seemed to hang right over the ship like a towering fragment of the everlasting night. On that enormous mass of blackness there was not a gleam to be seen, not a sound to be heard. It was gliding irresistibly toward us and yet seemed already within reach of the hand. I saw the vague figures of the watch grouped in the waist, gazing in awed silence.

"Are you going on, sir?" inquired an unsteady voice at my elbow.

I ignored it. I had to go on.

"Keep her full. Don't check her way. That won't do now," I said warningly.

"I can't see the sails very well," the helmsman answered me, in strange, quavering tones.

Was she close enough? Already she was, I won't say in the shadow of the land, but in the very blackness of it, already swallowed up as it were, gone too close to be recalled, gone from me altogether.

"Give the mate a call," I said to the young man who stood at my elbow as still as death. "And turn all hands up."

My tone had a borrowed loudness reverberated from the height of the land. Several voices cried out together: "We are all on deck, sir."

Then stillness again, with the great shadow gliding closer, towering higher, without a light, without a sound. Such a hush had fallen on the ship that she might have been a bark of the dead floating in slowly under the very gate of Erebus.[33]

"My God! Where are we?"

It was the mate moaning at my elbow. He was thunderstruck, and as it were deprived of the moral support of his whiskers. He clapped his hands and absolutely cried out, "Lost!"

"Be quiet," I said sternly.

He lowered his tone, but I saw the shadowy gesture of his despair. "What are we doing here?"

"Looking for the land wind."

He made as if to tear his hair, and addressed me recklessly.

"She will never get out. You have done it, sir. I knew it'd end in something like this. She will never weather, and you are too close now to stay. She'll drift ashore before she's round. O my God!"

I caught his arm as he was raising it to batter his poor devoted head, and shook it violently.

"She's ashore already," he wailed, trying to tear himself away.

"Is she? . . . Keep good full there!"

"Good full, sir," cried the helmsman in a frightened, thin, childlike voice.

I hadn't let go the mate's arm and went on shaking it. "Ready about, do you hear? You go forward"—shake—"and stop there"—shake—"and hold your noise"—shake—"and see these head sheets properly overhauled"—shake, shake—shake.

And all the time I dared not look toward the land lest my heart should fail me. I released my grip at last and he ran forward as if fleeing for dear life.

I wondered what my double there in the sail locker thought of this commotion. He was able to hear everything—and perhaps he was able to understand why, on my conscience, it had to be thus close—no less. My first order, "Hard alee!" re-echoed ominously under the towering shadow of Koh-ring as if I had shouted in a mountain gorge. And then I watched the land intently. In that smooth water and light wind it was impossible to feel the ship coming-to. No! I could not feel her. And my second self was making now ready to slip out and lower himself overboard. Perhaps he was gone already . . . ?

The great black mass brooding over our very

mastheads began to pivot away from the ship's side silently. And now I forgot the secret stranger ready to depart, and remembered only that I was a total stranger to the ship. I did not know her. Would she do it? How was she to be handled?

I swung the mainyard and waited helplessly. She was perhaps stopped, and her very fate hung in the balance, with the black mass of Koh-ring like the gate of the everlasting night towering over her taffrail. What would she do now? Had she way on her yet? I stepped to the side swiftly, and on the shadowy water I could see nothing except a faint phosphorescent flash revealing the glassy smoothness of the sleeping surface. It was impossible to tell—and I had not learned yet the feel of my ship. Was she moving? What I needed was something easily seen, a piece of paper, which I could throw overboard and watch. I had nothing on me. To run down for it I didn't dare. There was no time. All at once my strained, yearning stare distinguished a white object floating within a yard of the ship's side. White on the black water. A phosphorescent flash passed under it. What was that thing? . . . I recognized my own floppy hat. It must have fallen off his head . . . and he didn't bother. Now I had what I wanted—the saving mark for my eyes. But I hardly thought of my other self, now gone from the ship, to be hidden forever from all friendly faces, to be a fugitive and a vagabond on the earth, with no brand of the curse on his sane forehead to stay a slaying hand . . . too proud to explain.

And I watched the hat—the expression of my sudden pity for his mere flesh. It had been meant to save his homeless head from the dangers of the sun. And now—behold—it was saving the ship, by serving me for a mark to help out the ignorance of my strangeness. Ha! It was drifting forward, warning me just in time that the ship had gathered sternway.

"Shift the helm," I said in a low voice to the seaman standing still like a statue.

The man's eyes glistened wildly in the binnacle light as he jumped round to the other side and spun round the wheel.

I walked to the break of the poop. On the overshadowed deck all hands stood by the forebraces waiting for my order. The stars ahead seemed to be gliding from right to left. And all was so still in the world that I heard the quiet

---

[33] The dismal place through which souls must pass to get to Hades.

remark "She's round," passed in a tone of intense relief between two seamen.

"Let go and haul."

The foreyards ran round with a great noise, amidst cheery cries. And now the frightful whiskers made themselves heard giving various orders. Already the ship was drawing ahead. And I was alone with her. Nothing! no one in the world should stand now between us, throwing a shadow on the way of silent knowledge and mute affection, the perfect communion of a seaman with his first command.

Walking to the taffrail, I was in time to make out, on the very edge of a darkness thrown by a towering black mass like the very gateway of Erebus—yes, I was in time to catch an evanescent glimpse of my white hat left behind to mark the spot where the secret sharer of my cabin and of my thoughts, as though he were my second self, had lowered himself into the water to take his punishment: a free man, a proud swimmer striking out for a new destiny.

## Henry James
# THE BEAST IN THE JUNGLE

### I

What determined the speech that startled him in the course of their encounter scarcely matters, being probably but some words spoken by himself quite without intention—spoken as they lingered and slowly moved together after their renewal of acquaintance. He had been conveyed by friends, an hour or two before, to the house at which she was staying; the party of visitors at the other house, of whom he was one, and thanks to whom it was his theory, as always, that he was lost in the crowd, had been invited over to luncheon. There had been after luncheon much dispersal, all in the interest of the original motive, a view of Weatherend itself and the fine things, intrinsic features, pictures, heirlooms, treasures of all the arts, that made the place almost famous; and the great rooms were so numerous

THE BEAST IN THE JUNGLE: Reprinted from *The Better Sort,* by Henry James. Copyright, 1903, by Charles Scribner's Sons, 1931, by Henry James. Used by permission of the publishers.

that guests could wander at their will, hang back from the principal group, and, in cases where they took such matters with the last seriousness, give themselves up to mysterious appreciations and measurements. There were persons to be observed, singly or in couples, bending toward objects in out-of-the-way corners with their hands on their knees and their heads nodding quite as with the emphasis of an excited sense of smell. When they were two they either mingled their sounds of ecstasy or melted into silences of even deeper import, so that there were aspects of the occasion that gave it for Marcher much the air of the "look round," previous to a sale highly advertised, that excites or quenches, as may be, the dream of acquisition. The dream of acquisition at Weatherend would have had to be wild indeed, and John Marcher found himself, among such suggestions, disconcerted almost equally by the presence of those who knew too much and by that of those who knew nothing. The great rooms caused so much poetry and history to press upon him that he needed to wander apart to feel in a proper relation with them, though his doing so was not, as happened, like the gloating of some of his companions, to be compared to the movements of a dog sniffing a cupboard. It had an issue promptly enough in a direction that was not to have been calculated.

It led, in short, in the course of the October afternoon, to his closer meeting with May Bartram, whose face, a reminder, yet not quite a remembrance, as they sat, much separated, at a very long table, had begun merely by troubling him rather pleasantly. It affected him as the sequel of something of which he had lost the beginning. He knew it, and for the time quite welcomed it, as a continuation, but didn't know what it continued, which was an interest, or an amusement, the greater as he was also somehow aware—yet without a direct sign from her—that the young woman herself had not lost the thread. She had not lost it, but she wouldn't give it back to him, he saw, without some putting forth of his hand for it; and he not only saw that, but saw several things more, things odd enough in the light of the fact that at the moment some accident of grouping brought them face to face he was still merely fumbling with the idea that any contact between them in the past would have had no importance. If it had had no importance he scarcely knew why his actual impression of her should so seem to have so much; the answer to which, however, was that in such a life as they all appeared to be leading for the moment one could but take things as they came. He was satisfied, without in the least being able to say why, that this young lady might roughly have ranked in the house as a poor relation; satisfied also that she was not there on a brief visit, but was more or less a part of the establishment—almost a working, a remunerated part. Didn't she enjoy at periods a protection that she paid for by helping, among other services, to show the place and explain it, deal with the tiresome people, answer questions about the dates of the buildings, the styles of the furniture, the authorship of the pictures, the favourite haunts of the ghost? It wasn't that she looked as if you could have given her shillings—it was impossible to look less so. Yet when she finally drifted toward him, distinctly handsome, though ever so much older—older than when he had seen her before—it might have been as an effect of her guessing that he had, within the couple of hours, devoted more imagination to her than to all the others put together, and had thereby penetrated to a kind of truth that the others were too stupid for. She *was* there on harder terms than anyone; she was there as a consequence of things suffered, in one way and another, in the interval of years; and she remembered him very much as she was remembered—only a good deal better.

By the time they at last thus came to speech they were alone in one of the rooms—remarkable for a fine portrait over the chimney-place—out of which their friends had passed, and the charm of it was that even before they had spoken they had practically arranged with each other to stay behind for talk. The charm, happily, was in other things too; it was partly in there being scarce a spot at Weatherend with something to stay behind for. It was in the way the autumn day looked into the high windows as it waned; in the way the red light, breaking at the close from under a low, sombre sky, reached out in a long shaft and played over old wainscots, old tapestry, old gold, old colour. It was most of all perhaps in the way she came to him as if, since she had been turned on to deal with the simpler sort, he might, should he choose to keep the whole thing down, just take her mild attention for a part of her general business. As soon as he heard her voice, however, the gap was filled up and the missing link supplied; the slight irony he divined in her attitude lost its advantage. He almost jumped at it to get there before her. "I met you years and years ago in Rome. I remember all about it." She confessed to disappointment—she had been so sure he didn't; and to prove how well he did he began to pour forth the particular recollections that popped up as he called for them. Her face and her voice, all at his service now, worked the miracle—the impression operating like the torch of a lamplighter who touches into flame, one by one, a long row of gas jets. Marcher flattered himself that the illumination was brilliant, yet he was really still more pleased on her showing him, with amusement, that in his haste to make everything right he had got most things rather wrong. It hadn't been at Rome—it had been at Naples; and it hadn't been seven years before—it had been more nearly ten. She hadn't been either with her uncle and aunt, but with her mother and her brother; in addition to which it was not with the Pembles that *he* had been, but with the Boyers, coming down in their company from Rome—a point on which she insisted, a little to his confusion, and as to which she had her evidence in hand. The Boyers she had known, but she didn't know the Pembles, though she had heard of them, and it was the people he was with who had made them acquainted. The incident of the thunderstorm that had raged round them with such violence as to drive them for refuge into an excavation—this incident had not occurred at the Palace of the Cæsars, but at Pompeii, on an occasion when they had been present there at an important find.

He accepted her amendments, he enjoyed her corrections, though the moral of them was, she pointed out, that he *really* didn't remember the least thing about her; and he only felt it as a drawback that when all was made comfortable to the truth there didn't appear much of anything left. They lingered together still, she neglecting her office—for from the moment he was so clever she had no proper right to him—and both neglecting the house, just waiting as to see if a memory or two more wouldn't again breathe upon them. It had not taken them many minutes, after all, to put down on the table, like the cards of a pack, those that constituted their respective hands; only what came out was that the pack was unfortunately not perfect—that the past, invoked, invited, encouraged, could give them, naturally, no more than it had. It had made them meet—her at twenty, him at twenty-five; but nothing was so strange, they seemed to say to each other, as that, while so occupied, it hadn't done a little more for them. They looked at each other as with the feeling of an occasion missed; the present one would have been so much better if the other, in the far distance, in the foreign land, hadn't been so stupidly meagre. There weren't, apparently, all counted, more than a dozen little old things that had succeeded in coming to pass between them; trivialities of youth, simplicities of fresh-ness, stupidities of ignorance, small possible germs, but too deeply buried—too deeply (didn't it seem?) to sprout after so many years. Marcher said to himself that he ought to have rendered her some service—saved her from a capsized boat in the Bay, or at least recovered her dressing-bag, filched from her cab, in the streets of Naples, by a lazzarone [34] with a sti-letto. Or it would have been nice if he could have been taken with fever, alone, at his hotel, and she could have come to look after him, to write to his people, to drive him out in convalescence. *Then* they would be in possession of the some-thing or other that their actual show seemed to lack. It yet somehow presented itself, this show, as too good to be spoiled; so that they were re-duced for a few minutes more to wondering a little helplessly why—since they seemed to know a certain number of the same people—their reunion had been so long averted. They didn't use that name for it, but their delay from minute to minute to join the others was a kind of confession that they didn't quite want it to be a failure. Their attempted supposition of rea-sons for their not having met but showed how little they knew of each other. There came in fact a moment when Marcher felt a positive pang. It was vain to pretend she was an old friend, for all the communities were wanting, in spite of which it was as an old friend that he saw she would have suited him. He had new ones enough—was surrounded with them, for in-stance, at that hour at the other house; as a new one he probably wouldn't have so much as no-ticed her. He would have liked to invent some-thing, get her to make-believe with him that

___
[34] Ruffian.

some passage of a romantic or critical kind *had* originally occurred. He was really almost reach-ing out in imagination—as against time—for something that would do, and saying to himself that if it didn't come this new incident would simply and rather awkwardly close. They would separate, and now for no second or for no third chance. They would have tried and not suc-ceeded. Then it was, just at the turn, as he afterwards made it out to himself, that, every-thing else failing, she herself decided to take up the case and, as it were, save the situation. He felt as soon as she spoke that she had been consciously keeping back what she said and hoping to get on without it; a scruple in her that immensely touched him when, by the end of three or four minutes more, he was able to measure it. What she brought out, at any rate, quite cleared the air and supplied the link—the link it was such a mystery he should frivolously have managed to lose.

"You know you told me something that I've never forgotten and that again and again has made me think of you since; it was that tre-mendously hot day when we went to Sorrento, across the bay, for the breeze. What I allude to was what you said to me, on the way back, as we sat, under the awning of the boat, enjoying the cool. Have you forgotten?"

He had forgotten, and he was even more sur-prised than ashamed. But the great thing was that he saw it was no vulgar reminder of any "sweet" speech. The vanity of women had long memories, but she was making no claim on him of a compliment or a mistake. With another woman, a totally different one, he might have feared the recall of possibly even some imbecile "offer." So, in having to say that he had indeed forgotten, he was conscious rather of a loss than of a gain; he already saw an interest in the matter of her reference. "I try to think—but I give it up. Yet I remember the Sorrento day."

"I'm not very sure you do," May Bartram after a moment said; "and I'm not very sure I ought to want you to. It's dreadful to bring a person back, at any time, to what he was ten years before. If you've lived away from it," she smiled, "so much the better."

"Ah, if *you* haven't why should I?" he asked.

"Lived away, you mean, from what I myself was?"

"From what *I* was. I was of course an ass," Marcher went on; "but I would rather know from you just the sort of ass I was than—from the moment you have something in your mind—not know anything."

Still, however, she hesitated. "But if you've completely ceased to be that sort—?"

"Why, I can then just so all the more bear to know. Besides, perhaps I haven't."

"Perhaps. Yet if you haven't," she added, "I should suppose you would remember. Not indeed that *I* in the least connect with my impression the invidious name you use. If I had only thought you foolish," she explained, "the thing I speak of wouldn't so have remained with me. It was about yourself." She waited, as if it might come to him; but as, only meeting her eyes in wonder, he gave no sign, she burnt her ships. "Has it ever happened?"

Then it was that, while he continued to stare, a light broke for him and the blood slowly came to his face, which began to burn with recognition. "Do you mean I told you—?" But he faltered, lest what came to him shouldn't be right, lest he should only give himself away.

"It was something about yourself that it was natural one shouldn't forget—that is if one remembered you at all. That's why I ask you," she smiled, "if the thing you then spoke of has ever come to pass?"

Oh, then he saw, but he was lost in wonder and found himself embarrassed. This, he also saw, made her sorry for him, as if her allusion had been a mistake. It took him but a moment, however, to feel that it had not been, much as it had been a surprise. After the first little shock of it her knowledge on the contrary began, even if rather strangely, to taste sweet to him. She was the only other person in the world then who would have it, and she had had it all these years, while the fact of his having so breathed his secret had unaccountably faded from him. No wonder they couldn't have met as if nothing had happened. "I judge," he finally said, "that I know what you mean. Only I had strangely enough lost the consciousness of having taken you so far into my confidence."

"Is it because you've taken so many others as well?"

"I've taken nobody. Not a creature since then."

"So that I'm the only person who knows?"

"The only person in the world."

"Well," she quickly replied, "I myself have never spoken. I've never, never repeated of you what you told me." She looked at him so that he perfectly believed her. Their eyes met over it in such a way that he was without a doubt. "And I never will."

She spoke with an earnestness that, as if almost excessive, put him at ease about her possible derision. Somehow the whole question was a new luxury to him—that is, from the moment she was in possession. If she didn't take the ironic view she clearly took the sympathetic, and that was what he had had, in all the long time, from no one whomsoever. What he felt was that he couldn't at present have begun to tell her and yet could profit perhaps exquisitely by the accident of having done so of old. "Please don't then. We're just right as it is."

"Oh, I am," she laughed, "if you are!" To which she added: "Then you do still feel in the same way?"

It was impossible for him not to take to himself that she was really interested, and it all kept coming as a sort of revelation. He had thought of himself so long as abominably alone, and, lo, he wasn't alone a bit. He hadn't been, it appeared, for an hour—since those moments on the Sorrento boat. It was *she* who had been, he seemed to see as he looked at her—she who had been made so by the graceless fact of his lapse of fidelity. To tell her what he had told her—what had it been but to ask something of her? something that she had given, in her charity, without his having, by a remembrance, by a return of the spirit, failing another encounter, so much as thanked her. What he had asked of her had been simply at first not to laugh at him. She had beautifully not done so for ten years, and she was not doing so now. So he had endless gratitude to make up. Only for that he must see just how he had figured to her. "What, exactly, was the account I gave—?"

"Of the way you did feel? Well, it was very simple. You said you had had from your earliest time, as the deepest thing within you, the sense of being kept for something rare and strange, possibly prodigious and terrible, that was sooner or later to happen to you, that you had in your bones the foreboding and the conviction of, and that would perhaps overwhelm you."

"Do you call that very simple?" John Marcher asked.

She thought a moment. "It was perhaps because I seemed, as you spoke, to understand it."

"You do understand it?" he eagerly asked.

Again she kept her kind eyes on him. "You still have the belief?"

"Oh!" he exclaimed helplessly. There was too much to say.

"Whatever it is to be," she clearly made out, "it hasn't yet come."

He shook his head in complete surrender now. "It hasn't yet come. Only, you know, it isn't anything I'm to *do*, to achieve in the world, to be distinguished or admired for. I'm not such an ass as *that*. It would be much better, no doubt, if I were."

"It's to be something you're merely to suffer?"

"Well, say to wait for—to have to meet, to face, to see suddenly break out in my life; possibly destroying all further consciousness, possibly annihilating me; possibly, on the other hand, only altering everything, striking at the root of all my world and leaving me to the consequences, however they shape themselves."

She took this in, but the light in her eyes continued for him not to be that of mockery. "Isn't what you describe perhaps but the expectation—or, at any rate, the sense of danger, familiar to so many people—of falling in love?"

John Marcher thought. "Did you ask me that before?"

"No—I wasn't so free-and-easy then. But it's what strikes me now."

"Of course," he said after a moment, "it strikes you. Of course it strikes *me*. Of course what's in store for me may be no more than that. The only thing is," he went on, "that I think that if it had been that, I should by this time know."

"Do you mean because you've *been* in love?" And then as he but looked at her in silence: "You've been in love, and it hasn't meant such a cataclysm, hasn't proved the great affair?"

"Here I am, you see. It hasn't been overwhelming."

"Then it hasn't been love," said May Bartram.

"Well, I at least thought it was. I took it for that— I've taken it till now. It was agreeable, it was delightful, it was miserable," he explained. "But it wasn't strange. It wasn't what *my* affair's to be."

"You want something all to yourself—something that nobody else knows or *has* known?"

"It isn't a question of what I 'want'—God knows I don't want anything. It's only a ques-

tion of the apprehension that haunts me—that I live with day by day."

He said this so lucidly and consistently that, visibly, it further imposed itself. If she had not been interested before she would have been interested now. "Is it a sense of coming violence?"

Evidently now too, again, he liked to talk of it. "I don't think of it as—when it does come—necessarily violent. I only think of it as natural and as of course, above all, unmistakable. I think of it simply as *the* thing. *The* thing will of itself appear natural."

"Then how will it appear strange?"

Marcher bethought himself. "It won't—to *me*."

"To whom then?"

"Well," he replied, smiling at last, "say to you."

"Oh then, I'm to be present?"

"Why, you *are* present—since you know."

"I see." She turned it over. "But I mean at the catastrophe."

At this, for a minute, their lightness gave way to their gravity; it was as if the long look they exchanged held them together. "It will only depend on yourself—if you'll watch with me."

"Are you afraid?" she asked.

"Don't leave me *now*," he went on.

"Are you afraid?" she repeated.

"Do you think me simply out of my mind?" he pursued instead of answering. "Do I merely strike you as a harmless lunatic?"

"No," said May Bartram. "I understand you. I believe you."

"You mean you feel how my obsession—poor old thing!—may correspond to some possible reality?"

"To some possible reality."

"Then you *will* watch with me?"

She hesitated, then for the third time put her question. "Are you afraid?"

"Did I tell you I was—at Naples?"

"No, you said nothing about it."

"Then I don't know. And I should *like* to know," said John Marcher. "You'll tell me yourself whether you think so. If you'll watch with me you'll see."

"Very good then." They had been moving by this time across the room, and at the door, before passing out, they paused as if for the full wind-up of their understanding. "I'll watch with you," said May Bartram.

## II

The fact that she "knew"—knew and yet neither chaffed him nor betrayed him—had in a short time begun to constitute between them a sensible bond, which became more marked when, within the year that followed their afternoon at Weatherend, the opportunities for meeting multiplied. The event that thus promoted these occasions was the death of the ancient lady, her great-aunt, under whose wing, since losing her mother, she had to such an extent found shelter, and who, though but the widowed mother of the new successor to the property, had succeeded—thanks to a high tone and a high temper—in not forfeiting the supreme position at the great house. The deposition of this personage arrived but with her death, which, followed by many changes, made in particular a difference for the young woman in whom Marcher's expert attention had recognised from the first a dependent with a pride that might ache though it didn't bristle. Nothing for a long time had made him easier than the thought that the aching must have been much soothed by Miss Bartram's now finding herself able to set up a small home in London. She had acquired property, to an amount that made that luxury just possible, under her aunt's extremely complicated will, and when the whole matter began to be straightened out, which indeed took time, she let him know that the happy issue was at last in view. He had seen her again before that day, both because she had more than once accompanied the ancient lady to town and because he had paid another visit to the friends who so conveniently made of Weatherend one of the charms of their own hospitality. These friends had taken him back there; he had achieved there again with Miss Bartram some quiet detachment; and he had in London succeeded in persuading her to more than one brief absence from her aunt. They went together, on these latter occasions, to the National Gallery and the South Kensington Museum, where, among vivid reminders, they talked of Italy at large—not now attempting to recover, as at first, the taste of their youth and their ignorance. That recovery, the first day at Weatherend, had served its purpose well, had given them quite enough; so that they were, to Marcher's sense, no longer hovering about the head-waters of their stream, but had felt their boat pushed sharply off and down the current.

They were literally afloat together; for our gentleman this was marked, quite as marked as that the fortunate cause of it was just the buried treasure of her knowledge. He had with his own hands dug up this little hoard, brought to light—that is to within reach of the dim day constituted by their discretions and privacies—the object of value the hiding-place of which he had, after putting it into the ground himself, so strangely, so long forgotten. The exquisite luck of having again just stumbled on the spot made him indifferent to any other question; he would doubtless have devoted more time to the odd accident of his lapse of memory if he had not been moved to devote so much to the sweetness, the comfort, as he felt, for the future, that this accident itself had helped to keep fresh. It had never entered into his plan that anyone should "know," and mainly for the reason that it was not in him to tell anyone. That would have been impossible, since nothing but the amusement of a cold world would have waited on it. Since, however, a mysterious fate had opened his mouth in youth, in spite of him, he would count that a compensation and profit by it to the utmost. That the right person *should* know tempered the asperity of his secret more even than his shyness had permitted him to imagine; and May Bartram was clearly right, because—well, because there she was. Her knowledge simply settled it; he would have been sure enough by this time had she been wrong. There was that in his situation, no doubt, that disposed him too much to see her as a mere confidant, taking all her light for him from the fact—the fact only—of her interest in his predicament, from her mercy, sympathy, seriousness, her consent not to regard him as the funniest of the funny. Aware, in fine, that her price for him was just in her giving him this constant sense of his being admirably spared, he was careful to remember that she had, after all, also a life of her own, with things that might happen to *her,* things that in friendship one should likewise take account of. Something fairly remarkable came to pass with him, for that matter, in this connection—something represented by a certain passage of his consciousness, in the suddenest way, from one extreme to the other.

He had thought himself, so long as nobody

knew, the most disinterested person in the world, carrying his concentrated burden, his perpetual suspense, ever so quietly, holding his tongue about it, giving others no glimpse of it nor of its effect upon his life, asking of them no allowance and only making on his side all those that were asked. He had disturbed nobody with the queerness of having to know a haunted man, though he had had moments of rather special temptation on hearing people say that they were "unsettled." If they were as unsettled as he was—he who had never been settled for an hour in his life—they would know what it meant. Yet it wasn't, all the same, for him to make them, and he listened to them civilly enough. This was why he had such good —though possibly such rather colourless— manners; this was why, above all, he could regard himself, in a greedy world, as decently —as, in fact, perhaps even a little sublimely— unselfish. Our point is accordingly that he valued this character quite sufficiently to measure his present danger of letting it lapse, against which he promised himself to be much on his guard. He was quite ready, none the less, to be selfish just a little, since, surely, no more charming occasion for it had come to him. "Just a little," in a word, was just as much as Miss Bartram, taking one day with another, would let him. He never would be in the least coercive, and he would keep well before him the lines on which consideration for her—the very highest—ought to proceed. He would thoroughly establish the heads under which her affairs, her requirements, her peculiarities—he went so far as to give them the latitude of that name—would come into their intercourse. All this naturally was a sign of how much he took the intercourse itself for granted. There was nothing more to be done about *that*. It simply existed; had sprung into being with her first penetrating question to him in the autumn light there at Weatherend. The real form it should have taken on the basis that stood out large was the form of their marrying. But the devil in this was that the very basis itself put marrying out of the question. His conviction, his apprehension, his obsession, in short, was not a condition he could invite a woman to share; and that consequence of it was precisely what was the matter with him. Something or other lay in wait for him, amid the twists and the turns of the months and the years, like a crouching

beast in the jungle. It signified little whether the crouching beast were destined to slay him or to be slain. The definite point was the inevitable spring of the creature; and the definite lesson from that was that a man of feeling didn't cause himself to be accompanied by a lady on a tiger-hunt. Such was the image under which he had ended by figuring his life.

They had at first, none the less, in the scattered hours spent together, made no allusion to that view of it; which was a sign he was handsomely ready to give that he didn't expect, that he in fact didn't care always to be talking about it. Such a feature in one's outlook was really like a hump on one's back. The difference it made every minute of the day existed quite independently of discussion. One discussed, of course, *like* a hunchback, for there was always, if nothing else, the hunchback face. That remained, and she was watching him; but people watched best, as a general thing, in silence, so that such would be predominantly the manner of their vigil. Yet he didn't want, at the same time, to be solemn; solemn was what he imagined he too much tended to be with other people. The thing to be, with the one person who knew, was easy and natural—to make the reference rather than be seeming to avoid it, to avoid it rather than be seeming to make it, and to keep it, in any case, familiar, facetious even, rather than pedantic and portentous. Some such consideration as the latter was doubtless in his mind, for instance, when he wrote pleasantly to Miss Bartram that perhaps the great thing he had so long felt as in the lap of the gods was no more than this circumstance, which touched him so nearly, of her acquiring a house in London. It was the first allusion they had yet again made, needing any other hitherto so little; but when she replied, after having given him the news, that she was by no means satisfied with such a trifle, as the climax to so special a suspense, she almost set him wondering if she hadn't even a larger conception of singularity for him than he had for himself. He was at all events destined to become aware little by little, as time went by, that she was all the while looking at his life, judging it, measuring it, in the light of the thing she knew, which grew to be at last, with the consecration of the years, never mentioned between them save as "the real truth" about him. That had always been his own form of reference to it, but she adopted the form so quietly that, looking back at the end of a period, he knew there was no moment at which it was traceable that she had, as he might say, got inside his condition, or exchanged the attitude of beautifully indulging for that of still more beautifully believing him.

It was always open to him to accuse her of seeing him but as the most harmless of maniacs, and this, in the long run—since it covered so much ground—was his easiest description of their friendship. He had a screw loose for her, but she liked him in spite of it, and was practically, against the rest of the world, his kind, wise keeper, unremunerated, but fairly amused and, in the absence of other near ties, not disreputably occupied. The rest of the world of course thought him queer, but she, she only, knew how, and above all why, queer; which was precisely what enabled her to dispose the concealing veil in the right folds. She took his gaiety from him—since it had to pass with them for gaiety—as he took everything else; but she certainly so far justified by her unerring touch his finer sense of the degree to which he had ended by convincing her. *She* at least never spoke of the secret of his life except as "the real truth about you," and she had in fact a wonderful way of making it seem, as such, the secret of her own life too. That was in fine how he so constantly felt her as allowing for him; he couldn't on the whole call it anything else. He allowed for himself, but she, exactly, allowed still more; partly because, better placed for a sight of the matter, she traced his unhappy perversion through portions of its course into which he could scarce follow it. He knew how he felt, but, besides knowing that, she knew how he *looked* as well; he knew each of the things of importance he was insidiously kept from doing, but she could add up the amount they made, understand how much, with a lighter weight on his spirit, he might have done, and thereby establish how, clever as he was, he fell short. Above all she was in the secret of the difference between the forms he went through—those of his little office under Government, those of caring for his modest patrimony, for his library, for his garden in the country, for the people in London whose invitations he accepted and repaid—and the detachment that reigned beneath them and that made of all behaviour, all that could in the

least be called behaviour, a long act of dissimulation. What it had come to was that he wore a mask painted with the social simper, out of the eyeholes of which there looked eyes of an expression not in the least matching the other features. This the stupid world, even after years, had never more than half discovered. It was only May Bartram who had, and she achieved, by an art indescribable, the feat of at once—or perhaps it was only alternately—meeting the eyes from in front and mingling her own vision, as from over his shoulder, with their peep through the apertures.

So, while they grew older together, she did watch with him, and so she let this association give shape and colour to her own existence. Beneath *her* forms as well detachment had learned to sit, and behaviour had become for her, in the social sense, a false account of herself. There was but one account of her that would have been true all the while, and that she could give, directly, to nobody, least of all to John Marcher. Her whole attitude was a virtual statement, but the perception of that only seemed destined to take its place for him as one of the many things necessarily crowded out of his consciousness. If she had, moreover, like himself, to make sacrifices to their real truth, it was to be granted that her compensation might have affected her as more prompt and more natural. They had long periods, in this London time, during which, when they were together, a stranger might have listened to them without in the least pricking up his ears; on the other hand, the real truth was equally liable at any moment to rise to the surface, and the auditor would then have wondered indeed what they were talking about. They had from an early time made up their mind that society was, luckily, unintelligent, and the margin that this gave them had fairly become one of their commonplaces. Yet there were still moments when the situation turned almost fresh—usually under the effect of some expression drawn from herself. Her expressions doubtless repeated themselves, but her intervals were generous. "What saves us, you know, is that we answer so completely to so usual an appearance: that of the man and woman whose friendship has become such a daily habit, or almost, as to be at last indispensable." That, for instance, was a remark she had frequently enough had occasion to make, though she had given it at different times different developments. What we are especially concerned with is the turn it happened to take from her one afternoon when he had come to see her in honour of her birthday. This anniversary had fallen on a Sunday, at a season of thick fog and general outward gloom; but he had brought her his customary offering, having known her now long enough to have established a hundred little customs. It was one of his proofs to himself, the present he made her on her birthday, that he had not sunk into real selfishness. It was mostly nothing more than a small trinket, but it was always fine of its kind, and he was regularly careful to pay for it more than he thought he could afford. "Our habit saves you, at least, don't you see? because it makes you, after all, for the vulgar, indistinguishable from other men. What's the most inveterate mark of men in general? Why, the capacity to spend endless time with dull women—to spend it, I won't say without being bored, but without minding that they are, without being driven off at a tangent by it; which comes to the same thing. I'm your dull woman, a part of the daily bread for which you pray at church. That covers your tracks more than anything."

"And what covers yours?" asked Marcher, whom his dull woman could mostly to this extent amuse. "I see of course what you mean by your saving me, in one way and another, so far as other people are concerned—I've seen it all along. Only, what is it that saves you? I often think, you know, of that."

She looked as if she sometimes thought of that too, but in rather a different way. "Where other people, you mean, are concerned?"

"Well, you're really so in with me, you know—as a sort of result of my being so in with yourself. I mean of my having such an immense regard for you, being so tremendously grateful for all you've done for me. I sometimes ask myself if it's quite fair. Fair I mean to have so involved and—since one may say it—interested you. I almost feel as if you hadn't really had time to do anything else."

"Anything else but be interested?" she asked. "Ah, what else does one ever want to be? If I've been 'watching' with you, as we long ago agreed that I was to do, watching is always in itself an absorption."

"Oh, certainly," John Marcher said, "if you hadn't had your curiosity—! Only, doesn't it sometimes come to you, as time goes on, that your curiosity is not being particularly repaid?"

May Bartram had a pause. "Do you ask that, by any chance, because you feel at all that yours isn't? I mean because you have to wait so long."

Oh, he understood what she meant. "For the thing to happen that never does happen? For the beast to jump out? No, I'm just where I was about it. It isn't a matter as to which I can *choose,* I can decide for a change. It isn't one as to which there *can* be a change. It's in the lap of the gods. One's in the hands of one's law—there one is. As to the form the law will take, the way it will operate, that's its own affair."

"Yes," Miss Bartram replied; "of course one's fate is coming, of course it *has* come, in its own form and its own way, all the while. Only, you know, the form and the way in your case were to have been—well, something so exceptional and, as one may say, so particularly *your* own."

Something in this made him look at her with suspicion. "You say, 'were to *have* been,' as if in your heart you had begun to doubt."

"Oh!" she vaguely protested.

"As if you believed," he went on, "that nothing will now take place."

She shook her head slowly, but rather inscrutably. "You're far from my thought."

He continued to look at her. "What then is the matter with you?"

"Well," she said after another wait, "the matter with me is simply that I'm more sure than ever my curiosity, as you call it, will be but too well repaid."

They were frankly grave now; he had got up from his seat, had turned once more about the little drawing-room to which, year after year, he brought his inevitable topic; in which he had, as he might have said, tasted their intimate community with every sauce, where every object was as familiar to him as the things of his own house and the very carpets were worn with his fitful walk very much as the desks in old counting-houses are worn by the elbows of generations of clerks. The generations of his nervous moods had been at work there, and the place was the written history of his whole middle life. Under the impression of what his friend had just said he knew himself, for some reason, more aware of these things, which made him, after a moment, stop again before her. "Is it, possibly, that you've grown afraid?"

"Afraid?" He thought, as she repeated the word, that his question had made her, a little, change colour; so that, lest he should have touched on a truth, he explained very kindly, "You remember that that was what you asked *me* long ago—that first day at Weatherend."

"Oh yes, and you told me you didn't know— that I was to see for myself. We've said little about it since, even in so long a time."

"Precisely," Marcher interposed—"quite as if it were too delicate a matter for us to make free with. Quite as if we might find, on pressure, that I *am* afraid. For then," he said, "we shouldn't, should we? quite know what to do."

She had for the time no answer to this question. "There have been days when I thought you were. Only, of course," she added, "there have been days when we have thought almost anything."

"Everything. Oh!" Marcher softly groaned as with a gasp, half spent, at the face, more uncovered just then than it had been for a long while, of the imagination always with them. It had always had its incalculable moments of glaring out, quite as with the very eyes of the very Beast, and, used as he was to them, they could still draw from him the tribute of a sigh that rose from the depths of his being. All that they had thought, first and last, rolled over him; the past seemed to have been reduced to mere barren speculation. This in fact was what the place had just struck him as so full of—the simplification of everything but the state of suspense. That remained only by seeming to hang in the void surrounding it. Even his original fear, if fear it had been, had lost itself in the desert. "I judge, however," he continued, "that you see I'm not afraid now."

"What I see is, as I make it out, that you've achieved something almost unprecedented in the way of getting used to danger. Living with it so long and so closely, you've lost your sense of it; you know it's there, but you're indifferent, and you cease even, as of old, to have to whistle in the dark. Considering what the danger is," May Bartram wound up, "I'm bound to say that I don't think your attitude could well be surpassed."

John Marcher faintly smiled. "It's heroic?"

"Certainly—call it that."

He considered. "I *am,* then, a man of courage?"

"That's what you were to show me."

He still, however, wondered. "But doesn't the man of courage know what he's afraid of— or *not* afraid of? I don't know *that,* you see. I don't focus it. I can't name it. I only know I'm exposed."

"Yes, but exposed—how shall I say?—so directly. So intimately. That's surely enough."

"Enough to make you feel, then—at what we may call the end of our watch—that I'm not afraid?"

"You're not afraid. But it isn't," she said, "the end of our watch. That is it isn't the end of yours. You've everything still to see."

"Then why haven't *you?*" he asked. He had had, all along, to-day, the sense of her keeping something back, and he still had it. As this was his first impression of that, it made a kind of date. The case was the more marked as she didn't at first answer; which in turn made him go on. "You know something I don't." Then his voice, for that of a man of courage, trembled a little. "You know what's to happen." Her silence, with the face she showed, was almost a confession—it made him sure. "You know, and you're afraid to tell me. It's so bad that you're afraid I'll find out."

All this might be true, for she did look as if, unexpectedly to her, he had crossed some mystic line that she had secretly drawn round her. Yet she might, after all, not have worried; and the real upshot was that he himself, at all events, needn't. "You'll never find out."

III

It was all to have made, none the less, as I have said, a date; as came out in the fact that again and again, even after long intervals, other things that passed between them wore, in relation to this hour, but the character of recalls and results. Its immediate effect had been indeed rather to lighten insistence—almost to provoke a reaction; as if their topic had dropped by its own weight and as if moreover, for that matter, Marcher had been, visited by one of his occasional warnings against egotism. He had kept up, he felt, and very decently on the whole, his consciousness of the importance of not being selfish, and it was true he had never sinned in that direction without promptly enough trying to press the scales the other way.

He often repaired his fault, the season permitting, by inviting his friend to accompany him to the opera; and it not infrequently thus happened that, to show he didn't wish her to have but one sort of food for her mind, he was the cause of her appearing there with him a dozen nights in the month. It even happened that, seeing her come at such times, he occasionally went in with her to finish, as he called it, the evening, and, the better to make his point, sat down to the frugal but always careful little supper that awaited his pleasure. His point was made, he thought, by his not eternally insisting with her on himself; made for instance, at such hours, when it befell that, her piano at hand and each of them familiar with it, they went over passages of the opera together. It chanced to be on one of these occasions, however, that he reminded her of her not having answered a certain question he had put to her during the talk that had taken place between them on her last birthday. "What is it that saves *you?*"— saved her, he meant, from that appearance of variation from the usual human type. If he had practically escaped remark, as she pretended, by doing, in the most important particular, what most men do—find the answer to life in patching up an alliance of a sort with a woman no better than himself—how had she escaped it, and how could the alliance, such as it was, since they must suppose it had been more or less noticed, have failed to make her rather positively talked about?

"I never said," May Bartram replied, "that it hadn't made me talked about."

"Ah well then, you're not 'saved.' "

"It has not been a question for me. If you've had your woman, I've had," she said, "my man."

"And you mean that makes you all right?"

She hesitated. "I don't know why it shouldn't make me—humanly, which is what we're speaking of—as right as it makes you."

"I see," Marcher returned. " 'Humanly,' no doubt, as showing that you're living for something. Not, that is, just for me and my secret."

May Bartram smiled. "I don't pretend it exactly shows that I'm not living for you. It's my intimacy with you that's in question."

He laughed as he saw what she meant. "Yes, but since, as you say, I'm only, so far as people make out, ordinary, you're—aren't you?—no more than ordinary either. You help me to pass

for a man like another. So if I *am,* as I understand you, you're not compromised. Is that it?"

She had another hesitation, but she spoke clearly enough. "That's it. It's all that concerns me—to help you to pass for a man like another."

He was careful to acknowledge the remark handsomely. "How kind, how beautiful, you are to me! How shall I ever repay you?"

She had her last grave pause, as if there might be a choice of ways. But she chose. "By going on as you are."

It was into this going on as he was that they relapsed, and really for so long a time that the day inevitably came for a further sounding of their depths. It was as if these depths, constantly bridged over by a structure that was firm enough in spite of its lightness and of its occasional oscillation in the somewhat vertiginous air, invited on occasion, in the interest of their nerves, a dropping of the plummet and a measurement of the abyss. A difference had been made moreover, once for all, by the fact that she had, all the while, not appeared to feel the need of rebutting his charge of an idea within her that she didn't dare to express, uttered just before one of the fullest of their later discussions ended. It had come up for him then that she "knew" something and that what she knew was bad—too bad to tell him. When he had spoken of it as visibly so bad that she was afraid he might find it out, her reply had left the matter too equivocal to be let alone and yet, for Marcher's special sensibility, almost too formidable again to touch. He circled about it at a distance that alternately narrowed and widened and that yet was not much affected by the consciousness in him that there was nothing she could "know," after all, any better than he did. She had no source of knowledge that he hadn't equally—except of course that she might have finer nerves. That was what women had where they were interested; they made out things, where people were concerned, that the people often couldn't have made out for themselves. Their nerves, their sensibility, their imagination, were conductors and revealers, and the beauty of May Bartram was in particular that she had given herself so to his case. He felt in these days what, oddly enough, he had never felt before, the growth of a dread of losing her by some catastrophe—some catastrophe that yet wouldn't at all be *the* catastrophe: partly because she had, almost of a sudden, begun to strike him as useful to him as never yet, and partly by reason of an appearance of uncertainty in her health, coincident and equally new. It was characteristic of the inner detachment he had hitherto so successfully cultivated and to which our whole account of him is a reference, it was characteristic that his complications such as they were, had never yet seemed so as at this crisis to thicken about him, even to the point of making him ask himself if he were, by any chance, of a truth, within sight or sound, within touch or reach, within the immediate jurisdiction of the thing that waited.

When the day came, as come it had to, that his friend confessed to him her fear of a deep disorder in her blood, he felt somehow the shadow of a change and the chill of a shock. He immediately began to imagine aggravations and disasters, and above all to think of her peril as the direct menace for himself of personal privation. This indeed gave him one of those partial recoveries of equanimity that were agreeable to him—it showed him that what was still first in his mind was the loss she herself might suffer. "What if she should have to die before knowing, before seeing—?" It would have been brutal, in the early stages of her trouble, to put that question to her; but it had immediately sounded for him to his own concern, and the possibility was what most made him sorry for her. If she did "know," moreover, in the sense of her having had some—what should he think?—mystical, irresistible light, this would make the matter not better, but worse, inasmuch as her original adoption of his own curiosity had quite become the basis of her life. She had been living to see what would be to be seen, and it would be cruel to her to have to give up before the accomplishment of the vision. These reflections, as I say, refreshed his generosity; yet, make them as he might, he saw himself, with the lapse of the period, more and more disconcerted. It lapsed for him with a strange, steady sweep, and the oddest oddity was that it gave him, independently of the threat of much inconvenience, almost the only positive surprise his career, if career it could be called, had yet offered him. She kept the house as she had never done; he had to go to her to see her—she could meet him nowhere now, though there was scarce a corner of their loved old London in which she had not in the past, at one time or another, done so; and he found her always seated by her fire in the deep, old-fashioned chair she was less and less able to leave. He had been struck one day, after an absence exceeding his usual measure, with her suddenly looking much older to him than he had ever thought of her being; then he recognised that the suddenness was all on his side—he had just been suddenly struck. She looked older because inevitably, after so many years she *was* old, or almost; which was of course true in still greater measure of her companion. If she was old, or almost, John Marcher assuredly was, and yet it was her showing of the lesson, not his own, that brought the truth home to him. His surprises began here; when once they had begun they multiplied; they came rather with a rush: it was as if, in the oddest way in the world, they had all been kept back, sown in a thick cluster, for the late afternoon of life, the time at which, for people in general, the unexpected has died out.

One of them was that he should have caught himself—for he *had* so done—*really* wondering if the great accident would take form now as nothing more than his being condemned to see this charming woman, this admirable friend, pass away from him. He had never so unreservedly qualified her as while confronted in thought with such a possibility; in spite of which there was small doubt for him that as an answer to his long riddle the mere effacement of even so fine a feature of his situation would be an abject anticlimax. It would represent, as connected with his past attitude, a drop of dignity under the shadow of which his existence could only become the most grotesque of failures. He had been far from holding it a failure—long as he had waited for the appearance that was to make it a success. He had waited for a quite other thing, not for such a one as that. The breath of his good faith came short, however, as he recognised how long he had waited, or how long, at least, his companion had. That she, at all events, might be recorded as having waited in vain—this affected him sharply, and all the more because of his at first having done little more than amuse himself with the idea. It grew more grave as the gravity of her condition grew, and the state of mind it produced in him, which he ended by watching, himself, as if it had been some definite disfigurement of his outer person, may pass for another of his surprises. This conjoined itself still with another, the really stupefying consciousness of a question that he would have allowed to shape itself had he dared. What did everything mean—what, that is, did *she* mean, she and her vain waiting and her probable death and the soundless admonition of it all—unless that, at this time of day, it was simply, it was overwhelmingly too late? He had never, at any stage of his queer consciousness, admitted the whisper of such a correction; he had never, till within these last few months, been so false to his conviction as not to hold that what was to come to him had time, whether *he* struck himself as having it or not. That at last, at last, he certainly hadn't it, to speak of, or had it but in the scantiest measure—such, soon enough, as things went with him, became the inference with which his old obsession had to reckon: and this it was not helped to do by the more and more confirmed appearance that the great vagueness casting the long shadow in which he had lived had, to attest itself, almost no margin left. Since it was in Time that he was to have met his fate, so it was in Time that his fate was to have acted; and as he waked up to the sense of no longer being young, which was exactly the sense of being stale, just as that, in turn, was the sense of being weak, he waked up to another matter beside. It all hung together; they were subject, he and the great vagueness, to an equal and indivisible law. When the possibilities themselves had, accordingly, turned stale, when the secret of the gods had grown faint, had perhaps even quite evaporated, that, and that only, was failure. It wouldn't have been failure to be bankrupt, dishonoured, pilloried, hanged; it was failure not to be anything. And so, in the dark valley into which his path had taken its unlooked-for twist, he wondered not a little as he groped. He didn't care what awful crash might overtake him, with what ignominy or what monstrosity he might yet be associated—since he wasn't, after all, too utterly old to suffer—if it would only be decently proportionate to the posture he had kept, all his life, in the promised presence of it. He had but one desire left—that he shouldn't have been "sold."

## IV

Then it was that one afternoon, while the spring of the year was young and new, she met, all in her own way, his frankest betrayal of these alarms. He had gone in late to see her, but evening had not settled, and she was presented to him in that long, fresh light of waning April days which affects us often with a sadness sharper than the greyest hours of autumn. The week had been warm, the spring was supposed to have begun early, and May Bartram sat, for the first time in the year, without a fire, a fact that, to Marcher's sense, gave the scene of which she formed part a smooth and ultimate look, an air of knowing, in its immaculate order and its cold, meaningless cheer, that it would never see a fire again. Her own aspect—he could scarce have said why—intensified this note. Almost as white as wax, with the marks and signs in her face as numerous and as fine as if they had been etched by a needle, with soft white draperies relieved by a faded green scarf, the delicate tone of which had been consecrated by the years, she was the picture of a serene, exquisite, but impenetrable sphinx, whose head, or indeed all whose person, might have been powdered with silver. She was a sphinx, yet with her white petals and green fronds she might have been a lily too—only an artificial lily, wonderfully imitated and constantly kept, without dust or stain, though not exempt from a slight droop and a complexity of faint creases, under some clear glass bell. The perfection of household care, of high polish and finish, always reigned in her rooms, but they especially looked to Marcher at present as if everything had been wound up, tucked in, put away, so that she might sit with folded hands and with nothing more to do. She was "out of it," to his vision; her work was over; she communicated with him as across some gulf, or from some island of rest that she had already reached, and it made him feel strangely abandoned. Was it—or, rather, wasn't it—that if for so long she had been watching with him the answer to their question had swum into her ken and taken on its name, so that her occupation was verily gone? He had as much as charged her with this in saying to her, many months before, that she even then knew something she was keeping from him. It was a point he had never since ventured to press, vaguely fearing, as he did, that it might become a difference, perhaps a disagreement, between them. He had in short, in this later time, turned nervous, which was what, in all the other years, he had never been; and the oddity was that his nervousness should have waited till he had begun to doubt, should have held off so long as he was sure. There was something, it seemed to him, that the wrong word would bring down on his head, something that would so at least put an end to his suspense. But he wanted not to speak the wrong word; that would make everything ugly. He wanted the knowledge he lacked to drop on him, if drop it could, by its own august weight. If she was to forsake him it was surely for her to take leave. This was why he didn't ask her again, directly, what she knew; but it was also why, approaching the matter from another side, he said to her in the course of his visit: "What do you regard as the very worst that, at this time of day, *can* happen to me?"

He had asked her that in the past often enough; they had, with the odd, irregular rhythm of their intensities and avoidances, exchanged ideas about it and then had seen the ideas washed away by cool intervals, washed like figures traced in sea-sand. It had ever been the mark of their talk that the oldest allusions in it required but a little dismissal and reaction to come out again, sounding for the hour as new. She could thus at present meet his inquiry quite freshly and patiently. "Oh yes, I've repeatedly thought, only it always seemed to me of old that I couldn't quite make up my mind. I thought of dreadful things, between which it was difficult to choose; and so must you have done."

"Rather! I feel now as if I had scarce done anything else. I appear to myself to have spent my life in thinking of nothing *but* dreadful things. A great many of them I've at different times named to you, but there were others I couldn't name."

"They were too, too dreadful?"

"Too, too dreadful—some of them."

She looked at him a minute, and there came to him as he met it an inconsequent sense that her eyes, when one got their full clearness, were still as beautiful as they had been in youth, only beautiful with a strange, cold light—a light that somehow was a part of the effect, if it wasn't rather a part of the cause, of the pale,

hard sweetness of the season and the hour. "And yet," she said at last, "there are horrors we have mentioned."

It deepened the strangeness to see her, as such a figure in such a picture, talk of "horrors," but she was to do, in a few minutes, something stranger yet—though even of this he was to take the full measure but afterwards—and the note of it was already in the air. It was, for the matter of that, one of the signs that her eyes were having again such a high flicker of their prime. He had to admit, however, what she said. "Oh yes, there were times when we did go far." He caught himself in the act of speaking as if it all were over. Well, he wished it were; and the consummation depended, for him, clearly, more and more on his companion.

But she had now a soft smile. "Oh, far—!"

It was oddly ironic. "Do you mean you're prepared to go further?"

She was frail and ancient and charming as she continued to look at him, yet it was rather as if she had lost the thread. "Do you consider that we went so far?"

"Why, I thought it the point you were just making—that we *had* looked most things in the face."

"Including each other?" She still smiled. "But you're quite right. We've had together great imaginations, often great fears; but some of them have been unspoken."

"Then the worst—we haven't faced that. I *could* face it, I believe, if I knew what you think it. I feel," he explained, "as if I had lost my power to conceive such things." And he wondered if he looked as blank as he sounded. "It's spent."

"Then why do you assume," she asked, "that mine isn't?"

"Because you've given me signs to the contrary. It isn't a question for you of conceiving, imagining, comparing. It isn't a question now of choosing." At last he came out with it. "You know something that I don't. You've shown me that before."

These last words affected her, he could see in a moment, remarkably, and she spoke with firmness. "I've shown you, my dear, nothing."

He shook his head. "You can't hide it."

"Oh, oh!" May Bartram murmured over what she couldn't hide. It was almost a smothered groan.

"You admitted it months ago, when I spoke

of it to you as of something you were afraid I would find out. Your answer was that I couldn't, that I wouldn't, and I don't pretend I have. But you had something therefore in mind, and I see now that it must have been, that it still is, the possibility that, of all possibilities, has settled itself for you as the worst. This," he went on, "is why I appeal to you. I'm only afraid of ignorance now—I'm not afraid of knowledge." And then as for a while she said nothing: "What makes me sure is that I see in your face and feel here, in this air and amid these appearances, that you're out of it. You've done. You've had your experience. You leave me to my fate."

Well, she listened, motionless and white in her chair, as if she had in fact a decision to make, so that her whole manner was a virtual confession, though still with a small, fine, inner stiffness, an imperfect surrender. "It *would* be the worst," she finally let herself say. "I mean the thing that I've never said."

It hushed him a moment. "More monstrous than all the monstrosities we've named?"

"More monstrous. Isn't that what you sufficiently express," she asked, "in calling it the worst?"

Marcher thought. "Assuredly—if you mean, as I do, something that includes all the loss and all the shame that are thinkable."

"It would if it *should* happen," said May Bartram. "What we're speaking of, remember, is only my idea."

"It's your belief," Marcher returned. "That's enough for me. I feel your beliefs are right. Therefore if, having this one, you give me no more light on it, you abandon me."

"No, no!" she repeated. "I'm with you—don't you see?—still." And as if to make it more vivid to him she rose from her chair—a movement she seldom made in these days—and showed herself, all draped and all soft, in her fairness and slimness. "I haven't forsaken you."

It was really, in its effort against weakness, a generous assurance, and had the success of the impulse not, happily, been great, it would have touched him to pain more than to pleasure. But the cold charm in her eyes had spread, as she hovered before him, to all the rest of her person, so that it was, for the minute, almost like a recovery of youth. He couldn't pity her for that; he could only take her as she showed —as capable still of helping him. It was as if,

at the same time, her light might at any instant go out; wherefore he must make the most of it. There passed before him with intensity the three or four things he wanted most to know; but the question that came of itself to his lips really covered the others. "Then tell me if I shall consciously suffer."

She promptly shook her head. "Never!"

It confirmed the authority he imputed to her, and it produced on him an extraordinary effect. "Well, what's better than that? Do you call that the worst?"

"You think nothing is better?" she asked.

She seemed to mean something so special that he again sharply wondered, though still with the dawn of a prospect of relief. "Why not, if one doesn't *know?*" After which, as their eyes, over his question, met in a silence, the dawn deepened and something to his purpose came, prodigiously, out of her very face. His own, as he took it in, suddenly flushed to the forehead, and he gasped with the force of a perception to which, on the instant, everything fitted. The sound of his gasp filled the air; then he became articulate. "I see—if I don't suffer!"

In her own look, however, was doubt. "You see what?"

"Why, what you mean—what you've always meant."

She again shook her head. "What I mean isn't what I've always meant. It's different."

"It's something new?"

She hesitated. "Something new. It's not what you think. I see what you think."

His divination drew breath then; only her correction might be wrong. "It isn't that I *am* a donkey?" he asked between faintness and grimness. "It isn't that it's all a mistake?"

"A mistake?" she pityingly echoed. *That* possibility, for her, he saw, would be monstrous; and if she guaranteed him the immunity from pain it would accordingly not be what she had in mind. "Oh, no," she declared; "it's nothing of that sort. You've been right."

Yet he couldn't help asking himself if she weren't, thus pressed, speaking but to save him. It seemed to him he should be most lost if his history should prove all a platitude. "Are you telling me the truth, so that I sha'n't have been a bigger idiot than I can bear to know? I *haven't* lived with a vain imagination, in the most besotted illusion? I haven't waited but to see the door shut in my face?"

She shook her head again. "However the case stands *that* isn't the truth. Whatever the reality, it *is* a reality. The door isn't shut. The door's open," said May Bartram.

"Then something's to come?"

She waited once more again, always with her cold, sweet eyes on him. "It's never too late." She had, with her gliding step, diminished the distance between them, and she stood nearer to him, close to him, a minute, as if still full of the unspoken. Her movement might have been for some finer emphasis of what she was at once hesitating and deciding to say. He had been standing by the chimney-piece, fireless and sparely adorned, a small, perfect old French clock and two morsels of rosy Dresden constituting all its furniture; and her hand grasped the shelf while she kept him waiting, grasped it a little as for support and encouragement. She only kept him waiting, however; that is he only waited. It had become suddenly, from her movement and attitude, beautiful and vivid to him that she had something more to give him; her wasted face delicately shone with it, and it glittered, almost as with the white lustre of silver, in her expression. She was right, incontestably, for what he saw in her face was the truth, and strangely, without consequence, while their talk of it as dreadful was still in the air, she appeared to present it as inordinately soft. This, prompting bewilderment, made him but gape the more gratefully for her revelation, so that they continued for some minutes silent, her face shining at him, her contact imponderably pressing, and his stare all kind, but all expectant. The end, none the less, was that what he had expected failed to sound. Something else took place instead, which seemed to consist at first in the mere closing of her eyes. She gave way at the same instant to a slow, fine shudder, and though he remained staring—though he stared, in fact, but the harder—she turned off and regained her chair. It was the end of what she had been intending, but it left him thinking only of that.

"Well, you don't say—?"

She had touched in her passage a bell near the chimney and had sunk back, strangely pale. "I'm afraid I'm too ill."

"Too ill to tell me?" It sprang up sharp to him, and almost to his lips, the fear that she would die without giving him light. He checked himself in time from so expressing his question, but she answered as if she had heard the words. "Don't you know—now?"

" 'Now'—?" She had spoken as if something that had made a difference had come up within the moment. But her maid, quickly obedient to her bell, was already with them. "I know nothing." And he was afterwards to say to himself that he must have spoken with odious impatience, such an impatience as to show that, supremely disconcerted, he washed his hands of the whole question.

"Oh!" said May Bartram.

"Are you in pain?" he asked, as the woman went to her.

"No," said May Bartram.

Her maid, who had put an arm round her as if to take her to her room, fixed on him eyes that appealingly contradicted her; in spite of which, however, he showed once more his mystification. "What then has happened?"

She was once more, with her companion's help, on her feet, and, feeling withdrawal imposed on him, he had found, blankly, his hat and gloves, and had reached the door. Yet he waited for her answer. "What *was* to," she said.

v

He came back the next day, but she was then unable to see him, and as it was literally the first time this had occurred in the long stretch of their acquaintance he turned away, defeated and sore, almost angry—or feeling at least that such a break in their custom was really the beginning of the end—and wandered alone with his thoughts, especially with one of them that he was unable to keep down. She was dying, and he would lose her; she was dying, and his life would end. He stopped in the park, into which he had passed, and stared before him at his recurrent doubt. Away from her the doubt pressed again; in her presence he had believed her, but as he felt his forlornness he threw himself into the explanation that, nearest at hand, had most of a miserable warmth for him and least of a cold torment. She had deceived him to save him—to put him off with something in which he should be able to rest. What could the thing that was to happen to him be, after all, but just this thing that had begun to happen? Her dying, her death, his consequent solitude—*that* was what he had figured as the beast in the jungle, that was what had been in the lap of the gods. He had had her word for it as he left her; for what else, on earth, could she have meant? It wasn't a thing of a monstrous order; not a fate rare and distinguished; not a stroke of fortune that overwhelmed and immortalised; it had only the stamp of the common doom. But poor Marcher, at this hour, judged the common doom sufficient. It would serve his turn, and even as the consummation of infinite waiting he would bend his pride to accept it. He sat down on a bench in the twilight. He hadn't been a fool. Something had *been,* as she had said, to come. Before he rose indeed it had quite struck him that the final fact really matched with the long avenue through which he had had to reach it. As sharing his suspense, and as giving herself all, giving her life, to bring it to an end, she had come with him every step of the way. He had lived by her aid, and to leave her behind would be cruelly, damnably to miss her. What could be more overwhelming than that?

Well, he was to know within the week, for though she kept him a while at bay, left him restless and wretched during a series of days on each of which he asked about her only again to have to turn away, she ended his trial by receiving him where she had always received him. Yet she had been brought out at some hazard into the presence of so many of the things that were, consciously, vainly, half their past, and there was scant service left in the gentleness of her mere desire, all too visible, to check his obsession and wind up his long trouble. That was clearly what she wanted; the one thing more, for her own peace, while she could still put out her hand. He was so affected by her state that, once seated by her chair, he was moved to let everything go; it was she herself therefore who brought him back, took up again, before she dismissed him, her last word of the other time. She showed how she wished to leave their affair in order. "I'm not sure you understood. You've nothing to wait for more. It *has* come."

Oh, how he looked at her! "Really?"

"Really."

"The thing that, as you said, *was* to?"

"The thing that we began in our youth to watch for."

Face to face with her once more he believed her; it was a claim to which he had so abjectly little to oppose. "You mean that it has come as a positive, definite occurrence, with a name and a date?"

"Positive. Definite. I don't know about the 'name,' but, oh, with a date!"

He found himself again too helplessly at sea. "But come in the night—come and passed me by?"

May Bartram had her strange, faint smile. "Oh no, it hasn't passed you by!"

"But if I haven't been aware of it, and it hasn't touched me—?"

"Ah, your not being aware of it," and she seemed to hesitate an instant to deal with this—"your not being aware of it is the strangeness *in* the strangeness. It's the wonder *of* the wonder." She spoke as with the softness almost of a sick child, yet now at last, at the end of all, with the perfect straightness of a sibyl. She visibly knew that she knew, and the effect on him was of something co-ordinate, in its high character, with the law that had ruled him. It was the true voice of the law; so on her lips would the law itself have sounded. "It *has* touched you," she went on. "It has done its office. It has made you all its own."

"So utterly without my knowing it?"

"So utterly without your knowing it." His hand, as he leaned to her, was on the arm of her chair, and, dimly smiling always now, she placed her own on it. "It's enough if *I* know it."

"Oh!" he confusedly sounded, as she herself of late so often had done.

"What I long ago said is true. You'll never know now, and I think you ought to be content. You've *had* it," said May Bartram.

"But had what?"

"Why, what was to have marked you out. The proof of your law. It has acted. I'm too glad," she then bravely added, "to have been able to see what it's *not.*"

He continued to attach his eyes to her, and with the sense that it was all beyond him, and that *she* was too, he would still have sharply challenged her, had he not felt it an abuse of her weakness to do more than take devoutly what she gave him, take it as hushed as to a revelation. If he did speak, it was out of the foreknowledge of his loneliness to come. "If you're glad of what it's 'not,' it might then have been worse?"

She turned her eyes away, she looked

straight before her with which, after a moment: "Well, you know our fears."

He wondered: "It's something then we never feared?"

On this, slowly, she turned to him. "Did we ever dream, with all our dreams, that we should sit and talk of it thus?"

He tried for a little to make out if they had; but it was as if their dreams, numberless enough, were in solution in some thick, cold mist, in which thought lost itself. "It might have been that we couldn't talk?"

"Well"—she did her best for him—"not from this side. This, you see," she said, "is the *other* side."

"I think," poor Marcher returned, "that all sides are the same to me." Then, however, as she softly shook her head in correction: "We mightn't, as it were, have got across—?"

"To where we are—no. We're *here*"—she made her weak emphasis.

"And much good does it do us!" was her friend's frank comment.

"It does us the good it can. It does us the good that *it* isn't here. It's past. It's behind," said May Bartram. "Before—" but her voice dropped.

He had got up, not to tire her, but it was hard to combat his yearning. She after all told him nothing but that his light had failed—which he knew well enough without her. "Before—?" he blankly echoed.

"Before, you see, it was always to *come*. That kept it present."

"Oh, I don't care what comes now! Besides," Marcher added, "it seems to me I liked it better present, as you say, than I can like it absent with *your* absence."

"Oh, mine!"—and her pale hands made light of it.

"With the absence of everything." He had a dreadful sense of standing there before her for —so far as anything but this proved, this bottomless drop was concerned—the last time of their life. It rested on him with a weight he felt he could scarce bear, and this weight it apparently was that still pressed out what remained in him of speakable protest. "I believe you; but I can't begin to pretend I understand. *Nothing*, for me, is past; nothing *will* pass until I pass myself, which I pray my stars may be as soon as possible. Say, however," he added, "that I've eaten my cake, as you contend, to the last

crumb—how can the thing I've never felt at all be the thing I was marked out to feel?"

She met him, perhaps, less directly, but she met him unperturbed. "You take your 'feelings' for granted. You were to suffer your fate. That was not necessarily to know it."

"How in the world—when what is such knowledge but suffering?"

She looked up at him a while, in silence. "No—you don't understand."

"I suffer," said John Marcher.

"Don't, don't!"

"How can I help at least *that?*"

"*Don't!*" May Bartram repeated.

She spoke it in a tone so special, in spite of her weakness, that he stared an instant—stared as if some light, hitherto hidden, had shimmered across his vision. Darkness again closed over it, but the gleam had already become for him an idea. "Because I haven't the right—?"

"Don't *know*—when you needn't," she mercifully urged. "You needn't—for we shouldn't."

"Shouldn't?" If he could but know what she meant!

"No—it's too much."

"Too much?" he still asked—but with a mystification that was the next moment, of a sudden, to give way. Her words, if they meant something, affected him in this light—the light also of her wasted face—as meaning *all,* and the sense of what knowledge had been for herself came over him with a rush which broke through into a question. "Is it of that, then, you're dying?"

She but watched him, gravely at first, as if to see, with this, where he was, and she might have seen something, or feared something, that moved her sympathy. "I would live for you still —if I could." Her eyes closed for a little, as if, withdrawn into herself, she were, for a last time, trying. "But I can't!" she said as she raised them again to take leave of him.

She couldn't indeed, as but too promptly and sharply appeared, and he had no vision of her after this that was anything but darkness and doom. They had parted for ever in that strange talk; access to her chamber of pain, rigidly guarded, was almost wholly forbidden him; he was feeling now moreover, in the face of doctors, nurses, the two or three relatives attracted doubtless by the presumption of what she had to "leave," how few were the rights, as they were called in such cases, that he had to put forward, and how odd it might even seem that their intimacy shouldn't have given him more of them. The stupidest fourth cousin had more, even though she had been nothing in such a person's life. She had been a feature of features in *his,* for what else was it to have been so indispensable? Strange beyond saying were the ways of existence, baffling for him the anomaly of his lack, as he felt it to be, of producible claim. A woman might have been, as it were, everything to him, and it might yet present him in no connection that anyone appeared obliged to recognise. If this was the case in these closing weeks it was the case more sharply on the occasion of the last offices rendered, in the great grey London cemetery, to what had been mortal, to what had been precious, in his friend. The concourse at her grave was not numerous, but he saw himself treated as scarce more nearly concerned with it than if there had been a thousand others. He was in short from this moment face to face with the fact that he was to profit extraordinarily little by the interest May Bartram had taken in him. He couldn't quite have said what he expected, but he had somehow not expected this approach to a double privation. Not only had her interest failed him, but he seemed to feel himself unattended—and for a reason he couldn't sound —by the distinction, the dignity, the propriety, if nothing else, of the man markedly bereaved. It was as if, in the view of society, he had not *been* markedly bereaved, as if there still failed some sign or proof of it, and as if, none the less, his character could never be affirmed, nor the deficiency ever made up. There were moments, as the weeks went by, when he would have liked, by some almost aggressive act, to take his stand on the intimacy of his loss, in order that it *might* be questioned and his retort, to the relief of his spirit, so recorded; but the moments of an irritation more helpless followed fast on these, the moments during which, turning things over with a good conscience but with a bare horizon, he found himself wondering if he oughtn't to have begun, so to speak, further back.

He found himself wondering indeed at many things, and this last speculation had others to keep it company. What could he have done, after all, in her lifetime, without giving them both, as it were, away? He couldn't have made it known she was watching him, for that would

have published the superstition of the Beast. This was what closed his mouth now—now that the Jungle had been threshed to vacancy and that the Beast had stolen away. It sounded too foolish and too flat; the difference for him in this particular, the extinction in his life of the element of suspense, was such in fact as to surprise him. He could scarce have said what the effect resembled; the abrupt cessation, the positive prohibition, of music perhaps, more than anything else, in some place all adjusted and all accustomed to sonority and to attention. If he could at any rate have conceived lifting the veil from his image at some moment of the past (what had he done, after all, if not lift it to *her?*), so to do this to-day, to talk to people at large of the Jungle cleared and confide to them that he now felt it as safe, would have been not only to see them listen as to a goodwife's tale, but really to hear himself tell one. What it presently came to in truth was that poor Marcher waded through his beaten grass, where no life stirred, where no breath sounded, where no evil eye seemed to gleam from a possible lair, very much as if vaguely looking for the Beast, and still more as if missing it. He walked about in an existence that had grown strangely more spacious, and, stopping fitfully in places where the undergrowth of life struck him as closer, asked himself yearningly, wondered secretly and sorely, if it would have lurked here or there. It would have at all events *sprung; w*hat was at least complete was his belief in the truth itself of the assurance given him. The change from his old sense to his new was absolute and final: what was to happen *had* so absolutely and finally happened that he was as little able to know a fear for his future as to know a hope; so absent in short was any question of anything still to come. He was to live entirely with the other question, that of his unidentified past, that of his having to see his fortune impenetrably muffled and masked.

The torment of this vision became then his occupation; he couldn't perhaps have consented to live but for the possibility of guessing. She had told him, his friend, not to guess; she had forbidden him, so far as he might, to know, and she had even in a sort denied the power in him to learn: which were so many things, precisely, to deprive him of rest. It wasn't that he wanted, he argued for fairness, that anything that had happened to him should happen over again; it was only that he shouldn't, as an anticlimax, have been taken sleeping so sound as not to be able to win back by an effort of thought the lost stuff of consciousness. He declared to himself at moments that he would either win it back or have done with consciousness for ever; he made this idea his one motive, in fine, made it so much his passion that none other, to compare with it, seemed ever to have touched him. The lost stuff of consciousness became thus for him as a strayed or stolen child to an unappeasable father; he hunted it up and down very much as if he were knocking at doors and inquiring of the police. This was the spirit in which, inevitably, he set himself to travel; he started on a journey that was to be as long as he could make it; it danced before him that, as the other side of the globe couldn't possibly have less to say to him, it might, by a possibility of suggestion, have more. Before he quitted London, however, he made a pilgrimage to May Bartram's grave, took his way to it through the endless avenues of the grim suburban necropolis, sought it out in the wilderness of tombs, and, though he had come but for the renewal of the act of farewell, found himself, when he had at last stood by it, beguiled into long intensities. He stood for an hour, powerless to turn away and yet powerless to penetrate the darkness of death; fixing with his eyes her inscribed name and date, beating his forehead against the fact of the secret they kept, drawing his breath, while he waited as if, in pity of him, some sense would rise from the stones. He kneeled on the stones, however, in vain; they kept what they concealed; and if the face of the tomb did become a face for him it was because her two names were like a pair of eyes that didn't know him. He gave them a last long look, but no palest light broke.

## VI

He stayed away, after this, for a year; he visited the depths of Asia, spending himself on scenes of romantic interest, of superlative sanctity; but what was present to him everywhere was that for a man who had known what *he* had known the world was vulgar and vain. The state of mind in which he had lived for so many years shone out to him, in reflection, as a light that coloured and refined, a light beside which the glow of the East was garish, cheap and thin. The terrible truth was that he had lost—with everything else—a distinction as well; the things he saw couldn't help being common when he had become common to look at them. He was simply now one of them himself—he was in the dust, without a peg for the sense of difference; and there were hours when, before the temples of gods and the sepulchres of kings, his spirit turned, for nobleness of association, to the barely discriminated slab in the London suburb. That had become for him, and more intensely with time and distance, his one witness of a past glory. It was all that was left to him for proof or pride, yet the past glories of Pharaohs were nothing to him as he thought of it. Small wonder then that he came back to it on the morrow of his return. He was drawn there this time as irresistibly as the other, yet with a confidence, almost, that was doubtless the effect of the many months that had elapsed. He had lived, in spite of himself; into his change of feeling, and in wandering over the earth had wandered, as might be said, from the circumference to the centre of his desert. He had settled to his safety and accepted perforce his extinction; figuring to himself, with some colour, in the likeness of certain little old men he remembered to have seen, of whom, all meagre and wizened as they might look, it was related that they had in their time fought twenty duels or been loved by ten princesses. They indeed had been wondrous for others, while he was but wondrous for himself; which, however, was exactly the cause of his haste to renew the wonder by getting back, as he might put it, into his own presence. That had quickened his steps and checked his delay. If his visit was prompt it was because he had been separated so long from the part of himself that alone he now valued.

It is accordingly not false to say that he reached his goal with a certain elation and stood there again with a certain assurance. The creature beneath the sod *knew* of his rare experience, so that, strangely now, the place had lost for him its mere blankness of expression. It met him in mildness—not, as before, in mockery; it wore for him the air of conscious greeting that we find, after absence, in things that have closely belonged to us and which seem to confess of themselves to the connection. The plot of ground, the graven tablet, the tended flowers affected him so as belonging to him that he quite felt for the hour like a contented landlord reviewing a piece of property. Whatever had happened—well, had happened. He had not come back this time with the vanity of that question, his former worrying, "What, *what?*" now practically so spent. Yet he would, none the less, never again so cut himself off from the spot; he would come back to it every month, for if he did nothing else by its aid at least held up his head. It thus grew for him, in the oddest way, a positive resource; he carried out his idea of periodical returns, which took their place at last among the most inveterate of his habits. What it all amounted to, oddly enough, was that, in his now so simplified world, this garden of death gave him the few square feet of earth on which he could still most live. It was as if, being nothing anywhere else for anyone, nothing even for himself, he were just everything here, and if not for a crowd of witnesses, or indeed for any witness but John Marcher, then by clear right of the register that he could scan like an open page. The open page was the tomb of his friend, and *there* were the facts of the past, there the truth of his life, there the backward reaches in which he could lose himself. He did this, from time to time, with such effect that he seemed to wander through the old years with his hand in the arm of a companion who was, in the most extraordinary manner, his other, his younger self; and to wander, which was more extraordinary yet, round and round a third presence—not wandering she, but stationary, still, whose eyes, turning with his revolution, never ceased to follow him, and whose seat was his point, so to speak, of orientation. Thus in short he settled to live—feeding only on the sense that he once *had* lived, and dependent on it not only for a support but for an identity.

It sufficed him, in its way, for months, and the year elapsed; it would doubtless even have carried him further but for an accident, superficially slight, which moved him, in a quite other direction, with a force beyond any of his impressions of Egypt or of India. It was a thing of the merest chance—the turn, as he afterwards felt, of a hair, though he was indeed to live to believe that if light hadn't come to him in this particular fashion it would still have come in another. He was to live to believe this, I say, though he was not to live, I may not less definitely mention, to do much else. We allow him at any rate the benefit of the conviction, struggling up for him at the end, that, whatever might have happened or not happened, he would have come round of himself to the light. The incident of an autumn day had put the match to the train laid from of old by his misery. With the light before him he knew that even of late his ache had only been smothered. It was strangely drugged, but it throbbed; at the touch it began to bleed. And the touch, in the event, was the face of a fellow-mortal. This face, one grey afternoon when the leaves were thick in the alleys, looked into Marcher's own, at the cemetery, with an expression like the cut of a blade. He felt it, that is, so deep down that he winced at the steady thrust. The person who so mutely assaulted him was a figure he had noticed, on reaching his own goal, absorbed by a grave a short distance away, a grave apparently fresh, so that the emotion of the visitor would probably match it for frankness. This fact alone forbade further attention, though during the time he stayed he remained vaguely conscious of his neighbour, a middle-aged man apparently, in mourning, whose bowed back, among the clustered monuments and mortuary yews, was constantly presented. Marcher's theory that these were elements in contact with which he himself revived, had suffered, on this occasion, it may be granted, a sensible though inscrutable check. The autumn day was dire for him as none had recently been, and he rested with a heaviness he had not yet known on the low stone table that bore May Bartram's name. He rested without power to move, as if some spring in him, some spell vouchsafed, had suddenly been broken for ever. If he could have done that moment as he wanted he would simply have stretched himself on the slab that was ready to take him, treating it as a place prepared to receive his last sleep. What in all the wide world had he now to keep awake for? He stared before him with the question, and it was then that, as one of the cemetery walks passed near him, he caught the shock of the face.

His neighbour at the other grave had withdrawn, as he himself, with force in him to move, would have done by now, and was advancing along the path on his way to one of the gates. This brought him near, and his pace was slow, so that—and all the more as there was a kind of hunger in his look—the two men were for a minute directly confronted. Marcher felt him on the spot as one of the deeply stricken— a perception so sharp that nothing else in the picture lived for it, neither his dress, his age, nor his presumable character and class; nothing lived but the deep ravage of the features that he showed. He *showed* them—that was the point; he was moved, as he passed, by some impulse that was either a signal for sympathy or, more possibly, a challenge to another sorrow. He might already have been aware of our friend, might, at some previous hour, have noticed in him the smooth habit of the scene, with which the state of his own senses so scantly consorted, and might thereby have been stirred as by a kind of overt discord. What Marcher was at all events conscious of was, in the first place, that the image of scarred passion presented to him was conscious too—of something that profaned the air; and, in the second, that, roused, startled, shocked, he was yet the next moment looking after it, as it went, with envy. The most extraordinary thing that had happened to him—though he had given that name to other matters as well—took place, after his immediate vague stare, as a consequence of this impression. The stranger passed, but the raw glare of his grief remained, making our friend wonder in pity what wrong, what wound it expressed, what injury not to be healed. What had the man *had* to make him, by the loss of it, so bleed and yet live?

Something—and this reached him with a pang—that *he,* John Marcher, hadn't; the proof of which was precisely John Marcher's arid end. No passion had ever touched him, for this was what passion meant; he had survived and maundered and pined, but where had been *his* deep ravage? The extraordinary thing we speak of was the sudden rush of the result of this question. The sight that had just met his eyes named to him, as in letters of quick flame, something he had utterly, insanely missed, and what he had missed made these things a train of fire, made them mark themselves in an anguish of inward throbs. He had seen *outside* of his life, not learned it within, the way a woman was mourned when she had been loved for herself; such was the force of his conviction of the meaning of the stranger's face, which still flared for him like a smoky torch. It had not come to him, the knowledge, on the wings of experience; it had brushed him, jostled him, upset him, with the disrespect of chance, the insolence of an accident. Now that the illumination had begun, however, it blazed to the zenith, and what

he presently stood there gazing at was the sounded void of his life. He gazed, he drew breath, in pain; he turned in his dismay, and, turning, he had before him in sharper incision than ever the open page of his story. The name on the table smote him as the passage of his neighbour had done, and what it said to him, full in the face, was that *she* was what he had missed. This was the awful thought, the answer to all the past, the vision at the dread clearness of which he turned as cold as the stone beneath him. Everything fell together, confessed, explained, overwhelmed; leaving him most of all stupefied at the blindness he had cherished. The fate he had been marked for he had met with a vengeance—he had emptied the cup to the lees; he had been the man of his time, *the* man, to whom nothing on earth was to have happened. That was the rare stroke—that was his visitation. So he saw it, as we say, in pale horror, while the pieces fitted and fitted. So *she* had seen it, while he didn't, and so she served at this hour to drive the truth home. It was the truth, vivid and monstrous, that all the while he had waited the wait was itself his portion. This the companion of his vigil had at a given moment perceived, and she had then offered him the chance to baffle his doom. One's doom, however, was never baffled, and on the day she had told him that his own had come down she had seen him but stupidly stare at the escape she offered him.

The escape would have been to love her; then, *then* he would have lived. *She* had lived—who could say now with what passion?—since she had loved him for himself; whereas he had never thought of her (ah, how it hugely glared at him!) but in the chill of his egotism and the light of her use. Her spoken words came back to him, and the chain stretched and stretched. The beast had lurked indeed, and the beast, at its hour, had sprung; it had sprung in that twilight of the cold April when, pale, ill, wasted, but all beautiful, and perhaps even then recoverable, she had risen from her chair to stand before him and let him imaginably guess. It had sprung as he didn't guess; it had sprung as she hopelessly turned from him, and the mark, by the time he left her, had fallen where it *was* to fall. He had justified his fear and achieved his fate; he had failed, with the last exactitude, of all he was to fail of; and a moan now rose to his lips as he remembered she had prayed he mightn't know. This horror of waking—*this* was knowledge, knowledge under the breath of which the very tears in his eyes seemed to freeze. Through them, none the less, he tried to fix it and hold it; he kept it there before him so that he might feel the pain. That at least, belated and bitter, had something of the taste of life. But the bitterness suddenly sickened him, and it was as if, horribly, he saw, in the truth, in the cruelty of his image, what had been appointed and done. He saw the Jungle of his life and saw the lurking Beast; then, while he looked, perceived it, as by a stir of the air, rise, huge and hideous, for the leap that was to settle him. His eyes darkened—it was close; and, instinctively turning, in his hallucination, to avoid it, he flung himself, on his face, on the tomb.

## *Anonymous*
## SIR PATRICK SPENS

The king sits in Dumferling toune,
    Drinking the blude-reid wine:
"O whar will I get guid [35] sailor,
    To sail this schip of mine?"

Up and spak an eldern knicht,[36]
    Sat at the kings richt [37] kne:
"Sir Patrick Spens is the best sailor,
    That sails upon the se."

The king has written a braid [38] letter,
    And signed it wi his hand,                    10
And sent it to Sir Patrick Spens
    Was walking on the sand.

The first line that Sir Patrick red,
    A loud lauch [39] lauchèd he;
The next line that Sir Patrick red,
    The teir blinded his ee.

"O wha [40] is this has don this deid,[41]
    This ill deid don to me,
To send me out this time o' the yeir,
    To sail upon the se!                          20

---

[35] Good.        [36] Knight.        [37] Right.
[38] Broad, *i.e.,* official.        [39] Laugh.
[40] Who.        [41] Deed.

"Mak hast, mak haste, my mirry men all,
    Our guid schip sails the morne:"
"O say na sae,[42] my master deir,
    For I feir a deadlie storme.

"Late, late yestreen I saw the new moone,
    Wi the auld moone in hir arme,
And I feir, I feir, my deir master,
    That we will cum to harme."

O our Scots nobles were richt laith [43]
    To weet their cork-heild schoone; [44]       30
Bot lang owre a' the play wer playd,[45]
    Thair hats they swam aboone.[46]

O lang, lang may their ladies sit,
    Wi thar fans into their hand,
Or eir they se Sir Patrick Spens
    Cum sailing to the land.

O lang, lang may the ladies stand,
    Wi thair gold kems [47] in their hair,
Waiting for thair ain [48] deir lords,
    For they'll se thame na mair.                 40

Haf owre, haf owre to Aberdour,
    It's fiftie fadom [49] deip,
And thair lies guid Sir Patrick Spens,
    Wi the Scots lords at his feit.

---

[42] Say not so.          [43] Very loath, unwilling.
[44] Cork-heeled shoes.
[45] Long before the whole play was played.
[46] Above.          [47] Combs.          [48] Own.
[49] Fathom.

## *Alfred Lord Tennyson*
## ULYSSES

It little profits that an idle king,
By this still hearth, among these barren crags,
Matched with an agèd wife, I mete and dole
Unequal laws unto a savage race,
That hoard, and sleep, and feed, and know not
    me.
I cannot rest from travel: I will drink
Life to the lees: all times I have enjoyed
Greatly, have suffered greatly, both with those
That loved me, and alone; on shore, and when
Thro' scudding drifts the rainy Hyades [50]      10
Vext the dim sea: I am become a name;
For always roaming with a hungry heart

---

[50] A constellation supposed to rise with the beginning of the rainy season.

Much have I seen and known; cities of men
And manners, climates, councils, governments,
Myself not least, but honoured of them all;
And drunk delight of battle with my peers,
Far on the ringing plains of windy Troy.
I am a part of all that I have met;
Yet all experience is an arch wherethro'
Gleams that untravelled world, whose margin
    fades                            20
For ever and for ever when I move.
How dull it is to pause, to make an end,
To rust unburnished, not to shine in use!
As tho' to breathe were life. Life piled on life
Were all too little, and of one to me
Little remains: but every hour is saved
From that eternal silence, something more,
A bringer of new things; and vile it were
For some three suns to store and hoard myself,
And this gray spirit yearning in desire       30
To follow knowledge like a sinking star,
Beyond the utmost bound of human thought.
    This is my son, mine own Telemachus,
To whom I leave the sceptre and the isle—
Well-loved of me, discerning to fulfil
This labour, by slow prudence to make mild
A rugged people, and thro' soft degrees
Subdue them to the useful and the good.
Most blameless is he, centred in the sphere
Of common duties, decent not to fail        40
In offices of tenderness, and pay
Meet adoration to my household gods,
When I am gone. He works his work, I mine.
    There lies the port; the vessel puffs her sail:
There gloom the dark broad seas. My mariners,
Souls that have toiled, and wrought, and thought
    with me—
That ever with a frolic welcome took
The thunder and the sunshine, and opposed
Free hearts, free foreheads—you and I are old;
Old age hath yet his honour and his toil;     50
Death closes all: but something ere the end,
Some work of noble note, may yet be done,
Not unbecoming men that strove with Gods.
The lights begin to twinkle from the rocks:
The long day wanes: the slow moon climbs: the
    deep
Moans round with many voices. Come, my friends,
'Tis not too late to seek a newer world.
Push off, and sitting well in order smite
The sounding furrows; for my purpose holds
To sail beyond the sunset, and the baths     60
Of all the western stars, until I die.
It may be that the gulfs will wash us down:

It may be we shall touch the Happy Isles,
And see the great Achilles, whom we knew.
Tho' much is taken, much abides; and tho'
We are not now that strength which in old days
Moved earth and heaven; that which we are, we
    are;
One equal temper of heroic hearts,
Made weak by time and fate, but strong in will
To strive, to seek, to find, and not to yield.    70

## *Edwin Arlington Robinson*
# CLIFF KLINGENHAGEN

Cliff Klingenhagen had me in to dine
With him one day; and after soup and meat,
And all the other things there were to eat,
Cliff took two glasses and filled one with wine
And one with wormwood. Then, without a sign
For me to choose at all, he took the draught
Of bitterness himself, and lightly quaffed
It off, and said the other one was mine.

And when I asked him what the deuce he meant
By doing that, he only looked at me     10
And smiled, and said it was a way of his.
And though I know the fellow, I have spent
Long time a-wondering when I shall be
As happy as Cliff Klingenhagen is.

## *A. E. Housman*
# TO AN ATHLETE
# DYING YOUNG

The time you won your town the race
We chaired you through the market-place;
Man and boy stood cheering by,
And home we brought you shoulder-high.

To-day, the road all runners come,
Shoulder-high we bring you home,
And set you at your threshold down,
Townsman of a stiller town.

Smart lad, to slip betimes away
From fields where glory does not stay,     10
And early though the laurel grows
It withers quicker than the rose.

Eyes the shady night has shut
Cannot see the record cut,
And silence sounds no worse than cheers
After earth has stopped the ears.

Now you will not swell the rout
Of lads that wore their honors out,
Runners whom renown outran
And the name died before the man.     20

So set, before its echoes fade,
The fleet foot on the sill of shade,
And hold to the low lintel up
The still-defended challenge-cup.

And round that early-laurelled head
Will flock to gaze the strengthless dead,
And find unwithered on its curls
The garland briefer than a girl's.

## Vachel Lindsay

# ABRAHAM LINCOLN WALKS AT MIDNIGHT

It is portentous, and a thing of state
That here at midnight, in our little town
A mourning figure walks, and will not rest,
Near the old court-house pacing up and down,

Or by his homestead, or in shadowed yards
He lingers where his children used to play,
Or through the market, on the well-worn stones
He stalks until the dawn-stars burn away.

A bronzed, lank man! His suit of ancient black,
A famous high top-hat and plain worn shawl     10
Make him the quaint great figure that men love,
The prairie-lawyer, master of us all.

He cannot sleep upon his hillside now.
He is among us:—as in times before!
And we who toss and lie awake for long
Breathe deep, and start, to see him pass the door.

His head is bowed. He thinks on men and kings.
Yea, when the sick world cries, how can he sleep?
Too many peasants fight, they know not why,
Too many homesteads in black terror weep.     20

The sins of all the war-lords burn his heart.
He sees the dreadnaughts scouring every main.
He carries on his shawl-wrapped shoulders now
The bitterness, the folly and the pain.

He cannot rest until a spirit-dawn
Shall come;—the shining hope of Europe free:
The league of sober folk, the Workers' Earth,
Bringing long peace to Cornland, Alp and Sea.

It breaks his heart that kings must murder still,
That all his hours of travail here for men     30
Seem yet in vain. And who will bring white peace
That he may sleep upon his hill again?

## Andrew Marvell

# AN HORATIAN ODE UPON CROMWELL'S RETURN FROM IRELAND [51]

The forward [52] youth that would appear [53]
Must now forsake his Muses dear,
    Nor in the shadows sing
    His numbers languishing:

'Tis time to leave the books in dust,
And oil the unused armor's rust,
    Removing from the wall
    The corslet of the hall.

[51] Cromwell had returned from his victory in
Ireland late in May, 1650, to direct the campaign in
Scotland.
[52] Ambitious.
[53] Gain fame.

So restless Cromwell could not cease
In the inglorious arts of peace,     10
    But through adventurous war
    Urgèd his active star;

And like the three-forked lightning, first
Breaking the clouds where it was nursed,
    Did thorough his own side [54]
    His fiery way divide;

For 'tis all one to courage high,
The emulous or enemy;
    And with such to inclose
    Is more than to oppose. [55]     20

Then burning through the air he went,
And palaces and temples rent;
    And Cæsar's head at last
    Did through his laurels blast. [56]

'Tis madness to resist or blame
The force of angry heaven's flame;
    And if we would speak true,
    Much to the man is due,

Who, from his private gardens, where
He lived reservèd and austere     30
    (As if his highest plot
    To plant the bergamot [57]),

Could by industrious valor climb
To ruin the great work of time,
    And cast the kingdom old
    Into another mold;

Though Justice against Fate complain,
And plead the ancient rights in vain;
    (But those do hold or break,
    As men are strong or weak).     40

Nature, that hateth emptiness,
Allows of penetration [58] less,
    And therefore must make room
    Where greater spirits come.

What field of all the civil war,
Where his were not the deepest scar?
    And Hampton [59] shows what part
    He had of wiser art;

Where, twining subtle fears with hope,
He wove a net of such a scope     50
    That Charles himself might chase
    To Carisbrooke's [60] narrow case, [61]

That thence the royal actor borne
The tragic scaffold might adorn;
    While round the armèd bands
    Did clap their bloody hands.

He nothing common did, or mean,
Upon that memorable scene,
    But with his keener eye
    The axe's edge did try;     60

Nor called the gods with vulgar spite
To vindicate his helpless right;
    But bowed his comely head
    Down, as upon a bed.

This was that memorable hour
Which first assured the forcèd power:
    So, when they did design
    The Capitol's [62] first line,

A bleeding head, where they begun,
Did fright the architects to run;     70
    And yet in that the state
    Foresaw its happy fate.

And now the Irish are ashamed
To see themselves in one year tamed;
    So much one man can do
    That does both act and know.

They can affirm his praises best,
And have, though overcome, confessed
    How good he is, how just,
    And fit for highest trust.     80

---

[54] Through his own party. In 1647 Cromwell over-awed the Puritan Parliament by bringing his army to London.

[55] i.e., it is a greater deed to absorb rivals and enemies than to fight them.

[56] i.e., Cromwell destroyed Charles I despite his kingly crown.

[57] A species of pear.

[58] Occupation of one place by two bodies at one time.

---

[59] The Court Palace. Charles fled from here to the Isle of Wight.

[60] Castle on the Isle of Wight.

[61] Trap.

[62] The builders of the temple of Jupiter at Rome were said to have uncovered a human head (caput), which was looked upon as a sign of good fortune and led to naming the building the Capitol.

Nor yet grown stiffer with command,
But still in the republic's hand—
    How fit he is to sway
    That can so well obey!

He to the Commons' feet presents
A kingdom [63] for his first year's rents;
    And, what he may, forbears [64]
    His fame, to make it theirs;

And has his sword and spoils ungirt,
To lay them at the public's skirt:     90
    So when the falcon high
    Falls heavy from the sky,

She, having killed, no more does search
But on the next green bough to perch;
    Where, when he first does lure,
    The falconer has her sure.

What may not, then, our isle presume,
While victory his crest does plume?
    What may not others fear,
    If thus he crown each year?     100

A Cæsar he, ere long, to Gaul,
To Italy an Hannibal,
    And to all states not free
    Shall climacteric be.

The Pict [65] no shelter now shall find
Within his parti-colored [66] mind,
    But from this valor sad
    Shrink underneath the plaid;

Happy if in the tufted brake
The English hunter him mistake,     110
    Nor lay his hounds in near
    The Caledonian deer.

But thou, the war's and fortune's son,
March indefatigably on!
    And for the last effect,
    Still keep thy sword erect;

Besides the force it has to fright
The spirits of the shady night,
    The same arts that did gain
    A power must it maintain.     120

---

[63] Ireland.
[64] Minimizes as well as he can.
[65] Scot.
[66] Many-colored, like his plaid: *i.e.,* changeable in loyalty.

## John Milton
# LYCIDAS

Yet once more, O ye laurels, and once more,
Ye myrtles brown, with ivy [67] never sere,
I come to pluck your berries harsh and crude,
And with forced fingers rude
Shatter your leaves before the mellowing year.
Bitter constraint and sad occasion dear
Compels me to disturb your season due;
For Lycidas is dead, dead ere his prime,
Young Lycidas, and hath not left his peer.
Who would not sing for Lycidas? he knew     10
Himself to sing, and build the lofty rhyme.
He must not float upon his watery bier
Unwept, and welter to the parching wind,
Without the meed [68] of some melodious tear.
    Begin, then, Sisters [69] of the sacred well
That from beneath the seat of Jove doth spring;
Begin, and somewhat loudly sweep the string.
Hence with denial vain and coy excuse:
So may some gentle Muse
With lucky words favor *my* destined urn,     20
And as he passes turn,
And bid fair peace be to my sable shroud!
For we were nursed upon the self-same hill,
Fed the same flock, by fountain, shade, and rill.
    Together both, ere the high lawns appeared
Under the opening eyelids of the Morn,
We drove a-field, and both together heard
What time the grey-fly winds her sultry horn, [70]
Battening our flocks with the fresh dews of night,
Oft till the star [71] that rose at evening bright     30
Toward heaven's descent had sloped his westering
    wheel.
Meanwhile the rural ditties were not mute;
Tempered to the oaten flute,
Rough Satyrs danced, and Fauns with cloven heel
From the glad sound would not be absent long;
And old Damœtas [72] loved to hear our song.
    But, oh! the heavy change, now thou art gone,

---

[67] Laurel, myrtle, and ivy are sacred to the inspirers of poetry and traditionally were used in poet's crowns.
[68] Tribute.
[69] The Muses, who dwell near the Pierian spring at the foot of Mount Olympus.
[70] *i.e.,* in the middle of the day when insects buzz in the heat.
[71] Hesperus.
[72] Not definitely identified but probably a tutor of Milton and his friend.

Now thou art gone and never must return!
Thee, Shepherd, thee the woods and desert caves,
With wild thyme and the gadding [73] vine o'er-
  grown,                                          40
And all their echoes, mourn.
The willows, and the hazel copses green,
Shall now no more be seen
Fanning their joyous leaves to thy soft lays.
As killing as the canker [74] to the rose,
Or taint-worm to the weanling [75] herds that graze,
Or frost to flowers, that their gay wardrobe wear,
When first the white-thorn blows;
Such, Lycidas, thy loss to shepherd's ear.
  Where were ye, Nymphs, when the remorseless
    deep                                          50
Closed o'er the head of your loved Lycidas?
For neither were ye playing on the steep
Where your old bards, the famous Druids, lie,
Nor on the shaggy top of Mona [76] high,
Nor yet where Deva [77] spreads her wizard stream.
Ay me! I fondly dream
"Had ye been there"—for what could that have
    done?
What could the Muse [78] herself that Orpheus bore,
The Muse herself, for her enchanting son,
Whom universal nature did lament,              60
When, by the rout that made the hideous roar,
His gory visage down the stream was sent,[79]
Down the swift Hebrus [80] to the Lesbian shore? [81]
  Alas! what boots [82] it with uncessant care
To tend the homely, slighted, shepherd's trade,
And strictly meditate the thankless Muse?
Were it not better done, as others use,
To sport with Amaryllis [83] in the shade,
Or with the tangles of Neæra's hair?
Fame is the spur that the clear spirit doth raise 70
(That last infirmity of noble mind)
To scorn delights and live laborious days;
But the fair guerdon [84] when we hope to find,
And think to burst out into sudden blaze,

Comes the blind Fury [85] with the abhorrèd shears,
And slits the thin-spun life. "But not the praise,"
Phœbus replied, and touched my trembling ears:
"Fame is no plant that grows on mortal soil,
Nor in the glistering foil [86]
Set off to the world, nor in broad rumor lies,   80
But lives and spreads aloft by those pure eyes
And perfect witness of all-judging Jove;
As he pronounces lastly on each deed,
Of so much fame in heaven expect thy meed."
  O fountain Arethuse,[87] and thou honored flood,
Smooth-sliding Mincius, crowned with vocal reeds,
That strain I heard was of a higher mood.
But now my oat [88] proceeds,
And listens to the Herald of the Sea,[89]
That came in Neptune's plea.                     90
He asked the waves, and asked the felon winds,
What hard mishap hath doomed this gentle swain?
And questioned every gust of rugged wings
That blows from off each beakèd promontory.
They knew not of his story;
And sage Hippotades [90] their answer brings,
That not a blast was from his dungeon strayed:
The air was calm, and on the level brine
Sleek Panope,[91] with all her sisters, played.
It was that fatal and perfidious bark,           100
Built in the eclipse, and rigged with curses dark,
That sunk so low that sacred head of thine.
  Next, Camus,[92] reverend sire, went footing slow,
His mantle hairy,[93] and his bonnet sedge,[94]
Inwrought with figures dim, and on the edge
Like to that sanguine flower [95] inscribed with woe.
"Ah, who hath reft," quoth he, "my dearest
    pledge?" [96]
  Last came, and last did go,
The Pilot of the Galilean Lake; [97]

---

[73] Wandering.
[74] Cankerworm.
[75] Recently weaned.
[76] An island off the coast of Wales.
[77] The river Dee in Wales.
[78] Calliope, Muse of epic poetry and mother of Orpheus.
[79] He was torn to pieces by Thracian women for refusing to join their Bacchic orgy.
[80] River.
[81] i.e., the Isle of Lesbos, birthplace of many poets.
[82] Profits.
[83] A pastoral nymph, as is Neæra.
[84] Reward.

[85] Atropos, one of the three Fates, who cuts the thread of life.
[86] Shiny setting of a jewel.
[87] A fountain in Sicily associated with the birthplace of the ancient poet, Theocritus, as the Italian river Mincius was with that of Vergil.
[88] Flute made of oat straw; cf. line 33.
[89] The demigod Triton, who comes to defend Neptune against the charge of having purposely drowned Lycidas.
[90] Aeolus, god of the winds.
[91] A sea nymph.
[92] God of the river Cam which flows through Cambridge.
[93] As though embroidered with river grass.
[94] Grass along a river bank.
[95] Hyacinth.
[96] Young child.
[97] St. Peter.

Two massy keys he bore of metals twain      110
(The golden opes, the iron shuts amain [98]).
He shook his mitred locks, and stern bespake:—
"How well could I have spared for thee, young
  swain,
Enow of such as, for their bellies' sake,
Creep, and intrude, and climb into the fold! [99]
Of other care they little reckoning make
Than how to scramble at the shearers' feast,
And shove away the worthy bidden guest.
Blind mouths! that scarce themselves know how
  to hold
A sheep-hook, or have learned aught else the
  least                                         120
That to the faithful herdman's art belongs!
What recks it them? What need they? They are
  sped;
And when they list, their lean and flashy songs
Grate on their scrannel pipes [100] of wretched
  straw;
The hungry sheep look up, and are not fed,
But, swoln with wind and the rank mist they draw,
Rot inwardly, and foul contagion spread;
Besides what the grim wolf [101] with privy paw
Daily devours apace, and nothing said.
But that two-handed engine [102] at the door   130
Stands ready to smite once, and smite no more."
    Return, Alpheus; [103] the dread voice is past
That shrunk thy streams; return, Sicilian Muse,
And call the vales, and bid them hither cast
Their bells and flowerets of a thousand hues.
Ye valleys low, where the mild whispers use
Of shades and wanton winds and gushing brooks,
On whose fresh lap the swart star [104] sparely looks,
Throw hither all your quaint enameled eyes,
That on the green turf suck the honeyed
  showers,                                      140
And purple all the ground with vernal flowers.
Bring the rathe [105] primrose that forsaken dies,
The tufted crow-toe, and pale jessamine,
The white pink, and the pansy freaked [106] with jet,
The glowing violet,
The musk-rose, and the well-attired woodbine,

With cowslips wan that hang the pensive head,
And every flower that sad embroidery wears;
Bid amaranthus [107] all his beauty shed,
And daffadillies fill their cups with tears,     150
To strew the laureate hearse [108] where Lycid lies.
For so, to interpose a little ease,
Let our frail thoughts dally with false surmise.
Ay me! whilst thee the shores and sounding seas
Wash far away, where'er thy bones are hurled;
Whether beyond the stormy Hebrides,[109]
Where thou, perhaps, under the whelming tide
Visit'st the bottom of the monstrous world; [110]
Or whether thou, to our moist vows denied,
Sleep'st by the fable of Bellerus [111] old,     160
Where the great Vision of the guarded mount [112]
Looks toward Namancos and Bayona's [113] hold.
Look homeward, Angel,[114] now, and melt with
  ruth: [115]
And, O ye dolphins, waft the hapless youth.
    Weep no more, woeful shepherds, weep no
  more;
For Lycidas, your sorrow, is not dead,
Sunk though he be beneath the watery floor.
So sinks the day-star in the ocean bed,
And yet anon repairs his drooping head,
And tricks his beams, and with new-spangled
  ore                                           170
Flames in the forehead of the morning sky:
So Lycidas sunk low, but mounted high,
Through the dear might of Him that walked the
  waves,
Where, other groves and other streams along,
With nectar pure his oozy locks he laves,
And hears the unexpressive nuptial song,
In the blest kingdoms meek of joy and love.
There entertain him all the Saints above,
In solemn troops, and sweet societies,
That sing, and singing in their glory move,     180
And wipe the tears forever from his eyes.
Now, Lycidas, the shepherds weep no more;
Henceforth thou art the Genius of the shore,[116]

---

[98] Quickly and powerfully.

[99] i.e., corrupt Anglican clergymen.

[100] Harsh-sounding pipes.

[101] Either the Devil or the Roman Catholic Church.

[102] Not clearly identified but probably the sword of justice.

[103] River god.

[104] The black star; Sirius, the dog-star, so called because it was supposed to blacken vegetation.

[105] Early morning.

[106] Spotted.

[107] The flower which symbolizes immortality.

[108] i.e., laurel-crowned hearse.

[109] Islands west of Scotland.

[110] i.e., a world of monsters.

[111] The fabulous Bellerium, the Roman name for Land's End in Cornwall.

[112] Mount St. Michael, near Land's End, on which the Archangel supposedly sometimes appeared.

[113] Places on the coast of Spain from which an expedition against England would sail.

[114] i.e., let St. Michael turn from Spain to England.

[115] Compassion.

[116] i.e., the deity who is protector of the shore.

In thy large recompense, and shalt be good
To all that wander in that perilous flood.

    Thus sang the uncouth [117] swain to the oaks and
      rills,
While the still morn went out with sandals gray:
He touched the tender stops of various quills,
With eager thought warbling his Doric [118] lay.
And now the sun had stretched out all the hills, 190
And now was dropt into the western bay;
At last he rose, and twitched his mantle blue:
To-morrow to fresh woods, and pastures new.

---

[117] Unlearned and unknown.
[118] i.e., pastoral.

## Thomas Gray

# ELEGY WRITTEN IN A COUNTRY CHURCHYARD

The curfew tolls the knell of parting day,
The lowing herd wind slowly o'er the lea,
The plowman homeward plods his weary way,
And leaves the world to darkness and to me.

Now fades the glimmering landscape on the sight,
And all the air a solemn stillness holds,
Save where the beetle wheels his droning flight,
And drowsy tinklings lull the distant folds;

Save that from yonder ivy-mantled tower
The moping [119] owl does to the moon complain  10
Of such as, wandering near her secret bower,
Molest her ancient solitary reign.

Beneath those rugged elms, that yew-tree's shade,
Where heaves the turf in many a moldering heap,
Each in his narrow cell for ever laid,
The rude forefathers of the hamlet sleep.

The breezy call of incense-breathing morn,
The swallow twittering from the straw-built shed,
The cock's shrill clarion, or the echoing horn,
No more shall rouse them from their lowly bed.  20

For them no more the blazing hearth shall burn,
Or busy housewife ply her evening care:
No children run to lisp their sire's return,
Or climb his knees the envied kiss to share.

---

[119] Spiritless.

Oft did the harvest to their sickle yield,
Their furrow oft the stubborn glebe has broke;
How jocund did they drive their team afield!
How bowed the woods beneath their sturdy stroke!

Let not ambition mock their useful toil,
Their homely joys, and destiny obscure;        30
Nor grandeur hear with a disdainful smile
The short and simple annals of the poor.

The boast of heraldry, the pomp of power,
And all that beauty, all that wealth e'er gave,
Awaits alike th' inevitable hour:—
The paths of glory lead but to the grave.

Nor you, ye proud, impute to these the fault,
If memory o'er their tomb no trophies raise,
Where through the long-drawn aisle and fretted
    vault
The pealing anthem swells the note of praise.   40

Can storied urn or animated [120] bust
Back to its mansion call the fleeting breath?
Can honor's voice provoke the silent dust,
Or flattery soothe the dull, cold ear of death?

Perhaps in this neglected spot is laid
Some heart once pregnant with celestial fire;
Hands, that the rod of empire might have swayed,
Or waked to ecstasy the living lyre.

But knowledge to their eyes her ample page,
Rich with the spoils of time, did ne'er unroll;  50
Chill penury repressed their noble rage, [121]
And froze the genial current of the soul.

Full many a gem of purest ray serene
The dark unfathomed caves of ocean bear:
Full many a flower is born to blush unseen,
And waste its sweetness on the desert air.

Some village-Hampden, [122] that with dauntless
    breast
The little tyrant of his fields withstood;
Some mute inglorious Milton here may rest,
Some Cromwell, guiltless of his country's
    blood.                                        60

---

[120] Seeming alive.
[121] Enthusiasm, creative fervor.
[122] John Hampden, 1594–1643, one of the early
resisters to Charles, and hence a Puritan hero.

Th' applause of listening senates to command,
The threats of pain and ruin to despise,
To scatter plenty o'er a smiling land,
And read their history in a nation's eyes,

Their lot forbade: nor circumscribed alone
Their growing virtues, but their crimes confined;
Forbade to wade through slaughter to a throne,
And shut the gates of mercy on mankind;

The struggling pangs of conscious truth to hide,
To quench the blushes of ingenuous shame,    70
Or heap the shrine of luxury and pride
With incense kindled at the Muse's flame.

Far from the madding crowd's ignoble strife,
Their sober wishes never learned to stray;
Along the cool sequestered vale of life
They kept the noiseless tenor of their way.

Yet e'en these bones from insult to protect
Some frail memorial still erected nigh,
With uncouth rhymes and shapeless sculpture
   decked,
Implores the passing tribute of a sigh.    80

Their name, their years, spelt by th' unlettered
   Muse,
The place of fame and elegy supply:
And many a holy text around she strews,
That teach the rustic moralist to die.

For who, to dumb forgetfulness a prey,
This pleasing anxious being e'er resigned,
Left the warm precincts of the cheerful day,
Nor cast one longing, lingering look behind?

On some fond breast the parting soul relies,
Some pious drops the closing eye requires;    90
E'en from the tomb the voice of Nature cries,
E'en in our ashes live their wonted fires.

For thee, who, mindful of th' unhonored dead,
Dost in these lines their artless tale relate;
If chance,[123] by lonely contemplation led,
Some kindred spirit shall enquire thy fate,—

Haply some hoary-headed swain may say,
"Oft have we seen him at the peep of dawn
Brushing with hasty steps the dews away,
To meet the sun upon the upland lawn;    100

---

[123] *i.e.,* by chance.

"There at the foot of yonder nodding beech
That wreathes its old fantastic roots so high,
His listless length at noon-tide would he stretch,
And pore upon the brook that babbles by.

"Hard by yon wood, now smiling as in scorn,
Muttering his wayward fancies he would rove;
Now drooping, woeful-wan, like one forlorn,
Or crazed with care, or crossed in hopeless love.

"One morn I missed him on the 'customed hill,
Along the heath, and near his favorite tree;    110
Another came; nor yet beside the rill,
Nor up the lawn, nor at the wood was he;

"The next, with dirges due in sad array
Slow through the church-way path we saw him
   borne,—
Approach and read (for thou canst read) the lay
Graved on the stone beneath yon aged thorn."

### THE EPITAPH

Here rests his head upon the lap of earth
A youth, to fortune and to fame unknown;
Fair science frowned not on his humble birth
And melancholy marked him for her own.    120

Large was his bounty, and his soul sincere;
Heaven did a recompense as largely send:
He gave to misery all he had, a tear;
He gained from heaven ('twas all he wished) a
   friend.

No farther seek his merits to disclose,
Or draw his frailties from their dread abode,
(There they alike in trembling hope repose)
The bosom of his Father and his God.

## *Sophocles*
## ANTIGONE

### THE STORY

    *King Oedipus of Thebes unknowingly
slew his father, King Laios, and married his
mother, Iocaste. When the truth came to light,
he was exiled from Thebes by his own edict,
and the government of the city was assumed*

*by Iocaste's brother, Creon. Subsequently, Oedipus's sons, Polyneices and Eteocles, rebelled against Creon and against each other. When Eteocles received the support of most of the Thebans, Polyneices went to Argos for aid and returned with seven great captains to lay siege to his native city. Thebes withstood the assault, but the two brothers killed each other. Thereupon Creon, again master of the city, issued an edict refusing burial to Polyneices. Ismene and Antigone, the two remaining children of Oedipus, are discussing this as the play opens.*

## CHARACTERS

ANTIGONE
ISMENE
EURYDICE
CREON
HAIMON
TEIRESIAS
A SENTRY
A MESSENGER
CHORUS

SCENE: *Before the palace of* CREON, *King of Thebes. A central double door, and two lateral doors. A platform extends the length of the façade, and from this platform three steps lead down into the "orchestra," or chorus-ground.*
TIME: *dawn of the day after the repulse of the Argive army from the assault on Thebes.*

## PROLOGUE

[ANTIGONE *and* ISMENE *enter from the central door of the Palace.*

ANTIGONE.

Ismene, dear sister,
You would think that we had already suffered enough
For the curse on Oedipus:
I cannot imagine any grief
That you and I have not gone through. And now—
Have they told you of the new decree of our King Creon?

ISMENE.

I have heard nothing: I know
That two sisters lost two brothers, a double death

In a single hour; and I know that the Argive army
Fled in the night; but beyond this, nothing.   10

ANTIGONE.

I thought so. And that is why I wanted you
To come out here with me. There is something we must do.

ISMENE.

Why do you speak so strangely?

ANTIGONE.

Listen, Ismene:
Creon buried our brother Eteocles
With military honors, gave him a soldier's funeral,
And it was right that he should; but Polyneices,
Who fought as bravely and died as miserably,—
They say that Creon has sworn
No one shall bury him, no one mourn for him,   20
But his body must lie in the fields, a sweet treasure
For carrion birds to find as they search for food.
That is what they say, and our good Creon is coming here
To announce it publicly; and the penalty—
Stoning to death in the public square!
                                        There it is,
And now you can prove what you are:
A true sister, or a traitor to your family.

ISMENE.

Antigone, you are mad! What could I possibly do?

ANTIGONE.

You must decide whether you will help me or not.   30

ISMENE.

I do not understand you. Help you in what?

ANTIGONE.

Ismene, I am going to bury him. Will you come?

ISMENE.

Bury him! You have just said the new law forbids it.

ANTIGONE.

He is my brother. And he is your brother, too.

ISMENE.

But think of the danger! Think what Creon will
    do!

ANTIGONE.

Creon is not strong enough to stand in my way.

ISMENE.

Ah sister!
Oedipus died, everyone hating him
For what his own search brought to light, his
    eyes
Ripped out by his own hand; and Iocaste
    died,                                              40
His mother and wife at once: she twisted the
    cords
That strangled her life; and our two brothers
    died,
Each killed by the other's sword. And we are
    left:
But oh, Antigone,
Think how much more terrible than these
Our own death would be if we should go against
    Creon
And do what he has forbidden! We are only
    women,
We cannot fight with men, Antigone!
The law is strong, we must give in to the law
In this thing, and in worse. I beg the Dead   50
To forgive me, but I am helpless: I must yield
To those in authority. And I think it is danger-
    ous business
To be always meddling.

ANTIGONE.

                        If that is what you think,
I should not want you, even if you asked to
    come.
You have made your choice, you can be what
    you want to be.
But I will bury him; and if I must die,
I say that this crime is holy: I shall lie down
With him in death, and I shall be as dear
To him as he to me.                               60
                        It is the dead,
Not the living, who make the longest demands:
We die for ever . . .
                        You may do as you like,
Since apparently the laws of the gods mean
    nothing to you.

ISMENE.

They mean a great deal to me; but I have no
    strength
To break laws that were made for the public
    good.

ANTIGONE.

That must be your excuse, I suppose. But as for
    me,
I will bury the brother I love.

ISMENE.

                                Antigone,        70
I am so afraid for you!

ANTIGONE.

                        You need not be:
You have yourself to consider, after all.

ISMENE.

But no one must hear of this, you must tell no
    one!
I will keep it a secret, I promise!

ANTIGONE.

                        Oh tell it! Tell everyone!
Think how they'll hate you when it all comes
    out
If they learn that you knew about it all the time!

ISMENE.

So fiery! You should be cold with fear.

ANTIGONE.

Perhaps. But I am doing only what I must.   80

ISMENE.

But can you do it? I say that you cannot.

ANTIGONE.

Very well: when my strength gives out, I shall
    do no more.

ISMENE.

Impossible things should not be tried at all.

ANTIGONE.

Go away, Ismene:
I shall be hating you soon, and the dead will too,
For your words are hateful. Leave me my fool-
    ish plan:
I am not afraid of the danger; if it means death,
It will not be the worst of deaths—death with-
    out honor.

ISMENE.

Go then, if you feel that you must.
You are unwise,                                                      90
But a loyal friend indeed to those who love you.
      [*Exit into the Palace.* ANTIGONE *goes off,
      L. Enter the* CHORUS.


## PARODOS

CHORUS.                                                    [STROPHE 1

Now the long blade of the sun, lying
Level east to west, touches with glory
Thebes of the Seven Gates. Open, unlidded
Eye of golden day! O marching light
Across the eddy and rush of Dirce's stream,
Striking the white shields of the enemy
Thrown headlong backward from the blaze of
      morning!

CHORAGOS.

Polyneices their commander
Roused them with windy phrases,            100
He the wild eagle screaming
Insults above our land,
His wings their shields of snow,
His crest their marshalled helms.

CHORUS.                                                [ANTISTROPHE 1

Against our seven gates in a yawning ring
The famished spears came onward in the night;
But before his jaws were sated with our blood,
Or pinefire took the garland of our towers,
He was thrown back; and as he turned, great
      Thebes—
No tender victim for his noisy power—        110
Rose like a dragon behind him, shouting war.

CHORAGOS.

For God hates utterly
The bray of bragging tongues;
And when he beheld their smiling,
Their swagger of golden helms,
The frown of his thunder blasted
Their first man from our walls.

CHORUS.                                                    [STROPHE 2

We heard his shout of triumph high in the air
Turn to a scream; far out in a flaming arc

---

PARODOS: entrance-song of the Chorus.
96 *Dirce's stream:* river west of Thebes. *Choragos:*
leader of the Chorus.

He fell with his windy torch, and the earth
      struck him.                                               120
And others storming in fury no less than his
Found shock of death in the dusty joy of battle.

CHORAGOS.

Seven captains at seven gates
Yielded their clanging arms to the god
That bends the battle-line and breaks it.
These two only, brothers in blood,
Face to face in matchless rage,
Mirroring each the other's death,
Clashed in long combat.

CHORUS.                                                [ANTISTROPHE 2

But now in the beautiful morning of victory 130
Let Thebes of the many chariots sing for joy!
With hearts for dancing we'll take leave of war:
Our temples shall be sweet with hymns of
      praise,
And the long night shall echo with our chorus.


## SCENE I

CHORAGOS.

But now at last our new King is coming:
Creon of Thebes, Menoikeus' son.
In this auspicious dawn of his reign
What are the new complexities
That shifting Fate has woven for him?
What is his counsel? Why has he summoned 140
The old men to hear him?
      [*Enter* CREON *from the Palace, C. He ad-
      dresses the* CHORUS *from the top step.*

CREON.

   Gentlemen: I have the honor to inform you
that our Ship of State, which recent storms
have threatened to destroy, has come safely to
harbor at last, guided by the merciful wisdom
of Heaven. I have summoned you here this
morning because I know that I can depend
upon you: your devotion to King Laios was
absolute; you never hesitated in your duty to
our late ruler Oedipus; and when Oedi-    150
pus died, your loyalty was transferred to his
children. Unfortunately, as you know, his two
sons, the princes Eteocles and Polyneices, have
killed each other in battle; and I, as the next
in blood, have succeeded to the full power of
the throne.
   I am aware, of course, that no Ruler can
expect complete loyalty from his subjects until

he has been tested in office. Nevertheless, I say
to you at the very outset that I have    160
nothing but contempt for the kind of Governor
who is afraid, for whatever reason, to follow
the course that he knows is best for the State;
and as for the man who sets private friendship
above the public welfare,—I have no use for
him, either. I call God to witness that if I saw
my country headed for ruin, I should not be
afraid to speak out plainly; and I need hardly
remind you that I would never have any dealings with an enemy of the people. No one    170
values friendship more highly than I; but we
must remember that friends made at the risk
of wrecking our Ship are not real friends at all.

These are my principles, at any rate, and
that is why I have made the following decision
concerning the sons of Oedipus: Eteocles, who
died as a man should die, fighting for his country, is to be buried with full military honors,
with all the ceremony that is usual when the
greatest heroes die; but his brother Poly-    180
neices, who broke his exile to come back with
fire and sword against his native city and the
shrines of his fathers' gods, whose one idea was
to spill the blood of his blood and sell his own
people into slavery—Polyneices, I say, is to
have no burial: no man is to touch him or say
the least prayer for him; he shall lie on the
plain, unburied; and the birds and the scaveng-
ing dogs can do with him whatever they like.

This is my command, and you can see    190
the wisdom behind it. As long as I am King, no
traitor is going to be honored with the loyal
man. But whoever shows by word and deed
that he is on the side of the State,—he shall
have my respect while he is living, and my
reverence when he is dead.

CHORAGOS.

If that is your will, Creon son of Menoikeus,
You have the right to enforce it: we are yours.

CREON.

That is my will. Take care that you do your
    part.

CHORAGOS.

We are old men: let the younger ones carry it
    out.                                        200

CREON.

I do not mean that: the sentries have been
    appointed.

CHORAGOS.

Then what is it that you would have us do?

CREON.

You will give no support to whoever breaks
    this law.

CHORAGOS.

Only a crazy man is in love with death!

CREON.

And death it is; yet money talks, and the wisest
Have sometimes been known to count a few
    coins too many.

                        [Enter SENTRY from L.

SENTRY.

    I'll not say that I'm out of breath from run-
ning, King, because every time I stopped to
think about what I have to tell you, I felt like
going back. And all the time a voice kept    210
saying, "You fool, don't you know you're
walking straight into trouble?"; and then another voice: "Yes, but if you let somebody else
get the news to Creon first, it will be even
worse than that for you!" But good sense won
out, at least I hope it was good sense, and here
I am with a story that makes no sense at all;
but I'll tell it anyhow, because, as they say,
what's going to happen's going to happen,
and—                                         220

CREON.

Come to the point. What have you to say?

SENTRY.

    I did not do it. I did not see who did it. You
must not punish me for what someone else has
done.

CREON.

A comprehensive defense! More effective, per-
    haps,
If I knew its purpose. Come: what is it?

SENTRY.

A dreadful thing . . . I don't know how to put
    it—

CREON.

Out with it!

SENTRY.
            Well, then;
The dead man—
                  Polyneices—
[*Pause. The* SENTRY *is overcome, fumbles
for words.* CREON *waits impassively.*
                        out there—    230
                        someone,—
New dust on the slimy flesh!
            -       [*Pause. No sign from* CREON.
Someone has given it burial that way, and
Gone . . .
            [*Long pause.* CREON *finally speaks with
            deadly control:*

CREON.

And the man who dared do this?

SENTRY.
                        I swear I
Do not know! You must believe me!
                        Listen:
The ground was dry, not a sign of digging, no,
Not a wheeltrack in the dust, no trace of any-
      one.                               240
It was when they relieved us this morning: and
      one of them,
The corporal, pointed to it.
                        There it was,
The strangest—
            Look:
The body, just mounded over with light dust:
      you see?
Not buried really, but as if they'd covered it
Just enough for the ghost's peace. And no sign
Of dogs or any wild animal that had been there.

And then what a scene there was! Every man
      of us                              250
Accusing the other: we all proved the other
      man did it,
We all had proof that we could not have done
      it.
We were ready to take hot iron in our hands,
Walk through fire, swear by all the gods,
*It was not I!*
*I do not know who it was, but it was not I!*
            [CREON's *rage has been mounting steadily,
            but the* SENTRY *is too intent upon his story
            to notice it.*
And then, when this came to nothing, someone
      said
A thing that silenced us and made us stare

Down at the ground: you had to be told the
      news,
And one of us had to do it! We threw the dice,
And the bad luck fell to me. So here I am,   261
No happier to be here than you are to have me:
Nobody likes the man who brings bad news.

CHORAGOS.

I have been wondering, King: can it be that
      the gods have done this?

CREON.                              [*Furiously*
Stop!
Must you doddering wrecks
Go out of your heads entirely? "The gods!"
Intolerable!
The gods favor this corpse? Why? How had he
      served them?                       269
Tried to loot their temples, burn their images,
Yes, and the whole State, and its laws with it!
Is it your senile opinion that the gods love to
      honor bad men?
A pious thought!—
                  No, from the very beginning
There have been those who have whispered
      together,
Stiff-necked anarchists, putting their heads to-
      gether,
Scheming against me in alleys. These are the
      men,
And they have bribed my own guard to do this
      thing.
Money!                               [*Sententiously*
There's nothing in the world so demoralizing
      as money.                          280
Down go your cities,
Homes gone, men gone, honest hearts cor-
      rupted,
Crookedness of all kinds, and all for money!
                        [*To* SENTRY:
                        But you—!
I swear by God and by the throne of God,
The man who has done this thing shall pay for
      it!
Find that man, bring him here to me, or your
      death
Will be the least of your problems: I'll string
      you up
Alive, and there will be certain ways to make
      you
Discover your employer before you die;
And the process may teach you a lesson you
      seem to have missed:                290

The dearest profit is sometimes all too dear:
That depends on the source. Do you under-
    stand me?
A fortune won is often misfortune.

SENTRY.

King, may I speak?

CREON.

                    Your very voice distresses me.

SENTRY.

Are you sure that it is my voice, and not your
    conscience?

CREON.

By God, he wants to analyze me now!

SENTRY.

It is not what I say, but what has been done,
    that hurts you.

CREON.

You talk too much.

SENTRY.

                    Maybe; but I've done nothing.

CREON.

Sold your soul for some silver: that's all you've
    done.                                               301

SENTRY.

How dreadful it is when the right judge judges
    wrong!

CREON.

Your figures of speech
May entertain you now; but unless you bring
    me the man,
You will get little profit from them in the end.
                        [Exit CREON into the Palace.

SENTRY.

"Bring me the man"—!
I'd like nothing better than bringing him the
    man!
But bring him or not, you have seen the last
    of me here.
At any rate, I am safe!
                                        [Exit SENTRY.

## ODE I

CHORUS.                                    [STROPHE 1

Numberless are the world's wonders, but none
More wonderful than man; the stormgray sea
Yields to his prows, the huge crests bear him
    high;                                               312
Earth, holy and inexhaustible, is graven
With shining furrows where his plows have
    gone
Year after year, the timeless labor of stallions.

                                        [ANTISTROPHE 1

The lightboned birds and beasts that cling to
    cover,
The lithe fish lighting their reaches of dim
    water,
All are taken, tamed in the net of his mind;
The lion on the hill, the wild horse windy-
    maned,                                              319
Resign to him; and his blunt yoke has broken
The sultry shoulders of the mountain bull.

                                        [STROPHE 2

Words also, and thought as rapid as air,
He fashions to his good use; statecraft is his,
And his the skill that deflects the arrows of
    snow,
The spears of winter rain: from every wind
He has made himself secure—from all but one:
In the late wind of death he cannot stand.

                                        [ANTISTROPHE 2

O clear intelligence, force beyond all measure!
O fate of man, working both good and evil!
When the laws are kept, how proudly his city
    stands!                                             330
When the laws are broken, what of his city
    then?
Never may the anarchic man find rest at my
    hearth,
Never be it said that my thoughts are his
    thoughts.

## SCENE II

[Re-enter SENTRY leading ANTIGONE.

CHORAGOS.

What does this mean? Surely this captive
    woman
Is the Princess, Antigone. Why should she be
    taken?

SENTRY.

Here is the one who did it! We caught her
In the very act of burying him.—Where is
    Creon?

CHORAGOS.

Just coming from the house.

> [*Enter* CREON, *C.*

CREON.

                What has happened?
Why have you come back so soon?        340

SENTRY.                          [*Expansively*
                            O King,
A man should never be too sure of anything:
I would have sworn
That you'd not see me here again: your anger
Frightened me so, and the things you threat-
    ened me with;
But how could I tell then
That I'd be able to solve the case so soon?

No dice-throwing this time: I was only too glad
    to come!

Here is this woman. She is the guilty one:
We found her trying to bury him.        350
Take her, then; question her; judge her as you
    will.
I am through with the whole thing now, and
    glad of it.

CREON.

But this is Antigone! Why have you brought
    her here?

SENTRY.

She was burying him, I tell you!

CREON.                            [*Severely*
                    Is this the truth?

SENTRY.

I saw her with my own eyes. Can I say more?

CREON.

The details: come, tell me quickly!

SENTRY.

                    It was like this:
After those terrible threats of yours, King,
We went back and brushed the dust away from
    the body.        360

The flesh was soft by now, and stinking,
So we sat on a hill to windward and kept guard.
No napping this time! We kept each other
    awake.
But nothing happened until the white round sun
Whirled in the center of the round sky over us:
Then, suddenly,
A storm of dust roared up from the earth, and
    the sky
Went out, the plain vanished with all its trees
In the stinging dark. We closed our eyes and
    endured it.        369
The whirlwind lasted a long time, but it passed;
And then we looked, and there was Antigone!
I have seen
A mother bird come back to a stripped nest,
    heard
Her crying bitterly a broken note or two
For the young ones stolen. Just so, when this
    girl
Found the bare corpse, and all her love's work
    wasted,
She wept, and cried on heaven to damn the
    hands
That had done this thing.
                    And then she brought more dust
And sprinkled wine three times for her brother's
    ghost.        380

We ran and took her at once. She was not
    afraid,
Not even when we charged her with what she
    had done.
She denied nothing.
                    And this was a comfort to me,
And some uneasiness: for it is a good thing
To escape from death, but it is no great
    pleasure
To bring death to a friend.
                    Yet I always say
There is nothing so comfortable as your own
    safe skin!

CREON.                        [*Slowly, dangerously*
And you, Antigone,        390
You with your head hanging,—do you confess
    this thing?

ANTIGONE.

I do. I deny nothing.

CREON.                            [*To* SENTRY:
                    You may go.
                                [*Exit* SENTRY.

[*To* ANTIGONE:

Tell me, tell me briefly:
Had you heard my proclamation touching this
    matter?

ANTIGONE.

It was public. Could I help hearing it?

CREON.

And yet you dared defy the law.

ANTIGONE.

                              I dared.
It was not God's proclamation. That final
    Justice
That rules the world below makes no such
    laws.                                      400

Your edict, King, was strong,
But all your strength is weakness itself against
The immortal unrecorded laws of God.
They are not merely now: they were, and shall
    be,
Operative for ever, beyond man utterly.

I knew I must die, even without your decree:
I am only mortal. And if I must die
Now, before it is my time to die,
Surely this is no hardship: can anyone
Living, as I live, with evil all about me,    410
Think Death less than a friend? This death of
    mine
Is of no importance; but if I had left my
    brother
Lying in death unburied, I should have suffered.
Now I do not.
              You smile at me. Ah Creon,
Think me a fool, if you like; but it may well be
That a fool convicts me of folly.

CHORAGOS.

Like father, like daughter: both headstrong,
    deaf to reason!
She has never learned to yield.               419

CREON.

                        She has much to learn.
The inflexible heart breaks first, the toughest
    iron
Cracks first, and the wildest horses bend their
    necks
At the pull of the smallest curb.
                        Pride? In a slave?

This girl is guilty of a double insolence,
Breaking the given laws and boasting of it.
Who is the man here,
She or I, if this crime goes unpunished?
Sister's child, or more than sister's child,
Or closer yet in blood—she and her sister   430
Win bitter death for this!
                        [*To servants:*
                Go, some of you,
Arrest Ismene. I accuse her equally.
Bring her: you will find her sniffling in the
    house there.

Her mind's a traitor: crimes kept in the dark
Cry for light, and the guardian brain shudders;
But how much worse than this
Is brazen boasting of barefaced anarchy!

ANTIGONE.

Creon, what more do you want than my death?

CREON.

                              Nothing.
That gives me everything.                     441

ANTIGONE.

                    Then I beg you: kill me.
This talking is a great weariness: your words
Are distasteful to me, and I am sure that mine
Seem so to you. And yet they should not seem
    so:
I should have praise and honor for what I have
    done.
All these men here would praise me
Were their lips not frozen shut with fear of you.
                              [*Bitterly*
Ah the good fortune of kings,                 449
Licensed to say and do whatever they please!

CREON.

You are alone here in that opinion.

ANTIGONE.

No, they are with me. But they keep their
    tongues in leash.

CREON.

Maybe. But you are guilty, and they are not.

ANTIGONE.

There is no guilt in reverence for the dead.

CREON.

But Eteocles—was he not your brother too?

ANTIGONE.

My brother too.

CREON.

              And you insult his memory?

ANTIGONE.                          [*Softly*

The dead man would not say that I insult it.

CREON.

He would: for you honor a traitor as much as
    him.

ANTIGONE.

His own brother, traitor or not, and equal in
    blood.                                    460

CREON.

He made war on his country. Eteocles defended
    it.

ANTIGONE.

Nevertheless, there are honors due all the dead.

CREON.

But not the same for the wicked as for the just.

ANTIGONE.

Ah Creon, Creon,
Which of us can say what the gods hold
    wicked?

CREON.

An enemy is an enemy, even dead.

ANTIGONE.

It is my nature to join in love, not hate.

CREON.                     [*Finally losing patience*

Go join them, then; if you must have your love,
Find it in hell!

CHORAGOS.

But see, Ismene comes:                        470
              [*Enter* ISMENE, *guarded.*
Those tears are sisterly, the cloud
That shadows her eyes rains down gentle sor-
    row.

CREON.

You too, Ismene,
Snake in my ordered house, sucking my blood

Stealthily—and all the time I never knew
That these two sisters were aiming at my
    throne!
                       Ismene,
Do you confess your share in this crime, or
    deny it?
Answer me.

ISMENE.

Yes, if she will let me say so. I am guilty.

ANTIGONE.                          [*Coldly*

No, Ismene. You have no right to say so. 480
You would not help me, and I will not have
    you help me.

ISMENE.

But now I know what you meant; and I am
    here
To join you, to take my share of punishment.

ANTIGONE.

The dead man and the gods who rule the dead
Know whose act this was. Words are not
    friends.

ISMENE.

Do you refuse me, Antigone? I want to die with
    you:
I too have a duty that I must discharge to the
    dead.

ANTIGONE.

You shall not lessen my death by sharing it.

ISMENE.

What do I care for life when you are dead?  490

ANTIGONE.

Ask Creon. You're always hanging on his opin-
    ions.

ISMENE.

You are laughing at me. Why, Antigone?

ANTIGONE.

It's a joyless laughter, Ismene.

ISMENE.

                But can I do nothing?

ANTIGONE.

Yes. Save yourself. I shall not envy you.
There are those who will praise you; I shall
    have honor, too.

ISMENE.

But we are equally guilty!

ANTIGONE.

                    No more, Ismene.
You are alive, but I belong to Death.

CREON.                    [*To the* CHORUS:
Gentlemen, I beg you to observe these girls:
One has just now lost her mind; the other,    500
It seems, has never had a mind at all.

ISMENE.

Grief teaches the steadiest minds to waver,
    King.

CREON.

Yours certainly did, when you assumed guilt
    with the guilty!

ISMENE.

But how could I go on living without her?

CREON.

                    You are.
She is already dead.

ISMENE.

                    But your own son's bride!

CREON.

There are places enough for him to push his
    plow.
I want no wicked women for my sons!    510

ISMENE.

O dearest Haimon, how your father wrongs
    you!

CREON.

I've had enough of your childish talk of mar-
    riage!

CHORAGOS.

Do you really intend to steal this girl from your
    son?

CREON.

No; Death will do that for me.

CHORAGOS.

                    Then she must die?

CREON.                    [*Ironically*
You dazzle me.
                    —But enough of this talk!
                    [*To* GUARDS:
You, there, take them away and guard them
    well:
For they are but women, and even brave men
    run
When they see Death coming.    520
    [*Exeunt* ISMENE, ANTIGONE, *and* GUARDS.

## ODE II

CHORUS.                    [STROPHE 1
Fortunate is the man who has never tasted
    God's vengeance!
Where once the anger of heaven has struck,
    that house is shaken
For ever: damnation rises behind each child
Like a wave cresting out of the black northeast,
When the long darkness under sea roars up
And bursts drumming death upon the wind-
    whipped sand.

                    [ANTISTROPHE 1
I have seen this gathering sorrow from time
    long past
Loom upon Oedipus' children: generation from
    generation
Takes the compulsive rage of the enemy god.
So lately this last flower of Oedipus' line    530
Drank the sunlight! but now a passionate word
And a handful of dust have closed up all its
    beauty.

                    [STROPHE 2
What mortal arrogance
Transcends the wrath of Zeus?
Sleep cannot lull him, nor the effortless long
    months
Of the timeless gods: but he is young for ever,
And his house is the shining day of high
    Olympos.
    All that is and shall be,
    And all the past, is his.
No pride on earth is free of the curse of
    heaven.    540

                    [ANTISTROPHE 2
The straying dreams of men
May bring them ghosts of joy:
But as they drowse, the waking embers burn
    them;
Or they walk with fixed eyes, as blind men
    walk.

But the ancient wisdom speaks for our own
    time:
    *Fate works most for woe*
    *With Folly's fairest show.*
Man's little pleasure is the spring of sorrow.

## SCENE III

CHORAGOS.

But here is Haimon, King, the last of your
    sons.                                                      549
Is it grief for Antigone that brings him here,
And bitterness at being robbed of his bride?

                                   [*Enter* HAIMON.

CREON.

We shall soon see, and no need of diviners.

                                              —Son,
You have heard my final judgment on that girl:
Have you come here hating me, or have you
    come
With deference and with love, whatever I do?

HAIMON.

I am your son, father. You are my guide.
You make things clear for me, and I obey you.
No marriage means more to me than your con-
    tinuing wisdom.                                    559

CREON.

Good. That is the way to behave: subordinate
Everything else, my son, to your father's will.
This is what a man prays for, that he may get
Sons attentive and dutiful in his house,
Each one hating his father's enemies,
Honoring his father's friends. But if his sons
Fail him, if they turn out unprofitably,
What has he fathered but trouble for himself
And amusement for the malicious?

                                   So you are right
Not to lose your head over this woman.    570
Your pleasure with her would soon grow cold,
    Haimon,
And then you'd have a hellcat in bed and else-
    where.
Let her find her husband in Hell!
Of all the people in this city, only she
Has had contempt for my law and broken it.

Do you want me to show myself weak before
    the people?
Or to break my sworn word? No, and I will not.
The woman dies.

I suppose she'll plead "family ties." Well, let
    her.
If I permit my own family to rebel,          580
How shall I earn the world's obedience?
Show me the man who keeps his house in hand,
He's fit for public authority.

                    I'll have no dealings
With law-breakers, critics of the government:
Whoever is chosen to govern should be
    obeyed—
Must be obeyed, in all things, great and small,
Just and unjust! O Haimon,
The man who knows how to obey, and that
    man only,
Knows how to give commands when the time
    comes.                                                    590
You can depend on him, no matter how fast
The spears come: he's a good soldier, he'll stick
    it out.

Anarchy, anarchy! Show me a greater evil!
This is why cities tumble and the great houses
    rain down,
This is what scatters armies!

No, no: good lives are made so by discipline.
We keep the laws then, and the lawmakers,
And no woman shall seduce us. If we must lose,
Let's lose to a man, at least! Is a woman
    stronger than we?

CHORAGOS.

Unless time has rusted my wits,                600
What you say, King, is said with point and
    dignity.

HAIMON.                              [*Boyishly earnest*

Father:
Reason is God's crowning gift to man, and you
    are right
To warn me against losing mine. I cannot say—
I hope that I shall never want to say!—that you
Have reasoned badly. Yet there are other men
Who can reason, too; and their opinions might
    be helpful.
You are not in a position to know everything
That people say or do, or what they feel:
Your temper terrifies them—everyone          610
Will tell you only what you like to hear.
But I, at any rate, can listen; and I have heard
    them
Muttering and whispering in the dark about
    this girl.

They say no woman has ever, so unreasonably,
Died so shameful a death for a generous act:
"She covered her brother's body. Is this in-
    decent?
She kept him from dogs and vultures. Is this a
    crime?
Death?—She should have all the honor that
    we can give her!"

This is the way they talk out there in the city.

You must believe me:                              620
Nothing is closer to me than your happiness.
What could be closer? Must not any son
Value his father's fortune as his father does his?
I beg you, do not be unchangeable:
Do not believe that you alone can be right.
The man who thinks that,
The man who maintains that only he has the
    power
To reason correctly, the gift to speak, the
    soul—
A man like that, when you know him, turns out
    empty.
It is not reason never to yield to reason!    630

In flood time you can see how some trees bend,
And because they bend, even their twigs are
    safe,
While stubborn trees are torn up, roots and all.
And the same thing happens in sailing:
Make your sheet fast, never slacken,—and over
    you go,
Head over heels and under: and there's your
    voyage.
Forget you are angry! Let yourself be moved!
I know I am young; but please let me say this:
The ideal condition
Would be, I admit, that men should be right by
    instinct;                                    640
But since we are all too likely to go astray,
The reasonable thing is to learn from those who
    can teach.

CHORAGOS.

You will do well to listen to him, King,
If what he says is sensible. And you, Haimon,
Must listen to your father.—Both speak well.

CREON.

You consider it right for a man of my years
    and experience
To go to school to a boy?

HAIMON.

                            It is not right
If I am wrong. But if I am young, and right,
What does my age matter?                        650

CREON.

You think it right to stand up for an anarchist?

HAIMON.

Not at all. I pay no respect to criminals.

CREON.

Then she is not a criminal?

HAIMON.

The City would deny it, to a man.

CREON.

And the City proposes to teach me how to rule?

HAIMON.

Ah. Who is it that's talking like a boy now?

CREON.

My voice is the one voice giving orders in this
    City!

HAIMON.

It is no City if it takes orders from one voice.

CREON.

The State is the King!                          659

HAIMON.

                    Yes, if the State is a desert.
                                        [Pause.

CREON.

This boy, it seems, has sold out to a woman.

HAIMON.

If you are a woman: my concern is only for
    you.

CREON.

So? Your "concern"! In a public brawl with
    your father!

HAIMON.

How about you, in a public brawl with justice?

CREON.

With justice, when all that I do is within my
    rights?

HAIMON.
You have no right to trample on God's right.

CREON.                          [*Completely out of control*
Fool, adolescent fool! Taken in by a woman!

HAIMON.
You'll never see me taken in by anything vile.

CREON.
Every word you say is for her!

HAIMON.                          [*Quietly, darkly*
                              And for you.     670
And for me. And for the gods under the earth.

CREON.
You'll never marry her while she lives.

HAIMON.
Then she must die.—But her death will cause
    another.

CREON.
Another?
Have you lost your senses? Is this an open
    threat?

HAIMON.
There is no threat in speaking to emptiness.

CREON.
I swear you'll regret this superior tone of yours!
You are the empty one!

HAIMON.
                        If you were not my father,
I'd say you were perverse.                   680

CREON.
You girlstruck fool, don't play at words with
    me!

HAIMON.
I am sorry. You prefer silence.

CREON.
                        Now, by God—!
I swear, by all the gods in heaven above us,
You'll watch it, I swear you shall!
                        [*To the* SERVANTS:
                            Bring her out!

Bring the woman out! Let her die before his
    eyes!
Here, this instant, with her bridegroom beside
    her!

HAIMON.
Not here, no; she will not die here, King.
And you will never see my face again.     690
Go on raving as long as you've a friend to
    endure you.
                        [*Exit* HAIMON.

CHORAGOS.
Gone, gone.
Creon, a young man in a rage is dangerous!

CREON.
Let him do, or dream to do, more than a man
    can.
He shall not save these girls from death.

CHORAGOS.
                        These girls?
You have sentenced them both?

CREON.
                        No, you are right.
I will not kill the one whose hands are clean.

CHORAGOS.
But Antigone?                              700

CREON.                          [*Somberly*
                    I will carry her far away
Out there in the wilderness, and lock her
Living in a vault of stone. She shall have food,
As the custom is, to absolve the State of her
    death.
And there let her pray to the gods of hell:
They are her only gods:
Perhaps they will show her an escape from
    death,
Or she may learn,
                    though late,
That piety shown the dead is pity in vain.   710
                        [*Exit* CREON.


## ODE III

CHORUS.                          [STROPHE
Love, unconquerable
Waster of rich men, keeper

---

704 *custom:* it was believed that if food were placed
with a criminal who was being buried alive, his death
might be considered due to natural causes.

Of warm lights and all-night vigil
In the soft face of a girl:
Sea-wanderer, forest-visitor!
Even the pure Immortals cannot escape you,
And mortal man, in his one day's dusk,
Trembles before your glory.

[ANTISTROPHE

Surely you swerve upon ruin
The just man's consenting heart,               720
As here you have made bright anger
Strike between father and son—
And none has conquered but Love!
A girl's glance working the will of heaven:
Pleasure to her alone who mocks us,
Merciless Aphrodite.

## SCENE IV

CHORAGOS.        [As ANTIGONE enters guarded.

But I can no longer stand in awe of this,
Nor, seeing what I see, keep back my tears.
Here is Antigone, passing to that chamber
Where all find sleep at last.               730

ANTIGONE.                       [STROPHE 1

Look upon me, friends, and pity me
Turning back at the night's edge to say
Good-by to the sun that shines for me no longer;
Now sleepy Death
Summons me down to Acheron, that cold
    shore:
There is no bridesong there, nor any music.

CHORUS.

Yet not unpraised, not without a kind of honor,
You walk at last into the underworld;
Untouched by sickness, broken by no sword.
What woman has ever found your way to
    death?                                   740

ANTIGONE.                       [ANTISTROPHE 1

How often I have heard the story of Niobe,
Tantalos' wretched daughter, how the stone
Clung fast about her, ivy-close: and they say
The rain falls endlessly
And sifting soft snow; her tears are never done.
I feel the loneliness of her death in mine.

726 *Aphrodite:* goddess of love.  735 *Acheron:* river of
the underworld.  741 *Niobe:* wife of Amphion, king of
Thebes, who boasted that she had borne more children
than Leto, mother of Apollo and Artemis. In revenge,
Apollo and Artemis destroyed all of Niobe's children and
turned her to stone upon Mt. Sipylus.

CHORUS.

But she was born of heaven, and you
Are woman, woman-born. If her death is yours,
A mortal woman's, is this not for you
Glory in our world and in the world be-
    yond?                                    750

ANTIGONE.                       [STROPHE 2

You laugh at me. Ah, friends, friends,
Can you not wait until I am dead? O Thebes,
O men many-charioted, in love with Fortune,
Dear springs of Dirce, sacred Theban grove,
Be witnesses for me, denied all pity,
Unjustly judged! and think a word of love
For her whose path turns
Under dark earth, where there are no more
    tears.

CHORUS.

You have passed beyond human daring and
    come at last
Into a place of stone where Justice sits.     760
I cannot tell
What shape of your father's guilt appears in
    this.

ANTIGONE.                       [ANTISTROPHE 2

You have touched it at last: that bridal bed
Unspeakable, horror of son and mother min-
    gling:
Their crime, infection of all our family!
O Oedipus, father and brother!
Your marriage strikes from the grave to murder
    mine.
I have been a stranger here in my own land:
All my life
The blasphemy of my birth has followed
    me.                                      770

CHORUS.

Reverence is a virtue, but strength
Lives in established law: that must prevail.
You have made your choice,
Your death is the doing of your conscious hand.

ANTIGONE.                            [EPODE

Then let me go, since all your words are bitter,
And the very light of the sun is cold to me.
Lead me to my vigil, where I must have

747 *born of heaven:* Niobe's father, Tantalos, was a
son of Zeus.

Neither love nor lamentation; no song, but
silence.
                    [CREON *interrupts impatiently.*

CREON.

If dirges and planned lamentations could put off
death,
Men would be singing for ever.             780
                    [*To the* SERVANTS:
                    Take her, go!
You know your orders: take her to the vault
And leave her alone there. And if she lives or
dies,
That's her affair, not ours: our hands are clean.

ANTIGONE.

O tomb, vaulted bride-bed in eternal rock,
Soon I shall be with my own again
Where Persephone welcomes the thin ghosts
underground:
And I shall see my father again, and you,
mother,
And dearest Polyneices—
                    dearest indeed    790
To me, since it was my hand
That washed him clean and poured the ritual
wine:
And my reward is death before my time!

And yet, as men's hearts know, I have done no
wrong,
I have not sinned before God. Or if I have,
I shall know the truth in death. But if the guilt
Lies upon Creon who judged me, then, I pray,
May his punishment equal my own.

---

787 *Persephone:* queen of the underworld. 793 *And
my reward:* the translators have omitted a passage
of sixteen lines. The passage has been questioned by
some editors, but the consensus of modern scholarship
is against excluding it and against the simplification of
Antigone's character which results from excluding it. A
free prose translation of the omitted lines follows: "Yet
those who think rightly, Polyneices, know that I have
honored you rightly. Not even for children or husband
would I have done this deed against the will of the city.
On what principle do I say so? On the ground that if a
husband had died, I could have married another, and if
a child had died, I could have had another by another
man; but I could never have another brother, now that
my father and mother are in the grave. On this principle,
my brother, putting you above all other considerations,
I seemed in Creon's eyes to commit a crime and to be
fearless where I should have been afraid. So now, taking
me by force, he leads me away, without my ever having
known the marriage bed or marriage hymn, or the life
of marriage or the rearing of children: a wretched woman,
deserted by my friends, I go alive to the cave of the dead."

CHORAGOS.
                    O passionate heart,
Unyielding, tormented still by the same
winds!                                   800

CREON.

Her guards shall have good cause to regret their
delaying.

ANTIGONE.

Ah! That voice is like the voice of death!

CREON.

I can give you no reason to think you are
mistaken.

ANTIGONE.

Thebes, and you my father's gods,
And rulers of Thebes, you see me now, the last
Unhappy daughter of a line of kings,
Your kings, led away to death. You will re-
member
What things I suffer, and at what men's hands,
Because I would not transgress the laws of
heaven.
                    [*To the* GUARDS, *simply:*
Come: let us wait no longer.              810
                    [*Exit* ANTIGONE, *L., guarded.*

## ODE IV

CHORUS.                                [STROPHE 1

All Danaë's beauty was locked away
In a brazen cell where the sunlight could not
come:
A small room, still as any grave, enclosed her.
Yet she was a princess too,
And Zeus in a rain of gold poured love upon
her.
O child, child,
No power in wealth or war
Or tough sea-blackened ships
Can prevail against untiring Destiny!

---

*ODE IV:* the Chorus recalls in this ode three other
persons whose sufferings included imprisonment: Danaë,
Lycurgus, and Cleopatra of Thrace. Danaë was imprisoned
by her father because he had been told by an oracle that
if she ever bore a child, the child would kill him; but
Zeus penetrated the prison in a shower of gold and begot
Perseus. Lycurgus (*Dryas' son*) opposed the wild rites of
the god Dionysos and so was driven mad by the god and
imprisoned. Cleopatra of Thrace, daughter of the wind-
god Boreas, married King Phineus of Salmydessos and
bore him two sons. Phineus later put her away and imprisoned her, and then married a second wife who put
out the eyes of Cleopatra's sons.

[ANTISTROPHE 1
And Dryas' son also, that furious king,        820
Bore the god's prisoning anger for his pride:
Sealed up by Dionysos in deaf stone,
His madness died among echoes.
So at the last he learned what dreadful power
His tongue had mocked:
For he had profaned the revels,
And fired the wrath of the nine
Implacable Sisters that love the sound of the
    flute.

[STROPHE 2
And old men tell a half-remembered tale
Of horror done where a dark ledge splits the
    sea                        830
And a double surf beats on the gray shores:
How a king's new woman, sick
With hatred for the queen he had imprisoned,
Ripped out his two sons' eyes with her bloody
    hands
While grinning Ares watched the shuttle plunge
Four times: four blind wounds crying for re-
    venge,

[ANTISTROPHE 2
Crying, tears and blood mingled.—Piteously
    born,
Those sons whose mother was of heavenly
    birth!
Her father was the god of the North Wind
And she was cradled by gales,        840
She raced with young colts on the glittering
    hills
And walked untrammeled in the open light:
But in her marriage deathless Fate found means
To build a tomb like yours for all her joy.


SCENE V

[*Enter blind* TEIRESIAS, *led by a boy. The
opening speeches of* TEIRESIAS *should be
in singsong contrast to the realistic lines
of* CREON.

TEIRESIAS.
This is the way the blind man comes, Princes,
    Princes,
Lock-step, two heads lit by the eyes of one.

CREON.
What new thing have you to tell us, old
    Teiresias?

---

835 *Ares:* god of war, worshipped in Salmydessos.

TEIRESIAS.
I have much to tell you: listen to the prophet,
    Creon.

CREON.
I am not aware that I have ever failed to listen.

TEIRESIAS.
Then you have done wisely, King, and ruled
    well.                        850

CREON.
I admit my debt to you. But what have you to
    say?

TEIRESIAS.
This, Creon: you stand once more on the edge
    of fate.

CREON.
What do you mean? Your words are a kind of
    dread.

TEIRESIAS.
Listen, Creon:
I was sitting in my chair of augury, at the place
Where the birds gather about me. They were all
    a-chatter,
As is their habit, when suddenly I heard
A strange note in their jangling, a scream, a
Whirring fury; I knew that they were fighting,
Tearing each other, dying        860
In a whirlwind of wings clashing. And I was
    afraid.
I began the rites of burnt-offering at the altar,
But Hephaistos failed me: instead of bright
    flame,
There was only the sputtering slime of the fat
    thigh-flesh
Melting: the entrails dissolved in gray smoke,
The bare bone burst from the welter. And no
    blaze!

This was a sign from heaven. My boy described
    it,
Seeing for me as I see for others.

I tell you, Creon, you yourself have brought
This new calamity upon us. Our hearths and
    altars                        870

---

863 *Hephaistos:* god of fire.

Are stained with the corruption of dogs and
   carrion birds
That glut themselves on the corpse of Oedipus'
   son.
The gods are deaf when we pray to them, their
   fire
Recoils from our offering, their birds of omen
Have no cry of comfort, for they are gorged
With the thick blood of the dead.
        O my son,
These are no trifles! Think: all men make
   mistakes,
But a good man yields when he knows his
   course is wrong,
And repairs the evil. The only crime is
   pride.         880

Give in to the dead man, then: do not fight with
   a corpse—
What glory is it to kill a man who is dead?
Think, I beg you:
It is for your own good that I speak as I do.
You should be able to yield for your own good.

CREON.

It seems that prophets have made me their espe-
   cial province.
All my life long
I have been a kind of butt for the dull arrows
Of doddering fortune-tellers!
      No, Teiresias:  890
If your birds—if the great eagles of God himself
Should carry him stinking bit by bit to heaven,
I would not yield. I am not afraid of pollution:
No man can defile the gods.
        Do what you will,
Go into business, make money, speculate
In India gold or that synthetic gold from Sardis,
Get rich otherwise than by my consent to bury
   him.
Teiresias, it is a sorry thing when a wise man
Sells his wisdom, lets out his words for hire! 900

TEIRESIAS.

Ah Creon! Is there no man left in the world—

CREON.

To do what?—Come, let's have the aphorism!

---

897 *gold from Sardis:* electrum, an ore containing silver
as well as gold, was mined at Tmolus, south of Sardis.

TEIRESIAS.

No man who knows that wisdom outweighs
   any wealth?

CREON.

As surely as bribes are baser than any baseness.

TEIRESIAS.

You are sick, Creon! You are deathly sick!

CREON.

As you say: it is not my place to challenge a
   prophet.

TEIRESIAS.

Yet you have said my prophecy is for sale.

CREON.

The generation of prophets has always loved
   gold.

TEIRESIAS.

The generation of kings has always loved brass.

CREON.

You forget yourself! You are speaking to your
   King.         910

TEIRESIAS.

I know it. You are a king because of me.

CREON.

You have a certain skill; but you have sold out.

TEIRESIAS.

King, you will drive me to words that—

CREON.

        Say them, say them!
Only remember: I will not pay you for them.

TEIRESIAS.

No, you will find them too costly.

CREON.

        No doubt. Speak:
Whatever you say, you will not change my will.

TEIRESIAS.

Then take this, and take it to heart!
The time is not far off when you shall pay
   back         920
Corpse for corpse, flesh of your own flesh.

You have thrust the child of this world into
  living night,
You have kept from the gods below the child
  that is theirs:
The one in a grave before her death, the other,
Dead, denied the grave. This is your crime:
And the Furies and the dark gods of Hell
Are swift with terrible punishment for you.

Do you want to buy me now, Creon?

                              Not many days,
And your house will be full of men and women
  weeping,                                   930
And curses will be hurled at you from far
Cities grieving for sons unburied, left to rot
Before the walls of Thebes.

These are my arrows, Creon: they are all for
  you.

                              [*To* Boy:
But come, child: lead me home.
Let him waste his fine anger upon younger men.
Maybe he will learn at last
To control a wiser tongue in a better head.
                              [*Exit* Teiresias.
CHORAGOS.

The old man has gone, King, but his words
Remain to plague us. I am old, too,        940
But I cannot remember that he was ever false.

CREON.

That is true.... It troubles me.
Oh it is hard to give in! but it is worse
To risk everything for stubborn pride.

CHORAGOS.

Creon: take my advice.

CREON.

                              What shall I do?

CHORAGOS.

Go quickly: free Antigone from her vault
And build a tomb for the body of Polyneices.

CREON.

You would have me do this?

CHORAGOS.

                              Creon, yes!  950
And it must be done at once: God moves
Swiftly to cancel the folly of stubborn men.

CREON.

It is hard to deny the heart! But I
Will do it: I will not fight with destiny.

CHORAGOS.

You must go yourself, you cannot leave it to
  others.

CREON.

I will go.
    —Bring axes, servants:
Come with me to the tomb. I buried her, I
Will set her free.
                              Oh quickly!     960
My mind misgives—
The laws of the gods are mighty, and a man
  must serve them
To the last day of his life!
                              [*Exit* CREON.

## PÆAN

CHORAGOS.                              [STROPHE 1
God of many names

CHORUS.

                    O Iacchos
                        son
of Kadmeian Semele
                    O born of the Thunder!
Guardian of the West
                        Regent           970
of Eleusis' plain
                    O Prince of Maenad Thebes
and the Dragon Field by rippling Ismenos:

CHORAGOS.                              [ANTISTROPHE 1
God of many names

CHORUS.

                    the flame of torches
flares on our hills
                    the nymphs of Iacchos
dance at the spring of Castalia:

---

*PÆAN:* the Chorus now sings to Dionysos, also known
as Iacchos, son of Theban (*Kadmeian*) Semele by Zeus,
who visited her in thunder. The Chorus addresses him by
the names of places where his cult is honored (in the
West; at Eleusis in Attica; at the Castalian spring near
Delphi; on the vined slopes near Lysa in Euboea; on
Mt. Parnasos in Phocis), but keeps returning to the
thought that the center of his cult is Thebes, on the river
Ismene, home of his worshipping *Maenads,* land where
Cadmus, Thebes' founder, sowed the dragon's teeth from
which his people sprang.

from the vine-close mountain
         come ah come in ivy:   980
*Evohé evohé!* sings through the streets of
Thebes

CHORAGOS.                  [STROPHE 2

God of many names

CHORUS.

                 Iacchos of Thebes
heavenly Child
         of Semele bride of the Thunderer!
The shadow of plague is upon us:
                     come
with clement feet
            oh come from Parnasos
down the long slopes            990
         across the lamenting water

CHORAGOS.           [ANTISTROPHE 2

Io Fire! Chorister of the throbbing stars!
O purest among the voices of the night!
Thou son of God, blaze for us!

CHORUS.

Come with choric rapture of circling Maenads
Who cry *Io Iacche!*
            *God of many names!*

## EXODOS

            [*Enter* MESSENGER, *L.*

MESSENGER.

Men of the line of Kadmos, you who live
Near Amphion's citadel:
            I cannot say    1000
Of any condition of human life "This is fixed,
This is clearly good, or bad." Fate raises up,
And Fate casts down the happy and unhappy
    alike:
No man can foretell his Fate.
           Take the case of Creon:
Creon was happy once, as I count happiness:
Victorious in battle, sole governor of the land,

---

980 *ivy:* sacred to Dionysos.  981 *Evohé evohé:* cry of
Dionysos' worshippers, like *Io* in line 16.  992 *Fire:* the
climax of the Pæan associates the god with the elemental
fire of the stars, and perhaps also with the torches of his
worshippers.

*EXODOS:* conclusion.

999 *Amphion's citadel:* so called because Amphion was
said to have built the walls of Thebes by the music of
his lyre.

Fortunate father of children nobly born.
And now it has all gone from him! Who can say
That a man is still alive when his life's joy
    fails?             1010
He is a walking dead man. Grant him rich,
Let him live like a king in his great house:
If his pleasure is gone, I would not give
So much as the shadow of smoke for all he
    owns.

CHORAGOS.

Your words hint at sorrow: what is your news
    for us?

MESSENGER.

They are dead. The living are guilty of their
    death.

CHORAGOS.

Who is guilty? Who is dead? Speak!

MESSENGER.

                      Haimon.
Haimon is dead; and the hand that killed him
Is his own hand.          1020

CHORAGOS.

            His father's? or his own?

MESSENGER.

His own, driven mad by the murder his father
    had done.

CHORAGOS.

Teiresias, Teiresias, how clearly you saw it all!

MESSENGER.

This is my news: you must draw what conclu-
    sions you can from it.

CHORAGOS.

But look: Eurydice, our Queen:
Has she overheard us?
        [*Enter* EURYDICE *from the Palace, C.*

EURYDICE.

I have heard something, friends:
As I was unlocking the gate of Pallas' shrine,
For I needed her help today, I heard a voice
Telling of some new sorrow. And I fainted 1030
There at the temple with all my maidens about
    me.
But speak again: whatever it is, I can bear it:
Grief and I are no strangers.

MESSENGER.

                 Dearest Lady,
I will tell you plainly all that I have seen.
I shall not try to comfort you: what is the use,
Since comfort could lie only in what is not true?
The truth is always best.
                 I went with Creon
To the outer plain where Polyneices was
    lying,                      1040
No friend to pity him, his body shredded by
    dogs.
We made our prayers in that place to Hecate
And Pluto, that they would be merciful. And
    we bathed
The corpse with holy water, and we brought
Fresh-broken branches to burn what was left
    of it,
And upon the urn we heaped up a towering
    barrow
Of the earth of his own land.
               When we were done, we ran
To the vault where Antigone lay on her couch
    of stone.
One of the servants had gone ahead,    1050
And while he was yet far off he heard a voice
Grieving within the chamber, and he came back
And told Creon. And as the King went closer,
The air was full of wailing, the words lost,
And he begged us to make all haste. "Am I a
    prophet?"
He said, weeping, "And must I walk this road,
The saddest of all that I have gone before?
My son's voice calls me on. Oh quickly, quickly!
Look through the crevice there, and tell me
If it is Haimon, or some deception of the
    gods!"                      1060

We obeyed; and in the cavern's farthest corner
We saw her lying:
She had made a noose of her fine linen veil
And hanged herself. Haimon lay beside her,
His arms about her waist, lamenting her,
His love lost under ground, crying out
That his father had stolen her away from him.

When Creon saw him the tears rushed to his
    eyes
And he called to him: "What have you done,
    child? Speak to me.
What are you thinking that makes your eyes so
    strange?                 1070

---

1042 *Hecate; Pluto:* a goddess of the underworld and
its king.

O my son, my son, I come to you on my knees!"
But Haimon spat in his face. He said not a
    word,
Staring—
               And suddenly drew his sword
And lunged. Creon shrank back, the blade
    missed; and the boy,
Desperate against himself, drove it half its
    length
Into his own side, and fell. And as he died
He gathered Antigone close in his arms again,
Choking, his blood bright red on her white
    cheek.
And now he lies dead with the dead, and she is
    his                     1080
At last, his bride in the houses of the dead.
               [*Exit* EURYDICE *into the Palace.*

CHORAGOS.

She has left us without a word. What can this
    mean?

MESSENGER.

It troubles me, too; yet she knows what is best,
Her grief is too great for public lamentation,
And doubtless she has gone to her chamber to
    weep
For her dead son, leading her maidens in his
    dirge.

CHORAGOS.

It may be so: but I fear this deep silence.
                          [*Pause.*

MESSENGER.

I will see what she is doing. I will go in.
         [*Exit* MESSENGER *into the Palace.*

[*Enter* CREON *with attendants, bearing*
HAIMON'S *body.*

CHORAGOS.

But here is the King himself: oh look at him,
Bearing his own damnation in his arms.    1090

CREON.

Nothing you say can touch me any more.
My own blind heart has brought me
From darkness to final darkness. Here you see
The father murdering, the murdered son—
And all my civic wisdom!

Haimon my son, so young, so young to die,
I was the fool, not you; and you died for me.

CHORAGOS.

That is the truth; but you were late in learning it.

CREON.

This truth is hard to bear. Surely a god
Has crushed me beneath the hugest weight of
    heaven,                1100
And driven me headlong a barbaric way
To trample out the thing I held most dear.

The pains that men will take to come to pain!
    [*Enter* MESSENGER *from the Palace.*

MESSENGER.

The burden you carry in your hands is heavy,
But it is not all: you will find more in your
    house.

CREON.

What burden worse than this shall I find there?

MESSENGER.

The Queen is dead.

CREON.

O port of death, deaf world,
Is there no pity for me? And you, Angel of evil,
I was dead, and your words are death
    again.                1110
Is it true, boy? Can it be true?
Is my wife dead? Has death bred death?

MESSENGER.

You can see for yourself.
    [*The doors are opened, and the body of*
    EURYDICE *is disclosed within.*

CREON.

Oh pity!
All true, all true, and more than I can bear!
O my wife, my son!

MESSENGER.

She stood before the altar, and her heart
Welcomed the knife her own hand guided,
And a great cry burst from her lips for
    Megareus dead,
And for Haimon dead, her sons; and her last
    breath             1120
Was a curse for their father, the murderer of
    her sons.
And she fell, and the dark flowed in through her
    closing eyes.

---

1119 *Megareus:* killed defending Thebes in battle.

CREON.

O God, I am sick with fear.
Are there no swords here? Has no one a blow
    for me?

MESSENGER.

Her curse is upon you for the deaths of both.

CREON.

It is right that it should be. I alone am guilty.
I know it, and I say it. Lead me in,
Quickly, friends.
I have neither life nor substance. Lead me in.

CHORAGOS.

You are right, if there can be right in so much
    wrong.              1130
The briefest way is best in a world of sorrow.

CREON.

Let it come,
Let death come quickly, and be kind to me.
I would not ever see the sun again.

CHORAGOS.

All that will come when it will; but we, meanwhile,
Have much to do. Leave the future to itself.

CREON.

All my heart was in that prayer!

CHORAGOS.

Then do not pray any more: the sky is deaf.

CREON.

Lead me away. I have been rash and foolish.
I have killed my son and my wife.     1140
I look for comfort; my comfort lies here dead.
Whatever my hands have touched has come to
    nothing.
Fate has brought all my pride to a thought of
    dust.
    [*As* CREON *is being led into the house, the*
    CHORAGOS *advances and speaks directly to*
    *the audience.*

CHORAGOS.

There is no happiness where there is no wisdom;
No wisdom but in submission to the gods.
Big words are always punished,
And proud men in old age learn to be wise.

# READING AN ESSAY

IN THE Introduction, the main and distinguishing characteristics of each of the four basic modes of literature are briefly considered. In the following pages, we shall discuss in more detail the nature of each mode, beginning with the essay, and illustrating each discussion by reference to a particular example from this book.

An essay may be as short as a student's theme or as long as the longest article in a magazine. But diverse though this mode is, certain principles apply to all essays, and these are best understood by analysis of a single example. For this purpose let us consider "Love in America," by Raoul de Roussy de Sales, page 99.

## SUBJECT AND THESIS

The essential fact about an essay is that it lays a claim upon the reader's belief and purports to tell him what he did not already know, or know so well. Even if large parts of it are fanciful, as in "The Fable of the Vultures," page 168, it must have a point to make, a proposition or cluster of propositions to assert.

Like all literary works, an essay has a subject (what it is about) and a speaker, and it shows the speaker's attitude toward the subject. The subject is more often than not stated by the title—for example, love in America—al-

though sometimes the subject is referred to elliptically or figuratively in the title, as in Stevenson's "Æs Triplex," page 540, which means "triple brass"—courage in the face of death. The substance of the essay is what the speaker has to say about that subject.

A telephone directory or a chronological list of last year's main news items has a subject, but it is not an essay. An essay has to have a certain form, to be unified in some way; hence its contents must be organized around a central axis. This is true of both of the basic types of essay. In a narrative essay, the axis may be the point of a joke or the key to a human character; in a reflective essay, such as "Love in America," the central axis is a *thesis*.

Often the thesis of an essay is succinctly stated in it, perhaps near the beginning or end. The closest "Love in America" comes to such a statement is in the first paragraph of the last section, which might be paraphrased in this way:

The prevailing American attitude toward love, in contrast to the European attitude, is an unrealistic mixture of romantic perfectionism ("Ideal love can be successfully achieved....") and pseudo-scientific pragmatism ("...if we apply the right techniques").

686

This thesis is also summed up by the reference in the last paragraph to "love as Hollywood—or the professor—sees it."

The substance of "Love in America" is at the same time an illustration of this thesis—turning it over, developing it, clarifying it, and pointing it up—and an argument for the thesis. The general shape of a reflective essay can be considered from two points of view: it has a *logical structure* and it has a *rhetorical structure*.

## LOGICAL STRUCTURE

The logical structure of an essay is the way in which the statements in it are connected according to the rules of reasoning. From a logical point of view, an essay is a syllogism, or an inductive argument, or an analogical argument, or has some other logical form or combination of logical forms. The thesis of "Love in America" consists of two parts, each of which has to be supported by reasons. It asserts, first, that Americans tend to be perfectionists in their beliefs about love, and this generalization is supported by certain observations: that this belief prevails in American movies and popular songs; that Americans are continually changing their mates when their marriages develop strains, etc. Second, the essay asserts that Americans tend to think of love as something that can be made perfect by being tinkered with according to the advice of experts, and this generalization is supported by other observations: that there are popular books of advice to married couples; that American women have a compulsion to "talk things out" with their husbands, etc.

Note that in stating these two parts of the thesis we have used the phrase "tend to be." The author sometimes states his generalizations as though they were true of every single American, but he sometimes shows that he is only making a statistical claim: most Americans feel like this, or, at least, many. He speaks, for example, of "the great majority of the Americans of both sexes" (paragraph 2), and "the prevailing conception of love, in America" (paragraph 3), though, as the essay moves along, he is less careful to qualify: *e.g.,* "in America the idea seems to be" (paragraph 12), "the American woman entertains the delightful illusion" (section 2, paragraph 4), "the American woman does not want to be understood for the mere fun of it" (section 2, paragraph 9), "husbands and wives and lovers have no patience with their troubles" (section 4, paragraph 1).

The basis of this essay, then, is a set of observations of American customs; these observations are set forth in support of two generalizations about American attitudes; and it is the combination of these two generalizations that is the thesis. But the essay implies still another thesis, dependent upon the first one and never explicitly stated: that European skepticism about ideal love, and especially about attaining it by recipes and prescriptions, is more realistic and more likely to bring such human happiness in love as can be had. This thesis is not insisted upon, but suggested by the speaker's style and tone.

## RHETORICAL STRUCTURE

When an essayist has chosen the thesis that he will maintain, and decided what reasons to advance in support of it, he still has not imagined his essay concretely. For he must determine in what order to make his statements and how they are to be concretely embodied. The experience of reading an essay is more than the experience of understanding its logical structure; it involves, as well as intellectual activities, feelings of expectation and disappointment, surprise and pleasure, perhaps amusement or terror.

Suppose we wish to convince someone that Jones ought to be fired from his job; and our reason is that Jones has been lazy, incompetent, and dishonest. We can imagine writing out our argument in either of these ways:

### A

It has been increasingly clear in recent weeks that Jones is lazy, that his work is incompetent, and that he has even been dishonest. It is my recommendation that he be fired.

### B

Jones has simply got to be fired! We have put up long enough with his laziness, his incompetence, and his outright dishonesty!

We could think of other ways of stating this argument, but let us look at one fundamental difference between *A* and *B*. Both give the same reasons for the same conclusion, but in *A* the conclusion is stated last and in *B* the conclusion is stated first. Even apart from other differences, in tone and diction, this is an important difference in structure, for it is partly responsible for the contrast between *A's* air of reasonableness and caution, and *B's* bluntness and urgency.

Let us say that *A* and *B* have the same logical structure, because the reasons and conclusions are the same, but different rhetorical structures. The rhetorical structure is the essay as movement: its development in intensity, its changes of tone, its rise to a climax, its shifts of emphasis.

In analyzing the rhetorical structure of an essay, then, we may ask such questions as these: (1) In what way is the discussion begun? In some essays an introductory section leads into the main question, others open with a striking illustration; in some the thesis is stated at the beginning, in others it is allowed to appear only gradually as the essay develops. (2) How does the argument move? The steps may be formally announced, or each may lead casually into the next; the main points may be arranged in an order of increasing convincingness, so that the final point seems to clinch the argument, or they may be strung together with little or no regard for their logical force. (3) What is the climax of the argument? Simply as logical structure, an argument has no climax, but as a movement of ideas developed in time, it may reach a point where the force of the argument is most felt, or where the full implications of the thesis first become clear to the reader, or where the speaker is most emphatic —and such a point will be the climax.

"Love in America" opens with a flat, challenging, general statement in which the juxtaposition of "love" and "national problem" invites the reader to be somewhat startled and curious. This opening has its dramatic effect upon the entire essay, for the essay will fail as a persuasive or even entertaining piece of writing unless the rest of it shows why it is plausible to say that love *is* a "national problem" in America.

The character of "Love in America" is in part determined by the fact that it does not state its argument in a formal way. In fact, the whole process of discussion cuts across the logical structure and underemphasizes it. The opening is followed by a digression that runs through section 1 and over into section 2;

section 2 develops the first half of the thesis; section 3, on the influence of Freudianism, appears at first to be a digression on the historical background of the present American attitude, but then we discover that it prepares the way for a defense of the second half of the thesis. The suggested contrasts between America and Europe appear here and there, but the climax comes in section 5, in the very pointed contrast between French and American cookbooks. The point of this contrast is then abstractly stated in the first paragraph of section 6, which rounds out the discussion and concludes it.

So much for the general features of the rhetorical structure; to say more of it we must first examine the details of the work.

### Perspective

The *action* of an essay, like that of other literary works, implies more or less clearly a background of the possible human relations within which it takes place. In the essay, someone is saying something to somebody. There is a *speaker*—not necessarily the author, of whose actual life we need know no more than he tells us in the essay itself. There is a *spoken to:* the audience that the essayist appears to be writing for, or appealing to. And there are various aspects of his relations to his audience and his subject. Let us use the general term *perspective* for these aspects of the work.

One of the interesting features of "Love in America" is the perspective in which it is written. In section 1, the speaker takes pains to establish himself as one who looks at the behavior of Americans with the detached, faintly wondering, but sympathetic air of a foreigner. This gives a kind of man-from-Mars perspective, a device that allows a writer certain freedoms. For example, by pretending that he fails to understand why Americans believe in ideal love, he can say harsh things and yet make them sound less harsh because he appears not to realize how harsh they are. But at the same time, he risks being thought of by the reader as one who, because he is an outsider, is ignorant of what he is talking about, so that his opinion has no value. It is one of the delicate feats of this essay that the speaker establishes his independent perspective, while at the same time showing such familiarity with American movies, popular songs, feelings about European adventurers who marry American women, and the like, that the reader cannot think of him as an outsider.

Thus the audience is carefully kept in focus throughout the essay: the speaker is talking to Americans about their own customs, and asking them to look at themselves with some of the detachment and objectivity of a foreigner. He will tease them along a little without irritating them too much, making them a little embarrassed about their complacency, yet helping them to enjoy the spectacle of their own minor follies.

With his subject and audience in mind, the writer must be careful to control his *tone:* in this respect, "Love in America" is also very instructive. Taking it as a whole, the tone is light and easy-going. It is often ironic, but not heavily so; it is good-humored, with just a hint of sarcasm here and there—as when he calls the wife who likes talking things over with her husband a "good girl scout." But there are variations in the seriousness of tone throughout the essay. After a fairly serious opening, the speaker relaxes into a casual and humorous tone. Then, toward the end, with the audience prepared for a more assertive manner, he states his thesis frankly and explicitly.

The tone, of course, is primarily dependent upon the *style* of the essay, about which something must also be said.

## STYLE

If we were to read some other essays, one of them by the man who wrote "Love in America," should we be able to recognize it as the work of the same man? Even if it were on an entirely different subject, should we expect to find something similar in the style? And if we did recognize it, by what features would we recognize it?

One of the marks of a first-rate essayist, such as Bacon, Lamb, Hazlitt, or Bertrand Russell, is that he has, as we say, a style of his own. After one has read a good deal of any of these writers' works and become intimate with his style, one can recognize even a few sentences of his when someone reads them aloud. Yet it is difficult to analyze a style and to put into words exactly what is special about it.

In analyzing a style, we notice certain recurrent features of the texture of the work, certain types of diction or syntactical construction that the writer seems partial to. We are not, it is to be remembered, listing merely ornamental or decorative devices; we are discovering part of the meaning, characteristic turns of thought, associations, and ways of relating things. All these may be illustrated from "Love in America."

In this essay, de Sales employs a rather dignified though informal style, mingling occasional apt colloquialisms ("the de luxe model") and frequent concrete illustrations with more abstract phrases. The sentences are varied, the transitions generally smooth, the effect one of an easy-going flow of thoughtful reflections. There is a pervasive irony, kept alive by frequent ironic juxtapositions ("some unguent to cure heartaches or athlete's foot"), pointed references to American values ("love is always wholesome, genuine, uplifting, and fresh, like a glass of Grade A milk"), and epigrams ("In the American way of life there are no insoluble problems").

It is a somewhat pontifical style, as an ironic and epigrammatic style is likely to be, and perhaps the peculiar perspective it establishes could not be maintained successfully through a longer essay. But it is not allowed to get out of hand here, and in some paragraphs of section 6, the style changes to a more direct, serious, and personal one, so that a sense of the writer's concern for Americans accompanies his detached attitude.

## EVALUATION

We have considered various sorts of questions that might be asked about the form and meaning of an essay. The question of its value remains to be discussed. The qualities that make an essay good are complex, and we can touch on them only briefly.

Some of the questions to be asked in judging an essay are internal to it; that is, they are to be answered by a study of the essay itself and the relationships among its elements. Three of these are particularly important. (1) Is the thesis clear? A serious uncertainty about the thesis—ambiguity or vagueness—will weaken the whole essay. (2) Is the essay unified and well-organized? In some essays, the rhetorical structure works at cross-purposes to the logical structure, so that it is difficult if not impossible to determine what reasons are given for what conclusions. (3) Is the style suitable to the subject, thesis, and structure? If there is an incongruity among these elements, however interesting one of them may be by itself, the essay cannot provide a single absorbing experience.

We have seen that the thesis of "Love in America" can be gathered with reasonable certainty. The scope of the writer's generalizations is not precisely stated, but he does not claim strict accuracy for them, and his tone implicitly concedes that his rather impressionistic way of choosing the relevant evidence cannot establish exactly formulated conclusions, such as a social scientist would require. The style, on the whole, is quite clear; perhaps only the reference to "the dialectics of love" is at all obscure.

"Love in America" is given unity by the fact that it adheres for the most part to the same subject, with occasional digressions. It presents a single argument, and it has a dramatic shape, a beginning and a climax. The movement of thought does not sharply articulate the joints of the logical structure, so that there is some difficulty in seeing exactly what the argument is about; for example, the transition from arguing for the first half of the main thesis to arguing for its second half is not clearly marked. The essay would be better if the rhetorical structure emphasized the logical structure a little more.

The style of "Love in America" accords well, for the most part, with the other elements of the essay. Perhaps the style is somewhat pompous here and there, as though the speaker were talking down to the reader, which is inappropriate in view of the fact that the thesis cannot be set forth with great confidence on the basis of the evidence at hand. But the generally light tone is appropriate in reminding the reader that the thesis is not to be taken too seriously; the thesis is understood by the speaker to be less a solemn sociological theory than a peg on which to hang some observations of American customs.

Besides these internal matters, there are external questions that we cannot avoid asking of a reflective essay. In the end we also want to know how much belief to repose in it, and how seriously to take it as a piece of argu-ment. Even if we should decide that its thesis is false, it may still be an interesting and important essay, for it may give us insight into the point of view of someone with whom we disagree, and it may contain important information even if the conclusions it draws from that information are not acceptable. But ultimately, we must decide whether its conclusions are acceptable or not.

For all its sharp observations and insights, "Love in America" is not a very convincing essay as a whole. It does present a few specific examples of the kind of behavior that it asserts is typical of Americans, but such a short essay could not possibly find space for the amount of evidence that would really warrant such sweeping generalizations about American life and culture. Moreover, it would not be hard to think of other facts about American life that conflict with the writer's generalization: for example, the numerous movies, television scripts, and popular novels—as well as books of the sort that de Roussy de Sales mentions to show that Americans think ideal love may be obtained by the advice of experts—which imply that husbands and wives must accept each other for what they are worth, and not yearn for perfection. But perhaps this idea has become more widely accepted since 1938, when "Love in America" was first published. In that event the essay has lost some of its timeliness.

Good essays, however, derive much of their value from stimulating the reader to think about their subjects: perhaps to recognize his own follies, as "Love in America" may do. An essay may be valuable, that is, even if its generalizations should prove to be too broad, the evidence one-sided, the indictment exaggerated. Through its multiplicity of meaning, on more than one level of discourse, it may take on qualities that are enjoyable for their own sakes: wit, intense passion, pathos, purity of logic. Thus an essay, as a work of art— unlike telephone directories and almanacs— can act upon the reader in a number of ways, quite apart from informing or convincing him, and so afford an experience which, though complex, remains somehow a unity. If it can pass this test, we may be sure it is literature.

# READING A SHORT STORY

SHORT STORIES, being narratives, are members of a large family: the narrative family includes such diverse species as anecdotes, fairy tales, the parables of the New Testament, much of the contents of the popular weekly magazines, and novels—to name only a few. Narrative also embraces histories and biographies, which lay claim to factual truth, and stories told in verse; but we are here concerned only with prose fiction. Of all these, none is more familiar to most readers than the short story. It may seem surprising that many books have been written about the art of the short story, for do we not read stories simply to find out what happens in them? And when that is known, what more have they to tell us?

The happenings presented in a short story, which are indeed its first point of interest, can usually be grasped in a single reading. Yet some stories may be read and reread with increasing pleasure, for each new reading reveals more of that multiplicity of meaning which is a distinguishing mark of literature. If we are to enjoy a story to the full, we must appreciate the whole of its meaning, a process that is greatly assisted by familiarity with the names that have been devised for the various aspects of the form. Some of the terms used in analyzing short stories (*e.g., plot* and *characters*) are probably old acquaintances; others

may be less familiar. Since all of them become more understandable if defined with respect to a particular story, we shall illustrate them from Robert Penn Warren's story, "Blackberry Winter," page 18.

As we saw in the Introduction, prose fiction is told for the most part in the past tense, as though its events were already concluded; and while we are reading it we probably make-believe that they have actually occurred. Fiction is "pseudo-history." But a story is more than a record of imagined events, for the events and the rest of the subject are described by a speaker, who reveals an attitude toward the subject. He evaluates it, passes judgment on it. The writer, who is never identical with the speaker, has invented and shaped the subject so as to make the speaker's attitude intelligible. "Blackberry Winter" is narrated by a forty-four-year-old man named Seth. Its subject is the destruction of his childhood world, and his attitude combines affection for that vanished life with regret for its passing. Some of the elements of a short story are aspects of the subject; others are related to the speaker, and still others to the attitude that he reveals. In distinguishing these elements, we must keep in mind two warnings: first, the short story is such a varied form that not all of our terms will apply equally well to every story. Second, the separation of a story into its elements, though useful for analysis, is an artificial process. In reality, they cannot be separated, for each of them derives its existence from its relationship to the others. The elements of a successful short story, like those of any other work of art, compose an organic unity which makes the reading of it a single, harmonious experience.

## PLOT

Though a short story may be physically divided into parts as a book is divided into chapters, most stories are told in unbroken sequence. But they rely on two different methods of telling, which frequently alternate and form a pattern in the narrative. One of these narrative methods is the summarizing of the action, wholly in the past tense; the other is the presentation of action by means of *scenes.* In a scene, the action is described concretely, not summarized; it is presented in sharp focus, with enough detail to suggest the way in which an event actually happens, and a scene normally includes *dialogue,* or conversation in the form that it has when we hear it. The effect of a scene is to dramatize that part of the action and thus give it particular emphasis. A story consists of its scenes together with the narrative summary needed to connect them. "Blackberry Winter" begins with a scene of a boy standing before a fireplace, arguing with his mother about going barefoot. The scene ends as he sees a tramp appear from the woods and explains why it is strange for the man to come from that direction. Then follows a scene in the kitchen, as the boy and his mother discuss the meaning of what has just happened. Thus the narrative is developed step by step. As these examples suggest, the first stage in analyzing a short story is to distinguish its different scenes, for they are the units out of which the plot is developed.

*Plot* is conventionally defined as the chain of events that make up a story, but the metaphor of a chain suggests a linking of each event to the next which is not found in all stories. In "Blackberry Winter," if Seth had worn his shoes he would not have gone into Dellie's cabin—these events are linked as cause and effect; but the arrival of the tramp is not caused by the flood or any other event, nor does it produce the events at the creek or those in the cabin and the barn. It is a coincidence like those that we encounter in real life. By complicating the other events of the day, it sharpens their meaning, but the breakup of Seth's world would occur just the same if no stranger had entered it. The two sets of happenings harmonize to suggest the theme of the story; they are not otherwise chained together. The term *plot,* however, usefully describes that part of the subject that consists of related actions, even though the relationship is only a thematic one.

The writer is of course free to introduce as many events as he likes, whether they are caused by previous events or not. But he is restrained by two expectations on the part of the reader: one, that the events shall be related to the other elements of the story, as the actions of the tramp and of Dellie, though neither knows of the other's existence, are related to the theme. Second, we expect that each event shall contribute to the story's *progression:* the sense that it is moving steadily forward, without undue repetition of effect, and approaching nearer to its conclusion. The need for progression results from the fact that any good narrative creates *suspense:* doubt and curiosity as to its outcome. Its development causes questions to arise in our minds; and, though suspense is one of its most enjoyable qualities, we paradoxically wish to arrive at the answers to these questions so that the suspense will be ended.

What sort of questions should the development of the narrative produce? They are those that arise from its *contrasts* and *conflicts.* A contrast is a difference made striking by its presence in the same or similar persons or things or ideas; conflict results when a character's purpose encounters opposition. The arrival of the tramp in "Blackberry Winter" creates suspense simply because he is a stranger. The first of the many conflicts in which he is involved occurs when the dogs try to prevent him from approaching the house. This conflict is based upon the contrast that precedes it. Later on, the conflict of the tramp and Seth's father is underscored by the contrast between their shoes. As these examples show, the related elements of contrast and conflict give rise to the suspense that necessitates the progression of the story to its conclusion.

Not all of the conflicts in a story are marked by such tension as these: the argument be-

are firmly grounded in things as they are. And his attitude is not only rational but unified: it combines affection for his childhood world with regret for its passing, and these feelings are, of course, consistent with one another.

Identifying the attitude implicit in a story makes it necessary to discuss the speaker's *tone*—a term that has already been introduced in analyzing the perspective of "Love in America" (see page 689). When we hear words spoken in a special manner, we can usually identify the attitude that lies behind them. But it can be easily shown that printed words may have a tone as well as spoken ones. Consider the following sentence from "Blackberry Winter": "He glared at me for an instant out of the bloodshot eyes, then demanded in a low, harsh voice, 'What you looking at?'" If we were reading this sentence aloud, we should know approximately how to pronounce the question even if the phrase "in a low, harsh voice" had not been included. The preceding words, with their strong suggestion of the tramp's hostility, determine the tone of his question. Suppose the sentence had begun, "He glanced at me briefly, then asked. . . ." Its tone would then be neutral, expressive of no attitude, and we should not be sure how to read the question aloud.

Tone, then, results from the choice and arrangement of words—from their very rhythm. It is thus a function of the writer's style, as the style is made to express the attitude of the speaker towards the subject. Although style has been discussed on page 689, one of its most important elements, figurative language, must be touched on here because of the close connection between the tone of a passage and the figures of speech that appear in it. (The leading figures of speech are defined in the Introduction.) The last sentence of "Blackberry Winter"—"But I did follow him, all the years" —affords two examples of the connection between tone and style. First, the choice of the country phrase "all the years" recalls the speaker's attachment to his childhood. Second, the statement that Seth has followed the tramp is not literally true. It is a metaphor, expressive of Seth's regret for the rootless life that has been his as a result of the changes that Time has brought. Because metaphors and other figures of speech almost always convey sharp feelings, they often provide the key to the speaker's attitude.

## THEME

The *theme* of a story emerges from the interrelationships of all the other elements. It is the meaning or point, expressible in general terms, that comes to mind when these are considered organically. It can be expressed in general terms because it applies not only to the speaker and his subject but also to wider areas of human experience. The story may thus have "universal meaning." Since the theme grows out of the narrative elements, we have already referred to the theme of "Blackberry Winter" in discussing its plot, characters, and other aspects. It is a story about the destruction of the speaker's childhood world by the forces of change, which he recognizes as he grows to maturity. As the abstract form of this statement shows, the meaning of the story is not confined to Seth; it touches on the common experience of mankind. Although it is true that not everyone regrets the passing of his childhood world, yet a great many readers will find analogies between their own experience and that of Seth; such feelings are not his alone. Some persons are driven by circumstances into environments different in kind from the ones in which they grew up; others, although remaining where they were born, encounter such changes there and in themselves that they feel as lost as though they had left their native places forever. Both groups of readers will, as the saying is, see in the story something of themselves.

The fact that theme has been shown to arise from all the other elements of the story, and has consequently been discussed last, should not lead anyone to suppose that the quality of the story depends upon the novelty of its theme. As the example of "Blackberry Winter" suggests, many a successful story rings variations on a familiar theme. The value of the story may be to remind the reader powerfully of a universal truth. Its power derives not from its theme alone, however, but from the organic development of the theme by means of all the other elements. And though our judgment is not to be determined by the universality of the theme either, yet the pleasure of reading stories results partly from the recognition of likenesses between the experiences of their characters and the reader's own experience of reality. Stating the theme helps us to decide whether or not the story accords with what we know of life.

# READING A PLAY

SINCE PLAYS are narratives, they are made up of many of the same elements as short stories are: *e.g.,* plot, characters, and setting. A good exercise in literary analysis is to read *Arms and the Man,* page 191, and then decide which of the terms introduced in the discussion of "Blackberry Winter"—exposition, conflict, climax, and the rest—can usefully be applied to the play. But stories and plays also differ from each other in certain fundamental ways, and these differences make it necessary to give some attention to the special characteristics of the drama.

Stories are written to be read; most plays, including those printed in this book, are written in the first place to be put on the stage. Yet plays belong to the reader too: those by Shakespeare, for instance, are read by many more persons than ever see them performed, and modern playwrights, notably Shaw and Eugene O'Neill, often prepare special texts of their works for the reader, texts that differ markedly from those intended for the producer and the actors. The text of *Arms and the Man* in this book is a reading text rather than an acting text. Nevertheless, when an experienced reader enjoys a play in his armchair, he makes himself into an imaginary audience and acts out the play in his mind, visualizing it on a stage as though he were present in a theater

where it was being produced. The reading text is designed to help him to do this: the differences between it and the acting text are not in the dialogue but in the stage directions, which describe the appearance of the stage in detail, and indicate the way in which many of the characters' words should be spoken. The text of *Arms and the Man* affords many examples of both these aids to the reader's imagination. After one has read a few plays, it becomes almost automatic to visualize them on the stage of one's mind.

The need for this imaginative act results from what we saw in the introduction to be the drama's distinguishing trait: the perspective in which the playwright presents his action. Short stories are narrated predominantly in the past tense; they are "pseudo-histories." But the action of a play occurs in the present; past action has only secondary importance, for our attention is fixed on what is happening *now,* and on the future events that will unroll from this immediate present. The playwright may not in his own person provide a summary of past action nor of happenings that are supposed to connect the incidents of the present, nor does he himself tell us what sort of persons his characters are. We are made to know them almost entirely by what they say and what they do. For these and other reasons it is essential that the reader of a play should imagine it as happening before his mind's eye. In his imaginative creation of the play as it would be produced on a stage, he is assisted by all that he knows about the elements of dramatic technique.

## ACTS AND SCENES

Nearly all modern plays, those of the past four centuries, are divided into *acts;* these are the major divisions, corresponding to the chapters of a book. Shakespeare's plays are divided into five acts, as was the custom in his day and long afterwards. *Arms and the Man* is typical of recent plays in that it has three acts. The division into acts emphasizes the structure of the play. It is also convenient because, whenever the place represented by the stage is changed, or more time is supposed to pass than that taken up by the action, the action must of course be suspended—usually by lowering the curtain. An act division may or may not be followed by the representation of a new place; it nearly always means a lapse of time.

If the place or time is to be changed within an act, the act must be divided; and such subdivisions are called *scenes*. Since the theater of Shakespeare's day used little or no scenery, the plays written for it move very freely in place and time, and the acts of a Shakespearean play are regularly subdivided. In recent plays, which usually employ elaborate scenery, subdivision of the acts is uncommon. The term *scene,* however, is also applied, much as it is in discussing a story, to the unit of action marked off by the coming-in or going-out of an important character, even when the action is not otherwise interrupted. (In a film scenario, *sequence* is the term used; see *The Doctor and the Devils,* page 322.) Thus we should say that Act I of *Arms and the Man* begins with a scene between Raina and Catherine, followed by another scene involving them and the maid. *"They are interrupted by the entry of Louka,"* the stage direction tells us. Then follows the short scene in which Raina is alone, and then the important scene that is begun by Bluntschli's appearance on the balcony. In any play, the succession of scenes, in this second meaning of the word, marks the progress of the action; hence it deserves the same close attention that we give to the successive scenes of a story. (See page 692.)

## ACTION AND PROPERTIES

The audience of a play constitutes its "hearers," etymologically speaking; and no doubt the most important part of a play is the words that the characters are made to speak. But the hearers might equally well be called the spectators, for a good playwright addresses the eyes of the audience as well as their ears. Unless a story can be rendered by action as well as dialogue, it is scarcely suitable for dramatic representation. The action of a play is apt to be more restricted than that of a story or a film, but it is no less essential to the total impression. Raina's allowing Bluntschli to catch her hand at the end of *Arms and the Man* is just as much an action as Othello's murder of Desdemona.

Closely connected with the action are the *properties,* the tangible objects that the characters use in the course of it. Properties are distinct from the scenery, costumes, and furniture, though these also perform important parts in the visual impact of the play; properties are things small enough to be moved about, and frequently attention is drawn to them—and their significance emphasized—by the actors' moving them here and there. Like the objects that are named and discussed in stories and poems, stage properties are inclined to take on the multiple meanings of symbols. In Act I of *Arms and the Man* the stage direction calls for some paper-backed novels, a box of chocolate creams, and a portrait of Sergius on Raina's chest of drawers. At first these seem to be merely the realistic clutter of an inhabited room, but soon, as Raina picks them up or otherwise draws attention to them, they become full of meaning: from the novels her illusions about life have sprung, the portrait brings her fiancé's presence on the stage even though he is away at the war, and the chocolate creams (since this is a comedy) symbolize the reality of experience as represented by Bluntschli. They become identified with the chocolate that he carries in his cartridge box instead of ammunition, and in the end, when Raina agrees to marry him, he is her "chocolate cream soldier." The presence of the properties on the stage, where at the proper time each may be the focus of the audience's eyes, is vital to their success in conveying these multiple meanings.

## EXPOSITION

In a play as in a story, some of the narrative is conveyed indirectly, instead of happening before our eyes. We need information about the characters' supposed lives before the action begins, and usually about what is supposedly happening outside the action and in the intervals of the action. The process of imparting such information to the reader or audience is called *exposition*. The writer of a story attends to his exposition largely by speaking directly to the reader. In a play the exposition must be accomplished indirectly, by being made an inconspicuous part of the dialogue. *Arms and the Man* quite naturally informs the audience about the Bulgarian victory by having Catherine announce it to Raina, for Catherine, as the wife of a Bulgarian officer, would be among the first to hear the news. But from her fifth speech we also gather the important information that Raina, after long hesitation, has become engaged to Sergius—a fact with which both speakers are perfectly familiar. Further exposition occurs in Raina's speeches about herself and in the news brought by Louka, as well as in the dialogue at the beginnings of the other two acts. The skill of a playwright may often be judged by the way he manages his exposition without appearing to be intent upon it.

## PLOT

As the play begins and the necessary exposition is being supplied, the playwright must at the same time set his narrative in motion, developing simultaneously its interdependent parts: plot, characters, and setting. Although these may seem identical with the corresponding parts of a story, the fact that drama presents its action in present time makes necessary some special considerations of them as they figure in plays.

For several reasons, a noticeable amount of artifice enters into the plot of a play. Except where Destiny takes a hand, which rarely happens in modern plays, the plot must proceed from the intentions and decisions of the characters, and these must appear to be motivated with a clarity seldom found in life. Second, the evolution of the plot proceeds with preternatural rapidity: *e.g.,* Raina, from her first intention of giving Bluntschli up to his enemies, swings with scarcely realistic speed to a deter-

mination to save him. Third, the *resolution* occurs with a clear-cut decisiveness that is likewise seldom matched by reality. Prose fiction, presenting as it does a summation of events that supposedly have already occurred, approaches nearer to the often leisurely development of events in reality. The dramatization of present action must proceed with dispatch if the attention of the audience is to be held. During almost every scene more time seems to elapse than really does elapse. None of these departures from realism are to be regarded as faults, however; they are the very breath of life to a play.

## CHARACTERS

The interdependence of plot and characters is even more apparent in a play than in a story. As the events of a play proceed from the characters' purposes and decisions, so its characters are established by what they say and do. Bluntschli, wrote Shaw in his Preface, "is not a conventional stage soldier. He suffers from want of food and sleep; his nerves go to pieces after three days under fire." Shaw's characterization of him as a real soldier rather than a hero of romance is accomplished by having him gobble the chocolate creams, shy at Raina's cry of alarm, and collapse with fatigue when she leaves the room. Dramatic characterizations depend not upon assertion but upon action. As a result, plays seldom attempt to present more than half a dozen important characters, and these are individualized by only three or four striking traits. Although the genius of Shakespeare made possible a greater range of characterization, the playwright must as a rule content himself with fewer and more simply drawn characters than those of the novelist.

## SETTING

When *Arms and the Man* is produced, the stage is at different times made to represent two rooms and the garden of Major Petkoff's house. But the setting of the play consists not of these visible places alone; the Petkoff establishment is amplified by the dialogue until it comes to represent, seemingly, the whole of Bulgaria. It is a country under the influence of Vienna and St. Petersburg, at war with its neighbor, half-civilized—a country where social classes are rigidly stratified, and a staircase, a few books, and an electric bell are marks of aristocracy. Our conception of a play's setting should include both the actual stage sets and whatever else the dialogue causes us to imagine as surrounding the action.

The setting also contributes materially to the meaning of the play. *Arms and the Man* is memorable for its satire on current illusions about war, love, and aristocracy—satire that pointedly applied to the England for which the play was written. But there were obvious advantages to presenting these illusions as characteristic of a remote, rather unreal corner of the Balkans, where they could be mingled with jokes about the novelty of electric bells and the infrequency of baths. It is easier to recognize the absurdity of our own illusions when we find that they are cherished by a far-away, half-savage people.

## CONFLICT

If the intentions of two or more characters are opposed, or a character's intentions collide with some impersonal force such as war or Destiny, the result is *conflict:* the tension set up when one purpose is arrested by another. Conflict is so peculiarly characteristic of the drama, that we often praise stories and other literary works for being dramatic when we mean that they are based on conflicts that are strong and interesting. Shaw's Preface to the volume of plays containing *Arms and the Man* points out that "every drama is the artistic presentation of a conflict. The end may be reconciliation or destruction, or, as in life itself, there may be no end; but the conflict is indispensable: no conflict, no drama." In a well constructed play, the arrival on the stage of each new character supplies a new element in the conflict, so that the subject of the play is advanced and developed in every scene. Accordingly, to read a play with thorough understanding means above all to grasp the central conflict and its outcome. In fact, the conflict cannot be discussed without consideration of the theme or meaning of the play, as will be seen when we consider the theme of *Arms and the Man* below.

What are the reasons underlying the law formulated in Shaw's words, "No conflict, no drama"? The answer to this question is first of all a technical one. Conflict produces what is known as an *unstable situation:* the action cannot rest where it is, for the tension felt by the characters concerned leads on to further action as they struggle to gain the upper hand. But in addition to this structural function, the omnipresence of conflict in the drama reflects its inner meaning, the particular interpretation of life with which drama is concerned. For a play, even one so overshadowed by Destiny as the *Antigone* of Sophocles, portrays life as the action of characters who possess at least the illusion that their wills are free. Having purposes, they make decisions—or believe they make them—in order to realize their purposes, and their decisions inevitably bring them into collision with the purposes and decisions of others. It is through such conflicts that the playwright reveals the human values that he thinks are admirable or detestable, secure or fragile, and likely to be victorious or doomed in the long run.

## THEME

The definition of a play as "the artistic presentation of a conflict" implies that the interaction of plot, characters, and setting shall result in an implied point or meaning which, as we saw in discussing the short story, is called the *theme*. The theme of *Arms and the Man* lies in the conflict of illusions and reality, represented by the characters' varying conceptions of love, war, and the theory of aristocracy. The exposition in Act I introduces this theme when Raina recalls her hesitancy about becoming engaged to Sergius; its resolution comes about when she accepts the hand of Bluntschli, who is half-seriously called "the Emperor of Switzerland" and has proved his mastery of the art of war by demonstrating his skill in logistics. The vitality of the play arises from its movement to this final point through various subsidiary conflicts: Raina's scornful treatment of Bluntschli in their first scene, Louka's duels with Nicola and Sergius, and numerous others. At the beginning of the play, Raina is engaged to Sergius and Louka to Nicola; at the end, as a result of its conflicts, their relationships to one another have all been changed, and these changes are the visible manifestations of the changed conceptions of reality that the conflicts of the play have brought to pass. Thus the theme of the play is not so much expressed as dramatized by the struggle of the characters and its *resolution*.

# READING A POEM

POETRY is the form of literature in which the texture and the structure of sounds are most conspicuous. (These terms are explained in the general introduction, on pages xxi-xxxvii.) No absolute distinction between poetry and prose can be made because one shades off into the other. For instance, Churchill's speech entitled "Dunkirk" begins with a plain prose exposition of the Allies' defeat, then rises in its last paragraph to poetry-like language.[1] The difference is that the texture of the last paragraph forces the reader to attend to its sound as well as its sense. The rhythm, marked by heavier and more regular stresses, is emphasized by alliteration (as in "we shall not *f*lag or *f*ail") and repetition of words ("we shall fight . . ."). In sound-texture the passage resembles the translations of Hebrew poetry in the Old Testament, which may be considered either poetry or prose, as well as works like Whitman's *Leaves of Grass* that have neither rhyme nor meter yet are universally considered to be poetry. Meter and rhyme, though they regularly characterize poetry as song, are not essential to poetry in general. Those who would recognize poetry by their presence are right in seeking to identify it by means of sounds; they err only in defining a poetic sound-texture too narrowly.

---

[1] See page 168.

## POETRY VS. PROSE

Perhaps it is because of this and other misunderstandings that the popularity of poetry has waned. Like other literary forms, a poem consists of a speaker who confronts a subject and reveals an attitude toward it. The speakers, subjects, and attitudes that occur in poems resemble those in stories and other prose works; these terms and others already introduced, such as *scene, setting, resolution,* and *theme,* will be found equally useful in analyzing poems; but the fact remains that many readers who enjoy the presentation of a subject in prose are repelled by the presentation of the same or similar subjects in verse. Yet only in very recent times has prose surpassed poetry in popularity. Perhaps modern readers approach poems with mistaken expectations and are disappointed at not finding what never was there, while overlooking what has made poetry a source of pleasure for thousands of years.

At the same time, however, poetry in some forms is as popular as ever, and the modern reader who expresses a distaste for it is usually not expressing his feelings accurately. The words of popular songs are poems, though not often admirable ones; and comic verse, whether printable or not, has as good a chance of popularity as any prose production. When we find pleasure in the lyrics of a song ("The nightingale / Tells his fairy-tale") or Dryden's epitaph for his wife ("Here lies my wife, here let her lie! / Now she's at rest, and so am I") we are responding in large measure to the sound-texture, the distinctively poetic quality of these lines. A reader who says he dislikes poetry means the poems he has been asked to admire in the classroom. Yet these are the very ones that, instead of being quickly forgotten, continue to interest at least a few readers from one age to the next. Let us see how a reader of this kind reads a poem when he first encounters it.

## SOUND AND EMOTION

An experienced reader hardly expects to understand a great poem after reading it only once. The concentration of meaning that the poetic technique makes possible requires that it be read slowly and often if it is to be fully comprehended. What would occupy many pages if it could be expressed in prose cannot be grasped in a few minutes. Can we then say anything about the order in which the elements of a poem are mastered during the successive readings?

Though readers differ tremendously, it is likely that most of them on first reading a poem respond mainly to its sound-texture. They recognize the individual words, of course, and so understand some portions of the sense, but at this stage they are mainly aware of the rhymes, if there are any, and the rhythm, or pattern of stressed syllables, together with the support that these give to the fragments of the sense that are being taken in. A second reading will advance one's understanding of the sense, while at the same time one begins to identify the sound-structure: the rhyme-scheme and metrical form, if these are present. In subsequent readings one may notice the order of ideas from stanza to stanza, analyze the motivation given for the feelings expressed, as is done in reading a story, put the theme into satisfactory terms, and—last of all, perhaps—work out the complete implications of the figures of speech and their relevance to the subject. In some such way does the experienced reader arrive gradually at an understanding of the poem in all its organic complexity. While he is analyzing its parts, his awareness of its whole is maintained by the structure of its sound, which he remembers from his first readings.

Poetry differs from prose, then, chiefly in the greater organization of its sound. But since the meaning of words in combination is somewhat affected by their sound, it follows that the meaning of a poem cannot be duplicated in prose. It will always differ from even the closest paraphrase, chiefly because, as some of the famous descriptions of poetry suggest, one of the most important aspects of its subject matter is emotion.[2] This is especially the part of the meaning that eludes paraphrase, for the rendering of emotion is bound up with the more conspicuous sound-texture of poetry. We may observe evidence of this fact even in prose: the sound-texture of Churchill's speech becomes prominent at the very point where the sense becomes most emotional. It is in the last paragraph, when the speaker expresses his countrymen's resolve to continue fighting in the face of almost hopeless odds, that the language seems poetic; that is, the sound-texture has a more interesting pattern and the meaning is more emotional than is usually the case in prose.

Poetry must not be thought of, however, merely as emotional language, for emotions are important in most prose works, and actions, ideas, and other elements found in prose enter into the subject matter of many poems. Just as there is no absolute distinction where sound is concerned, so poetry and prose cannot be absolutely distinguished with respect to subject. Yet poetry tends to be more concerned with emotion, and to read a poem without regard to the emotions present in it is to overlook one of its essential elements.

The importance of sound in poetry makes it necessary to be familiar with the principal terms that are used to describe its sound effects. These terms will then be applied in the analysis of a particular poem; and, because prose and poetry differ little in subject matter, we shall see that the critical terms used in analyzing prose works are also applicable to a poem.

## RHYTHM

English sentences have rhythm because our words are made up of syllables that are not stressed equally when the words are spoken.

[2] Milton, for instance, observed that poetry is more simple, sensuous, and passionate (*i.e.,* emotional) than rhetoric; and Wordsworth stated that "poetry is the spontaneous overflow of powerful feelings; it takes its origin from emotion recollected in tranquillity."

For example, nearly all nouns, verbs, and adjectives—the words that contribute most to the meaning—have one stressed syllable, whereas articles and connectives are usually unstressed. In short, we tend to stress the important words and not the unimportant ones. Readers who are unable to distinguish the stressed syllables will find it helpful to notice in which syllables they clearly pronounce the vowel sounds, for these are stressed; the sentence before this one is pronounced almost as though it were written thus: *'n short, w'tend t'stress th'mport'nt words 'nd not th'un'mport'nt ones.* A less barbarous-looking method of indicating the stresses, however, is to mark them with accents: *In short, we ténd to stréss . . .* etc.

As words are arranged into sentences, most of the stressed syllables will be separated by one or more unstressed ones. If the words are arranged so that the stresses support the meaning rather than hinder it, the result will be pleasing though not perfectly regular. It will be rhythmical: that is, possess a quality somewhat like the beat in music or the motion of the waves of the sea. In an ordinary sentence, the stresses are not evenly spaced, not so much as musical beats or the motion of the waves; but in an emotional passage like the last paragraph of "Dunkirk" they become more than ordinarily regular. In some parts of this passage every second syllable is stressed: *wé shall not flág or fáil.* In others, a stressed syllable follows two or three unstressed ones: *wé shall fíght on the beáches, wé shall fíght on the lánding gróunds, we shall fíght in the fíelds and in the stréets.* The rhythm of the paragraph, however, is less regular than these examples imply. We have not marked the lesser stress on the word "we," and other parts of it exhibit neither of the above patterns. Though strongly rhythmical, the paragraph retains its essential prose character.

How, then, is its rhythm related to that of poetry? Arranging the passage just quoted in approximately equal groups of words, each with about the same number of stresses, would make the reader much more aware of its sound:

We shall fíght on the beáches,

We shall fíght on the lánding gróunds,

We shall fíght in the fíelds and in the stréets,

We shall fíght in the hills;

We shall néver surrénder. . . .

Although the sequence and the sense of the words are unchanged, it is now apparent that the structure and texture of their sound have been carefully devised, so as to give them as much regularity as is found in many poems. Compare, for instance, the opening lines of the poem "Musée des Beaux Arts" (page 388):

About súffering they were néver wróng,

The Óld Másters: how wéll they understóod

Its húman position; how it tákes pláce. . . .

The poem is not more rhythmical than the prose passage, but it has been printed in a way that accentuates its sound-structure. Churchill's passage is so nearly regular that its units of sound can almost be measured. That is, it comes near possessing what is called *meter.*

## METER

When the rhythm of a poem is irregular, as is that of "Musée des Beaux Arts," its lines are said to be *free verse.* (Free verse usually does not rhyme, but such free-verse poems as "Musée des Beaux Arts," "Dover Beach," page 127, and "The Love Song of J. Alfred Prufrock," page 270, have rhymes at irregular intervals.) When, however, the stressed syllables of a passage are so equally spaced that the rhythm approaches regularity, the passage is said to be metrical. Only in poems which demand prominence for their sound is this degree of regularity desirable; and not even in poems would it be desirable to have the rhythm perfectly regular, for that would remove the language of the poem too far from the language of ordinary life. But since the rhythm of a metered poem approaches regularity, by reading several lines we can perceive the pattern that is being approximated. Consider the beginning of Frost's "Birches" (page 31):

When Í see bírches bénd to léft and ríght

Acróss the línes of stráighter dárker trées,

I líke to thínk some bóy's been swínging thém.

If the ear did not tell us that these lines have a nearly regular rhythm, counting would show that each has ten syllables and that every even-numbered syllable is stressed. That is, we have only to ignore the stresses on *see* and the second *I* for a perfectly regular pattern to emerge. Ten-syllable lines stressed on the even-numbered syllables constitute by far the most common meter in poetry written in English. When there is no rhyme, this measure is called *blank verse*. (Sometimes "blank verse" is applied to any lines having meter but not rhyme.) In a terminology proper to Greek and Latin poetry, the meter of "Birches" is called *iambic pentameter*. This method involves imagining that the lines are divided into five pairs of syllables, each consisting of an unstressed syllable followed by a stressed one and known as an *iambic foot*. But English meter can be understood without a special set of terms if we think of it as regularity of line length, measured in syllables, plus regularity of stress position.[3]

Another meter found occasionally in English verse resembles the rhythm of the second quotation from "Dunkirk"; the stresses tend to fall on every third syllable instead of on every second one. This meter is usually treated with more freedom than that of "Birches," as in these lines from "Hellvellyn," by Walter Scott:

Lakes and mountains beneath me gleamed misty
and wide;
All was still, save by fits, when the eagle was
yelling. . . .

the first measure of each line is triple, the second duple, the third single. In

Now as / I was / young and / easy under the /
apple / boughs,

(the first line of "Fern Hill," by Dylan Thomas, p. 33) the first two words are not a complete measure, for they lack a stressed syllable; the first, second, and fourth measures are duple; the third is quintuple; and the fifth is duple, because the first syllable, *Ab-*, of the next line can be regarded as belonging to it.

It is important to remember that not all measures take exactly the same time to read, though the times will have to be nearly the same if the line is to sound metrical, and in a highly regular poem, such as "The Charge of the Light Brigade," the measures will be very close in length: for example, the voice lingers on the word *death* and pauses after it, so that this measure lasts as long as the next, *Into the,* which has three syllables. The stressed syllables, moreover, do not all receive exactly the same stress: in the last-quoted line *young* is stressed more than *I*; if the latter were stressed more strongly, the meaning of the line would be somewhat different. Yet unless the word *I* is stressed a little more than *as* and *was,* it will not sound like the beginning of a measure, and the beat of the rhythm will be lost.

One meter differs from another, then, in the kind of measures that make it up and in the number of measures in its lines. Since the lines quoted from "Birches" and "Fern Hill" have each five stresses to the line, they are alike in having five measures, though they differ in the kind of measures making up their lines. They are metrically more alike than either is like "The Charge of the Light Brigade," which has only three measures to the line. The number of measures to the line is denoted by the classical names listed above: "Birches" and "Fern Hill" are pentameter, "The Charge of the Light Brigade" trimeter.

---

[3] Since the meters of English poetry are often known by classical names, the reader may find it useful to have these tabulated. Here are the names of the principal feet, their adjective forms, and examples:

| | |
|---|---|
| *iamb, iambus* (*iambic*) | to·dáy |
| *anapaest* (*anapaestic*) | cig·a·rétte |
| *trochee* (*trochaic*) | éas·y |
| *dactyl* (*dactylic*) | yés·ter·day |
| *spondee* (*spondaic*) | swéet·héart |
| *amphibrach* (*amphibrachic*) | to·mór·row |

The number of feet to the line is denoted thus:

| | | | |
|---|---|---|---|
| 1 | monometer | 5 | pentameter |
| 2 | dimeter | 6 | hexameter |
| 3 | trimeter | 7 | heptameter |
| 4 | tetrameter | | |

The meter of "Hellvellyn," for example, is known as *anapaestic tetrameter;* that of "Lines Written among the Euganean Hills," as *trochaic tetrameter;* and that of *Evangeline* as *dactylic hexameter*.

A more fundamental method of describing English meters is provided by a system based on musical notation. The basic group of syllables, considered a *measure,* consists of a stressed syllable together with all the unstressed syllables that follow it before the next stress. In

A· / cross the / lines of / straighter / darker / trees

the measures are divided by vertical lines, each measure beginning on a stressed syllable.

Most measures are either *duple,* having two syllables, like those above, or *triple,* having three syllables. In

Into the / jaws of / death,
Into the / mouth of / hell, (page 180)

Still other meters result from reversing those of "Birches" and "Hellvellyn"; that is, when the lines begin with a stressed syllable, which is then followed by one or more unstressed ones:

/         /         /         /
In thine halls the lamp of learning,
/         /         /         /
Padua, now no more is burning. . . .

> (P. B. Shelley, "Lines Written among the Euganean Hills")

/         /         /         /         /
This is the forest primeval. The murmuring pines
/ /
and the hemlocks. . . .

> (H. W. Longfellow, *Evangeline*)

In the first of these, the last, unstressed syllable is often left off; and in the second, a stressed syllable occasionally replaces two unstressed ones, as in *hemlocks.*

Combinations of meters are also found, as in "The Charge of the Light Brigade."

Briefly, the meter of a poem is the result of (1) the number of syllables to the line, and (2) the position of the stressed syllables in the line. Determining meter, which is called *scansion,* is a useful activity because of the important part played by sound in the impression that a poem makes upon the reader. But in learning to scan, one should be wary of two common mistakes. One is to suppose that poems ought to have completely regular patterns of stressed and unstressed syllables. The fact is that the sentence rhythms in a metered poem have only been brought nearer to regularity than they ordinarily are in prose, and so the skilled reader is aware of a sort of rhythmical counterpoint—a harmonizing of the real sentence rhythms, determined by the normal pronunciation of words, with the ideal regularity of the metrical pattern.

The second mistake is to identify the poem with its meter. The aim of reading poetry should be not to discover the meter in which it is written, but to grasp its total meaning. Though its sound has an important influence on what it says, there are many other elements that constitute the poem in its entirety. Yet before coming to the subject of meaning, we must consider two other factors that may affect the sound by their presence in the poem.

## STANZAS

The sentences of a poem may be divided into paragraphs as prose sentences are, and this happens particularly often in blank verse. Or the lines may be arranged in equal (or nearly equal) units, called *stanzas.* This arrangement is not necessarily determined by the meaning; it is another method of calling attention to the sound. A poet may follow a traditional stanza form: A. E. Housman, for instance, often employed the four-line *ballad stanza,* as in "My Dreams Are of a Field Afar," page 183. Poets also invent new stanza forms, as Dylan Thomas did in writing "Fern Hill," page 33, the stanza of which is determined by stresses. (The first two lines have five stresses each, the next two have three, the middle line four; then the pattern of the first four lines is repeated.) This method is exceptional, however; normally the shape of a stanza is emphasized by rhymes, in some of its lines at least. Similarly, some poems have stanzas of unequal length (*e.g.,* "Poetry," by Marianne Moore, page 391); but normally the stanza form contributes to the shape of the poem by being exactly repeated. In many stanza forms, of course, the lines are of unequal length, as are those of the ballad stanza; but the pattern is repeated in each successive stanza.

## REPETITION OF SOUNDS; RHYME

Other devices which may be used to make sound prominent in a poem involve repetition of letter sounds. *Assonance* means repetition of vowel sounds; *consonance,* repetition of consonant sounds. Repetition at the beginnings of stressed syllables is called *alliteration.* Examples of assonance (*now, boughs, about, house*) and alliteration (*house, happy; grass, green*) are found in the first two lines of "Fern Hill." But these devices occur irregularly and often seem accidental. When the repetition of sounds is regularized, it is called *rhyme.*

Strictly defined, rhyme is a correspondence in sounds of this sort: the sounds must be identical from the last stressed vowel sound to the end, whereas the sounds before the vowel sound must be different. *Rhyme* rhymes with *chime,* but not with *rime*—and, of course, not with *line.* The rhyming syllable may occur earlier than the last syllable (*early, burly*) or in another word (*best of us, rest of us*); these are called *feminine rhymes.* They tend to be humorous, as in "The War Song of Dinas Vawr," page 181. In the poetry of the past, if the poet undertook to rhyme at all he was expected to rhyme strictly, except that by what is called *poetic licence* a few *near-rhymes* (*river, never; Heaven, even*) and *eye-rhymes* (*love, move*) were admitted. The greater the differences between two rhyming combinations, the more striking will be their identity of sound. The least interesting rhymes are those between the same parts of speech having the same terminal spelling: *sang, rang*. Such a rhyme as *debt, sweat* is more surprising. Rhymes normally occur at the ends of lines, but *internal rhyme* is also found, as in Shelley's "Cloud," which begins: "I bring fresh showers for the thirsting flowers."

Since the number of rhymes in English is limited compared with those in some other languages, many of them came to seem hackneyed; and recent poets have expanded the resources of the rhymer by admitting near-rhymes to equal status with perfect ones, *e.g.*, in "Ars Poetica," page 390, and "Sailing to Byzantium," page 562. Most near-rhymes vary the vowel sound while retaining the consonant sound (*seas, dies*), or else ignore the rule of stress (*sing, studying*). Only seldom are the consonant sounds varied (*time, climbs*). The use of near-rhymes, sometimes mistaken for carelessness, offers a middle course between repeating the familiar rhymes of earlier poems and abandoning rhyme entirely.

## SPEAKER, SUBJECT, ATTITUDE

Poems, then, differ from prose works in respect to sound: their rhythm is more pronounced, and most of them exhibit features involving the repetition of sounds, such as meter. But in all literary works, poems included, a subject is presented by a speaker who reveals an attitude toward that subject. What the reader of this book has learned about the content of stories and other prose works will therefore assist him in understanding poems. Accordingly, without repeating the explanations of terms introduced earlier, let us examine a specific poem which presents some difficulties of understanding: "Fern Hill," by Dylan Thomas, page 33.

On first reading a poem, as we have seen, the reader is apt to be more concerned with its sound than its sense. If he is wise, he will start by reading it aloud; and if it is "Fern Hill," he can assist his own reading by first listening to the admirable recording of it made by the poet himself. The long, flowing lines with which the stanzas begin will probably establish his first impression of "Fern Hill"; he will particularly notice the "liquid" quality of the rhythm, which results in part from the number of unstressed syllables that precede the stresses. There are few if any clusters of consonants or of stresses to arrest the voice; the sounds, urging the reader onwards, contribute to the feeling of zest with which the poem celebrates the joys of childhood. As to the sense, the reader will probably gather at this first reading that Fern Hill is the name of a farm, that the poem is partly about the speaker's memories of childish pleasures there (the games he played and the delights of simply going to sleep and waking up), and that the prominent words "dying" and "chains" in the final lines convey a wholly different emotion, one that will complete the basic contrast of the poem. Thus, even at this early stage, the reader begins to grasp the character of the speaker, the main outlines of the subject, and the contrasting emotions that enter into the speaker's attitude. If, later on, the structure of the stanzas is analyzed, it will be noticed that the contrast is reinforced by the meter: in general, the long, flowing lines are concerned with the joys of childhood, whereas the pathos of its passing is concentrated in the short six-syllable lines, three of which begin with the word "Time." This correspondence illustrates the close connection that may exist between meter and emotion.

Further readings make the reader's awareness of the remembered pleasures much more vivid and concrete. The speaker's claim that he was "happy as the grass was green" is supported by a series of images in which he describes the games that he played, the sensation of falling asleep while "the owls were bearing the farm away," the joy of waking to a world that seemed as fresh and new as on the day it was created. The poem, so far as it is a hymn to the delights of childhood, must stand or fall by the success with which it provides a solid basis for this emotion. But these remembered pleasures constitute only a part of the theme; for, paradoxically, the greater the happiness of childhood, the greater its pathos—the sadder is its passing. Like "Blackberry Winter," which it resembles in theme, "Fern Hill" asserts that for a child Time does not exist. Alas, however, Time is all the while carrying him out of his childhood, as later it will carry him from life into death. Yet the child is mercifully unconscious of what is happening to him. These reflections are suggested by the references to Time in the poem, though it is only after many readings that the full implications of such lines as "Time let me play and be Golden in the mercy of his means" can be grasped.

At some point in his reading, the reader will do well to notice the likenesses between the poem and a short story, for these will assist his understanding. The setting of "Fern Hill," as we have already seen, is essential to its meaning; except for Time, the characters are restricted to the speaker—which suggests, perhaps, the egocentricity of childhood; and a succession of scenes full of action and movement ("I was huntsman and herdsman"; "it was running"; "I ran my heedless ways"), which convey the intense though transitory vitality of the main character, correspond to the plot of a story. The point of view of "Fern Hill," the recollection of boyhood from the vantage point of maturity, is the same as that of "Blackberry Winter"—as might be expected from the likeness of their themes. (The reader will recall that novelty of theme is not often to be expected, since many works derive their value from the force with which they dramatize a universal experience.) Finally, a consideration of the progression in "Fern Hill" leads to an appreciation of its two most striking passages.

We have said that working out all the implications of the metaphors and symbols in a poem is one of the last stages in its reading. It is the symbols in the concluding stanza of "Fern Hill," particularly in the line "Up to the swallow thronged loft by the shadow of my hand," that suggest the analogy between passing from childhood to maturity and passing from life to death. But this aspect of the theme is not introduced abruptly in the last stanza: it has been prepared for by the progression that occurs at the middle of the poem. Having established the joyousness of childhood by mentioning its games and the sensations of sleeping and waking, the speaker sums up in

the striking metaphor, "it was Adam and maiden." The world of childhood, that is, resembles the Garden of Eden: all freshness and innocence, for the child knows neither sin nor death. Time will lead him out of this realm of grace, as the angel led Adam and Eve from Paradise, but he is as unaware of this fate as they were of theirs before their fall. Instead of resting in its expression of childish joys and the pathos of their passing, the poem proceeds to link these emotions with the joy and sorrow that, from the religious point of view, are central to man's condition. And the reader's understanding is prepared for the wider dimension that the concluding stanza will give to the subject; instead of merely repeating what has already been established, the final lines suggest that the poem is concerned not only with childhood, but with the whole human cycle of life and death.

We have suggested that some modern readers approach a poem with mistaken expectations. If a reader were to ask what the "thought" or "idea" of "Fern Hill" is, we should have to answer that it is merely that the child is unaware of the brevity of life, an answer that would probably cause disappointment. Such a reader has asked the wrong question. The reading of a poem is a complex experience in which understanding the idea may play only a minor part, as it does in reading "Fern Hill." Its fifty-four lines typify the concentration of meaning that characterizes all good poetry; and though we have discussed its sound, its speaker and subject, its figures of speech and the emotions that are interwoven with them, these prose paragraphs only begin to explore its riches. The essence of "Fern Hill" is not its thought, but the universal ironic contrast that the poem realizes by its concrete presentation of childhood pleasures and the sharp, subtle metaphors that ring in the reader's memory and unfold new meanings as they are turned over in the mind. The poem is pervaded by a feeling of controlled wild energy, by a joyous acceptance of the paradox of growth; and it is the intensity of these qualities, along with the complex, interrelated structure of its symbols, that makes the reading of "Fern Hill" a complete and satisfying experience.

# BIOGRAPHIES

ADDISON, Joseph (1672–1719). British essayist and poet. Prepared himself for diplomatic service and held a number of secretaryships under various Whig politicians. Contributed essays to Sir Richard Steele's *Tatler* (1709–1711), and during 1711 and 1712, with Steele's collaboration, produced the *Spectator,* a periodical devoted chiefly to social satire and literary criticism.

ANDERSON, Sherwood (1876–1941). American novelist and short story writer. Born in Camden, Ohio. Was a newspaperman and businessman before deciding to become a writer. Among his writings are *Windy McPherson's Son* (1916), *Winesburg, Ohio* (1919), *Poor White* (1920), *The Triumph of the Egg* (1921), *A Story Teller's Story* (1924), and *Dark Laughter* (1925).

ARNOLD, Matthew (1822–1888). British poet and critic. Son of Thomas Arnold, one of the great headmasters at Rugby. Educated at Oxford. Was Inspector of Schools (1851–1886); Professor of Poetry at Oxford (1857–1867). Poems include "The Scholar-Gipsy" (1853), "Sohrab and Rustum" (1853), "Rugby Chapel" (1869). Among his critical works are *On Translating Homer* (1861), *Culture and Anarchy* (1869), and *Literature and Dogma* (1873).

AUDEN, W(ystan) H(ugh) (1907–    ). English poet. Educated at Oxford. Married Erika Mann, daughter of Thomas Mann. Author of *Poems* (1930), *Orators* (1932), *On This Island* (1937), *Selected Poems* (1938), *Another Time* (1940), *The Double Man* (1941), and *Nones* (1951). Has collaborated with Christopher Isherwood on *Journey to a War* (1939) and *On the Frontier* (1939). Now lives in the United States.

AUGUSTINE, Saint (354–430). Early Christian church father and philosopher. Bishop of Hippo (Africa) from 396 to 430. Exercised, through books, letters, and sermons, an enormous influence on Christian world. A champion of orthodoxy, his most famous works are *The City of God* and his autobiographical *Confessions.*

BACON, Francis (1561–1626). English philosopher and writer. A politician and statesman, he was instrumental in having Essex convicted for treason (1601). Was commissioner for arranging union with Scotland (1604), and Lord Chancellor (1618). Was found guilty of bribery and corruption (1621) and banished from Parliament, but was later pardoned. *Essays,* first published in 1597, were published in complete form in 1621. Philosophical works include *Advancement of Learning* (1605), *Instauratio Magna* (unfinished), and *Novum Organum* (1620), in Latin, the key to his non-Aristotelian system of philosophy.

BETJEMAN, John (1906–    ). British poet and editor, educated at Oxford. His *Selected Poems,* published in 1948, won the Heinemann Award. Since then he has written *First and Last Loves* (1952) and *A Few Late Chrysan-*

707

*themums* (1954), his collected poems since 1948.

BIERCE, Ambrose (1847–1914?). American short story writer and journalist. Born in Ohio, he served in the Civil War. His reputation as a cynic was established by *The Fiend's Delight* (1872), *Cobwebs from an Empty Skull* (1874), and a column called "Prattle" in the San Francisco *Examiner* (1887–1896). Later works include *Tales of Soldiers and Civilians* (1891), *Can Such Things Be?*, and *The Devil's Dictionary* (1906). He disappeared into Mexico in 1913 and his fate is unknown.

BISHOP, John Peale (1892–1944). An American poet and critic. Born in West Virginia. Lived mostly in France after 1930. Author of *Green Fruit, Many Thousands Gone,* and *Now With His Love.*

BLAKE, William (1757–1827). English mystic, poet, and engraver. Illustrated his own *Songs of Innocence* (1789) and *Songs of Experience* (1794). Wrote several mystical and symbolic works, the best known of which are *Milton* (1804) and *Jerusalem* (1804–1818). At the time of his death he was preparing engravings for an edition of Dante's *Divine Comedy.*

BOSWELL, James (1740–1795). Scottish lawyer and writer. Son of Alexander Boswell (Lord Auchinleck, Lord Justiciary. An acquaintance of Rousseau, Voltaire, and other notables, he met Samuel Johnson in London in 1763. He became Johnson's close companion (1772–1784), and took voluminous notes on Johnson's conversation. Author of *Account of Corsica* (1768), *Journal of Tour to Hebrides* (1785), and the masterpiece of biography called *Life of Samuel Johnson* (1791).

BROOKS, Cleanth (1906–     ). American critic and educator. Born in Murray, Kentucky. Educated at Vanderbilt and Tulane; Rhodes Scholar at Oxford (1929–1932). Has been Professor of English at Yale since 1947. Author of *Understanding Poetry* (with R. P. Warren, 1938, 1950), *Understanding Drama* (with R. B. Heilman, 1945), *Understanding Fiction* (with R. P. Warren, 1948), and *The Well-Wrought Urn* (1947).

BROWNING, Robert (1812–1889). English poet. Began by writing long narrative poems *Pauline* (1833), *Paracelsus* (1835), and *Sordello* (1840). After writing a number of unsuccessful verse dramas, he achieved success with the dramatic monologues which appeared in *Men and Women* (1855), which includes "Fra Lippo Lippi," and *Dramatis Personae* (1864), which includes "Rabbi Ben Ezra" and

"Caliban upon Setebos." Eloped with Elizabeth Barrett in 1846 and spent most of the next fifteen years in Italy. *The Ring and the Book* (1864–1869), the story of an old Roman murder case told in twelve monologues by persons involved in the trial, is generally considered to be his masterpiece.

BURNS, Robert (1759–1796). Scottish poet. Educated by his father, a cotter, Burns wrote his early poetry—including "The Cotter's Saturday Night" and "Holy Willie's Prayer"—while farming with his brother Gilbert. A 1796 edition of his poems received great acclaim from Edinburgh literary circles; Burns's success enabled him to marry his sweetheart, Jean Armour, and to devote the rest of his life to writing poetry and collecting old Celtic ballads.

BYRON, George Gordon. Sixth Baron (1788–1824). English poet. Educated at Cambridge. Lived a tempestuous life, which included a disastrous marriage to an English heiress and love affairs with Jane Clairmont and an Italian countess. Died of malaria at Missolonghi, where he had gone to fight for Greek independence. Immensely popular in his own time for such narrative poems as *Childe Harold's Pilgrimage* (1812–17), *The Giaour, The Bride of Abydos, The Corsair*—and *Don Juan*, a satirical epic about a libertine in which Byron supposedly drew heavily on his own experiences.

CHAMBERS, Whittaker (1901–     ). American journalist. Attended Columbia University; traveled in Europe (1923); shortly thereafter became a member of the Communist Party. Served as foreign editor of the *Daily Worker*, editor of the *New Masses*. Broke with the Communist Party in 1938, and became a writer for *Time* magazine. It was on the basis of his evidence that Alger Hiss was convicted of perjury (1950). Chambers is the author of an autobiography, *Witness* (1952).

CHAUCER, Geoffrey (1340?–1400). English poet. The son of a vintner, he served as a page to the wife of Lionel, Duke of Clarence; later traveled extensively in Europe on diplomatic missions; eventually held official positions in the English government. Although his earlier writings—*The Book of the Duchess, The Parlement of Foules, Troilus and Criseyde*, etc.—show clearly the influence of French and Italian models, he gave primary attention to native English elements in his witty and realistic masterpiece, *The Canterbury Tales.*

CHEKHOV, Anton (1860–1904). Russian playwright and fiction writer. Began life as a doctor, but practiced little. His stories are noted for their psychological insight and realism; they include *The Chorus Girl* (1884), *Peasants* (1897, and *The Bishop* (1902). The most famous of his plays are *The Sea Gull* (1896), *The Three Sisters* (1901), and *The Cherry Orchard* (1904).

CHURCHILL, Winston (1874–    ). British statesman and author. The elder son of Lord Randolph Churchill, he served as a war correspondent in the Boer War, and became an M.P. in 1901. Served as colonel and minister of munitions during the First World War; became prime minister on May 10, 1940, and led England through the Second World War. Has written extensively on history, political problems, and his personal experiences—all three of which enter into his six-volume history of the Second World War, which began with *The Gathering Storm* (1948) and concluded with *Triumph and Tragedy* (1954).

COHEN, Morris (1880–1947). American philosopher and educator. Born in Minsk, Russia, he was brought to the U.S. at twelve. Received his Ph.D. at Harvard in 1906; was professor of philosophy at C.C.N.Y. and the University of Chicago. Among his works are *Reason and Nature* (1931), *Law and the Social Order* (1933), and *The Faith of a Liberal* (1946).

COLERIDGE, Samuel Taylor (1772–1834). English poet and critic. Educated at Cambridge. In his youth acquired the opium addiction which plagued him the rest of his life. Became a close friend of William Wordsworth in 1797, and collaborated with him on the *Lyrical Ballads* (1798). His most famous poems are "The Rime of the Ancient Mariner" (first printed in *Lyrical Ballads*), "Christabel," and "Kubla Khan." Among his prose works are *Biographia Literaria* (1817) and *Aids to Reflection* (1825).

CONRAD, Joseph (Teodor Józef Konrad Korzeniowski) (1857–1924). Novelist and short story writer. Born in the Ukraine, he served as a seaman and officer in the British merchant marine, and became a British subject in 1886. Most of his stories and novels make use of his personal knowledge of the sea and foreign lands. His short stories are collected in volumes called *Youth* (1902), *Typhoon* (1903), and *Tales of Hearsay* (1925). His novels include *Almayer's Folly* (1895), *Lord Jim* (1900), *Nostromo* (1904), *The Secret Agent* (1907), *Victory* (1915), and *The Shadow-Line* (1917).

COPLAND, Aaron (1900–    ). American composer. Born in Brooklyn, N.Y.; studied music and composition privately. Has lectured on music at the New School for Social Research, N. Y. C., and at Harvard; was Charles Eliot Norton professor of poetry at Harvard (1951–52). Received Pulitzer prize for music in 1944. Among his musical works are *A Dance Symphony* (1925), *El Salon Mexico* (1936), *Billy the Kid* (1938), *Rodeo* (1942), and *Appalachian Spring* (1944). His writings include *What to Listen for in Music* (1939), *Our New Music* (1941), and *Music and Imagination* (1952).

CRANE, Stephen (1871–1900). American novelist and short story writer. His first novel was *Maggie, A Girl of the Streets* (1893). His second, *The Red Badge of Courage* (1896), is a remarkably realistic account of an episode in the Civil War, written when Crane had never seen a battle. After writing it, he served as a war correspondent in Cuba and Greece. Among his stories are "The Open Boat" and "The Blue Hotel."

CROCKETT, David (1786–1836). American frontiersman, famed both as a marksman and as a humorist. Born in Tennessee, he served under Andrew Jackson in the Creek War (1813–1814), served as a member of the U.S. House of Representatives (1827–1831; 1833–1835), and was killed at the Alamo. His true character is obscured by the legends that began to grow up about him in his own time.

DAUDET, Alphonse (1840–1897). French novelist and short story writer. Born at Nîmes, he settled in Paris in 1857. His first great success was *Lettres de Mon Moulin* (1866); later works include *Le Petit Chose* (1868), *Tartarin de Tarascon* (1872), *Sapho* (1884), *Tartarin sur les Alpes* (1885), and *Soutien de Famille* (1898).

DAY, Clarence (1874–1935). American writer. Most famous for his books dealing with his family life and parents: *God and My Father* (1932), *Life with Father* (1935; dramatized by Howard Lindsay and Russel Crouse in 1939), and *Life with Mother* (published in 1937).

DE ROUSSY DE SALES, Raoul (1896–1942). French journalist and lecturer. Educated in Paris and England. Worked as French correspondent in America for several French newspapers and magazines from 1933 until the fall of France, when he became an ardent supporter of General De Gaulle. Author of *The Making of Tomorrow* (1942), a study of Western civilization in the 19th and 20th centuries, and numerous magazine articles interpreting American culture.

DICKENS, Charles (1812–1870). English novelist. After a childhood of hardship and humiliation, Dickens became the most popular author of his time. Among his chief works are the *Pickwick Papers* (1836–1837), *Oliver Twist* (1837–1839), *Martin Chuzzlewit* (1843–1844), *David Copperfield* (1849–1850), *Bleak House* (1852–1853), *A Tale of Two Cities* (1859), and *Great Expectations* (1860–1861).

DICKINSON, Emily (1830–1886). American poet. Lived a quiet, secluded life in Amherst, Massachusetts; none of her poetry was published during her lifetime. The first edition of her poems appeared in 1890, and additional volumes were published in 1891, 1896, 1914, 1929, and 1936.

DONNE, John (1573–1631). English poet; chief of the "metaphysical" poets. Brought up as a Roman Catholic, he studied law and wrote the frankly erotic *Songs and Sonnets* and *Elegies* (1593–1598). After sailing in Essex's expedition to Cádiz (1596), he was dismissed from private secretaryship to Thomas Egerton because he secretly married his patron's niece. Eventually he entered the Anglican Church, in which he became famous for his sermons and wrote the *Divine Poems* (1607) and *Holy Sonnets* (1618).

DRYDEN, John (1631–1700). English poet and satirist. Began his career as clerk to Cromwell's chamberlain; established his reputation as dramatist with *The Rival Ladies* (1663), *The Indian Queen* (1664), *The Indian Emperor* (1665), *Marriage-a-la-mode* (1673), *All for Love* (1678), and others. Wrote three great satires: *Absalom and Achitophel* (1681), *The Medal* (1682), and *Mac Flecknoe* (1682). Having defended Anglicanism in *Religio Laici* (1682), he justified his own conversion to Roman Catholicism in *The Hind and the Panther* (1687). As a result of his Catholicism, he lost his pensions in the Revolution of 1689. In his old age, he produced *Alexander's Feast* (1697) and *Fables, Ancient and Modern* (1699).

ELIOT, T(homas) S(tearns) (1888–      ). Poet, critic, and playwright. Born in St. Louis, Missouri; educated at Harvard, the Sorbonne, and Oxford. He has been a resident of London since 1914 and a British citizen since 1927. Received the Nobel prize for literature in 1948. Among his more famous poems are *The Waste Land* (1922), *Ash Wednesday* (1932), and *Four Quartets* (1944). His critical works include *The Sacred Wood* (1920), *The Use of Poetry and the Use of Criticism* (1933), and

*Selected Essays* (1951). His plays include *Murder in the Cathedral* (1935), *The Family Reunion* (1939), *The Cocktail Party* (1950), and *The Confidential Clerk* (1954).

FAULKNER, William (1897–      ). American novelist and short story writer. Born in Mississippi; served in the British Royal Air Force during the First World War. Received the Nobel prize for literature in 1949. Most of his novels deal with the problems of the South. They include *Soldier's Pay* (1926), *Sartoris* (1929), *The Sound and the Fury* (1929), *Sanctuary* (1931), *Absalom, Absalom!* (1936), *The Wild Palms* (1939), *Requiem for a Nun* (1951), and *A Fable* (1954).

FREUD, Sigmund (1856–1939). Austrian neurologist and founder of psychoanalysis. Studied with Charcot (1885–1886); was professor of neuropathology at the University of Vienna (1902–1938). Responsible for the theories of the unconscious, the id-ego-superego structure of the mind, and the significance of dreams as representations of repressed impulses. Some of his works which have been translated into English are *Three Contributions to the Sexual Theory* (1910), *Totem and Taboo* (1919), *Introductory Lectures on Psychoanalysis* (1922), *The Interpretation of Dreams* (1922, 1933), *The Future of an Illusion* (1928), *The Psychopathology of Everyday Life* (1938), and *Moses and Monotheism* (1939).

FROST, Robert (1875–      ). American poet. Educated at Dartmouth and Harvard. Has been professor of English at Amherst and Dartmouth. Received Pulitzer prize for poetry in 1924, 1931, 1937, and 1943. His books include *A Boy's Will* (1913), *North of Boston* (1914), *West-running Brook* (1924), *A Witness Tree* (1942), and *Collected Poems* (1930, 1939, 1949).

FRY, Roger (1866–1934). English painter and critic. Educated at Cambridge. Among his writings are *Vision and Design* (1920), *Henri Matisse* (1930), *Reflections on British Painting* (1934), and *Last Lectures* (published in 1939).

GIBBS, Wolcott (1902–      ). American drama critic and playwright. Born in New York City. Has been associated with the *New Yorker* since 1927; has been its drama critic since 1940. Author of *Bed of Neuroses* (1937) and *Season in the Sun* (1946).

GORDON, Caroline (Mrs. Allen Tate) (1895–      ). American novelist and short story writer. Born in Kentucky; has been a lecturer at Columbia University since 1946. Author of *The Forest of the South* (1945), *The House of*

*Fiction* (with Allen Tate, 1950), *The Strange Children* (1951).

GOSSE, Edmund (1849–1928). Poet and scholar. Lecturer at Cambridge (1895–1900); librarian to House of Lords (1904–1914). His *Collected Poems* appeared in 1911; his critical and scholarly works include *Seventeenth Century Studies* (1883), *A History of Eighteenth Century Literature* (1889), and studies of Donne (1899), Ibsen (1907), and Swinburne (1912, 1917). *Father and Son* (1907) is the best known of his autobiographical works.

GRAY, Thomas (1716–1771). English poet. Educated at Cambridge. Appointed professor of modern history at Cambridge in 1768. Besides the *Elegy Written in a Country Churchyard* (1751), his most famous work, he wrote *Ode on a Distant Prospect of Eton College* (1747), *Progress of Poesy* (1758), and *The Bard* (1758).

GREENE, Graham (1904–    ). English novelist and short story writer. Educated at Oxford. His novels include *Brighton Rock* (1938), *The Confidential Agent* (1939), *The Power and the Glory* (1940), *The Heart of the Matter* (1948), and *The End of the Affair* (1951).

GREENOUGH, Horatio (1805–1852). American sculptor. Educated at Harvard; spent most of his adult life in Italy. Some of his more famous statues are *Washington,* which is now in the Smithsonian Institution; *The Rescue,* a group which stands on a buttress of the portico of the capitol in Washington, D. C.; and *Angel and Child,* in the Boston Museum of Art.

HARDY, Thomas (1840–1928). English novelist and poet. His poetical works include *Wessex Poems* (1898), *Poems of the Past and Present* (1901), and the poetic drama *The Dynasts* (1904–1908). Among his novels are *The Return of the Native* (1878), *The Mayor of Casterbridge* (1886), *Tess of the D'Urbervilles* (1891), and *Jude the Obscure* (1895).

HAWTHORNE, Nathaniel (1804–1864). American short story writer and novelist. Educated at Bowdoin. A friend of Emerson, Thoreau, and Melville. His chief literary works include *Twice-Told Tales* (first series, 1837; second series, 1842), *Mosses from an Old Manse* (1846), *The Scarlet Letter* (1850), and *The House of the Seven Gables* (1851).

HAZLITT, William (1778–1830). English critic and essayist. Educated for the Unitarian ministry. Contributed numerous essays to the magazines of his time, and was popular as a lecturer on Shakespeare and the English drama. His works include *The Characters of Shakespeare's Plays* (1817), *Lectures on the Dramatic Literature of the Reign of Queen Elizabeth* (1821), and *The Spirit of the Age* (1825).

HEMINGWAY, Ernest (1899–    ). American short story writer and novelist. Born at Oak Park, Illinois; educated in public schools. Served in American ambulance unit in Italy during the First World War; served as war correspondent in the Second World War. Received Pulitzer prize in fiction in 1953; Nobel prize for literature in 1954. His stories are published in *The Fifth Column and the First Forty-Nine Stories* (1938); his novels include *The Sun Also Rises* (1926); *A Farewell to Arms* (1929), *To Have and Have Not* (1937), *For Whom the Bell Tolls* (1940), and *The Old Man and the Sea* (1952).

HERBERT, George (1593–1633). English poet and clergyman; one of the "metaphysical" poets. Educated at Cambridge; served as rector at Fugglestone and Bemerton, Wiltshire. His poems were published after his death under the title *The Temple; Sacred Poems and Private Ejaculations* (1633).

HERRICK, Robert (1591–1674). English poet and clergyman. Vicar of Dean Prior, in Devonshire; was removed from his office because of his Royalist sympathies in 1647; restored in 1662. His collected verse was published in *Hesperides, or the Works both Human and Divine of Robert Herrick, Esq.* (1648).

HOMER. Half-legendary Greek poet to whom the *Iliad* and the *Odyssey,* the two great Greek epic poems, are commonly attributed. It is now generally believed by scholars that neither poem was the work of a single man, but that each was the result of the efforts of a number of poets, who made additions and interpolations over a period of centuries.

HOPKINS, Gerard Manley (1844–1889). English poet and Jesuit priest. His poems, notable for their technical innovations, were published only after his death. They include "God's Grandeur," "Thou Art Indeed Just, Lord," "Pied Beauty," "The Leaden Echo," and "The Golden Echo."

HOUSMAN, A(lfred) E(dward) (1859–1936). English poet and classical scholar. Educated at Oxford; was professor of Latin at University College, London (1892–1911) and Cambridge (1911–1936). His poems may be found in *Collected Poems of A. E. Housman* (1940).

HUGO, Victor (1802–1885). French novelist, poet, playwright; leader of the romantic movement in French literature. His play *Hernani* (1830) set off clashes between romanticists and classicists at the Théâtre Français for nearly a hundred nights. He is best known in England and America for his novel *Les Misérables* (1862).

JAMES, Henry (1843–1916). American novelist; brother of the psychologist and philosopher William James. Attended Harvard Law School (1862). Lived in England after 1876, and became a British citizen in 1915. Among his many novels are *Daisy Miller* (1879), *The Princess Casamassima* (1886), *The Tragic Muse* (1890), *The Wings of the Dove* (1902), *The Ambassadors* (1903), and *The Golden Bowl* (1904).

JAMES, William (1842–1910). American psychologist and philosopher; brother of the writer Henry James. Graduated from Harvard Medical School (1869). Noted as a founder of the school of pragmatism. His works include *The Principles of Psychology* (1890), *The Will to Believe and Other Essays* (1897), *The Varieties of Religious Experience* (1902), and *Pragmatism* (1907).

JOHNSON, Samuel (1709–1784). English lexicographer, critic, and conversationalist. Famed chiefly for his English dictionary (1755) and for the conversations which Boswell recorded in his *Life of Samuel Johnson* (1791). Also wrote the poems *London* (1738) and *The Vanity of Human Wishes* (1749); the *Rambler* and *Idler* essays (1750–52, 1758–60); and *The Lives of the Poets* (1779–81).

JOYCE, James (1882–1941). Irish novelist and short story writer. Educated at Belvedere College and the Royal University at Dublin. Planned to enter the Catholic priesthood, but renounced both Catholicism and Ireland and turned to writing. His works include a volume of poetry, *Chamber Music* (1907); a collection of stories, *Dubliners* (1914); a novel, *A Portrait of the Artist as a Young Man* (1916); and two works of fiction whose unconventionality has aroused a storm of controversy— *Ulysses* (1922), and *Finnegan's Wake* (1939).

KAFKA, Franz (1883–1924). Austrian novelist and short story writer. His fiction is noted for its highly charged psychological and philosophical content. Among his chief longer works are the posthumously published *The Trial* (1925) and *The Castle* (1926).

KEATS, John (1795–1821). English poet. The son of a hostler, he studied medicine but did not practice. His first published verse was a sonnet in Leigh Hunt's *Examiner* on May 5, 1816. Died of tuberculosis in Rome at the age of twenty-five. Among his more famous poems

are *Endymion* (1817), "The Eve of St. Agnes" (1819), and the great odes "To Psyche," "To Indolence," "To a Grecian Urn," "To a Nightingale," "To Melancholy," and "To Autumn" (1819).

KINGLAKE, Alexander (1809–1891). English historian. Traveled in the East (1835) and wrote an account of his journey in *Eothen, or Traces of Travel Brought Home from the East* (1844). Having accompanied the British army to the Crimea in 1854, he wrote his eight-volume *Invasion of the Crimea* (1863–1887), at the invitation of Lady Raglan.

KIPLING, Rudyard (1865–1936). English short story writer, poet, novelist. Son of the curator of the Lahore Museum; educated at United Services College, North Devon. Worked as a newspaperman in Lahore, and began writing his stories and verse. Received Nobel prize for literature in 1907. Among his works are *Plain Tales from the Hills* (1887), *Soldiers Three* (1888), *The Light that Failed* (1891), *Barrack-Room Ballads* (1892), *The Jungle Book* (1894), and *Captains Courageous* (1897).

LATTIMORE, Richmond Alexander (1906– ). American scholar and translator. Born in Paotingfu, China. Educated at Dartmouth and University of Illinois; Rhodes scholar at Oxford (1929–1932). Has been professor of Greek at Bryn Mawr since 1948. Author of *Themes in Greek and Latin Epitaphs* (1943); translator of *The Odes of Pindar* (1947), *The Iliad of Homer* (1951), and *Aeschylus: Oresteia; Agamemnon, The Libation Bearers, The Eumenides* (1953).

LAWRENCE, D(avid) H(erbert) (1885–1930). English novelist, short story writer, poet. Born at Eastwood, Nottinghamshire; son of a coal miner. In 1914 married Frieda von Richthofen, sister of German military flyer in First World War. Author of *Sons and Lovers* (1913), *The Rainbow* (1915), *Kangaroo* (1923), *The Plumed Serpent* (1926), and *Lady Chatterley's Lover* (1928).

LEWIS, C(live) S(taples) (1898– ). English scholar and writer. Educated at Oxford; at present professor of Medieval and Renaissance English at Cambridge. Noted for his spirited defense of Christianity in our time. Among his writings are *The Pilgrim's Regress* (1933), *The Allegory of Love* (1936), *Out of the Silent Planet* (1938), *The Screwtape Letters* (1942), *Mere Christianity* (1952), and *English Literature in the Sixteenth Century* (1954).

LIEBLING, A(bbott) J(oseph) (1904– ). American journalist. Born in New York City;

educated at Dartmouth, Columbia, the Sorbonne. Has been on the staff of the *New Yorker* magazine since 1935. His books include *Back Where I Came From* (1938), *The Road Back to Paris* (1944), *The Wayward Pressman* (1947), and *The Honest Rainmaker* (1953).

LIMON, José (1908–    ). Concert dancer and choreographer. Born in Mexico, he came to the U. S. in 1915, attended the University of California, and studied art in New York City. Has made numerous concert tours in the U. S. and abroad, choreographed several Broadway shows, and participated as dancer, instructor, and choreographer at the American Dance Festival sponsored by Connecticut College.

LINDSAY, Vachel (1879–1931). American poet. Born in Springfield, Illinois, he attended Hiram College and studied art in Chicago and New York. Made a vagabond tour through the south and west, exchanging poems for bed and board; later made successful lecture and poetry-reading tours. His poems appeared in volumes titled *General William Booth Enters into Heaven and Other Poems* (1913), *The Congo and Other Poems* (1914), *The Chinese Nightingale* (1920), and others.

MACLEISH, Archibald (1892–    ). American poet. Educated at Yale and Harvard. Served in France during the First World War. Librarian of Congress (1939–1944), assistant secretary of state (1944–1945), Boylston Professor at Harvard since 1949. Author of *The Pot of Earth* (1925), *Nobodaddy* (1925), *Conquistador* (1932), *The Fall of the City* (1937), *Freedom Is the Right to Choose* (1951), *Collected Poems, 1917–1952* (1952). Received Pulitzer prize for poetry in 1932.

MANSFIELD, Katherine (1888–1923). English short story writer. Born in Wellington, New Zealand; married John Middleton Murry in 1913. Tuberculosis forced her to spend most of her later life in Italy, Switzerland, and France. Her stories were printed in *In a German Pension* (1911), *Prelude* (1918), *Bliss* (1920), *The Garden Party* (1922), *The Dove's Nest* (1923), and *Something Childish* (1924).

MARVELL, Andrew (1621–1678). English poet. Served as Milton's colleague in the Latin secretaryship (1657) under Cromwell; served also as M.P. (1660). Though he was a favorite of Charles II, he wrote pamphlets criticizing the government after the Restoration, and defended Milton. His poems include "Horatian Ode upon Cromwell's Return from Ireland," "Bermudas," and "The Garden."

MAUPASSANT, Guy de (1850–1893). French short story writer and novelist; student of Flaubert. Ranks as one of the great short story writers. Collections of his stories appeared under the titles *La Maison Tellier* (1881), *Mademoiselle Fifi* (1883), *Contes de la Bécasse* (1883), and *Contes et Nouvelles* (1885). His novels include *Une Vie* (1883), *Bel-Ami* (1885), and *Notre Coeur* (1890).

MCGINLEY, Phyllis (1905–    ). American writer of light verse. Born in Oregon, she worked as copy writer for a New York advertising agency and assistant editor of *Town and Country*. Her verse has appeared in the *New Yorker, Atlantic Monthly, Saturday Review of Literature,* and other magazines; it has been published in volumes titled *On The Contrary* (1934), *One More Manhattan* (1937), *Pocketful of Wry* (1940), and *Stones from a Glass House* (1946).

MENOTTI, Gian-Carlo (1911–    ). Composer. Born in Cadegliano, Italy; came to U.S. in 1928. Has composed chamber music, songs, and operas; among them *Amelia Goes to the Ball* (1936), *The Old Maid and the Thief, The Island God* (1942), *The Medium* (1946), *The Telephone* (1947), *The Consul* (1950), and *The Saint of Bleecker Street* (1954).

MEREDITH, George (1828–1909). British novelist and poet. Began as a journalist and contributor to periodicals. Married the daughter of Thomas Love Peacock (1849); nine years later she deserted him. His first important novel, *The Ordeal of Richard Feverel* (1859), won him the friendship of Swinburne and Rossetti. Other novels include *Rhoda Fleming* (1865), *The Egoist* (1879), and *Diana of the Crossways* (1885). As a poet he is chiefly known for the group of poems entitled *Modern Love* (1862).

MÉRIMÉE, Prosper (1803–1870). French writer and translator. Served as inspector general of historical remains in France (1841) and senator (1853). Best known in America for his novel *Carmen* (1845), which was made into an opera by Bizet in 1875.

MILTON, John (1608–1674). English poet. Educated at Cambridge; traveled in France and Italy (1638–1639). Played a vigorous part in the theological and political controversies of his time, and served as Cromwell's Latin secretary from 1649. Became blind in 1652, and in his last years produced his three greatest works: *Paradise Lost* (1667), *Paradise Regained* (1671), and *Samson Agonistes* (1671).

MOORE, Marianne (1887–    ). American poet. Born in St. Louis, Missouri; educated at

Bryn Mawr. Worked as teacher, librarian, and acting editor of the *Dial* (1925–1929). Received Pulitzer prize for poetry in 1951. Her volumes of poetry include *Poems* (1921), *Observations* (1924), *The Pangolin and Other Verse* (1936), *What Are Years* (1941), *Nevertheless* (1944), and *Collected Poems* (1951).

MORRISON, Theodore (1901–    ). American writer and educator. Born in New Hampshire; educated at Harvard. Has taught at Harvard since 1927. Among his writings are *Serpent in the Cloud* (1931), *Notes of Life and Death* (1935), *The Devious Way* (1944), *The Portable Chaucer* (1949), *The Dream of Alcestis* (1950), and *The Stones of the House* (1953).

MUMFORD, Lewis (1895–    ). American author. Born in Long Island; educated at C.C.N.Y., Columbia University, and New York University. Has written on a wide range of subjects: philosophy, history, city planning, literature. His books include *The Story of Utopias* (1922), *Sticks and Stones* (1924), *The Brown Decades* (1931), *The Culture of Cities* (1945), *Values for Survival* (1946), and *The Conduct of Life* (1951).

NASH, Ogden (1902–    ). American writer of light verse. Born in Rye, New York; attended Harvard. His verse has appeared in numerous magazines and in several volumes: *The Bad Parents' Garden of Verse* (1936), *I'm a Stranger Here Myself* (1938), *The Face Is Familiar* (1940), *Versus* (1949), and others.

NASHE, Thomas (1567–1601). English pamphleteer and dramatist. Engaged in a famous controversy with Gabriel Harvey, a friend of Edmund Spenser. His realistic prose romance *The Unfortunate Traveller, or the Life of Jack Wilton* (1594) is a forerunner of the novels of Defoe. Nashe was imprisoned for his satire of contemporary abuses in his comedy *The Isle of Dogs* (1597).

NIEBUHR, Reinhold (1892–    ). American clergyman; professor of applied Christianity at Union Theological Seminary since 1930. Editor of the magazines *Christianity and Society* and *Christianity and Crisis*. Author of *Does Civilization Need Religion?* (1927), *Moral Man and Immoral Society* (1932), *Beyond Tragedy* (1937), *The Nature and Destiny of Man* (volume I, 1941; volume II, 1943), and *Christian Realism and Political Problems* (1953).

ORWELL, George (Eric Blair) (1904–1950). British essayist and novelist. Fought on the side of the Loyalists in the Spanish Civil War. His writings include the allegorical *Animal Farm* (1945), the collection of essays *Dickens, Dali*

*and Others* (1946), the Utopia-in-reverse *1984* (1949) and several other novels.

OVID (Publius Ovidius Naso) (43 B.C.?–17 A.D.). Roman poet. Educated for the law, but turned to literature. Most famous for his elegies and for his *Metamorphoses,* a work in which he retells legends of miraculous transformations.

OWEN, Wilfred (1893–1918). English poet. Served in France during First World War; became company commander in 1918, and was killed shortly after. His poems were edited and published by his friend Siegfried Sassoon in 1920.

PEACOCK, Thomas Love (1785–1866). English novelist and poet; close friend of Shelley, and Shelley's executor. Best known for such satirical novels as *Headlong Hall* (1816), *Melincourt* (1817), *Nightmare Abbey* (1818), *Crotchet Castle* (1831), and *Gryll Grange* (1860).

PIRANDELLO, Luigi (1867–1936). Italian short story writer, novelist, and dramatist. Noted for his departures from convention in the drama. In America, his most famous work is the play *Six Characters in Search of an Author* (1918; produced in New York in 1922).

PLATO (427?–347 B.C.). Greek philosopher. A disciple of Socrates, with whom he studied in Athens until Socrates' trial and death (399 B.C.). Founded at Athens the Academy (387 B.C.), which is sometimes considered the first university. His works are written in the form of dialogues, in each of which Socrates plays a dominant role; among the most famous are the *Republic,* the *Laws,* the *Symposium,* and the *Timaeus.*

POE, Edgar Allan (1809–1849). American poet and short story writer. Attended University of Virginia for one quarter; entered West Point but was dismissed. Held a variety of editorial positions on American magazines. Died as a result of alcoholic excesses. Best known for his tales of the grotesque ("The Fall of the House of Usher," "The Tell-Tale Heart," etc.), his mystery stories ("The Gold Bug," "The Murders in the Rue Morgue," etc.), and his melancholy and melodious verse ("The Raven," "Ulalume," "Annabel Lee," etc.).

POPE, Alexander (1688–1744). English poet. Son of a Roman Catholic linen draper, he developed a physical deformity as a result of a severe illness at the age of twelve. *The Rape of the Lock* (1712), published when he was only twenty-four, won him a wide reputation.

His translations of the *Iliad* (1715–1720) and *Odyssey* (1725–1726) gained him financial independence. In the *Dunciad* (1728, 1742) he lampooned his literary enemies; and in *Imitations of Horace* (1733–1739) he satirized the followers of Walpole.

PORTER, Katherine Anne (1894–    ). American short story writer. Born in Texas, she has lived in New York, Mexico, and Europe. Her stories are collected in volumes titled *Flowering Judas and Other Stories* (1930), *Pale Horse, Pale Rider* (1939), and *The Leaning Tower* (1944).

PRESCOTT, W(illiam) H(ickling) (1796–1859). American historian. Educated at Harvard. Though handicapped by near-blindness as a result of an accident in a college course, he devoted himself to the study of Spanish history and produced four important works: a three-volume *History of the Reign of Ferdinand and Isabella the Catholic* (1838), a three-volume *History of the Conquest of Mexico* (1843), a *History of the Conquest of Peru* (1847), and a three-volume (unfinished) *History of the Reign of Philip the Second* (1855, 1858).

RANSOM, John Crowe (1888–    ). American educator and poet. Born at Pulaski, Tennessee. Rhodes scholar at Oxford (1910–1913). Has been professor of English at Kenyon College since 1937. His volumes of verse include *Poems about God* (1919), *Chills and Fever* (1924), *Grace after Meat* (1924), *Two Gentlemen in Bonds* (1926), and *Selected Poems* (1945).

RIESMAN, David (1909–    ). American lawyer, educator, and social scientist. Educated at Harvard. Was law clerk to Justice Brandeis of the U.S. Supreme Court (1935–1936); has been professor of social sciences at University of Chicago since 1949. Author of *Civil Liberties in a Period of Transition* (1942), *The Lonely Crowd* (1950), *Faces in the Crowd* (1952), and *Individualism Reconsidered, and Other Essays* (1954).

ROBINSON, Edwin Arlington (1869–1935). American poet. Born at Head Tide, Maine; lived in Maine and New York City. Received Pulitzer prize in 1921, 1925, and 1927. His books include *The Torrent and the Night Before* (1896), *The Man Against the Sky* (1916), *The Man Who Died Twice* (1924), *Tristram* (1927), and *Talifer* (1933). The final edition of *The Collected Poems of Edwin Arlington Robinson* appeared in 1937.

ROETHKE, Theodore (1908–    ). American poet. Born in Saginaw, Michigan; educated at the University of Michigan and Harvard. Has been professor of English at the University of Washington since 1947. Many of his poems have appeared in magazines; his books of poetry include *Open House* (1941), *The Lost Son and Other Poems* (1948), *Praise to the End* (1953) and *The Waking* (1953). He received the Pulitzer prize for poetry in 1954.

RUSSELL, Bertrand (1872–    ). English philosopher and mathematician. Educated at Cambridge. Received Nobel prize for literature in 1950. Among his works are *Principia Mathematica* (with A. N. Whitehead; 1910), *Mysticism and Logic* (1918), *The Conquest of Happiness* (1930), *Education and the Social Order* (1932), *Unpopular Essays* (1950), and *Satan in the Suburbs* (five short stories; 1953).

SAKI (Hector Hugh Munro) (1870–1916). British short story writer and novelist. Born in Burma; worked as correspondent in the Balkans, Russia, and Paris (1902–1908); killed in France in the First World War. He wrote one serious work, *The Rise of the Russian Empire* (1900), and two novels—*The Unbearable Bassington* (1912) and *When William Came* (1913)—but his fame rests primarily on his delightful short stories, which have been collected into one volume, *The Short Stories of Saki* (1930).

SHAKESPEARE, William (1564–1616). English poet and dramatist. Born in Stratford upon Avon; was established in London as an actor-playwright by 1592. During the next twenty years, he produced, besides the *Sonnets* (published in 1609), the series of histories, comedies, and tragedies which ranks as the greatest dramatic literature in English, and perhaps the greatest in world literature.

SHAPIRO, Karl (1913–    ). American poet. Born in Baltimore, Maryland; attended Johns Hopkins (1937–1939); served in the U.S. Army during the Second World War. Received the Pulitzer prize for poetry in 1945. Since 1950 he has been editor of *Poetry: A Magazine of Verse.* Author of *Poems* (1935), *Person, Place and Thing* (1942), *The Place of Love* (1942), *V-Letter and Other Poems* (1944), *Essay on Rime* (1945), and *Trial of a Poet* (1947).

SHAW, (George) Bernard (1856–1950). Irish playwright, novelist, and critic. Born in Dublin; began career as critic of music, art, and drama on London newspapers. Active as a Socialist and member of the Fabian Society. Received the Nobel prize for literature in 1925. His plays include *Mrs. Warren's Profession* (1898),

*Caesar and Cleopatra* (1900), *Man and Superman* (1903), *Major Barbara* (1905), *Pygmalion* (1912), *Saint Joan* (1923), and *The Apple Cart* (1929). Among his political writings are *Fabianism and the Empire* (1900) and *The Intelligent Woman's Guide to Socialism and Capitalism* (1928).

SHAW, Irwin (1913–    ). American short story writer, novelist, and playwright. Born in New York City; educated at Brooklyn College. His writings include *Bury the Dead* (1936), *The Gentle People* (1939), *Sailor Off the Bremen* (1940), *Act of Faith* (1946), *The Young Lions,* and *The Troubled Air* (1950).

SHELLEY, Percy Bysshe (1792–1822). English poet. Educated at Eton and at Oxford, from which he was expelled for circulating a pamphlet called *The Necessity of Atheism* (1811). Married Harriet Westbrook (1811); abandoned her to elope with Mary Godwin, whom he married after Harriet's suicide. His major works include *Queen Mab* (1813), *Revolt of Islam* (1817), *Prometheus Unbound* (1818–1820), *The Cenci* (1819), *Hellas* (1821; 1822), *Epipsychidion* (1821; 1822), and *Adonais* (1821).

SOCRATES (470?–399 B.C.). Greek philosopher. Born in Athens; son of the sculptor Sophroniscus. Developed a method of philosophic inquiry known as the "Socratic method," which involves asking a series of questions designed to elicit an answer which will represent universal truth. His contempt for convention angered the authorities in Athens, who brought him to trial for impiety and corrupting the youth; condemned, he drank hemlock and died. His philosophy is known only through the writings of his disciple, Plato.

SOPHOCLES (496?–406 B.C.). Greek tragic playwright. Sophocles, Aeschylus and Euripides are considered the greatest Greek dramatists. Only seven of Sophocles' hundred-odd plays are extant: *Oedipus Rex, Oedipus at Colonus, Antigone, Electra, Philoctetes, Ajax,* and *Maidens of Trachis.*

STEFFENS, Lincoln (1866–1936). American journalist. Born in California, he held editorial positions on *McClure's Magazine, The American Magazine* and *Everybody's Magazine.* Author of *The Shame of the Cities* (1904), *The Struggle for Self-Government* (1906), *The Least of These* (1910), and a highly readable *Autobiography* (1931).

STEVENSON, Robert Louis (1850–1894). Scottish essayist, novelist, and poet. Began his career by contributing essays to magazines and writing two travel books, *An Inland Voyage* (1878) and *Travels with a Donkey* (1879). Traveled to San Francisco, where he married the American widow Mrs. Osbourne; later returned to Scotland. There he produced his most famous works: *Treasure Island* (1883), *A Child's Garden of Verses* (1885), *Dr. Jekyll and Mr. Hyde* (1886), *Kidnapped* (1886), and others. Returned to America in 1888; set out for the South Seas, and remained in voluntary exile on Samoa until his death.

SWIFT, Jonathan (1667–1745). English poet and satirist. Born in Dublin; a cousin of John Dryden. While serving as secretary to Sir William Temple, he wrote the satiric *A Tale of a Tub* and *The Battle of the Books* (both published in 1704). Became a friend of Addison, Steele, Congreve, and Pope. Having taken orders in the Anglican Church in 1694, he was made dean of St. Patrick's, Dublin (1713). Published his most famous work, *Gulliver's Travels,* in 1726; championed the Irish people in the savagely ironic *A Modest Proposal* (1729), and died insane.

TAYLOR, Jeremy (1613–1667). English clergyman and author. Served as chaplain to Charles I; when monarchy was overthrown, he took refuge in Wales, opened a school, and produced the great religious works for which he is remembered: *The Liberty of Prophesying* (1646), *Holy Living* (1650), *Holy Dying* (1651), *The Golden Grove* (1655), and *Worthy Communicant* (1660).

TENNYSON, Alfred (First Baron Tennyson) (1809–1892). English poet. Educated at Cambridge. Earlier poems were published in *Poems by Two Brothers* (1827), *Poems, Chiefly Lyrical* (1830), and *Poems* (1832). His reputation was established by the two-volume *Poems* of 1842, which included "Ulysses," "Locksley Hall," and "Break, Break, Break"; it was enhanced by the publication of *In Memoriam* (1850), an elegy of Arthur Hallam, who had died in 1833. Appointed poet laureate on Wordsworth's death in 1850. Produced a series of historical dramas, and returned to Arthurian legend in his *Idylls of the King* (begun 1859; completed 1885). Buried in Westminster Abbey.

THOMAS, Dylan (1914–1953). British poet. Born in South Wales. Joined British Army in 1940. Made several lecture and poetry-reading tours in the U.S. Author of *Map of Love* (1939), *World I Breathe* (1939), *Portrait of the Artist as a Young Dog* (1940), *In Country Sleep* (1952), *Under Milk Wood* (published

1954), and *Adventures in the Skin Trade* (published 1955).

THOREAU, Henry David (1817–1862). American writer. Born in Concord, Massachusetts; educated at Harvard; worked as schoolteacher at Concord (1839–1841); lived at home of Ralph Waldo Emerson (1841–1843; 1847–1848); then lived in his father's house until his death. Two of his books were published in his lifetime: *A Week on the Concord and Merrimac Rivers* (1849) and *Walden, or Life in the Woods* (1854).

THURBER, James (1894–    ). American humorist and cartoonist. Born in Columbus, Ohio; attended Ohio State University. Worked on several newspapers; has been a contributor to the *New Yorker* since 1926. Author of *My Life and Hard Times* (1934), *The Middle-Aged Man on the Flying Trapeze* (1935), *Fables for Our Time* (1943), and *The Thurber Album* (1952). With E. B. White, he wrote *Is Sex Necessary?* (1929), and with Elliott Nugent, *The Male Animal* (1940).

TOLSTOI, Count Leo Nikolaevich (1828–1910). Russian novelist. Educated at Kazan. After serving in the Crimean War (1854–1856), he retired to his country estate to devote himself to study and writing. Underwent a spiritual transformation (1876), and tried to establish a new Christianity based on nonresistance to evil. His most famous works are *War and Peace* (1866) and *Anna Karenina* (1875–1877); others include *The Kreutzer Sonata* (1889), *The Power of Darkness* (1889), and *Master and Man* (1895).

TWAIN, Mark (Samuel Langhorne Clemens) (1835–1910). American humorist and novelist. Born in Missouri, he worked as a journeyman printer (1847–1855), a Mississippi river pilot (1857–1861), a prospector (1861), and a newspaper reporter (1862). Followed up his first great success, *The Jumping Frog of Calaveras County* (1865), with a travel book called *Innocents Abroad* (1869). In next two decades he produced, among other works, *The Gilded Age* (1873), *Tom Sawyer* (1876), *Huckleberry Finn* (1885), and *A Connecticut Yankee in King Arthur's Court* (1889). His later works, in which a note of bitterness is discernible, include *What Is Man?* (1906) and *The Mysterious Stranger* (published in 1916).

VAUGHAN, Henry (1622–1695). English mystic poet. Born in South Wales; practiced medicine. Best known for such religious verse as *Silex Scintillans* (1650) and "They are all gone into the world of light." Also wrote some non-religious verse and translations.

WALLER, Edmund (1601–1687). English poet. Addressed early poems to "Sacharissa" (Lady Dorothy Sidney). Conducted impeachment of Sir Francis Crawley (1641); was detected in plot to seize London for Charles II (1643), and banished. After the Restoration he became an M.P. (1661–1687) and a favorite at court. Author of *Poems* (1645), *St. James's Park* (1661), and *Divine Poems* (1685). Noted for making the heroic couplet popular.

WARREN, Robert Penn (1905–    ). Novelist, poet, critic, and educator. Born in Kentucky. Educated at Vanderbilt, University of California, Yale; Rhodes scholar at Oxford (1930). Has been professor of English at Yale since 1950. Received Pulitzer prize for fiction in 1947. Among his works are *Understanding Poetry* (with Cleanth Brooks, 1938, 1950), *Understanding Fiction* (with Cleanth Brooks, 1948), *All the King's Men* (1946), *World Enough and Time* (1950), and *Brother to Dragons* (1953).

WELTY, Eudora (1909–    ). American short story writer and novelist. Born in Jackson, Mississippi; educated at Mississippi State College for Women and the University of Wisconsin. Her stories have appeared in the *Atlantic Monthly, Harper's Bazaar,* the *New Yorker,* and other magazines; her books include *A Curtain of Green* (1941), *The Robber Bridegroom* (1942), *The Wide Net* (1943), *Delta Wedding* (1946), and *The Golden Apples* (1949).

WEST, Jessamyn (birth-date unknown). American fiction writer. Born in Indiana; graduated from Whittier College and attended the University of California. Her stories have appeared in the *New Yorker, Harper's, Atlantic Monthly,* and other magazines. Among her books are *The Friendly Persuasion* (1945), *Mirror for the Sky* (1945), *Witch Diggers* (1951), and *Cress Delahanty* (1953).

WORDSWORTH, William (1770–1850). English poet. Educated at Cambridge. Visited France in 1792; a love affair with Annette Vallon resulted in the birth of an illegitimate daughter (1792). On receiving a legacy he settled with his sister Dorothy at Racedown, Dorsetshire; later met Samuel Taylor Coleridge, with whom he collaborated on the *Lyrical Ballads* (1798), for which he wrote a preface that brought him the hostility of the critics and great notoriety. Became poet laureate in 1843. His later works include *The Prelude* (1805, published 1850);

*Poems* (1807), *The Excursion* (1814), and *Ecclesiastical Sonnets* (1822).

YEATS, William Butler (1865–1939). Irish poet and dramatist. Born near Dublin; began career by translating Gaelic tales and collecting Irish folklore. With George Moore, he was one of the leaders of the Irish literary revival; with Lady Gregory and Edward Martyn, one of the founders of the Irish Literary Theatre (1899), which became the Abbey Theatre (1904). His volumes of verse include *The Rose* (1893), *The Wind Among the Reeds* (1899), *Responsibilities* (1914), *The Wild Swans at Coole* (1919), *The Tower* (1928), and *Last Poems* (1936–1939). His poems are reprinted in *The Collected Poems of W. B. Yeats* (1950), and his plays in *The Collected Plays of W. B. Yeats* (1953). He received the Nobel prize in 1923.

# INDEX OF AUTHORS
# AND TITLES

719

# INDEX OF CRITICAL TERMS